Psychology

WITHDRAWN

Lester A. Lefton

Kent State University

Linda Brannon

McNeese State University

LIVERPOOL
JOHN MOORES UNIVERSITY
AVRIL ROBARTS LRC
TITHEBARN STREET
LIVERPOOL L2 2ER
TEL. 0151 231 4022

vango books

Boston   New York   San Francisco
Mexico City   Montreal   Toronto   London   Madrid   Munich   Paris
Hong Kong   Singapore   Tokyo   Cape Town   Sydney

Editor in Chief: Susan Hartman
Editorial Assistant: Courtney Mullen
Marketing Manager: Karen Natale
Production Editor: Patty Bergin
Composition Buyer: Linda Cox
Manufacturing Buyer: JoAnne Sweeney
Editorial Production Service and Electronic Composition: Elm Street Publishing Services
Cover Administrator: Elena Sidorova

For related titles and support materials, visit our online catalog at http://www.ablongman.com

Between the time Website information is gathered and then published, it is not unusual for some sites to
have closed. Also, the transcription of URLs can result in unintended typographical errors. The publisher
would appreciate notification where these errors occur so that they may be corrected in subsequent editions.

Library of Congress Cataloging-in-Publication Data

Lefton, Lester A., 1946–
 Psychology / Lester A. Lefton, Linda Brannon.—1st ed.
   p. cm.
   ISBN 978-0-205-59531-0   0-205-59531-6

 1. Psychology—Textbooks. I. Brannon, Linda, 1948– II. Title.
 BF121.L425 2008
  150—dc22

                                           2007042669

Printed in the United States of America

10 9 8 7 6 5 4 3 2 1 RRD-OH 11 10 09 08 07

Credits appear on pages 849–850, which constitute an extension of the copyright page.

CONTENTS

Preface to Instructors   x
About the Authors   xiii

1 What Is Psychology?   1

How Accurate Is the Image of Psychology?   2
Defining Psychology   3

How Did Psychology Begin?   3
The Early Traditions   3
The Behaviorist Revolution   6
Challenges to Behaviorism   7

What Trends Currently Shape Psychology?   8
The Changing Face of Psychology   9
Major Perspectives in Psychology   11
Current Trends in Psychology   15

**Who Are These People Called
Psychologists?**   17
Types of Mental Health Practitioners   17
What Psychologists Do   18
Making Psychology a Career   19

How Should You Use This Textbook?   22
Four Recurring Themes in Psychology   22

Summary and Review   23

2 The Science of Psychology   26

What Makes Psychology a Science?   26
Three Principles of Scientific Endeavor   27
The Scientific Method in Psychology   29

**What Research Methods Do
Psychologists Use?**   32
The Experimental Method   32
Descriptive Research Methods   35

**How Do Psychologists Evaluate
Their Research Findings?**   40
Using Statistics to Evaluate Research   41
Avoiding Bias in the Research Process   45

**What Ethical Principles Guide Psychology
Research?**   51

Summary and Review   52

3 Neuroscience: The Brain and Behavior 55

How Is the Nervous System Organized?   55
The Cellular Level   56
Divisions of the Nervous System   64
The Brain   68

How Does the Brain Function?   72
Monitoring Neural Activity   73
Brain Specialization   77
Plasticity and Change   80

What Effects Do Hormones Have on Behavior?   81

How Do Genetic Factors Affect Behavior?   84
The Issue of Nature versus Nurture   84
The Basics of Genetics   85
How Genes Affect Behavior   86
From Genetics to Genomics   88

**Does Our Evolutionary History Influence Our
Current Behavior?**   89
Natural Selection   90
Adaptations in Humans   90
Controversies about Evolutionary Psychology   92

Summary and Review   94

4 Child Development   98

What Are the Central Issues of Development?   99
Issues in Developmental Psychology   99
Research Designs   101

How Does Physical Development Proceed?   103
Prenatal Development   103
Harmful Environmental Effects   104
Newborns Are Ready to Experience
the World   106

How Does Thought Develop? 111

Jean Piaget's Insights 113

Vygotsky's Sociocultural Theory:
An Alternative to Piaget 120

Theory of Mind 122

Thought in a Social Context 123

How Do Social and Emotional Development Proceed? 124

Attachment: The Ties That Bind 124

Temperament 128

Moral Reasoning 130

What Environmental Factors Are Important for Social Development? 134

Early Social Development and Child Rearing 134

Gender Roles 137

Erik Erikson and the Beginning of the Search for Self 138

Summary and Review 141

5 Adolescence and Adulthood 145

How Do Adolescents Bridge the Gap to Adulthood? 146

Viewing Adolescence in Multiple Contexts 146

Physical Development in Adolescence 147

Cognitive Development in Adolescence 149

Emotional and Social Development in Adolescence 151

Who Am I? The Search for Gender Identity 154

Friendship and Sexual Behavior 157

Is Adulthood a Time of Stability or Change? 159

Physical Changes in Adulthood 160

Cognitive Changes in Adulthood 164

Social and Personality Development in Adulthood 165

Stage Theories of Adult Development 166

Do We Grow Older and Wiser in Late Adulthood? 170

Myths, Realities, and Stereotypes about Aging 171

Health in Late Adulthood 173

The Final Transition: Dying 175

Summary and Review 176

6 Sensation and Perception 180

How Are Stimulation and Perception Linked? 181

The Difference between Sensation and Perception 181

Psychophysics 183

Selective Attention 184

Restricted Environmental Stimulation 186

Inattentional Blindness 187

How Do We See the World? 188

The Structures of the Visual System 188

The Electrochemical Basis of Perception 194

How Do We Perceive Form and Substance? 202

Perception of Form: Constancy 202

Depth Perception 204

Illusions 207

Prosopagnosia: The Inability to Recognize Faces 210

Gestalt Laws of Organization 211

How Do We Perceive Sounds? 212

What Is Sound? 213

The Structure of the Ear 214

Theories of Hearing 216

Sound Localization 217

Hearing Impairments 218

Which Senses Are the Least Understood? 219

Taste 219

Smell 221

What Is the Relationship between Touch and Pain? 223

Touch 224

Pain 225

How Do We Keep Our Balance? 230

Does Extrasensory Perception Exist? 230

Summary and Review 231

7 Consciousness   236

What Is Consciousness?   236
Defining Consciousness   237
Theories of Consciousness   238

What Happens When We Sleep?   240
The Sleep–Wakefulness Cycle: Circadian Rhythms   240
Sleep Stages: REM and NREM Sleep   242
Sleep Deprivation   245
Why Do We Sleep?   247
Is There a Sleep Switch?   248
Sleep Disorders   249

What Are Dreams and What Do They Mean?   251
What Is a Dream?   251
The Content of Dreams   252
Dream Theories   252

Is It Possible to Control Consciousness by Using Biofeedback, Hypnosis, or Meditation?   257
Biofeedback   258
Hypnosis   258
Meditation   260

How Do Drugs Alter Consciousness?   261
Psychoactive Drugs   262
Drug Use and Abuse   266

Summary and Review   271

8 Learning   274

What Type of Learning Is Pavlovian, or Classical, Conditioning?   275
Terms and Procedures   276
Classical Conditioning in Humans   279
Higher-Order Conditioning   280

What Are the Key Variables in Classical Conditioning?   281
Strength, Timing, and Frequency   281
Predictability   282
Extinction and Spontaneous Recovery   282

Stimulus Generalization and Stimulus Discrimination   283
Classical Conditioning in Daily Life   286
Pavlov's Understanding Reinterpreted   289

What Type of Learning Is Operant Conditioning?   289
The Pioneers: E. L. Thorndike and B. F. Skinner   290
Reinforcement: A Consequence That Strengthens a Response   291
Two Reinforcement Strategies: Positive and Negative   291
The Skinner Box and Shaping   294
Punishment: A Consequence That Weakens a Response   295

What Are the Key Variables in Operant Conditioning?   298
Strength, Timing, and Frequency   298
Stimulus Generalization and Stimulus Discrimination   302
Extinction and Spontaneous Recovery   303
Operant Conditioning in Daily Life   304

Can Learning Occur through Observation?   307
The Power of Modeling   308
Key Processes in Observational Learning   309
Observational Learning in Daily Life   311
Other Types of Cognitive Learning   312

What Is the Biological Basis for Learning?   314
Are Evolutionary Theory and Learning Theory Incompatible?   314
Electrical Brain Stimulation and Reinforcement   315
Brain Changes and Learning   316

Summary and Review   317

9 Memory   321

How Does the Memory Process Begin?   322
The Brain as Information Processor   322
Encoding   323
Levels of Processing   323
Neuroscience and Encoding   324

What Are the Types of Memory Storage? **326**
Sensory Memory 326
Short-Term Storage 328
Long-Term Memory 332
Neuroscience and Storage 334

What Influences Memory Retrieval? **337**
Retention: Measures of Retrieval 337
Retrieval Success and Failure:
Encoding Specificity 338
What Facilitates Retrieval? 340
Flashbulb Memories 342
Gender and Memory 343
Culture and Memory 344

What Causes People to Forget? **345**
Early Studies 345
Key Causes of Forgetting 347
Special Types of Forgetting 349
Neuroscience and Forgetting: Studies
of Amnesia 352
Summary and Review **352**

10 Cognitive Psychology **356**
What Is Cognitive Psychology? **357**
**How Do We Form Concepts and Solve
Problems?** **357**
Concept Formation 358
Problem Solving 360
Barriers to Problem Solving 362
Avoid Barriers: Be a Critical Thinker 363
Creative Problem Solving 364

How Do We Reason and Make Decisions? **366**
Uncertainty: Estimating Probabilities 367
Barriers to Sound Decision Making 368
Culture and Reasoning 370
Evolution and Reasoning 370

**What Does Artificial Intelligence
Reveal about Cognition?** **371**
The Computer as Information Processor 371

Neural Networks 372
Robotics 374

What Is the Structure of Language? **375**
Language and Gender Stereotypes 376
Thought, Culture, and Language 377
Linguistics 378
Language Structure 378
The Biological and Evolutionary Basis of
Language 382

How Do We Acquire Language? **382**
Learning Theories 383
Biological Theories 383
Do Chimpanzees Use Language? 384
Do Dolphins or Whales Use Language? 387
Social Interaction Theory: A Little
Bit of Each 387
Summary and Review **388**

11 Intelligence **393**
**What Are the Origins and History
of Psychological Testing?** **393**
Binet's Intelligence Test 394
The Stanford–Binet Intelligence Scale 394
The Wechsler Scales 395
Group Intelligence Tests 397

What Is Intelligence? **399**
Theories of Intelligence—One Ability
or Many? 399
Emotions—A Different Kind
of Intelligence? 405

How Do Psychologists Develop Tests? **406**
Developing an Intelligence Test 407
Reliability 409
Validity 410

**How Do Biological and Environmental
Factors Contribute to Intelligence?** **412**
Biological Factors and Intelligence 412
Environmental and Cultural Factors
in Intelligence 415

The Interaction of Biological
and Environmental Factors 417

**What Is the Impact of Having
an Exceptional IQ?** 419
Giftedness 419
Intellectual Disability 421
Special Education: The IDEA 422

Summary and Review 423

12 Motivation and Emotion 428

What Is Motivation? 428
Definition of Motivation 429
Theories of Motivation 429

How Does Motivation Affect Behavior? 440
Hunger: A Physiological Need 441
Sexual Behavior: Physiology plus Thought 448
Social Needs 450

What Is Emotion? 455
Definition of Emotion 455
Theories of Emotion 456

How Does Emotion Affect Behavior? 463
Culture and Emotion 463
Gender and Emotion 464
Can We Control Emotions? 464

Summary and Review 466

13 Personality and Its Assessment 470

What Is Personality? 470
Definition of Personality 471
Personality in the Cultural Context 471

**What Is the Psychodynamic Approach
to Personality?** 473
The Psychoanalytic Theory
of Sigmund Freud 473
Adler and Individual Psychology 481
Jung and Analytical Psychology 484

Can Personality Be Learned? 485
The Power of Learning 485

Skinner and Behavioral Analysis:
Acquiring a Personality 486

**What Are Trait and Type Theories
of Personality?** 487
Allport's Personal Disposition Theory 487
Cattell's Trait Theory 488
Eysenck's Factor Theory 489
The Five-Factor Model 489

**What Characterizes the Humanistic
Approach to Personality?** 490
Maslow and Self-Actualization 491
Rogers and Self Theory 492
Positive Psychology 493

**What Is the Cognitive Approach
to Personality?** 495
Key Cognitive Concepts 495
Kelly and Personal Constructs 495
Rotter and Locus of Control 496
Bandura and Self-Efficacy 498
Mischel's Cognitive-Affective
Personality System 500

How Do Psychologists Assess Personality? 500
Projective Tests 502
Personality Inventories 503

Summary and Review 505

14 Social Psychology 510

What Is the Social Self? 511
The Self in Social Psychology 511
Thinking about Self and Others 512

How Are Attitudes Related to Behavior? 516
Dimensions of Attitudes 517
Do Attitudes Predict Behavior? 518
Does Behavior Determine Attitudes? 518
How Does Attitude Change Occur? 521

How Do People Relate to Each Other? 524
Attraction and Relationship Formation 524
Aggression and Violence 530
Prosocial Behavior 534

What Are the Effects of Identifying with a Group? 537

Group Performance 538

Identifying as a Group Member 542

How Do Others Affect the Individual? 546

Conformity 547

Compliance 548

Obedience to Authority 550

Summary and Review 553

15 Stress and Health Psychology 557

What Is Stress? 557

Definition of Stress 558

Sources of Stress 562

Responses to Stress 567

Stress and Health 569

How Do People Cope with Stress? 572

What Is Coping? 573

Factors That Influence Coping 573

Coping Strategies 575

What Is Health Psychology? 579

How Does Behavior Affect Health and Illness? 580

The Psychology of Being Sick 583

Adopting a Healthier Lifestyle 586

Health Psychology and the Future 589

Summary and Review 589

16 Psychological Disorders 592

What Is Abnormal Behavior? 592

A Definition 593

Perspectives on Abnormality 594

Diagnosing Psychopathology: The *DSM* 598

What Are Anxiety Disorders? 602

Defining Anxiety 602

Generalized Anxiety Disorder 603

Panic Disorder 603

Phobic Disorders 603

Obsessive-Compulsive Disorder 606

What Are Mood Disorders? 607

Depressive Disorders 608

Causes of Major Depressive Disorder 610

Bipolar Disorder 614

What Are Dissociative Disorders? 615

Dissociative Amnesia 616

Dissociative Identity Disorder: Multiple Personalities 616

What Is Schizophrenia? 617

Essential Characteristics of Schizophrenic Disorders 618

Types of Schizophrenia 619

Causes of Schizophrenia 621

What Are Personality Disorders? 624

How Are Violence and Mental Disorders Related? 626

Diagnoses Associated with Violence 626

Violence as a Risk for Developing Mental Disorders 628

Summary and Review 631

17 Therapy 635

What Is Psychotherapy, and What Types Are Available? 636

Is Psychotherapy Necessary and Effective? 637

Which Therapy, Which Therapist? 640

Are There Common Factors among Therapists? 641

What Roles Do Culture and Gender Play in Therapy? 643

Has Managed Care Changed Therapy? 645

How Do Psychodynamic Therapies Work? 647

Goals of Psychoanalysis 647

Techniques of Psychoanalysis 648

Criticisms of Psychoanalysis 649

What Do Humanistic Therapies Emphasize?   **650**

Techniques of Client-Centered Therapy   651

Criticisms of Client-Centered Therapy   653

**What Are the Methods
of Behavior Therapy?**   **654**

Assumptions and Goals
of Behavior Therapy   654

Operant Conditioning in Behavior
Therapy   656

Counterconditioning in Behavior Therapy   659

Modeling in Behavior Therapy   660

Why Is Cognitive Therapy So Popular?   **661**

Assumptions of Cognitive Therapy   661

Types of Cognitive Therapy   662

How Does Therapy in a Group Work?   **666**

Techniques of Group Therapy   666

Family Therapy   667

**How Do Psychologists Reach Out
to Communities?**   **669**

**How Do Biologically Based Therapies
Create Change?**   **671**

Drugs and the Therapeutic Process   671

Psychosurgery and Electroconvulsive
Therapy   675

Alternative Therapies   677

The Debate over Hospitalization   677

Summary and Review   **678**

18 Psychology in Action   683

**How Is Behavior Affected by the Work
Environment?**   **683**

Definition of Industrial/Organizational
Psychology   684

Human Resources   685

Motivation and Job Performance   692

Job Satisfaction   698

Teams and Teamwork   701

Leadership   701

The Future of I/O Psychology   706

How Do Human Factors Affect Performance?   **707**

Efficiency   707

Behavior-Based Safety   708

**How Do Psychology and the Law
Work Together?**   **710**

Psychologists in the Legal System   711

Crime and Punishment   712

The Law and Psychology:
An Uneasy Partnership   713

What Are the Goals of Sport Psychology?   **713**

Arousal and Athletic Performance   714

Anxiety and Athletic Performance   715

Intervention Strategies for Athletes   715

Putting It Together: Go with the Flow   716

The Future of Sport Psychology   717

Summary and Review   **717**

Appendix: Statistical Methods   720

References   739

Glossary   804

Name Index   817

Subject Index   835

Credits   849

Psychology, VangoBooks edition, is another exciting stop on a journey that began in 1979, when the idea of writing a textbook first became a reality. The amazing changes in the field of psychology since that time have provided fascinating opportunities for classroom discussion, debate, personal education, and application. Among the most important of these changes are the explosion of research in the areas of gender and culture and the changing faces of both students and instructors.

As psychologists, we continue to find our role as educators as important as our role as active learners in this ever-evolving field. Therefore, we revise each edition of this text with one goal in mind—empowering students to engage in the material presented, to understand the key concepts in psychology, and to apply their learning actively in the real world. In this edition, we have improved and strengthened the tools and features that encourage students to become active learners. Psychology is a story that we want to share with students. We've increased the number of Building Tables to help students synthesize concepts and make connections.

We are excited to have our textbook now available in the new VangoBook format. This is a very different type of psychology textbook—one that your students will want to read. It's also about half the cost of a traditional textbook. We understand what students need to learn, and what instructors need to teach—no more, no less. We believe you'll find that this VangoBook and its ancillary package present compelling content in an attractive format, without the sticker shock.

SUPPLEMENTS FOR INSTRUCTORS

All supplements are available electronically to qualified instructors only. Please contact your local Pearson representative for more information. To find your local representative please go to: http://www.ablongman.com/replocator.

Instructor's Manual   This teaching resource features helpful at-a-glance grids, handouts, lecture enhancements, detailed chapter outlines, activities for the classroom, and other valuable tools for new and experienced instructors. In addition, the Instructor's Manual suggests relevant reading, video, and Internet sources.

Test Bank   Written by Christopher Dula, of Eastern Tennessee State University, the test bank contains over 2,000 questions, including multiple choice, true/false, short answer, and essay (each with an answer justification). All questions are labeled with a page reference, a difficulty ranking, and a type designation.

PowerPoint Presentation   Erin Hardin, of Texas Tech University, has created an incredibly flexible PowerPoint package to be used by both new and experienced instructors. A robust version with detailed lecture outlines, art, and demonstrations is available to instructors who may be new to teaching the course and those who prefer a multimedia lecture format. A more scaled-back version is also available for those instructors who want the opportunity to modify their lectures to fit their classroom needs.

Pearson's **MyPsychKit** is the perfect online supplement for your classes. With an abundance of interactive activities, practice tests, chapter summaries, learning objectives, and access to Research Navigator, Pearson's MyPsychKit connects you to a world of resources beyond your textbook.

Organized by chapter, MyPsychKit site offers educational tools to help you fully understand the topic and study smarter. Learning Objects provide key chapter issues in a streamlined bullet-point format. Chapter Summary provides a detailed overview of the main ideas presented in each chapter. Interactive Activities feature engaging simulation quizzes and/or Internet games. The Multiple Choice and True/False sections provide a number of relevant test questions, while the Essay section offers a variety of sample essay questions. You can even submit the test questions and essays for immediate online grading! Web Links showcase 5-10 links to additional resources that can be used for further research. And the Flashcard section helps you brush up on your knowledge, pinpoint areas for further study, and review for a quiz or test.

Pearson's **Research Navigator**™ is the easiest way to start a research assignment or research paper. With access to exclusive databases of credible and reliable source material, including the EBSCO Academic Journal and Abstract Database, the New York Times Search by Subject Archive, "Best of the Web" Link Library, and Financial Times Article Archive and Company Financials, Research Navigator gives you all the tools you need to conduct online research for your projects and papers. In addition, Research Navigator offers extensive online content detailing the steps in the research process, helping you define topics, find sources, maximize your library time, start writing, and finish with endnotes and bibliography.

ACKNOWLEDGMENTS

We thank the following people who prepared both general and chapter specific reviews to assist us in gauging trends in the field and to provide us with their own valuable input to our draft manuscript of the ninth edition: Aneeq Ahmad, Henderson State University; Wade Arnold, University of Florida, Gainesville; David Baskind, Delta College; Aaron U. Bolin, Arkansas State University; David Brackin, Young Harris College; Michael C. Clayton, Jacksonville State University; David H. Dodd, University of Utah; Herb S. French, Portland Community College; Glenn Geher, State University of New York, New Paltz; Jamie Goldenberg, University of California, Davis; Rodney J.Grisham, Indian River Community College; Herman Huber, College of St. Elizabeth; Charles M. Huffman, Cumberland College; Heide Island, University of Montana; Brian Johnson, University of Tennessee at Martin; Amy Mitchell, Catawba Valley Community College; Alan Oda, Azusa Pacific University; Frank Provenzano, Greenville Technical College; N. Clayton Silver, University of Nevada,

Las Vegas; Barbara B. Simon, Midlands Technical College; Robert B. Stennett, Gainesville College, Oconee; Linda Tennison, College of Saint Benedict, St. John's University; David Tom, Columbus State Community College; Colin William, Ivy Tech State College; Karen Yanowitz, Arkansas State University.

Lester A. Lefton
Linda Brannon

I love teaching psychology. My teaching technique and style started to develop over three decades ago. My career in psychology began with a survey of sexual attitudes that I conducted in high school. I passed out questionnaires to the juniors and seniors, who were to respond anonymously. Then I spent days poring over and summarizing the data—which I, of course, found fascinating.

While in college, I worked as a counselor in a treatment center for emotionally disturbed children. Later, as a laboratory assistant, I collected and analyzed data for a psychologist doing research in vision. In contrast to my counseling experience, hunting for answers to scientific questions and gathering data were activities that held my interest. My graduate studies at the University of Rochester included research in perception. After earning my PhD, I became a faculty member at the University of South Carolina, where my research in cognitive psychology involved studying perceptual phenomena such as eye movements. My goal is to share my excitement about psychology in the classroom, in my textbooks, and in professional journals.

Lester A. Lefton

My career in psychology began when I kept taking psychology courses as an undergraduate at the University of Texas at Austin, where I received my undergraduate degree and then stayed to earn my PhD in human experimental psychology. Although I was fascinated by data collection and analysis, I got to teach a course in introductory psychology and discovered that I loved teaching. After receiving my doctoral degree, I went to McNeese State University in Lake Charles, Louisiana. This school emphasizes teaching, and I have taught a variety of courses, specializing in experimental psychology and biopsychology, as well as continuing to teach introductory psychology. In 1998, I was selected to be Distinguished Professor of the year at McNeese State University.

In the early 1980s, I began writing textbooks. My first book was *Health Psychology: An Introduction to Behavior and Health*, coauthored with Jess Feist, one of my colleagues at McNeese. My next book was *Gender: Psychological Perspectives*, which grew out of my interest in and research on gender issues. The course I teach on the psychology of gender is one of my favorites. I became coauthor of *Psychology* in its 8th edition, and now I get to tell the story of psychology to many more students.

Linda Brannon

CHAPTER 1

What Is Psychology?

How Accurate Is the Image
of Psychology?   2
   Defining Psychology

How Did Psychology Begin?   3
   The Early Traditions
   The Behaviorist Revolution
   Challenges to Behaviorism

What Trends Currently Shape
Psychology?   8
   The Changing Face of Psychology
   Major Perspectives in Psychology
   Current Trends in Psychology

Who Are These People Called
Psychologists?   17
   Types of Mental Health Practitioners
   What Psychologists Do
   Making Psychology a Career

How Should You Use This
Textbook?   21
   Four Recurring Themes in Psychology

Summary and Review   22

The psychological implications of the Internet, beliefs in UFOs and government conspiracies, social anxiety, and study skills are only a few of the topics that we will consider in this book. Psychology is a vast field with many areas of research and innumerable practical applications. However, psychology may be very different from what you imagine, since many people hold inaccurate views of this vast and fascinating field.

How Accurate Is the Image of Psychology?

When I (L.B.) had just completed my doctoral degree, my husband worked for a bank. We occasionally attended office parties at which he enjoyed introducing me to his colleagues using the title "Doctor" and saying that I was a psychologist. People usually reacted in one of two ways: They said either "I don't want to talk to you" or "I really want to talk to you." Both responses made me cringe inside as I smiled and tried to be polite. The ones who responded that they did not want to talk to me seemed to think that I could somehow read their minds and understand their innermost feelings through a casual conversation. Those who said that they really wanted to talk to me believed that I could solve their personal problems right then and there. My husband enjoyed watching the reactions of his colleagues a great deal more than I liked dealing with their misperceptions of psychology.

My husband's colleagues had never met a psychologist, and their views of psychology were based on popular culture, including movies and television. Unfortunately, the media have created and promoted some inaccurate and exaggerated ideas of what psychology is and what psychologists do. For example, a prominent image is that of a patient lying on a couch while a therapist, steeped in the theories of Sigmund Freud, listens and takes notes. This image only partly reflects reality: Freud was important in pioneering therapeutic methods for helping people understand and deal with psychological problems, and many psychologists do offer therapy to individuals. Yet the ideas of Freud reflect only one part of the history and theory of psychology, and few psychologists today use Freud's therapeutic techniques. I received no training to conduct any type of psychotherapy, so despite the prominence of the image that psychologists are professionals who provide help for people with problems, I did not fit that conceptualization.

Another image of a psychologist is a man in a white coat, running rats through a maze. Though such experiments do take place, today the researcher is almost as likely to be a woman (as I am), and the white coat is not a necessary part of the process. During the 1940s and 1950s, white rats were the most common experimental subjects in research on learning, the most popular focus of research at the time. But this situation has changed—humans have replaced rats as the most common participants in psychology research (Plous, 1996), and learning is only one of many areas of study for psychology researchers. My research participants are humans, and my husband's colleagues had a limited view of psychology that failed to include my research in thought and language. The role of the psychologist is much more varied than either of these popular images implies.

A third view holds that psychology is much less powerful than my husband's colleagues imagined. Indeed, those who hold this view believe that psychology is nothing more than common sense about how people behave. This view proposes that "everyone is a psychologist" because all people observe behavior and become experts by just interacting with others. What this view fails to acknowledge is the amount of hindsight and second guessing that people do when interpreting the behavior of others and the rigorous procedures that differentiate psychology research from common sense. The people who hold this view overlook how many times common sense fails to make correct predictions about behavior.

Defining Psychology

Psychology is the science of behavior and mental processes. Behavior includes a variety of overt actions such as walking and gesturing, social interactions such as talking to someone, and emotional reactions such as laughing or frowning. Certain physiological reactions, such as heart rate and patterns of brain activity, must be measured with instruments, but they still fit within the category of behavior. Mental processes include thoughts and ideas as well as more complex aspects of reasoning. Psychologists make inferences about mental processes by studying behavior.

Psychology ■ The science of behavior and mental processes.

Psychology differs from common sense precisely because it is a science. Rather than observing casually, psychologists use rigorous, systematic observation that yields comprehensive theories and reliable knowledge. The many subfields of psychological research have produced information on how people grow up and become independent, how people interact in relationships, and how they learn and remember, sleep and dream, perceive the world, and live fulfilling lives. Psychology also explores problem behaviors such as violence and drug abuse. Every day, this exciting field stretches the boundaries of what we know about people, their relationships, and their inner worlds of thoughts and feelings.

Psychology differs from its popular image by being both less and more than people imagine. Psychology is less than people like some of my husband's colleagues imagine because psychologists cannot perform feats of mind reading or telepathy. However, psychology is also more than some other people imagine because the field is so large and varied. Those who want to understand real human behavior and relationships need to look further than television and movies for their images of psychology. Taking a course in psychology and studying this book constitute a good way to begin. In this chapter, we introduce the discipline of psychology, beginning with how this science developed.

How Did Psychology Begin?

The history of psychology is short—going back just over 120 years—but the questions that interested early psychologists had ancient roots. For thousands of years, philosophers had considered questions such as "What is the nature of the mind?" and "How do people experience consciousness?" Then, beginning in the late 19th century, inquiry in philosophy evolved into psychology. At that point, psychology became a separate field. Even in its early years, psychology was characterized by schools of thought that viewed the emerging science in different ways. Some of those differences continue today. However, all of the early approaches shared the view that psychology had made a break with philosophy and had become a new field.

The Early Traditions

Structuralism

Before Wilhelm Wundt (pronounced "Voont"), psychology did not exist as a separate field. Wundt (1832–1920) intended to found a new science, and he did so by establishing a laboratory devoted to research on psychological topics (Boring, 1950). By

1879, Wundt's laboratory was set up in Leipzig, Germany, and the break between philosophical and scientific inquiry had occurred. Wundt taught his students to use the scientific method when asking psychological questions (Vermersch, 1999). He wanted to understand the mind by conducting research, and he attracted students from Europe and the United States who shared his interest in taking a scientific approach to studying the mind.

Englishman Edward B. Titchener (1867–1927) helped popularize Wundt's initial ideas, along with his own, in the United States and the rest of the English-speaking world. Titchener espoused *structuralism*, the school of psychological thought that considered the structure and elements of immediate, conscious experience to be the proper subject matter of psychology. Instead of exploring the broad range of behavior and mental processes that psychologists consider today, the structuralists tried to observe the inner workings of the mind to determine the simple elements of conscious experience. They felt that all conscious experience could ultimately be reduced to simple elements or blends of those elements.

Structuralism ■ The school of psychological thought that considered the structure and elements of immediate, conscious experience to be the proper subject matter of psychology.

To discover these elements, structuralists used the technique of *introspection*, or *self-examination* of one's mental processes. Using introspection, an individual describes and analyzes thoughts as they occur. With this technique, structuralists conducted some of the first experiments in psychology. For example, they studied the speed of thought by observing reaction times for simple tasks, reasoning that the speed of a person's reaction is a reflection of how much thought goes into processing the situation and deciding what to do. Psychologists today continue to use this technique.

Introspection ■ The self-examination of one's mental processes, a technique used by the structuralists.

By today's standards, the structuralists focused too narrowly on individuals' conscious experiences. And not only was the technique of introspection too limited, it was also biased because it required individuals to analyze their own thought processes as those occurred. People can report on their attitudes and behaviors, but thought processes occur too rapidly and automatically for people to understand. Thus, this school did not make the progress in describing the nature of the mind that its supporters had hoped for. Furthermore, the school of structuralist psychology not only excluded women and people from most ethnic groups from being researchers—almost all of whom were wealthy White men—but it also restricted the individuals whose minds were studied, excluding children, the mentally ill, and those with impaired mental capabilities (Schultz & Schultz, 2004; Shields, 1975). Thus, the minds that the structuralists sought to understand came from a narrow category of humans.

Functionalism

Functionalism ■ The school of psychological thought that was an outgrowth of structuralism and was concerned with how the mind functions and how this functioning is related to consciousness.

Before long, a new perspective developed, bringing with it a more active way of thinking about behavior. Built on the basic concepts of structuralism, *functionalism* was the school of psychological thought that tried to explore not just the mind's structures but how the mind *functions* and how this functioning is related to consciousness (Schultz & Schultz, 2004). Functionalists also sought to understand how people adapted to their environment, and this aspect of the field was strongly influenced by Charles Darwin's evolutionary theory.

With William James (1842–1910) at its head, this lively new school of psychological thought was the first American attempt to research the mind. Its practical orientation helped to make functionalism the dominant school of psychology in the United States. James, a physician and professor of anatomy at Harvard University, was charming, informal, outgoing, vivacious, and especially well liked by his students (Simon, 1998). He argued that knowing only the contents of consciousness, as the structuralists sought to do, was too limited and would never reveal the nature of the mind. Psychology needed to strive to understand how those contents functioned and worked together. Through such knowledge, psychologists could understand how the mind (consciousness) guided behavior. In 1890, James published *Principles of Psychology*, in which he described the mind as a dynamic set of continuously evolving elements. In this work, he coined the phrase "stream of consciousness," describing the mind as a river, always flowing, never remaining still.

James and the functionalists broadened the scope of psychology by studying nonhuman animals, by applying psychology in practical areas such as education, and by experimenting on overt behavior, not just mental processes. Despite this broadening, the definition of psychology remained the same—the study of consciousness.

Gestalt Psychology

Functionalism was an American movement that was never popular in Europe, where structuralism continued to be prominent until challenged by psychologists who wanted a different approach to understanding conscious experience. One such challenge came from *Gestalt psychology*, the school of psychological thought that argued that it is necessary to study a person's total experience, not just parts of the mind or behavior (*Gestalt* is a German word that means "configuration"). This school was a radical departure from structuralism in terms of its emphasis and its explanations of the mind. Gestalt psychologists such as Max Wertheimer (1880–1943) and Kurt Koffka (1886–1941) suggested that conscious experience is more than simply the sum of its individual parts. Gestalt psychologists argued that each person experiences the world in terms of perceptual frameworks, that each mind organizes the elements of experience into something unique by adding structure and meaning to incoming stimuli. They proposed that people mold simple sensory elements into patterns through which they interpret the world. For psychologists to understand the mind and its workings, they must analyze the whole experience—the patterns of a person's perceptions and thoughts.

Gestalt psychology exerted a major influence in several areas of psychology—especially social psychology, cognitive psychology, and therapy. The influence on social psychology resulted from Gestalt psychology's emphasis on perception, which affected theory and research on how people view each other and their social situations. The emphasis on perception's influence on thought provided the foundation for studies in cognitive psychology. A Gestalt-oriented therapist dealing with a "problem" family member might try to see how the "part" (the person seen as the problem) could be better understood in the context of the "whole" (the family configuration).

Gestalt [gesh-TALT] psychology ■ The school of psychological thought that argued that it is necessary to study a person's total experience, not just parts of the mind or behavior, since conscious experience is more than simply the sum of its parts.

The Gestalt school thrived in Germany during the 1920s and 1930s, but psychologists in other countries were not as receptive to this orientation, and its influence faded. This school no longer exists today. Indeed, the behaviorist revolution changed psychology in the United States to such an extent that although influences from these early schools of psychological thought remain, the individual schools do not.

Freud and Psychoanalysis

In the early 1900s, a Viennese neurologist named Sigmund Freud gained worldwide fame by promoting the idea that the mind consists of levels of consciousness. Freud (1900) argued that the part of the mind that we know about—the *conscious*—is only a small segment of mental functioning. A larger *unconscious* also contributes to thought and behavior by provoking slips of the tongue (Freudian slips) and by sending symbolic messages in dreams. In addition, Freud devised *psychoanalysis*, a therapy for people with mental problems. The concept of the unconscious and psychoanalytic treatment provoked great interest and debate among well-educated people of the time.

Although the psychologists of the time were interested in analyzing consciousness, Freud's conceptualization of the unconscious was not compatible with the views of structuralism or functionalism. Indeed, Freud's theory did not allow for analysis of the unconscious, except through psychoanalysis. The Freudian view eventually became influential in psychology, but the inaccessibility of the unconscious presented problems for psychologists who wanted to use a scientific approach, especially the behaviorists.

The Behaviorist Revolution

Structuralism, functionalism, and psychoanalysis focused on the mind, but many psychologists argued that these approaches did not create a science of psychology. The move toward a more objective science of psychology occurred in 1913, when John B. Watson (1878–1958) published a paper in which he contended that the subject matter of psychology should be behavior, rather than the contents of consciousness (Watson, 1913). Watson argued that psychology should focus on describing and measuring only what is observable, either directly or through assessment instruments. This new approach was called *behaviorism.*

Behaviorism ■ The approach to psychology that focuses on describing and measuring only what is observable, either directly or through assessment instruments.

Watson was an upstart—clever, brash, and defiant (Brewer, 1991). According to him, psychologists should study only activities that can be objectively observed and measured; prediction and control should be the goals of psychology. Watson rejected the work of Wundt and most other early psychologists, arguing that the field should abandon the study of consciousness. Behavior was the only proper subject matter of psychology, and only through the study of behavior could psychology become a science.

Watson's influence was profound. After Watson, other American researchers extended and developed behaviorism to such a degree that it became the dominant form of psychology in academia in the United States from the 1920s until the 1950s

(Schultz & Schultz, 2004). Certainly the most widely recognized among those supporting behaviorism was Harvard psychologist B. F. Skinner (1904–1990). In the 1940s, Skinner attempted to explain the causes of behavior by cataloging and describing the relationships among events in the environment (stimuli), a person's or animal's reactions (responses), and the establishing of the learned connection between the two (conditioning).

Skinner may be the most influential psychologist ever trained in the United States, and his views were extreme (Haggbloom et al., 2002). According to Skinner, our environment completely determines what we do—we control our actions about as much as a rock in an avalanche controls its path. It is possible to understand the factors that determine behavior, but that understanding requires an analysis of the effects of the environment. Skinner's behaviorism led the way for thousands of research studies on conditioning and human behavior, which focused on stimuli and responses and the controlling of behavior through learning principles.

The basic learning principles that Skinner developed are among the most prominent influences in psychology. One of the reasons for their importance is that they made it possible for psychology to fit within the definition of a science.

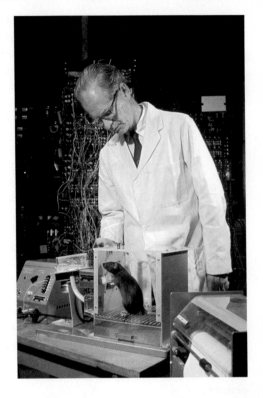

B. F. Skinner promoted the behaviorist position, emphasizing the importance of the environment in determining behavior.

Challenges to Behaviorism

The definition of behaviorism became broader than it was during the 1940s and 1950s as a result of challenges during the 1960s and 1970s. The dissatisfaction with behaviorism came from psychologists who objected to restricting the subject matter of psychology to overt behavior. Some of these psychologists wanted to expand the field so that it encompassed all facets of human potential; others believed that omitting cognitive and mental processes from the subject matter of psychology was to miss the point. Those who wanted to explore human potential were the humanistic psychologists; cognitive psychologists were those who objected to the exclusion of thought processes. Both challenges prompted changes in behaviorism.

Humanistic Psychology

The roots of humanistic psychology can be traced to the Gestalt movement of the 1920s and 1930s, but this approach flourished in the 1960s (Schultz & Schultz, 2004). *Humanistic psychology* was a reaction to behaviorism and its emphasis on the mechanistic nature of behavior. Advocates of humanistic psychology believed that behaviorism had dehumanized psychology, and they argued that psychology should be rehumanized (Clay, 2002). These psychologists concentrated on finding, emphasizing, and studying positive human values. The humanistic movement established its own

Humanistic psychology
■ The psychological perspective that emphasizes positive human values and people's inherent tendency toward personal growth.

journal, the *Journal of Humanistic Psychology*, founded its own association, and created a division within the American Psychological Association (APA).

Abraham Maslow (1908–1970), the spiritual father of humanistic psychology, envisioned a transformation of psychology through the inclusion of humanistic principles. Maslow attempted to combine psychological research with humanistic values, but this mixture was not a complete success (Schultz & Schultz, 2004). Maslow (1970) studied individuals he identified as motivated by *self-actualization*, the ultimate level of psychological development in which the self-actualizing person minimizes ill health, attains a superior perception of reality, feels a strong sense of self-acceptance, and functions fully as a human being. This concept captured popular interest, but Maslow's research was the target of criticism for lacking scientific rigor.

Humanistic psychology exerted a greater influence on therapy than on research. Psychologists such as Carl Rogers (1902–1987) brought humanistic values to the practice of therapy. Rogers's popular client-centered therapy (which we will examine in Chapter 17) emphasizes the empathic role of the therapist and people's inherent tendency toward personal growth.

Cognitive Psychology

Cognitive psychology The psychological perspective that focuses on the mental processes involved in perception, learning, memory, and thinking.

Like humanistic psychology, *cognitive psychology* held that behaviorism was too restrictive in concentrating exclusively on overt behavior. Cognitive psychologists argued that thought and mental processes are the essence of psychology; overlooking these essential elements misses the point of psychology. During the 1960s, this view of psychology began to gain supporters, and many spoke of a "cognitive revolution" (Schultz & Schultz, 2004).

Although important, the changes that the cognitive movement brought to psychology were not really revolutionary because cognitive psychologists retained the emphasis on measuring behavior. However, cognitive psychologists believed that behavior reflects underlying cognitive processes and that studying behavior makes it possible to understand those underlying thought processes. Therefore, cognitive psychologists enlarged the definition of psychology. Their challenge to behaviorism resulted in a change in the basic definition of psychology: Psychology is the science of behavior and mental processes. The addition of the phrase "and mental processes" may seem small, but its effects within psychology have been widespread. Today, many more psychologists have a cognitive orientation than a classic behaviorist orientation. But that change was only part of the developments that have affected psychology during the last 25 years. The trends that have influenced the field have made it more varied and more diverse.

What Trends Currently Shape Psychology?

In the 21st century, psychology will be more diverse than it was in the 20th century, both in terms of the individuals who are psychologists and in terms of the topics of interest to them. One important trend that has influenced psychology has been the increase in the numbers of women and members of various ethnic groups who have become psychologists. Other noteworthy trends are the development of positive psychology, the growth of industrial/organizational psychology, and the application of an evolutionary framework to understanding behavior and mental processes.

The Changing Face of Psychology

Until the 1970s, psychology was a profession made up principally of men, mostly White men. That situation has changed, and women and people of color have become a prominent part of the face of contemporary psychology.

Women in Psychology

Between 1920 and 1975, women received only 22.7% of all doctoral degrees in psychology (Keita, Cameron, & Burrwell, 2003). The first women in psychology received training similar to that of their male colleagues but were much less likely to achieve equivalent professional status (Task Force on Women in Academe, 2000). Women such as Mary Whiton Calkins and Margaret Floyd Washburn were leaders during the early years of psychology. William James, one of the first American psychologists, praised Calkins in 1895 for one of the best PhD examinations that he had ever seen, and Washburn served as president of the American Psychological Association (APA) in 1921. Leta Stetter Hollingworth was an eminent psychologist who made important contributions to the psychology of women, clinical psychology, and educational psychology (particularly the psychology of the highly gifted). Discrimination against women in academia made it difficult for these female psychologists to obtain faculty appointments and to establish careers in the field (Brannon, 2005). Thus, the achievements of these women are footnotes rather than headlines in the history of psychology.

But that situation has changed dramatically. Psychology now attracts, trains, and retains more women than men. Today, women earn 73% of bachelor's degrees and 70% of doctorates in psychology (Kohout & Wicherski, 2003). Seventy-three percent of new PhDs in clinical psychology but only 44% of experimental psychologists are women (Keita et al., 2003). About 35% of full-time faculty members in psychology departments are women (APA Research Office, 2001). In psychology, as in other fields, women are more likely than men to be employed on a part-time basis (Kohout & Wicherski, 2003), which has a negative impact on their career advancement.

Today, research by and about women is prominent in psychology. You will hear the voices of many female researchers throughout this text. Some of the more prominent ones are Judith Wallerstein and Mavis Hetherington, who have studied the impact of divorce on children; Florence Denmark, who has criticized sexist bias in research methods; Judith Rodin, who has done important work on eating and eating disorders; Elizabeth Loftus, who has studied the ability of eyewitnesses to remember accurately; Sandra Scarr, who studies intelligence; Kay Redfield Jamison, a national researcher, author, and advocate for those who suffer from mood disorders; Elizabeth Spelke, who studies infants' thought processes; and Patricia Goldman-Rakic, who studies the neural basis of learning. Women are presidents of national, regional, and local psychological organizations, and their work is prominent in psychological journals. In the APA's 112-year history, only 10 women have been elected president of the association: Mary Whiton Calkins (1905), Margaret Floyd Washburn (1921), Anne Anastasi (1972), Leona E. Tyler (1973), Florence L. Denmark (1980), Janet T. Spence (1984), Bonnie R. Strickland (1987), Dorothy W. Cantor (1996), Norine G. Johnson (2001), and Diane Halpern (2004).

Ethnic Diversity in Psychology

Ethnic minorities do not yet have as strong a presence in psychology as women do. Whites comprise 77% of the membership of the American Psychological Association (APA Research Office, 2001) and about 81% of recent recipients of doctoral degrees in psychology (Bailey, 2004). Despite vigorous recruiting efforts by universities, African Americans receive about 6%, Asian Americans about 4%, Latinos/Latinas about 7%, and Native Americans about 2% of the new doctoral degrees in psychology each year (Bailey, 2004).

Many early African American psychologists faced harsh discrimination when they sought admittance to training programs and tried to pursue careers in psychology. Still, some overcame the odds; they earned doctoral degrees, published scientific research, and made lasting contributions to the field (Guthrie, 2004). Gilbert Haven Jones was the first African American holder of a PhD to teach psychology in the United States. Jones received his training in Germany and taught psychology at several universities in the United States. Albert S. Beckham was a clinician who, in the 1930s, published studies of socioeconomic status and adolescence among ethnic minority groups. Inez Prosser and Howard H. Long are also among the distinguished African American psychologists who published in the 1930s.

Francis C. Sumner, who chaired the psychology department at Howard University, is considered the father of African American psychology. Beginning in the 1920s, Sumner built a program that trained African American psychologists during times when many universities refused to admit African Americans. One of Sumner's students, Kenneth Clark, went on to get a doctorate at Columbia University. Clark became the first African American to serve as president of the APA, achieved national prominence for his work on the harmful effects of segregation, and influenced the U.S. Supreme Court to overturn laws that allowed segregation in schools (Tomes, 2002). The works of Mamie Phipps Clark on self-esteem and racial identification (with her husband, Kenneth Clark) have become classics.

Today, African American Gail Elizabeth Wyatt conducts research in the United States and Jamaica and has been recognized for her distinguished contributions to research, scholarship, and writing in the areas of ethnicity and culture, especially her accounts of female sexuality among African Americans. Norman Anderson, a professor of health and social behavior at Harvard University, developed a career in both research and public health issues through his advocacy for the profession of psychology, his work to educate people about the importance of behavior in maintaining health, and his research on the topic of health disparities for African Americans (Martin, 2002). In 2002, he became the CEO of the APA.

Individuals of Latino/Latina origin also contribute to advances in psychology. Martha Bernal (1932–2002) was the first Latina to earn a PhD in psychology in the United States. She received her degree from Indiana University in 1962. Despite the discrimination she faced in finding a faculty appointment (Vasquez & Lopez, 2002), she established a research laboratory and turned part of her attention to researching and fighting against racism and sexism. Like Bernal, many other Latino/Latina psychologists have focused on issues relevant to the social situations of people of color. Manuel Barrera has done important work in community psychology, especially on social support systems. R. Diaz-Guerrero has examined cultural and personality variables among Latinos/Latinas. Jorge Sanchez conducted exemplary research on the role of education in the achievements of members of different ethnic minority groups and on bias in intelligence testing. Counseling psychologist Melba J. T. Vasquez has been an activist and educator. Psychologist Clarissa Pinkola Estés became the first Mexican American author to make the *New York Times* best-seller list with her 1992 book *Women Who Run with the Wolves: Myths and Stories of the Wild Woman Archetype*. Salvador Minuchin, along with his collaborator Jorge Colapinto, has a highly successful family therapy training program that emphasizes hands-on experience, online supervision, and the use of videotapes.

Diversity strengthens psychology. Research and theory become more complete when they embrace the multiculturality of human beings. On a practical level, the effectiveness of the helping professions is enhanced when practitioners understand their clients. The variety of psychologists' research interests and their wide-ranging ethnic backgrounds are contributing to a greater recognition of diversity—and this recognition is both a strength and a cause for celebration.

Major Perspectives in Psychology

Even though psychologists share the basic belief that psychology is a science, those working in various subfields have differing points of view—different ways of looking at human behavior and mental processes that are referred to as perspectives. These perspectives reflect the development of the field of psychology and continue to shape current psychological study and thought. **Table 1.1** provides a brief summary of these perspectives, but let's examine each one and its current influence.

The Psychoanalytic Perspective

Sigmund Freud's emphasis on the unconscious was only one of this pioneer's contributions to the treatment of emotional problems. Freud believed that sexual energy fuels day-to-day behavior and that childhood experiences influence future adult behaviors. Freud developed techniques to help people explore their unconscious processes in order to deal more effectively with their problems, and the provision of such help in the form of therapy is still prominently associated with psychology.

Freud created the *psychoanalytic approach*—the perspective that assumes that emotional problems are due to anxiety resulting from unresolved conflicts that reside in the unconscious. Psychoanalysis is the therapeutic technique that attempts to resolve these unconscious conflicts. By the 1920s, the United States was emerging

Psychoanalytic [SYE-ko-an-uh-LIT-ick] approach ■ The perspective developed by Freud, which assumes that emotional problems are due to anxiety resulting from unresolved conflicts that reside in the unconscious and treats these problems using the therapeutic technique of psychoanalysis.

Table 1.1

PERSPECTIVES ON PSYCHOLOGICAL ISSUES

Perspective	Main Idea	Main Emphasis or Technique
■ **Psychoanalytic**	Problems are a consequence of anxiety resulting from unresolved conflicts and forces of which a person may be unaware.	Techniques to explore unconscious processes that direct daily behavior
■ **Behaviorist**	Behavior can be predicted and controlled through the principles of learning.	The study of observable behavior focusing on conditioning and learning
■ **Humanistic**	Each human being's experience is unique, and humans are drawn toward becoming better.	Promoting self-actualization, which is the ultimate level of psychological development
■ **Cognitive**	Thoughts form the basis for human behavior.	The importance of thoughts, including attitudes, motivation, emotion, and behavior problems, in day-to-day behaviors
■ **Biopsychology**	The nervous system and heredity affect behavior and mental processes, including emotions, thoughts, and sensory experiences.	Central nervous system problems, brain damage, hormonal changes, neurotransmitters, and genetic abnormalities
■ **Social and Cultural**	Social and cultural context influences a person's behavior, thoughts, and feelings.	How culture and social setting affect psychological issues
■ **Evolutionary**	Over the course of generations, the human brain and behavior have adapted in ways that allow the species to survive.	The specialization, organization, and natural selection of neural structures

from some of the social and sexual strictures of the Victorian era, and the intellectual climate was open to the psychoanalytic approach, with its emphasis on sexuality. Interest in Freud and psychoanalysis spread rapidly, and this therapy became so popular that the image of the psychologist became the therapist rather than the researcher (Hornstein, 1992).

The psychoanalytic perspective emphasizes the role of the unconscious in behavior, the importance of early childhood experiences in forming personality, and the symbolism in dreams as a reflection of the unconscious. Psychologists are not the only ones influenced by this perspective; many people accept these views of human behavior. This perspective furnishes one of the most dominant images of psychology: a patient lying on a couch, talking to a therapist about problems. This accuracy of this image is explored in Chapter 13, which discusses Freud's theory of personality, and in Chapter 17, which describes the therapeutic technique of psychoanalysis.

The Behaviorist Perspective

The behaviorist perspective is based on behaviorism, the school of psychological thought that rejects the study of consciousness and cognitive processes and focuses on describing and measuring observable behavior. This perspective holds that by concentrating on observable behavior, psychology can describe, predict, and even control that behavior. As we've seen, behaviorism exerted a profound influence on psychology, especially in the United States. Indeed, this perspective furnished the image that is widely associated with experimental psychology—a researcher in a white lab coat making rats run through a maze. Today, behaviorists study a wider range of behavior than animal learning, including cognition, decision making, and maladjustment.

The Humanistic Perspective

Stressing individual free choice and a positive view of human nature, humanistic psychology became an influential movement within psychology in the 1960s. Humanistic psychologists see people as inherently good and creative, born with an innate desire to fulfill themselves; they believe that psychoanalytical theorists misread people as fraught with inner conflict and that behaviorists are too narrowly focused on stimulus–response reactions. The humanistic perspective emphasizes positive human values and offers an optimistic view of human behavior.

The humanistic movement had limited influence on academic psychology, but interest in humanistic psychology has recently increased. Citing a renewed emphasis on positive human values in psychology, humanistic psychologists are optimistic about the vitality of their approach and its continued importance within the field (Clay, 2002).

The Cognitive Perspective

Cognitive psychology is the perspective that focuses on the mental processes and activities involved in perception, learning, memory, and thinking. This perspective arose during the 1960s and 1970s as a challenge to behaviorism. The cognitive perspective asserts that ideas and thoughts are the basis for human behavior. Psychologists who adopt the cognitive perspective may be clinicians who work with troubled clients to help them achieve more realistic ideas about the world and then change their thoughts and behavior to adjust more effectively. For example, a cognitively oriented clinician might work to help a client realize that her distorted thoughts about her own importance are interfering with her ability to get along with coworkers. Psychologists who take the cognitive perspective may also be researchers who study intelligence, memory, perception, and other mental processes.

The Biopsychology Perspective

Researchers are increasingly turning to biology to explain behavior, acknowledging that biology and behavior interact in important ways. The *biopsychology perspective,* also referred to as the *neuroscience perspective*, examines how biological factors affect mental processes and behavior and how behavior can change brain function and structure. The biopsychology perspective often focuses on the molecular and cellular levels of the nervous system, for example, within the visual, auditory, or motor areas of the brain. Researchers with a biological perspective study behavior related to genetic abnormalities, central nervous system problems, brain damage, and hormonal changes.

Biopsychology perspective ■ The psychological perspective that examines how biological factors affect mental processes and behavior and how behavior can change brain function and structure; also known as the neuroscience perspective.

The U.S. Congress declared the years from 1990 to 2000 the Decade of the Brain because of technological developments that transformed the study of the brain (Cacioppo et al., 2003). Neuroscience researchers once relied on performing autopsies on humans or neurosurgery on nonhuman animals to understand the brain's structure and function. The development of brain-imaging technology allowed these researchers to examine living, functioning human brains, and this capability has made the biopsychology perspective even more prominent. Each day brings groundbreaking biopsychological research results.

The biopsychology perspective is especially important in studies of sensation and perception, memory, and many types of behavior problems. This approach has become prominent in research on psychological disorders such as schizophrenia, which has a genetic component, and alcoholism, which may also have biological underpinnings. Because the biopsychology perspective has attained such a prominent position in psychology, we will revisit it many times in later chapters.

The Social and Cultural Perspective

Today, most psychologists realize that complex relationships exist among the factors that affect both behavior and mental processes. Recognizing and paying attention to social and cultural factors allow researchers and practitioners to view psychological problems in new ways. For example, consider depression, the disabling psychological disorder that affects at least 10% of men and women in the United States at some time in their lives (American Psychiatric Association, 2000; Chapter 16 discusses depression at length). From a biological perspective, depression is related to changes in brain chemistry. From a behavioral point of view, people become sad and depressed as a result of faulty reward systems in their environment. From a psychoanalytic perspective, people become depressed because their early childhood experiences caused them to be unable to deal with negative events in their lives. From a cognitive perspective, depression is fostered by the interpretations (thoughts) an individual adopts about a situation. A psychologist sensitive to social and cultural factors recognizes the complex nature of depression, and how behaviors associated with depression occur in a social context and in response to social circumstances. For example, people experience depression after personal loss; the death of friends or family members is associated with depressed mood. Furthermore, women are typically expected and allowed to express sadness, whereas the male gender role restricts men from showing this emotion (Brannon, 2005). The social and cultural perspective takes such circumstances into account when considering depression.

Psychology in the early 21st century is diverse, in terms of both the perspectives it encompasses and the people it involves. The psychoanalytic perspective is no longer a major point of view in psychology, but its influence continues. The behaviorist orientation continues as a strong force in psychology; regardless of their research interests, many psychologists classify themselves as behaviorists. Cognitive psychology is another perspective that many psychologists identify as their own. The biopsychology perspective has grown more prominent and influential in recent years, and the social and cultural perspective also continues to exert widespread influence. A growing number of psychologists are attempting to combine perspectives.

In addition to having a number of perspectives, the field of psychology today is characterized by several developing trends.

Current Trends in Psychology

Psychology continues to grow and change, and several notable trends have developed within the past few years. These trends have their roots in psychology's past but also represent the continuing evolution of the field's theory and application.

Positive Psychology

The emphasis on positive human values that was the basis of the humanistic movement in psychology can be traced to Louis Terman's study of gifted children, which began in the 1920s (Terman, 1939). The emphasis on treating mental health and personal problems pushed these positive values aside, but they reappeared during the 1990s in the form of *positive psychology*. According to Seligman and Csikszentmihalyi (2000), "Psychology is not just the study of pathology, weakness, and damage; it is also the study of strength and virtue" (p. 7). This approach emphasizes the positive values of optimism, joy, well-being, and psychological health, but unlike the humanistic movement, positive psychology has a sound research base.

Proponents of positive psychology study how people develop wisdom (Sternberg, 2002), how optimism promotes health and longer life (Danner, Snowdon, & Friesen, 2001), and how people experience well-being (Diener, Lucas, & Oishi, 2003) and its effect on their lives (Ryan & Deci, 2001). Another goal of positive psychology is to find ways to assess attitudes and behaviors related to individuals' self-concept, self-worth, future orientation, and satisfaction with life (Bolt, 2003). This emphasis on research and assessment distinguishes positive psychology from the humanistic movement and promises that its contributions will become integrated into psychology, much more so than those of the humanistic movement.

Positive psychology ■ The subfield of psychology that combines an emphasis on positive human values such as optimism and well-being with an emphasis on research and assessment.

Industrial/Organizational Psychology

The subfield of *industrial/organizational (I/O) psychology* studies how individual behavior is affected by the work environment, by coworkers, and by organizational practices. The development of this trend in psychology can be traced back to the functionalist movement and its emphasis on individual differences (Schultz & Schultz, 2004). The use of psychological knowledge in the selection of

Industrial/organizational (I/O) psychology ■ The subfield of psychology that studies how individual behavior is affected by the work environment, by coworkers, and by organizational practices.

employees was one of the first applications of psychology to a practical problem, resulting in the development of *industrial psychology*. The integration of situational and social factors into the study of the workplace resulted in an expansion of the field to include *organizational psychology*.

Industrial/organizational psychology has been a prominent part of psychology since the 1940s, but it experienced a dramatic increase in programs and enrollment during the 1990s (Murray, 2002b). Much of this growth has been in programs granting master's degrees, but doctoral programs in I/O psychology have also expanded.

Part of the appeal of this subfield is, of course, its applied nature, but another asset is its good record in employment for students. Private businesses are the largest single type of employer for students who receive master's degrees in I/O psychology, but many also obtain employment in state and local governments and in colleges and universities (Murray, 2002b). Psychologists with training in this specialty do human resources management and personnel work in many companies, and the presence of good work environments is a positive factor for any city or region's workforce. Thus, the boom in I/O psychology is a promising trend not only for the employment of psychologists but also for businesses.

Evolutionary Psychology

Evolutionary psychology
■ The psychological perspective that seeks to explain and predict behaviors by analyzing how the human brain developed over time and how that evolutionary history affects human brain functions and behaviors today.

The work of Charles Darwin forms the basis for today's ***evolutionary psychology***. Darwin was the 19th-century naturalist who proposed that adaptation and survival of the fittest are mechanisms that produce the evolution of species, a theory that was influential for the functionalist movement in early psychology. Evolutionary psychology seeks to explain and predict behaviors by analyzing how the human brain developed over hundreds of thousands of years and how that evolutionary history affects human brain functions and behaviors today. Evolutionary psychology assumes that the behavioral tendencies that help organisms adapt, be fit, and survive are the ones that will be passed on to successive generations, because well-adapted, fit individuals have a greater chance of reproducing.

Evolutionary psychologists assume that the brain is a physical system whose operation is governed by biochemical processes, which can be modified (Pinker, 1997). They further assume that natural selection and evolutionary history have influenced how the brain currently operates. That is, the history of a species, over millennia, modifies the structure of the brains of its members. The design of the brain and its functioning have been shaped by previous experiences—not only those in an individual's lifetime, but also those of the species.

Evolutionary psychologists contend that many human mental abilities have evolved slowly over time, creating a human brain with specific abilities, such as the ability to learn and to acquire language (Caporael, 2001). Other common human behaviors that interest evolutionary psychologists include expression of humor and emotions, parenting behaviors, social interactions, and sex and mating behaviors. From an evolutionary perspective, passing on one's genes is the underlying motivation for many human behaviors.

For example, evolutionary psychologists hypothesize that mate-selection strategies lead to large differences between women's and men's behaviors (Buss, 2004). This view proposes that men seek out women who will be fertile and bear them children, and women seek out men who will be good providers, able to feed and shelter them and their children. This hypothesis is drawn from differences in reproductive biology: Women have few chances for reproduction because they produce few ova, but men have many opportunities because they produce millions of sperm. Evolutionary psychologists argue that these biological differences have implications for behavior, producing women who are selective in choosing sex partners and men who want to have sex with many women. These different strategies maximize the reproductive possibilities for both men and women but may also result in conflict between them. Evolutionary psychologists argue that this conflict is a side effect of our evolutionary heritage.

Who Are These People Called Psychologists?

Sometimes people mistakenly assume that all psychologists assist those experiencing personal problems or mental disorders, such as schizophrenia and severe depression. Actually, there is great variety in what psychologists do. Psychologists try not only to understand how people behave but also to help them lead happier, healthier, more productive lives. All psychologists consider research and theory to be the cornerstones of their efforts, but they work in different settings with different objectives (Kohout & Wicherski, 2003). Some psychologists have private practices or work in clinics or hospitals, testing patients and providing therapy, much like the popular image of their role. Other psychologists do research on a wide array of topics, such as social behavior, learning, memory, motivation, child development, and biopsychology. Many of these psychologists are employed in colleges or universities, where they conduct research and teach.

Types of Mental Health Practitioners

Psychologists, then, are professionals who study behavior and mental processes and use behavioral principles in scientific research or in applied settings. Most psychologists have an advanced degree, usually a PhD (doctor of philosophy). Many psychologists also train for an additional year or two in a specialized area such as mental health, behavioral medicine, or child development before they begin working in a university or clinical setting (Kohout & Wicherski, 2003).

People are often unsure about the differences among psychologists, psychiatrists, and psychoanalysts. All are mental health practitioners who help people with serious emotional and behavioral problems, but members of each profession tend to take a different perspective regarding the basis for behavior problems and the best approach for treating them. In addition, each profession requires different training. *Clinical psychologists* provide diagnosis and treatment of emotional and behavioral problems. These psychologists usually have a PhD in psychology and work in hospitals, clinics, or private practices. They typically hold a psychosocial view, believing that problems stem from emotional and social sources. *Counseling psychologists* also work with people who have emotional or behavioral problems. When counseling psychology began, these psychologists worked at helping people handle career planning and marriage, family, or parenting problems. In recent years,

Psychologist ■
Professional who studies behavior and mental processes and uses behavioral principles in scientific research or in an applied setting.

Clinical psychologist ■
Mental health practitioner who provides diagnosis and treatment of emotional and behavioral problems in hospitals, clinics, or private practices.

Counseling psychologist ■ Mental health practitioner who assists people who have emotional or behavioral problems, through the use of testing, psychotherapy, and other therapies; this profession is very similar to clinical psychology.

clinical psychology and counseling psychology have become more similar. Now, counseling psychologists use psychotherapy and other therapies as well as administering psychological tests. According to many practitioners and researchers, counseling and clinical psychology are converging (Brems & Johnson, 1997).

In contrast, *psychiatrists* are physicians (holding MD degrees) who have chosen to specialize in the treatment of mental or emotional disorders. Patients who see psychiatrists may have physical as well as emotional problems. As physicians, psychiatrists can prescribe medications and admit patients for hospitalization. The APA endorses the development of curricula to prepare psychologists to prescribe medications as well.

Psychiatrist ■ Physician (medical doctor) specializing in the treatment of mental or emotional disorders.

Clinical psychologists generally have more extensive training than psychiatrists do in research, assessment, and psychological treatment of emotional problems. Because their graduate training is within psychology rather than in general medicine, they have a nonmedical perspective that encourages them to examine social and interpersonal variables more than psychiatrists usually do. Psychiatrists are physicians and thus use a medical approach, which often involves making assumptions about behavior—for example, that abnormal behavior is like a disease—that psychologists do not make. Clinical psychologists and psychiatrists often see a similar mix of clients and often work together as part of a mental health team. Most clinical psychologists and psychiatrists support collaborative efforts. However, disagreements can arise because of their different points of view.

Psychoanalysts are the reason for the association of psychology, Freud, and couches. Ironically, most psychoanalysts are not psychologists (and neither was Freud). Instead, psychoanalysts are usually psychiatrists. In addition to medical school, they have training in the technique of psychoanalysis, which Freud developed as a way to help people understand and resolve emotional problems. This treatment involves the analysis of unconscious motivation and dreams, using the assumption that current life problems can be traced to the unconscious and to childhood experiences. To resolve these problems, patients must access unconscious conflicts and bring them to consciousness, which can be accomplished by lying on a couch and talking about one's life and problems. Strict Freudian psychoanalysis requires a course of daily therapy sessions, and a patient's treatment may last several years. Today, psychoanalytic institutes accept trainees who are not physicians, but the majority of psychoanalysts are medical doctors rather than psychologists.

Psychoanalyst ■ Mental health practitioner, generally a psychiatrist, who has studied the technique of psychoanalysis and uses it in treating people with mental or emotional problems.

As you may have gathered from these descriptions, the three kinds of practitioners may treat similar clients. However, their training and assumptions often vary, resulting in differences in their choice of treatment. Although the image of psychology as treatment is the most prominent one, psychology is much more.

What Psychologists Do

Psychologists work in a variety of settings, and their jobs include activities other than those that people associate with the role of therapist. Clinical and counseling psychologists provide services to people by using behavioral principles to conduct therapy, testing, and counseling. They try to help people solve problems and promote psychological and physical well-being. This image is what most people associate with the profession of psychology, but psychologists don't just help people with problems. In addition, school and community psychologists provide services such as career counseling and assistance with community projects. The jobs of psychologists also include providing services to well-adjusted people, helping individuals improve their interpersonal skills, and providing them with knowledge about self-help techniques. Working with professional athletes and musicians to improve their public performances is another service that some psychologists provide.

Psychologists also conduct research. Experimental psychologists try to identify and understand the basic elements of behavior and mental processes, whereas applied psychologists use research findings to solve practical problems. These two approaches share a set of research techniques for conducting their investigations, but their emphasis and content areas vary. Experimental psychologists focus on basic research issues such as how people learn, whereas applied psychologists orient their research toward the provision of practical help in specific situations, such as managing test anxiety to improve test performance. Most of the research that experimental psychologists conduct focuses on areas unrelated to mental disorders or problem behavior.

Table 1.2 shows a number of subfields of psychology that focus on providing human services or doing experimental or applied research.

Making Psychology a Career

As we saw at the beginning of this chapter, psychology is a field that encompasses both practice and research. Many psychologists help others directly through the delivery of mental health services. But an equal number of psychologists seek to generate knowledge, apply that knowledge, or do both; they focus on research and discovery. Psychologists ask research questions that ultimately inform practice.

Like many students, when I (L.L.) was first attracted to psychology as a career, it was because I had a desire to help others. Psychology is an optimistic profession—and psychologists unabashedly admit to this bias. Psychologists generally adopt the view that human beings can change and that trying to feel, do, or be better is productive. My goal was just that—to help people achieve more in life—and so psychology and I were a match.

When I (L.B.) was first attracted to psychology, I was interested in understanding people's thought processes. I was fascinated with designing experiments and collecting and analyzing data. Experimental psychologists are struck by the differences among people, by how they behave differently even in similar situations. I wanted to understand human behavior—and so psychology and I were also a match.

Psychology attracts many college students who like the idea of understanding human behavior and helping others. The causes and implications of behavior intrigue these students; they realize that psychology is part of the fabric of daily life. After business administration, psychology is the second most popular undergraduate major in the United States—every year, about 73,000 college graduates are psychology majors (Murray, 2002a). Today's psychology students are increasingly female and ethnically diverse; they are interested in a variety of subfields within psychology. Those who earn a bachelor's degree often go on to graduate school, but many find

Table 1.2

SUBFIELDS OF PSYCHOLOGY AND THEIR FOCUS

Subfield	Focus
■ **Human Services**	
Behavioral medicine	Helping people with physical illness cope with their condition and recover more quickly (see Chapter 15)
Clinical or counseling psychology	Helping people with behavior problems (see Chapter 17)
Community psychology	Helping communities develop resources and social support to promote health
School psychology	Administering and interpreting tests; developing communication among teachers, students, parents, and administrators
■ **Experimental Research**	
Biopsychology	Studies the relationship between nervous system and behavior (see Chapter 3)
Cognitive psychology	Studies thought processes, especially learning, memory, problem solving, and perception (see Chapter 10)
Developmental psychology	Studies the emotional, physical, and cognitive changes that occur through the lifespan (see Chapters 4 and 5)
Personality psychology	Studies traits and characteristics the underlie personality (see Chapter 13)
Social psychology	Studies how people interact, how groups affect individuals, how people form and change attitudes (see Chapter 14)
■ **Applied Research**	
Engineering psychology	Studies and improves the person–machine interface
Educational psychology	Studies and improves classroom learning and school performance
Forensic psychology	Consults with professionals in the legal system, including attorneys, court, and correctional system (see Chapter 18)
Health psychology	Studies and improves health-related behaviors (see Chapter 15)
Sport psychology	Studies psychological factors in athletic performance and helps prepare athletes for competition (see Chapter 18)
Industrial/organizational psychology	Studies and consults with business to improve personnel selection, employee motivation, work behavior, and management-labor relation; performs program evaluation (see Chapter 18)

jobs in business and teaching. The employment news is even better for students who go on to graduate school: Almost all of the approximately 3,900 recipients of a doctoral degree in psychology each year find jobs related to their training (Kohout & Wicherski, 2003). If you are considering the field of psychology, you'll be glad to hear that unemployment among psychologists is low and likely to remain so.

Training, of course, is the key to employment. For both research psychologists and clinical and counseling psychologists, obtaining a doctoral degree from an accredited university opens the door to many job opportunities. Completing an internship and obtaining licensure are important steps for clinical and counseling psychologists seeking employment in private practice, hospitals, or clinic settings. Some states grant credentials to psychologists with master's degrees, allowing them to provide services in the private and public sectors (MacKain et al., 2002). In those states that allow only psychologists with doctoral degrees to be licensed, a person with a master's or bachelor's degree may work in hospitals, clinics, or agencies under the supervision of a licensed psychologist. The salaries of those with master's degrees in psychology are comparable to those of professionals with master's degrees in similar fields but lower than those of individuals with doctoral degrees (Singleton, Tate, & Randall, 2003). The opportunities for research careers are quite limited for those with master's or bachelor's degrees.

The percentage varies slightly from year to year, but a recent survey showed that 36% of the members of the APA work in delivering human services (Singleton et al., 2003). About 21% are clinical psychologists, and another 7% are counseling psychologists who work in clinics, community mental health centers, health maintenance organizations, veterans' hospitals, public hospitals, and public and private mental health hospitals (see **Figure 1.1**). The remainder of psychologists delivering human services are private practitioners who maintain offices and work in schools,

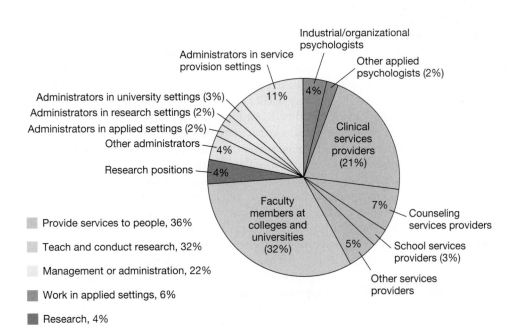

Figure 1.1
What Psychologists Do
Of the members of the American Psychological Association who work in the field of psychology, many are involved in the delivery of human services—as clinical, counseling, and school psychologists and as other types of human services providers. The rest focus on research, teaching, and applications in university settings, government, and business. (Source: Singleton, Tate, & Randall, 2003)

universities, businesses, and numerous other public and private settings. Most psychologists employed by hospitals spend their time in the direct delivery of human services, including individual and group therapy.

About 32% of the APA's members who are employed full-time work in colleges or universities, most of them as faculty members who combine teaching with conducting research (Singleton et al., 2003). Only about 4% work in facilities devoted exclusively to research. Business, industry, and other applied settings employ 6% of psychologists, and 22% do administrative work in government, business, university, or health care settings.

How Should You Use This Textbook?

You can use this textbook to learn about psychology and about yourself. To make the most of your psychology course, try to understand the abstract, research-based material and integrate it with the practical applications. To help you integrate the abstract and the practical, we have identified four themes within psychology that will be revisited repeatedly throughout this book. These themes provide a way to understand how the many content areas in psychology relate to each other and fit together.

Four Recurring Themes in Psychology

The first of the four key organizing themes involves the relationship between the brain and behavior. The structure and function of the brain, and the rest of the nervous system, have a huge impact on personality, communication, physical health, emotions, and many other areas of life. Current studies of the brain focus on how the brain changes over the life span, how drugs affect it (both positively and negatively), and what specific brain structures are involved in particular behaviors and abilities. Because the brain is so central to human thought and behavior, it has been (and continues to be) a "hot" topic in psychology.

The interaction of nature and nurture is the second theme that we will return to again and again. Nature (our biological and genetic composition) and nurture (the many elements of the environment we live in) both have important roles in shaping human thought and behavior. A lively debate concerning which is more influential, and how the two factors work together, has a long history in psychology, and continues today. This book will focus on how nature and nurture interact to affect intelligence, sexual behavior, and other areas, presenting the latest theories and research.

The third theme we will take into account as we study psychology is human diversity. Gender, ethnicity, social class, sexual orientation, age, religion, and other influences play important roles in shaping people's ideas and actions. Not too long ago, many psychologists focused their studies only on people of European or European American descent, believing that they set the norm for humanity. Fortunately, this bias is no longer prevalent. Today, psychologists try to understand how cultural context can affect areas such as child development, relationships, and personality. This book will often feature cross-cultural research and the experiences of diverse groups of people.

The final recurring theme emphasizes the action-oriented quality of research and practice in psychology. Psychologists generate knowledge and ideas, and then they put them to use. How can they help people improve their learning and memory to become better students? How can they help people achieve better social adjustment or manage relationships more successfully? Questions like these will be addressed in this book.

Summary and Review

HOW ACCURATE IS THE IMAGE OF PSYCHOLOGY?

What are some popular images of psychologists?

Popular images of psychologists include the mind reader, the Freudian analyst, and the white-coated lab researcher. Although many people have these inaccurate perceptions of psychologists, the field of psychology is much more varied than these limited images suggest. p. 2

What is the definition of psychology?

Psychology is defined as the science of behavior and mental processes. Psychologists observe many aspects of human behavior—overt actions, social interactions, emotional reactions, and physiological reactions. All of these actions are directly observable, but measuring instruments may be required for observation of physiological reactions such as heart rate and brain activity. From their observations of behavior, psychologists make inferences about mental processes. p. 3

HOW DID PSYCHOLOGY BEGIN?

What were the early traditions in psychology?

Psychology became a field of study separate from philosophy in the late 1800s. The early school of thought called *structuralism* focused on the elements of conscious experience and used the technique of *introspection*. Another early school, *functionalism*, emphasized how the mind works. *Gestalt psychology*, in contrast to structuralism, focused on perceptual frameworks and suggested that conscious experience is more than simply the sum of its individual parts. Freudian psychoanalysis also considered consciousness but emphasized the unconscious as a source of emotional problems. pp. 3–6

How did the school of behaviorism change psychology?

Behaviorism changed the definition of psychology to the science of behavior. This school became the dominant one in the United States and persists as an important force in psychology today, despite challenges from the humanist and cognitive movements. pp. 6–7

What movements challenged behaviorism?

Humanistic psychology and *cognitive psychology* challenged behaviorism. Cognitive psychologists broadened the definition of psychology by adding mental processes. pp. 7–8

WHAT TRENDS CURRENTLY SHAPE PSYCHOLOGY?

In recent years, more women have graduate training and careers in psychology, but African Americans and Latinos/Latinas remain underrepresented in the field. Recognizing the diversity among people is one of psychology's current strengths. pp. 8–11

Psychologists vary in their perspectives. The *psychoanalytic approach* developed by Freud assumed that psychological maladjustment is a consequence of anxiety resulting from unresolved conflicts and forces of which a person may be unaware. The behaviorist perspective holds that the proper subject of psychological study is observable behavior. Humanistic psychology arose in response to the psychoanalytic and behavioral views and stresses free will and self-actualization. Cognitive psychology focuses on perception, memory, learning, and thinking and asserts that human beings engage in both worthwhile and maladjusted behaviors because of their ideas and thoughts. The *biopsychology perspective* examines how biological factors affect mental processes and behavior and how behavior can change brain function and structure. The social and cultural perspective acknowledges that complex cultural and social factors affect behavior and mental processes. pp. 11–15

Current trends in psychology include the development of *positive psychology*, which combines the emphasis on positive human values that arose within humanistic psychology with research and assessment. The growth of the subfield *industrial/organizational (I/O) psychology* is another recent trend, as is the influence of *evolutionary psychology*, which integrates evolutionary theory into the explanation of human behaviors. pp. 15–17

WHO ARE THESE PEOPLE CALLED PSYCHOLOGISTS?

What are the differences among the various types of professionals in psychology?

Psychologists are professionals who study behavior and mental processes and use behavioral principles in scientific research or in applied settings. Most psychologists have an advanced degree, usually a PhD. *Clinical psychologists* provide services to people with emotional or behavioral problems; *counseling psychologists* provide similar services. A psychiatrist is a physician who specializes in the treatment of mental or emotional disorders. *Psychoanalysts* are usually *psychiatrists;* they have training in the use of the Freudian technique of psychoanalysis to help people with emotional problems. pp. 17–18

What are the differences among human services psychologists, applied researchers, and experimental psychologists?

Human services psychologists focus on helping individuals solve problems and on promoting their well-being. Applied researchers use research to solve practical problems. Experimental psychologists usually focus on teaching and basic research. p. 20

In what fields are psychologists likely to be employed?

About 36% of psychologists who are members of the APA work as human services providers in clinical, counseling, and school psychology. About 32% of the APA members work in colleges or universities, doing research and teaching. p. 21

HOW SHOULD YOU USE THIS TEXTBOOK?

What four themes can help integrate the study of psychology?

Four themes that recur in this textbook and help integrate the study of psychology are as follows: (1) Knowledge of the brain and its relationship to behavior are central to understanding psychology. (2) Human behavior results from a complex interaction of biological heritage and experience in the environment. (3) Behavior occurs within a cultural context, and diversity is an important part of psychology. (4) Psychology is an active, action-oriented discipline of research and practice. pp. 22–23

CHAPTER 2

The Science of Psychology

What Makes Psychology
a Science? 26
    Three Principles of Scientific Endeavor
    The Scientific Method in Psychology

What Research Methods Do
Psychologists Use? 32
    The Experimental Method
    Descriptive Research Methods

How Do Psychologists Evaluate Their
Research Findings? 40
    Using Statistics to Evaluate Research
    Avoiding Bias in the Research Process

What Ethical Principles Guide
Psychology Research? 51

Summary and Review 52

What Makes Psychology a Science?

Psychologists use scientific principles, methods, and procedures to develop an organized body of knowledge and to predict how people will behave. Psychologists often think of themselves as detectives, sifting through data and theories in an orderly way to uncover the causes of behavior (Smith & Davis, 2003). When psychologists conduct research, they follow a series of steps that define science. Those who follow these steps are considered to be "doing science"; those who do not, are not (McCain & Segal, 1988). Psychology is considered a social and behavioral science because it deals with both human behavior (as the behaviorists insist) and mental processes (as the cognitive psychologists insist). Overt behaviors include a range of actions: walking and gesturing, social interactions such as talking with someone, and emotional responses such as laughing. These behaviors are called overt because they are directly observable. Certain physiological responses, such as heart rate and patterns of brain activity, must be measured with instruments, which make these responses observable.

Psychologists place so much emphasis on behavior that they have declared the years from 2000 to 2010 the Decade of Behavior (McCarty, 1998). Through one of their national organizations, the American Psychological Association (APA), and with the support of more than a dozen other organizations, psychologists launched an initiative to focus attention on how the behavioral and social sciences can help address many of society's daunting challenges. Psychologists believe that the application of behavioral principles can achieve the goals of the Decade of Behavior—promoting a healthier, safer, better educated, more prosperous, and more democratic nation. Closely related to these goals are educating people to think critically, training workers to be more efficient and productive, and sensitizing people to the scope and impact of diversity. Achieving these goals will require the application of an extensive knowledge base, which psychologists have built through scientific research.

Like other modern sciences, psychology is based on two premises—empiricism and theory development. According to the premise of *empiricism,* knowledge must be acquired through careful observation rather than from logic or intuition. After gathering and studying data, psychologists are able to formulate theories. A psychological *theory* is a collection of interrelated ideas and observations that together describe, explain, and predict behavior or mental processes. Empirical observation leads to theories; thus, empirical data and theories are basic to the science of psychology.

Empiricism ▪ The idea that knowledge should be acquired through careful observation.

Theory ▪ A collection of interrelated ideas and observations that together describe, explain, and predict behavior or mental processes.

Three Principles of Scientific Endeavor

Psychology's commitment to empiricism requires researchers to follow three principles of scientific endeavor (see **Figure 2.1**). Careful observation requires setting aside

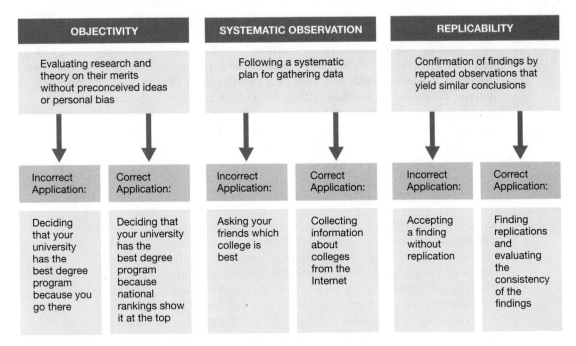

Figure 2.1
Three Principles of Scientific Endeavor

personal feelings and biases, gathering information systematically, and attempting to replicate results when studying behavior and mental processes. By following these basic principles of objectivity, systematic observation, and replicability and by maintaining a healthy skepticism, psychologists succeed as scientific researchers. These principles can also be helpful to people who are not scientists, allowing them to be critical thinkers in daily life.

Objectivity

For psychologists, objectivity means evaluating research and theory on their merits, without preconceived ideas and without allowing personal bias to affect evaluations. By becoming aware of and putting aside personal bias, researchers are better able to make objective observations and fair evaluations. Like everyone else, scientists are people, who have feelings and convictions and who live in particular social contexts. Setting aside personal biases is very difficult for anyone, but when researchers bring their biases into their research, they fail to be good scientists.

Although Alicia was trying to find a school that was right for her, she did have a bias in favor of one university because a friend of hers attended it. This bias caused her to examine this school more closely than others and to overlook some of its disadvantages. Her bias affected her evaluation of schools, just as researchers' biases can affect their results.

Unfortunately, the history of psychology (and other sciences) is filled with instances of bias. For example, during the 19th century, the intelligence of people of African descent was assumed to be lower than that of people of European backgrounds. This prejudiced view led some researchers to faulty conclusions. For example, a neurologist named Morton claimed to have found that people of African descent had smaller brains and were thus less intelligent than those of European descent (Gould, 1996; Guthrie, 2004). That claim was wrong; brain size does not vary with ethnic background. Morton saw what he expected to see rather than what his data showed. His research was contaminated because he failed to be objective, and his results were used to perpetuate racism and discrimination against people of African descent.

Systematic Observation

To do scientific research, one must be systematic—that is, one must make a plan for gathering data. People who gather information without a systematic plan are observing casually rather than collecting data scientifically. For example, Keisha formulated a systematic plan to gather information about colleges. In looking for the same information about each school so that she would be able to make direct comparisons, she was systematic. Alicia was not systematic in her approach to gathering information about colleges, and that error led to her main problem—she failed to collect important information that she needed to make her decision. A systematic method of collecting data is essential to good science, and many such methods exist. We discuss some of these later in this chapter.

Replicability

One needn't be a scientific researcher to realize that although life is full of incredible events, a one-time happening is not often an adequate basis for a scientific finding. A researcher has to be able to confirm findings through repeated observations, all of which lead to similar conclusions. In addition, replicability is not restricted to one researcher; when other researchers follow the same procedures, their findings must be similar to the original findings. This type of reliability gives scientists confidence in the accuracy of their results.

However, scientists also maintain an attitude of healthy skepticism, even about carefully conducted research with replicable results. That skepticism is another important part of the process of doing science. A cautious view of data, hypotheses, and theory until results are repeated, verified, and established over time—this healthy skepticism applies to all phases of scientific inquiry.

The Scientific Method in Psychology

As psychologists conduct research on behavior and mental processes, they use a method that is common to all sciences. The *scientific method* is the technique used in psychology to discover knowledge about human behavior and mental processes; it involves stating the problem, developing a hypothesis, designing a study, collecting and analyzing data, and drawing conclusions and reporting results. Let's consider these five basic steps of the scientific method as an overview of how psychologists (and other scientists) do their work. The steps are summarized in **Figure 2.2**.

Scientific method ■ The technique used in psychology and other sciences to discover knowledge about human behavior and mental processes.

State the Problem

Psychologists must first ask questions that can be answered, that is, questions that are stated in a way that allows investigation. The research process in psychology typically begins with a question that the researcher finds personally interesting; indeed, curiosity is a basic motivation for most researchers. The researcher must then narrow the question so that it is specific and defined in a clear way. For instance, if you ask a question such as "How do people learn?" you will make little headway toward an answer because this question is too broad and general. By contrast, a question such as "Does the timing of study sessions influence learning and memory?" or "Is repetition or analysis more effective in forming memories?" can be investigated. For prospective college students such as Keisha and Alicia, the question "What is the best college?" is too broad, but "Does this college have a premed program with a high acceptance rate to medical schools?" is a question that can be answered.

Develop a Hypothesis

In the second step of the scientific method, psychologists make an educated guess about the answer to the question they've posed. Such a formulation is called a *hypothesis*—a tentative statement or idea expressing a relationship between events or variables that is to be evaluated in a research study. A hypothesis might state that study sessions spaced over time will be more effective for learning than one long study session.

Hypothesis ■ A tentative statement or idea expressing a relationship between events or variables that is to be evaluated in a research study.

Figure 2.2
The Scientific
Method

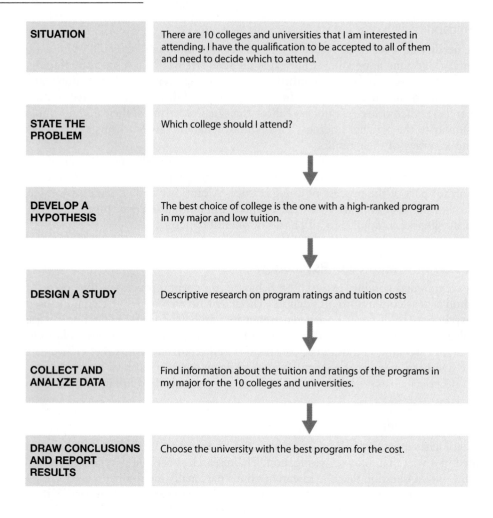

| SITUATION | There are 10 colleges and universities that I am interested in attending. I have the qualification to be accepted to all of them and need to decide which to attend. |

| STATE THE PROBLEM | Which college should I attend? |

| DEVELOP A HYPOTHESIS | The best choice of college is the one with a high-ranked program in my major and low tuition. |

| DESIGN A STUDY | Descriptive research on program ratings and tuition costs |

| COLLECT AND ANALYZE DATA | Find information about the tuition and ratings of the programs in my major for the 10 colleges and universities. |

| DRAW CONCLUSIONS AND REPORT RESULTS | Choose the university with the best program for the cost. |

Most often, a hypothesis emerges from a theory that psychologists have developed based on their current knowledge and past research. As previously defined, a theory is a collection of interrelated ideas and information that describes, explains, and predicts behavior or mental processes. For example, theories of learning address the effectiveness of practice spaced over time compared to practice massed into one session. To be useful, a theory must organize data so that the data make sense, and it must suggest testable predictions (hypotheses) that can be checked. Such testing usually occurs within the context of a well-designed research study.

Design a Study

Next, researchers choose the approach they will use to test the hypothesis. They identify key variables and then choose a suitable method for investigating them. Researchers must specify the variables they wish to investigate and decide how to measure these variables. Choosing a research design involves matching the topic of study and the hypothesis to the most appropriate method of investigation so that the results allow researchers to answer the question that prompted the study.

In investigating study strategies, for example, researchers must consider how they want to define and measure learning. Should they examine the process of studying and its relationship to learning or concentrate on the retention of the material studied? Researchers must decide how they want to define learning, and they must also consider whether they want to conduct the study in a natural context or in a more controlled laboratory setting. Another decision involves selecting participants—deciding how many will be required and who they will be. Thus, the process of designing a study includes many important decisions. Similarly, the process of selecting a college requires consideration of many variables, such as availability of financial aid and housing, cost of tuition, quality of departments and programs, possibilities for part-time jobs, opportunities for social activities, and many other variables. Alicia did not specify which variables were important to her before she started collecting data on schools, so she did not have the information she needed to make a decision.

Collect and Analyze Data

After researchers have specified the key variables, selected the participants, and chosen a design, they conduct the study, hoping it will yield interpretable, meaningful results. Researchers must choose the techniques for data collection carefully so as not to bias the results in one way or another. They must also organize, code, and analyze the data they collect in a way that allows them to know if the results really do support their hypothesis.

When a researcher has gathered 10,000 observations on 300 participants, it may be quite challenging to organize all that information. Psychologists usually use statistical methods to help summarize and condense the data they have collected. In addition, psychologists use statistics to help them understand the meaning of the data.

Data analysis was Keisha's problem in selecting a college. Because she had defined her variables and collected data systematically, she had the information she needed to make a good decision. However, she was unable to interpret her data because she felt overwhelmed by the amount of information she had. Some knowledge of statistical analysis would have helped her, and we will offer some suggestions for Keisha when we examine specific statistical techniques.

Draw Conclusions and Report Results

After the data are organized and the statistical analyses conducted, researchers begin to draw conclusions about the results and make predictions about behavior. They may make plans to apply their findings to change behavior in positive ways. Ultimately, researchers report their results to the scientific community by presenting them at a conference or by publishing them in a scientific journal—they report their findings along with their interpretations of what the results mean. To be accepted for presentation or publication, researchers' findings must be submitted in a paper, which is reviewed by other researchers who evaluate it critically. Critical thinking is an important part of evaluating psychology research.

What Research Methods Do Psychologists Use?

Like other scientists, psychologists can conduct several kinds of research studies. In order to conduct a sound study, psychologists face the challenge of choosing the method that will allow them to test the hypothesis in an appropriate way. Different situations lead researchers to choose different research methods. One of the basic considerations is whether the design will be an experiment or one of the descriptive research methods.

The Experimental Method

Experiment ■ A procedure in which a researcher systematically manipulates and observes elements of a situation in order to test a hypothesis and try to establish a cause-and-effect relationship.

Variable ■ A condition or a characteristic of a situation or a person that is subject to change or that differs either within or across situations or individuals.

Independent variable ■ The condition that the experimenter directly and intentionally manipulates to see what changes occur as a result of the manipulation.

Dependent variable ■ The behavior or response that is expected to change because of the manipulation of the independent variable.

Sample ■ A group of individuals who participate in a study and are assumed to be representative of the larger population.

Operational definition ■ A definition of a variable in terms of the set of methods or procedures used to measure or study it.

Psychological research often takes the form of an *experiment*—a procedure in which researchers systematically manipulate and observe elements of a situation in order to test a hypothesis and, ideally, to establish a cause-and-effect relationship.

All researchers must select the variables to include in a study. A *variable* is a condition or a characteristic of a situation or a person that is subject to change or that differs (it varies) either within or across situations or individuals. In experiments, there are two types of variables—independent variables and dependent variables. The *independent variable* is the condition or characteristic that the experimenter directly and intentionally manipulates to see what changes occur as a result of the manipulation. The *dependent variable* is the behavior or response that is expected to change because of the manipulation of the independent variable. For example, to test the hypothesis that spacing out study sessions will lead to better memory for material, a researcher might manipulate the length of the study sessions as the independent variable. The researcher could arrange for some students to study material in three 20-minute sessions and others in one 60-minute session. The dependent variable might be students' scores on an exam.

In addition, researchers must choose an appropriate sample of individuals to participate in the study. Researchers can test only a limited number of people (or nonhuman animals), so they choose a *sample*, a group of individuals who represent a larger group. The choice of individuals affects researchers' ability to extend their results to other individuals; that is, the composition of the sample affects whether or not the research results may be generalized beyond the individuals who participated in the experiment.

Researchers also try to be as precise as possible in the definitions and measurements associated with an experiment. To do so, they often use an *operational definition*, a definition of a variable in terms of the set of methods or procedures used to measure or study that variable. Saying that timing of study sessions is the independent variable is not very precise; many different timing patterns are possible. Using an operational definition, a researcher would specify the timing as, for example, 20-minute study sessions spaced over three days versus a single 60-minute session on one day. In addition, the researcher could operationalize the definition of the dependent variable, students' scores on an exam, by constructing an exam to administer or by choosing students in the same class who are all taking the same exam.

Researchers must determine whether it is the change in the manipulated variable—not some unknown, extraneous (outside) factor—that actually causes the change in the dependent variable. To allow for a proper comparison, researchers often use more than one group of participants. *Participants* are individuals who take part in experiments and whose behavior is observed and recorded. (Psychologists used to call such individuals *subjects*, but that term is now reserved for nonhumans.) In order to be compared, participants must have certain attributes in common, depending on what the experimenter is testing. For example, in the study on timing of study sessions, the participants must be students who are all studying the same material.

Once the participants are known to be comparable on important attributes, they are assigned randomly to either the experimental or the control (comparison) group. *Random assignment* means that the participants are assigned by lottery rather than on the basis of any particular characteristic, preference, or situation that might have even a remote possibility of influencing the outcome. The *experimental group* is the group of participants who receive some level of the independent variable as a treatment. (Thus, some psychologists refer to the experimental group as the *treatment group*.) The **control group** is the comparison group—the group of participants who are tested on the dependent variable in the same way as the experimental group but who receive the standard treatment. In the study on timing of study sessions, one group would experience study sessions spread over three days, while the others would study as college students typically do, in one long session.

If the researchers are confident that the two groups of students are equally capable of learning—that is, that the two groups are truly comparable—then they can conclude that the manipulation of the timing of study sessions is the cause of any change in the experimental group's exam scores. Unless the researchers use comparable groups, the effect of the change in timing of study sessions will not be clear, and no meaningful conclusion can be drawn from the data. In addition, if some extraneous, irrelevant variable is present, the experimental results can be impossible to interpret clearly. *Extraneous variables* are factors that affect the results of an experiment but that are not of interest to the experimenter. Examples of extraneous variables are the subject that the students are studying, the time of day when the study sessions occur, and the students' motivation to learn. When extraneous variables intrude during an experiment (or just before it), they may *confound* the results—make the data difficult to interpret. **Figure 2.3** summarizes the steps in an experiment.

Bias can enter the research process at many points, and researchers must be careful to minimize bias. They pay close attention to how the data are collected and to maintaining necessary controls for extraneous factors. To make meaningful causal inferences, researchers must create situations in which they can limit the likelihood of obtaining a result that was caused by irrelevant factors or is simply a chance occurrence. Only by using carefully formulated experiments can researchers make sound interpretations of results and cautiously extend them to other situations.

A carefully conducted experiment can allow researchers to make conclusions about cause and effect, and knowledge of this type of relationship is highly valued by scientists. Thus, an experiment is often the research method chosen when the situation allows researchers to designate and manipulate an independent variable and measure a dependent variable. However, not all variables of interest can be manipulated; sometimes,

Participant ■ An individual who takes part in an experiment and whose behavior is observed and recorded.

Experimental group ■ In an experiment, the group of participants who receive some level of the independent variable as a treatment.

Control group ■ In an experiment, the comparison group—the group of participants who are tested on the dependent variable in the same way as the experimental group but who receive the standard treatment.

Figure 2.3
Steps in
Conducting an
Experiment

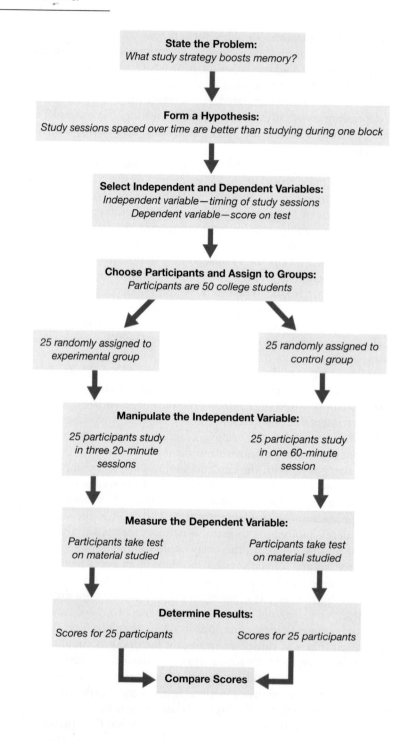

doing so would be unethical (such as manipulating brain damage in humans), impractical (such as manipulating income level), or impossible (such as manipulating age or sex). Thus, psychologists sometimes choose other research methods.

Descriptive Research Methods

Research methods other than the experimental method fall into the category of *descriptive research methods*. As the name implies, this type of research involves describing existing events rather than performing a manipulation of an independent variable and observing changes. This difference is critical: The manipulation of the independent variable while holding all other factors constant allows researchers to assess the effect of the systematic manipulation, including the determination of a cause-and-effect relationship between the independent and dependent variables. None of the descriptive research methods offers this possibility (Christensen, 2004). However, the descriptive methods allow researchers to test other types of hypotheses and to gather valuable observations about a great variety of situations. Keisha and Alicia were attempting descriptive research when they gathered information about a number of colleges.

Like experiments, descriptive research methods require researchers to choose and define variables, make systematic observations to collect data, and draw conclusions. However, rather than manipulating a situation, these methods study existing situations for which researchers hope to provide descriptions and analyses. There are several descriptive methods, and researchers choose which one to use based on the variables and the hypothesis they are investigating.

Descriptive research methods ■ The type of research that involves describing existing events rather than performing a manipulation of an independent variable and observing changes.

Case Studies

A *case study* is a descriptive research method that involves intensive observation and analysis of one individual. Psychologists choose to conduct a case study when they find a single person who is a suitable participant for in-depth study. They collect information about this person and the important factors related to the person's case. The individual is usually selected for study because either the person or his or her situation is unique and interesting; a thorough study of this individual will add to scientific knowledge.

For example, if researchers were interested in studying strategies and grades, they might select a college student who has a perfect grade point average and investigate that student's study habits, perhaps interviewing him or her and observing for an entire semester how, when, and for how long he or she studies. Prospective college students would be attempting the equivalent of a case study if they gathered information on only one school and evaluated it. Neither Keisha nor Alicia chose this approach.

The advantages of the case study include the extensive data that researchers can collect when they restrict an investigation to a single individual. However, one big disadvantage is an inescapable part of this method. Cases are usually chosen because they are unique, but this uniqueness prevents researchers from generalizing any of the findings to other cases. Information about a student with a perfect grade point average may not reveal much about students in general, and gathering information

Case study ■ A descriptive research method that involves intensive observation and analysis of a single individual.

about only one college is a poor plan for selecting a school. Thus, case studies are not a common type of descriptive research among psychologists (or wise students).

Naturalistic Observation

Naturalistic observation ■ A descriptive research method that involves observation of behavior in a naturally occurring situation rather than in a laboratory.

Observation is the basis of all research in psychology and other sciences, but researchers choose the method of **naturalistic observation** when they want to observe a behavior in a naturally occurring situation rather than in a laboratory. The goal of this method is to describe behavior as it occurs in its typical, or natural, context. This research method differs from the observations that people make every day in several ways, including the definition of variables of interest and the formulation of a specific plan to collect data in a systematic way. Alicia visited several college campuses as a way of forming an overall impression, by walking around and making observations. However, she failed to define the variables that were important to her or formulate a plan for collecting data. Thus, her observations did not constitute the method of naturalistic observation.

When researchers conduct naturalistic observation, they collect data without affecting participants' behavior or responses.

To use naturalistic observation, researchers must observe what occurs without changing the situation. When people know that they are being observed, they may change their behavior (behave in a way that was not natural in the situation), which would ruin the results. Thus, researchers using naturalistic observation must find ways to observe without attracting the awareness of those being observed. This requirement makes naturalistic observation more difficult than it might seem.

For example, if researchers were interested in students' study habits, they might go to a university library the week before final exams to observe whether students were studying alone or studying in groups. The researchers would need to specify what information they were going to collect and decide what they were going to do to "blend into the background" so that the observation would remain naturalistic. These researchers might simply count the number of individuals studying alone and the number and size of groups of students studying together, or they might try to determine how long the individuals studying in groups and those studying alone stayed on task. Those data could lead them to understand whether studying in a group or individually seems to result in longer study sessions.

Surveys

Survey ■ A descriptive research method in which a set of questions is posed to a large group of participants.

Another descriptive research method is the **survey**. Researchers use this method when they want to gather large amounts of information from many people. To conduct a survey, researchers may prepare a written questionnaire, or they may interview individuals on the telephone or face-to-face. Each of these approaches requires researchers to construct questions, choose a group of people to question, collect data from those participants, analyze the data, and formulate conclusions.

Students often imagine that the survey method is easy—everyone knows how to ask questions. However, this method requires researchers to make many decisions, each of which influences the survey results (Nardi, 2003). For example, the decision to use a written questionnaire rather than a face-to-face interview can affect the results because people are more likely to be honest when filling out an anonymous written questionnaire than when speaking with an interviewer. However, people are more likely to agree to participate in a face-to-face interview than to complete a written questionnaire. Researchers must carefully weigh these alternatives when they make decisions about how to carry out survey research, or they will not get the information they need.

Like other researchers, those who conduct surveys are concerned about the sample of participants they study. Researchers want to obtain a *representative sample* for a survey (Nardi, 2003). That is, they want the sample to reflect pertinent characteristics of the population from which it was drawn (see **Figure 2.4**). If the sample is representative, then the researchers will be able to generalize their results to the entire population. If the sample is not representative, then the researchers will know only about the people whom they surveyed, which is a severe limitation.

Representative sample ■
A sample that reflects pertinent characteristics of the population from which it was drawn.

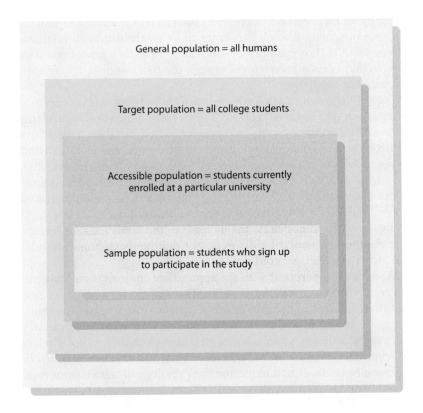

General population = all humans

Target population = all college students

Accessible population = students currently enrolled at a particular university

Sample population = students who sign up to participate in the study

Figure 2.4
Drawing a Sample from a Population

Survey research also has a built-in limitation in that it must rely on the self-reports of participants. Participants may have accurate memories and tell the truth when answering the questions on a survey, or they may not. Survey researchers have no way to validate participants' responses, so they must rely on these self-reports. For example, if a researcher were interested in knowing how much time students spend studying for exams and what their grades are, she might construct a questionnaire asking about these two things, distribute it to a large sample of students in a university, and tabulate the information from the returned questionnaires. This survey would be subject to problems from students' failure to report their study times (and possibly their grades) accurately.

The limitations on survey research make it a less common choice for psychologists. However, surveys are a good way to obtain a great deal of information from many people in a short length of time. Market researchers and those who conduct political polls rely heavily on this method. Keisha performed something like a survey: She applied a standard set of questions to each college she researched and collected a great deal of information that was comparable across institutions.

Correlational Studies

Correlational study ■ A descriptive research method that attempts to determine the strength of a relationship between two variables.

A *correlational study* is a type of descriptive research method that attempts to determine the strength of a relationship between two variables. A correlation exists between two variables when an increase in the value of one variable is regularly accompanied by an increase or a decrease in the value of a second variable. Researchers use this method when they want to know the degree of relationship between two variables. For example, if students make higher grades when they study more hours, then there is a correlation between the first variable, test grades, and the second variable, study time.

Knowing the degree of relationship between two variables is an important piece of information, but correlational studies have a crucial limitation. *Correlated events are not necessarily causally related.* That is, even if two variables have a strong relationship with each other, one may not cause the other, and correlational studies do not allow researchers to make conclusions about causality (Christensen, 2004). Correlated variables may be causally related, or they may not be. For example, during the 20th century, the divorce rate in the United States increased and so did the homicide rate, making these two variables correlated, as **Figure 2.5** shows. However, the rising divorce rate did not cause the increase in the homicide rate (except in rare cases where the murder involved a divorce), nor did the rising homicide rate cause divorces to increase (again, except in rare cases).

A well-conducted experiment with the appropriate controls is the only method that allows researchers to determine causality. Think of these two types of research methods as alternative instruments to examine behavior: A correlational study is like a magnifying glass, and an experimental design is like a microscope. If a causal relationship exists, a correlational study is not powerful enough to detect such a relationship, but an experimental design is. This limitation of correlational studies means that researchers must be cautious in interpreting their results and refrain from making conclusions about causality.

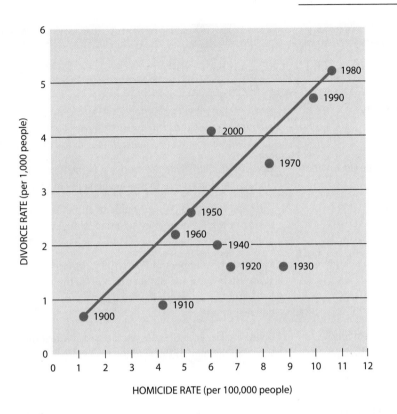

Figure 2.5
Correlation between Divorce and Murder in the United States, 1900–2000

Ex Post Facto Studies

An *ex post facto study* is another descriptive research method that allows researchers to describe differences among groups of participants. Researchers use this method when they want to know about differences among groups of individuals (Christensen, 2004). In an ex post facto study, researchers contrast groups of participants who differ naturally on some variable of interest, that is, on some existing characteristic such as gender, age, educational level, ethnicity, and so forth. This variable is called a *subject variable* or an *individual difference variable* because it describes a characteristic on which the subjects (individuals) in the study vary. Researchers divide participants into groups based on this characteristic and then test for differences among the groups of participants.

Recall that experiments also contrast groups of participants; this similarity between ex post facto studies and experiments can be confusing. Experiments include an *independent variable* that the experimenter manipulates so that it has at least two values. The manipulation of an independent variable versus the selection of a subject variable constitutes a critical difference: Independent variables are manipulated, whereas subject variables are selected. This difference puts ex post facto studies in the category of descriptive research methods, with the limitations of those methods. The most important limitation is the inability to reach any conclusion concerning causality.

Ex post facto study ■ A descriptive research method that allows researchers to describe differences among groups of participants.

Table 2.1

EXAMPLES OF DESCRIPTIVE RESEARCH METHODS

Method	Example
■ Case Study	Study a student with a perfect GPA, recording study habits, amount of study time, timing of study sessions, attitudes, living arrangements, and many details of the person's life.
■ Naturalistic Observation	Observe students who are studying in the library, comparing those who study alone to those who study in groups.
■ Survey	Question a representative sample of students at a university, asking how much time they spend on studying each week, broken down by day.
■ Correlational Study	Measure the numbers of hours that a group of students study each week and obtain their GPAs, then correlate the two variables to determine the degree of relationship between them.
■ Ex Post Facto Study	Divide a class according to gender, and contrast the test scores of the men to those of the women.

Ex post facto studies are very common in psychology research because psychologists are often interested in investigating variables that they cannot manipulate, for either ethical or practical reasons. For example, gender and ethnicity are variables that psychologists frequently study, and neither characteristic can be manipulated. When psychologists perform studies on gender differences, those studies are ex post facto studies with gender as the subject variable. For example, if a researcher were interested in whether women or men were better students, that researcher might contrast the grades of a group of women with those of a group of men who are taking the same classes. If the study revealed differences, the researcher might conclude that these two groups differ but may *not* make conclusions concerning the source of those differences.

Table 2.1 provides examples of how each of the descriptive research methods might be used to investigate factors related to effective study techniques.

How Do Psychologists Evaluate Their Research Findings?

Like Keisha, the prospective college student, psychology researchers collect large sets of data and are faced with the task of analyzing these data to find meaningful patterns. Without ways to analyze their data, researchers would be as overwhelmed as Keisha was. Fortunately, researchers know how to use statistics.

Using Statistics to Evaluate Research

Researchers use statistics to help them organize, evaluate, and understand the data they have collected in their studies. *Statistics* is the branch of mathematics that deals with classifying and analyzing data. The statistics that psychologists use fall into two categories: descriptive statistics and inferential statistics. We'll consider both of these here, and Appendix A provides some additional details.

Statistics ■ The branch of mathematics that deals with classifying and analyzing data.

Descriptive Statistics

Descriptive statistics include procedures to summarize, condense, and describe sets of data. As Keisha discovered, having a great deal of data can be overwhelming. Finding herself struggling to interpret her information, Keisha talked to her high school counselor, who suggested that Keisha bring in her folders so that they could work on them. Together, they planned an evaluation that included some simple statistics to help Keisha interpret the data she had gathered. In addition, the counselor asked Keisha to generate another piece of data for each college: her overall rating of how well she liked each school, on a scale from 1 to 10.

Descriptive statistics ■ A category of statistics that includes procedures to summarize, condense, and describe sets of data.

The first step for analyzing data is organization. Researchers often organize their data by arranging the numbers into a distribution of ordered scores. The organization may be from lowest to highest score or the other way around. Alternatively, an organization based on categories or groupings may be a good choice, as it was for Keisha. Her counselor advised her to extract several pieces of information from each of her folders so that she could compare schools at a glance.

Researchers usually want to know about characteristics of a group (or several subgroups), and measures of central tendency give them a way to summarize group characteristics. *Measures of central tendency* are statistics that tell which score best represents an entire set of scores. There are three commonly used measures of central tendency: mean, mode, and median. Each is a way to condense many scores for a group to one score.

Measure of central tendency ■ A descriptive statistic that tells which score best represents an entire set of scores.

The *mean* is the average of a set of scores. To obtain the mean, add the scores and divide by the number of scores in the group. Thus, a researcher who collects 300 test scores can calculate a mean and reduce 300 numbers to a single mean score, to which each score in the distribution has contributed. Keisha was interested in a medical career, so she collected information about the ratings of the premedical curricula for each of the 20 schools she considered. Those scores appear in **Table 2.2**, along with a calculation of the mean for each grouping of schools (public and private universities within and outside of the state) that she considered. That analysis shows that the private schools' premed curricula have higher ratings than state schools' curricula do, which may be important to Keisha.

Mean ■ A measure of central tendency that reflects the average of a set of scores.

Other measures of central tendency are the mode and the median. The *mode* is the most frequent score in a set of scores, and the *median* is the point in the ordered distribution of a set of scores that has 50% of the scores above it and 50% of the scores below it. Researchers may be interested in the mode because it represents the most popular score, or they may prefer the median as a measure of central tendency because it divides the distribution in half. Table 2.2 also shows these values for

Mode ■ The most frequent score in a set of scores.

Median ■ The point in the ordered distribution of a set of scores that has 50% of the scores above it and 50% of the scores below it.

Table 2.2

MEASURES OF CENTRAL TENDENCY FOR RATINGS OF THE PREMEDICAL CURRICULA OF IN-STATE AND OUT-OF-STATE PUBLIC AND PRIVATE UNIVERSITIES

Universities	Ratings of Premed Program (1–10)	Distribution of Ratings of Premedical Curricula	
In-State Public U #1	2	In-State Public U #1	2
In-State Public U #2	5	Out-of-State Public U #1	3
In-State Public U #3	6	Out-of-State Private U #1	3
In-State Public U #4	7	In-State Private U #1	4
In-State Public U #5	7	Out-of-State Public U #2	5
Mean	27 + 5 = 5.4	In-State Public U #2	5
Out-of-State Public U #1	3	Out-of-State Private U #2	5
Out-of-State Public U #2	5	In-State Public U #3	6
Out-of-State Public U #3	6	Out-of-State Public U #3	6
Out-of-State Public U #4	6	Out-of-State Public U #4	6
Out-of-State Public U #5	8		Median = 6.5
Mean	28 + 5 = 5.6	In-State Public U #4	7 ⎤
In-State Private U #1	4	In-State Public U #5	7
In-State Private U #2	7	Out-of-State Private U #3	7
In-State Private U #3	7	Out-of-State Private U #4	7 ⎬ Mode
In-State Private U #4	8	In-State Private U #2	7
In-State Private U #5	9	In-State Private U #3	7 ⎦
Mean	35 + 5 = 7.0	Out-of-State Private U #5	8
Out-of-State Private U #1	3	Out-of-State Public U #5	8
Out-of-State Private U #2	5	In-State Private U #4	8
Out-of-State Private U #3	7	In-State Private U #5	9
Out-of-State Private U #4	7		
Out-of-State Private U #5	8		
Mean	30 + 5 = 6.0		

Keisha's data. The mode and the median are less sensitive to extreme scores than the mean is, which gives these measures of central tendency an advantage in some situations. Keisha was interested that the mode for the schools she was considering was 7, which represents a very good score. She was encouraged by the high quality of programs at so many schools.

In addition to measures of central tendency, researchers are also interested in how much variability occurs in groups of scores. Do the scores cluster around the mean, or are they more spread out? One measure of variability is the *range,* calculated by subtracting the lowest score from the highest score. However, a more common measure of variability is the *standard deviation,* a measure of the variability of the scores in a set from the mean of the set. Keisha found that the four types of schools had an equal range of scores, as **Table 2.3** shows. Standard deviations for the types of schools are also given in Table 2.3. Notice that the private universities show a smaller standard deviation for ratings of their premed programs than the state universities do. This smaller standard deviation means that the programs at private universities are closer to the mean score than programs in state universities— they vary less as a group.

As we've noted, when researchers want to determine the degree of relationship between two variables, they conduct correlational studies, which involve measuring two variables within a group of individuals. After they have collected the whole set of these two measurements, researchers use a descriptive statistic called the *correlation coefficient* to assess the degree of relationship between the two variables. The calculation of a correlation coefficient produces a number that falls between -1.00 and $+1.00$. Coefficients closer to 1.00 (either positive or negative) indicate stronger relationships than values near 0. When the values of one variable increase in proportion to the increasing values of the other, the correlation is positive; when the values of one variable increase in proportion to the decreasing values of the other variable, the correlation is negative. For example, the school counselor obtained a correlation coefficient for Keisha's ratings of how well she liked each school and the cost of tuition at each school. Much to Keisha's disappointment, this correlation was positive, which indicated that higher liking ratings were associated with higher costs. Another correlation showed a negative relationship between liking rating and distance from her home town, which indicated that as the distance from home increased, Keisha's liking for the university decreased. This information was interesting to Keisha because she had not realized that distance from home was an important factor in her college choice, yet this correlation suggested that it might be. Keisha was also surprised at the results of a third correlation, which revealed that there was no relationship between her rating of how much she liked a school and how well its premed program was rated. Keisha is a serious student who thought she was paying attention to such information, but the lack of relationship between these two variables suggests that she may not have been.

Inferential Statistics and Decision Making

Researchers use descriptive statistics to summarize and interpret their data, but they also want to be sure that the differences they find are meaningful. They use *inferential statistics* to allow them to conclude whether the results they have obtained from experiments form meaningful patterns and confirm the hypotheses that prompted them to undertake the research. That is, researchers use inferential statistics to evaluate whether their experimental results are significant. For psychologists, a *significant difference* is a difference that is statistically unlikely to have occurred because of chance alone and is thus inferred to be most likely due to the systematic manipulation of a variable. For example, researchers might choose to

Range ■ A measure of the variability of a set of scores that is calculated by subtracting the lowest score from the highest score.

Standard deviation ■ A measure of the variability of the scores in a set from the mean of the set.

Correlation coefficient ■ A descriptive statistic used to assess the degree of relationship between the two variables of interest in a correlational study.

Inferential statistics ■ A category of statistics that allows researchers to conclude whether the results they have obtained from experiments form meaningful patterns.

Significant difference ■ A difference that is unlikely to have occurred because of chance alone and is thus inferred to be most likely due to the systematic manipulation of a variable in a research study.

Table 2.3

MEASURES OF VARIABILITY FOR RATINGS OF THE PREMEDICAL CURRICULA OF IN-STATE AND OUT-OF-STATE PUBLIC AND PRIVATE UNIVERSITIES

Universities	Ratings of Premedical Curricula (1–10)
In-State Public U #1	2
In-State Public U #2	5
In-State Public U #3	6
In-State Public U #4	7
In-State Public U #5	<u>7</u>
Mean	$27 \div 5 = 5.4$
Range	$7 - 2 = 5$
Standard deviation	$= 2.1$
Out-of-State Public U #1	3
Out-of-State Public U #2	5
Out-of-State Public U #3	6
Out-of-State Public U #4	6
Out-of-State Public U #5	<u>8</u>
Mean	$28 \div 5 = 5.6$
Range	$8 - 3 = 5$
Standard deviation	$= 1.8$
In-State Private U #1	4
In-State Private U #2	7
In-State Private U #3	7
In-State Private U #4	8
In-State Private U #5	<u>9</u>
Mean	$35 \div 5 = 7.0$
Range	$9 - 4 = 5$
Standard deviation	$= 1.5$
Out-of-State Private U #1	3
Out-of-State Private U #2	5
Out-of-State Private U #3	7
Out-of-State Private U #4	7
Out-of-State Private U #5	<u>8</u>
Mean	$30 \div 5 = 6.0$
Range	$8 - 3 = 5$
Standard deviation	$= 2$

manipulate the timing of study sessions while holding the total study time constant in order to determine the effect of session timing on exam scores. If the data indicated that study sessions spaced into three 20-minute sessions led to higher average exam scores than one 60-minute study session did, the researchers would want to conclude that the difference occurred because of the timing of the study sessions and that the difference is big enough to be important to students' grades. The different average exam scores would be significantly different only if they could not be due to chance, to the use of only one or two participants, or to individual differences among participants. If experimental results are not statistically significant, they do not confirm the study's hypothesis. (As Chapter 9 discusses, timing of study sessions is a factor in memory, and students who break up their studying into shorter sessions tend to learn and remember information better than students who cram all their studying into one long session.)

When people use the word *significant*, they often mean "important," but the concept of statistical significance is not the same as the concept of practical importance. A result is statistically significant when it is unlikely to have occurred on the basis of chance, which means that the result occurs in a meaningful pattern. However, statistically significant and meaningful differences may still be small. Indeed, they may be too small to have an impact on people's lives. For example, a number of researchers have found that performance of cognitive and motor tasks varies for women according to the phase of their menstrual cycle (Alexander et al., 2002). These differences represent statistically significant patterns that appear in well-controlled experiments in laboratories, but the effects are very small—too small to make a practical difference in women's performance in memorizing, judging, or reacting to situations in everyday life. A result that is not statistically significant will be unimportant, but having statistical significance does not guarantee that a result is important or has implications for people's lives. The size of the effect is a key consideration for evaluating its importance, and additional statistical analysis is required to determine effect size.

Although psychologists must use caution in interpreting their results and making conclusions or claims based on the statistical analyses they perform, statistics do help psychologists understand the data they collect. Psychologists use descriptive statistics to summarize the data they collect and inferential statistics to evaluate the results of their studies. Without statistics, psychologists would not be able to come to appropriate conclusions about their research.

Avoiding Bias in the Research Process

For nearly the first 75 years of the history of psychology, most research participants were 18-year-old, male, first-year college students, primarily with European American backgrounds. Researchers assumed that the differences between this sample and all other people were not important. In fact, this thinking was quite biased: Women do not respond in the same way as men do in many circumstances, and older adults and children don't respond in the same ways that 18-year-olds do. Also, members of various ethnic groups bring different perspectives to research situations. Eventually realizing that male European American college freshmen were not representative, psychologists sought to decrease the gender, age, and ethnic biases that characterized their research.

Because research studies are used to draw conclusions and make generalizations about people, it is important to understand that enormous differences exist among individuals and groups. The young and the old may behave differently under similar conditions; research done only on men may yield different results from research done only on women. People are not all alike and do not all behave in the same way, even when placed in the same situation. Avoiding the tendency to overgeneralize research results has become an important goal in psychology.

Ethnocentrism

Individuals, groups, and institutions often see the world only from their point of view and have trouble recognizing that their outlook is not the only vantage point. Individuals tend to believe that their own ethnic or cultural group is the standard, the reference point against which other people and groups should be judged; many even assume that their group is superior. Referred to as *ethnocentrism,* this type of bias should be avoided in research (and in life) because it leads to an inaccurate way of understanding the world, producing distortion and even prejudice. In addition, this type of bias can affect the research process (Huff, 1997).

People may be largely unaware that they hold ethnocentric (sometimes called *monocultural*) beliefs about their own superiority. Historically, psychology in the United States reflected such a bias; because most psychologists had European American backgrounds, they adopted a worldview largely based on that culture. Uncritically accepting the values of their culture, needless to say, affected earlier psychologists' views of child development, social relationships, and psychological abnormalities. Today, psychologists must be especially sensitive to ethnocentric biases and work to develop an awareness and understanding of ethnic and other forms of diversity. Without this sensitivity, research is subject to ethnocentric bias.

Ethnocentrism ■ The tendency to believe that one's own ethnic or cultural group is the standard, the reference point against which other people and groups should be judged.

Race, Ethnicity, Culture, and Social Class

The word *race* can mean dissimilar things to different groups. Some theorists— especially those who are biologically oriented—see natural, physical divisions among humans that are hereditary, are reflected in body type, and are roughly captured by terms such as Black, White, and Asian. According to a biological view, one's parents, body type, and skin color determine one's membership within a genetically defined racial group. Yet many observable traits or characteristics of human beings, for example, hair color and weight, are influenced by factors other than genetics. Furthermore, there is greater genetic variation within populations, for example, within those groups typically labeled Black and White, than between populations. There are no genetic characteristics possessed by all Blacks or by all Whites. Indeed, biologists have failed to find a genetic basis for race (Bamshad & Olson, 2003). For these reasons, race should be considered to be a construct or an abstraction rather than a physical reality. Although people use the term *race*, this term is less valuable to psychologists than *ethnicity*, which is a variable factor that affects behavior in fundamental ways.

Ethnicity refers to common experiences and allegiances, which are often culture-, religion-, or language-based, shared by a group of people. Although ethnic groups may be based on physical traits such as skin color, ethnicity is learned from family, friends, and experiences. The ethnic makeup of the U.S. population is changing rapidly. In the past decade, the Latino/Latina population has grown to almost 37 million people (out of a total U.S. population of about 290 million), largely of Mexican origin; the African American population also increased to over 36 million people; and the Asian American population grew to almost 11 million (U.S. Bureau of the Census, 2003). The portion of the U.S. population that is Native American has remained stable at less than 3 million. Like people in any large population, members of each of these ethnic groups exhibit a wide range of individual differences. However, people from all these ethnic groups contribute their worldviews to the American experience and to research studies in psychology. Rather than presenting research biases to be avoided, cultural differences have become topics of interest to psychologists.

Culture reflects a person's ethnic background, religious and social values, artistic and musical tastes, and scholarly interests. Culture is the unwritten social and psychological guidebook that each of us learns and uses to interpret our world. A number of cultural factors shape behavior, values, and even mental health; culture has a direct bearing on the functioning of families, especially the nurturing and upbringing of children.

Culture can also be described as promoting either an individualist or collectivist outlook. Individualist cultures (like those of the United States, Canada, and Australia) stress personal rather than group goals and value individual freedom and autonomy. Collectivist cultures (like those in many Asian countries) favor group needs (including those of family, coworkers, and religious and political groups) over individual ones (Nisbett, 2003). People in collectivist cultures value a tightly knit social fabric and a willingness to go along with the group (Oyserman, Coon, & Kemmelmeier, 2002). Such preferences often have religious origins, but they permeate many aspects of the culture (Sampson, 2000). An individualist or collectivist culture also has an impact on child-rearing techniques—individualist cultures stress exploration, creativity, and independence for children, whereas collectivist cultures foster duty, obedience, and conformity.

Of course, no society is made up entirely of people who adhere to a single set of cultural values. Most societies contain a variety of subcultures; for example, within the United States, the South is more collectivist (think family ties, church life, and a shared sense of oppression after the Civil War) than is the Mountain West, which tends to be more individualistic (think rugged, self-reliant farmers and cowhands) (Vello & Cohen, 1999). Furthermore, in today's world of global travel and communications, many societies are sharing values, ideas, and traditions. Thus, cultural values within a given society are strong but not homogeneous, and research on culture can help people understand both their differences and their commonalities.

Closely tied to culture is a person's social class, which refers to the combination of a person's education, income, and occupational status or prestige (Beeghley, 2000). The American class structure is not as rigid as it was in the 19th century or as it still is in some non-Western countries, but Americans do fall into several classes based on socioeconomic status. Among these classes are the lower class, whose members have below-average economic status and tend to be poorly educated; the working class, whose members work in skilled and semiskilled jobs such as contractor and mechanic; the middle class, which includes a wide range of income and educational levels; and the upper class, those individuals whose wealth comes from inheritance and who tend to be well educated. However, some people who are very wealthy, such as Bill Gates, do not belong to the upper class because their wealth is not inherited. In addition, some upper-class individuals may choose to obtain little education; thus, wealth and education are not perfectly related to social class.

Social class is not the same as ethnicity or culture; people in the same socioeconomic class may be of the same or different ethnicities and cultural backgrounds. For example, people who work in manufacturing automobiles on a production line are in the working class, and they may be from any ethnic background and have varying cultural values. Clearly, the concept of social class is complex, and individuals may vary from the generalizations. However, social class does affect people's view of the world and their behavior (Fine, 2002).

Participants in psychology research are often college students, and Americans in the lower class do not attend college as often as those in other social classes (U.S. Bureau of the Census, 2003). Therefore, psychologists have tended to overlook social class differences as research variables and have excluded people in the lower classes from much of their research (Fine, 2002). This exclusion can create bias. For example, socioeconomic class could be an important variable in a study of tobacco use among high school students; overlooking this factor might lead to conclusions that are not true or, at a minimum, not generalizable.

Gender

During the first three-quarters of the 20th century, women's roles in scholarship and academia were restricted because women were discriminated against both in terms of access to education and professional training and in terms of hiring and promotion (Brannon, 2005). Although some female faculty members taught and did research in psychology, they were rarely prominent in their departments. Nor was gender considered an important variable in psychology research.

Today, gender bias is less common in research; indeed, many psychologists conduct research in which gender is a variable. That research has shown that women may react differently than men in the same situations. For example, some early research on morality (Gilligan, 1982) showed that women see moral situations differently than men do; research on aggression (Knight et al., 2002), sexual attitudes and behavior (Peplau, 2003), and health-related behaviors such as smoking, drinking, and exercising (Kreeger, 2002) also has shown differences between men and women. In some situations, those differences are large. Further, more than half of the people seen by mental health practitioners are women—although this may be because men with mental health problems are less likely to seek therapy (Addis & Mahalik, 2003). Thus, gender can be a crucial factor to consider when choosing a research study sample. Today, psychology researchers seek to understand how, when, and why gender differences come to exist and to what extent they influence behavior.

Sexual Orientation

Sexual orientation is different from sexual behavior because it refers to self-perception and self-concept. Individuals may or may not express their sexual orientation in their behaviors. Three sexual orientations are commonly recognized: homosexual (attracted to individuals of one's own sex), heterosexual (attracted to individuals of the other sex), and bisexual (attracted to individuals of both sexes). People with a homosexual orientation are sometimes referred to as *gay* (both men and women) or *lesbian* (women only). Both the American Psychological Association and the American Psychiatric Association agree that being gay or lesbian in and of itself is unrelated to psychological disturbance or maladjustment—that is, sexual orientation is not a basis for a diagnosis of illness, mental disorder, or emotional problems. In 1973, the weight of empirical data, coupled with changing social standards and the development of a politically active gay community in the United States, led the American Psychiatric Association to remove homosexuality from its diagnostic manual. That decision was supported by a vote of the membership in 1987 and was reaffirmed by the organization's leadership in 1997.

People with homosexual or bisexual orientations have long been stigmatized, but the American Psychological Association has worked vigorously to eradicate that stigma (APA Division 44, 2000). It has sought to decrease *homophobia*—discomfort from being near or in contact with homosexuals. It has also sought to fight *heterosexism*—an ideological system that denies, denigrates, and stigmatizes any non-heterosexual form of behavior or identity. These goals are reflected in a growing body of research on the topic of sexual orientation and a decrease in bias due to heterosexism.

Age

Older people constitute a growing percentage of the general U.S. population, but they are not represented in psychologists' research as often as college students are. More than 30 million Americans are age 65 or older, and the aging of the baby boomer generation (those born between 1946 and 1964) means that the number of older Americans will continue to rise (U.S. Bureau of the Census, 2003). Psychologists are developing programs that focus on the special needs of older people for social support, physical and psychological therapy, and continuing education. They are also recognizing the need for including in their research people with a wider range of ages. The growing population of older people and the emphasis on healthy aging have created the opportunity for psychologists to include more older participants in their research, which is reducing bias due to ageism.

Disability

Disability is a concept that can be defined from different perspectives—medical, moral, and social. Most Western cultures view disability according to a medical model (for example, someone's medical condition requires the use of a wheelchair). A moral model regards disability as the result of sins or transgressions. Even today, in some cultures, disability is connected with feelings of guilt and shame, which may extend to the entire family. This model, which blames the disabled person for the disability, is not prevalent in the United States. Instead, the disability community employs a social model, which considers individuals as disabled in specific circumstances and in specific ways. This view emphasizes the context of the disability and the adaptations that individuals and institutions can make to allow disabled persons to function in society (American Association on Mental Retardation, 2002). People with disabilities need to be considered with care and sensitivity. Programs that focus on their special needs for social support, physical and psychological therapy, and continuing education are being developed by psychologists. Research today considers the sensibilities and voices of those with a broad array of disabilities—visual, hearing, cognitive, learning, psychiatric, and physical challenges. This consideration will increase inclusion and decrease bias.

Diversity Within and Between Groups

The differing perspectives on day-to-day behavior held by diverse ethnic and cultural groups have not always been appreciated, understood, or even recognized in psychological theory or research. For example, psychologists criticize Freud for developing a personality theory that can now be seen as clearly sexist. (We will be evaluating Freud's theory in Chapter 13.) In Freud's day, however, most people accepted sexist attitudes without much question. Further, ethnic minorities and older people were rarely—if ever—included in early psychological research studies, even though the studies were intended to represent the general population. Today, psychologists seek to study all types of individuals and groups in order to make valid conclusions based on scientific evidence. They see cultural diversity as an asset for both theorists and researchers; they also recognize that theories and knowledge about this diversity can help individuals optimize their potential. It is crucial to realize, though, that there are usually more differences within a group than between groups. For example, intelligence test scores differ more among Asian Americans than they do between Asian Americans and any other ethnic group (Geary et al., 1999).

Individual differences make generalizations risky. Sometimes individuals—even those who are members of special populations—behave just as members of the general population do; sometimes individual circumstances produce unique behavior. Psychology tends to focus on the individual rather than the group, and variables such as gender, sexual orientation, age, and disability status exert important effects on individuals. Although people are very much alike and share many common experiences and behaviors, every individual is unique; each person's behavior reflects his or her distinctive life experiences. Even human brains differ from one another (Brett, Johnsrude, & Owen, 2002). Psychology considers the influence of the group but concentrates on individual behavior and thought.

The emphasis on individuals has led psychologists to devise and implement a set of ethical guidelines for their research. Individuals who participate in psychology studies—both human and nonhuman animals—deserve to be treated with care and respect.

What Ethical Principles Guide Psychology Research?

In research, *ethics* consist of rules concerning proper and acceptable conduct that investigators use to guide their studies. These rules govern the treatment of nonhuman animals, the rights of human beings, and the responsibilities of researchers. Guided by images from movies and television, people sometimes imagine psychologists with evil motives, performing dangerous and painful experiments on human participants and nonhuman animals in secret laboratories, and avoiding the rules of ethical scientific conduct. Of course, this image is incorrect. Most research in psychology is conducted using human participants, and ethics is an important priority. Most psychologists work in university laboratories under rules of ethical conduct formulated by the U.S. government and the American Psychological Association (APA, 2002). The ethical guidelines from the APA were formulated in the 1960s and are continually revised in order to ensure that the rights and welfare of research participants are protected.

Before a study begins, participants must give the researcher their *informed consent*—their agreement to take part in the research study and their acknowledgment, through a signature on a document, that they have been fully informed about the general nature of the research, its goals, and its methods. By definition, informed consent has not been obtained unless the researcher has revealed the potential risks in the study so that participants may decide whether or not they wish to continue. Participants cannot be coerced to do things that would be physically harmful to them, that would have negative psychological effects, or that would violate standards of decency. The researcher is responsible for ensuring the ethical treatment of the participants in a study, and the participants are free to decline to participate or to withdraw at any time without penalty. In addition, any information gained in a study is considered strictly confidential. At the end of the study, the participants must go through an interview, a step sometimes referred to as *debriefing*. This interview informs participants about the full details of the study, including hypotheses, methods, and expected or potential results. Debriefing occurs after the experiment so that the validity of participants' responses is not affected by their knowledge of the experiment's purpose.

Is it ever acceptable for researchers to deceive human participants in psychological studies? Imagine a situation in which a researcher tricks a person into believing that she is causing another person pain. Is this deception acceptable? The answer to such questions is generally no, but researchers often withhold some details about a study so as not to bias participants' responses. (When participants know what the investigator is looking for, they tend to give that response, which biases the results.) However, withholding details about a study differs from misleading participants by giving them false information about the study. Misleading participants is considered deception, and researchers are restricted from using deception unless the study has overriding scientific, educational, or practical value (APA, 2002). Even then, two key procedures must be followed: obtaining informed consent and providing feedback about the true nature of the experiment.

Some psychologists believe that deception is unacceptable in research under any circumstances (Pittenger, 2002). Those psychologists assert that deception undermines the public's belief in the integrity of scientists and that its costs outweigh any

Ethics ■ Rules concerning proper and acceptable conduct that investigators use to guide their studies and that govern the treatment of animals, the rights of human beings, and the responsibilities of researchers.

Informed consent ■ The agreement of participants to take part in a research study and their acknowledgment, expressed through their signature on a document, that they have been fully informed about the general nature of the research, its goals, and its methods.

Debriefing ■ A procedure to inform participants about the true nature of a research study after its completion.

potential benefits. Other psychologists argue that deception is necessary to their research. For example, understanding the factors related to cheating is an important goal, but cheating is difficult to research if participants know that a study is focused on cheating. Most psychologists do not conduct research that involves deception, and those who do must obtain informed consent (psychologists are prohibited from using deception related to informed consent) and provide extensive feedback to participants to minimize potentially harmful effects. Whenever deception is necessary to achieve some legitimate scientific goal, psychologists must be especially careful to protect the well-being, rights, and dignity of participants—anything less is considered a violation of APA guidelines (Fisher & Fryberg, 1994).

Some psychologists study behavior by first observing it in nonhuman animals and then generalizing their findings to human behavior. Research with both nonhuman animals and human beings must be governed by ethical considerations. The use of nonhuman animals in research has become a controversial issue, and psychology is part of that debate.

Summary and Review

WHAT MAKES PSYCHOLOGY A SCIENCE?

Identify the two premises on which psychology (like other sciences) is based.

The premise of *empiricism* is that knowledge must be acquired through careful observation. Empirical observation in psychology leads to the development of a *theory*, a collection of interrelated ideas and observations that describe, explain, and predict behavior or mental processes. Theory development is the second premise on which psychology is based. pp. 26–27

Identify three key principles of scientific research.

Like research in other areas, psychology research is committed to objectivity, systematic observation, and replicability. As scientists, psychologists must strive to be objective, evaluating research and theory on their merits, without preconceived ideas. Psychologists are concerned with gathering data from the laboratory and the real world in systematic ways—that is, according to a plan rather than through casual observation. When scientists are able to replicate their results, they become more confident about the accuracy of those results. Psychologists also maintain a healthy skepticism: a cautious view of data, hypotheses, and theory until results are repeated, verified, and established over time. pp. 27–29

Describe the steps in the scientific method.

Psychologists use the *scientific method* to conduct their research. The scientific method's five basic steps are stating a problem clearly, developing a *hypothesis*, designing a study, collecting and analyzing data, and drawing conclusions and reporting results. pp. 29–31

WHAT RESEARCH METHODS DO PSYCHOLOGISTS USE?

Describe experiments, and indicate their key components.

Psychologists conduct *experiments*, systematic procedures aimed at discovering a cause-and-effect relationship between variables. A *variable* is a condition or a characteristic of a situation or person that is subject to change or that differs within or across situations or individuals. The experimenter directly and purposely manipulates the *independent variable* and observes the effect of this manipulation on the *dependent variable*. Experimenters must choose an appropriate *sample* of *participants*, individuals who take part in experiments and whose behavior is observed and recorded. They are usually divided into an *experimental group* and a *control group* for purposes of comparison. Researchers may use an *operational definition* to clarify a variable, and they must find ways to control extraneous variables, factors that may affect the results of the experiment but are not of interest to the experimenter. pp. 32–35

What descriptive research methods do psychologists use?

Psychologists also use a variety of *descriptive research methods*, including *case studies* (the intensive study of one individual), *naturalistic observation* (observation of behavior in a natural context), *surveys* (questioning a *representative sample* of individuals about their opinions, attitudes, or behaviors), *correlational studies* (finding a relationship between two variables), and *ex post facto studies* (contrasting groups of individuals who vary on some characteristic). pp. 35–40

HOW DO PSYCHOLOGISTS EVALUATE THEIR RESEARCH FINDINGS?

How do psychologists use statistics?

Psychologists use two kinds of *statistics* to help them understand and interpret the data they gather. *Descriptive statistics* include *measures of central tendency* (such as the *mean, median*, and *mode*) and measures of variability (such as the *range* and *standard deviation*). The *correlation coefficient* is a descriptive statistic that allows researchers to determine the degree of relationship between two variables. *Inferential statistics* allow researchers to determine if their results reveal significant patterns or differences. A *significant difference* is one that is statistically unlikely to have occurred because of chance alone. Understanding what a significant difference indicates is important in interpreting research results. pp. 40–45

What types of bias must psychologists try to avoid when conducting research?

Ethnocentrism is the tendency to believe that one's own group is the standard, the reference point against which other people and groups should be judged. Psychologists currently strive to eliminate ethnocentrism as well as bias based on gender, sexual orientation, age, and disability. Psychologists also emphasize individual differences and keep in mind that differences among individuals are typically larger than differences between groups. pp. 45–50

WHAT ETHICAL PRINCIPLES GUIDE PSYCHOLOGY RESEARCH?

Ethics in research consists of rules of conduct that investigators use to guide their research; these rules concern the treatment of nonhuman animals, the rights of human beings, and the responsibilities of researchers. The APA has strict ethical guidelines for psychology research. Human participants cannot be coerced to do things that would be physically harmful, that would have other negative effects, or that would violate standards of decency. In addition, any information gained in a study is considered strictly confidential. Human participants must give *informed consent* to a researcher and must undergo *debriefing* after the study is over so that they understand the true nature of the research. In general, researchers must not use deception unless a study has overriding scientific, educational, or practical value. The use of nonhuman animals in research is controversial. Ethical research guidelines also protect nonhuman animals. pp. 51–52

Neuroscience: The Brain and Behavior

How Is the Nervous System
Organized? 55
  The Cellular Level
  Divisions of the Nervous System
  The Brain

How Does the Brain Function? 72
  Monitoring Neural Activity
  Brain Specialization
  Plasticity and Change

What Effects Do Hormones Have
on Behavior? 81

How Do Genetic Factors Affect
Behavior? 84
  The Issue of Nature versus Nurture
  The Basics of Genetics
  How Genes Affect Behavior
  From Genetics to Genomics

Does Our Evolutionary History
Influence Our Current Behavior? 89
  Natural Selection
  Adaptations in Humans
  Controversies about Evolutionary Psychology

Summary and Review 94

The human nervous system directs an enormous variety of reactions and behaviors, and to begin to understand it, we must examine both its structure and function.

How Is the Nervous System Organized?

The nervous system provides a means of communication within the body as well as an interface for communication with the outside world. In some ways, the nervous system acts like an air traffic controller—watching, sending, receiving, processing, and interpreting vital information. Even the simplest task we perform requires smooth functioning of the nervous system, the swift integration and transmission of electrical and chemical signals in individual nerve cells. By studying how the nervous system's components work together and how they are integrated, psychologists learn a great deal about the nature and diversity of behavior.

Nervous system ■ The structures and organs that facilitate electrical and chemical communication in the body and allow all behavior and mental processes to take place.

Neurons ■ The type of cell that is the basic building block of the nervous system and functions through specialized structures, including dendrites (which receive neural signals), an axon (which transmits neural signals), and axon terminals (which relay signals to adjacent neurons); also known as a *nerve cell*.

Afferent neurons ■ Neurons that send messages to the spinal cord and brain; sensory neurons.

Efferent neurons ■ Neurons that send messages from the brain and spinal cord to other structures in the body; motor neurons.

Interneurons ■ Neurons that connect sensory neurons to motor neurons.

Glial cells ■ Cells in the nervous system that nourish the neurons and provide support functions.

Myelin sheath ■ A thin, white, fatty layer that covers some large motor neurons and speeds neural transmission.

Overall, the *nervous system* has two subdivisions: the central nervous system (the brain and spinal cord) and the peripheral nervous system (all the nerves in the body outside the brain and spinal cord). We'll consider these two subdivisions shortly and examine the brain in some detail. First, however, you need to understand how communication in the nervous system proceeds at the cellular level.

The Cellular Level

The nervous system is composed of billions of individual nerve cells called *neurons.* Each of these receives information from hundreds or thousands of others. Let's examine neurons and their communication process more closely.

The Neuron

The neuron is the basic building block of the nervous system. There are billions of neurons throughout the body (as many as 100 billion in the brain alone), which differ in shape, size, and type. Neurons are often grouped together in bundles; these bundles of neurons are called *nerves* if they are in the peripheral nervous system and *tracts* if they are in the central nervous system.

Neurons vary according to the direction in which they relay information. Nerve pathways allow signals to flow (1) to the brain and spinal cord from the sense organs and muscles, and (2) from the brain and spinal cord to the sense organs and muscles, carrying messages that initiate reactions and behaviors. Three types of neurons are involved in this two-way information flow: *afferent neurons* (from the Latin *ad*, "to," and *ferre*, "carry"), or *sensory neurons*, carry messages to the spinal cord and brain; *efferent neurons* (from the Latin *ex*, "out of," and *ferre*, "carry"), or *motor neurons*, carry messages from the brain and spinal cord to other structures in the body (see **Figure 3.1**). *Interneurons* connect sensory neurons to motor neurons and outnumber both of these other types. Interneurons are also connected to each other, forming a network that allows interaction.

The billions of neurons in the nervous system are surrounded by *glial cells,* which nourish the neurons and provide support functions. Glial cells are small—and ten times more numerous than neurons. These cells constitute about 90% of the cells in the brain and are important in forming connections between neurons (Ullian et al., 2001). Other functions of glial cells include protecting the brain from toxins and helping in the formation of the *myelin sheath,* a thin, white, fatty layer that covers some large motor neurons and insulates them from other neurons. Myelinated neurons conduct signals faster than unmyelinated neurons, which speeds reactions. Multiple sclerosis causes loss of the myelin, and people with this disease experience movement and coordination problems as a result.

Neurons have structures found in all cells, including a cell membrane, cell body, nucleus, and cytoplasm. In addition, neurons have three specialized structures that allow them to carry out their function of communication: dendrites,

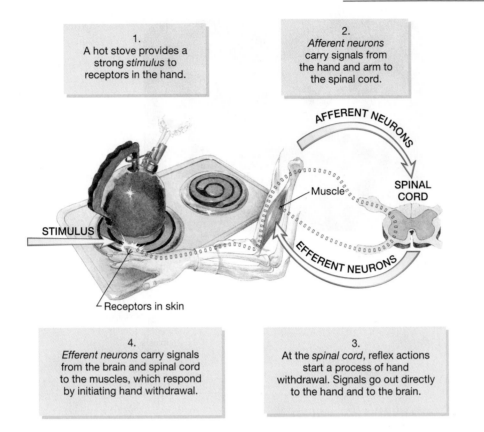

1.
A hot stove provides a strong *stimulus* to receptors in the hand.

2.
Afferent neurons carry signals from the hand and arm to the spinal cord.

AFFERENT NEURONS

Muscle

SPINAL CORD

STIMULUS

EFFERENT NEURONS

Receptors in skin

4.
Efferent neurons carry signals from the brain and spinal cord to the muscles, which respond by initiating hand withdrawal.

3.
At the *spinal cord*, reflex actions start a process of hand withdrawal. Signals go out directly to the hand and to the brain.

Figure 3.1
The Action of Afferent and Efferent Neurons

an axon, and axon terminals (see **Figure 3.2** on p. 58). *Dendrites* (from the Greek word for "tree," because of their many branches) are thin, bushy, widely branching fibers that extend outward from the neuron's cell body. Dendrites are the principal signal reception sites for a neuron—receiving signals from neighboring neurons and carrying them to the cell body (Kennedy, 2000). From the cell body, the signals continue to travel along the *axon,* a thin, elongated structure that transmits signals to its terminals (end points). Each axon branches near its end and thus has a number of terminals, from which neural signals can be relayed to many other neurons.

Neurons do not actually touch each other, but the *synapse,* the space between neurons, is microscopically small—about 1/4000 as thick as a sheet of paper (see **Figure 3.3** on p. 58). The synapse is the space between the axon terminals (the buttonlike structures at the ends of branches) of one neuron and the dendrites, cell body, or axons of other neurons. You can think of many neurons strung together in a long chain as a relay team passing signals from one to another, which convey information or initiate some action in a cell, muscle, or gland. But the image of a chain is too simplistic; each neuron actually receives information from hundreds or even thousands of neighboring neurons and has an average of 10,000 synapses between its terminal branches and other neurons (Whalley, 2001). These many interconnections make complex actions possible.

Dendrites ■ Thin, bushy, widely branching fibers that extend outward from a neuron's cell body and that receive signals from neighboring neurons and carry them back to the cell body.

Axon ■ A thin, elongated structure that transmits signals from a neuron's cell body to the axon terminals, which pass the signals on to adjacent neurons.

Synapse [SIN-apps] ■ The microscopically small space between the axon terminals of one neuron and the dendrites, cell body, or axons of other neurons.

Figure 3.2

The Basic Components of a Neuron

There are several types of neurons, but all possess the basic structures shown here: a cell body, an axon (with myelin sheath and axon terminals), and dendrites.

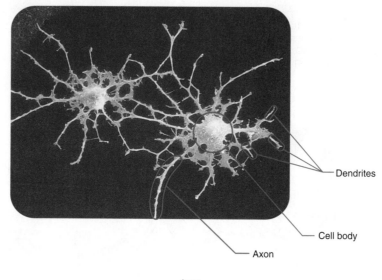

Dendrites

Cell body

Axon

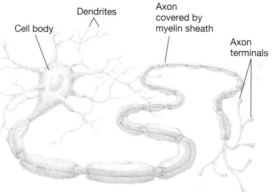

Cell body

Dendrites

Axon covered by myelin sheath

Axon terminals

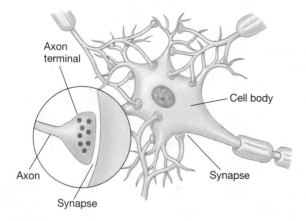

Axon terminal

Cell body

Axon

Synapse

Synapse

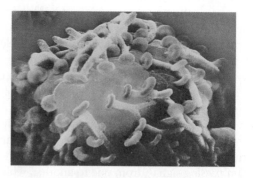

Figure 3.3

The Synapse

The synapse is very small. Neurotransmitters released by the axon terminals cross the synapse to stimulate receptors on the cell body or the dendrites of another neuron.

The Functioning of Neurons

Exactly how do neurons communicate? Neuroscientists know that the neural impulse, or signal, is electrochemical in nature—a combination of electrical and chemical activity. Within neurons, the activity is electrical; between neurons, the activity is chemical. Understanding the electrochemical processes of neural transmission is essential to understanding the role of neurons in behavior.

The electrical part of a neural impulse arises from the permeability of the extremely thin cell membrane (only 1/10,000 as thick as a piece of paper). That is, there are channels, or "gates," in this membrane through which some particles can pass but others cannot. This partial permeability causes some charged particles to be trapped either inside or outside the neuron. Thus, in their resting state, neurons are negatively charged on the interior (relative to the exterior). The difference in electrical charge between the inside and the outside of a neuron creates a state of *polarization* across its cell membrane. Because of this polarization, the neuron is charged, ready and waiting to activate.

Each neuron has a ***threshold,*** a level of stimulation required for activation. When a neuron is stimulated by other neurons enough to reach its threshold, changes occur very rapidly. At this point, the "gates" of the cell membrane open, and the membrane becomes fully permeable to all particles. Positively charged ions rush through the membrane into the neuron, and a rapid reversal of electrical polarity occurs (see **Figure 3.4**). This reversal is called *depolarization*, and it initiates an action potential. The ***action potential,*** or *spike discharge*, is an electrical current that travels along the axon of a neuron, initiated by the rapid reversal of the polarization of the cell membrane. This event is often described as "firing," and the image is a good one to describe this explosive discharge.

Threshold ■ A level of stimulation required for activation of a neuron.

Action potential ■ An electrical current that travels along the axon of a neuron and is initiated by a rapid reversal of the polarization of the cell membrane; also known as a *spike discharge*.

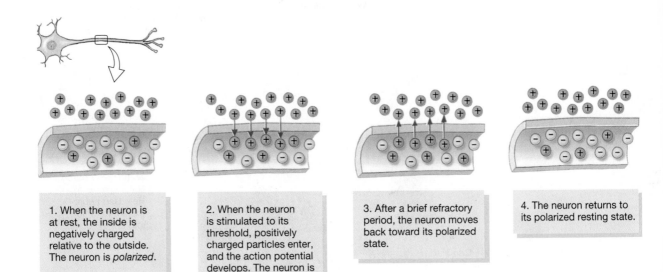

1. When the neuron is at rest, the inside is negatively charged relative to the outside. The neuron is *polarized*.

2. When the neuron is stimulated to its threshold, positively charged particles enter, and the action potential develops. The neuron is *depolarized*.

3. After a brief refractory period, the neuron moves back toward its polarized state.

4. The neuron returns to its polarized resting state.

Figure 3.4
Generation of an Action Potential

A neuron does not necessarily fire, or produce an action potential, every time it is stimulated. If the stimulation does not reach a neuron's threshold, the neuron will not fire; the level of stimulation is crucial for firing. For example, a bright flash from a camera stimulates more cells in the visual areas of the brain than the flicker of a candle does. However, when any neuron fires, or generates an action potential, it does so in an *all-or-none* fashion—that is, a neuron, like a gun, either fires at full strength or not at all. Action potentials occur rapidly, in 2 to 4 milliseconds (thousandths of a second). After each firing, a neuron needs time to recover, generally just a few thousandths of a second. This necessary recovery time is called the *refractory period*. During this period, normal levels of stimulation will not produce an action potential. This limitation means that neurons cannot normally fire more than 500 times per second.

Neurotransmitters and Behavior

The electrical signal of the action potential does not cross the synapse; instead, communication between neurons is chemical. When an action potential reaches the end of an axon, it initiates the release of *neurotransmitters*—chemical substances stored in *synaptic vesicles,* small structures found in every axon terminal. Neurotransmitters are the basis of the chemical part of neural transmission. These chemicals are released into the synapse, move across the synaptic space, and bind to receptor sites on adjacent neurons. The binding of a neurotransmitter to a receptor site conveys a chemical message to the neuron on which the site is located (see **Figure 3.5**). We'll examine the types of neurotransmitters shortly.

All-or-none ▪ Either at full strength or not at all; the basis on which neurons fire.

Refractory period ▪ The time needed for a neuron to recover after it fires; during this period, an action potential will not occur.

Neurotransmitter ▪ Chemical substance that is stored within a synaptic vesicle in the axon terminal vesicles and that, when released, moves across the synaptic space and binds to a receptor site on an adjacent cell.

Synaptic vesicles ▪ Small structures that are found in every axon terminal and store neurotransmitters.

Figure 3.5
Major Steps
in Neuronal
Transmission

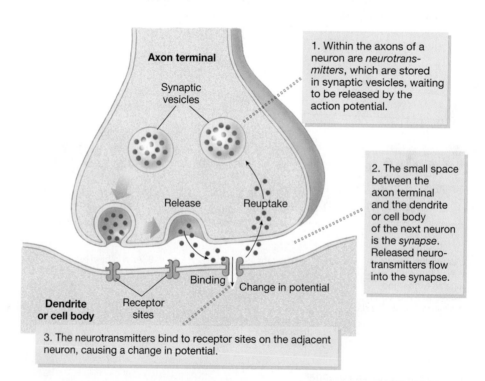

Axon terminal

Synaptic vesicles

1. Within the axons of a neuron are *neurotransmitters*, which are stored in synaptic vesicles, waiting to be released by the action potential.

Release   Reuptake

2. The small space between the axon terminal and the dendrite or cell body of the next neuron is the *synapse*. Released neurotransmitters flow into the synapse.

Binding   Change in potential

Dendrite or cell body   Receptor sites

3. The neurotransmitters bind to receptor sites on the adjacent neuron, causing a change in potential.

Neurotransmitters act on receiving neurons in one of two ways: either exciting them, causing them to fire more easily, or inhibiting them, causing them to fire less easily. This excitatory or inhibitory action of a neurotransmitter produces a change in the polarization of the receiving neuron; this change is called a *postsynaptic potential*. An ***excitatory postsynaptic potential (EPSP)*** pushes the receiving neuron toward its threshold for firing; an ***inhibitory postsynaptic potential (IPSP)*** pushes the neuron away from its threshold, making it less likely to fire. Because each neuron has hundreds (or even thousands) of synapses, it can receive many EPSPs and IPSPs simultaneously (Abbott et al., 1997). When a neurotransmitter has affected an adjacent neuron, it has accomplished its mission. The neurotransmitter is then neutralized, either by being broken down by an enzyme or by being taken back up by the neuron that released it (in a process called *reuptake*). **Table 3.1** summarizes the key steps in the process of neural transmission.

There are a large number of types of neurotransmitters; at least 50 have been identified. Further, each type of neurotransmitter is associated with several types of receptor sites. Therefore, each neurotransmitter can produce different effects, depending on the receptor it reaches. The reception of neurotransmitters is critical for neural functioning and thus for behavior.

Excitatory postsynaptic potential (EPSP) ■ Postsynaptic change in the polarization of a neuron that pushes the neuron toward its threshold and firing.

Inhibitory postsynaptic potential (IPSP) ■ Postsynaptic change in the polarization of a neuron that pushes the neuron away from its threshold, making it less likely to fire.

Table 3.1

SEQUENCE OF EVENTS IN NEURAL TRANSMISSION FROM ONE NEURON TO ANOTHER

■ **First Neuron**
- Resting potential
  Occurs when the neuron is not stimulated
  Includes neural membrane polarized by difference in electrical charge of ions
- Action potential
  Forms if threshold is reached
  Produces depolarization
  Occurs in an all-or-none fashion
- Neurotransmitters
  Released by the action potential
  Flow across the synapse

■ **Second Neuron**
- Neurotransmitters
  Occupy receptors on neuron, which is at resting potential
- Postsynaptic potentials affect likelihood of neuron's developing action potential
  EPSP pushes neuron toward threshold
  IPSP pushes neuron away from threshold
- Threshold is reached = action potential forms in neuron
- Threshold is not reached = neural impulse does not continue

Acetylcholine ■ An excitatory neurotransmitter that was the first to be identified and is the most well-studied.

Neuroscientists have researched the action of some neurotransmitters more thoroughly than others. The most well-studied neurotransmitter, and the first to be identified, is *acetylcholine* (Julien, 2004). Acetylcholine receptors appear in many parts of the brain and throughout the body, indicating that this neurotransmitter is involved in many functions. Its effect is typically excitatory, and its action is crucial to excitation of the skeletal muscles, the muscles that allow you to move. It is also important in functions such as memory and learning (Power, Vazdarjanova, & McGaugh, 2003). In fact, some research indicates that the production of acetylcholine in specific brain structures is associated with different learning strategies (McIntyre, Marriott, & Gold, 2003). The memory problems associated with Alzheimer's disease (to be discussed in Chapter 9) may be related to insufficient production of acetylcholine (Sabbagh et al., 2002).

Gamma-aminobutyric acid (GABA) ■ An important inhibitory neurotransmitter.

Gamma-aminobutyric acid (GABA) is an important inhibitory neurotransmitter (Julien, 2004). It is involved in a wide variety of behaviors, as well as being associated with some behavior problems. Research has linked GABA to the experience of anxiety, and it has also been implicated in alcohol abuse, seizure disorders, and sleep disorders.

Serotonin ■ One of the monoamine neurotransmitters that plays a role in sleep, mood, and appetite.

Another important neurotransmitter is *serotonin,* which is a substance derived from the amino acid tryptophan. This amino acid is a component of many foods, so it is possible (but not easy) to change the amount of serotonin in the brain by eating certain foods (Young, Hoffer, & Jones, 2002). Serotonin is involved in many behaviors: It plays an important role in sleep regulation and in appetite, especially appetite for carbohydrates. The mood-regulating functions of serotonin have become the subject of intensive study in recent years. Serotonin levels appear to be related to anxiety (Schneier, 2003) and depression (Greenshaw, 2003). Many antidepressant drugs affect the metabolism of this neurotransmitter.

Serotonin is classified as one of a family of neurotransmitters called *monoamines* because they all share a similar chemical structure, having one (*mono*) of a chemical grouping called an *amine*. The neurotransmitters *dopamine* and *norepinephrine* are other members of the monoamine family. Dopamine is involved in movement, thought processes, emotion, and feelings of reward and pleasure (Self, 2003). In addition, dopamine has been implicated in a variety of behavior problems, including schizophrenia (Javitt & Coyle, 2004), attention-deficit/hyperactivity disorder (Viggiano et al., 2003), and drug abuse (Julien, 2004). Norepinephrine plays a role in arousal reactions and acts in several parts of the brain, increasing heart rate, respiration, sweating, and dilation of the pupils in the eye (Julien, 2004). Norepinephrine may also be involved in hunger, eating, and sexual activity.

Dopamine ■ One of the monoamine neurotransmitters that plays a role in movement, thought processes, emotion, feelings of reward and pleasure, and several behavior problems.

Norepinephrine ■ One of the monoamine neurotransmitters that plays a role in arousal reactions and possibly in hunger, eating, and sexual activity.

Endorphins ■ One of the neuropeptides that exerts effects similar to those of opiate drugs.

Table 3.2 (on p. 63) summarizes these five important neurotransmitters and their effects. In addition to neurotransmitters, cells contain other substances that act in similar ways. For example, chemicals called *neuropeptides* act much like neurotransmitters. The effects of one type of naturally produced neuropeptide called *endorphins* are similar to those of morphine (Julien, 2004; Pert & Snyder, 1973). Indeed, opiate drugs such as morphine and heroin exert their effects by occupying endorphin receptors on neurons in the brain. Endorphin receptors are particularly plentiful in parts of the brain that affect pain perception and emotional experiences. We will examine pain, endorphins, and pain management in more detail in Chapter 6.

Table 3.2

FIVE KEY NEUROTRANSMITTERS

Neurotransmitter	Location	Effects
■ Acetylcholine	Brain, spinal cord, autonomic nervous system, selected organs	Excitation in brain and autonomic nervous system; excitation or inhibition in certain organs
■ Norepinephrine	Brain, spinal cord, selected organs	Inhibition in brain; excitation or inhibition in certain organs
■ Dopamine	Brain	Inhibition
■ Serotonin	Brain, spinal cord	Inhibition
■ GABA	Brain, spinal cord	Inhibition

Neurotransmitters, Drugs, and Behavior

The study of how drugs affect the body is called *pharmacology*, and *psychopharmacology* is the study of how drugs affect behavior. By studying many types of drugs to learn the physiological mechanisms that underlie their effects, researchers have discovered that many common drugs alter the amount of a neurotransmitter released at synapses; for example, the drug MDMA (Ecstasy) causes a massive release of serotonin. Other drugs increase the production of neurotransmitters; for example, the drug L-dopa increases the supply of dopamine and thus is used in treating Parkinson's disease, which is caused by a deficit of that neurotransmitter. Still other drugs change the rate at which neurotransmitters are disabled after they are released; for example, antidepressants such as Prozac and Zoloft affect the reabsorption of serotonin. A drug that changes the rate of release of an excitatory neurotransmitter increases the number of action potentials that result, which will produce a stimulant effect. When a drug affects an inhibitory neurotransmitter in a similar way, it decreases the number of action potentials; this produces a sedative effect.

Psychopharmacology may hold the key to treating many behavior problems, since research in this area has the potential to discover drugs that can alter the brain's chemistry in beneficial ways. Such research may even reveal ways to effectively block the addictive properties of drugs such as cocaine and thus lead to more successful forms of treatment for addiction (Robinson & Berridge, 2000).

One of the goals of psychopharmacology research is to understand how some drugs either mimic or facilitate the action of neurotransmitters and how other drugs block the action of neurotransmitters. Chemicals that mimic or facilitate the actions of neurotransmitters are called *agonists*. When an agonist is present, receptor sites on neurons respond as if the neurotransmitter itself had been released. Chemicals that act as *antagonists* oppose the actions of specific neurotransmitters. When an

Psychopharmacology ■ The study of how drugs affect behavior.

Agonist [AG-oh-nist] ■ Chemical that mimics or facilitates the actions of a neurotransmitter.

Antagonist ■ Chemical that opposes the actions of a neurotransmitter.

antagonist is present, receptor sites for a particular neurotransmitter are blocked, and the neurotransmitter cannot exert its usual effect.

There are both agonists and antagonists for each of the neurotransmitters we have discussed, and these drugs produce effects that may be beneficial or harmful. For example, cobra snake venom is an antagonist of acetylcholine—it blocks the action of acetylcholine and prevents it from having its typical excitatory effect. The results are paralysis and death. Nicotine, the active drug in tobacco, is an acetylcholine agonist, binding to acetylcholine receptors and mimicking the effect of this neurotransmitter by producing stimulant effects (Julien, 2004).

Alcohol affects GABA receptors (and possibly other types of receptors as well), producing slowed reactions and altered thought processes (Julien, 2004). The effects of alcohol are similar to those of GABA: Both slow a person's reactions, produce lower response levels, and, in sufficient quantities, induce sleep and unconsciousness.

Altering the function of the monoamine class of neurotransmitters has proven to be beneficial for some people. Schizophrenia, a disabling mental disorder, is often treated with dopamine antagonists. Neurons that normally respond to dopamine are blocked from doing so by the presence of these antagonists, thereby diminishing the symptoms of schizophrenia (Julien, 2004). (We will discuss dopamine and its role in schizophrenia in more detail in Chapter 16.) Another strategy, that of blocking the reuptake of serotonin and norepinephrine, has proved highly useful in drug treatments for depression (Davidson et al., 2002), one of the most common and debilitating mental disorders in the world.

We've discussed the firing of individual neurons and the action of neurotransmitters to give you a close-up look at the function of the nervous system. To understand the relationship between brain and behavior, you need a wider view of brain structure and the organization of the nervous system.

Divisions of the Nervous System

It is a dark, wet evening; you are driving down a deserted road, listening to some 1980s oldies. A car appears out of nowhere, heading straight toward you. You swerve, brake, swerve again, pump the brakes, and then pull over to the side of the road—all within a matter of seconds. Your nervous system controls each of these reactions on a second-by-second basis, allowing you to avoid a crash. Such rapid perceptions and reactions require a high degree of organization, which your nervous system has. This organization starts with two general divisions: the central nervous system, consisting of the brain and spinal cord, and the peripheral nervous system, which connects the central nervous system to the rest of the body. Let's see how these parts of your nervous system work together to allow you to perform a wide variety of behaviors, including avoiding oncoming cars.

Peripheral [puh-RIF-er-al] nervous system ■ The part of the nervous system that carries information to and from the central nervous system through spinal nerves attached to the spinal cord and through 12 cranial nerves.

The Peripheral Nervous System

The *peripheral nervous system* is the part of the nervous system that carries information to and from the central nervous system through spinal nerves attached to the spinal cord and through 12 cranial nerves, which carry signals directly to and from the brain. The peripheral nervous system contains all the nerves that are not in the central nervous system; its nerves lie in the *periphery*, or outer parts, of the body. It is subdivided into two divisions: the somatic nervous system and the autonomic nervous system.

The *somatic nervous system* is the part of the peripheral nervous system that both responds to the senses of sight, hearing, touch, smell, and taste and acts on the outside world. Most of the actions and reactions mediated by this division of the nervous system are under the individual's voluntary control. The somatic nervous system is involved in perceptual processing (processing information gathered through the senses) and in controlling movement and muscles. The somatic nervous system consists of both sensory (afferent) neurons and motor (efferent) neurons, carrying information from the sense organs to the brain and from the brain and spinal cord to the muscles under conscious control. It is the somatic nervous system that allows you to see an oncoming car and get out of its way.

The *autonomic nervous system* is the part of the peripheral nervous system that controls physiological actions and reactions that proceed automatically, such as heart rate, digestive processes, the regulation of blood pressure, and the functioning of internal organs. In contrast to the somatic nervous system, the autonomic nervous system operates continuously and without a person's voluntary control. (The technique of biofeedback, discussed in Chapter 7, allows a person to learn how to exert partial voluntary control of this system.) The system is called *autonomic* (from the Greek word meaning "independent") because many of its subsystems are self-regulating. The autonomic nervous system consists of two divisions: the sympathetic nervous system and the parasympathetic nervous system, which work together to control the activities of muscles and glands (see **Figure 3.6** on p. 66).

The *sympathetic nervous system* is the part of the autonomic nervous system that responds to emergency situations like a possible head-on collision with a car by activating certain physiological changes to prepare the body to respond to the emergency. This activation results in a sharp increase in heart rate and blood pressure, a slowing of the digestive processes, and dilation of the pupils. Together, these bodily changes are sometimes called the *fight-or-flight response*. This pattern of changes is usually accompanied by an increased flow of *epinephrine* (also called *adrenaline*), which is a substance released by the adrenal gland and regulated by a set of neurons in the hypothalamus and the brain stem. Increased activity of the sympathetic nervous system is what makes your heart pound and your mouth go dry when your car narrowly misses hitting an oncoming car.

When the body is in a fight-or-flight state, the somatic nervous system is also activated. For example, when you are attempting to avoid a crash with another car, the adrenal gland is stimulated by the sympathetic nervous system; the burst of energy produced by the epinephrine released by the adrenal gland affects the somatic nervous system, which makes your muscles respond strongly and rapidly, initiating motor movements to steer, brake, and possibly shift gears. Thus, changes in the sympathetic nervous system can produce rapid changes in the somatic nervous system. These types of changes are also associated with emotional and stress reactions (discussed in detail in Chapters 12 and 15).

Somatic [so-MAT-ick] nervous system ■ The part of the peripheral nervous system that carries information from sense organs to the brain and from the brain and spinal cord to skeletal muscles, and thereby allows bodily movement; it controls voluntary sensory and motor functions.

Autonomic [autoe-NOM-ick] nervous system ■ The part of the peripheral nervous system that controls physiological actions and reactions that proceed automatically, such as heart rate, digestive processes, regulation of blood pressure, and the functioning of internal organs.

Sympathetic nervous system ■ The part of the autonomic nervous system that responds to emergency situations by activating certain physiological changes to prepare the body to respond.

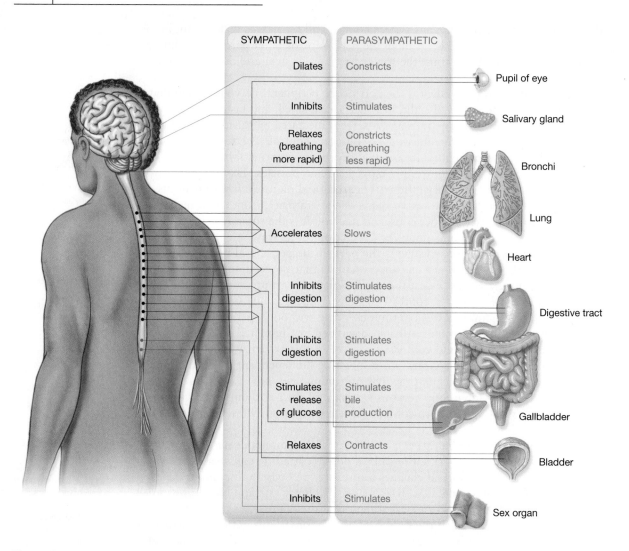

SYMPATHETIC	PARASYMPATHETIC	
Dilates	Constricts	Pupil of eye
Inhibits	Stimulates	Salivary gland
Relaxes (breathing more rapid)	Constricts (breathing less rapid)	Bronchi / Lung
Accelerates	Slows	Heart
Inhibits digestion	Stimulates digestion	Digestive tract
Inhibits digestion	Stimulates digestion	
Stimulates release of glucose	Stimulates bile production	Gallbladder
Relaxes	Contracts	Bladder
Inhibits	Stimulates	Sex organ

Figure 3.6
The Two Divisions of the Autonomic Nervous System

Parasympathetic [PAIR-uh-sim-puh-THET-ick] nervous system ■ The part of the autonomic nervous system that controls the normal operations of the body, including digestion, blood pressure, and respiration.

The *parasympathetic nervous system,* which is active most of the time, is the part of the autonomic nervous system that controls the normal operations of the body, including digestion, breathing, normal heart rate, and other functions. This system keeps the body running smoothly in ordinary circumstances and brings responses back to normal after an emergency. Because you are not experiencing an emergency right now, your parasympathetic nervous system is probably currently in control.

The Central Nervous System

The *central nervous system* is the other major division of the nervous system. Consisting of the brain and the spinal cord, it serves as the body's main processing system for information (see **Figure 3.7**). Millions of brain cells are involved in the performance of even simple activities. When you walk, for example, the visual areas of the brain are active so you can see where you're going, the brain's motor areas help make your legs move, and the cerebellum helps you keep your balance.

The brain is the control center, but it receives much of its information from the *spinal cord,* the main communication line to the rest of the body, and from the cranial nerves. The spinal cord, contained within the spinal column, receives signals from the sensory organs, muscles, and glands and relays these signals to the brain. *Spinal reflexes*—automatic responses that are controlled almost solely by the spinal cord—do not involve the brain. The knee jerk reflex, elicited by a tap on the tendon below the kneecap, is a spinal reflex. However, spinal reflexes represent only a fraction of the activity that occurs in the spinal cord. Most sensory signals make their way up the spinal cord to the brain for further analysis. In addition, motor impulses that originate in the brain make their way down the spinal cord and then to the peripheral nervous system, where they stimulate glands and muscles.

The spinal cord's most important function is relaying information to and from the brain. When a person's spinal cord is severed, the information exchange between the brain and the muscles and glands stops below the point of damage. Spinal reflexes still operate, but individuals who suffer spinal cord damage, like actor Christopher Reeve, lose voluntary control over muscles in the parts of their

Central nervous system ■ One of the two major divisions of the nervous system, consisting of the brain and the spinal cord.

Spinal cord ■ The portion of the central nervous system that is contained within the spinal column and relays signals from the sensory organs, muscles, and glands to the brain, controls reflexive responses, and transmits signals from the brain to the peripheral nervous system.

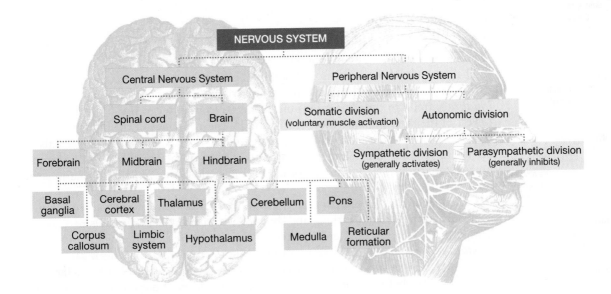

Figure 3.7
The Basic Divisions of the Nervous System

bodies below the site of the injury. This shows that the spinal cord serves a key communication function between the brain and the rest of the body; it is the chief trunk line for neuronal impulses. However, the brain is much more important for behavior.

The Brain

Brain ■ The part of the central nervous system that is located in the skull and that regulates, monitors, processes, and guides other nervous system activity.

A person's intelligence, personality traits, and ability to communicate through language reside in a relatively small organ protected by the skull—the *brain*. The human brain is highly evolved, complex, and specialized. It is this specialization that allows humans—in contrast to nonhuman animals—to think about the past and the future and to communicate using language. Scientists have studied the structures and interconnections of the brain and the effects of brain damage, yet they still do not fully understand how the brain functions.

During the prenatal period, the brain initially forms three divisions—hindbrain, midbrain, and forebrain. Later, the forebrain and the hindbrain divide again, so the fully developed brain has five divisions. As a general principle, the structures in the hindbrain tend to be responsible for more biologically basic and reflexive functions, whereas those in the forebrain are involved in more complex and abstract cognitive functions. Consistent with that principle, the cortex—the deeply fissured gray layer that covers the surfaces of the cerebral hemispheres at the very top of the brain—is the location of the most complex functioning, including thought and language. The hindbrain controls functions that are more basic to survival. Let's examine the brain from the bottom to the top, looking for evidence of this general principle as well as specific functions.

The Hindbrain and Midbrain

Hindbrain ■ The lowest of the three main divisions of the brain, consisting of the medulla, the reticular formation, the pons, and the cerebellum.

Every time Tiger Woods wins another golf tournament, the victory is a tribute to his cerebellum, one of the structures of the hindbrain. If his cerebellum functioned even slightly less proficiently, he would be a duffer rather than a champion. The *hindbrain* (refer to the illustrations on the inside front cover of this book) is the lowest of the three main divisions of the brain. The structures of the hindbrain receive signals from other parts of the brain and from the spinal cord. The signals are interpreted and then either relayed to other parts of the brain or translated into immediate action. The hindbrain consists of the medulla, the reticular formation, the pons, and the cerebellum.

Medulla [meh-DUH-lah] ■ The part of the hindbrain that controls heartbeat and breathing.

Reticular formation ■ An interconnected network of nerve cells that stretches from the hindbrain into the midbrain, with connections to the pons and projections toward the cortex, and that is involved in the regulation of arousal.

The *medulla* is a dense package of nerves lying just above the spinal cord that controls heartbeat and breathing and through which many neural signals pass. Within the medulla is an interconnected network of nerve cells, the *reticular formation,* which helps regulate a person's state of arousal. Damage to it can result in coma, and its normal function focuses on arousal and sleeping. The reticular formation stretches from the hindbrain into the midbrain; it has connections to the pons and projections toward the cortex.

Pons ■ A structure in the hindbrain that provides a link to the rest of the brain and that affects sleep and dreaming.

The *pons* provides a link between the hindbrain and the rest of the brain, and many tracts of nerves from the midbrain and forebrain go through the pons and then to the spinal cord. Like the medulla, the pons is involved in sleep and dreaming. The *cerebellum* (or "little brain"), a structure in the hindbrain, influences balance, coordination, and movement, including single joint actions such as the flexing of an elbow or a knee. The cerebellum constitutes only 10% of the total volume of the brain but contains more than half of its neurons! People with damage to the cerebellum have difficulties in performing discrete movements that require coordination (Spencer et al., 2003). Alcohol disrupts the activity of the cerebellum, and the field sobriety tests that police officers administer assess the types of coordination that the cerebellum directs. The cerebellum is also involved in learning and memory for coordinated motor skills (Petrosini et al., 2003). The healthy functioning of the cerebellum allows you to walk in a straight line, type accurately, and coordinate the many movements involved in dancing—and, if you're Tiger Woods, hit a golf ball better than almost anyone. The cerebellum may also play a role in emotions; some individuals with damage to the cerebellum experience emotional changes that are severe and disruptive, such as depression or explosive anger (Margolis, 2002).

The *midbrain* (refer to the inside front cover) consists of nuclei (collections of cell bodies) that receive neural signals from other parts of the brain and from the spinal cord. Like the hindbrain, the midbrain interprets the signals and either relays the information to the forebrain or causes the body to act at once. Different portions of the midbrain govern smoothness of movement, temperature regulation, and reflexive movement. Movements of the eyeball in its socket, for example, are controlled by the *superior colliculus*, a structure in the midbrain. The reticular formation continues into the midbrain.

The Forebrain

At the top of the brain is the *forebrain,* the largest and most complex brain structure in humans. Part of the complexity of the forebrain lies in the interconnections among its structures, which allow for enormous variability in behavior and responses.

The *thalamus* (refer to the inside front cover) acts primarily as a routing station for sending information to other parts of the brain, although it probably also performs some interpretive functions. For example, nearly all sensory information coming from the body proceeds through this structure (which is about the size of a hen's egg) before going to other areas of the brain. The *hypothalamus* is much smaller than the thalamus (it is only the size of a pea) and is located just below it. Despite its small size, the hypothalamus has numerous connections with the rest of the forebrain and with the midbrain and affects many complex behaviors, such as eating, drinking, and sexual activity. We will examine its influence on eating in more detail in Chapter 12.

One of the least understood structures of the brain is the *limbic system* (see **Figure 3.8** on p. 70). This system in the forebrain consists of an interconnected group of structures (including parts of the cortex, thalamus, and the hypothalamus) that influence emotions, memory, social behavior, and brain disorders such as epilepsy. Included within the limbic system are the hippocampus and the amygdala.

Cerebellum [seh-rah-BELL-um] ■ A structure in the hindbrain that influences balance, coordination, and movement.

Midbrain ■ The second of the three main divisions of the brain, which receives neural signals from other parts of the brain and from the spinal cord, interprets the signals, and either relays the information to the forebrain or causes the body to act at once.

Forebrain ■ The largest and most complex of the three main divisions of the brain, which has many interconnected structures, including the thalamus, hypothalamus, limbic system, basal ganglia, corpus callosum, and cortex.

Thalamus ■ A large structure of the forebrain that acts primarily as a routing station for sending sensory information to other parts of the brain but probably also performs some interpretive functions.

Hypothalamus ■ A relatively small structure of the forebrain, lying just below the thalamus, that affects many complex behaviors, such as eating, drinking, and sexual activity.

Limbic system ■ An interconnected group of structures in the forebrain that includes parts of the cortex, the thalamus, and the hypothalamus and that influences emotions, memory, social behavior, and brain disorders such as epilepsy.

Figure 3.8
Principal
Structures
of the Limbic
System

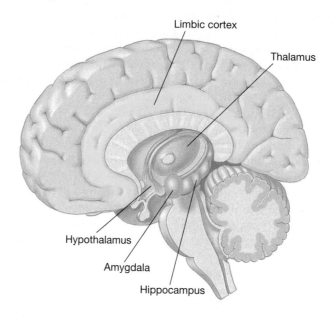

The *hippocampus* is involved in learning and memory (Prickaerts et al., 2004), navigating in the environment (Silvers et al., 2003), and some emotional functions (Ma & Leung, 2004; Maguire et al., 1998).

The *amygdala*, one of a pair of olive-shaped structures in the forebrain, is also involved in emotional behaviors (Damasio, 1999; 2003; Davidson, 2003). Stimulation of the amygdala in animals, for instance, produces attack responses, and surgical removal of the amygdala was once a radical way of treating people who were extremely violent. The amygdala is now considered important in learning, in the recognition of fear, and in a wide range of other emotions.

Stimulation of several areas of the limbic system in rats produces what appear to be highly pleasurable sensations. James Olds and Peter Milner (1954) discovered that rats that received small doses of electrical current in some limbic areas as a reward for bar pressing chose bar pressing over eating, even after having been deprived of food for long periods. The researchers called the areas of the brain being stimulated *pleasure centers*, but more recent research has demonstrated a link between addictive behaviors and stimulation of these areas (Volkow et al., 2002; Wise, 1996).

The *basal ganglia* are a series of nuclei that are located deep in the forebrain to the left and right of the thalamus and that link the thalamus and the cortex. These nuclei control movements and posture, and their degeneration is associated with Parkinson's disease (Purves et al., 2001). Parts of the basal ganglia influence muscle tone and initiate commands to the cerebellum and to parts of the forebrain. Damage to this neurological center can have severe consequences, including muscular rigidity and tremors. In addition, parts of the basal ganglia are involved in cognitive functions.

The topmost part of the human brain and the largest structure in it is the *cerebrum*. The cerebrum consists of the left and right halves called *cerebral hemispheres* and a covering called the *cortex*. The two sides of the brain are connected by the corpus callosum. Each of these structures is important for psychology.

Hippocampus ■ A structure in the forebrain that is part of the limbic system and is involved in learning and memory.

Amygdala ■ One of a pair of oval structures in the forebrain that are part of the limbic system and are involved in emotional behaviors.

The exterior covering of the hemispheres, or the *cerebral cortex* (or the *neocortex*), is about 2–3 millimeters thick and consists of six thin layers of cells. It is convoluted, or wrinkled. The *convolutions,* or folds in the cortical tissue and in the underlying cerebral hemispheres, create more surface area within a small space, allowing a relatively large cerebral cortex to fit in a small skull. The overall surface area of the human cortex is at least 1.5 square feet. Human beings have a highly developed cortex, but most other mammals' brains are less deeply convoluted. Following the general principle of brain organization, as the topmost part of the brain, the cortex controls the most complex and abstract cognitive function: thought.

The cerebral cortex is divided into several lobes, or areas, named after the overlying cranial bones—frontal, parietal, temporal, and occipital. The four lobes are well defined by prominent *sulci* (folds) and fissures (very deep folds)—the lateral fissure, the longitudinal fissure, and the central sulcus. These easily recognizable fissures are like deep ravines that run among the convolutions, separating the lobes. The *frontal lobe* is in front of the central sulcus; the *parietal lobe* is behind it. Below the lateral fissure and the parietal lobe on each side of the brain is the *temporal lobe*. And at the back of the head, behind the parietal and temporal lobes, is the *occipital lobe*. **Figure 3.9** illustrates the various lobes.

Cerebral cortex ■ The convoluted exterior covering of the brain's hemispheres, which is about 2–3 millimeters thick and is divided into several lobes.

Convolutions ■ Folds in the cortical tissue and in the underlying cerebral hemispheres.

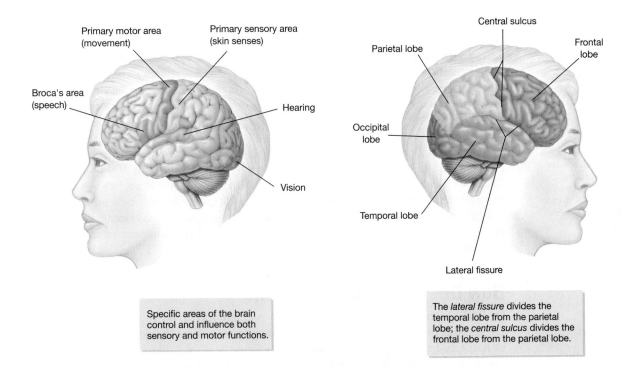

Primary motor area (movement)

Primary sensory area (skin senses)

Broca's area (speech)

Hearing

Vision

Central sulcus

Parietal lobe

Frontal lobe

Occipital lobe

Temporal lobe

Lateral fissure

Specific areas of the brain control and influence both sensory and motor functions.

The *lateral fissure* divides the temporal lobe from the parietal lobe; the *central sulcus* divides the frontal lobe from the parietal lobe.

Figure 3.9
The Cortex and the Lobes of the Brain
The cortex is the exterior covering of the cerebral hemispheres. It consists of four major lobes that contain specific sensory and motor areas. The cortex is the uppermost part of the brain and is involved in more abstract and complex thought processes.

Table 3.3

THE LOBES OF THE BRAIN

Lobe	Location	Function
■ Frontal lobe	In front of the central fissure; contains the motor cortex and Broca's area	Memory, movement, speech and language production
■ Parietal lobe	Behind frontal lobe	Sense of touch and body position
■ Temporal lobe	Below lateral fissure and parietal lobe	Speech, hearing, and some visual information processing
■ Occipital lobe	Back of the brain, next to and behind parietal and temporal lobes	Visual sensing

The location of the cerebral cortex—just beneath the skull—makes it easier to study than other parts of the brain. During the 1940s, neurosurgeon Wilder Penfield (1977) began to map the cerebral cortex during surgery to the brain, stimulating the lobes of the cerebral cortex with low levels of electrical current. Penfield found that the stimulation of some areas produced sensations, whereas stimulation of other areas produced movement. Penfield's work prompted others to conduct similar investigations, and a picture began to emerge of specific sensory and motor areas in the cerebral cortex. **Table 3.3** lists the sensory and motor functions of the lobes of the brain.

Corpus callosum ■ A thick band of nerve fibers that forms the main connection between the left and right cerebral hemispheres.

The *corpus callosum*, the structure that connects the cerebral hemispheres, is important to their function. The callosum is a thick band of about 200 million nerve fibers, which provide connections that convey information between the two cerebral hemispheres. Damage to the corpus callosum results in essentially two separate brains within one skull. Studies of this type of damage, which has occurred almost exclusively as the result of surgery, has helped to reveal the functions of the cerebral hemispheres. We'll discuss these functions in the next section.

How Does the Brain Function?

In the 18th century, phrenology was a very popular way to try to understand something about the brain's functioning. Phrenologists measured the size and proportions of heads and analyzed the locations of bumps and other prominent features; their reasoning was that features on the skull were associated with certain kinds of thoughts. Today, scientists are still striving to understand the brain and how it works, but the methods of study have changed. Knowledge of the brain's structure forms the basis for understanding its function, but it is not enough. A complete understanding of brain function requires knowledge of the activities that each structure performs.

One strategy for understanding what brain structures perform what activities is to investigate the results of brain damage. By studying the brains of people who have died of tumors, brain diseases, or trauma (injury) to the brain, researchers attempt to relate the type and location of brain damage to the loss of specific abilities, such as speaking, moving, reading, or even recognizing faces (Willingham & Dunn, 2003). This approach led to the identification of the first area of the brain to be associated with a specific function. In the middle of the 19th century, a country doctor named Paul Broca treated a patient who did not speak (Springer & Deutsch, 1998). Broca believed that the man could not speak because he had experienced a stroke that damaged his brain. Broca was correct. After the patient died, an autopsy revealed damage to the man's left frontal lobe. Damage to this area of the cortex, now called *Broca's area*, consistently creates problems in language production. Several years after Broca made his observations, a German neurologist named Karl Wernicke found that an area in the left temporal lobe is important for language comprehension. This area of the cerebral cortex is known as *Wernicke's area*. Thus, by studying many individuals with various types of brain damage, neurologists established that the left hemisphere is specialized for language. This strategy has been used to understand the relationship between behavior and damage to specific parts of the brain.

An alternative strategy involves a technique called *ablation*, in which the brain is intentionally damaged to determine the effects of the damage. In ablation studies, after anesthetizing an animal (the ethical rules of research with nonhuman animals require anesthesia for surgery to prevent unnecessary pain), researchers remove or destroy a portion of the animal's brain; then they study the animal's behavior to determine changes. Of course, ablation studies are not conducted on human participants. Ablation is more precise than studying people with brain damage, because the researchers create the damage and know its precise location and extent. However, the goal is similar: to determine the relationship between behavior and brain damage.

Today, in addition to observations of brain-damaged individuals and ablation studies on nonhuman animals, researchers can use a variety of techniques to study living brains without harming the participants in their studies. It is now possible to study the functioning human brain using EEGs, MRIs, and CT and PET scans.

Broca's area ■ The area of the left frontal lobe that Paul Broca discovered to be critical for language production.

Wernicke's area ■ The area of the left temporal lobe that Karl Wernicke discovered to be important for language comprehension.

Monitoring Neural Activity

Researchers have taken several approaches to the task of monitoring neural activity, from recording the function of a single neuron to using sophisticated technology to observe the brain as it works.

Single-unit recording is a technique in which researchers implant a thin wire, needle, or glass tube containing a chemical solution into or next to a single neuron and leave it there to measure the neuron's electrical activity (Willingham & Dunn, 2003). Scientists usually perform this type of study on rats, cats, or monkeys, because such studies are invasive and damaging, and it would be considered unacceptable to perform them on humans. The researchers typically use anesthesia or other medications to minimize any potential pain or discomfort the animals might experience. When the animal recovers, a recording of the neuron's electrical activity is made as the animal behaves and responds to a variety of stimuli. Because neurons fire extremely rapidly, the information from the recording is often fed into a computer, which averages the number of times the cell fires in 1 second or 1 minute.

Another technique for studying neural activity involves the use of an *electroencephalograph*, which measures electrical activity in the nervous systems of either nonhuman animals or humans. As the photo shows, this technique produces a graphical record of brain-wave activity called an ***electroencephalogram, or EEG*** (*electro* means "electrical," *encephalon* means "brain," and *gram* means "record"). Small electrodes placed on the scalp record the activity of thousands of neurons beneath the skull to produce an EEG (Uttal, 2001). Researchers usually use computers to analyze these recordings, which can show patterns consistent with diagnoses of brain damage, epilepsy, tumors, and other abnormalities. Detecting such abnormalities has been the major use of EEGs, although researchers investigating sleep also use these recordings.

EEGs of healthy human beings show a variety of characteristic brain-wave patterns, depending on the level and kind of mental activity that is occurring. Researchers usually describe brain waves in terms of their *frequency* (the number of waves in a unit of time) and *amplitude* (the relative height or size of the waves). If people are awake yet relaxed, their EEGs primarily show *alpha waves*, which occur at a moderate rate (frequency) of 8 to 12 cycles per second and are of moderate amplitude. When people are excited, their brain waves consist of *beta waves*, which are of high frequency and low-amplitude. At different times during sleep, people show varying patterns of high-frequency and low-frequency waves correlated with dreaming activity and nondreaming sleep, both of which are discussed in Chapter 7.

Electroencephalogram [ee-LECK-tro-en-SEFF-uh-low-gram] (EEG) ■ A graphical record of brain-wave activity obtained through electrodes placed on the scalp.

MRI (magnetic resonance imaging) ■ Imaging technique that uses magnetic fields to produce scans of great clarity and high resolution, distinguishing brain parts as small as 1 or 2 millimeters.

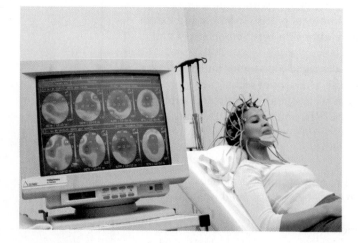

An electroencephalogram (EEG) provides a graphic record of the electrical activity of the brain.

Newer techniques for measuring the activity of the nervous system include CT scanning, MRI, and PET scanning. CT (computerized tomography) scans are computer-enhanced X-ray images of the brain (or any area of the body). The computer enhancement builds a series of images into a three-dimensional picture of the scanned area (Uttal, 2001). CT scans are especially helpful in locating specific damaged areas or tumors in the brain. However, since people must be very still while being scanned, this technique is much more useful in showing structure than in revealing function.

MRI (magnetic resonance imaging) uses magnetic fields instead of X-rays to produce brain scans that have far greater clarity and resolution than CT scans (Uttal, 2001). MRI scans can distinguish brain parts as small as 1 or 2 millimeters, providing highly detailed images of the brain's tissue that can reveal many kinds of abnormalities. MRIs are not invasive—nothing needs to be injected—and no radiation is involved, making MRI scans preferable to CT scans in many situations.

A variation of MRI allows observation of functioning brains. *Functional MRI (fMRI)* is an imaging technique that registers changes in the metabolism (energy consumption) of neurons. A person is often asked to perform a particular task while the imaging is taking place. The area of the brain involved in performing this task experiences an increase in metabolism that shows up on the fMRI image, typically as a color change. By having a person perform different tasks, it is possible to locate the regions of brain activation corresponding to these tasks (Reichle, Carpenter, & Just, 2000; Willingham & Dunn, 2003). Advances in fMRI have allowed researchers to track changes in brain activity over time (Kim & Ogawa, 2002; Mitchell et al., 2000). The newest fMRI techniques both locate areas of active neurons and detect the release of neurotransmitters in order to study both electrical and chemical aspects of brain activity (Thiel, 2003).

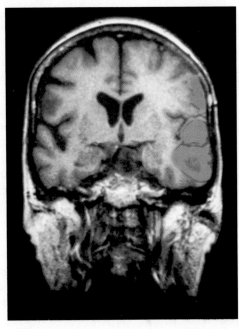

PET (positron emission tomography) takes an alternative approach to localizing brain function. PET tracks radioactive substances injected into the bloodstream and allows researchers to see which areas of the brain become more active in response to the experience of different sensations, perceptions, emotions, and cognitive tasks (Uttal, 2001). For example, PET scans allowed one team of researchers to find a relationship between blood flow and performance on an attention task in people with brain damage and in those whose brains were intact; the results indicated that the right frontal cortex is active during performance of tasks involving attention (Koski & Petrides, 2001). Other studies using PET have shown that specific brain regions are associated with specific types of memory or thought processes (Anderson et al., 2000) and that specific areas show more blood flow for some tasks (for example, recall compared to recognition) than do other areas (Cabeza & Nyberg, 2000). PET scans have several disadvantages, including the fact that the scan patterns are too indistinct to locate activated brain regions precisely. In addition, PET scans expose participants to radiation, and the equipment is expensive and not widely available. However, the advantages of PET scans outweigh the disadvantages for many researchers.

Both fMRI and PET have become important techniques for investigating brain function. For example, researchers have studied learning and memory formation (Zeineh et al., 2003), differences in the activation of the brains of people with and without mental disorders (Gur et al., 2003), and language and speech comprehension and production (Bookheimer, 2002). One study even used fMRI to examine the changes that occur in the brain as a result of psychotherapy (Paquette et al., 2003). This study compared the patterns of brain activation of 12 people with a phobia (an unreasonable fear) of spiders before and after they had undergone psychotherapy for their phobia. In addition, the study recorded the brain activation of a group of

This MRI shows brain damage that may produce problems in using language or interpreting sensory stimulation.

fMRI (functional magnetic resonance imaging) ■ Imaging technique that allows observation of functioning brains by registering changes in the metabolism (energy consumption) of neurons.

PET (positron emission tomography) ■ Imaging technique that tracks radioactive substances injected into the bloodstream, allowing researchers to view how brain activity varies in response to different sensations, perceptions, emotions, and cognitive tasks.

people with no phobia to provide an appropriate comparison for those participants with spider phobias. Using fMRI to image the brains of both types of participants as they watched a video of spiders, the researchers found differences in brain activation between the two groups. The observed differences may have been related to managing thoughts about fear of spiders (higher activity in the frontal lobe) and memories of spiders (higher activity in part of the hippocampus). After therapy, the two groups showed fewer differences in brain activation patterns, demonstrating the effectiveness of the therapy for the phobic participants. This study demonstrates the ability of brain imaging to reveal the activity involved with thought processes and behavioral problems as well as to confirm that changes in the brain occur as a result of psychological treatment.

Table 3.4 summarizes the four important brain-imaging techniques. Despite the impressive results and great promise of these techniques, remember that PET and fMRI do not detect mental activity directly—rather, they measure changes in blood flow or metabolism that are related to energy consumption by brain cells. Psychologists must be cautious in how they interpret results from these techniques (Willingham & Dunn, 2003). Just because there is a correlation between two events (in these cases, brain activity and behavior) does not mean one causes the other in any direct way. Results from PET and fMRI studies must be analyzed with caution, because many parts of the

Table 3.4

FOUR IMPORTANT IMAGING TECHNIQUES

Technique	Function and Application
■ CT (computerized tomography)	Produces computer-enhanced, three-dimensional, X-ray images of the brain (or any part of the body), essentially a series of X-rays showing slices of the brain (or other part of the body)
■ PET (positron emission tomography)	Tracks radioactive markers injected into the bloodstream, enabling researchers to monitor variations in cerebral activity, which correlate with mental processes
■ MRI (magnetic resonance imaging)	Uses magnetic fields instead of X-rays to produce highly detailed images of brain tissue that have far greater clarity and resolution than CT scans; can distinguish brain parts with sizes as small as 1 or 2 millimeters
■ fMRI (functional MRI)	Registers changes in the metabolism (energy consumption) of cells in various regions of the brain, allowing observation of activity in the brain as it takes place

brain are active simultaneously and are interconnected. The temptation to conclude that behavior can be reduced to specific patterns of localized brain activity is strong, but such a conclusion is not warranted. The interactions among brain areas are complex, and many psychological constructs such as intelligence and personality may not be reducible to particular brain activity.

Brain Specialization

Are there specific places in the brain that control specific behaviors and thoughts? Are some areas in the brain devoted to one function? As you've seen, these questions have prompted neuroscientists to investigate the connection between brain locations and behaviors using a wide range of techniques. Researchers have even investigated the difference in function between the two cerebral hemispheres and the possibility that women's and men's brains function differently.

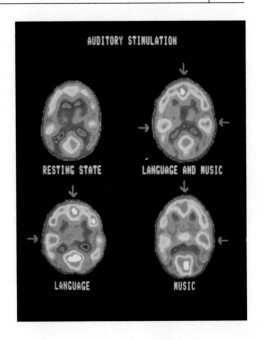

PET scans allow researchers to determine what areas of the brain are active during various types of stimulation.

Splitting the Brain

Many parts of the body, such as arms, legs, and kidneys, are bilaterally symmetrical—the same on each side—but the cerebral hemispheres are not. Broca discovered this asymmetry in the 1860s, when he found that the left frontal lobe contains an area that is important for language production, whereas the right frontal lobe does not. Several years later, Wernicke found another structure in the left cerebral hemisphere that is important for language comprehension. Thus, the left hemisphere contains two centers specialized for language. The full extent of the differences in function of the two hemispheres became apparent when psychologists began to study people whose brains had been surgically split, separating the two cerebral hemispheres.

Beginning in the 1960s, Nobel Prize winner Roger Sperry (1913–1994) and Michael Gazzaniga have been at the forefront of research in cerebral organization, studying what happens when the two cerebral hemispheres are surgically severed (Gazzaniga, 1967; 2000). The participants in these studies are individuals who have undergone surgery that severs the corpus callosum, the band of fibers that connects the left and right hemispheres of the brain, as a means of reducing uncontrollable seizures. This surgery can be successful because the seizures can no longer spread to both hemispheres. After the operation, the two hemispheres cannot communicate with each other; the *split-brain individuals* seem to have two distinct, independent brains, each with its own abilities. Studies of these individuals have revealed how the two cerebral hemispheres function together and separately.

To understand this fascinating research, it is necessary to know that each cerebral hemisphere is connected neurologically to the opposite side of the body; thus, the left hemisphere controls the right side of the body and vice versa (Johnson, 1998).

Split-brain individuals ■ People whose corpus callosum, which normally connects the two cerebral hemispheres, has been surgically severed.

The split-brain operation does not affect the crossing over of information between the sides of the body and the brain, which occurs at the level of the pons in the hindbrain, but it does limit the communication between the two hemispheres. Split-brain individuals are unable to access the speech and language capabilities located in the left cerebral hemisphere to describe activities carried out by the right one. When stimulus information is presented exclusively to a participant's right visual field (and thus to the left hemisphere) while the person stares straight ahead, the person can name or describe the stimulus in essentially normal ways. But when the same stimulus is presented exclusively to the left visual field (and thus to the right cerebral hemisphere), the person is unable to describe the stimulus verbally (a left-hemisphere task), because the splitting of the corpus callosum prevents the right hemisphere from accessing the language capabilities of the left. (See **Figure 3.10.**)

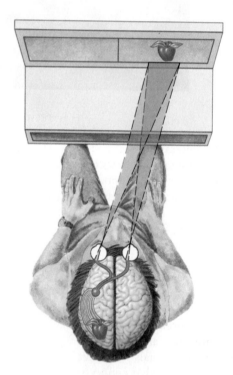

"I saw an apple."

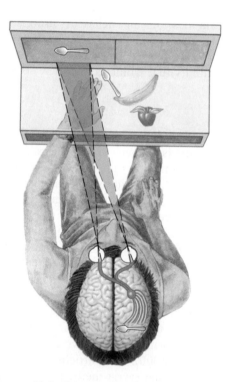

"I don't know what the image is."

Figure 3.10

The Effects of Severing the Corpus Callosum

A man whose corpus callosum has been severed is staring directly before him at a screen. A picture of an apple appears on the right side of the screen, in the man's right visual field. This image travels to the man's left hemisphere, which contains language centers. He is able to name the image as an apple. When an image of a spoon flashes on the left side of the screen, in the man's left visual field, the image travels to the man's right hemisphere, which does not have language centers. The man cannot say that he saw a spoon. However, he can identify the spoon as the object he saw by touching or picking it up with his left hand, controlled by the right hemisphere.

Although the right hemisphere has limited language functions, it has other functions that the left hemisphere lacks (Vogel, Bowers, & Vogel, 2003). This half of the cerebrum predominates during spatial tasks that rely on the ability to deal with the size, shape, and position of objects in space. Your right hemisphere, more so than your left, is activated when you are drawing, putting together jigsaw puzzles, reading maps, and other tasks that require spatial skills.

The division of abilities to the left or right hemisphere is referred to as *lateralization* of function. There is no doubt that human beings as well as other animals exhibit such lateralization. Unfortunately, the popular press and TV newscasters oversimplify this characteristic and, in some cases, overgeneralize its significance to account for school problems, marital problems, artistic abilities, and even baseball batting averages. One example of a popular misconception of hemispheric specialization is that the right hemisphere is "creative." This belief is an overgeneralization of the right hemisphere's role in spatial visualization and drawing. The right hemisphere is dominant for drawing, but it is not necessarily more creative than the left hemisphere. For example, the right hemisphere alone cannot produce creative writing, and both hemispheres must work together to produce poetry—the left hemisphere must find the words and the right hemisphere must construct the meter. Typically, the two hemispheres work together in everyday tasks. For example, the left side of the brain may recognize a stimulus, but the right side puts that recognition into context (Doty, 1999).

In addition, sophisticated brain-imaging studies have led to a more complex picture of hemispheric specialization. Performance on some tasks may depend on one hemisphere or the other, but many more abilities draw from a complex interconnection of structures (Metcalfe, Funnell, & Gazzaniga, 1995; Walsh, 2000). The growing body of brain-imaging research shows that many activities that were once considered exclusively left-brain functions (such as listening to someone speaking) or right-brain functions (such as listening to music) actually involve both hemispheres (Bookheimer, 2002; Doty, 1999; Waldie & Mosley, 2000). Brain specialization is clearly more complex than researchers once believed, but brain-imaging technology is beginning to help neuroscientists understand that complexity.

Gender and the Brain

People's misconceptions of hemispheric specialization have also led to theories on gender differences in brain function. Although there are studies indicating that men's and women's cerebral hemispheres may show some differences in functioning, the findings do not support the conclusion that there are masculine and feminine sides of the brain. This unwarranted conclusion, which typically portrays the left side as logical and rational (and thus masculine) and the right side as emotional and holistic (and thus feminine), is mistaken not only in its gender stereotyping but also in its overgeneralization of the findings on the brain's hemispheres.

Over the past several decades, some research has indicated that men's and women's brains may differ in the way their cerebral hemispheres are organized. Evaluations of a great deal of research show that women's brains are less lateralized than men's (Josse & Tzourio-Mazoyer, 2004; Medland, Geffen, & McFarland, 2002).

In men, language functions are more strongly lateralized in the left hemisphere and spatial functions in the right, whereas in women, both abilities are represented in both hemispheres. However, a study of a large group of men and women using fMRI showed that both genders had strong left hemisphere lateralization for language (Frost et al., 1999). Another study that focused on spatial tasks (Georgopoulos et al., 2001) found gender differences in brain activation during a task involving imagining how pieces of a puzzle fit together: Men's right hemispheres were more active than their left hemispheres, whereas women's left hemispheres showed greater activation. Apparently, gender differences related to activity of the left and right hemispheres are small and limited to a few tasks.

Do these small differences indicate that women's and men's brains function differently? And if so, does one gender's brain function "better"? Researchers have not agreed about the implications of the findings, so the first question is difficult to answer. Some researchers believe that the small differences produce large differences in mental abilities; others hold that the differences exist but are too small to be meaningful. The second question is far easier to answer: Few of the brain-imaging studies have shown a performance difference in the tasks they have measured. For example, one study using a word recognition task (Walla et al., 2001) showed different patterns of brain activation during the task but similar performance accuracy by women and men. Patterns of activation may represent differences in organization and may affect the efficiency of functioning. For example, one study showed that people who were better at a spatial task showed lower levels of brain activation than those who performed more poorly (Unterrainer et al., 2000). However, both men and women were able to perform the task equally well. Thus, there is some evidence for one type of gender difference in cerebral organization but little evidence for superiority of function in either gender.

Plasticity and Change

Does your brain stay the same from birth to death, or can it change through experience or simply from the passage of time? Neuroscientist Michael Merzenich emphasizes the brain's capability for change by saying, "The brain was constructed to change" (in Holloway, 2003, p. 78). Although the basic organization of the human brain is established well before birth, the brain remains capable of growth and development throughout the life span—a capability referred to as *plasticity*. Plasticity can result from changes in the process of neural conduction or at the level of the synapse, or it can be due to *neurogenesis*, the formation of new neurons. All of these processes produce adaptations in the brain.

Plasticity ■ The capability of the brain to grow and develop throughout the life span.

Although the brain can create new neurons, neurogenesis is not typically the means by which people recover from most brain injuries. In mature brains, neurogenesis mainly occurs in the area around the hippocampus, the structure in the forebrain that is involved in learning and memory. The exact mechanism for the creation of new neurons remains poorly understood, but the hippocampal area has definitely been implicated both as an area in which neurogenesis occurs and as an area associated with the formation of new memories (Prickaerts et al., 2004).

Several factors influence plasticity. Experience with specific stimuli reinforces the development of neural structures. You can liken the developing brain to a highway system that expands with use. Less-traveled roads are abandoned, but popular ones are broadened and new ones are built. When neural structures are used, reused, and constantly updated, they become faster and more easily accessed (Martin et al., 2000). The majority of neural interconnections are established during fetal development and early infancy (Neville & Bavelier, 2000). If these links are not used, they disappear (Colman, Nabekura, & Lichtman, 1997). The links that are used not only become reinforced but also proliferate. For example, rats raised in a complex, stimulating environment develop more synapses in their cerebral cortexes than rats raised in an unstimulating environment (Greenough & Chang, 1989). This finding demonstrates how experience can affect the brain by prompting it to change—that is, by encouraging plasticity.

Age is also a factor in plasticity. Changes in the brains of young organisms are not surprising, but plasticity is less expected in aging ones. As human beings grow older, their central nervous systems do not function as well. For example, the numbers of neurons and receptors decrease (Whalley, 2001). In addition, some learning tasks become more difficult for aging animals, including humans. Diseases may affect aging brains, producing problems for brain function. However, even aging animals have some plasticity and experience changes in their cerebral cortexes when they live in a stimulating environment (Kolb, Gibb, & Gorny, 2003).

The occurrence of plasticity in mature and even aging people and nonhuman animals suggests that damage done to the nervous system can be repaired. Injury to the brain can be devastating, but the extent and permanence of the damage depend on the nature of the injury, the age of the organism when the injury takes place, and whether the organism is exposed to positive factors, such as an enriched environment, training, and practice, which can prompt the brain to compensate for the damage (Kolb & Gibb, 1999). According to Merzenich (in Holloway, 2003), behavior is the key to producing brain changes, and problems such as reading disabilities, schizophrenia, and autism may someday be treated with techniques that induce brain changes. Other researchers acknowledge the potential for prompting brain changes but also see limits to this application of plasticity.

The research on how experience affects brain plasticity illustrates an important point: Brain and behavior interact in both directions. We tend to think of the brain directing behavior, but this research demonstrates how behavior can affect the brain. Hormones also affect neural plasticity (Kolb, Gibb, & Robinson, 2003), as well as various functions of the nervous system and other parts of the body.

What Effects Do Hormones Have on Behavior?

People imagine that hormones control many behaviors, from sexual activity to cravings for sugar. Indeed, defense lawyers have argued that hormones make people commit crimes. What are hormones, what do they do, and how do they affect behavior?

Figure 3.11

The Endocrine Glands

The endocrine glands are situated throughout the body. Though small in size, they secrete hormones that exert powerful influences on behavior.

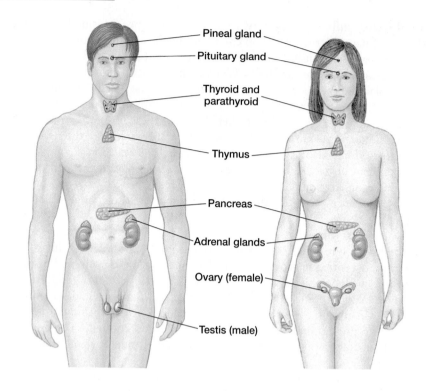

Pineal gland

Pituitary gland

Thyroid and parathyroid

Thymus

Pancreas

Adrenal glands

Ovary (female)

Testis (male)

Hormones ■ Chemicals that are produced by the endocrine glands and that regulate the activities of specific organs or cells.

Endocrine [END-oh-krin] glands ■ Ductless glands that secrete hormones into the bloodstream (rather than into a duct that goes to the target organ).

Pituitary [pit-YOU-ih-tare-ee] gland ■ The body's so-called master gland, which is located at the base of the brain and closely linked to the hypothalamus and which regulates the actions of many other endocrine glands.

Hormones are chemicals that are produced by the endocrine glands and that regulate the activities of specific organs or cells. A hormone travels through the bloodstream to target an organ containing cells that respond specifically to that hormone. *Endocrine glands* are ductless glands that secrete hormones into the bloodstream (rather than into a duct that goes to the target organ). **Figure 3.11** shows the locations of several endocrine glands.

The endocrine system is similar to the nervous system in that it provides a means of internal communication using chemical signals, although hormone action tends to be slower than neurotransmitter action. Also, the endocrine system is closely involved with nervous system functioning. For example, the brain initiates the release of hormones, which affect the target organs, which in turn affect behavior, which in turn affects the brain, forming a complex interaction of systems.

The *pituitary gland* is often called the body's "master gland" because it regulates the actions of many other endocrine glands. The pituitary is located at the base of the brain and is closely linked to the hypothalamus (see **Figure 3.12** on p. 63). The pituitary produces hormones that act on other glands such as the thyroid gland, which regulates body metabolism; the gonads, which produce the steroid hormones that influence reproductive physiology and sexual behavior; and the adrenal glands, which produce epinephrine to mobilize the body in emergency situations.

The steroid hormones called *androgens* and *estrogens* are produced by the gonads—the ovaries and testes. These hormones affect sexual behavior, beginning before birth. They control the prenatal development of the reproductive system,

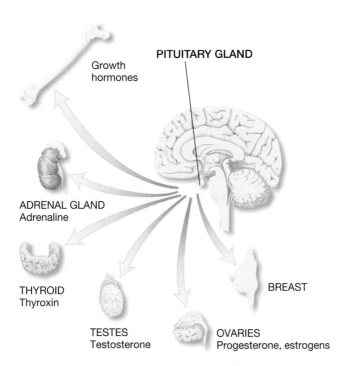

PITUITARY GLAND

Growth
hormones

ADRENAL GLAND
Adrenaline

THYROID
Thyroxin

TESTES
Testosterone

OVARIES
Progesterone, estrogens

BREAST

Figure 3.12
The Pituitary Gland
The pituitary gland is often called the body's master gland because its actions regulate many of the other endocrine glands. Located at the base of the brain, this pea-sized gland affects behavior both indirectly through control of other glands and directly through release of hormones—including growth hormones and sex hormones—into the bloodstream.

prompt the onset of puberty and sexual maturity, and are essential for fertility. People often assume that androgens, especially testosterone, are the basis for aggression and believe that men are more aggressive than women because men have higher levels of testosterone. But the relationship between testosterone and aggression is complex. For example, individuals with high levels of testosterone are not necessarily more violent or more aggressive than those with average levels (Booth et al., 2003). In addition, aggression and competition may increase testosterone levels, rather than the other way around (Wagner, Flinn, & England, 2002). Thus, the relationship between testosterone and aggression is not a simple one.

The adrenal glands, located just above the kidneys, produce adrenaline (epinephrine), which has a dramatic effect on behavior. Imagine that, in your next chemistry class, the instructor announces "pop quiz"—and you haven't even looked at the chapter. Prompted by this stress, the sympathetic division of your autonomic nervous system goes into action. It stimulates your adrenal glands to produce epinephrine, which allows you to react quickly and leads to the state of activation known as the fight-or-flight response.

The pancreas is an endocrine gland involved in regulating the body's sugar levels through the production of *insulin*, the hormone that facilitates the transport of sugar (glucose) from the bloodstream into body cells. When the blood sugar level is high, people feel energetic; a low level results in fatigue and weakness. Diabetes and hypoglycemia are two problems associated with insulin, and both can influence behavior. *Diabetes mellitus* occurs when the pancreas fails to produce insulin, and

Insulin ■ Hormone that is produced by the pancreas and that facilitates the transport of sugar (glucose) from the bloodstream into body cells.

the body can no longer metabolize sugar. The overproduction of insulin by the pancreas results in *hypoglycemia*, a condition characterized by low blood sugar levels and accompanying feelings of fatigue and weakness.

Therefore, hormones affect behavior, both directly, by prompting responses such as the fight-or-flight response, and indirectly, by acting on the nervous system and blood sugar levels. This interaction of the nervous and endocrine systems is just one facet of the complex biological foundation of behavior. These systems and all the others in the body are also affected by heredity. That is, the basic plans for building a brain (and a body) come from genes. Next, we examine how genetic factors affect behavior.

How Do Genetic Factors Affect Behavior?

Genetics ▪ The study of heredity, the process through which physical traits and behavioral characteristics are transmitted from parents to offspring.

Does a person's genetic makeup set him or her up to be depressed, schizophrenic, or violent? Biologists first began to examine this question, and many similar ones, through research in the field of *genetics*, the study of heredity. Heredity is the process by which physical traits and behavioral characteristics are transmitted from parents to offspring. Geneticists study how traits such as blue eyes, brown hair, height, and a tendency to develop diabetes or high blood pressure are transmitted from one generation to the next and are investigating the possibility that depression, schizophrenia, and violence may have genetic components. The question of the relative contributions of genetics and environment constitutes one of the recurring themes in psychology—the issue of nature versus nurture.

The Issue of Nature versus Nurture

Nature ▪ A person's biological makeup, including inherited characteristics determined by genetics.

Psychologists know that biological factors, including heredity, play a role in shaping human behavior. However, there is a complex interplay between biology and experience, between inherited genes and encounters in the world—that is, between nature and nurture. The term *nature* refers to a person's biological makeup, including inherited characteristics determined by genetics; *nurture* refers to a person's experiences in the environment.

Nurture ▪ A person's experiences in the environment.

Those who consider nurture more important than nature suggest that experience, training, and effort are more significant than genetic inheritance in determining behavior. John B. Watson, a pioneer in the field of behaviorism (which we examined in Chapter 1 and will examine further in Chapter 8) believed that nurture was all-important. Watson's strong opinion of the importance of nurture is not shared by most contemporary psychologists, who acknowledge that both nature and nurture contribute to behavior (Crabbe, 2002).

Many people think of nature and nurture as opposites, but biopsychologist John Pinel (2003) expressed the impossibility of separating the two by offering an analogy: When you hear music being played, do you assume that its source is the instrument or the musician? You cannot say that the source is the instrument, because no music comes from an instrument that no one is playing. You cannot say that the source is the musician, because no music comes from a musician who has no instrument. Music requires both. Separating nature and nurture is similarly impossible; without the combination of the two, no individual would develop.

However, we can discuss genetic factors and environmental factors that contribute to behavior, just as we might examine the characteristics of a musical instrument separately from those of the musician who plays it. Psychologists know that genetic inheritance affects people's behavior—but how important is it? How might genes be translated into behavior? To understand the genetic component of behavior, it is necessary to understand the basics of genetics.

The Basics of Genetics

With two exceptions (sperm cells and egg cells), each human cell normally contains 23 pairs of chromosomes (46 chromosomes in all). *Chromosomes* are microscopic strands of deoxyribonucleic acid (DNA) found in the nucleus (center) of every cell in the body (see **Figure 3.13** on p. 86). Chromosomes carry the genetic information in the functional units of hereditary transmission, known as *genes*—thousands of which line up along each chromosome. Genes provide templates for protein production; that is, genes furnish the "blueprints" for building all the components of a body and assembling those components. Genes control various aspects of a person's physical makeup, including eye color, hair color, and height—and they influence behavior as well.

The mechanism of gene inheritance basically works like this: Each parent's sperm or ovum (egg) cells contain 23 chromosomes—half of the total of 46 contained in all other body cells. Of the 23 pairs of chromosomes in humans, 22 carry the same types of genetic information in both men and women, and the 23rd pair determines a person's sex. In women, the 23rd pair consists of two X chromosomes; in men, it includes one X and one Y chromosome. At the moment of conception, a sperm and an ovum, each containing 23 chromosomes, combine, and the chromosomes form 23 new pairs. These pairings contain the genetic plans for a new and unique individual.

Genetically determined characteristics are controlled by pairs of genes, located in parallel positions on a pair of chromosomes. Both of the genes in a pair influence the same trait, but they may carry different forms of the genetic code for that trait. One gene is the dominant gene; the other gene is the recessive gene. The dominant gene is expressed in the person's physical makeup, and the recessive gene is not. For example, if an individual's two genes for eye color carry the genetic codes for blue and brown, the person will have brown eyes, because the brown version of the gene is dominant. Only when both genes in the pair are the recessive versions will that recessive gene exert its influence (resulting in blue eye color).

A *genotype* is a person's genetic makeup, which is fixed at conception, but a genotype may or may not be evident in a person's *phenotype*, his or her observable characteristics. Consider eye color again. A mother and a father may both have brown eyes, but they may each also carry a recessive gene for blue eyes. Thus, their genotype includes a gene for blue eyes, but their phenotype is brown-eyed. There are

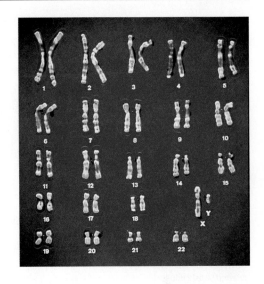

The Y chromosome in these 23 pairs of human chromosomes means that the person is a male.

Chromosomes ■ Microscopic strands of DNA that are found in the nucleus of every cell in the body and that carry the genetic information in the genes.

Gene ■ The functional unit of hereditary transmission, which provides a template for protein production.

Genotype ■ A person's genetic makeup, which is fixed at conception.

Phenotype ■ A person's observable characteristics.

Figure 3.13
Building Blocks of Genetics
Each of the trillions of cells in the human body (except the eggs and sperm) has 23 pairs of chromosomes in its nucleus. Each chromosome is essentially a long, threadlike strand of DNA, a giant molecule consisting of two spiraling and cross-linked chains. Resembling a twisted ladder and referred to as a double helix, each DNA molecule carries thousands of genes—the basic building blocks of the genetic code—which direct the synthesis of all the body's proteins.

Mutations ■
Unexpected changes in genes that result in unusual, and sometimes harmful, characteristics of body or behavior.

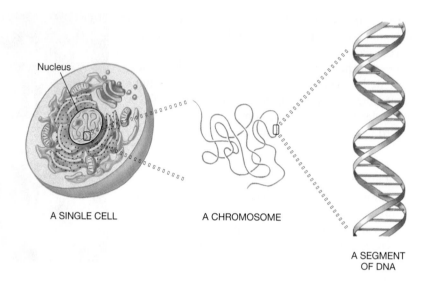

Nucleus

A SINGLE CELL   A CHROMOSOME

A SEGMENT
OF DNA

many more brown-eyed people than blue-eyed people because the brown-eye gene is dominant and is usually expressed in the phenotype when it is present in the genotype. The two brown-eyed parents may have offspring with brown eyes (very likely) or with blue eyes (less likely). Sometimes genotypes change in ways that are not expected and that result in unusual characteristics of body or behavior. These unexpected changes in genes are known as **mutations**. Mutations are principal sources of diversity in the human gene pool. Some mutations result in desirable changes, but most do not.

How Genes Affect Behavior

DNA is a double-stranded molecule built of four simple chemical building blocks, called *bases*. Resembling a twisted ladder and referred to as a double helix, the DNA molecule has pairs of these bases joining its two strands. Genes are sequences of the chemical bases that direct the production of proteins. How, then, can genes affect behavior? The basic answer to this question is that genes can affect behavior only indirectly (Pinker, 2002). As evolutionary psychologist Douglas Kenrick and his colleagues (Kenrick, Ackerman, & Ledlow, 2003, p. 116) explained, "genes do not determine anything except in interaction with other genes and developmental experience. Genes interact with other genes to produce cells, which interact with other cells to produce organs, which interact with other organs to produce organisms, which interact with one another to produce emergent social structures such as ant colonies, chimpanzee hierarchies, the Bon Jovi fan club, and the European Union." Therefore, genetic influences on behavior are indirect and are moderated by environmental effects. The interaction between the two types of influences is very complex.

The field of *behavioral genetics* focuses on the influence of genes on behavior. Behavioral geneticists ask questions about whether human behaviors and characteristics such as aggression, shyness, and impulsiveness have a genetic, inherited basis. If they do, then how do environmental factors, especially learning and experience, interact with genes to produce behavior? That is, what are the contributions of nature and nurture to behaviors?

Psychologists interested in the contributions of genetics know that some traits and behaviors show a fairly high degree of *heritability*, defined as the proportion of a trait's variation among individuals in a population that is genetically determined. The heritability of some physical traits such as height is fairly obvious. Children with two tall parents have a high probability of being tall, but even a highly heritable trait like height depends on the environment to develop. Even a good diet will not make people born to average-height or short parents as tall as those whose parents are tall—but children of tall parents will be tall only if they get proper nutrition while they are growing. When scientists say that a trait is heritable and attach a percentage to that heritability—for example, 50%—they mean that 50% of the variation (difference) within a group of people is attributable to heredity. However, this number does not mean that 50% of a given person's height is genetic and the other 50% is due to environment. Heritability reflects the variation within a population, not within an individual.

A common approach to the study of genetic influences on behavior has made use of the genetic similarity of twins (Plomin et al., 2003a). *Fraternal twins* (dizygotic twins) occur when two sperm fertilize two ova (eggs) and the two resulting fertilized ova implant in the uterus and grow alongside each other. The genes of these twins are not identical, so the twins are no more genetically similar than other brothers and sisters. *Identical twins* (monozygotic twins) occur when one fertilized ovum splits into two identical cells, which then begin to divide and form two individuals. Thus, identical twins have exactly the same genes. They also begin their lives in the same uterine environment and share similar patterns of nutrition and prenatal influences. Twins raised together continue to share similar environments; those adopted into different families share genes, but factors in their environments may vary. Studying pairs of identical twins who were raised together or apart allows behavioral geneticists to study the relative influence of environmental and genetic factors. These researchers have succeeded in estimating the heritability of intelligence, behavior and learning disorders, and personality traits (Hamer, 2002).

Although behavioral geneticists have established that genes play a role in many behaviors, they have been largely unsuccessful at identifying single genes that influence behavior (Crabbe, 2002). Instead, the genetic influences on behavior occur through an interaction between genes and environment. A study by Avshalom Caspi and his colleagues (2002) that demonstrated this gene–environment interaction explored the role of child abuse and maltreatment in the development of antisocial behavior. Researchers have been aware that some children who are mistreated exhibit unacceptable violence and aggression, whereas others do not. Caspi and his colleagues found that the two outcomes seem to be related to a gene variation that affects the metabolism of a group of neurotransmitters in the brain. **Figure 3.14** on page 88 shows the possibilities for the interaction of genes and environment that this study

Heritability ■ The proportion of a trait's variation among individuals in a population that is genetically determined.

Fraternal twins ■ Twins who occur when two sperm fertilize two eggs and who are no more genetically similar than other brothers and sisters; dizygotic twins.

Identical twins ■ Twins who occur when one fertilized egg splits into two identical cells, which then develop independently into twins with exactly the same genes; monozygotic twins.

Figure 3.14
An Example of an Interaction between Genes and the Environment
Source: Based on results from Caspi et al., 2002

MISTREATED OR ABUSED AS CHILDREN?

CARRY GENE FOR FAULTY METABOLISM OF NEUROTRANSMITTER?		No	Yes
	No	Unlikely to show antisocial behavior	Elevated risk for antisocial behavior
	Yes	Unlikely to show antisocial behavior	Twice as likely to show antisocial behavior

revealed. Boys whose brain chemistry was affected by this gene variation were not likely to become violent if their families were supportive and nurturing. Boys who were victims of abuse had a slightly elevated risk of becoming antisocial but were not certain to do so if their genetic makeup did not include the variation of the neurotransmitter metabolism gene. However, the combination of childhood maltreatment plus the genetic variation in neurotransmitter metabolism made boys about twice as likely to receive a diagnosis of conduct disorder during adolescence and about three times more likely to be arrested for a violent crime by age 26. The interaction of genes and environment observed in this study demonstrated that both nature and nurture are important.

Other problem behaviors that are influenced by genes are alcoholism and substance abuse: Some people are at much higher genetic risk of becoming addicted than are others (Crabbe, 2002). But this genetic vulnerability may or may not lead to substance abuse problems. The key to what happens lies in the interaction between a person's genetic endowment and the environment that the person experiences.

From Genetics to Genomics

Genome ■ The total sequence of the genes on an organism's DNA.

Genomics ■ The study of the entire pattern of genes in an individual.

In 2001, researchers completed a preliminary map of the human *genome,* the total sequence of the genes on our DNA (Venter et al., 2001). With the completion of that massive task, the focus of behavioral genetics research shifted from demonstrating the existence of genetic influences to exploring the genome and how it functions. This new approach is known as *genomics,* the study of the entire pattern of genes in an individual; *behavioral genomics* is the study of the behavioral effects of the genome (McGuffin, Riley, & Plomin, 2001). Recent technological advances are allowing researchers to study the influence of genes on behavior "from the bottom up," from the smallest level of molecules to the level of behavior. Traditional methods, such as twin studies, investigate genetic influences "from the top down," attempting to trace behavior back to the level of chemical sequences of genes. The application of both research strategies to the investigation of links between genes and behavior offers exciting possibilities (Plomin et al., 2003b). The bottom-up approach and the top-down approach must meet in the brain, which is the organ through which genes are capable of affecting behavior.

Genetic effects are guaranteed to be complex. Behavioral genomics researchers such as Robert Plomin and his colleagues (Plomin et al., 2003a) argue that because most traits are determined by multiple genes, scientists cannot expect to find single genes that underlie complex behaviors. Indeed, as we noted earlier, the search for single genes that affect behavior has had disappointing results. Behavioral genomics will concentrate on identifying the multiple genes that control various proteins and finding out how those proteins affect the brain, and thus behavior.

So far, behavioral genomics research has tended to concentrate on disorders (Crabbe, 2002; Plomin & McGuffin, 2003). But many researchers in this area see a bright future as the expanding knowledge of genetics and the human genome will be combined with behavioral findings to explore both disorders and normal development (Plomin et al., 2003b; Plomin & McGuffin, 2003). However, these researchers face troubling questions of what to do with the expanding knowledge of the human genome. When scientists understand both basic genetic and biological mechanisms and their relationship to behavior, they will be better able to predict situations in which maladjustment and disorders may occur. Yet this ability to predict will no doubt create some difficult dilemmas for both health care professionals and people who carry genes that make them vulnerable to disorders. If a particular pattern of genes is found to be associated with schizophrenia, for example, how should society respond? Would it be desirable or ethical to screen newborns to identify those at risk of developing schizophrenia? Could this information be used to justify terminating pregnancies? Along with advances in genetics and genomics must come ethical deliberations and guidelines (and possibly even legislation) to guard people's rights and privacy. Those who engage in the ethical debate must acknowledge that genetics only establishes the framework for behavior; research in behavioral genetics and genomics indicates that genes create risks and vulnerabilities but do not determine any behavior.

Does Our Evolutionary History Influence Our Current Behavior?

The current human genome is the product of a long history; human beings have evolved, and that process has given our genes their present configuration. If you accept the evidence that human behavior is influenced by our genes, then you will likely concede that understanding human evolutionary history is an important aspect of learning about behavior. *Evolutionary psychology* is the psychological perspective that seeks to explain and predict behaviors by analyzing how the human brain developed over time and how evolutionary history affects the behavior of humans today. The emphasis of evolutionary psychology differs from that of behavioral genetics and genomics, which emphasize individual differences and how genes and gene combinations affect behavior. Evolutionary psychologists are interested in what humans have in common rather than their differences. They want to understand how evolution has created similarities in all humans—that is, has yielded universals of human behavior.

Evolutionary psychology ■ The psychological perspective that seeks to explain and predict behaviors by analyzing how the human brain developed over time and how evolutionary history affects the behavior of humans today.

Human brains have evolved over tens of thousands of years to meet environmental demands; the result is a highly organized, complex brain that controls behavior. Evolutionary psychologists argue that human behavior patterns have endowed the human brain with many specialized modules that govern abilities in the areas of perception, learning, acquiring language, relating to other people, and choosing suitable mates. According to evolutionary psychologist Steven Pinker (2002, p. 197), "The human brain equips us to thrive in a world of objects, living things, and other people. Those entities have a large impact on our well-being, and one would expect the brain to be well suited to detecting them and their powers." Evolutionary psychology relies on natural selection as a critical concept.

Natural Selection

Evolutionary theory assumes that natural selection is a key factor in biological changes that appear in different organisms over time. *Natural selection* is the principle that those characteristics and behaviors that help organisms adapt, be fit, survive, and reproduce are the ones that will be passed on to successive generations; flexible, fit individuals have a greater chance of reproducing. Evolutionary psychologists such as Steven Pinker (1997; 2002), Leda Cosmides and John Tooby (1997; 2000), and David Buss (2004) have extended the principles of evolutionary theory to psychology. They argue that natural selection has acted over thousands of years to perpetuate certain traits and behavior patterns, which have created distinct physiological mechanisms in humans that push them toward certain behaviors and away from others. Evolutionary psychologists explain changes in traits and behaviors in terms of *adaptations*.

When a trait or inherited characteristic has increased in a population, evolutionary psychologists say that an adaptation has occurred—and that it arose to help solve a problem of survival or reproduction. An adaptation allows individuals to better fit with the environment in which the adaptation occurred, and offspring who inherit this adaptation are more likely to survive in that environment. **Figure 3.15** shows how evolution, genetics, and experience may interact to shape current behavior, and how behavior may influence evolution and genes.

Adaptations in Humans

Evolutionary psychologists are trying to identify human traits and behaviors that are inherited and have evolved over time, and they have several candidates. For example, evolution has created an instinct in human beings to protect their offspring from danger; there is a natural tendency—in fact, evolutionary psychologists assert, a genetically coded tendency—for parents to protect their young from danger (Geary, 2000; Hrdy, 1999). In doing so, parents ensure that their genes are passed on—that their children live long enough to reproduce.

Another example comes from the development of communication: In the early stages of human evolution, communication consisted merely of grunts. But through the course of generations, those who grunted good commands, advice,

Natural selection ■ The principle that those characteristics and behaviors that help organisms adapt, be fit, and survive will be passed on to successive generations, because flexible, fit individuals have a greater chance of reproducing.

Adaptation ■ A trait or inherited characteristic that has increased in a population because it solved a problem of survival or reproduction.

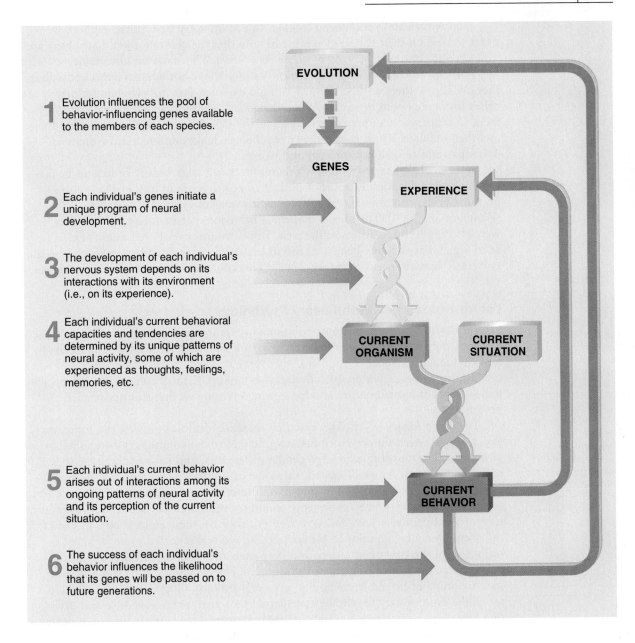

1 Evolution influences the pool of behavior-influencing genes available to the members of each species.

2 Each individual's genes initiate a unique program of neural development.

3 The development of each individual's nervous system depends on its interactions with its environment (i.e., on its experience).

4 Each individual's current behavioral capacities and tendencies are determined by its unique patterns of neural activity, some of which are experienced as thoughts, feelings, memories, etc.

5 Each individual's current behavior arises out of interactions among its ongoing patterns of neural activity and its perception of the current situation.

6 The success of each individual's behavior influences the likelihood that its genes will be passed on to future generations.

EVOLUTION

GENES

EXPERIENCE

CURRENT ORGANISM

CURRENT SITUATION

CURRENT BEHAVIOR

Figure 3.15
The Interactions among Behavior, Experience, Genes, and Evolution

and other ideas were more likely to survive in difficult circumstances. Those who lived taught their children their successful communication strategies, and over succeeding generations, language developed and was ultimately encoded in the human genome.

Jealousy is also hypothesized to have an evolutionary base (Buss, 2000a). In order to pass on their genes, men must be sure that the children their mates bear are indeed theirs, and not fathered by some other man. This parental uncertainty is hypothesized to be basis of sexual jealousy in men, but not women (who know that they are the mothers of their offspring). Buss explains that, for women, jealousy arises from emotional betrayals. When their mates develop an emotional commitment to other women, this behavior signals the risk that the men will abandon them and their children. Thus, evolutionary psychology makes differential predictions about patterns of jealousy for men and women.

Some evolutionary psychologists maintain that a wide variety of human behaviors, including devotion to sports teams, the need to be right (rather than wrong), personal pride, and even arrogance, are expressions of evolved tendencies (Zimmerman, 2000). The idea is that these behaviors persist today because they were effective as adaptations in the past. Some evolutionary psychologists go so far as to argue that so many behaviors are traceable to evolved tendencies that there is a universal "human nature" (Pinker, 2002). This contention has created controversies.

Controversies about Evolutionary Psychology

Several controversies concerning evolutionary psychology are ongoing. One of these concerns the assertions by evolutionary psychologists that certain traits and behaviors are human universals. Another controversy revolves around the methods of establishing evidence within evolutionary psychology. A third controversy relates to the concepts of human nature and biological determinism that this perspective proposes.

The evolutionary psychology research on sexual jealousy reflects the controversy about hypothesized universals of behavior. In addition, evolutionary psychologists' views of jealousy hypothesize large gender differences, and such hypotheses often create controversy. As we discussed, this view of jealousy holds that men and women experience jealousy in response to different behaviors (Buss, 2000); men feel sexual jealousy and women experience jealousy over emotional infidelities. However, tests of this hypothesis have failed to find evidence for these contentions. In a study of college students (Nannini & Meyers, 2000), women reported more jealousy, regardless of the type of situation, and both men and women said that sexual infidelities were the source of greater jealousy than emotional betrayals were. A comparative study of heterosexual and homosexual jealousy (Sheets & Wolfe, 2001) tested the evolutionary psychology prediction that men, regardless of sexual orientation, experience greater sexual jealousy than women. This pattern did not appear; sexual orientation and gender both affected ratings of jealousy, and emotional infidelity was more distressing to all groups except to heterosexual men, who rated sexual infidelity as more distressing.

The failure to confirm predictions about jealousy points up a weakness of evolutionary psychology that underlies another of the controversies associated with it: Evolutionary psychology seeks to predict current behavior but looks into the distant past for explanations, so evolutionary psychologists depend on a different type of evidence than other psychologists do. Evolutionary psychologists such as Buss (1999, 2000), Kenrick (2001), and Cosmides and Tooby (1999, 2000) assert that this new approach helps explain unanswered questions of human nature by looking into the distant past for analyses of such behaviors as jealousy and aggression. However, this view is vulnerable to the criticism that it is impossible to observe and test past behaviors. Patricia Gowaty (2001, p. 55) commented, "After all, we do not yet have a time machine." And Jerry Coyne (2000, p. 27) differentiated evolutionary biology from evolutionary psychology by saying, "Unlike bones, behavior does not fossilize, and understanding its evolution often involves concocting stories that sound plausible but are hard to test." To establish itself as a legitimate approach, evolutionary psychology must meet this criticism with research from the present and better examples of human universals of behavior.

A third controversy surrounding evolutionary psychology concerns the issue of human nature and determinism. If the human brain has evolved to feel jealousy and to be aggressive under certain circumstances, then how much free will do humans have? If our behavior is the result of evolutionary programming, do we have no responsibility for our actions? If I kill someone, may I urge my attorney to claim that my genes made me do it? Steven Pinker (2002) discusses these questions and argues that such a defense will not and should not be successful. Understanding the factors that determine behavior is not the same as saying that behavior is predetermined and that humans have no ability to decide about their actions.

Evolutionary psychologists are quick to point out that their approach does not assert that evolutionary history determines behavior in an inalterable way (Caporael, 2001; Gowaty, 2001). Evolutionary history does not provide excuses for misbehavior (such as promiscuity) or criminal behavior (such as killing a neighbor). Instead, evolutionary history provides a framework for interpreting current behavior in the context of how adaptive it was for human survival and reproduction 100,000 years ago. If the evolutionary psychology perspective is correct, then we all possess certain evolved tendencies, and they affect our behavior on a daily basis. They influence our ability to cope with situations that did not arise in the human environment in the distant past, such as living in a city, driving an automobile, operating a computer, and meeting romantic partners over the Internet.

What is exciting about evolutionary psychology is that it addresses questions that psychology has previously ignored. Evolutionary psychologists not only want to understand mating and reproduction—behaviors closely associated with natural selection—but also human coping mechanisms, self-esteem, creativity, problem-solving abilities, and even self-awareness, or consciousness. In some ways, evolutionary psychology is going beyond the question of how the mind works, asking how it evolved to work the way it does, why, and where might it go next.

Like all appealing theories, that of evolutionary psychology will go through refinements and changes in focus; if it is a good, workable theory that explains data and phenomena well, it will stand the test of time (Ketelaar & Ellis, 2000). For now, evolutionary psychology, like behavioral genomics, is opening up more questions than it can answer.

Summary and Review

HOW IS THE NERVOUS SYSTEM ORGANIZED?

Describe the structures and processes that allow communication in the nervous system.

The basic unit of the *nervous system* is the *neuron*, or nerve cell, which has *dendrites*, a cell body, an *axon*, and axon terminals. *Afferent (sensory)* neurons carry messages to the spinal cord and brain; *efferent (motor)* neurons carry messages from the brain and spinal cord to organs and muscles. *Interneurons* connect sensory motor neurons. *Glial cells* provide support for neurons and help form the *myelin sheath* that covers some motor neurons. The space between one neuron's axon terminals and another neuron is the *synapse*. pp. 55–57

An *action potential* occurs when the stimulation of a neuron reaches its *threshold*. The neuron fires in an *all-or-none* fashion and then enters a *refractory period*, during which it cannot fire. The action potential moves along the axon and stimulates the release of *neurotransmitters*, chemicals that reside in each axon terminal's synaptic vesicles. The neurotransmitters move across the synaptic space and bind to receptor sites on neighboring neurons, thereby conveying information to them. pp. 59–60

How do neurotransmitters function and affect behavior?

Neurotransmitters may be excitatory, producing an *excitatory postsynaptic potential (EPSP)*, or inhibitory, producing an *inhibitory postsynaptic potential (IPSP)*. p. 61

Researchers know that neurotransmitters exert complex effects. *Acetylcholine* acts as an excitatory neurotransmitter to activate muscles, and *gamma-aminobutyric acid (GABA)* acts as an inhibitory neurotransmitter and is associated with anxiety. The family of monoamine neurotransmitters includes *serotonin*, which is important in mood regulation; *dopamine*, which is involved in feelings of reward and pleasure; and *norepinephrine*, which plays a key role in arousal reactions. p. 62

Psychopharmacology is the study of how drugs affect behavior. Research often focuses on *agonists*, chemicals that mimic the action of neurotransmitters by occupying receptor sites, and *antagonists*, chemicals that oppose the action of neurotransmitters by blocking receptor sites. Opiate drugs such as morphine act as *endorphin* agonists, occupying receptor sites and producing pain-relieving effects. pp. 63–64

Identify the subdivisions of the nervous system.

The nervous system has two major divisions: the central nervous system and the peripheral nervous system. The *central nervous system* consists of the brain and the spinal cord. The *peripheral nervous system* carries information to and from the spinal cord and brain through spinal and cranial nerves. The peripheral nervous system is further subdivided into the *somatic* and *autonomic* nervous systems. The autonomic nervous system has two subdivisions: the *sympathetic* and *parasympathetic* nervous systems, which have different functions. pp. 64–66

What are the major divisions and main structures of the brain?

The brain is divided into the hindbrain, the midbrain, and the forebrain (which includes the cortex). The *hindbrain* has four main structures: the *medulla,* the *reticular formation,* the *pons,* and the *cerebellum.* The *midbrain* is made up of nuclei that receive afferent signals from other parts of the brain and from the spinal cord, interpret them, and either relay the information to other parts of the brain or cause the body to act at once. The *forebrain* is the largest and most complex brain structure; it comprises the *thalamus* and the *hypothalamus,* the *limbic system* (including the *amygdala* and *hippocampus),* and the *basal ganglia.* The topmost part of the brain is the *cerebral cortex,* with its many *convolutions,* and the underlying *cerebral hemispheres,* which are connected by the *corpus callosum.* The cortex is divided into four lobes. pp. 68–72

HOW DOES THE BRAIN FUNCTION?

Describe several techniques for studying brain activity and functions.

One technique for studying nervous system function involves relating brain damage to loss of function. The areas that relate to speech and language abilities, *Broca's area* and *Wernicke's area,* were identified using this method. Another technique is the single-unit recording, in which scientists record the activity of a single cell by placing an electrode within or next to the cell. Another technique uses graphical records of brain-wave patterns, called *electroencephalograms (EEGs),* to assess neurological disorders and the types of activities that occur during thought, sleep, and other behaviors. pp. 72–73

More recent techniques for measuring the activity of the nervous system are CT (computerized tomography) and *magnetic resonance imaging (MRI).* These scanning techniques reveal more about structure than about function, but *functional magnetic resonance imaging (fMRI)* and *PET (positron emission tomography)* allow researchers to observe brain activity as it takes place, while a participant performs a task. pp. 73–77

How is brain function specialized?

Research shows that in most human beings, one cerebral hemisphere—usually the left—is specialized for processing speech and language; the other—usually the right—appears better able to handle spatial tasks and drawing. The cerebral hemispheres are normally connected to each other by the corpus callosum. *Split-brain individuals* have had their cerebral hemispheres disconnected surgically, and as a result, their left hemisphere language functions cannot be accessed by their right hemisphere and their right hemisphere spatial capabilities are not available to their left hemisphere. pp. 77–79

Women's and men's brains may differ, especially in terms of lateralization of functions to left and right hemispheres. Gender differences may also exist in the functioning of men's and women's brains when they perform certain tasks. Research does not support the view that one gender has superior brain function. pp. 79–80

Brains are capable of change, a capability called *plasticity*. Plasticity may be due to growth at the level of synapses or to the generation of new neurons (neurogenesis). Plasticity allows people to recover from brain injury. pp. 80–81

WHAT EFFECTS DO HORMONES HAVE ON BEHAVIOR?

The *endocrine glands* are a set of ductless glands that affect behavior by secreting *hormones* into the bloodstream. The pituitary gland is appropriately referred to as the master gland because of its central role in regulating other glands. Hormones can affect behavior. Androgens and estrogens, secreted by the testes and the ovaries, affect fertility and sexual behavior. Epinephrine, secreted by the adrenal gland, is important in reactions to emergency situations. Insulin is secreted by the pancreas and regulates the body's blood sugar levels. pp. 81–84

HOW DO GENETIC FACTORS AFFECT BEHAVIOR?

Which is more influential—nature or nurture?

Psychologists generally assert that human behavior is influenced by both nature (heredity) and nurture (environment). Psychologists study the biological bases of behavior to better understand how these two sets of variables interact. pp. 84–85

What is genetics, and how is it important in psychology?

Genetics is the study of heredity—the biological transmission of traits and characteristics from parents to offspring. Chromosomes contain thousands of *genes*, the basic units of heredity, made up of DNA. Chromosomes from each parent combine to provide the blueprints for building an offspring's body. The *genotype* is one's genetic makeup, which is fixed at conception; the *phenotype* consists of one's observable characteristics. Unexpected changes in genes produce *mutations*, which are the principal source of genetic diversity. pp. 85–86

How can genes affect behavior?

Genes provide the directions that body cells use to manufacture proteins, which can affect the growth and development of the brain. Genes can also affect behavior by affecting brain structure or brain function through the effects of neurotransmitters. The field of psychology that studies the influence of genes on behavior is behavioral genetics, which studies *heritability*, defined as the proportion of a trait's variation that is due to genetic factors. Investigators study *identical twins* and *fraternal twins* to attempt to establish the role of genetics and environment in behavior. Behavior cannot usually be traced to single genes; it is more likely that combinations of genes and the interaction of genes and environment are responsible for genetic influences on behavior. pp. 86–88

What is genomics, and how does this field relate to psychology?

The *genome* is the total DNA blueprint of heritable traits contained in every cell of the body, and *genomics* is the study of the genome. Behavioral genomics researchers suggest that it is necessary to understand the complex interactions of genes in order to understand the influence of genes on behavior. However, expanding genetic knowledge has serious implications for privacy and health care decisions. pp. 88–89

DOES OUR EVOLUTIONARY HISTORY INFLUENCE OUR CURRENT BEHAVIOR?

What is the main idea of evolutionary psychology?

Evolutionary psychology is the psychological perspective that seeks to explain and predict behaviors by analyzing how the human brain developed over time, how it functions, and how input from the social environment affects human behaviors; it considers human behavior from the vantage point of evolutionary biology. p. 89

Evolutionary theory assumes that physiology and behavior are shaped by *natural selection*, the principle that those behaviors that help organisms adapt, be fit, and survive are the ones that will be passed on to successive generations because fit individuals have a greater chance of reproduction. p. 90

When a trait or inherited characteristic increases in the population, *adaptation* has occurred. Human adaptations may include the drive to protect one's children and the development of language and sexual jealousy. pp. 90–92

What controversies surround evolutionary psychology?

Controversies surrounding evolutionary psychology concern doubts about the existence of human universals, problems in confirming that current behavior has explanations in the distant past, and questions concerning free will and determinism. pp. 92–93

Child Development

What Are the Central Issues
of Development?   99
   Issues in Developmental Psychology
   Research Designs

How Does Physical Development
Proceed?   103
   Prenatal Development
   Harmful Environmental Effects
   Newborns Are Ready to Experience the World

How Does Thought Develop?   111
   Jean Piaget's Insights
   Vygotsky's Sociocultural Theory: An Alternative
     to Piaget
   Theory of Mind
   Thought in a Social Context

How Do Social and Emotional
Development Proceed?   124
   Attachment: The Ties That Bind
   Temperament
   Moral Reasoning

What Environmental Factors
Are Important for Social
Development?   134
   Early Social Development and Child Rearing
   Gender Roles
   Erik Erikson and the Beginning of the Search
     for Self

Summary and Review   141

In this chapter, we'll examine normal developmental processes in children, including physical, cognitive, moral, emotional, and social development. We will also see how genetic makeup interacts with the environment to produce individuals who are unique. A child's physical development sets up the framework for his or her psychological development. Children who are extremely short, who have problems with weight, or who have unique musical or athletic gifts face challenges and opportunities that may be experienced as positive or negative and may have effects extending into adolescence and adulthood. So we study normal development, and we begin with physical development, to see how that framework helps set the stage for other aspects of development.

What Are the Central Issues of Development?

Developmental psychology is the study of lifelong, often age-related processes of change in the physical, cognitive, moral, emotional, and social domains of functioning; such changes are rooted in biological mechanisms that are genetically controlled (for example, maturational processes involved in the growth of the nervous system), but they are also strongly influenced by social interactions. Developmental psychologists are interested in how people grow from infants into mature adults and to learn what factors affect the course of human development.

Developmental psychologists recognize that development involves gains and losses over time, because people can respond in either positive or negative ways to life's experiences. They also recognize that development must be viewed from multiple perspectives and within historical and cultural contexts. They acknowledge that the interaction of genetics and the environment is complex and that there is considerable diversity in developmental processes. In general, developmental psychologists have focused on a few key issues, theories, and research methods to unravel the causes of behavior. Their goal is always the same: to describe, explain, predict, and potentially help manage human development.

Developmental psychology ▪ The study of the lifelong, often age-related processes of change in the physical, cognitive, moral, emotional, and social domains of functioning; such changes are rooted in biological mechanisms that are genetically controlled but are also influenced by social interactions.

Issues in Developmental Psychology

Several key issues help developmental researchers form their questions and shape their point of view. Five of the most important of these issues are nature versus nurture, stability versus change, activity versus passivity, continuity versus discontinuity, and the influence of culture.

Nature or Nurture?

One way to look at individual development is to consider to what extent the developing person's abilities, interests, and personality are determined primarily by biological influences (*nature*) or primarily by environmental influences (*nurture*). The question of the impacts of nature and nurture underpins many of the issues we will be discussing. Separating biological from environmental causes of behavior is a complex matter. The answer to any specific question about human behavior usually involves the interaction of nature and nurture.

To assess the roles played by genes and environment, researchers have studied identical twins who have been raised in different surroundings. They have found extraordinary similarities between such siblings, in such characteristics as whether the twins are conscientious or sloppy, anxious or relaxed, or antagonistic or friendly (Pinker, 2002). In one such study (Lykken et al., 1992), researchers found an identical twin who was an accomplished storyteller with a collection of amusing anecdotes. When his twin brother, whom the researchers located later, was asked if he knew any funny stories, he leaned back with a practiced air and launched into one. Other twins shared an interest in dogs, smoked the same kind of cigarettes, or had the same political opinions. One pair of twins shared a phobia of the ocean; at the beach, both would enter the water backward, and only up to their knees. This study included twin firefighters, twin gunsmiths, and twins who obsessively counted things. Another twin study by McCourt and colleagues (1999) argues that genetic makeup plays an especially important role in human development.

Evolutionary psychologists go a step further. They suggest that development of an individual from birth through maturity involves the expression of a biological heritage that evolved in prehistoric times and unfolds through an interaction with the social environment. These psychologists assume that adaptations are necessary at different times in the course of development, and they conclude that individual differences in development are the result of predictable, adaptive responses to environmental pressures that existed in human prehistory, and not the result of random events (Bjorklund & Pellegrini, 2000; Pinker, 2002). Intelligence is fostered and develops in response to environmental demands. Mothers and fathers spend different amounts of time and energy on their children, and the children's responses to the attention are adaptive—those who have been nurtured more have a greater chance of surviving and reproducing. According to this view, attachment, gender roles, mate choices—all developmental events—have evolved to help human beings adapt (Geary & Bjorklund, 2000; Plomin & Colledge, 2001).

But not all psychologists or parents agree with the view that nature is all-important (Lickliter & Honeycutt, 2003). Many psychologists believe that environment plays an equally crucial role. Their idea is that *unique* experiences in and outside of the home affect an individual's development in profound ways (Reiss et al., 2000). Many parents think that enhancing their children's environment will optimize the likelihood of their living successful and satisfying lives; but, of course, the opposite can (and sometimes does) occur. And sometimes parenting is ineffectual and elicits antisocial behavior from children—the consequence is often a family torn by strife and anxiety. When this occurs, it is hard to discern who is "at fault." Thus, many researchers think of the family as a system and view the interactions among the family members according to a *transaction model* in which parents, children, and situations mutually influence one another (Little, 2000).

Stability or Change?

Do individuals stay pretty much the same throughout their lives—cognitively, emotionally, and socially—or do they change and adapt in response to events in their environment? The issue of stability versus change is an important theme in developmental psychology. It is closely associated with the nature–nurture issue, because when a researcher assumes that developmental stability exists, he or she often assumes that stable traits—for example, shyness—are inherited and genetically determined. Those who favor an environmental view are more likely to believe that people change over the course of a lifetime because of unique life events—for example, the loss of a sibling in a car accident.

Activity or Passivity?

A third issue developmental researchers consider is whether people are active or passive in exploring the world. A child who seeks out stimulation, new toys, and interactions with peers is seen and treated differently by parents, teachers, and friends than is a child who lets the world go by as if looking through a window. An active child seeks out problems, asks questions, and explores intellectual frontiers. A passive child works on what he or she is given, listens attentively, but seeks no new challenges. Both are affected by the environment, but the active individual has a "take charge" personality, and the passive individual lets the world take charge.

Continuity or Discontinuity?

A fourth important developmental issue is whether development is continuous or discontinuous. Some see development as continuous, a process of gradual growth and change, with skills and knowledge added a bit at a time and one skill building on another. But development can also be viewed as discontinuous, with maturation and understanding of the world advancing during various critical periods and with changes appearing abruptly. For example, one day a child cannot walk, but the next day she takes several steps.

Culture

There is one last key influence on development that has perhaps the strongest effects—culture. All humans grow up within a context, a culture. Culture is a key determinant of how people ultimately behave. Some people grow up in an *individualistic culture*, like that of the United States; others grow up in a *collectivist culture*, like that of Japan. Studying a person's growth and development can rarely be done outside of cultural considerations, because every society has prevailing ideas, events, and expectations that combine to acculturate individuals. Culture may be more dominant than any other variable in influencing a person's response to his or her genetic endowment or environment. A child who grows up in a culture that stresses self-reliance, individualism, and a take-charge approach is going to view the world differently than a child brought up to believe that her circumstances—her poverty, her minority status, being female, and living in the inner city—predispose her to failure.

The big picture of developmental psychology focuses on change in the physical, cognitive, moral, emotional, and social lives of human beings. Some people are affected more by heredity than others ("Sylvia is just like her mom"); some people stay basically the same throughout their lives ("Good old Joe, you can always count on him"). Some people are constantly exploring new avenues ("Joe is a real risk taker"); others grow in leaps and spurts ("Sylvia has changed so much in college, and it's all for the better"). Individuals are just that—unique entities who grow up in particular cultures and families. The relative influences of genetic makeup, parenting and family dynamics, and social and cultural environments on individuals are what interest developmental psychologists. They explore these variables through research, and there are key research designs that they use to guide this exploration.

Research Designs

Good researchers know that the method they use to study a problem often influences the results. In order to interpret the meaning of results, a researcher must take into account the particular research design used. In developmental research, two

Cross-sectional research design ■ A method for conducting a research study that compares individuals of different ages to determine if and how they differ on some dimension.

Longitudinal research design ■ A method for conducting a research study that follows individuals over a period of time to examine changes that have occurred with aging.

widely used designs are known as cross-sectional and longitudinal. A psychologist using a *cross-sectional research design* compares many individuals of different ages to determine if and how they differ on some dimension. A psychologist using a *longitudinal research design* studies a specific group of individuals at diffferent ages to examine changes that have occurred over a long period of time. **Figure 4.1** compares the cross-sectional and longitudinal research designs.

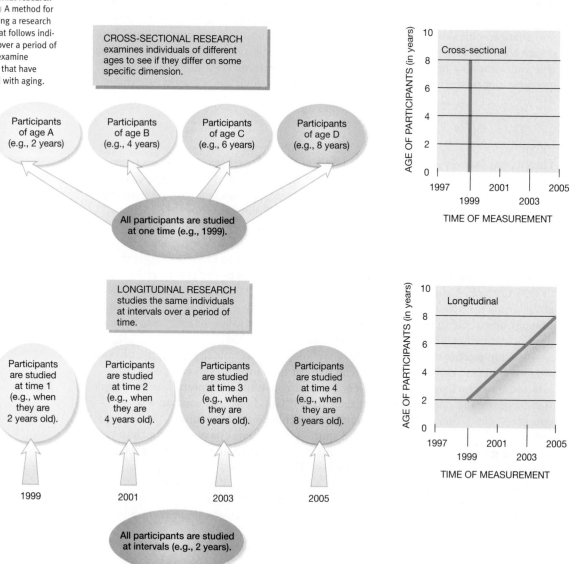

Figure 4.1
Cross-Sectional and Longitudinal Research Designs

Each of these research designs has its advantages and disadvantages. For example, the cross-sectional design suffers from the fact that the participants' backgrounds differ; they may have learned various things in different ways. Further, a participant's behavior, performance on a specific task, or level of ability may reflect a predisposition, a liking for the task, or some other variable unrelated to changes that come from development or aging. Most important, the age groups that are being examined may have had different life experiences—for example, one generation may have received substantially less education than the next, and education level affects results on standardized tests. Individual differences are impossible to assess with the cross-sectional design.

But the longitudinal research design also has problems. For one thing, it requires that a researcher have access to the same people repeatedly, even though some participants may move, withdraw from the study, or even die. Also, after repeated testing on the same task, participants may do better simply because of practice (even if the tests are months or years apart). Moreover, longitudinal research sometimes takes years to complete; during that time, important changes may occur in the participants' personal or social environments. Finally, such research is time-consuming and expensive.

Now that you know the basics about the study of developmental psychology let's really begin our exploration of development by focusing on how physical development proceeds.

How Does Physical Development Proceed?

Psychologists refer to developmental events that occur before birth as prenatal; those that occur in the month after birth are neonatal. Both terms derive from the Latin word *natus*, meaning "born."

Prenatal Development

The lifelong process of human development begins with conception. Conception occurs when an ovum and a sperm join in a woman's fallopian tube to form a *zygote*—a fertilized egg. Within 10 hours of conception, the zygote divides into four cells. During the next 5 days or so, the zygote floats down the fallopian tube and implants itself in the wall of the uterus. From implantation until the 49th day after conception, the organism is called an *embryo*. Then, from the 8th week until birth, it is referred to as a *fetus*. On the average, maturation and development of a full-term human infant require 266 days, or about 9 months; this length of time is often divided into three *trimesters* (3-month periods). **Table 4.1** summarizes the prenatal (before birth) and postnatal (after birth) periods of human development.

Although the prenatal environment—especially the mother's diet (Galloway et al., 2002)—can have an influence, many of a person's characteristics are established at conception; these include the color of the hair and eyes, the sex, the likelihood that the person will be tall or short, a tendency to be fat or thin, and perhaps basic intellectual abilities and personality traits. Once the zygote implants in the uterus, the cells

Zygote [ZY-goat] ■ A fertilized egg.

Embryo [EM-bree-o] ■ The prenatal organism from the 5th through the 49th day after conception.

Fetus [FEET-us] ■ The prenatal organism from the 8th week after conception until birth.

Table 4.1

LIFE STAGES AND APPROXIMATE AGES IN HUMAN DEVELOPMENT

Life Stage	Approximate Age
■ **Prenatal Period**	
Zygote	Conception to day 5 to 7
Embryo	To day 49
Fetus	Week 8 to birth
■ **Postnatal Period**	
Infancy	Birth to 18 months
Toddlerhood	18 months to 3 years
Early childhood	3 to 6 years
Middle childhood	6 to 13 years
Adolescence	13 to 20 years
Young adulthood	20 to 40 years
Middle adulthood	40 to 65 years
Late adulthood	65 and older

Placenta [pluh-SENT-uh] ■ A mass of tissue that is attached to the wall of the uterus and connected to the developing fetus by the umbilical cord; it supplies oxygen, nutrients, and antibodies and eliminates waste products.

begin the process of *differentiation*: Organs and other parts of the body begin to form. Some cells form the *umbilical cord*—a group of blood vessels and tissues that connect the zygote to the placenta. The *placenta* is a mass of tissue that is attached to the wall of the uterus and acts as the life support system for the fetus. It supplies oxygen, food, and antibodies and eliminates wastes—all by way of the mother's bloodstream. **Table 4.2** summarizes the major physical developments during the prenatal period.

Harmful Environmental Effects

The behavior of a pregnant woman affects prenatal development. Today, we can dismiss the ill-informed fears about these effects that were perpetuated in the past—for example, medieval European doctors advised pregnant women that uplifting thoughts would help a baby develop into a good, happy person, whereas fear, despondency, and negative emotions might disrupt the pregnancy and possibly result in a sad or mean-spirited child. However, research with animals does show that stress during pregnancy has effects on the later development of offspring (DiPietro, 2004; Lin, 2000). In an effort to produce a child who is easily soothed or to introduce an unborn child to his or her parents' voices, some pregnant women and their partners talk, sing, and/or play music for their child in the womb in the hope that the child will gain a benevolent perspective on the outside world.

While a fetus may not be affected by the mother's emotional states to the extent suggested by medieval doctors, the quality of the life support system provided by the mother does influence the embryo and fetus from conception until birth.

Table 4.2

MAJOR DEVELOPMENTS DURING THE PRENATAL PERIOD

Age	Size	Physical Development
■ First Trimester (1–12 weeks)		
1 week	150 cells	Zygote attaches to uterine lining.
2 weeks	Several thousand cells	Placental circulation established.
3 weeks	1/10 inch	Heart and blood vessels begin to develop. Basic components of brain and central nervous system form.
4 weeks	1/4 inch	Kidneys and digestive tract begin to form. Rudiments of ears, nose, and eyes are present.
6 weeks	1/2 inch	Arms and legs develop. Jaws form around mouth.
8 weeks	1 inch, 1/30 ounce	Bones begin to develop in limbs. Sex organs begin to form.
12 weeks	3 inches, 1 ounce	Gender can be distinguished. Kidneys are functioning, and liver is manufacturing red blood cells. Fetal movements can be detected by a physician.
■ Second Trimester (13–24 weeks)		
16 weeks	6 1/2 inches, 4 ounces	Heartbeat can be detected by a physician. Bones begin to calcify.
20 weeks	10 inches, 8 ounces	Mother feels fetal movements.
24 weeks	12 inches, 1 1/2 pounds	Vernix (white waxy substance) protects the body. Eyes open; eyebrows and eyelashes form; skin is wrinkled. Respiratory system is barely mature enough to support life.
■ Third Trimester (25–38 weeks)		
28 weeks	15 inches, 2 1/2 pounds	Fetus is fully developed but needs to gain in size and strength, and systems must mature.
32 weeks	17 inches, 4 pounds	A layer of fat forms beneath the skin to regulate body temperature.
36 weeks	19 inches, 6 pounds	Fetus settles into position for birth.
38 weeks	21 inches, 8 pounds	Fetus arrives at full term—approximately 266 days after conception.

4 weeks

11 weeks

20 weeks

Critical period ■ A time in the development of an organism when it is especially sensitive to certain environmental influences; outside of that period, the same influences will have far less effect.

Teratogen [ter-AT-oh-jen] ■ Substance that can produce developmental malformations (birth defects) during the prenatal period.

Fetal alcohol syndrome ■ A set of physical, mental, and neurobehavioral birth defects that is associated with alcohol consumption during pregnancy and is the leading known and preventable cause of mental retardation.

Environmental factors such as diet, infection, radiation, and drugs affect both the mother and the baby. The developing child is especially vulnerable in certain *critical periods*, during which it is maturing rapidly and is particularly sensitive to the environment. Although the basic architecture of the brain is in place well before birth, individual connections between neurons are subject to considerable influence or damage in infancy.

Substances that can produce developmental malformations (birth defects) during the prenatal period are known as *teratogens*. The impact of a teratogen changes over the course of the prenatal period and is dependent on the dose. For example, if a mother drinks alcohol in early and middle pregnancy, her baby is more likely to be born prematurely, to have a lower birth weight, and to suffer from mental retardation or attention-deficit/hyperactivity disorder (Ponnappa & Rubin, 2000). Each year, about 10,000 infants are born with physical signs or cognitive disabilities associated with maternal drinking (Jacobson, 1997; Ohio State University, 2004). Maternal drinking during pregnancy may even result in fetal alcohol syndrome. *Fetal alcohol syndrome* is a set of physical, mental, and neurobehavioral birth defects associated with alcohol consumption during pregnancy; it is the leading known and preventable cause of mental retardation. Alcohol in a pregnant woman's bloodstream crosses the placenta and thus circulates into the fetus's bloodstream. There, the alcohol interferes with the fetus's ability to receive sufficient oxygen and nourishment for normal cell development. Research shows that mothers who drink *more* than 3 ounces of 100-proof liquor (a 12-ounce can of beer, a 5-ounce glass of wine, and a 12-ounce wine cooler contain about the amount of alcohol and the same intoxication potential as 11/2 ounces of liquor) per day during pregnancy are significantly more likely to have children who show deficits in intelligence test scores at age 4 (Kelly, Day, & Streissguth, 2000) and who may even show alcohol-related problems later in life (Baie et al., 2003).

Studies show that many drugs affect prenatal development. High doses of aspirin, caffeine, or tobacco all have negative effects (Barr et al., 1990). Cigarette smoking constricts the oxygen supply to the fetus. Babies born to mothers who smoke cigarettes tend to be smaller and may be at increased risk for cleft palate, a slightly lower IQ, and hyperactivity (Kotimaa et al., 2003). In addition, one study found that babies born to mothers who smoked were more likely to develop asthma than those born to mothers who did not (Lewis et al., 1995). Certain drugs, including tranquilizers, can produce malformations of the head, face, and limbs as well as neurological disorders. Drugs may have an especially strong influence during the embryonic stage of development, when the mother may not realize she is pregnant; this is usually considered a critical period.

Newborns Are Ready to Experience the World

It is hard not to appreciate newborns; they change so much and so quickly, and most people marvel at their rapid growth. Newborns grow seemingly overnight— and they are not nearly as helpless as many people believe. At birth, infants can hear, see, smell, and respond to the environment in adaptive ways; in other words, they have good sensory systems (Cassia et al., 2002). They are also directly affected by experience. Psychologists try to find out exactly how experiences affect infants' perceptual development—to discover how infants think, what they perceive, and how they react to the world. Researchers are interested in answers to various questions about newborns' perceptual world: What are a child's inborn abilities and reflexes? When do inborn abilities become evident? How does the environment affect the emergence of inborn abilities? And how are sensory and motor development interrelated?

Growth

An infant who weighs 7.5 pounds at birth may weigh as much as 20 or 25 pounds by 12 months. At 18 months, a child is usually walking and beginning to talk (Carruth et al., 2004). Infancy continues until the child begins to represent the world abstractly through language. Thus, *infancy* is the period from birth to about 18 months.

The rapid growth that occurs in the early weeks and months after birth is quite extraordinary and mirrors embryonic development in important ways. A newborn's head is about one-fourth of its body length; a 2-year-old's is only one-fifth. The head develops early, and motor development, control, and coordination progress from the head to the feet. This pattern of growth is called the *cephalocaudal trend* (from the Greek word *kephalé,* "head," and the Latin word *cauda,* "tail"). Following another pattern—the *proximodistal trend*—maturation and growth progress from the center (the *proximal* part) of the body outward to the extremities (the more distant, or *distal,* part). That is, the head and torso grow before the arms, legs, hands, and feet do. Thus, a newborn's head is about the same circumference as the torso, and an infant's arms and legs are quite short, relatively speaking—but these proportions change very quickly (see **Figure 4.2**).

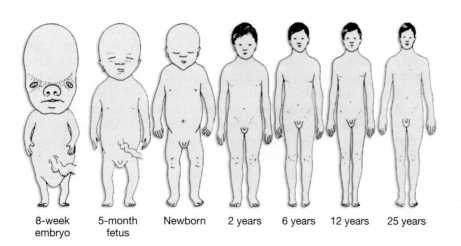

8-week embryo   5-month fetus   Newborn   2 years   6 years   12 years   25 years

Figure 4.2
The Cephalocaudal Trend of Growth
Body proportions change dramatically from fetal stages of development until adulthood. (Berk, 1994)

Figure 4.3
Development
of Motor Skills
in the First Two
Years
Infants typically
develop motor
skills in the
sequence shown
here. Normal,
healthy infants may
reach any of these
milestones earlier
or later than these
average ages.

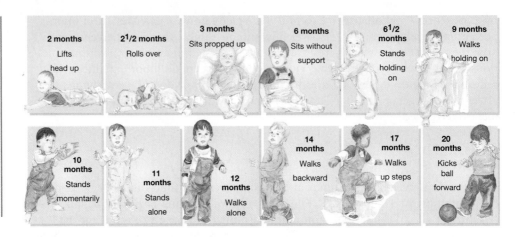

Babinski reflex ■ Reflex that causes a newborn to fan out the toes when the sole of the foot is touched.

Moro reflex ■ Reflex that causes a newborn to stretch out the arms and legs and cry in response to a loud noise or an abrupt change in the environment.

Rooting reflex ■ Reflex that causes a newborn to turn the head toward a light touch on lip or cheek.

Sucking reflex ■ Reflex that causes a newborn to make sucking motions when a finger or nipple is placed in the mouth.

Grasping reflex ■ Reflex that causes a newborn to grasp vigorously any object touching the palm or fingers or placed in the hand.

During the period of infancy and childhood (through about age 13 years), the child grows physically from a being that requires constant care, attention, and assistance to a nearly full-sized, independent person. By 13 months, children can walk, climb, and manipulate their environment—skills that often lead to the need for a variety of safety features in the home. There is significant variability in the age at which children begin to walk or climb. Some do so early; others are slow to develop these abilities. The age at which these specific behaviors first occur seems unrelated to any other major developmental milestones. **Figure 4.3** shows the major achievements in motor development in the first 2 years. While infants change and grow in fits and starts, all newborns are born with certain built-in responses, or reflexes.

Newborns' Reflexes

Touch the palm of a newborn baby, and you'll probably find one of your fingers held in the surprisingly firm grip of a tiny fist. The baby is exhibiting a reflexive reaction. Babies are born with innate *primary reflexes*—unlearned responses to stimuli. Some responses, such as the grasping reflex, no doubt helped ensure survival in humanity's primate ancestors; most of these reflexes disappear over the course of the first year of life. Physicians use the presence or absence of primary reflexes to assess neurological status at birth and to evaluate rate of development during infancy. One primary reflex exhibited by infants is the *Babinski reflex*—a fanning out of the toes in response to a touch on the sole of the foot. Another is the *Moro reflex*—outstretching of the arms and legs and crying in response to a loud noise or an abrupt change in the environment. Newborns also exhibit the *rooting reflex*—turning the head toward a light touch (such as of a breast or hand) on their lip or cheek. They show the *sucking reflex* when a finger or nipple is placed in their mouth and the vigorous *grasping reflex* in response to an object touching the palms of their hands or their fingers.

At first, an infant's abilities and reflexes are biologically determined. Gradually, learned responses, such as reaching for desired objects, replace reflexive reactions. The baby's experiences in the environment become more important in determining

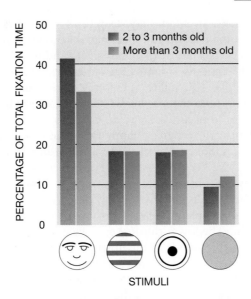

Figure 4.4
Results of Fantz's Study
Using a viewing box to observe newborns' eye movements, Fantz (1961) recorded the total time infants spent looking at various patterns. He found that they looked at faces or patterned material much more often than they looked at plain fields.

development. The complex interactions between nature and nurture follow a developmental timetable that continues throughout life.

Infant Perception: Fantz's Viewing Box

A mountain of research on infant perception shows that newborns have surprisingly well-developed perceptual systems. Robert Fantz (1961) did some of the earliest work on infant perception. Fantz designed a viewing box in which he placed an infant; he then had a hidden observer or camera record the infant's responses to stimuli (see **Figure 4.4**).

The exciting part of Fantz's work was not so much that he asked interesting questions but that he was able to get "answers" from the infants. By showing infants various patterns and pictures of faces and recording their eye movements, he discovered their visual preferences. He recorded how long and how often the infants looked at each pattern or picture. Because the infants spent more time looking at pictures of faces than at patterns of random squiggles, Fantz concluded not only that they could see different patterns but also that they preferred faces.

Other researchers confirm that infants prefer complex visual fields over simple ones, curved patterns over straight or angular ones, and normal human faces over random patterns or faces with mixed-up features (Cassia, Simion, & Umiltà, 2001; Turati, 2004). In addition, newborns pay more attention to elements in the upper part of an image than to those in the lower part (Turati et al., 2002). Even in the first few months of life, babies can discriminate among facial features and prefer attractive faces to less attractive ones (Slater et al., 2000). Newborns look at pictures of their parents more than at pictures of strangers (Fullmer, 1999). Babies as young as 3 months can discern a caregiver's shift of attention by observing the person's eyes and can then shift their own attention to the same object or event (Brooks & Meltzoff, 2002).

At about 4 to 8 weeks, an infant may sleep for 4 to 6 hours during the night, uninterrupted by the need to eat, a change that weary parents usually welcome. When awake, infants smile at their caregivers and listen attentively to human voices. Between 6 and 9 months, infants begin to crawl, giving them more freedom to seek out favorite people. The ability to crawl is accompanied by important changes in behavior; in fact, some researchers assert that crawling is what allows critical behavior changes to occur (Bertenthal, Campos, & Kermoian, 1994).

By 7 months, infants can recognize happy faces and sounds and can discriminate among them (Soken & Pick, 1999). According to Arlene Walker-Andrews (Montague & Walker-Andrews, 2001), they recognize emotional expressions at an early age—in some cases as young as 4 months. Using a procedure similar to Fantz's, Walker-Andrews (1986) observed 5- and 7-month-old infants who saw films of people with angry or happy facial expressions making angry or happy sounds. (The lower third of each face was covered so that the infants could not match the sounds to the lips.) She recorded which images the infants looked at and how long they looked at them as an index of their interest and of whether they perceived incongruity between face and sound. Results showed that 7-month-old infants could tell when the sound and facial expression did not match, but 5-month-olds could not. This research suggests that there is a timetable by which infants develop the ability to discriminate among facial expressions.

You can see that infants' perceptional development follows a maturational timetable, with some discontinuities. At first, babies attend to the most prominent features in the world; as time passes, they attend to, recognize, and respond to the world based on their recognition of people and situations— they begin to make more cognitive-based perceptual decisions (Reznick, Chawarska, & Betts, 2000). Depth perception is another ability that infants develop early, as studies of the visual cliff show.

The visual cliff method allows researchers to study infants' depth perception.

The Visual Cliff

Gibson and Walk conducted a classic developmental research study in 1960. They devised the *visual cliff method* to determine the extent of infants' depth perception. In this method, a researcher places an infant who is able to crawl on a glass surface, half of which is covered with a checkerboard pattern. The same checkerboard pattern appears several feet below the transparent half of the glass surface. Infants can crawl easily from the patterned area onto the transparent area. Infants with poorly developed depth perception should be willing to crawl onto the transparent side as often as onto the patterned side. Conversely, infants with well-developed depth perception should refuse to crawl onto the transparent side, even when encouraged to do so by their mothers. Gibson and Walk found that 9-month-olds avoided the transparent surface, thus demonstrating that depth perception is well developed at this age. Recent research (Durand, Lecuyer, & Frichtel, 2003) using other methodology suggests that this ability develops even earlier—as much as 4 months earlier.

Evolution and Newborn Preparedness

Newborns enter the world with the ability to experience, respond to, and learn from the environment. Their sensory systems are well formed but still developing; this development is strongly shaped by experience, which ultimately alters brain connections permanently (Simion & Butterworth, 1998). Newborns are thus biologically equipped and ready to perceive and experience the world; as their brains develop, neurons interconnect, and this neuronal development continues for several years. Recall from Chapter 3 that most of the neuronal connections are present at birth; however, the proper functioning of the nervous system is sensitive to and depends on experience. Without varied perceptual experiences, brain development is less than optimal. So, while evolution may have prepared a newborn to experience the world, the infant's interactions with the world shape her or his ability to cope effectively. And infants are active explorers of their world, not passive vessels into which experience is poured. Infants experiment, infants explore, and infants learn—it is this active, cognitive maturation that allows for and promotes survival, growth, and cognitive development. We explore the course of cognitive maturation next.

How Does Thought Develop?

Why are some cars made with child-proof locks and windows? Why do parents use gates to guard stairs and gadgets to keep kitchen cabinets closed? Why are young children's toys made so that small parts cannot come off? Because children are inquisitive and much more intelligent than many people give them credit for. Even 3-month-olds can learn the order of a list of items and, when given age-appropriate prompts, remember that information a day later (Morrongiello, Lasenby, & Lee, 2003).

Infants' physical development is visible and dramatic; for example, to the delight of caregivers, babies sometimes respond by imitating their facial expressions (pursed lips, stuck-out tongues) (Forman & Kochanska, 2001) The cognitive changes that occur in slightly older children are sometimes less visible, but no less dramatic. Children are continually developing, both physically and cognitively, learning to cope with an ever-expanding world. As they mature, they can determine causes of events. Much of this ability is cognitively based and develops according to a timetable that is rooted in brain growth and development (Peltzer-Karpf & Zangel, 2001). **Figure 4.5** (on p. 112) shows some of the many cognitive milestones of the first 12 months.

1 week

- See patterns, light, and dark
- Are sensitive to the location of a sound
- Distinguish volume and pitch
- Prefer high voices
- Will grasp an object if they touch it accidentally
- Stop sucking to look at a person momentarily

1 month

- Become excited at the sight of a person or a toy
- Look at objects only if in their line of vision
- Prefer patterns to plain fields
- Coordinate eyes sideways, up, and down
- Follow a toy from the side to the center of the body

2 months

- Prefer people to objects
- Stare at human faces; become quiet at the sound of a human voice
- Are startled at sounds and make a facial response
- Perceive depth
- Coordinate eye movements
- Reach out voluntarily instead of grasping reflexively
- Discriminate among voices, people, tastes, and objects

3 months

- Follow moving objects
- Glance from one object to another
- Distinguish near objects from distant objects
- Search with eyes for the source of a sound
- Become aware of self through exploration
- Show basic signs of memory

4 to 7 months

- See the world in color and with near-adult vision
- Pull dangling objects toward them
- Follow dangling or moving objects
- Turn to follow sound and vanishing objects
- Visually search out fast-moving or fallen objects
- Begin to anticipate a whole object when shown only part of it
- Deliberately imitate sounds and movements
- Recall a short series of actions
- Look briefly for a toy that disappears

8 to 12 months

- Put small objects into containers and pull them out of containers
- Search behind a screen for an object after they see it hidden there
- Hold and manipulate one object while looking at another object
- Recognize dimensions of objects

Figure 4.5

Infants' Perceptual and Cognitive Milestones
(Clarke-Stewart, Friedman, & Koch, 1985)

Without question, the 20th-century's leading researcher and theorist on the cognitive development of children and adults was Jean Piaget; his work laid the foundation for an understanding of the development of thought.

Jean Piaget's Insights

Swiss psychologist Jean Piaget (1896–1980) came to believe that the fundamental development of all cognitive abilities takes place during the first 2 years of life, and many psychologists and educators agree. Piaget devised ingenious procedures for examining the cognitive development of young children; he looked at what children did well, what mistakes they made, and when and how they gained insights into the world. Piaget's theory focuses on *how* people think instead of on *what* they think, making it applicable to people in all cultures. Perhaps Piaget's greatest strength, however, was his description of how a person's inherited capacities (nature) interact with the environment (nurture) to produce cognitive functioning. What Piaget did best was focus on the details of children's cognitive development; he observed children at great length and noted advances in their abilities at various ages. Piaget's explanations of cognitive development focus, to a great extent, on its direction. He explains how a person changes from a self-centered infant to an independent thinker as an adolescent (Piaget, 1936, 1970, 1980).

Although psychologists were initially skeptical of Piaget's ideas, and some criticisms persist, many researchers have shown that his assumptions are generally correct and can be applied cross-culturally. But there are some dissenters (notably Russian psychologist Lev Vygotsky, whose theories we will consider a bit later) who stress society's role in shaping thought processes. Piaget put considerable emphasis on biology, asserting that cognitive development depends on the interaction between biological changes that take place within a child and the child's experiences and that this development follows the same path in all social environments.

Piaget's Central Concepts

Piaget believed that what changes during development is the child's ability to make sense of experience. He called a set of organized ways of interacting with the environment and experiencing the world a *schema* (plural, *schemata*). Think of a schema as a *mental structure*, a way of organizing thoughts and categorizing things and actions. For example, suppose you are playing with a 3-year-old at one of those little toy toolbenches that has multicolored nuts and bolts and easy-to-grasp hammers, pliers, and other tools. You say, "I need a whatchamacallit," and then pause. With only a slight hesitation, the child hands you the plastic wrench. Researchers assert that the child (and you) are using a schema to refer to some type of device that can grab a bolt and turn it. In a way, a schema is a generalization a person makes based on comparable occurrences of various actions, usually physical, or motor, actions. Schemata guide thoughts based on prior experiences; they thus serve as the building blocks of cognitive growth.

Piaget argued that a schema could change through three processes: adaptation, assimilation, and accommodation. Initially, children develop schemata for simple

Schema ■ In Piaget's view, a specific mental structure; an organized way of interacting with the environment and experiencing it; a generalization a child makes based on comparable occurrences of various, usually physical or motor, actions (plural, *schemata*).

motor behaviors; for example, they realize that reaching out and touching an object will cause it to move. Basic schemata are combined to yield more complex ones. Schemata develop because a child discovers that action brings results; those results, in turn, may affect the child's future behavior. For example, a child reaches out and touches a mobile, the bells that are attached to the mobile make a sound, the mobile changes position—and the child observes that a specific action has influenced the world. This entire process is called *adaptation*. As adaptation continues, a child organizes his or her schemata into more complex mental representations, linking one schema with another. Ultimately, children develop schemata about play, make-believe, and the permanence of objects. To develop these schemata and more complex mental structures, children must be capable of two other important processes: assimilation and accommodation. The complexity of a child's schemata depends on how well and how much the child assimilates and accommodates information (Spelke, 2000).

Both children and adults use assimilation and accommodation to establish new schemata. *Assimilation* is the process by which a person absorbs new ideas and experiences and incorporates them into existing mental structures and behaviors. *Accommodation* is the process of modifying previously developed mental structures and behaviors to adapt them to new experiences. A child who learns to grasp a ball demonstrates assimilation by later grasping other round objects. This assimilated behavior then serves as a foundation for accommodation. That is, the child can learn new behaviors such as grasping forks, crayons, and sticks by modifying the earlier response—for example, by widening or narrowing the grasp. According to Piaget, the two processes of assimilation and accommodation alternate in an ongoing cycle of cognitive development that has certain identifiable stages. These developmental processes and stages are part of an active construction of reality—babies and young children piece together their own view of the world, rather than just absorbing what adults teach them. Piaget thus asserted that children play an active role in their own cognitive development.

Assimilation ■
According to Piaget, the process by which new ideas and experiences are absorbed and incorporated into existing mental structures and behaviors.

Accommodation ■
According to Piaget, the process by which existing mental structures and behaviors are modified to adapt to new experiences.

Piaget's Stages of Cognitive Development

Four stages of cognitive development are central to Piaget's theory. Piaget believed that just as standing must precede walking, some stages of cognitive development must precede others. For example, if a parent presents an idea that is too advanced, a child will not understand, and no real learning will take place. A 4-year-old who asks how babies are made will probably not understand a full, biologically accurate explanation and will not remember it. If the same child asks the question a few years later, a more realistic and complex explanation will be more meaningful and more likely to be remembered. Piaget's stages are associated with approximate ages. The exact ages for each stage vary from person to person, but children in all cultures go through the series of stages. Piaget acknowledged the complex interaction of environmental influences and genetic inheritances; nevertheless, he felt strongly that the stages always occurred in the same order. The four developmental stages he proposed are the sensorimotor stage, the preoperational stage, the concrete operational stage, and the formal operational stage.

THE SENSORIMOTOR STAGE. Piaget considered the *sensorimotor stage*, which extends from birth to about age 2, to be the most significant, because the foundation for all cognitive development is established during this period. Consider the enormous changes that take place during the first 2 years of life. Newborns are totally dependent and mostly reflexive organisms. Within a few weeks, infants learn some simple habits. They smile at their mothers or caregivers; they seek visual or auditory stimulation; they anticipate events in the environment, such as being presented with the mother's breast or a bottle. At 2 to 3 months, infants develop some motor coordination skills (Thelen, 2000) and a memory for past events, and they are able to predict future visual events (Diedrich et al., 2001). According to Piaget, the acquisition of memory is a necessary foundation for further cognitive development.

By the age of 6 to 8 months, infants seek new and more interesting kinds of stimulation. They can sit up and crawl. No longer content to merely watch what goes on around them, they begin to attempt to manipulate their environment. Piaget called this attempt "making interesting sights last"—that is, infants try to make events that intrigue them recur. Karen Wynn (Wynn, Bloom, & Chiang, 2002) suggests that even at this age, infants have some very basic numerical abilities that form the foundation for further development of arithmetical reasoning. At about 8 months, infants have intentions, and they attempt to overcome obstacles in order to reach goals. They can crawl to the other side of a room to reach a cat or a toy or follow a parent into the next room. They have developed good recognition memory (Rose, Feldman, & Jankowski, 2003).

From about 9 months on, babies develop *object permanence*—the realization that objects continue to exist even when they are out of sight (see **Figure 4.6**). Prior to the development of object permanence, when the caregiver leaves the room and the baby

Sensorimotor stage ■
The first of Piaget's four stages of cognitive development (covering roughly the first 2 years of life), during which the child develops some motor coordination skills and a memory for past events.

Object permanence ■
The realization that objects continue to exist even when they are out of sight.

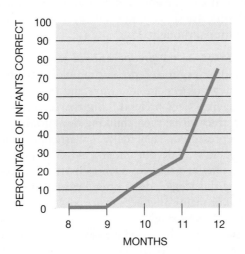

Figure 4.6
Object Permanence
Object permanence is the ability to know that an object continues to exist even when out of view. Research shows that the ability to remember the location of an object that is subsequently hidden improves over time. Most 1-year-olds can remember where an object has been hidden even after a delay of 7 seconds. (Fox, Kagan, and Weiskopf, 1979)

can no longer see her or him, the caregiver no longer exists. After object permanence develops, the baby realizes that the caregiver is just out of view. Although the exact age at which object permanence becomes evident has not yet been established, Renée Baillargeon (Hespos & Baillargeon, 2001) has shown the existence of this capability in some 4-month-olds—a younger age than Piaget believed possible (see also von Hofsten, Feng, & Spelke, 2000). In general, researchers assert that infants have knowledge of the physical world and a specialized learning ability that guides their acquisition of such knowledge, with various aspects of object permanence evolving gradually throughout the sensorimotor stage (Meltzoff & Moore, 2001).

In the second half of the sensorimotor stage (from about 12 to 24 months), children begin to walk, talk, and use simple forms of logic. Object permanence is more fully developed; a child can now follow a ball that rolls away, can search for a caregiver who has left the room, and realizes that objects just out of view are still there (Berthier et al., 2000). Children also begin to use signing and language to represent the world, an ability that takes them beyond the concrete world of visual imagery. Elizabeth Bates's research has shown that language and even gesturing are evident at early ages (Bates & Dick, 2002; Bates et al., 1989). At 1 year, an infant can gesture a desire for water or food by tapping the head with the hand, for example. Joseph Garcia (2002) has focused on this ability in his best-selling self-help book for parents called *Sign with Your Baby: How to Communicate with Infants before They Can Speak*. By age 2, a child can talk about "dolly," "doggy," cookies, going "bye-bye," and other people, objects, and events. No longer an uncoordinated, reflexive infant, the child has become a thinking, walking, talking human being. Simultaneously, children may become manipulative and difficult to deal with. Parents often describe this stage as the "terrible twos"; it is characterized by the overuse of the emphatic "No!" The child's behavior may vacillate between charming and awful. This vacillation and the emergence of annoying new habits, such as being difficult to dress and bathe, are signs of normal development, marking the beginning of the stage of preoperational thought.

Preoperational stage ■ Piaget's second stage of cognitive development (lasting from about age 2 to age 6 or 7), during which the child begins to represent the world symbolically.

THE PREOPERATIONAL STAGE. In the *preoperational stage*, which lasts from about age 2 to age 6 or 7, children begin to represent the world symbolically. As preschoolers, they play with objects in new ways and try to represent reality through symbolic thought, by playing "let's pretend." But they continue to think about specifics rather than abstract ideas; their thinking does not incorporate concepts that are not easily visually represented. They make few attempts to make their speech more intelligible to listeners who do not understand or to justify their reasoning, and they may develop behavior problems such as inattentiveness, belligerence, or temper tantrums. During this stage, adults often begin trying to teach children how to interact with others, but major advances in social development do not become fully apparent until Piaget's next stage.

Egocentrism [ee-go-SENT-rism] ■ Inability to perceive a situation or event except in relation to oneself; self-centeredness.

A key element of the preoperational stage—one which affects a child's cognitive and emotional behavior—is *egocentrism*, or self-centeredness. Present in the sensorimotor stage, but becoming especially apparent in the preoperational stage, egocentrism is the inability to perceive a situation or event except in relation to oneself. Children are unable to understand that the world does not exist solely to reflect their interests and satisfy their needs. They respond to questions such as "Why does it snow?" with answers such as "So I can play in it." Children in the preoperational stage cannot put themselves in anyone else's position.

At the end of Piaget's preoperational stage, children are just beginning to understand the difference between their ideas, feelings, and interests and those of others. *Decentration,* or the process of changing from a totally self-oriented point of view to one that recognizes other people's feelings and viewpoints, continues for several years. The concepts of egocentrism and decentration are widely recognized as central to Piaget's theory. However, few contemporary researchers have incorporated these ideas into their conceptions of how development proceeds.

Piaget held that children's understanding of space and their construction of alternative visual perspectives are limited during the preoperational stage. Recent evidence, however, suggests that Piaget may have underestimated the spatial-perceptual abilities of children. Researchers have found that even 5-year-olds can solve certain visual and spatial problems previously thought to be solvable only by children 9 to 10 years old or older (Newcombe & Huttenlocher, 2000). Also, 4-year-olds are able to represent and remember the past, as when they recall their visit to a theme park or the good chocolate cake they had at their birthday party.

THE CONCRETE OPERATIONAL STAGE. The *concrete operational stage* is Piaget's third stage of cognitive development, lasting from approximately age 6 or 7 to age 11 or 12. During this stage, a child develops the ability to understand constant factors in the environment, rules, and higher-order symbolic systems such as arithmetic and geography. Children in this stage attend school, have friends, can dress and feed themselves, and may take on household responsibilities. They can look at a situation from more than one viewpoint. They have gained sufficient mental maturity to be able to distinguish between appearance and reality and to think ahead one or two moves in checkers or other games. During this stage, children discover constancy in the world; for example, a child learns not to build a sandcastle right at the ocean's edge, because the rising tide will inevitably destroy it. They can also learn rules and understand the reasons for them.

Cognitive and perceptual abilities continue to develop as children mature and, slowly and in different ways, comprehend ever more difficult concepts. For example, at around age 7, children come to realize the connectedness of their thoughts, and they become especially conscious of their inner mental life and its unpredictability at times (Flavell, Green, & Flavell, 2000).

The hallmark of this stage is the acquisition of *conservation*—the ability to recognize that objects can be transformed in some way, visually or physically, yet still be the same in number, weight, substance, or volume. This concept has been the subject of considerable research. In a typical conservation task, a child is shown three beakers or glasses. Two are short and squat and contain the same amount of liquid (water or juice); the other is tall, narrow, and empty (see **Figure 4.7** on p. 118). The experimenter pours the liquid from one short, squat glass into the tall, narrow one and asks the child, "Which glass has more juice?" A child who does not understand the principle of conservation will claim that the taller glass contains more, because it is "large" or because the act of pouring somehow adds volume. A child who is able to conserve liquid quantity will recognize that the same amount of liquid is in both the tall glass and the short glasses.

Decentration ■ Process of changing from a totally self-oriented point of view to one that recognizes other people's feelings and viewpoints.

Concrete operational stage ■ Piaget's third stage of cognitive development (lasting from approximately age 6 or 7 to age 11 or 12), during which the child develops the ability to understand constant factors in the environment, rules, and higher-order symbolic systems.

Conservation ■ Ability to recognize that objects can be transformed in some way, visually or physically, yet still be the same in number, weight, substance, or volume.

Figure 4.7
Development of Conservation
Conservation is the ability to recognize that an object that has been transformed is still the same object, regardless of any changes it has undergone.

1. A child examines two glasses of juice and sees that they are the same.

2. A researcher pours the contents of one glass into a taller and narrower glass.

3. The child is asked to choose the glass that has "more" in it. Children who have not yet developed the ability to conserve choose the taller glass and often declare, "It has more in it; it's bigger."

A child who has mastered one type of conservation (for example, conservation of liquid quantity) often cannot immediately transfer that knowledge to other conservation tasks. For example, the child may not understand that two weights stacked one on top of the other weigh the same as when they are placed side by side. A child who masters conservation realizes that specific facts are true because they follow logically, not simply because they are observed. That is, the child infers that the tall glass must contain the same amount of liquid as the short glass because no liquid was added or taken away when the contents of the short glass were poured into the tall one.

Formal operational stage ■ Piaget's fourth and final stage of cognitive development (beginning at about age 12), during which the individual can think hypothetically, can consider future possibilities, and can use deductive logic.

THE FORMAL OPERATIONAL STAGE. The *formal operational stage* is Piaget's fourth and final stage of cognitive development (beginning at about age 12), during which the individual can think hypothetically, can consider future possibilities, and can use deductive logic. Unlike children in the concrete operational stage, whose thoughts are still tied to immediate situations, adolescents can engage in abstract thinking. They can form hypotheses that allow them to think of different ways to represent situations, organizing them into various possible relationships and outcomes. The cognitive world of adolescents is full of informal theories of logic and ideas about life; they are able to undertake scientific experiments requiring the formation and testing of hypotheses.

By age 12, at about the beginning of adolescence, the egocentrism of the sensorimotor and preoperational stages has for the most part disappeared, but another form of egocentrism has developed. According to Inhelder and Piaget (1958), "The adolescent goes through a phase in which he [or she] attributes an unlimited power to his [or her] own thoughts so that the dream of a glorious future or of transforming the

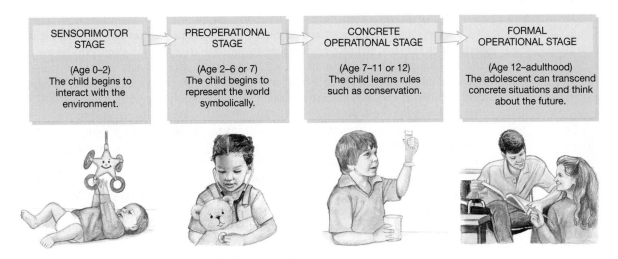

Figure 4.8
Piaget's Stages of Cognitive Development

world through ideas (even if this idealism takes a materialistic form) seems to be not only fantasy, but also an effective action which in itself modifies the empirical world" (pp. 345–346). The egocentrism and naive hopes of adolescents eventually decrease as they face and deal with the challenges of life.

Piaget's stages of cognitive development are summarized in **Figure 4.8**.

Putting Piaget in Perspective

Parents, educators, and psychologists can enhance children's cognitive development by understanding how mental abilities develop. Piaget recognized that parental love and parent–child interactions are always important to a child's development, but he asserted that they are essential in the first 2 years of life. For a child to develop object permanence, to learn how to make interesting events recur, and to develop the rudiments of numerical reasoning, it is necessary for caregivers to provide abundant physical and cognitive stimuli, especially stimuli that move and change color, shape, and form. Research confirms that children and animals given sensory stimulation during their early months develop more quickly, both cognitively and socially, than those lacking such stimulation. From Piaget's point of view, stimulation and manipulation optimize children's potential. Parents and educators who agree with Piaget try to ensure that during children's first years of life, stimulation is plentiful, curiosity is encouraged, and opportunities for exploration are maximized. A child in an enriched environment has the freedom to manipulate objects and see them from many vantage points; expensive toys are not necessary—variety is the key. In one research study, fifth-grade students who received special lessons and activities designed to increase abilities in concrete and abstract thinking showed remarkable gains (Bakken et al., 2001).

Although Piaget's ideas have had an enormous influence on developmental psychology, some researchers have problems with his approach on three fronts: He may have underestimated the rate and extent of children's cognitive development; he miscalculated the ages of transitions; and he placed too great an emphasis on the individual and de-emphasized much of the social world. Further, psychologists today see development as a continuous process rather than a series of discrete stages (Courage & Howe, 2002). Psychologist Rochel Gelman argues that Piaget also tended to underestimate younger children's abilities. For example, Shatz and Gelman (1973) found that 2-year-olds change the length of their sentences depending on whom they are talking to, using shorter sentences, for example, when speaking to younger children. The researchers point out that being decentered enough to make such a shift in point of view is a sign of cognitive maturity. Many other researchers claim that Piaget may have overestimated the degree of egocentrism in young children. Baillargeon asserts that Piaget also underestimated the spatial-perceptual abilities of infants. For example, she holds that understanding what actually happens to objects when they are hidden, which Piaget saw as developing at 18 months, can be seen in infants 6 months old (Luo et al., 2003; Miller & Baillargeon, 1990). Similarly, other research shows that infants have abilities to make inferences earlier than previously thought (Diamond, Lee, & Hayden, 2003). Baillargeon (1998; Baillargeon & Wang, 2002) has argued that infants are born with specialized learning mechanisms that allow for the acquisition of knowledge about the physical world. Other researchers agree, pointing out strong genetic effects on early cognitive development (Price et al., 2000). This is an interesting assertion that needs further research.

A biological emphasis was the underpinning of Piaget's view of cognitive development. But others, especially ecological psychologists, focus more on the environment.

Ecological Systems Theory

Perhaps the newest developmental theory to have had a wide impact is *ecological systems theory*. Developed by a number of researchers, with Urie Bronfenbrenner (1979) at the forefront, this approach argues that children develop within a system of complex human relationships that encompass both immediate environments such as families and neighborhoods and larger environments such as communities, states, and countries. Bronfenbrenner calls this layered interactive system a *context of development*. The ecological systems approach stresses the role of culture and of social relationships between individuals and within the larger society. According to this approach, behavior and development must be studied cross-culturally, because people do not live in a social vacuum. Next, we'll see that Bronfenbrenner is not alone in espousing a socially oriented approach. Lev Vygotsky, who stressed that dialogues between children and other members of their society fuel child development, argued the same thing over 70 years ago.

Vygotsky's Sociocultural Theory: An Alternative to Piaget

Piaget saw the child as an organism that is self-motivated to understand the world. The child, he held, is a busy constructor of reality, making interesting sights last, inventing games, and learning abstract rules. But Lev Vygotsky (1896–1934) saw the child as developing not alone, but as part of a social world filled with communication, both with the self and with others. Vygotsky believed that children are constantly trying to extract meaning from the social world and to master higher-order concepts (Lindblom & Ziemke, 2003). At first, children's mental life expresses itself in interactions with other people. Later, children engage in private speech (talking to themselves) to plan and guide their own behavior; when they use such speech, they do better at various tasks (Winsler, Carlton, & Barry, 2000). It is important to note that Piaget believed that private speech was egocentric and did not involve taking the perspective of others. Vygotsky suggested just the opposite: Private speech helps a child understand his or her world and that of other people. For Vygotsky (1934/1962), even the earliest speech is essentially social and useful; in fact, he asserted that social speech comes first, followed by private speech, then inner speech (thinking in words). Vygotsky wrote: "The most significant moment in the course of intellectual development . . . occurs . . . when speech and practical activity, two previously completely independent lines of development, converge" (Vygotsky, 1930/1978, p. 24).

To a great extent, Vygotsky's work focused on trying to understand what he called "culturally patterned dialogue." Vygotsky emphasized the extraction of meaning from the world, especially through verbal interchanges, and he was particularly interested in examining the culture and the situation—the context—through which meaning is extracted. Vygotsky's approach can be considered sociocultural (Bruner, 1997).

Vygotsky was especially concerned—perhaps overly concerned, according to Bruner (1997)—with how adults provide information about culture to children. From a Vygotskian perspective, skills and knowledge are culture-bound (Duncan & Tarulli, 2003). According to Vygotsky, when children are presented tasks that are outside of their current abilities, they need the help of culture and society—usually parents—to accomplish them. Vygotsky referred to the gap or difference between a child's current abilities and what he or she might accomplish with the help and guidance of a more skilled individual as the *zone of proximal (or potential) development*. When a more skilled individual helps a child, the child is able to incorporate new skills and ideas into his or her repertoire of behavior. In this interactive process, which Vygotsky called *scaffolding*, an adult sets up a structure for a child. For example, suppose a parent is helping his daughter learn to add columns of numbers. In summing up a column of three-digit numbers, he helps the child come to understand the procedure for carrying over digits from one column to the next. Once this concept is mastered, he may make the task slightly more difficult by making the column of numbers longer and by increasing their size to four digits. This task is marginally more difficult, and the child is challenged a bit more. Mastery is usually achieved within a few tries, and the procedure is repeated with longer columns of even larger numbers. Each attempt by the child is a scaffolded learning event, slightly harder but not out of her reach. The adult gradually provides less help or makes the task slightly more challenging so that the child engages in more complex analysis and learning (Meadows, 1998).

Zone of proximal development ■ The gap or difference between a child's current abilities and what he or she might accomplish with the help and guidance of a more skilled individual.

Vygotsky's theory requires that researchers and teachers pay attention to what children bring to interactions, what goes on during those interactions, and the cultural contexts of the individuals involved (Scrimsher & Tudge, 2003). It is important to remember that what one learns in one context does not necessarily transfer easily to another. Many children have difficulty transferring their informal knowledge of, say, language or logic to classroom situations, because they have to shift from one context to another. Children need to be capable of *decontextualized thought*—they must learn to shift from a problem in which a context is evident to more abstract thought that is devoid of a context. In practical terms, most researchers and teachers believe that it would be beneficial to be aware of a child's zone of proximal development, to use scaffolding as a teaching technique, to pay attention to context, and to use slightly more skilled peers as teachers—by doing all of this, in Vygotsky's view, children can learn more and more efficiently (Vygotsky, 1985).

Piaget investigated how and when children develop intellectual abilities; Vygotsky extended the study of children's intellectual development by considering its social context. Recently, developmental theorists have been focusing on how and when children acquire theories about causation, including the causes of human behavior.

Theory of Mind

Adults use their knowledge of the world to construct informal and formal theories to explain behavior, other people's and their own. Adults are aware of their theories of human behavior and can articulate them: They say that people do what they do because of internal mental states, such as desires and beliefs. Tomas climbed up on the kitchen counter because he "wanted" cookies; Maria looked for her glasses in the study because she "thought" she left them on her desk. Thus, adults possess and apply a *theory of mind*—a set of ideas about mental states such as feelings, desires, beliefs, and intentions and about the causal role they play in human behavior.

Theory of mind ■ A set of ideas about mental states such as feelings, desires, beliefs, and intentions and about the causal role they play in human behavior.

When do children first develop a theory of mind? Research indicates that children have little awareness of their own and other people's mental processes until about age 3 (Wellman, Phillips, & Rodriguez, 2000). A typical research study of children's theory of mind might take the form of the following situation: A child and two adults are in a room where some object such as a ball is in a box. One adult leaves the room and the other moves the object somewhere else—into a basket, for example. The child is then asked where the person who left the room will expect the object to be when he or she returns. A child who has developed a theory of mind will correctly predict that the person will look for the object where it last was (in the box), because the person will believe that it should still be there, not knowing that it was moved. A younger child, who has not yet developed a theory of mind, will say that the person coming back into the room will look for the object in its new location (in the basket). Before the age of 2 or 3, children are not able to set aside their own knowledge of the situation and realize that the person who left the room does not know that the object was moved. Developmental researchers say that these young children don't yet have a theory of mind.

The concept of theory of mind has stimulated many lines of research, including studies of infant and child attention, infant desires, and the role of brain development in cognitive maturation. But, according to some researchers, acquisition of a theory of mind is not an automatic developmental process. Astington (1999) asserts that children do not acquire such an understanding on their own; rather, through participation in social activities, they come to share their culture's view of people's relations to one another and to the world. How and when children develop a theory of mind is partly determined by their interactions with others, especially family—a key variable in the development of intelligence (Cutting & Dunn, 1999). But theory of mind develops in all cultures, although not necessarily at the same age (Tardif & Wellman, 2000). Thus, the notion that social relationships play a crucial role in cognitive development—which, as we saw earlier, was first introduced by Vygotsky—continues to influence developmental theory and research. As we'll see next, the psychologists who advised the federal government to begin Project Head Start in the 1960s agreed that an enriched social environment could help children develop cognitively (Haskins & Sawhill, 2003).

Thought in a Social Context

Does growing up in an enriched environment facilitate learning and discovery? Can tutoring children one-on-one give them a leg up? Today, programs like JUMPSTART attempt to do just that (Garnet, 1998). Such programs assume that giving a child individual help and a supportive environment makes a difference. The pioneer effort in this area was Project Head Start, which was initiated in the 1960s in an effort to break the poverty cycle by raising the social and educational competency of disadvantaged preschool children. Today, Head Start enrolls about 750,000 children a year, mostly African American (65%) and from lower socioeconomic classes (Schnur, Brooks-Gunn, & Shipman, 1992). Although Head Start has served 13 million children and is often referred to as a milestone in educational psychology (Kisker et al., 2002), it is still considered an underutilized resource (Beauchesne et al., 2004).

Project Head Start gives preschool children an enriched environment. Children attend a school with a low teacher–student ratio and are provided nutritional and medical services. They receive focused, individual attention; efforts are made to build their self-confidence and self-esteem. The emphasis is on basic skills that may lead to more complex learning strategies and on helping preschoolers experience the joy of learning. Parent involvement is central; parents work on school boards and in the classroom and also receive related social services such as family counseling.

Research on programs like Head Start has led to important conclusions about early interventions and their effects on children's lives. Children who live in a cycle of poverty and in poor neighborhoods are less likely to achieve academic success and/or social maturity (Chall & Jacobs, 2003; Evans, 2004; Leventhal & Brooks-Gunn, 2000). Head Start is an important beginning, as Ramey (1999) claims in his study on the importance of intervention programs to help improve achievement and life experiences for some children. He found that interventions need to begin early in development and continue for a long period of time, that intensive programs (more hours per week) are better than nonintensive ones, that direct intervention (rather than intervention through parental training) works best, that programs that use multiple routes to enhance development are especially effective, that individual differences must be emphasized, and so it is essential to find the right fit between children and programs, and that environmental support at home and in the community is necessary. Working together, psychologists and educators are improving the effectiveness of Head Start and other similar intervention programs for children, such as Sure Start (Caputo, 2003; Ness Research Team, 2004). Sure Start is a government program in England that aims to achieve better outcomes for children, parents, and communities by increasing the accessibility of child care, improving health, schooling, and emotional development for young children, and supporting parents in their goals for employment. Modeled after Head Start, its focus is to boost the chances of young children in poorer areas, and initial results are quite positive (Ness Research Team, 2004).

How Do Social and Emotional Development Proceed?

In the diary that survived her, Anne Frank, the young Jewish girl who was hidden for a time from the Nazis during World War II, wrote extensively about all her feelings—her hopes, her fears, and her gratitude toward the people who were making sacrifices and putting their lives at risk to help her family. For a teenage girl, Anne showed extraordinary emotional maturity. And what is even more amazing is that she attained this maturity while in hiding, where her connections with others were limited. Although emotional maturity may be attained in adolescence, the process of emotional development begins long before—shortly after birth with the attachments that infants form with caregivers.

Attachment: The Ties That Bind

Attachment The strong emotional bond or connection that a person feels toward special people in his or her life.

Socialization The process by which a person's behaviors, values, skills, plans, and attitudes conform to and are adapted to those desired by society.

Attachment is the formal term psychologists use to describe the strong emotional bond or connection that a person feels toward special people in his or her life. Such bonds are usually enduring and long-lasting; they often involve comfort, soothing, or pleasure; and the loss of the individual (or the threat of such loss) brings intense distress. Many developmental psychologists study attachment because they believe that forming attachments is among the first key steps in socialization. *Socialization* is the process by which a person's behaviors, values, skills, plans, and attitudes conform to and are adapted to those desired by society.

People's ability to form attachments develops from birth through adulthood. Strong attachments often arise during adolescence and adulthood, when people form close, loving bonds with others. Because attachment behaviors appear in all cultures (e.g., Livingston, 1998), most researchers consider these behaviors to have a biological basis, though they unfold slowly over the first year of life and are reinforced by caregivers.

Classic Work: Attachment in Rhesus Monkeys

To find out how people develop attachment behaviors, Harry Harlow (1905–1981), a psychologist at the University of Wisconsin, focused on the development of attachment in rhesus monkeys. Harlow's initial studies were on the nature of early interactions among monkeys. But he found that monkeys raised from birth in isolated bare-wire cages, away from their mothers, did not always survive, even though they were well fed. Other monkeys, raised in the same conditions but with scraps of terry cloth in their cages, survived. Terry cloth hardly seems likely to be a critical variable in the growth and development of monkeys, yet its introduction into a wire cage made the difference between life and death for Harlow's subjects. (Harlow, 1958). Harlow inferred that the terry cloth provided some measure of security or comfort. That conclusion led him to attempt to discover whether infant monkeys had an inborn desire for love or warmth.

In a classic experiment, Harlow placed infant monkeys in cages along with two wire-covered shapes resembling adult monkeys. One figure was covered with terry cloth; the other was left bare. Both could be fitted with bottles to provide milk. In some cases, the wire mother surrogate had the bottle of milk; in other cases, the terry-cloth mother surrogate had the bottle. Harlow found that the infant monkeys clung to the terry-cloth mother surrogate whether or not that surrogate provided milk. He concluded that the wire mother surrogate, even with a bottle of milk, could not provide the comfort that the terry-cloth mother surrogate could (Harlow & Zimmerman, 1958).

Another of Harlow's findings was that neither group of monkeys grew up to be totally normal. Harlow's monkeys were more aggressive and fearful than monkeys raised normally. They were also unable to engage in normal sexual relations. In addition, some of the infants raised with wire mother surrogates exhibited self-destructive behaviors (Harlow, 1962). These findings suggest that attachment to and interaction with others during infancy is critically important for normal development.

Attachment in Infants

John Bowlby (1907–1990) was one of the first modern psychologists to study the close attachment between mothers and their newborns. Bowlby (1977) argued that the infant's emotional tie with the mother (or whoever is the principal caregiver) evolved because it promotes survival. Bowlby asserted that an infant's very early interactions with parents are crucial to normal development. Some psychologists consider the establishment of a close and warm parent–child relationship to be one of the major accomplishments of the first year of life. Formation of attachment is considered a pivotal developmental event that helps an infant acquire basic feelings of security.

By the age of 7 or 8 months, attachment to the caregiver may become so strong that his or her departure from the room causes a fear response, especially to strangers; this response is known as *separation anxiety* and reflects insecurity on the part of the infant. When infants fear that the principal caregiver, usually the mother, may not be consistently available, they become clingy and vigilant (Ainsworth, 1979; Bowlby, 1988). Separation anxiety can come and go, though usually in less strong forms, throughout childhood.

In attempting to analyze attachment to parents, researchers have used a procedure called the *strange situation technique,* in which infants 12 to 24 months old are observed with parents, separated from them briefly, and then reunited; the goal is to assess attachment patterns. Although attachment theory has been criticized for being largely based on behaviors observed during stressful situations that are somewhat artificial, research with the strange situation technique shows that most babies (about 60%) are *secure;* they are distressed by a parent leaving but are easily comforted when reunited with the parent. Other babies (about 20%) are neither distressed by

Separation anxiety ■ The distress or fear response that children feel when they are separated from a primary caregiver.

Strange situation technique ■ A procedure in which infants are observed with parents, separated from them briefly, and then reunited with then reunited with them in order to assess attachment patterns.

separations nor comforted by reunions—these babies are categorized as *avoidant* and are considered to have an insecure attachment. Still other babies (about 15%) are *resistant;* these babies seek closeness with the parent, become angry when separated from the parent, and then show mixed feelings when reunited. Last, some babies (about 5%) are characterized as *disoriented;* they show confused, contradictory attachment behaviors and may act angry, sad, or ambivalent at any time. Of course, like most things, this classification system is imperfect, as a child may be neither secure nor resistant, but may fall somewhere in between. How to best classify children in terms of attachment is being studied intensively (Fraley & Spieker, 2003; Sroufe, 2003).

Researchers find that spending time with babies enables secure attachments (Bakermans-Kranenburg, van IJzendoorn, & Juffer, 2003; Scher & Mayseless, 2000) and that secure babies have caregivers who are affectionate and highly responsive (McCartney et al., 2004). According to some researchers, having such a caregiver makes cognitive and emotional development smoother (Call, 1999). Not all researchers agree, and cross-cultural studies show significant variations in attachment among cultures. For example, in some cultures, children may attach to more than one person, and each can have a different effect later in the child's life (e.g., Suizzo, 2002; Tronick, Morelli, & Ivey, 1992).

Children who have not formed warm, close attachments early in life lack a sense of security and become anxious and overly dependent. Those who have close attachments require less discipline and are less easily distracted (Foote, Eyberg, & Schuhmann, 1998).

Once established, early attachment is fairly stable. Babies are resilient, and brief separations from parents, as in child-care centers, do not adversely affect attachment (Waters, Hamilton, & Weinfield, 2000). Influential psychologist Mary Ainsworth (1979) asserts that early attachment patterns affect a child's later friendships, relations with relatives, and enduring adult relationships; other research confirms that people's relationships as adults are related to the attachment styles they had as children (Brennan, Clark, & Shaver, 1998).

There is little doubt that attachment is important, but does it determine who we become? Human beings have an amazing ability to adapt, survive, and negotiate the future. Michael Lewis (1998) cautions that researchers often overestimate the long-term effects of attachment, and that separation anxiety at age 1 has little to do with adjustment at age 18, let alone at age 35. Lewis studied a group of individuals at age 1 and again at age 18, looking at participants' attachment to family and friends; he found that secure attachment did not protect children from later maladjustment, nor did insecure attachment predict later trouble. Thus, early attachment probably doesn't *determine* adjustment as an adult, because too many life events, chance circumstances, and good and bad decisions can also affect the life course. Yet a good secure attachment as a child is certainly a plus. When researchers examined relationships between older children and mothers, they found a positive correlation between good interactions and ratings of attachment by the caregivers (McCartney et al., 2004).

Regardless of children's early attachment status, research shows that divorce affects their social development (Lewis, Feiring, & Rosenthal, 2000). The truth is that when there is conflict between parents, child adjustment suffers (Grych et al., 2000).

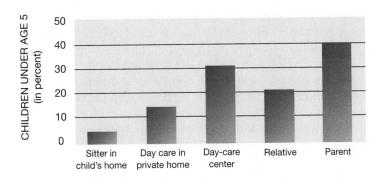

Figure 4.9
Arrangements for Child Care in the United States
This figure shows the types of child-care arrangements used in the United States in 1995 for children under age 5 who were not in school. (Scarr, 1998)

Although there is significant variation, and some children are more vulnerable than others, divorce and separation usually have negative effects on feelings of attachment. As adults, children of divorced parents trust less and have diminished expectations about relationships as well as shorter marriages (Quinlan, 2003; Wallerstein, Lewis, & Blakeslee, 2000).

Attachment and Child Care

When single parents or both parents in a family work outside of the home, they must rely on nonparental child care, including after-school programs, family, friends, and day care. In the United States, day-care centers currently provide care for about 30% of preschool children whose parents are employed outside the home (Harrison & Ungerer, 2002) (see **Figure 4.9**).

Psychologists are studying the differences in development of children who are cared for at home by a parent and those who receive some form of nonparental caregiving (Brooks-Gunn, Han, & Waldfogel, 2002). Many variables influence the success of day care, including the child's age, the security of the child's attachment to parents, and the stability (and quality) of the child-care arrangement (Love et al., 2003). The majority of studies have found that children who participate in day care experience minimal negative effects (Fuller et al., 2002; Harrison & Ungerer, 2002). In fact, Broberg and his colleagues (1997) assert that being in day care does not place children at any disadvantage. Other research found virtually no difference in personality or attachment between children cared for at home and children who had received day care (Erel, Oberman, & Yirmiya, 2000). Many believe that any negative effects of time in child care are overestimated (Booth et al., 2002).

A comprehensive, multiyear study by Harvey (1999) assessed the cognitive, academic, behavioral, and emotional development of more than 6,000 children whose parents were both employed outside the home. The study tracked 12,600 mothers and their children, interviewing them each year starting in 1979, and it concluded that there were no permanent negative effects on those children who were cared for by people other than their parents. The large sample size and the longitudinal nature of the study make its results an important piece of evidence that parental employment and child-care arrangements do not have significant negative effects—if the care is of high quality. Some research shows that children from both rich and poor backgrounds can do as well in high-quality day care as in home care (Loeb et al., 2004). And Sandra Scarr (Phillips et al., 2000; Scarr, 1998, p. 95) concludes: "Widely varying qualities of child care have been shown to have only small effects on children's current development and no demonstrated long-term impact, except on disadvantaged children, whose homes put them at developmental risk." Of course, like most complex issues, this one is not straightforward; for example, Newcombe (2003) argues that the use of child care is closely linked with maternal employment, which increases family income and decreases maternal depression, which in turn are linked to children's socioemotional adjustment. Whether a child is at home with a parent or in day care, early childhood interactions, especially positive ones, are important—and this appears to be true cross culturally (Loeb et al., 2004; NICHD Early Child Care Research Network, 2003; Posada et al., 2002).

Nearly this entire discussion has focused on the impact of environment on development, but evolutionary psychologists suggest that environment is not the whole story.

Evolutionary Perspective and Attachment

In a very real sense, one of the seminal figures in attachment theory, John Bowlby, was an evolutionary psychologist. Evolutionary psychologists assert that attachment is an evolved adaptation that facilitates a reproductive strategy. Bowlby argued that the infant's attachment to the caregiver evolves because it promotes survival. Children who have strong attachments to their parents are more likely to grow up to be confident adults, to form attachments to other people, to reproduce, and to pass on their genes to another generation. But, of course, as with so many human characteristics, the environment certainly has an effect on attachment. Poverty, malnutrition, war, famine, and disease can all influence childhood attachment. Environmental conditions and biological factors also affect a child's temperament, which has often been closely linked to attachment.

Temperament

My (L.L.'s) daughter Jesse was born an inspector—she touched and tasted everything within reach, climbed out of her crib, and dangerously explored her world. As soon as she could navigate, she examined everything and everyone, including her sister! She and her sister got along well; both had and still have fairly easygoing dispositions and have never had any major quarrels. They read each other's moods well. But conflicts between siblings are common, and on occasion quite pronounced. The truth is that because of differences in temperament, siblings often don't get along, and some parents can't or don't know how to smooth things over (Brody, 1998). One of the surprising conclusions from years of behavioral genetics research is that being reared together in the same home by the same parents does not tend to make children more alike psychologically—evidence of a strong genetic component in temperament (Lykken et al., 1993).

Temperament is the early-emerging and long-lasting pattern in an individual's disposition and in the intensity and especially the quality of his or her emotional reactions. Some psychologists believe that each person is born with a specific

Temperament ■ Early-emerging and long-lasting pattern in an individual's disposition and in the intensity and especially the quality of his or her emotional reactions.

temperament—easygoing, willful, outgoing, or shy, for example. Newborns, infants, and children, like the adults they will eventually become, are all different. Generalizations from one child to all children are impossible, and even generalizations from a sample of children must be made with caution. So many variables can affect a child's growth and development that researchers must painstakingly try to separate out the important ones.

Alexander Thomas and Stella Chess (1977; Chess & Thomas, 1996), in their pioneering work in the New York Longitudinal Study, which began in 1956 and continues today, point out that temperament is not fixed and unchangeable. The findings from this systematic investigation into the concept of temperament (including temperamental profiles of infants, children, adolescents, and adults) show specific individual behavioral character traits. Children tend to fall into four broad categories:

- Easy children are happy-go-lucky and adapt easily to new situations (40% of children).
- Difficult children are resistant to environmental change and often react poorly to it (10% of children).
- Slow-to-warm-up children respond slowly, have low-intensity responses, and are often negative (15% of children).
- Many children are unique, showing a varied blend of emotional reactions (35% of children).

Nevertheless, along with many other researchers, Thomas and Chess argue that temperament is a complex set of processes—not a single thing—and it refers to the way in which behavior is expressed, independent of the content of behavior or the motivation for behavior. Temperament is biologically based, moderately stable across time and over situations, but not necessarily invariant across time or situations. Further, the expression of temperament can be influenced by biological, developmental, and contextual factors.

Many researchers contend that some specific temperamental characteristics may be biologically based. For example, Jerome Kagan and his colleagues found that 2- and 3-year-olds who were *extremely* inhibited—that is, cautious and shy—tended to remain that way for 4 more years. They also found physiological evidence that these children may be especially responsive (showing an increase in autonomic nervous system activity, for example) to change and unfamiliarity (Woodward et al., 2000). During the earliest months of life, some infants smile or reach out to a new face and readily accept being held or cuddled. Others are more inhibited. Still others exhibit extreme reticence, even distress, in the presence of strangers. Such xenophobic infants (those who fear strangers) may turn out to be inhibited, meek, and wavering as adults (Caspi & Roberts, 2001). Researchers know, however, that infant behaviors are not necessarily stable over time and may not be evident in later behavioral styles (except for very extreme cases—intense shyness or diffidence, for example). Further, what parents observe (social wariness with unfamiliar people) is different from the shyness that teachers observe (concern about social evaluation by peers); thus, shyness—social inhibition with accompanying anxiety—varies in different situations (Eisenberg et al., 1998).

Biological factors play a key role in shyness (McEwen, 1999). Studies of identical twins on a range of emotional dimensions, especially temperament, support a strong genetic component for shyness (DiLalla & Jones, 2000; Stroganova et al., 2000). Maternal actions, such as time spent in daylight during pregnancy, may also have an effect on shyness. Gortmaker and colleagues (1997) found that short exposure to daylight during pregnancy was associated with a higher likelihood of shy behavior in off-spring. Further evidence for a biological predisposition comes from studies of basic physiological responsivity—infants' heart rates in response to a distracting stimulus are known to predict temperament (Huffman et al., 1998). However, shyness is also influenced by culture. In one cross-cultural study, researchers found that shyness in native Chinese students helps them gain acceptance from teachers; the opposite tends to be true for students in Western countries (Chen, 2000).

In addition, there is a relationship between temperament and parenting. Imagine a child who is shy or diffident and not easy to coax into social situations. Researchers today suggest that such a disposition will affect parent–child interactions and parental discipline practices, and, ultimately, the child's socialization. The fit between the temperament of an infant and that of the caregiver is critical. Some caregivers can do well with a calm infant but are overwhelmed by an irritable one. Sometimes an interaction style that a caregiver developed with one child may not be suitable with another child. The shared irritation can impair good socialization. Yet, as Greenspan (2003) argues, the qualities we value more than any others—empathy, creativity, honor, the ability to love and trust—stem from relationships, not genes; thus, how caregivers relate to their children over time will affect such qualities. Indeed, researchers assert that a child's conscience emerges because of interactions with caregivers and the growth of self-understanding (Stilwell, Galvin, & Kopta, 2000).

Clearly, a child's temperament affects his or her interactions with parents in important ways and may determine in part how the parents treat the child—there is a reciprocal and mutually reinforcing influence. Parents know whether their children are easy or difficult compared to others. Parents are aware that they affect their child's temperament and personality (Hesse & Main, 2000). Parents assume that their child-rearing practices strongly influence development and recognize that a child who might be categorized as "difficult" may, if treated with patience, become "easy" as an adolescent. But researchers also know that children with aggressive or difficult temperaments are more likely to use and abuse drugs in their teenage and adult years (Chassin et al., 2001). The choice to use drugs may also be affected by a person's ability to make moral decisions.

Moral Reasoning

Few children make it to adolescence without squabbling with a sibling or a friend over the "borrowing" of a sweater, a toy, or a couple of dollars. The adult in charge usually tells them to stop fighting and makes it clear that the behavior that gave rise to the squabble is unacceptable. As children grow, they develop the capacity to assess for themselves what is right or wrong, acceptable or unacceptable. From childhood on, individuals develop *morality*—a system of learned attitudes about social practices, institutions, and individual behavior used to evaluate situations and behavior as right or wrong, good or bad.

Children learn from their parents the behaviors, attitudes, and values considered appropriate and correct in their family and culture. Morality is also nurtured by teachers, by religious and community leaders, and by friends. But it is especially nurtured by daily interactions with caregivers in dialogues and interactions of all kinds (Laible & Thompson, 2000; Walker, Hennig, & Krettenauer, 2000). As children mature, they acquire attitudes that accommodate an increasingly complex view of reality. Your moral views when you were a 10-year-old probably differ from those you hold today. The U.S. Supreme Court has restricted adolescents' rights to make important life decisions such as whether to undergo life-threatening surgery to alleviate some medical condition—in part because the court believes adolescents lack moral maturity. But do they? Or are the reasoning and judgment of a preteen or an adolescent as sound as an adult's? Researchers are showing that children and teenagers can and should be involved in making good decisions about their own health care (Ranelli, Bartsch & London, 2000).

> **Morality** ■ A system of learned attitudes about social practices, institutions, and individual behavior used to evaluate situations and behavior as right or wrong, good or bad.

Piaget and Kohlberg

Piaget examined children's ability to analyze moral issues and found the results to be consistent with his ideas about cognitive development. Young children's ideas about morality are rigid and rule-bound; children expect justice to depend on particular actions. When playing a game, a young child will not allow the rules to be modified. Older children, on the other hand, recognize that rules are established by social convention and may need to be altered, depending on the situation. They have developed a sense of *moral relativity*, which allows them to recognize that situational factors affect the way things are perceived and that people may or may not receive their just reward or punishment (Piaget, 1932).

According to Piaget, as children mature, they move away from inflexibility and toward relativity in their moral judgments. They begin to develop new cognitive structures and assimilate and accommodate new ideas. When young children are questioned about lying, for example, they respond that it is always bad, under any circumstances—a person should never lie. At some time between the ages of 5 and 12, however, children come to recognize that lying may be permissible in some circumstances—for example, lying to a bully so that he will not hurt a friend.

Piaget's theory of moral development was based on descriptions of how children respond to specific kinds of questions and the ages at which they switch to other forms of answers. The research of Harvard psychologist Lawrence Kohlberg (1927–1987) grew out of Piaget's work. Kohlberg believed that moral development generally proceeds through three levels, each of which is divided into two stages. The central concept in Kohlberg's theory is that of justice. In his studies of moral reasoning, Kohlberg presented stories involving moral dilemmas to people of various ages and asked them to describe what the stories meant to them and how they felt about them (Kohlberg, 1969). **Table 4.3** shows the correspondence between Piaget's developmental stages and Kohlberg's levels of moral development.

Table 4.3

PIAGET'S DEVELOPMENTAL STAGES AND KOHLBERG'S STAGES OF MORAL DEVELOPMENT

Piaget: Developmental Stages	Kohlberg: Moral Development Stages
Sensorimotor and preoperational (birth–6 or 7 years)	Level 1—*Preconventional morality* Stage 1: Obedience and punishment orientation Stage 2: Egocentric orientation
Concrete operational (7–11 or 12 years)	Level 2—*Conventional morality* Stage 3: Good-child orientation Stage 4: Authority and social order
Formal operational (12 years and beyond)	Level 3—*Postconventional morality* Stage 5: Contractual-legalistic orientation; societal needs considered Stage 6: Conscience or principle orientation

In one of Kohlberg's stories, Heinz, a poor man, stole a drug for his wife, who would have died without it. Presented with the story of Heinz, children at Kohlberg's level 1, *preconventional morality*, either condemn Heinz's behavior as unacceptable or they come up with some reason why it is acceptable. They base their decisions about right and wrong on the likelihood of avoiding punishment and obtaining benefits. A child in this stage might say that Heinz should not have taken the drug because he might get caught. Individuals at level 2, *conventional morality*, have internalized society's rules and say that Heinz broke the law by stealing and should go to jail. School-aged children who are at level 2 conform in order to avoid the disapproval of other people. At this stage, a 10-year-old might choose not to try cigarettes because his parents and friends disapprove of smoking. Considerations of the implications of a person's behavior also govern level 2 judgments: Why did the person act a particular way? What will the consequences be for that person and for others? Does the act violate important laws and rules? Only people who have reached level 3, *postconventional morality*, can see that although Heinz's action was illegal, the ethical dilemma is complex (see **Figure 4.10**). As individuals move toward level 3, they become better able to look beyond fixed rules and laws and focus on principles. At level 3, people make moral judgments on the basis of their perception of the needs of society, with the goal of fulfilling social contracts and maintaining community welfare and order.

Not all adults reach level 3. In the advanced stage of level 3, people make judgments on the basis of personally created moral principles rather than societal teachings. People at this stage may express moral objections to legally sanctioned behaviors—for example, a person can believe that it is morally wrong to kill for any reason, even to execute a person convicted of a capital crime. Research shows that such reasoning may incorporate a sense of virtue and religiosity (Walker & Pitts, 1998). But research also shows some differences in moral reasoning between men and women—our next topic.

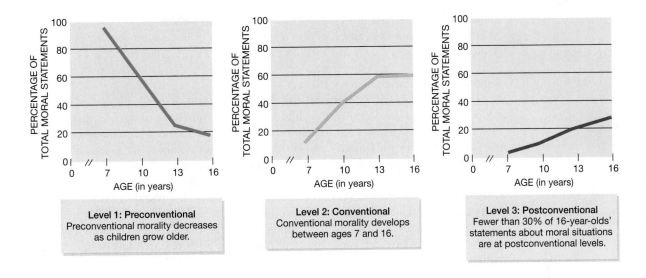

Figure 4.10

Development of Morality over Time

In Kohlberg's theory of morality, a distinct progression of moral development emerges over a child's life. Children do not often achieve the highest, or postconventional, levels of moral reasoning.

Men and Women: Carol Gilligan's Work

Criticisms of Kohlberg's pioneering research came from Carol Gilligan (1982, 1995), who believed it was a serious flaw that Kohlberg based his theory solely on research with boys and men. When Gilligan studied women, she found gender differences in moral reasoning.

Differences between men and women on behaviors or mental processes are referred to as *gender differences*. Psychologists used to refer to such differences as sex differences, but now make a distinction between the terms *sex* and *gender*. *Sex* refers to the biologically based categories of male and female. *Gender*, by contrast, refers to a socially and culturally constructed set of distinctions between masculine and feminine behaviors that are promoted and expected by society. Although there is a complicated relationship between sex and gender, because biologically based characteristics are affected by cultural factors (Lobel et al., 2001), the distinction is widely used (Fausto-Sterling, 2000).

Gilligan noted differences between girls and boys in their inclinations toward caring and justice. She found that girls are more concerned with caring, relationships, and connections with other people—she hypothesized a feminine orientation to moral issues. According to Gilligan, as younger children, girls gravitate toward a morality of caring, whereas boys gravitate toward a morality of justice. Gilligan asserts that the difference between boys' and girls' approaches to morality is established by gender and by the child's relationship with the mother. Because of the gender difference between boys and their mothers, boys feel essentially different from other people, whereas girls develop a belief in their similarity (connectedness) to others. Gilligan asserts that the

Sex ■ The biologically based category of male or female.

Gender ■ A socially and culturally constructed set of distinctions between masculine and feminine behaviors that are promoted and expected by society.

transition to adolescence is a crucial time, during which girls develop their own voice—"a voice too often muted and suppressed" (Gilligan, 1997). Gilligan showed that boys respond to Kohlberg's story of Heinz by indicating that sometimes people must act on their own to do the right thing; girls tend to say that Heinz's relationship with his wife is more important than obeying the law.

Like Kohlberg, Gilligan argues that the development of a morality of caring takes place over time: Initially, the child feels caring only toward herself, then later toward others as well, and ultimately (in some people) a more mature stage of caring for truth develops. Gilligan's work has influenced psychologists' evaluations of morality. Yet her approach fosters a continuation of gender stereotyping—women as nurturing, men as logical—and despite widespread acceptance of her view that Kohlberg's work is biased against women, surprisingly little research evidence supports that view (Cook, Larson, & Boivin, 2003; Fisher & Bredemeier, 2000). Moreover, Gilligan's work has been limited to White, middle-class children and adults; it needs a broader, more multicultural basis. Such research has been initiated with a wide range of populations, including Hispanic men and women (Gump, Baker, & Roll, 2000).

Nevertheless, Gilligan's work highlights an important element of moral reasoning: People think about other people in a caring, human way, not just from a legalistic point of view, as Kohlberg suggested. Both men and women can and do emphasize caring when they face dilemmas involving relationships; similarly, both are likely to focus on justice when confronting issues involving others' rights. Women and men are more alike than they are different when it comes to caring and justice, and the type of moral reasoning a man or woman uses is highly dependent on the context and content of the dilemma the individual faces. If theories of human development are to reflect real experiences, then they must be assembled with the complexity and multiplicity of such experiences in mind (Jaffee & Hyde, 2000).

What Environmental Factors Are Important for Social Development?

Any bookstore has shelves lined with how-to books on child rearing, written by physicians, parents, psychologists, and others. The variety of approaches and the number of experts show that ideas about child rearing are complicated and constantly changing. As society changes, so do beliefs and practices related to children's social development and ideas about how children form a sense of identity and self. As children move cognitively from being egocentric to perceiving themselves as different from the rest of the world, they also develop the ability to think about social relationships. As we will see, children develop socially in not one but many environments.

Early Social Development and Child Rearing

The family is the first social environment. Regardless of culture, parents respond positively to what they judge as good behaviors in children and negatively to bad ones. Although cultural differences exist (for example, French parents' extensive scheduling of daytime childhood behaviors contrasts with Swedish parents' noninterference), parents worldwide respond to their children in similar ways (McDermott, 2001). Although parents exert a powerful influence on children and a positive early relationship between parents and children is very important (Belsky et al., 2001), other influences play a role. Some researchers, such as Harris (1998), assert that a child has many environments, especially his or her play groups, which exert profound effects on social development.

Social development begins soon after birth, with the development of attachment between parents and their newborn. The nature of a child's early interactions with parents is a crucial part of personality development. Infants have a great need to be hugged, cuddled, nurtured, and made to feel good. Nurturing affects children's ideas and attitudes about everything from friends to food choices, political attitudes, and ideas about race and ethnicity (O'Connor, Brooks-Gunn, & Graber, 2000). Volumes of research show that even watching movies and television affects a child's (and later the adult's) behavior (Bushman & Anderson, 2001; Bushman & Cantor, 2003). Ultimately, the most important job for parents is teaching their children how to become independent and how to interact with others.

The Role of Fathers

I (L. L.) think of myself as a good dad. I often took charge of child care, changed diapers, and attended to my daughters' needs. But I probably didn't spend as much time with them as my wife did, and I may not have been as communicative as she was. Typical patterns of how mothers and fathers interact with their children are indeed changing. During the past three decades, more families have two employed parents, and this has resulted in some challenges to the traditional structure of family life. Both parents are struggling to balance work and family, but is one parent or the other carrying more of the child-care responsibilities than the other?

In 1991, the National Institute of Child Health and Human Development (NICHD) established a Study of Early Child Care and recruited more than 1,300 families and their newborn children at ten locales throughout the country for a longitudinal study to determine the relationship between children's early experiences and their developmental outcomes. Research from this study shows that receiving affection from both parents is important to a child (Jayakody & Kalil, 2002; NICHD Early Child Care Research Network, 2000).

Today, more fathers are present in the delivery room when their children are born than was true in previous generations. In general, fathers are affectionate and responsive caregivers; they are concerned with their children's welfare (Fagan, 2001). Still, some men view parenting as a voluntary activity and themselves as helpers or assistants to their partners, whom they consider the primary caregivers. Fathers sometimes assert that although they spend limited time with their children, the time is "quality" time. Research shows that in two-parent families, child care is affected by shifting caregiving roles and responsibilities over the course of years. For example fathers increase their engagement with infants between 6 and 15 months (Wood & Repetti, 2004).

Research on the quality and quantity of interactions between fathers and their children showed that some fathers spend significant time with their children, and the amount depends on a whole array of variables including patterns of family members' interaction and their emotional styles, parents' jobs, and the hours that parents work (Quinlan, 2003; Wood & Repetti, 2004). Some fathers spend quality time (time devoted to active involvement with a child, as opposed to merely being present in the room with the child); others do not. Play turns out to be a prominent feature of the time men spend with their infants. Some studies have found that men are twice as likely to be involved in play as in basic caregiving activities (Tulananda & Roopnarine, 2001).

The quality of the time a father spends with his children is affected by the mother's attitudes and her work hours (NICHD Early Child Care Research Network, 2000). For example, if mothers are highly supportive of a father's involvement, father involvement may be high or low, depending on the father, his work schedule, as well as his spouse's work schedule, and his predispositions. But if a mother opposes or does not support father involvement (some mothers actually discourage father involvement in some activities), the father will not be involved, regardless of his predisposition.

Ethnicity is also a factor in fathering. African American families have their own unique ways of dealing with child care, as do Latino/Latina, Asian American, and European American families, and more cross-cultural research is needed to understand these patterns. For example, fathers' perceptions of their abilities, their gender role, and the family's requirements may combine to influence their involvement in child care (Sanderson & Thompson, 2002). So, a father from a family in which three generations have college educations may take special pride in his status as a role model. By contrast, a father recently released from a drug rehabilitation facility or one who is estranged from his family for any of a variety of reasons may desire to be a role model and participate, but may live in another state. Other factors, such as work schedules, also enter the picture—a resident father's involvement has as much to do with each parent's work schedule as anything else (Averett, Gennetian, & Peters, 2000; Jayakody & Kalil, 2002).

The First Two Years

Parenting is especially important in the first two years of life when social interactions among children are limited. In the first year of life, infants are largely egocentric and are basically unable to recognize any needs other than their own. As previously discussed, by about 6 months, infants exhibit strong attachments to parents and other caregivers, along with fear of strangers. As early as 9 months, children show that they like to play games by indicating their unhappiness when an adult stops playing with them (Ross & Lollis, 1987). They play by themselves; then, as they grow older, especially after 2 years of age, they engage in more social play with other children (Maccoby, 2002).

By age 2, children have begun to understand that they are separate from their parents—they are developing a sense of self. They begin to learn to interact with other people. They may play alongside other children, but they prefer to play with an adult rather than with another 2-year-old. Gradually, however, they begin to socialize with their peers (Scott, Mandryk, & Inkpen, 2003).

Sharing

The noted pediatrician Benjamin Spock once said that the only things children will share willingly are communicable diseases and their mother's age. Actually, from age 2 until they begin school, children vacillate between quiet conformity and happy sharing, on the one hand, and stubborn negative demands and egocentric behavior, on the other. Because sharing is a socially desirable behavior, learning to share becomes a top priority when children enter a day-care center, nursery school, or kindergarten (Lee, 2001; Rayna, 2001).

Although very young children know that people experience mental states (they can tell when Dad or Mom is in a bad mood, for example) (Wellman, Phillips, & Rodriguez, 2000), they do not understand the concept of sharing—particularly the idea that if you share with another child, the other child is more likely to share with you. In a laboratory study of sharing (Levitt et al., 1985), researchers observed pairs of children separated by a gate. Initially, one child was given toys and the other wasn't; then the situation was reversed. The researchers found that none of the children shared spontaneously; however, 65% shared a toy when their mothers asked them to. Moreover, a child who was deprived of a toy after having shared one often approached the child who now had the toy. One child even said, "I gave you a toy. Why don't you give me one?"

Children do not initiate sharing at a young age; but once they share, they seem to exhibit knowledge about reciprocal arrangements. Of course, sharing is more likely among children who are friends because they have more frequent social interaction and make more attempts at conflict resolution (Newcomb, Bukowski, & Bagwell, 1999). Sharing is also more likely after entry into kindergarten, which helps lead to a breakdown of egocentrism. It is also affected by culture. Research by Mosier and Rogoff (2003) observed U.S. middle-class mothers and Guatemalan Mayan mothers, their 14- to 20-month-old toddlers, and the toddlers' 3- to 5-year-old siblings while the siblings and toddlers both sought access to attractive objects. The U.S. children seemed to engage in fair competition for resources (reflecting individual rights and freedom) and skillful negotiation to take turns and share. By contrast, sharing by the Mayan children seemed based on a cultural model that children's voluntary cooperation is fostered when their freedom of choice is respected.

Gender Roles

Earlier we drew a distinction between sex and gender—between biological traits that affect reproduction (sex) and behavioral and mental processes that are constructed and reinforced by society (gender). Everyone acknowledges that women and men are different—but both women *and* men are powerful, resourceful, sensitive, intuitive, and analytical. Yet they exhibit those abilities in different circumstances. To an important extent, the study of gender differences is an investigation of when, how, and under what circumstances people reveal those abilities.

When people conform to a gender role, they are conforming to society's expectations for men and women. Psychologists define a ***gender role*** as a set of expectations in a given society about behaviors and responsibilities that are appropriate for

Gender role ■ A set of expectations in a given society about behaviors and responsibilities that are appropriate for males or females.

males or females—expectations about the ways in which men or women are supposed to behave based on their sex. Historically, many Western parents tended to encourage "masculine" traits such as athletic prowess in their sons and "feminine" traits such as popularity in their daughters. Parents accepted, promoted, and vigorously reinforced gender-based social environments. Today, many parents try to de-emphasize gender-based interests in their children, seeking to reduce or eliminate society's tendency to stereotype people on the basis of sex (Sleeter & Grant, 2002).

Researchers must place gender differences within meaningful contexts in order to analyze them (Maccoby, 2002). This means looking at how parents treat children as a function of their biological sex, how schools and religious institutions establish and reinforce gender-specific behaviors, and how society views the influence of gender in the daily life of children and young adults (Hannover, 2000; Rowe, 2001; Tiedemann, 2000). Also, children are active learners, even when it comes to gendered behaviors.

Because of modern medical technology, parents who want to can find out the sex of their child during prenatal development, which allows them to begin treating the child on the basis of gender roles before the child is born. Thus, from the beginning, girls and boys have different life experiences. As Collins (Collins et al., 2000) suggests, parental influences on child development are neither unambiguous nor insubstantial. They have a strong impact from the beginning (Martin & Ruble, 2004). For example, relatively few American adults have gender-neutral names such as Pat, Terry, Chris, or Lee (Pine & Nash, 2003). Moms and dads agonized over picking just the right gender-appropriate name. However, in the last decade, more parents are choosing gender-neutral names than ever before—names like Madison, Miller, Jesse, and Taylor, for example.

Some psychologists assert that the way parents talk to and treat boys and girls creates special emotional and learning problems (Tiedemann, 2000). For example, some (Dickhaeuser & Stiensmeier-Pelster, 2003; Pollack, 1998) argue that parents have such strong expectations about how boys should behave—they should be independent, strong, tough, computer-literate—that the pressure of these expectations puts boys at risk for various psychological problems. Many parents put similar, but different, pressure on girls—to be independent and strong, yet feminine. Children today are sometimes sent mixed messages, and they certainly have high expectations placed on them, far more than in the past, when children were expected to be "seen but not heard" (Maccoby, 1998). The effects of gender roles are important; for example, boys, who have flexible views about gender roles and relationships, tend to have fewer relationship problems as adults (Blazina & Watkins, 2000).

Erik Erikson and the Beginning of the Search for Self

Emotional growth and the discovery of who one is are lifelong processes. Adults are generally aware that their identities and roles in family and in society can be greatly affected by outside influences. This process of becoming aware of one's identity and roles begins when a person is a young child.

Developing an awareness of the self as different from others is an important step in social development in early childhood. Self-perception begins when the child recognizes that he or she is separate from other people, particularly the mother. The self becomes more differentiated as a child develops an appreciation of his or her inner mental world. Ideally, as children develop a concept of themselves, they develop self-esteem and significant attachments to others. Such cognitive, and then social, changes do not take place in isolation. They are influenced by the nature of a child's early attachments, by the cultural world surrounding the child, by the family's and society's child-rearing practices, and by how the child is taught to think about the causes of events in the world (Teichman, 2001; Waters, Hamilton, & Weinfield, 2000). The construction of an identity—a self—occurs slowly and gradually and is affected by many variables.

Perhaps no one studied the challenges of social development and self-understanding more closely than the psychoanalyst Erik H. Erikson (1902–1994). With sharp insight, a linguistic flair, and a logical, coherent approach to analyzing human behavior, Erikson, who studied with Freud in Austria, developed a theory of *psychosocial stages of development*. Each of his stages contributes to the development of a unique self, a person with a particular role, attitudes, and skills as a member of society. According to Erikson, a series of basic psychological conflicts determines the course of development. His theory is noted for its integration of individual disposition and the environment in the shaping of the self. Erikson's theory describes a continuum of stages, each involving a dilemma, through which all individuals must pass. Each stage can have either a positive or a negative outcome. New dilemmas emerge as a person grows older and faces new responsibilities, tasks, and social relationships. A person may experience a dilemma as an opportunity and face it positively or may view the dilemma as a catastrophe and fail to cope with it effectively.

Table 4.4 lists the first four psychosocial stages in Erikson's theory, with their age ranges and the important events associated with each (Erikson, 1964, 1975, 1984). These four stages cover birth through age 13. We will look at Erikson's later stages, covering adolescence and adulthood, in Chapter 5.

Stage 1 (birth to 12–18 months) involves the dilemma of *basic trust versus basic mistrust*. During their first months, according to Erikson, infants make distinctions about the world and decide whether it is a comfortable, loving place in which they can feel basic trust. At this stage, they develop beliefs about people's essential trustworthiness. If their needs are adequately met by caregivers, they learn that the world is a predictable and safe place. Infants whose needs are not met learn to distrust people and the world in general.

During stage 2 (18 months to 3 years), toddlers must resolve the dilemma of *autonomy versus shame and doubt*. Success in toilet training and other tasks involving control leads to a sense of autonomy and more mature behavior. Difficulties in gaining some control in their lives during this stage result in fears and a sense of shame and doubt.

Stage 3 of Erikson's theory (3 to 6 years) involves the dilemma of *initiative versus guilt;* in this stage, children begin to exercise their own inventiveness, drive, and enthusiasm. They either gain a sense of independence and begin to feel good about themselves or develop a sense of guilt, lack of acceptance, and negative feelings about themselves. If children learn to dress themselves, clean their rooms and accomplish other similar tasks, and develop friendships with other children, they can feel a sense of mastery; otherwise, they may be dependent or regretful.

Table 4.4

ERIKSON'S FIRST FOUR STAGES OF PSYCHOSOCIAL DEVELOPMENT

Stage	Approximate Age	Important Event	Description
■ **1.** Basic Trust versus Basic Mistrust	Birth to 12–18 months	Feeding	The infant must form a loving, trusting relationship with the caregiver or develop a sense of mistrust.
■ **2.** Autonomy versus Shame and Doubt	18 months to 3 years	Toilet training	The child's energies are directed toward the development of physical skills, including walking and controlling the sphincter. The child learns control but may develop shame and doubt if his or her efforts to be in control are not successful or are not handled well.
■ **3.** Initiative versus Guilt	3 to 6 years	Gaining independence	The child continues to become more assertive and to take more initiative but may be chastised for being too forceful, which can lead to guilt feelings.
■ **4.** Industry versus Inferiority	6 to 12 years	Beginning school	The child must deal with learning many new skills or risk a sense of inferiority, failure, and incompetence.

During stage 4 (6 to 12 years), children must resolve the dilemma of *industry versus inferiority*. They either develop feelings of competence and confidence in their abilities or experience inferiority, failure, and feelings of incompetence.

Erikson's theory asserts that children must go through each stage, resolving its dilemma as best they can (Erikson, 1964, 1975, 1984). Many factors have a bearing on the successful navigation of these stages. Of course, children grow older whether they are ready for the next stage or not. A person may have unresolved conflicts and dilemmas at any age. These can cause anxiety and discomfort and make it more difficult to advance to other stages. Because adolescence is such a crucial stage for the formation of a firm identity, the environment surrounding an adolescent becomes especially important. We will turn to this topic in the next chapter.

Summary and Review

WHAT ARE THE CENTRAL ISSUES OF DEVELOPMENT?

What is developmental psychology?

Developmental psychology is the study of the lifelong, often age-related processes of change in the physical, cognitive, emotional, moral, and social domains of functioning. These changes are rooted in genetically controlled biological mechanisms as well as in social interactions. p. 99

What are the key issues in developmental psychology and the main methods of studying development?

A key issue in developmental psychology involves the extent to which a person's abilities, interests, and personality are determined by biological or genetic influences (nature) or by environmental influences (nurture). The issue of stability versus change is closely associated with that of nature versus nurture. Many researchers assume that stable traits are inherited and genetically determined, whereas others believe that people change with life's events, that environmental influences are important. Children can also be seen as active or passive in their approach to life. Last, some view development as a continuous process of gradual growth and change, but others see it as discontinuous, with maturation and understanding of the world advancing during various key periods and with changes appearing abruptly. The influence of culture on individual development is also important. pp. 99–101

With a *cross-sectional research design*, researchers compare individuals of different ages to determine if and how they differ on some important dimension. With a *longitudinal research design*, researchers study a group of individuals over a period of time to examine changes that have occurred. pp. 101–103

HOW DOES PHYSICAL DEVELOPMENT PROCEED?

Describe key steps and features of prenatal development.

Conception occurs when an ovum and a sperm join in a woman's fallopian tube to form a *zygote*—a fertilized egg. The *placenta* is a mass of tissue that is attached to the wall of the uterus and acts as the life-support system for the fetus. From about the 5th through the 49th day after conception, the prenatal organism is called an *embryo;* from that point until birth, it is called a *fetus.* pp. 103–104

During a *critical period* of development, an organism is especially sensitive to environmental influences. In the first months of development, an embryo is especially sensitive to teratogens. A *teratogen* is a substance that can produce developmental malformations; alcohol, which can cause *fetal alcohol syndrome*, and other drugs are teratogens. p. 106

How is a newborn equipped to deal with the world?

A newborn comes prepared with a set of primary reflexes, among them the *Babinski reflex*, the *Moro reflex*, the *rooting reflex*, the *sucking reflex*, and the *grasping reflex*. Newborns also have surprisingly well-developed perceptual systems. pp. 106–109

HOW DOES THOUGHT DEVELOP?

What is the difference between Piaget's concepts of assimilation and accommodation?

Piaget's theory focuses on *how* people think, instead of on *what* they think. His theory includes the concept of a *schema*, a mental structure that helps a child make sense of experience. Piaget identified the process of adaption, which enables the individual to gain new knowledge through either assimilation or accommodation. *Assimilation* is the process of incorporating new information into existing understanding. *Accommodation* is the process of modifying one's existing thought processes and framework of knowledge in response to new information. pp. 111–113

Describe Piaget's stages of cognitive development.

Piaget believed that cognitive development occurs in four stages, each of which must be completed before the next stage begins. In the *sensorimotor stage*, covering roughly the first 2 years of life, the child develops some motor coordination skills and a memory for past events; the foundation for cognitive development is established. *Object permanence* is the understanding that objects continue to exist even when they are out of sight. pp. 114–116

The *preoperational stage* lasts from about age 2 to age 6 or 7, when the child begins to represent the world symbolically. *Egocentrism*, the inability to perceive a situation or event except in relation to oneself, flourishes in this stage. At the end of the preoperational stage, children begin the process of *decentration*, gradually moving away from self-centeredness. pp. 116–117

The *concrete operational stage* lasts from approximately age 6 or 7 to age 11 or 12; the child develops the ability to understand constant factors in the environment, rules, and higher-order symbolic systems. *Conservation* is the ability to recognize that objects can be transformed in some way, visually or physically, yet still be the same in number, weight, substance, or volume. pp. 117–118

The *formal operational stage* begins at about age 12, when the child can think hypothetically, consider future possibilities, and use deductive logic. pp. 118–119

How is Vygotsky's approach different from Piaget's?

Vygotsky saw the child as part of an active social world. Communication with others and self-speech (private speech) help the child understand his or her world and that of other people. Vygotsky held that when children are presented with tasks that are outside of their current abilities, they need the help of society to accomplish them. He referred to the gap between a child's current abilities and what he or she might accomplish with the help and guidance of a more skilled individual (usually an adult) as the child's *zone of proximal development*. pp. 120–122

What is a theory of mind?

Children have little awareness of their own and other people's mental processes until about age 3. Adults possess and apply a *theory of mind*—ideas about mental states such as feelings, desires, beliefs, and intentions and about the causal role they play in human behavior. pp. 122–123

HOW DO EARLY SOCIAL AND EMOTIONAL DEVELOPMENT PROCEED?

What is attachment, and why is it Important?

Attachment is the strong emotional bond that a person feels toward special people in his or her life. Bowlby was one of the first to study the close attachment between mothers and their babies and to show that babies separated from their mothers exhibit characteristic responses he identified as secure, avoidant, resistant, and disoriented. Once established, early attachment is fairly permanent. Verbal exchanges between child and caregiver help establish ties, teach language, inform infants about the world, and socialize them. pp. 124–128

What is temperament?

Temperament refers to the early-emerging and long-lasting pattern in an individual's disposition and in the intensity and especially the quality of his or her emotional reactions. Temperament is not fixed and unchangeable, although many researchers contend that some specific initial temperamental characteristics may be biologically based. pp. 128–130

How do Piaget's, Kohlberg's, and Gilligan's views on the development of morality differ?

Morality is a system of learned attitudes about social practices, institutions, and individual behavior that people use to evaluate situations and behavior as right or wrong, good or bad. Both Piaget and Kohlberg studied moral reasoning, focusing on how people make moral judgments about hypothetical situations. Piaget thought of the stages of moral development as discrete, whereas Kohlberg viewed them as overlapping and proposed that children's interactions with parents and friends may influence their conceptions of morality. pp. 130–133

Whereas Kohlberg showed that young children base their decisions about right and wrong on the likelihood of avoiding punishment and obtaining rewards, Gilligan found that children also focused on caring, relationships, and connections with other people. Most important, Gilligan found some differences between boys and girls. According to Gilligan, as young children, girls gravitate toward a morality of caring, while boys tend toward a morality of justice. pp. 133–134

WHAT ENVIRONMENTAL FACTORS ARE IMPORTANT FOR SOCIAL DEVELOPMENT?

What advances characterize early social development?

Fathers spend significant amounts of time with their young children, often engaging in play. The amount and quality of father–child interactions do vary among families, depending on factors such as emotional style and financial situation. pp. 134–136

By the end of their second year, children have begun to understand that they are separate from their parents—they are developing a sense of self. Very young children do not understand the concept of sharing—particularly the idea that sharing with another child makes the other child more likely to share, too. pp. 136–137

What are gender roles and stereotypes?

A *gender role* is a set of expectations in a given society about behaviors and responsibility that are appropriate for males or females. A *gender stereotype* is a fixed, overly simple, and sometimes incorrect idea about traits, attitudes, or behaviors of males or females; it can give rise to discrimination. Parents reinforce children selectively, based on their gender to some extent, especially at young ages, but gender differences in behavior are small and are apparent only in certain situations, such as on the playground and in groups. pp. 137–138

Describe Erikson's stage theory of psychosocial development.

Erikson characterized psychosocial development throughout life as a series of stages during which people resolve various basic dilemmas. His theory suggests that at each stage, resolution of a dilemma (whether successful or unsuccessful) determines personality and social interactions. The first four of Erikson's stages are basic trust versus basic mistrust, autonomy versus shame and doubt, initiative versus guilt, and industry versus inferiority. pp. 138–141

Adolescence and Adulthood

How Do Adolescents Bridge the Gap to Adulthood?   146
  Viewing Adolescence in Multiple Contexts
  Physical Development in Adolescence
  Cognitive Development in Adolescence
  Emotional and Social Development in Adolescence
  Who Am I? The Search for Gender Identity
  Friendship and Sexual Behavior

Is Adulthood a Time of Stability or Change?   159
  Physical Changes in Adulthood
  Cognitive Changes in Adulthood

Social and Personality Development in Adulthood
Stage Theories of Adult Development

Do We Grow Older and Wiser in Late Adulthood?   170
  Myths, Realities, and Stereotypes about Aging
  Health in Late Adulthood
  The Final Transition: Dying

Summary and Review   176

Human experience and development are influenced by numerous factors, including a person's biological inheritance, life experiences, and thoughts—and, to a certain extent, by chance. There is great variability in how specific events—when children are born, a decline in a parent's health, the opening of a job opportunity—affect individuals. For example, moving from one school to another changes children's lives; a divorce is unsettling; and a death in the family can be devastating. So, in addition to normal, predictable developmental changes, once-in-a-lifetime events can permanently alter physical, social, and personality development. Normative life events are those that are typical for most men and women in a culture. They are commonly experienced major events, such as having children, retiring from work, or helping aging parents. Other life events are idiosyncratic; they are unique to an individual, such as the death of a sibling or a major health problem. Idiosyncratic life events are often compelling, but psychological theories have focused on normative life events because they affect most people.

This chapter discusses some of the normative developmental changes that occur during adolescence and adulthood and traces the psychological processes underlying these changes. As you read, remember that a person's *chronological age* (how old the person is in years) is sometimes different from his or her *functional age* (how old the person acts or seems). For example, some adolescents act older and wiser than their peers of the same chronological age.

How Do Adolescents Bridge the Gap to Adulthood?

In Western culture, the transition from childhood to adulthood brings dramatic cognitive, social, and emotional changes. Generally, this transition occurs between the ages of 12 and 20, a period known as adolescence, which bridges childhood and adulthood but is like neither of those states. *Adolescence* is the period extending from the onset of puberty to early adulthood. *Puberty* is the period during which the reproductive system matures. It begins with an increase in the production of sex hormones, which signals the end of childhood. Although adolescents are like adults in many ways—they are nearly mature physically and mentally, and their moral development is fairly advanced—their emotional development may be far from complete, and generally they have not yet become self-sufficient economically. Their stages of development—physical, cognitive, social, and emotional—are often mismatched.

Adolescence ■ The period extending from the onset of puberty to early adulthood.

Puberty ■ The period during which the reproductive system matures; it begins with an increase in the production of sex hormones, which signals the end of childhood.

Viewing Adolescence in Multiple Contexts

Adolescence is often thought of as a time of storm and stress brought on largely by raging hormones—and for some adolescents, this is the case. It is a popular stereotype that adolescents are in a state of conflict resulting in part from a lack of congruity among the various aspects of their development—physical, cognitive, social, and emotional. In fact, most adolescents normally have some conflicts, such as with parents, and some have atypical problems, such as poverty or parental alcoholism. What may compound these problems is that adolescents' coping mechanisms, or ways of dealing with such stressors, may not yet have developed sufficiently (Compas et al., 2001). Consider alcohol use. Most adolescents know that underage drinking is illegal and that drinking is potentially deadly when combined with driving. Yet many are not mature enough to stand up to peer pressure and make a conscious decision not to drink—especially those youths who are at high risk because of multiple stressors, such as poverty, absent parents, and/or alcoholism in the home (Branje, van Aken, & van Lieshout, 2002; Chassin, Pitts, & Prost, 2002; Taubman-Ben Ari, 2000).

Storm and stress do not give the whole picture of adolescence. Most adolescents go through this period of multiple changes without significant psychological difficulty (Larson, 2000). Although spurts of hormones do affect adolescents' reactions, nonbiological factors seem to be especially important in moderating the effects of these hormones on moods (Archibald, 2000). Adolescence may be a challenging life period, just as adulthood is, but relatively few adolescents have serious difficulties (Roesser, Eccles, & Sameroff, 2000), and most psychologists agree that adolescence is not typically marked by great psychological turmoil. This does not mean that adolescence is conflict-free or that parent–child relationships do not change during this period. What it does mean is that adolescence does not have to be a stressful time (Galambos & Tilton-Weaver, 2000), especially when parents are willing and able to modify their parenting style to fit the situation (Bumpus, Crouter, & McHale, 2001; Mounts, 2002). Most adolescents experience healthy emotional and social development, and the frequency and intensity of conflicts decrease as they grow older

(Collins & Laursen, 2000). And most adolescents have good relationships with parents, rely on them for advice, embrace their values, and feel respected and loved.

While it is almost a cliché for a teenager in the United States to feel that "no one understands me," it is difficult to imagine a teenager growing up in the jungle of New Guinea expressing the same sentiment; her focus during the teen years is not on self-expression but on learning specific skills. Thus, the problems of adolescence must be considered in a cultural context. Even adolescents who grow up in the same country experience life's joys and disappointments in different ways. Some American teenagers come from disadvantaged economic groups, whereas others have advantaged economic backgrounds. Some teenagers are exposed to racial prejudice, alcohol and other drug abuse, violence, nonsupportive families, or other stressors that lead them to feel a lack of control over their lives (Kilpatrick et al., 2000; Leventhal & Brooks-Gunn, 2000). Ultimately, the culture in which a teen matures affects his or her overall view of the world, attitudes, and specific behaviors (Farver, Narang, & Bhadha, 2002). In addition, spirituality is a cornerstone of many people's lives—and whether you feel that religion and nature are inseparable, see life as an unending process, or view men and women as equals is determined by your culture (Banks-Wallace & Parks, 2004).

Unfortunately, most research on adolescence has been conducted on White, middle-class American teenagers. But researchers now understand that the life experiences of various ethnic and cultural groups are not alike. Each year, more studies compare the experiences of different groups, and both professionals and the public are becoming more sensitive to cultural differences among groups as well as to the diversity that exists within groups. Remember, there is often more diversity within a given group than between groups.

Physical Development in Adolescence

The words *adolescence* and *puberty* are often used interchangeably, but in fact they mean different things. As we noted earlier, puberty is the period during which the reproductive system matures. The age when puberty begins varies widely; some girls begin to mature physically as early as age 8, and some boys at 9 or 10 (Wilson, 1992). The average age at which individuals reach sexual maturity—the first menstruation for a girl, the first ejaculation for a boy—is 13, plus or minus a year or two. (On average, girls enter puberty a year or two before boys.) Just before the onset of sexual maturity, boys and girls experience significant *growth spurts*, gaining as much as 5 inches in height in a single year.

By the end of the first or second year of the growth spurt, changes have occurred in body proportions, fat distribution, bones and muscles, and physical strength and agility. In addition, the hormonal system has begun to trigger the development of secondary sex characteristics. *Secondary sex characteristics* are the genetically determined physical features that differentiate the sexes but are not directly involved with reproduction. These characteristics help distinguish men from women—for example, beards and chest hair in men, breasts in women. (*Primary sex characteristics* are the external genitalia and their associated internal structures, all of which are present at birth.) Boys experience an increase in body mass and a

Secondary sex characteristics ■ The genetically determined physical features that differentiate the sexes but are not directly involved with reproduction.

deepening of the voice, as well as the growth of pubic, underarm, and facial hair. Girls experience an increase in the size of the breasts, a widening of the hips, and the growth of underarm and pubic hair. The first ejaculation for boys and the first menstrual cycle for girls (called *menarche*) are usually memorable events. The order and sequence of the physical changes associated with puberty are predictable, but, as noted earlier, the age at which puberty begins and the age at which secondary sex characteristics emerge varies widely from person to person. The age of first menstruation for girls seems to have leveled off in the United States at the end of the 20th century, although the first appearance of other signs of sexual maturity, such as breasts and pubic hair, is still declining a bit. This decline is thought by some to be a consequence of the prevalence of obesity and/or the presence of estrogen in the environment—for example, from discarded birth control pills (Cray et al., 2000).

Puberty has received a good deal of research attention. For example, researchers have found that boys feel more positive about their bodies during puberty, whereas girls are more likely to have negative feelings (Craft, Pfeiffer, & Pivarnik, 2003). Puberty itself does not create psychological maladjustment, but the social and sexual changes during adolescence require significant adjustment. New forces affect the adolescent's self-image, and although these forces create new stresses, most adolescents perceive their new status as desirable. While they may eventually attain independence and clear thinking, research shows that adolescents sometimes make bad decisions, take risks, and are vulnerable to abuse of alcohol and other drugs (Novins & Baron, 2004; Wilson & Donenberg, 2004), as well as to eating disorders.

Physical maturation has implications for social development, because young people often gravitate to environments and activities that complement their physical abilities and traits as well as their personality predispositions—toward shyness, for example (Collins et al., 2000). Researchers find that in junior high school, early-maturing adolescents enjoy several advantages, including increased confidence, superior athletic prowess, greater sexual appeal, and higher expectations from teachers and parents (Prokopcakova, 1998). But some early-maturing adolescents seem to be at a disadvantage, in part because peers often treat them as outsiders (Archibald, 2000), and they tend to be at risk for substance abuse (Lanza & Collins, 2002). Such differences in adolescence seem to have few long-term negative consequences. In fact, the stresses of maturing early or late may help teenagers become adept at coping. Many who were at a disadvantage during their school years become self-assured adults (Ge, Conger, & Elder, 2001). Actually, so many factors go into the making of a self-assured adult that psychologists are still not sure how significant the long-term impact of early or late maturation is.

During the teen years, the brain continues to form neuronal networks for various abilities—physical ones like catching baseballs, mental ones like doing algebra problems, and artistic ones like playing piano. It is important to remember that the brain is still maturing during the adolescent years, making new connections and interconnections. In young adulthood, the brain continues to prune neural cells that are no longer useful and reorganize the most often used circuits (Casey, Giedd, & Thomas, 2000). In a real way, it is organizing itself to operate more efficiently.

Cognitive Development in Adolescence

As children mature, their cognitive development makes great advances, though often in fits and starts. Piaget and Vygotsky showed that children's cognitive development has both biological and social components (see Chapter 4). Cognitive development does not stop in adolescence. Most adolescents are in Piaget's stage of formal operations. Because they can think about the world abstractly and develop hypotheses, they learn new cognitive strategies. Teenagers expand their vocabularies, seek out creative solutions, and make full use of their higher mental functions. Problem solving often becomes a focus for adolescent thought. In addition, many adolescents become egocentric, idealistic, and critical of others—at least for some time.

Developing new cognitive abilities—moving into Piaget's stage of formal operations—is quite liberating for adolescents. But their newfound ability to understand the world and its subtleties is not always easy for adolescents, and they sometimes become argumentative and difficult. Part of the problem, from Piaget's view, is that teenagers become wrapped up in themselves and in their own thoughts—in short, quite egocentric. This egocentrism leads to two cognitive distortions. The first is the *imaginary audience*—the feeling adolescents have that they are always "on stage." "Everyone will be watching," thinks a teenager, referring to his or her first date, dance, or debate. The imaginary audience has been explained as an outcome of adolescent egocentrism (Vartanian, 2001). Adolescents who egocentrically believe that the world is looking critically at their lives may go to great lengths to avoid calling attention to themselves (Vartanian & Powlishta, 2001).

Not only do adolescents believe that they are always on stage, but they can also develop an inflated sense of their own importance. This cognitive distortion is called the *personal fable*—the belief adolescents have that they are so special and unique that other people cannot understand them and that risky behaviors, such as unsafe sex, which might harm other people, will not harm them. The personal fable can lead to tragedy, such as when teens think that they can drive after drinking. According to Inhelder and Piaget (1958), adolescents go through a phase in which they attribute an unlimited power to their own thoughts.

The imaginary audience and the personal fable may be not so much a return to childhood egocentrism as a side effect of cognitive development and the ability to think about thinking. Adolescent egocentrism may be a bridging mechanism that allows adolescents to take on new roles, break away from parents, and integrate new views of the self—processes that even adults may continue to go through (Franken-Berger, 2000).

Cognitive differences between male and female adolescents are minimal. There are some observed differences—for example, on certain tests (such as the SAT), males as a group outperform females in mathematics (Park, Bauer, & Sullivan, 1998). However, when certain socioeconomic and cultural variables and varying testing situations are controlled for, these differences are very small (Gallager, Bridgeman, & Cahalan, 2002; Hyde & Kling, 2001). It's also important to remember that these are overall group differences, having no bearing on any individual's achievements. As we'll see next, cultural background can be another factor influencing some adolescents' cognitive development (Piaget, 1970).

Imaginary audience ■ A cognitive distortion experienced by adolescents, in which they feel that they are always "on stage" with an audience watching.

Personal fable ■ A cognitive distortion experienced by adolescents, in which they believe that they are so special and unique that other people cannot understand them and that risky behaviors will not harm them.

Are There Ethnic Differences in Academic Success?

Which group does best in school: Latinos/Latinas, Asian Americans, European Americans, or African Americans? Stereotypes hold that students of Asian descent perform better because of cultural values that stress achievement. Researchers have found that this belief is accurate. Culture does affect school achievement in direct and indirect ways. Students in Asian nations spend more classroom time on academic subjects than do students in the United States; it is not surprising that their math scores are higher (Stigler & Baranes, 1988). Further, families and teachers in Asian societies tend to treat all students as equal, emphasizing effort more than innate ability—whereas in many Western cultures, more attention is given to innate cognitive strengths. In addition, in Asian and other non-Western societies, success in school and other aspects of life is often attributed to external factors and failure is attributed to internal factors such as ability; the reverse is true in Western societies (Bernardo, Zhang, & Callueng, 2002; Kivilu & Rogers, 1998; Yu & Miller, 2003). But cultural variables other than ethnicity are more important—poverty, for one. Low income is an extraordinarily strong predictor of school achievement. In the United States, non-White families are heavily represented among those with low incomes. Schools with predominately White, low-income students have achievement levels more like those of schools with non-White, low-income populations than like those of schools with White, high-income populations (Abbott & Joireman, 2001).

Parental behavior is also important in an adolescent's academic success. Adolescents whose parents are *authoritative*—not rigidly authoritarian but accepting, warm, democratic, and firm—achieve more in school than do peers whose parents are either rigid and demanding or too permissive (Steinberg et al., 1992). And peer interactions can also be facilitative; strong peer support for academic achievement can make up for a lack of positive parenting (Farmer et al., 2003; Ungar, 2000).

Regardless of ethnic background, adolescents with authoritative parents functioned better socially than those with permissive or neglectful ones (Steinberg et al., 1992). In school performance, Steinberg found a slight difference among ethnic groups: Authoritative parenting seemed to make more of a difference to White American teenagers than to African American or Asian American ones.

Why would authoritativeness, however it is defined, benefit one ethnic group more than another? For example, why might authoritativeness benefit African Americans and Asian Americans less in academic performance than in social development? This difference may have to do with sharply differing attitudes about education. Researchers found that all of the students in one study (Steinberg et al., 1992) believed that a good education would pay off, but the Asian Americans in particular had been taught to fear the consequences of a poor education. In contrast, the African American students, many of whom were from a lower income bracket, were more likely to be optimistic and to believe that life could have positive outcomes despite a poor education. Obviously, students who believe that they can succeed without doing well in school will devote far less energy to academic pursuits than will those who are more fearful of the negative consequences of school failure.

One research study showed that adolescents raised by authoritative parents tended to consult with their parents regarding moral and informational decisions, while those raised by authoritarian, permissive, or neglecting-rejecting parents more often turned to their peers for help with moral and informational decisions (Bednar & Fisher, 2003). Overall, according to Steinberg (2001, p. 1), "there is enough evidence to conclude that adolescents benefit from having parents who are authoritative: warm, firm, and accepting of their needs for psychological autonomy." A child's attitudes, taught by his or her parents and reinforced by peers, shape success in many domains, including academics (Cross, 2003). Thus, distinctly different cultural views and parenting styles may alter motivation and academic performance, affecting later success in life and work, and emotional and social development, which we turn to next.

Emotional and Social Development in Adolescence

Show me (L.L.) ten teenagers, and I will show you ten distinct personalities. American teenagers have grown up in a society that values individual expression rather than conformity. Today's teenagers also have parents who have divorced at alarming rates, and they live in a society in which the economic gap between the very rich and the very poor has widened. Seventy-three percent of the wealth in the United States is held by the richest 10% of the population, and the economic gap tends to reflect racial and ethnic divisions. While poverty has decreased for all ethnic groups, the overall income gap between the richest and poorest Americans is still huge (Finegold & Wherry, 2004). Racial disparity in educational attainment, income, health, housing opportunity, and political power has remained one of the most pressing social issues in the United States (Giddens, Dunier, & Applebaum, 2003).

Clearly, early childhood social interactions, as well as advances in cognitive development, profoundly affect adolescent social adjustment. Teenagers in the United States spend a great deal of time alone—more so than in previous generations—whether listening to music, surfing the Internet, or watching television. They have an unprecedented number of opportunities to succeed or fail—as well as to be lonely and to feel isolated (Sanders et al., 2000). Children whose early emotional or social adjustment is poor are less likely to make good adjustments as adolescents. One research effort, the Carolina Longitudinal Study (Cairns & Cairns, 2000; Mahoney, Cairns, & Farmer, 2003), tracked 695 young people growing up over a 14-year period. The participants were 364 girls and 331 boys living in the southeastern United States who were originally recruited in 1981–1983. Participants were interviewed in the 4th grade (Group 1) or the 7th grade (Group 2) and were tracked annually to 12th grade. Participants were later interviewed again when they were approximately 20 years old. Approximately 25% of the sample was African American. Cairns and Cairns saw early patterns of social adjustment manifest themselves as the years went by. These researchers argue that the trajectories of social development do not change much. Troubled boys and girls tend to stay troubled, and happy and well-adjusted children are more likely to remain so. But, as mentioned earlier, regardless of their previous adjustment, teenagers' egocentrism—taking the form of the imaginary audience and the personal fable—complicates their emotional and social adjustment, and the strong impact of peers often reinforces aggression when it occurs (Xie et al., 2002).

Ethnic Identity

Adolescents develop a self-image based on beliefs about themselves that are both cognitively and emotionally based, but other people also form expectations and beliefs about adolescents, which have an impact on their self-image (Cairns & Cairns, 1994, 2000). Thus, an adolescent's personality and sense of self-esteem are affected by childhood experiences, events such as the timing of puberty and how peers and parents react to that timing, and stage of cognitive development. Self-esteem is also affected by ethnic identity, religion, and involvement in community service (McClellan & Youniss, 2003; Youniss et al., 2002).

Ethnic identity ■ A feeling of membership in an ethnic or cultural group.

A sense of *ethnic identity*—a feeling of membership in an ethnic or cultural group—helps individuals develop a sense of cultural belonging. However, having a sense of ethnic identity can place some individuals in a difficult position. Their sense of ethnic identity may keep them alienated from the larger society. For example, having an immigrant family that has strong cultural traditions—even something as simple as always speaking the native language at home—may be at odds with a high school student's goals of speaking articulate English, doing well on standardized tests, and having new friends able to communicate with family members without a language barrier getting in the way. The society at large can help minority youth develop ethnic identity, strong self-esteem, and mainstream values by ensuring that teens of all backgrounds are respected in school, are mainstreamed in classes with peers of similar ethnicity, and are encouraged to explore their ethnic pride and its meaning within contemporary society.

Parents and teachers can help teens—normal or troubled, early- or late-maturing—develop a stronger sense of self-esteem. For example, research shows that involvement in athletics can be a buffer against the initially negative feelings about body image that can sometimes arise during this period (Kirkcaldy, Shephard, & Siefen, 2002). For both girls and boys, playing sports is associated with higher satisfaction with body image and higher self-ratings on strength and attractiveness. Physical activity is associated with higher achievement, weight reduction, improved muscle tone, and stress reduction, all of which foster a positive self-image (Hagger et al., 2003; Stunkard, Faith, & Allison, 2003).

There are sharp individual differences in the development of adolescent self-esteem. In contrast to middle or later adolescence, early adolescence is associated with lower self-esteem and with feelings of insecurity, inadequacy, and shyness (Robins et al., 2002). Roy Baumeister and others (Baumeister, Smart, & Boden, 1996) argued that aggression and violence are more likely when highly favorable views of self are disputed by some person or circumstance. Later research is supporting this claim (Costello & Dunaway, 2003).

It is commonly believed that low self-esteem affects girls more than boys, but research shows that gender differences in self-esteem are small and do not exist at all in some countries and ethnic groups (Huurre, Aro, & Rahkonen, 2003). Adolescent girls face many barriers to later achievement, including wage disparities and institutional discrimination, but very low self-esteem is not a big problem.

Two important sources of influence on self-esteem and personality are parents and peers. There is no question that adolescents are responsive to parental influence (Bosacki, 2003; Otto, 2000). Psychologists and parents disagree about the relative importance of peers versus parents (Harris, 1998), but most studies indicate that adolescents' attitudes fall somewhere between those of their parents and those of their peers (Vazsonyi, Hibbert, & Snider, 2003). The influence of peer groups is especially strong in the middle years of adolescence. Peer groups are made up of individuals who identify with and compare themselves to one another. They often consist of people of the same age, gender, ethnicity, and even skin color, although adolescents may change their peer group memberships and may belong to more than one peer group (Thompson & Keith, 2001). As adolescents spend more time away from parents and home, they experience increasing pressure to conform to their peer groups' values and preferences regarding politics, religion, fashion, music—and even fast-food restaurants. The desire for conformity is especially evident in same-sex peer relations (Eagan & Perry, 2001). Peers constantly pressure one another to conform to behavioral standards, including standards for dress, social interaction, and even forms of rebellion, such as shoplifting and drug taking. Most important, peers influence the adolescent's developing self-concept. Adolescents are vulnerable; those who are unpopular can be victimized, which further erodes self-esteem and can lead to withdrawal and a range of problems (Kilpatrick Demaray & Kerres Malecki, 2003).

Parents and their child-rearing style undoubtedly affect an adolescent's self-esteem and self-confidence (Neumark-Sztainer et al., 2000). Are parents nurturing and firm, or are they heavy-handed and dictatorial, or perhaps more interested in being their child's pal and thus too permissive? Both parents and peers set standards by which the adolescent judges his or her own behavior. These three sources of influence (parents, peers, and self-interpretation) can establish self-esteem and self-confidence and allow an individual to attain good social and emotional adjustment.

Suicide

What about those whose adjustment is not good, those who become depressed, need medication, or become suicidal? Much has been written about suicide and teenagers. Most who are suicidal also show other symptoms, including substance abuse, eating disorders, or antisocial behavior. The truth is that adults are more likely to commit suicide than are teenagers, but teenagers are more likely to attempt suicide—even multiple times. That such attempts are cries for help is well known; if they are ignored, the attempts often continue until one of them is successful.

Suicide is the eighth leading cause of death for all U.S. men (Anderson & Smith 2003), and men are four times more likely to die from suicide than women (Centers for Disease Control and Prevention, 2004). Girls are more likely than boys to attempt suicide, but boys are far more likely to succeed. Among teens, African Americans and Latinos are less likely than White Americans to commit suicide, but Native Americans have strikingly higher suicide rates (Centers for Disease Control and Prevention, 2004). Over the last three decades, the suicide rate has increased for American teens—regardless of ethnicity—probably as a result of increased stress, pressure, and use of drugs and decreased family or social supports. Although the rate increase has leveled off recently, overall rise has captured public notice, and that is why so much media attention is given to teen suicide. If someone tells you he or she is thinking about suicide, you should take the claim seriously and help the person obtain counseling from a professional.

Teen suicide is a distressing phenomenon, but it is important to remember that most adolescents lead relatively happy lives and become competent, well-adjusted, happy adults. The process of adjustment and the search for happiness and identity turn out be affected by one's sex and gender-based characteristics, as we'll discover next.

Who Am I? The Search for Gender Identity

Sex and gendered behaviors matter a great deal in both childhood and adulthood (Maccoby, 1998, 2000). Being a man or a woman in any culture carries with it certain roles. Men and women have different expectations for themselves and for members of the other sex, and those expectations often create inequality. Discrimination against women has decreased but persists. For example, a wage gap favoring men still exists (Ostroff & Atwater, 2003). Women still experience serious disparities in employment opportunities, pay, status, and access to leadership roles (U.S. Department of Labor, 2004). This problem stems from society's definition and valuing of gender roles, which vary from culture to culture (Tiggemann & Ruutel, 2004).

We saw in Chapter 4 that gender differences are differences between males and females in behavior or mental processes. Extensive research has revealed that behavioral and cognitive differences between the sexes are smaller than many people assume (Geary, 1998; Halpern, 2000). Although girls often reach developmental milestones earlier than boys do, this difference between the sexes usually disappears by late adolescence (Cohn, 1991). On the other hand, experience and learning—the ways in which a person is raised and taught—have a profound impact on behaviors.

Gender Identity

Gender identity ■ A person's sense of being male or female.

As noted earlier, a key feature of adolescence is that it is a period of transition and change. Adolescents must develop their own identity, a sense of themselves as independent, mature individuals. One important aspect of identity is *gender identity*—a person's sense of being male or female. The process of forming one's gender identity begins in childhood and continues through adolescence and adulthood. Children develop some sense of gender identity by age 3. By age 4 or 5, most children realize that their gender is permanent; that is, they know that they will always be the sex that they are. However, children as old as 6 or 7 can be confused about gender constancy (Martin, Ruble, & Szkrybalo, 2002). Some children in early elementary school believe that changing their hair, clothing, or behavior will alter their sex.

Gender intensification ■ The exaggeration of traditional male or female behaviors seen in some adolescents.

Adolescents must confront gender issues when their bodies change very rapidly. During the transition to adulthood, adolescents often try out various types of behaviors, including those relating to male–female relationships and dating. Some adolescents become extreme in their orientation toward maleness or femaleness. This exaggeration of traditional male or female behaviors, called *gender intensification*, is often short-lived, and it may be related to the increased self-esteem that many boys feel during adolescence and the decreased self-esteem that some girls experience (Aube et al., 2000; Kremen & Block, 1998). Interestingly, both boys and girls experience pressure with regard to their appearance, including pressure to make sure their bodies are sporty, strong, and "hard." The failure to do this and the experience of being excluded and/or devalued if they do not rise to the challenge may have as much to do with socioeconomic status and ethnicity as with gender (Frost, 2003).

Many psychologists believe that while children and adolescents are developing their gender identity, they attempt to bring their behavior and thoughts into conformity with generally accepted gender-specific roles. ***Gender schema theory*** asserts that children and adolescents use gender as an organizing theme to classify and interpret their perceptions about the world and themselves (Bem, 1985; Maccoby, 2000). (A *schema* is a conceptual framework that organizes information and helps a person make sense of the world.) See **Figure 5.1** for a description of gender schema theory. Young children decide on appropriate and inappropriate gender behaviors by processing a wide array of social information. They develop shorthand concepts of what boys and girls are like; they then try to behave in ways that are consistent with those concepts (Levy, 1999). Thus, they show preferences for sex-typed toys, activities, and vocations. In fact, children's—and adolescents'—self-esteem and feelings of worth are often tied to their gender-based perceptions about themselves, many of which are determined by identification with the same-gender parent or by what they see as society's view of gender roles (Hudak, 1993).

Gender schema theory ■ The theory that children and adolescents use gender as an organizing theme to classify and interpret their perceptions about the world and themselves.

Gender Roles and Stereotypes

The transition to adulthood has always included the adoption of gender-related behaviors sanctioned by the person's society. Today, knowing which behaviors are socially acceptable for one's gender is more complicated. In the last century, roles for women have changed: previously limited to marriage and homemaking, which were considered full-time jobs, women can now enter many of the same careers as men—although the career may be interrupted for child rearing. And men's plans often

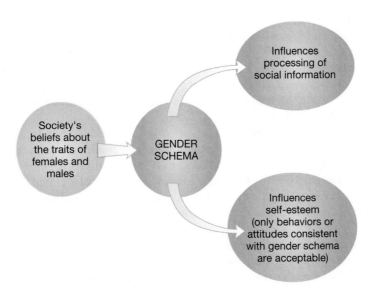

Figure 5.1
Gender
Schema Theory
According to gender schema theory, children and adolescents use gender as an organizing theme for classifying and interpreting their perceptions about the world.

include not only careers but also active involvement in raising their children. Many women and men today are in the process of developing new attitudes about gender roles—many of which incorporate the best characteristics of traditionally masculine and traditionally feminine behaviors. Behaviors that represent a blend of stereotypically male and stereotypically female characteristics are labeled *androgynous*. Men and women can fix cars, pursue careers, do housework, and help care for children. They can be both assertive and emotionally sensitive. Several studies have found that people who rate high in androgynous characteristics tend to feel more fulfilled and more competent (Bem, 1993; Woodhill & Samuels, 2003).

Androgynous ■ Having both stereotypically male and stereotypically female characteristics.

The challenges facing today's adolescents are difficult, as adult society asks them to be strong, sensitive, and competent, as well as occasionally docile and vulnerable, but also independent. They are expected to develop all of these abilities, but often to express only some of them—the ones that are considered gender appropriate (Faludi, 1999). This creates confusion.

In families that place a high value on traditionally gendered behaviors, boys may be urged to mask their emotional vulnerability. They are expected to cut themselves off from feelings that are seen as unacceptable for males and to wear a mask of cheerfulness and resiliency—to appear to be masters of their universe. Pollack (1998) calls this the "Boy Code" and argues that it puts boys, teens, and later men into emotional straitjackets. According to Sanchez (2002), the result is that many men never learn how to deal with hurt or pain. They are either punished for expressing such emotions or are encouraged to express them in aggressive ways (e.g., in physical fights or reckless behaviors). As adults, they have difficulty identifying their feelings or knowing how to manage them.

Girls, teens, and women are similarly tied, but with a different set of knots. One problem is that vulnerable, sexual, strong, independent, and competent don't always go together—and certainly not for all girls or women (Khan, 2003; Najjar, 2003). Another is that, while women have fully entered the workforce, they work for lower wages and face corporate glass ceilings (American Psychological Association, 2003; U.S. Department of Labor, 2004). That is, women have not achieved equality in the workplace. They experience less satisfaction and pride in their work than men do (Hodson, 2004). For many women, work does not define them, as it does for men, and this different attitude may arise from gender distinctions still reinforced in childhood (Heyman & Legare, 2004). As young women make the transition from high school to university, many may still be actively closing off possibilities for their own futures, straitjacketing themselves (Lips, 2004).

In the end, traditional gender stereotypes hold men and women to a near-impossible standard of manhood or womanhood. The challenge for parents, educators, and psychologists is to allow teenagers to blossom fully, to emerge as adults unhindered by the destructive emotional straitjackets that exaggerated gender stereotyping creates. Real boys and girls, real men and women all need to be able to be strong and independent and to express their emotions openly, whether they are happy, sad, lonely, or unhappy. They have to be allowed to express their humanity as individuals, not in a highly gendered, emotionally constricted context.

In the face of all of the stress potentially involved in becoming a mature man or woman, most adolescents grow up, seek friends and then lovers.

Friendship and Sexual Behavior

In this first decade of the new millennium, more high school students and college students than ever are having sexual relationships outside of a romantic relationship. Although widely discussed on daytime talk shows in terms like "friends with benefits," sexual relationships between high schoolers who are primarily friends have been little researched. How might such a relationship begin? It clearly starts with friendship.

Some people have many friends; others have only a few. But most people, at one time or another, find someone with whom they share values, ideas, and interests. We seek friends who share our interests, and those may be shaped heavily by popular culture that reinforces our day-to-day behavior. Research shows that people in our lives also make a huge difference—for example, older siblings, extended family members, family friends, community- or school-based informal mentors (Stanton-Salazar & Spina, 2003).

At its simplest, a friendship is a close emotional tie between two peers (Kerns, 1998). Most teenagers report having between three and five good friends. As much as 29% of adolescents' waking hours are spent with friends; among adults, for a whole range of reasons, the time spent interacting with friends drops to 7%. If you had lots of friends as a child, you are more likely to have lots of them as an adult, even if you don't spend a great deal of time with each one of them. The number of friendships a child or adolescent has is uniquely associated with prosocial skills. Elementary school children tend to form same-gender friendships; most prefer playmates with styles of play or interaction that are similar to their own, and this preference facilitates gender segregation (Hoffmann & Powlishta, 2001). Cross-gender friendships are rare. Research shows that social skills that facilitate peer relationships emerge in the preschool years and develop during adolescence, during which time peer groups become structured with respect to friendship groups, gender, and dominance relations (Hay, Payne, & Chadwick, 2004).

There are some important developmental consequences of having or not having friends (Gest, Graham-Bermann, & Hartup, 2001). Children and adolescents who have friends tend to be more socially competent than those who do not. A friend is someone to confide in, to be afraid with, and to grow with, and friendship sets the stage for intimacy in adulthood (Furman et al., 2002). From a developmental point of view, friends are an important resource from childhood through old age, both cognitively and emotionally (Hartup & Stevens, 1997). Adolescent friendships can contribute to sharing and intimacy, although they can also be filled with conflict over social or political issues, drugs, gangs, and sexual behavior (Keefe & Berndt, 1996).

Many researchers report that intimacy and shared values are the key variables that define a friendship. Ideally, close friends participate as equals, enjoy each other's company, have mutual trust, provide mutual assistance, accept each other as they are, respect each other's judgment, feel free to be themselves with each other, understand each other in fundamental ways, and are intimate and share confidences (Bender, 1999). Among today's teens, the intimacy of friendship sometimes includes sex.

Sex fascinates and captivates. It is biological and it is cultural. It is important to recognize and appreciate the fact that girls and women and boys and men tend to view sex and sexual behavior somewhat differently. For example, you will get many different answers if you ask adolescent boys and girls and adult men and women the following questions:

- What constitutes sex?
- Is oral sex actually sex?
- How many partners do you want to have in a lifetime?
- How often do you have sex?

American adolescents view sexual intimacy as an important and normal part of growing up, and premarital heterosexual activity has become increasingly common among adolescents. Adolescents are having sexual experiences at younger ages than in previous decades, in part because knowledge and use of contraception are becoming more widespread, thus reducing the fear of pregnancy and diseases. Today, Western adolescents consider sexual behavior normal in an intimate relationship (Graber, Britto, & Brooks-Gunn, 1999). In the United States, 55% of male teenagers have intercourse by age 18, and the same percentage of White female adolescents do so by just a year later, age 19 (Gates & Sonenstein, 2000). Among African Americans, 60% of boys have intercourse by age 16, and 60% of girls do so by age 18. However, there are great individual differences with regard to age at first intercourse and the subsequent frequency of intercourse. The gender differences are notable. Research shows that across many different studies and measures, men have more frequent and more intense sexual desires than women, as reflected in spontaneous thoughts about sex, frequency and variety of sexual fantasies, desired frequency of intercourse, desired number of partners, among other measures (Baumeister, Catanese, & Vohs, 2001). But thoughts and desires do not necessarily translate into overt behavior.

More accepting attitudes about adolescent sexual behavior have brought about increased awareness of the problems of teenage pregnancy. Each year in the United States, 500,000 adolescents under age 19 become pregnant, according to the Centers for Disease Control and Prevention (2004). Adolescent pregnancy rates vary substantially with ethnicity; for example, White Americans have substantially lower rates than do Latinos/Latinas or African Americans (Coley & Chase-Lansdale, 1998). The more engaged students are with schooling, the less likely they are to become pregnant (Manlove, 1998). Further, young women who indicated a high degree of religiosity were significantly more likely to report that they felt able to communicate with partners and refuse unwanted or unsafe sexual encounters (Guttmacher Institute, 2003).

The consequences of childbearing for teenage mothers are serious. Teenage mothers are more likely to smoke and to have low-birthweight infants; they are also less likely to receive timely prenatal care (National Center for Health Statistics, 2004b). Furthermore, a young woman's chances of obtaining education and employment become more limited if she becomes a mother, and many young mothers are forced to rely on public assistance.

Current studies show that, despite the threat of AIDS, high school and college students still engage in regular sexual activity, often without appropriate protection (National Center for Health Statistics, 2004b). Comprehensive school-based health care programs that present a complete picture of sexuality (focusing not only on facts but also on attitudes, motivation, and behavior) reduce the risks of pregnancy in teenagers. But, for many parents and teenagers, such programs are controversial; they see discussing contraception and safe sex as condoning immoral activity.

Being a teenager can be difficult; today's teenagers will vouch for increased pressure, a desire for social mobility, and standards that seem to move beneath their feet. Teens must decide daily about many behaviors, including whether to engage in risky behaviors that involve sex or drugs. Some youths are better at navigating the choices than others. Making these choices is never easy—but it can be easier for children and teens who mature in a stable family that is supportive and encourages schooling and friendships and in which ethnicity and strong identity are valued. A teen has to separate from family and form friends and loving relationships, and the influences of family and friends shift. It is indeed a great deal of change in a few years.

Change is not limited to the teenage years. In fact, adolescent changes are just the beginning. As teens become adults, they quickly see that adulthood may involve fewer physical changes but many more emotional and social changes.

Is Adulthood a Time of Stability or Change?

The life experience of an American adult today is different from that of adults two generations ago or adults in most other cultures. You may have heard that "today's 60 is the new 40"—meaning that today's 60-year-olds resemble the 40-year-olds of a generation ago. The same is true in some other Western cultures, but less likely in developing countries, where good education, nutrition, and health care are less readily available. In truth, psychologists know less about developmental processes in other cultures than they would like. In addition, until the 1970s, developmental psychologists in the United States concentrated largely on White middle-class infants and children rather than on a full range of ethnicities and ages. Today, psychologists are aware that immigration is strongly affecting the composition of the young adult population in the United States. According to some researchers (Brown, Moore, & Bzostek, 2003), new immigrants are expected to account for over 60% of the U.S. population growth among 25-year-olds between now and 2025. Latino/Latina and Asian populations in this age group are expected to increase by over 75%.

Psychologists are now focusing on development throughout the lifespan *and* across cultures. They are recognizing that a person encounters new challenges in every stage of life, regardless of his or her cultural background or experience. Researchers study adult development by looking at the factors that contribute to stability or change, to a sense of accomplishment or feelings of despair, and to physical well-being or diminished functioning (Brown, Moore, & Bzostek, 2003). Think about the years after retirement, which can be a time of stability, bringing feelings of completion and well-being, or a difficult, unhappy time, full of physical and emotional troubles. Researchers also examine a range of differences between men and women, and they realize that a career is often a defining characteristic of adulthood. Many adults spend an enormous amount of time and energy on their careers, and up until recently this aspect of adulthood had been examined relatively infrequently. Careers are important because adults' financial status affects physiological well-being, mental health, and overall quality of life. Without adequate financial assets, the physical and mental health of older adults is in danger of declining.

The good news is that as people move from adolescence to adulthood, and ultimately to old age, they become psychologically healthier (Jones & Meredith, 2000). Today, a higher percentage of people live well into their 70s and beyond, but psychologists know relatively little about those middle years from 20 to 70. Psychologists study childhood physical development extensively but pay much less attention to adult physical development. **Building Table 5.1** summarizes the major changes in important functional domains during young adulthood, early adulthood, and middle adulthood.

Physical Changes in Adulthood

One hundred years ago, only about half of all Americans who reached age 20 lived beyond age 65. Demographers predict that by 2050, one in five people worldwide

Building Table 5.1

MAJOR CHANGES IN IMPORTANT DOMAINS OF ADULT FUNCTIONING

Age	Physical Change	Cognitive Change	Work Roles	Personal Development	Major Tasks
Young Adulthood, Ages 18–25	Peak functioning in most physical skills	Cognitive skills high on most measures	Choice of career, which may involve several job changes	Conformity; task of establishing intimacy	Separate from parents; form partnership; begin family; find job; create individual life pattern
Early Adulthood, Ages 25–40	Good physical functioning in most areas; health habits during this time establish later risks	Peak period of cognitive skill on most measures	Rising work satisfaction; major emphasis on career or work success; most career progress steps made	Task of passing on skills, knowledge, love (generativity)	Rear family; establish personal work pattern and strive for success
Middle Adulthood, Ages 40–65	Beginning signs of physical decline in some areas (strength, elasticity of tissues, height, cardiovascular function)	Some signs of loss of cognitive skill on timed, unexercised skills	Career reaches plateau, but higher satisfaction with work is likely	Increase in self-confidence, openness	Launch family; redefine life goals; redefine self outside of family and work roles; care for aging parents

will be over age 60, and in that year, there will be 2.2 million people age 100 or older. Over one-third of the older population lives in China, India, and the United States (Hawkins, 1999). As researchers at the Center on Aging and Aged (2004) point out, within the next 50 years, a rapid rise in the proportion of older adults in less developed countries will strain economic and social welfare systems.

Fitness Changes

Most of the adult years are characterized by health and fitness; the leading cause of death, for example, for people aged 25–44 is accidental injury—in motor vehicle crashes, for example (Disaster Center, 2004). Psychologists often speak of fitness as involving both a psychological and a physical sense of well-being. Physically, human beings are at their peak of agility, speed, and strength between ages 18 and 30. From 30 to 40, there is some loss of agility and speed. Between 40 and 60, even greater losses occur (Merrill & Verbrugge, 1999). In general, strength, muscle tone, and overall fitness deteriorate gradually from age 30 on. People become more susceptible to disease because their immune systems lose efficiency and thus the ability to fight disease. Respiratory, circulatory, and blood pressure problems are more apparent; lung capacity and physical strength are significantly reduced. Decreases in bone mass and strength occur, especially in women after menopause; the result is often *osteoporosis*, a condition characterized by low bone mass and deterioration of bone tissue, which increases the risk of a break or fracture. A fracture of the hip almost always requires major surgery. It impairs a person's ability to walk and may cause prolonged or permanent disability. Although the risk of disease and disability clearly increases with advancing age, people are generally healthy in most of adulthood. Failing health is not an inevitable result of growing older (Centers for Disease Control and Prevention, 2004).

Osteoporosis ■ A condition characterized by low bone mass and deterioration of bone tissue, which increases the risk of a break or fracture.

Sensory Changes

In early adulthood, most sensory abilities remain fairly stable. As the years pass, however, adults must contend with almost inevitable sensory losses. Reaction time slows. Vision, hearing, taste, and smell require a higher level of stimulation than they did at a younger age. Older people, for example, usually are unable to make fine visual discriminations regarding signs at a distance or read the fine print on medicine bottles without the aid of glasses; they have limited capacity to adapt to darkness, and are at greater risk for glaucoma, cataracts, and retinal detachment. Older adults often have some degree of hearing loss, especially in the high-frequency ranges. People age 65 and older are more likely than any other age group to have hearing loss. By age 65, many people can no longer hear very high-frequency sounds, and some are unable to hear ordinary speech. Hearing loss is more common for men than for women, and with each passing year the disparity grows. Further, Whites are proportionately overrepresented among people with hearing loss (National Academy on an Aging Society, 1999). Sensory losses as people age in general do not disable them, however.

Sexual Changes

In adults of both sexes, advancing years bring changes in sexual behavior and desire as well as physical changes related to sexuality. For example, in the child-rearing years, women's and men's sexual desires are sometimes moderated by the stresses of raising a family and juggling a work schedule. Women often experience an increase in sexual desire in their 30s and 40s, but men achieve erections less rapidly at that age. Interestingly, Roy Baumeister and Dianne Tice (2001) point out that men tend to estimate and women tend to count when it comes to calculating sexual encounters; the former approach results in high numbers of partners and encounters, the latter approach, to low numbers. Any careful reading of the facts shows discrepancies, and so data about human sexual behaviors—especially data about frequency—must be analyzed carefully and critically.

For women, midlife changes in hormones lead to the cessation of ovulation and menstruation at about the age of 50, a process known as *menopause*. Menopause is generally seen as a transition, after which women no longer have to deal with birth control issues; some women, however, perceive it as the beginning of old age and an end to youthful femininity (Avis, 1999). Many people incorrectly believe that all women experience depression, anxiety, and other psychological problems at menopause (Matlin, 2003). After menopause, many women feel freer to focus on relationship status and quality (Winterich, 2003). At about the same age as women are experiencing menopause, men's testosterone levels decrease, their ejaculations become weaker and briefer, and their desire for sexual intercourse typically decreases from adolescent levels. Like menopause, men's decline in gonadal function is a gradual one (Seidman, 2003).

Older men and women continue to engage in sexual activities and to find them enjoyable, and significant percentages find their sexual activities more satisfying than when they were younger (National Council on Aging, 1998). According to the National Council on Aging, sex remains a significant part of life for many older Americans. Nearly half of all Americans age 60 or older engage in sexual activity at least once a month. Drugs such as Viagra are now available to help older men with erectile problems achieve erections. And pharmaceutical companies are working on drugs that will increase sexual responsiveness for those women who have desire/responsiveness problems. If older people are not active sexually, it is usually because they lack a partner or have a disabling medical condition. As with their younger counterparts, however, there is considerable variation from person to person.

Researchers realize that much of the illness and disability associated with aging is avoidable through prevention. This means practicing a healthy lifestyle, for example, by being physically active, and taking advantage of early detection practices such as cancer screening tests. But is there a satisfactory theory of aging?

The Evolutionary View of Adult Sexual Behavior

Evolutionary psychologists assert that those whom we seek out as mates and have children with is, at least in part, under evolutionary control. In their view, men seek out as many women as they can to mate with, especially women who are fertile—men are *polygamous* (Hinsz, Matz, & Patience, 2001). Women have evolved to seek out a man who can provide status, wealth, and security for them and their offspring; accordingly, they will be far more selective about whom they mate with, and will tend to be *monogamous* and to remain in long-term relationships (Schmitt et al., 2002). Further, men and women draw different conclusions and ascribe different priorities and attributes to sex and love (Cramer et al., 2002). The conclusion from an evolutionary perspective is that this difference in sexual behavior is due to natural selection.

Critics of evolutionary approaches are quick to point out that evolutionary psychology is nondevelopmental in its nature—it does not track changes in individuals over time, nor does it explain how evolution may express itself differently in different environments (for example, in cities versus agrarian societies). In addition, humans' environment has grown more complex than ever before, and evolution may be able to exert only a modest influence on sexual behavior.

Theories of Aging

Psychologists and physicians have been examining the behaviors and physiological changes that accompany aging only since the early 1970s. Three basic types of theories—based on heredity, external factors, and physiology—have been developed to explain aging, although it is likely aging results from a combination of all three causes.

Genes determine much of a person's physical makeup; thus, it is probable that *heredity*, to some extent, determines how a person ages and how long he or she will live. There is much evidence to support this claim. For example, long-lived parents tend to have long-lived offspring. However, researchers still do not know exactly how heredity exerts its influence on the aging process; they only know that there are multiple mechanisms of aging, some of them hereditary (Jazwinski, 1996).

One promising area of study has focused on *apoptosis*, the process by which cells kill themselves. Normal human cells have a limited capacity to proliferate, which is most likely mediated by telomeres. *Telomeres* are end segments of the chromosomes found within every cell (Bodnar et al., 1998). After a certain finite number of cell divisions, time on the biological clock runs out; the cells stop dividing. The research shows that human cells grow older each time they divide because their telomeres shorten; in a way, they are "chewed up" just a bit with each successive cell division. If a chromosome does not have telomeres of the proper length, the cell it is in will not divide. This recent finding holds promise for an explanation of aging.

External, or lifestyle, factors also affect how long a person will live. For example, people who live on farms live longer than those in cities, probably because they get more exercise and are exposed less to pollutants; normal-weight people live longer than overweight people because excess weight taxes the cardiovascular system; and people who do not smoke cigarettes, who are not constantly tense, who wear seatbelts, and who are not exposed to disease or radiation live longer than those who do or are. Because these data on external factors are often obtained from correlational studies, cause-and-effect statements cannot be based on them; it is reasonable to assume, however, that external factors such as disease, smoking, and obesity affect a person's life span (Centers for Disease Control and Prevention, 2004).

There is no doubt that older people tend to have more long-term, chronic illnesses—such as arthritis, diabetes, high blood pressure and heart disease—than younger people. Several theories use *physiological explanations* to account for aging and its related diseases. Because a person's physiological processes depend on both hereditary and environmental factors, these theories rely on both concepts. *Genetic theory* doesn't entirely explain how long one is going to live. Aging is only partially determined by the genes—very few identical twins die at exactly the same age. The *wear-and-tear theory* of aging claims that the human organism simply wears out from overuse, like a machine (Hayflick, 1996). The wear begins at the cellular level. The DNA that makes up our genes sustains repeated damage from toxins, radiation, and ultraviolet light. Our bodies can repair DNA damage, but not all repairs are accurate or complete. Thus, the damage progressively accumulates. This idea has intuitive appeal but little research support. Some research that focuses on how the body uses its energy stores has indicated that the more active a life a person lives, the less efficient the body's use of energy may be and the faster the aging process (Levine & Stadtman, 1992). A related theory, the *homeostatic theory*, suggests that the body's ability to adjust to stress and other variations in internal conditions decreases with age. For example, as the ability to maintain a constant body tempera-ture decreases, cellular and tissue damage occurs, and aging results. Similarly, when the body can no longer control the use of sugar through the output of insulin, signs of aging appear. On the other hand, aging may be the cause of the deviations from homeostasis, rather than the result.

It is also important to distinguish between primary and secondary aging. *Primary aging* is the normal, inevitable change that occurs in every human being and is irreversible and progressive. Such aging happens despite good health, and it can make a person more vulnerable to American society's fast-paced and sometimes stressful lifestyle. *Secondary aging* is aging that is due to extrinsic factors such as disease, environmental pollution, and smoking. Lack of good nutrition is a second-ary aging factor that is a principal cause of poor health among the lower-income elderly in the United States (Weddle & Fanelli-Kuczmarski, 2000). And poor nutri-tion can also adversely affect cognitive functioning.

Cognitive Changes in Adulthood

Changes in intellectual functioning that occur with age are minimal. Up to the age of 65, there is little decline in learning or memory. Motivation, interest, and recent educational experience (or lack of it) are more important than age in affecting a per-son's ability to master complex knowledge (Willis & Schaie, 1999). Although many people believe that age-related declines in intellectual functioning are drastic and universal, they are not. Researchers do agree that certain cognitive abilities, espe-cially in mathematics and memory functions, begin to deteriorate in many people after age 65.

Although most research indicates that cognitive abilities and memory functions typically decrease in old age (Anstey et al., 2001; Chen, Han, & Wang, 2003), many of the changes are of little importance for day-to-day functioning (Salthouse, 1999; Schaie, 2000). For example, overall vocabulary decreases only slightly. Moreover, some of the changes observed in laboratory tasks (e.g., reaction-time tasks) are small and can be forestalled or reversed through cognitive interventions. Yet there is no doubt that the brain of a young person encodes information differently than the brain of an older person does.

Researchers generally acknowledge that some age-related decrements do occur, especially after age 65 (e.g., DeBeni and Palladino, 2004; Salthouse, Atkinson, & Berish, 2003). However, such effects are often less apparent in cognitively active individuals. Most researchers would tell older individuals to "use it or lose it"; active adults who continue to flex their intellectual muscle seem to stay intellectually acute (Kliegl et al., 2001). When deficits do occur, older individuals can compensate to optimize their performance. The truth is that most Americans are aging well. With appropriate health care and social support systems, older individuals can do just fine in everyday situations (Centers for Disease Control and Prevention, 2004), including social ones involving family and friends.

Social and Personality Development in Adulthood

Social changes in adulthood follow a fairly predictable order. Younger adults focus on developing a sense of identity, a career direction, an intimate relationship, and often parenthood. Middle-age adults focus on caring for children and older parents, dealing with role changes, and planning for retirement. Older adults must address changing roles, retirement, loss of friends or spouse, changing friendships and relationships, physical change, and eventual death.

A basic tenet of most social and personality theories is that, regardless of day-to-day variations, an individual's personality remains stable over time. That is, the way a person copes with events and experiences tends to remain fairly consistent throughout her or his lifetime. But personality may also be sensitive to the unique experiences of the individual, especially during the adult years. The adult years are filled with great personal challenges and opportunities and therefore require innovativeness, flexibility, and adaptability. Positive changes during adulthood—the development of a sense of generativity, the fulfillment of yearnings for love and respect—usually depend to some degree on success during earlier life stages. Adults who continue to have an especially narrow outlook are less likely to experience personality growth in later life.

Women have undergone special scrutiny from psychologists since the early 1970s. As we have seen, researchers now recognize that the profession of psychology was dominated by males through the 1950s and that many personality theories were based on studies of men. Not surprisingly, these failed to address women's personality and development issues. Personality researchers acknowledge that contemporary women face challenges in the workplace and the home that were not conceived of three decades ago. These challenges have given rise to the "supermom" phenomenon—the woman who tries to achieve family, career, and personal satisfaction, all within the same span of years. This is a tough task, and today's working mothers rarely feel that their lives are in balance; instead, the competing needs of work and children often make women feel they are "spread too thin" (Talbot, 2002). Of course, how one perceives the stress and hassles of daily life is determined by a whole range of personality variables that are discussed in further detail in Chapter 13.

Some people—perhaps the more poetic—think of life and the development of our social selves as a journey along a road from birth to death. The concept of a journey has similarities to the theoretical view of development as progressing in stages.

Stage Theories of Adult Development

Stage theories of development suggest that people progress through distinct stages from the beginning of life to the end. We examined the childhood aspects of Erik Erikson's stage theory in Chapter 4; we continue to explore it here as it relates to adult development.

Erikson Revisited

An important aspect of Erikson's stage theory is that people progress through well-defined stages of psychosocial development and at each of these they must resolve a particular dilemma. People move toward greater maturity as they pass from stage to stage. Stages 1–4 focus on childhood. Let's now consider the stages that begin with adolescence.

Erikson's stage 5, *identity versus role confusion*, marks the end of childhood and the beginning of adolescence. According to Erikson, the growth and turmoil of adolescence create an "identity crisis." The major task for adolescents is to resolve that crisis successfully by forming an identity—a sense of who they are and what their place in the world is. Adolescents have to form a multifaceted identity that includes vocational choices, religious beliefs, gender roles, sexual behaviors, and ethnic customs. The task is quite daunting, which is one reason why adolescence is such a critical stage of development. In Erikson's view, failure to form an identity leaves the adolescent confused about adult roles and unable to cope with the demands of adulthood, including the development of mature relationships with members of the opposite sex (Erikson, 1963, 1968). The special problems of adolescence—which may include rebellion, suicidal feelings, and drug abuse—must also be dealt with at this stage and are tied up with forming an identity (Belgrave, Brome, & Hampton, 2000).

Stage 6 (young adulthood) is *intimacy versus isolation*. Young adults begin to select others with whom to form intimate, caring relationships. Ideally, they learn to relate emotionally to others and to commit to a lasting relationship; the alternative is to become isolated.

In stage 7 (middle adulthood), *generativity versus stagnation*, people become more aware of their mortality and develop a concern for future generations. They develop the urge to convey information, love, and security to the next generation, particularly their own children. They do so through caring acts that foster growth, such as career mentoring (Bradley & Marcia, 1998). They try to influence their family and the world; otherwise, they stagnate and become self-absorbed. Generativity is, of course, not limited to middle adulthood. Research shows that people in early adulthood also experience it (Stewart & Vanderwater, 1998).

In stage 8 (late adulthood), *ego integrity versus despair*, people conduct a life review and assess whether their lives have been meaningful, happy, and cohesive or wasteful and unproductive. Many individuals never arrive at stage 8, and some who do are filled with regrets and a feeling that time is too short. Those who successfully resolve the conflict inherent in this stage feel fulfilled, with a sense that they understand, at least partly, what life is about.

Table 5.1 summarizes the last four stages of Erikson's theory. (The first four stages were summarized in Table 4.4.) An alternative to Erikson's theory—one that has received significant media attention—has been proposed by Levinson.

Levinson's Life Structures

Noted theorist Daniel Levinson has devised a stage theory of adult development similar to Erikson's in that it proposes that people go through stages and have similar experiences at key points in their lives. Unlike Erikson, however, Levinson does not see life as a journey toward some specific goal such as ego integrity or inner harmony. Rather, he believes that there are general eras during which individuals work

Table 5.1

ERIKSON'S LAST FOUR STAGES OF PSYCHOSOCIAL DEVELOPMENT

Stage	Approximate Age	Important Event	Description
■ 5. Identity versus role confusion	Adolescence	Peer relationships	The teenager must achieve a sense of identity that encompasses occupation, gender roles, sexual behavior, and religion.
■ 6. Intimacy versus isolation	Young adulthood	Love relationships	The young adult must develop intimate relationships or suffer feelings of isolation.
■ 7. Generativity versus stagnation	Middle adulthood	Parenting and work	Each adult must find some way to contribute to and support the next generation.
■ 8. Ego integrity versus despair	Late adulthood	Reflection on and acceptance of one's life	Ideally, the older adult arrives at a sense of acceptance of self and a sense of fulfillment.

out various developmental tasks. These tasks may not be the same for all individuals and do not lead to a specific end.

Levinson (1978) suggests that as people grow older, they adapt to the demands and tasks of life. He describes four basic eras in the adult life cycle, each with distinctive qualities and different problems, tasks, and situations. The four eras outlined by Levinson are adolescence, early adulthood, middle adulthood, and late adulthood.

During *adolescence* (ages 4–17), young people enter the adult world but are still immature and vulnerable. During *early adulthood* (ages 18–45), they make their first major life choices regarding family, occupation, and style of living. The much-discussed *midlife crisis* occurs at the end of early adulthood. Levinson calls particular attention to this crisis, asserting that most adults experience it in their early 40s. At this time, people often realize that their lives are half over—that if they are to change their lives, they must do so now. (This era is similar to Erikson's stage of generativity versus stagnation.) The term *midlife crisis* may be a misnomer. Levinson himself (1980) suggests that it should more properly be called a *midlife transition*—a change that may be more difficult for some individuals than others. The word *transition* suggests that a person has reached a time in life when old ways of coping are giving way to new ones. A person in transition faces new challenges and responsibilities and is able to reassess and reappraise his or her life and develop new skills. A *crisis*, in contrast, occurs when old ways of coping become ineffective but a person is helpless, not knowing what to do or how to acquire different coping strategies. Crises are often perceived as painful turning points in people's lives. Not everyone experiences the infamous midlife crisis, but most people pass through at least one midlife transition (Rosenberg, Rosenberg, & Farrell, 1999).

Middle adulthood spans the years from age 46 to 65. Adults who have gone through a midlife transition learn to live with the decisions they made during early adulthood. Career and family are usually well established. People experience either a sense of satisfaction, self-worth, and accomplishment or a sense that much of their life has been wasted. Levinson's fourth and final stage, *late adulthood*, covers the years from age 65 on. During retirement, many people relax and enjoy the fruits of their labors. Children, grandchildren, and even great-grandchildren can become the focus of an older person's life.

Levinson's stage theory specifies ages more explicitly than does Erikson's, and it focuses on developmental tasks, or themes. Levinson realizes that not all adults succeed in every era or achieve feelings of independence. Who does and under what conditions are not clear. Levinson's theory is an alternative to Erikson's, but both suffer from being hard to evaluate experimentally and difficult to apply in making predictions about future behavior. A major shortcoming of Levinson's theory is that it was based on information gathered from a small sample of 40 middle-class men between the ages of 35 and 45 over several years. He interviewed the men weekly for several months and again after 2 years, collecting extensive biographical data. Levinson also interviewed the men's wives, but his original study did not include women as participants.

Gender Differences in Adult Stages

In Levinson's view, women follow life stages similar to those of men. But as children, women are taught different values, goals, and approaches to life, which are often reflected later in their choices of vocations, hobbies, and intellectual pursuits. Women have traditionally sought different careers, although this is changing. For example, women now comprise about half of all law school students (Werner, 2004). However, female attorneys often choose careers that do not follow the traditional path chosen by men. In his book *The Seasons of a Woman's Life* (1996), Levinson described the complexities of women's lives, based on interviews with a small sample of women. According to Levinson, women must deal with multiple roles and responsibilities, which make their lives more complex than men's. Career women and homemakers go through the same sequence of stages, but these stages differ in their details.

Among adults, friendships between women differ from those between men; and both differ from a friendship between a man and a woman (Werking, 1997). In Western cultures, expectations for specific gender-based behaviors often control male–female interactions in friendship. Women talk more about family, personal matters, and doubts and fears than men do; men talk more about sports and work than do women. Women in general find friendships more satisfying than men do (Bleske & Buss, 2000). Nevertheless, men experience and seek intimacy and support in friendships (Botschner, 1996).

Women experience midlife transitions differently than men; whereas some men view age 40 as a last chance to hold on to their youth, many women see it as a time to reassess, refocus, and revitalize their creative energies (Apter, 1995; Levinson, 1996). Stewart and Ostrove (1998) suggest that midlife brings women an increased sense of personal identity, personal efficacy, and capacity for generativity—women of this age feel both vigorous and well adjusted. Ostrove also found that identity, generativity, confidence, and concern about aging all were more prominent among women in middle age (the 40s) than in early adulthood (the 30s) (Stewart, Ostrove, & Helson, 2001; Zucker, Ostrove, & Stewart, 2002). Not only that, but work is often not as important for some women, who place greater weight on fulfillment in their family life.

Women's lives are complicated when they have careers because women still face discrimination in the workplace, and society continues to be ambivalent in its expectations for women. They still have the primary burden of family responsibilities, especially child care; in the aftermath of a divorce, the woman usually gets physical custody of any children. Women often must juggle multiple roles, which can bring great satisfaction but also enormous burdens (Kubicek, 2000; Napholz, 2000; Park & Liao, 2000). Taking on sole responsibility for child care after divorce has serious economic consequences that alter a woman's lifestyle, mental health, and course of life stages.

Obvious life-stage differences exist for men and women—regardless of class—but even greater differences exist within groups of demographically similar men or women. The truth is that life isn't always an orderly sequence of planned events for either men or women—it's sometimes random.

Critique of Stage Theories

Many events are unplanned, chance happenings. A chance encounter or an acciden-tal occurrence may lead to an outcome that is not anticipated. It may generate new ideas, relationships, and careers; it may result in a change in direction in a person's life. Small events may have a big impact.

Researchers have come to understand that to varying degrees, adults of all ages think about issues of identity, intimacy, generativity, and integrity identified by Erikson and Levinson. Such thoughts may be particularly intense during some peri-ods, may take different forms at different ages, and may vary for men and for women (Kroger, 2000; Zucker, Ostrove & Stewart, 2002). Developmental changes may occur at any point in life—and those changes do not *have* to take place in order. Different circumstances and influences will result in individual variations. The idea that there are predictable, fixed, and stable stages or phases of development must be viewed with some skepticism and an acknowledgment that people differ, circumstances differ, men and women differ, and that sometimes circumstances weigh in heavily. Some people just seem to understand what life is about at fairly young ages. Others never seem to grow wiser. Or do they?

Do We Grow Older and Wiser in Late Adulthood?

As we grow older, we age experientially as well as physically; that is, we gather experiences and usually expand our worldview. Nevertheless, in Western society, growing older is not always easy, especially because of the negative stereotypes associated with the aging process. Today, however, people are healthier than ever before, are approaching their later years with vigor, and often look forward to second and sometimes third careers. In general, being over age 65 brings with it new developmental tasks—retirement, coping with health issues, and maintenance of an adequate standard of living.

How people view themselves depends in part on how society treats them, and this is true for older adults as well as for young men and women. Many Asian and African cultures greatly respect the elderly for their wisdom and maturity; in such societies, gray hair is a mark of distinction, not an embarrassment. In contrast, the United States is a youth-oriented society in which people spend a fortune on every-thing from hair dyes to facelifts to make themselves look younger. However, because the average age of Americans is increasing, how the elderly are perceived by their fellow Americans and how they perceive themselves may be changing.

Approximately 12% of the U.S. population—or more than 37 million Americans—are 65 years old or older. According to the U.S. Census Bureau (2004), the proportion of elderly Americans is expected to increase to between 20% and 25% of the total population by 2030, and the number of Americans over age 65 will exceed 60 million by that year and 78 million by 2050 (see **Figure 5.2**). At present, the average *life expectancy* at birth—the average number of years a new-born can expect to live—in the United States is about 77 years, and the oldest of the old—those over 85—are the most rapidly growing elderly age group. Life expectancy is different for men and women, however. Women live about 6 years

Life expectancy ■ The average number of years a newborn can expect to live.

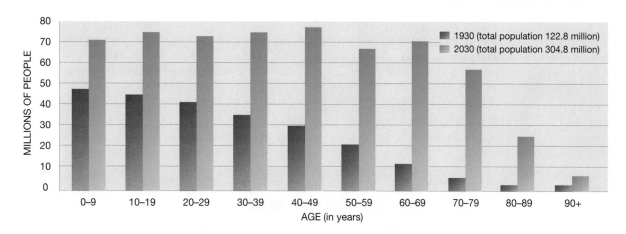

Figure 5.2
A Nation Growing Older
In the year 2030, the U.S. population will be distributed fairly evenly among 10-year age groups ranging from birth through 69. However, the number of elderly people in the United States will have increased sharply with the aging of the baby boomers.

longer than men, on average. There are also ethnic differences, probably due to more limited access to adequate health care and to the fact that African Americans are more likely to work in jobs where accidents are more apt to happen. On average, African Americans live 2 fewer years than European Americans—but Latinos/Latinas live 2 years longer than European Americans, despite facing some of the same problems of health-care accessibility faced by African Americans (U.S. Census Bureau, 2004). The reasons for this discrepancy are not understood.

For many people of all ethnicities, the years after age 65 are filled with new activities and interests. Both men and women enjoy doing things that they may have had to forgo earlier because of family commitments. Financially, two-thirds of American retirees are covered by pension plans provided by their employers, and virtually all receive Social Security checks. Socially, most older people maintain close friendships, stay in touch with family members, and are quite stable emotionally (Carstensen & Charles, 1998; Jones & Meredith, 2000). Some, however, have financial problems, and others experience loneliness and isolation because many of their friends and relatives have died, or they have lost touch with their families. In the United States, there are about as many people over the age of 65 as there are under the age of 7, yet funding for programs to support the health and psychological well-being of older people is relatively limited (U.S. Census Bureau, 2004). The truth is that most older American are getting by and they are doing it with the help of family, savings, and cutting back—they defy a great many fairytales about aging.

Myths, Realities, and Stereotypes about Aging

There is a widely held myth that older people are less intelligent than younger people, less able to care for themselves, inflexible, and sickly. The reality is that many elderly people are as competent and capable as they were in earlier adulthood. They work, play, socialize, and stay politically aware and active. Most older adults maintain a regular and satisfying sex life (Bretschneider & McCoy, 1988) and good mental health. Some people live their lives in a disorganized manner, even when young; others, although chronologically old, are youthful and vigorous (Carstensen & Charles, 1998; Jones & Meredith, 2000). How engaged in life older adults remain is a key factor; the willingness to persevere, cope, and stay involved seems central to happiness in one's later years (Nair, 2000). Building Table 5.2

Building Table 5.2

MAJOR CHANGES IN IMPORTANT DOMAINS OF ADULT FUNCTIONING

Age	Physical Change	Cognitive Change	Work Roles	Personal Development	Major Tasks
Young Adulthood, Ages 18–25	Peak functioning in most physical skills	Cognitive skills high on most measures	Choice of career, which may involve several job changes	Conformity; task of establishing intimacy	Separate from parents; form partnership; begin family; find job; create individual life pattern
Early Adulthood, Ages 25–40	Good physical functioning in most areas; health habits during this time establish later risks	Peak period of cognitive skill on most measures	Rising work satisfaction; major emphasis on career or work success; most career progress steps made	Task of passing on skills, knowledge, love (generativity)	Rear family; establish personal work pattern and strive for success
Middle Adulthood, Ages 40–65	Beginning signs of physical decline in some areas (strength, elasticity of tissues, height, cardiovascular function)	Some signs of loss of cognitive skill on timed, unexercised skills	Career reaches plateau, but higher satisfaction with work is likely	Increase in self-confidence, openness	Launch family; redefine life goals; redefine self outside of family and work roles; care for aging parents
Late Adulthood, Ages 65–75+	Decline in many areas	Small declines on some skills for virtually all adults	Retirement	Integration of ideas and experiences, perhaps self-actualization; task of ego integrity	Cope with retirement; cope with declining health; redefine life goals and sense of self

extends the earlier overview of major changes in important functional domains through late adulthood.

Ageism

Stereotypes about the elderly have given rise to *ageism*—prejudice toward, stereotyping of, and/or discrimination against any person or persons solely because of age. Ageism is prevalent in the job market, in which older people are not given the same opportunities as their younger coworkers, and in housing and health care. It is exceptionally prevalent in the media and in everyday language (Schaie, 1993). Palmore (2001) showed that ageism was widespread and frequently experienced among the elderly. Participants in Palmore's study reported several incidents of ageist treatment, and over half of the incidents were reported to have occurred "more than once." The most frequent incidents involved disrespect for older people and assumptions about ailments or frailty caused by age.

Schmidt and Boland (1986) examined everyday language to learn how people perceive older adults. They found interesting contrasts. For example, "elder statesman" implies that a person is experienced, wise, or perhaps conservative. However, "old statesman" might suggest that a person is past his prime, tired, or useless. The phrase "old people" may allude to positive traits of older adults—for example, being the perfect grandparent—or to negative qualities such as grouchiness or mental deficiencies. What does *old* mean to you?

Older people who are perceived as representing negative stereotypes are more likely to suffer discrimination than those who appear to represent more positive stereotypes (McConatha et al., 2003). That is, an older person who appears healthy, bright, and alert is more likely to be treated with the same respect shown to younger people (Kaufman & Phua, 2003); by contrast, an older adult who *appears* less capable may not be given the same treatment as younger adults (McVittie, McKinlay, & Widdicombe, 2003). In Chapter 14, you'll see that first impressions have a potent effect on people's behavior. This seems to be particularly true of impressions of older people. Ageism can be reduced if people recognize the diversity that exists among aging populations.

Ageism ■ Prejudice toward, stereotyping of, and/or discrimination against any person or persons solely because of age.

Health in Late Adulthood

Many people lead happy and healthy lives well into late adulthood. Of course, as people age, they endure various aches, pains, and a certain slowing of responses. In some people, blood pressure rises, cardiac output decreases, and the likelihood of stroke increases, often as a result of cardiovascular disease, which also affects intellectual functioning by decreasing blood flow to the brain (Riegel & Bennett, 2000). Although there have been twin studies of health and aging, little evidence suggests that genetics, more than lifestyle or environmental variables, is a determining factor in age-related deficits (Pedersen & Svedberg, 2000).

Older people may sleep less and not as well; they are more likely to suffer from arthritis, and osteoporosis makes them more susceptible to accidents. With advancing age, the heart beats more slowly, the lungs lose capacity, arteries become less flexible, and digestive processes become less efficient. Further, slowing of cell division reduces the response of the immune system, making it less effective. Thus, infections are more likely to occur, and latent illnesses can be activated.

While some older people have serious problems with arthritis or hypertension or have orthopedic problems, many lead active, relatively healthy lives. Some older individuals may experience cognitive problems, one of which is dementia.

Many cognitive deficits are caused by brain disorders, sometimes termed *dementias*, which occur only in *some* older people. A ***dementia*** is an impairment of mental functioning and global cognitive abilities in an otherwise alert individual, causing memory loss and related symptoms; typically, dementia is progressive in nature (that is, the condition grows worse over time). Dementia usually involves a loss of function that significantly interferes with a person's daily activities and affects at least two of the following areas of behavior: language, memory, visual and spatial abilities, and judgment. The most important risk factors for dementia are old age and a family history of dementia. However, it is important to point out that dementia is not a normal part of the aging process. Dementias are caused by abnormal disease processes and can affect younger as well as older persons. Only 0.4% of people aged 60 to 65 suffer from dementias. The percentage increases to 3.6% of people aged 75 to 79 and to 23.8% of those aged 85 to 93 (Selkoe, 1992). Those who suffer from dementia often lose their memory for recent events first and their memory for past events later. Additional symptoms of dementia include loss of language skills, reduced capacity for abstract thinking, personality changes, and loss of a sense of time and place. Severe and disabling dementias affect about 1.5 million Americans. With the increasing number of elderly citizens, this statistic is on the rise.

Reversible dementias, which can be caused by malnutrition, alcoholism, or toxins (poisons), usually affect younger people. *Irreversible dementias* are of two types: multiple infarct dementia and Alzheimer's disease. About 75% of people who are diagnosed with dementia have either Alzheimer's or multiple infarct dementia, or a combination of the two. *Multiple infarct dementia* is usually caused by two or more small strokes (often by ruptures of small blood vessels in the brain); it results in damage to the brain and a loss of function. According to the National Institutes of Health (2004), multiple infarct dementia affects approximately 4 out of 10,000 people. *Alzheimer's disease* is a chronic and progressive disorder of the brain that is the most common cause of degenerative dementia in the United States. According to the National Institutes of Health (2004), as many as 4 million Americans and nearly 20 million people worldwide currently suffer from Alzheimer's disease. Named after Dr. Alois Alzheimer, a German physician who first studied its symptoms, it could well be the most widespread neurological disorder of all time (see **Figure 5.3**).

People of all kinds can be victims of Alzheimer's disease, and all confront an unkind fate. In addition to memory loss, the disease is responsible for language deterioration, poor visual/spatial skills, and indifferent attitudes. It accounts for about 50% of the cases of progressive memory loss in aging individuals. (Multiple infarct dementia and other similar disease processes account for 10%–20%, and depression for about 1%–5%. The other causes are metabolic, infectious, traumatic, inflammatory, and mass lesion disorders.)

Dementia ■ An impairment of mental functioning and global cognitive abilities in an otherwise alert individual, causing memory loss and related symptoms and typically having a progressive nature.

Alzheimer's [ALTZ-hymerz] disease ■ A chronic and progressive disorder of the brain that is the most common cause of degenerative dementia in the United States.

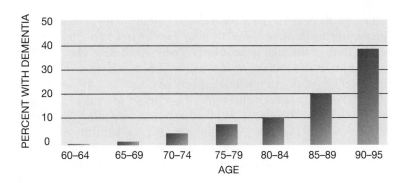

Figure 5.3
Incidence of Dementia, by Age, Caused by Alzheimer's Disease or Strokes

As the U.S. population grows older, the number of cases of Alzheimer's disease will increase. In addition, there are an untold number of undiagnosed cases. Because Alzheimer's is a degenerative disease, its progression cannot be stopped; it is irreversible and ultimately ends in death. The National Institutes of Health (2004) acknowledges that there is no cure for Alzheimer's disease as yet. The goals in treating Alzheimer's disease include slowing the progression of the disease, managing behavior problems, confusion, and agitation, modifying the home environment, and supporting family members and other caregivers. Several drugs are available that appear to slow the progression of Alzheimer's disease and possibly improve the person's mental capabilities.

Scientific findings about possible causes of the disease come from a wide variety of sources, and it is generally argued that there are multiple causes for the disease. Research is showing that there may be specific genes on specific chromosomes that cause nearly all of the cases of early-onset familial Alzheimer's; such research may lead to an understanding of the biochemical causes of the disease (Sherrington et al., 1995). The discovery of these genes may lead to diagnostic tests that can be offered individuals who are at risk because of family history.

The Final Transition: Dying

If you are young (particularly if you are an adolescent), you are more likely than older people to die from an auto accident or AIDS. But the majority of people die at an older age, and the leading causes of death in the United States are heart disease, cancer, strokes, and accidents. In fact, 7 out of 10 older Americans die from one of the first three of these causes (National Center for Health Statistics, 2004a). The number of Americans who succumb to heart disease has decreased because of improved health, reduced smoking, and positive lifestyle changes. Rates of strokes are significantly lower among men and women who do not smoke, who manage their high blood pressure, and who regularly exercise. But cancer remains the second leading cause of deaths; despite good cure rates, half of all cancers are found in men and women over the age of 65. A healthy lifestyle decreases the likelihood of disease, and research shows that older adults who exercise experience increases in self-esteem (Tiggemann & Williamson, 2000). Some individuals experience what is known as *terminal drop*—a rapid decline in intellectual functioning in the year before death.

However, although there is evidence for the terminal drop, no satisfactory method exists for predicting death on the basis of poor performance on intelligence or neuropsychological tests or through genetic tests (Pedersen & Reynolds, 1998).

Thanatology ■ The study of the psychological and medical aspects of death and dying.

In part because of the increasing age of the U.S. population, *thanatology*, the study of the psychological and medical aspects of death and dying, has become an interdisciplinary specialty. Researchers and theorists in several areas—theology, law, history, psychology, sociology, and medicine—are working together to better understand death and dying. For psychologists, dealing with the process of dying is especially complicated, because people often do not like to talk or think about it. Nevertheless, considerable progress has been made toward understanding the psychology of dying.

Summary and Review

HOW DO ADOLESCENTS BRIDGE THE GAP TO ADULTHOOD?

What is the difference between puberty and adolescence?

Puberty is the period during which the reproductive system matures; it signals the end of childhood. There is considerable variation among individuals as to its time of onset. *Adolescence* is the period extending from the end of childhood (often defined as the onset of puberty) to early adulthood. p. 146

What are the major physical and cognitive changes experienced by adolescents?

Adolescents develop *secondary sex characteristics*, the genetically determined physical features that differentiate the sexes but that are not directly involved with reproduction. Examples are bodily hair patterns and a deepening of the voice. pp. 147–148

Cognitive differences between male and female adolescents are minimal, especially when certain socioeconomic and cultural variables and differences in testing situations are controlled. Adolescents also develop cognitive distortions, especially *the imaginary audience* and the *personal fable*, in which they see themselves as "on stage" all the time and so special and unique that other people cannot understand them. The challenges of adolescence, however, must be considered in a cultural context, because most of the research on adolescence has been conducted with White, middle-class, American teenagers, who are clearly not representative of all adolescents. Culture can affect school achievement. pp. 149–151

What are some factors that influence emotional and social development in adolescence?

Changes in intellectual abilities, body proportions, and sexual urges (together with changing relationships with parents and peers) create enormous challenges for adolescents. For some, the changes are emotionally troubling. Adolescents develop a self-image based on a set of beliefs about themselves; other people also generate expectations and beliefs about adolescents, and these beliefs affect them. A sense of *ethnic identity* can be important to social development, as can a sense of self-esteem. pp. 152–153

Gender identity is a person's sense of being male or female. It begins to develop in early childhood, and the process continues through adolescence. Some adolescents experience a short period of *gender intensification* in which they exaggerate traditional male or female behaviors. *Gender schema theory* asserts that children and adolescents use gender as an organizing theme to classify and interpret their perceptions about the world and themselves. pp. 154–155

Gender roles, which assign some behaviors as appropriate and acceptable for each gender, are strongly reinforced by society. Androgyny, the presence of some stereotypically male and some stereotypically female characteristics in one individual, is more common and accepted today than in the past. pp. 155–156

What is friendship?

Friendship is a close emotional tie between peers. Close friends ideally interact as equals, enjoy each other's company, have mutual trust, provide mutual assistance, accept each other as they are, respect each other's judgment, and feel free to be themselves with each other, understand each other, and share confidences. Teenagers typically report having three to five good friends. Adolescents spend as much as 29% of their waking hours with friends. pp. 157–158

How have adolescent sexual behavior and attitudes changed in recent years?

More so than previous generations, today's adolescents view sexual intimacy as a normal part of growing up. Premarital heterosexual activity has become more common among adolescents younger than 18. Although there is increased awareness among adolescents about the use of contraception, teen pregnancy is still widely prevalent. pp. 158–159

IS ADULTHOOD A TIME OF STABILITY OR CHANGE?

What are some of the important effects of aging?

Physical development and aging continue throughout adulthood. Although most of the adult years are characterized by good health, in general, strength, muscle tone, and overall fitness do deteriorate from age 30 on. *Osteoporosis*, a condition characterized by low bone mass and bone deterioration, can develop in middle age, especially in women after menopause. As the years pass, adults must contend with sensory changes. Sexual behavior and desire typically change as adults grow older, and physical changes related to sexuality occur in adults of both sexes. pp. 159–164

Researchers know that heredity influences the aging process, but they do not know exactly how. Lifestyle factors also affect how long a person will live. Primary aging is the normal, inevitable change that occurs with age and is irreversible, progressive, and universal. Secondary aging is aging that is due to extrinsic factors such as disease, environmental pollution, or smoking. pp. 163–164

Most research indicates that cognitive abilities decrease somewhat with advancing age, but many such late-life changes are of little importance for day-to-day functioning and affect only some people. pp. 164–165

What are Erikson's stages of psychosocial development for adolescents and adults?

Erikson's stage 5, identity versus role confusion, marks the end of childhood and the beginning of adolescence; adolescents must decide who they are and what they want to do in life. Stage 6 (young adulthood) is intimacy versus isolation; young adults begin to select others with whom to form intimate, caring relationships. In stage 7 (middle adulthood), generativity versus stagnation, people become more aware of their mortality and develop a particular concern for future generations. Finally, in stage 8 (late adulthood), ego integrity versus despair, people decide whether their lives have been meaningful, happy, and cohesive or wasteful and unproductive. pp. 166–167

How does Levinson's theory of adult development describe the life course?

According to Levinson's stage theory, all adults live through the same developmental eras (periods), though people go through them in their own ways. His theory of adult development (which was generated from data on men) describes four basic eras: adolescence, early adulthood, middle adulthood, and late adulthood. Each era has distinctive qualities and different life problems, tasks, and situations. pp. 167–168

What is the difference between a midlife transition and a midlife crisis?

Nearly everyone has a midlife transition, but not everyone experiences it as a crisis. A transition suggests that a person has reached a time in life when old ways of coping are giving way to new ones. A crisis occurs when old ways of coping become ineffective, and a person feels helpless and frustrated. p. 169

Do women's life stages parallel men's?

Women do not necessarily follow the same life stages as men. Women tend to experience transitions and life events at later ages and in less orderly sequences than those reported by Levinson for men. Among adults in Western cultures, expectations for specific gender-based behaviors often control male–female interactions in friendship. p. 169

DO WE GROW OLDER AND WISER IN LATE ADULTHOOD?

How is life different in late adulthood?

Approximately 12% of the U.S. population—more than 37 million Americans—are age 65 or older. Currently, Americans' *life expectancy* is about 77 years. *Ageism* is discrimination on the basis of age, often resulting in the denial of rights and services to the elderly. pp. 170–174

Brain disorders called *dementias* involve loss of cognitive abilities and mental functioning. Currently, there are about 4 million diagnosed Alzheimer's patients in the United States. *Alzheimer's disease* is a degenerative disorder whose progression cannot be stopped; it is irreversible and ultimately ends in death. Individuals who suffer from Alzheimer's disease slowly lose their memory. Within months, or sometimes years, they lose their speech and language functions. Eventually, they lose all bodily control. pp. 174–175

What is thanatology?

Thanatology is the study of the psychological and medical aspects of death and dying. This interdisciplinary specialty involves researchers and theorists from theology, law, history, psychology, sociology, and medicine. p. 176

CHAPTER 6

Sensation and Perception

How Are Stimulation and Perception Linked?   181
The Difference between Sensation and Perception
Psychophysics
Selective Attention
Restricted Environmental Stimulation
Inattentional Blindness

How Do We See the World?   188
The Structures of the Visual System
The Electrochemical Basis of Perception
Color Vision

How Do We Perceive Form and Substance?   202
Perception of Form: Constancy
Depth Perception
Illusions
Prosopagnosia: The Inability to Recognize Faces
Gestalt Laws of Organization

How Do We Perceive Sounds?   212
What Is Sound?
The Structure of the Ear
Theories of Hearing
Sound Localization
Hearing Impairments

Which Senses Are the Least Understood?   219
Taste
Smell

What Is the Relationship between Touch and Pain?   223
Touch
Pain

How Do We Keep Our Balance?   230

Does Extrasensory Perception Exist?   230

Summary and Review   231

Attention and what you look at, hear, or smell are all part of the study of sensation and perception. Perception is vital because it aids our survival by letting us create a likeness of the world in our mind—it keeps us from having traffic accidents, from falling over mountain cliffs, and from eating spoiled food; it also allows us to understand the needs of a crying of a baby and appreciate the delights of music.

How Are Stimulation and Perception Linked?

Whenever you are exposed to a stimulus in the environment—a word on a page, a sound from an MP3 player, or a breeze through your hair—the stimulus initiates an electrochemical change in sensory receptors in your body. (A sensory receptor is a nerve cell that transforms stimulus energy into an electrical signal.) That change in turn initiates the processes of sensation and perception. Psychologists study sensation and perception because what people sense and perceive determines how they understand and interpret the world. Such understanding depends on a combination of stimulation, past experiences, and current interpretations. Although the relationship between perception and culture has not been extensively researched, it is clear that culture can affect perception—by establishing what people pay attention to or ignore, expect, and feel comfortable with in their environments. For example, composers have long known that a person exposed only to Western music will find non-Western melodies unfamiliar and dissonant.

The Difference between Sensation and Perception

Psychologists have studied sensation and perception together, although they can be thought of as different processes. *Sensation* is the process in which the sense organs' receptor cells are stimulated and relay initial information to the brain for further processing. *Perception* is the process by which an organism selects and interprets sensory input so that it acquires meaning. Thus, sensation provides the stimulus for further perceptual processing. For example, when light striking your eyeball initiates electrochemical changes, you experience the sensation of light. But your interpretation of the pattern of light and its resulting neural representation (the pattern of neuronal activity in the brain) as an image are part of perception. Thus, sensation and perception are both crucial to knowing about the world, and they are the subject of the emerging field of *cognitive neuroscience.*

Some researchers who examine the processes of sensation and perception start at the most fundamental level of sensation—where a stimulus meets receptors—and work up to more complex perceptual tasks involving interpretation. This approach is often called *bottom-up analysis.* Other researchers examine perceptual phenomena by starting from the more complex level—not surprisingly, called *top-down analysis.* Top-down analysis focuses on aspects of the perceptual process such as attention, concentration, and decision making. A bottom-up analysis starts with stimulus information arriving from the sensory receptors (the bottom level of processing) and analyzes the processes that combine that information so that a person can identify more complex patterns. By contrast, top-down analysis looks at how knowledge about and memory of the world help a person identify stimulus patterns or elements of patterns. Perception is thus more than a reflexive process of discriminating individual stimuli; rather, it involves integration of current sensory experiences with past experiences and even cultural expectations (Maner et al., 2003). **Figure 6.1** compares top-down and bottom-up processing.

Sensation ■ Process in which the sense organs' receptor cells are stimulated and relay initial information to the brain for further processing.

Perception ■ Process by which an organism selects and interprets sensory input so that it acquires meaning.

Bottom-up analysis ■ Analysis of the perceptual process that begins at the most fundamental level of sensation—where a stimulus meets receptors—and works up to more complex perceptual tasks involving interpretation.

Top-down analysis ■ Analysis of perceptual phenomena that begins at the more complex level of the perceptual process, with aspects such as attention, concentration, and decision making, to see how these affect the identification of sensory stimuli.

Figure 6.1
Bottom-up and Top-down Processing
Bottom-up processing builds from an analysis of individual stimuli to perception. Top-down processing begins with a perception, then determines how it arises from an organization of sensory stimuli.

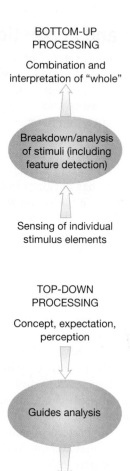

BOTTOM-UP
PROCESSING

Combination and interpretation of "whole"

Breakdown/analysis of stimuli (including feature detection)

Sensing of individual stimulus elements

TOP-DOWN
PROCESSING

Concept, expectation, perception

Guides analysis

Interpretation of stimuli

These two approaches, from the top down and from the bottom up, are both useful, because sensation and perception are not accomplished by the firing of a single neuron or even a few neurons but rather involve whole sets of neurons, through stimulation that occurs at the eyes, ears, or other sense organs. Sensation and perception together form the entire process through which an organism acquires sensory input, converts it into electrochemical energy, and interprets it so that it gains organization, form, and meaning. Through this complex process, people explore the world and discover its rules. The whole process involves the nervous system and one or more of the perceptual or sensory systems: vision, hearing, taste, smell, and touch (Macaluso, Frith, & Driver, 2000). Of course, the relationship between physical stimuli and people's conscious experiences of them is not always immediately apparent, as we'll see in our examination of psychophysics.

Psychophysics

Although the various perceptual systems differ, they share a common process. In each, the environment provides an initial stimulation. Receptor cells translate that stimulus into neural impulses, and the impulses are then sent to specific areas of the brain for further processing. Psychologists who study this process are using *psychophysics*—the subfield of psychology that focuses on the relationship between physical stimuli and people's conscious experiences of them. (Psychophysics is distinct from, but often confused with, *metaphysics*, which is a branch of philosophy.)

Psychophysical studies attempt to relate the physical dimensions of stimuli to psychological experiences. This effort often begins with a study of sensory thresholds. A *threshold* can be thought of as a dividing line, a point at which something becomes different. In perception, a threshold is the point at which a stimulus becomes noticeable; it is the value of a sensory event (such as the wattage of a light or the volume of a radio) at which the environment is perceived as different. Early researchers, such as Ernst Weber and Gustav Fechner, investigated the minimum levels of stimulation necessary to excite a perceptual system, such as vision. They asked, for example, what minimum intensity of light is necessary to make a person say "I see it" or what minimum pressure is necessary for a person to feel something against the skin. It turns out that a true minimum, or absolute threshold, is impossible to determine, because no two individuals see, hear, or feel at exactly the same intensity. The absolute threshold for vision, or any other sense, is thus an average of the responses of a range of normal people. So, for a psychologist, the *absolute threshold* is the statistically determined minimum level of stimulation necessary to excite a perceptual system (see **Figure 6.2**). When perception takes place below the threshold of awareness, it is said to be *subliminal perception*.

Closely related to the absolute threshold is the *difference threshold*—the amount of change necessary for an observer to report 50% of the time that a value of a stimulus (say, a sound) has changed (has become louder or softer) or is different from another value (is the chirping of a cricket rather than of a bird).

Psychophysics ■
Subfield of psychology that focuses on the relationship between physical stimuli and people's conscious experiences of them.

Absolute threshold ■
The statistically determined minimum level of stimulation necessary to excite a perceptual system.

Subliminal perception ■
Perception that occurs below the threshold of awareness.

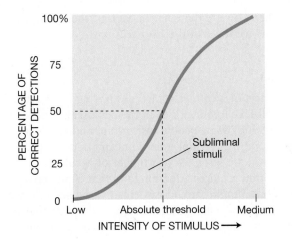

Figure 6.2
Absolute Threshold
Stimuli that are detectable less than 50% of the time are considered subliminal.

Psychologists have devised a variety of methods for studying perceptual thresholds. In one—the *method of limits*—various values of a signal are presented in ascending order (each time slightly higher or more intense) or in descending order (each time slightly lower or less intense). For example, a psychologist may present a light of very low intensity, then one of slightly higher intensity, and so on. A participant's task is to say when he or she finally sees the light (or, in the case of descending limits, no longer sees it). In another method—the *method of constant stimuli*—values of a signal are presented in random order; the participants' task is to respond "yes" or "no," indicating that they have detected a stimulus or have not.

Both the method of limits and the method of constant stimuli have methodological weaknesses—they do not allow for key factors in the human observer. In the past few decades, researchers studying thresholds have applied signal detection theory. *Signal detection theory* holds that an observer's perception depends not only on the intensity of a stimulus but also on the observer's motivation, on the criteria he or she sets for the stimulus, and on the background noise. For example, when you are worried about a loved one being late, you listen especially carefully for cars coming down the street. Your perception also depends on the criteria you set for determining that a signal is present—the criteria that lead you to say "Yes, I detect the signal—the sound of a car." Finally, your perception also depends, according to signal detection theory, on the noise (the unstructured, constant background activity) in the environment. For example, the noise of children playing in the street, birds chirping, and a TV in the next apartment all make it more difficult to detect the sound of a car. In addition to manipulating the actual signal intensity, therefore, researchers have manipulated motivation levels (by offering varying rewards for detection), discrimination criteria (for example, by telling participants to be very sure before they say they can detect the signal), and levels of noise. It turns out that each variable affects a person's willingness to say "Yes, I detect the signal." This important finding lends support to the idea that there is no finite or absolute threshold—individuals' responses to stimuli vary, although each individual is consistent within a specific type of situation. The situation in which a stimulus is perceived turns out to be really important—your threshold for seeing a dim light is very different when you are falling asleep, when you have just had a glass of wine, or when you are dancing. In each of these cases, your attention is focused differently, as we'll see in the next section.

Selective Attention

People behind the wheel of a car are sometimes paying more attention to their CD player, iPod, Palm Pilot, cell phone, kids in the back seat, lunch, or even the sports page than to their driving. Some people eat, primp, and conduct business while driving at 65 miles per hour. If you think that you can attend to the road just because your eyes are open, you are wrong—the number of accidents caused by inattention is frightening. Perception requires attention, and that is an active process. Attending to too many things or failing to attend can create accidents (Gray & Regan, 2000).

Consider what happens when you face competing tasks that require attention. For example, have you ever tried to study while listening to quiet music? You may

---

Signal detection theory ■ Theory that holds that an observer's perception depends not only on the intensity of a stimulus but also on the observer's motivation, on the criteria he or she sets for the stimulus, and on the background noise.

have thought that the music barely reached your threshold of awareness. Yet you may have found your attention wandering. Did melodies or words start to interrupt your studying? Research on attention shows that human beings constantly extract signals from the world around them (Domijan, 2003) and select some stimuli over others; this allows us to perform multiple tasks in a coordinated manner (Vecera & Rizzo, 2003). Although we receive many different sensory messages at once, we can usually attend to only a single selected one. *Selective attention* is the purposeful focusing of conscious awareness on a specific stimulus or event in the environment to the (relative) exclusion of others. As Sterr (2004) has asserted, selective attention acts as the mind's "gatekeeper" by regulating and prioritizing the stimuli to be processed by the central nervous system. Because people can pay attention to only one or two things at a time, psychologists sometimes call the study of attention the study of selective attention. Early researchers in this area discovered the *cocktail party phenomenon*—the fact that a person who cannot discern the content of conversations across a crowded and noisy room can nevertheless hear his or her name mentioned by someone in the crowd.

Selective attention ■
The purposeful focusing of conscious awareness on a specific stimulus or event in the environment to the (relative) exclusion of other stimuli or events.

Perceptual psychologists are interested in the complexities of the processes through which people extract information from the environment. These psychologists hope to determine which stimuli people choose to attend to. They focus on the *allocation* of a person's attention. For example, in selective-listening experiments (e.g., Asbjornsen et al., 2003; Hugdahl et al., 2004; Osorio et al., 2003), participants wearing a pair of headphones receive a different message in each ear simultaneously. Their task is often to shadow, or repeat, the message heard in one ear. Typically, they report that they are able to listen to a speaker, and provide information about the content and quality of that speaker's voice, in one ear or the other, but not both.

Selective-attention studies show that human beings *must* select among the available stimuli. It is impossible, for example, to pay attention to four lectures at once. A listener can extract information from only one speaker at a time. Admittedly, you can do more than one task at a time if the tasks use different sensory and motor systems—for example, you can drive a car and sing along to your favorite CD—but you cannot use the same sensory channel (such as vision) for several tasks simultaneously. You cannot drive a car, read a book, and look at photographs at the same time, because you have to direct your attention (Kastner et al., 1998).

Focusing on one stimulus or activity while trying to ignore other stimuli can be hard, but it is not impossible. In the 1996 Summer Olympics, gymnast Kerri Strug executed a near-perfect vault while ignoring severe ligament pain by focusing her attention on the sight of the apparatus; Strug's efforts indicate that we can "reject" some inputs while focusing on others, and research shows that this is indeed possible (Martino & Marks, 2000). Clearly, both the auditory and visual systems have limited capacities. But we do process information from more than one sensory modality at the same time (sight and hearing, for example), and the modalities affect one another (McDonald & Ward, 2000; Yeung & Monsell, 2003). In fact, some cells in the brain are responsive to two kinds of stimulation, such as vision and touch—these neurons are said to be *bimodal* or *multimodal* (Graziano, Hu, & Gross, 1997). Like many psychological phenomena, selective attention is complex, because under *some* conditions (for example, when saying a word in response to hearing it) you can do two things at once (Greenwald, 2003). However, what happens when it is not necessary to divide your attention? What occurs when stimuli in the environment are restricted?

Restricted Environmental Stimulation

Imagine utter darkness and silence, a complete lack of light and sound. Being in an isolation tank in such conditions was the situation described in a compelling novel by Paddy Chayefsky called *Altered States*. I (L.L.) recommend it to all of my students; it raises provocative questions about human perceptual systems and consciousness—and the relationship between the two.

Psychosocial researchers have examined human functioning in isolated, confined environments (ICEs) and extreme and unusual environments (EUEs), such as space vehicles or polar research stations, to find people who are more likely to do well in those environments (Suedfeld, 2001). In 1954, neurophysiologist John Lilly enlisted modern technology to investigate what would happen if the brain were deprived of all sensory input—if a person were to be placed in a situation much like that described in Chayefsky's novel. Lilly constructed an isolation tank that excluded all

An isolation tank removes all external stimuli and may promote a sense of profound relaxation in some people.

light and sound and was filled with heavily salted water, which helps the body to float. In this artificial sea, deprived of all external stimuli, Lilly experienced dreams, reveries, hallucinations, and other altered mental states. Throughout the ages, mystics of all kinds have claimed to achieve such trance states by purposely limiting their sensory experiences—taking vows of silence, adhering to austere lifestyles, meditating while sitting as still as a stone for hours, and so on. Benedictine monks and nuns such as the Oblates of Mary, a traditional Catholic community of sisters, work hard to cultivate an atmosphere for prayer and insist on silence—except in cases of grave necessity, all speech is forbidden.

Psychologists refer to the limited sensory input that Lilly experienced as *restricted environmental stimulation*. Some researchers argue that psychological benefits such as a sense of rest or peace can be derived from sensory restriction (deprivation)—isolation from sights, sounds, smells, tastes, and most tactile stimuli. The benefits may be exaggerated, but such restriction can have profound effects on animals and humans. One team of researchers (Bexton, Heron, & Scott, 1954) studied the effects of sensory restriction by isolating individual college students in a comfortable but dull room. The researchers allowed the students to hear only the continuous hum of an air conditioner; the participants wore translucent plastic visors to limit their vision and tubes lined with cotton around their hands and arms to limit sensory input to their skin. The results were dramatic. Within a few hours, the participants' performance on tests of mental ability was impaired. The students became bored and irritable, and many said they saw "images."

Several fascinating follow-up studies placed participants in the same conditions, except that these participants were told that the sensory restriction would serve as an aid to meditation. How do you think this information affected their responses? The participants did not hallucinate or become irritable; in fact, their mental abilities actually improved (Lilly, 1956; Zuckerman, 1969). These studies suggest that people do not necessarily become bored because of lack of stimulation. Rather, when people evaluate their situation as monotonous, they become bored. Given the opportunity to relax in a quiet place for a long time, many people meditate; they find the "deprivation" relaxing. Such findings indicate a need for caution in interpreting data from sensory deprivation studies involving human beings, because participants approach these situations with powerful expectations.

Sensory restriction clearly has positive effects on some people (Harrison & Barabasz, 1991). Many experience a profound relaxation in an environment of extreme sensory restriction (Suedfeld, 1998, 2003); this relaxation can be highly effective in modifying some habits such as smoking and in treating problems such as obesity and addiction (Borrie, 1991). Men, older individuals, and people with strong religious backgrounds may be more likely to benefit than others. Further, previous experience with sensory restriction may produce a cumulative effect; that is, each time a person experiences the restricted environment, it may have a greater effect. In general, the benefits of restricted environmental stimulation are probably underestimated (Suedfeld, 2001, 2003).

Sensory restriction is purposeful in most cases. But, as we'll see next, unless we focus our attention, we can miss even the most noticeable events around us.

Inattentional Blindness

When you drive down the road, listen to a concert, or watch a favorite movie, you display an inability to detect unexpected objects—a phenomenon called *inattentional blindness*. Research on inattentional blindness shows that unless you pay attention, you can miss even the most conspicuous events around you (Mack, 2003; Scholl, 2000). In one experiment, while participants paid close attention to a visual scene with sports figures in it, a figure in a gorilla suit appeared, pounded its chest, and then disappeared—but it was completely unnoticed by most of the participants (Most et al., 2001)!

Experimental research on attention shows that when you pay concentrated attention to an object, a scene, or an event, other (unexpected) events go unnoticed (Simons, Franconeri, & Reimer, 2000). This means that a bicyclist or motorist, closely attending to traffic on the road ahead, may completely miss an unanticipated automobile approaching from the left. Similarly, if you are intently focused on a video game, you may not notice someone coming into the room. The more you pay attention to the main event, the less likely you will be to notice the unexpected one (Most et al., 2001). Further, the more the unexpected event differs from what you are attending to or accustomed to, the more likely you will be to miss it (Lachter, Durgin, & Washington, 2000; Simons & Chabris, 1999).

Inattentional blindness is proof that the brain can do only so much at one time—it can encode only so much. This fact brings up questions that we will examine later in the chapter: What information will get coded? What happens to the stimuli that our brains do not register? These questions require us to look more closely at the visual system itself.

How Do We See the World?

You understand the environment because of perception—you don't make direct contact with trees at a distance, cars ahead of you on the road, or the vivid colors of a shirt across the room. Instead, your perceptual processes link you indirectly to the environment. Imagine that you are in an unfamiliar house at night when the power goes out. Left in total darkness, you hear creaking sounds but have no idea where they are coming from. You stub your toe on the coffee table, and then grope along the walls until you reach the kitchen, where you fumble through the drawers in search of a flashlight. You quickly come to a full appreciation of the sense of sight when you suddenly lack it as a mediator of perception.

Human beings derive more information through sight than through any other sense. By some estimates, the eyes contain 70% of the body's sense receptors. Although the eyes do sense pressure, the appropriate stimulus for vision is *electromagnetic radiation*—the entire spectrum of waves initiated by the movement of charged particles. The electromagnetic spectrum includes gamma rays, X-rays, ultraviolet rays, visible light, infrared rays, radar, radio waves, microwaves, and AC currents (see **Figure 6.3**). Note that the *light* that is visible to the human eye is a very small portion of the electromagnetic spectrum. Light may come directly from a source or may be reflected from an object.

The impact of light is complex and affects about 30 areas of the brain that are involved in sensation and perception. We'll analyze the visual system from the bottom up, looking first at the sensory structures of the eye.

The Structures of the Visual System

Figure 6.4 shows the major structures of the human eye. Light first passes through the *cornea*—a small, transparent bulge covering both the *pupil* (the dark opening in the center of the eye) and the pigmented *iris*. The iris either constricts to make the

Electromagnetic [ee-LEK-tro-mag-NET-ick] radiation ■ The entire spectrum of waves initiated by the movement of charged particles.

Light ■ The small portion of the electromagnetic spectrum that is visible to the human eye.

Figure 6.3
The Electromagnetic Spectrum
People can perceive only a small part of the total electro-magnetic spectrum.

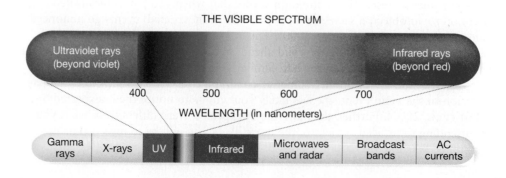

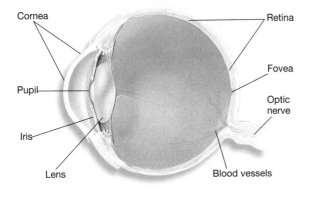

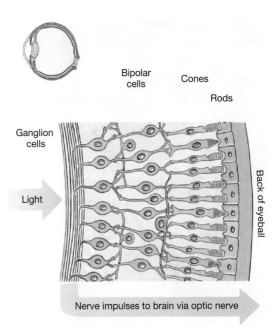

Figure 6.4

The Main Structures of the Eye

The photoreceptors of the retina are connected to the brain through the optic nerve. Light filters through layers of retinal cells before hitting the receptors (rods and cones), located at the back of the eyeball and pointed away from the incoming light. The rods and cones pass an electrical impulse to the bipolar cells, which in turn relay the impulse back out to the ganglion cells. The axons of the ganglion cells form the fibers of the optic nerve. (Dowling & Boycott, 1966)

pupil smaller or dilates to make it larger. Behind the pupil is the *lens*, which is about 4 millimeters thick. Together, the cornea, the pupil, the iris, and the lens form images in much the same way as the shutter and lens of a camera do. The ***retina***, which lines the back of the eyeball, is like the film in a camera: It captures the image. It is a complex network of neurons that generate signals in response to light. Constriction of the iris makes the pupil smaller, which improves the quality of the image on the retina and increases the depth of focus—the distance from the lens to the part of the visual field that is in sharp focus. The action of the lens also helps control the amount of light entering the eye.

Poets have claimed that the eyes are the windows to the soul, but two researchers are suggesting that the transparent cornea that covers the front of the eyeball actually holds an image of what the person is looking at—of the external world. Nishino and Nayar (2004) have recorded images of what the corneas reflect while a person is viewing an object. They point out that the panorama on the corneas in these photographs is far more than what falls on the retina and thus is subsequently seen. They ask, "What does an image of an eye reveal about the world and the person and how can this information be extracted?" They have just begun their exciting work, but you can no doubt think of the applications it may have.

Retina ■ A multilayered network of neurons that line the back of the eyeball and generate signals in response to light.

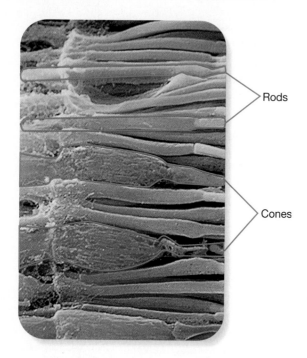

Rods

Cones

When people's eyeballs are not perfectly shaped, their vision is affected. People whose eyeballs are deeper than normal, from front to back, are **myopic**, or *nearsighted;* they see things that are close clearly but have trouble seeing objects at a distance, because the images fall short of the retina. **Hyperopic**, or *farsighted*, people have shortened eyeballs. They see objects at a distance clearly but have trouble seeing things up close, because the image of an object is focused behind the retina.

Some vision losses, such as farsightedness, are age-related and normal, but *macular degeneration*—a loss of the ability of the central part of the retina to process information—impairs the vision of thousands. In fact, it is responsible for most (90%) severe loss of vision. There are approximately 200,000 new cases of macular degeneration in the United States each year.

The *retina* consists of ten layers of neurons. Of these cells, the most important are the *photoreceptors* (the light-sensitive cells), the *bipolar cells*, and the *ganglion cells*. After light passes through several layers of bipolar and ganglion cells, it strikes the photoreceptor layer, which consists of *rods* (rod-shaped receptors) and *cones* (cone-shaped receptors). In this layer, the light breaks down *photopigments* (light-sensitive chemicals), which causes an electrochemical change in the rods and cones. The process by which the perceptual system converts stimuli into electrical impulses is **transduction**, or *coding*. After transduction of the light stimulus by the photoreceptors in the retina, the resulting electrical impulse is transferred back to the adjacent layer of bipolar cells.

Most of the cones are packed tightly in the center of the retina and used for day vision and color vision; rods are found in the rest of the retina and are used predominantly for night vision.

Myopic [my-OH-pick] ■ Able to see things that are close clearly but having trouble seeing objects at a distance; nearsighted.

Hyperopic [HY-per-OH-pick] ■ Able to see objects at a distance clearly but having trouble seeing things up close; farsighted.

Photoreceptors ■ The light-sensitive cells in the retina—the rods and the cones.

Rods and Cones

Each eye contains more than 120 million rods and 6 million cones. These millions of photoreceptors do not have individual pathways to the areas of higher visual processing in the brain. Instead, through **convergence**, electrochemical signals from many rods come together onto a single bipolar cell. Convergence is the synapsing of many signals onto one bipolar cell. At the same time, signals from many cones converge onto other bipolar cells. From the bipolar cells, electrochemical energy is transferred to the ganglion cell layer of the retina. There are about 1 million ganglion cells, and signals from dozens of bipolar cells synapse and converge onto each of them. The axons of the ganglion cells make up the *optic nerve*, which carries visual information that was initially received by the rods and cones to the brain.

The *duplicity theory of vision* (sometimes called the *duplexity theory*), which is now universally accepted, was the first to identify two separate receptor systems in the retina, the rods and the cones, as structurally different and responsible for different tasks. Cones are for the most part tightly packed in the center of the retina, at the fovea, and

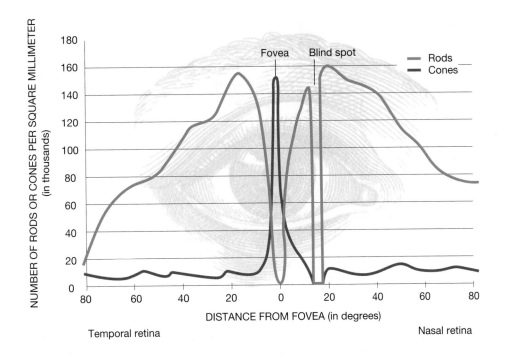

Figure 6.5

The Distribution of Rods and Cones and the Blind Spot

The center of the retina (the fovea) contains only cones. At a distance of about 18° from the fovea, there are no receptors at all. This is the place where the optic nerve leaves the eye, called the *blind spot*. Because the blind spot for each eye is on the side of the eyeball toward the nose, the two blind spots do not coincide (Pirenne, 1967).

are used for day vision, color vision, and fine visual discrimination. Rods (together with some cones) are found in the rest of the retina (the periphery) and are used predominantly for night vision (see **Figure 6.5**). The functioning of the cones is demonstrated in the test of *visual acuity* that you take when you apply for a driver's license. Such a test measures the resolution capacity of the visual system—its ability to see fine details. Cones principally mediate this ability. You do best on such a test in a well-lit room (cones operate at high light levels) and when looking directly at the test items (because more cones are in the center of the retina than in any other place).

Both rods and cones are sensitive to light, but they are less sensitive in a well-lit room than they are after having been in the dark. **Dark adaptation** is the increase in sensitivity to light that occurs when the illumination level changes from high to low. In dark adaptation, the photopigments in the rods and cones regenerate, increasing the eyes' sensitivity to light. If you go from a well-lit lobby into a dark theater, for example, you experience a brief period of low light sensitivity, during which you are unable to distinguish empty seats. Your ability to discern objects and people in the theater increases with each passing moment. Within 30 minutes, your eyes will have almost fully adapted to the dark; they will have become far more light-sensitive. Of course, when leaving a dark theater and emerging into afternoon sunlight, you must squint or shade your eyes until they become adapted to the light.

Rods ■ Rod-shaped receptors in the retina that are primarily responsible for vision at low levels of illumination and are not especially responsive to either fine details or variations in wavelength (color).

Cones ■ Cone-shaped receptors in the retina that are primarily responsible for vision at high levels of illumination and are responsive to fine details and to variations in wavelength (color).

Transduction ■ Process by which a perceptual system converts stimuli into electrical impulses; also known as coding.

Convergence ■ The synapsing of electrochemical signals from many rods or cones onto one bipolar cell.

Dark adaptation ■ The increase in sensitivity to light that occurs when the illumination level changes from high to low, causing the photopigments in the rods and cones to regenerate.

Figure 6.6
A Dark
Adaptation
Curve
The dashed line represents a typical overall dark adaptation curve. The two solid lines represent separate dark adaptation curves for rods and cones. Dark adaptation of cones occurs in about 10 minutes. Rods, however, continue to adapt for another 20 minutes, reaching greater levels of sensitivity.

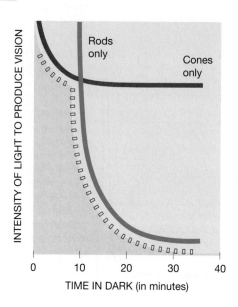

Figure 6.6 shows a dark adaptation curve. The cones determine the first part of the curve; the second part is determined by the rods. (The data for such curves are obtained from experiments with participants who possess only rods or cones.) The speed at which the photopigments in these receptors regenerate determines the shape of the two parts of the curve. Typically, a participant is first shown bright light for 2 minutes. The light is then turned off, and the participant waits in a totally dark room for 15 seconds. Next, a very dim spot of light is turned on for half a second, and the participant is asked if he or she sees it. Usually, the participant will report seeing the spot only after several successive presentations, because dark adaptation occurs gradually. This is why, when you are driving at night, you may have trouble seeing clearly for a brief time after a car drives toward you with its high beams on; the photopigments in the rods take some time to regenerate (Theeuwes, Alferdinck, & Perel, 2002).

Pathway to the Brain

When electrical impulses leave the retina through the optic nerve, they proceed to the brain, first to the lateral geniculate nucleus and then to the *visual cortex* (also called the *striate cortex*) (see **Figure 6.7**). Further coding of the visual information from the eyes takes place in the visual cortex, the most important area of the occipital lobe. Knowledge about the way visual structures are connected to the brain aids not only psychologists but also physicians, who can determine, for example, whether a stroke victim with poor vision has a blood clot that is obstructing circulation in one hemisphere of the brain.

Each eye is connected to both hemispheres of the brain, with half of its optic nerve fibers going to the left side of the brain and the other half connecting to the

Visual cortex ■ The most important area of the brain's occipital lobe, which receives and further processes visual information from the lateral geniculate nucleus; also known as the striate cortex.

right side. The point at which the crossover of half the optic nerve fibers from each eye occurs is called the *optic chiasm* (see **Figures 6.7 and 6.8**). This crossover of nerve fibers allows the brain to process two sets of signals from an image and helps human beings perceive form in three dimensions. Severing of the optic nerves at the optic chiasm results in *tunnel vision*—a condition in which peripheral vision is

Optic chiasm [KI-azm] ▣
The point at which half of the optic nerve fibers from each eye cross over and connect to the other side of the brain.

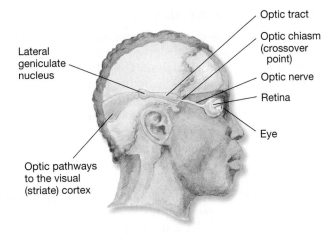

Lateral geniculate nucleus

Optic tract

Optic chiasm (crossover point)

Optic nerve

Retina

Eye

Optic pathways to the visual (striate) cortex

Figure 6.7
The Major Components of the Visual System

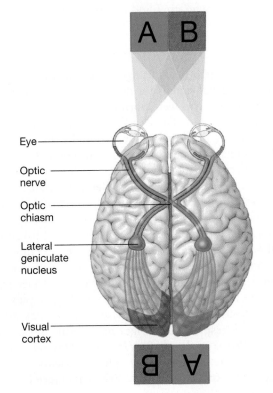

Eye

Optic nerve

Optic chiasm

Lateral geniculate nucleus

Visual cortex

Figure 6.8
A Visual Image Projected to Both Hemispheres of the Brain

severely impaired and a person can see only objects whose images fall on the central area of the retina, the fovea.

The anatomy of the visual system is only part of the equation; to understand the whole process of visual perception, we have to consider electrochemical activity of that system.

The Electrochemical Basis of Perception

Vision and all other perceptual processes are electrochemical in nature. When receptors in the perceptual systems are stimulated, the information is coded and sent to the brain for interpretation and further analysis. Using this basic information about electrochemical stimulation, researchers are working on a visual prosthesis—a device to help the blind see—that bypasses the eyes and directly stimulates the visual cortex (Schmidt et al., 1996). Many of these efforts focus on electrode arrays implanted on or under the retina, around the optic nerve, and on or in the visual cortex (Sommerhalder et al., 2003). The most promising results, however, have come from researchers focusing on developing an interface that can convey signals directly from a device mounted on a pair of glasses to the visual cortex. This device would act as if it were an "eye" and would be linked to the brain. Signals would stimulate selected electrodes in the visual cortex to produce spots of light, called *phosphenes*. The researchers hope that the resulting neural representation will match the shape of an object in the environment (DeMarco et al., 1999). Such a device could benefit millions of people who are blind or suffer severe visual impairment.

Receptive Fields

Scientists in a wide range of related fields have carried out research on the organization of the brain's coding of visual signals for decades. In 1932, Von Senden reported case histories of people who were born with cataracts (which cloud vision) and had them removed in adulthood. These individuals, seeing clearly for the first time as adults, experienced several problems. For example, they were unable to recognize simple forms presented in an unfamiliar color or context.

Receptive fields ∎
Areas of the retina that, when stimulated, produce a change in the firing of cells in the visual system.

Current knowledge about how the brain processes electrochemical signals comes from studies of single cells and of receptive fields. *Receptive fields* are areas of the retina that, when stimulated, produce a change in the firing of cells in the visual system. For example, specific cells in the retina will fire, or become active, in response to a vertical line but not to a horizontal line. Many perceptual psychologists refer to these stimulated visual system cells as *feature detectors*. David Hubel and Torsten Wiesel (1962, 2000) found receptive fields that are sensitive to features of a stimulus line such as its position, length, movement, color, and intensity (see **Figure 6.9**). Hubel and Wiesel characterized feature detectors as simple, complex, or hypercomplex cells. *Simple cells* respond to the shape and size of lights that stimulate the receptive field. *Complex cells* respond most vigorously to the movement of light in one direction (e.g., W. R. Taylor et al., 2000). *Hypercomplex cells* are the most specific; they respond only to a line of a specific length and orientation that moves in a particular direction (e.g., J. S. Anderson et al., 2000; Blakemore & Campbell, 2000).

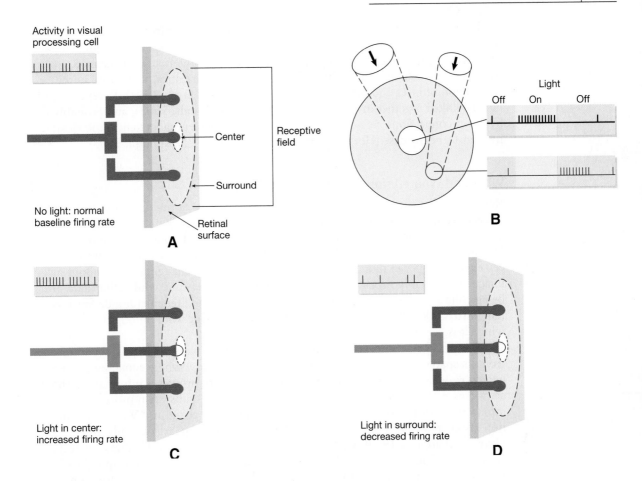

Figure 6.9
Receptive Fields
Hubel and Wiesel (1962) found that receptive fields in the retina are often circular, with a center-surround arrangement (A). Light striking the center of the field produces the opposite result of light striking the surround (B). Light hitting the center produces increased firing in the visual cell (C), and light hitting the surround produces decreased firing (D).

From Hubel and Wiesel's point of view, electrochemical coding becomes increasingly more complex as information proceeds through the visual system (Anderson et al., 2000; Sonnenborg, Andersen, & Arendt-Nielson, 2000). Hubel and Wiesel's work earned them a Nobel Prize in 1981 and has been supported and extended by other noted researchers (e.g., Hinkle & Connor, 2002).

Scientists now know that receptive fields also help link visual perception of space to body movements—as when Jackie Chan judges just the right time to leap from a helicopter to a floating barge, or when you see a ball and then slide to catch it (Peper et al., 1994). Receptive fields are associated not only with every area of the visual cortex but with some nonvisual areas of the brain as well (Hurlbert, 2003; Polonsky et al., 2000); for example, receptive fields stimulate cells in the parietal cortex, which is adjacent to the visual cortex and is associated with the control of movement (Corbetta & Vereijken, 1999). Not only do receptive fields help you recognize vertical and horizontal lines and balls flying through the air (Oelveczky, Baccus, & Meister, 2003; Zhang et al., 2003), they also seem to be critically involved in the recognition of faces and other common objects (Allison et al., 1994). Receptive fields may be linked together in complex ways (Gawne & Woods, 2003), and probably not by direct connections between individual cells—the perceptual system is too flexible for that to be the case (Heeger, 1999; Lee, 2002; Sato & Nakamura, 2003).

What and Where Information

Remember that the task of perception is difficult; a face, a building, a flower may all be seen from different angles and distances, and these can change from moment to moment. Yet an image of the president from any view still looks like the president. Herein lies a central problem for perception researchers: How does the brain perceive constancy even though sensory input is constantly changing? Data about an image are probably kept in a storage location for a brief time while other data are being collected, and then all the data are integrated (e.g., Tenenbaum, de Silva, & Langford, 2000). Part of these data is information about what an object is and where it is.

The visual system processes an object's form and color (what it is) separately from its spatial location (where it is). A person can know where something is but not know what it is. In general, the "what" subsystem processes information about attributes such as size, color, and texture. The "where" subsystem processes spatial information, or information about motion, depth, and position. "What" information affects our ability to make "where" discriminations (Carlson-Radvansky, Covey, & Lattanzi, 1999). Furthermore, some neurons seem to be able to detect either "what" information or "where" information; others seem to respond to both what an object is and where it is. Kilgard and Merzenich (1998) have found high degrees of "what" and "where" specificity for cells in the prefrontal cortex and suggest that these cells may hold the key to how we get around in the world, by linking objects (what) to places (where), as in following directions that rely on landmarks such as "the drugstore at the corner of 2nd and Main" (Rybak et al., 1998).

Research on electrochemical changes in the visual system shows that the brain simultaneously processes many components of an image—what it is, where it is, when it is perceived, colors, movement, and so on (Deco & Schürmann, 2000). Such simultaneous and coordinated processing of information in multiple locations in the brain is referred to as *parallel processing;* it can be contrasted to *serial processing,* which occurs in a step-by-step, linear fashion. Parallel processing allows for fast recognition of complexities in the world; it also explains why brain-damaged individuals can recognize some elements of a scene and not others. And it helps explain why people with reading disabilities can be intelligent and astute, able to play the piano and draw, but unable to make sounds correspond to letters. The representation and interpretation of the world happen in multiple brain locations, and some of those locations may not be operating at peak efficiency in people with such disabilities (Frey & Hinton, 1999; Kreiman, Koch, & Fried, 2000).

Gender Differences—An Evolutionary Perspective

Males and females are more alike than different in most visual abilities. But males have an edge when it comes to spatial abilities—tasks that require the perception of a relationship of parts to a whole, such as mental rotation of three-dimensional objects and perhaps map reading and navigating mazes (McBurney et al., 1997). When it comes to seeing and remembering where something is, females excel. And there are some specific other differences; for example, research shows that females were more precise when listening with the left ear, while males did better with the right (Lewald, 2004). Early researchers thought that some of these gender differences might have emerged because men were exposed to and trained in map reading and other tasks—a strong environmental point of view. But evolutionary researchers have asserted that as human beings evolved into hunter-gatherers, men predominately hunted while women foraged. Over time and through the process of natural selection, these hunter-gatherer activities fostered spatial skills (hunting) in men and spatial remembering skills (gathering) in women (Silverman et al., 2000).

These differences may have implications for everyday life today. For example, women and men tend to use different strategies to find their way around. Men's strategies rely more on geography and directions, whereas women use landmarks in navigation (Schmitz, 1999). After studying routes on a map, females tend to give directions that feature landmarks and left/right turns, whereas males include more cardinal information (north, south, east, west) and distance information (MacFadden, Elias, & Saucier, 2003). Men's use of geography and directions may be related to their proficiency in spatial orientation. The results from some studies show that men are more confident and learn to find their way around an unfamiliar place faster than women do (Schmitz, 1999; Silverman et al., 2000), but other studies indicate that, despite the difference in strategies, women and men do equally well in navigating the world (Gwinn et al., 2003; Malinowski, 2001). Overall, support for gender differences based on evolutionary theory is not clear, although clearly some differences exist in how men and women perceive the world. Some of that perception depends on how we scan the world for changes in the environment, and we can see that in a person's eye movements.

Eye Movements

Your eyes are constantly in motion. They search for familiar faces in a crowded classroom, scan the headlines on a page in a newspaper, or follow a baseball hit high into right field for a home run. You notice when someone is eyeing something over your shoulder or gazing at a spot on the top of your head. Research on eye movements reveals what people are looking at, how long they look, and perhaps where they will look next. This research can reveal a great deal about cognitive processes in general, and about reading, language, and memory in particular (Radach & Kennedy, 2004). It also helps psychologists understand the link between visual and auditory processing and sentence production (Griffin & Bock, 2000) and the cause of some problems such as reading disabilities. Zangwill and Blakemore (1972) studied the eye movements of a man who had difficulty reading. They found

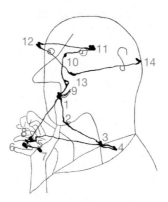

Saccades [sack-ADZ] ■
Rapid voluntary movements of the eyes.

that he was moving his eyes from right to left across the page, rather than in the usual left-to-right direction. Eye movements also depend on the context in which they are measured. The eye movements of a reader are different from those of someone keyboarding text, even when both are examining the same material. The keyboarder is processing the text merely in order to transcribe it, while the reader is trying to absorb its meaning (Inhoff, Starr, & Shindler, 2000). When researchers study eye movements, they work from the bottom up, from the physiology and nature of the movements to the functions they perform (Schiller, 1998).

Saccades are rapid voluntary movements of the eyes that you make when you are reading, driving, or looking for an object. They are the most common type of eye movement—in fact, your eyes make at least 100,000 saccades per day, at a rate of up to 4 or 5 saccades each second. Each movement of the eye takes only about 20 to 50 milliseconds, but there is a delay of about 200 to 250 milliseconds before the next movement can be made. During this delay, the eye fixates on some part of the visual field. (See **Figure 6.10**.) People use eye *fixations* to form representations of the visual world, probably by integrating successive glances into memory. This integration requires that observers exert careful, systematic control over eye movements and pay attention to key elements of a visual scene (Rayner, Reichle, & Pollatsek, 2000; Rayner et al., 2003).

People use eye movements to form images of the world, but what makes those images even more complex is that they are typically in color.

Color Vision

Think of all the different shades of blue there are—navy blue, sky blue, baby blue, royal blue, turquoise, aqua, to name a few. If you're like most people, you have no trouble discriminating among a wide range of colors. Color depends on the wavelengths of the visible light that stimulates the photoreceptors. Color has three perceptual, or psychological, dimensions: hue, brightness, and saturation. These dimensions correspond to three physical properties of light: wavelength, intensity, and purity.

When people speak of the color of an object, they are referring to its *hue*—whether the light reflected from the object looks red, blue, orange, or some other

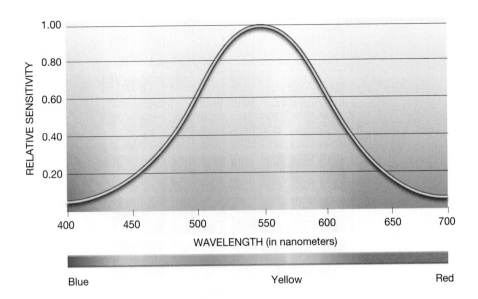

Figure 6.11
Spectral Sensitivity Curve
The curve in the graph is a *spectral sensitivity curve*. It illustrates that the average observer in daylight is most sensitive to light with a wavelength of about 550 nanometers. Thus, the normal human eye is more sensitive to yellow light than to red or blue.

color. **Hue** is a psychological term, because objects themselves do not possess color. Rather, a person's perception of color is determined by how the eyes and the brain sense and interpret the reflected light of various wavelengths. In the visible spectrum, a different hue is associated with each range of wavelengths. Light with a wavelength of 400–450 nanometers looks blue, light with a wavelength of 700 nanometers looks red, and so on.

The second psychological dimension of color is *brightness*—how light or dark the hue of an object appears. Brightness is determined by three variables: (1) the greater the intensity of reflected light, the brighter the object; (2) the longer the wavelength of reflected light, the less bright the object; and (3) the nearer the wavelength of reflected light to the range 500–600 nanometers, the more sensitive the photoreceptors are to it (see **Figure 6.11**). This is why school buses are often painted yellow—it makes them more visible to motorists.

The third psychological dimension of color is *saturation*, or *purity*—the depth and richness of the hue, determined by the homogeneity of the wavelengths of the reflected light. Few objects reflect light that is totally pure. Usually objects reflect a mixture of wavelengths. Nearly pure saturated light is made up of a narrow range of wavelengths, and thus is perceived as an intense color. A saturated red light with no blue, yellow, or white in it, for example, appears as a very intense red. Unsaturated colors are produced by a wider band of wavelengths. Unsaturated red light can appear to be light pink, dark red, or rusty brown, because its wider range of wavelengths makes it less pure (see **Figure 6.12**).

Hue ▪ The psychological property referred to as "color," determined by the wavelengths of reflected light.

Brightness ▪ The lightness or darkness of a hue, determined in large part by the intensity of reflected light.

Saturation ▪ The depth and richness of a hue, determined by the homogeneity of the wavelengths of the reflected light; also known as purity.

Theories of Color Vision

How does the brain code and process color? Two 19th-century scientists, Thomas Young and Hermann von Helmholtz, working independently, proposed that

Figure 6.12
Hue,
Brightness, and
Saturation
These colors have the same dominant wavelength (or hue) but differing saturation and brightness.

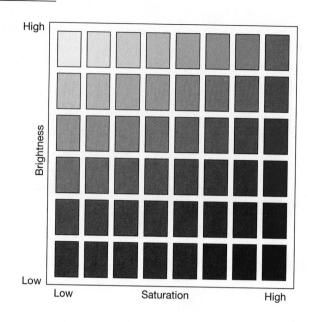

Trichromatic [try-kroe-MAT-ick] theory ■
Theory that proposed that different types of cones provide the basis for color coding in the visual system and that all colors can be made by mixing three basic colors (red, green, and blue); also known as the Young-Helmholtz theory.

different types of cones provide the basis for color coding in the visual system. *Color coding* is the ability to discriminate among colors on the basis of differences in the wavelength of light. According to the **trichromatic theory**, or the *Young-Helmholtz theory*, all colors are made by mixing three basic colors—red, green, and blue. (*Trichromatic* means "having three colors"—*tri*, "three," and *chroma*, "color.") All cone cells in the retina are assumed to respond to all wavelengths of light; but there are three types of cones that are especially responsive to red, green, or blue wavelengths, respectively (see **Figure 6.13**). The combined neural output of

Figure 6.13
Three Types of Cones
Each of the three types of cones in the retina has peak sensitivity in a different area of the visible spectrum. That is, cones are more responsive to some wave-lengths of light than to others. (MacNichol, 1964)

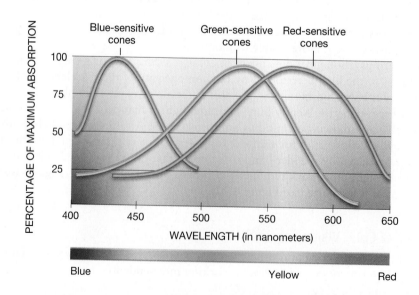

the red-sensitive, green-sensitive, and blue-sensitive cones provides the information that enables a person to distinguish colors. If the neural output from one type of cone is sufficiently greater than that from the others, that type of color receptor will have a stronger influence on a person's perception of a color. Because each person's neurons are unique, it is likely that each of us sees colors somewhat differently.

Unfortunately, the trichromatic theory does not account for some specific visual phenomena. It does not explain why some colors look more vivid when placed next to other colors (color contrast). It does not explain why people asked to name the basic colors nearly always name more than three. Further, the trichromatic theory does not do a good job of explaining aspects of *color blindness*—the inability to perceive different hues (described below). For example, many people with color blindness cannot successfully discriminate colors in two areas of the visual spectrum. In 1887, to address some of the problems left unsolved by the trichromatic theory, Ewald Herring proposed another theory of color vision—the *opponent-process theory*. This theory assumes that there are six basic colors to which people respond and three types of paired color receptors: red–green, blue–yellow, and black–white. Every receptor fires in response to all wavelengths of light; but in each pair of receptors, one responds more strongly to one wavelength. Frequent firing in response to red light, for example, is accompanied by slower firing in response to green light. Opponent-process theory explains color contrast and color blindness better than the trichromatic theory does.

Both the trichromatic theory and the opponent-process theory have received research support (e.g., Hurvich & Jameson, 1974). Physiological studies of the retina do show three classes of cones. Thus, the trichromatic theory seems to describe accurately the color coding at the retina (Marks, Dobell, & MacNichol, 1964). Support for the opponent-process theory comes from microelectrode studies of the lateral geniculate nucleus in monkeys. Retinal ganglion cells transmit information to the visual cortex through the lateral geniculate nucleus. Cells in this nucleus respond differently to various wavelengths. When the eye is stimulated with light of a wavelength between 400 and 500 nanometers, some cells in the lateral geniculate nucleus decrease their rate of firing. If the eye is stimulated with light of a longer wavelength, these cells' firing rate increases (DeValois & Jacobs, 1968). This change is predicted by the opponent-process theory. Exactly how color information is transferred from the retina to the lateral geniculate nucleus remains to be discovered (Engel, 1999).

Color blindness ■ The inability to perceive different hues.

Opponent-process theory ■ Theory, proposed by Herring, that there are six basic colors and color is coded by varying responses of three types of paired receptors: red–green, blue–yellow, and white–black.

Color Blindness

In 1794, John Dalton, formulator of the atomic theory of matter, believed that he had figured out why he couldn't distinguish his red stockings from his green ones. He reasoned that something blue in his eyeball absorbed red light and prevented him from seeing red. Although Dalton was the first to try to describe color blindness scientifically, he was not the first—or the last—person to suffer from it. In fact, about 30 million Americans have some type of color perception problem (Loop et al., 2003; Neitz & Neitz, 2001).

Trichromats [TRY-kroe-MATZ] ■ People who can perceive all three basic colors and thus can distinguish any hue.

Monochromats [MON-o-kroe-MATZ] ■ People who cannot perceive any color, usually because their retinas lack cones.

Dichromats [DIE-kroe-MATZ] ■ People who can distinguish only two of the three basic colors.

Most human beings have normal color vision and can distinguish among about 100 different hues; they are considered trichromats. *Trichromats* are people who can perceive all three basic colors and thus can distinguish any hue. A very few people (less than 1%) do not see any color. These people, known as *monochromats*, are totally color-blind and cannot discriminate among light of different wavelengths, often because they lack cones in their retinas (Boynton, 1988). What does the world look like to a person who is a monochromat? Such a person sees all the colors in a range of the electromagnetic spectrum as similar. Fortunately, most people with color vision deficiencies (about 8% of men and 1% of women) are only partially color-blind (Nathans, 1989). *Dichromats* are people who can distinguish only two of the three basic colors; they usually have difficulty distinguishing between red and green. About 2% of men cannot discriminate between red and green (Loop et al., 2003; Neitz & Neitz, 2001; Wyszecki & Stiles, 1967).

The role of genetics in color blindness is not completely clear, but this perceptual problem is transmitted genetically from mothers to their male offspring. The fact that more men than women are color-blind is due to the way genetic information is coded and passed from one generation to the next. Color blindness results from inherited alterations in the genes that are responsible for cone pigments; these genes are located on the X chromosome. Since girls have two X chromosomes and boys have only one, a girl will be color-deficient only if she inherits the defective gene from both parents. Boys who inherit an X chromosome with a defective gene get the X chromosome from their mother and will have deficient color vision.

When the brain processes information on color, position, movement, and size, we see form and substance.

How Do We Perceive Form and Substance?

Perception is a creative process; the reality is that we create our visual world. Many perceptual experiences depend on past events as well as current stimulation. Integrating previous experiences with new events makes perceptual encounters more meaningful. Sometimes those previous experiences only allow us to estimate what a particular stimulus is or might be. For example, only through experience do children learn that an object stays the same size and shape when it is moved farther away from them. Let's consider a range of visual perceptual phenomena that rely heavily on the integration of past and current experiences.

Perception of Form: Constancy

If a friend is wearing dark glasses that conceal much of her face, you will probably still recognize her. Similarly, impressionist artists count on people's ability to infer a complete scene from dots or daubs of paint on canvas, and cartoonists use exaggerated features to portray well-known people. Perception of form involves the interpretation of stimuli conveying information about size, shape, and depth to create a unified image. Two important aspects of form perception are recognizing forms that appear to have changed size or shape and recognizing forms at a distance.

Size Constancy

People can generally judge the size of an object, even if the size of its image on the retina changes. For example, you can estimate the height of a 6-foot man who is standing 50 feet away, casting a small image on the retina; you can also estimate his height from only 5 feet away, when he casts a much larger image on the retina. *Size constancy* is the ability of the visual perceptual system to recognize that an object remains constant in size regardless of its distance from the observer or the size of its image on the retina. Infants develop size constancy by the age of 6 months and probably as early as 4 months.

Three variables affect the perception of size constancy: (1) previous experience with the true size of an object, (2) the distance between the object and the person, and (3) the presence of surrounding objects. As an object moves farther away, the size of its image on the retina decreases and its perceived distance from the viewer increases (see **Figure 6.14**).

Size constancy ■ Ability of the visual perceptual system to recognize that an object remains constant in size regardless of its distance from the observer or the size of its image on the retina.

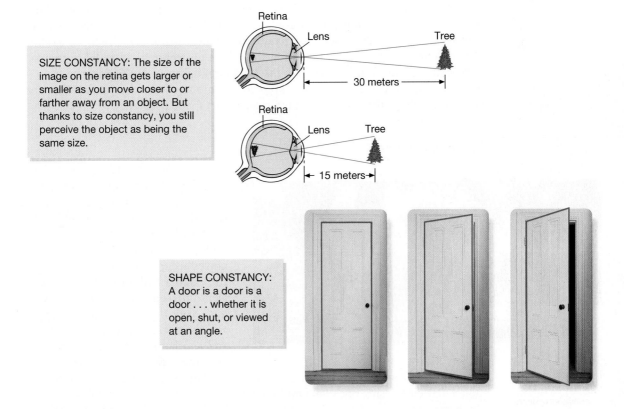

SIZE CONSTANCY: The size of the image on the retina gets larger or smaller as you move closer to or farther away from an object. But thanks to size constancy, you still perceive the object as being the same size.

SHAPE CONSTANCY: A door is a door is a door . . . whether it is open, shut, or viewed at an angle.

Figure 6.14

Perceptual Constancies

Size constancy is the perceptual system's ability to recognize that an object remains the same size regardless of its distance from an observer or the size of its image on the retina.

Shape constancy is the perceptual system's ability to recognize a shape despite changes in the angle or position from which it is viewed.

These two effects always work together. Moreover, as an object moves away, its perceived size does not change in relation to that of objects around it. This is why knowing the size of surrounding objects helps people determine a perceived object's distance from them as well as its actual size. Hollywood special effects artists have used the brain's tendency to judge an object's size by comparing it with surrounding objects to convince moviegoers that a 6-inch clay model of an ape is the giant King Kong.

Shape Constancy

Another important aspect of form perception is *shape constancy*—the ability of the visual perceptual system to recognize a shape despite changes in its orientation or the angle from which it is viewed (see **Figure 6.14***). For example, even though you usually see trees standing perpendicular to the ground, you can recognize a tree that has been chopped down and is lying in a horizontal position. Similarly, an ice cream cone looks triangular when you view it from the side; yet you perceive it as an ice cream cone even when you view it from above, where it appears more circular than triangular. But shape constancy doesn't always hold up; in some instances, distance makes a difference. When we view paintings in which features are reduced to small squares—that is, the squares taken together make up features—our ability to perceive shapes (for example, eyes, mouths, or doors) depends on the distance from which we view them (Pelli, 1999). Psychologists are not sure why yet, but this phenomenon violates the widely accepted rules about shape constancy.

Depth Perception

Zen landscape artists apply the principles of depth perception when they create seemingly expansive, rugged gardens on small plots of land.

For centuries, Zen landscape artists have used the principles of depth perception to create seemingly expansive, rugged gardens out of tiny plots of land. Although a Zen landscape can fool the eye, you normally judge distances accurately when you drive a car, catch a ball, or take a picture. Depth perception allows you to estimate your distance from an object and the distance between that object and another one. Closely associated with these two abilities is the ability to see in three dimensions—that is, to perceive height, width, and depth. Both monocular cues (using one eye) and binocular cues (using two eyes) are used in depth perception. Binocular cues predominate at close distances, and monocular cues are used for distant scenes and two-dimensional fields of view, such as paintings. These cues are operative even in infants (Sen, Yonas, & Knill, 2001). Because the visual system is still plastic (modifiable) early in life, where and how information on depth perception is coded depends on an infant's experiences. Research shows that binocular depth information is coded at different places in the brain than is typical if a child is deprived of depth experiences (Berardi et al., 2003; Trachtenberg, Trepel, & Stryker, 2000).

Monocular Depth Cues

Depth cues that do not depend on the use of both eyes are ***monocular depth cues*** (see **Figure 6.15** on p. 206). Two important monocular depth cues arise from the effects of motion on perception. The first cue, *motion parallax*, occurs when a moving observer stares at a fixed point. The objects behind that point appear to move in the same direction as the observer; the objects in front of the point appear to move in the opposite direction. So, if you stare at a fence while riding in a moving car, the trees behind the fence seem to move in the same direction as the car (forward) and the bushes in front of the fence seem to move in the opposite direction (backward). Motion parallax also affects the speed at which objects appear to move. Objects at a greater distance from the moving observer appear to move more slowly than objects that are closer. The second monocular depth cue derived from movement is the *kinetic depth effect*. Objects that look flat when stationary appear to be three-dimensional when set in motion. When two-dimensional projections—such as images of squares or rods shown on a computer screen—are rotated, they appear to have three dimensions.

Monocular [mah-NAHK-you-ler] depth cues ■ Cues for depth perception that do not depend on the use of both eyes.

Other monocular depth cues arise from the stimulus itself; these are often seen in photographs and paintings. For example, because of the depth cue of *linear perspective*, larger or taller objects are usually perceived to be closer than smaller ones, particularly in relation to surrounding objects. In addition, because distant objects appear to be closer together than nearer objects, a painter shows distance by making parallel lines converge as they recede. Another monocular cue for depth is *interposition*. When one object blocks out part of another, the first appears to be closer. A third monocular depth cue is *texture gradient;* surfaces that have little texture or detail seem to be in the distance. Artists often use the cue of *shading*, either highlighting or shadowing, to convey depth. Highlighted (lighter) objects appear close; shadowed (darker) objects appear to be farther away. In addition, the

Mountains in the distance often look blue because of a monocular depth cue known as atmospheric perspective. And Michelangelo's figures seem to float off the ceiling of the Sistine Chapel because he used color so effectively to portray depth.

Figure 6.15
Depth
Perception
The ability to see in
three dimensions—
to perceive height,
width, and depth—
depends on both
monocular and
binocular cues.

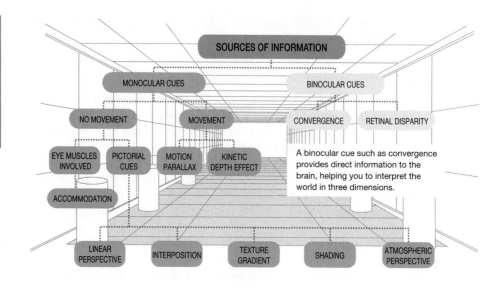

SOURCES OF INFORMATION

MONOCULAR CUES

BINOCULAR CUES

NO MOVEMENT

MOVEMENT

CONVERGENCE

RETINAL DISPARITY

EYE MUSCLES INVOLVED

PICTORIAL CUES

MOTION PARALLAX

KINETIC DEPTH EFFECT

A binocular cue such as convergence provides direct information to the brain, helping you to interpret the world in three dimensions.

ACCOMMODATION

LINEAR PERSPECTIVE

INTERPOSITION

TEXTURE GRADIENT

SHADING

ATMOSPHERIC PERSPECTIVE

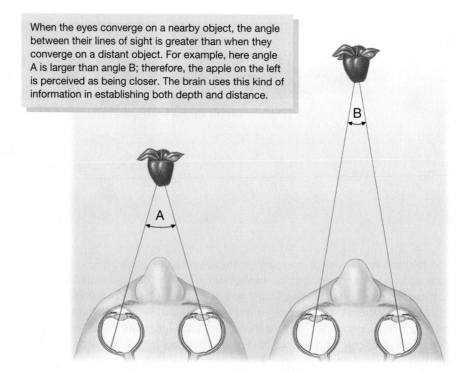

When the eyes converge on a nearby object, the angle between their lines of sight is greater than when they converge on a distant object. For example, here angle A is larger than angle B; therefore, the apple on the left is perceived as being closer. The brain uses this kind of information in establishing both depth and distance.

B

A

perceptual system picks up other information from shading, including the curvature of surfaces (Cavanagh & Leclerc, 1989). Still another monocular depth cue is *atmospheric perspective*, which relates to the wavelengths of reflected light. Distant mountains often look blue because long (red) wavelengths are scattered more as they pass through the air, allowing more short (blue) wavelengths to reach our eyes. Leonardo da Vinci used this phenomenon in his paintings; he even developed an equation for how much blue pigment to mix with the normal color for an object to make the object appear as far away as he wished. Similarly, Michelangelo's figures seem to float off the ceiling of the Sistine Chapel because he used color so effectively to portray depth.

Another monocular depth cue that is not derived from the stimulus is accommodation. *Accommodation* is the change in the shape of the lens of the eye that enables the observer to keep an object in focus on the retina when the object is moved or when the observer focuses on an object at a different distance. Muscles attached to the lens control this change and provide information about the shape of the lens (and thus the distance of the object from the viewer) to the brain. Accommodation cues are provided by each eye separately.

Accommodation ■ The change in the shape of the lens of the eye that enables the observer to keep an object in focus on the retina when the object is moved or when the observer focuses on an object at a different distance.

Binocular Depth Cues

Most people, even infants, also use *binocular depth cues*—cues for depth perception that require the use of both eyes. One important binocular depth cue is *retinal disparity*, which is the slight difference between the visual images projected on the two retinas. Retinal disparity occurs because the eyes are physically separated (by the bridge of the nose), which causes them to see an object from slightly different angles. To see how retinal disparity works, hold a finger up in front of your face and look at some object across the room first with one eye and then with the other eye; your finger will appear in different positions relative to the object. The closer objects are to the eyes, the farther apart their images on the retinas will be—and the greater the retinal disparity. Viewing objects at a great distance produces little retinal disparity.

Another binocular depth cue is convergence. *Convergence* is the turning of the eyes inward, toward each other, in order to keep visual stimulation at corresponding points on the retinas as an object moves closer to the observer. Like accommodation, convergence is controlled by eye muscles that convey information to the brain. When a person looks at objects beyond 20 or 30 feet away, the eyes are aimed pretty much in parallel, and the effect of convergence diminishes. Of course, from time to time our brain misperceives visual information, creating an illusion.

Binocular depth cues ■ Cues for depth perception that require the use of both eyes.

Retinal disparity ■ The slight difference between the visual images projected on the two retinas.

Convergence ■ The movement of the eyes inward, toward each other, to keep visual stimulation at corresponding points on the retinas as an object moves closer to the observer.

Illusions

No doubt you've had the experience of seeing what looks like water ahead on the road, only to find it has disappeared when you drive by that point. You most likely also have seen railroad tracks that appear to converge in the distance. When normal visual perceptions seem to break down, you experience an *optical illusion*. An

Figure 6.16
Four Well-Known Illusions
In the Müller-Lyer and Ponzo illusions, lines of equal length appear to differ in length. The photos with the Müller-Lyer illusion show how the lines can be viewed as corners that are projecting toward or receding away from the viewer. In the Zollner illusion, the short lines make the longer ones seem not parallel, even though they are. In the Wundt illusion, the two horizontal lines are parallel, even though they appear bent.

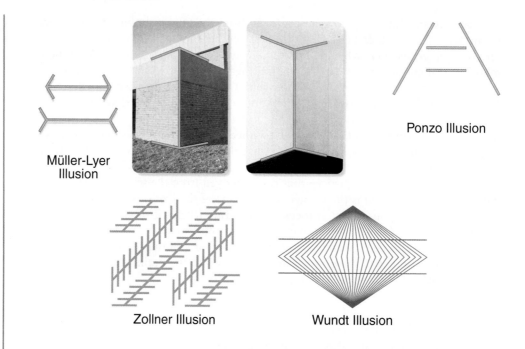

Müller-Lyer Illusion

Ponzo Illusion

Zollner Illusion

Wundt Illusion

Illusion ■ A perception of a physical stimulus that differs from measurable reality or from what is commonly expected.

illusion is a perception of a physical stimulus that differs from measurable reality or from what is commonly expected.

One fairly well-known illusion is the *Müller-Lyer illusion*, in which two lines of equal length with arrows on the ends appear to be of different lengths. A similar illusion is the *Ponzo illusion* (sometimes called the *railroad illusion*), in which two horizontal lines of the same length, bracketed by slanted lines, appear to be of different lengths. (See **Figure 6.16** for examples of these and other illusions.) The moon illusion is a *natural illusion*. Although the actual size of the moon and the size of its image on the retina do not change, the moon appears about 30% larger when it is near the horizon than when it is overhead. The moon illusion is quite striking—in just a few minutes, the moon appears to change from quite large to quite small. The moon illusion can even be seen in photographs and paintings (Suzuki, 1998).

Why are our eyes and brains fooled by visual illusions? No completely satisfactory explanations have been found. Recent theories account for these illusions in terms of the backgrounds against which the objects are seen. These explanations assume that the observer has had previous experiences with a particular stimulus and has well-developed perceptual constancies. For example, the moon illusion is explained by the fact that, when seen overhead, the moon is against a featureless background, whereas when it is near the horizon, other objects are close to it in the observer's field of vision. Objects in the landscape provide cues about distance that change the observer's perception of the size of the moon (Baird, Wagner, & Fuld, 1990; Restle, 1970). To see how the moon illusion depends on landscape cues, try this: When the moon is at the horizon, bend over and look at it from between your legs. Since that position screens out some of the landscape cues, the magnitude of the illusion is reduced.

The Ponzo illusion is similarly accounted for by the linear perspective cue provided by the slanted background lines. The Müller-Lyer illusion occurs because of the angles of the short lines attached to the ends of the longer lines. Short lines angled like arrow tails are often interpreted as far corners—corners receding away from the observer. Short lines angled like arrow heads are commonly interpreted as corners projecting toward the observer. Therefore, lines with arrow tails on them appear longer because the observer judges their length in a context of distance.

Some researchers (Prinzmetal & Beck, 2001) assert that the perception of body orientation is more influenced by visual cues than by cues resulting from the force of gravity. These researchers predicted that the strength of some visual illusions would increase when observers were tilted 30°. Perception of the Zollner and Ponzo illusions substantially increased when observers were tilted. In contrast, the Müller-Lyer illusion and another size constancy illusion, which are not related to orientation perception, were not affected by body orientation.

These are not the only ways of explaining illusions. Some researchers assert that the moon appears to be a different size at the horizon than it is overhead because people judge its size the same way they judge that of other moving objects that pass through space. Because the moon does not get any closer, they assume it is moving away. Objects that move away get smaller; hence, the illusion of a change in the size of the moon (Reed, 1984). This explanation focuses on constancies but also takes account of movement and space.

Cross-Cultural Research on Illusions

Each person brings a lifetime of experiences to his or her perceptions. This becomes especially clear from research conducted cross-culturally. Cross-cultural research on illusions, for example, shows that the Müller-Lyer and Ponzo illusions are perceived differently in different cultures. Leibowitz (1971) conducted a series of studies on the Ponzo illusion, using both American participants and participants from Guam, where there are no railroads and perspective cues are far less prevalent than in the United States. Leibowitz presented the Ponzo illusion to participants in simple line drawings and also in photographs. He found that the illusion was more pronounced for the American participants as he added more pictorial cues. The participants from Guam showed few differences when more pictorial cues were added. There were other differences between the groups; for example, the participants from Guam viewed depth differently than did their American counterparts. People from different cultures view the world in dissimilar ways (Pani & Parida, 2000).

Other illusions have been investigated with different cultural groups. For example, Pedersen and Wheeler (1983) compared the reactions of two groups of Navajos to the Müller-Lyer illusion. One group lived in rectangular houses; these participants had extensive experience with corners, angles, and oblique lines. The other group lived in traditional Navajo round houses, and their early experiences included far fewer encounters with angles. The researchers found that those who lived in angular houses were more susceptible to the Müller-Lyer illusion, which depends on angles. Some researchers say such illusions depend on the *carpenter effect*, because in Western cultures carpenters use straight lines and angles to build houses.

Cross-cultural research is exciting and illuminating, although still limited in extent. For psychologists to develop truly comprehensive theories of perception, they must incorporate cross-cultural differences into their research.

Prosopagnosia: The Inability to Recognize Faces

Jennifer Lopez, Leonardo DeCaprio, and Denzel Washington all have distinctive faces. Faces define and differentiate people. Whether a person's eyes, teeth, and hair represent facial "landmarks" is unclear, but the perception of faces is a unique process. We all engage in the perceptual task of discerning, analyzing, remembering, and recognizing faces. Even in the first weeks of life, newborns are able to distinguish faces from other objects, and they quickly develop the ability to recognize their principal caregiver's face (Mondloch et al., 1999).

Research on brain structure shows that there is something about face perception that distinguishes it from other kinds of perception. Some interesting evidence comes from studies of *agnosia*. People with **agnosia** have normal, intact perceptual systems for detecting color, shape, and motion, and they have no verbal, memory, or intellectual impairment. And yet they are unable to recognize things the way they should be able to. Agnosia usually occurs because of injury to the brain from an accident, or perhaps from a stroke. A patient who has agnosia can see stimuli but cannot name them. When presented with an object—a cup or a candle, for example—a person with object agnosia is unable to name the object. Some visual agnosias are very specific—for example, color agnosia or movement agnosia.

Agnosia ■ An inability to recognize a sensory stimulus that should be recognizable, despite having normal, intact perceptual systems for detecting color, shape, and motion and no verbal, memory, or intellectual impairments.

Is it possible that deficiencies in particular regions of the brain are responsible for *prosopagnosia*—the inability to recognize faces (from the Greek words *prosopon*, "person," and *agnosia*, "ignorance")? Does the brain include a "face detector"? There are several lines of evidence supporting this notion. First, research shows that certain brain cells are activated by facial stimuli and not by other stimuli (Renault et al., 1989). Some individual cells (around the temporal lobes) have been found that respond best to faces, sometimes even to faces in a particular orientation, such as facing forward or in profile. Unfortunately, the idea of "one face, one neuron" is flawed, because we simply do not have enough neurons in our brains to ensure that every face, every object, every scene, is represented by an individual neuron. People are normally skilled at recognizing faces, but when faces are distorted, turned upside-down, or otherwise altered from the usual perspective, face recognition is far more difficult (Farah et al., 1998; McNeil & Warrington, 1993), though still possible.

Researchers study agnosia in general, and prosopagnosia in particular, because it helps them understand specific areas of the brain. But such study also leads to the conclusion that the visual system is made up of interacting and interdependent parts that create a whole visual experience. Face perception requires a holistic, interactive analysis that depends on both sides of the brain (Rumiati & Humphreys, 1997) and on the brain as a whole (Macaluso, Frith, & Driver, 2000). The whole-versus-part distinction as it relates to prosopagnosia is the focus of cutting-edge research that may ultimately help specify relationships between brain and behavior. Interestingly, the whole-versus-part perceptual issue was raised by Gestalt psychologists 75 years ago.

Gestalt Laws of Organization

Remember from Chapter 1 that Gestalt psychologists suggested that conscious experience is more than the sum of its parts. They argued that the mind organizes the elements of experience to form something unique; each individual views the world in terms of perceptual frameworks. Analyzed as a whole experience, the patterns of a person's perceptions make sense. The first Gestalt psychologists—including Max Wertheimer, Kurt Koffka, and Wolfgang Köhler—greatly influenced early theories of form perception (Koffka, 1935; Köhler, 1947; Wertheimer, 1923). These psychologists assumed (wrongly) that human perceptual processes *solely* reflect brain organization and that they could learn about the workings of the brain by studying perception (Herrmann & Bosch, 2001). Researchers now know, of course, that the relationship between brain structure and function is much more complex—perception is a process that not only represents stimuli but reflects past experiences as well (Chen, 1999; Spelke et al., 1993).

The early Gestaltists focused their perceptual studies on how people experience form and grouping. These early researchers believed people organize each complex visual field into a coherent whole rather than seeing individual, unrelated elements. That is, they believed people see groups of elements, not fragments or parts. According to this idea, called the *law of Prägnanz*, items or stimuli that can be grouped together and seen as a whole, or a form, will be seen that way; viewers see the simplest shape consistent with available information. So, for example, people tend to see the series of 16 dots in the lower left portion of **Figure 6.17** on (p. 212) as a square.

The law of Prägnanz was based on principles of organization for the perception of figures, especially contours, which help define *figure–ground relationships*. Gestalt psychologists focused on the nature of these relationships, contending that people perceive figures (the main objects of sensory attention—the foregrounds) as distinct from the grounds (the backgrounds) on which they are presented. Gestalt psychologists developed the following series of laws, the first three of which are illustrated in the upper part of **Figure 6.17**, for predicting which areas of an ambiguous pattern would be seen as the figure (foreground) and which as the ground (background):

Law of Prägnanz [PREG-nants] ■ The Gestalt notion that when items or stimuli can be grouped together and seen as a whole, they will be.

- *Law of proximity:* Elements close to one another in space or time will be perceived as groups.
- *Law of similarity:* Similar items will be perceived in groups.
- *Law of continuity:* A string of items will project the probable location of the next item.
- *Common fate principle:* Items that move or change together will be perceived as a whole.
- *Law of closure:* Parts of a figure that are not presented will be filled in by the perceptual system.

Beck (1966) conducted a well-known study that examined Gestalt principles (see the lower right part of **Figure 6.17**). However, Beck's work showed that Gestalt principles are vague: They apply whether participants choose orientation or shape to break up the figure, but they do not explain why orientation predominated in Beck's study. Apparently, not all people use the same criteria when perceiving the same figures. Nor

Figure 6.17
Gestalt Laws
Gestalt laws are the organizing principles humans use to group perceptual fragments into the coherent wholes by which they perceive the world. (Beck, 1966)

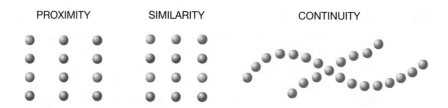

PROXIMITY   SIMILARITY   CONTINUITY

According to the Gestalt law of proximity, the circles on the left appear to be arranged in vertical columns because items that are close together tend to be perceived as a unit. According to the law of similarity, the red and blue circles in the middle appear to be arranged in horizontal rows because similar items tend to be perceived in groups. According to the law of continuity, an observer can predict where the next item should occur in the arrangement on the right because the grouping of items projects lines into space.

The law of Prägnanz: Items or stimuli that *can* be grouped together as a whole *will* be. These 16 dots are typically perceived as a square.

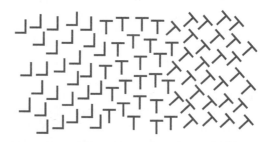

In a study asking people to divide these objects into two groups, Beck (1966) found that participants generally placed the boundary between upright and tilted *Ts* rather than between the backward *Ls* and the upright *Ts* because the latter appear more similar. Beck argued that this result supports the law of Prägnanz.

are Gestalt laws always consistent with current knowledge of brain organization—for example, when viewing a figure made up of other smaller figures, people vary a good deal as to whether they pay attention to the larger figure or the smaller ones (Han, Humphreys, & Chen, 1999; Rock & Palmer, 1990). Furthermore, the fact that cells that process "what" and "where" information are located throughout the brain shows that visual processing is multistage and complex. Nevertheless, early investigations by Gestaltists offered enough glimpses into the true nature of perception that they continue to influence perceptual psychologists, serving as springboards to further research. Some of this new research focuses on how we perceive sounds.

How Do We Perceive Sounds?

It's often said that blind people can hear better than sighted individuals—and at least on some tasks, that turns out to be true (Bavelier et al., 2000; Rosenbluth, Grossman, & Kaitz, 2000). Although our sense of sight is powerful, we rely enormously on our sense of hearing for many perceptual experiences, even more than on sight. And, although most of us take hearing for granted, the task of listening can be exceedingly complex. Consider music by a composer such as Aaron Copland—although intriguing, it can be a real challenge to listen to, because so much is going on at once and the sounds often seem dissonant. The listener must simultaneously process the sounds, rhythms, and intensities produced by more than 20 instruments playing at once. Like seeing, hearing is a complex process that involves converting physical stimuli into a psychological experience and that is affected by past experiences and cultural background.

What Is Sound?

When a tuning fork is struck or a stereo system booms out a bass note, sound waves are created and air is moved. You can place your hand in front of a stereo speaker and feel the displacement due to the sound waves when the volume rises. The movement of the air and the accompanying changes in air pressure (physical stimuli) cause a listener's eardrum to move back and forth rapidly. The movement of the eardrum triggers a series of electromechanical and electrochemical changes that the person experiences as sound. *Sound* is the perceptual, or psychological, experience that occurs when changes in air pressure affect the receptive organ for hearing. Like light waves, sound waves vary in frequency and amplitude. Sound is often thought of in terms of two psychological aspects, pitch and loudness, which are associated with the two physical attributes of frequency and amplitude.

As shown in **Figure 6.18** (on p. 214), *frequency* is the number of complete sound waves passing a point (such as the entrance to the ear canal) during a given unit of time. Within 1 second, for example, there may be 50 complete waves (50 cycles per second) or 10,000 complete waves (10,000 cycles per second). Frequency is usually measured in hertz (Hz); 1 Hz equals 1 cycle per second. Frequency determines the pitch, or *tone*, of a sound; *pitch* is the psychological experience that corresponds with the frequency of an auditory stimulus. High-pitched tones usually have high frequencies. When a piano hammer strikes a short string on the right-hand end of a piano keyboard, the string vibrates at a high frequency and the resulting sound is high in pitch; when a long string (at the left-hand end) is struck, it vibrates less frequently and the sound is low in pitch.

Amplitude, or *intensity*, is the total energy of a sound wave, which determines the loudness of the sound. High-amplitude sound waves have more energy than low-amplitude waves; they apply greater force to the ear (see **Figure 6.18** on p. 214). Amplitude is measured in *decibels*. Every increase of 20 decibels corresponds to a tenfold increase in perceived intensity. (Decibels are measured on a logarithmic scale, which is exponential, not linear; thus, increases in sound intensity of only a few decibels are quite large.) As **Figure 6.19** on page 215 shows, normal conversation has an amplitude of about 60 decibels, and sounds above 120 decibels are painfully loud.

Amplitude and frequency are not correlated. A low-frequency sound can be very loud or very soft; that is, it can have either high or low amplitude. Middle C on a piano, for example, can be played loudly or softly. The frequency (and thus the pitch) of the sound stays the same—it is still middle C; only its amplitude

Sound ■ The psychological experience that occurs when changes in air pressure stimulate the receptive organ for hearing.

Frequency ■ The number of complete sound waves passing a point per unit of time; measured in hertz (Hz), or cycles per second.

Pitch ■ The psychological experience that corresponds with the frequency of an auditory stimulus; also known as tone.

Amplitude ■ The total energy of a sound wave, which determines the loudness of the sound; also known as intensity.

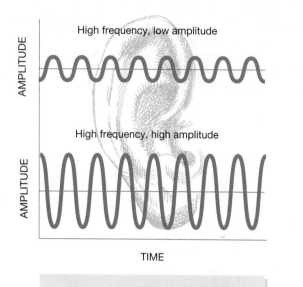

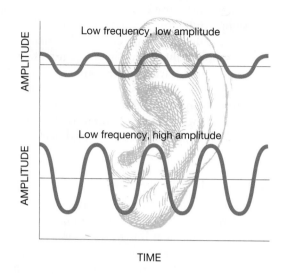

High-frequency sound waves have a large number of complete cycles per second and a high pitch; they can be of low amplitude (soft sound) or high amplitude (loud sound).

Low-frequency sound waves have a small number of complete cycles per second and a low pitch; they can be of low amplitude (soft sound) or high amplitude (loud sound).

Figure 6.18
The Frequency and Amplitude of Sound Waves
A person's perception of sound depends on the frequency and amplitude of sound waves.

(and corresponding loudness) varies. The perception of loudness depends on other factors, such as background noise and whether the listener is paying attention to the sound. Another psychological dimension, *timbre*, is the quality of a sound—the specific mixture of amplitudes and frequencies that make up the sound. People's perceptions of all these qualities depend on the physical structure of their ears.

The Structure of the Ear

The receptive organ for *audition*, or hearing, is the ear: it translates physical stimuli (sound waves) into electrical impulses that the brain can interpret. The ear has three major parts: the outer ear, the middle ear, and the inner ear (see **Figure 6.20**). The tissue on the outside of the head is part of the outer ear. The eardrum (*tympanic membrane*) is the boundary between the outer and middle ear. When sound waves enter the ear, they produce changes in pressure on the eardrum. The eardrum responds to these changes by vibrating.

The middle ear is quite small. Within it, tiny bones (*ossicles*) known as the *hammer, anvil,* and *stirrup* help convert the relatively large forces striking the

PSYCHOLOGICAL RESPONSE

EXAMPLES

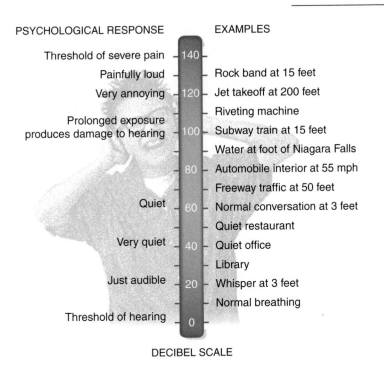

Threshold of severe pain — 140

Painfully loud — Rock band at 15 feet

Very annoying — 120 — Jet takeoff at 200 feet

Riveting machine

Prolonged exposure produces damage to hearing — 100 — Subway train at 15 feet

Water at foot of Niagara Falls

80 — Automobile interior at 55 mph

Freeway traffic at 50 feet

Quiet — 60 — Normal conversation at 3 feet

Quiet restaurant

Very quiet — 40 — Quiet office

Library

Just audible — 20 — Whisper at 3 feet

Normal breathing

Threshold of hearing — 0

DECIBEL SCALE

Figure 6.19
Psychological Responses to Various Sound Intensities
High-amplitude sound waves, such as those generated by a rock band, have greater energy than low-amplitude waves and a greater impact on the sensitive structure of the ears.

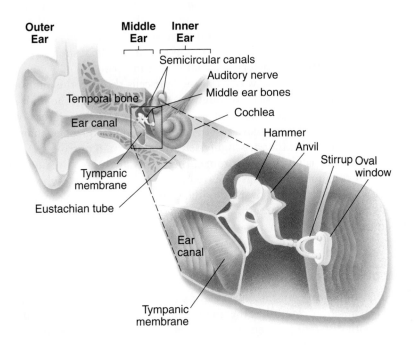

Outer Ear   **Middle Ear** **Inner Ear**

Semicircular canals

Auditory nerve

Temporal bone

Middle ear bones

Ear canal

Cochlea

Hammer

Anvil

Stirrup Oval window

Tympanic membrane

Eustachian tube

Ear canal

Tympanic membrane

Figure 6.20
The Major Structures of the Ear

Figure 6.21
The Basilar
Membrane
In this view, the
cochlea has been
unwound and cut
open to reveal the
basilar membrane,
which is covered
with thousands of
hair cells.
Oscillations caused
by sound waves
travel along the
basilar membrane,
stimulating the hair
cells.

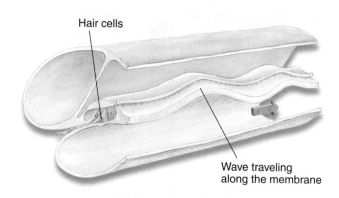

eardrum into small forces. Two small muscles are attached to the ossicles; these muscles contract involuntarily when they are exposed to intense sounds. They help protect the delicate mechanisms of the inner ear from the damaging effects of an intense sound that could overstimulate them (Borg & Counter, 1989). Ultimately, the middle ear bones stimulate the *basilar membrane*, which runs down the middle of the *cochlea*, a spiral tube in the inner ear. **Figure 6.21** depicts the basilar membrane.

In the cochlea, which is shaped like a snail's shell and comprises three chambers, sound waves of different frequencies stimulate different areas of the basilar membrane. These areas, in turn, stimulate the hair cells, which initiate the coding of the sound waves. That is, these cells are responsible for the transduction of mechanical energy into electrochemical energy—neural impulses. The hair cells are remarkably sensitive. Hudspeth (1983), for example, found that hair cells respond when they are displaced as little as 100 picometers (trillionths of a meter).

Neural impulses make their way from the hair cells through the auditory system to the brain. The impulses proceed through the auditory nerve to the midbrain and finally to the auditory cortex. Studies of single cells in the auditory areas of the brain show that some cells are more responsive to certain frequencies than to others. Katsuki (1961) found cells that are highly sensitive to certain narrow frequency ranges; if a frequency is outside their range, these cells might not fire at all. This finding is analogous to the findings reported by Hubel and Wiesel, who discovered receptive visual fields in which proper stimulation brought about dramatic changes in the firing of cells; cellular organization in the auditory system is highly structured, like that in the visual system.

Theories of Hearing

Most theories of hearing fall into two major classes: place theories and frequency theories. *Place theories* claim that the analysis of sound occurs in the basilar membrane, with different frequencies and intensities affecting different parts (places) of the membrane. Such theories assert that each sound wave causes a traveling wave on the basilar membrane, which in turn causes displacement of hair cells on the membrane. The displacement of individual hair cells triggers specific information about pitch. Think of ripples on still water: A strong stimulus like a rock thrown into the water creates a larger ripple (displacement) than does a weaker stimulus like a leaf falling onto the surface.

In contrast, *frequency theories* maintain that the analysis of pitch and intensity occurs in the brain, in the auditory area of the cortex, and that the basilar membrane merely transfers information from the ear for further processing. These theories suggest that the entire basilar membrane is stimulated and its overall rate of responding somehow provides information to the brain for analysis.

Both place theories and frequency theories have shortcomings. Neither type of theory explains all the data about pitch and loudness. For example, the hair cells do not act independently (as place theories suggest) but instead act together (as frequency theories suggest). And the rate at which hair cells fire is not fast enough to keep up with sound waves (which typically have frequencies of 1,000 to 10,000 cycles per second), as frequency theories suggest. To get around the difficulties, modern researchers have developed theories of auditory information processing that attempt to explain pitch in terms of both specific action in parts of the basilar membrane and generalized frequency analysis in the brain. Theories that seem at odds can often be combined to explain complex phenomena.

Sound Localization

How does a mother know where to turn when she hears her baby crying? Although they are not as sensitive as many animals to the direction from which a sound arrives, human beings have efficient sound-localization abilities. Researchers have learned much about these abilities by presenting sound through headsets, with one sound going to one ear and another sound to the other ear. Such experiments have revealed that two key factors influence sound localization: *interaural time differences* and *interaural intensity differences*. You have two ears, and a sound produced to the left of your head will arrive at the left ear before it arrives at the right. Thus, you have an interaural time difference. In addition, a sound produced to your left will have different intensities when it reaches the two ears. It will be perceived as slightly more intense by the left ear than the right; thus, there is an interaural intensity difference (Bernstein et al., 2001; Cook et al., 2003; Fujiki et al., 2002). These time and intensity differences are analyzed in the brain at nuclei (collections of cell bodies) that are especially sensitive to them.

Time and intensity differences are not the sole factors that determine sound localization, however. What happens when the sound source is just in front of you, and thus is equidistant from your two ears? It turns out that head and body movements help resolve the source of a sound. You rotate your head and/or move your body when you are unsure of the source of a sound. In addition, the external ear has ridges and folds that bounce sounds around just a bit, creating slight delays that help you localize sounds. Finally, visual cues and previous experiences also help you with sound localization.

Hearing Impairments

Sixteen percent of adults and more than one-third of people over age 60 have a hearing loss. In total, about 13 million people in the United States have hearing impairments, ranging from minor hearing loss to total deafness (National Institute on Deafness and Other Communication Disorders, 2004). Individuals are often discriminated against because of their hearing problems. But, although hearing loss or deafness is a real challenge, students with hearing impairments have academic outcomes that are very similar to those of students with no declared disability (Richardson & Woodley, 2001). According to some researchers, for hearing-impaired college students, the major obstacles to success are difficulties in communication and not the academic demands of their courses. The numerous causes of hearing impairments include both environmental and genetic factors, which result in varying degrees of conduction deafness, sensorineural deafness, or a combination of the two (Vahava et al., 1998).

Conduction deafness ■
Deafness resulting from interference with the transmission of sound to the inner ear.

Conduction deafness is deafness resulting from interference with the transmission of sound to the inner ear. The interference may be caused by something temporary, such as a head cold or a buildup of wax in the ear canal. Or it may be caused by something far more serious, such as hardening of the tympanic membrane, destruction of the tiny bones within the ear, or diseases that create pressure in the middle ear. If sound can somehow be transmitted past the point of the conduction problem, hearing can be improved.

Sensorineural [sen-so-ree-NEW-ruhl] deafness ■ Deafness resulting from damage to the cochlea, the auditory nerve, or auditory processing areas in the brain.

Sensorineural deafness is deafness resulting from damage to the cochlea, the auditory nerve, or auditory processing areas in the brain. The most common cause of this type of deafness is ongoing exposure to very high-intensity sound, such as that of gunshots, industrial noise, orchestras, rock bands, or jet planes. Musicians are at high risk, but listening to even moderately loud music for longer than 15 minutes a day can cause permanent hearing loss. Cochlear implants can help in some cases of sensorineural deafness.

An *audiometer*, which presents sounds of different frequencies through a headphone, is used to evaluate hearing; results are presented as an *audiogram*, which is a graph showing hearing sensitivity at selected frequencies. The audiogram of the person whose hearing is being tested is compared with that of an adult with no known hearing loss. One less technical way to assess hearing is to test a person's recognition of spoken words. In a typical test of this sort, a person listens to a tape recording of speech sounds that are standardized in terms of loudness and pitch. Performance is rated by counting the number of words the participant can repeat correctly at various intensity levels. Nonmedical personnel often administer these types of tests and then refer individuals who may have hearing problems to a physician.

You can easily see that there are many similarities in the perceptual mechanisms for hearing and vision. In both perceptual systems, physical energy is transduced into electrochemical energy, coding takes place at several locations in the brain, and impairments can affect people's abilities. The auditory system, like the visual system, is plastic and can recover functioning to some extent after an accident or other trauma, especially in young animals or humans (Klinke et al., 1999).

Which Senses Are the Least Understood?

Smell is the sense that people appreciate the least, and yet it has an enormous impact on behavior. In mere seconds, a scent can enter the nose, stimulate sensory receptors, and then further activate emotions and even memories. There are many ways to experience the world through the senses, but few offer such subtle discriminations and delights as smell and its close associate, taste. Tastes and smells evoke feelings. We become enchanted with the scent of a lover, the smell of a home cooked meal, or the taste of a gourmet dessert. Tastes and smells evoke memories of past events—Thanksgiving dinner, gnocchi during that summer in Italy, or the dentist's office. Perfume makers mingle dozens of substances to make perfumes that will evoke pleasant thoughts and feelings—and make some money!

Try the following experiment. Cut a fresh onion in half and inhale its odor while holding a piece of raw potato in your mouth. Now chew the potato. You'll most likely find that the potato tastes like an onion. This experiment demonstrates that taste and smell are closely linked. Food contains substances that act as stimuli for both these senses.

There is one taste most people have a special fondness for—sweetness. People of all ages, from babies to great-grandmothers, prefer sweet foods. But researchers know that a sweet tooth, a preference for candy, cake, ice cream, and sometimes liquor, involves a craving for more than the taste of sugar (Damak et al., 2003). People's bodies perceive the sweetness and learn that it is associated with many foods that are high in carbohydrates, which act almost as sedatives. So, your cravings for a substance—your desire to eat, drink, or smell it—are affected by a number of variables, including the chemical composition of the substance, what it ultimately does to you, and your previous experiences with it.

Taste

I remember the first time I (L.L.) was in a wine store. My father wanted some wine to serve with dinner. I was overwhelmed by the quantity of wines, and the store owner allowed me (and I was only 16) to sample a variety: Cabernet Sauvignon, Merlot, Syrah, and Pinot Noir. The Cabernet was too strong, and I found the Syrah and the Pinot Noir bland in comparison. Dad finally decided on a white wine; it was a Chardonnay, and it tasted of oak.

Taste is so complex that it is usually studied from the bottom up. Taste is a chemical sense. Food placed in the mouth is partially dissolved in saliva, which releases chemicals in the food that stimulate the *taste buds*, the primary receptors for taste stimuli (see **Figure 6.22** on p. 220). When substances contact the taste buds, you experience taste. The taste buds are found on small bumps on the tongue called *papillae* (the singular is *papilla*). Each hill-like papilla is separated from the next by a tiny trench, almost like a moat; located on the wall of this trench are the taste buds, which can be seen only under a microscope. Each taste bud (human beings have about 10,000 of them) consists of 5 to 150 *taste cells*. These cells last only about 10 to 14 days and are constantly being renewed.

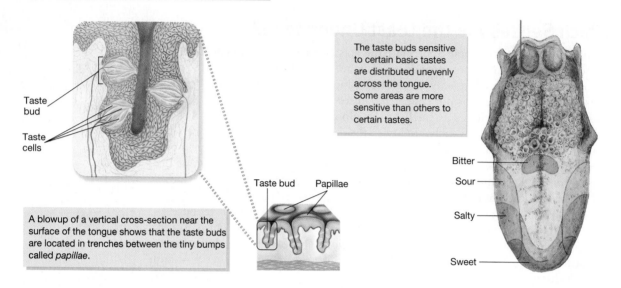

Taste bud

Taste cells

The taste buds sensitive to certain basic tastes are distributed unevenly across the tongue. Some areas are more sensitive than others to certain tastes.

Taste bud   Papillae

A blowup of a vertical cross-section near the surface of the tongue shows that the taste buds are located in trenches between the tiny bumps called *papillae*.

Bitter

Sour

Salty

Sweet

Figure 6.22
Taste Buds on the Surface of the Tongue

Although psychologists do not know exactly how many tastes there are, most agree that there are four basic ones: sweet, sour, salty, and bitter. Most foods contain more than one primary taste; Hawaiian pineapple pizza, for example, offers a complex array of taste stimuli and also stimulates the sense of smell. All taste cells are sensitive to all taste stimuli, but some cells are more sensitive to some stimuli than to others. (In this regard, they are much like the cones in the retina, which are sensitive to all wavelengths but are especially sensitive to a specific range of wavelengths.) By isolating stimuli that initiate only one taste sensation, psychologists have found that some regions of the tongue seem to be more sensitive than others to particular taste stimuli. The tip of the tongue, for example, is more sensitive to sweet tastes than the back of the tongue is, and the sides are especially sensitive to sour tastes (Hoon et al., 1999; McBurney, Collings, & Glanz, 1973; McMahon, Shikata, & Breslin, 2001).

Taste sensitivity seems to be genetically determined, and some people are more sensitive to tastes than others. In fact, there are great differences in this sensitivity—some individuals are considered to be nontasters, most are medium tasters, and some seem to be supertasters. Well-known taste researcher Linda Bartoshuk (Bartoshuk, 2000) investigated the taste buds at the tip of the tongue in individuals in these groups. She found that nontasters had as few as 11 taste buds per square centimeter, whereas supertasters had as many as 1,100 taste buds per square centimeter. Supertasters taste sweet things as too sweet, bitter things as too bitter, and so forth. Nontasters cannot distinguish among basic tastes and require additional samplings to discern a flavor. Interesting, and not yet explained, is the finding that women are more likely to be supertasters. Not too surprisingly, smokers have impaired tasting abilities (De Jong et al., 1999).

The taste of a particular food depends not only on its chemical makeup and the number of taste buds you have, but also on your past experiences with this or similar foods, on how much saliva is being mixed into the food as you chew, and on how long you chew the food. Food that is chewed well has a stronger taste. Food that rests on the tongue for a long time loses its ability to stimulate. This phenomenon is called *sensory adaptation*, or the temporary decrease in responsiveness of a receptor, often due to sustained or repeated high levels of stimulation. A food that loses its texture by being mashed up, or blended, with other foods has less taste and is less appealing to most adults. A taste experience, much like other perceptual experiences, depends not only on a sensory stimulus but also on the frequency and intensity of past experiences (Friedrich & Laurent, 2001).

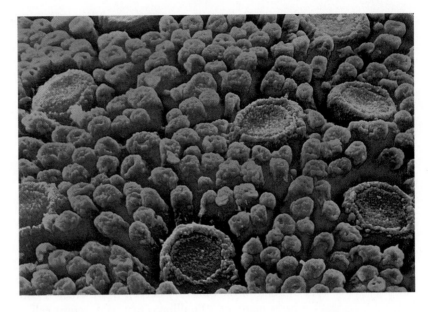

Each taste bud consists of 5 to 150 taste cells. These cells last only about 10 to 14 days and are constantly being renewed.

Smell

There's a good reason, other than etiquette, not to talk when your mouth is full: You lose some of the smells that help you experience the taste of food. The nose is the external section of the olfactory system, and it houses a complex array of receptors that transmit signals to key areas of the brain and allow us to smell (Scott et al., 2001; Vroon, 1997). Try eating chunks of raw potato and raw onion while holding your nose, and you will quickly see that they taste alike, as do chunks of pear and apple. Like the sense of taste, *olfaction*—the sense of smell—is a chemical sense. That is, the stimulus for smell is a chemical in the air. The human olfactory system is remarkably sensitive: Humans can distinguish approximately 10,000 different scents and can recognize a smell from as few as 40 or 50 molecules of the chemical. For the sensation of smell to occur, the molecules must move toward the receptor cells located on the walls of the nasal passage. This happens when you breathe molecules in through your nostrils or take them in through the back of your throat when you chew and swallow. When a chemical substance in the air moves past the receptor cells, it is partially absorbed into the mucus that covers the cells, thereby initiating the process of smell.

For human beings to perceive smell, information must be sent to the brain. At the top of the nasal cavity is the *olfactory epithelium* (see **Figure 6.23** on p. 222), a layer of cells that contains the *olfactory receptor cells*—the neurons that process

Olfaction [ole-FAK-shun] ■ The sense of smell.

Figure 6.23
The Olfactory
System

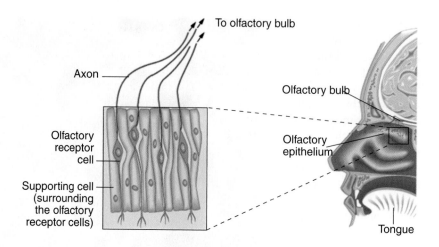

odors and transmit information about smell to the *olfactory bulbs* (enlargements at the end of the olfactory nerve), from which it continues on to the brain. There can be as many as 30 million olfactory receptor cells in each nostril, which is what makes the olfactory system so sensitive and the electrochemical coding so complicated (Laurent, 1999; Scott et al., 2001; Wilson, 2000).

The sensitivity of the human sense of smell is dramatically illustrated by perfume manufacturing, which is a complex process. Perfume makers combine dozens of substances to make a perfume; many perfumes have the same basic scent, varying only slightly. The manufacturer's task is to generate a perfume that has a distinctive *top note*—the first smell that makes an impact. Other substances in the mixture produce a middle note and an end note. The middle note follows after the top note fades away; the end note is long-lasting and persists for some time after the top and middle notes have disappeared.

Theories of smell involve both the stimulus for smell and the structure of the olfactory system. Some theories posit a few basic smells; others suggest that there are many—including flowery, foul, fruity, resinous, spicy, and burned. Psychologists have not agreed on a single classification system for smells, nor do they completely understand how odors affect the receptor cells. Research into the coding of smell is intense, and biopsychologists make headway each year. For example, they have shown that our memory for odors is long-lasting, that odors can evoke memories of past events and childhood, and that the memory of smells is affected by language and the emotions associated with particular times in our lives (Engen & Engen 1997). So, a smell experience depends not only on a sensory stimulus but also on past experiences, including their frequency and intensity (Friedrich & Laurent, 2001). Researchers are also studying whether and how odors affect human behavior. We consider this issue next.

Smell and Communication

Animals secrete *pheromones* (pronounced FER-uh-moans)—chemical substances that are detected as scents by other animals and act as a means of communication.

In fact, scents released by one animal may even influence the physiology of another animal.

Pheromones are widely recognized as initiators of sexual activity among animals. For example, female silkworms release a pheromone that can attract male silkworms from miles away. Similarly, when female salamanders are sexually receptive, they emit a highly odorous substance that attracts males (Rollmann, 2000); rats and elephants also have such pheromones (Fornai & Orzi, 2001; Rasmussen & Krishnamurthy, 2000). Many animals emit pheromones to elicit specific behavioral reactions; others, notably dogs and cats, use scents in their urine and scent glands to maintain territories and identify one another. Beavers attempt to keep strangers out of their territory by depositing foul-smelling substances emitted by sacs near the anus. Reindeer have scent glands between their toes that leave a trail for the rest of the herd. Communication via pheromones is found throughout the animal world. But do human beings share this ability?

Although people have always believed that a kind of "chemistry" exists between close friends, few really believed that one person's secretions might alter another person's behavior. Until relatively recently, scientists assumed that human beings do not communicate through smell. However, ground-breaking research in the 1970s began to change psychologists' thinking about smell and communication. McClintock (1971) found that the menstrual periods of women who were living in a college dormitory and were either roommates or close friends became roughly *synchronous*. That is, after the women lived together for several months, their menstrual cycles began and ended at about the same time. McClintock began to question whether the synchronization of the menstrual cycles was due to some type of chemical message. More recent experimental research (Jacob & McClintock, 2000; Stern & McClintock, 1998) found that women emit a whole array of chemical signals that affect menstrual synchronicity and other behavior.

The effects of pheromones on animals are profound, but the role pheromones may play in human behavior remains somewhat obscure and even controversial. Nevertheless, perfume makers have been working frenetically to make a perfume with pheromonelike capabilities. Is it reasonable for them to assert that perfumes, like pheromones, can attract members of the other sex? Probably not. Pheromones are not likely to be as powerful for human beings as they are for animals, because so many other environmental stimuli affect human behavior, attitudes, and interpersonal relations (Cacioppo et al., 2000).

What Is the Relationship between Touch and Pain?

I (L.L.) have a picture of six-time Tour de France winner Lance Armstrong on my bulletin board, where it gives me a bit of inspiration every day. Some days, I'm inspired because of Armstrong's sheer talent as an athlete (something that I'm not); other days, it's because Armstrong learned a valuable lesson about life (that it's not all about winning) at a young age; on still other days, I think about his ability to withstand pain and adversity during his illness (cancer) and his bike races (the longest and toughest known). Armstrong used psychological processes to overcome the difficulties and pain of chemotherapy, surgery, and the punishing Tour de France. Most people know that pain is a signal of damage to the body or impending damage, but Armstrong was able to turn his pain off or endure it—it was a matter of mind over body. Armstrong's courageous achievements show that one's situation, culture, family background, and beliefs all affect the ability to endure or overcome pain. (Armstrong's autobiography, *It's Not About the Bike* [2000], explains how to harness some of the techniques he used in times of adversity and competition.)

Pain can be either visceral (felt in the internal organs) or initiated at the level of the skin. Your skin, an organ of your body, contains a wide range of receptors for relaying information about the skin senses—including pain, touch, and temperature. In each case, a stimulus is converted into electrochemical energy transmitted by neurons, and then the brain interprets that energy as a psychological experience. Skin receptors ultimately send information to the somatosensory cortex of the brain.

Touch

The skin is more than just a binding that holds your body together. It is the location of your sense of touch—your tactile system. The skin of an adult human being measures roughly 2 square yards and comprises three layers: the epidermis, the dermis, and the hypodermis. The top layer, the *epidermis* (*epi* means "outer" and *derma,* "skin"), consists primarily of dead cells and varies in thickness. It is thin on the face and quite thick on the elbows and the heels. The epidermis is constantly regenerating; in fact, all of its cells are replaced every 28 days or so. The layer underneath the epidermis, the *dermis,* contains live skin cells as well as a supply of nerve endings, blood, hair cells, and oil-producing (sebaceous) glands. The dermis and the epidermis are resilient, flexible, and quite tough. They protect the body against quick changes in temperature and pressure, and the epidermis guards against pain from small scratches, cuts, and bumps. The deepest layer of the skin—the *hypodermis* (*hypo* means "under")—is a thick, insulating cushion.

The specialized receptors for each of the skin senses—pain, touch, and temperature—vary in shape, size, number, and distribution. For example, the body has many more cold receptors than heat receptors; it has more pain receptors behind the knee than on the top of the nose. The most sensitive areas of the hand have as many as 1,300 pain receptors per square inch.

The skin sense receptors appear to interact with one another; sometimes one sensation seems to combine with or change to another. Thus, increasing pressure can become pain. Similarly, an itch seems to result from a low-level irritation of nerve endings in the skin; however, a tickle can be caused by the same stimulus and can produce a response that seems reflexive but is actually highly dependent on psychological and social variables, as we'll see in the next subsection. Further, people are far more sensitive to pressure on some parts of their bodies than on other parts (compare your fingers to your thigh); the more sensitive areas, such as the neck and the back of the knees, have more receptors than do the less sensitive areas. Complicating matters further, women have greater sensitivity to some pain stimuli than do men and are better able to discriminate among painful stimuli (Berkley, 1997).

Many of your determinations of how something feels are relative. When you say a stimulus is cold, you mean it is cold compared to normal skin temperature. When you say an object is warm, you mean it feels warmer than normal skin temperature. When you feel a child's head with the back of your hand and say the child has a fever, you are comparing normal skin temperature to a sick child's elevated skin temperature (and you wouldn't make such a determination immediately after coming indoors on a winter day when it was 20°F outside).

Being Tickled

There's no one who hasn't been tickled at some point in his or her life. Some of us are especially ticklish. We smile, laugh, squirm, and sometimes howl when tickled. But why?

In the 19th century, it was suggested that people laugh when tickled because of a "pleasant state of mind." But recent research is showing that the response to tickling is only partly physical and mostly psychological. People respond to a light touch on the sole of the foot or on the spine, but if they anticipate the touch, if they are with a friend or relative, or if there is an element of surprise, the response is much stronger. That's why people can't tickle themselves—there is no element of surprise, and tickling depends on a social interaction and a psychological tension that requires at least two people (Claxon, 1975; Fogel et al., 2000; Panksepp, 2000).

Think back to your childhood. When your mom or dad said, "I'm going … to … tickle you!" and started to wiggle her or his fingers, you were likely to squirm and giggle even before you were touched. Once you were actually tickled, you may have convulsed in laughter. Those of us who laugh easily at humor are more likely to respond to tickling (Harris & Christenfeld, 1997), our physiological responses to tickling are likely to be stronger when we are with friends (Christenfeld et al., 1997), and we are more likely to experience touching as tickling if we feel comfortable with our bodies and are disposed to perceive pleasurable stimuli (Ruggieri et al., 1983).

The response to humor and the ability to be tickled seem to be somewhat related. Both of these responses are universal behaviors found in human beings and in some chimpanzees. They occur at an early age and can be linked to specific neural pathways—characteristics that are indicative of an evolved response. Indeed, the responses to both humor and tickling may serve an evolutionary purpose. Some evidence suggests that those with a humorous outlook on life may live longer (Weisfeld, 1993). Be tickled and live longer? Even if not—you'll have more fun!

Pain

For most of us, pain comes and then goes, leaving us thankful for the relief. Pain is a perceptual experience with particularly negative qualities (Wall, 2000). It is the most common symptom that doctors must deal with; everyone has experienced acute pain at one time or another—from a severe headache, a broken bone, a dental procedure, arthritis, or perhaps a kidney stone or appendicitis. Despite its association with illness and disease, pain is adaptive and necessary. In rare cases, children are born without the ability to feel pain, which places them in constant danger. Their encounters with caustic substances, violent collisions, and deep cuts elicit no painful responses that could teach them to avoid such experiences. Further, they do not recognize serious conditions that would send most of us to the doctor for attention—for example, broken bones, deep burns, or the sharp pains that signal appendicitis.

Studying pain is difficult, because pain can be elicited in so many ways. For example, hunger or the flu may cause stomach pains, a cavity or an abscess can cause a toothache, and headaches can be caused by stress or eyestrain. There are many kinds of pain—including sunburn pain, pain from terminal cancer, labor pains, lower back pain, pain from frostbite, and even pain in a "phantom limb" after amputation. Psychologists use several kinds of stimuli to study pain; among these are chemicals, extreme heat and cold, and electrical stimulation.

Most researchers believe that the receptors for pain are free nerve endings (Lidow, 2002; Rainville, 2002; Sandkuehler, 2002). *Free nerve endings* are the microscopic ends of afferent neurons that are distributed throughout the body and are not connected to any specific sensory organ. There are various types of these receptors, each especially sensitive to a certain type of intense or potentially harmful stimulation. Some areas of the body are more sensitive to pain than others. For example, the sole of the foot and the ball of the thumb are less sensitive than the back of the knee and the neck. Also, though each individual's pain threshold remains fairly constant, different individuals show varying sensitivities to pain. Some people have a low threshold for pain; they will describe a comparatively low-level stimulus as painful. Others have a fairly high pain threshold. When you experience pain, you know where it hurts, how much it hurts, and the quality of the pain (sharp, burning, localized); a moderate to high level of pain will activate your autonomic nervous system, and you will experience increased heart rate and blood pressure, sweating, and so forth. You will then, in turn, respond in a certain way, depending on whether you are frightened, anxious, or merely annoyed.

You can see that the perception of pain is both physical and psychological; it depends to a great extent on a person's attitudes, previous experiences, and culture (Jensen, Turner, & Romano, 2001; Pincus & Morley, 2001). For example, athletes often report not feeling the pain of an injury until after the competition has ended. Some cultures, such as that of India, teach individuals to be stoical about pain and to endure individual suffering without complaint; in Western cultures, many people believe that pain and suffering are ennobling (Raj, Steigerwald, & Esser, 2003). When there are ethnic, cultural, or language differences between a patient and a doctor, the practitioner must use specialized knowledge and skill to treat pain and to communicate about it with the patient and family (Cervantes & Lechuga, 2004). Researchers also argue that older people who suffer from pain are often under treated or excluded from treatment because of inaccurate beliefs or ageist stereotypes about the elderly (Yonan & Wegener, 2003). Also, in Western cultures, boys and girls are often taught to respond differently to pain (Wall, 2000) (see **Table 6.1**). As adults, women in laboratory studies typically report lower pain thresholds, lower pain tolerance, and higher

Table 6.1		
VARIABLES THAT AFFECT THE PERCEPTION OF PAIN		
Biological	**Psychological**	**Environmental**
Stimulation of free nerve endings	Cognitive factors involving beliefs about meaning of pain	Environmental stressors that increase or decrease pain perception through release of hormones
Heightened sensitivity because of lowered thresholds	Beliefs and expectations about how to react to difficult situations, including pain	Cultural experiences that produce beliefs and expectations
Actions of endorphins		Painful physical stimuli including accidents and toxins

pain ratings than do men, according to Fillingim (2003). Fillingim contends that hormones, pain modulatory systems, family history, stereotypic sex roles, and cognitive factors place women at increased risk for pain and increase its severity. Thus, pain is not completely physiological.

What allows pain suppression? How does the body process, interpret, and stop pain? The neuromatrix theory may offer an answer.

Neuromatrix Theory

One explanation of how the body processes pain is the *neuromatrix theory* developed by Ronald Melzack (1999). The theory takes into account the sizes, level of development, and interplay of cells that initiate pain sensations, as well as inhibitory cells that can diminish those sensations. The theory contends that the brain has a widely distributed and largely inborn neural network, the *body–self neuromatrix* (BSN), which integrates sensory and other inputs to produce an output pattern that we experience as pain. Melzack refers to this output pattern of the neuromatrix as a *neurosignature,* a pattern of nerve impulses of varying temporal and spatial dimensions. Multiple inputs affect the neuromatrix, including (1) inputs from pain receptors, (2) visual and other sensory inputs that influence the interpretation of a situation, (3) emotional inputs from other areas of the brain, (4) neural self-modulation, and (5) the activity of the body's stress-regulation systems.

If Melzack's theory is correct (and research is still being done), the brain has been prewired to realize, for example, that the body has a right arm. Even if the right arm is amputated, the brain still believes that the arm is there (because its circuits for that arm are intact). Since the limb is not there, and the brain receives no sensory feedback, it will increase the strength of its stimulation, thus causing what is referred to as *phantom pain* (Schultz & Melzack, 1999).

Endorphins

There have been some exciting breakthroughs in research on pain receptors and the nature of pain. Consider, for example, the study of endorphins. *Endorphins* (from *endogenous*, meaning "naturally occurring," and *morphine*, an opiate drug) are painkillers that are produced naturally in the brain and the pituitary gland. There are many kinds of endorphins, and they help regulate several bodily functions, including blood pressure and body temperature (Koob, Wall, & Bloom, 1989). Endorphins also can produce euphoria and a sense of well-being. During and after running, runners often report experiencing "runner's high," a sensation many believe is related to the body's increased endorphin level. Exercise can increase endorphin levels, but intense exercise is required—and many who experience "runner's high" may actually be exhilarated about their accomplishment rather than affected by endorphins.

Endorphins bind themselves to receptor sites on neurons in the brain and spinal cord, thereby preventing pain signals from affecting those neurons. (Morphine occupies these same receptor sites in the nervous system and is extremely effective in controlling pain.) Some endorphins increase tolerance to pain, and others actually reduce pain sensations. *Enkephalin*, for example, is a brain endorphin that blocks pain signals (Blum et al., 2000; Samoriski & Gross, 2000). Another endorphin, *nocistatin*, is being tested on a variety of painful conditions, and scientists may eventually be able to produce it synthetically (Okuda-Ashitaka et al., 1998).

Acupuncture

Many people who suffer chronic pain have sought help from acupuncture (Olausson & Sagvik, 2000). Initially developed in China thousands of years ago, *acupuncture* is a technique that uses long, slender needles, inserted into the body at specific locations, to relieve particular kinds of pain. Controlled studies of acupuncture have yielded varying results. Acupuncture seems to help when needles are placed near the site of pain; this contrasts to the traditional Chinese view that the key sites for placement of acupuncture needles are located along particular lines called life-force meridians (Wall, 2000). It is possible that the needles stimulate endorphins that may help block the pain signals (Murray, 1995) or alter serotonin levels that affect pain (Nash, 1996). For some people, acupuncture may be a reasonable and effective option for pain treatment (Pan et al., 2000). The National Institutes of Health (1997) concludes that acupuncture may be effective with some kinds of pain—such as from migraines, arthritis, and postoperative pain from dental surgery—but that more research is needed because controlled studies on acupuncture are inconclusive.

Pain Management

Usually the pain resulting from a headache, toothache, or small cut is temporary and can be alleviated with a simple pain medication such as aspirin. For millions of people, however, aspirin is not enough (Ezzo et al., 2000). For those who suffer from constant pain caused by back injury, arthritis, or cancer, drug treatment either is not effective or is dangerous because of the high dosages required; in addition, each type of pain may require a different treatment (Fishbain, 2000). Sometimes doctors do not prescribe painkillers because of fear of addiction—a fear that is often exaggerated by caring, well-meaning family and friends who wrongly assume that taking medication for serious pain will lead to addiction (Friedman, 1990; Wall, 2000).

New technologies emerge every few years to help people manage pain. Leaders in pain research reason that something must happen at the site of an injury to trigger endorphin production. What if a drug could stop the whole pain-perception process at the place where the injury occurred? In an effort to find such a compound, researchers are studying the pain receptors in skin tissue and observing how chemicals bind to them. The compounds they discover may not relieve pain completely but may be effective in combination with other pain medications, such as aspirin (Graven-Nielsen & Mense, 2001; Mas Nieto et al., 2001; Uhl, Sora, & Wang, 1999).

Practitioners who deal with pain recognize that although it may arise initially from a physical cause, it sometimes continues even after that problem abates because it provides other benefits to the sufferer (Gatchel & Turk, 1999). For example, pain may get the sufferer attention, which is reinforcing, or it may act as a distraction from other problems. In Chapter 15, we'll discuss pain management that focuses on helping people cope with pain regardless of its origins and on increasing their pain-controlling skills.

Hypnosis (which we'll examine in more detail in Chapter 7) has been used to treat pain. Patients may be instructed to focus on other aspects of life and may be told that their pain will be more bearable after the hypnotic session. Hypnosis can help—but hypnotic treatments that fail to take into consideration the many-sided and complex nature of pain often don't work. The effect of hypnosis could be enhanced if clinicians who used it had more comprehensive understanding of pain (Patterson & Jensen, 2003). Although some researchers claim that two-thirds of patients who are considered highly susceptible to suggestion can experience some relief of pain through hypnosis, a more conservative and realistic estimate is 15–20% (Agarguen, Oener, & Akbayram, 2001; Flammer & Bongartz, 2003; Ginandez et al., 2003; Harandi, Esfandani, & Shakibaei, 2004).

Anxiety and worry can make pain worse. People who suffer from migraine headaches, for example, often make their condition worse by becoming fearful when they feel a headache coming on. Researchers find that biofeedback training, which teaches people how to relax and cope more effectively, can give some relief to those who suffer from chronic pain or migraine headaches—although, again, results are mixed. (Biofeedback will be discussed further in Chapter 7.) Other treatments, closely related to biofeedback, involve cognitive coping strategies (discussed in Chapter 17). A negative attitude can make pain worse. Cognitive coping strategies teach patients to have a better attitude about their pain. Patients learn to talk to themselves in positive ways, to divert attention to pleasant images, and to take an active role in managing their pain and trying to transcend it.

How Do We Keep Our Balance?

If you are a dancer or any type of athlete, you must have constant awareness and control of hand, arm, and leg movements. You try to keep your balance, be graceful, and move smoothly and with coordination. Two sensory systems allow for skilled, accurate, and smooth movement—the not well-known, but vitally important, kinesthetic and vestibular systems.

Kinesthesis is the awareness aroused by movements of the muscles, tendons, and joints. It is what allows you to touch your finger to your nose with your eyes closed, leap over hurdles during a track-and-field event, and dance without stepping on your partner's feet. The kinesthetic system provides information about bodily movements. The movements of muscles around your eye, for example, help you know how far away objects are. Kinesthesia and other internal sensations (such as an upset stomach) are *proprioceptive cues* (kinesthesia is sometimes called *proprioception*)—sensory cues that come from within the body.

The *vestibular sense* is the sense of bodily orientation and postural adjustment. It helps you keep your balance and sense of equilibrium. The structures essential to these functions are in the ear. Vestibular sacs and semicircular canals, which are linked indirectly to the body wall of the cochlea, provide information about the orientations of the head and the body. The vestibular sense allows you to walk on a balance beam without falling off, to know which way is up after diving into water, and to sense that you are turning a corner when riding in a car, even when your eyes are closed. It involves the integration of multiple modalities of sensation and perception (Carello & Turvey, 2004). Rapid movements of the head bring about changes in the semicircular canals. These changes induce eye movements to help compensate for head changes and changes in bodily orientation. The movements may also be accompanied by physical sensations ranging from pleasant dizziness to unbearable motion sickness. Studies of the vestibular sense help scientists understand what happens to people during space travel and under conditions of weightlessness.

Does Extrasensory Perception Exist?

Sights, sounds, tastes, smells, and touches, even pains, are all part of human beings' normal sensory and perceptual experiences. Some people, however, claim there are other perceptual experiences that not all human beings recognize as normal. People have been fascinated by extrasensory perception (ESP) for hundreds of years. The British Society for the Study of Psychic Phenomena has investigated reports of ESP since the 19th century. Early experimenters tested for extrasensory perception by asking participants to guess the symbols on what are now called ESP cards, each marked with a star, a cross, a circle, a square, or a set of wavy lines. One of the most consistently successful guessers once guessed 25 cards in a row, an event whose odds of happening by chance are nearly 300 quadrillion to 1.

ESP is a broad term that encompasses several phenomena: telepathy, clairvoyance, precognition, and psychokinesis. *Telepathy* is the transfer of thoughts from one person to another. *Clairvoyance* is the ability to recognize objects or events, such as the contents of a message in a sealed envelope, that are not discernible by normal

Kinesthesis [kin-iss-THEE-sis] ■ The awareness aroused by movements of the muscles, tendons, and joints.

Vestibular [ves-TIB-you-ler] sense ■ The sense of bodily orientation and postural adjustment.

sensory receptors. *Precognition* is unexplained knowledge about future events, such as knowing when the phone is about to ring. *Psychokinesis* is the ability to move objects using only one's mental powers.

Experimental support for the existence of ESP is generally weak, and confirming results have not been repeated very often (Sanders & Delin, 2000). Moreover, ESP phenomena such as reading people's minds or bending spoons through mental power cannot be verified by experimental manipulations in the way that other perceptual events can be. The National Research Council has denounced the scientific merit of most experiments undertaken to study ESP (Alcock, 1988). These criticisms do not mean that ESP does not exist. Recent research uses techniques such as sophisticated electronic detection devices (Alcock, Burns, & Freeman, 2003; Rao, 2001; Steinkamp, 2000). Some attempts to relate ESP phenomena to traditional psychology are underway (especially in nations of the former Soviet bloc). However, most psychologists see so much trickery in demonstrations of ESP and so many design errors in and falsification of data from ESP experiments that they remain skeptical.

Summary and Review

HOW ARE STIMULATION AND PERCEPTION LINKED?

What is the difference between sensation and perception?

Sensation is the process in which the sense organs' receptor cells are stimulated and relay initial information to higher brain centers for further processing. *Perception* is the process through which an organism selects and interprets sensory stimuli so that they acquire meaning. Although perceptual systems are different, they share common processes. *Bottom-up analysis* starts with stimulus information arriving from the sensory receptors and analyzes the processes that combine that information so that a person can identify more complex patterns. By contrast, *top-down analysis* looks at how knowledge about and memory of the world help a person identify stimulus patterns or elements of patterns. pp. 181–182

What is psychophysics?

Psychophysics is the study of the relationship between physical stimuli and people's conscious experience of them. Psychophysical techniques allow researchers to study and approximate the *absolute threshold*—the statistically determined minimum level of stimulation necessary to excite a perceptual system. If a visual or auditory stimulus is presented so quickly or at such a low level that a person cannot consciously perceive it, psychologists say that it is presented subliminally. Research on *subliminal perception* is controversial, and many researchers maintain that it can be explained in terms of nonperceptual variables such as motivation, previous experience, and unconscious or critical censoring processes. pp. 183–184

What is selective attention?

The cocktail party phenomenon, which allows a person to hear his or her name spoken across a crowded and noisy room, is a result of *selective attention*. Studies show that people have a limited capacity to pay attention to numerous stimuli at once. pp. 184–186

Describe the effects of restricting environmental stimulation.

Studies of sensory deprivation and especially of sensory restriction have shown that an environment of extreme sensory restriction can bring on profound relaxation. pp. 186–187

What is inattentional blindness?

Research on attention shows that when a person pays concentrated attention to an object, scene, or event, other (unexpected) events go unnoticed. This phenomenon is *inattentional blindness*. pp. 187–188

HOW DO WE SEE THE WORLD?

Describe the structures of the visual system.

The main structures of the eye are the cornea, pupil, iris, lens, and retina. The *retina* is made up of ten layers, of which the most important are the *photoreceptors* (*rods* and *cones*), the bipolar cells, and the ganglion cells. The axons of the ganglion cells make up the optic nerve. The duplicity theory of vision states that rods and cones are structurally unique and are used to accomplish different tasks. Cones are specialized for color, day vision, and fine acuity, and rods are specialized for low light levels but contribute little to color vision or acuity. pp. 188–194

What are receptive fields?

Receptive fields are areas on the retina that, when stimulated, produce changes in the firing of cells in the visual system. These cells are sometimes called feature detectors, and some of them are highly specialized—for example, for detecting motion or color. pp. 194–196

What are the trichromatic and opponent-process theories of color vision?

The three psychological dimensions of color are *hue, brightness*, and *saturation*. They correspond to the three physical characteristics of light: wavelength, intensity, and purity. Young and Helmholtz's *trichromatic theory of color vision* states that all colors can be made by mixing three basic colors (red, green, and blue) and that the retina has three types of cones. Herring's *opponent-process theory* states that color is coded by a series of receptors that respond either strongly or weakly to different wavelengths of light. *Color blindness* is the inability to perceive different hues; many people with color blindness cannot successfully discriminate colors in two areas of the visual spectrum. pp. 198–202

HOW DO WE PERCEIVE FORM AND SUBSTANCE?

What are size constancy and shape constancy?

Size constancy is the ability of the perceptual system to recognize that an object remains constant in size regardless of its distance from the viewer or the size of the retinal image. *Shape constancy* is the ability of the visual perceptual system to recognize a shape despite changes in its orientation or the angle from which it is viewed. pp. 202–203

What kinds of cues help people see depth?

The *monocular depth cues* include motion parallax, the kinetic depth effect, linear perspective, interposition, texture gradient, shading, atmospheric perspective, and *accommodation*. The two major *binocular depth cues* are *retinal disparity* and *convergence*. pp. 204–207

What is an illusion?

An *illusion* is a perception of a physical stimulus that differs from measurable reality or from what is commonly expected. pp. 207–210

What is an agnosia?

People with an *agnosia* have normal, intact perceptual systems for detecting colors, shapes, and motion, but they are unable to recognize things the way they should be able to. Prosopagnosia is the inability to recognize faces. p. 210

What did the Gestalt psychologists contribute to scientists' understanding of perception?

According to a Gestalt idea called the *law of Prägnanz*, stimuli that can be grouped together and seen as a whole, or a form, will be seen that way. Based on the law of Prägnanz, Gestalt psychologists developed principles of organization for the perception of figures, especially figure–ground relationships. pp. 211–212

HOW DO WE PERCEIVE SOUNDS?

What are the key characteristics of sound?

Sound refers to the psychological experience of changes in air pressure that affect the auditory system. The *frequency* and *amplitude* of sound waves determine in large part how a listener will experience a sound. pp. 212–214

Describe the anatomy of the ear.

The ear has three main parts: the outer ear, the middle ear, and the inner ear. The eardrum (tympanic membrane) is the boundary between the outer ear and the middle ear. Tiny bones (ossicles) in the middle ear stimulate the basilar membrane in the cochlea, a tube in the inner ear. pp. 214–216

What are two major theories of hearing?

Place theories of hearing claim that the analysis of sound occurs in the inner ear; frequency theories claim that the analysis of pitch and intensity takes place in the brain. pp. 216–217

How does sound localization work?

Because you have two ears, you can locate the source of sound. A sound produced to the left of the head will arrive at the left ear before it arrives at the right. This creates an interaural time difference. In addition, a sound produced to the left will be slightly more intense at the left ear than the right; thus, there is an interaural intensity difference. p. 217

Distinguish between conduction deafness and sensorineural deafness.

Conduction deafness results from interference in the delivery of sound to the neural mechanism of the inner ear. *Sensorineural deafness* results from damage to the cochlea, the auditory nerve, or higher auditory processing centers. p. 218

WHICH SENSES ARE THE LEAST UNDERSTOOD?

Describe the anatomy of the tongue and how it is related to taste.

The tongue contains thousands of bumps, or papillae, each of which is separated from the next by a trench. The taste buds are located on the walls of these trenches. Each taste bud has many taste receptors. All taste cells are sensitive to all taste stimuli, but certain cells are more sensitive to some stimuli than to others. pp. 219–221

Why are taste and smell called chemical senses?

For taste or smell to occur, chemicals must come into contact with the receptor cells. The receptors for the sense of smell (*olfaction*) are located on the walls of the nasal passage. When a chemical substance in the air moves past these receptor cells, it is partially absorbed into the mucus that covers the cells, thereby initiating the process of smell. The olfactory epithelium contains the olfactory receptor cells—the nerve fibers that process odors and enable an individual to perceive smell. pp. 221–223

WHAT IS THE RELATIONSHIP BETWEEN TOUCH AND PAIN?

Describe the anatomy of the skin.

The skin is made up of three layers. The top layer is the epidermis. The layer underneath the epidermis is the dermis. The deepest layer, the hypodermis, is a thick insulating cushion. The skin sense receptors appear to interact with one another; sometimes one sensation seems to combine with or change to another. pp. 224–225

What is one theory of pain that is currently being investigated?

One recent explanation of how pain sensations are processed is that a neural network in the brain, the body–self neuromatrix (BSN), integrates various inputs to produce the output pattern perceived as pain. pp. 225–227

What are the body's naturally produced painkillers?

Endorphins are painkillers that are produced naturally in the brain and the pituitary gland. They help regulate several bodily functions, including blood pressure and body temperature. Stress, anticipated pain, and athletic activities may increase the body's level of endorphins. pp. 228–229

HOW DO WE KEEP OUR BALANCE?

Keeping one's balance involves senses that detect the movement and the orientation of the entire body. *Kinesthesis* is the awareness that is aroused by movements of the muscles, tendons, and joints. The *vestibular sense* is the sense of bodily orientation and postural adjustment—which helps you keep your balance and sense of equilibrium. p. 230

DOES EXTRASENSORY PERCEPTION EXIST?

The "sixth sense" known as extrasensory perception (ESP) encompasses telepathy, clairvoyance, precognition, and psychokinesis. Psychologists remain skeptical about the existence of ESP because experiments on it have been characterized by trickery, falsification of data, and design errors. pp. 230–231

CHAPTER 7

Consciousness

What Is Consciousness? 236
   Defining Consciousness
   Theories of Consciousness

What Happens When We Sleep? 240
   The Sleep–Wakefulness Cycle: Circadian Rhythms
   Sleep Stages: REM and NREM Sleep
   Sleep Deprivation
   Why Do We Sleep?
   Is There a Sleep Switch?
   Sleep Disorders

What Are Dreams, and What Do
They Mean? 251
   What Is a Dream?
   The Content of Dreams
   Dream Theories

Is It Possible to Control
Consciousness by Using Biofeedback,
Hypnosis, or Meditation? 257
   Biofeedback
   Hypnosis
   Meditation

How Do Drugs Alter
Consciousness? 261
   Psychoactive Drugs
   Drug Use and Abuse

Summary and Review 271

What Is Consciousness?

> Introduction to Psychology: The theory of human behavior ... Is there a split between mind and body, and, if so, which is better to have? Special consideration is given to a study of consciousness as opposed to unconsciousness, with many helpful hints on how to remain conscious. (Allen, 1983)

This humorous description of an introductory psychology course includes several elements that are actually relevant to the consideration of consciousness. It refers to the mind–body distinction and the concept of the unconscious, both of which are important issues. However, its definition of psychology as the theory of human behavior is a modern one; early psychologists, such as Wilhelm Wundt and William James, focused on the study of consciousness (Schutz & Schultz, 2004). In the late 1880s, psychologists asked participants to report their level of conscious experience while sitting still, while working, and while falling asleep. At the turn of the century, Sigmund Freud (whom we will study in more depth in Chapter 13) extended the study of consciousness by dividing consciousness into levels. He proposed that the conscious level of the mind was small in comparison to the unconscious, which houses a person's underlying needs and wishes. According to Freud (1900/1953), people are aware of the information in their conscious minds but not of what is in the unconscious, although that strongly influences feelings and behavior.

Then, in the 1920s, behaviorists such as John B. Watson argued that consciousness should be eliminated as a subject of psychological study, because it is not a physical structure or a behavior that can be examined and measured. The behavioral approach came to dominate American psychology, and the study of consciousness and thought was all but abandoned (Baars, 2003). In the 1960s and 1970s, the emergence of cognitive psychology led psychologists to reconsider the phenomenon of consciousness. During the 1990s, research advances in neuroscience spurred even greater interest in consciousness among psychologists.

Defining Consciousness

The recent resurgence of interest in consciousness has led to a new definition of *consciousness* as the general state of being aware of and responsive to events in the environment, as well as one's own mental processes. Almost all psychologists agree that a person who is conscious is aware of the immediate environment; for example, you are conscious when you listen to a lecture (at least we instructors hope so!). But consciousness also refers to inner awareness and includes your awareness of your feelings (*sentience*) and of your thoughts and memories (Roth, 2004).

Consciousness ■ The general state of being aware of and responsive to events in the environment, as well as one's own mental processes.

The humorous description of the psychology course mentions a concept that has a long tradition: the notion that the mind and the body are separable. This *doctrine of dualism* dates back to the 17th-century French philosopher René Descartes, who asserted that the mind and body are completely separate things that interact to only a limited degree. The idea of dualism is widely accepted and has even crept into the English language. For example, the statement "These athletes are prepared in both mind and body" suggests that mind and body are separate entities requiring different preparations. However, almost all psychologists reject this dualistic notion, asserting that the mind does not exist independent of the body. The view that mental life has a physiological basis rooted in the brain is referred to as *materialism*. However, some theorists (Chalmers, 2002) consider this explanation to be inadequate because it is *reductionist*: It tries to explain one level of function (mental) by reducing it to another level (physical). To such theorists, knowing that consciousness arises from the functioning of the brain still does not answer the question of *why* consciousness arises.

Materialism dominates over dualism among today's psychologists and neuroscientists. They also take a complex view of levels of consciousness, acknowledging that people are more aware of certain mental processes and less aware of others (Coward & Sun, 2004; Roth, 2004). For example, when you drive along a very familiar route, you may suddenly realize that you've gone several miles seemingly without being aware of what you passed. You know the route so well that you can drive it almost automatically. You don't even have to attend to events to be influenced by them. Recent research has indicated that people can be influenced by stimuli of which they are not consciously aware (Erdelyi, 2004) and that perception can be guided by information that people do not notice consciously (Roser & Gazzaniga, 2004). For example, if we were fully aware of our perceptual processes, we would never be fooled by perceptual illusions, which tend to persist even when we consciously understand the basis for them (see Chapter 6).

Most psychologists—including the early psychologists, Freud, and today's neuroscientists and evolutionary psychologists—have acknowledged that people experience different levels of consciousness. Consciousness can be seen as a continuum—ranging from the alert attention required to read this textbook through various other levels, including the "automatic pilot" state described above, dreaming, hypnosis, or drug-induced states. According to this view of consciousness, a person who is not paying attention or is not alert may be said to be conscious, but not at the same level as one who is vigilant and alert. A person who is in a state of consciousness that is dramatically different from ordinary awareness and responsiveness is said to be in an *altered state of consciousness*, which assumes that the standard state of consciousness is alert and awake.

Not only are there various levels of consciousness, but some people are more able than others to think about and regulate their own thinking—a process called *metacognition*—which may allow them to access levels of consciousness or thought processes that are not available to other people. Self-awareness requires attention, memory, and possibly language (Premack, 2004). Nonhuman animals clearly possess some levels of self-awareness, but they are not capable of metacognition. Indeed, one group of researchers hypothesized that these abilities are specifically human and develop between 12 and 15 months of age (Perner & Dienes, 2003). However, metacognition is not initially under an individual's control, and its development continues even in adulthood (Kuhn, 2000).

Theories of Consciousness

As in other areas of psychology, theory guides the research on consciousness, and opposing views have generated a great deal of controversy. Some theorists maintain that consciousness will never be explained; the mind is beyond human comprehension. Others assert that consciousness comes from the workings of the brain; that is, consciousness is what the brain does. This latter view is a materialist one, because it holds that consciousness can be understood in terms of the physical apparatus of the brain. Between these two views is another, which holds that consciousness can be understood, but that a new approach is needed (Chalmers, 1996, 2002). That is, neither science nor philosophy has yet formulated principles that can explain consciousness, but more work may bring success.

Theorists who believe that consciousness is beyond understanding are the intellectual descendants of René Descartes, and they can be termed *mysterians* (Chalmers, 2002). One theorist who fits into this category is Colin McGinn (1999), who contends that consciousness is the ultimate mystery. Humans will never understand the mind because their minds are not built to do so; the human mind cannot analyze itself.

Many theorists who have taken the materialist view of consciousness come from the neuroscience perspective. Holding that the mind and consciousness emerge from the brain at work, these theorists reject dualism and make no distinction between the workings of the brain and the mind. Antonio Damasio's *Descartes' Error* (1994), as its title suggests, argues that Descartes was wrong to believe that the mind and body function according to different principles. Damasio (1994, 2003) contends that the mind is firmly grounded in the brain and that highly complex brains become conscious. Daniel Dennett (1991, 1996, 2003) asserts that human beings have access to many sources of information, which together create conscious experiences. He argues that the brain creates multiple drafts (copies) of experiences, which are constantly being reanalyzed. According to Dennett, the brain develops consciousness as well as a sense of self through this constant updating and reanalysis of experience. Taking this argument even further, Allan Hobson (1999) contends that not only the brain but the entire body is part of conscious experience. In complete opposition to Descartes' dualism, this view holds that consciousness and the body form a seamless, functioning whole.

Consciousness has also been considered from the evolutionary perspective. In addition to taking the materialist position that the mind is what the brain does, evolutionary psychologists explain consciousness as an adaptation that gave humans a survival advantage (Cosmides & Tooby, 1997; LeDoux, 2002; Pinker, 1997). According to this view, the mind is a set of systems for computation, developed through natural selection to solve the kinds of problems our ancestors faced as hunters and gatherers. Evolutionary psychologists (Gaulin & McBurney, 2001; Pinker, 1997) argue that consciousness has three aspects: sentience, access, and self-knowledge. *Sentience* refers to subjective experience and awareness—feelings. *Access* refers to the ability to report on the content and product of rational thought—to take deliberate, reasoned actions based on memory, rational ideas, and past experiences. *Self-knowledge* refers to the ability of individuals to recognize that their experiences are uniquely their own and to be aware that they are experiencing as they are doing it. Sentience is difficult to assess, but access and self-knowledge are cognitive activities that can be analyzed in a variety of ways, including fMRI scans and even biofeedback. From a scientist's point of view, such objective analysis is crucial; it is the only way to investigate consciousness that avoids focusing on subjective experience.

Evolutionary psychologists see consciousness as only part of what the mind does; their view is that much of the mind's function arises from brain activity that is outside awareness (Cosmides & Tooby, 1997; LeDoux, 2002). Complex neural circuits underlie processes such as vision, which is largely automatic, and emotion, which seems more complex but is not usually under conscious control. We are not aware of some of the processes based in the brain, but we have conscious awareness of others. Thus, evolutionary psychologists see a variety of levels of consciousness, all of which can be traced to neural circuitry that has evolved over human history.

The puzzle of the origin of consciousness is a classic one in philosophy, and some philosophers do not believe that neuroscience is on the right track to solve it. David Chalmers (1996, 2002) is one of those philosophers. He contends that the problems that neuroscience can solve are the "easy problems," whereas the origin of human consciousness is the "hard problem." Chalmers considers consciousness a problem of another order, separate from considerations of physiology, but he does not believe that the problem is unsolvable, as the mysterians do.

Thus, the larger issues related to consciousness are difficult even to frame as questions, much less to answer. To work toward a more complete understanding of consciousness, researchers often focus on particular states of consciousness. In the remainder of this chapter, we will look at many of those states. Some people choose to alter their conscious experience through hypnosis, meditation, or the use of drugs. However, there's a more commonplace way to alter your consciousness, one you experience daily—sleep.

What Happens When We Sleep?

Most people—indeed, most creatures—sleep. Some animals are awake during daylight and asleep at night; others have the opposite cycle. But cycles of sleep and waking are the rule.

The Sleep–Wakefulness Cycle: Circadian Rhythms

In the casinos of Las Vegas, it is difficult to tell night from day. Activity is at fever pitch 24 hours a day, and there are no windows and few clocks. It is as if there is no day or night. The casinos want business around the clock, and slot machines never sleep. But even in Las Vegas, people do. Sleep is inescapable. Humans and other animals seem to have an internal biological clock that controls the sleep–wakefulness cycle. This clock runs on about a 24-hour cycle; thus, it is referred to as *circadian* (from the Latin *circa diem*, "around a day"). **Circadian rhythms** are internally generated patterns of body functions, including hormone levels, sleep and wakefulness, blood pressure, and body temperature, which vary over approximately a 24-hour cycle. Even in places such as Las Vegas, when normal cues about whether it is day or night are missing, circadian rhythms still operate.

Light is not essential for maintaining circadian rhythms, but it is a very important cue. Light helps synchronize the biological clock through signals that go to the **suprachiasmatic nucleus**, a structure that is part of the anterior hypothalamus, located just above where the two optic nerves meet and cross in the brain (Pace-Schott & Hobson, 2002). Several genes have been identified that synthesize proteins that affect the suprachiasmatic nucleus, regulating changes in sleep and waking. When time cues (clocks, natural light, temperature changes as the sun goes down) are missing from the environment for a long time, circadian rhythms still operate with only a few minutes variation in the 24-hour cycle (Lavie, 2001).

You can see the impact of circadian rhythms when your routine is thrown off, for example, by having to work through the night and sleep during the day. Under these circumstances, your work schedule is at odds with your biological clock. This kind of disruption is common among airline pilots, police, and health-care workers—some of the approximately 10 million Americans who work at night (Beers, 2000). Even small adjustments, such as the beginning of Daylight Savings

Circadian [sir-KAY-dee-an] rhythms ■ Internally generated patterns of body functions, including hormone levels, sleep and wakefulness, blood pressure, and body temperature, which vary over approximately a 24-hour cycle and occur even in the absence of normal cues about whether it is day or night.

Suprachiasmatic nucleus ■ A structure in the anterior hypothalamus, just above where the two optic nerves meet and cross in the brain.

Time, can have negative effects (Valdez, Ramirez, & Garcia, 2003). When you put in long hours that stretch through the night and into the dawn, and especially when you do so irregularly, you become less attentive, think less clearly, and may even fall asleep on the job. Employers, workers, and consumers need to be aware of the potential decreases in efficiency of night workers who vary their schedules, especially airline pilots (Ariznavarreta et al., 2002) and health-care workers (Hill, 2004), whose inattentiveness and errors can have serious safety consequences. Research shows that light therapy can help. Exposure to bright light, even during sleep, can help reset circadian rhythms (Lowden, Åkerstedt, & Wibom, 2004; Yan & Silver, 2004). This possibility offers relief for those whose jobs require them to constantly readjust their internal clocks.

Another problem caused by disruption of circadian rhythms is jet lag. If you travel by jet from, say, New York City to London, the trip will take about 6 hours. If you leave at 9:00 p.m., you will arrive in London 6 hours later—at 3:00 a.m., as far as your body is concerned. But the local time will actually be 8:00 a.m. You will probably experience the exhaustion and disorientation that are typical of jet lag. You might have the urge to sleep during the first day, which will make you feel better, but it might also make you stay up the next night and keep your circadian rhythms out of sync with London time. Traveling east from New York to London is likely to produce more unpleasant symptoms than going west to Hawaii, because it is easier to lengthen your day than to shorten it (Herxheimer, 2004). Jet lag can affect performance in ways similar to a shifting work schedule.

What should you do to minimize the effects of a shifting schedule or jet lag? Your body's circadian rhythms adjust slowly, so there is no instant cure (Herxheimer, 2004). But you can make adjustments that ease a transition. Your adjustment will be more successful if your schedule shifts slowly or if you are able to work nights all the time rather than shifting back and forth from day shift to night shift. (The shifting prevents adaptation.) Getting over jet lag also takes time, but a trip may be too short for your body to make the adjustment. In that case, the best course may be to stay on your home time schedule and try to schedule your activities to accommodate your body's established rhythms (Dement, 1999).

If your trip is long enough that you need to adjust your time schedule, you can speed up the adjustment process in several ways. One way is to expose yourself to light, which promotes wakefulness. Any level of light can be helpful, but the best is bright sunlight. Be careful to get lots of light exposure when you want to be more alert and to limit light exposure, even room lighting, when you are preparing to sleep (Boivin & James, 2002). To promote sleep, the hormone melatonin may be useful. This hormone is produced by the pineal gland in the brain; its level rises before people fall asleep. Synthetic melatonin has the same effect as the hormone produced in the body. Although researchers know that melatonin is involved in keeping the biological clock in sync (Middleton, Arendt, & Stone, 1997), not all people find taking melatonin helpful in easing the symptoms of jet lag (Herxheimer, 2004; Waterhouse et al., 2002). Exercise helps some people, and good health habits such as eating right and limiting alcohol intake may be even more important while adjusting to a different time schedule than they typically are. Those good habits are also conducive to normal sleep.

Sleep Stages: REM and NREM Sleep

Until the 1950s, scientists assumed that humans had two levels of consciousness: awake and asleep. Then sleep researchers Eugene Aserinsky, Nathaniel Kleitman, and William Dement studied the sleep–wakefulness cycle and surprised the world with their discovery that sleep consists of different levels of consciousness. By using *electroencephalograms (EEGs)*—graphic records of brain-wave activity obtained through electrodes placed on the scalp and the forehead—these researchers were able to identify these levels.

Researchers working in sleep laboratories make EEG recordings by attaching electrodes to participants' scalps and allowing the participants to sleep (no easy task for some!). The electrodes measure the electrical activity of neurons in the brain, and the wave-forms reflect the brain's activity. EEG waves vary in two ways: in frequency and in amplitude. The frequency is the number of waves per second, and the amplitude is the height of the waves. Both of these factors are important in determining brain activity and stages of sleep. Recordings of the brain waves of sleeping participants have revealed five different stages of sleep, which occur in a cycle throughout a night.

The most dramatic finding of early sleep research was the discovery of *rapid eye movement (REM) sleep*—characterized by high-frequency, low-amplitude brain-wave activity and rapid eye movements (Aserinsky & Kleitman, 1953). The stage of REM sleep occurs only after people go through four stages of *non–rapid eye movement (NREM) sleep*.

Figure 7.1 shows the distinctive brain-wave patterns of wakefulness, the four stages of NREM sleep, and the stage of REM sleep. Note that the brain-wave patterns of REM sleep are similar to the pattern that appears during waking. The waking brain-wave pattern exhibits high-frequency, low-amplitude waves; such a pattern is typical when the brain is engaged in many types of activity. Stages 1 through 4 of NREM sleep involve decreasing body arousal and slower EEG activity. During NREM sleep, heart rate slows, blood pressure lowers, respiration slows, and EEG activity indicates lower levels of brain arousal (Siegel, 2003). In addition, people become more difficult to awaken as they progress through the stages of NREM sleep.

In stage 1 NREM sleep, light sleep, brain waves have low amplitude and mixed frequencies. Stage 2 sleep shows low-amplitude, nonrhythmic brain-wave activity, but sleepers in stage 2 are in deeper sleep than those in stage 1. Stage 3 sleep shows brain waves that have lower frequencies and higher amplitudes than

Electroencephalogram [eel-ECK-tro-en-SEFF-uh-low-gram] (EEG) ■ Graphical record of brain-wave activity obtained through electrodes placed on the scalp and the forehead.

Rapid eye movement (REM) sleep ■ Stage of sleep characterized by high-frequency, low-amplitude brain-wave activity, rapid eye movements, more vivid dreams, and postural muscle paralysis.

Non–rapid eye movement (NREM) sleep ■ Four distinct stages of sleep during which no rapid eye movements occur.

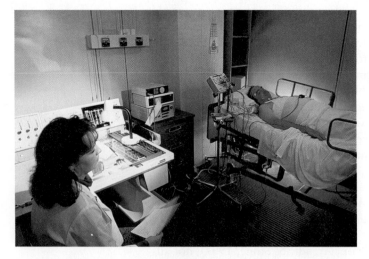

Researchers in sleep laboratories study the EEG patterns of sleeping participants.

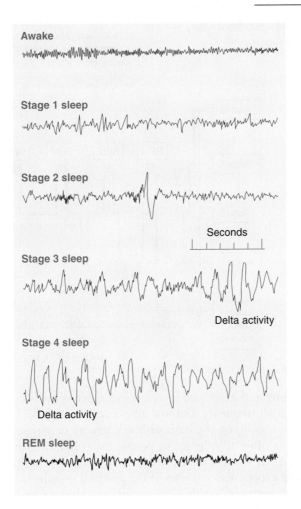

Awake

Stage 1 sleep

Stage 2 sleep

Seconds

Stage 3 sleep

Delta activity

Stage 4 sleep

Delta activity

REM sleep

Figure 7.1

EEG Activity during Sleep

An EEG recording shows characteristic patterns of brain waves when a person is awake and during stages 1–4 of NREM sleep and REM sleep. After the onset of sleep, the EEG pattern changes progressively from low-amplitude, high-frequency waves to high-amplitude, low-frequency waves.

those in stage 2, including some low-frequency, high-amplitude waves called *delta waves*. These big, slow waves result from many brain neurons firing in synchrony. Stages 3 and 4 together are referred to as *slow wave sleep* because of the dominance of these slow waves. In stage 4 sleep, the deepest sleep, the EEG pattern shows over 50% delta waves. This stage of sleep is the lowest level of arousal that people normally experience.

Sleepers take about 30 to 40 minutes to go through these NREM stages, as **Figure 7.2** shows. When sleepers leave stage 4, they move back through stages 3, 2, and 1 before going into REM sleep. During an 8-hour period of sleep, people typically progress through five full cycles of stages, with each cycle lasting approximately 90 minutes. The cycles earlier in the night usually include the REM stage and the four NREM stages, but as Figure 7.2 shows, later cycles may omit some NREM stages.

REM sleep is very different from NREM sleep, not only because of the presence of eye movements but also in the level of arousal (Hobson & Pace-Schott, 2002). In

Figure 7.2
The Course of
Sleep Stages
during 8 Hours
of Sleep
Most people com-
plete about five
sleep cycles per
night, which occur
in a regular pattern
of stages 1–4 of
NREM sleep and
REM sleep.
(Dement, 1972)

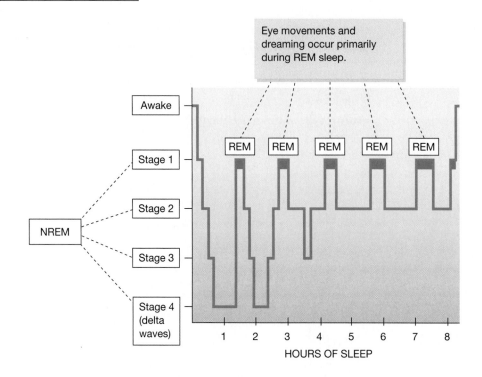

REM sleep, breathing and heart rate increase, eye movements become rapid, and EEG waves are of high frequency and low amplitude. Indeed, REM sleep is difficult to distinguish from waking on the basis of brain activity or physiological arousal (as **Figure 7.1** shows). But in some sense, people are even more soundly asleep during REM sleep than at other times, because they are more difficult to awaken. In addition, people experience paralysis of the postural muscles during REM sleep; they make small movements, but they cannot sit up, stand, or walk during this sleep stage. These seemingly contradictory indications led researchers to coin the term *paradoxical sleep* to describe REM sleep (Jouvet, 1999).

When awakened from REM sleep, people are more likely to report that they were dreaming than when they are awakened from other stages. Early research on sleep and dreaming suggested that dreams occur only during REM sleep, but later research demonstrated that REM sleep and dreaming do not always coincide (Solms, 2003). Indeed, sleepers report dreams when awakened from all stages of sleep (Domhoff, 2004; Foulkes, 1996). However, REM dreams tend to be more vivid, to last longer, and to involve more detail and movement than dreams occurring in NREM sleep. Sleepwalking, however, cannot take place during REM sleep—the postural muscle paralysis prevents walking, so the popular notion that sleepwalkers are acting out dreams is wrong.

Sleep cycles develop before birth, and they continue to change into adulthood. Initially, sleeping fetuses show no eye movements. Later, they show eye, facial, and bodily movements, but not the five distinct stages of sleep (Dement, 1999; Winson, 2002). Newborns spend nearly half their sleep time in REM sleep. From age 1 to age 10, the ratio of REM sleep to stage 4 sleep decreases dramatically; by age 10, REM sleep accounts for only about 25% of sleep. In later adulthood, sleep patterns become more fragmented; older people have trouble sleeping through the night, and they experience a further decrease in the proportion of REM sleep (see **Figure 7.3**).

Sleep researchers have established the cyclic pattern that occurs during sleep by testing people in sleep laboratories. Therefore, almost everything psychologists know about sleep comes from studies of people in Western, industrialized societies,

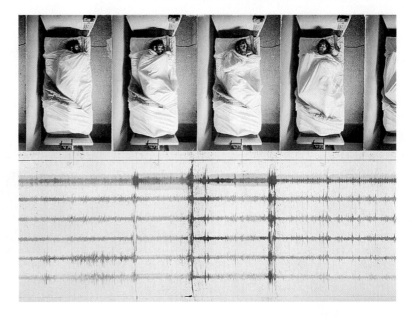

During REM sleep, breathing and heart rate increase, eye movements become rapid, and EEG waves are high frequency and low amplitude.

and their conclusions may be biased. Anthropologist Carol Worthman studies sleep in other cultures, and she has found that Western sleep patterns and habits are not universal (Worthman & Melby, 2002). People in traditional tribal cultures in Africa, Paraguay, Pakistan, and Indonesia have sleep habits very different from those of people in the United States. In these societies, sleep is more social, and people sleep in groups rather than alone or in couples; babies sleep with their mothers. Noise is part of the sleep environment, and there are no thick, comfortable mattresses. Yet people in these cultures sleep well—they tend to complain about getting too much rather than too little sleep. In addition, people in these cultures experience the five stages of sleep, but they spend more time in stages 1 and 2 and less in the deeper stages, 3 and 4. This difference may allow them to wake more easily in less protected environments. Such cross-cultural research shows how easy it can be to overgeneralize laboratory research and how variable even biologically based activities like sleep can be.

Sleep Deprivation

In January 1964, at age 17, Randy Gardner made history and set a world record by staying awake for more than 260 hours—just short of 11 days. He enlisted two friends to help keep him awake, and he took no stimulants, not even coffee. After 2 days, sleep researcher William Dement began supervising Gardner's progress, much to the relief of his parents. Although Gardner did not suffer any serious physical symptoms, there were marked psychological effects. On day 2, he had trouble focusing his eyes. On day 3, he experienced mood changes. On day 4, he was irritable and uncooperative, and he began to hallucinate. By day 6, Gardner had some memory lapses and difficulty speaking. By day 9, his thoughts and speech were sometimes incoherent. On day 10, blurred vision became more of a problem, and he was regularly forgetting things.

Figure 7.3

Changes in Sleep Patterns over a Lifetime

Children spend more time in REM sleep than adults do; the proportion of time spent in REM sleep decreases every year. NREM sleep accounts for nearly half of a newborn's sleep time. In adulthood, 80–85% of sleep is NREM sleep. (Roffwarg, Muzio, & Dement, 1966)

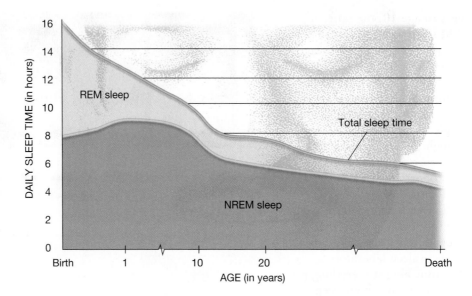

Dement followed up on Randy's marathon of sleep deprivation by monitoring and observing him for several days to see how well he recovered, what happened to his sleep patterns, and whether he made up for the sleep he had lost. Dement found that for three nights following his deprivation, Gardner slept an extra 6.5 hours; on the fourth night, he slept an extra 2.5 hours (Gulevich, Dement, & Johnson, 1966; Johnson, Slye, & Dement, 1965). Therefore, Randy did not make up all the sleep that he lost in his 11 days of sleep deprivation.

Randy Gardner's experience was unusual in terms of the length of his sleep deprivation, but going without sleep is a part of many people's lives. According to the National Sleep Foundation (Harvey, 2000), 67% of adults in the United States get less than the recommended amount of sleep; 43% say that sleepiness interferes with activities in their lives, including work performance. People cut short their sleep in order to work, as well as to have fun, by partying and watching TV, for example. What are the effects of sleep deprivation? How much harm is caused by going without sleep, especially by giving up a few hours per night, as many people do? If Randy Gardner's experience is typical, missing a few hours' sleep doesn't cause many problems, but many hours of deprivation produce major problems in functioning.

The results of research on sleep deprivation point to how drastically sleep deprivation can affect performance. The obvious result is that the longer people go without sleep, the sleepier they get and the worse their performance becomes (Devoto et al., 1999). One night of total sleep deprivation affects motor performance and memory (Forest & Godbout, 2000). But even a few hours of missed sleep can affect performance. A study that made this point in a dramatic way compared the driving performance of people who were deprived of various amounts of sleep to that of people who had drunk various amounts of alcohol (Arnedt et al., 2001). The results showed that even low levels of alcohol impair driving ability and that sleep deprivation is comparable to drinking in its effects on driving. Indeed, driving skills worsen after a person stays awake only 3 hours longer than usual.

These results about sleep deprivation and driving suggest an underlying reason for many traffic accidents. Research with long-haul truckers suggests that sleep deprivation is a serious safety problem (Mitler et al., 1997). The truckers averaged just over 5 hours of sleep per 24-hour period, which is about 2 hours less than what they reported as their ideal amount of sleep. The monitoring revealed that sleepiness was a substantial problem. For 7% of the time they were actually driving, drivers exhibited signs of being in the first stage of sleep, and a majority experienced extended periods of serious drowsiness. Truckers are not the only people who engage in activities that can be dangerous if one is sleep-deprived. Airline and ship pilots, health-care workers, police, and workers at nuclear facilities can endanger the lives of others by their sleepiness. Millions of other people endanger their own and others' lives by driving while drowsy; 60% of young adults admit that they have done so, and 17% say they have dozed off while driving (Harvey, 2000).

Lack of sleep is not confined to any age group or any nationality. Many young adolescents in the United States (Fredriksen, Reddy, & Way, 2004) and many Japanese high school students (Tagaya et al., 2004) report that they get too little sleep to perform optimally. Pioneering sleep researcher William Dement (1999) describes this problem as *sleep debt*. To understand this concept, think of your sleep needs as a checkbook that should be in balance at the end of a week. After sleep deprivation, you owe your body sleep time. If you don't make it up, you pay the price in terms of sleepiness, difficulty with concentration and attentiveness, poor mood, and lack of judgment, which may put you in danger. When combined with other risks, the dangers multiply. For example, the sleep deprivation, stress, and substance use that college students commonly experience create an increased risk for depression (Voelker, 2004).

What about complete sleep deprivation? What happens when people do not sleep at all? For obvious reasons of ethics, researchers cannot completely deprive people of sleep to see what happens. But they do know what happens to rats who are not permitted to sleep and to those with fatal familial insomnia: They die. Rats die after 2 to 3 weeks of complete sleep deprivation (Rechtschaffen & Bergmann, 2002). Some of the symptoms in sleep-deprived rats are similar to those experienced by humans who have FFI—they show signs of terrible exhaustion, they lose the ability to regulate body temperature, and they lose weight. These studies indicate that sleep is obviously important, but what does it do?

Why Do We Sleep?

The distressing consequences of sleep deprivation suggest that sleep is essential, but none of the research has provided an answer to the basic question: *Why* is sleep necessary? Several theories have addressed this question, but some answers are more satisfactory than others (Occhionero, 2004). The most obvious answer is that we sleep because we are tired—sleep provides some type of restorative function. If so, researchers have not identified what sleep restores. Fatigue does not relate directly to the need for sleep. Bedridden hospital patients, for example, sleep about the same amount of time as people who are on their feet all day. Heavy exercise seems to increase the need for sleep on a particular day, but the variation is not large (Youngstedt, O'Connor, & Dishman, 1997). One recent version of the restorative theory (Siegel, 2003) holds that sleep, and especially REM sleep, produces neuro-chemical changes that allow the brain to repair itself and permit the body to reestablish optimal control of many of its systems. This view is consistent with the many problems that arise from sleep deprivation, including the deaths from FFI.

The evolutionary approach encounters problems in explaining sleep. One evolutionary view is that lowered activity levels conserve energy and forced unconsciousness keeps creatures out of danger (Pace-Schott & Hobson, 2002). Having a means to lower energy use *would* be an adaptive advantage, but spending hours per day unconscious and vulnerable to predation is difficult to interpret as a survival advantage. In addition, people who are asleep are not able to do other things that would increase their chances of survival and reproduction, such as gather food, care for children, or have sex (Rechtschaffen, 1998). Therefore, considering the evolutionary role of sleep fails to answer the question of why we sleep.

Another theory conceptualizes sleep as part of circadian rhythms and emphasizes the brain mechanisms underlying the regulation of sleep and waking (Lavie, 2001). This circadian theory of sleep takes a broad approach, examining the cross-species differences and similarities in amount of sleep and sleep stages. This theory explains the mechanisms of sleep better than it answers the question of why sleep is necessary (Pace-Schott & Hobson, 2002).

Some theories of sleep concentrate on the stages of sleep, especially on REM sleep. One theory that takes this approach holds that REM sleep is important to memory formation (Hobson & Pace-Schott, 2002), but two opposing camps disagree about how REM sleep and memory are related. One version proposes that REM sleep is necessary to eliminate unnecessary neural connections formed during waking (Crick & Mitchison, 1983), whereas another version hypothesizes that REM activity is important to memory formation (Stickgold, James, & Hobson, 2000). Another theory holds that REM sleep plays an essential role in neural maturation, pointing to the finding that infants and babies spend more time in REM sleep than adults and older people do (Dement, 1999; Siegel, 2003).

No single theory has yet explained why we sleep, and perhaps none ever will. One theory might be inadequate for the task, anyway: Sleep probably serves multiple functions, and thus, several theories may be necessary to explain those functions (Rechtschaffen, 1998).

Is There a Sleep Switch?

What makes you go to sleep, and what wakes you? If your life is like mine (L.B.'s), you probably answer "exhaustion" to the first part of that question and "the alarm clock" to the second. Although those answers may be applicable to many of us, they don't tell the whole story. If we could sleep whenever we wanted, we would still go to sleep and wake up on a fairly regular schedule. Indeed, research on circadian rhythms shows that people maintain a rhythmic cycle of sleeping and waking, even when they are removed from their normal lives and deprived of cues about day and night (Czeisler et al., 1999). Is there a physiological structure that regulates and initiates sleep and wakefulness?

Research suggests that there are brain systems that "turn on" sleep and "turn on" waking. As we discussed earlier, the suprachiasmatic nucleus (SCN) of the anterior hypothalamus is essential to the regulation of circadian rhythms. This structure provides control of the sleep–wake cycle, and the selective activity of its cells promote the cyclic experience of waking and sleeping (Pace-Schott & Hobson, 2002).

The "sleep on" switch may be located in the front region of the hypothalamus, called the *ventrolateral preoptic area*, or the VLPO. Cells in this area of the brains of sleeping rats seem to fire or not fire, depending on the stage of sleep (Sherin et al., 1996). Researchers found that in rats that were deprived of sleep for 9 to 12 hours, a certain protein was present throughout most of the brain but not in the VLPO. In contrast, in rats that were not sleep-deprived, the protein was found in the VLPO but not in the rest of the brain. Further research has confirmed the importance of the VLPO in promoting sleep and perhaps regulating wakefulness and has suggested how this area might work (Gallopin et al., 2000; Pace-Schott & Hobson, 2002). Neurons in the VLPO produce GABA, an inhibitory neurotransmitter (see **Table 3.1**). In addition, these neurons have connections to other locations in the brain.

Other areas toward the back of the hypothalamus are important to wakefulness and alertness (Pace-Schott & Hobson, 2002). The waking system acts to inhibit the sleep-promoting system, and it involves interconnected neurons that extend from the brain stem to the forebrain. The neuropeptide *orexin* stimulates this system and promotes wakefulness (Siegel, 2004). Discovered by researchers trying to understand and treat the sleep disorder narcolepsy (discussed later in this chapter), orexin-producing neurons are found in several regions of the lateral hypothalamus, and they project to the *locus coeruleus*, lower in the brain.

In summary, systems within the brain act like switches that control both sleep and waking. These brain systems consist of interconnected neurons controlled by a complex set of neurochemicals. The mechanisms that control sleeping and waking may also be the source of problems with these functions. Some people fall asleep when they want to stay awake; others have trouble sleeping.

Sleep Disorders

Do you fall asleep easily, or does it take you half an hour or more to get to sleep? Do you fall asleep at inappropriate times, such as during class, while driving, or at work? Have you ever walked in your sleep? If you answer yes to either the second or third question, you very likely have a sleep disorder. Your condition may not be unusual; there are many sleep disorders. Some are not dangerous, but others are life-threatening.

People who experience sudden, uncontrollable episodes of sleep have a disorder known as *narcolepsy*. In addition to these episodes of daytime sleepiness, people with narcolepsy experience muscle weakness as they fall asleep. This disorder affects about 1 in 2,000 people and severely restricts their lives—they never know when they will have an attack (Naumann & Daum, 2003). Narcolepsy has a genetic component (Takahashi, 1999), and effective drug treatment has recently been developed (Tentative approvals, 2004).

Narcolepsy ■ A sleep disorder characterized by sudden, uncontrollable episodes of sleep.

Sleep apnea ■ A life-threatening sleep disorder in which airflow into the lungs stops for at least 15 seconds, causing the sleeper to choke and then awaken briefly.

Another sleep disorder, *sleep apnea*, is even more serious. This sleep disorder causes airflow into the lungs to stop for at least 15 seconds; the sleeper stops breathing and chokes, and then wakens briefly. Rather than choking awake, however, some choke and die. Loud snoring is a symptom of sleep apnea (Young, Skatrud, & Peppard, 2004). People with this disorder may have as many as 100 apnea episodes in a night. Because their sleep is interrupted so often, people with apnea get poor-quality sleep and feel exceedingly sleepy much of the time. They may have memory losses, severe headaches, and work-related accidents. As much as 33% of the population experience symptoms that suggest sleep apnea (Netzer et al., 2003). Middle-aged, overweight men are at particular risk, but even children can have this disorder (Chan, Edman, & Koltai, 2004). Several therapies have been effective in treating apnea, including a minor surgical procedure or use of a machine that affects airway pressure. Both approaches help ensure that people can breathe normally during sleep.

Insomnia ■ Problems in getting to sleep or remaining asleep.

Insomnia, problems getting to sleep or remaining asleep, is a very common sleep disorder. Ten percent of the population experiences insomnia at some time in their lives, often caused by anxiety or depression. Some people who complain about insomnia have trouble going to sleep, tossing and turning for hours. Others may be able to go to sleep but then wake up too soon and can't get back to sleep. They may actually sleep as much as those who do not complain of insomnia, but their quality of sleep tends to be poor and they do not feel rested (Dement, 1999). People with insomnia tend to be listless and tired during the day and desperate to get some sleep, which may lead them to try sleeping pills or other drugs. In the past, sleeping pills were usually *barbiturates*, which produced dependence and altered the stages of sleep by reducing the proportion of REM sleep (Webb & Agnew, 1975). Today's sleeping pills are safe for short-term use, but drugs are not generally a good solution for those who have chronic insomnia (Gibson, 2004). Various researchers have proposed behavioral methods that do not rely on drugs to help people manage their sleep problems. Among these methods are relaxation training, thought restructuring, and self-hypnosis.

Night terrors ■ A sleep disorder in which a person experiences a high degree of arousal and symptoms of panic that occur within 60–90 minutes after he or she falls asleep.

Night terrors are a sleep disorder in which a person experiences a high degree of arousal and symptoms of panic that occur within 60–90 minutes after falling asleep. A person suffering night terrors may sit up abruptly, scream, breathe rapidly, and appear to be in a state of total fright, yet he or she is not fully conscious (Wills & Garcia, 2002). Night terrors are not vivid nightmares; they occur in NREM sleep, usually in stage 4. They are especially common in young children between the ages of 3 and 8 but usually disappear as a child grows older. Although night terrors appear to be extremely frightening to children, they are not symptoms of any psychological disorder and are often forgotten (except by the startled and concerned parents). The cause of night terrors is not fully established, but they may be a result of an electrochemical overload of some part of the brain during NREM sleep.

Sleepwalking is a disorder that tends to run in families and is more common among children than adults (Wills & Garcia, 2002). A sleepwalker appears both asleep and awake at the same time—a sleepwalking child may reach out to a parent for a hug, navigate a darkened room, avoid a piece of furniture, walk into the street, or seem to be trying to accomplish a task—yet still be asleep. More boys sleepwalk than girls, and children who sleepwalk tend to outgrow it as they mature. The brain activity of sleepwalkers, when recorded with an EEG, indicates stage 4 sleep. Research also shows that different parts of a sleepwalker's brain display different levels of activity: Motor areas of the brain are active; areas of higher-level cognitive functioning show little activity. Contrary to popular belief, there is no danger in waking a sleepwalker. However, it's unlikely that you will be able to do so because he or she is so deeply asleep (Dement, 1999).

Sleepwalking can result in an injury if the sleepwalker does dangerous things (such as fall down stairs or walk into the street), but the disorder itself does not signal a problem and causes no direct damage. Sleep disorders like apnea are very dangerous, however. Not only are people with apnea at risk of dying in their sleep, but they also experience sleepiness that can cause other dangers. Research indicates that sleep disorders are more common than many people imagine, which contributes to their underdiagnosis. For example, it may take years for a person with narcolepsy or apnea to be correctly diagnosed and receive treatment (Morrish et al., 2004; Netzer et al., 2003).

What Are Dreams, and What Do They Mean?

Do you dream every night, or rarely? Do you have trouble remembering your dreams? Have you wondered what dreams mean and if they contain hidden symbols that would be important if only you could interpret them? People have probably tried to interpret dreams for thousands of years. The meaning of dreams has been debated by psychologists for over 100 years, but only since the 1950s have dreams come under close scientific scrutiny. The short history of scientific research on dreaming is attributable to the difficulty of this type of research. Dream researchers have to overcome problems inherent in studying participants' internal, personal events—and they have to stay awake while participants are sleeping so that they can awaken the participants and ask about dreaming.

What Is a Dream?

A *dream* is a state of consciousness that occurs during sleep and is usually accompanied by vivid visual imagery, although the imagery may also be tactile or auditory. Dreams are associated with REM sleep—about 80% of the time when people are awakened from REM sleep, they report a dream. Dreams also occur during NREM sleep, but these tend to be less visual and less bizarre and to contain less action imagery (Casagrande et al., 1996; Schwartz & Maquet, 2002). Dreaming during NREM sleep tends to involve more focused thought, while REM dreams have more visual imagery, especially during the first several hours of a night's sleep (Fosse, Stickgold, & Hobson, 2004).

Although we cannot assume that REM sleep guarantees dreaming (Pagel, 2003), research from sleep labs suggests that people tend to forget dreams when they do not wake during them or soon after. It is likely that most people dream every night, probably several times. REM dreams last from a few seconds to several minutes. The first REM period (and likely the first dream) of a typical night occurs about 90 minutes after a person has fallen asleep and lasts for about 10 minutes (Winson, 2002).

Dream ■ A state of consciousness that occurs during sleep, usually accompanied by vivid visual, tactile, or auditory imagery.

More dreaming occurs near the end of the night than at the beginning. Assuming that the average person dreams in 80% of REM periods, he or she will have three or four dreams per night, 365 days per year, for a total of more than 100,000 dreams in a lifetime. However, people remember only a few of their dreams. Usually, they recall a dream because they woke in the middle of it or because the dream had powerful emotional content or imagery.

The Content of Dreams

Sometimes the content of a dream is related to day-to-day events, sometimes to an unfulfilled desire, and other times to an unpleasant or anxiety-provoking experience. Some people experience the same dream or a sequence of related dreams over and over again. Dreams are mostly visual, and most are in color (Occhionero, 2004). Most dreams focus on events and people with whom the dreamer comes into contact frequently—family, friends, or coworkers (Schredl & Hofmann, 2003). Sounds and other sensations from the environment that do not awaken a sleeper are often incorporated into a dream. For example, one team of researchers sprayed water on the hands of sleepers, and 42% of those who did not awaken immediately later reported dreaming about swimming pools, baths, or rain (Dement & Wolpert, 1958).

The results from brain-imaging studies using PET scans or fMRI show that areas of the brain that are active during REM sleep are consistent with participants' reports of their experiences in their dreams (Occhionero, 2004). For example, the visual association areas are active during REM sleep, which is consistent with the visual imagery that accompanies dreaming. Parts of the frontal cortex show low levels of activity, which probably reflects the lack of integration among the images in dreams and their bizarre, disconnected nature. Also consistent with the experience of dreaming is the activation of brain areas involved with emotion.

When my (L.L.'s) younger daughter was 6 years old, she told me about a dream in which she was being chased by a monster. In the dream, she realized that she was dreaming, and so she turned around and made friends with the monster. Like my daughter, people sometimes report that they are aware of dreaming while it is happening. This type of dream is called a *lucid dream*. Most people have had a lucid dream at one time or another, particularly as children. Most lucid dreams, but not all, occur during REM sleep (Watanabe, 2003). Often people who have experienced a lucid dream report that they felt as though they were in the dream and looking on from outside at the same time. Stephen LaBerge has worked on understanding and developing people's ability to experience lucid dreams, claiming that many benefits accompany the ability to control your dreams (LaBerge & Gackenbach, 2000).

Lucid [LOO-sid] dream
■ Dream in which the dreamer is aware of dreaming while it is happening.

Dream Theories

Psychologists have developed a number of theories to explain what dreams mean. Some believe that dreams express desires and thoughts that may be unacceptable to the conscious mind and must be expressed in symbolic form in dreams. Others believe that dreams reveal a more ordinary level of thought, and still others find the content of dreams less important than the neural activities during REM and NREM sleep. Thus, theories of dreaming vary. The suggested meaning of a dream depends on the psychologist's orientation. (See **Table 7.1**.)

Table 7.1

COMPARISON OF THEORIES OF DREAMING

The Dream: Many people have an anxiety-filled dream in which they are late for an important exam or appointment, but no matter how hard they try to get there, things keep diverting and delaying them.

Basic Orientation	Interpretation of the Dream
■ **Freudian Theory**	
Freud viewed dreams as expressions of desires, wishes, and unfulfilled needs that exist in the unconscious.	The dream is expressing the dreamer's anxiety about potential failure, but the symbolic message from the unconscious is that the dreamer will succeed in the task that is causing anxiety (which may not be an exam or appointment), just as he or she has done in similar situations in the past.
■ **Jungian Theory**	
Jung saw dreams not only as expressions of needs and desires, but as reflections of the collective unconscious.	The dream may be expressing deeper messages from the collective unconscious, with symbols for the trickster archetype, a clever villain who creates problems and does harm.
■ **Cognitive View**	
Cognitive theorists view dreams as continuations of waking cognitive processes; dreams have no hidden meaning and reflect people's everyday concerns.	The dream is expressing anxiety that exists in the dreamer's everyday waking life; the dreamer has a problem in meeting some obligation and is worried about this situation.
■ **Physiological View**	
The activation-synthesis theory of dreaming views dreams as combinations of neural signals that are generated by brain activity during REM sleep.	The content of the dream is the product of the forebrain, which synthesizes the neural impulses generated during the stages of sleep, especially REM sleep, into meaningful episodes.
■ **Evolutionary View**	
The evolutionary perspective views dreams as an opportunity for rehearsal of threatening events.	The dreamer is rehearsing the threatening possibility experienced in the dream, which allows him or her to better manage such situations in waking life.

Psychodynamic Views

Sigmund Freud described dreams as "the royal road to the unconscious." For Freud, a dream expressed desires, wishes, and unfulfilled needs that exist in the unconscious (see Chapter 13 for more on Freud and the unconscious). In his book *The Interpretation of Dreams* (1900/1953), Freud spoke about the manifest and latent content of dreams. The *manifest content* of a dream consists of its overt story line, characters, and setting—the obvious, clearly discernible events of the dream. The *latent content* of a dream is its deeper meaning, usually involving symbolism, hidden meaning, and repressed or obscure ideas and wishes. These wishes might make the dreamer uncomfortable if they were expressed overtly because of their sexual or aggressive nature. Freud would say that at the latent level, a dream about a tunnel is definitely not about a tunnel. You will see in Chapters 13 and 17 that Freud used dreams extensively in his theory of personality and in his treatment approach.

Carl G. Jung (1875–1961) was trained in the Freudian approach to therapy and personality analysis, and he, like Freud, considered dreams a crucial means for understanding human nature. However, Jung believed that an individual's dreams expressed his or her deepest feelings in an uncensored form; they were a dreamer's attempt to make sense of life's tasks, compensate for unconscious urges, and predict the future (McLynn, 1997). In addition, Jung asserted that dreams give visual expression to instincts that all humans share in the *collective unconscious*, a storehouse of primitive ideas and images inherited from our ancestors. Jung called these inherited ideas and images *archetypes*, and noted that they are sometimes represented in dreams. Archetypes are emotionally charged and rich in meaning and symbolism. The photo shows one especially important archetype—the *mandala*, a mystical symbol, often with a circular pattern, that in Jung's view represents a person's inner striving for unity. Dream analysis, with a focus on understanding and accepting one's humanity, is important in Jungian therapy. We will consider this approach in more detail in our study of personality in Chapter 13.

Today, psychodynamic interpretations of dreams (those based on the ideas of Freud and Jung) are not as popular as they once were, but some researchers see recent findings in neuroscience as confirming Freud's basic conceptualization that dreams are expressions of unconscious wishes and desires (Solms, 2004; Solms & Turnbull, 2002). Other scholars have found similarities between the psychodynamic approach and the view of dreaming held in many Native American cultures (Krippner & Thompson, 1996; Tedlock, 2004). Many Native American religions place high importance on dreams; dreams are seen as a route to empowerment and insight. Native Americans do not make as drastic a separation between states of consciousness as Europeans do, but rather accept the dream state as an alternative reality that can reveal wisdom and insight. That is, it can be an experience much like the Western concept of lucid dreaming.

Manifest content ■ The overt story line, characters, and setting of a dream—the obvious, clearly discernible events of the dream.

Latent content ■ The deeper meaning of a dream, usually involving symbolism, hidden meaning, and repressed or obscure ideas and wishes.

Collective unconscious ■ Jung's concept of a shared storehouse of primitive ideas and images (archetypes) that humans have inherited from our ancestors and that are emotionally charged and rich in meaning and symbolism.

Jung believed that the mandala represents a person's inner striving for unity.

Other researchers disagree with approaches that emphasize the role of the unconscious in dreaming (Domhoff, 2004; Hobson, 2004). Instead, these researchers tend to promote the view that dreams represent another way of thinking about life's problems.

Cognitive View

Theorists who hold the cognitive view argue that dreams are connected to waking thought processes, have meaning, and even have a "grammar" of their own, but they have no hidden, or latent, content. Cognitive researchers (e.g., Cicogna & Bosinelli, 2001; Foulkes, 1985, 1996) suggest that dreams reflect the same kind of thinking that people do when they are awake—dreams express current wishes or desires or involve issues with which a person is dealing. Foulkes (1990) argues that the creation of a dream depends on active, integrative cognition and that studying the content of dreams allows researchers to learn more about development, intelligence, and language, as well as about how cognitive processes develop. According to this view, not only do we dream of what currently concerns us, but our culture and language affect dream content. For example, the dream content of those who are bilingual is related to the language that was dominating their waking hours before sleep (Foulkes et al., 1993).

In support of the cognitive view, a cross-cultural study demonstrated that life events affect dream content (Punamäki & Joustie, 1998). This study compared the dreams of Finnish and Palestinian children, whose cultures vary a great deal in attitudes toward dreams (as well as in many other ways). The study also compared the dreams of Palestinian children living in Gaza, an area where opposition to Israeli occupation is strong and where residents often experience violence and the threat of violence, to those of children living in Galilea, a peaceful area. The study found few differences in the children's dreams that were related to the differing values of the two cultures, but the children's life events made a difference in the content of their dreams. As expected, the Palestinian children living in violent neighborhoods reported far more dreams of persecution and aggression than did the Palestinian children from nonviolent areas or the Finnish children. Thus, daily life experiences influence dream content for individuals, but there is a great deal of cross-cultural consistency in the characters, interactions, and situations that appear in dreams (Schredl et al., 2003).

Building Table 7.1 contrasts the psychodynamic view of dreaming with the cognitive view.

Biological Views

Theorists who emphasize the biological basis of dreaming have investigated what happens in the brain when people experience REM sleep. Two researchers from Harvard Medical School, Allan Hobson and Robert McCarley (1977), proposed that dreams (and, for that matter, all consciousness) have a physiological basis. For them, dream content has no hidden meaning; indeed, the meaning of dreams is not

Building Table 7.1

PSYCHODYNAMIC AND COGNITIVE THEORIES OF DREAMING

Dream Theory	Theorist	Dream Origins	Psychological Explanation	Physiological Explanation
Psychodynamic	Freud	Unconscious wishes and desires	Latent content is more important than manifest content.	None
	Jung	Messages from the unconscious	Dreams are messages from the unconscious, including the collective unconscious.	None
Cognitive	Foulkes	Cognitive integration of physiological activity produced by sleep stages	Conscious factors, including problems, worries, and anxiety, drive dream content.	Brain activation during sleep stages is critical for dreaming.

the focus of their research or theory. Instead, they are interested in how levels of brain activation during sleep lead to the cyclic variation of stages of sleep and how the brain synthesizes this activation to yield dreams (Hobson, 1989, 1999; Hobson, Pace-Schott, & Stickgold, 2003). Thus, their view was aptly named the *activation–synthesis theory of dreaming.*

Research supports both the activation and the synthesis parts of the theory. A growing body of research (Maquet et al., 2003; Stickgold, James, & Hobson, 2000) shows that REM activity is important to memory formation. Thus, the neural activity of REM sleep may be essential to information processing in the cerebral cortex, scanning previous memories, refreshing storage mechanisms, and maintaining active memories. Brain-imaging research (Ogawa, Nittono, & Hori, 2002) indicates that REM sleep initiates cognitive processing rather than the other way around, which is consistent with the synthesis part of the theory.

Evolutionary psychologists have also proposed biologically based theories of dreaming. One such theory hypothesizes that dreaming evolved as a way to help people deal effectively with threatening situations by allowing them to process threats during sleep (Revonsuo, 2003). According to this theory, dreams tend to involve unpleasant and anxiety-provoking situations that are similar to the ones we encounter in our lives. Experiencing such situations in dreams allows us to become more proficient in dealing with them in waking life. That is, dreams are practice for real threats. Those who benefited from this type of sleep tended to survive and reproduce more than those who did not, leaving all humans with an inherited tendency to have threatening dreams. **Building Table 7.2** (on p. 257) adds the biological view to the psychodynamic and cognitive views of dreams.

Building Table 7.2

PSYCHODYNAMIC, COGNITIVE, AND BIOLOGICAL THEORIES OF DREAMING

Dream Theory	Theorist(s)	Dream Origins	Psychological Explanation	Physiological Explanation
Psychodynamic	Freud	Unconscious wishes and desires	Latent content is more important than manifest content.	None
	Jung	Messages from the unconscious	Dreams are messages from the unconscious, including the collective unconscious.	None
Cognitive	Foulkes	Cognitive integration of physiological activity produced by sleep stages	Conscious factors, including problems, worries, and anxiety, drive dream content.	Brain activation during sleep stages is critical for dreaming.
Biological	Hobson and colleagues	Activation of brain centers and synthesis of information from activated areas	Dreams have no underlying meaning.	Brain activation prompts synthesis, thus causing dreaming.
	Evolutionary theorists	Practice in threat avoidance	Instinctive fears are inherited, and dreaming about them provides preparation for real threats.	The REM stage evolved to allow special processing during sleep.

Is It Possible to Control Consciousness by Using Biofeedback, Hypnosis, or Meditation?

Can you learn to control your own consciousness? Can you manipulate your mental states to achieve certain bodily reactions? Some people's personal experience suggests that this is possible, and as surprising as it might be, research confirms these possibilities. For centuries, people have learned to relax and breathe in special ways to decrease the experience of pain—for example, during childbirth. Intense mental concentration has allowed people to win marathons and endure difficult physical ordeals. Laboratory research also shows that people can bring some other autonomically controlled responses, such as blood pressure, heart rate, and blood vessel constriction, under conscious control through the technique of biofeedback.

Biofeedback

Imagine a special clinic where people are taught how to treat themselves for headaches, high blood pressure, stress-related illnesses, even nearsightedness, through conscious control of what are normally involuntary reactions. Although such a clinic may be imaginary, biofeedback can help some people with such problems.

Biofeedback ■ A process through which people receive information about the status of a physical function and use this feedback to learn to alter that function.

Physicians and psychologists once assumed that most biological functions, especially those involving the autonomic nervous system, could not be controlled voluntarily though they could be altered through drugs or surgery. Since the 1960s, however, studies have explored the extent to which people can learn to control these functions through biofeedback. *Biofeedback* is a process through which people receive information about the status of a physical function and use this feedback to learn to alter that function somehow. The process usually uses electronic equipment to monitor the status of a function, such as blood pressure, and to give the person immediate feedback about the activity level. A well-known psychologist, Neal E. Miller, was one of the first researchers to train rats to control certain physical responses, such as heart rate. Miller's research (1969) indicated that rats can be trained to either raise or lower their heart rate, and Miller suggested that human beings might be able to learn the same techniques and benefit from them.

Even though we do not normally have any conscious awareness of physiological processes such as brain activity or heart rate, biofeedback machines provide that awareness, which allows us to learn to consciously control such processes. A relaxed person viewing his or her own brain waves on a monitor, for example, can increase the frequency of those waves by responding appropriately to feedback. Similarly, a participant whose heart rate is displayed on a monitor can see the rate decrease as he or she relaxes, thereby learning about the physiological states that accompany relaxation. The person can learn which behaviors relax the heart and lower blood pressure and, in time, can learn to reproduce those behaviors to control heart rate and blood pressure.

Biofeedback studies use electronic equipment to monitor a physical function, such as blood pressure or heart rate, and give feedback on its status. Such feedback allows a person to learn to alter the function.

How useful is biofeedback? The technique has been used to treat a variety of disorders, including chronic headaches, muscle tension problems, back pain, and high blood pressure. However, biofeedback is not practical as the sole strategy for managing high blood pressure (Kranitz, 2004). Its greatest success has been in helping people manage chronic headaches, especially migraine headaches (Astin, 2004). Other techniques for controlling consciousness, including hypnosis, are sometimes as effective as biofeedback.

Hypnosis

"You are falling asleep. Your eyelids are becoming heavy. The weight on your eyes is becoming greater and greater. Your muscles are relaxing. You are feeling sleepier and sleepier. You are feeling very relaxed." These instructions are typical of those used in *hypnotic induction*—the process used to hypnotize people. *Hypnosis* is a state of consciousness during which a person's sensations, perceptions, thoughts, or behaviors change because of suggestions made to the person. The induction procedure is fairly standard, but almost everything else about hypnosis is controversial, including whether it actually *is* an altered state of consciousness.

Hypnosis was first used to treat people in the late 18th century in France by Franz Anton Mesmer. His work was discredited, and hypnosis fell into disfavor. Since that time, hypnosis has gone through cycles of acceptance and rejection. Today, opinions are divided not only on what hypnosis is but also on its uses. There is more agreement about the characteristics associated with the hypnotic state.

The movie image of hypnosis, which contributes to public misperceptions, differs from the actual hypnotic state (Green, 2003). In the movies, the hypnotist swings a gold watch in front of a person's eyes, while saying, "You are getting sleepy," and the weak-willed person loses the ability to maintain control, falling completely under the power of the hypnotist. Almost everything about this image is incorrect; the only accurate part is that hypnotic inductions usually contain the suggestion that the participant is getting sleepy. Despite that suggestion, the hypnotic state is not the same as any stage of sleep (Rainville et al., 1999).

People who are hypnotized are not weak-willed or unintelligent. Those who are good hypnotic participants tend to have a strong ability to visualize images and are able to become absorbed in imaginative experiences (Lichtenberg et al., 2004). The ability to concentrate is also related to how easily people can be hypnotized, so intelligence is positively rather than negatively related to this characteristic. In the movies, people usually fall into a deep trance immediately, but in real life, most people do not. Practice is a factor in hypnosis. Even good hypnotic participants need practice to attain a deep hypnotic state, and those who are not good at it at first can improve with practice (Patterson & Jensen, 2003).

Suggestibility is also a characteristic of the hypnotic state, but there is controversy over whether hypnosis produces increased suggestibility or whether those who can be hypnotized are more suggestible than average. This difference of opinion relates to the controversy about the definition of hypnosis However, the popular image of the extent of suggestibility during hypnosis is also incorrect. Suggestibility does increase when a person is hypnotized (Braffman & Kirsch, 1999; Poulsen & Matthews, 2003), but most people will not do bizarre or unconventional things suggested to them when under hypnosis. And the increased suggestibility does not extend beyond hypnosis. The power of *posthypnotic suggestion*, a suggestion that a participant in hypnosis should perform a particular action after the hypnotic session has ended, is not as strong as people imagine. That is, when a hypnotist makes suggestions about behaviors to

Hypnosis ■ A state of consciousness during which a person's sensations, perceptions, thoughts, or behaviors change because of suggestions made to the person.

Posthypnotic suggestion ■ A suggestion that a participant in hypnosis should perform a particular action after the hypnotic session has ended.

Most people do not achieve a hypnotic state as easily as the popular image suggests, and most hypnotized people will not do bizarre or unconventional things.

be performed at a later time, the hypnotized person does not inevitably carry out those suggestions. In one study, participants who were not hypnotized responded at a higher rate to a verbal request from the experimenter than did participants who were hypnotized to a posthypnotic suggestion (Barnier & McConkey, 1998). Therefore, hypnosis is not very effective in helping people lose weight, stop smoking, or break other bad habits because posthypnotic suggestions are not very effective in altering behavior.

Other effects popularly associated with hypnosis are also less powerful than most people believe. Heightened memory is supposedly associated with hypnosis, but the evidence for this effect is weak, especially for *age regression* under hypnosis. In the movies, hypnotized people sometimes recall early childhood experiences that they had thought they had forgotten, but these effects are most likely re-creations of those experiences rather than memories of them (Spiegel, 1998). In fact, the increased suggestibility associated with hypnosis can make a hypnotized person vulnerable to suggestions by the hypnotist concerning imagery, which can result in memory distortion. For this reason, hypnosis is a poor choice for helping witnesses recall details of a crime—they may remember things that they did not see (Loftus, 2000). The problem of memory distortion during hypnosis has become extremely controversial in connection with the *recovered memories* of women who have, often while under hypnosis, remembered childhood sexual abuse (a topic we'll consider in Chapter 9).

What uses, then, does hypnosis have? The technique is used in psychotherapy and in health-care settings to help people relax and to assist in pain control. A great deal of research on hypnosis and pain has indicated that the technique does work to reduce pain, including pain due to injuries and surgery as well as pain from chronic headaches (Patterson & Jensen, 2003). Hypnosis has also been used to help people control other types of pain, ranging from childbirth and dental pain to burn and cancer pain. Hypnosis is sometimes used in combination with other treatments to help people cope with stress, focus energy, and deal with anxiety and traumatic experiences (Astin, 2004). Brain-imaging studies indicate that hypnotized people show changes in the somatosensory cortex (where body sensations are perceived) as well as in areas of the brain associated with emotions (which may relate to the emotional component of the experience of pain) (Patterson & Jensen, 2003). These results show that hypnosis is capable of producing physical changes. Therefore, hypnosis offers benefits for people trying to manage stress or pain. Meditation is another possible aid for those with such problems.

Meditation

Meditation has become an important daily routine for one of my (L.B.'s) former students. He had been arrested, had problems with drug use, and had behaved impulsively in a number of ways. He was in prison when he decided that meditation would allow him to think and behave in a more productive way. Now he has a college degree and holds a management-level job. He says that meditation is an important part of his life, and he meditates every day. He is not alone in believing in the benefits of meditation.

Meditation is the use of a variety of techniques, including concentration, restriction of incoming stimuli, and attention to breathing and muscle tension, to produce a state of consciousness characterized by a sense of detachment and deep relaxation. All meditation techniques aim to induce an altered state of awareness and to direct the focus of attention away from the outside world through intense concentration. Those who meditate take a variety of approaches and use a variety of positions—sitting, lying down, or reclining. For centuries, meditation has been used to help relieve health problems. Practitioners report that it can reduce anxiety, tension headaches, backaches, asthma, and the need for sleep, and research has confirmed some of these benefits. Meditation can also increase self-awareness and feelings of inner peace (Andresen, 2000). Meditation is not relaxation—rather, relaxation is a by-product of meditation.

Practitioners distinguish among several types of meditation, but much of the research done by psychologists has concentrated on *mindfulness meditation* (Kabat-Zinn, 1993). A person begins mindfulness meditation by trying to empty the mind and just be still. As random and intrusive thoughts arise, the person notices them (becomes mindful of their content) without reacting to them, judging them, or dwelling on them. They eventually become mere wisps of thought that pass through consciousness, while the meditator remains serene. Eventually, a mindful meditator becomes aware that reactions to thoughts cause suffering, and that one can entertain thoughts without having to react.

In *concentrative meditation*, a meditator concentrates on a visual image or a *mantra* (a word or a phrase repeated over and over). When a thought enters the mind, the meditator brings the mind back to the image or the mantra, without paying attention to the content of the thought. With this style of meditation, the image or the mantra is the important thing. Concentrative meditation is closely tied to religions such as Tibetan Buddhism, Zen Buddhism, and Hinduism.

Supporters of meditation claim that it is a practice that induces a unique state and that it is capable of causing profound physiological and psychological changes. They argue that mindfulness meditation produces a different mode of cognitive processing, by training people to maintain awareness of ongoing events and increase their attention. Research has indicated that this technique produces changes in brain activation and in immune system functioning (Davidson et al., 2003) and that it is beneficial in the management of heart disease (Tacon et al., 2003). Detractors argue that meditation is nothing more than relaxation and that the positive results are due to a combination of factors, not just the meditation (Smith, 2004).

> **Meditation** ■ The use of a variety of techniques, including concentration, restriction of incoming stimuli, and attention to breathing and muscle tension, to produce a state of consciousness characterized by a sense of detachment and deep relaxation.

Meditation involves concentration and deep relaxation.

How Do Drugs Alter Consciousness?

Like many people in the United States, you may have ingested some type of drug within the past 24 hours. If you have taken a pain-relieving tablet, smoked a cigarette, or drunk any beverage containing caffeine or alcohol, then you are among a large group of drug users. More than half of the people in the United States over age 12 regularly use some kind of drug that changes both brain activity and behavior (Substance Abuse and Mental Health Services Administration [SAMHSA], 2003). Drugs may be legal or illegal; they may be used responsibly or abused with tragic consequences. A *drug* is any chemical substance that, in small amounts, alters biological or mental processes, or both. Many widely used drugs are *psychoactive drugs*, which affect biochemical reactions in the nervous system, thereby altering behavior, thought, or perception, and thus consciousness.

The use of psychoactive drugs is not limited to the United States, of course. Using drugs to alter consciousness is common in almost all cultures (Adrian, 2002). Some cultures restrict drug use to ceremonial or religious occasions, whereas others permit drug use as a way to manage emotions and moods. Some cultures allow drugs to be used in order to increase social interaction or to improve performance. Drugs that are condoned by one culture may be condemned by another, but drug use occurs throughout the world and has existed throughout history. Problems associated with drug use are related to certain effects of taking the drugs.

Many psychoactive drugs lead to tolerance or dependence, or both. *Tolerance* is the condition in which higher and higher doses of a drug are required to produce the same effect. *Dependence* occurs when a drug becomes part of the body's functioning in such a way that the drug user suffers withdrawal symptoms when the drug is discontinued. *Withdrawal symptoms* are effects experienced when someone stops using a drug that produces dependence. Tolerance and dependence can be dangerous, especially in combination. The term *addiction* is usually used to describe the combination of tolerance and dependence. But drug use and abuse are determined by more than drugs' effects. Societal attitudes, family circumstances, genetic background, friends' drug use, and personal attitudes influence a person's reasons for using (or avoiding) drugs (SAMHSA, 2003). In addition, not all people who use drugs abuse them. Therefore, drug use and abuse are products of complex individual and social circumstances. Let's first consider psychoactive drugs and their effects and then examine drug use and abuse.

Psychoactive Drugs

If a drug is to alter behavior and cognitive processes, it must affect the nervous system. Most do so by influencing the action of neurotransmitters in the brain. These drugs cross the **blood–brain barrier**, a mechanism that prevents certain molecules from entering the brain but allows others to cross. In the brain, psychoactive drugs can produce a variety of effects, ones that involve inhibiting, stimulating, or altering neural activity. These effects result from the drugs' influence on neurotransmitter action. Drugs can cause a more rapid release of a type of neurotransmitter or slow the breakdown or reuptake of another type. In addition, some drugs can occupy the same receptor sites on neurons in the brain as neurotransmitters do, which allows them to mimic the effects of the neurotransmitters. Psychoactive drugs, then, alter consciousness by affecting brain chemicals and neural transmission (see Chapter 3). There are many different types of psychoactive drugs, but they can be classified according to their effects.

Drug ■ Any chemical substance that, in small amounts, alters biological or mental processes, or both.

Psychoactive [SYE-koh-AK-tiv] drug ■ A drug that affects biochemical reactions in the nervous system, thereby altering behavior, thought, or perceptions and thus consciousness.

Tolerance ■ The condition in which higher and higher doses of a drug are required to produce the same effect.

Dependence ■ The condition that occurs when a drug becomes part of the body's functioning in such a way that the user suffers withdrawal symptoms when the drug is discontinued.

Withdrawal symptoms ■ The reactions experienced when a person with a drug dependence stops using the drug.

Blood–brain barrier ■ A mechanism that prevents certain molecules from entering the brain but allows others to cross.

Sedative–Hypnotics

Drugs that have inhibitory effects are classified as **sedative–hypnotics**, a class of drugs that relax and calm a user and, in higher doses, induce sleep; sometimes these are referred to as **sedatives** or **depressants**. Sedative–hypnotics depress (lower) brain activation. Many widely used (and abused) drugs fit into this classification, including alcohol, tranquilizers, barbiturates, and opiates. Alcohol is clearly the most commonly used drug in this category. About half of Americans use alcohol regularly, including 29% of adolescents, who are too young to drink legally (SAMHSA, 2003). Indeed, alcohol is so commonly used and legally available that many people do not realize that it is a drug.

Alcohol meets the definition of a psychoactive drug: It crosses the blood–brain barrier and can produce both tolerance and dependence. Alcohol molecules can pass into the brain and depress its overall functioning. Alcohol's effects include a dampening of arousal and a decrease in inhibitions—allowing some behaviors that are normally under tight control to occur (McKim, 2003). For example, it may diminish people's social inhibitions and make them less likely to restrain aggressive impulses. This disinhibition can cause problems, but alcohol's effects on coordination and reaction time are its main hazards. These effects vary, depending on the amount of alcohol in the bloodstream and the gender and weight of the user (see **Figure 7.4**). After equal alcohol consumption, women have higher blood alcohol levels than men do, even allowing for differences in body weight; the difference may relate to differences in the enzymes that break down alcohol in the stomach (Frezza et al., 1990; McKim, 2003).

With increasing amounts of alcohol in the bloodstream, people typically exhibit progressively slower responses. They often show severe motor disturbances, such as staggering and slurred speech. A blood alcohol level greater than 0.10 (0.1 milligram of alcohol per 100 milliliters of blood) usually indicates that the person has consumed too much alcohol to function responsibly, but lower levels of alcohol also affect

Sedative–hypnotic Any of a class of drugs that relax and calm a user and, in higher doses, induce sleep; also known as a *sedative* or a *depressant*.

Sedatives Another term for sedative–hypnotics.

Depressants Another term for sedative–hypnotics, used because these drugs depress many body responses.

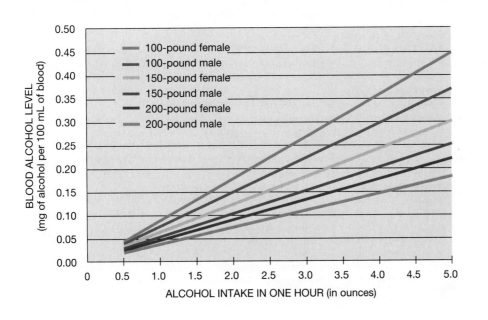

Figure 7.4
Relationship between Alcohol Consumption and Blood Alcohol Level, by Gender and Weight
Note that 1.0 ounce of alcohol is equivalent to two glasses of wine, two cans of beer, or one mixed drink. (Ray & Ksir, 1993)

behavior. Some states use 0.10 as the level to define intoxication, but 0.08 is the standard level in other states. **Table 7.2** shows the behavioral effects associated with various blood alcohol levels.

Other drugs in the sedative–hypnotic class are barbiturates, tranquilizers, and opiates. These are not as widely used as alcohol, but their effects are similar: In low doses, they relax or calm people, and in high doses, they induce sleep, unconsciousness, or even death. All have legitimate medical uses and are legally available with a prescription, but they are also used illegally for their psychoactive effects. Some people experience euphoria (a "high") when they use sedative–hypnotics, but others find their effects unpleasant (Julien, 2004).

Opiates are drugs derived from the opium poppy, including opium, morphine, and heroin. Methadone, oxycodone (OxyContin), and hydrocodone (Vicodin) were created in laboratories to be chemically similar to opiates and have similar effects. Because of their opiate effects, the illegal use of OxyContin and Vicodin has been increasing in recent years (SAMHSA, 2003). Medically, opiates are used for pain relief, for which they are the most effective drugs. In the brain, opiates exert their effects by occupying endorphin receptors. Endorphins are chemicals that the brain manufactures, providing a natural means of pain relief. When opiates occupy endorphin receptors, they mimic the effect of endorphins. Opiates are likely to produce tolerance and dependence, and many of those who use these drugs for pleasure become addicted. (Few people who receive opiates in the hospital for pain relief become addicted.)

Opiates ■
Sedative–hypnotic drugs that are derived from the opium poppy and include opium, morphine, and heroin.

Table 7.2

BEHAVIORAL EFFECTS ASSOCIATED WITH VARIOUS BLOOD ALCOHOL LEVELS

Blood Alcohol Level*	Behavioral Effects
0.05	Lowered alertness, impaired judgment, release of inhibitions, feelings of well-being or sociability; slowed reaction time and impaired motor function
0.10	Markedly slowed reaction time and impaired motor function, less caution
0.15	Large, consistent increases in reaction time
0.20	Marked depression in sensory and motor capability, decidedly intoxicated behavior
0.25	Severe motor disturbance and impairment of sensory perceptions
0.30	In a stupor, with no comprehension of events in the evironment, although still conscious
0.35	Lack of consciousness equivalent to that induced by surgical anesthesia; lethal dose for about 1% of adults
0.40	Lethal dose for about 50% of adults

*In milligrams of alcohol per 100 milliliters of blood

Stimulants

A *stimulant* is any drug that increases alertness, reduces fatigue, and elevates mood. Drugs in this category also tend to increase blood pressure, heart rate, and metabolic rate and to decrease appetite (Julien, 2004). When they think of stimulants, people tend to think of amphetamines and cocaine, but the category also includes two of the most commonly consumed drugs: caffeine and nicotine. Stimulants act on the peripheral nervous system as well as the central nervous system, and they can lead to tolerance and dependence. People who need a cup of coffee to wake up in the morning rarely think of themselves as drug addicts, but they may be dependent on the caffeine in coffee and may experience withdrawal when coffee is unavailable. These symptoms meet the definition of drug dependence (Bernstein et al., 2002). Dependence on caffeine may be socially acceptable and easy to satisfy, but it is a dependence on a psychoactive drug.

People who are dependent on caffeine experience fewer problems than those who are dependent on nicotine, amphetamines, or cocaine. *Nicotine* is the addictive drug in tobacco. Tobacco use is the leading cause of preventable deaths in the United States and many other countries (Mokdad et al., 2004). Nicotine is not the main health risk associated with tobacco, but it is the ingredient that makes quitting tobacco use so difficult (Julien, 2004). Nicotine does not produce strong tolerance, but dependence on it is strong, and withdrawal symptoms are unpleasant. People continue to smoke to alleviate those symptoms.

Not only do *amphetamines* create a strong dependence, but users very readily develop tolerance to these drugs (Julien, 2004). Like other stimulants, amphetamines produce arousal and alertness. People often take them for these effects, or as an appetite suppressant. Some people react strongly to amphetamines, getting more than they wanted—prolonged wakefulness and agitation rather than alertness. Continued use can lead not only to dependence but also to altered thoughts, especially unfounded suspiciousness and even symptoms like those of schizophrenia (see Chapter 16 for a description of these symptoms).

Like other stimulants, cocaine produces increased alertness, but it also acts as an anesthetic (Julien, 2004). Those properties were actually the reason for its initial use in Europe and the United States, but its potential for abuse soon became evident. A smokable form of cocaine called *crack* is less expensive and thus more widely used (the name comes from the crackling sound that the drug emits when it is heated). Cocaine takes effect rapidly and produces positive feelings, and these two attributes can lead to abuse. Because the effects are short-lived, people have the urge to use more cocaine.

Psychedelic Drugs

A *psychedelic drug* is a consciousness-altering drug that affects moods, thoughts, memory, judgment, and perception and that is consumed for the purpose of producing those results. (The term *psychedelic* means "mind-expanding"; it comes from two Greek words: *psyche*, for "soul," and *deloun*, "to show.") Psychedelic drugs are sometimes called *hallucinogens*, although many psychedelic drugs do not cause hallucinations. Their principal action is creating altered perceptions and producing vivid imagery. The impact of psychedelics varies widely, depending on the individual user, the situation, and the drug.

Stimulant ■ A drug that increases alertness, reduces fatigue, and elevates mood.

Psychedelic drug ■ Consciousness-altering drug that affects moods, thoughts, memory, judgment, and perception and that is consumed for the purpose of producing those results.

The class of psychedelics includes a range of drugs from LSD to Ecstasy. *Lysergic acid diethylamide*, or *LSD*, produces altered perceptions of visual and auditory stimuli and sometimes changes in time and distance perception. *Ecstasy* (also called Adam, X-TC, X, or E) is the common name for methylene-dioxymethamphetamine, or MDMA. It is a psychedelic, although it is derived from methamphetamine, a stimulant. MDMA was synthesized over 80 years ago but became popular in the 1980s as part of the "rave scene" at nightclubs around the world (Hunt & Evans, 2003). Ecstasy produces feelings of well-being, happiness, and kinship with others by bringing on a massive release of the neurotransmitter serotonin. Many claim that the drug is very dangerous, and the controversy over its hazards became more heated when a prominent researcher, who reported on the brain-damaging effects of MDMA, was forced to retract a paper because of inaccuracies in his research (Bartlett, 2004). There is some evidence of lasting negative effects, however, including prolonged problems with the brain's ability to regulate levels of serotonin (Reneman et al., 2001), which may be related to risks of depression and memory problems among long-term users (Hanson, 2004).

In contrast to synthetic Ecstasy, marijuana is completely natural; it is the dried leaves and flowering tops of the *Cannabis sativa* plant, whose active ingredient is *tetrahydrocannabinol (THC)*. Marijuana is even more controversial than Ecstasy, mostly because its use is more widespread. Marijuana is the most widely used of the illicit drugs; 37% of adolescents and adults in the United States have used it (U.S. Bureau of the Census, 2003). People's reactions to marijuana vary even more than their reactions to other psychoactive drugs. Some people experience elation and a feeling of well-being; some just feel sleepy; others experience feelings of paranoia and nausea. Like alcohol, marijuana affects judgment and coordination; thus, it can be dangerous to use it while driving or in other situations requiring quick responses and decisiveness.

Researchers agree that marijuana produces neither tolerance nor dependence in the strictest sense. Some people use marijuana to the point that it interferes with their lives; they seem to have a dependence on it despite the fact that it does not create physical dependence. Marijuana has been said to produce psychological dependence, but psychological dependence is hard to quantify and difficult to measure, and this claim has lost support (Pinel, 2003).

Millions of people have used marijuana and believe that its risks are equivalent to those of alcohol. Many of these people see no reason why marijuana is illegal while alcohol is legal. One faction is pushing for the legalization of marijuana, pointing to its benefits and medical uses. Others believe that marijuana is a "gateway" drug that leads to the use of other, more dangerous drugs and argue that it should remain illegal (National Institute on Drug Abuse, 2002).

Table 7.3 lists commonly used drugs and their effects.

Drug Use and Abuse

Although U.S. society is filled with drug users, most of those people do not consider themselves drug abusers. Part of their reasoning depends on the legality and acceptability of the drug they use, and those two factors are related. People often reserve the classification of "drug" for the substances that require prescriptions or are obtained

Table 7.3

COMMONLY USED AND ABUSED DRUGS

Type of Drug	Examples	Effects	Produces Tolerance?	Produces Physiological Dependence?
■ Sedative–hypnotics	Alcohol	Reduces inhibitions; slows reactions	Yes	Yes
	Barbiturates (e.g., Seconal)	Reduce tension; induce sleep	Yes	Yes
	Tranquilizers (e.g., Valium)	Alleviate tension; induce relaxation	Yes	Yes
	Opium, morphine, heroin	Alleviate pain and tension; alter perception	Yes	Yes
■ Stimulants	Caffeine	Increases alertness	Yes	Yes
	Amphetamines	Increase excitability, alertness, and talkativeness; decrease appetite	Yes	Yes
	Cocaine	Increases alertness; decreases fatigue; stimulates sexual arousal	Yes	Yes
	Nicotine	Increases alertness and metabolism	Yes	Yes
■ Psychedelics	Marijuana	Changes mood and perception	No	No
	LSD	Changes perception	No	No
	Ecstasy	Produces sense of well-being and connection to others	No	Possibly

illegally, and they have trouble thinking of other substances, particularly alcohol, tobacco, and over-the-counter medications, as drugs. This thinking leads people to overestimate the dangers of the substances they consider drugs and to underestimate those of the substances they do not classify as drugs. Both errors can lead to problems.

One problem with discounting the hazards of legally available and socially acceptable substances is that people overlook the problems associated with alcohol and tobacco. These two substances create the biggest drug problems in the United States (and in many other countries). The legal availability and social acceptability of alcohol and tobacco contribute to their widespread use. For example, about 82% of adolescents and adults in the United States have tried alcohol and 67% have tried cigarettes; 48% are current drinkers and 25% are current smokers (U.S. Bureau of the Census, 2003). Adults between the ages of 21 and 39 are the heaviest drinkers, but young adults between 18 and 25 are more likely to be binge drinkers, who consume at least 5 drinks on one occasion, a pattern of drinking that is especially dangerous. Among adolescents, boys are more likely than girls to drink, but the rate of smoking among teens is similar for both sexes. Italian adolescents are very similar to Americans in the percentage of alcohol use and the gender difference (Gerra et al., 2004).

Usage rates for illegal drugs are much lower than those for these legal drugs. Marijuana is the most commonly used illegal drug—37% of Americans have tried it, and about 6% are current users (SAMHSA, 2003). By contrast, amphetamines, cocaine, sedatives, tranquilizers, opiates, hallucinogens, and prescription pain medication together are currently used illegally by a total of only 4.0% of Americans aged 12 and older. (See **Figure 7.5**.)

Those numbers may not sound right to you—it may seem as if practically everyone you know has tried some illegal drug, and many are current users. Adolescents and young adults use both legal and illegal drugs at higher rates than the general population, and that fact affects your perception of the frequency of drug use. For example, 50% of 18- to 25-year-olds have tried marijuana, and 16% are current users; 13% have tried cocaine, and 2% are current users (U.S. Bureau of the Census, 2003). These numbers indicate that illegal drug use is more widespread among adolescents and young adults than among younger or older people

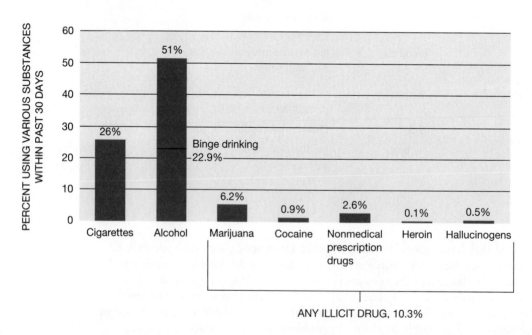

Figure 7.5

Percent of Americans over Age 12 Who Have Used Various Drugs within the Past 30 Days
(U.S. Bureau of the Census, 2003)

(for example, less than 20% of those younger than 18 have tried marijuana). The small percentage of people who use illegal drugs can cause big problems, but the use of legal, socially acceptable drugs is a much larger social and health problem.

Some psychoactive drugs produce physical damage directly, but most of the problems associated with drug use are indirect effects of the drug. For example, nicotine is not an especially dangerous drug, but smoking tobacco is a major cause of disease and death (Mokdad et al., 2004). The major hazards of using most psychoactive drugs come largely from changes in perception and the resulting changes in reactions, judgment, and behavior. For example, alcohol use can cause liver damage, but the primary hazard of using alcohol is that it increases the risk of accidents. Smoking marijuana is more damaging to the lungs than smoking tobacco, but again, increased risk of accidents is the greatest danger of marijuana use. These risks are substantial—unintentional injury is the leading cause of death for people under age 35, and drug use contributes significantly to accidental injury and death (U.S. Bureau of the Census, 2003). Therefore, any psychoactive drug use can present dangers.

What Is Substance Abuse?

What is the difference between drug use and drug abuse? Some authorities consider the use of any illegal drug to be substance abuse. However, some of those who use illegal drugs experience few problems, while others ruin their lives and the lives of those around them. The impact on people's lives is one way to distinguish substance use from abuse: People who experience ongoing negative effects as a result of their drug use cross the line into abuse.

Substance abuse is overuse of and reliance on a drug in order to deal with everyday life. Most substance abusers use alcohol or tobacco, but the whole range of psychoactive drugs and combinations of these drugs presents possibilities for abuse. A person is a substance abuser if all three of the following statements apply:

Substance abuse ▪
Overuse of and reliance on a drug in order to deal with everyday life.

- The person has used the substance for at least a month.
- The use has caused legal, personal, social, or vocational problems.
- The person repeatedly uses the substance even in situations when doing so is hazardous, such as when driving a car.

Missing work or school, spending more than one can afford on the drug, having problems in personal relationships, and getting into legal trouble are all signs of substance abuse. When substance abusers try to decrease or quit their drug use, they experience withdrawal symptoms if the substance is one that tends to cause dependence. Withdrawal symptoms are typically the opposite of the drug's effects. For example, the effects of alcohol are decreased levels of activation, so the withdrawal effects are increased levels of activation, including agitation and physical arousal (the "shakes"). Although substance abusers usually like the effects of the drug they use, the opposite effects are not as pleasant. Of course, one way to stop these unpleasant symptoms is to use more drugs. Repeated drug use often results in addiction.

A great variety of social and individual factors have an impact on drug use and abuse; among these are family members' drug use, peer group drug use, personal beliefs about the dangers of drugs, age, and education. With every category of drug, men more often have problems than women do, making gender another important factor in substance abuse (American Psychiatric Association, 2000). Ethnicity is also a factor in drug use (SAMHSA, 2003). Although many people believe that African Americans and Latino/Latinas use illicit drugs at higher rates than other ethnic groups, this perception is inaccurate. The rate of drug use is similar for African Americans, Latino/Latinas, and Whites (Adrian, 2002). Native Americans, however, have a higher rate of drug use than other ethnic groups, and Asian Americans have a lower rate (SAMHSA, 2003). All of these demographic factors (and many more) relate to drug use, but none specifically predicts who will become a drug abuser and who will use drugs in socially accepted, responsible ways.

The possibility that genetic factors play a role in drug abuse, especially alcohol abuse, has received a great deal of recent publicity. Alcoholism is not inherited, but certain factors related to the metabolism of alcohol are genetic. One study demonstrated the importance of the neurotransmitter GABA in alcohol dependence and identified genes that control its production; these genes exhibit variations in families with a history of alcoholism (Edenberg et al., 2004). Such genetically based metabolic factors create what is known as a *genetic predisposition*, an inherited tendency to be susceptible to or to develop a problem. A genetic predisposition differs from a direct inheritance. Characteristics that are inherited, such as eye color, require no set of environmental circumstances for their expression: People with two recessive genes for blue eyes will have blue eyes. However, people who inherit genes that predispose them to problem drinking will not necessarily develop drinking problems. For example, people who do not drink cannot have drinking problems; thus, those who live in cultures that forbid alcohol are less likely to develop problem drinking, regardless of any genetic predisposition (Bloomfield et al., 2003). Indeed, cultural factors are very important in alcohol use and abuse, affecting patterns of drinking in those of different ages and genders as well as the types of alcoholic beverages consumed. Therefore, a genetic predisposition is a risk factor for alcohol abuse (and possibly other drug problems), but it does not specifically predict problem drug use.

Why, then, do people use (and abuse) drugs? From an evolutionary point of view, drug use (and especially abuse) seems difficult to explain (Lende & Smith, 2002; Nesse, 1997). If consciousness is an adaptive advantage, then alterations to consciousness are maladaptive. Psychoactive drugs have a variety of effects that put people in danger, which is clearly maladaptive. Yet people in almost every culture in the history of the world have used some consciousness-altering substance. One possible evolutionary explanation relies on the observation that drugs employ naturally existing brain chemicals and pathways in ways other than their primary function. That is, the consciousness-altering effects of drugs occur through existing neural mechanisms, the brain's "reward circuit." Thus, our brains seem to be built to respond to psychoactive drugs. Also, today's societies, unlike the environments in which we evolved, have a high availability of drugs. This combination of factors explains the drug use problem faced by many societies. This explanation suggests that getting people to refrain from using drugs may be almost impossible, and that decreasing the amount of harm that drugs can cause is a more feasible strategy (Duff, 2003).

Summary and Review

WHAT IS CONSCIOUSNESS?

Consciousness is a general state of being aware of and responsive to events in the environment, as well as one's own mental processes. Consciousness can range from alert attention to dreaming, being hypnotized, or being in a drug-induced state. Theories of consciousness attempt to explain the underlying basis of self-awareness, some by relying on philosophy and others by relying on neuroscience. pp. 236–240

WHAT HAPPENS WHEN WE SLEEP?

Describe the sleep–wakefulness cycle.

Circadian rhythms are internally generated patterns of body functions, including the sleep–wakefulness cycle. The *suprachiasmatic nucleus* in the anterior hypothalamus in the brain is the control center for this cycle. When time cues such as daylight and clocks are removed from the environment, circadian rhythms still operate. Disruptions of the sleep–wakefulness cycle such as travel and those that occur with shift work lead to problems. pp. 240–241

What are the stages of sleep?

Recordings of the brain waves of participants in sleep research called *electroencephalograms (EEG)* have revealed distinct cycles of sleep. Each cycle has four stages of *non–rapid eye movement (NREM) sleep* plus a stage of *rapid eye movement (REM) sleep*. During NREM sleep, levels of activation and arousal in the brain and body decrease. During REM sleep, the brain and body experience high levels of arousal, including rapid eye movements. A full sleep cycle lasts about 90 minutes, so five complete sleep cycles occur in an average night's sleep. pp. 242–245

What are the effects of sleep deprivation?

The effects of sleep deprivation include increased sleepiness, difficulty concentrating, slowed reaction times, and poorer decision making. pp. 245–247

Why do we sleep?

The distressing consequences of sleep deprivation suggest that sleep is essential, but the reason for sleep remains a mystery. pp. 247–248

Is there a sleep switch?

Brain structures are important for sleeping and waking. The ventrolateral preoptic area (VLPO) of the hypothalamus seems to act as a "sleep on" switch, and neurons toward the back of the hypothalamus appear to maintain wakefulness and alertness. p. 248–249

What are the characteristics of common sleep disorders?

People who fall asleep suddenly and uncontrollably have a sleep disorder known as *narcolepsy*. Loud snoring is a symptom of *sleep apnea*. *Insomnia* is the inability to fall asleep or to remain asleep throughout the night. *Night terrors* are a sleep disorder in which a person experiences high arousal and symptoms of panic during sleep. Sleepwalking can put the sleepwalker at risk of injury but is otherwise not dangerous. pp. 249–251

WHAT ARE DREAMS, AND WHAT DO THEY MEAN?

What is a dream?

A *dream* is a state of consciousness that occurs during sleep and is usually accompanied by vivid visual imagery, although the imagery may also be tactile or auditory. Dreams are associated (although not totally) with REM sleep, and REM dreams tend to be vivid. The first dream of a typical night occurs 90 minutes after a person has fallen asleep and lasts for approximately 10 minutes. Individuals tend to dream about events and people in their daily lives. Some people experience *lucid dreams*, in which they are aware that they are dreaming. pp. 251–252

How have key theorists explained dreaming?

Freud believed that a dream expressed desires, wishes, and unfulfilled needs that exist in the unconscious; he referred to dreams as "the royal road to the unconscious." Freud made a distinction between a dream's *manifest content* (its obvious story line, characters, and settings) and its *latent content* (its deeper, hidden meaning, usually expressed in symbolic form). pp. 252–254

Like Freud, Jung accepted the idea that a dream is nature's way of allowing humans access to their own unconscious, but Jung saw dreams as more complex. He asserted that each person shares in the *collective unconscious*, a storehouse of primitive ideas and images in the unconscious that are inherited from our ancestors and that all humans share. pp. 254–255

Cognitive theorists believe that dreams show the same type of cognitive processes that occur during waking, and dream content reflects areas of concern to the dreamer. p. 255

Biological theorists believe that, during periods of REM sleep, the parts of the brain responsible for long-term memory, vision, audition, and perhaps even emotion are activated. The cortex attempts to synthesize the stimulation, producing a dream. An evolutionary view holds that dreams allow humans to rehearse for threatening situations. pp. 255–256

IS IT POSSIBLE TO CONTROL CONSCIOUSNESS BY USING BIOFEEDBACK, HYPNOSIS, OR MEDITATION?

Describe the characteristics of three techniques for controlling consciousness.

Biofeedback is a process through which people receive information about the status of a physical function and use this feedback to learn to alter that function. Learning conscious control of autonomic processes is possible, and biofeedback has been used as a therapeutic technique, especially to control headaches. pp. 257–258

Hypnosis remains controversial; even its definition is debated. Some authorities see it as an altered state of consciousness, but others do not. Hypnosis can produce effects such as relaxation, increased concentration, and pain reduction, but *posthypnotic suggestion* is less effective in altering behavior, and it can distort rather than enhance memory. pp. 258–260

Meditation produces a state of consciousness characterized by a sense of detachment and deep relaxation. Meditators may practice either mindfulness or concentrative meditation. Meditation techniques are often used to help manage stress. pp. 260–261

HOW DO DRUGS ALTER CONSCIOUSNESS?

What are the properties of drugs?

A *drug* is any chemical substance that alters biological or mental processes, or both. A *psychoactive* drug is a drug that alters behavior, thought, or perceptions, and thus consciousness, by crossing the *blood–brain barrier* and affecting biochemical reactions in the nervous system. Some drugs produce *tolerance*, the condition in which higher and higher doses of a drug are required to produce the same effect, or *dependence*, the condition that occurs when a drug becomes part of the body's functioning in such a way that the drug user suffers *withdrawal symptoms* when the drug is discontinued. Drugs that produce the combination of tolerance and dependence are said to be addictive. pp. 261–262

How do psychoactive drugs affect the nervous system and behavior?

Sedative–hypnotics (also called *sedatives* or *depressants*) include alcohol, barbiturates, and *opiates*. These drugs all relax and calm users, and they produce both tolerance and dependence. *Stimulants* are drugs that increase alertness, reduce fatigue, and elevate mood. This class of drugs includes caffeine, nicotine, cocaine, and amphetamines, all of which can produce tolerance and dependence. *Psychedelic drugs*, such as LSD, Ecstasy, and marijuana, are consciousness-altering drugs that affect moods, thoughts, memory, judgment, and perception and that are consumed for the purpose of producing those results. These drugs do not produce tolerance or dependence, but are still abused and may be dangerous. pp. 262–266

What is the difference between substance use and substance abuse?

Many people use various substances, but not all users are abusers. *Substance abuse* is overuse of and reliance on a drug in order to deal with everyday life. A person is a substance abuser if she or he has used a drug for at least 1 month; has experienced legal, personal, social, or vocational problems as a result of the drug use; and has used the drug in situations when doing so is hazardous. Many drug abusers experience withdrawal symptoms if they are dependent on the drug they abuse. Many social and personal factors relate to substance use and abuse. Brain mechanisms involving the neurotransmitter dopamine may be a factor in drug abuse. pp. 266–270

Learning

What Type of Learning Is Pavlovian, or Classical, Conditioning?   275
Terms and Procedures
Classical Conditioning in Humans
Higher-Order Conditioning

What Are the Key Variables in Classical Conditioning?   281
Strength, Timing, and Frequency
Predictability
Extinction and Spontaneous Recovery
Stimulus Generalization and Stimulus Discrimination
Classical Conditioning in Daily Life
Pavlov's Understanding Reinterpreted

What Type of Learning Is Operant Conditioning?   289
The Pioneers: E. L. Thorndike and B. F. Skinner
Reinforcement: A Consequence That Strengthens a Response
Two Reinforcement Strategies: Positive and Negative
The Skinner Box and Shaping
Punishment: A Consequence That Weakens a Response

What Are the Key Variables in Operant Conditioning?   298
Strength, Timing, and Frequency
Stimulus Generalization and Stimulus Discrimination
Extinction and Spontaneous Recovery
Operant Conditioning in Daily Life

Can Learning Occur through Observation?   307
The Power of Modeling
Key Processes in Observational Learning
Observational Learning in Daily Life
Other Types of Cognitive Learning

What Is the Biological Basis for Learning?   314
Are Evolutionary Theory and Learning Theory Incompatible?
Electrical Brain Stimulation and Reinforcement
Brain Changes and Learning

Summary and Review   317

Learning ■ A relatively permanent change in an organism that occurs as a result of experiences in the environment.

Psychologists define ***learning*** as a relatively permanent change in an organism that occurs as a result of experiences in the environment and that is often exhibited in overt behavior. This definition of learning includes several important concepts: (1) permanence, (2) experience, (3) change, and (4) overt behavior. Learning cannot be considered completely permanent because organisms forget things they have learned, but it is relatively permanent. Experience is the basis of learning, rather than instinct or growth and development (although these can also lead to changes in behavior). To assess learning, psychologists must confirm that change has taken place. In addition, learning is an internal process that cannot be seen, but psychologists must find ways to study the results of learning. To do so, they may examine overt behavior such as solving an algebra problem or throwing a ball. They may also assess learning by measuring physiological changes such as brain-wave activity or blood flow to specific areas of the brain.

The factors that affect learning are often studied by using nonhuman animals as subjects, because the genetic heritage of these animals is easy to control and manipulate and because all details of their life history and environmental experiences can be known. Although some psychologists claim that different processes underlie animal and human learning, most believe—and experiments show—that the processes are similar. Differences do become apparent, however, when complex behaviors and the use of language are involved.

As you read this chapter, think about the range of learned associations that shape your daily behavior and interactions. For example, do you favor particular study spots or associate fear or other emotions with specific places? You will see how your experiences and the resulting associations illustrate the three basic learning processes that are covered in this chapter: classical conditioning, operant conditioning, and observational learning.

What Type of Learning Is Pavlovian, or Classical, Conditioning?

Psychologists often use the term conditioning in a general sense, to mean learning. But more precisely, *conditioning* is a systematic procedure through which associations and responses to specific stimuli are learned. Conditioning is one of the simplest forms of learning. For example, consider what generally happens when you hear the theme from *Friends*. You expect that something amusing will appear on your TV screen, because the music introduces a program that usually includes comedy—and if you're a fan of the show, you probably feel a pleasant sense of anticipation. You have been conditioned to feel that way. In the terminology used by psychologists, the *Friends* theme is the stimulus, and your pleasure and anticipation are the response. A *stimulus* is an event, usually a detectable sensory input (music, for example), that has an impact on an organism; a *response* is the reaction of an organism to a stimulus (pleasant anticipation or fear, for example).

When psychologists first studied conditioning, they found relationships between specific stimuli and responses. They observed that each time a certain stimulus occurred, the same reflexive response, or behavior, followed. For example, the presence of food in the mouth leads to salivation; a tap on the knee results in a knee jerk; shining a bright light in the eye produces contraction of the pupil and an eye blink. A *reflex* is an automatic behavior that occurs involuntarily in response to a stimulus, without prior learning, and usually shows little variability from one instance to another. Conditioned behaviors, in contrast, are learned. Dental anxiety—fear of dentists, dental procedures, and even the dentist's chair—is a common conditioned response (Merckelbach et al., 1999; White, 2000). Many people have learned to respond with

Conditioning ■ A systematic procedure through which associations and responses to specific stimuli are learned.

Reflex ■ Automatic behavior that occurs involuntarily in response to a stimulus, without prior learning, and usually shows little variability from one instance to another.

When your eye is exposed to intense light, it responds by reflex—the pupil contracts and you blink.

fear to the stimulus of sitting in a dentist's chair, since they associate the chair with pain (Liddell & Locker, 2000). A chair by itself (a neutral stimulus) does not elicit fear, but a chair associated with pain becomes a stimulus that can prompt fear. This is an example of conditioning. This type of associative learning was studied by an Austrian physiologist named Alois Kreidl in the 1830s, but Kreidl's work did not make history (Logan, 2002). When Russian physiologist Ivan Pavlov rediscovered conditioning in the late 1800s, it did.

In 1927, Ivan Pavlov (1849–1936) summarized a now-famous series of experiments in which he discovered the basic principles of conditioning. His study began as an investigation of saliva and gastric secretions in dogs. He knew it is normal for dogs to salivate when they eat (salivation is a reflexive behavior that aids digestion), but he found that the dogs were salivating before they tasted their food. Pavlov knew that the response (salivation) cannot come before the stimulus (food), so he reasoned that some association had occurred. When he examined the situation, he found that the dogs had learned to associate stimuli such as the sight of the food dish, the trainers who brought them food, and even the sound of the trainers' footsteps with the food itself. Anxious to know more about this form of learning, Pavlov abandoned his research on dogs' digestive processes and redirected his efforts to studying their salivary reflex.

Terms and Procedures

Classical conditioning ■ Conditioning process in which an originally neutral stimulus, through repeated pairing with a stimulus that naturally elicits a response, comes to elicit a similar or even identical response; also known as *Pavlovian conditioning*.

Unconditioned stimulus ■ A stimulus that normally produces an involuntary response.

Unconditioned response ■ An unlearned or involuntary response to an unconditioned stimulus.

The terminology and procedures associated with Pavlov's experiments can seem confusing, but the basic ideas are actually quite straightforward. Let's explore them systematically. What Pavlov described is known as *classical conditioning*, or *Pavlovian conditioning*, in which an originally neutral stimulus, through repeated pairing with a stimulus that naturally elicits a response, comes to elicit a similar or even identical response. For example, when a bell, buzzer, or light (a neutral stimulus) is associated with the presentation of food, a stimulus that normally brings about a response (salivating), the neutral stimulus comes to elicit the same response as the normal stimulus if the two are paired many times. Pavlov termed the stimulus that normally produces the involuntary response the *unconditioned stimulus* (as its name implies, it elicits the relevant response without conditioning). He termed the response to this stimulus the *unconditioned response*. The unconditioned response occurs involuntarily, without learning, in response to the unconditioned stimulus.

Pavlov started his study of conditioning in dogs with a relatively simple experiment—teaching the dogs to salivate in response to the sound of a bell. First, he surgically moved the duct for each dog's salivary gland to the outside of the dog's cheek to make the secretions of saliva accessible. He attached tubes to the relocated

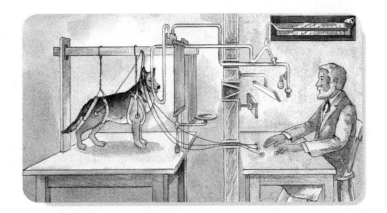

Figure 8.1
Pavlov's
Experimental
Setup

salivary duct so that he could collect and then measure precisely the amount of saliva produced by the food; that is, so that he could measure the unconditioned response. The dog was restrained in a harness and isolated from all distractions in a cubicle (see **Figure 8.1**). Then Pavlov introduced the bell sound—the new stimulus (see **Figure 8.2**). He called the sound of the bell a *neutral stimulus,* because that sound is not normally associated with salivation and generally elicits only attentiveness or an

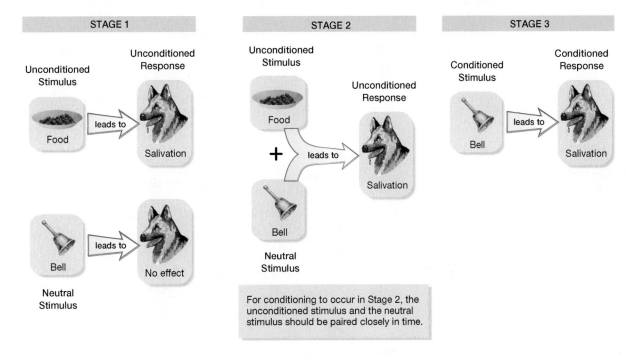

Figure 8.2
The Three Stages of Classical Conditioning

orientation response (an attempt to locate the sound). The dog did not salivate in response to the sound of the bell. Pavlov then began the conditioning process by ringing the bell and immediately placing food in the dog's mouth. After he did this several times, the dog salivated in response to the sound of the bell alone.

Pavlov reasoned that the dog had associated the bell with the arrival of food. He termed the sound of the bell, which elicited (or produced) salivation as a result of learning, a conditioned stimulus. A *conditioned stimulus* is a neutral stimulus that, through repeated association with an unconditioned stimulus, becomes capable of eliciting a response. As its name implies, a conditioned stimulus becomes capable of eliciting a response because of its pairing with the unconditioned stimulus. The salivation—the learned response to the sound of the bell—is a *conditioned response* (the response elicited by a conditioned stimulus). (Pavlov originally called the conditioned response a "conditional" response because it was conditional on—it depended on—events in the environment. An error in translating his writings created the term used most often today—conditioned response.) From his experiments, Pavlov discovered that the conditioned stimulus (the sound of the bell) brought about a similar but somewhat weaker response than the unconditioned stimulus (the food). The process of classical conditioning is outlined in Figure 8.2.

The key characteristic of classical conditioning is the use of an originally neutral stimulus (here, a bell sound) to elicit a response (salivation) through repeated pairing with an unconditioned stimulus (food) that elicits the response naturally. On the first few trials of such pairings, conditioning is unlikely to occur. With additional trials, the association becomes stronger. After dozens or even hundreds of pairings, the neutral stimulus yields the conditioned response. Psychologists generally refer to this process as an *acquisition process* and say that an organism has acquired a response. **Figure 8.3** shows a typical acquisition curve.

Classical conditioning occurs regularly in the everyday world. You may have learned to associate the distinctive spicy smell of a certain aftershave with a boyfriend

Conditioned stimulus ■ A neutral stimulus that, through repeated association with an unconditioned stimulus, begins to elicit a conditioned response.

Conditioned response ■ The response elicited by a conditioned stimulus.

Figure 8.3
A Typical
Acquisition
Curve

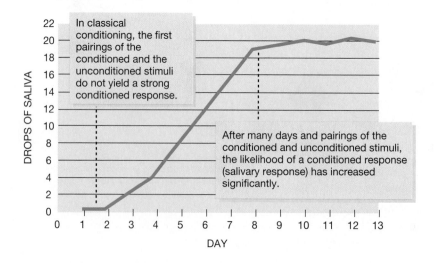

In classical conditioning, the first pairings of the conditioned and the unconditioned stimuli do not yield a strong conditioned response.

After many days and pairings of the conditioned and unconditioned stimuli, the likelihood of a conditioned response (salivary response) has increased significantly.

DROPS OF SALIVA

DAY

or a particular flowery perfume with a girlfriend. If you walk into a room and smell this distinctive fragrance, you may think of this person or expect him or her to be there. Classical conditioning doesn't always involve associations of positive things. When you enter a dentist's office, your heart rate may increase and you may begin to feel anxious because you have learned associations with this place. When classical conditioning occurs, behavior changes, which indicates that learning has occurred.

Classical Conditioning in Humans

After Pavlov's success with conditioning in dogs, psychologists were able to see that conditioning also occurs in human beings. Marquis (1931) showed that classical conditioning occurs in infants. Marquis knew that when an object touches an infant's lips, the infant immediately starts sucking; human infants are programmed by evolution to respond with the sucking reflex when something touches their lips, because the object is usually a nipple. The nipple, an unconditioned stimulus, elicits sucking, an unconditioned response. By repeatedly pairing a sound or light with a nipple, Marquis conditioned infants to suck when only the sound or light was presented.

Sucking is only one of many reflexive behaviors of human beings; thus, many responses can be conditioned. For example, newborns (and the rest of us) respond reflexively to loud noises. (We examined newborns' reflexes in Chapter 4.) A loud noise naturally elicits a *startle response*—an outstretching of the arms and legs and associated changes in heart rate, blood pressure, and breathing. Through conditioning, all kinds of neutral stimuli can become conditioned stimuli that elicit reflexive responses of this sort. Another example is a puff of air delivered to the eye, which produces the unconditioned response of an eye blink. When a light or a sound (a conditioned stimulus) is paired with the puff of air (the unconditioned stimulus), the light or sound will eventually elicit the eye blink by itself. This conditioned eye blink is a robust response, one that is retained for a long time (Clark, Manns, & Squire, 2002), particularly among younger adults (Solomon et al., 1998). Humans are not the only ones subject to this conditioning effect—it can be produced in many other animals.

The process of learning depends on a wide array of events in addition to conditioned and unconditioned stimuli, including an organism's past experiences with the stimuli. It appears that classical conditioning can even occur outside conscious awareness; we can learn connections between stimuli without even being aware that such learning is taking place (Clark et al., 2002; Knight, Nguyen, & Bandettini, 2003). In addition, a person can be conditioned to have either pleasant or unpleasant emotional responses. For example, if a child is repeatedly frightened by a sudden loud noise while playing with a favorite toy, the child may be conditioned to be afraid rather than happy each time she or he sees the toy.

John B. Watson and Rosalie Rayner (1920) explored the conditioning of such a negative emotional response in a now-famous experiment with an 11-month-old infant named Albert. (Today, such an experiment would be considered unethical.) Albert was given several toys and a live white rat to play with. One day, as Albert reached for the rat, the experimenters suddenly made an ear-splitting noise that

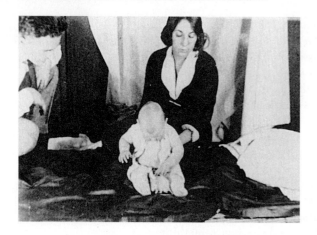

In their now-famous experiment, Watson and Rayner gave baby Albert a white rat to play with. However, after Watson and Rayner repeatedly paired the rat (the conditioned stimulus) with a loud noise (the unconditioned stimulus), Albert learned to associate the two and grew afraid of the rat.

Higher-order conditioning ■ The process by which a neutral stimulus takes on conditioned properties through pairing with a conditioned stimulus.

frightened the child. After repeated pairing of the rat (conditioned stimulus) and the noise (unconditioned stimulus), Albert learned to associate the two. The rat began to evoke a conditioned response of fear in Albert. Researchers believe that this type of learning is the primary source for most fears and anxiety in children (Ressler & Davis, 2003).

As another example, television commercials for cars apply conditioning principles by featuring attractive people enjoying and being admired for driving a particular model. The producers of such commercials hope that when viewers associate the specific car (a neutral stimulus) with an unconditioned stimulus that naturally elicits a positive emotional response (the admiration of others), the car will elicit a similar positive response. In other words, the producers hope to condition people to feel good whenever they think about a particular model of car.

Higher-Order Conditioning

After a neutral stimulus becomes a conditioned stimulus, it elicits the conditioned response whenever it is presented. Once that relationship is established, it is possible to pair another neutral stimulus with the conditioned stimulus. The new, neutral stimulus begins to take on the same conditioned properties as that conditioned stimulus. This phenomenon is called *higher-order conditioning*—the process by which a neutral stimulus takes on conditioned properties through pairing with a conditioned stimulus. Suppose a dog has been conditioned to associate the sound of a bell with food. On hearing the bell, the dog will salivate; the bell is a conditioned stimulus that elicits the salivation response. If a light is now paired with or presented just before the bell sounds, the new stimulus (the light) can also start to elicit the same response as the conditioned stimulus (the bell). After repeated pairings, the dog associates the two events (the bell and the light), and either event by itself will elicit a salivation response. When a third stimulus—say, an experimenter in a white lab coat—is introduced, the dog may learn to associate the experimenter with the bell or the light. After enough trials, the dog may show a salivation response to each of the three stimuli: the light, the bell, and the experimenter (Pavlov, 1927; Rescorla, 1977, 1998, 2001a, 2001b).

Thus, higher-order conditioning permits increasingly remote associations, which can result in a complex network of conditioned stimuli and responses. At least two factors determine the extent of higher-order conditioning: (1) the similarity between the new stimulus and the original conditioned stimulus, and (2) the frequency and consistency with which the two stimuli are paired. You can see that successful pairing of conditioned and unconditioned stimuli—that is, successful classical conditioning—is influenced by many variables.

What Are the Key Variables in Classical Conditioning?

Although classical conditioning is a simple type of learning, it is not a simple process. As noted earlier, such learning is not automatic; it depends on an array of events, including an organism's past experiences with the conditioned and unconditioned stimuli as well as key variables related to those stimuli. For example, how loud does the warning bell in your car have to be to prompt you to remember to take the keys out of the ignition? How sinister must movie music be to give you goose bumps? How many times must someone experience pain in a dentist's chair, and how strong does the pain have to be, before the person develops a fear of dentists? As with other psychological phenomena, situational variables affect whether and under what conditions classical conditioning will occur. Although the principles of conditioning are the same throughout the world, cultural variables play a role in this type of learning. For example, learning what foods are desirable occurs through the process of classical conditioning, but what constitutes a desirable food varies from culture to culture and even from person to person (Rozin & Zellner, 1985).

Some of the most important variables in classical conditioning are the strength of the unconditioned stimulus and the timing and frequency of its pairings with the neutral stimulus. When these variables are at optimal levels, conditioning occurs easily and sometimes very rapidly.

Strength, Timing, and Frequency

Strength of the Unconditioned Stimulus

A puff of air delivered to the eye will easily elicit a conditioned response to a neutral stimulus paired with it, but only if the puff of air (the unconditioned stimulus) is sufficiently strong. Research shows that when the unconditioned stimulus is strong and constantly elicits the reflexive (unconditioned) response, conditioning to a neutral stimulus is likely to occur. On the other hand, when the unconditioned stimulus is weak, it is less likely to elicit the unconditioned response, and so conditioning does not take place. Thus, pairing a neutral stimulus with a weak unconditioned stimulus will not reliably lead to conditioning.

Timing of the Unconditioned Stimulus

For conditioning to occur, an unconditioned stimulus must usually be paired with a neutral stimulus close enough in time for the two to become associated; that is, they must be temporally contiguous (close in time). For optimal conditioning, the neutral stimulus should occur a short time before the unconditioned stimulus (many researchers say one-half second) and should overlap with it, particularly for reflexes such as the eye blink. (In Pavlov's experiment, conditioning would not have occurred if the bell had rung an hour before the food was presented.) The two stimuli may be presented together or separated by a brief interval. Some types of conditioning can occur despite fairly long delays, but the optimal time between the two stimuli varies from one study to another and depends on many things, including the type of conditioned response (e.g., Cunningham et al., 1999).

Frequency of Pairings

Occasional or rare pairings of a neutral stimulus with an unconditioned stimulus, even at close intervals, usually do not result in conditioning. Generally speaking, frequent pairings that establish a relationship between the unconditioned and conditioned stimuli are necessary. If, for example, food and the sound of a bell are paired on every trial, a dog will be conditioned more quickly than if the stimuli are paired on every other trial. The frequency of the natural occurrence of the unconditioned stimulus is also important. If the unconditioned stimulus does not occur frequently but is always associated with the conditioned stimulus, more rapid conditioning is likely, because one stimulus predicts the other (Rescorla, 1988). Once the conditioned response has reached its maximum strength, additional pairings of the stimuli do not increase the likelihood of a conditioned response. There are exceptions to this general rule, though, situations in which one-time pairings can produce learning. For example, touching a hot stove once is typically sufficient.

Predictability

A key factor determining whether conditioning will occur is the predictability of the association of the unconditioned and conditioned stimuli. Closeness in time and regular frequency of pairings promote conditioning, but these are not enough. *Predictability*—the likelihood that the occurrence of the unconditioned stimulus can be anticipated—turns out to be a critical factor in facilitating conditioning (Rescorla, 1988).

Pavlov thought that classical conditioning depended mostly on timing. Research has shown, however, that if the unconditioned stimulus (such as the appearance of food) can be predicted by the conditioned stimulus (such as a bell), then conditioning is rapidly achieved. Conditioning depends more on the reliability with which the conditioned stimulus predicts the unconditioned stimulus. Pavlov's dogs learned that bells were good predictors of food. The conditioned stimulus (bell) reliably predicted the unconditioned one (food), and so conditioning was quickly achieved.

In Rescorla's view, what an organism learns through conditioning is the predictability of some event—a bell predicting food, light predicting a puff of air to the eye, a dentist's chair predicting pain. An organism learns that there is some sort of relationship between the conditioned and unconditioned stimuli. Human beings and many animals make predictions about the future based on past events in a wide range of circumstances (Siegel et al., 2000). As you will see in the next two chapters (on memory and cognition), such predictions are based on simple learning but their formation is more complex than that. The predictability and relationship of events is also important in extinction and spontaneous recovery, which we consider next.

Extinction and Spontaneous Recovery

Some conditioned responses last for a long time; others disappear quickly. The durability of such a response depends to a great extent on whether the conditioned stimulus continues to predict the unconditioned one. Consider the following: What

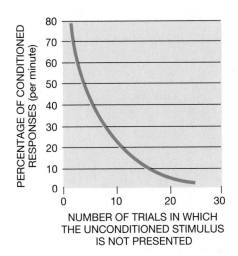

Figure 8.4
A Typical Extinction Curve
Numerous experiments have demonstrated that the occurrence of a conditioned response decreases if the unconditioned stimulus is not presented over a number of trials. When presentation of the unconditioned stimulus alone no longer elicits the conditioned response, the response has been extinguished.

would have happened to Pavlov's dogs if Pavlov had rung the bell each day but never followed it with food? What would happen if you went to the dentist every day for 2 months, but the dentist only cleaned your teeth with pleasant-tasting toothpaste and never gave you injections or drilled?

If a researcher duplicates Pavlov's experiment but continues by presenting the conditioned stimulus (bell) but no unconditioned stimulus (food), the likelihood of a dog's displaying the conditioned response (salivation) decreases with every trial, until it disappears. In classical conditioning, *extinction* is the procedure of withholding the unconditioned stimulus while presenting the conditioned stimulus alone. This procedure gradually reduces the probability (and often the strength) of a conditioned response. Imagine a study in which a puff of air is associated with a buzzer so that the buzzer consistently elicits the conditioned eye-blink response. If the unconditioned stimulus (the puff of air) is no longer delivered in association with the buzzer, the likelihood that the buzzer will continue to elicit the eye-blink response decreases over time (see **Figure 8.4**). When presentation of the buzzer alone no longer elicits the conditioned response, psychologists say that the response has been extinguished (Rescorla, 2001a, 2001b).

An extinguished conditioned response may not be gone forever. It can return, especially after a rest period, and this recurrence is termed *spontaneous recovery*. If the dog whose salivation response has been extinguished is placed in the experimental situation again after a rest period of 20 minutes, its salivary response to the bell will recur briefly (although less strongly than before). This behavior shows that the effects of extinction are not permanent and that the dog does not totally forget the learned association (see **Figure 8.5**).

Stimulus Generalization and Stimulus Discrimination

When Watson and Rayner (1920) conditioned Little Albert to fear the white rat, they also assessed the degree to which Albert responded to similar objects.

Extinction ▪ In classical conditioning, the procedure of withholding the unconditioned stimulus and presenting the conditioned stimulus alone, which gradually reduces the probability that the conditioned response will occur.

Spontaneous recovery ▪ The recurrence of an extinguished conditioned response, usually following a rest period.

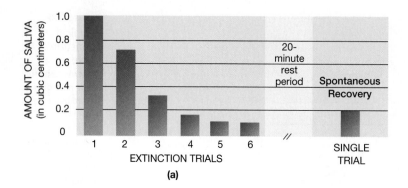

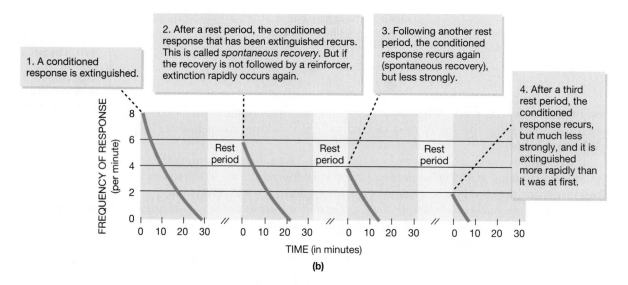

Figure 8.5

The Process of Spontaneous Recovery

Part (a) shows a graph of some of Pavlov's actual data from an experiment published in 1927. Pavlov brought about extinction in a series of six trials by omitting the presentation of the unconditioned stimulus; but after a 20-minute rest period, spontaneous recovery occurred.

Stimulus generalization
■ The process by which a conditioned response becomes associated with a stimulus that is similar but not identical to the original conditioned stimulus.

Watson and Rayner observed that Albert showed a fear response, similar to his conditioned response to the white rat, when he saw other white, fuzzy objects such as a rabbit, some cotton, and a white fur piece. The process known as *stimulus generalization* occurs when an organism develops a conditioned response to a stimulus that is similar but not identical to the original conditioned stimulus. The extent to which an organism responds to a stimulus similar to the original one depends on how alike the two stimuli are. If, for example, a loud tone is the conditioned stimulus for an eye-blink response, somewhat less loud but similar tones will also produce the response. A totally

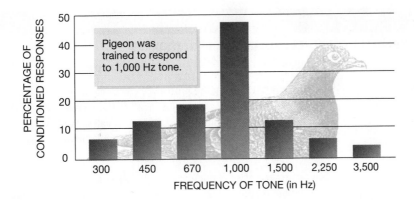

PERCENTAGE OF CONDITIONED RESPONSES

Pigeon was trained to respond to 1,000 Hz tone.

FREQUENCY OF TONE (in Hz)

Figure 8.6
Stimulus Generalization
Stimulus general-ization occurs when an animal or a human being exhibits a condi-tioned response to a stimulus that is similar but not identical to the original condi-tioned stimulus. In this experiment, a pigeon was trained to respond to a tone of 1,000 Hz by pecking a key. Later, the pigeon was presented with tones of different frequencies. Results showed that the percentage of responses decreased as the tone's frequency became increas-ingly different from that used during the training. (Jenkins & Harrison, 1960)

Stimulus discrimination
◼ The process by which an organism learns to respond only to a spe-cific stimulus and not to other similar stimuli.

dissimilar tone will produce little or no response. See **Figure 8.6** for another example of stimulus generalization.

Many psychologists believe that irrational fears develop because of stimulus generalizations that people make from one area of life to another (Ressler & Davis, 2003). Some people with phobias (unreasonable fears) develop them after first suf-fering from spontaneous panic attacks—feelings of intense, overwhelming terror accompanied by symptoms such as sweating, shortness of breath, or faintness. These attacks seem to occur randomly and without warning, making it impossible for a person to predict what situation will trigger such a reaction. The person then gener-alizes from the set of circumstances that was associated with the panic attack to other similar situations.

Stimulus discrimination is the process by which an organism learns to respond only to a specific stimulus and not to other similar stimuli. Pavlov showed that animals that have learned to differentiate between pairs of stimuli display frustration or even aggression when discrimination is difficult or impossible. He trained a dog to discriminate between a circle and an ellipse and then, on successive trials, changed the shape of the ellipse to look more and more like the circle. Eventually, the animal was unable to discriminate between the shapes but randomly chose one or the other; it also became aggressive.

Human beings also exhibit disorganized behavior when placed in situations in which they feel compelled to make a response but don't know how to respond correctly. On occasions when choosing a response becomes difficult or impossible, behavior can become stereotyped and limited in scope. People may choose either not to respond to the stimulus at all or always to respond in the same way (Lundin, 1961; Maier & Klee, 1941). For example, a husband who has not learned to discriminate between his wife's anger and her sadness may withdraw from the situation by leaving the room when his wife "gets emotional." Such a limited behavioral response may become a problem and may be a reason to seek help; therapists often help people learn to be more flexible in their responses.

Table 8.1 (on p. 286) summarizes four important concepts in classical condi-tioning: extinction, spontaneous recovery, stimulus generalization, and stimulus discrimination.

Table 8.1		

FOUR IMPORTANT CONCEPTS IN CLASSICAL CONDITIONING

Concept	Definition	Example
■ Extinction	The process of reducing the probability of a conditioned response by withholding the unconditioned stimulus	A dog conditioned to salivate to the sound of a bell stops salivating when the unconditioned stimulus of food is removed.
■ Spontaneous recovery	The recurrence of an extinguished conditioned response following a rest period	After a rest period, a dog whose conditioned salivary response has been extinguished again salivates in response to the conditioned stimulus, though less than before.
■ Stimulus generalization	The occurrence of a conditioned response to stimuli that are similar but not identical to the original conditioned stimulus	A dog conditioned to salivate in response to a high-pitched tone also salivates in response to a somewhat lower-pitched tone.
■ Stimulus discrimination	The process by which an organism learns to respond only to a specific stimulus	A dog is conditioned to salivate only in response to lights of high intensity, not to lights of low intensity.

Classical Conditioning in Daily Life

When I (L.B.) was about 8 years old, I had to take some type of medicine that had an artificial strawberry flavor. I got sick and threw up a few hours later. The medicine may not have been what made me sick; after all, I was ill, so the illness itself may have been the culprit. But I know that I developed an immediate dislike for things with artificial strawberry flavoring. Real strawberry flavor is fine (I make this stimulus discrimination), but I can pick out the artificial flavoring just by the smell. The accidental pairing of the taste of artificial strawberry flavoring and being sick to my stomach conditioned me; more than 40 years later, I still avoid anything with that flavor. My experience is not unusual, and psychologist John Garcia has investigated this particular type of classical conditioning.

The Garcia Effect

My association of artificial strawberry flavoring and nausea is an example of a *conditioned taste aversion*. In a famous experiment, John Garcia gave animals specific foods or drinks and then induced nausea (usually by injecting a drug or by exposing the animals to radiation). He found that after only one pairing of a food or drink (the conditioned stimulus) with the drug or radiation (the unconditioned stimulus), the animals avoided the food or drink that preceded the nausea (e.g., Garcia & Koelling, 1971; Linberg et al., 1982).

Two aspects of Garcia's work startled other researchers. First, Garcia showed that a conditioned taste aversion could be established even if the nausea was induced several hours *after* the food or drink had been consumed. This finding contradicted the general rule that the time interval between the unconditioned stimulus and the conditioned stimulus must be short, especially for conditioning to occur quickly. More recent research (as well as my personal experience) has confirmed Garcia's finding (De La Casa & Lubow, 2000; Grigson, 2000).

The second of Garcia's startling findings was that not all stimuli were equally easily associated. Garcia tried to pair bells and lights with nausea to produce a taste aversion in rats, but he was unable to do so—learning depended on the relevance of the stimuli to each other. The taste of food is relevant to the experience of nausea, but lights or sounds are not. These findings led Garcia to conclude that "strong aversions to the smell or taste of food can develop even when illness is delayed for hours after consumption [but] avoidance reactions do not develop for visual, auditory, or tactile stimuli associated with food" (Garcia & Koelling, 1971, p. 461). This type of association of stimuli may depend on whether they "belong" together in nature. Smells and nausea are far more likely to be related in the real world, and so a smell might quickly become a conditioned stimulus for nausea (Hollis, 1997). Garcia's work demonstrated that conditioning could occur after only one trial. He also showed that the principles of classical conditioning apply to naturally occurring associations.

Conditioned taste aversion, sometimes called the *Garcia effect*, has survival value for individuals as well as practical applications. There is survival value in learning to avoid food that makes one ill, and both humans and nonhuman animals learn this easily. Garcia demonstrated the practical use of conditioned taste aversion by teaching coyotes to stop their practice of attacking sheep and lambs (e.g., Garcia et al., 1976). Garcia taught them not to do so by lacing samples of lamb meat with a substance that causes a short-term illness. He put the lamb meat on the outskirts of sheep ranchers' fenced-in areas, and coyotes that ate it became sick and developed an aversion to it. After this experience, they approached the sheep and lambs as if ready to attack but nearly always backed off.

Learning and Chemotherapy

Cancer patients also learn taste aversions. They often undergo chemotherapy, and an unfortunate side effect of this therapy is vomiting and nausea. Patients often show a lack of appetite and lose weight. Is it possible that they lose weight because of a conditioned taste aversion? According to researchers, some cancer patients become conditioned to avoid food (Montgomery et al., 1998; Montgomery & Bovbjerg, 1997). Schafe and Bernstein (1996) reported on research with children and adults who were going to receive chemotherapy. This research showed that patients who ate before receiving chemotherapy developed specific aversions to whatever they ate; patients in control groups who did not eat before their therapy did not develop taste aversions.

Knowing about the association between chemotherapy and nausea is not sufficient to override the conditioning that takes place. Patients develop food aversions even when they know that it is the chemotherapy that induces the nausea. Bernstein suggested an intervention based on learning theory: Patients could be given a "scapegoat" food, such as candies with a particular flavor, just before chemotherapy; then, any conditioned taste aversion that developed would be to an unimportant and easily avoided food rather than to other nutritious foods. When Bernstein (1988, 1991) tried this procedure, she found that both children and adults were far less likely to develop general food aversions.

Conditioning of the Immune System

Classical conditioning explains a wide range of human behaviors, including some physical responses to the world, such as accelerations in heart rate and changes in blood pressure. However, research indicates that biological processes can be affected by conditioning even when we are not aware of them (Clark et al., 2002). This type of conditioning applies to many biological processes, including responses of the immune system, the body's defense against infection and disease.

Substances such as pollen, dust, animal dander, and mold initiate allergic reactions in many people; cat fur, for example, may elicit the allergic reaction of sneezing. In people with asthma, however, allergens like cat fur can initiate a cascade of reactions including constriction of the airway and difficulty in breathing. Allergic reactions and asthma attacks, like other responses, can be conditioned (Lehrer et al., 2002). For example, if Libby has asthma attacks in response to the cat fur in her friend Lindsay's house (a regular pairing), classical conditioning theory predicts that even if all the cat hair is removed, Libby may have an allergic reaction when she enters Lindsay's house. The house has become a conditioned stimulus, and the allergic reaction is a conditioned response. Researchers have shown that people with severe allergies can have an allergic reaction after merely seeing a cat, even if they have had no contact with cat fur, or upon entering a house where a cat used to live, though the cat (and its fur) are gone.

Even the body's immune system can be conditioned. Normally, the body releases disease-fighting antibodies when toxic substances appear in the blood. This response is an involuntary activity that is not directly controlled by the nervous system. In a person with a type of disorder called *autoimmune disease*, the immune system is overactive, which is a problem. Thus, suppressing immune system activity may be beneficial in this situation. In a striking series of studies, animals that had a fatal autoimmune disease were classically conditioned in a way that lowered their immune system activity (Ader, 1997, 2001; Ader & Cohen, 1975, 1993). The experimenters paired a sweet solution with a drug that produced nausea and, as a side effect, also suppressed the immune response. Later, tasting the sweet solution alone produced a reduction in the animals' immune system response. This series of experiments demonstrated that conditioning applies to the immune system and has the potential to affect health and disease. This intriguing finding demonstrates how many responses can be affected by classical conditioning.

Pavlov's Understanding Reinterpreted

When Pavlov was busy measuring salivation, he had no reason to consider the complex array of variables that psychologists now think about in connection with classical conditioning. Pavlov thought in terms of simple associations between paired stimuli. Today, researchers also consider the relevance of a stimulus, as well as its appropriateness, predictability, context, and ability to create higher-order associations. Pavlov laid the foundation for later studies of emotion and thought because he showed that organisms learn associations about events in the environment. But these associations are more complex than Pavlov realized.

Pavlov focused on actual, observable stimuli and responses. Today, researchers are considering how imagined stimuli—thoughts that we have about events—can evoke a response (Dadds et al., 1997). For example, do thoughts about airplane disasters cause people to avoid air travel? This broader view of conditioning may lead to a better understanding of how behavior can be established and maintained by thoughts, images, and anticipation of events, all of which can lead to conditioned responses, sometimes nonproductive or even abnormal ones.

Building Table 8.1 summarizes some of the key elements of classical conditioning. Although classical conditioning explains a wide range of phenomena, not all behaviors are the result of such conditioning. Many complex behaviors arise from another form of learning—operant conditioning—which focuses on behavior and its consequences.

What Type of Learning Is Operant Conditioning?

An organism can be exposed to bells, whistles, or lights and may form associations between stimuli that prompt responses—but in these kinds of situations the organism—the learner—has little control over the stimulus or the response. A light flashes before food appears, and an association is formed between the two. But what happens when a child is scolded for playing with and breaking a valuable camera or receives a pat on the back after doing well in class? Do these situations lead to learning? From the point of view of many psychologists, the consequences of a person's behavior have powerful

Building Table 8.1			
TYPES OF LEARNING: CLASSICAL CONDITIONING			
Type of Learning	**Procedure**	**Result**	**Example**
Classical conditioning	A neutral stimulus (such as a bell) is paired with an unconditioned stimulus (such as food).	The neutral stimulus becomes a conditioned stimulus—it elicits the conditioned response.	A bell elicits a response from a dog.

Operant [OP-er-ant] conditioning ■ Conditioning in which an increase or decrease in the probability that a behavior will recur is affected by the delivery of reinforcement or punishment as a consequence of the behavior; also known as *instrumental conditioning*.

Skinner believed so strongly in controlled environments that he devised a living space for his infant daughter. This "baby box" allowed Skinner to shape his daughter's behavior in certain ways, for example, to determine how she would respond if she was uncomfortable. Although Skinner's daughter grew up quite normally, ethical questions were raised about manipulating a child in this way.

effects that change the course of subsequent behavior. Unlike classical conditioning, this change in behavior occurs when the organism as actively operating on and within the environment and is thus experiencing rewards or punishments for voluntary (rather than reflexive) behavior.

According to psychologist B. F. Skinner (1904–1990), more behaviors can be explained through operant conditioning than through classical conditioning. *Operant conditioning*, or *instrumental conditioning*, is conditioning in which an increase or decrease in the probability that a behavior will recur is affected by the delivery of reinforcement or punishment as a consequence of the behavior. (Skinner used the word *operant* because the organism *operates* on the environment in performing the behavior.) This type of conditioning differs from classical conditioning in two important ways. First, the conditioned behavior is usually voluntary rather than reflexive. Second, a consequence follows, rather than coexists with or precedes, the behavior. Investigation into this type of conditioning began early in the history of psychology, and it became the most prominent type of learning studied by psychologists.

The Pioneers: E. L. Thorndike and B. F. Skinner

American psychologist E. L. Thorndike (1874–1949) pioneered the study of operant conditioning during the 1890s and first reported on his work in 1898. Thorndike placed hungry cats in boxes and put food outside the boxes. Each cat could escape from the box and get the food by hitting a lever that opened a door in the box. The cats quickly performed the behavior Thorndike was trying to condition (hitting the lever), because doing so—at first by accident and then deliberately—gave them access to food. Because the response (hitting the lever) was essential to (instrumental in) obtaining the reward, Thorndike used the term *instrumental conditioning* to describe the process and called the behaviors *instrumental behaviors*.

Describing this process further under the name *operant conditioning* was only one of B. F. Skinner's many contributions to the study of learning. In the 1930s, Skinner began to change the way psychologists think about conditioning and learning, researching and expanding the concept and importance of operant conditioning. Skinner's 1938 book, *The Behavior of Organisms*, continues to have an impact on studies of conditioning. In a survey of eminent psychologists of the 20th century, Skinner was placed at the top (Haggbloom et al., 2002).

Although Skinner called it operant conditioning and Thorndike instrumental conditioning, the two terms are often used interchangeably. What is important

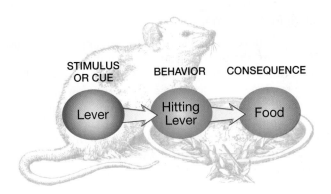

Figure 8.7
The Process of Operant Conditioning
Operant conditioning differs from classical conditioning in that the behavior to be conditioned (such as hitting a lever) is reinforced after it occurs.

is that both Skinner and Thorndike acknowledged that the behavior occurs first and then a consequence (for example, a reward) follows. This is unlike classical or Pavlovian conditioning, in which there is first a change in the environment (for example, a bell and food are paired) and then the conditioned behavior (usually a reflexive response) is elicited (see **Figure 8.7**).

Behavior can have any of three consequences: It may be reinforced, punished, or ignored. Behavior that is ignored is not likely to change in frequency, but reinforcement and punishment both change the likelihood that a behavior will be repeated. Let's examine both concepts in some detail because they are the keys to understanding operant conditioning.

Reinforcement: A Consequence That Strengthens a Response

To psychologists, a *reinforcer* is any event that increases the probability of a recurrence of the response that preceded it. Thus, a behavior followed by a desirable event is likely to recur. Examples of reinforcement abound in daily life: A person works hard at her job and is rewarded with high pay; a student studies long hours for an exam and is rewarded with a top grade; a young man asks a young woman out on a date, and she accepts; children behave appropriately and receive affection and praise from their parents. The specific behaviors of working hard, studying, asking for a date, and behaving appropriately become established because of reinforcement.

Some reinforcers are more powerful than others, and a reinforcer that rewards one person may not have reinforcing value for another. A smile from an approving parent may be a powerful reinforcer for a 2-year-old; high grades may be the most effective reinforcer for a student; money may be effective for one adult, a trip to Hawaii for another, or prestige or status for someone else. The power of reinforcers varies not only among individuals but also among cultures: In some cultures, money and individual achievement are valued and are therefore reinforcing; in other cultures, the approval of family and group harmony are more likely to reinforce behaviors.

Reinforcer ■ Any event that increases the probability of a recurrence of the response that preceded it.

Two Reinforcement Strategies: Positive and Negative

The likelihood that a behavior will recur can be increased by using one or both of two strategies for reinforcement: positive reinforcement and negative reinforcement.

Pet owners can use shaping to teach animals to obey. Each time this dog makes a closer approximation to sitting, the owner rewards it with a treat.

Positive reinforcement
■ Presentation of a stimulus after a particular response in order to increase the likelihood that the response will recur.

Negative reinforcement
■ Removal of an unpleasant stimulus after a particular response in order to increase the likelihood that the response will recur.

Positive Reinforcement

Most people have no problems understanding and even using *positive reinforcement*, the presentation of a stimulus after a particular response in order to increase the likelihood that the response will recur. When you are teaching your dog tricks, you reward it with a biscuit or a pat on the head. A parent who is toilet training a 2-year-old may applaud when the child uses the toilet. The dog biscuit and the applause are reinforcers. The dog and the child are likely to repeat the behaviors because they have been rewarded with something desirable—their behaviors have been positively reinforced.

Negative Reinforcement

Negative reinforcement is more difficult to understand than positive reinforcement because "negative" and "reinforcement" are concepts that don't seem to fit together. But they do. Whereas positive reinforcement increases the probability of a response through delivery of a pleasant stimulus, *negative reinforcement* increases the probability of a response through removal of an unpleasant stimulus. Negative reinforcement is reinforcement because it strengthens or increases the likelihood of a response being repeated; its reinforcing properties are associated with removal of an unpleasant stimulus.

Did you take an aspirin or some other type of pain reliever the last time you had a headache? If you did, you learned to do so through negative reinforcement. You have learned that the behavior of taking medication removes the unpleasant stimulus of headache pain; so, when you experience a headache, you are likely to repeat the response of taking that medication. As another example, consider a child who is told to go to his room until he apologizes to his sister for breaking her toy. Assuming that the child does not want to be isolated in his room (that is, that situation is unpleasant to him), he can escape the situation by apologizing. The reinforcement is the termination of the unpleasant stimulus of being confined to his room. In this case, termination of the unpleasant stimulus increases the probability of the response (apologizing), because that response ends the confinement.

If this boy's parents use this strategy of controlling his behavior, the child may learn how to escape from his room very quickly; that is, he may learn *escape conditioning*. Indeed, he may learn how to avoid being confined to his room altogether through a process called *avoidance conditioning*. If the child learns that he can apologize before he is confined to his room, he may avoid the consequences of his behavior (damaging his sister's toys). In avoidance conditioning, an organism learns to respond in such a way that a negative or unpleasant stimulus is never delivered. Other examples of such learning include studying for an exam in order to avoid a bad grade and avoiding air travel to prevent being afraid on an airplane. Thus, avoidance conditioning can explain both adaptive behaviors, such as studying before an exam, and irrational behaviors, such as refusing to travel by air.

Both positive and negative reinforcement increase the likelihood that an organism will repeat a behavior. If the reinforcement is strong enough, is delivered often enough, and is important enough to the organism, it can help maintain behaviors for long periods.

The Nature of Reinforcers

The precise nature of reinforcers is not completely clear. Early researchers recognized that anything that satisfies biological needs is a powerful reinforcer. Later researchers found that the satisfaction of various nonbiological needs can also be reinforcing—for example, conversation relieves boredom, and attention is gratifying. However, researchers make a distinction between reinforcers that satisfy biological needs and those that do not.

A *primary reinforcer* is a reinforcer that has survival value for an organism, such as food, water, or the termination of pain. The reinforcement value does not have to be learned. Food is a primary reinforcer for a hungry person, water for a thirsty one. A *secondary reinforcer* is a neutral stimulus (such as money or grades) that initially has no value for an organism but that becomes rewarding when linked with a primary reinforcer. Many things that people enjoy are secondary reinforcers that have acquired value; for example, leather coats keep us no warmer than cloth ones, and sports cars take us where we want to go no more effectively than four-door sedans. However, many of us work hard so that we can acquire leather coats and sports cars.

Secondary reinforcers can be very powerful in modifying human behavior. Approving nods, unlimited use of the family car, job promotions, and friends' acceptance are secondary reinforcers that can establish and maintain a wide spectrum of behaviors. People work very hard for money, which they cannot eat, drink, or wear to keep warm. However, people can use money to satisfy their survival needs, and it is a powerful incentive for human behavior.

However, as was mentioned earlier, something that acts as a reinforcer for one person may not do so for another person (especially if that person is from a different culture) or for the same person on another day. Therefore, those who want to use reinforcement to change behavior must be very careful about identifying what will be an effective reinforcer. If someone wanted to persuade you to perform some fairly difficult task, what would be the most effective reinforcer? Your answer may not apply to others, and you may give a different answer next week than you do today.

In addition, the effectiveness of reinforcers may change with a person's age and experiences and may depend on how often the person has been reinforced. A reinforcer that is known to be successful may work only in specific situations. The delivery of food pellets to a hungry rat that has just pressed a lever increases the likelihood that the rat will press the lever again. But this reinforcer is most effective when the rat is hungry. For people, food is also a more powerful reinforcer when they are hungry (Epstein et al., 2003). Today, researchers are trying to discover what reinforcers will work best in practical settings such as the home and the workplace (Farmer-Dougan, 1998).

Primary reinforcer ■
Reinforcer (such as food, water, or the termination of pain) that has survival value for an organism.

Secondary reinforcer ■
Any neutral stimulus that initially has no value for an organism but that becomes rewarding when linked with a primary reinforcer.

The Skinner Box and Shaping

Much of the research on operant conditioning has used an apparatus that most psychologists call a Skinner box—even though Skinner himself never approved of the name. A *Skinner box* is a box that contains a responding mechanism and a device capable of delivering a consequence to an animal in the box whenever it makes a desired response (one the experimenter has chosen). In experiments that involve positive reinforcement, the delivery device is often activated by a small lever or bar (the responding mechanism) in the side of the Skinner box. When the animal presses the lever or bar, the box releases a piece of food.

In a traditional operant conditioning experiment, a rat that has been deprived of food is placed in a Skinner box. The rat moves around the box, seeking food or a means of escape. Eventually, it stumbles on or climbs on the lever, pressing it. Immediately following that action, the experimenter delivers a pellet of food into a feeding cup near the lever. The rat moves about some more and happens to press the lever again, so another pellet of food drops into the cup. After a few trials, the rat learns that pressing the lever brings food. A hungry rat will learn to press the lever many times in rapid succession to obtain food. Today, psychologists use computerized devices to keep records of bar pressing and to track the progress an organism makes in learning a response.

For some complex behaviors, reinforcement of the desired response is not possible because the organism will not perform the response spontaneously. However, complex behaviors can be taught in small steps, through shaping. *Shaping* is the gradual process of selective reinforcement of behaviors that gradually come closer and closer to (approximate) a desired response. Dolphins do not naturally play basketball, but some dolphins have been taught to do so through shaping. Initially, the dolphin receives a food reward for approaching the ball as it floats in the water. Then, the dolphin must touch the ball to receive a reward. After that behavior is established, the dolphin must touch the ball with its nose, then bounce the ball off its nose, and so forth. At each stage, the reinforced behavior more closely approximates the desired behavior (making a goal with the ball). With sufficient shaping, the animal performs the sequence of approaching the ball, balancing it on the nose, and bouncing it into the hoop for a goal. The sequence of stages used in shaping to elicit increasingly closer approximations of a desired behavior is sometimes called the *method of successive approximations*. This procedure is used to train most animals to do tricks or to perform work that is not based on their natural behavior.

Shaping is also helpful in teaching people new behaviors. For example, if you learned how to hit a baseball, you were probably first taught, with reinforcing praise from your coach, how to hold the bat correctly, then how to swing it, then how to make contact with the ball, how to shift your weight, how to follow through, and so on. Similarly, a parent who wants a child to make his or her bed neatly will at first reinforce any attempt at bed making, even if the results are sloppy. Over time, the parent will reinforce only the better attempts, until finally only neat bed making receives reinforcement. Patience is important when using shaping, because it is essential to reinforce all steps toward the desired behavior, no matter how small.

Skinner box ■ Named for its developer, B. F. Skinner, a box that contains a responding mechanism and a device capable of delivering a consequence to an animal in the box whenever it makes a desired response.

Shaping ■ Selective reinforcement of behaviors that gradually come closer and closer to (approximate) a desired response.

Shaping embodies a central point of behaviorism: Reinforced behaviors recur. Skinner was responsible for forcefully advancing that notion, and psychologists attribute to him the idea that various consequences can redirect the natural flow of behavior. Reinforcement is most important in this process of operant conditioning, but punishment is also a factor.

Punishment: A Consequence That Weakens a Response

We have seen how reinforcement can establish new behaviors and maintain them for long periods. How effective is punishment in manipulating behavior? *Punishment* is the process of presenting an undesirable or noxious stimulus, or removing a desirable stimulus, in order to decrease the probability that a preceding response will recur. Punishment, unlike reinforcement, aims to *decrease* the probability of a particular response. Thus, people commonly use this technique to try to teach children and pets to control their behavior. For example, when a dog growls at visitors, its owner may scold it. When a child writes on the walls with crayons, the parents may reprimand her harshly or make her scrub the walls. In both cases, someone delivers a stimulus intended to suppress an undesirable behavior.

Researchers use the same technique to decrease the probability that a behavior will recur. They can use either positive or negative punishment. Adding something unpleasant to a situation is *positive punishment*. When researchers deliver a noxious or unpleasant stimulus to an organism that displays an undesirable behavior, they are using positive punishment. If an animal receives positive punishment for a specific behavior, the probability that it will continue to perform that behavior decreases. For example, if a rat receives a shock when it presses the lever in a Skinner box, it is less likely to push the lever again.

Another form of punishment is *negative punishment*, which involves removal of a pleasant stimulus. For example, if a teenager stays out past her curfew (an undesirable behavior, at least from her parents' point of view), she may be grounded for a week. If a child misbehaves, he may not be allowed to watch television that evening. One effective negative punishment is the *time-out*, in which an individual is removed from an environment containing positive events or reinforcers. For example, a child who hits and kicks may have to sit alone in a corner with no toys, television, books, or other diversions for a specified length of time.

Thus, punishment comes in positive and negative versions, just as reinforcement does. But the goal of both types of punishment is to decrease the repetition of a behavior, whereas the goal of both types of reinforcement is to increase the frequency of a behavior. (See **Figure 8.8** for a summary of the effects of adding or subtracting a reinforcer or punisher; see **Figure 8.9** for a comparison of punishment and negative reinforcement.)

The Nature of Punishers

Like reinforcers, punishers can be primary or secondary. A *primary punisher* is a stimulus that is naturally painful or unpleasant to an organism. Two examples are a very high-pitched sound (which is painful to an animal) and a spanking (which is painful to

Punishment ■ Process of presenting an undesirable or noxious stimulus, or removing a desirable stimulus, in order to decrease the probability that a preceding response will recur.

Primary punisher ■ Any stimulus that is naturally painful or unpleasant to an organism.

	ADDITION OF A STIMULUS	REMOVAL OF A STIMULUS	
REINFORCEMENT	Positive reinforcement: Delivery of food, money, or some other reward	*or* Negative reinforcement: Removal of shock or some other aversive stimulus	Establishes or increases a specific behavior
PUNISHMENT	Positive punishment: Delivery of electric shock, a slap on the hand, or some other aversive stimulus	*or* Negative punishment: Removal of automobile, television, or some other pleasant stimulus	Suppresses or decreases a specific behavior

Figure 8.8
Effects of Reinforcement and Punishment

Secondary punisher ■
Any neutral stimulus that initially has no negative value for an organism but acquires punishing qualities when linked with a primary punisher.

a child). A *secondary punisher* is any neutral stimulus that initially has no negative value for an organism but acquires punishing qualities when linked with a primary punisher. Examples are the word "no," a shake of the head, or an angry expression. Secondary punishers can be effective means of controlling behavior, especially when used in combination with reinforcers for desired behaviors. But, as with reinforcement, what is punishing for one person or in one culture may not have the same properties for another person or in another culture. An angry facial expression may punish some behaviors for some people, but other individuals will not care about such a display of displeasure. Fathers may be more powerful disciplinarians in some cultures, and mothers in others. Similarly, guilt is used as a punishing device in some cultures more than in others. In collectivist societies, which focus on group cohesiveness and agreement, the disapproval of one's group may be far more powerful than it would be in individualist societies, which focus on individual effort and self-esteem.

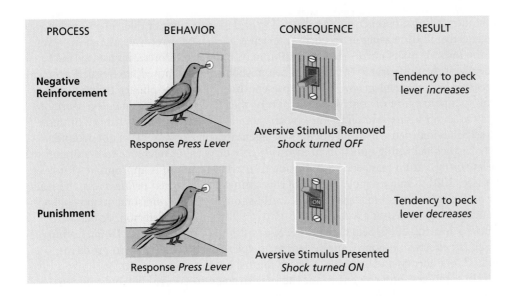

| PROCESS | BEHAVIOR | CONSEQUENCE | RESULT |

Negative Reinforcement

Response *Press Lever*

Aversive Stimulus Removed
Shock turned OFF

Tendency to peck lever *increases*

Punishment

Response *Press Lever*

Aversive Stimulus Presented
Shock turned ON

Tendency to peck lever *decreases*

Figure 8.9
Comparison of Negative Reinforcement and Punishment
Punishment involves the presentation of an unpleasant stimulus to decrease the likelihood that a behavior will recur. Negative reinforcement encourages a behavior by removing an aversive stimulus. Thus, punishment and negative reinforcement have opposite effects on behavior.

Limitations of Punishment

A serious limitation of punishment as a behavior-shaping device is that it only suppresses behaviors; punishment does not have the potential to establish new, desired behaviors. Punishment also has serious social consequences (Clutton-Brock & Parker, 1995; Rodriguez, 2003). If parents use excessive punishment to control a child's behavior, for example, the child may try to escape from the home so that punishment cannot be delivered. Rather than associating the punishment with the behavior, the child learns to associate the punishment with the punisher. Further, children who are physically punished often demonstrate increased levels of aggression when they are away from the punisher (Gershoff, 2002). Punishment may control a child's immediate behavior, but it may also damage the child's relationship with the parents and fail to control behavior in the long run.

Research also shows that children imitate aggression (Bandura, 2001). Thus, parents who punish children physically are likely to have children who are physically aggressive (Gershoff, 2002; Grusec, Goodnow, & Kuczynski, 2000). A child may strike out at the person who administers punishment in an attempt to eliminate the source of discomfort, sometimes inflicting serious injury. Punishment can also bring about generalized aggression and has been shown to be related to delinquent behavior (Gershoff, 2002). For example, people who have been punished frequently tend to be hostile and aggressive toward other members of their group and to act on this hostility. This phenomenon is especially evident in prison inmates, whose hostility is well recognized, and in schoolyard bullies, who are often the children most strictly disciplined by their parents or teachers.

Psychologists argue about the effects of punishment (Kazdin & Benjet, 2003), but Skinner (1988) believed that punishment is unnecessary and harmful in schools. Instead, he advocated the use of nonpunitive disciplinary techniques, which might involve developing strong bonds between students and teachers and reinforcing school activities at home (Comer & Woodruff, 1998). Ignoring undesirable behavior can also be effective in decreasing its frequency. When a misbehavior receives attention—even in the form of punishment—that attention may act as a reinforcer, increasing the frequency of the undesirable behavior. When misbehavior is ignored, its frequency may decrease because reinforcement is not present. In general, disciplinary techniques that lead to a perception of control on the part of the child being disciplined—a sense of how to avoid future discipline—are much more likely to prevent recurrence of undesired behavior, even when the disciplining agent (teacher or parent) is not around.

Further, delivering punishment inconsistently or without reference to the organism's behavior or culture may lead to confusion over what response is appropriate (Rudy & Grusec, 2001). An extreme outcome of this confusion is *learned helplessness*, the reaction of a person or animal that feels powerless to control the punishment and so stops making any response at all (LoLordo & Taylor, 2001; Maier, Peterson, & Schwartz, 2000; Schwartz, 2000; Seligman, 1976; Shatz, 2000; Springer, 2000). Doing nothing is rarely an effective response, and so learned helplessness usually leads to problems. Indeed, one theory of depression is based on this concept (see Chapter 16).

In summary, punishment is not the best strategy to control behavior. It can suppress undesirable behavior, but it does not create desirable behavior. In addition, punishment must be delivered consistently, and it must be moderately severe but not too severe. Severe punishment creates problems.

Learned helplessness ■
The reaction of a person or animal that feels powerless to control punishment or negative consequences and so stops making any response at all.

Punishment Plus Reinforcement

Psychologists have long known that punishment by itself is not an effective way to control or eliminate behavior (Gershoff, 2002). Punishment can suppress simple behavior patterns; once the punishment ceases, however, humans and nonhuman animals often return to their previous behavior patterns. If punishment is to be effective, it must be paired with reinforcement of desired alternative behavior. This strategy suppresses the undesirable response while creating a more desirable one. For example, those who study children's classroom behavior suggest that a combination of punishment for undesirable, antisocial behaviors and public praise for cooperative, prosocial behaviors may be an effective method for controlling classroom behavior (Shukla-Mehta & Albin, 2003).

What Are the Key Variables in Operant Conditioning?

Like classical conditioning, operant conditioning is affected by many variables. Most important are the strength, timing, and frequency of consequences (either reinforcement or punishment).

Strength, Timing, and Frequency
Strength of Consequences

Studies that vary the amount of reinforcement show that the greater the reward, the harder, longer, and faster a person will work to complete a task (see **Figure 8.10**).

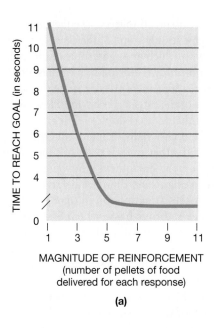

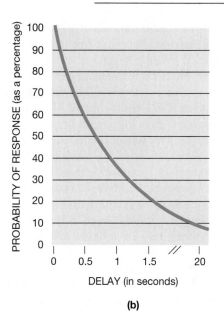

Figure 8.10
The Magnitude and Delay of Reinforcement
(a) As the amount of a reinforcer (its strength or magnitude) increases, the time it takes an organism to reach a goal usually decreases. (b) When there is a delay between a response and reinforcement, the probability that a behavior will occur decreases. Short delays (or no delays) between a response and reinforcement increase the chances that a behavior will recur.

For example, if you ran a lawn-mowing company, the more money you received for mowing lawns, the more lawns you would want to mow. Similarly, the stronger the punishment, the more quickly a behavior can be suppressed. If you knew you would get a $200 ticket for speeding, you would be far more likely to obey the speed limit.

The strength of a consequence can be measured in terms of either how long it continues or how forceful it is. For example, the length of time a teen is grounded can affect how soon and for how long an unacceptable behavior will be suppressed. That is, for a given teen, a weekend might not be as effective as a week. Likewise, a polite "Please don't do that, sweetie" is not as effective as a firm "Don't do that again."

Punishment, whatever its form, is best delivered in moderation (Baumrind, Larzelere, & Cowan, 2002); too much may be as ineffective as too little. Too much punishment may cause panic, decrease the likelihood of the desired response, or even elicit behavior that is contrary to the punisher's goals.

Timing of Consequences

Just as the interval between presenting the conditioned stimulus and presenting the unconditioned stimulus is important in classical conditioning, the interval between exhibiting a behavior and experiencing the consequence (reward or punishment) is important in operant conditioning. Generally, the shorter the interval, the greater the likelihood that the behavior will be learned (again, see Figure 8.10).

Frequency of Consequences

How often do people need to be reinforced? Is a paycheck once a month a good incentive? Will people work better if they receive reinforcement regularly or if they receive it at unpredictable intervals? Up to this point, we have assumed that a consequence follows each response. But what if people receive reinforcement only some of the time, not continually? When a researcher varies the frequency with which an organism is reinforced, the researcher is manipulating the ***schedule of reinforcement***—the pattern of presentation of a reinforcer over time. The simplest and easiest reinforcement pattern is *continuous reinforcement*—reinforcement for every occurrence of the targeted behavior. However, most researchers (or parents or animal trainers, for that matter) do not reinforce a behavior every time it occurs. Rather, they reinforce occasionally or intermittently.

Schedules of reinforcement generally are based either on intervals of time or on frequency of response. Some schedules establish a behavior quickly; however, quickly established behaviors are more quickly extinguished than are behaviors that are slower to be established. (We'll look more closely at extinction in operant conditioning later in this chapter.) Researchers have devised four basic schedules of reinforcement; two are interval schedules (based on time periods), and two are ratio schedules (based on rate of responding or on work output).

Interval schedules can be either fixed or variable. Imagine that a rat in a Skinner box is being trained to press a bar in order to obtain food. If the experiment is on a ***fixed-interval schedule***, the reward will follow the first bar press that occurs after a specified interval of time, perhaps every 15 seconds. That is, the rat will be given a reinforcer if it presses the bar at least once after 15 seconds have passed and will receive the same reward regardless of whether it pressed the bar repeatedly or just once. As **Figure 8.11** shows, a fixed-interval schedule produces a scalloped graph,

Schedule of reinforcement ■ The pattern of presentation of a reinforcer over time.

Fixed-interval schedule ■ A schedule of reinforcement in which a reinforcer (reward) is delivered after a specified interval of time, provided that the required response occurs at least once in the interval.

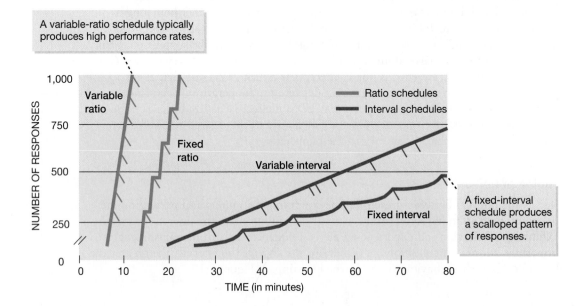

Figure 8.11
The Four Basic Types of Reinforcement Schedules
Each tick mark indicates presentation of a reinforcer. Steep slopes represent high response rates. In general, the rate of response is higher with ratio schedules than with interval schedules.

which reflects an uneven pattern of responding. Just after reinforcement (shown by the tick marks in the figure), both animals and humans typically respond slowly, but just before the reinforcement is due, performance increases.

Under a *variable-interval schedule*, the reinforcer is delivered after predetermined but varying amounts of time, as long as an appropriate response is made at least once after each interval. The organism may be reinforced if it makes a response after 10 seconds, after 30 seconds, and then after 15 seconds. Rats reinforced on a variable-interval schedule work at a slow, regular rate; the graph of a variable-interval schedule does not have the scalloped effect reflecting the uneven performance of a fixed-interval graph. The work rate is relatively slow because the delivery of the reinforcer is tied to time intervals rather than to output.

Ratio schedules are based on output instead of time, and these schedules can also be either fixed or variable. In a *fixed-ratio schedule*, the organism is reinforced for a specified number of responses—that is, for the amount of work performed. For example, a rat in a Skinner box might be reinforced after every 10th bar press. In this case, the rat will work at a fast, regular rate. It has learned that hard work brings regular delivery of a reinforcer. Variable-ratio schedules can bring about an even higher rate of response. A *variable-ratio schedule* reinforces the organism for a predetermined but variable number of responses (amount of work). For example, a rat receives a food pellet for every 10 bar presses on average (say, a pellet is delivered three times during a span of 30 presses, at the 4th, 13th and 29th presses) rather than at exactly every 10th bar press (a pellet is delivered on press 10, press 20, and press 30). Thus, a rat learns that hard work produces a reinforcer, but it cannot predict exactly when the reinforcer will be delivered. Therefore, the rat's best bet is to work at a regular, high rate, thereby generating the highest available rate of response. People gambling at slot machines behave very much like rats on a variable ratio schedule—they pour quarters into slot machines because they never know when they will be reinforced with a jackpot. **Table 8.2** summarizes the four schedules of reinforcement.

Is it possible to have the best of both types of reinforcement schedules? That is, is it possible to create responses quickly and to have those responses persist? Lasting responses cannot be created quickly using a single schedule of reinforcement—but combining schedules can work. An efficient way to teach a response is to begin with a continuous schedule of reinforcement, then switch to a fixed-ratio schedule, and finish with a variable-ratio schedule. For example, a rat can initially be reinforced on every trial so that it will learn the proper response quickly. It can then be reinforced after every other trial, then after every fifth trial, and then after a variable number of trials. Once the rat has learned the desired response, very high response rates can be obtained even with infrequent reinforcement. These schedules can easily be combined for maximum effect, depending on the targeted behavior (e.g., Worsdell et al., 2000; Zarcone et al., 1999).

Psychologists use the principles of reinforcement to answer frequently asked questions such as these: How can I change my little brother's bratty behavior? How can I get more work out of my employees? How do I learn to say no? How do I get my dog to stop chewing my shoes? To get your brother to shape up, you can shape his behavior. Each time he acts in a way you like, reward him with praise or affection. When he behaves annoyingly, withhold attention or rewards

Variable-interval schedule ■ A schedule of reinforcement in which a reinforcer (reward) is delivered after predetermined but varying amounts of time, provided that the required response occurs at least once after each interval.

Fixed-ratio schedule ■ A schedule of reinforcement in which a reinforcer (reward) is delivered after a specified number of responses has occurred.

Variable-ratio schedule ■ A schedule of reinforcement in which a reinforcer (reward) is delivered after a predetermined but variable number of responses has occurred.

Table 8.2

TYPES OF REINFORCEMENT SCHEDULES

Schedule	Description	Effect
■ Fixed-interval	Reinforcement is given for the first response after a fixed time.	Response rate drops right after reinforcement but then increases near the end of the interval.
■ Variable-interval	Reinforcement is given for the first response after a predetermined but variable interval.	Response rate is slow and regular.
■ Fixed-ratio	Reinforcement is given after a fixed number of responses.	Response rate is fast and regular.
■ Variable-ratio	Reinforcement is given after a predetermined and variable number of responses.	Response rate is regular and high.

and ignore him. Continue this pattern for a few weeks. Remember, reinforced behaviors tend to recur.

Most workers get paid a fixed amount each week. They are on a fixed-interval schedule—regardless of their output, they get their paycheck. One way to increase productivity is to place workers on a fixed-ratio schedule. A worker who is paid by the piece—by the report, by the page, or by the widget—is going to produce more reports, pages, or widgets than one who is paid by the hour and whose productivity therefore does not make a difference. Automobile salespeople, who are known for their persistence, work for commissions; their pay is linked to their ability to close a sale. Research in both the laboratory and the workplace shows that when pay is linked to output, people generally work harder.

Stimulus Generalization and Stimulus Discrimination

Stimulus discrimination and *stimulus generalization* occur in operant conditioning much as they do in classical conditioning. In operant conditioning, reinforcement is delivered only after the organism correctly discriminates between stimuli. For example, suppose an animal in a laboratory is shown either a vertical or a horizontal line and is given two keys to press—one if the line is vertical, the other if the line is horizontal. The animal gets rewards for correct responses. The animal will usually make errors at first. After repeated presentations of the vertical and horizontal lines, with reinforcement only for correct responses, the animal will learn to discriminate between the stimuli. Stimulus discrimination can also be established with colors, tones, and more complex stimuli.

Stimulus generalization occurs when the individual behaves similarly in situations similar to the one in which it has been reinforced or punished. A child

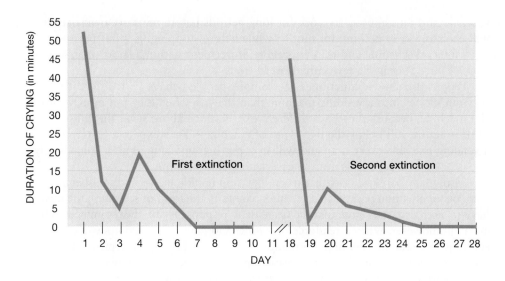

Figure 8.12
The Process of Extinction
When an organism's behavior is no longer reinforced, the likelihood that the organism will continue to respond decreases; psychologists say that the behavior has undergone extinction. In one study, C. D. Williams (1959) found that a child was throwing tantrums at bedtime to get attention. Williams instructed the parents to pay no attention to the tantrums. After several days, the number of minutes the child cried decreased to zero. A week later, an aunt put the child to bed; when the child made a fuss (spontaneous recovery), the aunt reinforced the child with attention. The parents then had to initiate a second extinction process.

who has been bitten by a dog may avoid all dogs, and possibly even all small, four-legged animals. The processes of stimulus generalization and discrimination are evident daily. The natural tendency is to generalize, but discrimination can be learned. We often make mistakes by overgeneralizing. For example, a young child whose family has a pet cat knows that cats have four legs and a tail and may call all four-legged animals "cat," generalizing incorrectly. With experience and with guidance, the child will learn to discriminate between dogs and cats, based on body size, shape, fur, and sounds. When you are introduced to a type of music with which you are unfamiliar, you may have trouble distinguishing among various musicians or groups, but further experience allows you to make distinctions even among those whose style is similar. Similarly, you may be unaware of distinctions among various impressionist artists, but after several viewings, you can learn to recognize the works of Renoir, Monet, and Pissarro.

Extinction and Spontaneous Recovery

In operant conditioning, if a reinforcer or punisher is no longer delivered—that is, if a consequence does not follow an instrumentally conditioned behavior—the behavior either will fail to become well established or, if it is already established, will undergo extinction (see **Figure 8.12**). In operant conditioning, *extinction* is the process by which the probability of an organism's emitting a response is reduced when reinforcement no longer follows the response. One way to measure the extent of conditioning is to measure how resistant a response is to extinction. *Resistance to extinction* is a measure of how long it takes, or how many trials are necessary, before extinction occurs. Suppose, for example, that a pigeon is trained to peck a key whenever it hears a high-pitched tone. Pecking in response to the high-pitched tone brings reinforcement. If the reinforcement process ceases entirely, the pigeon will eventually stop pecking the key. If the pigeon has been on a variable-ratio

Extinction ■ In operant conditioning, the process by which the probability of an organism's emitting a response is reduced when reinforcement no longer follows the response.

schedule and thus expects to work for long periods before reinforcement occurs, it will probably keep pecking for quite a while before stopping. If it has been on a fixed-interval schedule and thus expects reinforcement within a short time, it will stop pecking after just a few unreinforced trials.

People also show extinction. For example, people behave very differently when they put money into a vending machine than they do when they put money into a slot machine, because they have different expectations about what the consequences of their action will be for the two types of machines. They expect a reinforcer from a vending machine every time and will stop putting money in almost immediately if one is not delivered; this is not the case with a slot machine.

Also, many parents know that when they stop reinforcing a child's misbehavior with lots of attention (even if that attention comes in the form of scolding), the misbehaviors often decrease. Note that the decrease in response is not always immediately apparent, however. When a reinforcer is withheld, organisms sometimes work harder—showing an initial increase in performance. In such cases, the curve depicting the extinction process shows a small initial increase in performance, followed by a decrease.

As with classical conditioning, *spontaneous recovery* also occurs with operant conditioning. If an organism's conditioned response has undergone extinction and the organism is given a rest period and then retested, the organism will show spontaneous recovery of the response. If the organism is put through this sequence several times, its overall response rate in each session will decrease. After one rest period, the organism's rate will almost equal what it was when the conditioned response was reinforced. However, after about a dozen rest periods (with no reinforcements), the organism may make only one or two responses; the level of spontaneous recovery will have decreased markedly. Eventually, the response will disappear completely.

People also show spontaneous recovery. When you answer a question in class, reinforcement or punishment often follows: The instructor may praise you for your intelligence or grill you about your lack of understanding. However, if the instructor stops reinforcing correct answers or does not call on you when you raise your hand, you will probably stop responding (your behavior will be extinguished). After a vacation, you may start raising your hand again (spontaneous recovery), but you will quickly stop if your behavior remains unreinforced. Instructors learn early in their careers that if they want to have lively classes, they need to reinforce not just correct answers but also attempts at correct answers. In doing so, they help shape their students' behavior.

Table 8.3 (on p. 305) summarizes four important concepts in operant conditioning: extinction, spontaneous recovery, stimulus generalization, and stimulus discrimination. **Building Table 8.2** compares key points about classical and operant conditioning.

Operant Conditioning in Daily Life

Our world is full of reinforcers and punishers. We can work for rewards such as money, praise, and chocolate. We can volunteer our time for worthy causes such as the Red Cross, homeless shelters, and AIDS research. Sometimes people feel helpless in the face of punishers: The cost of living keeps rising; random violence seems to increase; the environment is in serious trouble. But, by and large, most of us feel in control of many of the important reinforcers and punishers in our lives. We know

Table 8.3

FOUR IMPORTANT CONCEPTS IN OPERANT CONDITIONING

Concept	Definition	Example
• Extinction	The process of reducing the probability of a conditioned response by withholding the reinforcer after the response	A rat trained to press a bar stops pressing when this behavior is no longer reinforced.
• Spontaneous recovery	The recurrence of an extinguished conditioned response following a rest period	After a rest period, a rat whose conditioned bar-pressing behavior has undergone extinction again presses the bar.
• Stimulus generalization	The process by which an organism learns to respond to stimuli that are similar but not identical to the original conditioned stimulus	A cat presses a bar when presented with either an ellipse or a circle.
• Stimulus discrimination	The process by which an organism learns to respond only to a specific reinforced stimulus	A pigeon presses a key only in response to red lights, not to blue or green ones.

that many rewards and punishments are contingent on our behaviors. Each of us experiences operant conditioning in daily life in many ways.

Superstitious Behaviors

Because reinforcement plays a key role in the learning of new behaviors, people often use reinforcement to change behavior—their own and that of others. But what happens when a person or animal is accidentally rewarded for a

Building Table 8.2

TYPES OF LEARNING: CLASSICAL CONDITIONING AND OPERANT CONDITIONING

Type of Learning	Procedure	Result	Example
Classical conditioning	A neutral stimulus (such as a bell) is paired with an unconditioned stimulus (such as food).	The neutral stimulus becomes a conditioned stimulus—it elicits the conditioned response.	A bell elicits a response from a dog.
Operant conditioning	A behavior is followed by a consequence, either reinforcement or punishment.	The behavior increases or decreases in frequency.	A rat will press a bar 120 times per hour to achieve a reward or to avoid punishment.

Superstitious behavior
■ Behavior learned through its coincidental association with reinforcement.

behavior—when a reward has nothing to do with the behavior that immediately preceded it? In this case, *superstitious behavior* may develop—behavior learned through its coincidental association with reinforcement. Superstitious behavior often represents an attempt to gain some control of a situation that may be unpredictable. For example, a baseball player may try to extend his hitting streak by always using the same "lucky" bat or engaging in small, often repetitive rituals (Bleak & Frederick, 1998).

Many superstitious behaviors—including fear responses to the number 13, black cats, and walking under ladders—are centuries old. Such beliefs have strong cultural associations. For example, in Asian cultures, the number 4 is considered unlucky instead of 13 (Phillips et al., 2001). Individual superstitious behaviors generally arise from the purely random, coincidental association of some object or event and a particular behavior. Thus, a person who happens to wear the same pair of socks in three bicycle races and wins the races may come to believe there is a causal relationship between wearing that pair of socks and winning.

Intrinsically Motivated Behavior

Psychologists have shown that reinforcement is effective in establishing and maintaining behavior. But some behaviors are intrinsically rewarding—they are pleasurable in themselves. People are likely to repeat intrinsically motivated behaviors for their own sake. For example, they may work on craft projects for the feeling of satisfaction they bring; they may learn to dance for the feeling of pleasure and accomplishment in dancing well. In contrast, people generally perform extrinsically motivated behaviors, such as working for a paycheck, for the sake of the external reinforcement alone.

Interestingly, if a person is offered reinforcement for an intrinsically motivated behavior, performance may actually decrease. Imagine, for example, that a man does charity work because it makes him feel good. Being paid could actually cause the man to lose interest in the work because it would no longer offer the intrinsic reinforcement of feelings of selflessness. A student pianist may lose her desire to practice if her teacher enters her in a competition; practice sessions become ordeals, and the student may wish to stop playing altogether. Remember—for every person and in every culture, reinforcers differ and are determined by a host of learning experiences. (Chapter 12 further considers the interesting paradox of the potential hidden costs of rewards.)

Behavioral Self-Regulation

Behavioral regulation theorists assume that people and animals will, if possible, choose activities that seem optimal to them. Rats, for example, will spend their time eating, drinking, and running on a wheel—activities they find pleasurable. An experiment by Bernstein and Ebbesen (1978) showed that human beings readjust their activities in a systematic manner. The researchers paid participants to live in an isolated room 24 hours a day, 7 days a week, for several weeks. The room had all the usual amenities of a home—bed, tables, bathroom, books, cooking utensils, and so forth. The experimenters observed the participants through a one-way mirror and recorded their baseline activity—the frequency of their specific behaviors when no restrictions were placed on them. The researchers found, for example, that one participant spent nearly twice as much time knitting as studying. The experimenters used each participant's baseline activity to determine the reinforcer—in this case, knitting.

The experimenters then imposed a contingency on the participants' behavior. In the case of the participant who liked to knit, for example, they insisted that she study for a specific amount of time before she could knit. If she studied only as much as she did before, she would be able to knit for much less time than she preferred. As a consequence, the woman altered her behavior so that she could spend more time knitting. She began to study for longer periods of time—eventually more than doubling the time she spent studying. This type of behavior analysis and application of reinforcement can allow you to manage your study habits and regulate your behavior.

Other techniques of behavioral self-regulation are derived from the basic learning principles of reinforcement. According to Rena Wing and her colleagues (Jeffery et al., 2000; Tate, Wing, & Winett, 2001; Wing & Jeffery, 1999), individuals with medical conditions that require daily attention will benefit from regulating their health-related behaviors. To do so, they must observe, evaluate, and then reinforce their own behaviors. These researchers assert that when people observe their own target behavior, such as adhering to a low-fat diet, they are better able to evaluate their own progress. After evaluating their progress, it is crucial that they receive reinforcement for adhering to their medical regimen—perhaps by going out to a concert with a friend or buying themselves a present. When these procedures are followed, adherence to the medical regimen improves. This procedure can also help you regulate your behavior, including studying. When you make a study schedule, plan a reward; after you stick to a study schedule, make sure you give yourself that reward.

Behavioral self-regulation has other practical applications. It is effective in classrooms (Winsler, Carlton, & Barry, 2000) and in other social situations where it can modulate disruptive behavior (Cavalier, Ferretti, & Hodges, 1997). Members of the diet program Weight Watchers may be told to keep track of when and what they eat, when they have the urge to eat, and what feelings or events precede those urges. The program tries to help people identify the events that lead to eating so that they can control it. The aim is to help people think clearly, regulate their behavior, and thus manage their eating.

Another factor that can be useful in changing the behavior of one individual is the behavior of others. Behavior occurs in a social context, and other people provide not only reinforcement and punishment but also examples of actions and responses.

Can Learning Occur through Observation?

A truly comprehensive learning theory of behavior must be able to explain how people learn behaviors that are not taught through reinforcement. If we were limited to learning behaviors for which we received direct reinforcement or punishment, our range of behaviors would be much more limited than it is. For example, everyone knows that smoking cigarettes presents a significant health risk. Very few parents encourage their children to smoke, and most actively discourage this behavior. Nonetheless, 12-year-olds light up anyway. However, this first smoking experience is rarely pleasurable; they inhale, cough for several minutes, and feel nauseated. There is no doubt that it is a punishing experience for them, but many try again. Over time, they master the technique of inhaling and, in their view, look "cool" smoking a cigarette. That's the key to the whole situation: The 12-year-olds observe other people with cigarettes, think they look cool, want to look cool themselves, and therefore imitate the smoking behavior.

Such situations present a problem for traditional learning theorists, whose theories give a central role to the concept of reinforcement. There is little reinforcement in establishing smoking behavior; instead, the coughing and nausea that accompany the first cigarette are definitely punishment, and young smokers may also face punishment from parents. Nonetheless, the behavior recurs. To explain this type of learning, Stanford University psychologist Albert Bandura has contended that the principles of classical and operant conditioning are only two of the many ways in which people learn. They also learn through observation of others.

The Power of Modeling

Social learning theory
■ Bandura's theory that suggests that organisms learn new responses by observing the behavior of a model and then imitating it; also known as observational learning theory.

Modeling ■ The process, critical to observational learning, in which an observer matches his or her behavior to that of the model through an internal representation of the behavior, which is stored in memory in symbolic form.

During the past 40 years, Bandura has expanded the range of behaviors that can be explained by learning theory (Bandura, 1986, 2004; Woodward, 1982). His *social learning theory* (also known as *observational learning theory*) suggests that organisms learn new responses by observing and modeling the behavior of others. *Modeling* is a process that includes more than imitation; it involves an observer matching his or her behavior to that of the model through an internal representation of the behavior, which is stored in memory in symbolic form. That is, modeling is a cognitive process. One source of models in Western societies is the media, and portrayals of smoking in the media are influential in prompting adolescents to try cigarettes (Wakefield et al., 2003).

Bandura and his colleagues have conducted important research that confirms the idea that people can learn by observing and that modeling is important for subsequent behavior (Bandura, 1969, 1977b; Bandura, Ross, & Ross, 1963). In their early studies, these researchers manipulated the aggressive content of programs that they showed to groups of children and observed the results. One group of children saw a film with aggressive content (an adult punched and did other violent actions to an inflated doll known as a "Bobo doll"); another group saw an animated version of the same content. A third group saw the same content performed by live actors; a fourth group of children saw a film that had no aggressive content (Bandura et al., 1963). The researchers then compared the play behavior of the four groups. They found that the children who had viewed the film with aggressive content tended to play more aggressively afterward, imitating the model's aggression and also coming up with novel aggressive responses of their own. One of the most distressing findings was that the children who had seen the animated version were the most strongly influenced, which initiated concern about how violent media portrayals affect children (and adults). Even children who failed to respond aggressively during the play session were later able to demonstrate that they had learned how to do so: When offered candy for showing how the model treated the Bobo doll, every child could do so.

Subsequent studies have confirmed that observing aggression teaches children how to be aggressive, and that observing violence in the media and in the family creates and perpetuates violence by teaching aggressive responses. In other words, observation and modeling are important for aggression, which gets passed down in families through the process of observing family violence (Conger et al., 2003; Straus & Yodanis, 1996). **Building Table 8.3** (on p. 310) compares observational learning with classical and operant conditioning.

Laboratory studies of observational learning show that people can learn new behaviors merely by observing them, without being reinforced. For example, in a study by Bernal and Berger (1976), participants watched a film of people being conditioned to produce an eye-blink response. The people in the film had a puff of air delivered to their eyes; this stimulus was paired with a tone. After a number of trials, the people in the film showed an eye-blink response to the tone alone. This result is not surprising; it is an example of classical conditioning. What is more surprising is that the participants who watched the film also developed an eye blink in response to a tone. That is, they had learned this association through their observation of the people in the film. Hundreds of studies from the 1960s onward have demonstrated that observational learning applies to a variety of behaviors and that children as young as 12 months learn through observation (Elsner & Aschersleben, 2003). Furthermore, observational learning is not restricted to humans but occurs in many nonhuman species, including rats, dogs, cats, ravens, and even octopuses (Zentall, 2003).

After watching an adult take aggressive action against a Bobo doll, children imitated the aggressive behavior.

A study that used brain-imaging techniques examined the brains of people who were performing a task and those who were observing; the results showed that the brains of the observers showed similar activation to the brains of those who were performing the task, including the area in the middle of the forebrain that is associated with learning (van Schie et al., 2004). These results are consistent with Bandura's view that people learn through observing in much the same way as they learn by acting. Bandura believes that certain processes are essential in observational learning.

Key Processes in Observational Learning

Bandura's theory focuses on the role of thought and cognition in establishing and maintaining behavior. Four processes are important in observational learning: attention, representation, behavioral production, and motivation. *Attention* is important to observational learning because individuals must attend to a model to learn from that model. Thus, people tend to model those with whom they associate the most. Parents often encourage modeling in their children by saying things like "Now watch me..." and "See how your sister is doing that." They provide innumerable

Building Table 8.3

TYPES OF LEARNING: CLASSICAL CONDITIONING, OPERANT CONDITIONING, AND OBSERVATIONAL LEARNING

Type of Learning	Procedure	Result	Example
Classical Conditioning	A neutral stimulus (such as a bell) is paired with an unconditioned stimulus (such as food).	The neutral stimulus becomes a conditioned stimulus—it elicits the conditioned response.	A bell elicits a response from a dog.
Operant Conditioning	A behavior is followed by a consequence, either reinforcement or punishment.	The behavior increases or decreases in frequency.	A rat will press a bar 120 times per hour to achieve a reward or to avoid punishment.
Observational Learning	An observer watches a model and learns a behavior.	The observer is likely to produce the learned behavior if the model was reinforced for that behavior and if the situation is similar to the observed situation.	After watching violence in a television program, children are more likely to show aggressive behaviors.

examples for children to watch and copy, and then reinforce the children for modeling (Masia & Chase, 1997). However, individuals are selective about attention, and factors such as power and attractiveness influence attention. Attractive, powerful models are more influential than models who are less attractive and less powerful, but characteristics that models have in common with observers also play a role in attention and influence (Bandura, 1986). For example, age peers may be more influential models than adults (Ryalls & Ryalls, 2000). In a classroom, children are more likely to participate with and imitate peers whom they see as powerful, dominant, and like themselves (or like they want to be).

Bandura's (1986) second key process in observational learning is *representation*. For observation to become learning, observers must represent the information in memory. Bandura believes that they do so in an abstract or even symbolic form that is not necessarily an exact replication of what they observed. For humans, language furnishes a system of symbols that may influence the process of representation.

Whether or not an observed behavior will be reproduced by the learner depends on whether the learned information can be readily translated into action and on whether the learner is motivated to do so. *Behavioral production* refers to the process of converting the cognitive representation of the learned behavior into action. Behavioral production may include cognitive rehearsal—thinking about what one is going to do—and evaluation of how well one is performing. The cognitive processes that accompany behavioral production work better for information than for skills, which profit from motor practice. Indeed, observation is not an effective strategy for learning skills unless it is accompanied by direct practice (Deakin & Proteau, 2000).

Motivation is also a critical process in observational learning. Behaviors may be learned yet not produced because the individual is not motivated to do so. Bandura (1986) argues that reinforcements and punishments have a large impact on whether a learned behavior is performed. That is, we may know how to perform a behavior yet refrain from doing so because we have not been rewarded or we have been punished for doing so. In addition, when we see others receive reinforcement or punishment for their behavior, those vicarious experiences affect our behavior. For example, a 2-year-old may see another child throw a temper tantrum in the store. According to the observational learning view, the 2-year-old observer learns how to throw a tantrum but may not do so if the child who had the tantrum was not reinforced or was punished for that behavior. However, the 2-year-old now knows how to throw a tantrum and may do so when a similar situation arises in the future. Learning how to have a tantrum is only one of many examples of observational learning in daily life.

Observational Learning in Daily Life

Although observational learning occurs in many aspects of daily life, it is particularly important in gender role development and in learning cultural values. There is a clear biological component that underlies each person's identification as male or female, but the characteristics of masculinity and femininity are more variable (Maccoby, 1998). Male and female infants become masculine and feminine children, adolescents, and adults, and Bandura and his colleagues (Bussey & Bandura, 1999) hypothesize that observation is a major factor in this process.

Within their families and the broader society, young children have many opportunities to observe what their culture considers appropriate behavior for women and men; however, what constitute appropriate gender-related behaviors vary from culture to culture. For example, women are associated with food preparation in many cultures, such as the United States, but in some Asian cultures, this association is not as strong. Indeed, the strength of the association of gender and cooking has changed over the past 50 years in the United States, and today, cooking is less sharply gendered. However, children who observe gender differences in their parents' performance of household tasks learn that these chores are gendered, and such experience in childhood has long-lasting effects on behavior as adolescents and young adults (Cunningham, 2001).

Cooking and household chores provide only one example; differences in gender roles are evident in behaviors as inconsequential as painting fingernails and lips and as important as choosing acceptable careers. In general, many more opportunities exist for children to observe parents and other adults behaving in ways that are consistent with traditional gender roles than to observe departures from those roles. Thus, adults tend to transmit gender stereotypes to children.

Parents are not the only models who are influential; siblings and peers also send gender messages. Siblings may be even more influential models for younger children than parents are (McHale, Crouter, & Whiteman, 2003; McHale et al., 2001).

Siblings and peers may convey that flexibility about gender-appropriate behavior is acceptable, but more often, they provide models that promote sharply gendered behavior and discourage crossing gender boundaries. During childhood, children tend to segregate themselves according to gender—girls associating with other girls and boys with other boys (Maccoby, 1998). Adults sometimes enforce this division, but children are often more vigorous enforcers than adults are. Elementary and middle-school children provide few models for deviating from these standards and many examples of adhering to them. Indeed, peers often act as the "gender police" and punish children who cross the line (Blakemore, 2003).

Observational learning is as important in learning cultural values as in gender role development. The transmission of what is valued and important begins during infancy, with how babies are treated and what they see. Research confirms that observational learning begins as early as 12 months of age (Elsner & Aschersleben, 2003), so very young children see what is acceptable and expected and receive reinforcement and punishment for their behavior. Although all members of a given culture share the tasks of transmitting values to children in the culture (Greenfield et al., 2003), specific values vary a great deal, and parents, siblings, peers, teachers, and public figures are especially important as models.

Bandura's emphasis on observation and modeling represents only one type of cognitive learning. Psychologists have studied several other types of cognitive learning that do not fit the definition of conditioning.

Other Types of Cognitive Learning

"Enough!" Patrick shouted, after 4 grueling hours of trying to write a program for his personal computer. The program wouldn't work, and Patrick didn't know why. After dozens of trial-and-error changes, Patrick turned off the computer and went off to study for his history exam. Then, while staring at a page in the text, he noticed a phrase set off by commas—and suddenly he realized his programming mistake. He had put commas in his program's if–then statements. It was correct English, but not correct computer syntax.

Patrick solved his problem by thinking in a new way. His solution to his programming problem would be difficult to explain using the concepts of conditioning or observational learning, yet it was based on his experience. His sudden realization of how to fix his program is only one type of cognitive learning that humans (and other animals) experience.

Insight

Insight ■ The process of finding a solution to a problem by thinking about the problem in a new way.

When you discover a relationship among a series of events that you did not recognize before, insight has taken place. *Insight* is the process of finding a solution to a problem by thinking about the problem in a new way. Patrick's discovery of his extra commas is a typical example of someone who agonizes over a problem for a long time and then suddenly sees the solution.

Discovering the sources of insight was the goal of researchers working with animals during World War I. Wolfgang Köhler (1927), a Gestalt psychologist and researcher, showed that chimpanzees were capable of achieving insights about how to retrieve food that was beyond their reach. The chimps discovered that they could pile up boxes or make a long stick out of several shorter ones. They were never reinforced for these specific behaviors; insight showed them how to get the food. Insight results from thought, without direct reinforcement. Once a chimp learns how to pile up boxes, or once Patrick realizes his comma error, the insight is not forgotten, and no further instruction or training is necessary. The role of insight is often overlooked in studies of learning; however, it is an essential element in problem solving (discussed in Chapter 10).

Latent Learning

After a person has an insight, learns a task, or solves a problem, the new learning is not necessarily evident. Researchers in the 1920s placed hungry rats in a maze and recorded how many trials these rats needed to reach a particular spot, where food was hidden (Tolman & Honzik, 1930). After many days and many trials, the hungry rats learned the mazes well. Other hungry rats were put into the maze but were not reinforced with food on reaching the same spot; instead, they were merely removed from the maze. Rats in a third group were not reinforced at first, but after 10 days of running the maze, they were given food on reaching the goal. Surprisingly, after 1 day of receiving reinforcement, the rats in the third group were reaching the goal with few errors. During the first 10 days of maze running, they must have been learning something but not showing it. Receiving a reward gave them a reason to use what they had learned.

Researchers such as Edward C. Tolman (1886–1959) argued that the rats were exhibiting *latent learning*—learning that occurs in the absence of direct reinforcement and that is not necessarily demonstrated through observable behavior. Tolman showed that when a rat is given a reason (such as food) to show learning, the behavior becomes evident. In other words, a rat (or a person) that is given no motivation to do so may not demonstrate learned behavior. Tolman's work with rats led him to propose the idea that animals and human beings develop (or generate) a kind of mental map of their world.

Latent learning ■
Learning that occurs in the absence of direct reinforcement and that is not necessarily demonstrated through observable behavior.

Cognitive Maps

Some people are easily disoriented when visiting a new city; others seem to acquire an internal map quickly. These internal maps are sometimes called *cognitive maps*—mental representations that enable people to navigate from a starting point to an unseen destination. Tolman contended that this type of internal representation develops in rats as well as in humans.

During the 1940s, Tolman (1948) conducted a series of experiments in which he taught rats to run various types of mazes. The mazes were complex, and sometimes the shortest routes were blocked, but the rats received reinforcement for reaching the goal box through the complex, circuitous route. However, Tolman discovered that when the shortest routes were unblocked, the rats were able to take this more efficient, alternative route to the goal box. This finding led Tolman to conclude that

Cognitive maps ■
Mental representations that enable people to navigate from a starting point to an unseen destination.

the rats had learned a cognitive map of the maze rather than learning a series of turns. He believed that rats learn to navigate the world in much the same way that humans do, by building a mental representation of the geography of their environment.

For both rats and humans, cognitive maps are not just memories of specific turns and signs but also involve a building up of a cognitive representation of the overall environment. Research has continued in this area, and findings about route learning indicate that people use visual information to build a cognitive map of an area (Allen, 2000a). People pay attention to landmarks, and they orient by mapping the information they gather with their existing cognitive map of the area. However, research suggests that women and men tend to use different strategies to accomplish this task and that there may be gender differences in the types of cognitive maps that people build.

Tolman (1948) believed that in the course of learning, something like a working map becomes established in the rat's (or human's) brain. However, he did not investigate the neurology of learning. Others, however, have done so, beginning at about the same time that Tolman was running his rats through mazes and continuing today, with contemporary techniques for imaging functioning human brains.

What Is the Biological Basis for Learning?

The idea that humans and other animals learn from their experiences in the environment—that experience shapes behavior—seems to contradict the view of evolutionary psychologists that many behaviors have their basis in evolved adaptations. Let's examine how biology affects learning by first considering how the evolutionary perspective, with its emphasis on nature, accounts for the obvious experiential basis for learning, its strong connection to nurture.

Are Evolutionary Theory and Learning Theory Incompatible?

We defined learning as a relatively permanent change in an organism that occurs as a result of experiences in the environment. Evolutionary theory, with its emphasis on innate mechanisms that govern behavior, seems almost the opposite of learning theory. Part of this apparent difference lies in the emphasis of each theory. Changes that occur in an organism due to experiences in life are not the primary focus of evolutionary theory. Rather, this approach concentrates on the distant past of human history and prehistory to explain current behavior. This type of explanation leads to the identification of factors that can be described as *ultimate causes*, whereas learning theory focuses on the more immediate causes, or *proximate causes*, of behavior (Gannon, 2002). That is, the two theories differ in focus, with evolutionary theory emphasizing the mechanisms that caused behavioral tendencies to become incorporated into the human genome.

Evolutionary theory does not rule out learning, and evolutionary theorists acknowledge that evolution does not strictly determine behavior—the genome does not code for any specific behavior (Kenrick et al., 2003; Petrinovich, 1997).

Indeed, humans and other animals must be capable of learning, or they would not be very good at adapting. In addition, genetically determined tendencies are modified by the environment, and so evolutionary theory recognizes differences in cultures and in individuals. Although all human beings everywhere in the world exhibit some characteristics—for example, all human beings smile—they do not smile at the same things.

The ability to learn and adapt is a key evolved psychological mechanism. This mechanism helps human beings survive and look toward the future, evaluate the past, and plan for different outcomes and contingencies. However, evolutionary psychologists believe that psychology has placed too much emphasis on learning, giving the impression that humans are infinitely adaptable when they are not. For example, evolutionary psychologist Steven Pinker (2002) argues that humans are not "blank slates" that develop and differentiate only through the process of learning. Pinker believes that humans come equipped with the ability to learn certain behaviors or tasks more easily than others rather than with a general ability to learn. The acquisition of a conditioned taste aversion (explained earlier) is consistent with this view of learning.

Thus, evolutionary theory accepts learning as an important process for human behavior. Humans who could not learn also could not adapt to their environments, which would make them vulnerable. But evolutionary theory holds that the processes of conditioning and learning are not sufficient to explain human behavior. So, the learning approach and the evolutionary approach are not incompatible, but they differ in their emphases and assumptions about behavior.

Electrical Brain Stimulation and Reinforcement

Until the 1950s, researchers assumed that reinforcers were effective because they satisfied some need or drive in an organism, such as hunger. Then James Olds (1955, 1969) found an apparent exception to this assumption. He discovered that rats find direct electrical stimulation of specific areas of the brain to be rewarding. Olds implanted an electrode in the hypothalamus of rats and attached the electrode to a stimulator that provided a small voltage. The stimulator was activated only when the rat pressed a lever in a Skinner box. Olds found that the rats pressed the lever thousands of times in order to continue the self-stimulation. In one study, the rats pressed it at a rate of 1,920 times per hour (Olds & Milner, 1954). Rats even crossed an electrified grid to get to the lever and obtain this stimulation. Animals that received brain stimulation performed better in a maze, running faster with fewer errors. Hungry rats often chose the self-stimulation over food.

During the 1950s and 1960s, researchers did not know why the stimulation of these brain sites produced what seemed like reinforcement, but later research on the topic of neurotransmitters has clarified this point. What Olds had tapped into was a brain system that involved the neurotransmitter *dopamine* (LeDoux, 2002). This neurotransmitter is important to the experience of reinforcement. Drugs that block dopamine's effect in the brain also decrease rats' motivation to stimulate electrodes implanted in their hypothalamus. A system of dopamine-producing neurons, which runs from the brain stem to the forebrain, is important to many types of reinforcement. Indeed, it may be how the brain represents reinforcement.

However, neurotransmitters are only part of the story of how learning actually occurs in the nervous system. Another way to consider the role of biology in learning is to examine how the brain changes when learning occurs. The brain must form a record of experience, and researchers are using the sophisticated technology of brain imaging to begin to understand this process. However, an interest in the brain processes involved in learning is not recent; investigation of these processes began in the 1950s.

Brain Changes and Learning

Whenever learning occurs, there is a relatively permanent change in behavior, and this change must be reflected in the nervous system in some way. Donald O. Hebb (1904–1985), a Canadian psychologist, was one of the first to suggest that, with each learning situation, the structure of the brain changes. He argued that certain groups of neurons act together, and their synaptic transmissions and general neural activity form a recurring pattern—he referred to such a group of coordinated neurons as a *reverberating circuit*. The more stimulation to a circuit that represents a concept or an experience, the better that concept or experience will be remembered and the more the structure of the brain is altered.

Remember that learning is a process that occurs because of unique interactions among hundreds of thousands of neurons in the brain. Hebb (1949) suggested that stimulation of particular groups of neurons causes them to form specific patterns of neural activity. The transformation of a temporary neural circuit into a more permanent circuit is known as *consolidation*. According to Hebb, consolidation serves as the basis of learning and memory. If Hebb is correct, only temporary changes take place in neurons when people first sense a new stimulus. Repetition of the stimulus causes consolidation—the temporary circuit becomes a permanent one.

Hebb's theory seemed like a good explanation, but only with advances in neurology have psychologists had the means to attempt to confirm it. In 1973, research revealed that stimulation of neurons produces changes that extend beyond the point of stimulation and that persist after stimulation stops (Bliss & Lømø, 1973). This type of change is referred to as *long-term potentiation (LTP)*, which occurs in many parts of the brain. It fits with Hebb's theory—it occurs when neurons have been stimulated in a specific sequence, and it lasts for weeks.

Other changes also occur in the brain when learning takes place. Those changes involve the synthesis of proteins, which seem essential for learned events to be turned into memories; that is, for learning to leave a record in the brain (Hernandez, Sadeghian, & Kiley, 2002). In addition, structural changes occur at the level of synapses. These changes include the growth of *dendritic spines*, which allow neurons to form more connections with neighboring neurons. In other words, stimulating a neuron over and over again may cause it to add synaptic connections. These findings may indicate that when neurons are stimulated, the events that cause the stimulation are better remembered and more easily accessed—this may be part of the reason why practice makes permanent (or at least tends to) (McGaugh, 1999; O'Mara, Commins, & Anderson, 2000). Most of the research on this topic has been done on nonhuman animals, but Jacobs and his colleagues (1993) found that people with more education have more dendritic spines. In addition, Scheibel's research team (1990) found that parts of the body that are used more (say, fingers versus the wall of the chest) are controlled by areas of the brain in which there is more elaborate dendritic organization.

Neuroscientists are also focusing on how genes affect the brain changes that underlie learning and the formation of memories. The expression of genes may be important for changes that occur at the synaptic level. This research began with the isolation of a gene, dubbed the *CREB gene*, which is crucial in the consolidation process (Barco, Alarcon, & Kandel, 2002). Without this gene, certain proteins are not activated and memories are fleeting rather than lasting (Duman et al., 2000; Kida et al., 2002). Additional research has identified 13 other genes that may be involved in activating the chemical mechanisms necessary for the consolidation of learning into memory (Edelheit & Meiri, 2004).

The types of changes that occur in the brain as a result of learning are one of the major types of *plasticity* that adult brains exhibit—our brains change every day to allow us to store new information in permanent form. The amount of new information coming in each day is substantial, and the brain must respond by making connections that may be temporary while also preparing to consolidate some of the information for permanent memory (Munk, 2003). A great deal of research has focused on one brain structure, the hippocampus (Abraham & Williams, 2003). In the brains of adults, this structure is more capable of changing (that is, it is more *plastic*) than any other structure, and researchers have explored its role in learning and memory. A great deal of evidence suggests that the hippocampus is critical to the brain changes that turn learning into memory. Without these changes, we would not be able to remember what we learned. Thus, learning furnishes material for memory, and in the next chapter, we will come back to the important issue of what happens in the brain as memories are formed.

Summary and Review

WHAT TYPE OF LEARNING IS PAVLOVIAN, OR CLASSICAL, CONDITIONING?

Define learning, and differentiate it from reflexes.

Learning is a relatively permanent and stable change in an organism that occurs as a result of experiences in the environment. *Conditioning* is a systematic procedure that connects responses with specific stimuli. In contrast, *reflexes* are behaviors that occur involuntarily and without prior learning. pp. 275–276

Describe the process of classical conditioning.

Classical conditioning involves the pairing of a neutral, *conditioned stimulus* (for example, a bell tone) with an *unconditioned stimulus* (for example, food) so that the *unconditioned response* (for example, salivation) becomes a *conditioned response*. In *higher-order conditioning*, a neutral stimulus becomes associated with the conditioned stimulus. pp. 276–280

WHAT ARE THE KEY VARIABLES IN CLASSICAL CONDITIONING?

What are the most important variables in classical conditioning?

The most important variables in classical conditioning are the strength, timing, and frequency of the unconditioned stimulus. For classical conditioning to occur, the unconditioned stimulus and the conditioned stimulus must usually be presented in rapid succession. The predictability of the association of the unconditioned and conditioned stimuli is also critical. pp. 281–282

How may conditioned responses vary, depending on the situation?

Extinction is the process of reducing the likelihood of a conditioned response by withholding the unconditioned stimulus (not pairing it with the conditioned response). *Spontaneous recovery* is the recurrence of an extinguished conditioned response, usually following a rest period, which shows that previously learned associations are not totally forgotten. pp. 282–283

Stimulus generalization is the process by which a conditioned response becomes associated with a stimulus similar to, but not the same as, the original conditioned stimulus. In contrast, *stimulus discrimination* is the process by which an organism learns to respond only to a specific stimulus and not to other, similar stimuli. p. 283

What are the key findings in studies of conditioned taste aversion?

It takes only one pairing of a food or drink (the conditioned stimulus) with a nausea-inducing substance (the unconditioned stimulus) to make organisms avoid the food or drink that preceded the nausea—to develop a conditioned taste aversion. The finding that a taste aversion can be learned even if the nausea is induced several hours after the food or drink has been consumed is important, because learning theorists had previously assumed that it was essential for the two events to occur close together in time. pp. 286–288

WHAT TYPE OF LEARNING IS OPERANT CONDITIONING?

What is the difference between classical and operant conditioning?

Operant conditioning is a process that increases or decreases the probability that a behavior will recur because of its consequences. This type of conditioning can be done with voluntary behaviors, whereas classical conditioning involves reflexive responses. pp. 289–290

How do reinforcement and punishment work?

A *reinforcer* is any event that increases the probability that the response that preceded it will recur. *Positive reinforcement* increases the probability that a desired response will occur by introducing a rewarding or pleasant stimulus. *Negative reinforcement* increases the probability that a desired behavior will occur by removing an unpleasant stimulus. pp. 291–293

Primary reinforcers have survival value for an organism; their value does not have to be learned. *Secondary reinforcers* are neutral stimuli that initially have no value for the organism but that become rewarding when they are paired with a primary reinforcer. *Shaping* is a way to use reinforcement to create a new behavior by selectively reinforcing approximations to a desired behavior. Many studies on operant conditioning are conducted on nonhuman animals in a device called a *Skinner box*. pp. 293–295

Punishment, unlike reinforcement, decreases the probability of a particular response. Positive punishment is the process of presenting an undesirable or noxious stimulus, and negative punishment involves removing a desirable stimulus. Both types of punishment decrease the probability that a preceding response will recur. A primary punisher is naturally painful or unpleasant, whereas a secondary punisher comes to be so through learning. pp. 295–296

When punishment continues regardless of an organism's response, the organism may display *learned helplessness*, in which it stops making any response at all. p. xxx

WHAT ARE THE KEY VARIABLES IN OPERANT CONDITIONING?

The most important variables affecting operant conditioning are the strength, timing, and frequency of consequences. Strong consequences delivered quickly yield high response rates. But consequences do not have to be continuous. The *schedule of reinforcement* is a key factor. Studies have shown that consequences, especially reinforcers, can be intermittent. *Fixed-interval* and *variable-interval schedules* provide reinforcement after fixed or variable time periods; *fixed-ratio* and *variable-ratio schedules* provide reinforcement after fixed or variable numbers of responses. Variable-ratio schedules produce the highest response rates; fixed-interval schedules induce the lowest response rates. pp. 297–298

When reinforcement is discontinued, *extinction* occurs. Learned behavior that occurs through a coincidental association between the behavior and a reinforcer is called *superstitious behavior*. pp. 303–306

CAN LEARNING OCCUR THROUGH OBSERVATION?

How does social learning theory explain how some learning occurs?

Social learning theory, or observational learning theory, suggests that organisms learn new responses by observing and *modeling* the behavior of others. This theory has expanded the range of behaviors that can be explained by learning theorists, and it focuses on the role of thought in establishing and maintaining behavior. The similarity of models to an observer as well as the models' attractiveness and power determine their influence. Observational learning applies to many behaviors, including gender role development and learning of cultural values. pp. 308–312

What other types of cognitive learning are possible?

Cognitive learning psychologists focus on thinking processes such as insight, latent learning, and the formation of cognitive maps. Discovering a solution to a problem by thinking about the problem in a new way is *insight*. *Latent learning* is learning that occurs in the absence of any direct reinforcement and that is not necessarily demonstrated through observable behavior, though it has the potential to be exhibited. *Cognitive maps* are mental representations that allow people and other animals to navigate through the environment successfully. pp. 312–314

WHAT IS THE BIOLOGICAL BASIS FOR LEARNING?

Are learning theory and evolutionary psychology incompatible?

Evolutionary theory does not propose genetic determinism, but it does emphasize influences on behavior that acted in the distant past, whereas learning theory emphasizes more immediate causes. However, learning from the environment is one process important to adaptation, and so evolutionary psychologists acknowledge the importance of learning in behavior. pp. 314–315

What is the basis in the brain for reinforcement and learning?

The effect of the neurotransmitter dopamine in a specific brain system forms the basis for many types of reinforcement. The neural basis for learning seems to be similar to the reverberating circuits described by Hebb. The evolution of a temporary neural circuit into a more permanent circuit occurs through consolidation. When learning occurs, changes occur that affect protein synthesis and synaptic connections in the brain, and these changes form the basis for memory. pp. 315–317

CHAPTER 9

Memory

How Does the Memory Process Begin? 322
    The Brain as Information Processor
    Encoding
    Levels of Processing
    Neuroscience and Encoding

What Are the Types of Memory Storage? 326
    Sensory Memory
    Short-Term Storage
    Long-Term Memory
    Neuroscience and Storage

What Influences Memory Retrieval? 337
    Retention: Measures of Retrieval

Retrieval Success and Failure: Encoding
    Specificity
What Facilitates Retrieval?
Flashbulb Memories
Gender and Memory
Culture and Memory

What Causes People to Forget? 345
    Early Studies
    Key Causes of Forgetting
    Special Types of Forgetting
    Neuroscience and Forgetting: Studies of Amnesia

Summary and Review 352

Chapter 8 pointed out that learning is a relatively permanent change in an organism that occurs as a result of experience and is often, but not always, expressed in overt behavior. *Memory* is the ability to recall past events, images, ideas, or previously learned information or skills. Memory is also the storage system that allows a person to retain and retrieve previously learned information. Learning and memory are two facets of the process of acquiring information, storing it, and using it. The acquisition part is learning, and the storage and accessing of learned information comprise memory.

Memory ■ The ability to recall past events, images, ideas, or previously learned information or skills; the storage system that allows for retention and retrieval of previously learned information.

How Does the Memory Process Begin?

Traditionally, psychologists have considered memory as a type of storage and have sought to understand its structure and limits. Studies of memory at the beginning of the 20th century focused on factors related to how quickly people learned and forgot lists of nonsense words (Robinson-Riegler & Robinson-Riegler, 2004). Physiological psychologists sought to discover locations in the brain corresponding to the functions of memory. During the 1950s, research became more practical, focusing on variables such as how the organization of material affects retention. Today, research still focuses on understanding the complex processes of memory but also considers practical issues, including how people can code information and use memory aids, imagery, and other learning cues to retrieve information from memory more effectively. Researchers are also using brain-imaging techniques to pinpoint the specific areas in the brain that become more active when people are in the process of remembering.

The Brain as Information Processor

In this age of computers and information technology, it is not surprising that psychologists have likened the brain to a computer—an information processor. This analogy has influenced the study of memory since the 1960s and 1970s, when researchers began to recognize the brain's complex interconnections and information-processing abilities. Psychologists use the term *information processing* to refer to organizing, interpreting, and responding to information coming from the environment (Lachman, Lachman, & Butterfield, 1979). Of course, human brains are not computers—no computer has yet come close to the sophistication of the human brain. In addition, brains do not work exactly as computers do. Brains make mistakes, and they are influenced by biological, environmental, and interpersonal events. Computers complete some operations much faster than brains can, and they always get the same answer when they are given a problem repeatedly. Nevertheless, there are enough similarities between human brains and computers for psychologists to discuss perception, learning, and memory in terms of information processing.

The information-processing approach typically focuses on the flow of information, beginning with the sensory systems, where information from the outside world first impinges on the body. This approach describes and analyzes a sequence of stages for key memory processes and assumes that the stages and processes are related but separate. Although psychologists once considered memory a step-by-step, linear process, they now recognize that many of the steps take place simultaneously, in parallel (Rumelhart & McClelland, 1986).

Virtually every approach to understanding memory offered by researchers has proposed that memory involves three key processes. The names of these processes derive from information technology and will sound familiar to you if you know how computers work. The first process is *encoding*, the second is placement of information in some type of *storage* (either temporary or permanent), and the third is making the information available through *retrieval*. We'll use this three-process model to guide our exploration of memory.

Encoding

I (L.B.) tell my students to think of their memory as a filing cabinet, and I point out that how well a filing cabinet works depends on several factors. A filing cabinet can be very useful if you have a good system of organization so that when you put papers away, you will know how to retrieve them. You need folders and a system of labels that will allow you to find each folder in the cabinet. If you put papers in a folder and file it away in the cabinet without labeling it, your filing cabinet will be useful as a place to move folders off your desk, but little more. Labeling, or coding, the folders is critical.

The conversion of sensory stimuli into neural impulses is a type of coding, the first step of establishing a memory. *Encoding* is the organizing of sensory information so that the nervous system can process it, much as a computer programmer devises code that a computer can understand. The sensory information can be of any type: visual, auditory, olfactory, and so on. The type and extent of encoding affect what we remember. Encoding is not a discrete step that happens all at once. Rather, some levels of encoding happen quickly and easily, whereas others take longer and are more complex. Your brain may continue to encode information while storing previously encoded information.

Attention is important for encoding (Brown & Craik, 2000; Craik, 2002). In general, *attention* refers to the process of directing mental focus to some features of the environment and not to others. People can focus their attention on one idea, one event, one person, or one memory task, or they can shift their attention among several tasks or events. Dividing one's attention during encoding interferes with the process, and people who are forced to divide their attention during encoding tend to perform more poorly during retrieval—they experience a type of memory problem known as *encoding failure*. Such failures are very common, because many stimuli compete for a person's attention.

Encoding ■ The organizing of sensory information so that the nervous system can process it.

Levels of Processing

Does the human brain encode and process different kinds of information in different ways? Do thinking processes depend on different types of analysis? Researchers Fergus Craik and Robert Lockhart (1972) argued that the brain encodes and processes stimuli (information) in different ways, to different extents, and at different levels. They called their theory the *levels-of-processing approach*. According to this view of encoding, how information is processed determines how it will be stored for later retrieval.

Cognitive psychologists equate the level of processing with the depth of analysis involved. When the level of processing becomes more complex, they theorize, the code goes deeper into memory.

The levels-of-processing approach has generated an enormous amount of research (Craik, 2002). It explains why you retain some information, such as your family history, for long periods, whereas you quickly forget other information, such as the dry cleaner's phone number. It shows that when people are asked to encode information in only one way, they do not encode it in other ways. However, the levels-of-processing approach focuses on encoding and largely

Levels-of-processing approach ■ Theory of memory that suggests that the brain encodes and processes stimuli (information) in different ways, to different extents, and at different levels.

ignores retrieval, which led to the development of alternative views of how information is processed.

Transfer-appropriate processing ■ Processing of information that is similar for both encoding and retrieval of the information.

One variation is the idea of *transfer-appropriate processing,* which occurs when the processing for encoding of information is similar to the process for retrieval of the information. When there is a close relationship between the form of the information encoded (whether it is visual, auditory, or in some other form) and the processing required to retrieve it, retrieval improves. For example, when researchers give participants instructions to encode words for sound and then ask participants to recall the meaning of the words, performance is worse than when participants are asked to code for sound and to recall sound (Franks et al., 2000; Morris, Bransford, & Franks, 1977; Rajaram, Srinivas, & Roediger, 1998).

Encoding specificity principle ■ The principle that the effectiveness of a specific retrieval cue depends on how well it matches up with the originally encoded information.

Other researchers also questioned the levels-of-processing approach, suggesting that differences in recall originate from how memories are elaborated on, or made distinctive. The *encoding specificity principle* explains the link between encoding and retrieval by stating that the effectiveness of a specific cue for retrieving information depends on how well it matches up with the originally encoded information (Tulving & Thompson 1973). The more sharply such cues are defined and the more closely they are paired with memory stores, the better your recall will be and the less likely you will be to experience retrieval failures. For example, my (L.B.'s) students sometimes fail to recognize me when they meet me in the grocery store or at the movies, but they always recognize me on campus. On campus, the circumstances in which we meet match those in which they first knew me, but off campus, the circumstances are different. Thus, some of them experience retrieval difficulties because of the type of encoding they have done.

The research on the levels-of-processing approach and its subsequent refinements and extensions have influenced the study of memory by emphasizing the importance of encoding. Researchers are aware that the encoding process is flexible. This process is affected by both the cues provided and the demands of the retrieval tasks, as well as by people's preconceived biases. Humans tend to notice and encode information that confirms beliefs they already hold—a tendency called *confirmation bias* (Jonas et al., 2001). This tendency to "see what you expect to see" is a powerful force in allowing people to retain inaccurate beliefs.

Neuroscience and Encoding

Memories are retained because they take some form in the brain. Many researchers are using brain-imaging techniques to explore the neurobiological bases of memory. Positron emission tomography (PET) and functional magnetic resonance imaging (fMRI) (described in Chapter 3) have allowed researchers to examine the brain during the process of encoding.

A general rule about brain functioning is that structures toward the top of the brain tend to control functions that are more complex and abstract. This principle has led researchers to concentrate on the cerebral cortex in their efforts to understand memory. Specifically, researchers have directed their attention to the prefrontal lobes with their overlying cortex—the large areas on the left and right at the top front of the brain, behind the forehead.

In the view of Endel Tulving and his colleagues, the left prefrontal cortex is used more in the encoding of new information into memory, whereas the right prefrontal cortex is involved more in memory retrieval (Habib, Nyberg, & Tulving, 2003; Nyberg, Cabeza, & Tulving, 1996). Research using PET and fMRI imaging shows that when participants engage in various tasks, brain scans of the left and right hemispheres are quite different—that is, patterns of blood flow differ in different portions of the prefrontal cortex. These differences are generally consistent with Tulving's view—the left prefrontal cortex is more active when people encode information, especially meaningful verbal information (Otten, Henson, & Rugg, 2002). The left prefrontal cortex is also more active during encoding of information that is later recalled correctly than during encoding of information that is not recalled correctly (Casino et al., 2002; Reynolds et al., 2004).

Researchers have long known that the temporal lobes of the cerebral cortex are related to memory (Squire & Kandel, 1999), and brain-imaging studies have furnished more specific knowledge of how the temporal lobes interact with other brain structures. (**Figure 9.1** shows several of the brain structures that are important to memory.) An fMRI study demonstrated that the anterior (front) part of the medial (middle) temporal lobes is activated during the process of successfully encoding information in memory (Jackson & Schacter, 2004). This type of association is critical for learning associations, for example, between a name and a face or a car and a parking space. Indeed, the medial temporal lobes may be important for encoding information about setting and context (Davachi, Mitchell, & Wagner, 2003).

One study that used PET scanning of the brain during encoding showed that more of the brain was activated when people encode fact-based information than when they merely listened to sentences (Maguire & Frith, 2004). The areas of greater activation included several regions of the prefrontal cortex, part of the thalamus, and the temporal cortex. Reasonably enough, your brain works harder when

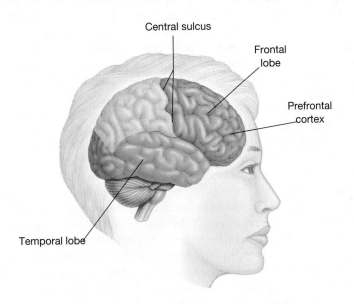

Central sulcus

Frontal lobe

Prefrontal cortex

Temporal lobe

Figure 9.1

Areas of the Brain Involved in Encoding
The prefrontal cortex and the temporal lobes are involved in the process of encoding.

you are encoding information than when you are listening passively. Just as the levels-of-processing approach predicts, people's brains are activated in different ways when they process information on a superficial level than when they process it on a deeper level (Weiser & Weiser, 2003).

Learners encode information to store it. If they do a good job of encoding, then they will be able to retrieve the information from storage. Thus, encoding is the first step in the flow of information through the memory system. Storage is the next step.

What Are the Types of Memory Storage?

Storage ■ The process of maintaining or keeping information readily available, as well as the locations where information is held, also known as *memory stores.*

If you think of memory as a filing cabinet, its storage capacity consists of the drawers of the cabinet. Once a folder is created and labeled, it is filed away in a drawer. *Storage* is the process of maintaining or keeping information readily available. It also refers to the locations where information is held, which researchers call memory stores. The duration of storage may be a few seconds or many years, but whenever people have access to information they no longer sense, memory is involved. For example, if you look up a telephone number, go to the telephone, and dial the number while no longer looking at it, then memory is involved, even if only for seconds.

Researchers have conceptualized a three-stage model for memory storage: (1) sensory memory, (2) short-term storage, and (3) long-term memory. Each type of storage has different characteristics and limits.

Sensory Memory

Sensory memory ■ The mechanism that performs initial encoding of sensory stimuli and provides brief storage of them; also known as the *sensory register.*

Sensory memory, sometimes called the *sensory register*, is the mechanism that performs initial encoding of sensory stimuli and provides brief storage of them. When you hear a song, see a photograph, or touch a piece of silk, sensory memory starts. This very brief storage allows the attention and coding processes to begin. The brief image of a stimulus appears the way lightning does on a dark evening: The lightning flashes, and you retain a brief visual image of it.

Research on sensory memory can be traced back to the early 1960s, when George Sperling (1960) briefly presented research participants with a visual display consisting of three rows of letters, which they saw for only a fraction of a second. He asked the participants to recite the letters, and they typically responded by reciting three or four letters from the first row. This limit on their performance suggests that they recorded only three or four items in their sensory register. But when Sperling cued them (with a tone that varied for each row), he found that participants were able to recall three out of four letters from *any* of the rows. This result suggests that the sensory register records a complete picture but that the image fades too rapidly for people to "read" the information before it fades. When Sperling delayed the cue that signaled which row to report, recall decreased, which again suggests a picture that fades rapidly (see **Figure 9.2**). From Sperling's studies and others that followed, researchers concluded that humans have a brief (250 milliseconds, or 0.25 second), rapidly fading sensory memory for visual stimuli. Current research on sensory memory concentrates on finding the underlying neural basis for the immediate processing of this type of stimuli (Schall et al., 2003; Ulanovsky, Lars, & Nelken, 2003).

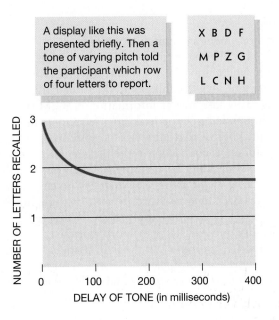

A display like this was presented briefly. Then a tone of varying pitch told the participant which row of four letters to report.

X B D F
M P Z G
L C N H

Figure 9.2
Sperling's Discovery of a Visual Sensory Memory
The graph plots participants' accuracy in reporting a specified row of letters. At best, participants recalled about three out of the four letters in a row. As the tone was delayed, the accuracy of recall decreased. But note that there were no further decreases in accuracy when the tone was delayed more than 200 milliseconds. (Based on data from Sperling, 1960, p. 11.)

Sensory memory captures a visual, auditory, tactile, or chemical stimulus (such as an odor) in a form the brain can interpret. In the visual system, the initial coding usually contains information in the form of a picture stored for 0.25 second in a form almost like a photograph. This visual sensory representation is sometimes called an *icon*, and the storage mechanism is called *iconic storage*. For the auditory system, the storage mechanism is called *echoic storage*, which holds an auditory representation for about 3 seconds.

Sensory memory lasts very briefly. Once information is established there, it must be transferred elsewhere for additional encoding and storage, or it will be lost. For example, when you locate a phone number on a computer screen or phone book page, the number is established in your visual sensory memory (in iconic storage), but unless you quickly transfer it to short-term storage by repeating it over and over to yourself, writing it down, or associating it with something else in your memory, you will forget it. **Building Table 9.1** summarizes key processes in sensory memory.

Building Table 9.1

KEY PROCESSES IN SENSORY MEMORY

Stage	Encoding	Storage	Retrieval	Duration	Forgetting
Sensory Memory	Visual or auditory (iconic or echoic storage)	Brief, fragile, and temporary	Information is extracted from stimulus and transferred to short-term storage.	Visual stimuli: 250 milliseconds; auditory stimuli: about 3 seconds	Rapid decay of information; interference is possible if a new stimulus is presented.

Short-Term Storage

Once captured in sensory memory, stimuli either fade or are transferred to a second stage—short-term storage. This storage is similar to a computer's random access memory (RAM)—it is where information is held for processing. Another similarity between your memory and your computer's RAM is their fragility—information in short-term storage is easily lost, just as information in RAM is when the electricity goes off unexpectedly. Similarly, if you look up a telephone number but do not dial it immediately, you quickly lose that information. In terms of our filing cabinet analogy, short-term storage is equivalent to the process of creating folders for the papers on your desk, and deciding what to use as labels on the folders.

Initially, researchers spoke of *short-term memory*, to emphasize its brief duration. After extensive research demonstrated its active nature, however, some began to call it *working memory*. Both terms apply to the brief, fragile storage that occurs between sensory memory and long-term memory, but the two terms have slightly different meanings to some researchers in the field (Baddeley, 2002; Kail & Hall, 2001). This text uses *short-term storage* as a general term to refer to this type of brief memory; the terms *short-term memory* and *working memory* are used when discussing research on those specific topics.

Early Research on Short-Term Memory

Thousands of researchers have studied the components and characteristics of storage in short-term memory. Early research focused on its duration, its capacity, and its relationship to rehearsal. In 1959, Lloyd and Margaret Peterson presented experimental evidence for the existence of a separate memory store they called short-term memory. In a laboratory study, the Petersons asked participants to recall a three-consonant sequence, such as *xbd*, either immediately following its presentation or after a time interval ranging from 1 to 18 seconds. During the interval, the participants had to count backward by threes to prevent them from repeating (rehearsing) the consonant sequence. The Petersons wanted to examine recall when rehearsal was not possible. **Figure 9.3** shows that, as the interval between presentation and recall increased, accuracy of recall decreased until it fell to levels that could have been due to chance. The Petersons' experiment, like many others that followed, showed that information contained in short-term memory is available for 20–30 seconds at most. After that, the information must be transferred to long-term memory, or it will be lost.

In 1956, George Miller argued that human beings can retain about seven (plus or minus two) items in short-term memory. The number of items that a person can reproduce from short-term memory is the **memory span**. But what constitutes an "item" is not consistent. For example, a person can recall about five letters, about five words, and about five sentences. Therefore, people can group information in ways that expand short-term memory capacity. The groupings are called *chunks*—manageable and meaningful units of information organized in a familiar way for easy encoding, storage, and retrieval. Short-term memory will hold one or two chunks. Many people remember their Social Security number in three chunks (a really difficult task for short-term memory) and telephone numbers in two chunks (a much easier task). When ten-digit

Memory span ■ The number of items that a person can reproduce from short-term memory, usually consisting of one or two chunks.

Chunks ■ Manageable and meaningful units of information organized in a familiar way for easy encoding, storage, and retrieval.

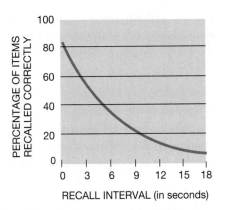

RECALL INTERVAL (in seconds)

Figure 9.3
Results of Peterson and Peterson's Classic Experiment
Peterson and Peterson (1959) found that when they delayed the report of three-letter syllables by having participants count backward, accuracy of recall decreased over the first 18 seconds.

telephone numbers came into existence, people had trouble remembering them because of their short-term memory limit. But because they could think of the area code as a chunk, people got around that limit and dealt with ten-digit dialing. Chunks can be organized on the basis of meaning, past associations, rhythm, or some arbitrary strategy a person devises to help encode large amounts of data (Brown & Craik, 2000). Determining what constitutes a chunk is sometimes difficult, though, because it varies according to each individual's perceptual and cognitive groupings.

Psychologists agree that a key operation—rehearsal—is especially important in memory (Robinson-Riegler & Robinson-Riegler, 2004). *Rehearsal* is the process of repeatedly verbalizing, thinking about, or otherwise acting on or transforming information in order to keep that information active in memory. Rehearsal usually involves more than simply repeating information. Psychologists distinguish two important types of rehearsal: maintenance rehearsal and elaborative rehearsal. *Maintenance rehearsal* is the repetitive review of information with little or no interpretation. This shallow form of rehearsal focuses only on the physical stimuli, not their underlying meaning. It generally occurs just after initial encoding has taken place—for example, when you repeat a phone number just long enough to dial it. *Elaborative rehearsal* involves repetition plus analysis, in which the stimulus may be associated with (linked to) other information and further processed. When a grocery shopper attempts to remember the things he needs in order to make dinner, he may organize them in a meaningful mental pattern, such as the ingredients required for each recipe. Elaborative rehearsal, during which information is made personally meaningful, is especially important in the encoding processes. Maintenance rehearsal alone is usually not sufficient to allow information to be permanently stored, but elaborative rehearsal allows information to be transferred into long-term memory. In general, information held in short-term memory is either transferred to long-term memory or lost.

For example, you can repeat the term *suprachiasmatic nucleus* until you can recognize it and connect it with the regulation of circadian rhythms, but to remember this term and its meaning beyond the date of the test on Chapter 7, you need to do more. One strategy would be to analyze the term, breaking it down into parts and developing an understanding of each one. *Chiasm* means "intersection," and it refers to the place in the brain where the optic nerves from the two eyes come

Rehearsal ■ The process of repeatedly verbalizing, thinking about, or otherwise acting on or transforming information in order to keep that information active in memory.

Maintenance rehearsal ■ Repetitive review of information with little or no interpretation.

Elaborative rehearsal ■ Rehearsal involving repetition and analysis, in which a stimulus may be associated with (linked to) other information and further processed.

together. *Supra* means "above," and *nucleus* is a formation of neurons within the brain. So the term *suprachiasmatic nucleus* describes a brain structure that lies above the optic chiasm. Though it requires some work, this level of elaboration will boost memory for this information.

The Emergence of Working Memory

Working memory ■ The storage mechanism that temporarily holds current or recent information for immediate or short-term use.

Until the 1970s, psychologists used the term *short-term memory* to refer to memory that lasts for less than a minute. In the 1970s researchers Alan Baddeley and Graham Hitch (1974; Baddeley, 2002) began to reconceptualize short-term memory as a more complex type of brief storage they called **working memory**, the storage mechanism that temporarily holds current or recent information for immediate or short-term use. Their model conceives of working memory as several substructures that operate simultaneously to maintain information while it is being processed. The concept of working memory goes beyond individual stages of encoding, storage, and retrieval to describe the active integration of both conscious processes (such as repetition) and unconscious processes. This model of memory emphasizes how human memory meets the demands of real-life activities such as listening to the radio, reading, and mentally calculating the sum of 74 plus 782.

In working memory, information is not simply stored; it is further encoded and then maintained for about 20–30 seconds while active processing takes place. A person may decide that a specific piece of information is important; if it is complicated or lengthy, the person will need to actively rehearse it to keep it in working memory. The addition of new information may interfere with the recall of other information in working memory. Baddeley and Hitch (1974) demonstrated the limited capabilities of several components, or subsystems, of working memory by having participants recall digits while doing some other type of reasoning task. If one subsystem is given a demanding task, the performance of the others will suffer.

One subsystem in working memory is the phonological loop, which encodes, rehearses, and holds auditory information such as a person's name or phone number. Another subsystem is a visual-spatial "scratchpad," which stores visual and spatial information, such as the appearance and location of objects, for a brief time and then is erased to allow new information to be stored. A third subsystem is an episodic buffer that holds integrated episodes or scenes and provides a limited-capacity storage system. Each of these subsystems also receives information from long-term memory. A fourth subsystem is a central executive mechanism; it balances the information flow, controlling attention. Research confirms the existence of these four separable components of working memory and also shows that they are functioning by the time a child is 6 years old (Gathercole et al., 2004).

Figure 9.4 illustrates the current form of the model of short-term storage as working memory (Baddeley, 2002). **Building Table 9.2** summarizes key processes in the first two stages of memory. Recent research on working memory has concentrated on the brain activity that underlies this type of processing (Bor et al., 2003) and on the episodic buffer, which allows a better explanation of how working memory relates to long-term memory (Baddeley, 2002).

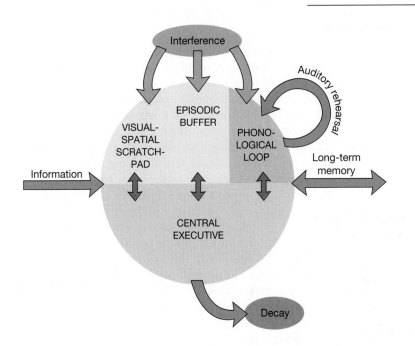

Figure 9.4
Working Memory
Active processing occurs in working memory. Information is held in the visual-spatial scratchpad, the episodic buffer, or the phonological loop, depending on the type of input. This information is monitored by the central executive.

Building Table 9.2

KEY PROCESSES IN THE FIRST TWO STAGES OF MEMORY

Stage	Encoding	Storage	Retrieval	Duration	Forgetting
Sensory Memory	Visual or auditory (iconic or echoic storage)	Brief, fragile, and temporary	Information is extracted from stimulus and transferred to short-term storage.	Visual stimuli: 250 milliseconds; auditory stimuli: about 3 seconds	Rapid decay of information; interference is possible if a new stimulus is presented.
Short-Term Storage	Visual and auditory	Repetitive rehearsal maintains information in storage, in either visual or verbal form, so that further encoding can take place.	Maintenance and elaborative rehearsal can keep information available for retrieval; retrieval is enhanced through elaboration and further encoding.	No more than 30 seconds, probably less than 20 seconds; depends on specific task and stimulus	Interference and decay affect memory; new stimulation causes rapid loss of information unless it is especially important.

Long-Term Memory

In a computer, information is stored for long periods of time on the hard drive. In the brain, information is stored in **long-term memory**, the storage mechanism that keeps a relatively permanent record of information from which a person can recall, retrieve, and reconstruct previous experiences. Names, faces, dates, places, smells, and events are stored in long-term memory. In contrast to the limitations of sensory memory and short-term storage, long-term memory may last a lifetime, and its capacity seems unlimited. Using our filing cabinet analogy, we can say that long-term memory includes all the folders in the cabinet. Like folders in a filing cabinet, information in long-term memory can be lost (misfiled) or unavailable for some other reason (the drawers can get stuck). However, unlike a filing cabinet, human long-term memory is an active rather than a passive storage system that is subject to distortion—as if the information on the papers in the folders developed errors while in the filing cabinet.

A wide variety of information is stored in long-term memory—the words to "The Star-Spangled Banner," the meaning of the word *sanguine*, how to operate a CD player, where your psychology class meets, what you did to celebrate your high school graduation—the list is endless and, of course, unique for each individual. Different types of information seem to be stored and called on in different ways. Based on how information is stored and retrieved, psychologists have made a number of distinctions among types of long-term memories.

Procedural and Declarative Memory

Procedural memory is memory for skills, including the perceptual, motor, and cognitive skills required to complete complex tasks (see **Figure 9.5** on p. 333). Driving a car, riding a bike, or cooking a meal involves a series of steps that include perceptual, motor, and cognitive skills—and thus procedural memories. Acquiring such skills is usually time-consuming and difficult at first; but once the skills are learned, they are relatively permanent and automatic. *Declarative memory* is memory for specific information, such as what Abu Gharaib is (an American prison camp in Iraq), who tore off Janet Jackson's costume during halftime at the 2004 Superbowl (Justin Timberlake), and the meaning of the word *sanguine* (hopeful and confident). Declarative memories may be established quickly, but the information is more likely to be forgotten over time than is the information in procedural memory. Some researchers subdivide declarative memory into episodic memory and semantic memory.

Episodic and Semantic Memory

Episodic memory is memory for specific personal events and situations (episodes), tagged with information about time (Tulving, 1972, 2002). An episodic memory includes where and when the episode occurred; the chronological dating, or tagging, lets you know the sequence of events within your episodic memory. Examples of episodic memories include memories of having breakfast this morning, seeing a movie last night, and being on vacation two summers ago. Episodic memory is often highly detailed: You may recall not only the plot of the movie you saw last night and who starred in it, but also the temperature of

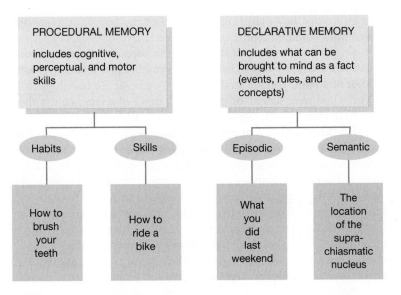

Figure 9.5
Procedural and
Declarative
Long-Term
Memory

the theater, the smell of the popcorn, what you were wearing, who accompanied you, and many other details of the experience.

Episodic memories about ourselves—our own personal stories—are called *autobiographical memories*. In some sense, we *are* our autobiographical memories; we need these memories to construct our sense of self (Nelson & Fivush, 2004). Cognitive abilities such as understanding time are required for the development of autobiographical memory, and this capacity develops during early childhood. People's autobiographical memories can last for many years (Neisser & Libby, 2000), and when people lose autobiographical memory, they lose some of their sense of self. This type of long-term memory storage is durable and fairly easy to access if a helpful retrieval cue, such as a smell associated with an event, is available. These memories are also subject to a variety of distortions (which we'll consider in a later section).

Semantic memory is memory for ideas, rules, words, and general concepts about the world. It is your set of generalized knowledge, based on concepts about the world, about previous events, experiences, and learned information (Tulving, 1972, 2002). It is not time-specific. Semantic memory contains knowledge that may have been gathered over days or weeks, and it continues to be modified and expanded over a lifetime. Your knowledge of what a horse typically looks like comes from semantic memory, whereas your knowledge of your last encounter with a horse is episodic memory. Semantic memory develops earlier in childhood than does episodic memory (Wheeler, 2000).

Semantic memory ■
Memory for ideas, rules, words, and general concepts about the world.

Explicit and Implicit Memory

Explicit memory is conscious memory that a person is aware of, such as a memory of a word in a list or an event that occurred in the past. Both semantic and episodic memories are explicit, resulting from voluntary, active memory storage. When you tap semantic memory to recall, for example, the year the Declaration of Independence was signed, you are accessing explicit memory. In contrast, *implicit memory* is memory a

Explicit memory ■
Conscious memory that a person is aware of.

Implicit memory ■
Memory a person is not aware of possessing.

person is not aware that he or she possesses. Implicit memory is accessed automatically and sometimes unintentionally.

For example, you may remember things you are supposed to remember (explicit memories), but you are also likely to recall things you did not deliberately attempt to learn—the color of a book you are studying or the name of the book's publisher, the size of a piece of cake you were served, or perhaps the make of a computer in the office of a professor you have visited. Such implicit memories are formed without conscious awareness, which demonstrates that people can learn without intentional effort (Boronat & Logan, 1997). What they learn explicitly and how they are asked to recall it may affect their implicit memories (Nelson, McKinney, & Gee, 1998). The hippocampus and structures in the medial temporal lobe are necessary for the formation of most explicit memories but are not necessary for all implicit memories (Adeyemo, 2002). For example, people with damage to the hippocampus can still learn skills and motor associations. That different brain structures are required for forming explicit versus implicit memories confirms that these types of memory are separable.

The distinction between explicit and implicit memory adds another dimension to researchers' understanding of long-term memory, suggesting that this storage is varied and complex. The distinction also suggests that these different types of memory may have differing representations in the brain and that the functioning of each system is independent of others.

Practice

Obviously, practice is a factor in storage, but research indicates that the timing of practice is also an important factor. One early study (Baddeley & Longman, 1978) investigated which of two types of practice resulted in more optimal learning and retention: intensive practice at one time (massed practice) or the same amount of practice divided into several intervals (distributed practice). To answer this question, the researchers taught postal workers to type.

The participants were divided into four groups, each member of which practiced the same number of hours but spread over different numbers of days, to create either distributed practice or massed practice. One group practiced typing for 1 hour a day; the second practiced for 2 hours a day; the third practiced for 1 hour twice a day; the fourth practiced for 2 hours twice a day. Given the same total number hours of practice, did the distribution of those practice hours over days make a difference? The dependent variable was how well participants learned to type—that is, the number of accurate keystrokes per minute. A typing test showed that distributed practice (typing 1 hour a day for several days) was most effective. From this experiment and others, researchers have learned that the effectiveness of distributed practice depends on many variables, but it is typically more effective than massed practice. Distributed practice is especially effective for perceptual motor skills, where eye–hand coordination is important.

Neuroscience and Storage

Using both PET and fMRI, researchers can now monitor the neural machinery that underlies brain functions, and this technology has been applied to the study of both working memory and long-term memory. Brain-imaging studies of working memory reveal a complex pattern of activity in several different brain regions, which is compatible with the phonological loop and visual-spatial scratchpad of Baddeley's model (Wagner & Smith, 2003). Other research suggests that various parts of the frontal cortex as well as parts of the parietal cortex (see **Figure 3.9**) are activated when working memory is being used (Collette & Van der Linden, 2002). This diffusion of function is consistent with the concept of a central executive function that draws on several parts of the brain.

One patient with brain damage has been very important in understanding the brain mechanisms underlying the transition of information from short-term storage to long-term memory. Brenda Milner (1966) reported the case of H.M., a man whose brain was damaged as a result of surgery to control his epilepsy. His short-term storage was intact, but he was unable to form new long-term declarative memories. As long as H.M. was able to rehearse information and keep it in short-term storage, his recall performance was normal. For example, he could recall a telephone number as long as he kept repeating it. However, as soon as he could no longer rehearse, his recall became poor. His ability to shift information from short-term to long-term storage was impaired. He would have no memory that he had even heard the phone number 5 minutes after hearing it. (His procedural memory was not so severely affected, and he was able to learn new motor skills such as tracing and coordination tasks, but much more slowly than people with no brain damage.) Milner's account of this case provides support for a neurological distinction between short-term and long-term memory and focused researchers' attention on the role of the *hippocampus*, a brain structure in the medial (middle part of the) temporal lobes. Subsequent research has shown that this brain structure is an important component in memory formation, especially the transfer of information from short-term to long-term storage (Zeineh et al., 2003).

The process of changing a temporary memory to a permanent one is called *consolidation*. This concept plays an important role in one of the leading theories of storage, formulated by psychologist Donald Hebb. Hebb (1949) suggested that when groups of neurons are stimulated, they form patterns of neural activity. When specific groups of neurons fire frequently, this activity establishes regular neural circuits through the process of consolidation. According to Hebb, this process must occur for short-term memory to become long-term memory. When key neurons and neurotransmitters are repeatedly stimulated by various events, those events tend to be remembered and more easily accessed—this may be part of the reason that practiced behaviors are so easily recalled (Kandel, 2001).

If a neuron is stimulated, the biochemical processes involved make it more likely to respond again later. This increase in responsiveness is referred to as *long-term potentiation*, and it is especially evident in areas of the brain such as the hippocampus. In addition, clear evidence exists that specific proteins are synthesized in the brain just after learning and that long-term memory depends on this synthesis (Kandel, 2001). Psychologists now generally accept the idea that synapses undergo structural changes after learning, and especially after repeated learning experiences. As Hebb (1949) said, "Some memories are both instantaneously established and permanent. To account for the permanence, some structural change seems necessary" (p. 62).

If the physical changes in the brain that form the basis for memory occur at the level of the synapse, then no particular brain structure should be specifically associated

Consolidation [kon-SOL-ih-DAY-shun] ■ The process of changing a temporary (short-term) memory to a permanent (long-term) one.

Long-term potentiation ■ An increase in responsiveness of a neuron after it has been stimulated.

with long-term memory. This conclusion seems true. Researchers worked for years try-ing to find a structure in the cerebral cortex associated with the formation of memory. They failed (Lashley, 1950). Although complete agreement has not been reached, many researchers accept that memory is distributed throughout the brain rather than local-ized in one spot. As we have seen, structures in the medial temporal lobe, including the hippocampus, are critically important to long-term storage, but the temporal lobes are not the site of long-term memory (Markowitsch, 2000). Memories are distributed over the cerebral cortex and other brain structures, and their encoding and retrieval activate pathways that include the prefrontal cortex and the medial temporal lobes.

Building Table 9.3 summarizes key processes in the three stages of memory.

Building Table 9.3

KEY PROCESSES IN THE THREE STAGES OF MEMORY

Stage	Encoding	Storage	Retrieval	Duration	Forgetting
Sensory Memory	Visual or auditory (iconic or echoic storage)	Brief, fragile, and temporary	Information is extracted from stimulus and transferred to short-term storage.	Visual stimuli: 250 milli-seconds; auditory stimuli: about 3 seconds	Rapid decay of information; interference is possible if a new stimulus is presented.
Short-Term Storage	Visual and auditory	Repetitive rehearsal main-tains informa-tion in storage, in either visual or verbal form, so that further encoding can take place.	Maintenance and elaborative rehearsal can keep information available for retrieval; retrieval is enhanced through elabora-tion and further encoding.	No more than 30 seconds, probably less than 20 seconds; depends on specific task and stimulus	Interference and decay affect memory; new stimula-tion causes rapid loss of information unless it is especially important.
Long-Term Memory	Important informa-tion processed by short-term storage is transferred into long-term memory through elaborative rehearsal.	Storage is organized on logical and semantic lines for rapid recall; organization of information by categories, events, and other structures aids retrieval.	Retrieval is aided by cues and care-ful organization; errors in retrieval can be intro-duced: long-term memory is fallible.	Indefinite: many events will be recalled in great detail for a lifetime.	Both decay and interference contribute to retrieval failure.

What Influences Memory Retrieval?

If memory is like a filing cabinet, then retrieval is like the process of opening the drawer and finding a folder. The retrieval operation usually goes smoothly: You know which drawer to open and you can find the folder, pull it out, and look at the information, which matches the coded label. Likewise, most memory retrieval is fairly easy: We consciously and deliberately try to remember something, and it becomes available with little effort. But things *can* get in the way of remembering—you realize this when you take a test and cannot remember a fact or a concept, even though you know you have it "filed away." Like everyone, you experience many retrieval failures, situations in which you know that you know the information—it's "on the tip of your tongue," yet you cannot access it (Brown, 1991).

Retrieval is the process by which stored information is recovered from memory. Recalling your Social Security number, remembering the details of an assignment, and listing the names of all Seven Dwarfs are retrieval tasks. Information may be encoded quickly, dealt with in working memory, and entered into long-term memory, but then the person must be able to retrieve the information and use it in a meaningful way. It turns out that the ability to retrieve information depends on how retention is measured and how the information is encoded and stored.

Retrieval ■ The process by which stored information is recovered from memory.

Retention: Measures of Retrieval

Are you a fan of *Jeopardy*, or did you tune in regularly to *Who Wants to Be a Millionaire?* Does your preference relate to the difference in difficulty of the two? These two television shows are similar—both require participants to retrieve information that they have stored in memory. They differ in rules and format, but a major difference is the way that each asks participants to access information. *Jeopardy* asks participants to recall information by reproducing it, whereas *Who Wants to Be a Millionaire?* required participants to recognize information. Psychologists use these two measures of *retention*, as well as another called *relearning*, in studies of memory retrieval.

Recall

In memory tasks using *recall*, participants have to retrieve previously presented information by reproducing it. In addition to *Jeopardy*, fill-in-the-blank and essay exams require the recall of information. In experiments, the information to be recalled usually consists of strings (lists) of digits or letters. A typical study might ask participants to remember 10 items, one of which appears on a screen every half-second. The participants would then try to repeat the list of 10 items at the end of the 5-second presentation period.

Recall ■ A method of measuring memory in which participants have to retrieve previously presented information by reproducing it.

Three widely used recall tasks involve free recall, serial recall, and paired associates. In *free recall tasks*, participants may recall items in any order, much as you might recall the items on a grocery list. *Serial recall tasks* are more difficult, because the items must be recalled in the order in which they were presented, as when recalling the digits in a telephone number. In *paired associate tasks*, participants must learn the association of items in pairs and be able to produce the second item in each pair when cued with the first item. For example, in the learning phase of a paired associate study, the experimenter might pair the words *tree* and *shoe*. In the testing phase, participants would be presented with the word *tree* and would have to respond with the correct answer, *shoe*.

Recognition

Recognition ■ A method of measuring memory in which participants select previously presented information from other unfamiliar information.

On *Who Wants to Be a Millionaire?* people must recognize the correct information from a set of four possibilities. Psychologists study ***recognition*** by using memory tasks that also require participants to select previously presented information from other unfamiliar information, as in a multiple-choice test. Recognition tasks are better than recall tasks for showing subtle differences in memory ability. Although a person may be unable to recall the details of previously learned material, he or she may recognize them (Robinson-Riegler & Robinson-Riegler, 2004). If a question involved the identity of the capital of Maine, more people would succeed on *Millionaire* than on *Jeopardy*. The chance of answering correctly is better when presented with four names to choose from: Columbus, Annapolis, Helena, or Augusta. (Final answer: Augusta.)

Relearning

Relearning ■ A method of assessing memory by measuring how long it takes participants to relearn material they have learned previously.

No game show uses ***relearning*** as a memory task—it wouldn't make a very exciting program. A relearning task assesses memory by measuring how long it takes a participant to relearn material that was learned previously. The rationale for this assessment is that rapid relearning indicates some residual memory. For example, let's say you receive a list of 12 words to memorize, and you study them until you can recite them perfectly. You report back two days later and are asked to recall the list. Unless you have rehearsed the list during the two-day interval, your performance will be far from perfect. However, you will probably relearn the material more quickly than you originally learned it, indicating that you have some memory of the items, even though you cannot recall them.

Retrieval Success and Failure: Encoding Specificity

Some contemporary researchers assert that every memory is retained but that some memories are less accessible than others. Think of the filing cabinet analogy: You may be unable to find some of the folders in the cabinet (perhaps because they are misfiled, or perhaps the drawer is stuck temporarily), making retrieval difficult or impossible. When retrieval of information is blocked, the information is effectively forgotten. It is not gone, however—just inaccessible.

Research on retrieval focuses on how people encode information and on the cues that help them recall it—on the interaction between encoding and retrieval. If you are given a cue for retrieval that relates to some aspect of the originally stored information, retrieval will be easier, faster, and more accurate. For example, if asked what stage of sleep is usually associated with dreams, you might find it fairly easy to recall because you may have known about the association between REM sleep and dreaming even before you studied Chapter 7. But recalling which brain structure is associated with the regulation of the sleep–wakefulness cycle would likely be harder for you, because the term *suprachiasmatic nucleus* is much less familiar than the concept of REM sleep.

Retrieval cues make recall easier. This evidence supports the *encoding specificity principle*, which asserts that the effectiveness of a specific retrieval cue depends on how well it matches up with information in the original encoded memory. This principle predicts that people who encode information under one set of circumstances will find it easier to retrieve that information under the same circumstances. This prediction is supported by studies of state-dependent learning and retrieval.

State-Dependent Learning and Retrieval

Psychologist Gordon Bower (1981) used the following story to describe a phenomenon known as *state-dependent learning*:

> When I was a kid I saw the movie *City Lights* in which Charlie Chaplin plays the little tramp. In one very funny sequence, Charlie saves a drunk from leaping to his death. The drunk turns out to be a millionaire who befriends Charlie, and the two spend the evening together drinking and carousing. The next day, when sober, the millionaire does not recognize Charlie and even snubs him. Later the millionaire gets drunk again, and when he spots Charlie, treats him as his long-lost companion. So the two of them spend another evening together carousing and drinking and then stagger back to the millionaire's mansion to sleep. In the morning, of course, the sober millionaire again does not recognize Charlie, treats him as an intruder, and has the butler kick him out by the seat of his pants. The scene ends with the little tramp telling the camera his opinion of high society and the evils of drunkenness. (p. 129)

State-dependent learning ■ The tendency to recall information learned while in a particular physiological or emotional state most accurately when one is again in that state.

The millionaire remembers Charlie only when he is intoxicated, the same state he was in when he originally met him. Psychologists find that information learned while a person is in a particular physiological or emotional state is recalled most accurately when the person is again in that state. This phenomenon is known as *state-dependent learning*. This dependence of retrieval on learning state is associated not only with alcohol but also with caffeine (Kelemen & Creeley, 2003), with emotional states (Lang et al., 2001), and with language spoken (Schrauf, 2000). Mood is an example of an emotional state that affects learning and recall.

In a typical study of state-dependent learning, Weingartner and colleagues (1976) had four groups of participants learn and recall lists of words. Participants in the control group learned and recalled the words while they were sober; those in a second group learned and recalled while they were intoxicated; a third group learned while sober and recalled while intoxicated; a fourth group learned while intoxicated and recalled while sober. The results showed that participants recalled the words best when they were in the state in which they had learned them. (This does not mean your memory works better when you're drunk! All else being equal, recall is better in sober individuals.) The finding that certain states affect retrieval brings up questions about what makes retrieval easier.

What Facilitates Retrieval?

Long-term memory studies have brought forth some interesting findings about retrieval and have generated hundreds of other studies focusing on factors that can facilitate or inhibit accurate recall. Two of these factors are (1) primacy and recency effects and (2) imagery.

Primacy and Recency Effects

In a typical memory experiment, a participant is asked to do some type of memory task, such as study a list of words and recall as many of the items as possible so that the researcher can determine whether the information was transferred from short-term storage to long-term memory. If the list is 30 or 40 items long, such experiments typically show an overall recall rate of 20%, but the recall rate is not even throughout the list. Recall is higher for words at the beginning of a series than for those in the middle, a phenomenon termed the ***primacy effect*** (Robinson-Riegler & Robinson-Riegler, 2004). This occurs because when a person begins a new memory task, no information related to the task is already in short-term storage, and so attention to new stimuli is at its peak. In addition, words at the beginning of a series get to be rehearsed more thoroughly, allowing them to be transferred to long-term memory.

However, recall is *even higher* for words at the end of a series—a phenomenon termed the ***recency effect*** (Robinson-Riegler & Robinson-Riegler, 2004). These more recently presented items are still being held in short-term storage, where they can be actively rehearsed without interference. These items are easy to retrieve from short-term storage. **Figure 9.6** is a graph showing the recall rate for words in various positions in a list. It is called a ***serial position curve*** and presents the probability of recall as a function of an item's position in a list (series) of presented items.

There is an exception to the serial position curve: When one item in a list differs from the others—for example, an adjective in a series of common nouns or a longer

Primacy effect ■ The more accurate recall of items presented at the beginning of a series.

Recency effect ■ The more accurate recall of items presented at the end of a series.

Serial position curve ■ A bow-shaped curve that represents the probability of recall as a function of an item's position in a list (series) of presented items.

Figure 9.6
A Serial Position Curve
The probability of recalling an item is plotted as a function of its position in a series (list) of items. Generally, the first several items are fairly likely to be recalled (the primacy effect), and the last several are recalled very well (the recency effect).

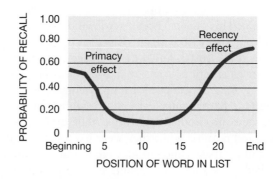

word in a series of short ones—the different item is learned more easily (Hunt &
Lamb, 2001). This phenomenon is called the *von Restorff effect*.

Imagery

People use perceptual imagery every day as an aid to long-term memory retrieval.
Imagery is the creation or re-creation of a mental picture of a sensory or perceptual
experience. People constantly invoke images to recall things they did, said, read, or
saw. People's imagery systems can be activated not only by visual stimuli but also by
auditory stimuli (Tranel et al., 2003) or olfactory stimuli (Kosslyn, 2003). Imagery
helps you answer questions such as these: Which is darker green, a pea or a
Christmas tree? Which is bigger, a tennis ball or a baseball? Does the person you
met last night have brown eyes or blue?

    One technique researchers use to study imagery is to ask participants to imagine
objects of various sizes—for example, an animal such as a rabbit next to either an
elephant or a fly. In a 1975 study by Stephen Kosslyn of Harvard University, participants reported that when they imagined a fly, plenty of room remained in their mental image for a rabbit. However, when they imagined an elephant, it took up most of
the space. One particularly interesting result was that the participants required more
time and found it harder to see a rabbit's nose when the rabbit was next to an
elephant than when it was next to a fly, because the nose appeared to be extremely
small in the first instance (see **Figure 9.7**).

Imagery ■ The creation
or re-creation of a mental
picture of a sensory or
perceptual experience.

Figure 9.7
Kosslyn's
Imagery
Studies
(Kosslyn, 1975)

Kosslyn had subjects imagine
elephants, flies, and rabbits. An
imagined rabbit appeared small
in size next to an elephant.

Next to a fly, however, an
imagined rabbit appeared
large in size.

Imagery is an important aid for retrieval of perceptual memories. In fact, a large body of evidence suggests that it is a means of preserving perceptual information that might otherwise decay. According to Allan Paivio (1971), a person told to remember two words may form an image combining those words. Someone told to remember the words *house* and *hamburger*, for example, may form an image of a house made of hamburgers or of a hamburger on top of a house. When the person is later presented with the word *house*, the word *hamburger* will be easy to retrieve because the imagery will aid retrieval. Paivio suggests that words paired in this way become conceptually linked, with the image as the crucial factor. How images facilitate recall and recognition is not yet fully understood, but one possibility is that an image may provide an easy way to elaborate information, which relates to effective encoding (Willoughby et al., 1997).

Figure 9.8 presents an overall view of the memory processes of encoding, storage, and retrieval. However, some extreme situations seem to create memories that are exceptions to the typical processes of memory.

Flashbulb Memories

Where were you when you heard about the attacks on the World Trade Center and the Pentagon on September 11, 2001? How did you hear about these events? What were you doing? What were your first thoughts? Do you remember those details more vividly than you remember what you had for lunch two days ago? These terrorist attacks made a life-long impression on most Americans as well as on many people around the world. Are these public, dramatic events the basis of a special kind of memory?

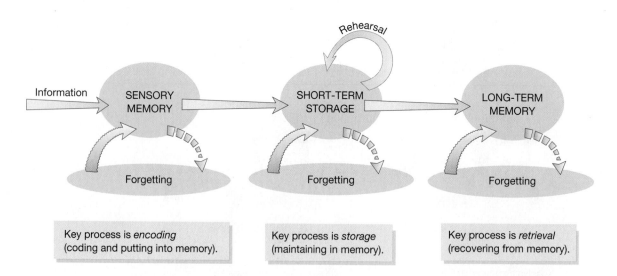

Figure 9.8
Encoding, Storage, and Retrieval in Memory
Information proceeds from sensory memory to short-term storage and then to long-term memory.

Your memory of first hearing about the terrorist attacks may be the type referred to as a *flashbulb memory*, a detailed memory of circumstances at the time of some dramatic major event. Such memories are vivid, and people have great confidence that they are accurate (Talarico & Rubin, 2003).

Brown and Kulik (1977) were the first to research this type of memory. They argued that there is a special type of memory for events that have a critical level of emotional impact. Most people immediately understand the concept of flashbulb memories and can identify personal examples. In addition to the attacks on the World Trade Center, the Columbine shootings and the death of Princess Diana were also dramatic, public events about which many people have flashbulb memories. The types of events that are likely to create flashbulb memories vary among individuals and even among countries. For example, people living in the United Kingdom are more likely to have such a memory for the death of Princess Diana than are people living in Italy (Kvavilashvili et al., 2003). Not only has there been a great deal of research on the concept of flashbulb memories, there has also been debate over its validity.

The concept of flashbulb memory holds that people will have complete, detailed, accurate memories about dramatic events. Brown and Kulik claimed that a special memory mechanism creates flashbulb memories, which explains their special characteristics. Other psychologists argue that the processes of encoding and retrieval can account for flashbulb memories, just as for other memories (Schooler & Eich, 2000). The emotional component of these memories makes them more distinctive (affecting encoding), and research has confirmed distinctiveness as a characteristic of flashbulb memories (Edery-Halpern, & Nachson, 2004).

Another point of debate involves the accuracy of flashbulb memories. Brown and Kulik argued that the special mechanism for creating these memories should make them very accurate—just as a photograph made with a flashbulb accurately captures details of a scene. Researchers have focused on collecting people's memories of various public events that generated emotion (assassinations, the space shuttle *Challenger* explosion, the September 11 terrorist attacks) and comparing their detail and accuracy to those of other memories and assessing these factors over time. Results indicate that flashbulb memories are far from perfectly accurate, and they change over time. For example, an examination of President George W. Bush's reports of the terrorist attacks showed evidence of changes over time (Greenberg, 2004). People retain a feeling of vividness associated with these memories, and they believe that these memories are more accurate than memories of other information, but this confidence is misplaced (Talarico & Rubin, 2003). Thus, flashbulb memories are probably created by the same mechanisms that form other memories and are subject to the same type of forgetting. They are certainly vivid, but they are probably not a unique type of memory.

Flashbulb memory ▦
A detailed memory for circumstances at the time of some dramatic event.

Gender and Memory

The emotional vividness of flashbulb memories may be the component that relates to gender differences in this type of memory. When asked to report their most vivid memories, women and men show some differences (Niedzwienska, 2003). Gender differences also appeared in a study of autobiographical memory among older people; women's reports were more vivid, contained more details, and were longer than men's (Pillemer et al., 2003). Perhaps these gender differences do not indicate that women have better memories than men but rather that women attend better to emotional factors or are more willing to report them than men are, making their memory reports more detailed and longer.

Several studies confirm how memory can be influenced by gender stereotypes. For example, one study asked women and men to memorize a shopping list and the directions to a particular place (Herrmann, Crawford, & Holdsworth, 1992). The results showed the expected stereotypical differences: Women performed slightly better on the shopping list and men on the directions. But the study also showed that memory performance could be manipulated along stereotypical lines. Among the participants who were told that the shopping list related to groceries, women did better at remembering its items, but among participants who were told that the list pertained to hardware, men remembered the items better. A similar study (Colley et al., 2002) showed that both men and women were affected by being told that either men or women were better at the memory task being studied. Therefore, memory is influenced by gender-stereotypical information and by gender-related expectations.

When memory tests do not evoke gender stereotypes, gender differences in memory are very small or nonexistent. For example, some studies have found small gender differences in favor of women for memory related to verbal information (Larsson, Lövdén, & Nilsson, 2003) and in favor of men for memory related to the position of objects in space (Postma et al., 2004). Other studies have failed to find gender differences. For example, no gender difference appeared in one study of short-term memory in children and adolescents (Lowe, Mayfield, & Reynolds, 2003). Another study found no gender differences when women and men recalled pictures and words (Ionescu, 2000). Thus, gender differences in memory are likely to be based on differences in attention and motivation related to the specific tasks.

Culture and Memory

The effects of culture on memory may be stronger than those of gender. Many of the studies on culture and memory explore the differences between people in individualist Western cultures and those in collectivist Asian cultures. These studies examine the possibility that these differing cultural views become personalized in ways that affect memory. For example, Asian Canadians were slower to recognize individual traits but quicker to recognize collective traits than European Canadians, suggesting that culture influences what information becomes encoded into long-term memory or how it is encoded (Wagar & Cohen, 2003).

This cultural difference also appears in examinations of the types of information that individuals from the United States and China recall in their personal memories (Lang, 2001). People from China tend to give brief accounts that focus on collective activities, whereas people from the United States tend to give longer reports in which the individual is the center of the story. In addition, an individualistic or collectivist orientation may also influence the development of memory. One study showed that adults from an individualist Western culture reported childhood memories from earlier ages than did adults from a collectivist Asian culture, suggesting that an emphasis on the individual made a difference in the early organization of memory during childhood (MacDonald, Uesiliana, & Hayne, 2000). On an even more profound level, research using brain-imaging technology showed that Chinese and American participants exhibited different patterns of brain activity during a memory recall task, even when their behavioral performance was alike (Grön et al., 2003). Therefore, individuals from different cultures may have the same memory ability, but what they remember and how they recall this information is influenced by their culture.

What Causes People to Forget?

Quick! Name your first-grade teacher. Recite your Social Security number. Tell where you went on your last vacation. Did you have any problems remembering what you needed to answer these questions? In general, our memories function well, but we tend to take good memory for granted and to complain about memory lapses. Everyone experiences memory failures, and forgetting has been a focus of research in psychology since its early years.

Early Studies

Starting with pioneering work over 100 years ago, in the late 19th century, many psychologists have studied forgetting—and their work has not been forgotten! Such research has revealed a great deal, not only about forgetting in particular, but about memory processes in general. Some of the memory tasks used in the early studies required paper and pencil, but most merely involved the experimenter, a participant, and some information to be learned.

Ebbinghaus and Forgetting

Hermann Ebbinghaus (1850–1909) studied how well people retain stored information. Ebbinghaus earnestly believed that the contents of consciousness could be studied by scientific methods. He tried to quantify how quickly participants could learn, relearn, and forget information. Ebbinghaus (1885) was the first person to investigate memory scientifically and systematically, which made his technique as important as his findings.

In his early studies, in which he was both researcher and participant, Ebbinghaus assigned himself the task of learning lists of letters in order of their presentation. First, he strung together groups of three letters to make nonsense syllables such as *nak*, *dib*, *mip*, and *daf*, because he believed that these would carry no previous associations to contaminate the measurement of learning. Next, he recorded how many times he had to present lists of these nonsense syllables to himself before he could remember them perfectly. Ebbinghaus found that when the lists were short, his learning was nearly perfect after one or two trials. When the lists contained more than seven items, however, he had to present them over and over to achieve accurate recall.

Later, Ebbinghaus did learning experiments with other participants, using the technique of *relearning*. He had the participants learn a list of syllables and then,

**Figure 9.9
Ebbinghaus's
Forgetting
Curve**
Ebbinghaus found
that most forgetting
occurs during the
first 9 hours after
learning.

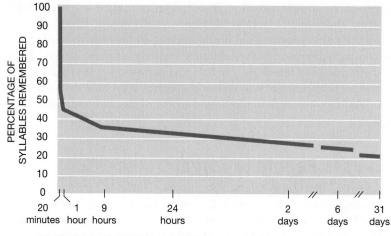

ELAPSED TIME BETWEEN LEARNING OF SYLLABLES AND MEMORY TEST

after varying amounts of time, measured how quickly they relearned the original list. He called this method the *savings method*, because it revealed what was saved in memory from the initial learning. Ebbinghaus's research showed that forgetting occurs very rapidly. Recall falls from 100% to less than 50% correct within 20 minutes. After the first several hours, forgetting levels off and shows a very slow decrease after that, indicating that most forgetting occurs quickly. (See **Figure 9.9**, which shows Ebbinghaus's "forgetting curve.")

Bartlett and Forgetting

In 1932, English psychologist Sir Frederick Bartlett reported that when college students tried to recall stories they had just read, they changed the stories in several interesting ways. First, they shortened and simplified details, a process Bartlett called *leveling*. Second, they focused on or emphasized certain details, a process he called *sharpening*. Third, they altered facts to make the stories fit their own views of the world, a process he called *assimilation*. In other words, the students constructed memories of the stories that distorted their details.

Contemporary explanations of this distortion have centered on the reconstructive nature of the memory process—the idea that memory retrieval is more like a reconstruction than a replay. Reconstruction may have to be the means for retrieval because memory formation often relies on a *schema*—a conceptual framework that organizes information and allows a person to make sense of the world. Because people cannot remember *all* the details of an event or situation, they retain key facts and lose minor details. Schemas group together key pieces of information. In general, people try to fit an entire memory into some framework to make it more readily available for later recall. Distortion is important in forgetting, but so is the type of decay that Ebbinghaus researched.

Schema [SKEEM-uh] ■
A conceptual framework
that organizes informa-
tion and allows a per-
son to make sense of
the world.

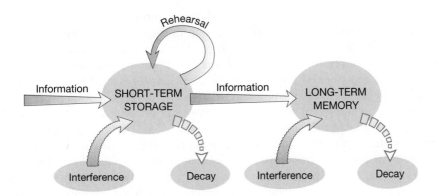

Figure 9.10

Decay and Interference in Short-Term Storage and Long-Term Memory

The transfer of information from short-term storage to long-term memory is crucial for accurate recall. Note that decay and interference affect both stages of memory.

Key Causes of Forgetting

Daniel Schacter (2001) wrote about the types of problems that can plague memory, referring to them as "sins of memory." Schacter's memory sins include the reasons that people fail to retrieve information when they need it and the processes that make memory inaccurate. Two such processes—decay and interference—can affect both short-term storage and long-term memory. (See **Figure 9.10.**)

Decay of Information

Decay is the loss of information from memory as a result of disuse and the passage of time. Decay theory asserts that unimportant events fade from memory, and details become lost, confused, or fuzzy if not called up from time to time. Another way to look at decay theory is to think of a memory as existing in the brain in a physiological form known as a *memory trace*. With the passage of time and a lack of active use, the trace disintegrates or fades and is lost. Despite the logic of disuse leading to decay, research indicates that decay is not the main way that information in memory is lost. Decay does affect information in short-term storage more than that in long-term memory (Robinson-Riegler & Robinson-Riegler, 2004). However, decay is less important to forgetting than other processes, such as interference.

Decay ■ Loss of information from memory as a result of disuse and the passage of time.

Interference in Memory

Interference is the suppression of one bit of information by another that is received either earlier or later or the confusion caused by the input of more than one piece of information. Interference theory suggests that the limited capacity of short-term storage makes it susceptible to interference when stimuli are coming in at a high rate. That is, when competing information is stored in short-term storage, the crowding that results affects a person's memory for particular items. The person experiences *encoding failure*—a memory failure attributable to encoding problems. For example, if you look up a friend's home telephone number and then her cell phone number as well, the second number will probably interfere with your ability to remember the first one. Moreover, interference in memory is more likely to occur

Interference ■ The suppression of one bit of information by another that is received either earlier or later or the confusion caused by the input of more than one piece of information.

when a person is presented with a great deal of new information, such as meeting a group of new people and trying to remember all of their names. Situations that present an overload of information tend to produce encoding failures.

A person's memory for information learned at a specific time will be influenced by information encountered both before and after that learning. For example, if you studied French on Tuesday morning and Spanish on Tuesday night and took a test on Wednesday morning, you would likely experience some interference on your exam, depending on which language you were tested on. Psychologists call these interference effects proactive and retroactive interference (or inhibition). ***Proactive interference***, or *proactive inhibition*, is a decrease in accurate recall of information as a result of the effects of previously learned or presented information (the interference you experience from studying French before you studied Spanish). ***Retroactive interference***, or *retroactive inhibition*, is a decrease in accurate recall of information as a result of the subsequent presentation of different information (the interference you experience from studying Spanish after you studied French). The similarities of these two languages make the interference worse. **Figure 9.11** illustrates both types of interference. Proactive and retroactive interference help explain most failures to recall information from long-term memory.

The effects of proactive and retroactive interference apply to many situations. For example, suppose you hear a series of speeches, each 5 minutes long. According to research on interference, you will be most likely to remember the first and last speeches. There will be no proactive interference with the first speech and no retroactive interference with the last speech. Your memory of the middle speeches, however, will suffer from both proactive and retroactive interference. Political campaign managers attempt to capitalize on these effects in scheduling their candidates' speeches. For example, they urge the candidates to speak both very early in the

Proactive [pro-AK-tiv] interference ▪ A decrease in accurate recall of information as a result of the effects of previously learned or presented information; also known as *proactive inhibition*.

Retroactive [RET-ro-AK-tiv] interference ▪ A decrease in accurate recall of information as a result of the subsequent presentation of different information; also known as *retroactive inhibition*.

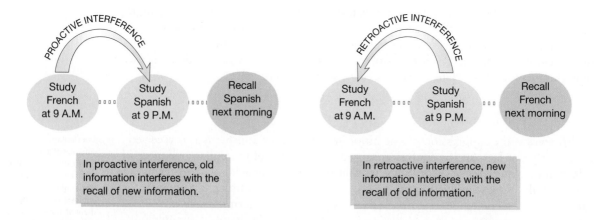

In proactive interference, old information interferes with the recall of new information.

In retroactive interference, new information interferes with the recall of old information.

Figure 9.11
Proactive and Retroactive Interference
Proactive and retroactive interference occur when information interferes with (inhibits recall of) other information in memory.

campaign and very late, just before people vote. If several candidates are to speak in succession at one event, knowledgeable campaign managers try to schedule their candidate either first or last.

Interference with Attention

According to Schacter (2001), interference with attention is responsible for one of the most annoying types of memory failure—absentmindedness. This problem plagues almost everyone, even people who have excellent memories, because this type of interference prevents information from getting into long-term memory. That is, absentmindedness is encoding failure. You really can't remember where you put your keys because that information is not there to retrieve. This problem is common, because the competition for our attention leads us to ignore some stimuli at critical points in the flow of information through the memory system. Thus, we do not remember where we put our keys, whether we locked the car, what time we agreed to meet a friend for coffee, and so on.

When people try to attend to more than one thing at a time, their attention is divided, which is another way that interference affects attention. Divided attention presents a problem for both encoding and retrieval processes, but these effects are not equal: Distraction during encoding is a much bigger problem than distraction during retrieval (Brown & Craik, 2000; Fernandes & Moscovitch, 2002).

For many years, interference with attention was used to explain what is called the *Stroop effect* (Stroop, 1935). In the Stroop test, people are presented with the names of colors, printed in different colors of ink. When reading the color names in column A aloud, most people find it difficult to attend to the word and ignore the color of ink (the Stroop effect). Their performance for column A is slower and has more errors than when they read column B, where all the words are printed in black ink, or when they read column C, where all the words are printed in the color of ink that matches the name of the color. The color of the ink produces interference. This explanation seems reasonable, but a more recent explanation of the Stroop effect has focused on a more complex interaction of selective attention and cognitive processing (Melara & Algom, 2003).

Special Types of Forgetting

Psychologists have learned that some kinds of forgetting are not easily explained by decay or interference. Sometimes the problem is not an inability to retrieve information from memory, but rather, remembering incorrectly.

Eyewitness Testimony

The police and the courts have generally accepted *eyewitness testimony* as some of the best evidence. Eyewitnesses are people who saw a particular crime occurring, often have no bias or grudge, and are sworn to tell (and to recall) the truth. Eyewitness testimony is considered very credible, and both jurors and judges place confidence in eyewitnesses (Wise & Safer, 2004). But research indicates that eyewitnesses are far from accurate, both in experimental studies (Yarmey, 2004) and in the recalling of actual crimes (Wagstaff et al., 2003). Approximately 75% of all wrongful convictions are based on eyewitness testimony (Wells & Olson, 2003).

Beginning in the 1970s, psychologists such as Elizabeth Loftus (1975, 1979) investigated the accuracy of eyewitness testimony and the circumstances that lead witnesses to make mistakes. She discovered that people who witness an event may have inaccurate memories of it. One of her early studies presented a video of a traffic accident and asked people to answer questions about what they saw. Loftus found that the wording of questions influenced witnesses' reports. For example, witnesses who answered the question "How fast were the cars going when they *contacted* each other?" gave significantly lower speed estimates than the witnesses who answered the question "How fast were the cars going when they *crashed into* each other?" All participants saw the same videotape, but their responses were influenced by the wording of the questions. This distortion of memory is sometimes referred to as the *misinformation effect*, and it is not the only type of memory distortion that eyewitnesses experience.

Someone who witnesses (or is the victim) of a crime may not get a good look at the culprit but may be strongly motivated (and even urged by authorities) to identify a suspect. Research indicates that repeated and prolonged attempts to remember details of an event can actually blur the details rather than sharpen them (Henkel, 2004). Thus, being presented with leading questions and making repeated attempts to remember can create false memories and lead eyewitnesses to mistakenly identify suspects. In addition, witnesses who make mistakes tend to believe their self-generated misinformation, and after time has passed, they no longer know what they have constructed and what they have actually observed (Pickel, 2004).

Mistakes in witness identification occur with similar frequency in women and men and in all age groups, although young children and older individuals are somewhat less accurate than those of other ages (Wells & Olson, 2003). Unfortunately, accuracy and confidence in one's accuracy are not strongly associated: People can have a great deal of confidence that they saw something when, in fact, they did not (Wells, Olson, & Charman, 2002). However, confidence tends to sway juries and judges, creating additional potential for wrongful convictions. Research indicates that speed of identification is a better indicator of accuracy than confidence is (Dunning & Perretta, 2002). Witnesses who identify culprits (from photos or police lineups) within 10 seconds are 90% accurate, whereas those who take longer than 12 seconds are only 50% accurate.

Research on eyewitness testimony suggests that memory is routinely inaccurate. People reconstruct events, and those reconstructions may vary sharply from what actually occurred. This type of error is definitely one of the "sins of memory," highlighting the need for applying research findings from psychology to the procedures of the criminal justice system. A related memory issue has generated a great deal of controversy: Can traumatic events lead people to experience a special type of forgetting in which the memory is buried in the unconscious but then later recovered?

Motivated Forgetting

Freud (1964/1933) was the first to propose the occurrence of *motivated forgetting*—that frightening, traumatic events might be forgotten simply because people want (or need) to forget them. He stated that such memory loss occurs through *repression*—the burying of traumatic events in the unconscious, where they remain but are inaccessible to conscious memory. The concept of repressed memories caught the public's attention when the topic of sexual abuse of children began to get widespread media publicity.

Repression ■ The burying of traumatic events in the unconscious, where they remain but are inaccessible to conscious memory.

Confirming the existence of motivated forgetting has been a challenge. Research on this topic presents ethical and practical problems—it would be unethical to attempt to traumatize participants, and it would require follow-ups over time to determine if an experience had resulted in repression. Therefore, researchers have been restricted to creating false memories of incidents that are not traumatic. Studies have succeeded in demonstrating false memories for a variety of situations in college-aged students, including false memories of the occurrence of a specific childhood event (Lindsay et al., 2004) and for the existence of a nonexistent friend during adolescence (Nourkova, Bernstein, & Loftus, 2004).

Other evidence of motivated forgetting of traumatic events comes from clinical psychologists who study people who have lived through such events, in childhood and later in life. However, some researchers are reluctant to accept this type of clinical evidence (Pope, 2000). Thus, that motivated forgetting occurs as a result of repression is controversial within psychology, and many psychologists are critical of claims of recovered memories of childhood abuse.

To further complicate this complex issue, repression is not necessary for the creation of false memories, nor are repressed memories limited to traumatic experiences.

Why are memories so vulnerable to interference, distortion, and error? The adaptive benefits of memory are obvious (Klein et al., 2002). In addition, the existence of multiple memory systems and their relative independence are consistent with the view that each system evolved to solve some specific adaptive problem during evolution. Evolutionary psychologists approach the study of memory by trying to understand the function of memory rather than by concentrating on its many capabilities. However, some of the evolutionary benefit of a complex memory system is negated by memory problems.

Examined another way, perhaps the problems of memory are not so serious (Anderson & Schooler, 2000). The processes that produce memory problems may have advantages; or, alternatively, these problems are not damaging enough to hamper reproductive success. For example, most of the information that we cannot recall is not critically important, at least not life-threatening, and we seem to be able to retrieve the information that is important at any given time. We might forget information that we need to remember during a test, but we do not forget that walking into traffic is dangerous. Indeed, even people with profound types of memory loss rarely lose memory to the extent that they endanger themselves.

Neuroscience and Forgetting: Studies of Amnesia

Amnesia [am-NEE-zhuh] ■ Inability to remember information (typically all events within a specific period), usually because of physiological trauma.

Retrograde [RET-ro-grade] amnesia ■ Inability to remember events and experiences that preceded a blow to the head or other event causing brain damage.

Anterograde amnesia ■ Inability to remember events and experiences that occur after brain damage.

Much of the early work on the neuroscience of memory began with the study of patients who for one reason or another had developed *amnesia,* the inability to remember information, usually because of physiological trauma. Popular beliefs about amnesia contain a number of inaccuracies, many created by media portrayals. There are two basic kinds of amnesia: retrograde and anterograde.

Retrograde amnesia is the inability to remember events and experiences that preceded a damaging event, such as a blow to the head. The loss of memory can cover a period ranging from a few minutes to several years. Recovery tends to begin quickly, and memory returns over a period of days to weeks, with earlier events being remembered before more recent ones.

Anterograde amnesia is the inability to remember events and experiences that occur *after* an injury or brain damage; that is, anterograde amnesia is the inability to form new memories. People suffering from anterograde amnesia are stuck in the lives they lived before being injured because they cannot form new memories. H.M., discussed earlier in the chapter, had anterograde amnesia. People with anterograde amnesia are able to learn some new information, but they tend to be much better at forming new procedural memories than declarative memories (Squire & Kandel, 1999). H.M. could meet someone for the hundredth time and still believe the individual to be a perfect stranger, but he was able to learn new motor skills. Interestingly, he would have no recall of the experience of practicing a new skill, so he would believe that he could not perform it even though he could.

The existence of different types of amnesia produced by different types of brain damage supports the view that memory includes many types of coding and creates many types of memories. The range of events that affect memory suggests that memory is a complex process rather than a single thing.

Summary and Review

HOW DOES THE MEMORY PROCESS BEGIN?

What is memory, and what is the information-processing view of memory?

Memory is defined as the ability to remember past events, images, ideas, or previously learned information or skills; it is also the storage system that allows retention and retrieval of information. p. 321

The information-processing approach assumes that each stage of learning and memory is separate, though related, and that information flows through this series of stages. p. 322

What is the encoding process in memory?

Encoding is the organizing of sensory information so that the nervous system can process it. The extent and type of encoding affect what we remember. p. 323

What are the underlying assumptions of the levels-of-processing approach?

The *levels-of-processing approach* holds that the brain encodes and processes stimuli (information) in different ways, to different extents, and at different levels. The deeper the level of processing, the better the retrieval of the memory. The *encoding specificity principle* asserts that the effectiveness of a specific retrieval cue depends on how well it matches up with the originally encoded information. The more clearly and sharply retrieval cues are defined, the better recall will be. *Transfer-appropriate processing* is an alternative explanation of this effect. pp. 323–324

What is the neurological basis of encoding?

PET and fMRI brain-imaging techniques indicate that the left prefrontal cortex and areas in the medial temporal lobes are involved in encoding, but different areas are activated during retrieval. pp. 324–326

WHAT ARE THE TYPES OF MEMORY STORAGE?

Describe the role of sensory memory.

Storage refers to the process of maintaining information as well as the locations where information is held. *Sensory memory* is the mechanism that performs initial encoding and brief storage of sensory information. Once information is established in sensory memory, it must be transferred elsewhere for additional encoding or it will be lost. pp. 326–327

Describe short-term storage.

Short-term storage, initially conceptualized as short-term memory, maintains a limited amount of information (seven plus or minus two items) for about 20–30 seconds. The limited number of items that can be reproduced easily after presentation is called the *memory span*. *Chunks* are manageable and meaningful units of information. *Rehearsal* is the process of repeatedly verbalizing, thinking about, or otherwise acting on or transforming information in order to remember it. *Maintenance rehearsal* is the repetitive review of information with little or no interpretation; this shallow form of rehearsal involves the physical stimulus, not its underlying meaning. *Elaborative rehearsal* involves repetition and analysis in which the stimulus may be associated with other information and further processed. This type of rehearsal is usually necessary to transfer information to long-term memory. pp. 328–330

Working memory is a more recent conceptualization that is seen as consisting of four subsystems: a phonological loop to encode and rehearse auditory information, a visual-spatial scratchpad, an episodic buffer, and a central executive to balance the information flow. p. 330

What is long-term memory, and what are the different types of long-term storage?

Long-term memory is the storage mechanism that keeps a relatively permanent record of information. It is divided into procedural memory and declarative memory. *Procedural memory* is memory for the perceptual, motor, and cognitive skills necessary to complete complex tasks; *declarative memory* is memory for specific facts, which can be subdivided into episodic and semantic memory. p. 332

Episodic memory is memory for specific personal events and situations, including their time sequence. *Semantic memory* is memory for ideas, rules, words and general concepts about the world, based on experiences and learned information. pp. 332–333

Explicit memory is conscious memory that a person is aware of, such as memory of a word in a list or an event that occurred in the past; generally speaking, most recall tasks require participants to recall explicit information. Explicit memory is a voluntary, active memory store. In contrast, *implicit memory* is memory a person is not aware of possessing; implicit memory occurs unintentionally and almost automatically. pp. 333–334

What is the neurological basis of memory storage?

Structures in the frontal cortex and the parietal cortex are important for working memory, and the hippocampus, a structure in the medial temporal lobes, is critical in transferring memories from short-term to long-term storage. *Consolidation* is the transformation of temporary memory into permanent memory. The repeated stimulation of neurons may produce changes in the synapses of neurons and *long-term potentiation*, which may be the underlying neurological basis for memory. pp. 334–336

WHAT INFLUENCES MEMORY RETRIEVAL?

How do psychologists measure retrieval?

Retrieval is the process by which stored information is recovered from memory. Recall, recognition, and relearning can be used to assess retrieval success. *Recall* is a type of memory task that requires reproducing previously presented information (usually without any cues or aids). *Recognition* requires distinguishing information that one has previously encountered from other, unfamiliar information. After information has been learned, *relearning* can determine how long it takes to reacquire the information. pp. 337–339

What is state-dependent learning?

Physiological and emotional states affect retrieval. *State-dependent learning* is the tendency to recall information learned in a particular physiological or emotional state most accurately when one is again in that state. p. 339

What factors facilitate retrieval?

Timing influences retrieval. The *primacy effect* is the more accurate recall of items presented first in a series; the *recency effect* is the more accurate recall of items presented last. A combination of these two effects produces the *serial position curve*, a graph illustrating the probability of recall of different items in a list. *Imagery*, the cognitive process of creating a mental picture of a sensory event (visual, auditory, or olfactory), can facilitate memory. pp. 340–342

What are flashbulb memories?

Flashbulb memories are vivid memories associated with some dramatic major event. Their formation and recall are subject to the same factors as other memories. pp. 342–343

Are gender and culture factors in memory?

Gender is not a very important factor in memory, but gender stereotypes have an impact on attention, which can affect memory. pp. 343–344

Culture has an influence on memory, and reports of personal memories of people from collectivist cultures are less self-centered than those of people from individualistic cultures. pp. 344–345

WHAT CAUSES PEOPLE TO FORGET?

What factors influence memory failures?

Distortions of memory are common and occur in part because people develop a *schema*, a way to organize information, that fails to include all details of a situation. pp. 346–347

Decay may result in forgetting, but *interference* is a more common source of memory failure. *Proactive interference* is a decrease in accurate recall as a result of the effects of previously learned or presented information. *Retroactive interference* is a decrease in accurate recall as a result of the subsequent presentation of different information. Interference may also affect attention, which influences memory. pp. 347–349

What do eyewitness testimony and false memories reveal about the memory process?

Both eyewitness testimony and false memories show that memory is subject to errors, including distortion and suggestibility. These errors indicate that memory is more of a reconstruction than a replay. An extreme type of memory distortion is motivated forgetting through *repression*. Everyone is subject to these memory problems, but memory is an evolutionary adaptation that has many more advantages than disadvantages. pp. 349–351

Distinguish retrograde from anterograde amnesia.

Amnesia is the inability to remember information, usually because of some physiological trauma (such as a blow to the head). *Retrograde amnesia* is the inability to remember events that preceded a traumatizing event. *Anterograde amnesia* is the inability to form new memories after the trauma has occurred. p. 352

CHAPTER 10

Cognitive Psychology

What Is Cognitive Psychology?   357

How Do We Form Concepts and
Solve Problems?   357
Concept Formation
Problem Solving
Barriers to Problem Solving
Avoid Barriers: Be a Critical Thinker
Creative Problem Solving

How Do We Reason and Make
Decisions?   366
Uncertainty: Estimating Probabilities
Barriers to Sound Decision Making
Culture and Reasoning
Evolution and Reasoning

What Does Artificial Intelligence
Reveal about Cognition?   371
The Computer as Information Processor
Neural Networks
Robotics

What Is the Structure
of Language?   375
Language and Gender Stereotypes
Thought, Culture, and Language
Linguistics
Language Structure
The Biological and Evolutionary Basis
of Language

How Do We Acquire Language?   382
Learning Theories
Biological Theories
Do Chimpanzees Use Language?
Do Dolphins or Whales Use Language?
Social Interaction Theory: A Little Bit of Each

Summary and Review   388

Every day, each of us tries to sort out problems—both small and large. Researchers attempt to learn how we do this, to better understand thought processes and to help people maximize their potential. Researchers try to break down thought and language into their components, analyzing each part separately. In searching for a comprehensive theory of psychology—one that accounts for individual differences—researchers have recognized that thought and language are separate, but closely related, aspects of human behavior. Thought allows human beings to reflect on and assess the past and to develop new ideas and plans. Language provides human beings with a unique vehicle for expressing thoughts about the past, present, and future. This chapter therefore covers both cognition (thought) and language, the symbolic system that people use to communicate their thoughts verbally.

What Is Cognitive Psychology?

How are a tiger and a domestic cat similar? Who is the U.S. Secretary of State? How do you make an omelet? Answering each of these questions requires a different mental procedure. To answer the first question, you probably formed mental images of both felines and then compared the images. In answering the second question, you may simply have recalled the right name from recent news stories. The third question may have required you to mentally review the preparation of an omelet and describe each step. The thinking you used to answer these questions involved the use of knowledge, language, and perceptual images.

Cognitive psychology is the study of the related phenomena of perception, learning, memory, and thought, with an emphasis on how people attend to, acquire, transform, store, and retrieve knowledge. Cognitive psychology includes the topics of consciousness, learning, perception, and memory, which we discussed in earlier chapters, and it is basic to other topics, such as intelligence (Chapter 11). In this chapter, we'll focus on two core subjects of cognitive psychology: thought and language. The word *cognition* derives from the Latin *cognoscere*, "to know." Cognitive psychologists are interested primarily in mental processes that influence the acquisition and use of knowledge as well as the ability to *reason*—to generate logical and coherent ideas, evaluate situations, and reach conclusions. Cognitive researchers assume that mental processes exist, that people are active processors, and that their mental processes can be studied using techniques that measure the speed and accuracy of responses. Basic research in cognitive psychology can lead to applications relevant to day-to-day life, and research on applications often brings better understanding of the principles of cognition. While human beings are excellent and efficient thinkers, our memory and perceptual systems are subject to error, and we are easily distracted. All in all, we are pretty good at cognition, but not perfect!

The study of how human beings go about thinking began in the early part of the 20th century. In the 1920s, behaviorism—with its focus on directly observable behavior—became the main force in psychology, and little attention was paid to internal cognitive processes. Discussion of and research on such "mentalistic" phenomena as imagery were avoided. In the decades after World War II, during the late 1950s and early 1960s, the brain itself began to be compared to a computer, and research into thought began again in earnest. This research was incredibly wide-ranging and attempted to answer questions that the behaviorists of the 1920s could not address adequately. One such question concerns concept formation, which is crucial for all cognition.

Cognitive psychology The study of the related phenomena of perception, learning, memory, and thought, with an emphasis on how people attend to, acquire, transform, store, and retrieve knowledge.

How Do We Form Concepts and Solve Problems?

Each day, we all solve problems, make decisions, and reason logically, often following steps that are complicated but orderly. Many researchers conceive of reasoning itself as a systematic process that takes place in discrete steps, one set of ideas leading to another. To perform this process, people need to be able to form, manipulate, transform, and interrelate concepts. From there, they go on to solve problems.

Concept Formation

Concept ■ A mental category people use to classify events or objects according to their common properties or features.

Concepts are the mental categories people use to classify events or objects according to their common properties or features. Many objects with four wheels, a driver's seat, and a steering wheel are automobiles; "automobiles" is a concept. More abstract is the concept of "justice," which has to do with legality and fairness. "Animal," "computer," and "holiday" are all examples of concepts that have a large number of *exemplars*, or specific instances—for example, there are many kinds of animals. The study of *concept formation* is the examination of the way people classify events and objects, usually in order to solve problems.

Concepts make people's experience of the world more meaningful by helping them organize their thinking. Individuals develop progressively more complex concepts throughout life. Early on, infants learn the difference between "parent" and "stranger." Within a year, they can discriminate among objects, colors, and people and can comprehend simple concepts such as "animal" and "flower." By age 2, they can verbalize these differences.

Much of what young children learn involves *classification*—the process of organizing things into categories—which is crucial to understanding the world (see **Figure 10.1**). Think back to your early school years and to television shows that taught basic language skills. You learned the letters of the alphabet, different colors, the names of farm animals and their sounds, and shapes such as triangles, circles, and squares through song, animation, and repetition. This process of developing concepts through classification continues throughout life. It involves separating dissimilar objects or events, finding commonalities, and then grouping similar items together (Ariely, 2001). But what is the best way to study the processes by which children and adults classify and organize information?

As a type of thinking, concept formation is relatively easy to study in controlled laboratory situations. Psychologists design laboratory studies whose objective is to observe participants forming and using concepts through a wide range of tasks. If you were a participant in such an experiment, you might be asked to respond to simple questions, such as "Is this card red, blue, or yellow?" Other tasks become more complex—"Is a bicycle a toy or a vehicle?" (Well, it depends on whether it is a kid's bike or a motorized one.) In even more complicated concept formation tasks,

Figure 10.1
Classification
Tasks
These tasks require choosing from alternatives that share certain properties. For example, in a typical classification task for children, the objective is to circle the picture that is most like the sample.

SAMPLE

subtleties between categories are hard to discern—for example, you could be asked to distinguish between a big house and a mansion, or a street, a drive, and a boulevard. The experimenter might time your responses and also ask you to express your thought processes out loud. In truth, when you take an IQ test or the SAT, many questions require such concept formation—think about test items like this one: "A cat is to a house as a bee is to a _____." You have to understand that bees often live in hives, just as cats often live in houses.

A key requirement for laboratory studies of concept formation is that participants be able to form rules—statements of how stimuli are related. A researcher might ask a participant to say when she observes a characteristic under study (this is a *positive instance*) and when she does not observe a characteristic under study (this is a *negative instance*). So, in one common task used in laboratory investigations of concept formation, the experimenter tells the participants that something about the stimuli to be presented makes them similar. Participants are asked to identify this characteristic—this rule about the relationship between the stimuli. Each time a stimulus is presented, participants are told whether or not the item has the particular characteristic. For example, suppose the first stimulus is a picture of a large bird. The experimenter says that it is a positive instance. The participant now knows that the concept being studied is possibly largeness or being a bird. The second stimulus is a picture of a small red bird; the experimenter says that this, too, is a positive instance. The participant now knows that size is not important. The third stimulus is a picture of a large blue bird; it, too, is a positive instance. Although the concept could be the ability to fly or being an animal, the participant may guess that the relevant concept is being a bird. When the fourth picture presented is of a small blue toy car and the experimenter says that it is a negative instance (not an example of the concept), the participant can say with conviction that "bird" is the concept being presented.

The laboratory procedure we have just considered allows careful examination of how people form or recognize concepts. But concepts are not always clear-cut. For example, you know that a professor is a teacher and a high school instructor is a teacher, but are ministers teachers? How about den leaders of scout troops or the president of the United States? Each of these individuals acts as a teacher from time to time. Or, consider the concept "family." One concept of a family is mom, dad, and 2.4 kids. But what about single-parent families, blended families, adoptive families, communal families, single-gender families, and extended families? Some researchers consider a family to be any group of people who care about each other in significant ways. You can see that concepts are often fuzzy. You must think about such concepts carefully to understand and define them.

Eleanor Rosch has asserted that people tend to define *fuzzy concepts* through the use of prototypes, or best examples of the class of items (Rosch, 1978). A *prototype* is an abstraction, an idealized pattern of an object or idea that is stored in memory and used to decide whether similar objects or ideas are members of the same class of items. A high school English teacher may be a prototype of "teacher"; ministers, den leaders, and psychologists are also examples, but not best examples. Some concepts have easily defined prototypes; others are hard to define. When you think about the concept "furniture," you easily recognize that chairs, sofas, and

Prototype ■ An abstraction, an idealized pattern of an object or idea that is stored in memory and used to decide whether similar objects or ideas are members of the same class of items.

Problem solving ■ The behavior of individuals when confronted with a situation or task that requires insight or determination of some unknown elements.

Algorithm [AL-go-rith-um] ■ A procedure for solving a problem by implementing a set of rules over and over again until the solution is found.

tables are good examples (or exemplars). But telephones, stoves, pianos, and mirrors are all furniture as well; therefore, finding a prototype that truly embodies the essence of "furniture" is not an easy task. The concept "computer modem" is much less fuzzy; there may be a few shapes and sizes, but nearly all computer modems do the same thing, in pretty much the same way. Of course, many variables affect how easily concepts are defined, including the properties of the class of objects or ideas as well as an individual's unique experiences with the exemplars from that class. These experiences help people build strategies and solve problems.

Problem Solving

You are generally unaware of your cognitive processes; you don't usually think about thinking. And yet you are thinking all the time—sorting through choices, deciding where to go, what to do, and when to do it. Thinking encompasses a wide variety of activities, from daydreaming to planning your next few steps on a mountain path.

Most humans have learned many associations, have distinct memories, and are able to categorize and distinguish among objects, events, and concepts. We might, for example, have exemplars of various kinds of physics problems (or algebra or chemistry, for that matter). When presented with a new problem, we recall an example problem and see if its solution (or one very similar to it) will work. As another example, a coach who realizes that a zone defense works against weak offensive teams in basketball might use the same overall approach in football to solve the problem of how to keep an opposing team at bay. So, our concept formation abilities often form the basis for our problem-solving abilities.

Human beings are wonderful at *problem solving*—confronting and resolving situations that require insight or determination of some unknown elements. Because you can form concepts and group things together in logical ways, you are able to organize your thoughts and attack a problem. How can you manage to study for your psychology exam when you have an English paper due tomorrow? How can you fit all your clothes and other belongings into your tiny closet?

Coaches use heuristics when considering the plays they believe are most likely to succeed, based on past experience. A coach might ask, "What move has usually enhanced our strategic position in the game?"

What should you do when your car gets a flat tire on the interstate? These are all problems to be solved. Your approaches to these dilemmas represent some of the highest levels of cognitive functioning. Psychologists believe the process of problem solving has four general stages, summarized in **Figure 10.2** (e.g., Knoblich & Ohlsson, 1999).

There are huge differences in people's problem-solving abilities, but psychologists can help individuals improve their skills in this area. It turns out that when people (or machines, for that matter) solve problems, they tend to use two basic approaches: algorithms and heuristics. An *algorithm* is a procedure for solving a problem by implementing a set of rules over and over again until the solution is found. An algorithm, if

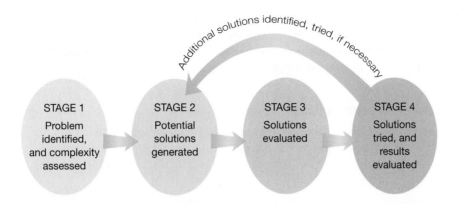

Additional solutions identified, tried, if necessary

STAGE 1

Problem identified, and complexity assessed

STAGE 2

Potential solutions generated

STAGE 3

Solutions evaluated

STAGE 4

Solutions tried, and results evaluated

Figure 10.2
Stages in Problem Solving
Problem solving can be conceived of as a four-stage process.

performed correctly, *guarantees* a correct solution. Many mathematics problems (for example, finding a square root) can be solved by using an algorithm. Algorithms are also used for a wide variety of real-life tasks, from increasing the yield of a recipe (say, by doubling each ingredient) to writing a computer program (even a relatively simple program requires several algorithms). To implement an algorithm, you follow rules that specify which task to implement at which point in the procedure. For example, an algorithm for doubling a recipe might be as follows: "Find the recipe's list of ingredients. Find the amount of a given ingredient, multiply that amount by 2, and use the product as the new amount for that ingredient. Repeat this procedure for each ingredient listed in the recipe." It's monotonous, but it works. However, because you *must* follow every step in an algorithm in order to use it, the time and effort required make algorithms impractical for some purposes. Human problem solvers learn to use rules of thumb so that they do not have to follow algorithms rigidly. These rules of thumb are integral to heuristic problem-solving strategies.

Heuristics are sets of strategies that serve as flexible guidelines—not strict rules and procedures—for discovery-oriented problem solving. A heuristic *may* lead you quickly to a correct solution, but it does not guarantee one. Heuristics reflect the processes used by the human brain; they involve making rough guesses and subjective evaluations that might be called hunches or intuitions. For example, the coach of a hockey team might evaluate the team's poor first-period performance and intuit that different plays might better its chances for a win. Such intuitions are highly accessible and relatively effortless compared to deliberate, thoughtful analysis (Kahneman, 2003); most types of heuristics, including intuitions, are adaptive (Bröder, 2003).

Most heuristics focus on the goal that is to be achieved. In one procedure called *subgoal analysis*, a problem is taken apart or broken down into several smaller steps, each of which has a subgoal. For example, the writing of an essay could be broken into subgoals such as formulating the problem, doing library research, and drafting an outline. In *means–end analysis*, a person compares the current situation or position with a desired goal (the *end*) to determine the most efficient way (the *means*) to get from one to the other—for example, she might recognize that getting out of debt means first cutting up her credit cards. The objective is to minimize the number of steps needed to reach the goal. A *backward search* involves working back from the goal, or endpoint, to the current position, in order to analyze the problem and reduce

Heuristics [hyoo-RISS-ticks] ◼ Sets of strategies that serve as flexible guidelines for discovery-oriented problem solving.

Subgoal analysis ◼ Heuristic procedure in which a problem is broken down into smaller steps, each of which has a subgoal.

Means–end analysis ◼ Heuristic procedure in which the problem solver compares the current situation or position with a desired goal to determine the most efficient way to get from one to the other.

Backward search ◼ Heuristic procedure in which a problem solver works back from the goal to the current position, in order to analyze the problem and reduce the steps needed to get to the goal.

the steps needed to get to the goal. Some problems are most easily solved by starting at the objective and working backward toward the beginning position. People often solve puzzles using this approach, because there are usually a smaller number of choices at the end than at the beginning of a puzzle.

Barriers to Problem Solving

People's problem-solving abilities vary, and they may be subject to certain limitations, among which are functional fixedness and mental set. Researchers study these limitations to gain a better understanding of the processes of problem solving.

Functional Fixedness: Cognition with Constraints

When my (L.L.'s) daughter Sarah was 4 years old, we went on a camping trip. It was raining, and she wanted to sleep in the car but complained that there was no pillow. I took her raincoat out of the back seat and rolled it up—it instantly became a pillow, and she slept soundly. When she complained about not having a pillow, Sarah was exhibiting a basic human characteristic—functional fixedness. *Functional fixedness* is the inability to see that an object can have a function other than its stated or usual one. When people are functionally fixed, they have limited their conceptual framework; they see too few functions for an object. In many ways, this fixedness constitutes a barrier to problem solving.

Functional fixedness ■ The inability to see that an object can have a function other than its stated or usual one.

Studies of functional fixedness show that the name given to an object or tool or its typical use often limits its function in people's minds (German & Defeyter, 2000). In a typical study, a research participant is presented with a task and provided with tools that can be used in various ways. One laboratory problem used to show functional fixedness is the two-string problem (see **Figure 10.3**). In this task, a person is put in a room that has two strings hanging from the ceiling and some objects lying on a table. The task is to tie the two strings together, but it is impossible to reach one string while holding the other. The only solution is to tie a weight (one of the objects on the table) to one string and set it swinging back and forth, then take hold of the second string and wait until the first string swings within reach. This task is difficult for some people, because their previous experiences with the objects on the table may prevent them from considering them as potential tools in an unusual situation.

Mental Set

Psychologists have found that most individuals are flexible in their approaches to solving problems. In other words, they do not use preconceived, or set, solutions but think about objects, people, and situations in new ways. A flexible approach would allow an astronaut to make a life-saving air-filtering device out of duct tape and other spare parts (as in a scene from the film *Apollo 13*). This kind of solution requires limber thought processes. However, sometimes people develop rigid approaches to certain types of problems (Wiley, 1998).

Mental set ■ Limited ways of thinking about possibilities and a tendency to approach situations the same way because that way worked in the past.

Creative thinking requires breaking out of one's *mental set*—limited ways of thinking about possibilities and a tendency to approach situations the same way because

Figure 10.3
The Two-String Problem
In the two-string problem, the person must set one string in motion in order to tie the strings together. The solution illustrates that sometimes, in order to solve problems, people need to overcome functional fixedness and use tools in new ways.

that way worked in the past. Having a mental set is the opposite of being creative. Prior experience predisposes a person to make a particular response in a given situation. In an increasingly complex and changing world, such limitations are problematic.

Another example of mental set is the basis of this well-known riddle. A boy is rushed into an emergency room at the local hospital. Dr. Suarez cries out, "That's my son! What happened?" A few seconds later, Dr. Sonnenschein looks at the same child and says something similar, such as "Oh no, my son!"

Whose child is he? Did the hospital make a mistake? Or is Dr. Suarez a woman who is married to Dr. Sonnenschein, a man? Or did a gay couple adopt the child? Mental sets about physicians and about the traditional composition of nuclear families limit the ability to solve this riddle easily.

Avoid Barriers: Be a Critical Thinker

Every day, you have to make judgments, classify ideas, and follow logic—that is, engage in reasoning—to solve problems. Being able to think critically will improve your reasoning and thus your problem-solving skills. In addition to the guidelines presented in Chapter 1, several other tips can make you a better critical thinker:

- *Don't fixate on availability*. Things that come to mind quickly are not necessarily the best solutions to problems. Don't choose the first answer just because it's there and it might apply (Kahneman, 2003).

- *Don't generalize too quickly*. Just because most elements in a group follow a pattern does not mean that all elements in the group will follow the pattern. For example, just because the florist removed the thorns from most of the red roses you bought for Valentine's Day does not mean he didn't miss one—watch out!
- *Don't settle for an easy solution*. People often settle for a solution that works, even though other solutions may work even better. Look at all the alternatives; try a totally different approach.
- *Don't choose a solution just because it fits preexisting ideas*. People often accept too quickly solutions that conform to their previously held views. This is a serious mistake for researchers, who need to be open to new ideas, a state of mind that often requires a conscious effort to look for alternative, and possibly better, answers or solutions.
- *Don't fail to consider any possible solution*. If you do not evaluate all of the available alternatives, you are likely to miss the correct, or most logical, answer.
- *Don't be emotional*. Sometimes people become emotionally tied to a specific idea, premise, or conviction. When this happens, the likelihood of being able to critically evaluate the evidence drops sharply. Critical thinkers are cool and evaluative, not headstrong and emotional; they work through all the options analytically.

For example, suppose an actor is to appear in the first scene of a local theater company production. He needs to be at the theater long before the performance will begin, but he waits until the last minute to leave, and then finds that his car won't start. He panics and becomes fixated on getting the car going—he spends precious minutes repeatedly trying to start it, looking under the hood and fiddling with wires; next, he wastes more time calling his mechanic (who doesn't answer), and then he goes back to frantically trying to start the car. Emotion has triumphed over reason. Some cool-headed evaluation of the situation would allow the actor to realize that there are workable alternative solutions to his problem: riding his bike, calling a cab, asking a neighbor or a friend for a lift, or even, as a last resort, thumbing a ride.

Creative Problem Solving

The owners of a high-rise professional building were deluged with complaints that the building's elevators were too slow. The owners called in a consultant, who researched the problem and discovered that, indeed, tenants often had to wait several minutes for an elevator. Putting in new, faster elevators would cost tens of thousands of dollars, more than the owners could afford. Eventually, the consultant devised a creative solution that ended the complaints but cost only a few hundred dollars: He installed a mirror on the wall at each elevator stop. Evidently, being able to check out one's appearance while waiting made the time go faster.

Picasso's creativity broke the traditional mold for painting; furniture designer Mies van der Rohe, composer Phillip Glass, architect Frank Lloyd Wright, and Olympic ice skater Oksana Baiul did the same in their own fields. *Creativity* is the ability, related to thought and problem solving, to generate or recognize high-quality ideas that are original, novel, and appropriate, along with the tendency to do so (Sternberg, 2001b). An *original response* to a problem is one that doesn't copy or

Creativity ■ The ability to generate or recognize high-quality ideas that are original, novel, and appropriate, along with the tendency to do so.

imitate another response; that is, it originates from the problem solver. A *novel response* is a response that is new or that has no precedent. Unless an original and novel response is also an appropriate response to a given problem, however, psychologists do not call it creative. An *appropriate response* is a response that is reasonable in terms of the situation. Two important questions that researchers are studying are how people can become more creative in their thinking and who is likely to be creative (Mumford et al., 2001; Sternberg, 2000a).

According to well-known creativity researcher Mihalay Csikszentmihalyi (pronounced "chick-sent-ME-high"), creative individuals are those who have changed the surrounding culture in some way that involves original thinking. Csikszentmihalyi (2001) asserts that creativity is the process of redefining or transforming a domain (a professional field or an area of interest, such as gardening, music, or painting) or creating a new domain. But he also acknowledges, and indeed stresses, that individuals work and create within a culture; creativity is culture dependent—it is often measured as a work product in Western cultures but often seen as a process of finding inner truth in Eastern ones (Lubart, 1999).

When people sort through alternatives to try to solve a problem, they attempt to focus their thinking, discarding inappropriate solutions until a single appropriate option is left. In this way, they *converge* on an answer (or use convergent thinking skills). *Convergent thinking* involves narrowing down choices and alternatives to arrive at a suitable solution. *Divergent thinking*, in contrast, means widening the range of possibilities and expanding the options for solutions; doing so lessens the likelihood of being limited by functional fixedness or mental set. Guilford (1967) defined creative thinking as divergent thinking. According to other psychologists, any solution to a problem that can be worked out by anyone given enough time and practice is not a creative solution.

To foster creativity, people need to rethink their whole approach to a task. Successful executives and entrepreneurs know this to be the case, and those who develop new technologies, products, and services are often well rewarded for their creativity. One technique for stimulating creative problem solving is brainstorming. In *brainstorming*, people consider all possible solutions without making any initial judgments about the worth of those solutions. This procedure can be used to generate alternative solutions to problems as diverse as how a city can dispose of its waste and what topic should be selected for a group project. The rationale behind brainstorming is that people will produce more high-quality ideas if they do not have to evaluate the suggestions immediately. Brainstorming attempts to release the creative potential of the participants so as to increase the diversity of ideas; it is especially useful in generating hypotheses about solving problems (McGlynn et al., 2004). Related to brainstorming is *brainsketching*, in which people sketch their ideas on large sheets of paper—not necessarily better than brainstorming, this alternative mechanism serves basically the same purpose (van der Lugt, 2002)

Convergent thinking ■ In problem solving, the process of narrowing down choices and alternatives to arrive at a suitable solution.

Divergent thinking ■ In problem solving, the process of widening the range of possibilities and expanding the options for solutions.

Brainstorming ■ A problem-solving technique that involves considering all possible solutions without any initial judgments about the worth of those solutions.

Expertise in Problem Solving

There is a difference between people who are creative problem solvers and those who are expert problem solvers. Creative problem solvers often use domain-free knowledge—they just have good overall, creative strategies for problem solving.

Expert problem solvers have domain- or area-specific knowledge, which is often—but not always—an advantage (Wiley, 1998). The idea is that experts (such as experts in computers or auto maintenance) have spent hundreds of hours learning everything they can about their specific area of interest (computers or cars). They can often see nuances that a novice won't be aware of. Their problem solving is "grounded" in experience and training.

The Investment Theory of Creativity

Psychologist Robert Sternberg has developed a novel approach to studying creativity. He argues that a problem solver can use a number of interactive resources: intelligence, thinking style, knowledge, personality, motivation, and environment. Sometimes problem solving requires promoting an idea; other times it involves inventing a new solution or challenging pre-existing ideas. Some people use their creativity to develop a solution that others have ignored or dismissed when dealing with a problem. These creative thinkers may later promote, or "sell," their idea, and their independent work may pay off. This notion of working on undervalued problem solutions and marketing them to others for implementation led Sternberg to call this approach an *investment theory of creativity* (Sternberg & Lubart, 1999). Sternberg contrasts this approach with the traditional definition of creativity as resulting from exceptionally high levels of certain personality attributes. To be creative, you have to be intelligent and willing to redefine problems, analyze ideas, take some sensible risks, see clever connections between ideas, and convince other people that the ideas are good—unexamined ideas produce little societal change (Sternberg, 2001a). Thus, creativity relies to some extent on reasoning, our next topic.

How Do We Reason and Make Decisions?

Whether to go for a run at lunchtime, have a sandwich and a soft drink, or catch up on my email is a daily decision for me (L.L.). Each choice carries with it benefits, and each has costs. Because I make this decision day in and day out, however, the process usually occurs quickly. And more often than not, I choose the sandwich and drink over the other options. But how do I make this and other decisions? When cognitive psychologists study *thinking*, they generally attempt to study the systematic day-to-day processes of reasoning and decision making. *Reasoning* is the purposeful process by which a person generates logical and coherent ideas, evaluates situations, and reaches conclusions. The system of principles of reasoning that is used to reach valid conclusions or make inferences is called *logic*. Reasoning can be either a highly ordered process or a relatively unstructured one in which ideas and beliefs are continuously updated—both types of reasoning are valid and useful.

> **Reasoning** ■ The purposeful process by which a person generates logical and coherent ideas, evaluates situations, and reaches conclusions.

> **Logic** ■ The system of principles of reasoning that is used to reach valid conclusions or make inferences.

> **Decision making** ■ Assessing and choosing among alternatives.

Decision making means assessing and choosing among alternatives. Some decisions involve determining the probability of some event (Will my friends want to go on this trip with me?); others involve assessing expected value (How important is this trip to me?). Your decisions vary from the trivial to the complex—what to eat for breakfast, which courses to take, what career to pursue. The trivial decisions are usually made quickly, without much effort or even conscious thought. The complex ones require conscious, deliberate, effortful consideration.

Imagine a person who decides to become a physician. The person recognizes that to achieve this goal, she has to get good grades in high school, get into a good college, prepare well, get terrific grades, and potentially do volunteer work. Figuring out how to achieve all this is problem solving—discovering the best way to get to a goal. In decision making, you make a choice between at least two alternatives—for example, between going to law school and going to medical school, or perhaps between two good medical schools in different parts of the country. Some students have trouble with the distinction between problem solving and decision making. Think of it like this: Both focus on reaching a good rational solution, but problem solving involves generating your own options and choosing the best one, while decision making often involves narrowing down options presented to you.

Psychologists have devised numerous approaches for looking at decision-making processes. Let's first consider estimating probabilities, an approach used in situations in which the answer or decision is uncertain.

Uncertainty: Estimating Probabilities

How do people decide what to wear, where to go on vacation, or how to answer a question on the SAT? How do they decide when something is bigger, longer, or more difficult than something else? Many decisions are based on formal logic, some on carefully tested hypotheses, and some on educated guesses. An *educated guess* is one based on knowledge gained from past experience—often using a prototype (discussed earlier in this chapter). When you see dark thunderheads, for example, you may guess that it will rain (perhaps, in your mind, a prototypical rainy day begins with dark thunderheads)—but you cannot be 100% sure. Weather forecasts express the likelihood of rain as a percentage—that is, as a probability, based on past experiences.

People make probability estimates about all types of events and behaviors. They guess about the likelihood of a Democratic or a Republican victory in an election or about their favorite team's chances in the playoffs. On the basis of past experience, they estimate the probability that they will stay on their diet or get stuck in a traffic jam on the way to work. People can judge whether a particular event increases or decreases the probability of another event. When several factors are involved, they may either compound or mitigate one another to alter the probability of an outcome. For example, the probability that there will be rain when there are dark clouds, high winds, and low barometric pressure is much higher than the probability of rain when it is merely cloudy.

Research participants asked to make probability judgments about the real world, particularly about fairly rare events such as airplane crashes, are less likely to make accurate judgments than are participants who are given problems in a laboratory (Chase, 2000). In the real world, people do not always behave logically; because of their mood or lack of attention, they may act irrationally, ignore key pieces of data, and thus make bad (or irrational) decisions that are not based on probability. The further in the future an event is, and the more variables that could come into play, the more likely people will be to make bad predictions (Olsen, 1997). Sometimes, people's worldviews color their decision making. For example, having strong religious or political views can influence a person's probability estimates.

Finally, people are not machines or computers; their past experiences, personalities, and cultural backgrounds can influence their thought processes—sometimes in unpredictable ways. However, cognitive psychologists have discovered ways for individuals to become more efficient learners and thinkers; they have found that people can be taught to weigh costs and benefits more accurately and to be less influenced by their frames of reference (Bayster & Ford, 2000; Blount & Larrick, 2000). One way to break out of limiting frames of reference is to use analogies. When researchers examined how students could best learn scientific concepts, they found analogies and metaphors to be especially useful. Students can learn factual details well through traditional teaching methods, but analogies—especially creative ones—provide conceptual bridges that facilitate learning of unfamiliar or complex concepts. Such conceptual bridges facilitate decision making, but what are the barriers to good decisions?

Barriers to Sound Decision Making

Just as people's problem solving can be hampered by mental sets, their decision making can be hindered by certain kinds of stumbling blocks. By studying and learning about those limitations, it is possible to overcome some of them.

The Gambler's Fallacy

Gambler's fallacy ■ The belief that the chances of an event's occurring increase if the event has not recently occurred.

If you know about probability, you know that people have misconceptions about the probabilities of events. One common misconception is the *gambler's fallacy*—the belief that the chances of an event's occurring increase if the event has not recently occurred. This fallacy has brought millions of dollars to the casinos of Las Vegas and Atlantic City. In reality, *every time* you flip a coin, the chance of getting heads is 1 in 2, or 0.5—regardless of what happened on the last flip, or the last ten flips. And *every pull* of a slot machine handle has the same likelihood of making you a winner, regardless of what happened—or didn't happen—on the last pull. And even when people are given explicit instruction and knowledge about such outcomes, they continue to bet and to invoke the gambler's fallacy (Boynton, 2003).

Belief in Small Numbers

Belief in small numbers ■ The willingness to draw conclusions from a small sample and to assume that such a sample is representative.

Limiting the number of observations we make because of the belief in small numbers also contributes to poor decision making. The *belief in small numbers* is the willingness to draw conclusions from a small sample and to assume that such a sample is representative. A small sample of observations is likely to be highly variable and not reflective of the larger population. However, the truth is that people are willing to draw conclusions from a small sample—say, ten neighbors—and assume that such a sample is representative of an entire town, state, or country.

The Availability Heuristic

Although my (L.L.'s) wife knows that flying in planes is quite safe—safer than walking through the parking lot of a nearby shopping mall—she is still hesitant to fly for fear of an (unlikely) malfunction and subsequent crash. Like my wife, most people overestimate the probability of unusual events occurring in their lives and may make poor decisions based on those probabilities. The overestimation of this probability is largely due to the wide media attention given to infrequent catastrophic events; information about them is more available than information about other events, and it is easy to think of examples. Thus, people often exhibit the *availability heuristic*—the tendency to judge the probability of an event by how easy it is to think of examples of it (Cioffi, 2001; Oppenheimer, 2004). The number of fatalities due to plane crashes, tornadoes, and encounters with icebergs is overestimated, given the actual rate of occurrence of these events (Perrow, 1999). For example, Americans are far more likely to be in a car crash than to be bitten by a shark (over 6 million car accidents occur in the United States annually but fewer than 60 shark attacks); yet people have nightmares and worry excessively about the shark attacks.

Availability heuristic ■ The tendency to judge the probability of an event by how easy it is to think of examples of it.

Overconfidence Phenomenon

People often overestimate the soundness of their judgments and the accuracy of their knowledge. Such overconfidence is another major stumbling block to sound decision making. The *overconfidence phenomenon* occurs when individuals are so committed to their ideas and beliefs, especially political ones, that they are often more certain than correct and, when challenged, may become even more rigid and inflexible. For example, a person who believes that the only solution to local traffic problems is to construct new roads may refuse to even consider mass transit as an alternative solution. Imagine the surprise of a student when he was rejected from the only law school he applied to. He neglected to apply to other schools because he was sure—convinced—that he would get into his first choice.

Overconfidence phenomenon ■ The tendency of individuals who are highly committed to their ideas and beliefs, especially political ones, to be more certain than correct and, when challenged, to become even more rigid and inflexible.

The Confirmation Bias and Belief Perseverance

Perhaps the greatest barrier to making good decisions is the tendency to cling to beliefs despite contradictory evidence; psychologists call this phenomenon the *confirmation bias*—the tendency of people to discount information that does not fit with their pre-existing views. People rarely dwell on the fact that they missed an opportunity to save money by purchasing an inexpensive car; more often, they seek to confirm their good judgment by boasting that they bought a terrific, well-made piece of machinery. As you will see when we study social psychology in Chapter 14, reliance on past experience and reluctance to seek (or listen to) information that might disconfirm one's beliefs leads to stereotypes and prejudices that are often ill-informed and wrong. This phenomenon is closely related to *belief perseverance*—people's tendency, once they have decided to believe something, to keep on accepting it as true, even in the face of conflicting data.

Confirmation bias ■ The tendency of people to discount information that does not fit with their pre-existing views.

Belief perseverance ■ People's tendency, once they have decided to believe something, to keep on accepting it as true, even in the face of conflicting data.

Culture and Reasoning

Problem solving, reasoning, and decision making are universal thought processes. Everybody experiences difficult situations and tough decisions and faces barriers to good decision making and problem solving. But we don't all go about reasoning in the same way.

It turns out that the intellectual traditions of the East and the West are quite different, and so are the reasoning and decision-making approaches of people with different cultural backgrounds (Peng & Nisbett, 1999). For example, when given contradictory statements to rationalize, people from China prefer to compromise; European Americans prefer not to compromise. Chinese tradition holds that reality is a process, that it does not stand still but is in constant flux. That tradition recognizes that there are contradictions in life and accepts that such contradictions must be embraced. It further asserts that all things are in one way or another connected. Western European and American traditions use reasoning that is analytical and logical. Reality is considered objective, fixed, and identifiable; it is also precise and constant, and many aspects of it are independent of one another. So when Easterners and Westerners are seeking to solve a trade conflict, a border dispute, or an immigration problem, their traditions may collide, at least at first. Easterners may see ambiguities and may allow for a "sometimes yes, sometimes no" solution; Westerners often see things in black and white and are unwilling to accept compromises.

Such different worldviews affect how people in the East and the West solve problems; they think about problems differently. Therefore, it should not be surprising that the behaviors of Eastern business leaders, politicians, and soldiers puzzle Westerners. Psychologists will learn more about cognition by studying such cultural variation. One potentially illuminating line of research will be to study multicultural individuals. How does a person who is raised in one culture but then moves to another reason? How long will she live in the new culture before she adopts a new mode of thinking? Is it even possible for people to switch modes of thinking? While cultural identity is learned at a very young age (Tomasello, 2000), Hong and colleagues (2000) have found that people are able to adjust their thinking, especially about recently acquired ideas. Much more study of multicultural individuals, who constitute a growing segment of the world's population, is likely to be carried out in the future. Another area that will be explored more fully is how thought and reasoning develop and to what extent the ability to reason is determined by genetics and evolution.

Evolution and Reasoning

How do evolutionary theorists and researchers account for reasoning? Remember that evolutionary psychologists assume that people have specific abilities because those abilities have helped them be fit, survive, and reproduce. The world is a complex place, and people are faced with many decisions. Evolutionary psychologists believe that humans have built-in mechanisms to help them sift through information and make decisions, especially those decisions that are most relevant for survival and reproduction. Most psychologists believe that cognition is shaped by general mechanisms, or processes, which are ways of handling information that apply to situations both simple and complex—finding a misplaced key or finding a cure for a disease. Evolutionary psychologists, in contrast, argue that human brains have specific "programs," or specialized ways of handling certain information, that shape cognition and reasoning (Cosmides & Tooby, 1997; Lickliter & Honeycutt, 2003). Thus, some of our reasoning is determined by the type of information processing that our brains are set up to do. This type of reasoning is easier for us than other types, such as the reasoning required by certain logic problems.

The evolutionary perspective has been widely discussed, and researchers debate how the environment and learning may interact with evolution and genetics to give rise to thought, language, and concept formation (Geary & Huffman, 2002; Lickliter & Honeycutt, 2003). Some evolutionary psychologists assert that cognitive psychologists have focused too much on problems that are difficult for humans, such as analogies and syllogisms, and have paid too little attention to the types of reasoning the human brain is programmed to do, such as figuring out how to use a tool or drawing a map to find a source of food.

What Does Artificial Intelligence Reveal about Cognition?

Because human beings invented computers, it is not surprising that computers handle information in much the same way the human brain does—though the brain has far more options and strategies for information processing than a computer does. By simulating specific models of the brain, computers help psychologists understand human thought processes. For example, computers help in developing hypotheses about information processing and perception, in investigating how people solve problems, and in testing models of certain aspects of behavior, such as memory. Computers also perform many tasks that humans find too time-consuming or complicated. Computer programs that mimic some type of human cognitive activities are said to apply *artificial intelligence (AI)*, the branch of computer science concerned with making a device or machine (a computer) behave like a human being, especially in reasoning abilities. While many computers have been trained to play games and exhibit language-like abilities, no computer exhibits full artificial intelligence.

Artificial intelligence (AI) ▪ The branch of computer science concerned with making a device or machine (a computer) behave like a human being, especially in reasoning abilities.

The Computer as Information Processor

The information-processing approach to perception, memory, and problem solving is a direct outgrowth of computer simulations. The *information-processing approach* proposes that information is processed and stored in three stages of memory (refer back to Chapter 9). According to this approach, information is processed in a sequential manner as it moves from one stage to the next. Flowcharts showing how information from sensory memory reaches short-term storage and then long-term memory rely implicitly on a computer analogy. Those who study memory extend the computer analogy further by referring to storage areas as "buffers" and information-processing mechanisms as "central processors." Although popular, the information-processing approach has come under attack because it tends to reduce complex memory processes to simple mechanistic elements.

Information-processing approach ▪ A model of human memory that proposes that information is processed and stored in three stages, moving in a sequential manner from one stage to the next.

The most widely investigated aspect of artificial intelligence is problem solving. The problem most often addressed is the game of chess. Researchers use chess for two key reasons. First, the solution is well defined—to capture the king—and thus, the scope of the problem is clear. Second, by understanding how humans and machines solve a relatively straightforward problem like chess, researchers hope to generalize and gain insights into more complex forms of problem solving.

Playing chess was one of the first human activities that researchers tried to duplicate with computers. Ever since then, human beings like master chess player Garry Kasparov have been challenging computers for dominance—with some modest successes and some notable failures. Computers have been programmed to play other games, such as checkers and backgammon, and to solve simple number-completion tasks. They can also solve complicated problems involving large amounts of memory, such as deciphering the tens of thousands of genes in the human genome. The most sophisticated computer programs mimic aspects of human memory and decision making and have been used to solve a wide array of problems, including those involved in the design of computer chips and the management of human resources (Lawler & Elliot, 1996).

Although computers can be programmed to process information the way human beings do, they lack human ingenuity and imagination. In addition, computers cannot interpret information by referring to or analyzing its context.

Neural Networks

One of the most interesting areas of research in cognitive psychology is focusing on the brain's ability to represent information in a number of locations simultaneously. Take a moment and think of a computer. You may conjure up an image of an IBM or a Macintosh, a laptop or a mainframe. You may also start thinking about programming code, monitor screens, or even your favorite computer game. Your images of a computer and representations of what it can do are stored and coded at different places in your brain. That is, you don't have a "computer corner," where all information about computers is stored. Since the various pieces of information are stored in different parts of your brain, they must be combined at some point, in some way, for you to use the word *computer*, understand it, and visualize what it stands for.

According to University of Iowa researcher Antonio Damasio (Adolphs & Damasio, 2000; Damasio, 2000; Parvizi & Damasio, 2001), a *convergence zone*, or center, is what mediates and organizes information from various brain locations. Signals from widely separated clusters of neurons come together in convergence zones to evoke words and allow a person to develop sentences and fully process ideas and images about the subject at hand. That convergence zones are not located in the same place as specific pieces of information helps explain why some stroke victims and patients with brain lesions (injuries) can tell you some things about a given subject—say, pianos—but not everything they once knew. For example, a stroke victim may look at a picture of a piano and be able to tell you that it has keys and pedals but be unable to say that it is a picture of a piano. According to Damasio's view, in such a case, a key convergence zone has been corrupted.

The idea of convergence zones has led to the development of models of how the brain represents the world, develops concepts, solves problems, and performs day-to-day tasks like reading and listening (Posner & Pavese, 1998). It also helps explain why a person whose visual cortex has been damaged (who has incurred localized brain damage) can sometimes have knowledge of things that she or he is unaware of having seen (Place, 2000; Ward & Jackson, 2002). For example, a patient may be unable to see objects, but if pressed to guess at their location may point at them with reasonable accuracy. This residual vision—sometimes referred to as *blindsight*—is attributed to secondary, less important visual pathways, although people with blindsight often claim to be merely "guessing." Such knowledge of the world—showing a reliance on multiple sources of input—supports the existence of convergence zones and levels of processing.

In recent years, mathematicians, physiologists, and psychologists have joined forces to develop specific models of how neural structures represent complicated information (e.g., Crosson, 2000). Their work is often based on the concept of *parallel distributed processing* (PDP), the idea that many operations take place simultaneously and at many locations within the brain. Most personal computers can perform only one operation at a time—admittedly very quickly, but still only one at a time. In contrast, the largest of modern computers operate hundreds or even thousands of processors at once. These supercomputers perform many operations simultaneously (in parallel) to solve problems. PDP models of the human brain assert that it too can process many events simultaneously, store them, and compare them to past events. PDP models also incorporate perception and learning: Data from studies of eye movements, hearing, the tactile senses, and pattern recognition are combined into a coherent view of how the brain integrates information to make it meaningful. PDP models even allow for nodes, units, or (in Damasio's terminology) convergence zones that store or process different types of information in different ways.

To study parallel distributed processing, researchers have devised artificial neural networks. These networks are typically composed of interconnected units that serve as model neurons. Each unit, or artificial neuron, receives signals that vary in intensity just like the signals that are received by a real neuron. Activity generated by a unit is transmitted as a single outgoing signal to other units. Both input to and output from units can be varied, as can the interconnections among units. Units can be connected in layers, and the output of one layer may be the input to another.

Researchers often use computers to create electronic neural networks that simulate specific activities. For example, some electronic neural networks have sophisticated pattern-recognition abilities and can recognize handwritten letters and other simple patterns. In addition, such a network can learn to recognize a range of forms that look like specific letters—say, the letter A. In this case, the network applies a *prototype*—a standard or a generalized pattern. Prototypes constitute the basis of the network's form and letter perception.

An interesting aspect of networks is what happens when one portion of a network is destroyed. The network does not crash, as a hard drive in a computer does, but it makes some mistakes, much as the brain would. When portions of the brain are surgically destroyed or removed or injured in an accident, the person is still able to complete some tasks. (Remember the split-brain patients who could name an object presented to one hemisphere but could only point to the object presented to the other hemisphere—refer to Figure 3.10.)

Neural networks learn by changing the connections between their units in response to the level of activity and intensity of signals. Sophisticated networks learn quickly and easily and modify their connections based on experience. Also, most neural network models suggest that those units that are frequently activated will have a lower threshold of activation and will be more easily accessed in the future. This access is part of the retrieval process; easy access means easy retrieval, and both are dependent on clear, unambiguous learning. Thus, a network that has learned a game may learn a similar game more easily, faster, and with fewer errors.

Controlling robots with brain waves is no longer science fiction: Researchers have implanted electrodes that allow this type of monkey to control this robotic arm.

Robotics

Imagine a mechanical soldier with the brains of a human being, the strength of a tank, and a willingness to do what ever it is told. Perhaps you could think of such a soldier as a robot. People have always been fascinated by the idea of robotic devices that could do things for them. This idea is becoming a reality. One team of researchers trained monkeys to manipulate a joystick that operates a robot. This is not new, but what is new is that the researchers implanted electrodes in the brains of the monkeys and hooked the electrodes to the robot (Carmena et al., 2003). After the monkeys were trained with the joystick, the joystick was removed. The monkeys were able, simply by thinking, to generate signals that made the robotic arm move.

What about human beings? Could a robotic device work with humans who are paralyzed and unable to perform ordinary chores or drive an automobile? Some researchers (e.g., Carmena et al., 2003) propose that a paralyzed person could indeed be helped to function by such a device, and that ultimately, skilled operation will lead users to perceive the device as an integral part of their own bodies. This is a dream for the future, but so was landing on the moon at one time.

Although robots can operate efficiently and can already perform some tasks they do not have the creativity and personality that human beings possess. They lack a sense of humor and the ingenuity that arises from perseverance, motivation, and intelligence. And neural networks help us understand human cognition, reasoning, and language acquisition, but they merely provide models of these human activities. As you will see in the next section, language in particular is enormously complex, with built-in components, and is considered by most researchers to be uniquely human.

What Is the Structure of Language?

When someone says "cat," how do you know she is referring to a four-legged furry creature? Are you sure she is referring to an animal? Or might she be saying "cap"—as in headgear? Perhaps she said "cab," meaning a taxi? The truth is, you know she is referring to a pet because of the context in which the word is used; context clues allow you to decide whether the utterance was *cat* or *cap* or *cab*. They sound similar, but the sentence the word is used in, the discussion that preceded the use of the word, and the setting where the word is used all help you identify it correctly. Linguists have a name for the study of how the social context in which words are used affects their meaning—*pragmatics*.

A *language* is a system of symbols, usually words, that convey meaning; in addition to the symbols, a language also has rules for combining symbols to generate an infinite number of messages, usually sentences. The key elements of this definition are that language is symbolic, rule-governed, used to represent meaning, and *generative*—that is, it allows an infinite number of messages to be created. Language is clearly rule governed—the rules are called *grammar* (more on it later). And knowledge of a language's rules allows a user to generate an almost infinite number of meaningful ideas and sentences (Premack, 2004). Further, languages can be examined at multiple levels (the level of sounds, words, or sentences), and they are in a constant state of change. In English, for example, we add new words and convert nouns into verbs, as in "Let's TiVo *American Idol* tonight" or "I'll Google him."

Acquiring, processing, and producing language are essentially human capabilities: All normal human beings speak; no nonhuman animal does. Many animals use signs of various kinds, but none uses language. Think about how amazing it is that we can refer to objects that are not present or that don't even exist; we are able to talk about abstractions such as future career goals, places we want to see, and concepts such as justice and creativity that have no distinct physical reality. No other form of communication used by any other animal (not whales, dolphins, bees, or chimps) allows these things. Not surprisingly, the uniqueness of language suggests an evolutionary heritage (Fitch & Hauser, 2004).

For most of us, language is first conveyed through spoken words, and then later in writing. But it is important to remember that other means of communication also exist. For example, many deaf individuals communicate through American Sign Language, or ASL. ASL is visual rather than auditory; it is a system of precise hand shapes and movements. It is the native language of many deaf men and women, as well as some hearing children born to deaf parents. Like spoken languages, ASL is capable of communicating subtle, complex, and abstract ideas. It has its own distinct grammatical structure that is not like that of English. In fact, ASL has more in common with spoken Japanese than it does with English. The rules and grammar of ASL must be mastered in the same way as the grammar of any other language; ASL is a true human language, fully distinct from spoken languages, with its own literature and culture.

Languages reflect people's cultures; they allow individuals within a culture to share ideas and values almost effortlessly. Thus, language is a social tool. Language takes place in a context, and the same words can have different meanings depending

Pragmatics ■ The study of how the social context in which words are used affects their meaning.

Language ■ A system of symbols, usually words, that convey meaning, along with a set of rules for combining the symbols to generate an infinite number of messages, usually sentences.

on who says them and when, whether they are said with a smile, with a grunt, or in a song (Trimble, 2000). Language is often also expressed with gestures. The French and the Italians are well known for speaking with their hands when excited.

Recognizing that language and culture are intertwined, some researchers have wondered whether two people who speak the same language but use different expressions to describe the same event or situation actually think about the world in different ways. Does language determine thought, or do all people think alike, regardless of their language (Premack, 2004)? Is language gendered? Ultimately, what is the influence of culture on language? Let's start by looking at gender and language.

Language and Gender Stereotypes

In general, the English language has evolved in such a way that its words define many roles as male, except for certain traditionally female roles (nurses, teachers) that are considered softer, weaker, and less powerful (Lakoff, 2000). However, in churches, synagogues, and mosques around the country, people are trying out, and getting used to, gender-neutral language. In some liturgies, God is no longer referred to as "father," and "forefathers" are called "ancestors." Research shows that such changes affect listeners' responses to liturgy and sermons (Wharry, 2003).

Language with a sexist bias expresses stereotypes and role expectations about men and women. For example, men are often described using active, positive words (*successful, strong, independent,* and *courageous*). Women have traditionally been described with words implying passiveness (such as *gentle, loving,* or *patient*), or even with negative terms (*the weaker sex, timid, frail*). Even in the 21st century, some people still consider it incongruous to use words like "strong" and "courageous" to describe a woman, and when they want to compliment a woman for being logical or decisive, they say, "She thinks like a man."

Lakoff (2000) asserts that many people still see the world through a gendered frame of reference—usually a male one—and that male values are assumed to be preferable. This frame of reference affects and is affected by language. Research supports the idea that men and women are perceived, referred to and treated differently; furthermore, they speak differently (Ladegaard & Bleses, 2003). If people believe in and speak of gender-specific abilities, they are likely to apply that belief to their decision making. Frable (1989) found that people with strong gender-typed ideas were especially likely to pay attention to the gender of job applicants and then to devalue the interview performance of the women.

Gender differences in language use are usually context-dependent—the differences between men and women's use of language must be considered within a larger context involving ethnicity, class, age, social norms, personality, and even marital status (Tannen, 2003). For example, research shows that women pay more compliments than men; in talk with same-sex peers, women use many more "politeness" strategies than men do; women are also more likely than men to apologize, to soften criticism, or to express thanks (Hobbs, 2003). Deborah Tannen (2002) suggests that when people become aware of their style of language use, they become more effective communicators. For example, in talk within a family, it is crucial to learn to separate word meanings, or messages, from deeper meanings, or what Tannen refers to as "heart meanings," or "metamessages." According to Tannen, these unstated but powerful meanings that come from the history of relationships and the way things are said are often gendered. Tannen further asserts that growing up male or female (or as an older or younger sibling) results in different language experiences that persist throughout life. Research shows that people can adapt their language style depending on whom they talk to; that is, they "gender" their language depending on whether the listener is a man or a woman (Thomson, Murachver, & Green, 2001).

Although gender stereotypes persist, some women and men accept the value of *androgyny,* behavior and attitudes that incorporate qualities traditionally considered masculine as well as those traditionally considered feminine. People are becoming more accepting of individuals whose behaviors or roles are not gender-stereotyped, for example, men who are nurses and women who are engineers. Even more important, people are becoming more sensitive to how language shapes their concept of the world and their problem-solving abilities.

Androgyny ■ Behavior and attitudes that incorporate qualities traditionally considered masculine as well as those traditionally considered feminine.

Thought, Culture, and Language

In the 1950s, researchers thought that language shaped thinking. In the view of some researchers, the structure of the language that people speak directly determines their thoughts and perceptions. But consider the perception of odors: Human beings are very sensitive to odors; we can detect them easily, and we can think about them. But odors are difficult to describe. We have a limited language structure to describe them, and our descriptions are often based on personal experiences and sometimes reflect a biographical event—for example, we might say that something smells like Aunt Maria's attic. The language used to describe odors is determined by factors other than simply olfactory perceptions. In other words, language may influence thought, but language does not determine thought.

Certainly language and thought interact. And culture has a great influence on both. In France, for example, fairly rigid linguistic customs reflect hundreds of years of history; so, in the French language, there are formal and informal means of address. With friends, for example, the word for "you" is *tu;* in more formal settings, one uses *vous.* Japan has even greater culturally determined distinctions in formality of language; who a person is in the workplace—boss, manager, supervisor, worker—affects how he or she is addressed and whether he or she will be shown deference. (In Chapter 18, we will consider workplace psychology in more detail.)

As Matsumoto (2000) asserts, language and culture are intertwined. Along with studies of culture, we know that language does not determine thought, but rather, subtly influences it. Thoughts about ideas and events help shape language, which is used to express those thoughts. And the language people speak is influenced by an unspoken but agreed-to set of rules for conversation. For example, conversationalists take turns, they stick to a topic, they are informative (not too informative), they say what is true and do not exaggerate, and they are clear, brief, and try not to interrupt (Grice, Cole, & Morgan, 1975). These implicit conversational rules are learned over time, and they are heavily affected by culture (Cutting, 2001; Louis & Taylor, 2001). Think about conversations between Nia Vardalos's character Toula and her family in *My Big Fat Greek Wedding*—the implicit rules for conversation in her family all focused around her Windex-bearing father Gus Portokalos. When helping people from different cultures, therapists must be sensitive to their use of language and that of their clients—a topic we will consider in Chapter 17.

Americans are in a minority, in that most speak only one language; in other developed countries, many people are bilingual or multilingual. Although bilingualism promotes cognitive flexibility, research shows that when bilingual people are asked to respond to a question, take a personality test, or otherwise interact in the world, they do so in a culturally bound way—depending on the language in which they respond. For example, when responding to a personality inventory or to a list of physical symptoms, native speakers of Chinese are likely to reflect Chinese values if the test or list is written in Chinese; their responses to an English version of the same personality test or list are more likely to reflect Western values (Dinges, Atlis, & Vincent 1997). However, it is worth noting that when children are raised in a bilingual home, the acquisition of early reading skills in either language is not affected in any fundamental way (Lesaux & Siegel, 2003; Nicol & Greth, 2003).

Linguistics

Linguistics [ling-GWIS-ticks] ■ The study of language, including speech sounds, meaning, and grammar.

Psycholinguistics ■ The study of how language is acquired, perceived, understood, and produced.

Linguistics is the study of language, including speech sounds, meaning, and grammar. *Psycholinguistics* is the study of how language is acquired, perceived, understood, and produced. Among other things, psycholinguists seek to discover how children so readily learn the complicated rules necessary to speak correctly. Psycholinguistic studies dating back to the early 1970s show that children first acquire the simple aspects of language and then learn progressively more complex elements and capabilities. Studies have also revealed *linguistic structures*—the rules and regularities that exist in a language and make it possible to learn it.

Language Structure

We'll examine three major components of a language: *phonology*, the study of the sounds of language; *semantics*, the study of the meanings of words and sentences; and *syntax*, the study of the relationships among words and how they combine to form sentences. In each of these areas, researchers have tried to identify universal characteristics that apply to all languages, not just English.

Phonology

Phonology ■ The study of the patterns and distribution of speech sounds in a language and the commonly accepted rules for their pronunciation.

The gurgling, spitting, and burping noises infants first make are caused by air passing through the vocal apparatus. At about 6 weeks, infants begin to make speechlike cooing sounds. During their first 12 months, babies' vocalizations become more varied and frequent, until they eventually become words. As psychologists have studied people's speech patterns, they have helped define the field of *phonology:* the study of the patterns and distribution of speech sounds in a language and the commonly accepted rules for their pronunciation.

The basic or smallest units of sound that compose the words in a language are called *phonemes.* Some English phonemes are sounds represented by *b, p, f,* and *v* and simple combinations of sounds, such as *th* in *these.* All the sounds in the English language are combinations of just 45 phonemes; of those, just 9 make up nearly half of all words. Phonemes are cognitive and perceptual abstractions and are considered separate from and independent of a writing system—so phonemes are not the same as the sounds of the letters in a language's alphabet. Researchers argue that the structure of the mouth, tongue, and throat—the biomechanical properties of speech—play a key role in the initial production of phonemes (MacNeilage & Davis, 2000).

Words consist of *morphemes,* the basic units of meaning in a language. A morpheme consists of one or more phonemes combined into a meaningful unit. The morpheme *do,* for example, consists of two phonemes, the sounds *d* and *o.* Adding prefixes and suffixes to morphemes can form other words. Adding *un-* or *-er* to the morpheme *do,* for example, creates *undo* or *doer. Morphology* is the study of these meaningful sound units. Linguists call the entire set of morphemes in a language or in an individual's linguistic inventory a *lexicon.*

No matter what language people speak, one of their first meaningful utterances is the morpheme *ma.* It is coincidental that *ma* is a word in English. Other frequently heard early words of English-speaking children are *bye-bye, dada,* and *baby.* Spanish-speaking children's earliest words tend to be sounds of animals and names of objects. In any language, the first words often refer to a specific person or object, especially food, toys, or animals.

At about 1 year of age, children make the first sounds that can be classified as communicative speech. Initially they may utter only one word, but soon they are saying as many as four or five. Children are astonishingly adept at understanding and using the basic rules of spoken language. Even children only 18 months old, who have vocabularies of perhaps 50 words, understand what people say to them. Psychologists say that young children's *receptive vocabulary* is greater than their *productive vocabulary*—but that changes quickly. A 3-year-old, noticing that many nouns can be turned into verbs by the addition of a suffix, may say "It sunned today," meaning it was a sunny day. Once children have mastered about 100 words, there is a rapid increase in the size of their vocabulary. Interestingly, there is considerable variation in when this "vocabulary spurt" takes place; some children exhibit it far earlier than others, and it depends in part on how much interaction they have with caregivers. In the second year, a child's vocabulary may increase to more than 200 words, and by the end of the third year, to nearly 900 words. By the time most English-speaking people reach adulthood, they recognize about 40,000 words. **Figure 10.4** (on page 380) shows vocabulary growth through age 7.

Semantics

At first, babies do not fully understand what their parents' speech means but they react to the tone, facial expression, and sounds. But as more words take on meaning, the growing child develops semantic capability. *Semantics* is the analysis of the meaning of language, especially of individual words, the relationships among them, and their significance within particular contexts.

Phoneme [FOE-neem] ■ A basic unit of sound that combines with others to compose the words in a language.

Morpheme [MORE-feem] ■ A basic unit of meaning in a language.

Lexicon ■ The entire set of morphemes in a language or in an individual's linguistic inventory.

Semantics [se-MAN-ticks] ■ The analysis of the meaning of language, especially of individual words, the relationships among them, and their significance within particular contexts.

Figure 10.4
Vocabulary Changes in Childhood
The average size of children's vocabulary increases rapidly from age 1½ until age 6, when children have a vocabulary of more than 2,500 words. (Moskowitz, 1978)

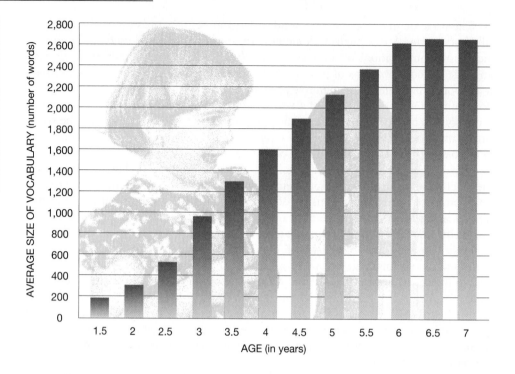

Consider how a 4-year-old child might misconstrue what her mother says to her father: "I've had a terrible day. First, the morning traffic made me a nervous wreck. Then, I got into an argument with my boss, and he almost fired me." The child might think her mom got into a car accident and was nearly set on fire. In trying to understand what is being said, a child must decipher not only the meanings of single words but also their relationships to other words. As everyone who has attempted to learn a new language knows, the meaning of a sentence is not always determined by the definitions of the individual words in it. Although children acquire words daily, the words can mean different things, depending on their context. Of course, even adults use only a small set of words over and over again; most other words are used rarely. People who learn a new language usually concentrate on the most widely used words; teachers of foreign languages rarely ask students to learn the words for *syllogism* or *modality*. The focus tends to be on basic, utilitarian vocabulary and syntax such as names of days of the week, food names, body parts, and directions.

Syntax

Telegraphic speech ■ A condensed form of speech used by young children, which often consists of almost all nouns and verbs, arranged in an order that makes sense; also called *telegraphese*.

Young children start out by using single words to represent whole sentences or ideas. They say "peas" or "truck," and adults understand that they mean they want more peas or they see a truck. Such one-word utterances are known as *holophrases*. Next, children begin to combine words into short sentences, such as "Mama look" or "truck go." This kind of slightly expanded, but still condensed, speech in which words are left out is referred to as **telegraphic speech**, or *telegraphese*. Telegraphic speech sounds like a telegram or an instant message and often consists of almost all nouns and verbs arranged in an order that makes sense. Eventually, children show syntactic capability. *Syntax* is the way words and groups of words can be combined to form phrases, clauses, and sentences. Syntactic capability enables children to convey more meaning. For example, children acquire a powerful new way of making their demands known when they learn to combine the words "I want" or "Give me" with appropriate nouns. Suddenly, they can ask for cookies, toys, or Mommy, without any of them being within pointing range. The rewards that such linguistic behavior bring children are powerful incentives to learn more language, although external rewards are not necessary for language learning. Children begin to use sentences at different ages; but once they begin, they tend to improve at similar rates (Brown, 1970). Moreover, the average length of sentences increases at a fairly regular rate as children grow older.

Early studies of children's short sentences suggested that their speech could be characterized by descriptions of the positions and types of words they used. However, later investigations showed these descriptions to be inadequate and suggested that young children possess an innate grammar and that they use grammatical relationships in much the same ways as adults do (McNeill, 1970). *Grammar* is the linguistic description of how a language functions, especially the rules and patterns used for generating appropriate and comprehensible sentences. A key point about language—any language—is that a limited set of units (phonemes and morphemes) and syntactic rules allow an almost infinite number of sentences and ideas to be produced. **Table 10.1** summarizes some of the early linguistic milestones in a child's life.

Syntax [SIN-tacks] ■ The way words and groups of words can be combined to form phrases, clauses, and sentences.

Grammar ■ The linguistic description of how a language functions, especially the rules and patterns used for generating appropriate and comprehensible sentences.

Table 10.1

EARLY LINGUISTIC MILESTONES

Age	Language Activity
12 weeks	Smiles when talked to; makes cooing sounds spontaneously
16 weeks	Turns head in response to human voices
20 weeks	Makes vowel and consonant sounds while cooing
6 months	Vocal expressions change from cooing to babbling
12 months	Imitates sounds; understands some words
18 months	Uses from 3 to 50 words (some babies use very few words at this age—as few as 3—while others use as many as 100); understands basic speech
24 months	Uses from 50 to 250 words; uses two-word phrases
30 months	Uses new words daily; has good comprehension of speech; vocabulary of about 500 words
36 months	Has vocabulary of more than 850 words; makes grammatical mistakes, but many fewer each week

The Biological and Evolutionary Basis of Language

In 1957, linguist Noam Chomsky began the development of an idea that has found wide support. His idea was that human beings have an inborn, biologically based, universal grammar that allows them to easily master the language of their caregivers. This universal grammar, he asserted, is an innate word–sound–sentence generating mechanism that guides the formation of meaningful sentences. You can think of this universal grammar as a set of built-in "super-rules" that are instinctive and unconscious.

Evidence for the biological readiness of human beings to learn a language comes from studies of the physiology of the brain, which show that infants—even very young ones—begin to respond physiologically to the language to which they are first exposed (Werker & Vouloumanos, 1999). This means that the infant brain must be programmed at birth and ready to adapt to the sounds and meanings of speakers.

Evidence also exists from studies of congenitally deaf infants and children who have never been taught a sign language. For example, Zheng and Goldin-Meadow (2002) found that deaf children in the United States and in the Republic of China (Taipei) generated unprompted signing as a communication device—despite the fact that parents tried to communicate through lip reading and speech. Not only did the children spontaneously use signs, but they did so in a consistent, grammatically coherent pattern. Their gestures were in the form of sentences rather than single signs, and the sentences did not conform to the grammars of English or Mandarin. This is more evidence for an innate (signing) grammar (Goldin-Meadow, 2000).

Contemporary researchers assert that there is but one human grammar, which is innate and thus biologically based in our genes and which underpins the specific grammars of English, Swahili, Hebrew, and so on (Chomsky, 1999; Pinker, 1999; Premack, 2004). From an evolutionary point of view, language has enormous adaptive value. Pinker points out that humans have an instinctive tendency to speak, babble, and acquire knowledge and words. Research on young children, including twin studies, shows that this is indeed the case (Colledge et al., 2002) and provides evidence that language, like other cognitive abilities, has a substantial genetic component and is well established by age 4. But once your first language is established, what happens if you want, or need, to learn a second?

How Do We Acquire Language?

That human beings acquire language is one of their defining characteristics. Acquiring language is a major achievement in the life of a child, and language continues to define us as adults and separates us from other species (Bickerton, 1998). All our cultural achievements, including the arts and advances in science, technology, and even warfare, depend on the use of language. Language development is an individual achievement, but it is also a social process that involves people communicating with one another.

Since language is a unique human ability, was there some evolutionary turn of events that set humans apart in this respect (Premack, 2004)? If language were solely an evolutionary development, the story would be simple, but research shows that language is sensitive to both genetic inheritance (nature) and experience (nurture). As in other areas of human behavior, the debate continues about the relative contribution of each factor. If evolution and biology make the dominant contribution, two things should be true: (1) Many aspects of language ability should be evident early in life, and (2) all children, regardless of their culture or the language they are exposed to, should develop grammar (an understanding of language patterns) in a similar way. If environmental factors are more important in accounting for language acquisition, the role of learning should be preeminent. Let's explore a range of evidence that tries to sort this out.

Learning Theories

The learning approach to language acquisition is straightforward. People speak and understand language because specific language behaviors are continually reinforced from the moment of birth. Babies attend in a focused way, listening intently and repeating the sounds they hear, especially those they have heard before (Houston, Santelmann, & Jusczyk, 2004). As parents become better able to make sense of a baby's babbling, they often repeat the baby's sounds in the proper form so that the baby can hear them pronounced correctly. Parents often then reinforce the baby by responding in some way to the baby's utterances. A baby might say, "Daddy, baby, wasue," and the parent may reply, "You want Daddy to give you water?" The baby smiles, receives a drink, and the process continues—until eventually, over days and weeks, the baby learns correct pronunciation and proper word order. Thus, learning approaches use both operant conditioning and social and observational learning theories to explain the acquisition of language.

Biological Theories

Learning theories emphasize the role of environmental influences, or nurture, in language acquisition. The basic idea is that language is acquired in a process that reflects traditional concepts of learning. But people have the ability to generate an almost infinite number of correctly formed sentences in their native language. Because this ability cannot be acquired solely through imitation or instruction, many researchers, such as psychologist George Miller (1965), assert that human beings are born equipped with an innate, unique capacity to acquire and develop language. Referred to as *nativist*, such a view assumes that human beings possess an inborn *language acquisition device* (LAD), to process and facilitate the learning of language.

Although neither Miller nor Chomsky (1957) excludes experience as a factor in shaping children's language, they claim that human biology, through the LAD, allows children to pay attention to language in their environment and ultimately to use it. Nonetheless, even the strongest proponents of the nature (biological) argument do not contend that a specific language is inborn. Rather, they agree that a predisposition toward language use exists and that human beings are born with a "blueprint" for language. As a child matures, this blueprint provides the framework through which the child learns a specific language and its rules. Evidence from studies of brain structure and lateralization and from studies of learning readiness supports the nature side of the nature–nurture debate.

Brain Structure and Lateralization

Even as early as 1800, researchers knew that the human brain was specialized for different functions. At that time, researchers began mapping the brain and discovering that if certain areas were damaged (usually through accidents), the injured person exhibited severe disorders in language abilities. Later work, some of it by Norman Geschwind (1972), led to the idea of *lateralization*—the localization of a particular brain function primarily in one hemisphere. As Chapter 3 showed, considerable evidence suggests that the left and right hemispheres of the brain (normally connected by the corpus callosum) have some distinctly different functions. Some researchers argue that the brain has unique processing abilities in each hemisphere. For example, many language functions are predominantly, but not exclusively, left-hemisphere functions (Corina et al., 2003). However, the available data do not make an airtight case; each hemisphere seems to play a dominant role in some functions and to interact with the other hemisphere in the performance of others (Kroll et al., 2003; Long & Baynes, 2002).

lateralization ■ The localization of a particular brain function primarily in one hemisphere.

Learning Readiness

Researcher Eric Lenneberg (1921–1975) claimed that human beings are born with a grammatical capacity and a readiness to produce language (Lenneberg, 1967). Lenneberg believed that the brain continues to develop from birth until about age 13, with the greatest developmental leap taking place around age 2. During this period, children develop grammar and learn the rules of language. After age 13, there is little change in an individual's neurological structures. Lenneberg supported his argument with the observation that brain-damaged children can relearn some speech and language, whereas brain-damaged adolescents or adults who lose speech and language are unable to regain them. Lenneberg's view is persuasive, but some of his original claims have been seriously criticized—particularly his idea of the role of a critical period for language development, although critical periods for learning have been established for some animals, such as birds and fish (e.g., Hakuta, Bialystok, & Wiley, 2003; Stevens, 2004; Tchernichovski et al., 2001).

Some researchers claim that not only human beings but also other animals—for example, chimpanzees—are born with a grammatical capacity and a readiness for language.

Do Chimpanzees Use Language?

Whales communicate with clicks, wails, squeaks, and groans; monkeys use various sounds to signal one another; wolves howl—the examples are nearly endless. Clearly, many animals communicate with one another. But do animals communicate with one another through language? If they do, is that language similar to or totally different from the language of human beings? Most important, what can scientists learn from animals about the inborn aspects of language?

The biological approach to language suggests that human beings are born with a capacity for language. Experience is the key that unlocks this preprogrammed capacity and allows its development. The arguments for and against the biological view of language acquisition use studies showing that chimpanzees naturally develop some language abilities. Chimpanzees are generally considered among the most intelligent animals; in addition, genetically, they resemble human beings more closely than any other animal does. Playful and curious, chimps share many physical and mental abilities with human beings. Their brains have a similar organization; and some of their languagelike functions may even be lateralized (Mazur, 2002). This is an important and interesting finding, because psychologists have generally believed that only human beings exhibited brain asymmetries related to lateralization of language functions. Researchers are not sure what this lateralization in chimps means, but it will most likely provide some hints about their language abilities. What it does *not* mean is that chimps have human language—a similarity in structure does not necessarily imply the same function.

Chimps are especially valuable as research subjects because researchers can control and shape the environment in which chimps learn language, something they cannot do in studies involving human beings. Thus, chimpanzees have been the species of choice among psychologists who study language in animals.

However, all attempts to teach animals to talk have failed. This failure has led most psycholinguists to conclude that only human beings have the capacity to acquire language. However, several major research projects have showed that even though chimpanzees lack the physical vocal apparatus necessary to produce speech, they can learn to use different methods to communicate with humans. Scientists have studied chimpanzees both in near-natural environments and in laboratory settings using computer technology. With results from sharply different environments, clear conclusions are emerging.

Washoe

From age 1, the chimpanzee Washoe was raised like a human child by Allen and Beatrice Gardner (1969). Rather than being taught to speak words, Washoe was taught American Sign Language, and she was able to make signs that stood for specific objects and events as well as simple concepts and commands (for example, *more, come, give me, flower, tickle,* and *open*). She was able to generalize these signs and to combine them in meaningful order to make sentences. There is no proof, however, that she used a systematic grammar to generate novel kinds of sentences.

Sarah

The chimp Sarah was raised in a cage, with more limited contact with human beings than Washoe had. Psychologist David Premack (1971) used magnetized and colored plastic icons to teach Sarah words and sentences (see **Figure 10.5**). Sarah gradually developed a small but impressive vocabulary. She learned to make compound sentences, to answer simple questions, and to substitute words in a sentence construction. There is no evidence, however, that she could generate a new sentence.

Figure 10.5
Icons Used by Sarah in Premack's Study
Sarah learned to construct sentences using pieces of magnetized plastic of various colors and shapes.
(Premack, 1971)

Lana

The chimp Lana learned to interact with a computer at the Yerkes Primate Research Center at Emory University. Researchers Rumbaugh, Gill, and Von Glaserfeld (1973) gave Lana 6 months of computer-controlled language training. Lana learned to press a series of keys imprinted with geometric symbols. Each symbol represented a word in an artificial language the researchers called Yerkish. The computer varied the location of each Yerkish word and the color and brightness of the keys. Through conditioning, Lana learned to demonstrate some of the rudiments of language acquisition. However, Lana did not show that she could apply grammatical rules in meaningful and regular ways.

These studies of chimps showed that their language usage is similar to that of very young children: It is concrete, specific, and limited. However, chimps do not show the ability to generate an unlimited number of grammatically correct sentences, an ability that human beings begin to acquire at a fairly young age.

Nim

Columbia University psychologist Herbert Terrace reports significant differences between chimp language and the language of young children. Terrace taught his chimp, Nim Chimpski (a word play on the name of the famous linguist Noam Chomsky), to communicate using manual signs. Terrace found that Nim's signed communications did not increase in length, as young children's sentences do. Nim acquired many words, but only 12% of Nim's utterances were spontaneous; the remaining 88% were responses to her teacher. Terrace points out that a significantly greater percentage of children's utterances are spontaneous. Terrace also found no evidence of grammatical competence in either his own data or those of other researchers.

Chimp Language?

Unlike young children, who spontaneously learn to name and to point at objects (often called *referential naming*), chimps do not spontaneously develop such communication skills. Terrace (1985) agrees that the ability to name is a basic part of human consciousness. Chimps can be taught some naming skills, but the procedure is long and tedious. Children, on the other hand, develop these skills easily and spontaneously at a young age. Accordingly, researchers generally assert that chimps do not interpret the symbols they use in the same way that children do. They question the comparability of human and chimp language.

Although they do communicate with humans, chimps do not transmit sign language culturally from ape to ape (Bodamer & Gardner, 2002; Povinelli et al., 2003). They do not show referential naming, nor do they have the ability to be generative—to form new words, sentences, and ideas. So chimps do not use language the way human beings do. The answers to questions about language acquisition in animals are far from complete. And in some ways the questions being asked today and the research endeavors are new; for example, Taglialatela, Savage-Rumbaugh, and Baker (2003) are investigating vocal output of apes; other researchers are examining different kinds of learning of languagelike activities by chimpanzees (Jensvold & Gardner, 2000). The research is exciting and is being extended to other species, including sea lions (Reichmuth & Schusterman, 2002).

Do Dolphins or Whales Use Language?

It is widely known that dolphins communicate with one another through squeaks and groans. It is also well accepted that dolphins learn quickly and well. But do they have language? The answer is no, not in the sense that humans do. Dolphins have no vocal cords, and they do not gesture. Nevertheless, dolphins do communicate with one another and with human beings (Herman, Richards, & Wolz, 1984). They repeat signals from other dolphins—which is one aspect of language use; Vincent Janik (2000) showed that wild bottlenose dolphins listened to and learned the whistles of other dolphins, and repeated those signals; Marino (2002) found similar results. This ability to replicate sounds is a part of early language development.

Researchers Miller and Bain (2000) presented evidence that whales not only communicate with one another, but they do so with flair. He found that whales repeat sounds, like dolphins, but do so with inflections, almost like a tone of voice among human beings. Miller and Bain found that whales, their offspring, and even the third generation possess some calls or sounds that are distinct to their families. Do dolphins or whales have language? The answer is no. Do they have communicative abilities? The answer is surely yes.

Social Interaction Theory: A Little Bit of Each

The debate over language acquisition is a wonderful example of how issues in psychology emerge, grow, and contribute to an understanding of human behavior. Early learning theorists took an unbending view of the role of reinforcement in language development. Later, biologically based researchers assumed that the evidence for biological and genetic underpinnings of language was just too strong to deny. But neither view by itself is correct. Children are born with a predisposition to language—there is no doubt about that. And nearly everybody agrees that children are reinforced for their language behavior. But children's use of language takes place within a social and emotional setting that changes daily; the child's differing moods and needs may be met by different caretakers with their own moods and needs. So language is in part innate and in part reinforced—and polarized views that overemphasize innate grammars or reinforced behaviors are probably too limited to fully explain language acquisition (Haskell, MacDonald, & Seidenberg, 2003).

Like so many other behaviors, language use is affected by the context in which it occurs. At feeding time, babies are far more likely to express hunger vocally. While playing, babies are far more likely to be self-centered, making utterances that do not necessarily have communicative functions. Parents often go into "teaching mode" and articulate words, sentences, and emotional expressions especially strongly when talking to a child, because they want the child to learn something particular. In the early months of life, infants acquire phonetic properties of their native language by listening to adults speak (through social and observational learning). Interestingly, mothers exaggerate—they produce more extreme versions of vowel sounds—when talking with infants (Liu, Kuhl, & Tsao, 2003).

A key to understanding language acquisition is to consider not only the structure of language, but also its function and the context in which it is learned, expressed, and practiced. Human beings are very much social organisms, and language serves a vital function as a way for children to get attention and make their needs known. In the end, although a child may be biologically programmed for language acquisition and reinforced for using language correctly, language nearly always is used in a social setting—whose importance cannot be overestimated.

Summary and Review

WHAT IS COGNITIVE PSYCHOLOGY?

Cognitive psychology is the study of the related phenomena of perception, learning, memory, and thought, with an emphasis on how people attend to, acquire, transform, store, and retrieve knowledge. Cognitive psychologists study thinking; they assume that mental processes exist and can be studied scientifically. p. 357

HOW DO WE FORM CONCEPTS AND SOLVE PROBLEMS?

What is involved in the process of concept formation?

Concepts are the mental categories people use to classify events or objects according to their common properties or features. Concept formation involves classifying events or objects by grouping them with or isolating them from others on the basis of shared characteristics. In laboratory studies of concept formation, participants are presented with stimuli that are either positive or negative instances of a concept and are asked to identify the concept. pp. 357–359

A *prototype* is an abstraction, an idealized pattern of an object or idea that is stored in memory and used to decide whether similar objects or ideas are members of the same class of items. pp. 359–360

What are some approaches people use in solving problems?

Problem solving involves confronting and resolving situations that require insight or determination of some unknown elements. *Algorithms* are problem-solving procedures that implement a particular series of steps repeatedly. *Heuristics* are sets of strategies that serve as flexible guidelines, not strict rules, for problem solving. In *subgoal analysis*, a problem is broken down into several smaller steps, each of which has a subgoal. In *means–end analysis*, a current situation or position is compared with the desired end in order to determine the most efficient means for getting from one to the other. A *backward search* involves working back from the goal to the current position, in order to analyze the problem and reduce the steps needed to get to the goal. pp. 360–362

What are some barriers to effective problem solving?

Functional fixedness is the inability to see that an object can have a function other than its stated or usual one. It has been shown to be detrimental to problem solving. A *mental set* consists of limited ways of thinking about possibilities and a tendency to approach situations the same way because that way worked in the past. pp. 362–363

What characterizes creativity?

Creativity is the ability to generate or recognize high-quality ideas that are original, novel, and appropriate, along with the tendency to do so. According to Guilford, creative thinking is divergent thinking. *Divergent thinking* is the process of widening the range of possible solutions. In contrast, *convergent thinking* involves reducing the number of possible options until one option remains as the answer. To solve problems creatively, some people use the technique of *brainstorming*. Sternberg's investment theory of creativity focuses on working on undervalued solutions to problems, marketing them, and implementing them. pp. 364–366

HOW DO WE REASON AND MAKE DECISIONS?

Differentiate between reasoning and decision making.

Reasoning is the purposeful process by which a person generates logical and coherent ideas, evaluates situations, and reaches conclusions. The system of principles of reasoning that is used to reach valid conclusions or make inferences is called *logic*. *Decision making* is the assessment of alternatives and selection of the best one; some decisions involve determining the probability of occurrence of an event or assessing the expected value of the outcome. Psychological factors, especially previous events, affect how people estimate probabilities of behaviors and events. pp. 366–368

What are some barriers to sound decision making?

There are five major barriers to sound decision making. The *gambler's fallacy* is the belief that the chances of an event's occurring increase if the event has not recently occurred. Limiting the number of observations made because of a *belief in small numbers* also contributes to poor decision making. The *availability heuristic* is the tendency to judge the probability of an event by how easy it is to think of examples of it. *Confirmation bias* is the tendency of people to discount information that does not fit with their pre-existing views. And *belief perseverance* is the tendency of people, once they have decided that they believe something, to keep on accepting it as truth, even in the face of conflicting data. pp. 368–369

What is the effect of culture on reasoning?

The intellectual traditions of the East and the West are quite different, and so are the reasoning and decision-making approaches of people in different cultures. Different worldviews affect how people in the East and West solve problems. p. 370

How does the evolutionary perspective account for the ability to reason?

Evolutionary psychologists assert that the human ability to reason is a direct consequence of evolution. Reasoning is an adaptation to a complex world. pp. 370–371

WHAT DOES ARTIFICIAL INTELLIGENCE REVEAL ABOUT COGNITION?

What is artificial intelligence?

Artificial intelligence (AI) is the branch of computer science concerned with making a device or machine (a computer) behave like a human being, especially in reasoning abilities. A computer analogy of perception and reasoning has been the model for most studies of AI. The *information-processing approach* proposes that information is processed and stored in three stages of memory in a sequential manner, moving from one stage to the next. pp. 371–372

Describe how neural networks work.

Information about any thing or event may be stored in multiple locations throughout the brain. However, the locations are connected through convergence zones, or centers that mediate and organize the information. The concept of parallel distributed processing (PDP) suggests that many operations take place simultaneously and at many locations in the brain. This concept is applied to create electronic neural networks that simulate specific cognitive activities, including recognizing patterns, and spatial layouts. Neural networks learn and remember by noting changes in the intensity of signals and the level of activity associated with various connections between their units. Those units that are frequently activated have lower thresholds of activation and can be more easily accessed. pp. 372–374

WHAT IS THE STRUCTURE OF LANGUAGE?

What is language, and what is pragmatics?

A *language* is a system of symbols, usually words, which convey meaning; in addition, a language also has rules for combining the symbols to generate an infinite number of messages (usually sentences). *Pragmatics* is the study of how the social context of a sentence affects its meaning. pp. 375–376

How is language related to gender?

The English language has evolved in such a way that its words define many roles as male; many people still see the world through a male frame of reference and assume that this is the preferred value system. Although gender stereotypes persist, some women and men accept the value of *androgyny*. pp. 376–377

How are language, thought, and culture interrelated, and what are the key elements of language?

Research shows that language structure alone is unlikely to account for the way people think, because culture also influences language and thought. pp. 372–378

Linguistics is the study of language, including speech sounds, meaning, and grammar. *Psycholinguistics* is the study of how people acquire, perceive, understand, and produce language. *Phonology* is the study of the patterns and distribution of speech sounds in a language and the commonly accepted rules for their pronunciation. *Phonemes* are the basic units of sounds in a language; *morphemes* are the basic units of meaning. Linguists call the entire set of morphemes in a language or in a person's linguistic inventory a *lexicon*. *Semantics* is the study of the meaning of language components. A condensed form of speech used by young children, in which most words except nouns and verbs are left out, is referred to as *telegraphic speech*, or *telegraphese*. *Syntax* describes the way words and groups of words are related and how words are arranged into phrases and sentences. *Grammar* is the linguistic description of a language's rules and patterns for generating comprehensible sentences. pp. 378–381

Is there a biological and evolutionary basis of language?

Chomsky first proposed that human beings have an inborn, biologically based, universal grammar that allows them to easily master language. This universal grammar, he asserted, is an innate word–sound–sentence mechanism that makes us capable of generating meaningful sentences. Contemporary researchers assert that there is but one human grammar, which is innate and thus biologically based in our genes. p. 382

HOW DO WE ACQUIRE LANGUAGE?

How do theorists explain language acquisition?

Learning plays an important part in language acquisition. However, people have the ability to generate an unlimited number of correctly formed sentences in their native language. This ability cannot be acquired solely through imitation or instruction, which suggests the existence of an innate language ability. pp. 382–383

Biological theorists assert that the brain has specific language-processing areas, some of which are lateralized. *Lateralization* is the localization of a brain function in one brain hemisphere or the other. pp. 382–384

Do animals use language?

Studies of language ability in chimpanzees have produced some impressive results, although few psychologists are completely convinced that chimps use language in the same way that humans do. Dolphins and whales communicate extensively with others of their species. Both use sounds, and whales even use inflections, almost like tones of voice. These communicative abilities do not constitute language, however. pp. 384–387

What does social interaction theory emphasize about language acquisition?

A key to understanding language acquisition is to consider not only the structure of language, but also its function and the context in which it is learned, expressed, and practiced. Communication serves a vital function and nearly always takes place in an interactive, social setting. pp. 387–388

CHAPTER 11

Intelligence

What Are the Origins and History
of Psychological Testing? 393
  Binet's Intelligence Test
  The Stanford–Binet Intelligence Scale
  The Wechsler Scales
  Group Intelligence Tests

What Is Intelligence? 399
  Theories of Intelligence—One Ability or Many?
  Emotions—A Different Kind of Intelligence?

How Do Psychologists
Develop Tests? 406
  Developing an Intelligence Test
  Reliability
  Validity

How Do Biological and
Environmental Factors Contribute
to Intelligence? 412
  Biological Factors and Intelligence
  Environmental and Cultural Factors in Intelligence
  The Interaction of Biological and Environmental
    Factors

What Is the Impact of Having
an Exceptional IQ? 419
  Giftedness
  Intellectual Disability
  Special Education: The IDEA

Summary and Review 423

In this chapter, we consider intelligence and intelligence testing, examining theories, tests, and controversies. We differentiate intelligence tests from the other types of tests that have become so important in the educational system. In addition, we examine two special populations: those who are gifted and those who are intellectually disabled. First, let's look at the history of intelligence tests and some examples of these tests, which will reveal how intelligence and scholastic tests came to be confused. Then, we'll tackle the basic but difficult question of what intelligence is.

What Are the Origins and History of Psychological Testing?

The goal of assessing mental abilities was established in the early years of psychology, in the work of Sir Francis Galton (1822–1911), who formulated a series of tests designed to measure intelligence (Schultz & Schultz, 2004). Galton conceptualized intelligence in terms of the senses and believed that people with better sensory ability were more intelligent. He gathered information from over 9,000 individuals in England, but his measurements did not show a high relationship between sensory ability and school achievement. Thus, his version of intelligence testing quickly lost favor, but another approach was more successful.

Binet's Intelligence Test

In the early years of the 20th century, a young French psychologist named Alfred Binet (1857–1911) was approached by the French Ministry of Public Instruction and asked to formulate a test (Boake, 2002). The Paris school system had undergone reform, and many students who had not previously attended school were doing so. Some students were doing poorly and dropping out. The school administrators needed a test that would allow them to determine which children would profit from education in regular classes and which needed special attention. To formulate this test, Binet enlisted the help of a young psychiatrist, Theodore Simon (1873–1961). Binet and Simon (1905) delivered a 30-item test that focused on language skills, judgment, comprehension, reasoning, and memory. The assessment required that the test administrator interact individually with the child, and testing took about 40 minutes.

The Binet-Simon test was successful for the Paris school system and generated a great deal of interest among psychologists across Europe and in the United States (Benjamin & Baker, 2004). A major revision appeared in 1908, in which the concept of mental age was added to the assessment. *Mental age* is the age at which children of average ability were able to perform various tasks on the test, and this measure allowed a comparison of children of different ages and a way to gauge individual children's ability. Although Binet believed that this measure was in itself of little general significance, soon the Binet-Simon test was the model for intelligence tests (Boake, 2002). American psychologist H. H. Goddard (1866–1957) translated Binet's test into English and began to use it to diagnose mental retardation in children. However, Lewis Terman, another American psychologist, also translated Binet's test into English, and Terman's version of the test became the standard.

Mental age ■ The age at which children of average ability are able to perform various tasks on an intelligence test.

The Stanford–Binet Intelligence Scale

From 1912 to 1916, Lewis M. Terman revised and developed the test now known as the Stanford–Binet Intelligence Scale (Terman, 1916). (Terman was teaching at Stanford University when he revised the test.) For his revision, Terman used an alternative to the concept of mental age—he coined the term *intelligence quotient (IQ)*, which he defined as a child's mental age (intellectual ability) divided by the child's chronological age and multiplied by 100. **Table 11.1** gives examples of this calculation.

The Stanford–Binet has traditionally been a good predictor of academic performance, and many of its simplest subtests correlate highly with one another. However, as the popularity of the IQ concept spread, the perception of IQ test scores as a predictor of academic performance became less prominent, and people

Intelligence quotient (IQ) ■ A child's mental age (intellectual ability) divided by the child's chronological age and multiplied by 100.

Table 11.1

TRADITIONAL CALCULATION OF INTELLIGENCE QUOTIENT FOR THREE PEOPLE

	Person 1	Person 2	Person 3
Mental Age (MA)	6 years	15 years	15 years
Chronological Age (CA)	6 years	18 years	12 years
MA + CA	6 + 6 = 1	15 + 18 = 0.83	15 + 12 = 1.25
(MA + CA) × 100	1 × 100 = 100	0.83 × 100 = 83	1.25 × 100 = 125
IQ	100	83	125

began to think of the IQ arrived at by the Stanford–Binet as a general measure of intelligence. But Binet and Simon's original test was never intended to be used that way. Their original commission was to devise a test for the Paris school system that was to be used to assess academic abilities, not general intelligence. Lewis Terman's use of the term IQ gave rise to the confusion, and it persists today. *Intelligence tests* are tests designed to measure general mental abilities rather than specific learned content.

> **Intelligence tests** ■ Tests designed to measure general mental abilities rather than specific learned content.

Revisions of Terman's test continue to be used. The fifth edition of the Stanford–Binet Intelligence Scales, published in 2003, tests five major factors: fluid reasoning, knowledge, quantitative reasoning, visual-spatial processing, and working memory. The major subscales contain various subtests that vary greatly in content (see **Figure 11.1** on p. 396 for examples). The Stanford–Binet can be used to test anyone from age 2 through age 85, yielding one overall IQ score but also allowing for assessments of specific abilities. The test administration time varies with the examinee's age, because the number of subtests given is determined by age. All examinees first take two subtests that allow administrators to proceed to other tests. The tester begins by using entry-level items and continues until the test taker fails a prescribed number of items. Although the Stanford–Binet Intelligence Scale can be used over a wide range of ages and abilities, it is not the most widely used individual assessment of intelligence—that distinction goes to the Wechsler scales.

The Wechsler Scales

The most popular individual assessment of IQ originated with David Wechsler (1896–1981), a Rumanian immigrant to the United States. During World War I, Wechsler administered intelligence tests for the Army (Boake, 2002). After a variety of experiences in psychology clinics, he earned a doctoral degree in psychology from Columbia University and, in 1932, was appointed chief psychologist at Bellevue Hospital in New York City. Wechsler's experience in intelligence testing had convinced him that the Stanford–Binet was inadequate for testing adults and that the test was too heavily weighted with verbal items.

> The Wechsler Intelligence Scale for Children groups test items by content. The score on each subtest is calculated and converted to a standard score, adjusted for the test taker's age.

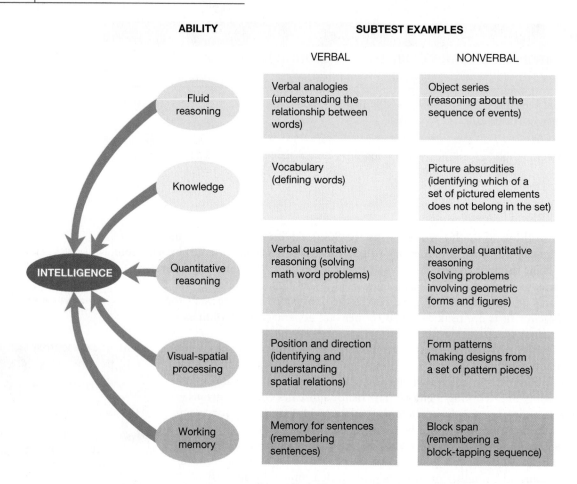

ABILITY

SUBTEST EXAMPLES

VERBAL

NONVERBAL

INTELLIGENCE

Fluid reasoning

Verbal analogies (understanding the relationship between words)

Object series (reasoning about the sequence of events)

Knowledge

Vocabulary (defining words)

Picture absurdities (identifying which of a set of pictured elements does not belong in the set)

Quantitative reasoning

Verbal quantitative reasoning (solving math word problems)

Nonverbal quantitative reasoning (solving problems involving geometric forms and figures)

Visual-spatial processing

Position and direction (identifying and understanding spatial relations)

Form patterns (making designs from a set of pattern pieces)

Working memory

Memory for sentences (remembering sentences)

Block span (remembering a block-tapping sequence)

Figure 11.1
The Modern Stanford–Binet Intelligence Scale
The most recent version of the Stanford–Binet Intelligence Scale measures intelligence with a composite score made up of five scores on tests of broad types of mental activity: fluid reasoning, knowledge, quantitative reasoning, visual-spatial processing, and working memory. Each score is obtained through a series of subtests that measure specific mental abilities.

Wechsler began working on a test that would separate verbal from performance assessments. *Performance skills* include the ability to assemble blocks in a manner something like a jigsaw puzzle, find the pieces missing from pictures, and arrange pictures in the correct sequence. (**Figure 11.2** gives examples of some items on this test.) Wechsler believed that assessing a combination of verbal and performance skills would yield a more valid measure of intelligence than relying on verbal skills alone (Boake, 2002). The inclusion of performance subtests moved this test away from a school-based definition of intelligence toward a broader conceptualization.

Wechsler also grouped test items by content. For example, all the information questions are presented together, all the arithmetic problems appear together, and so on. The Wechsler–Bellevue Intelligence Scale appeared in 1939. In 1955, the Wechsler Adult Intelligence Scale (WAIS) was published; it eliminated some technical difficulties

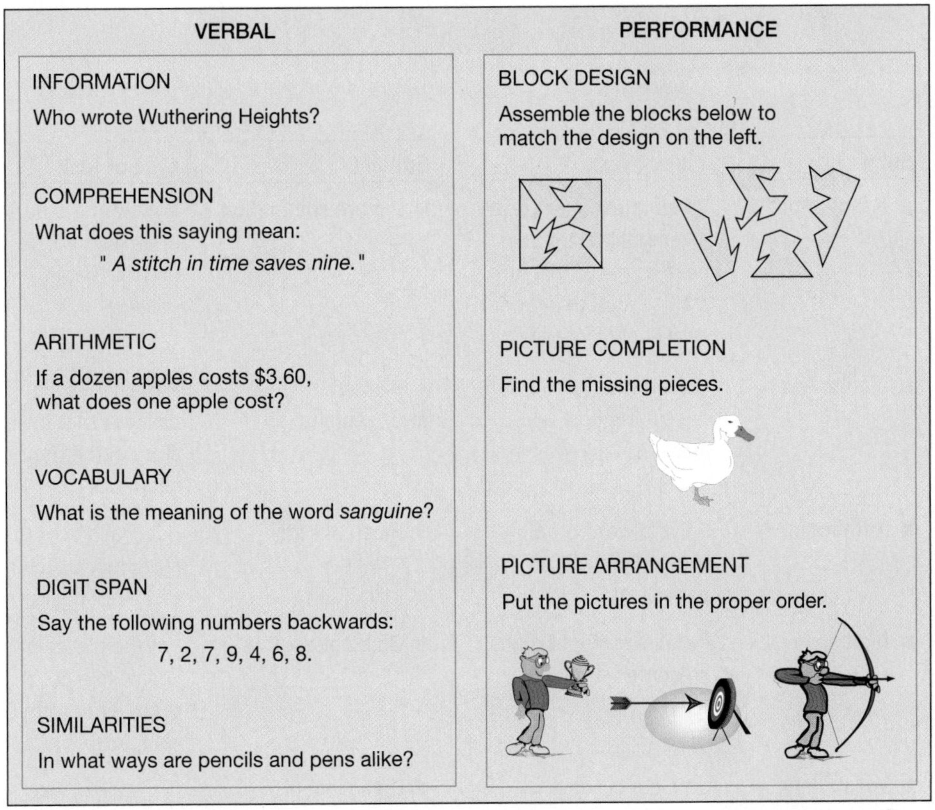

Figure 11.2

Items from the WAIS–III Verbal and Performance Subtests

VERBAL

INFORMATION

Who wrote Wuthering Heights?

COMPREHENSION

What does this saying mean:
  "*A stitch in time saves nine.*"

ARITHMETIC

If a dozen apples costs $3.60, what does one apple cost?

VOCABULARY

What is the meaning of the word *sanguine*?

DIGIT SPAN

Say the following numbers backwards:
  7, 2, 7, 9, 4, 6, 8.

SIMILARITIES

In what ways are pencils and pens alike?

PERFORMANCE

BLOCK DESIGN

Assemble the blocks below to match the design on the left.

PICTURE COMPLETION

Find the missing pieces.

PICTURE ARRANGEMENT

Put the pictures in the proper order.

inherent in the Wechsler–Bellevue scale. The most recent revision of the test is the WAIS–III, which appeared in 1997. **Table 11.2** lists some of the subtests on the WAIS. Wechsler also developed assessments for children, including the Wechsler Intelligence Scale for Children (WISC). The latest version of this test, the WISC-IV Integrated, appeared in 2004 and can be used to assess children aged 6 through 16. The Wechsler Preschool and Primary Scale of Intelligence (WPPSI) covers younger children, those from age 4 through age 6½.

All the Wechsler tests require a trained test administrator and a one-to-one testing situation. This testing situation allows test administrators to ensure the cooperation of the individual being tested and to be sensitive to his or her situation and responses. However, it limits the number of people who can be tested and increases the cost of testing. For these reasons, group intelligence tests were developed.

Group Intelligence Tests

Group intelligence testing started during World War I, when the U.S. Army needed to assess thousands of recruits. A committee of psychologists developed two group tests, the Alpha and Beta versions of the Army Intelligence Test. The two versions were for recruits who were fluent in English (Alpha) and those who were not (Beta). David Wechsler was one of the psychologists who worked on these tests, and many of the items on the Alpha version later appeared on Wechsler's original test (Boake, 2002).

Table 11.2

TYPICAL SUBTESTS OF THE WAIS

Verbal Test		Performance Test	
Subtest	**Type of Task**	**Subtest**	**Type of Task**
■ **Information**	When questioned, recall a general fact that has been acquired in a formal (school) or informal (non-school) setting	■ **Picture completion**	Point out the part of an incomplete picture that is missing
■ **Similarities**	Use another concept in describing how two ideas are alike	■ **Picture arrangement**	Put a series of pictures that tell a story in the right sequence
■ **Arithmetic**	Solve a word problem without pencil and paper	■ **Block design**	Use real blocks to reproduce a picture of a block design
■ **Digit span**	Recall a string of digits presented orally	■ **Object assembly**	Put the pieces of a jigsaw-like puzzle together to form a complete object
■ **Vocabulary**	Define a vocabulary word	■ **Digit symbol**	Given a key that matches numbers to geometric shapes, fill in a form with the shapes that go with the listed numbers
■ **Comprehension**	Answer a question requiring practical judgment and common sense		

The formation of The Psychological Corporation in 1921 laid the foundation for the commercial publication of intelligence tests. Once group tests were available for use in education and industry, intelligence testing became part of American life. People accepted the conclusion that IQ tests measured intelligence. Psychologists such as Lewis Terman and David Wechsler were also convinced that IQ tests measured general intelligence, despite the origin of these tests as scholastic assessments. Despite this widespread acceptance of IQ tests, debates over what they measure and over the definition of intelligence raged within psychology.

What Is Intelligence?

Although people around the world (and most psychologists) accept the idea that intelligence exists, there is widespread disagreement over what intelligence is. It has been described quite differently, not only by various psychologists, but also in various societies. For example, Mandarin Chinese has no word that corresponds to the English word *intelligence*; the translation of the word the Chinese do use is something closer to *wisdom* (Yang & Sternberg, 1997). The Chinese conceptualization of intelligence, like the Western view, emphasizes learning and a life-long dedication to learning, but the Chinese believe that the quality of humility is essential to intelligence, whereas Westerners do not. Many African societies emphasize interpersonal skills in their conceptualization of intelligence (Ruzgis & Grigorenko, 1994). In Chinese and African societies, intelligence is not limited to academic skills but includes other cognitive and social skills. Even within the United States, definitions of intelligence show some variation with ethnicity (Okagaki & Sternberg, 1993). Asians and Whites emphasize cognitive skills, whereas Latinos/Latinas view the social dimension as important to intelligence. Thus, there is considerable variation in what people include in their definitions of intelligence.

Psychologists also disagree over the definition of intelligence. For some, intelligence refers to the entire range of mental abilities. For others, it is the basic general factor necessary for all mental activity. For still others, it is a group of specific abilities. Most agree, however, that intelligence is a capacity. These differing points of view make defining intelligence difficult, but here is a working definition: *Intelligence* is the overall capacity of an individual to act purposefully, to think rationally, and to deal effectively with the environment. This general capacity includes learning and understanding. By this definition, people express their intelligence in their behavior; intelligence is evident in a person's actions and abilities to learn new things and to use previously learned knowledge. Most important, intelligence has to do with a person's ability to adapt to the social and cultural environment. Intelligence is a capacity that is affected by a person's day-to-day experiences in the world. Intelligence is *not* a person's IQ, which is merely a score derived from a test.

Intelligence ■ The overall capacity of an individual to act purposefully, to think rationally, and to deal effectively with the environment.

Theories of Intelligence—One Ability or Many?

Clearly, all people are not equally intelligent, and a given person does not act equally intelligently all of the time. Individual differences apply to all areas of behavior, and from its beginnings, psychology has had to take these individual differences into consideration. In formulating theories of intelligence, psychologists want to study individual behavior and how it varies over time and in different circumstances, but they also want to make generalizations about human behavior.

The different conceptualizations of intelligence vary in terms of whether intelligence has one or many components. Is intelligence a singular property, or does it consist of many more-or-less independent factors? Does intelligence extend beyond intellect to social and emotional factors? Psychologists have defined intelligence in terms of one general factor, many factors, cognitive structures or processes, biological processes, and interacting systems (Sternberg, Lautrey, & Lubart, 2003). Let's examine some of these approaches and evaluate their strengths and weaknesses.

Factor Theories

Factor theories of intelligence use the correlation technique of factor analysis to explore what makes up intelligence. *Factor analysis* is a statistical procedure designed to discover the independent elements (factors) in any set of data. Applied to intelligence testing, factor analysis is used to find a cluster of items that measure a common ability. Results on tests of verbal comprehension, spelling, and reading speed, for example, usually correlate highly, suggesting that some attribute of verbal abilities (a factor) underlies a person's scores on those three tests.

> **Factor analysis** ■ A statistical procedure designed to discover the independent elements (factors) in any set of data.

In the early 20th century, Charles E. Spearman (1863–1945) used factor analysis to show that intelligence consists of two parts: a general factor affecting all tasks, which he termed the *g* factor, and specific factors associated with particular tasks. According to Spearman, some amounts of both the general factor and the appropriate specific factor(s) were necessary for the successful performance of any task. This view of intelligence is known as the *two-factor theory of intelligence*. Those who endorse this approach assert that a general factor underlies diverse cognitive abilities, and some researchers argue that there is physiological evidence for a general factor of intelligence (Duncan et al., 2000; Plomin, 2003).

Louis L. Thurstone (1887–1955) further developed Spearman's work by postulating a general factor analogous to Spearman's, along with seven basic factors, each representing a unique mental ability: verbal comprehension, word fluency, number facility, spatial visualization, associative memory, perceptual speed, and reasoning. Known as the *factor theory of intelligence*, Thurstone's theory included a computational scheme for sorting out the seven basic factors. The factor theory is not universally accepted. Spearman argued that all of Thurstone's factors were intercorrelated, that is, not truly independent (Sternberg, 2003b). Other objections to the factor approach came from psychologists who took a completely different view of intelligence.

Vygotsky's View

Lev Vygotsky (1896–1934) was a Russian psychologist who believed that intellectual development depends on a social context that includes communication, with the self and with others. Intelligence is the development of cognitive structures, which are interwoven. Children, for example, engage in *private speech*—essentially, talking to themselves, to plan their own actions and behavior. When they use such speech, they do better at various intellectual tasks. Vygotsky suggested that private speech helps a child understand his or her world, and the internalization of this speech is an important part of cognitive development. For Vygotsky (1934/1962), even the earliest speech is essentially social and useful and a key part of intelligence. He asserted that social speech comes first, followed by egocentric (self-centered) speech, then private speech.

Vygotsky held that children need the help of society to accomplish the many tasks that are beyond their current abilities. Parents and other adults help children accomplish these tasks, and their assistance allows children to succeed. Since many tasks are involved, intelligence is not so much a product as a process. The child continually incorporates new skills into his or her repertoire of behaviors and thus shows intelligence. Vygotsky believed that psychologists must examine not only the result of intellectual growth, but the process as well. His approach places intelligence within a social and cultural context and emphasizes changes in cognitive structures. Other theorists have concentrated on the biological basis for intelligence.

Biological Theories of Intelligence

Viewed from an evolutionary perspective, intelligence is an adaptive trait that allows for wider behavioral flexibility. Such flexibility would be an advantage in uncertain environments where individuals could not rely on one fixed pattern of responding. Thus, some evolutionary psychologists see human intelligence as part of our evolutionary heritage. This reasoning is difficult to dispute, but for genes inherited from our ancestors to get translated into intelligent, adaptive behavior requires some biological mechanisms that are evident in humans today. Theorists have suggested several such biological mechanisms, including the possibility that the overall size of the brain is important for intelligence.

One biological approach ties hemispheric specialization to the performance of different tasks (see Chapter 3). For example, language abilities tend to be localized in the left hemisphere, whereas spatial tasks are a specialization of the right hemisphere. In separating the assessment of intelligence into verbal and performance tests, Wechsler's intelligence tests draw on these differences in hemispheric function.

Another possible biological basis for intelligence is that some human brains function more efficiently than others at the level of the neuron (Neubauer, 2000). According to this view, some brains work both faster and more efficiently than others. According to studies using brain-imaging techniques (Neubauer, Fink, & Schrausser, 2002), more intelligent individuals show less brain activity when performing various tasks than less intelligent individuals do—their brains operate more efficiently, so accomplishing the task requires less activation. Therefore, the biology of brain activity may relate to intelligence in specific ways.

As Sternberg (2003b) points out, biological theories of intelligence offer interesting ways to look at individual differences and also provide a framework for understanding the development of human intelligence. However, biological theories alone will never be sufficient to answer the important questions in intelligence—it is not really possible to reduce intelligence to biological processes. But theoretical approaches may draw from biology, as Gardner's and Sternberg's theories do.

Gardner's Multiple Intelligences

Howard Gardner has proposed that there are multiple types of intelligences, which traditional intelligence tests do not measure (1983/1993, 1999, 2003; Gardner & Hatch, 1989). In hypothesizing these multiple types, Gardner uses a systems approach, which leads to a more complex view of intelligence than factor, cognitive, or biological theories.

Gardner argues that human competencies, of which there are many, do not all lend themselves to measurement on a standard test. He maintains that people have multiple intelligences—an "intelligence" being an ability to solve a problem or create a product within a specific cultural setting. Gardner sees the need to hypothesize multiple types of intelligence to capture the full range of human abilities. He originally proposed seven types (Gardner, 1983), but later added one more and discussed the possibility of two others (Gardner, 1999). For example, one of his multiple intelligences is *linguistic intelligence*, which is the capability measured by most IQ tests and scholastic achievement tests. Another type of intelligence is *bodily-kinesthetic*, which is the type of intelligence that allows skilled motor movements. Gardner's 10 types of intelligences are summarized in **Table 11.3** on p. 403.

Gardner's approach has been praised for its recognition of the cultural context of intelligence, its consideration of multiple human competencies, and the framework it offers in which to analyze intelligence in school and other applied settings (Kornhaber, Fierros, & Veenema, 2004). The criticisms of his approach focus on terminology—for example, are talents one type of intelligence? Some critics assert that Gardner's "intelligences" are not as independent as he claims but rather are highly correlated with one another, essentially measuring the same thing. Others claim that the intelligences seem to resemble learning and personality styles, not competencies. Gardner's theory represents an important contribution to thinking about intelligence as a broader system of abilities. Another theory that takes the systems approach is Sternberg's theory of successful intelligence.

Sternberg's Theory of Successful Intelligence

Robert J. Sternberg maintains that traditional tests used by colleges to make admissions decisions—including the SAT, the GRE, and even IQ tests—measure only limited aspects of behavior and do not predict future success very well (Sternberg, Grigorenko, & Bundy, 2001; Sternberg & Williams, 1997). Such tests often do not look at the person within his or her sociocultural context, and they fail to consider the various dimensions of intelligence. Sternberg says that testing involves the same populations and the same tasks in the same contexts and gets the same results—which are often wrong and not generalizable to all people (Sternberg & Grigorenko, 2000b).

Sternberg (2003b, 2003c) asserts that a comprehensive theory of intelligence must focus on *successful intelligence*, or "the ability to achieve success in life in terms of one's personal standards, within one's sociocultural context" (Sternberg, 2003b, pp. 55–56). Sternberg believes that psychologists should investigate not how much intelligence people have, but how they use it. A theory that focuses on successful intelligence is applicable not only to a wide variety of people but also to cultures around the world. Sternberg (2003b, 2003c; Sternberg, Castegon, et al., 2001) has proposed that successful intelligence consists of three dimensions: analytic, practical, and creative (see **Figure 11.3**). And it also depends on balancing these factors, drawing on one's strengths and compensating for one's weaknesses.

The *analytic dimension* of intelligence involves an individual's ability to solve problems in specific situations where there is one right answer. This part of

Table 11.3

GARDNER'S MULTIPLE INTELLIGENCES

Gardner originally proposed the first seven intelligences listed here. He later added naturalistic intelligence and is considering the addition of spiritual and existential intelligences.

Type of Intelligence	Exemplar	Core Components
■ Linguistic	Poet Journalist	Sensitivity to the sounds, rhythms, and meanings of words; sensitivity to the different functions of language
■ Logical-mathematical	Scientist Mathematician	Sensitivity to and capacity to discern logical or numerical patterns; ability to handle long chains of reasoning
■ Musical	Composer Violinist	Ability to produce and appreciate rhythm, pitch, and timbre; appreciation of the forms of musical expressiveness
■ Spatial	Navigator Sculptor	Capacity to perceive the visual–spatial world accurately and to perform transformations on initial perceptions
■ Bodily-kinesthetic	Dancer Athlete	Ability to control bodily movements and to handle objects skillfully
■ Interpersonal	Therapist Salesperson	Capacity to discern and respond appropriately to the moods, temperaments, motivations, and desires of other people
■ Intrapersonal	Person with detailed, accurate self-knowledge	Ability to access one's own feelings and to discriminate among them and draw on them to guide behavior; knowledge of one's own strengths, weaknesses, desires, and intelligence
■ Naturalistic	Botanist Chef	Ability to make fine discriminations among the flora and fauna of the natural world or the patterns and designs of human artifacts
■ Spiritual	Religious leader Person with deep spiritual beliefs	Ability to master abstract concepts about being and also the ability to attain a certain state of being
■ Existential	Philosopher	Capacity to understand one's place in the universe and the nature of being in both physical and psychological terms

Source: Gardner, 1999; Gardner & Hatch, 1989

Figure 11.3
Sternberg's
Theory of
Successful
Intelligence
Includes Three
Dimensions

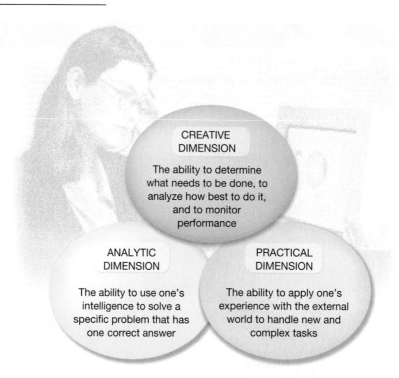

CREATIVE DIMENSION

The ability to determine what needs to be done, to analyze how best to do it, and to monitor performance

ANALYTIC DIMENSION

The ability to use one's intelligence to solve a specific problem that has one correct answer

PRACTICAL DIMENSION

The ability to apply one's experience with the external world to handle new and complex tasks

Sternberg's theory focuses on how people shape their environments so that their competencies can be used to best advantage. In Western societies, analytical intelligence is measured on tests and valued in classrooms. For example, a student might divide an argument into parts and think of a counterargument for each component part. The analytic dimension does not refer to any specific mental operations required to carry out problem solving, and thus it may be culture-free. The analytic dimension may be used by an African herdsman weaving leaves to build walls for a dwelling, a machinist cleaning a lathe, or a student solving a problem in long division. However, the emphasis on the analytic dimension is stronger in Western society than in Asian societies, especially China (Tweed & Lehman, 2002).

The *practical dimension* has to do with a person's application of his or her experiences in the external world and with everyday tasks. This part of Sternberg's successful intelligence includes the ability to adapt, shape, and select environments to enhance one's performance, often so that one can function smoothly without thinking consciously about the situation. An example of such mastery through experience is learning time management during one's first year of college. Managing one's time to include studying is a skill different from studying itself, but this practical dimension of intelligence is necessary for college success. Initially, skills based on the practical dimension usually require a lot of attention and may be difficult to develop, but practice makes them nearly automatic (Sternberg & Grigorenko, 2000a).

The *creative dimension* of successful intelligence is the factor that differentiates Sternberg's theory from other theories of intelligence. Most theories of intelligence (and most intelligence tests) do not include such a dimension, but Sternberg considers creativity an essential component of intelligence. The creative dimension includes the ability to deal with novel situations and to think about solutions in new ways. It also includes the ability to make successful transitions between conventional and unconventional ways of thinking. This is the aspect of intelligence necessary to write a love poem or a computer program. Tasks that tap creative intelligence include solving novel verbal analogies and number operations, applying new rules to prior knowledge, and imagining unknown situations, complete with consistent details.

Few behaviors engage all three dimensions of intelligence, so Sternberg asserts that various tasks measure intelligence to differing extents. Thus, from Sternberg's point of view, new batteries of tests are needed to fully analyze the three basic dimensions of intelligent behavior (Sternberg, 2003b). Good predictors of a person's academic achievement should take into account knowledge of the world—practical intelligence or common sense—in addition to verbal comprehension and mathematical reasoning (Sternberg, 2000b). Some people develop practical intelligence on their own, but too often, children do poorly in school and in life despite having obvious intellectual skills. These individuals often do not know how to allocate their time or how to work effectively with other people. Such skills need to be taught. As Ceci (2000) asserts, schools foster the learning of specific skills, not necessarily general problem-solving abilities. In addition, schools tend to promote specific ways of thinking about problems, often neglecting the creative component of intelligence. Researchers and intelligence tests need to value alternative modes of thought and creativity. As Sternberg (2003b, p. 69) suggests, "The time perhaps has come to expand . . . everyone's notion of what it means to be intelligent."

Gardner's multiple intelligences include interpersonal intelligence, and Sternberg's successful intelligence has the ability to interact effectively as part of the practical dimension. This ability has been popularized as the concept of emotional intelligence.

Emotions—A Different Kind of Intelligence?

Being highly intelligent (as assessed by IQ tests) is no guarantee of success in life. It is true that doing well in school is important, but there is more to success—in work and in life—than superior cognitive ability. You probably know people who are quite bright intellectually but who have few leadership skills, insufficient motivation, or poor "people skills." In 1990, Peter Salovey and John Mayer proposed that knowing how emotions work and being able to regulate one's emotions effectively contribute to success in ways that differ from the contributions of intellectual ability. In 1995, Daniel Goleman popularized this concept in his book *Emotional Intelligence*.

Emotional intelligence is the ability to both perceive and express emotions in accurate and adaptive ways (Salovey & Pizarro, 2003). Individuals who are high in emotional intelligence are able to regulate their own emotions and to perceive the emotions of others so that they get along well in a variety of situations. According to Salovey and his colleagues (Mayer & Salovey, 1997; Salovey & Pizarro, 2003), emotional intelligence has four aspects: (1) the ability to perceive emotions in oneself

Emotional intelligence ■
The ability to both perceive and express emotions in accurate and adaptive ways.

and in others, (2) the ability to use emotions to facilitate thought, (3) the ability to understand emotional information and its impact, and (4) the ability to manage emotions, both one's own and those of others. According to this view, emotion is a dimension omitted from traditional definitions of intelligence, which are therefore inadequate as theoretical conceptualizations and as predictors of people's abilities.

Cognitive ability and emotional intelligence are not mutually exclusive. Highly intelligent people can be high in emotional intelligence, but they can also be insensitive to their own emotions and those of others, unable to manage their emotions, and oblivious to the effect of emotions in their lives—that is, low in emotional intelligence. Both Salovey and his colleagues and Goleman contend that, all other things being equal, those with high emotional intelligence will nearly always do better than those with low emotional intelligence—independent of cognitive abilities. Mayer, Salovey, and Caruso (2000) argue that people can learn to regulate their emotions. These researchers separate the effects of emotion and intelligence and assert that each affects the other. They contend that Goleman's popularization of the concept of emotional intelligence focuses too much on the motivational properties of emotional states.

The concept of emotional intelligence is beginning to gain research support. A study with college students (Brackett, Mayer, & Warner, 2004) found that a measure of emotional intelligence was related to problems experienced by those students: Male students whose emotional intelligence was low were more likely than other students to experience alcohol and drug problems. A study with British secondary school students found similar results relating to risks for problem behavior and also showed that high emotional intelligence scores predicted academic success (Petrides, Frederickson, & Furnham, 2004). Another study found that emotional intelligence was a predictive factor for academic success among first-year university students (Parker et al., 2004). Studies have also shown that emotional intelligence relates to success in the workplace, both for effective leaders (Palmer, Gardner, & Stough, 2003) and for workers (Stough & De Guara, 2003). Emotional intelligence was related to workers' creativity and innovation in solving problems as well as to their ability to work in teams. These results seem to support the idea that emotional intelligence is an additional aspect of intelligence, separate from academic and intellectual capacity.

How Do Psychologists Develop Tests?

Of the dozens of tests that you have taken during your years of school, one or more may have been intelligence tests, but most were achievement or aptitude tests. *Achievement tests* are tests designed to measure how well students have learned specific content. Schools administer achievement tests, often at the beginning and end of the academic year, to assess how well students have learned during the year. Achievement tests differ from *aptitude tests*, which are psychological tests designed to measure the ability to learn specific types of material. These two types of tests concentrate on specific content or ability rather than general intelligence. In addition to failing to measure general intelligence, neither of these types of tests measures other characteristics that are important to success, such as motivation, creativity, and leadership skills.

Achievement tests ■
Tests designed to measure how well students have learned specific content.

Aptitude tests ■
Psychological tests designed to measure the ability to learn specific types of material.

Whether or not you were aware of the results of achievement and aptitude tests you took, those results may have determined your educational track from elementary school onward. But psychologists are among the first to admit that intelligence, achievement, and aptitude tests have shortcomings. Understanding how psychologists develop tests can help you see the limitations of tests.

Developing an Intelligence Test

Imagine you are a 7-year-old child taking an intelligence test, and the test administrator asks you "Which one of the following tells you the temperature?" and then shows you pictures of the sun, a radio, a thermometer, and a pair of mittens. Is the thermometer the only correct answer? If there are no thermometers in your home, but you often hear the temperature given on radio weather reports, or if you estimate the temperature each morning by stepping outside to feel the sun's strength, or if you know it's cold outside when your parents tell you to wear mittens, then you may choose a picture of something other than the thermometer. Does this choice indicate lower intelligence or different experiences?

What Does a Test Measure?

In general, a *test* is a standardized device for examining a person's responses to specific stimuli, usually questions or problems. Because responses to some test questions can be based on experiences—which reflect social and cultural biases—developing intelligence tests free of cultural bias is a challenge. Because there are many potential pitfalls in creating a test, psychologists follow an elaborate set of guidelines and procedures to make certain that questions are properly constructed. These steps include deciding what the test is to measure, constructing items, and then standardizing the test. Standardization is a process common to all psychological and educational tests.

Standardization

Standardization is the process of developing uniform procedures for administering and scoring a test and for establishing norms. *Norms* are the scores and corresponding percentile ranks of a large and representative sample of individuals from the population for which the test is designed. A *representative sample* is a sample of individuals who match the larger population for which the test is designed with regard to key variables such as socioeconomic status and age. Thus, a test designed for all first-year U.S. college students might be given to a sample of 2,000 first-year students, including an equal number of men and women, who graduated from large and small high schools, come from different areas of the United States, are of various ages, and represent different ethnic groups and socioeconomic levels.

Standardization ensures that there is a basis for comparing all future test results with those of the standard reference group. Establishing norms by testing a representative sample of the population allows psychologists and educators to be able to interpret future test results properly. Norms serve as a reference point for comparing individual scores.

Standardization ■ The process of developing uniform procedures for administering and scoring a test and for establishing norms.

Norms ■ The scores and corresponding percentile ranks of a large and representative sample of individuals from the population for which a test was designed.

Representative sample ■ A sample of individuals who match the larger population for which a test is designed with regard to key variables such as socioeconomic status and age.

Figure 11.4
A Normal
Distribution
The bell-shaped
curve shows a stan-
dard normal distri-
bution. In normal
distributions of
height, weight, and
even intelligence,
very few people
appear at the
extremes.

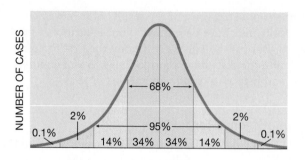

The Normal Curve

Test developers generally plot the scores of the representative sample on a graph that shows how frequently each score occurs. On most tests, some people score very well, some score very poorly, and most score in the middle. Psychologists say that test scores distributed in this way are *normally distributed* or that they fall on a normal curve. A **normal curve** is a bell-shaped graphic representation of normally distributed data that shows the percentage of the population that falls under each part of the curve. As **Figure 11.4** shows, most people fall in the middle range, with a few at each extreme. Psychologists often devise tests so that individual scores can be placed within a normal distribution. (The Appendix discusses the normal distribution in more detail.)

Normal curve ■ A bell-shaped graphic representation of normally distributed data that shows the percentage of the population that falls under each part of the curve.

Scores

The simplest score on a test is the *raw score*—the number of correct answers, not converted or transformed in any way. The raw score, however, may be difficult to interpret. Raw scores on many tests, particularly intelligence tests, are transformed into *standard scores*—scores that express each individual's position relative to those of other test takers, based on the mean score and on how scores are distributed around it. If, for example, a 100-item intelligence test is administered to 8-year-olds and 16-year-olds, test developers expect 16-year-olds to answer more items correctly than 8-year-olds. To adjust for such differences, scoring procedures allow each individual's score to be compared to the score typically achieved by others the same age. A standard score is generally a *percentile score*—a score indicating what percentage of the population taking the test obtained a lower score. If, for example, someone's percentile score is 84, then 84% of those taking the test obtained a lower score than that person did.

Another way to accomplish this type of comparison of scores on IQ tests is to convert the number of correct items into a *deviation IQ*—a standard IQ test score whose mean and standard deviation remain constant for all ages. If a child of 8 and an adolescent of 16 each have a deviation IQ of 116, they are in the same percentile relative to others of their respective ages who have taken the same IQ test.

Raw score ■ A test score that simply gives the number of correct answers not converted or transformed in any way.

Standard score ■ A score that expresses an individual's position relative to those of other test takers, based on the mean score and on how scores are distributed around it.

Percentile score ■ A score indicating what percentage of the population taking a test obtained a lower score.

Deviation IQ ■ A standard IQ test score whose mean and standard deviation remain constant for all ages.

Reliability

Reliability is a test's ability to yield very similar scores for the same individual over repeated testings. That is, reliability refers to the consistency of test scores. (When a researcher says that test scores have consistency, the researcher is assuming that the person taking the test is in approximately the same emotional and physiological state each time the test is administered.) If a test's results are not consistent over several testing sessions or for two comparable groups of people, useful comparisons are impossible. A test is rarely perfectly reliable, but it should be generally consistent and yield similar results from multiple administrations.

There are several ways to determine whether a test is reliable, but the simplest is the *test–retest method*. To determine test–retest reliability, the same test is administered to the same person on two or more occasions. If, for example, the person achieves a score of 87 one day and 110 another, the test is not very reliable (see **Table 11.4**). Of course, the person might have remembered some of the items from one test session to the next. Retesting individuals after long periods of time avoids the memory problem but raises the issue of the stability of test scores. IQ scores do not remain the same over the life span. Adults' scores remain relatively stable, but the IQ scores of infants do not correlate well with their IQ scores when they are of school age (Bayley, 1969). In general, psychologists have shown that intelligence test scores increase with age during childhood, then level off in adulthood, only to decline somewhat in late adulthood (Deary et al., 2004). This decline may be due to diseases that affect the brain rather than a general cognitive decline related to aging. Interestingly, this decline associated with aging affects women more than men.

To establish reliability within a shorter time frame, testers use the *alternative-form method* of determining reliability, which involves giving two different versions of the same test. If the two versions test the same characteristics and content and differ only in the specific items they contain, both should yield very similar results. Another way to evaluate reliability is to use the *split-half method*, which involves dividing a test into two parts; the scores from the two halves of a reliable test yield similar, if not identical, results.

Reliability ■ The ability of a test to yield very similar scores for the same individual over repeated testings.

Table 11.4

TEST–RETEST RELIABILITY

Test–retest reliability indicates whether people who are given the same or a similar test on repeated occasions achieve similar scores each time.

	Test with High Reliability		Test with Low Reliability	
	Score from First Testing	Score from Second Testing	Score from First Testing	Score from Second Testing
■ Person 1	92	90	92	74
■ Person 2	87	89	87	96
■ Person 3	78	77	78	51

Validity

If a psychology exam included questions such as "What is the square root of 647?" and "Who wrote *The Grapes of Wrath*?" that test would not be a valid measure of test takers' knowledge of psychology. That is, it would not be measuring what it is supposed to measure. To be useful, a test must have not only reliability, but also *validity*—the ability to measure only what it is supposed to measure and to predict only what it is supposed to predict.

Validity ▪ The ability of a test to measure only what it is supposed to measure and to predict only what it is supposed to predict.

Types of Validity

Content validity is a test's ability to measure the knowledge or behavior it is intended to measure; content validity is determined through a detailed examination of the contents of the test items. A test designed to measure musical aptitude should not include items that assess mechanical aptitude or personality characteristics.

In addition to content validity, a test should have *predictive validity*—the ability to predict a person's future achievement with some degree of accuracy. IQ tests such as the Stanford–Binet and the Wechsler scales and aptitude tests such as the SAT are not always accurate predictors of people's performance, even in school situations. Tests cannot take into account high levels of motivation or creative abilities. Nevertheless, many colleges use standard scores from such tests to decide which high school students should be admitted—thus assuming that the scores accurately predict the students' ability to do college-level work.

Content validity ▪ The ability of a test to measure the knowledge or behavior it is intended to measure, determined through a detailed examination of the contents of the test items.

Predictive validity ▪ The ability of a test to predict a person's future achievement with at least some degree of accuracy.

Criticisms of Intelligence Test Validity

Critics cite many problems concerning the validity of intelligence tests. One major criticism is that intelligence cannot be measured precisely because no clear definition of intelligence has been agreed on. The defense against this argument is that, even though different intelligence tests seem to measure different abilities, the major tests are good, if not perfect, predictors of scholastic ability (Kuncel et al., 2001). However, scholastic ability includes many skills, and it is important to remember that it is not the same thing as general intelligence.

A second criticism is that intelligence test items usually refer to *learned information* and therefore reflect the quality of an individual's schooling rather than his or her underlying intelligence. The response to this point is that people learn most vocabulary items on intelligence tests in their general environment, not only in school. Moreover, the ability to learn vocabulary and facts seems to depend on a general ability to reason verbally. But as important as verbal reasoning is, it is not the same as general intelligence.

A third criticism is that the administration of intelligence tests in school settings may adversely affect test scores—not only because the tests are often administered inexpertly, but also because of the halo effect (e.g., Darley and Gross, 2000). The *halo effect* is the tendency for one noticeable characteristic of an individual (or a group) to influence the evaluation of other characteristics. A test administrator may

Halo effect ▪ The tendency for one noticeable characteristic of an individual (or a group) to influence the evaluation of other characteristics.

develop a positive or negative feeling about a person, a class, or a group of students that may influence the administration of tests or the interpretation of test scores. People who defend intelligence tests against this charge acknowledge that incorrectly administered tests are likely to result in inaccurate scores, but they claim that errors in administration occur less often than critics think. However, bias in administration or scoring is a threat to test validity and has the potential to lead to discrimination against particular groups of students.

Another criticism is that test takers' scores are affected by their own expectations for their performance, and their per-formance can decrease as a result of *stereotype threat*. As we saw at the beginning of the chapter, Claude Steele (1999; Steele & Aronson, 2000) has argued that whenever members of ethnic or other minorities concentrate explicitly on a scholastic task, they worry about confirming negative stereotypes about their group. This burden may drag down their performance. Stereotype threat applies to many individuals in a variety of testing situations and can be aroused by several kinds of cues, even subtle ones (Mayer & Hanges, 2003). For example, one study demonstrated the effect of stereotype threat by telling women who were about to take a math test that women typically perform more poorly than men on this type of test, a statement that explicitly activated stereotype threat (Smith & White, 2002). These women performed more poorly than women who were told that women and men score the same on the test, a statement designed to counteract any stereotype threat the women might have felt. When women were administered the same math test without being told explicitly how women perform compared to men, they performed worse than men, which demonstrates Steele's point about stereotype threat—the stereotype is always present and threatens the performance of individuals from stereotyped groups.

Stereotype threat ■ The fear that one's performance on a task will confirm a negative stereotype about one's group.

One final criticism of the validity of intelligence tests refers to the sociocultural context: Economic and social success in the United States is heavily influenced by academic achievement and the opportunities that emerge from completing college. But entry into college is determined by success on standardized tests, which is influenced by other educational and intelligence tests (Sternberg, 2000b). All standardized test results are affected by schooling. Thus, the system is self-reinforcing and circular. So the criticism is that the society *creates* the correlation between academic success and intelligence test scores. The defense against this criticism, again, is that the test scores also correlate with measures of intelligence that seem independent of schooling, but the counter-criticism is that very few measures of intelligence are free of such influences.

Interpretation of scores is also an important component of the validity of tests. Remember that intelligence tests are generally made up of different subtests or subscales, each yielding a score. There may also be one general score for the entire test. All these scores require knowledgeable interpretation. In addition, test scores must be put into a context that is relevant to the situation of the test taker (Daniel, 2000). Without such a context, a score is little more than a number. The interpretation of test scores is crucial—without correct interpretation, a single score can be biased, inaccurate, or misleading. **Table 11.5** summarizes some misconceptions about intelligence tests and testing.

Table 11.5	
SOME MISCONCEPTIONS ABOUT INTELLIGENCE TESTS AND TESTING	
Misconception	**Reality**
Intelligence tests measure innate intelligence.	IQ scores measure some of an individual's interactions with the environment; they never measure only innate intelligence.
IQs never change.	People's IQs change throughout life, but especially from birth through age 6. Even after this age, significant changes can occur.
Intelligence tests provide perfectly reliable scores.	Test scores are only estimates. Every test should be reported as a statement of probability, such as "There is a 90% chance that the test taker's IQ falls within a 6-point range of the reported score (from 3 points above to 3 points below)."
Intelligence tests measure all aspects of a person's intelligence.	Most intelligence tests do not measure the entire spectrum of abilities related to intellectual behavior. Some stress verbal and nonverbal intelligence but do not adequately measure other areas, such as mechanical skills, creativity, or social intelligence.
A battery of tests reveals everything necessary to make judgments about a person's competence.	No battery of tests can give a complete picture of any person. A battery can only illuminate various areas of functioning.

Source: Sattler, 1992

How Do Biological and Environmental Factors Contribute to Intelligence?

The varying opinions concerning what intelligence is and the political, cultural, and scientific issues related to measuring intelligence have created controversies. These are complicated by findings about ethnic differences in IQ scores. Along with some psychologists and educators, minority groups have challenged the usefulness of IQ tests by pointing to their biases. However, underlying both the public concern and the scientific debate is the fundamental question of the extent to which intelligence is due to heredity (nature) or to upbringing and culture (nurture).

Biological Factors and Intelligence

Biology (nature) has the potential to influence intelligence in at least two ways: through evolutionary heritage and through specific genetic inheritance. Although these two mechanisms are not entirely independent, their patterns of influence may operate differently.

Evolution and Intelligence

A fundamental assumption of evolutionary psychology is that human behaviors can be explained as efforts to fulfill some evolutionary goal, which typically involves adaptations that increase the chances for reproduction. From an evolutionary perspective, then, intelligence develops in specific ways. In general, our smarter ancestors were able to avoid predators, develop the use of tools, and plant crops that provided nutrition. Over the course of generations, smarter individuals predominated. In this way, over hundreds of generations, the elements of complex intellectual functioning are acquired.

Evolutionary psychology does not concentrate on the development of general intelligence. Rather, this approach focuses on the evolution of mental adaptations oriented toward solving specific problems that were important in human prehistory (Cosmides & Tooby, 2002; Tooby & Cosmides, 1997). For example, the ability to acquire language provided specific advantages in communication. The evolution of specialized "mental modules" is the focus of intelligence for evolutionary psychologists; the general factors of intelligence are less important than these specific adaptations (Kanazawa, 2004).

Although evolutionary psychologists acknowledge the existence of general human intelligence (Cosmides & Tooby, 2002), they tend to see it as a property that emerged from the combination of the specialized modules rather than the other way around. According to this view, general intelligence exists, but its existence is an incidental outcome of evolution rather than the focus (Kanazawa, 2004). Thus, the view of evolutionary psychologists differs from that of psychologists who have developed intelligence tests and also that of psychologists who study the genetic component of intelligence.

Genetic Contributions to Intelligence

If you came from a well-bred, upper-class family and had access to schooling and appropriate family connections, you would likely be smart. Or so thought Sir Francis Galton in the 19th century. Galton was among the first to speculate that genetics was a factor in intelligence, arguing that intelligence—a measurable trait or ability—is passed from generation to generation. Today, some psychologists have extended and refined Galton's notions, attempting to understand how genetic factors contribute to intelligence.

The main goal of these behavioral genetics researchers has been to determine the *heritability* of intelligence, the genetically determined proportion of the trait's variation among individuals in a population. As we discussed in Chapter 3, the heritability of some traits is more obvious than for others. For example, height is a highly heritable trait. Children who have two tall parents have a strong likelihood of being tall—the heritability of height is high. When behavioral geneticists say that a trait is heritable, especially when they attach a percentage to that heritability—for example, 50%—they mean that 50% of the variation (difference) among a group of people in

Heritability ■ The genetically determined proportion of a trait's variation among individuals in a population.

that trait is attributable to heredity. Note that this is *not* the same as saying that 50% of a specific person's intelligence, height, or any other trait is determined by heredity. Also note that even highly heritable traits, such as height, can be modified by the environment. Deprive the child of tall parents of a nutritious diet during the growth years, and the child will likely not be as tall as she or he could have been. This is an example of an interaction between nature (genes for height) and nurture (nutrition during childhood).

Estimates of the heritability of intelligence vary, partly because of variations in the research techniques that attempt to measure it. To establish how much of intelligence is heritable, one strategy is to study twins. Identical twins are genetically identical, so any variation in their intelligence must be due to environment, not heredity. If the intelligence test scores of identical twins are more similar than those of fraternal twins, of other siblings, of parents and children, and of unrelated people, this similarity is evidence for a genetic component for intelligence (Petrill, 2003). **Figure 11.5** summarizes the correlation between the IQ scores of related and unrelated children and adults found in different studies. If genetics were the sole determinant of IQ scores, the correlation for identical twins would be 1.00 whether they were reared together or apart. However, identical twins, whether raised together or apart, do not have identical IQ scores—although their scores are similar. Over 50 years of research on this topic has led researchers to conclude that about 50% of the similarity in the IQ test scores of identical twins can be accounted for by heredity (Plomin & Spinath, 2004).

Another strategy for estimating the role of heredity in intelligence involves studying adopted children who are raised by adults other than their biological

Figure 11.5
Correlations between IQ Scores of Persons of Varying Relationships
The closer the biological relationship of two individuals, the more similar their IQ scores—providing strong support for a genetic component to intelligence. (Based on data from Bouchard & McGue, 1981, and Erlenmeyer-Kimling & Jarvik, 1963.)

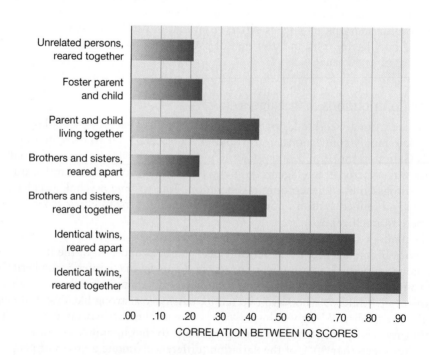

parents (e.g., Finkel et al., 1998; McGue & Bouchard, 2000). Behavioral geneticists compare an adopted person's intelligence test scores and other measures of cognitive ability with those of biological parents, adoptive parents, biological siblings, and adoptive siblings. The goal is to see if the adopted individual's scores more closely resemble those of biological relatives or adoptive relatives. Results suggest that the biological mother's IQ score has a more important effect on an adopted child's IQ score than the adoptive home environment. As time passes, the correlation between the IQ score of an adopted child and those of the adoptive parents decreases, and the correlation with the IQ scores of the child's biological parents increases (Plomin & DeFries, 1999; Plomin et al., 1997; Stoolmiller, 1999). Eysenck (1998) explains this finding by asserting that when an adopted child is young, his or her environment is determined solely by the adoptive parents, resulting in a correlation with their IQ scores. But as the child grows older, he or she becomes less subject to parental environmental influences. His or her biological predispositions become more evident, and the result is a greater correlation with the IQ scores of the biological parents.

Therefore, the evidence is clear that genetic factors play a role in intelligence, at least when it is defined as the scores on IQ tests such as the Stanford–Binet and the Wechsler tests. Because the correlation between the IQ scores of identical twins is far from perfect, twin and adoption studies also indicate that the environment is an important factor in intelligence.

Environmental and Cultural Factors in Intelligence

Factors in an individual's immediate environment influence intelligence, but the broader culture is also important. Indeed, as we noted earlier, even the definition of intelligence varies by culture (Sternberg, 2003b). The history of intelligence testing has been marked by numerous accusations that these tests are culturally biased. That is, people from various groups feel that intelligence tests such as the Stanford–Binet, the WISC, and the WAIS test for information that is related to culture, not intelligence.

Accusations of Cultural Bias

The accusations of cultural bias in intelligence tests assert that these tests are effective in assessing people who resemble the test makers, who are usually White, male, middle-class suburbanites. If this group is the only one for which the tests are valid, then the tests are culturally biased. A test item or subscale is considered culturally biased if, with all other factors held constant, its content is more difficult for members of one group than for those of other groups. To understand how a test item can be culturally biased, imagine that the young child of impoverished migrant workers is asked the question about temperature that we considered earlier. If the child is unfamiliar with thermometers and radios, the child might choose the sun as the best answer. But if the test designer has deemed "thermometer" the correct answer, the child's answer will be counted wrong.

Accusations of cultural bias have some basis in fact. For example, Lewis Terman, who adapted the Binet–Simon test for use in the United States, was enthusiastic about using the test to find mentally defective individuals so that they could be prevented from having children (Leslie, 2000). His standardization of the test excluded Asian American, Hispanic American, and African American children, yet the test was used to classify children from all ethnic groups. This is a clear instance of cultural bias.

Since the early 1970s, educators and psychologists have scrutinized the weaknesses of IQ tests and have attempted to eliminate cultural biases by creating better tests and establishing better norms that include a representative sample of individuals from all ethnic groups. However, despite attempts to control for the influences of different cultural backgrounds, tests tend to reflect the values of the dominant culture. One conclusion is strikingly clear: *Rather than measuring innate intellectual capacity, IQ tests measure the degree to which people have adapted to the culture in which they live.* In many cultures, to be intelligent is to be socially adept. In Western society, because social aptitude is linked with schooling, the more schooling you have, the higher your IQ score is likely to be (Ceci & Williams, 1997).

All individuals have special capabilities (not necessarily intellectual ones), and how those capabilities are regarded depends on the social environment. Being a genius in traditional African cultures may be defined as being a good storyteller; in the United States, it is often associated solely with high academic achievement. Concern about the implications of this limited conception of intelligence is one reason why some American educators are placing less emphasis on IQ scores.

Even if intelligence tests are not intentionally culturally biased, the content of any test reflects the culture in which the test was developed. All tests originate within a culture, and tests cannot be completely free of that culture. Environment and culture inevitably contribute to intelligence and to scores on intelligence, aptitude, and achievement tests.

Environmental Factors That Influence Intelligence

Considering the history of intelligence testing and the relationship between intelligence and school-related abilities, it comes as no surprise that IQ scores show a positive correlation with level of education (Colom et al., 2002; Wechsler, 1958). People with more education tend to score higher on intelligence tests. But is their higher education the reason for their higher IQ scores, or does their higher intelligence allow them to be more successful and to continue longer in school? This dilemma highlights the problem of interpreting a correlation—it is impossible to say which variable (if either) causes the other. However, the correlation confirms the overlap between the types of skills that are required to do well in school and on intelligence tests.

In addition to the relationship between intelligence and education, there is a correlation between a child's IQ and that child's parents' level of education (Neiss & Rowe, 2000). Parents with more education tend to have children with higher IQs. Again, this relationship is difficult to analyze. Do smart parents have smart children because of heredity, because they create family environments that foster the development of their children's abilities, or because they value intellectual achievement and urge their children to excel? Each of these factors may contribute.

Family environment, including how large the family is, plays a role in the development of intelligence (Downey, 2001). In addition, the birth order of each child within the family has an effect on IQ (Zajonc, 1976, 2001). Larger families tend to have children with lower IQs than do smaller families, and first-born children tend to have higher IQs than later-born children. Of course, all children within a large family may be very intelligent, and the older child in a family with two children may not be very smart, but averaged over thousands of families, these effects appear. Although difficult to interpret, these effects illustrate the many environmental factors that may contribute to intelligence.

The Interaction of Biological and Environmental Factors

In addition to the interaction between heredity and environment within families, nature and nurture play interacting roles in several other areas that relate to intelligence. Debate about the relative influence of nature and nurture on intelligence has began to focus on specific factors. As Stephen Petrill (2003, p. 81) put it, "research has begun to move beyond asking *whether* genes or environments are important to intelligence to an examination of *how* genes and environments influence the relationship among differing cognitive skills across development." Let's look at some research related to gender, socioeconomic status, and recent increases in IQ scores.

Gender and Intelligence

People have argued for centuries over who is smarter, men or women, and that controversy extends to specific cognitive abilities as well as overall intelligence. Research on gender differences in cognitive abilities clearly shows the influence of both biological and cultural factors. When Lewis Terman adapted the Stanford–Binet for use in the United States in the early years of the 20th century, it was widely assumed that women were less intelligent than men, so it came as a surprise to many psychologists (and most people) that women's IQ scores were as high as men's (Lewin, 1984). Although societal opinions have changed to some degree, this prejudice persists; people still tend to judge women's intelligence to be lower than men's (Furnham, Reeves, & Budhani, 2002). However, the standardization procedures for intelligence tests include equating scores for women and men, so overall, their IQ scores are equal.

Equal IQ scores do not necessarily mean equality in all cognitive abilities, and stereotypes of women and men hold that women have better verbal abilities, whereas men do better at mathematics. Parents and teachers have long encouraged boys to engage in spatial, mechanical, and mathematical tasks but have emphasized verbal interactions with girls. That encouragement prompts differences in the development of these abilities in boys and girls. Thus, gender stereotyping in the culture affects the expression of these abilities.

However, there are actually only small gender differences in performance on verbal and mathematical tasks (Hyde, 1996; Jaffee & Hyde, 2000; Plant et al., 2000). Decreasing gender-based stereotyping has led to more equal encouragement, and girls and boys now enroll in the same number of math classes, on average (Bae et al., 2000). The female advantage in verbal performance began to decline during the 1980s, and the male advantage in mathematics started to diminish during the 1990s (American Association of University Women, 1998). For these cognitive abilities, individual differences are much larger than gender differences. However, cultural stereotypes have contributed to maintaining gender differences in performance.

Socioeconomic Status and Intelligence

Other evidence of an influence on intelligence arising from interaction between genes and the environment comes from a study that examined the IQ scores of twins but also considered the factor of socioeconomic status (whether the children lived in poverty or in better-off homes). The results of this study (Turkheimer et al., 2003) showed that genetic factors accounted for most of the variation in IQ scores of the wealthier children but that environmental factors accounted for most of the variation in IQ scores of the children growing up near or below the poverty level. These results mean that the effect of heredity on IQ scores is not constant. Some environments promote optimal development, so the variation that appears in those environments will be due more to heredity. But some environments prevent adequate development. In those situations, the individual effects due to heredity are proportionally smaller than they are in more favorable environments.

Increases in Intelligence Test Scores

An interaction of biological and environmental factors may explain one of the most intriguing trends revealed by research on intelligence: the recent overall increases in IQ scores. James Flynn (1987, 1999) documented that IQ scores have been rising over the past 60 years in countries around the world. The increases have been substantial—about 20 IQ points gain within the past 30 years. These gains have been too rapid and dramatic to be due to genetic factors, so environment must be causing them.

But what environmental changes might be responsible for a 20-point increase in population IQ over 30 years? Has better nutrition promoted more optimal brain development? Has the growing complexity of technological society forced people to learn skills that boost their scores on IQ tests? Better nutrition does boost intelligence (Grigorenko, 2003), but this factor alone is not sufficient to account for the increases. Increasingly complex technology has changed the environment and prompted us to learn new skills, but this change is also not enough to account for the increased intelligence test scores.

Although neither heredity nor environment alone seems to be the reason for the increase, William Dickens and James Flynn (2001) argue that the interaction between the two underlies it. As the environment has become more complex, individuals make choices about their own situations and these choices amplify their inherent abilities and talents. The fit between abilities and situations multiplies the influence of the improved environment, boosting IQ at a rapid rate. An increasingly complex, technological society offers (and possibly demands) a wider range of complex skills, and people respond by refining the abilities they possess. However, people whose situations offer limited opportunities benefit less from this effect, so not everyone benefits equally from the changes in society.

Dickens and Flynn offered the increase in basketball performance as an analogy for how an interaction between genetic ability and environment can occur. The level of skill among basketball players has increased dramatically since the 1930s, partly because better nutrition has produced taller players and partly because society has promoted basketball through the broadcasting of games, the increase in salaries for professional players, and the wider range of opportunities to play the game at a higher level of skill. Those with high ability are able to play a better game today than was played 40 years ago because social factors have interacted with biological factors to select individuals with aptitude in this area and to develop their skill. Dickens and Flynn argue that the increases in IQ scores are due to a similar interaction of genetic and environmental forces.

What Is the Impact of Having an Exceptional IQ?

The American educational system is oriented toward testing for and teaching special or exceptional children. At the beginning of first grade, most children take some kind of test that assesses their reading readiness. By the end of fourth grade, students are usually classified and labeled with respect to their projected future development, largely on the basis of their scores on aptitude, achievement, and possibly intelligence tests. The results of these assessments are important for children's futures: "Individuals with advanced intellectual abilities are said to be *gifted* and in extreme cases are referred to as *geniuses*. Conversely, individuals who cannot complete common everyday cognitive tasks, or who can only complete them with partial success, are often said to be individuals with *mental retardation, cognitive delays*, or *intellectual disabilities*" (Thompson, McGrew, & Bruininks, 2002, p. 24). The impact of having an exceptionally high or low IQ varies, but deviating from the norm either way makes a difference.

Giftedness

Gifted individuals represent one end of the continuum of intelligence and talent. The phenomenon of giftedness has been recognized and discussed for centuries. Some, like Duke Ellington or Billie Holiday, display their giftedness musically. Others, like Serena Williams or Tiger Woods, display it in athletics; still others display it in science or in literature. Many great scientists, like Albert Einstein, made their most important theoretical discoveries very early in their careers, and Mozart's incredible musical talent was apparent when he was still a child. The attempt to identify giftedness in the young springs from the urge to allow gifted children to develop and use their full potential. However, just as there is no universally agreed-on definition of intelligence, there is no universally accepted definition of giftedness (Renzulli, 2002). Definitions that rely entirely on IQ restrict the number of individuals identified as gifted, often discriminating against ethnic groups. Definitions that include a variety of talents and mental abilities lead to identification of a wider group. Section 902 of the U.S. government's Gifted and Talented Children's Act of 1978 offers a liberal definition:

> The term *gifted and talented* means children and, whenever applicable, youth who are identified at the preschool, elementary, or secondary level as possessing demonstrated or potential abilities that give evidence of high performance responsibility in areas such as intellectual, creative, specific academic or leadership ability, or in the performing or visual arts and who by reason thereof require services or activities not ordinarily provided by the school.

Joseph Renzulli (2002) argues that you have to consider three key factors to determine giftedness: above-average ability, task commitment, and creativity. *Ability*, according to Renzulli, refers to both specific abilities and general capacity—which is not high IQ test scores but rather high levels of abstract thinking and rapid accurate, automatic thinking processes. *Task commitment* refers to a focused form of motivation—persistence, a drive to achieve, and a capacity for perseverance and dedicated practice. The third factor, *creativity*, refers to originality of thought, flexibility, curiosity, and an ability to set aside established or commonly accepted ideas. Renzulli argues that it is a combination of these three factors that creates the gifted individual. And the factors are often overlapping—a person who possesses all three is most likely to be considered truly gifted.

Gifted students need special opportunities to develop their abilities and talents fully, and many parents of gifted children believe that U.S. public schools fail to provide these opportunities (Hertzog & Bennett, 2004). Schools may fail to challenge gifted children to such an extent that the children lose interest in academics or develop behavioral problems. However, the image of gifted students as "troubled geniuses," loners, and problem students is inaccurate; research indicates that these students are at least as well adjusted as other students (Reis & Renzulli, 2004).

Although there is some disagreement over what types of programs best suit gifted students, individualized instruction and tailoring of programs is preferable (and probably for most children, not just the gifted) (Tieso, 2003). When special programs are available, most gifted students take advantage of the opportunity, earning advanced placement and college credit during high school (Lubinski et al., 2001).

Nearly every state has special programs for gifted students. However, some local school systems have none, and others provide special instruction only in brief periods or to small groups. These efforts may not be sufficiently challenging for most gifted students and certainly not for the extraordinarily gifted (Renzulli, 2004). Special schools for children with superior cognitive abilities, performing talents, or science aptitude have been successful, but their availability is limited. Failure to nurture gifted and talented students is a loss for the individuals and for society.

Intellectual Disability

The term *intellectual disability* refers to mental impairments and problems in learning and reasoning. This term is beginning to replace *mental retardation*, but both terms are used by some experts, and both are controversial. Recall that Binet and Simon developed a test for the Paris school system to identify students who needed special help to succeed in school (Boake, 2002). That identification was based on scores on the Binet–Simon test, but the definition of and range of behaviors that characterize "intellectual disability" have varied both over time and across cultures. In characterizing such disability, some cultures emphasize social skills, and others concentrate on intellectual abilities (Oakland et al., 2003).

Consistent with its origins in intelligence testing, the concept of mental retardation is often defined in terms of scores on an IQ test, but other behaviors may also be included. The American Association on Mental Retardation (2002) defines **mental retardation** as "a disability defined by significant limitations both in intellectual functioning and in adaptive skills." This definition also specifies that the disability must be identified before the individual is 18 years old and that the assessment procedure should take into account the individual's social and linguistic context. In addition, the definition states that mentally retarded individuals have strengths as well as limitations and that they require support to function in their environment.

Mental retardation ■ A disability defined by significant limitations in both intellectual functioning and adaptive skills.

When the definition of mental retardation is framed in terms of the type of support required, the estimate of the number of disabled individuals varies more than when IQ is the sole criterion (Leonard & Wen, 2002). But even when IQ scores are used as the basis for classification, the number of people identified as mentally retarded varies, because the overall increase in IQ scores affects how many individuals score in the lower part of the distribution of those scores (Kanaya, Scullin, & Ceci, 2003). Therefore, it is difficult to obtain precise estimates of how many people are affected by intellectual disabilities. However, according to a recent study in the United States (National Center on Birth Defects and Developmental Disabilities, 2004), about 1% of children between ages 3 and 10 years old are affected. Older children are more likely than younger children to be identified as intellectually disabled, and boys are more likely to be affected than girls. These differences appear in other countries, including Australia, France, and Zimbabwe (Oakland et al., 2003). The reason for the gender difference is that some of the causes of mental retardation affect boys more often than girls.

There are a variety of causes of mental retardation, including deprived environments, genetic abnormalities, infectious diseases, and physical trauma, which can be damage to the fetus caused by drugs taken during pregnancy, trauma produced by problems during delivery, or injury during infancy and childhood (Leonard & Wen, 2002). Three of the major known causes of mental retardation are the genetic conditions of Down syndrome and fragile X syndrome and the environmentally caused fetal alcohol syndrome. Fragile X syndrome only affects males. Fetal alcohol syndrome is the result of a woman's consuming alcohol during pregnancy, and it affects both genders. For some cases of mental retardation, no cause is ever identified.

Levels of mental retardation were once defined in terms of IQ scores, but now the classification is based on the amount of support the individual requires. The resources and strategies necessary to promote the education, development, and well-being of people with intellectual disabilities vary (American Association on Mental

Table 11.6

TYPES OF SUPPORT REQUIRED FOR INDIVIDUALS WITH INTELLECTUAL DISABILITIES

Level of Support	Description	Examples of Areas Where Assistance May Be Needed
■ Intermittent	Person sometimes needs support to accomplish some activities	Registering for school (but not going to school) Getting a job (but not doing the job)
■ Limited	Person needs consistent support, but not on a daily basis	Job training Finding appropriate housing Obtaining legal services Making financial decisions
■ Extensive	Person needs consistent, daily support in some but not all environments	Transportation Shopping and purchasing food Housekeeping and cleaning Taking medication
■ Pervasive	Person needs extensive, daily support in all life areas	Dressing Bathing and personal care Communicating with others

Retardation, 2002). **Table 11.6** lists the levels of support and gives examples of each. With appropriate support, most mentally retarded individuals are able to lead productive lives. Since the mid-1970s, the trend has been to integrate these individuals into school classrooms and workplaces—to give them the opportunity to receive an appropriate education and to participate as productive members in society.

Special Education: The IDEA

The Individuals with Disabilities Education Act (IDEA), Public Law 102-119, guarantees a free appropriate public education to children with disabilities in the United States. Similar laws have been passed in many other countries, especially industrialized countries with requirements for education (Oakland et al., 2003). Fundamental to the IDEA is the basic assumption that all children can achieve, that schools need to set reasonable and attainable achievement goals for all children, that parents should be involved in the education of their children, that special programs must be provided to build teachers' skills in working with special needs children, and that local municipalities must provide for the education of children with disabilities. Among the disabilities addressed by the IDEA are intellectual disability, hearing impairments, speech impairments, visual impairments, emotional impairments, orthopedic impairments, autism, and specific learning disabilities, as well as delayed development.

The IDEA has changed the lives of people with disabilities by providing legal guarantees for their education and protection against discrimination in employment.

Prior to the 1980s, thousands of children received neither special education nor special attention. Today, under IDEA, all school-age children must be provided with an appropriate, free public education. After testing, children with special needs are not to be grouped separately unless their conditions necessitate it.

The act requires the evaluation of the "whole child" by a multidisciplinary team, which may include a school psychologist, speech pathologist, classroom teacher, and occupational therapist. Parents, the school, or a doctor may request an evaluation of a child with the ultimate aim of developing an *Individualized Education Program (IEP)*, a written statement that establishes learning goals and states the methods that the school will implement to help the child meet those goals. Parents have to be involved in the development of IEPs and can take an active role in tracking their child's progress. Further, IEPs must be as close as possible to the programs for other children, considering the unique needs of each child. The No Child Left Behind Act of 2001 reinforces the rights of disabled children and makes it clear that school districts are responsible for meeting the goals set forth in IEPs.

The passage of laws protecting people with disabilities increased the emphasis on *mainstreaming*, or **inclusion**—the integration of children with special needs into regular classroom settings, whenever appropriate, with the support of professionals who provide special education services. Students with disabilities are placed in the least restrictive or least unusual environment feasible so that school life is as normal as possible while they and their teachers and classmates cope with their current skill levels and try to expand them as much as possible. The policy of inclusion dramatically changed the school experience for disabled students beginning in the late 1970s. By 1999, almost half of these students spent 80% of their school time in regular classrooms rather than in special education or restricted classrooms (U.S. Department of Education, 2003).

Inclusion can be a great benefit to children with disabilities. In addition, the inclusion of these children in regular classrooms allows their classmates who are not disabled to know them as peers, furthering acceptance of diversity. The success of inclusion depends on support by teachers as well as by administrators, and the inclusion of disabled students presents challenges to classrooms and school systems (Villa & Thousand, 2003). Some school districts find it difficult to afford the modifications needed to meet the requirements of the IDEA. Some teachers are more comfortable than others with modifying their classes to include students with various types of disabilities. However, school systems and faculty with a commitment to diversity are more successful in including intellectually disabled students in their classrooms. And this success benefits everyone.

Inclusion ■ The integration of children with special needs into regular classroom settings, whenever appropriate, with the support of professionals who provide special education services.

Summary and Review

WHAT ARE THE ORIGINS AND HISTORY OF PSYCHOLOGICAL TESTING?

The origins of psychological testing go back to Binet's test to identify children in the Paris school system who needed special attention. p. 394

Binet's test used the concept of *mental age* to compare children. When Binet's test was adapted to the United States, it became the Stanford–Binet Intelligence Scale. This widely accepted test used the concept of an *intelligence quotient*, a ratio of mental age to chronological age, multiplied by 100. David Wechsler developed an alternative test, including a version for adults. The development of group tests allowed testing to spread into educational and employment settings. The application of testing in school settings produced confusion over the differences between *intelligence tests* and aptitude or achievement tests. Despite the similarities in these types of tests, all differ in their goals. pp. 394–398

WHAT IS INTELLIGENCE?

Different cultures emphasize different components of intelligence, but most Western cultures emphasize academic abilities. *Intelligence* is the overall capacity of an individual to act purposefully, to think rationally, and to deal effectively with the environment. p. 399

Describe several different theoretical perspectives on intelligence.

A factor approach to intelligence concentrates on *factor analysis*, a correlational technique to determine which tasks are involved in intellectual ability. In factor analysis, the assumption is that tasks with high correlations test similar aspects of intellectual functioning. pp. 399–400

Vygotsky argued that the development of speech is important for intellectual development but that children develop intelligence within a social context, with the help of adults. pp. 400–401

Biological theories of intelligence emphasize brain functions, brain specialization, or the role of heredity in intelligence. p. 401

Gardner maintains that people have multiple intelligences (at least 8 and possibly 10). An intelligence is an ability to solve a problem or create a product within a specific cultural setting. He argues that not all human intelligences, or competencies, lend themselves to measurement by a test. pp. 401–402

Sternberg takes a systems approach to intelligence. Like Gardner's view that intelligence has many parts, Sternberg's theory of successful intelligence divides intelligence into three dimensions: analytic, practical, and creative. Sternberg's theory focuses on adaptation to the world. pp. 402–405

Are emotions another dimension of intelligence?

The concept of *emotional intelligence* expands the definition of intelligence to include emotional and motivational factors that are not typically captured by traditional IQ tests. Advocates argue that such an expanded definition of intelligence is useful. pp. 405–406

HOW DO PSYCHOLOGISTS DEVELOP TESTS?

Psychologists develop *achievement tests* to measure how well students have learned specific content. *Aptitude tests* are designed to measure the ability to learn specific types of material. pp. 406–407

What criteria must be addressed in order to develop a fair and accurate intelligence test?

Standardization is the process of developing uniform procedures for administering and scoring a test. This includes developing *norms*—the scores and corresponding percentile ranks of a large and representative sample of test takers from the population for which the test was designed. A *representative sample* is a sample of individuals who match the larger population for which a test is designed with regard to key variables such as socioeconomic status and age. p. 407

A *normal curve* is a bell-shaped graphic representation of normally distributed data, showing what percentage of the population falls under each part of the curve. The simplest score on a test is the *raw score*—the number of correct answers unconverted or transformed in any way. Scores are commonly expressed in terms of a *standard score*—a score that expresses an individual's position relative to those of others, based on the mean and on how scores are distributed around the mean. A standard score is generally a *percentile score*—a score indicating what percentage of the test population obtained a lower score. Another way to express standard test scores uses the concept of a *deviation IQ* to compare individuals. p. 408

What is reliability?

There are several types of *reliability*. A test is considered reliable if it yields a very similar score for the same individual over repeated testings. All tests are unreliable to some degree, and determining the reliability of intelligence tests may be difficult because intelligence is not completely stable over the life span. p. 409

What is validity?

A test's *validity* is its ability to measure what it is supposed to measure. *Content validity* relates to the content of the items, whereas *predictive validity* relates to the ability of the test to predict future behavior. If a test does not have validity, no inferences can be drawn from test results. p. 410

There are several basic criticisms of—and defenses of—the validity of intelligence tests and testing. The first is that there is no agreed-on definition of intelligence. The second is that intelligence tests measure learned information rather than intelligence. The third is that school settings may adversely affect IQ test results through the *halo effect*, and *stereotype threat* may reduce some people's scores. In addition, people's IQ test scores may depend on their motivation to succeed. Finally, some claim that society helps create the correlation between academic success and IQ test scores by using test scores as criteria for admissions to schools. Interpretation of scores is also critical; that is, test scores must be considered in the context of the individual test taker. Without such a context, a test score is little more than a number. pp. 410–411

HOW DO BIOLOGICAL AND ENVIRONMENTAL FACTORS CONTRIBUTE TO INTELLIGENCE?

What biological factors influence intelligence?

Evolutionary psychology emphasizes the influence of human prehistory on modern cognitive processes. Rather than concentrating on general cognitive factors, evolutionary psychologists emphasize the evolution of specialized mental modules that guide certain behaviors. pp. 412–413

Behavioral genetics investigates the influence of heredity on behavior, often by performing twin and adoption studies to determine the relative contributions of genes and environment. The *heritability* of a trait is the genetically determined proportion of a trait's variation within a population of individuals. Results from many studies indicate that heredity (nature) contributes to a person's intelligence but does not fix it; heredity sets a framework within which intelligence is shaped by the environment (nurture). pp. 413–415

What is the role of environmental and cultural variables in influencing intelligence?

Culture influences intelligence in many ways, including in the way intelligence is defined. Intelligence tests have been the focus of accusations of cultural bias. Although the history of IQ testing is filled with cultural bias, developers of current tests have made efforts to eliminate overt bias from their tests. However, IQ tests measure the degree to which people adapt to the culture in which they live. Environmental factors such as amount of education, family size, and birth order also affect IQ scores. pp. 415–417

How do biology and environment interact to affect intelligence?

Biological and environmental factors can interact to influence intelligence test scores. Cultural stereotypes have prompted differential development of abilities in boys and girls and contributed to differences in IQ scores. However, in fact there are only small differences between the genders in cognitive abilities. Socioeconomic status is one environmental factor that interacts with biological endowment. One study indicates that the environment affects IQ scores for poor children more than for wealthier ones. Also, the worldwide increase in IQ scores may be attributable to the choices made by individuals with specific skills and talents of situations that allow them to develop their abilities. pp. 417–419

WHAT IS THE IMPACT OF HAVING AN EXCEPTIONAL IQ?

Having an IQ at either extreme of the distribution has an impact on a person's life. p. 419

What is giftedness?

Giftedness is superior cognitive, interpersonal, or creative abilities. Efforts to identify gifted children spring from the urge to allow them to develop their talents. pp. 419–420

What is mental retardation?

Mental impairments or problems in learning and reasoning that are reflected in low IQ scores have been referred to as *mental retardation*, but a more modern term is *intellectual disability*. In addition to low IQ scores, the criteria for determining that a person has an intellectual disability include limitations in adaptive functioning and the need for support. The level of support required is one way to classify the severity of the disability. pp. 421–422

What has been the effect of the IDEA?

The Individuals with Disabilities Education Act (IDEA) mandates that disabled children receive a free, appropriate public education in the least restrictive environment, through the development of an Individual Education Plan (IEP). This legislation has changed the educational experience for disabled children, putting many into regular classrooms. *Inclusion* is the integration of all children with special needs into regular classroom settings wherever appropriate, with the support of special services. The purpose of inclusion is to help normalize the life experiences of children with disabilities. It has also promoted diversity. pp. 422–423

CHAPTER 12

Motivation and Emotion

What Is Motivation?   428
   Definition of Motivation
   Theories of Motivation

How Does Motivation
Affect Behavior?   440
   Hunger: A Physiological Need
   Sexual Behavior: Physiology plus Thought
   Social Needs

What Is Emotion?   455
   Definition of Emotion
   Theories of Emotion

How Does Emotion
Affect Behavior?   463
   Culture and Emotion
   Gender and Emotion
   Can We Control Emotions?

Summary and Review   466

In this chapter, we explore the topics of motivation and emotion, including the rules that apply to the display of emotion and how those rules vary by gender and culture. First let's consider motivation—why people do the things they do.

What Is Motivation?

The question of why people do what they do and why some people's motivations seem so different from those of others interested people long before the science of psychology existed. Motivation has been a research topic since the early years of psychology, as scientists have tried to understand the enormous variations in motivation from person to person. Why do some cancer survivors experience continuing fears and allow the disease to rule their lives, whereas Lance Armstrong and others develop a philosophy that every second counts (Armstrong, 2003)? What makes some people with spinal cord injuries feel hopelessly resigned to their condition, whereas Christopher Reeve was motivated to fight for funding to discover a cure? Psychologists have devoted much effort to studying what compels people to take various actions—from simple, biologically based actions such as eating to complex actions such as competing in world-class athletic events and raising funds for spinal cord research.

Definition of Motivation

The word *motivation* derives from the Latin *movere*, meaning "to move." *Motivation* is a condition, usually an internal one, that initiates, activates, or maintains an organism's goal-directed behavior. Let's examine the four basic parts of this definition of motivation.

First, motivation is usually an *internal condition*, which means that it cannot be directly observed. Regardless of whether motivation develops from physiological needs and drives or from complex desires, such as the desire to help others, to obtain approval, or to earn a higher income, the source for motivation is internal. For example, if you really want to make a good grade on your next biology exam, your motivation is internal. Initially, no one but you knows about it.

Second, motivation is *inferred* to be the link between a person's internal condition and external behavior. An observer can only infer the presence of motivation from the behavioral effects. When you begin to study a week before the biology exam, the people around you may conclude that you are motivated to get a good grade, but they are making an inference rather than observing your motivation directly.

Third, motivation *initiates*, *activates*, or *maintains* behavior. If you want to make a good grade in biology, that motivation will require that you attend class, study, and maintain (or develop) good test-taking skills.

Finally, motivation generates *goal-directed behavior*. Individuals' goals vary widely. Some are concrete and immediate—for example, to get a snack, to remove a painful stimulus, or to make a good grade on your next biology exam. Other goals are more abstract—the behavior of someone who studies hard, for example, may be motivated by a desire to learn more, to obtain the approval of parents, or to get a good job after graduation.

The study of motivation can be considered the study of what people choose to do, why they choose to do it, and how much energy they expend in doing it. Several theories have shaped research on this and have allowed psychologists to explain how motivation affects behavior.

Motivation ■ Any condition, usually an internal one, that initiates, activates, or maintains an organism's goal-directed behavior.

Theories of Motivation

Many theories of motivation have been developed to explain human behavior. These theories fall into five broad categories, each of which has generated research activity: evolutionary theories, drive theory, arousal theory, cognitive theories, and humanistic theory. Let's examine each of these categories.

Evolutionary Theories

In the early days of psychology, instinct was a popular explanation for motivation. The popularity of this explanation can be traced to the influence of Charles Darwin (1859, 1872), who proposed that instinct was an important force underlying the behavior of humans and nonhuman animals. An *instinct* is a fixed behavioral pattern that occurs in all members of a species and appears without learning or practice. In the early part of the 20th century, psychologists made lists of instincts, and the length of the lists grew, but the explanation of motivation in terms of instinct faded when psychologists began to emphasize learning as a factor in motivation (Schultz & Schultz, 2004).

Instinct ■ A fixed behavioral pattern that occurs in all members of a species and appears without learning or practice.

The evolutionary perspective has revived interest in the concept of instinct, claiming that the behavior of humans and other animals is motivated by many instincts. Rather than hypothesizing that humans are less controlled by instinct than other animals, evolutionary psychologists believe that humans have *more* instincts. These instincts give humans a variety of built-in modules that control behaviors that were adaptive at some time in evolutionary history. Many of these built-in behaviors occur automatically, without conscious thought or decision making. This view of humans as having many automatic behaviors is not widely accepted in psychology. However, Leda Cosmides and John Tooby (1997) claim that the majority of psychologists are "instinct blind," unable to see how prominent and important instincts are in human behavior.

In the evolutionary view, motivation and emotion are inseparable (Gaulin & McBurney, 2001). Motivation pushes people toward various behaviors, possibly more than one at a time, but emotion sets priorities about what to do at any particular time. A person who is motivated to eat and even moving toward food, will change that motivated behavior to another very quickly upon hearing a threatening noise in the next room.

Evolutionary psychologists examine motivation in the framework of understanding how it helps organisms survive and reproduce. According to the evolutionary view, situations that produce pleasure or pain will be motivating because these feelings relate to survival. Thus, eating, drinking, pain avoidance, temperature regulation, and reproductive behaviors are all of interest to evolutionary psychologists, who assume that these behaviors have built-in bases.

Critics of the evolutionary view argue that the concept of instinct is as problematic now as it was in the early years of psychology and that finding evidence for behavior that occurred in prehistory is impossible (Gannon, 2002). Much of the evidence presented by evolutionary psychologists consists of observations of the universality of a particular human motivation or emotion, and this criterion is one to keep in mind in evaluating the evidence for various motivations and emotions.

Drive theory ■ An explanation of behavior that assumes that an organism is motivated to act because of a need to attain, reestablish, or maintain some goal that aids survival.

Drive Theory

Some of the most influential and best-researched motivation theories are forms of drive theory, which arose as part of the behaviorist approach (Hull, 1943, 1951). *Drive theory* is an explanation of behavior that assumes that an organism is motivated to act because of a need to attain, maintain, or reestablish some goal that aids survival. Stimuli such as hunger and pain energize and initiate such behavior. A person who is hungry is *driven* to seek food.

A *drive* is an internal aroused condition that directs an organism to satisfy some physiological need. Drive theory focuses on *need*—a state of physiological imbalance that is usually accompanied by arousal. (This arousal component prompted the development of an alternative view of motivation, which we'll explore in the next subsection.) According to drive theory, physiological needs cause on organism to operate almost like a machine, because the organism is pushed and pulled by them. An organism motivated by a need is said to be in a *drive state*. In such a state, animals and human beings show goal-directed behavior. A *motive* is a specific (usually internal) condition, typically involving some form of arousal, which directs an organism's behavior toward a goal. Unlike a drive, a motive does not necessarily have a physiological basis.

The ultimate goal of each organism is *homeostasis*—maintenance of a steady state of inner stability or balance. The processes by which homeostasis is achieved are a key part of drive theory. For example, a thirsty animal will seek out water to reestablish its body fluid balance. Motivation theorists often refer to the goal that satisfies a need as an *incentive*. Incentives can be positive and lure us, as does food or a sexually attractive person, or they can be negative and repel us, as when we avoid a painful situation or someone we dislike. Behaviors such as eating or drinking, which reduce biological needs and promote homeostasis, are reinforced when the goal is attained and the drive is reduced. Such behaviors are therefore especially likely to recur. Behaviors such as yodeling or juggling, which do not reduce a biological need, are less likely to recur. (See **Figure 12.1** for an overview of drive theory and examples of drives.)

Physiologically based behaviors such as eating and drinking offer clear examples that fit the drive-reduction point of view. In the 1940s and 1950s, theorist Clark Hull (1943, 1951) asserted that the actions of reinforcers in developing stimulus–response associations were in part determined by the motivational drive state of the organism. In his elaborate, mathematically based theory of motivation and learning, Hull attempted to reduce the behavior of organisms to operations similar to those of machines. Hull argued that only hungry organisms find food a good reinforcer and are thus motivated to engage in tasks that lead to food. Organisms are also motivated to avoid pain, and escaping from situations with negative consequences can be strong motivation. The possibility that a person can experience drives both toward and away from certain goals can result in conflict.

When people (or other animals) face competing motives, they may experience conflict. *Conflict* is the emotional state or condition that arises when a person must make a choice between two or more competing motives, behaviors, or impulses. Consider a student who must choose between two equally desirable academic courses, both of which are required for graduation but which meet at the same time, or a person faced with a dessert menu that offers both cheesecake and chocolate torte. These people experience conflict.

Drive ■ An internal aroused condition that directs an organism to satisfy a physiological need.

Need ■ A state of physiological imbalance that is usually accompanied by arousal.

Motive ■ A specific (usually internal) condition, typically involving some form of arousal, which directs an organism's behavior toward a goal.

Homeostasis ■ Maintenance of a steady state of inner stability or balance.

Conflict ■ The emotional state or condition that arises when a person must choose between two or more competing motives, behaviors, or impulses.

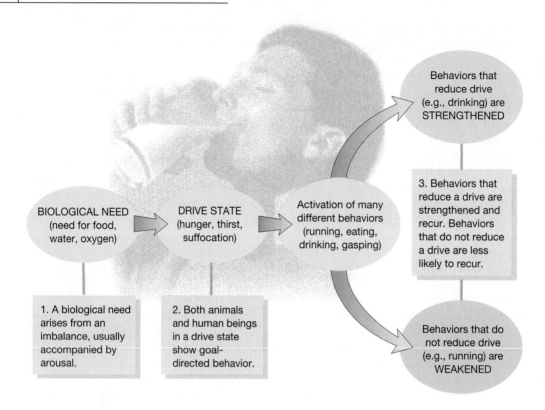

Figure 12.1
An Overview of Drive Theory

One of the first psychologists to describe and quantify such conflict situations was Neal Miller (1944, 1959). Miller developed hypotheses about how animals and human beings behave in situations that have both positive and negative aspects. In general, he described three types of conflicts that result when situations involve competing goals or demands: (1) approach–approach conflict, (2) avoidance–avoidance conflict, and (3) approach–avoidance conflict.

Approach–approach conflict results when a person must choose between two attractive alternatives (for example, receiving acceptance notices from two good universities or reading the dessert menu creates this type of conflict). Because both alternatives are pleasant, such situations don't really present much of a conflict (Dollard & Miller, 1950). *Avoidance–avoidance conflict* results from having to choose between two distasteful alternatives. For example, did your parents ever give you a choice of punishment, such as being grounded for a week versus having to do extra chores? This type of choice is an avoidance–avoidance situation in which you must choose between the lesser of two evils. *Approach–avoidance conflict* results when one is facing a single alternative that has both attractive and unappealing

Approach–approach conflict ■ Conflict that results from having to choose between two attractive alternatives.

Avoidance–avoidance conflict ■ Conflict that results from having to choose between two distasteful alternatives.

Approach–avoidance conflict ■ Conflict that results when facing a single alternative that has both attractive and unappealing aspects.

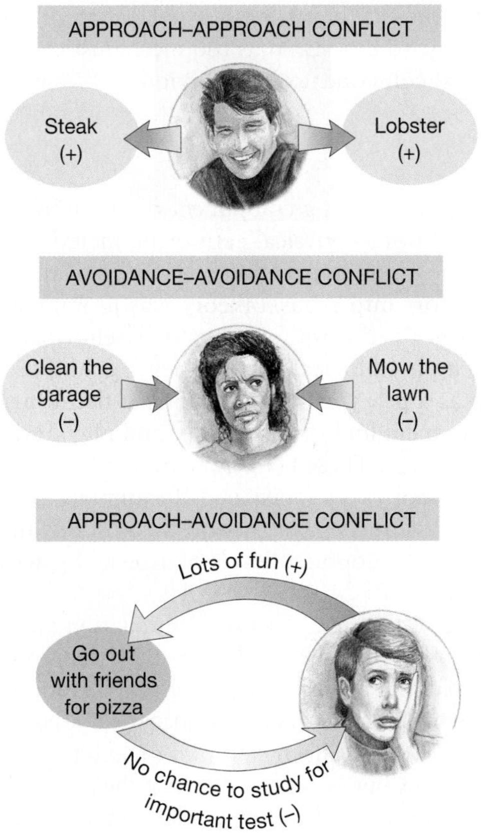

Figure 12.2
Three Types of Conflict
In approach–approach conflict, people have to choose between equally appealing alternatives. In avoidance–avoidance conflict, people have to choose between equally distasteful alternatives. In approach–avoidance conflict, people are faced with a single alternative that is both appealing and distasteful.

aspects. For example, a young woman is good at math and science and wants to be an engineer because she finds this field interesting, but her friends maintain that engineers are nerds. As **Figure 12.2** shows, these three types of conflicts lead to different degrees of distress.

Miller also developed principles to predict behavior in conflict situations, particularly in approach–avoidance conflicts: (1) The closer a person is to achieving a goal, the stronger the tendency is to approach the goal. (2) When two incompatible responses are available, the stronger one will be expressed. (3) The strength of the tendency to approach or avoid is correlated with the strength of the motivating drive. (The young woman may decide to become an engineer when she learns the starting salaries for engineers.)

Drive theory does not work well as a comprehensive theory of motivation. It does not explain all, or even most, motivated behavior. In addition, concepts such as *need* and *hunger* are difficult to define and vary from person to person. Although Hull's theory influenced the study of learning and motivation for decades, it was too focused on reducing concepts to formulas and behaviors to machine-like actions to be useful in accounting for diverse human behaviors. Although we can all think of examples of conflicts like those Miller hypothesized, trying to understand motivation in terms of drives came to be viewed as too mechanistic. Theorists began to concentrate on the arousal component of motivation.

Arousal Theory

Arousal ■ Physical activation, including activation of the central nervous system, the autonomic nervous system, and the muscles and glands.

According to drive theory, arousal is a component of all motivated behaviors. *Arousal* is generally thought of as physical activation, including activation of the central nervous system, the autonomic nervous system, and the muscles and glands. The evolution of drive theory into arousal theory was prompted by the finding that deprivation or conflict is not necessary for motivated behavior. An animal does not have to be experiencing a physiological need to seek a goal. For example, if you ever had a hamster or gerbil as a pet, you probably noticed that it had a strong motivation to explore its environment and to run, climb, and play in the tunnels, wheels, and chambers of its home cage. These behaviors are not always oriented toward seeking food or water—it looks very much as if the animals are playing (Sheldon, 1969). Some motivational theorists have concentrated on this finding and suggest that organisms seek to maintain optimal levels of arousal by actively varying their exposure to sensory stimuli.

Unlike hunger and thirst, the lack of sensory stimulation does not result in a physiological imbalance; yet both humans and other animals seem motivated to seek such stimulation. When deprived of a normal amount of visual, auditory, or tactile stimulation, some people become irritable and may consider their situation unpleasant ("I'm so bored") (Kjellgren et al., 2004). This motivation to seek novel stimulation is not unique to hamsters or humans but occurs throughout the animal kingdom—kittens like to explore their environment, and young monkeys investigate mechanical devices and play with puzzles.

Arousal theory attempts to explain the link between a behavior and a state of arousal. R. M. Yerkes and J. D. Dodson were among the first to scientifically explore the link between performance and arousal in 1908. They described a relationship involving arousal and performance that has become known as the *Yerkes–Dodson principle*. This principle suggests that arousal and level of task difficulty are related. On easy tasks, moderate to high levels of arousal produce maximum performance; on difficult tasks, low levels of arousal yield better performance and high arousal decreases performance (Hebb, 1955). For example, if the task is stepping on a pedal as quickly as possible when a light comes on, a high state of arousal will be a benefit. But if the task is driving a car during an ice storm, too much arousal may yield poor decision making—for example, causing oversteering and braking too soon. Optimal performance requires matching the level of arousal to the task's requirements. **Figure 12.3** illustrates this relationship between level of arousal and level of performance.

People who do not care about what they are doing have little anxiety, but they also have low arousal and therefore usually perform poorly. If arousal increases to the point of high anxiety, performance suffers. Many students know the answers to test questions but have trouble responding correctly because they are anxious when taking the test. The Yerkes–Dodson principle explains why it is easier to make free

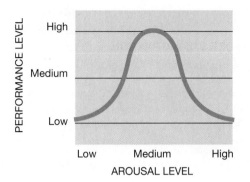

PERFORMANCE LEVEL

High

Medium

Low

Low   Medium   High
AROUSAL LEVEL

Figure 12.3
Performance and Arousal
Performance is at its peak when arousal is at moderate levels; too much or too little arousal results in low performance levels.

throws in practice or a scrimmage, when pressure is moderate, than during an important game, when pressure is high. It also explains why essentially the same task brings different levels of arousal at different times. It is important to realize that the stimulus itself (for example, taking the SAT, playing in the World Series, or going on a blind date) does not produce arousal. Rather, it is the internal response to a stimulus that determines how a person behaves.

Researcher Donald Hebb (1904–1985) suggested that behavior varies from disorganized to effective, depending on a person's level of arousal. He argued that human functioning is most efficient when people are at an optimal level of arousal (Hebb, 1955). By suggesting that it is unsatisfactory to equate motivation with biological need and that other factors, such as arousal and attention, are also important, Hebb anticipated the influence of cognitive theory on psychology. The development of optimal-arousal theories helped psychologists explain the variation in people's responses in terms of their states of internal arousal. This shift in emphasis marked a subtle but important transition from a strictly mechanistic drive-reduction theory toward learning, expectancy, and even cognitive theories. (See **Building Table 12.1** for a comparison of evolutionary, drive, and arousal theories.)

Cognitive Theories

What motivates you to attend class? In many courses, the professor does not take attendance, so there is no immediate negative consequence for missing class. Many students consider class attendance a chore, yet they attend regularly. Their motivation may be explained best by cognitive theories of motivation. *Cognitive theories* of motivation focus on goals that people actively determine and how they achieve them. For cognitive theorists, thought is an initiator and determinant of behavior. For some, expectation about reaching a goal is a key factor in motivation. For others, the source of the motivation is critical.

Explanations of behavior that focus on people's expectations about reaching a goal and their need for achievement are known as *expectancy theories*. Such theories connect thought and motivation. As expressed by achievement researcher David McClelland (1961), who formulated an early expectancy theory, and by Jacquelynne Eccles and Allan Wigfield (2002), who have proposed a

Cognitive theories ■
In the study of motivation, explanations of behavior that assert that people use thought processes to actively determine their own goals and the means of achieving them.

Expectancy theories ■
Explanations of behavior that focus on people's expectations about reaching their goals and their need for achievement.

Building Table 12.1

EVOLUTIONARY, DRIVE, AND AROUSAL THEORIES OF MOTIVATION

Theory	Theorist(s)	Focus of Theory	Key Idea	View of Behavior
Evolutionary Theory	Cosmides and Tooby	Instincts that improve survival and reproductive ability	Humans are even more driven by instincts than other animals are.	Behavior is strongly influenced by human evolutionary history.
Drive Theory	Hull	Stimulus–response associations and drive reduction	The organism seeks physiological balance, or homeostasis.	Behavior is largely mechanistic.
	Miller	Conflict among motivations	Conflicts can be categorized as approach–approach, avoidance–avoidance, and approach–avoidance.	Behavior is largely mechanistic.
Arousal Theory	Hebb	The optimal level of arousal is the level that matches the requirements of a task.	Performance depends on level of arousal.	Behavior is determined by the level of physiological arousal.

contemporary version, a key element of these theories is thought. Both models hold that people's thoughts—their expectations—guide their actions and help regulate their behaviors.

Expectations are based on experience that occurs in a social context, and some expectancies originate in social needs. A *social need* is an aroused condition that directs people to behave in ways that allow them to feel good about themselves and others and to establish and maintain relationships. The needs for achievement and affiliation are examples of social needs, which are determined by many factors, including socioeconomic status and ethnicity. For example, many Asian American families stress school achievement very strongly, so Asian American children fulfill both the need for achievement and the need for acceptance by their families by doing well in school. Consistent with these values, Asian American students tend more often than European American students to choose achievement-related goals over activities that are immediately pleasurable (Diener, Oishi, & Lucas, 2003). (We'll explore the need for achievement in more detail later in this chapter and also in Chapter 14.)

People seem motivated to engage in some behaviors yet require coaxing for others. For example, a child may love doing puzzles, coloring in coloring books, or playing video games, yet need to be urged or ordered to practice the piano or

Social need ■ An aroused condition that directs people to behave in ways that allow them to feel good about themselves and others and to establish and maintain relationships.

do homework. Why do some activities seem like fun, while others seem like work?

Psychologists talk about the types of activities that require prompting versus those that are naturally fun in terms of *extrinsic* versus *intrinsic* motivation. **Extrinsic motivation** is motivation that comes from the external environment in the form of rewards or threats of punishment. Praise, a high grade, and payment for a particular behavior are extrinsic rewards. Such rewards can strengthen existing behaviors, provide people with information about their performance, and increase feelings of self-worth and competence. In contrast, behaviors engaged in for no apparent reward except the pleasure and satisfaction gained from the activity itself arise from **intrinsic motivation**. Edward Deci (1975) suggests that people engage in such behaviors for two reasons: to obtain cognitive stimulation and to gain a sense of accomplishment, competence, or mastery over the environment. For example, many of your high school behaviors may have been extrinsically motivated, with parents and teachers offering praise, feedback, and punishment on a daily basis (Thompson & Thornton, 2002). However, college requires more intrinsic motivation: You can attend class or not; tests are less frequent, so you may not know how you are doing; you may be in a class with 300 other students in which the professor does not even know your name. Students who want to learn and who find intrinsic rewards in the college experience are more likely to be successful than those who require frequent rewards supplied by others. Some students have trouble making the transition from high school to college, and a lack of intrinsic motivation may be a factor.

Individuals vary in the activities they find intrinsically motivating. Some people can play basketball or tennis for hours, whereas others find such games awkward and unsatisfying. Some people become so absorbed in their work that they lose track of time and may even forget to go to lunch, whereas others watch the clock, waiting for quitting time. Psychologist Mihaly Csikszentmihalyi (1997, 2000; Nakamura & Csikszentmihalyi, 2002) calls the experience of becoming completely and pleasurably absorbed in an intrinsically motivated behavior *flow*. Only intrinsically motivated behaviors can give rise to flow, but even those do not always produce it.

A funny thing happens when people receive extrinsic rewards for behaviors they find intrinsically interesting: They become less motivated to perform those

For some artists, intrinsic motivation (and not extrinsic rewards) leads them to create.

Extrinsic [ecks-TRINZ-ick] motivation ■ Motivation supplied by rewards or threats of punishment that come from the external environment.

Intrinsic [in-TRINZ-ick] motivation ■ Motivation that arises from the pleasure and satisfaction gained by engaging in a particular behavior.

Flow ■ The experience of becoming completely and pleasurably absorbed in an intrinsi-cally motivated b

behaviors (Deci, Koestner, & Ryan, 1999). Studies that present rewards to some participants who already find an activity intrinsically interesting (such as solving puzzles or playing video games) but not to others find that the rewarded participants lose some of their motivation to perform the activity. This effect, known as the *overjustification effect*, is the decrease in likelihood that an intrinsically motivated task, after having been extrinsically rewarded, will be performed when the reward is no longer given.

Research on the overjustification effect has been extensive and controversial. The earliest studies focused on the basic finding that extrinsic rewards can have detrimental effects. When a task is interesting, providing tangible rewards can decrease intrinsic motivation, and this effect applies to a variety of tangible rewards, from candy to dollar bills. However, later research suggests that these detrimental effects occur only in certain situations (Eisenberger & Cameron, 1996; Pittenger, 1997; Snelders & Lea, 1996) or perhaps not at all (Roane, Fisher, & McDonough, 2003). Thus, researchers differ on whether there are risks associated with the delivery of rewards. Some caution that, for example, even verbal praise for children's accomplishments may have negative as well as positive effects (Henderlong & Lepper, 2002).

The overjustification effect applies only to inherently *interesting* tasks— activities that people would do even without reward. The value of reward in encouraging performance of uninteresting tasks is not part of this controversy. Reward is a way to get both children and adults to work at a task they find inherently uninteresting. However, the reward becomes the motivation, and people do not have the opportunity to learn to self-regulate those rewarded behaviors. For example, when parents offer their children money for making good grades, they may be focusing on the goal of good grades so much that they fail to realize that their children need to develop a sense of accomplishment by mastering school subjects. The delivery of the monetary reward can block the development of the intrinsic motivation to learn.

Humanistic Theory

Humanistic theory is an explanation of behavior that emphasizes the entirety of life rather than individual components of behavior. It focuses on human dignity, individual choice, and self-worth. One of the appealing aspects of humanistic theory is that it incorporates some of the best elements of the drive, arousal, and cognitive approaches to explain motivation and behavior. Humanistic psychologists believe that a person's behavior must be viewed within the framework of the person's environment and values.

As you learned in Chapter 1, one of the founders and leaders of the humanistic approach was Abraham Maslow (1908–1970), who assumed that people are essentially good—that they possess an innate inclination to develop their potential and to seek beauty, truth, and harmony. Maslow (1970) believed that people are innately open and trusting and capable of experiencing the world in healthy ways. In his words, people are naturally motivated toward self-actualization. *Self-actualization* is the highest level of psychological development, in which a

---

Overjustification effect ■ The decrease in likelihood that an intrinsically motivated task, after having been extrinsically rewarded, will be performed when the reward is no longer given.

Humanistic theory ■ An explanation of behavior that emphasizes the entirety of life rather than individual components of behavior and focuses on human dignity, individual choice, and self-worth.

Self-actualization ■ In humanistic theory, the highest level of psychological development, in which one strives to realize one's uniquely human potential—to achieve everything one is capable of achieving.

Figure 12.4
Maslow's Hierarchy of Needs
Physiological needs are at the base of the ladder. Successively higher levels represent needs that are increasingly learned or social ones.

person strives to realize his or her uniquely human potential—to achieve everything he or she is capable of. This level of motivation includes attempts to attain a clear perception of reality, to be independent of others' influence and yet fit into society, and to feel a strong sense of self-acceptance along with a dedication to others.

Maslow's influential theory conceives of motives as forming a hierarchy, which can be represented as a ladder, with fundamental physiological needs at the bottom, followed by the needs for safety, love and belongingness, and esteem, with self-actualization at the top (see **Figure 12.4**). According to Maslow (1970), as lower-level needs are satisfied, people begin to be motivated by the next higher level need. Maslow believed that only a small percentage of people attain self-actualization, mostly because of circumstances: People who are hungry or in danger cannot be motivated by the drive to achieve their fullest potential, because they must instead focus on their very survival—their most basic needs. Although Maslow's theory provides an interesting way to think about many aspects of motivation and behavior, it is difficult to test experimentally. In addition, Maslow's theory has received criticism for being too tied to the individualistic values of Western culture (Hanley & Abell, 2002). **Building Table 12.2** (on p. 440) adds the cognitive theory and Maslow's humanistic theory to the comparative summary of motivation theories.

Building Table 12.2

EVOLUTIONARY, DRIVE, AROUSAL, COGNITIVE, AND HUMANISTIC THEORIES OF MOTIVATION

Theory	Theorist(s)	Focus of Theory	Key Idea	View of Behavior
Evolutionary Theory	Cosmides and Tooby	Instincts that improve survival and reproductive ability	Humans are even more driven by instincts than other animals are.	Behavior is strongly influenced by human evolutionary history.
Drive Theory	Hull	Stimulus–response associations and drive reduction	The organism seeks physiological balance, or homeostasis.	Behavior is largely mechanistic.
	Miller	Conflict among motivations	Conflicts can be categorized as approach–approach, avoidance–avoidance, and approach–avoidance.	Behavior is largely mechanistic.
Arousal Theory	Hebb	The optimal level of arousal is the level that matches the requirements of a task.	Performance depends on level of arousal.	Behavior is determined by the level of physiological arousal.
Cognitive Theory	McClelland	Achievement motivation	Humans learn the need to achieve.	Behavior is based on expectation of outcome.
	Deci	Intrinsic motivation	Intrinsic motivation is self-rewarding because it makes people feel competent.	Extrinsic rewards can decrease inherent motivation for interesting tasks.
Humanistic Theory	Maslow	A hierarchy of motives, from basic physiological needs through needs for safety, love and belongingness, esteem, and needs for fulfillment and self-actualization	Humans can seek self-actualization, the highest level of psychological development, only after basic needs for food and security are fulfilled.	Behavior is mostly directed by cognition.

How Does Motivation Affect Behavior?

Now that we've examined how theorists explain motivation, let's look at how motivation affects behavior. All of us have been hungry, felt sexually aroused, and wanted to be around others. These three motivators—food, sex, and social needs—can illustrate how motivation affects a variety of behaviors and how motives can have a range of sources. Let's begin with hunger, which would seem to have a straightforward biological basis. You will see that this motivation, like other psychological phenomena, arises from a complex interplay between biology and experience. Even hunger and eating are not as simple as they seem.

Hunger: A Physiological Need

The basis of eating and hunger may seem very clear—we need energy to fuel our bodies, and eating furnishes this fuel. When depleted of energy, our bodies send out signals that prompt us to seek food. The first part is correct: We need energy in the form of calories to fuel our bodies, and we get that energy as well as other nutrients from food. But an explanation that views hunger as energy depletion and eating as the automatic response to low fuel levels is too simple (Woods et al., 2000; Woods & Seeley, 2002). Not only is this biologically based motivation physiologically complex, it is also influenced by learning and culture.

The Physiological Determinants of Hunger

Physiological explanations of hunger have focused on the concept of *homeostasis*, which we encountered earlier in this chapter. Applied to eating and hunger, homeostasis is a balance of energy intake and output that results in a stable body weight. Thus, food intake is only one factor in the weight maintenance equation. To maintain body weight, a person's energy expenditure must equal energy intake. Energy is expended in physical activity and through basal metabolism, which involves the maintenance of basic cellular and body functions. When you burn as many calories as you eat, your weight remains the same.

Many adults maintain a relatively stable weight for years, which led researchers to look for a homeostatic system for weight control. Weight stability is consistent with the concept of a *set point*—a predetermined weight that the body maintains. Such a system requires a mechanism to set the weight and another to signal when it moves away from the set point. Richard Nisbett (1972) proposed that fat cells determine the body's set point. Fat cells vary as a result of both genetic and environmental factors; the number of fat cells an infant has can increase during the first several years of life. Have you noticed the similarity in body shape among family members? This similarity is a result of the inheritance of a particular pattern of fat cell distribution throughout the body, creating a similar body shape (Price, Li, & Kilker, 2002). The other component needed in a homeostatic weight control system is a mechanism that detects a nutritional excess or deficit and sends signals that prompt an increase or decrease in food intake. Researchers have proposed that both glucose and fats circulating through the blood act as these signals, but the physiology of digestion is not consistent with these hypotheses (Woods et al., 2000).

Within the past 10 years, several hormones have been discovered to be important in maintaining body weight (Halford, Cooper, & Dovey, 2004). These include (1) *insulin*, which is produced by the pancreas and allows glucose to be taken into and used by body cells, (2) *leptin*, which is produced by fat cells, (3) *cholecystokinin*, which is produced by the intestines and contributes to the feeling of having eaten enough, (4) *ghrelin*, which is produced mainly by the stomach and whose level rises until eating begins, and (5) *peptide YY*, which may provide the signal to quit eating. The discovery that a number of hormones are involved indicates how complex the signaling system between the brain and the body is. Although the system is not fully understood, the hypothalamus (see Chapter 3) plays an important role in receiving the hormonal signals and in communicating with other brain structures. Because the system functions on a cellular level in your brain and body, you aren't aware of most of its operations. You only know whether you feel hungry or full.

Researchers have known for years that the hypothalamus influences eating, because surgery on this brain structure alters eating behavior. Surgery that damages the ventromedial hypothalamus produces extreme overeating, and surgery that damages the lateral hypothalamus produces a drastic decrease in eating (see **Figure 12.5**). Using the functional brain-imaging technique of fMRI, researchers have found that neurons in the hypothalamus become more active when a person eats (Liu et al., 2000) The actions of hormones in the brain produce a complex cascade of events that appear to signal hunger and satiety (feelings of fullness), but psychological cues may be more important than bodily signals in producing hunger and in prompting eating (Scientists study body's hunger signals, 2003).

Learning to Be Hungry: Environmental and Cultural Influences

The physiological mechanisms that underlie eating are not the whole story of hunger. We do not eat because we are energy deficient—we eat *before* we are. We *feel* hungry, and that feeling prompts us to seek food. Research shows that learning and experience are important in feeling hungry. Stimuli in the environment associated with food can be signals to eat, and there is evidence that these signals are learned (Changizi, McGehee, & Hall, 2002). One of those powerful stimuli is time of day. Most of us feel hungry at specific times. You have probably missed a meal and had the experience of feeling very hungry for an hour or so, but then your hunger diminishes. This experience shows how

Figure 12.5

The Effects of the Hypothalamus on Eating Behavior

The stimulation or destruction of part of a rat's hypothalamus alters the rat's eating behavior; the location of the hypothalamic stimulation or damage—in the ventromedial or the lateral hypothalamus— affects the results.

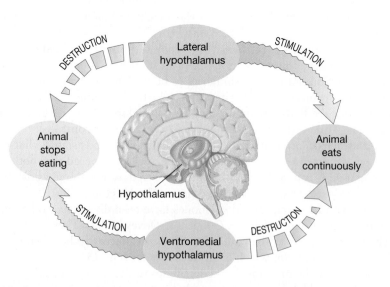

eating at regular times leads to feeling hungry at those times. Both rats and humans are susceptible to being trained to eat on a schedule.

We also learn what to eat, and the enormous cultural variations as to what constitute desirable and forbidden foods reflect the strength of this learning. People even show different physiological responses to foods that are familiar or unfamiliar in their cultures (Lokko, Kirkmeyer, & Mattes, 2004). Almost every substance that has nutritional value is eaten by the people of some culture in some part of the world (Rozin, 1999). Fried grasshoppers or other insects might not be considered desirable foods by most college students in the United States, but in some cultures, insects are a favorite. And many American favorites are not accepted worldwide. For example, an extensive advertising campaign attempted unsuccessfully to market corn flakes to Spanish children. Because the Spanish do not pour milk over any foods before eating them, however, cultural tradition made corn flakes a hard sell in Spain (Visser, 1999).

Cultural experiences are not the only learned factor in food preferences; individuals also develop personal likes and dislikes. Those preferences are guided in part by innate factors and in part by family, peer, and advertising influences. In human prehistory, foods with sweet or salty tastes were usually safe and nutritious, whereas bitter foods often contained poisonous toxins. Thus, human evolution has led to an inborn preference for sweet and salty foods and a tendency to avoid bitter foods (Rozin, 1999). Another component of food preferences is sensitivity to various tastes, and some taste sensitivities have a genetic component (Tepper, 1998). For example, vegetables in the broccoli and cabbage family contain a chemical to which people have varying hereditary sensitivities. So, if you dislike broccoli, it may be in your genes.

Early family experiences, peer pressure, and advertising also play a role in individual food choices. For example, television advertisements prompt increased eating by children, and overweight children are more strongly influenced by food advertisements than children of normal weight are (Halford, Gillespie, et al., 2004).

Sometimes hunger is not even a factor in eating; people also eat for pleasure. When tasty food is available, people eat, even if they are not hungry (Pinel, Assanand, & Lehman, 2000). Almost everyone has had the experience of yielding to the temptation of a luscious dessert after eating a large meal. Despite being full (perhaps uncomfortably so) from the meal, we find the dessert just too good to resist. We would not be tempted to eat more of the food that we had just consumed, but a different food can prompt us to eat more. Clearly, variety is a factor in eating (Raynor & Epstein, 2001; Sokolov, 1999). Being presented with a variety of tasty foods can produce overeating in both rats and humans, and variety is a key factor in the pleasure of eating. Even your favorite food—turkey with dressing, pepperoni pizza, a ripe peach, chocolate—would eventually become unappealing if it were the only thing you could eat. These observations bring up a question about overeating: Is the wide variety of foods available to most people in the United States a factor in overeating and obesity?

Eating and Obesity

Despite indications of health consciousness (low-fat and low-carb foods, health clubs, strong sales of sports gear), it seems there is an ever-growing tendency for Americans to be ever growing. Over one-third of Americans are overweight, and

22.5% of the population is clinically obese—a proportion almost twice as high as it was two decades ago (Wadden, Brownell, & Foster, 2002). No one tries to be obese—indeed, most people want to be slim. Is it the ever-increasing variety of junk food, excessive time spent watching television, not enough exercise? What is the underlying reason for obesity? Both physiological and psychological explanations have been offered to account for it.

One explanation for obesity comes from an examination of evolutionary history. For humans and other animals, food scarcity and potential starvation were serious threats. A good fat supply was one way to diminish that threat, so animals with a tendency to develop fat stores had a survival advantage. This interpretation suggests that humans and other animals have a tendency to get fat when food is readily available (Walker, Walker, & Adam, 2003). That hypothesis is confirmed by obesity rates in industrialized countries. In the United States and many other countries, the food supply is steady and plentiful, and these countries have a much higher obesity rate than poorer countries. Yet the evolutionary explanation of obesity leaves some unanswered questions. For example, why do most people maintain a stable weight even when they have access to lots of food? Also, why is there such variation in weight among people?

The individual variation in body weight may be partly due to the inherited tendency to store fat, which varies among people. Some researchers insist that obesity has a genetic basis and that behavioral and physiological patterns affecting the distribution of body fat are inherited (Price et al., 2002). If you have an overweight parent, your likelihood of being overweight as an adult increases dramatically, even if your weight was normal as a youngster. The possibility of a genetic predisposition for obesity is based partly on the observation that fat cell distribution is inherited; however, eating habits also run in families. Studies of identical twins indicate a genetic component for obesity in the form of inherited factors that affect metabolism and fat distribution (Ukkolal & Bouchard, 2004). The research that has resulted in the identification of hormones related to eating suggests that genetic factors may be involved in weight regulation through effects on these hormones (Woods et al., 2000).

Further, some studies suggest that people can inherit both a tendency to overeat and a slow metabolism. A person with a slow metabolism has a lower basal metabolic rate, which means that the person's body uses available energy (calories) from food efficiently and stores unused calories as fat. A slow metabolism is an advantage in protecting against starvation, but obesity tends to be the result when people with a low metabolic rate eat what would otherwise be a normal diet. For example, the Pima Indians of Arizona are prone to obesity; 80–90% of the tribe's young adults are dangerously overweight, and related health problems such as diabetes are unusually prevalent. According to Ravussin and his colleagues (Ravussin et al., 1988; Stephan et al., 2002; Tataranni et al., 2003), the Pima have unusually low metabolic rates. During any 24-hour period and with the same level of physical activity, the typical Pima burns about 80 calories less than the average European American. Ravussin's view is that the Pima, whose ancestors spent generations in a desert environment where they went through periods of famine, developed a metabolism that adapted to this on-again, off-again pattern of food availability. But in the 20th century, the Pima abandoned their traditional low-fat diet and began to eat like other

Americans. Their "thrifty" metabolism, which had become disposed to storing fat, became a liability as the proportion of fat in their diet increased.

Even people with low metabolic rates are not destined to be obese. They can match their food intake to their metabolic rate or increase their energy output by exercising. Nor are people with a normal metabolic rate guaranteed lifelong thinness. Americans are bombarded with food-oriented messages that have little to do with nutritional needs (Halford, Gillespie, et al., 2004). Advertisements proclaim that merriment can be found at a restaurant or a supermarket. Parents coax good behavior from their children by promising them desserts or snacks. Thus, eating acquires a significance that far exceeds its role in satisfying physiological needs: It becomes a center for social interaction, a means to reward good behavior, and a way to fend off unhappy thoughts and reduce stress (Puhl & Schwartz, 2003). In addition to promoting excessive food intake, American culture glorifies physical activity but offers multiple opportunities to avoid it.

The basic problem is that the human body has developed effective mechanisms for gaining weight and weak ones for shedding pounds that are no longer needed (Hill & Peters, 1998). Researchers have identified four key factors that contribute to overeating in the United States:

- Food is readily available—from drive-through windows and vending machines, restaurants and street vendors, at home, at work, and everywhere in between.
- Portion sizes are growing bigger—fast-food restaurants "supersized" meals, which may be supersizing their customers (Young & Nestle, 2002).
- The average person's diet—especially if it is a low-carb one—is higher in fat than ever before, and fat provides nearly twice the calories per gram as protein or carbohydrates.
- Most children and adults do not engage in regular, sustained physical activity.

Put all of this together—low physical activity, eating too much, too often, of the wrong things—and the result is an overweight population that has trouble losing weight.

To make the situation even worse, being thin has become increasingly desirable, especially for women. So, dieting has become a way of life for many Americans. Indeed, more people are dieting than are overweight. Most dieters are in the normal weight range, but not all overweight people are dieting (U.S. Bureau of the Census, 2003). The majority of normal-weight dieters in the United States are women who want to attain the very thin body that has become the cultural ideal. This ideal has led to chronic dieting and other eating disorders, such as anorexia and bulimia. Although eating disorders are more common among women, in recent years, an increasing number of men are developing them (Morrison, Morrison, & Hopkins, 2003).

The quest for thinness is often unsuccessful; dieters often gain back the weight they lost. A longitudinal study of dieting among adolescents indicated that dieters tended to be heavier 3 years later than they were when they began to diet and also tended to be at risk for engaging in unhealthy eating behaviors such as binge eating (Field et al., 2003). Even for successful dieters, the same factors that lead to obesity push toward regaining lost weight. This evidence supports the notion of a set point for weight. However, increasing obesity rates in the United States and other industrialized countries provide evidence that set point is not the only factor in weight maintenance. If it were, when people gained weight, they should soon lose the weight to return to their set point.

The increasing number of obese people is evidence for psychological and social factors in eating and weight gain. In other words, even the motivation to eat is not purely physiological. And some motivations are even more influenced by psychological factors.

Sexual Behavior: Physiology plus Thought

Sex is often in the media—in reports on sex scandals involving entertainers or politicians, in advertisements for Viagra, sexual lubricants, and condoms, and even in sexually suggestive advertisements for products that have nothing to do with sex. Ads for everything from toothpaste to automobiles, from sports equipment to orange juice, feature attractive, often scantily clad models. Advertisers use learning principles to pair attractive people and situations with products in the hope that the products will take on an arousing glamor—and to hint that if you use the product, you may become as alluring as the models. The advertisers are seeking to initiate buying activity by activating the sexual drive. They know, of course, that people's thoughts direct buying behavior.

No matter how fascinating it is, sex is not physiologically necessary to sustain a person's life. You won't die if you don't have sex (no matter what your dates tell you). Thus, there is an important difference between sexual behavior and food seeking. In many animals, sexual behavior is controlled largely by physiology. In human beings, the degree of physiological control of sex is less clear, because ideas, past behaviors, emotions, expectations, and goals all enter into human sexual behavior. The relative contributions of these factors vary widely. For some people, sights, sounds, and smells are triggers for sexually motivated behavior. For others, thoughts, feelings, and fantasies initiate or, in many cases, satisfy sexual needs.

Sexual behavior varies with age, gender, religion, and cultural background. The diversity among cultures is enormous—what one culture considers forbidden, another deems acceptable or even necessary (Ford & Beach, 1951). For example, to the British, sexual indiscretions by politicians are primarily titillating; in contrast, Americans generally find such behavior difficult to condone. Recognizing this diversity, let's look at some of the initiators of human sexual behavior, at the physiology of that behavior, and then at its range.

Sex Hormones versus Sights, Sounds, Smells, and Fantasy

Sex hormones are important for sexual behavior in humans, beginning before birth. Both males and females produce both *androgens* (the "male" hormones) and *estrogens* (the "female" hormones), but in different proportions. In males, the testes are the principal producers of androgens. In females, the ovaries are the principal producers of estrogens. During prenatal development, the presence of testosterone, an androgen, prompts the development of the male reproductive organs; its absence allows development of the female organs. The release of androgens and estrogens initiates the emergence of the secondary sex characteristics in developing teenagers (see Chapter 5). The presence of these hormones is important for the development of sexual desire, and their regulation is essential for fertility. Women's levels of sex hormones vary according to their menstrual cycles and then decrease at menopause, whereas men's levels of sex hormones do not vary as much or in any cyclic fashion. However, men's levels of testosterone do decline as they age. Thus, for humans, hormone levels are important to but not directly responsible for sexual behavior (Bancroft, 2002).

In the animal kingdom, the relationship between sex hormones and sexual behavior is much clearer. Female rats, for example, are sexually responsive only when they are fertile (when they are "in heat"), and both sexual receptivity and fertility are regulated by a complex series of hormones released into the bloodstream. If the testes of male rats are removed, the animals show a marked decrease in sexual interest and performance. Most sexual responses in nonhuman animals do not occur without hormonal activation. Human beings, on the other hand, can choose whether or not to respond sexually at any given time. The removal of hormone-generating organs affects sexual interest and behavior in human beings, but not as much as in nonhuman animals.

In nonhuman animals, a receptive female may show her receptivity by releasing pheromones; the pheromones trigger sexual activity in the male (see Chapter 6). A specific action or set of actions may also signal female receptivity and trigger sexual behavior from the male animal. But human beings, because they are not so directly under hormonal control, can be sexually aroused by the sight or sound or smell of something with erotic associations. Thought plays an enormous role in human sexuality. People's thoughts, fantasies, and emotions initiate and activate sexual desire and behavior. Brain-imaging studies have identified specific areas of the brain that are activated when people are experiencing sexual arousal (Mouras et al., 2003).

The Sexual Response Cycle

When human beings become sexually aroused and engage in sexual activity, they go through a series of four phases (stages). Together known as the *sexual response cycle*, they include the excitement, plateau, orgasm, and resolution phases.

The *excitement phase* is the first phase of the cycle, during which there are increases in heart rate, blood pressure, and respiration. A key characteristic of this phase is *vasocongestion*—engorgement of the blood vessels, particularly in the genital area, due to increased blood flow. In women, the breasts and clitoris swell, the vaginal lips expand, and vaginal lubrication increases. In men, the penis becomes erect. The excitement phase may last from a few minutes to a few hours.

The *plateau phase* is the second phase of the sexual response cycle, during which physical arousal continues to increase as the partners' bodies prepare for orgasm. Autonomic nervous system activity increases, causing a faster heart rate. In women, the clitoris withdraws, the vagina becomes engorged and the vaginal lips fully expanded. In men, the penis becomes fully erect, turns a darker color, and may secrete a bit of fluid, which may contain sperm.

The *orgasm phase* is the third phase of the sexual response cycle. During this phase, autonomic nervous system activity reaches its peak, and muscle contractions

Excitement phase ■ The first phase of the sexual response cycle, during which there are increases in heart rate, blood pressure, and respiration.

Vasocongestion ■ Engorgement of the blood vessels, particularly in the genital area, due to increased blood flow.

Plateau phase ■ The second phase of the sexual response cycle, during which physical arousal continues to increase as the partners' bodies prepare for orgasm.

Orgasm phase ■ The third phase of the sexual response cycle, during which autonomic nervous system activity reaches its peak and muscle contractions occur in spasms throughout the body, but especially in the genital area.

occur in spasms throughout the body, especially in the genital area. An *orgasm* is the peak of sexual activity. In men, muscles throughout the reproductive system contract to help expel semen; in women, muscles surrounding the vagina contract. An orgasm lasts only a few seconds and is an all-or-none response; once the threshold for orgasm is reached, the orgasm occurs. Although men experience only one orgasm during each sexual response cycle, women are capable of multiple orgasms.

The ***resolution phase*** (also called the *refractory period*) is the fourth phase of the sexual response cycle, following orgasm. Now, the body returns to its resting, or normal, state, which takes from one to several minutes. During this phase, men are usually unable to achieve an erection.

Like many other physiological and psychological phenomena, the sexual response cycle is subject to considerable variation, with longer or shorter phases and different signs of arousal, depending on the person and his or her age.

Resolution phase ■ The fourth phase of the sexual response cycle, following orgasm, during which the body returns to its resting, or normal, state.

Understanding Human Sexual Behavior

Although American culture is saturated with sexually suggestive advertisements and sexually explicit movies, it is also characterized by considerable reluctance to talk about sexual behavior frankly or examine it scientifically. Efforts to study sexuality in a systematic way are often viewed with skepticism or reluctance. For example, in 1994, the U.S. Congress sought to ensure that a federally funded sex survey was not conducted.

Despite this opposition, various researchers have studied sex, mostly by conducting sex surveys. The first and most famous were surveys conducted by a biologist, Alfred Kinsey, and his colleagues (Kinsey, Pomeroy, & Martin, 1948; Kinsey et al., 1953). For years, the Kinsey surveys were the main source of information about American sexual attitudes and behavior, but researchers such as Morton Hunt (1974), William Masters, Virginia Johnson, and Robert Kolodny (1994), and Edward Laumann and his colleagues (1994; Michael et al., 1998) have conducted more recent and more well-designed sex surveys. Comparisons of their results allow conclusions about how sexual behavior has changed over the past 50 years.

When Kinsey and his colleagues conducted their sex surveys, they found substantial differences between women's and men's sexual behavior. Later surveys have revealed a decrease in those differences. For example, the percentages of women and of men who engage in masturbation, premarital sex, and extramarital sex are more similar now than they were in the 1950s (Dekker & Schmidt, 2002). This decreasing gender difference appears in other industrialized countries, such as Great Britain, but not in many Asian, Latin American, and African countries, where social norms for women's and men's sexuality differ sharply (Singh et al., 2000). Men and women in the United States are more likely today than in the 1950s to have intercourse before marriage, and there was a slow and steady decrease in the age of first intercourse for both boys and girls from the 1950s to the mid-1990s (Wellings et al., 2001).

Today, people express their sexuality more often and more openly—and want to understand their sexual feelings and behaviors. Laumann's research team (Laumann et al., 1994; Michael et al., 1998) reported a wide variety in sexual behaviors among Americans, relative to other cultures, and a decline in the differences between male and female sexuality. The incidence of masturbation and the acceptance of casual sex remain higher for men than women in the United States, as well as in other countries around the world (Schmitt et al., 2003). However, there are smaller differences in many other sexual behaviors and attitudes, such as attitudes about the acceptability of oral sex, masturbation, and same-gender sexuality (Hyde & Oliver, 2000).

The development of sexuality begins before birth and continues throughout life (DeLamater & Friedrich, 2002). Sex hormones direct the prenatal development of the reproductive organs. Children experience sexual feelings, and engage in exploratory sexual play and masturbation. Because children spend so much time with peers of the same gender, their sexual explorations may be with same-gender children, but this behavior does not indicate homosexuality. Sexual activity, which may include intercourse, typically begins during adolescence (Singh et al., 2000). Learning to engage in physical and emotional intimacy is one of the major tasks for this developmental period (DeLamater & Friedrich, 2002). In the United States and many other societies, marriage is the primary context of sexuality, and despite the media image of rampant sex among singles, married people in the United States engage in sexual activity more often than unmarried people (Laumann et al., 1994).

As people age, several types of changes may affect their sexuality. Divorce or the death of a spouse tends to decrease sexual activity, especially for women. Older women are also less likely to have sexual partners than older men are. The frequency of sexual activity tends to decline, even for people who have sexual partners, but many older individuals continue to engage in sexual behaviors and have satisfying sex lives.

The picture of sexuality in the United States is not a completely positive one. Compared with other industrialized countries, individuals in the United States begin sexual activity at younger ages, and although the pregnancy rate among American adolescents has fallen recently, that rate is substantially higher in the United States and the United Kingdom than in other developed countries (Kmietowicz, 2002). Other negative aspects of American sexual behavior include a high incidence of sexually transmitted diseases, the continuing spread of AIDS (discussed in Chapter 15), and the prevalence of risky sexual behaviors, such as not using condoms (Singh et al., 2000). The rates of *sexual dysfunction* (any disorder or problem related to sexual behavior) are relatively high: 33% for women and 14% for men (Johnson, Phelps, & Cottler, 2004). Young women and older men are more likely to suffer from sexual dysfunction, including inability to experience orgasm, low sexual desire, problems attaining an erection in men, and painful intercourse in women. Despite the existence of such problems, most people report their sex lives as being satisfactory (Laumann et al., 1994).

Sexual problems have both health-related and psychological components (Laumann, Paik, & Rosen, 1999). Unfortunately, embarrassment prevents many people from seeking treatment, which is a bad decision. Many types of sexual problems may signal general health problems. Seeking help is wiser.

Sexual Orientation

One's sexual orientation is the direction of one's sexual interest. A person with a *heterosexual orientation* has an erotic attraction to and preference for members of the other sex as partners; a person with a *homosexual orientation* has an erotic attraction to and preference for members of the same sex as partners. A *bisexual orientation* is an erotic attraction to members of both sexes. Kinsey and his colleagues (1948) introduced the idea of a continuum of sexual behaviors ranging from exclusively homosexual behaviors through some homosexual behaviors, to mostly heterosexual behaviors, to exclusively heterosexual behaviors. These researchers also recognized that a sexual experience with someone of the same sex does not make an individual homosexual. In addition, a person may have a homosexual or bisexual orientation without ever having had a sexual experience with someone of the same sex. It is thus an overgeneralization to define a person's sexual orientation based solely on a single, or even on multiple, sexual encounters (Haslam, 1997).

The Kinsey survey of male sexual behavior reported that 37% of men had had at least one same-sex sexual experience and that 10% of men were primarily homosexual in orientation (Kinsey et al., 1948). Other surveys reported lower rates, and most sex researchers consider the Kinsey statistics to be overestimates. The Laumann study (1994) found that 2.8% of men and 1.4% of women identified themselves as primarily homosexual, and other studies confirm these low figures (Cameron & Cameron, 1998; Sell, Wells, & Wypij, 1995).

People who are not heterosexual experience discrimination and censure in some cultures, but not in others. In the United States, gays, lesbians, and bisexuals face discrimination, censure, harassment, and threats of violence, which have a negative impact on these individuals' mental health (Meyer, 2003). Many gay and lesbian adolescents have to endure taunts and harassment in school, which may underlie their higher dropout rates and higher numbers of suicide attempts (Lock & Steiner, 1999). The continuing controversy over sexual orientation has even led to a movement to pass a constitutional amendment to ban same-sex marriages. Underlying this controversy is confusion over the basis of sexual orientation. Gay, lesbian, and bisexual individuals have the same motivation to be accepted as other individuals—that is, they have the same social needs.

Social Needs

Do you consider yourself an overachiever? Would you rather win awards than win friends? What would you be willing to sacrifice to succeed—marriage, children, friends? What would you do to be accepted by others? Your answers to these questions may reveal your level of certain social needs: the ***need for achievement***, which is the need that directs a person to strive for excellence and success, and the ***need for affiliation***, which is the need to be with and to establish positive relationships with others. Humans have many other social needs, but these two have a long research history that reflects their importance in motivating a range of behaviors.

Need for achievement The social need that directs a person to strive for excellence and success.

Need for affiliation The social need that motivates a person to be with and to establish positive relationships with others.

The Need for Achievement and Mastery

The need for achievement can be explained by expectancy theories of motivation, which hypothesize that people engage in behaviors that satisfy their desires for success, mastery, and fulfillment. Tasks that do not further these goals are less motivating for people with a high need for achievement, and these individuals either do not undertake such tasks or perform them with less energy or commitment (Chusmir, 1989). For example, many people bicycle for fun but do not race. And even among bicycle racers, few are motivated to train for and compete in an event as intense as the Tour de France, as Lance Armstrong has.

One of the leaders in studies of achievement motivation was David C. McClelland (1917–1998), whose early research focused on the idea that people have strong social motives for achievement (McClelland, 1958). McClelland showed that achievement motivation is learned in the home environment during childhood. People with a high need for achievement had parents who stressed excellence and who provided physical affection and emotional rewards for high achievement. Such people also generally walked early, talked early, and had a high need for achievement even in elementary school (Teevan & McGhee, 1972). A high need for achievement is typically strongest in first-born children, perhaps because parents typically have more time to give them direction and praise.

Culture is also a factor in achievement motivation. Many Asian cultures, for example, stress the value of achievement, and Asian American parents encourage their children to achieve in school and to pursue higher education (Okagaki & Bojczyk, 2002). However, certain factors that relate to achievement in Asian cultures differ from those in Western cultures. One such factor is independence, which is positively related to achievement in Western cultures but not in Asian cultures, which are more collectivist than individualist. Interdependence is highly valued in Asia, and the need for achievement and the need for affiliation are positively correlated there (Nisbett, 2003). In Western cultures, factors emphasizing the individual, including a willingness to leave family and country, are more strongly related to achievement needs. The need for achievement was found to be positively related to willingness to emigrate for students in Albania, the Czech Republic, and Slovenia (Frieze et al., 2004). Not surprisingly, these achievement-oriented students had lower affiliation needs than their peers who were unwilling to emigrate. Therefore, need for achievement occurs in both Asian and European cultures, but other characteristics that relate to this need vary among these cultures.

Achievement motives are usually measured in one of two ways: either by analyzing the thought content of imaginative stories or by asking people to report their motives. The two methods of measurement do not always yield the same results, because some people are not fully aware of their underlying motivations (Sokolowski et al., 2000). Thus, both approaches can be valuable. The studies that measure people's underlying motivation by analyzing the content of imaginative stores often use the *Thematic Apperception Test (TAT)*. In this test, people are presented with pictures of scenes in which what is happening is unclear, making the pictures open to interpretation. Test takers are instructed not to think in terms of right or wrong answers but to answer four basic questions for each scene:

1. What is happening?
2. What has led up to this situation?

3. What are those in this situation thinking?
4. What will happen next?

The TAT involves a complex scoring system, and some researchers criticize it as being too subjective and open to the interpretations of different administrators (Wood et al., 2002). Some researchers have devised alternative tests, such as the Oshodi Sentence Completion Index (OSCI; Oshodi, 1999), which asks participants to complete a series of sentences to assess their achievement needs, and the Multi-Motive Grid (MMG; Sokolowski et al., 2000), which asks participants to react to pictures by checking which statements in a grid most closely match their evaluation of the pictures. In general, all of these assessments show that people with higher levels of achievement motivation attach importance to success, getting ahead, and competition (Oshodi, 1999; Sokolowski et al., 2000; Spangler, 1992).

In an early study on achievement (Lowell, 1952), participants who were asked to rearrange scrambled letters (such as *wtse*) to construct a meaningful word (*west* or *stew*) varied in their performance according to their achievement motivation. Participants with a low need for achievement improved only slightly at the task over successive testing periods, but those with a high need for achievement showed increasing improvement over several periods of testing (see **Figure 12.6**). This improvement may reflect a constant striving toward better performance and a belief in the importance of effort among those with a high need for achievement (Carr, Borkowski, & Maxwell, 1991; McClelland, 1961).

Self-efficacy ■ A person's belief that she or he can successfully engage in and execute a specific behavior.

People motivated by the need for achievement also tend to be high in *self-efficacy*, the belief that they can successfully engage in and execute a specific behavior (Bandura, 1977a). Self-efficacy is based on a person's belief that she or he has specific skills that will allow the accomplishment of a particular task; it differs from the more general concept of self-esteem in being task-specific (Maddux, 2002). Many studies have demonstrated how self-efficacy relates to success in performing various tasks. One example involved an examination of a number of factors related to success in college, defined as having a passing grade-point average or higher and staying in school (Robbins et al., 2004). The factors the researchers considered were study skills, social support, academic goals, achievement motivation, and academic self-efficacy. They found that academic self-efficacy was the best predictor and achievement motivation was the second-best predictor of grade-point average. The research supports the idea that belief in the ability to succeed at particular tasks relates to success on those tasks.

Recent theory and research in the area of achievement have been influenced by *positive psychology* (see Chapter 1), which has emphasized mastery (Franken, 2002). This orientation stresses competence and striving to do well but does not view attaining recognition from others as essential to success. Thus, achievement and mastery are related but not identical. It is possible to attain high levels of success without actual mastery or to master a subject or skill without being

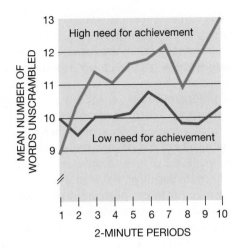

Figure 12.6
Performance on a Scrambled-Letter Task
The graph shows performance on a scrambled-letter task for successive 2-minute periods. Performance is affected by a person's overall approach to achievement-related tasks. Participants with a low need for achievement improved overall; however, those with a high need for achievement improved even more. (Based on data from Lowell, 1952.)

recognized for that achievement. Mastery and achievement also differ in terms of their sources. Mastery tends to be an intrinsic motivation, whereas achievement may be either intrinsic or extrinsic (see the discussion of intrinsic and extrinsic motivation earlier in the chapter). For example, the desire for either mastery or achievement may motivate a person to spend long hours practicing a sport or a musical instrument. The motivation for mastery comes from within the person, whereas the motivation for achievement may come from a desire for recognition or from parental pressure.

The need for achievement is one important type of social motivation, but another important social need is affiliation.

The Need for Affiliation and Belonging

If you like to drink beer, do you prefer to drink at a bar or a party or to buy a six-pack and have a few beers alone at home? Many beer drinkers have a strong preference for one of these choices, and their preference relates to their *need for affiliation*. People who enjoy going out for drinks demonstrate their motivation to be with others. Indeed, many people drink alcohol only when they are socializing, and interaction with others is part of their enjoyment. For these people, affiliation is one of their motivations for drinking. However, the motivation to seek the company of others extends to many other human behaviors. We are social creatures.

The motivation to seek the company of others can be traced to infancy and attachment to caregivers who are important to survival (see Chapter 4). However, in older children and adults, the company of others is not essential for survival, making affiliation a social need. As the drinking example illustrates, this motivation varies among individuals. Indeed, some people prefer solitary activities over those that involve interacting with others (Leary, Herbst, & McCrary, 2003). However, even those people who are drawn to solitary activities typically seek the company of others under some circumstances.

Early research on the need for affiliation was similar to that on the need for achievement (McClelland, 1985). It concentrated on assessing the need for affiliation using the TAT and then determining other characteristics of individuals with a high need for affiliation (Chusmir, 1989; McClelland & Koestner, 1992) and identifying situations that prompt affiliative behaviors (Schachter, 1959). People with a high need for affiliation may join organizations, engage in many social activities, value relationships over achievement, and prefer work situations that include friendly interactions with others. The imagery that they describe when taking the TAT reveals themes of seeking to be with others and displeasure at being alone or isolated.

The need to be with people takes many forms. Seeking the company of other people may represent a desire to socialize, but it may also reveal wanting to be accepted, to belong to a group, or to establish an intimate connection with others. The need to belong has been hypothesized as a basic human need, and research points to the strength of this motivation and the diversity of its expression in cultures around the world (Baumeister & Leary, 1995). One complicating facet of the need for affiliation is that people have both positive and negative feelings about being with others. At the same time as they feel the need to be with others, they fear rejection (Cantwell & Andrews, 2002). Seeking the company of others may represent the resolution of a conflict between being accepted and being rejected.

One classic series of studies (Schachter, 1959) demonstrated some of the circumstances that prompt the tendency to affiliate, revealing that some people tend to affiliate when they feel anxious and stressed. More recent research supports the notion that the tendency to seek support from others can be an effective strategy for coping with many types of problems (Brannon & Feist, 2004). *Social support* is assistance from others, in the form of either emotional support, such as comforting or reassurance, or tangible help, such as money or advice about how to solve a problem. Individuals with a network of people to provide social support tend to be not only more satisfied with life but also healthier than those with fewer sources of such support (Cohen et al., 2003; Kiecolt-Glaser & Newton, 2001; Wills, 1998).

Recently, positive psychology has influenced theory and research on affiliation by emphasizing the motives, benefits, and difficulties involved in establishing and maintaining satisfying connections with other people (Reis & Gable, 2003). Whether described as the need for belongingness or the need for relatedness, the desire to establish positive connections with others is clearly an important social need. Being with others provides some of life's greatest pleasures and takes a high priority across the life span. This need may be satisfied through early childhood relationships with family, the formation of childhood and adolescent friendships, the search for romantic love, and the bond with children. Thus, throughout the life-span, personal relationships are an important component of people's happiness and feelings of well-being (Keyes & Magyar-Moe, 2003). Many people also feel a need to make connections with others beyond family and friends, to experience a sense of community, and some feel a strong motivation to achieve a sense of connection through relationships they form in their workplaces (Burroughs & Eby, 1998; Hodson, 2004).

Although some people are more strongly motivated by the need for affiliation than others, almost no one is immune to it. Despite the problems involved in forming

Social support ■
Assistance from others, in the form of either emotional support or tangible help.

and maintaining satisfactory relationships, belonging may be considered a basic human motivator (Baumeister & Leary, 1995).

What Is Emotion?

When U.S. presidential contender Howard Dean came in third in the Iowa primary in January 2004, he was understandably upset. However, his reaction was much more emotional than most people considered appropriate, including his own campaign workers (Thompson, 2004). Dean's emotional reaction was seen as a "meltdown" for his campaign. Nor was he the first presidential contender to experience negative consequences after a public emotional reaction. Senator Edmund Muskie withdrew from the 1972 campaign shortly after he cried in public.

The experience of emotion is private and personal, but the expression of emotion is observable behavior. Even though Howard Dean experienced very strong emotions at his loss, people would not have known how upset he was had he behaved differently. The negative reactions were not to the emotions themselves but to his display of emotion, which was not considered "presidential." *Display rules* are the rules that govern the display of emotions, and these rules vary according to age, culture, and gender, creating wide differences in what kinds of emotional expression are expected and even allowed (Ekman & Friesen, 1975). Not only Dean's campaign workers but also the American public agreed that his emotional display was inappropriate. Temper tantrums are generally unacceptable behavior, but these displays are more expected from 3-year-olds than from a presidential hopeful.

Display rules ■ The rules that govern the display of emotion, which vary according to age, culture, and gender, thus creating wide differences in emotional expression.

Definition of Emotion

Anger can cause you to lash out at a friend, to hurl an object across a room, or to yell at coworkers. When a loud noise startles you, you may freeze up. Happiness can make you smile all day or stop to help a motorist with a flat tire. Although emotions, including love, joy, and fear, can motivate behavior, they remain difficult to define precisely (Panksepp, 2000).

The word *emotion* refers to a wide range of subjective states, such as love, fear, sadness, and anger. We all have emotions, talk about them, and possibly even agree on what they are—but these categorizations are not scientific. The psychological investigation of emotion has led to a more specific definition. Most psychologists acknowledge that emotion has three elements: feeling, physiological response, and behavior. An *emotion* is a subjective response (a feeling), accompanied by a physiological change, which is interpreted in a particular way by the individual and often leads to a change in behavior. The elements often fit together, but they are separable. A person who comes across a large bear while hiking in the woods is likely to experience fear. This situation is likely to be accompanied by faster breathing, sweating, and decreased salivation (dry mouth) on the physiological level. The person is likely to admit to being afraid or at least startled. Despite these physical experiences and feelings, the person who has encountered the bear might mask the experience of emotion by maintaining control of facial expression and restraining the impulse to

Emotion ■ A subjective response, accompanied by a physiological change, which is interpreted in a particular way by the individual and often leads to a change in behavior.

run. That is, the person might feel fear without showing behaviors associated with fear. Viewing emotion as having three components has resulted in a variety of theoretical approaches to understanding and studying it.

Theories of Emotion

Psychologists focus on different aspects of emotional behavior. Some early researchers attempted to catalogue and describe basic emotions (Bridges, 1932; Wundt, 1896). Others focused on the physiological bases of emotion (Bard, 1934) and created theories based on their conceptualization of emotion. More recent theories have explored the evolutionary basis of emotion or emphasized its cognitive component.

Physiological Theories of Emotion

Researchers who have a physiological orientation believe that happiness, rage, and even romantic love can be traced to a common physiological basis. They argue that the wide range of human emotions is in large part controlled by the brain and expressed by the reactions of the sympathetic division of the autonomic nervous system. Two major physiological approaches to the study of emotion dominated for decades: the James–Lange theory and the Cannon–Bard theory. They differ in their assumptions about whether physiological change or emotional feelings occur first. More recent physiological theories of emotion have focused on finding specific brain structures that are related to the experience of emotion.

According to a theory proposed by both William James (1842–1910) and Carl Lange (1834–1900) (who are given joint credit because their approaches were so similar), people experience physiological changes and *then* interpret them as emotional states. People do not run because they are afraid; they feel afraid after they start running. In other words, the James–Lange theory says that people do not experience an emotion until after their bodies become aroused and begin to respond with physiological changes; feedback from the body produces feelings or emotions (James, 1884; Lange, 1922). For this approach, in its most simplified form, *feeling* is the essence of emotion. Thus, James (1890) wrote, "Every one of the bodily changes, whatsoever it be, is felt, acutely or obscurely, the moment it occurs" (p. 1006).

A modern physiological approach suggests that facial movements, by their action, can create emotions. This *facial feedback hypothesis* suggests that sensations from the face provide signals to the brain that act as feedback to help a person determine an emotional response (Tourangeau & Ellsworth, 1979). In some ways, this approach derives from the James–Lange theory. William James suggested that we don't cry because we are sad, but rather, we are sad because we cry. According to this theory, a facial movement such as a smile may release the appropriate emotion-linked neurotransmitters (Ekman, 1993; Izard, 1990; Soussignan, 2002). Facial action is not necessary for the experience of emotion, but facial expression may influence the occurrence of emotions, actually creating an emotion that would not have otherwise occurred (Abel & Hester, 2002; Soussignan, 2002). That is, putting on a happy face may actually make you happier.

Some physiologists, notably Walter Cannon (1871–1945), were critical of the James–Lange theory. Cannon and his colleague Philip Bard argued that the physiological changes associated with many different emotional states are identical. They wondered how people are able to determine their emotional state from physiological changes since increases in blood pressure and heart rate accompany feelings of both anger and joy. What allows people to make the distinction? Cannon spoke of *undifferentiated arousal*, asserting that the physiological reactions underlying the fight-or-flight response (the body's response to emergency situations that includes activating resources needed to fight or to flee) are the same as those for all emotions. Cannon argued that simultaneous stimulation of the brain and the sympathetic nervous system produce feelings and physiological reactions. According to Cannon (1927), emotional feelings *accompany* physiological changes rather than produce or result from such changes. (**Building Table 12.3** contrasts these two physiological approaches to emotion.)

The nonspecific nature of the reaction to emotion presents a problem with the use of the *polygraph*. This device is better known as a lie detector, but it does not detect lies. Instead, it measures the physiological reactions that occur when a person experiences emotion and the sympathetic division of the autonomic nervous system goes into action. The measurements taken by a polygraph typically include blood pressure (which increases with the experience of emotion), breathing (which becomes more rapid and shallow), and galvanic skin response (a measure from the palms of the hands, which sweat). A polygraph operator first obtains baseline measurements using neutral questions and then asks questions that may elicit the emotional reaction typical of a person telling a lie. A skilled operator can distinguish the changes that differentiate truth from lying, but even skilled operators are far from 100% accurate in their assessments (National Research Council, 2002). Inaccurate assessments may lead to the conclusion that a person is lying when the person is telling the truth or that a person is telling the truth when the person is actually lying. Both types of errors can create major problems when polygraphs are used for employment or security screening, and a national review panel concluded that the polygraph is unsuitable for these uses. If emotions were more physiologically

Building Table 12.3

PHYSIOLOGICAL THEORIES OF EMOTION

Theory	Theorist(s)	The Role of Physiology	The Role of Cognition	The Role of the Situation
Physiological Theories	James and Lange	Arousal precedes interpretation of events.	People interpret bodily arousal as emotion.	Not relevant
	Cannon and Bard	Physiological arousal and interpretation occur simultaneously.	Cognition supplies an interpretation, which occurs at the same time as arousal.	Not relevant

distinct, this problem would not occur. However, as the Cannon–Bard theory proposed, emotions are physiologically similar.

When Cannon and Bard were formulating their theory, they knew relatively little about how the brain functions. They did know that certain brain structures were related to the experience of emotion. Bard (1934) found that the removal of portions of the cortex of cats produced sharp emotional reactions to simple stimuli such as a touch or a puff of air. The cats would hiss, claw, bite, arch their backs, and growl—but their reactions did not seem directed at any specific person or target. Bard referred to this behavior as *sham rage*, a behavior sequence that showed the signs of emotion in the absence of any appropriate motivation.

Later research discovered that the cortex of the brain was involved in integrating information involved in the experience of emotion. Then, structures deeper within the brain, especially the limbic system, which is composed of cells in the hypothalamus, the amygdala, and other areas in and below the cerebral cortex, became the focus of research. Recent research has concentrated on the role of the amygdala. Another recent approach to understanding emotion—the evolutionary theory—goes back to the beginning.

Evolutionary Theory of Emotion

Evolutionary psychologists see complex behavior as a series of specialized modules that are called into action by specific situations (Barrett, Dunbar, & Lycett, 2002; Cosmides & Tooby, 2000). Emotions have a prominent role in evolutionary psychology. Repeated situations in human prehistory led to modules organized around emotions; when specific situations arise now, emotions occur, and along with them, the behaviors governed by these modules. In this view, emotional responses arise from the brain's neural circuits, and subjective feelings follow them. Fear responses—such as freezing up at the sight of a natural predator—occur automatically without thought and have adaptive advantages that caused these behavioral sequences to become part of human biology. Joseph LeDoux has investigated the physiological bases of emotions. LeDoux's view of fear includes the hypothesis that evolution has prepared humans (and other animals) to respond in certain basic emotional ways to some stimuli. Through the process of natural selection, the human brain has evolved the ability to be very sensitive to fear-inducing situations and to respond rapidly to avoid any danger. Indeed, the situations that elicit such an alert do not have to produce fear—any new or unusual stimulus should provoke a response that focuses the organism on this new element. The stimulus could be trouble, or alternatively, it could be food (Cacioppo & Gardner, 1999).

Not all feared stimuli occur equally frequently, and evolutionary psychologists have examined fear and other emotional reactions for their adaptive utility. Humans seem programmed to fear some objects and situations but not others—for example, heights, snakes, and insects rather than trees, chickens, and books (Öhman & Mineka, 2003). Encountering any of these fear-provoking stimuli can be dangerous, and having built-in responses to them can be adaptive. Of course, the modern environment is drastically different from that of our distant ancestors, and such instinctive fears may now be unreasonable—tall buildings are typically safe, and people see snakes more often in zoos or as pets than in the street. Thus, some of our programmed adaptations are not nearly as useful in the modern world as they were in our prehistory. Indeed, this discrepancy may be one source of discontent and maladjustment in modern life (Buss, 2000b).

Although evolutionary psychology emphasizes negative over positive emotions (Reis & Gable, 2003), this orientation also explains that humans have the capacity to experience a range of positive emotions (Buss, 2000b). Humans lived in groups during prehistory and formed close mating bonds, which evolved into a predisposition to form personal relationships and to derive great satisfaction from them (Barrett et al., 2002). That is, evolutionary psychologists see love, friendship, and social relationships as part of our evolved history. Indeed, these kinds of relationships should be the basis for many people's most satisfying experiences, and studies of happiness confirm this view (Diener & Seligman, 2004; Myers, 2000; Reis & Gable, 2003).

Evolutionary psychologists have also been interested in identifying "basic" emotions and determining if these emotions are evident among all humans, and even among all primates. Facial expressions, because they are easily observed and interpreted, have provided a means to this goal. Paul Ekman and his colleagues (1992; Keltner & Ekman, 2000; Keltner, 2004) conducted cross-cultural studies of the perception of emotion, finding a great deal of consistency among cultures in people's ability to interpret facial expressions. In addition, people are extremely good at detecting changes in facial expressions (Edwards, 1998; Farah et al., 1998)—with the exception of individuals with damage to specific areas of the brain (Adolphs & Tranel, 2003, 2004) and those with mental disorders such as depression (Surguladze et al., 2004) or schizophrenia (Sachs et al., 2004). However, claims for universality of facial expressions are the target of criticism (Russell, Bachorowski, & Fernandez-Dols, 2003). In addition, of course, facial expressions do not always reflect people's feelings. People can "put on a happy face" to mask sadness or adopt a "poker face" to conceal excitement. The experience of emotion is not the same as the expression of emotion.

In addition, some cultural variations exist in both the interpretation of expressions and the situations that elicit them (Keltner & Ekman, 2000). For example, laughter is common at funerals in some cultures but very unusual in others. Individuals from Southeast Asia show a wider variety of facial expressions to reflect embarrassment than do people in the United States. The frequency of certain emotions and their intensity of experience also vary across cultures (Scollon et al., 2004). For example, people in Asian cultures report more experiences of unpleasant emotions than do people in Western cultures.

Building Table 12.4 summarizes the physiological and evolutionary theories of emotion.

Cognitive Theories of Emotion

Fear, sadness, anger, and surprise all have readily recognizable behavioral and physiological manifestations, but these emotions are also accompanied by thoughts and feelings. But why are some people frightened by a situation that angers others, such as almost being hit by a bicycle? The differences lie in beliefs and expectations—that

Building Table 12.4

PHYSIOLOGICAL AND EVOLUTIONARY THEORIES OF EMOTION

Theory	Theorist(s)	The Role of Physiology	The Role of Cognition	The Role of the Situation
Physiological Theories	James and Lange	Arousal precedes interpretation of events.	People interpret bodily arousal as emotion.	Not relevant
	Cannon and Bard	Physiological arousal and interpretation occur simultaneously.	Cognition supplies an interpretation, which occurs at the same time as arousal.	Not relevant
Evolutionary Theories	LeDoux	Physiological changes occur in the amygdala and other brain structures first.	Subjective interpretation is mediated by a different, slower pathway in the brain.	The situation can affect an emotion by stimulating memories and interpretation.
	Cosmides and Tooby	The brain contains a series of specialized programs for basic emotions.	Cognition follows the reactions of the brain and the body.	A given situation brings forth the appropriate programs.

is, in thoughts about the situation. Cognitive theories of emotion focus on mental interpretation as well as on physiology. The importance of cognition in the experience of emotion was demonstrated in a classic experiment by Stanley Schachter and Jerome Singer.

Schachter and Singer (1962) formulated a cognitive approach to emotion that focuses on emotional activation and incorporates elements of both the James–Lange and the Cannon–Bard theories. Schachter and Singer argued that people interpret physical sensations within a specific context and that the context is important to the interpretation. They knew that bodily states, including chemically induced states brought on by alcohol or other drugs, can change moods. But observers cannot interpret what a person's emotional behavior means unless they know the situation in which it occurs. If a man cries at a funeral, observers think he is sad; if he cries at his daughter's wedding, they conclude that he is joyful. Thus, according to the Schachter–Singer view, an emotion is created by cognitive factors as a person tries to account for a state of perceived activation (Lang, 1994).

To demonstrate their contention, Schachter and Singer designed a complex but clever experiment in which they manipulated participants' level of physiological arousal in addition to the emotional climate of their surroundings. To manipulate arousal, Schachter and Singer injected volunteers with epinephrine (adrenaline), a powerful stimulant that increases physiological arousal by increasing heart rate and blood pressure and even creating sensations of "butterflies in the stomach." These participants were compared to a group who received a saline injection, which has no physiological effects. To see if they could influence how participants interpreted their aroused state, Schachter and Singer manipulated the settings in which the volunteers experienced their arousal. The researchers hired confederates, undergraduate students trained to act either happy or angry. The hired confederates pretended that they were volunteers in the drug study, but they were actually behaving according to a script; their emotional behavior was strictly an act. The "happy" confederates played at throwing wads of paper into a wastebasket and flew paper airplanes around the room. The "angry" ones complained about the questionnaire they had to fill out and voiced their dissatisfaction with the experiment.

Schachter and Singer found that both manipulations were successful. The experimental participants who received epinephrine injections and who interacted with the happy confederates reported that the drug made them feel good; those who interacted with the angry ones reported feeling anger. Schachter and Singer reasoned that when people have no label for the cause of their physiological arousal (especially when arousal levels are low), they will label their feelings in terms of the thoughts available to them—in this case, thoughts stimulated by their interactions with the confederates.

Schachter and Singer were correct: Arousal does intensify emotions. However, it does not work alone. People don't live in an experiential vacuum. For example, when people first smoke marijuana or take other psychoactive drugs, they tend to approach the experience with definite expectations. If told the drug gives people the "munchies," new users report feeling hungry; if told the drug is a "downer," new users often interpret their bodily sensations as depressed. In Schachter and Singer's view, people experience internal arousal, become aware of the arousal, seek an explanation for it, identify an external cue, and then label the arousal. In an important way, arousal provides the fuel—the energy—for the physiological reaction, but the labeling determines the feeling.

These findings have been the target of criticism of several types, including that they rely too much on physiological arousal to explain emotion. That is, some critics believe that thoughts alone are sufficient to produce emotion (Reisenzein, 1983). And many physiological theorists argue that brain arousal or excitation of the autonomic nervous system is the controlling factor in the experience of emotion, but generally accept that cognitions are influential in the experience of emotion.

Richard Lazarus (1991) formulated a theory of emotion that also relies heavily on cognition. Like Schachter and Singer, Lazarus considered both physiology and cognition important in emotion, and he also believed that the situation is critical in people's experience of emotion. Lazarus argued that cognition affects emotion through people's appraisal of the situation and its impact on them. *Appraisal* is a person's evaluation of the significance of a situation or an event in term's of the person's well-being. Thus, people's evaluation of a situation in personal terms is important for emotion. For example, a hiker will not always appraise the sighting of a bear as threatening. I (L.B.) once saw two bears while hiking, but they were cubs that were running away from the group of hikers I was with, so I felt no fear. (I did give some thought to the location of their mother, and I subsequently learned that

Appraisal ■ A person's evaluation of the significance of a situation or an event in terms of the person's well-being.

I *should* have been afraid of the mother bear. But I didn't know that at the time, so I did not appraise the situation as dangerous.) Lazarus's cognitive theory of emotion is controversial, but his insistence on the importance of thoughts and personal appraisal in the experience of emotion fits well with the varieties of emotional experience that occur.

Building Table 12.5 contrasts the key elements of physiological, evolutionary, and cognitive theories of emotion.

Building Table 12.5

PHYSIOLOGICAL, EVOLUTIONARY, AND COGNITIVE THEORIES OF EMOTION

Theory	Theorist(s)	The Role of Physiology	The Role of Cognition	The Role of the Situation
Physiological Theories	James and Lange	Arousal precedes interpretation of events.	People interpret bodily arousal as emotion.	Not relevant
	Cannon and Bard	Physiological arousal and interpretation occur simultaneously.	Cognition supplies an interpretation, which occurs at the same time as arousal.	Not relevant
Evolutionary Theories	LeDoux	Physiological changes occur in the amygdala and other brain structures first.	Subjective interpretation is mediated by a different, slower pathway in the brain.	The situation can affect an emotion by stimulating memories and interpretation.
	Cosmides and Tooby	The brain contains a series of specialized programs for basic emotions.	Cognition follows the reactions of the brain and the body.	A given situation brings forth the appropriate programs.
Cognitive Theories	Schachter and Singer	Physiological arousal requires a cognitive interpretation before it is experienced as emotion.	Cognitive labels determine the experience of emotion.	The situation is a key determinant of emotion, because the situation affects how people interpret their experience.
	Lazarus	Physiological reaction is less important than cognition.	Cognition affects emotion through appraisal of the situation.	A situation must be appraised before a person experiences emotion.

How Does Emotion Affect Behavior?

Over the years, researchers have tried to identify the "basic" emotional expressions of feeling. One noted researcher (Izard, 1997) isolated 10 such basic emotions (joy, interest, surprise, sadness, anger, disgust, contempt, fear, shame, and guilt), but an observational study of facial expressions in college students (Rozin & Cohen, 2003) found that these "basic" emotions were not the ones most commonly expressed on the students' faces. Emotional responses are also molded by strong cultural expectations. Fear, for example, can be praised or punished, depending on the culture, and children may learn to hide some emotions. One person's sense of joy may differ from another's, and the ways of expressing joy differ from individual to individual and from culture to culture.

Culture and Emotion

Most emotions are expressed in most cultures, indicating some type of cross-cultural commonality. But emotional expressions vary in degree and especially in the circumstances under which they occur. Thus, emotions show both consistency and variation among cultures. Questions about cultural variation in emotion are important to theorists who argue that emotions are universal and biologically based. Research indicates that some cultural and individual variation exists even for "basic" emotions such as disgust, fear, and happiness (Keltner & Ekman, 2000; Kobayashi, Schallert, & Ogren, 2003; Scherer, 1997; Scollon et al., 2004). For example, people are better at interpreting expressions of people within their own culture than those of individuals from other cultures, and the more similar the cultures, the more accurate the interpretation (Elfenbein & Ambady, 2002, 2003). Individuals from different cultures also vary in how intense they judge the emotion underlying a particular facial expression to be (Matsumoto et al., 2002). In addition, different cultures allow the display of very different emotions in similar situations. For example, Japanese children are taught to smile when an elder scolds or corrects them (they should be grateful for this useful information). Children in the United States are not taught to frown and pout when they are scolded, but they learn that these responses are accepted.

One survey (Scherer, 1997) found that the greatest differences among cultures came from people's evaluations of the situations and events that provoke emotion. This survey revealed both differences among geopolitical regions and similarities within them. Other research confirms these findings, including studies that have concentrated on the similarity of emotional perceptions among people in similar cultures (Elfenbein & Ambady, 2002). The more similar the cultures, the more consistent the interpretation of emotion. People's very different interpretations of a situation can lead to misunderstandings. For example, if a person believed that an action was unfair, then the person would be justified in feeling angry. If someone from another region evaluated the same situation as fair, he or she would see the first person's anger as unprovoked and even irrational. These differing interpretations have implications for international travelers, businesspeople, politicians, and diplomats.

One of the most frequently studied topics in cross-cultural research is the distinction between individualist and collectivist cultures. (As you learned in Chapter 1, individualist cultures stress the individual, whereas collectivist cultures stress how the individual fits within a group and within society.) People living in these different types of cultures show some variations in emotionality (Matsumoto et al., 2002). A study contrasting people from collectivist cultures in Surinam and Turkey with those from the individualist culture of the Netherlands showed that people from the collectivist cultures were more likely than those from the individualist culture to see emotion as reflecting reality rather than their own individual experience (Mesquita, 2001). In addition, the collectivist cultures tended to foster the attitude that emotion resides in the interaction between people rather than within the person.

Emotions are also differently valued by collectivist and individualist cultures. A study of people in 61 countries (Suh et al., 1998) found that the relationship between positive emotions and life satisfaction was stronger in individualist than in collectivist cultures. In collectivist cultures, life satisfaction was more closely related to achieving the culture's norm for happiness. This result suggests that people in individualist cultures use their own emotions as the standard to judge their happiness, whereas people in collectivist cultures use social standards to make that judgment. Subsequent research has confirmed this interpretation (Cohen & Gunz, 2002). People in individualist cultures are not necessarily more satisfied with life or happier than those in collectivist cultures, but the life situations and feelings that correlate with reported happiness differ for these two types of cultures (Diener et al., 2003). For example, self-esteem and self-respect are more strongly related to happiness in individualist than in collectivist cultures. One factor that does not affect people's judgments of their own happiness is gender (Myers, 2000), but women and men show other differences in emotion.

Gender and Emotion

Most people believe that women are more emotional than men, but in making that assumption, they are concentrating on some emotions and overlooking others. People are thinking of sympathy, fear, and sadness when they associate women with emotion, but are overlooking anger when they consider men unemotional (Shields, 2002). Research shows that the degree to which these stereotypes reflect reality may be due to the power of stereotypes to shape reality. People who fail to conform to generally held beliefs may be punished with social rejection, and people who do conform are rewarded for such behaviors. In addition, people have a tendency to notice and recall examples that conform to their stereotypes and to ignore and forget examples that do not. Both the reinforcements and the memory biases help to shape and perpetuate gender stereotypes of emotionality. Also, people interpret situations that are not clear in stereotypical terms. Thus, gender stereotypes continue to limit both men's and women's full expression of their emotionality.

Consider, for example, the gender stereotype that men experience more anger than women. This stereotype is largely inaccurate, but it persists because it focuses on the behavioral expression of anger through aggression while ignoring the expression of anger in other ways. Research on the experience of anger indicates that there are few gender differences in feelings of anger (Simon & Nath, 2004). Women often verbalize anger more intensely and for longer periods of time than men do—especially women who are in close heterosexual relationships. Men in a similar situation more frequently "stonewall"—they limit their facial expressions and minimize their listening behaviors and eye contact (Gottman, 1998). Yet the physiological reactions of men and women in these situations are much more similar than their behaviors indicate. Even in situations that require less personal involvement, such as viewing an emotion-arousing movie, the physiological reactions of women and men are similar (Kring & Gordon, 1998). Thus, the feelings of anger (and other emotions) are probably very similar for men and women.

Display rules for emotionality in many cultures hold that women can be more emotional, giving them the freedom to express a wider variety of emotions than men can. However, women are restricted in their expression of anger, so even though they feel anger as frequently and as intensely as men, they display it verbally or indirectly rather than in direct, physical confrontations. Men are similarly restricted in their expressions of sadness, fear, affection, and most emotions other than anger. Men's and women's displays of emotion differ in most cultures, depending on the display rules that govern these behaviors (Fischer et al., 2004). In many cultures, men tend to display emotions associated with power (such as anger), whereas women show emotions related to powerlessness (such as sadness and fear). However, these tendencies vary with women's status in the culture, and there are fewer gender differences in the expression of emotions in cultures in which women have more status and power.

Women and men learn to conform to the display rules deemed appropriate to their gender in their society. This role that learning plays suggests that expressions of emotion can change—that is, people can learn to control their emotions. But if one component of emotion involves brain and nervous system arousal, how can this be accomplished?

Can We Control Emotions?

The extent to which emotions can be controlled depends on which of the three components of emotion—physiology, feelings, or behavior—is the focus of the attempt. Control of the physiological component of emotion is quite difficult. The activation that occurs in brain structures and the resulting responses of the peripheral nervous system and changes to hormone levels happen automatically and largely outside the level of conscious thought. Controlling these physiological reactions is possible but difficult (see the discussion on biofeedback in Chapter 7).

Changing one's feelings and behavior are more likely ways of managing emotions. If cognitions are an important component of emotional experience, then changing how one thinks about a situation should produce alterations in the emotion one feels. Indeed, the notion that cognitions can change emotions is the basis for the cognitive approach to psychotherapy (see Chapter 17). Changing feelings by reappraising or reevaluating a situation is more constructive than suppressing or concealing those feelings (Richards, 2004). Indeed, suppressing or denying feelings may take more effort than reevaluating the situation, detracting from one's ability to think about and deal with other problems. When people learn to think about their problems and situations in different ways, they can change their feelings about their lives.

Although it may seem that some people cannot control their emotions, research indicates that such behavior is not the result of inability to exert control but rather attributable to immediate, personal priorities. Dianne Tice and her colleagues (2001) studied breakdowns of impulse control in an effort to understand the origin of these (often problem) behaviors. Rather than seeing people with impulse control problems as self-destructive or poor at self-regulation, these researchers considered the possibility that people indulge themselves in behaviors that may be unacceptable as a strategy to make themselves feel better in times of emotional distress. When people feel bad, they want to do something to feel better, which may include behaviors that are unwise, socially inappropriate, or even dangerous. Tice and her colleagues found that people who feel bad are more likely than those in a better mood to eat unhealthy snacks, to choose an immediate rather than a delayed gratification, and to put off a tedious task. Ethical restrictions kept the researchers from including behaviors that were violent or dangerous in this study, but the results imply that emotional reactions are not beyond control. Rather, people make choices to behave in ways that they believe will make them feel better immediately (if you feel bad, do it). That is, we can control our emotional reactions, but we do not always choose to do so.

Summary and Review

WHAT IS MOTIVATION?

What are the important elements of the definition of motivation?

A *motivation* is any condition, usually internal, that initiates, activates, or maintains an organism's goal-directed behavior. Motivation is inferred from behavior rather than directly observed. pp. 428–429

What are the major theories of motivation?

Evolutionary psychologists believe that humans have many *instincts*, fixed behavioral patterns that occur in all members of the species. These instincts motivate people as a result of adaptations related to survival and reproduction throughout evolutionary history. pp. 429–430

Drive theory is an explanation of behavior that assumes that an organism is motivated to act because of a need to attain, reestablish, or maintain some goal that aids survival. A *drive* is an internal arousal condition related to a *need*, a state of physiological imbalance. A drive explanation of behavior views the organism as being pushed and pulled by needs. A *motive* is typically an internal condition, involving some form of arousal, that directs an organism's behavior toward a goal. The goal of many drives is *homeostasis*, the maintenance of a steady state of inner stability or balance. Goals can also cause *conflict*. *Approach–approach conflict* arises when a person must choose between two equally pleasant alternatives, such as going to a party or to a movie. *Avoidance–avoidance conflict* occurs when a choice involves two equally distasteful alternatives, such as mowing the lawn or cleaning the garage. *Approach–avoidance conflict* results when a single alternative has both attractive and undesirable aspects, such as accepting an invitation to go out with friends, which prevents you from studying for an important exam. pp. 430–434

According to arousal theory, individuals seek an optimal level of stimulation. The Yerkes–Dodson principle asserts that behavior varies from disorganized to effective to optimal, depending on the person's level of *arousal*. Contemporary researchers have studied how arousal and anxiety that are too high or too low affect performance, especially on complex tasks. pp. 434–435

Cognitive theories explain behavior by emphasizing the role of thoughts in people's active decision making regarding goals and the means of achieving them. *Expectancy theories* are cognitive theories of motivation that focus on people's expectations about reaching their goals and their need for achievement. Needs can be learned, and a *social need* directs people to behave in ways that allow them to feel good about themselves and to establish and maintain relationships. pp. 435–437

Extrinsic motivation is supplied by rewards that come from the external environment. *Intrinsic motivation* gives rise to behaviors that a person performs in order to obtain pleasure and satisfaction from the behavior itself. On some occasions, people involved in intrinsically motivated behaviors will experience *flow*—complete and pleasurable absorption in an activity—but this experience is not routine. The *overjustification effect* is the decrease in likelihood that an intrinsically motivated task that has been extrinsically rewarded will be performed once the reward is no longer given. pp. 437–438

Humanistic theory focuses on human dignity, individual choice, and self-worth. Maslow described how motivation can be arranged in a hierarchy, ranging from physiological needs to the need for *self-actualization*, or fulfilling one's full human potential. pp. 438–439

HOW DOES MOTIVATION AFFECT BEHAVIOR?

What causes hunger?

People do not eat because their energy levels are low; they eat before energy deficits occur. A variety of hormones, including insulin, leptin, cholecystokinin, ghrelin, and peptide YY, provide signals to the brain, which the brain interprets as hunger or satiation. pp. 441–442

Learning is also important for hunger and eating. The initiation of eating is affected by habit and learning, and food preferences are strongly influenced by cultural factors and individual taste preferences. pp. 442–443

Why is obesity becoming more prevalent?

The increasing prevalence of obesity is evidence against a completely genetic basis for body weight, but genetic factors do contribute to fat-cell distribution and to the tendency to gain weight. A person's history with food, the availability of a variety of tasty food, and low levels of physical activity all contribute to the development of obesity. pp. 443–446

How do physiology and thought contribute to sexual behavior?

Sexual behavior in human beings is in part under hormonal control, and the balance of sex hormones differs for men and women. In men, androgens produced by the testes predominate, and in women, estrogens produced by the ovaries do. These sex hormones control prenatal development of the reproductive organs and prompt the onset of sexual behavior and fertility during puberty. p. 446

Thought plays an enormous role in the sexual behavior of human beings; thoughts, fantasies, and images can initiate and activate sexual desire and activity. pp. 446–447

What are the phases in the sexual response cycle?

When human beings become sexually aroused and engage in sexual activity, they go through a series of four phases, which together are known as the sexual response cycle: the *excitement phase* (characterized by *vasocongestion*), the *plateau phase*, the *orgasm phase*, and the *resolution phase*. pp. 447–448

How have Americans' sex lives changed over the past 50 years?

The sex survey by Laumann and his colleagues, the most recent of the comprehensive studies of sexual behavior, showed that women's and men's sexual attitudes and behaviors are more similar than they were 50 years ago. However, some gender differences remain. Married women and men have sex more often than unmarried people do. Most Americans are satisfied with their sex lives. pp. 448–449

A person with a heterosexual orientation has an erotic attraction and preference for members of the other sex; a person with a homosexual orientation has an erotic attraction and preference for members of the same sex. According to the Laumann study, only 2.8% of men and 1.4% of women identify themselves as exclusively homosexual in orientation. These figures are substantially lower than Kinsey reported in the 1950s. pp. 449–450

What are some important social needs?

The *need for achievement* is a social need that directs a person to strive for excellence and success. According to expectancy theories, people engage in behaviors that satisfy their desires for success, mastery, and fulfillment. Tests such as the TAT have been used to measure need for achievement. Achievement values vary among and within cultures, and a person's *self-efficacy* is related to his or her need for achievement. The *need for affiliation* is the social need that motivates a person to be with and to establish positive relationships with others. Building a *social support* network is one healthy way to satisfy this need. pp. 450–455

WHAT IS EMOTION?

What is the definition of emotion?

An *emotion* is a subjective response (a feeling), accompanied by a physiological change, which is interpreted in a particular way by the individual and often leads to a change in behavior. The three components of an emotion—feeling, physiological response, and behavior—usually function together but are separable.

Display rules govern the expression of emotion and vary according to age, gender, and culture. pp. 455–456

What are the important theories of emotion?

Physiological theories of emotion include the James–Lange theory and the Cannon–Bard theory. The James–Lange theory states that people experience physiological changes and then interpret those changes as emotions. The Cannon–Bard theory states that when people experience emotions, an emotional response and physiological changes occur simultaneously. Recent research has identified brain structures that are important to the experience of emotion. This research has concentrated on the limbic system, especially the amygdala, which has some role in fear. pp. 456–458

Evolutionary theory views emotion as an adaptive response to specific situations that increases survival and reproductive advantages. Facial expressions have been used as a way to assess universal emotional experience, as hypothesized by evolutionary theory, but claims of universality of emotion are controversial. pp. 458–459

According to cognitive theories of emotion, for example, the Schachter–Singer approach and Lazarus's approach, thoughts and an appraisal of the situation are an important and even a determining component of emotion. p. 459

HOW DOES EMOTION AFFECT BEHAVIOR?

How does culture affect emotion?

Researchers have tried to identify basic emotions that are universal, but culture affects the expression of emotion through its influence on display rules. Thus, emotions show both consistency and variation among cultures. pp. 463–464

Are there gender differences in emotion?

Women and men experience similar feelings or physiological reactions when they experience emotion, but women and men are governed by different display rules that lead to different behavioral expression of emotion. Culture and gender interact to influence the display of emotion in women and men. pp. 464–465

Can emotions be controlled?

The extent to which people can control their emotions depends on whether we consider the physiology, the feelings, or the behavior associated with emotion. Physiology is difficult to control, but programs that teach people how to control their emotions, such as anger-management programs, target feelings and behaviors. Failure to control emotions may be due to unwillingness rather than to inability to do so. pp. 465–466

CHAPTER 13

Personality and Its Assessment

What Is Personality?   470
  Definition of Personality
  Personality in the Cultural Context

What Is the Psychodynamic Approach to Personality?   473
  The Psychoanalytic Theory of Sigmund Freud
  Adler and Individual Psychology
  Jung and Analytical Psychology

Can Personality Be Learned?   485
  The Power of Learning
  Skinner and Behavioral Analysis: Acquiring a Personality

What Are Trait and Type Theories of Personality?   487
  Allport's Personal Disposition Theory
  Cattell's Trait Theory
  Eysenck's Factor Theory
  The Five-Factor Model

What Characterizes the Humanistic Approach to Personality?   490
  Maslow and Self-Actualization
  Rogers and Self Theory
  Positive Psychology

What Is the Cognitive Approach to Personality?   495
  Key Cognitive Concepts
  Kelly and Personal Constructs
  Rotter and Locus of Control
  Bandura and Self-Efficacy
  Mischel's Cognitive-Affective Personality System

How Do Psychologists Assess Personality?   500
  Projective Tests
  Personality Inventories

Summary and Review   505

To explore questions about personality, we first need to define the term. Then we'll look at how the cultural context may influence people's personalities.

What Is Personality?

Although personality psychologists may disagree on the meaning of the term *personality*, most agree that it originated from the Latin *persona*, the word for a theatrical mask worn by Roman actors in dramas. Despite the origins of the word, psychologists now view personality as something more than simply the role people play.

Definition of Personality

Personality is a pattern of relatively permanent traits, dispositions, or characteristics that give some consistency to an individual's behavior. Your personality is what leads you to behave at least somewhat consistently in different environmental situations. But the definition of personality must also allow for some inconsistency in behavior. For example, you may behave aggressively in one situation but submissively in another, depending on the presence of other people, the behavior of those people, and your own mood and motivation.

Personality ■ A pattern of relatively permanent traits, dispositions, or characteristics that give some consistency to an individual's behavior.

The individual traits, dispositions, or characteristics that make up your personality may be unique to you, common to your particular cultural group, or shared with all other people. Thus, you are identical to no other person, yet similar to others in your cultural group and akin to all other people in some ways.

What causes people to have particular personality dimensions? Personality theorists differ in their answer to this question. Some, such as Freud, focus on unconscious conflicts that originated during childhood. Others, such as Skinner, see human personality as largely learned from the environment. Still others, such as Allport, emphasize the *patterns* of traits that characterize individuals. Still others, such as Cattell and Eysenck, look for genetic influences that motivate behavior and shape personality. Another group of theorists, including Rogers and Maslow, see humans as moving toward fulfillment or self-actualization, and, finally, some personality theorists, such as Bandura and Kelly, emphasize various cognitive factors that influence personality.

Like all theories, personality theories should generate research as well as organize, explain, and predict data. The data amassed by personality theorists help psychologists answer questions such as these:

- Does nature or nurture play a greater role in personality development?
- Do unconscious processes direct behavior?
- What accounts for the development of stable behavior patterns in humans?
- Does a person's behavior depend on the situation?
- Do people behave consistently throughout their lives?
- What is the impact of culture on personality?

Personality in the Cultural Context

Like other behaviors, personality must be viewed in a cultural context. *Culture,* as we have seen, refers to the norms, ideals, values, rules, patterns of communication, and beliefs adopted by a group of people. Culture is significant for many psychological phenomena because it shapes how people raise their children, what values they teach, and what family life is like. However, the role of culture in shaping personality is controversial.

Some researchers have tried to investigate this issue by focusing on the differences among cultures. For example, many cultures in North America and Western Europe are individualist, valuing competitiveness, autonomy, and self-reliance and focusing on the individual (Triandis & Suh, 2002). In contrast, many cultures in Asia, Africa, and South America are collectivist, valuing interdependence and cooperation and focusing more on group interactions and social hierarchy. Further, within large and diverse countries, such as the United States, there are significant variations in values and social norms among different ethnic and cultural groups. Another dimension of difference is how tightly or loosely cultures enforce their rules. One culture may value conformity, strict adherence to religious values, and obedience to parental authority. Another culture may have similar rules but looser standards for their enforcement.

These sorts of cultural differences have obvious effects on behavior, but do they affect personality (Rozin, 2003)? The answer to that question depends in part on how personality is defined. Some researchers have searched for differences in behaviors that relate to cultural dimensions. For example, independence and interdependence are related to the individualist versus collectivist dimension. Some cultures emphasize family and social group as the foundation for personality, whereas others emphasize establishing independence as the basis for personality. Nor are all individualist or all collectivist cultures the same. For example, American individualism varies from Swedish individualism (Triandis & Gelfand, 1998). The correlation between the individualist or collectivist dimension and certain personality traits has a great deal of research support (Triandis & Suh, 2002). For example, conformity is higher, and the desire to be distinctive is lower, among individuals from collectivist cultures than among those from individualist cultures (Bond & Smith, 1996; Kim & Markus, 1999; Tafarodi, Marshall, & Katsura, 2004).

Some personality researchers contend that culture makes very little contribution to personality traits. This view is prominent among evolutionary psychologists, who tend to see personality as the expression of biological traits and who look for the commonalities across cultures, the underlying dimensions of personality that all humans share (Hofstede & McCrae, 2004; McCrae et al., 2000). Some evolutionary psychologists even contend that personality is not restricted to humans, that traits common to humans appear in other primates (King, 2003). One personality theorist, Robert McCrae (2004), even argues that personality traits furnish one of the bases of culture, rather than the other way around.

The line of research that looks for universal personality traits has been productive (Hendriks et al., 2003). These results mean that people's personalities can be analyzed in terms of the same traits, but not that people in different cultures have the same traits to the same extents. Indeed, personality traits vary substantially across cultures (Hendriks et al., 2003; Lynn & Martin, 1997). For example, people in China are much lower in the trait of extraversion (how outgoing a person is) than people in the United States, and many people in China have a trait that does not appear in people from North America (Triandis & Suh, 2002). In some cultures, women are higher in extraversion than men, but men are higher in this trait than in most. In all cultures, there is a lot of individual variation in personality. Indeed, individual variation within cultures is so large that it presents a problem for personality theorists (Rozin, 2003).

In examining theories of personality, we must keep in mind that each theory arose in a particular cultural context, which influenced the person who created the theory and thus the theory's conceptualization of personality. The theories we will examine are rooted in Western philosophical assumptions about humans (Markus, 2004). In addition, some of these theories originated over 100 years ago, and they reflect the culture of their time and place. The psychodynamic theory of Sigmund Freud is a good example of a theory of personality that is biased by the cultural context in which it arose.

What Is the Psychodynamic Approach to Personality?

Let's begin our consideration of personality theories by examining examples of *psychodynamic theory*—an approach to personality that focuses on how unconscious processes direct day-to-day behavior and affect personality formation. The most famous, and perhaps the most widely disputed, of the psychodynamic theories, is that of Sigmund Freud. Freud's psychoanalytic theory gave rise to two other psychodynamic theories: the individual psychology of Alfred Adler and the analytical psychology of Carl Jung.

Psychodynamic theory
■ An approach to personality that focuses on how unconscious processes direct day-to-day behavior and affect personality formation.

The Psychoanalytic Theory of Sigmund Freud

Sigmund Freud (1856–1939) was an Austrian physician whose influence on psychology was so great that some of his basic concepts are now taken for granted. Such terms as *ego, oral fixation, death wish, anal retentive, Freudian slip, unconscious motivation,* and *Oedipus complex* are part of everyday language. However, when Freud introduced his ideas in the late 19th century, they were seen as strange and radical. Freud's exploration of the unconscious and his suggestion that children have sexual experiences were, to say the least, revolutionary ideas.

Freud developed his theory by treating people with emotional problems (Breger, 2000), using hypnosis, and later, a process known as *free association.* (We'll discuss free association in Chapter 17.) Most of his patients were from the middle and upper classes of European society; thus, cultural context was important in shaping Freud's theory and also limited it. Many of Freud's patients were married women of wealth and position who, because they lived in a repressive society, had limited opportunities for the release of anxiety and tension. Freud noticed that many of them wanted to discuss their personal problems and often felt better after having done so.

From his therapeutic work with these patients, Freud began to formulate a theory of behavior that centered on early childhood experiences and fantasies. Originally, Freud believed that the symptoms of his adult patients sprang from their experiences of being sexually seduced in childhood by some older person, often a parent (Freud, 1985). However, he soon abandoned this seduction theory and replaced it with the *Oedipus complex*, which places responsibility for childhood sexual experiences on the child's fantasies rather than a parent's or other adult's behavior. Over time, Freud developed an elaborate theory of personality and an accompanying approach to therapy called *psychoanalysis.*

Psychoanalytic theory rests on several key assumptions:

■ Human experience takes place on three *levels of consciousness*—the conscious, the preconscious, and the unconscious, with the unconscious dominating the other two.

- Human functioning is influenced by three basic *structures of the mind*—the id, the ego, and the superego.
- The foundation of personality is shaped mostly by *early childhood experiences*.
- Punishment of a child's *sexual and aggressive behaviors* results in repression of at least part of these experiences and leads to psychological conflict.
- Unconscious psychological conflict creates anxiety, and all people learn to protect themselves against anxiety by adopting a variety of *defense mechanisms*.

Levels of Mental Life

Conscious ■ According to Freud, the level of the mind that consists of those experiences that a person is aware of at any given time.

Freud assumed that mental life takes place on three levels: conscious, preconscious, and unconscious (Freud, 1915/1957, 1933/1964). The *conscious* occupies a relatively minor place in psychoanalytic theory; it consists of those experiences that we are aware of at any given time. It is the only level of mental life directly available to us.

Preconscious ■ According to Freud, the level of the mind that contains those experiences of which a person is not currently conscious but may become so, with varying degrees of difficulty.

The *preconscious* is the level of the mind that contains those experiences of which we are not currently conscious but may become so, with varying degrees of difficulty. You can probably bring your social security number to conscious awareness very easily, but you may have much difficulty dredging up some date in history that you learned four years ago. Both the social security number and the date are in your preconscious, but one is easily recalled whereas the other is quite difficult or even impossible to remember.

Unconscious ■ According to Freud, the level of the mind that consists of thoughts, urges, and memories that are not within a person's awareness.

The *unconscious* contains thoughts, urges, and memories that, by definition, are beyond the realm of awareness. They are not like the history date, which is simply forgotten; they must remain unconscious because they would bring too much anxiety. However, unconscious urges may become preconscious, or even conscious, in a form that prevents us from recognizing their true nature. For example, thoughts about harming a despised rival may be too anxiety-provoking, so we suppress these thoughts by behaving in an overly friendly manner toward that person. This façade may slip, and we may say or do something that reflects our true feelings of hostility. These *Freudian slips* reveal our true but unconscious thoughts (Freud, 1901/1960).

The Structure of the Mind

Id ■ In Freud's theory, the region of the mind that is the source of a person's instinctual energy and that works mainly on the pleasure principle.

According to Freud's theory, the primary structural elements of the mind and personality are three regions of the mind (not physical structures of the brain) that reside, fully or partially, in the unconscious: the id, the ego, and the superego (Freud, 1933/1964). Each force accounts for a different aspect of functioning (see **Table 13.1** on p. 475).

The *id* is the source of a person's instinctual energy; according to Freud (1933/1964), the energy of the id is either sexual or aggressive. The id works mainly according to the *pleasure principle*; that is, it tries to maximize immediate gratification through the satisfaction of raw impulses. Residing deep within the unconscious, the demanding, irrational, and selfish id seeks pleasure—without regard for reality or morality.

Ego ■ In Freud's theory, the region of the mind that seeks to satisfy instinctual needs in accordance with reality

While the id seeks to maximize pleasure and obtain immediate gratification, the *ego* is the region of the mind that seeks to satisfy the individual's instinctual needs in

Table 13.1

COMPARISON OF FREUD'S THREE SYSTEMS OF PERSONALITY

	Id	Ego	Superego
■ Level of Mind	Unconscious	Primarily conscious and preconscious	Primarily preconscious
■ Principle	Pleasure principle	Reality principle	Morals and ideals from parents and society
■ Purpose	Seek pleasure and avoid pain	Adapt to reality while controlling the id and the superego	Distinguish right from wrong
■ Aim	Immediate gratification	Safety, compromise, and delayed gratification	Perfection

accordance with reality—working according to the *reality principle*. Whereas the id strives to achieve immediate gratification, the ego attempts to check the power of the id and delay gratification. The ego acts as a manager, adjusting cognitive and perceptual processes so as to control the id and keep the person in touch with reality. For example, when a 4-year-old boy in a grocery store sees candy, his id says, "Take the candy." However, his ego may recognize that he is likely to be caught and punished. His decision to leave the candy alone is *not* based on morality but on reality; his ego tells him, "If I take the candy, I will be caught and punished."

Freud's third region of the mind is the *superego,* which embodies ideals and morals. As children grow older, their superego develops and provides them with both an *ego ideal* and a *conscience*. A somewhat older boy with a developed superego would behave according to his ego ideal or his conscience with regard to the tempting candy. The ego ideal says, "I'm not a person who steals candy," and the conscience says, "I would feel guilty if I took something that did not belong to me." The ego and superego thus attempt to moderate the demands of the id and direct it toward appropriate ways of behaving.

The superego in Freud's theory has something in common with the id—neither is in touch with reality. In other ways, however, they are direct opposites. The id seeks instant pleasure without regard for what is wise or possible, while the superego tells a person not to do anything that would be pleasurable. (**Figure 13.1** illustrates Freud's levels of consciousness and structures of the mind.)

Superego [sue-pur-EE-go] ■ In Freud's theory, the region of the mind that comprises the ego ideal (what a person would ideally like to be) and the conscience (taught by parents and society).

Development of Personality

Freud believed that the core aspects of personality are established early, remain relatively stable throughout life, and are changed only with great difficulty. He argued that all people pass through five critical *psychosexual stages* of personality

Psychosexual stages ■ The oral, anal, phallic, latency, and genital stages of personality development described by Freud, through which all people pass.

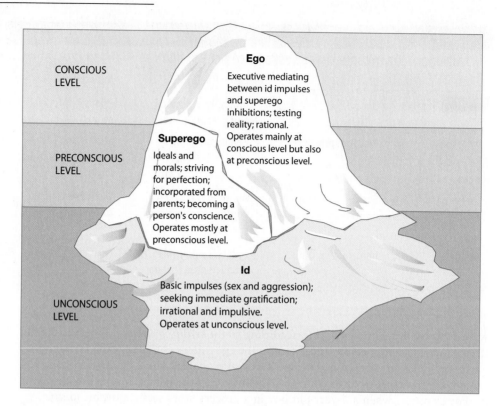

Figure 13.1
Freud's View of Levels and Regions of the Mind
Freud viewed the mind as having three levels: the conscious, the preconscious, and the unconscious. Freud theorized that just as the greater part of an iceberg is hidden beneath the surface of the sea, so most of the contents of the mind are below the level of conscious awareness. The *ego* is a region of the mind mainly in conscious and the preconscious. The *superego* operates mostly in the preconscious. The *id* operates solely at an unconscious level.

Oral stage ■ Freud's first stage of personality development, from birth to about age 2, during which the instincts of the infant are focused on the mouth as the primary pleasure center.

development: oral, anal, phallic, latency, and genital (see **Table 13.2**). At each of these stages, Freud (1933/1964) asserted, people experience conflicts and issues associated with *erogenous zones*—areas of the body that give rise to erotic or sexual sensations when they are stimulated.

Freud believed that the psychosexual stages begin at birth and that babies experience sexual feelings and impulses. Although his concept of infantile sexuality was quite controversial, Freud had an expanded view of sexuality. To him, sexual pleasure was not limited to the genital areas of the body but could be derived from stimulation of the mouth, anus, and other erogenous zones.

The concept of the *oral stage* is based on the fact that the instincts of infants (from birth to about age 2) are focused on the mouth as the primary pleasure center. Infants receive oral gratification through feeding, thumb sucking, and cooing during the early months of life, when their basic feelings about the world are being established. Relying heavily on symbolism, Freud (1933/1964) contended that adults who consider the world a bitter place (analogous to tasting something bitter) probably had difficulty during the oral stage of development and may have traits associated with passivity and hostility. Their problems tend to focus on their need for nurturing, warmth, and love. Adults who continue to remain attached to the oral stage or who revert to this stage during times of intense anxiety will display the traits of an oral personality. They may take pleasure in biting objects (or making biting comments), smoking, overeating, or using the mouth for sexual pleasure.

Table 13.2

FREUD'S FIVE PSYCHOSEXUAL STAGES OF PERSONALITY DEVELOPMENT

Stage	Erogenous Zone	Conflicts/Experiences	Adult Traits Associated with Problems (Especially Fixations) at a Stage
■ Oral stage (birth to 2 years)	Mouth	Infant achieves gratification through oral activities, such as feeding, thumb sucking, and cooing.	Optimism, gullibility, passivity, hostility, substance abuse
■ Anal stage (2 to 3 years)	Anus	The child learns to respond to some parental demands (such as for bladder and bowel control).	Excessive cleanliness, orderliness, messiness, rebelliousness
■ Phallic stage (4 to 7 years)	Genitals	The child experiences the Oedipus complex.	Flirtatiousness, vanity, promiscuity, chastity
■ Latency stage (7 to puberty)	None	The child continues developing but sexual urges are relatively quiet.	Not specified
■ Genital stage (puberty onward)	Genitals	The growing adolescent shakes off old dependencies and learns to deal maturely with the other sex.	Not specified

The *anal stage* is Freud's second stage of personality development, from age 2 to about age 3, during which children learn to control the immediate gratification they obtain through defecation and to become responsive to the demands of society. In this stage, children learn to respond to some of parents' and society's demands. One parental demand is that children control their bodily functions and become toilet trained. This stage therefore establishes the basis for conflict between the id and the ego—between the desire for immediate gratification of physical urges and the demand for controlled behavior. Freud claimed that during the anal stage, children might develop certain lasting personality characteristics related to control. Children who rebel against the parents' demands for cleanliness and control may develop the anal expulsion personality pattern and become exceedingly sloppy, messy, and rebellious. On the other hand, children who do not rebel against parents' attempts to toilet train them may acquire an anal retentive personality pattern characterized by compulsive needs for orderliness, miserliness, and stubbornness. Thus, adults who had difficulty in the anal stage tend to have problems that focus on orderliness (or lack of it) and also might be compulsive in many behaviors.

The *phallic stage* is Freud's third stage of personality development, from about age 4 through 7, during which children obtain gratification primarily from the genitals (Freud, 1933). At about age 4 or 5, children become aware of their genitals and the pleasure that comes from them. During the phallic stage, children pass

Anal stage ■ Freud's second stage of personality development, from about age 2 to about age 3, during which children learn to control the immediate gratification they obtain through defecation and to become responsive to the demands of society.

Phallic [FAL-ick] stage ■ Freud's third stage of personality development, from about age 4 through age 7, during which children obtain gratification primarily from the genitals.

Oedipus [ED-i-pus] complex ■ A group of unconscious wishes to have sexual intercourse with the parent of the opposite sex and to kill or remove the parent of the same sex, which arise during Freud's phallic stage and are ultimately resolved through identification with the parent of the same sex.

through what Freud termed the **Oedipus complex.** According to Freud, this complex is a group (or complex) of unconscious wishes to have sexual intercourse with one parent and to kill or remove the other parent. Freud derived the term *Oedipus complex* from the story of Oedipus, as told by the Greek playwright Sophocles. Oedipus killed his father and married his mother without realizing who they were.

In boys, the Oedipus complex usually involves feelings of rivalry toward the father and sexual love for the mother. The boy develops feelings of hostility toward his father and believes that his attraction to his mother makes his father jealous. This rivalry produces *castration anxiety*, the fear that the father will remove the boy's penis as a punishment. Freud argued that the Oedipus complex follows a slightly different course for girls than it does for boys. In girls, the Oedipus complex typically involves hostile feelings for the mother and sexual love for the father. Freud held that when a girl realizes that she has no penis, she develops what he called *penis envy* and the desire to acquire a penis. Freud suggested that the little girl could symbolically acquire a penis by forming a relationship with her father. A young girl might ask her father to marry her so that they can raise a family together. Thus, the behavior of children who are experiencing the Oedipus complex produces uneasiness within the family and causes anxiety for the children.

For both boys and girls, the Oedipus complex is resolved through identification with the parent of the same sex and the acquisition of a developing superego, one based on the child's perception of the same-sex parent's morals and ideals. A young boy begins to identify with and model his behavior on his father, and the young girl takes her mother as a role model. When the Oedipus complex is properly resolved, children will accept the authority of the same-sex parent and surrender the sexual nature of their love for the other-sex parent. Adult traits associated with problems in the phallic stage usually involve sexuality and may include vanity, promiscuity, or excessive worry about chastity. Some research indicates that, as adults, people choose characteristics in their mates that they see as similar to those of their other-sex parent, which is consistent with the Freudian view (Geher, 2000).

The Oedipus complex is controversial and widely debated, especially because many people find the idea insulting to women. There is no doubt about Freud's view of women—he saw them as morally weaker and inferior to men. Most researchers now believe that Freud's notion of penis envy was imaginative but lacking in credibility (Breger, 2000; Webster, 1995). Does the concept of the Oedipus complex provide a good explanation of the family dynamics between parents and 4- or 5-year-olds? Most researchers have doubts.

Latency [LAY-ten-see] stage ■ Freud's fourth stage of personality development, from about age 7 until puberty, during which sexual urges are inactive.

The *latency stage* follows the phallic stage and lasts from about age 7 until puberty. During this period, children develop physically, but sexual urges are inactive (latent). Much of children's energy is channeled into social or intellectual activities.

Genital [JEN-it-ul] stage ■ Freud's last stage of personality development, from the onset of puberty through adulthood, during which the sexual conflicts of childhood resurface (at puberty) and are often resolved (during adolescence).

Freud's last stage of personality development, the **genital stage,** begins at the onset of puberty and continues through adolescence into adulthood. When individuals reach this stage, sexuality re-emerges, along with fears and repressed feelings from earlier stages. Repressed sexual feelings toward one's parents may also resurface at puberty. Over the course of the genital stage, the adolescent learns to deal socially and sexually with members of the other sex in mature ways. Members of the other sex, who were ignored during the latency stage, are now seen as attractive. Many unresolved conflicts and repressed urges affect behavior during this stage. Ideally, if people have passed successfully through previous psychosexual stages, they will develop heterosexual relationships. If not, they may continue to have unresolved unconscious conflicts throughout their adult lives.

As children proceed from one psychosexual stage to the next, they adjust their views of the world. Successfully passing through a stage requires resolution of that stage's principal conflict. Freud likened the process to military troops moving from battle to battle—a failure to successfully resolve one conflict weakens an army at its next.

Sex and Aggression: The Two Great Drives

Freud (1920/1966) theorized that people are energized to act the way they do because of two basic instinctual drives: the drive toward *life*, which is expressed through sex and sexual energy, and the drive toward *death*, which is expressed through aggression. These instincts are buried deep within the unconscious, and their expression is not always socially acceptable. Freud wrote little about aggression until late in his life; he focused mainly on energy from the sexual instinct, which he termed the *libido*—the instinctual (and sexual) life force that, working on the pleasure principle and seeking immediate gratification, energizes the id.

Libido [lih-BEE-doe] In Freud's theory, the instinctual (and sexual) life force that, working on the pleasure principle and seeking immediate gratification, energizes the id.

When people exhibit socially unacceptable behaviors or have feelings that they consider socially unacceptable, especially sexual feelings, they often experience self-punishment, guilt, and anxiety—all forms of inner conflict. Freud's theory thus describes a conflict between a person's instinctual (often unconscious) need for gratification and society's demand that each individual be socialized. In other words, it paints a picture of human beings caught in a conflict between basic sexual and aggressive desires and socialization. Personality functions as a delicate balancing act, with sexual and aggressive desires weighed against the demands of society, and the person attempting to satisfy both.

Defense Mechanisms

To defend itself against the anxiety brought about by sexual and aggressive drives, the ego adopts one or more *defense mechanisms*—unconscious attempts to reduce anxiety by distorting perceptions of reality. Freud (1926/1959) made several key assumptions about defense mechanisms:

Defense mechanism An unconscious way of reducing anxiety by distorting perceptions of reality.

- They are normal and universal reactions.
- When carried to extremes, they may lead to compulsive, unhealthy behaviors.
- They operate on an unconscious level.
- They protect the ego against anxiety.
- They are helpful to the individual and generally harmless to society.
- They all have some elements of repression.

Repression Defense mechanism by which anxiety-provoking thoughts and feelings are forced into the unconscious.

Thus, *repression*, or the forcing of anxiety-provoking thoughts and feelings into the unconscious, is the basic Freudian defense mechanism.

What types of experiences are most likely to be repressed? Freud believed that childhood experiences with sex and aggression are often unacceptable to the parents and eventually are denied or repressed by the child. For example, the Oedipal feelings of sexual attraction toward one parent and aggression toward the other are not acceptable to most parents in Western societies. After parents suppress their child's sexual and aggressive behaviors by either punishing or withholding reward for these behaviors, the child begins to develop anxiety about certain sexual and aggressive impulses and therefore forces them into the unconscious. In addition to repression, Freud identified several other defense mechanisms with specific functions.

Rationalization is the defense mechanism by which people reinterpret undesirable feelings or behaviors in terms that make them seem acceptable. For example, a shoplifter may rationalize that no one will miss the things she steals or that she needs the things more than other people do. A student may cheat, asserting to himself that his failing the course would hurt his parents far too much for them to bear.

Fixation is a defense mechanism by which a person develops an excessive attachment to another person, object, or behavior that was appropriate only at an earlier stage of development. For example, a person with an oral fixation continues to receive pleasure from talking, biting, drinking, eating, smoking, and other oral functions. A person with an anal fixation might hold on to his money or opinions just as he originally held in his feces when being toilet trained.

Regression is the defense mechanism by which a person returns to an earlier stage of psychosexual development. During periods of extreme anxiety, a person may regress or move backward to an earlier stage, typically the oral stage. For example, older children who suck their thumbs express their oral needs, despite having progressed far beyond this stage.

Projection is a defense mechanism by which people attribute their own undesirable traits to others. A friend who inexplicably asks "Are you mad at me?" may actually be mad at you but afraid to admit it to himself. Instead, he sees *your* behavior as angry. Similarly, a person with deep aggressive tendencies may see other people as acting in an excessively hostile way.

Reaction formation is the defense mechanism by which people behave in a way opposite to what their true (but anxiety-provoking) feelings would dictate. A classic example of reaction formation is the behavior of a person who has strong sexual urges but whose behavior is extremely chaste. Similarly, a person with strong but unconscious hostile feelings for her boss may behave in an overly friendly manner to him or her. Reaction formations can be detected by other people because they produce behavior that is exaggerated or overly dramatic.

Displacement is the defense mechanism by which people divert sexual or aggressive feelings for one person onto another person or thing. For example, a woman who is mistreated by her boss may repress her hostility toward that person but take it out on her husband, children, pets, or even a stuffed animal. Displacement differs from reaction formation in that the behaviors are not exaggerated or overdone.

Denial is the defense mechanism by which people refuse to accept reality or recognize the true source of anxiety. For example, a person with drinking or drug problems may deny that these behaviors are causing problems.

Rationalization ■ Defense mechanism by which people reinterpret undesirable feelings or behaviors in terms that make them seem acceptable.

Fixation ■ An excessive attachment to some person, object, or behavior that was appropriate only at an earlier stage of development.

Regression ■ Defense mechanism by which a person is driven by anxiety to return to an earlier stage of psychosexual development.

Projection ■ Defense mechanism by which people attribute their own undesirable traits to others.

Reaction formation ■ Defense mechanism by which people behave in a way opposite to what their true (but anxiety-provoking) feelings would dictate.

Displacement ■ Defense mechanism by which people divert sexual or aggressive feelings for one person onto another person or thing.

Denial ■ Defense mechanism by which people refuse to accept reality or recognize the true source of anxiety.

Family Constellations

Adler believed that psychologists can learn about people's personality from an understanding of their *family constellation,* which involves the birth order of siblings as well as their age differences, genders, and health. Adler and others have observed some traits typical of people in each of four family positions: only child, first-born, second-born, and last-born. (See **Table 13.3**.) A first-born child, for example, is likely to have different early relationships with people in her or his family than a second-born child does and is thus likely to develop a different style of life. Only children may be socially mature but may demand to be the center of attention. First-borns are pushed by parents toward success, leadership, and independence and so tend to have a high need for achievement. Their early experiences make it likely that they will choose careers reflecting that need for achievement, such as corporate executive or politician. Second-born children, on the other hand, are usually more relaxed about achievement. If they feel competitive with an older sibling (as Adler did toward his older brother), however, they may develop a strong need for achievement that will drive them toward public success. Youngest children are often pampered and allow older siblings to take care of them.

Early Recollections

Adlerian therapists are much more likely to use *early recollections* rather than birth order to discover a person's style of life. With this technique, they simply ask the person to describe the earliest experience she or he can remember. The objective validity of the memory is not important; the crucial factor is the person's interpretation of the event.

Although Adler believed that early recollections yield clues for understanding current style of life, he did not believe that the events recollected cause the style of life. Rather, people reconstruct their early experiences to make them consistent with some

Table 13.3

SOME OF ADLER'S HYPOTHESIZED CHARACTERISTICS ARISING FROM BIRTH ORDER

Birth Order	Hypothesis
■ Only child	The center of attention, dominant, often spoiled because of parental timidity and anxiety
■ First-born	Driven to success, independent, high need for achievement, high levels of anxiety, protective toward others
■ Second-born	Actively struggling to surpass others, often competitive (especially with older sibling)
■ Last-born	The most pampered (the smallest and weakest), dependent on others, may excel by being different

theme that runs through their life. To illustrate this point, Adler (1929) reported the case of one of his patients, a young man who was about to be married but who deeply and inexplicably distrusted women, including his fiancée. When asked his earliest recollection, the young man recalled that he was "going with my mother and little brother to market. Suddenly it began to rain and my mother took me in her arms, and then, remembering that I was the older, she put me down and took up my younger brother" (p. 123). This seemingly insignificant memory related to the man's current distrust of women. Having first gained the favorite position with his mother, he quickly lost it to his younger brother. Although women may initially love him, they cannot be trusted to continue their love. In the Adlerian interpretation, the man's present style of life continues to reshape the way he perceives his early experiences.

Adler's theory is less influential than Freud's and less prominent in psychology today. Most Adlerians apply the theory as a guide to counseling. Carl Jung's influence was not as strong as Freud's, but his theory is currently more prominent than Adler's.

Jung and Analytical Psychology

The second important theorist to break with Freud's psychoanalytic theory was Swiss psychiatrist Carl Gustav Jung (1875–1961). Jung had an intense personal relationship with Freud but ultimately broke away over several key issues. Compared to Freud, Jung placed relatively little emphasis on sex. He saw people's behavior as less rigidly fixed and determined than Freud described. Jung also emphasized the search for meaning in life and focused on religiosity.

Jung's *analytical psychology* held that people are ultimately motivated to attain self-realization or perfection, but the journey toward self-realization is an exceedingly difficult one that includes many obstacles and several tests of courage (Jung, 1954/1959). Like Freud, Jung believed in the importance of the unconscious. However, his concept of the unconscious differs from Freud's in that it includes a *collective unconscious,* a shared storehouse of primitive ideas and images that reside in the unconscious and are inherited from one's ancestors (Jung, 1937/1959). These inherited ideas and images, called *archetypes,* are emotionally charged with rich meaning and symbolism. Jung believed that the archetypes of the collective unconscious emerge in art, in religion, and especially in dreams (Jung, 1961).

One important archetype is the *shadow,* or the dark side of the personality (Jung, 1954/1959). The shadow represents those personal tendencies we find distasteful and attempt to hide from ourselves and others. For example, we may enjoy reading about serial killers and other criminals because it allows us to project our shadow onto other people while denying it in ourselves. On the quest for self-realization, the first test of courage is to recognize our own shadow; that is, to come to grips with the darkness and ugliness within ourselves. The second test of courage for men is to recognize their anima, or the feminine side of their personality, and for women, it is to make peace with their animus, or the masculine side of their personality. Many men, especially young men, have difficulty coming to grips with their feminine side. Often, they behave in ultra-masculine ways to convince themselves and others that they are totally masculine.

Collective unconscious ■ In Jung's theory, a shared storehouse of primitive ideas and images that reside in the unconscious and are inherited from one's ancestors.

Archetypes [AR-ki-types] ■ In Jung's theory, the inherited ideas and images that exist within the collective unconscious and are emotionally charged with rich meaning and symbolism.

Two other archetypes are the *great mother* and the *wise old man* (Jung, 1954/1959). The great mother is the archetype that embodies or symbolizes both nourishment and destruction. Just as our real mother and "Mother Nature" can either nourish us or destroy us, the great mother archetype includes these two qualities. In fairy tales and legends, the great mother may appear as a fairy godmother, a witch, or Mother Earth. The wise old man is the archetype of wisdom, but this wisdom is often shallow, with no substance. The Wizard of Oz is a good example—he seemed to be quite wise, but his wisdom, at best, was merely common sense. The wise old man is seen in dreams and legends as a father, grandfather, philosopher, doctor, priest, or rabbi.

The most important archetype is the *self*, the archetype of completion and wholeness (Jung, 1951/1959). The self encompasses all other archetypes as well as the opposing aspects of personality, such as extraversion and introversion, masculinity and femininity, conscious and unconscious, light and dark forces, and so on. The final test of courage we all face is to realize the self—to bring all the opposing parts of the personality together. The self is ultimately symbolized by the *mandala,* a mystical symbol, generally circular in form, that in Jung's view represents a person's inward striving for unity. Jung pointed out that many religions have mandala-like symbols; indeed, Hinduism and Buddhism use such symbols as aids to meditation.

Jung's ideas are widely known but not widely accepted among psychologists. Although they had a significant impact on psychodynamic theory, these ideas never achieved prominence in psychological thought because they are so difficult to verify (Feist & Feist, 2006). Some theorists view them as poetic speculation; others see them as attractive but untestable hypotheses. Some psychologists reject the entire notion of the unconscious and turn to learning theory as a more empirical way to study personality.

Can Personality Be Learned?

Behaviorists look at personality very differently than do any of the theorists described so far. They generally do not concern themselves with thoughts and feelings; rather, they concentrate on overt behavior. Behavioral approaches are often viewed as a reaction to the conceptual vagueness of traditional psychodynamic personality theories. Behavioral personality theorists assert that personality develops as people learn from their environments. The key word is *learn.* According to behaviorists, personality characteristics are not fixed traits; instead, they are learned and subject to change. Thus, for behaviorists, personality is the sum of a person's learning.

The Power of Learning

The concept of *operant conditioning* is critical in a behavioral analysis of personality. As we saw in Chapter 8, *reinforcement* is any condition within the environment that strengthens a response. Punishment may also be a factor in operant conditioning; *punishment* tends to decrease the probability that a response will be repeated. Thus, reinforcement strengthens and punishment weakens any specific behavior. According to learning theorists, the application of reinforcement and punishment determines behavior, including the pattern of stable behaviors that is considered to constitute personality.

How can we tell the difference between reinforcement and punishment? If any given behavior increases in frequency, then we know that it has been reinforced. For example, if a teacher scolds a child for misbehaving in class, and the child's rowdy behavior increases, then we know that the scolding is reinforcement for that child, not punishment. The teacher may have meant to punish, but that was not the result. If a 12-year-old boy hides when his affectionate aunt comes for a visit, then we know that the aunt's affectionate behaviors serve as a punishment for the boy, not reinforcement.

Behaviors that are reinforced tend to recur, which can build a strong tendency for those behaviors to become response patterns. Learning theories of personality rely on this explanation of why people develop patterns of behavior that are stable over time: People's reinforcement history creates these patterns. Thus, the learning theory approach to personality draws on past experiences to explain personality development; however, unlike psychodynamic theorists, learning theorists believe that early childhood experiences are no more important than adolescent or adult experiences. Personality is subject to change at any time during a person's life.

Skinner and Behavioral Analysis: Acquiring a Personality

B. F. Skinner (1904–1990), the foremost American behaviorist, applied the principles of learning to all facets of behavior, including personality. Behaviorists argue that speculating about private, unobservable behavior is fruitless. They further assert that inner drives, psychic urges, and levels of consciousness are concepts that are impossible to define and should play no role in psychological theories.

Theorists who use behavioral analysis believe that, in addition to being influenced by the individual's experiences with reinforcement and punishment, personality is affected by natural selection and cultural evolution (Skinner, 1987). Human behaviors have been partially shaped by the contingencies of survival. Throughout human history, those behaviors that were helpful to the species tended to survive, whereas those that were merely beneficial to an individual were not so likely to survive. For example, natural selection has favored people who formed cooperative communities to protect themselves from outside forces. Today, cooperation remains an important human behavior.

The evolution of cultures is also responsible for at least some human behaviors. Perhaps the two strongest contributors to modern life are the development of symbolic language and the continuing expansion of technology (Premack, 2004). Thus, your facility with language contributes somewhat to your personality. Similarly, your experiences with many modern inventions have greatly shaped your life, making you much different from any of your ancestors who lived thousands of years ago.

Skinner and others who provide behavioral analysis reject many of the concepts that other personality theorists use. Skinner emphasized learning, and personal learning history was the foundation for his approach to personality. Through experiences, people form stable tendencies to behave in similar ways over time. These tendencies, not underlying dimensions of personality, are the basis for behavior. This approach is in sharp contrast to the psychodynamic view, as **Building Table 13.1** shows.

Building Table 13.1					
PSYCHODYNAMIC AND BEHAVIORAL APPROACHES TO PERSONALITY					
Approach	**Major Proponent**	**Basis of Personality**	**Structure of Personality**	**Development**	**Cause of Problems**
Psychodynamic Approach	Freud	The id maximizes gratification while minimizing punishment or guilt; instinctual unconscious urges direct behavior.	Id, ego, superego	Five stages: oral, anal, phallic, latency, genital	Conflicts between the id, ego, and superego, resulting in fixations
Behavioral Approach	Skinner	Patterns of behaviors are learned through experience with the environment.	Responses to stimuli	Process of learning new responses	Faulty or inappropriate behaviors learned through experience with the environment

What Are Trait and Type Theories of Personality?

Ancient philosophers and medieval physicians believed that the proportions of various fluids (called *humors*) in the body determined a person's temperament and personality. Cheerful, healthy people, for example, were said to have a *sanguine* (hopeful and self-confident) personality, because blood was their primary humor, whereas those who had a preponderance of yellow bile were considered hot-tempered.

Cheerful and hot-tempered could be considered traits. A ***trait*** is any readily identifiable stable quality that characterizes how an individual differs from other individuals. For example, someone might characterize one politician as energetic and forward-looking and another as tough and patriotic. Such characterizations present specific ideas about a person's *disposition*—the way that person is likely to behave across a wide range of circumstances and situations as well as over time. Traits can be placed on a continuum—for example, people can be extremely shy, very shy, shy, or mildly shy. For some personality theorists, traits are the elements of which personality is made. When several related traits are combined, the result is a ***type***, a category or broad collection of personality traits that are loosely interrelated.

We'll examine the trait and type theories of Gordon Allport, Raymond Cattell, and Hans Eysenck, as well as a newer model of traits, the Five-Factor Model.

Trait ▪ Any readily identifiable stable quality that characterizes how an individual differs from other individuals.

Type ▪ A category or broad collection of personality traits that are loosely interrelated.

Allport's Personal Disposition Theory

Psychologist Gordon Allport (1897–1967) suggested that each individual has a unique set of personality traits, which he called *personal dispositions*. Allport counted several thousand trait names in an English dictionary, and these formed the bases for the way he and other psychologists have studied traits.

Allport (1961) divided traits into three categories: cardinal, central, and secondary. *Cardinal traits* are so dominant that a person's entire personality reflects that trait, like Severus Snape in the Harry Potter books. Most people do not have a cardinal trait, but those who do are ruled by it. Some words in the English language reflect the cardinal traits of real or fictional people—for instance, *sadism* (from the Marquis de Sade), *narcissism* (from the mythical Greek figure Narcissus), and *Scrooge* (from Dickens's character).

Although most people do not have a cardinal trait, each of us has from 5 to 10 *central traits,* or qualities that characterize our daily interactions. It is the *pattern* of a person's central traits that is crucial. Two people could possess the same set of traits, such as self-control, apprehensiveness, self-assertiveness, forthrightness, and practicality, but the manner in which one person's self-control relates to her apprehensiveness, self-assertiveness, and so on may be quite different from the way the other person's self-control relates to these other central traits.

Secondary traits are characteristics that are exhibited in response to specific situations. For example, a person might have a secondary trait of xenophobia—a fear and intolerance of strangers or foreigners. This trait might become obvious only when the person was approached by a foreign tourist seeking directions. Secondary traits are more easily modified than central traits and are not necessarily exhibited daily. People have many more secondary traits than central traits.

Everyone has different combinations of traits, which is why Allport claimed that each person is unique. To identify a person's traits, Allport recommended an in-depth study of that individual through an analysis of personal diaries, letters, and interviews over a lengthy period of time.

Cattell's Trait Theory

Allport's study of traits was based mostly on nonmathematical procedures, as well as common sense. In contrast, Raymond B. Cattell (1905–1998) used a mathematical technique called *factor analysis*—a statistical procedure for analyzing groups of variables (factors) to detect which are related—to show that groups of traits tend to cluster together. For example, researchers find that people who describe themselves as warm and accepting also tend to rate themselves as high in nurturance and tenderness and low in aggression, suspiciousness, and apprehensiveness. Cattell termed obvious, day-to-day traits *surface traits,* and he called higher-order traits *source traits.*

Cattell (1950) used factor analysis to identify 35 specific traits. These 35 traits can be broken down into 23 normal and 12 abnormal primary source traits. (Sixteen of the normal traits are the basis for Cattell's personality test, which is described later in the chapter.) With further factor analysis, Cattell identified eight second-order traits. One of these is the extraversion–intraversion dimension, which also appears in Eysenck's theory and in the Five-Factor Model.

Factor analysis ■
A statistical procedure for analyzing groups of variables (factors) to detect which are related.

Eysenck's Factor Theory

Whereas Allport and Cattell focused on traits, Hans Eysenck (1916–1997) focused on higher levels of trait organization, or what he called *types*. Each type incorporates lower-level elements (traits), and each trait incorporates still lower-level qualities (habits). Eysenck (1970) argued that all personality traits could be assigned to one of three basic bipolar dimensions: extraversion–introversion (E), neuroticism–emotional stability (N), and psychoticism–superego function (P).

Extraverts are sociable and impulsive, and they enjoy new and exciting experiences, including meeting new people. In contrast, *introverts* are unsociable and cautious, prefer routine activities, and do not enjoy meeting new people. People who are on the *neuroticism* end of Eysenck's second dimension are not necessarily pathological, but they do have high levels of anxiety, tend to overreact emotionally, and experience difficulty calming down after emotional arousal. They frequently complain of physical difficulties, such as headache or back pain, and are often overconcerned about matters they cannot change. People on the opposite end of this dimension are *emotionally stable* and are able to control their feelings. They are often spontaneous, genuine, and warm. Eysenck's third dimension, psychoticism–superego function, is sometimes called tough-mindedness or tender-mindedness. High levels of *psychoticism* do not necessarily indicate psychopathology, but they do suggest a person who is cold, self-centered, nonconforming, hostile, aggressive, and suspicious. People who fall on the other end of this dimension (toward *superego function*) tend to be altruistic, highly socialized, caring, cooperative, and conventional.

Eysenck (1994) argued that personality has a biological basis, although he believed that learning and experience also help shape an individual's behavior. He said that introverts and extraverts experience different levels of arousal in the cortex of the brain. Accordingly, persons of each type seek the amount of stimulation necessary to achieve their preferred level of arousal. For example, a person who prefers a low level of arousal, in which stimulation is less intense, might become a librarian, whereas a person who prefers a high level of arousal might become an emergency room physician. Many people who prefer high levels of arousal might be characterized as *sensation seekers;* they climb mountains, ride dirt bikes, gamble, take drugs, or engage in any number of exciting and/or potentially dangerous activities.

The Five-Factor Model

Because trait and type theories follow a common-sense approach, researchers today still find them attractive. However, rather than speaking of hundreds of traits or of a few types, many theorists agree that there are five broad trait categories. These categories have become known as the Five-Factor Model or the Big Five (McCrae & Costa, 1999):

- *Neuroticism–stability,* the extent to which people are worried or calm, nervous or at ease, insecure or secure
- *Extraversion–introversion,* the extent to which people are social or unsocial, talkative or quiet, affectionate or reserved

- *Openness to experience,* the extent to which people are open to experience or closed, independent or conforming, creative or uncreative, daring or timid
- *Agreeableness–antagonism,* the extent to which people are good-natured or irritable, courteous or rude, flexible or stubborn, lenient or critical
- *Conscientiousness–undirectedness,* the extent to which people are reliable or undependable, careful or careless, punctual or late, well organized or disorganized

Researchers think of these five factors as "supertraits," the important dimensions that characterize every personality (McCrae & Costa, 1999). Research has supported the idea of the Five-Factor Model (Busato et al., 1999) and shown the accuracy of the categories (Borkenau & Ostendorf, 1998; McCrae et al., 2002). In addition, a growing amount of cross-cultural research supports the Five-Factor Model (Hofstede & McCrae, 2004; McCrae & Allik, 2002; McCrae et al., 1998; McCrae et al., 2000; McCrae et al., 2004). Some research suggests there may be genetic bases for the categories. The Five-Factor Model may also apply to children's personalities (Shiner, 1998) and may explain the stability of personality from childhood to adolescence (McCrae et al., 2002).

The Five-Factor Model is easy to understand (Sneed, McCrae, & Funder, 1998) and has been adapted to psychological assessment (Costa & McCrae, 1992; McCrae & Costa, 2004). However, not all researchers agree on the categories (Benet-Martinez & Waller, 1997; Zuckerman, 2004), and certain elements of personality are not well identified by the Five-Factor Model (Schinka, Dye, & Curtiss, 1997).

Like other trait theories, the Five-Factor Model is a description rather than an explanation of personality, but McCrae and Costa (2003) are working toward developing the model into a theory that consists of three core and three peripheral components. Their core components are basic tendencies, which are biologically based and stable over time; characteristic adaptations, which are acquired personality structures that allow people to adapt to their environments; and self-concept, which consists of all knowledge of the self. These core components and the peripheral components interact in dynamic ways to form unique individual personalities. Individual uniqueness is also an important emphasis in humanistic theories.

What Characterizes the Humanistic Approach to Personality?

Some psychologists have objected to psychodynamic, behavioral, and type theories of personality because they believe these approaches have *dehumanized* people, describing them as ruled by their unconscious (Freud and Jung), little different from other animals (Skinner), or best understood by measuring their types and traits (Cattell and Eysenck). These psychologists, led by Abraham Maslow and Carl Rogers, have attempted to humanize the study of personality by focusing on humans' unique qualities. Humanistic theorists are interested in people's conceptions of themselves and what they would like to become. In general, *humanistic theories* assume that people are motivated by internal forces to achieve personal goals. Humanistic psychology focuses not on maladjustment or abnormal behavior but on well-adjusted individuals who are basically decent (although some of their specific behaviors may not be). Moreover, humanistic theories enable theoreticians and practitioners to make predictions about specific behaviors.

Humanistic theories usually take a *phenomenological approach,* meaning that they focus on the individual's unique experiences with and ways of interpreting the things and people in the world (phenomena). These approaches are more likely to examine immediate experiences than past ones and are more likely to deal with an individual's perception of the world than with a researcher's perception of the individual. Finally, such approaches focus on self-determination. Humanistic theories assert that people create their own destinies, from their own vantage points and in their own ways. And although many psychologists regard Freud's disciple Alfred Adler as the first humanistic theorist, Abraham Maslow is best known for promoting this view.

Maslow and Self-Actualization

No single individual is more closely associated with humanistic psychology than Abraham Maslow (1908–1970). In Chapter 12, we examined Maslow's theory of motivation, which states that human needs are arranged in a step-by-step hierarchy, like a ladder. On the lowest level are physiological needs, which are powerful and drive people toward fulfilling them. In the middle are the needs for safety, belongingness, and self-esteem. At the top of the ladder is the need for *self-actualization,* or the need to realize one's full human potential. The higher a need is in the hierarchy, the more distinctly human it is.

Self-actualization ■ In humanistic psychology, the realization of one's full human potential.

As a humanist, Maslow (1950, 1970) focused on psychologically healthy people rather than on disturbed individuals. He studied both living people and historical figures who he believed were self-actualizing, and he found that these people shared several important characteristics: (1) Self-actualizing people, who make up a very small percentage of the population, have a more efficient perception of reality—they are not easily fooled by phony people. (2) They accept themselves, others, and nature. (3) They are spontaneous, simple, and natural. (4) They are problem-centered rather than person-centered—a good idea is a good idea regardless of who thought of it first. (5) They are able to feel comfortable when they are alone, but they genuinely like at least some people. (6) They are autonomous and are unmoved by either flattery or unjust criticism. (7) They are almost childlike in their continual appreciation of the world around them. (8) They have high levels of what Adler called *social interest,* or a feeling of oneness with all humanity and a genuine concern and caring for all people; they enjoy profound interpersonal relations. (9) They can clearly discriminate between ends and means—they recognize that a desirable end product does not justify using unlawful means to attain it. (10) They have a philosophical sense of humor and are not amused by contrived stories. (11) They are creative in the broad meaning of the term—a hand-picked bouquet of flowers may be more creative than a popular work of art. (12) They have the ability to transcend a particular culture— they don't do things merely because "everyone else is doing it." Maslow believed that each of us has the potential for self-actualization, but to reach that stage of psychological health, our lower-level needs must be at least mostly satisfied.

Maslow's theory is vulnerable to criticism—his notions are fuzzy and his approach was romantic rather than objective (Feist & Feist, 2006). Also, his theory is virtually untestable, because he provided little explanation of the nature of self-actualizing tendencies. Carl Rogers formulated a more complete and scientific humanistic approach to personality.

Rogers and Self Theory

Carl Rogers (1902–1987) began to formulate his personality theory during the first years of his practice as a clinician in Rochester, New York. He listened to thousands of patients and was one of the first psychologists to tape-record and transcribe his interactions with patients. What his patients said about their experiences, their thoughts, and themselves led Rogers to make three basic assumptions about behavior: (1) Behavior is goal-directed; (2) people have the potential for growth; and (3) how individuals see their world determines how they will behave.

Rogers (1961) believed that personal experiences provide an individual with a unique and subjective internal frame of reference and worldview. He believed that *fulfillment*—an inborn tendency directing people toward actualizing their essential nature and thus attaining their potential—is the force that motivates personality development. However, people do not move inevitably toward fulfillment but must experience three essential conditions to grow and develop. The necessary and sufficient conditions for growth are *empathy* and *unconditional positive regard* received in a relationship with a *congruent* partner or therapist. You experience empathy when you perceive that another person accurately senses your feelings. You receive *unconditional positive regard* when you sense that another person accepts you completely and unconditionally. Both empathy and unconditional positive regard must be received from a partner who is congruent, or psychologically healthy.

The Self-Concept and the Ideal Self

Rogers's theory of personality is structured around the concept of the *self*—your view of yourself and of your relationships to other people and to various aspects of life (Rogers, 1959). Your *self-concept* is how you see your own behavior and internal characteristics. In addition to your self-concept, you have a picture of what you would like to be, that is, your *ideal self*. Incongruence, or psychological stagnation, results when your ideal self is severely out of line with your self-concept. According to Rogers, people are generally happy when there is agreement between their self-concept and their ideal self. Great discrepancies between the two selves create unhappiness, dissatisfaction, and, in extreme cases, maladjustment. These discrepancies are perceived only by the individual, not by others. Rogers stressed that each person evaluates her or his own situation using a personal (internal) frame of reference, not any external framework that is provided by society or others.

When your self-concept and ideal self are in agreement, you will move naturally toward *self-actualization*—that is, toward becoming fully functioning. People who are fully functioning have a clear perception of reality and feel a strong sense of self-acceptance. When your self-concept is not what you would like it to be, you may

Fulfillment ■ In Rogers's theory of personality, an inborn tendency directing people toward actualizing their essential nature and thus attaining their potential.

Unconditional positive regard ■ Complete and unconditional acceptance by another person.

Self ■ In Rogers's theory of personality, the perception an individual has of himself or herself and of his or her relationships to other people and to various aspects of life.

Self-concept ■ In Rogers's theory of personality, how a person sees his or her own behavior and internal characteristics.

Ideal self ■ In Rogers's theory of personality, the self a person would ideally like to be.

become anxious. Rogers saw anxiety as useful because it motivates people to try to actualize their best selves, to become all they are capable of being.

Psychological Stagnation

People with rigid self-concepts guard themselves against potentially threatening feelings and experiences. Rogers (1959) suggested that such people become unhappy and psychologically stagnant when their behavior does not mesh with their existing self-concept. They then distort their perceptions of their behavior in order to make these perceptions compatible with the self-concept. A man whose self-concept includes high moral principles, rigid religious values, and strict self-control, for example, might become anxious when he feels greed, because such a feeling is inconsistent with his self-concept. To avoid anxiety, he denies or distorts what he is truly experiencing. He may deny that he feels greed, or he may insist that he is entitled to the object he covets.

The Fully Functioning Person

People who have received empathy and unconditional positive regard from a congruent partner or therapist develop healthy self-concepts and will move in a positive direction, toward becoming fully functioning. Rogers (1961, 1980) suggested several characteristics of the fully functioning person. Such people are in a constant state of change—they welcome new experiences and have little reason to deny or distort their view of self. Even unpleasant or repugnant experiences are viewed as opportunities to learn and to grow. They trust in their *organismic self*, which means that they act on deeply felt emotions such as love, disgust, joy, anger, fear, and so on. They do not waste time in wishful thinking and have a clear perception of their own values. Finally, fully functional people establish harmonious relations with others. Because they like themselves, they behave in likable ways, which in turn, makes it easier for other people to like them.

Positive Psychology

Humanistic psychologists are correct in contending that psychology has tended to concentrate on problems and maladjustment and to neglect studying positive human qualities. However, the humanistic approach did not bring about a shift in emphasis in psychology to positive factors such as self-actualization, congruence, and fulfillment. Nor did the humanistic movement generate a body of research to provide confirmation for its contentions (Seligman & Csikszentmihalyi, 2000). The developing field of *positive psychology* strives to do so, focusing its research on well-being, contentment, hope, optimism, and happiness.

An important difference is the positive psychologists' emphasis on research. These psychologists strive to collect information using the scientific method. Martin Seligman and Mihaly Csikszentmihalyi (2000) explain the emphasis of this developing field: "Psychology is not just a branch of medicine concerned with illness or health; it is much larger. It is about work, education, insight, love, growth, and play. And in this quest for what is best, positive psychology does not rely on wishful thinking, faith, self-deception, fads, or hand waving; it tries to adapt what is best in the scientific method to the unique problems that human behavior presents to those who wish to understand it in all its complexity" (p. 7).

Positive psychology examines topics that other psychologists address, such as self-esteem, personal relationships and love, creativity, and moral reasoning (Snyder & Lopez, 2002). In addition, positive psychology strives to reformulate many concepts within psychology—for example, promoting a shift from intelligence to wisdom, from motivation to commitment, from learning to self-control and self-regulation, and from emotion to well-being and happiness (Bolt, 2003). Researchers in this developing field have conducted studies on topics that other psychologists have neglected, such as happiness and personal well-being (Diener, Lucas, & Oishi, 2002), optimism (Carver & Scheier, 2002; Peterson & Chang, 2003), spirituality (Pargament & Mahoney, 2002), humility (Tangney, 2002), and hope (Snyder, Rand, & Sigmon, 2002).

Optimism is one of the concepts that positive psychology researchers have studied. Optimists are people who believe that the outcomes of situations will be good (Carver & Scheier, 2002). Pessimists, on the other hand, expect bad things to happen. This difference in general outlook may be considered a personality dimension, and variations on this dimension are related to other differences in attitudes and behaviors. For example, optimists tend to cope with problems more effectively and to have better health than pessimists. Although too much optimism can lead to coping failures and health problems resulting from inaction, negative thoughts are more damaging than positive ones. Not surprisingly, optimism is related to happiness, which is another topic of research for positive psychologists.

Personality traits such as extraversion and neuroticism are related to happiness and subjective well-being, but culture also influences feelings of well-being (Diener, Oishi, & Lucas, 2003). That is, people in some cultures report higher levels of happiness on average. Even within countries, ethnicity is related to happiness; for example, European Americans report higher levels of happiness than Asian Americans. This finding extends to nations; for example, people in Asia are not as happy as those in the United States. National differences in happiness show a relationship to national wealth, but other characteristics of wealthier nations (such as greater equality and human rights) may be more important than individual income (Diener & Biswas-Diener, 2002). A rise in income tends to increase happiness when it boosts individuals from serious poverty but not when it lifts them from a middle income level to wealth. Indeed, some research suggests that experiences are more important than possessions in creating happiness (Van Boven & Gilovich, 2003). Thus, research in positive psychology confirms the saying that money can't buy happiness. However, it also shows that poverty can lower happiness.

Culture may also influence happiness in terms of the emotions that are believed to be acceptable or important to experience and express—in some cultures, individuals are expected to be happy (Diener et al., 2003). Despite these patterns of differences among cultures, in terms of happiness, individuals vary more within each culture than cultures differ from one another.

Positive psychology has begun to fulfill its goal of emphasizing positive human values in research that is firmly grounded in the scientific method. This field has the same emphasis as humanistic psychology, but it has already exerted a greater impact on psychology. And it promises to add more to psychologists' understanding of the positive side of human behavior.

What Is the Cognitive Approach to Personality?

Cognitive approaches to personality have become increasingly popular among psychologists. Cognitive theorists generally reject psychodynamic theories, which have their origins in therapy. Cognitive theorists are also in disagreement with the behaviorists, especially the early behaviorists, who were single-minded in their belief that psychology should limit itself to studying only observable, measurable behavior. Human beings clearly have an inner mental and psychic life, thinking about things and reacting emotionally. Those thoughts and feelings are not always evident in observable behavior but are still influential.

Cognitive theories emphasize the interaction of thoughts and behavior. They affirm the uniqueness of human beings, especially their thought processes, and assume that human beings are decision makers, planners, and evaluators of their own behavior. Rather than viewing people as having stable traits, cognitive theorists assume that people are fluid and dynamic in their behavior and responses to the world. Many contemporary cognitive therapists claim that people can change their behavior, their conceptions of themselves, and thus their personalities, if they change their thoughts.

Key Cognitive Concepts

From the point of view of cognitive psychologists, the mere association of stimuli and responses is not enough for conditioning and learning to occur in humans—thought processes also have to be involved. According to the cognitive approach, whether a person exhibits learned behavior depends on the situation and the person's needs at the particular time. If thought and behavior are closely intertwined, then something that affects the person's thoughts should also affect his or her behavior.

Over the years, a number of cognitive theories have been developed, dealing with how people perceive themselves and their relationship with the world. We'll consider four concepts from cognitive personality theories: Kelly's concept of personal constructs, Rotter's concept of locus of control, Bandura's concept of self-efficacy, and Mischel's concept of cognitive social learning. Each of these concepts is an integral part of a different cognitive personality theory.

Kelly and Personal Constructs

George Kelly (1905–1967) formulated a theory of personality that relies almost entirely on cognition. Kelly (1955) contended that people's interpretation and anticipation of events guide their behavior. Kelly believed that people work toward building *personal constructs*, ways of understanding the world based on individual interpretation. People form these constructs by combining experience with personal explanation. Kelly believed that the process of forming personal constructs is similar

Personal constructs ■
Ways of understanding the world based on personal interpretation.

to the process used by scientists in gathering and explaining data. However, people are not objective and unbiased (and Kelly suggested that scientists aren't, either). Instead, each individual constructs a view of the world that may be terribly distorted or relatively accurate, but that construction is that person's reality.

This construction is vital to each individual's view of all events, including events anticipated to occur in the future. Kelly's basic postulate is that each person's anticipation of events channels that individual's personal processes (Kelly, 1955). This postulate gives primary emphasis to cognition, and Kelly's corollaries to this basic postulate specify how individual thought processes modify and maintain personal constructs. For example, people differ from each other in terms of their personal constructs, which means that the ways in which they organize and think about the world differ. However, each person tends to see events through a lens of his or her own personal constructs, producing consistency for each individual from situation to situation. Thus, personal differences in forming constructs give rise to uniqueness from other individuals and provide internal consistency within each individual.

In this emphasis on the phenomena of perception and construction of reality, Kelly is similar to the humanistic theorists of personality. However, his emphasis on the importance of cognition in forming a view of the self and the world allies Kelly with other cognitive theorists. Indeed, his theory has influenced Rotter and Bandura indirectly and Mischel more directly (Feist & Feist, 2006).

Rotter and Locus of Control

Patients who seek the help of a therapist frequently say they feel "a lack of control." Psychotherapy often involves helping clients realize what forces are shaping events in their lives and what they can do to gain a sense of control. One widely studied cognitive–behavioral concept that therapists often apply is locus of control, introduced in the 1950s by Julian Rotter (1954). *Locus of control* involves the extent to which individuals believe that a reinforcer or an outcome is contingent on their own behavior or personal characteristics rather than being a function of external events that are not under their control or are simply unpredictable (Lefcourt, 1992; Rotter, 1990). Rotter focused on whether people place their locus of control inside themselves (an internal locus of control) or in their environments (an external locus of control). Locus of control influences how people identify the causes of successes or failures in their lives. In an important way, locus of control reflects people's personalities—their views of the world and their reactions to it.

To examine locus of control, Rotter (1966) developed an inventory consisting of a series of statements about oneself and other people. **Table 13.4** gives some examples of the kinds of statements included in Rotter's inventory. (If you agree with more of the statements on one side, you may have that kind of locus of control.) People with an internal locus of control (shown by their choice of statements on Rotter's inventory) feel a need to control their environment. They are more likely to engage in proactive behavior, such as taking preventive health measures and dieting, than are people with an external locus of control. People who endorse most, but not all, of the statements indicating an internal locus of control have the highest level of health; those who endorse all of those statements feel anxious and guilty because

Table 13.4	
STATEMENTS REFLECTING INTERNAL VERSUS EXTERNAL LOCUS OF CONTROL	
Internal Locus of Control	**External Locus of Control**
People's misfortunes result from the mistakes they make.	Many of the unhappy things in people's lives are partly due to bad luck.
With enough effort, we can wipe out political corruption.	It is difficult to have much control over the things politicians do in office.
There is a direct connection between how hard I study and the grade I get.	Sometimes I can't understand how teachers arrive at the grades they give.
What happens to me is my own doing.	Sometimes I feel that I don't have enough control over the direction my life is taking.

they see themselves as responsible for everything, even the things they actually cannot control. People who agree with most of the statements indicating an external locus of control feel little responsibility for their actions.

Locus of control is associated with differences in many behaviors, including those important to school and achievement. For example, locus of control is a factor in pursuing education. African American high school students with a higher internal locus of control are more likely to plan to attend college than those with a higher external locus of control (Flowers, Milner, & Moore, 2003). Once they enter college, students characterized as having an internal locus are more likely than others to show high academic achievement (Lefcourt & Davidson-Katz, 1991). In contrast, a college student characterized as having an external locus may attribute a poor grade to a lousy teacher, feeling there was nothing he or she could have done to get a good grade. Such a student is more likely than those with an internal locus of control to procrastinate on a project (Janssen & Carton, 1999). External locus of control is associated with high levels of competitiveness but lower grade-point averages (Frederick, 2000). Individuals who develop an internal locus of control, on the other hand, believe that hard work will allow them to make their best grades. External locus of control has also been found to relate to thoughts of suicide in university students, especially in those who believe that they are poor students (Labelle & Lachance, 2003). Therefore, students with an internal locus of control have advantages over those with an external locus of control.

People develop expectations based on their beliefs about the sources of reinforcement in their environment. These expectations lead to specific behaviors. Reinforcement of these behaviors in turn strengthens expectancy and leads to increased belief in either internal or external control (see **Figure 13.2** on p. 498). The concept of locus of control integrates personality theory, expectancy theories, and reinforcement theory. It describes several specific behaviors but is not comprehensive enough to explain all, or even most, of an individual's behavior. Bandura's theory is more comprehensive.

Figure 13.2
Locus of
Control

A person's general
expectancies about
life are determined
in a three-part
process: specific
expectancies
result in specific
behaviors, which
are reinforced. This
cycle eventually
leads to a general
expectancy about
life, which under-
lies either an inter-
nal or an external
locus of control.

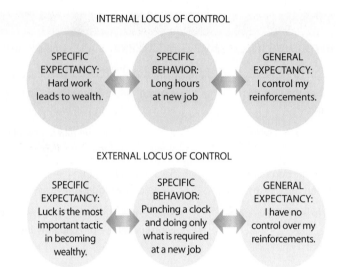

INTERNAL LOCUS OF CONTROL

SPECIFIC EXPECTANCY: Hard work leads to wealth. ⟷ SPECIFIC BEHAVIOR: Long hours at new job ⟷ GENERAL EXPECTANCY: I control my reinforcements.

EXTERNAL LOCUS OF CONTROL

SPECIFIC EXPECTANCY: Luck is the most important tactic in becoming wealthy. ⟷ SPECIFIC BEHAVIOR: Punching a clock and doing only what is required at a new job ⟷ GENERAL EXPECTANCY: I have no control over my reinforcements.

Bandura and Self-Efficacy

While teaching psychology at Stanford University, Albert Bandura developed one of the most influential cognitive theories of personality. His conception of personality began with observational learning theory and the idea that human beings observe, think about, and imitate behavior, which accounts for their learning both acceptable and unacceptable behaviors. Bandura has played a major role in reintroducing thought processes into learning and personality theory.

Bandura argued that people's expectations of mastery and achievement and their convictions about their own effectiveness determine the types of behaviors they will engage in and the amount of risk they will undertake (Bandura, 1977a). He used the term *self-efficacy* to refer to a person's belief about whether he or she can successfully engage in and execute a specific behavior. Judgments about self-efficacy determine how much effort people will expend and how long they will persist in the face of obstacles (Bandura, 2001; Bandura & Locke, 2003).

Self-efficacy ■
A person's belief about whether he or she can successfully engage in and execute a specific behavior.

A strong sense of self-efficacy allows people to feel that they influence and even create the circumstances of their lives. Also, people's perceived self-efficacy in managing a specific situation heightens their sense that they can control it (Conyers, Enright, & Strauser, 1998). People who have a high level of self-efficacy are more likely than others to attribute success to variables within themselves rather than to chance factors, making them more likely to pursue their own goals (Bandura, 1999, 2000, 2004). Because people can think about their motivation, and even about their own thoughts, they can effect changes in themselves, persevere during tough times, and do better at difficult tasks (Bandura & Locke, 2003).

Bad luck or nonreinforcing experiences can damage a developing sense of self-efficacy. For example, students with learning disabilities have lower self-efficacy because they have a history of not being reinforced for studying and completing school assignments (Hampton & Mason, 2003). The observation of positive models or the experience of receiving reinforcement, on the other hand, can help learning-disabled people develop a strong sense of self-efficacy that will encourage them in specific behaviors related to school work.

Self-efficacy both determines and flows from feelings of self-worth. Thus, people's sense of self-efficacy may determine how they present themselves to other people. For example, a man whom others view as successful may not share that view, whereas a man who has received no public recognition may nevertheless consider himself a capable and worthy person. Each of these men will present himself as he sees himself (as a failure or as a worthy person), not as others see him. Growing up male may be one factor that affects these feelings.

Gender, Culture, and Self-Efficacy

In Bandura's view, gender has a major impact on personality, and gender is reinforced through modeling and observational learning. Boys and girls receive rewards for different gender-typed behaviors: Girls tend to be reinforced for behaviors considered feminine (such as acting nurturant and looking pretty), and boys for behaviors considered masculine (such as being competitive and independent). Girls and boys also observe women and men being rewarded for gender-typical behaviors and being punished for behaviors that are not typical of their gender (Bussey & Bandura, 1999). Their environment is filled with stereotypical models in the family, the schools, and the media. This stereotyping has effects on self-efficacy.

Self-efficacy is specific to a given task or activity, and people tend to have higher self-efficacy for activities that are typed as appropriate for their gender. However, women show lower expectancies for success on a stereotypically masculine task (such as a math test) than on a stereotypically feminine one (such as an English test) or a neutral one (such as a history test), but this imbalance is not seen in men (Beyer, 2002). In other words, beginning with interactions with parents (Tenenbaum & Leaper, 2003), many women receive messages about their abilities in some areas such as math and science, which affect their sense of self-efficacy for those kinds of tasks. These experiences may be a factor in the low number of women who choose careers involving math or science (Bleeker & Jacobs, 2004). Girls who believe that girls are not good at math will be less likely to enroll in advanced mathematics courses and will not consider math-related careers (Nosek, Banaji, & Greenwald, 2002).

Small gender differences also appeared in a cross-cultural exploration of self-efficacy (Scholz et al., 2002), which measured self-efficacy among college students in 25 countries from around the world. The researchers found evidence that this concept applies universally but also noted some differences between men and women, including lower levels of self-efficacy among women in some cultures. More dramatic differences appeared in two Asian cultures, those of Japan and Hong Kong, where women showed substantially lower levels of self-efficacy than in other cultures. That finding was confirmed by a review of cross-cultural research, which indicated that people in Asian societies tend to report lower levels of self-efficacy than people in Western societies do (Klassen, 2004). Therefore, the collectivist versus individualist dimension of cultures may contribute to the development of self-efficacy.

Mischel's Cognitive-Affective Personality System

Like Bandura, Walter Mischel claims that thought is crucial in determining human behavior and that both past experiences and current reinforcement are important. But Mischel is an *interactionist*—he focuses on the interaction between people's stable personality traits and the situation (Mischel, 1999, 2004). Mischel and other cognitive theorists argue that people respond flexibly to various situations; that is, they change their responses on the basis of their past experiences and their assessments of current situations (Mischel & Ayduk, 2002). This process of adjustment is called *self-regulation*. For example, people make adjustments in their tone of voice and overt behaviors (aspects of their personality), depending on the context in which they find themselves. Those who tend to be warm, caring, and attentive, for example, can in certain situations become hostile and dismissive.

Mischel believes that a given individual's behaviors are relatively inconsistent from one situation to another but basically consistent over time. He and his colleagues (Mischel & Shoda, 1999; Shoda, LeeTiernan, & Mischel, 2002) suggest that relatively permanent personal dispositions interact with cognitive-affective personality units to produce behavior. Cognitive-affective personality units include *competencies* (what people know and can do), *encoding strategies* (the way they process, attend to, and select information), *expectancies and beliefs* (their prediction of the outcomes of their actions), *personal goals and values* (the importance they attach to various aspects of life), and *affective responses* (their feelings and emotions that accompany their physiological responses).

Mischel's views have had a great impact on psychological thought because he has challenged researchers to consider the idea that traits alone cannot predict a person's behavior. The context of the situation must also be considered—not only the immediate situation but also the culture in which the person lives and was raised, as well as other variables such as the person's gender and age. According to this view, day-to-day variations in behavior should not be seen as aberrations, but rather as meaningful responses to changing circumstances (Brown & Moskowitz, 1998). Mischel's view of personality takes situation and culture into account more than other theories of personality do.

Building Table 13.2 presents an overall summary of the personality theories we have considered. Theories that attempt to account for differences and similarities in personality must be evaluated by measuring personality and personality traits. This goal has been part of psychology from the early years, and it has inspired psychologists to devise a large variety of personality assessments, which we examine next.

How Do Psychologists Assess Personality?

Assessment ■ The process of evaluating individual differences among human beings by means of tests, interviews, observations, and recordings of physiological responses.

When you think to yourself that your mom is an affectionate person, that your brother is conscientious, or that your neighbor is sociable, you are making assessments of their personalities. Most people make these types of evaluations, but for psychologists, assessment requires a more thorough and systematic approach.

Assessment is the process of evaluating individual differences among human beings by means of tests, interviews, observations, and recordings of physiological

Building Table 13.2

PSYCHODYNAMIC, BEHAVIORAL, TRAIT AND TYPE, HUMANISTIC, AND COGNITIVE APPROACHES TO PERSONALITY

Approach	Major Proponent	Basis of Personality	Structure of Personality	Development	Cause of Problems
Psychodynamic Approach	Freud	The id maximizes gratification while minimizing punishment or guilt; instinctual unconscious urges direct behavior.	Id, ego, superego	Five stages: oral, anal, phallic, latency, genital	Conflicts between the id, ego, and superego, resulting in fixations
Behavioral Approach	Skinner	Patterns of behaviors are learned through experience with the environment.	Responses to stimuli	Process of learning new responses	Faulty or inappropriate behaviors learned through experience with the environment
Trait and Type Approaches	Allport Cattell Eysenck	Traits organize a person's responses in characteristic modes.	Traits and types	Genetic factors and learning	Having learned faulty or inappropriate traits
Humanistic Approaches	Maslow Rogers	The individual enhances the experiences of life through the process of self-actualization.	The self	Process of cumulative self-actualization and development of sense of self-worth	Incongruence between self-concept and ideal self
Cognitive Approaches	Kelly Rotter Bandura Mischel	Ways of thinking and acting develop in response to a changing environment.	Responses determined by thoughts	Process of thinking about new responses	Inappropriate thoughts or faulty reasoning

responses. Psychologists who conduct personality assessments usually have one of two goals: either to explain behavior or to diagnose and classify people with behavioral problems. Psychologists who are motivated by the first goal have developed hundreds of personality tests, which can be grouped according to the personality theory that prompted their development. Psychologists who want to diagnose psychological disorders use some of the same tests that personality researchers do, but they also have tests that are oriented toward specific types of psychological disorders. Rather than relying on a single test, clinicians often use information from a battery of tests to make diagnoses. The purpose of the testing determines the type and number of tests administered, but the two major types of personality tests are projective tests and personality inventories.

Projective Tests

Projective tests ◼
Assessment instruments made up of a standard set of ambiguous stimuli that are presented to examinees, who are asked to respond to the stimuli in their own way.

Projective tests are assessment instruments made up of a standard set of ambiguous stimuli that are presented to examinees, who are asked to respond to the stimuli in their own way. The examinees are assumed to use the defense mechanism of projection and to impose their unconscious feelings, drives, and motives onto the ambiguous stimuli. The fundamental idea underlying the use of projective tests for assessing personality is that they will uncover a person's unconscious motives, which direct his or her thoughts and behavior, a belief that can be traced back to Freud's theory of personality. Projective tests are most often used by clinical psychologists to diagnose problems. Clinicians with a psychodynamic orientation often use these tests when they feel that a client is trying to hide something. The use of projective tests has become very controversial. Systematic evaluations of these tests indicate that their accuracy is limited (Lilienfeld, Wood, & Garb, 2000; Wood et al., 2002). They typically have not undergone the rigorous development or standardized scoring procedures associated with IQ tests, and they are less reliable than personality inventories. However, some psychologists defend the use of these tests (Wagner, 2003).

The Rorschach Inkblot Test

A classic projective test is the *Rorschach Inkblot Test* (see **Figure 13.3**). The test taker sees 10 inkblots, one at a time. The blots are symmetrical, with distinctive forms; five

Figure 13.3
The Rorschach Inkblot Test
In a Rorschach Inkblot Test, the psychologist asks a person to describe what he or she sees in an inkblot such as this one. From the person's descriptions, the psychologist makes inferences about the person's drives, motivations, and unconscious conflicts.

are black and white, two also have some red ink, and three have various pastel colors. Test takers tell the clinician what they see in each design, and a detailed report of the responses is made for later interpretation. Aiken (1988, p. 390) reports a typical response:

> My first impression was a big bug, a fly maybe. I see in the background two facelike figures pointing toward each other as if they're talking. It also has a resemblance to a skeleton—the pelvis area. I see a cute little bat right in the middle. The upper half looks like a mouse.

The examiner usually prompts the examinee to give additional information, by making a comment such as "Describe the facelike figures."

This test dwindled in usage in the face of growing criticism, but a new scoring system revived its popularity during the 1970s (Exner, 1974). However, that system has also been criticized, and research evidence indicates that the test is limited in its usefulness for diagnosing psychological problems (Lilienfeld et al., 2000). Despite that evidence, some psychologists believe that the Rorschach yields useful information and continue to use it.

The Thematic Apperception Test

The *Thematic Apperception Test* (TAT) is much more structured than the Rorschach but suffers from some of the same problems (Lilienfeld et al., 2000). (The TAT was discussed in Chapter 12 as one way to assess need for achievement.) The TAT consists of black-and-white pictures, each depicting one or more people in an ambiguous situation. Examinees are asked to tell a story describing the situation. Specifically, they are asked what led up to the situation, what will happen in the future, and what the people are thinking and feeling. There are several scoring systems to standardize the administration of this test, but most psychologists who administer it do not use any standardized system, leading to a lack of consistency in the information obtained.

Projective tests have a bad reputation in terms of their accuracy and reliability. Critics argue that the interpretation of pictures is prone to errors in scoring and that projective tests are not standardized well enough for clear interpretation. Practicing clinicians, even those who use projective tests, often rely more heavily on personality inventories to assess people with problems, and personality researchers rarely use projective techniques.

Personality Inventories

Next to intelligence tests, the most widely administered psychological tests are *personality inventories,* generally consisting of true/false or multiple-choice items to which people respond. The aims of personality inventories vary, but each major approach to personality has generated assessment instruments tied to its theoretical basis. Well-constructed personality tests turn out to be valid predictors of performance in a wide array of situations, including school, work, and personal interactions, and for men and women from various ethnic groups (Ones & Anderson, 2002).

The Myers–Briggs Type Indicator (MBTI; Myers, 1962) is a test based on Jung's theory of personality. Jung proposed that each individual favors specific *modalities,* or ways of dealing with and learning about the world, and that a person's preferred modalities define her or his personality type. The MBTI asks a test taker to choose between pairs of statements that deal with preferences or inclinations and scores the responses so that the test taker is characterized as predominantly at one pole or another on four distinct dimensions: extraversion–introversion (E or I), sensing–intuition (S or N), thinking–feeling (T or F), and judging–perceptive (J or P). The MBTI is a quick and easy way to gather information about personality, but its uses are limited (Hunsley, Lee, & Wood, 2003). This test was developed using students in grades 4 through 12 and is best used with individuals in that age range. For example, results from the MBTI correlate with critical thinking ability among high school students (Yang & Lin, 2004) and are useful in career counseling (Kennedy & Kennedy, 2004).

Trait theories of personality have generated the majority of personality inventories. Each of these tests requires test takers to respond to many items (often more than 100 and in some cases over 500) that measure the personality traits in the associated theory. These items have been tested on groups of people so that the responses not only reflect the traits in the theory but also allow comparisons among individuals. The process allows an assessment of how people vary along these dimensions of personality.

The Sixteen Personality Factor Test (16 PF) was developed by Raymond Cattell (1949). Using the technique of factor analysis, Cattell constructed a test of personality traits based on his theory of personality. People taking this test respond to 187 items, choosing one of three choices for each item. The result of the test is a score for each of the 16 factors, so test administrators can compare the person being tested to others on each dimension.

In contrast to the many traits in the 16 PF, Hans Eysenck conceptualized personality as consisting of only three broad factors, or types: extraversion–introversion, neuroticism–emotional stability, and psychoticism–superego function. The Eysenck Personality Questionnaire (Eysenck & Eysenck, 1993) includes scales that measure each of these types.

The Five-Factor Model (or Big Five model) of personality also prompted the development of a personality inventory, the Revised NEO-Personality Inventory (NEO-PI-R; Costa & McCrae, 1995). This test consists of 240 items, which yield measures on the five factors proposed by the theory as well as on six traits related to each of the five factors. The traits revealed on the 16 PF and the NEO-PI-R correlate with each other (Rossier, Meyer de Stadelhofen, & Berthoud, 2004). In addition, results from the NEO-PI-R correlate with several of the types measured by the Myers-Briggs Type Indicator (Furnham, Moutafi, & Crump, 2003). These intercorrelations suggest that these tests are measuring the same personality dimensions.

Humanistic personality theory prompted the development of the Personal Orientation Inventory (POI), based on Maslow's theory of personality (Shostrom, 1974). This test is oriented toward assessing self-actualization. The POI consists of 150 items for which people must choose one of two alternatives, for example: (a) "Two people can get along best if each concentrates on pleasing the other" versus (b) "Two people can get along best if each person feels free to express himself." The items are scored in terms of 2 major scales and 10 subscales. Higher scores indicate agreement with self-actualizing values.

One of the most widely used and researched personality tests is the Minnesota Multiphasic Personality Inventory (MMPI), now in its 2nd edition (MMPI–2). Unlike inventories designed to assess personality in terms of various theories, the MMPI was designed as a diagnostic instrument to detect abnormal behavior. The MMPI–2 consists of 567 true/false statements that focus on the test taker's attitudes, feelings, motor disturbances, and bodily complaints. Its norms are based on the profiles of thousands of normal people and smaller groups of psychiatric patients. Each scale compares test takers' responses to those of the normal people and those of the psychiatric patients. In general, a score significantly above normal may be considered evidence of psychopathology. The test has built-in safeguards to detect untruthful responses to the items. Interpretation of the MMPI–2 generally involves looking at patterns of scores, rather than at a person's score on a single scale.

Students who want to know about their personalities are often anxious to take the MMPI. I (L.B.) always discourage my students from doing so; the test is designed to diagnose pathological problems, making it unsuitable for students interested in learning about testing or their own personalities. Other personality tests are typically better choices for these goals than the MMPI.

Personality tests were once used in a variety of settings, such as in the screening of job applicants or prospective students, but the lack of research supporting their ability to predict who will be a good employee or student has limited this use (Flynn, 2002). Personality tests continue to be used extensively in the diagnosis of psychopathology by clinicians in hospitals, in private practice, and within the legal system. Personality tests are also used to test people with no psychopathology as part of research on personality and to assess people as part of career counseling.

Summary and Review

WHAT IS PERSONALITY?

How do psychologists define personality?

Personality is a set of relatively enduring traits, dispositions, or characteristics that give consistency to a person's behavior. p. 471

What are the effects of culture on personality?

All personality theories developed within cultural contexts, but the influence of culture was not considered in personality theory until recently. Some psychologists look for cross-cultural differences in personality, such as variation on the individualistic–collectivist dimension, and others search for the universal personality traits. pp. 471–473

WHAT IS THE PSYCHODYNAMIC APPROACH TO PERSONALITY?

Psychodynamic theory is an approach to personality that focuses on how unconscious processes direct day-to-day behavior and affect personality formation. p. 473

What are the basics of Freud's psychoanalytic theory?

Freud's structure of the mind includes three levels: the *conscious*, the *preconscious*, and the *unconscious*. The primary structural elements of the mind and personality—the id, the ego, and the superego—are three forces that reside, completely or partially, in the unconscious. The *id*, which works through the pleasure principle, is the source of a person's instinctual energy. The *ego* tries to satisfy instinctual needs in accordance with reality. The *superego* includes the ego ideal and the conscience and provides the moral aspect of mental functioning. pp. 474–475

Freud described the development of personality in terms of five *psychosexual stages:* oral, anal, phallic, latency, and genital. In the *oral stage*, newborns' and young children's instincts are focused on the mouth—their primary pleasure-seeking center. In the *anal stage*, children learn to control the immediate gratification obtained through defecation and to become responsive to the demands of society. In the *phallic stage*, children obtain gratification primarily from the genitals. During this stage, children experience the *Oedipus complex*, which results in identification with the same-sex parent. In the *latency stage*, sexual urges are inactive. The *genital stage*, Freud's last stage of personality development, is the stage in which the sexual conflicts of childhood resurface (at puberty) and are resolved (in adolescence). pp. 475–479

The energizing force underlying personality comes from two instinctual drives: the sexual instinct (the *libido*) and the instinct for aggression. p. 479

What is the fundamental function of Freud's defense mechanisms?

A *defense mechanism* is a distorted perception of reality that arises as a defense against the anxiety caused by drives toward sex and aggression. For Freud, the most important defense mechanism was *repression*—the removal of anxiety-provoking feelings from conscious awareness into the unconscious. Other defense mechanisms are *rationalization, fixation, regression, projection, reaction formation, displacement, denial,* and *sublimation*. Defense mechanisms allow the ego to deal with anxiety. pp. 479–481

How did Adler and Jung differ from Freud in their views of personality?

Adler and Jung modified some of Freud's basic ideas. These theorists attributed a greater influence to cultural and interpersonal factors than Freud did. Adler argued that Freud overemphasized sex and ignored social issues; he formulated the concept of *social interest* as a foundation of his view of personality. Adler theorized that feelings of inferiority prompt people to strive for superiority or success. According to Adler, individuals develop a style of life that allows them to express their goals in the context of human society. pp. 481–484

Jung emphasized unconscious processes as determinants of behavior and believed that each person houses past events in the unconscious. The *collective unconscious* is a shared collection of *archetypes*, emotionally charged ideas and images that have rich meaning and symbolism and are inherited from one's ancestors. pp. 484–485

CAN PERSONALITY BE LEARNED?

What approach to personality do learning theorists take?

The behavioral approach to personality centers on overt behavior and learning. Behavioral psychologists try to discover behavior patterns. Personality is basically an overall set of these patterns that develops as a person learns while responding to his or her environment. p. 485

Describe Skinner's view of personality.

According to Skinner, personal learning history is the foundation for stable patterns of behavior, which are the basis of personality. However, Skinner used not only behavioral learning principles but also the concepts of natural selection and evolution of culture to explain personality. p. 486

WHAT ARE TRAIT AND TYPE THEORIES OF PERSONALITY?

Distinguish between a trait and a type.

A *trait* is any readily identifiable stable quality that characterizes how an individual differs from others; a *type* is a category or broad collection of personality traits that are loosely interrelated. A person can be said to *have* a trait or to *fit* a type. p. 487

Describe the ideas of Allport, Cattell, and Eysenck regarding traits.

Allport proposed the concepts of cardinal traits, enduring characteristics that determine the direction of a person's life; central traits, the qualities that characterize a person's daily interactions; and secondary traits, characteristics that are exhibited in response to specific situations. Cattell used the technique of *factor analysis* to show that groups of traits tend to cluster together. Cattell called obvious, day-to-day traits surface traits and higher-order traits source traits. Eysenck focused on types, which are higher levels of trait organization. Eysenck argued that all personality traits can be assigned to one of three basic bipolar dimensions: neuroticism–emotional stability, extraversion–introversion, and psychoticism–superego function. pp. 487–489

What is the Five-Factor Model?

Although there may be hundreds of personality traits, researchers think of the factors in the Five-Factor Model as "supertraits," the important dimensions that characterize every personality. The five factors are neuroticism–stability, or the extent to which people are nervous or at ease; extraversion–introversion, or the extent to which people are social or unsocial; openness to experience, or the extent to which people are independent or conforming; agreeableness–antagonism, or the extent to which people are good-natured or irritable; and conscientiousness–undirectedness, or the extent to which people are reliable or undependable. pp. 489–490

WHAT CHARACTERIZES THE HUMANISTIC APPROACH TO PERSONALITY?

What are the motivating forces of personality development, according to Maslow's and Rogers's theories?

In Maslow's theory, *self-actualization* is the process of realizing one's innate human potential. The process of realizing one's potential, and of growing, is the process of becoming self-actualizing. pp. 490–492

The humanistic approach of Rogers views *fulfillment* as the motivating force of personality development. Rogers focuses on agreement between *self-concept* (how a person sees her or his own behavior and internal characteristics) and *ideal self* (who a person would ideally like to be). For personal growth, people must experience a relationship with a congruent partner or therapist that includes empathy and *unconditional positive regard*. pp. 492–493

What is positive psychology?

Positive psychology is a developing movement within psychology that focuses on positive human characteristics such as happiness and optimism. In contrast to humanistic psychology, positive psychology is generating research that confirms the existence and benefits of these qualities. pp. 493–495

WHAT IS THE COGNITIVE APPROACH TO PERSONALITY?

What are the key ideas of the cognitive approach to personality?

The cognitive approach emphasizes the interaction of a person's thoughts and behavior. Cognitive theories assert that people make rational choices in trying to predict and manage events in the world. p. 495

How do the concepts of personal constructs, locus of control, self-efficacy, and the cognitive-affective personality system reflect the cognitive approach?

Personal constructs, according to Kelly, are personal ways of understanding reality that guide a person's interpretation of events and shape personality. pp. 495–496

Locus of control, according to Rotter, is the extent to which individuals believe that a reinforcement or an outcome is contingent on their own behavior or personal characteristics, rather than being a function of external events that are not under their control or are unpredictable. People with an internal locus of control feel in control of their environment and future; people with an external locus of control believe that they have little control over their lives. pp. 496–497

Self-efficacy, in Bandura's theory, is a person's belief about whether he or she can successfully engage in and execute a specific behavior. Judgments about self-efficacy determine how much effort people will expend to achieve a goal and how long they will persist in the face of obstacles. A strong sense of self-efficacy allows people to feel free to influence and even construct the circumstances of their lives. pp. 498–499

Mischel's cognitive-affective personality system focuses on how people interpret the situations in which they find themselves; the interpretation may prompt them to alter their behavior. Mischel argues that people adjust their responses based on their past experiences and their assessment of the current situation. This process of adjustment is called self-regulation. p. 500

HOW DO PSYCHOLOGISTS ASSESS PERSONALITY?

What are the purpose and uses of personality testing?

Assessment is the process of evaluating individual differences among human beings by means of tests, interviews, observations, and recordings of physiological responses. Psychologists use personality tests as part of an assessment process. Some psychologists use these tests to research personality, and others use them to diagnose psychological problems. pp. 500–502

What is a projective test?

Projective tests such as the Rorschach Inkblot Test and the TAT ask examinees to respond to ambiguous stimuli in their own way. Examinees are thought to project unconscious feelings, drives, and motives onto the ambiguous stimuli. pp. 502–503

What are personality inventories?

Personality inventories are tests consisting of questions test takers answer or statements to which they respond. The responses yield assessments of personality in terms of the traits measured by the specific test. Various tests are based on specific theories of personality, such as the 16 PF and the NEO-PI-R. The MMPI–2 is a personality test that is used for diagnosis of psychological disorders. pp. 503–505

CHAPTER 14

Social Psychology

What Is the Social Self?   511
   The Self in Social Psychology
   Thinking about Self and Others

How Are Attitudes Related to
Behavior?   516
   Dimensions of Attitudes
   Do Attitudes Predict Behavior?
   Does Behavior Determine Attitudes?
   How Does Attitude Change Occur?

How Do People Relate to
Each Other?   524
   Attraction and Relationship Formation

Aggression and Violence
Prosocial Behavior

What Are the Effects of Identifying
with a Group?   537
   Group Performance
   Identifying as a Group Member

How Do Others Affect
the Individual?   546
   Conformity
   Compliance
   Obedience to Authority

Summary and Review   553

Social psychology ■
The scientific study of
how individual
thoughts, feelings, and
behaviors are influenced
by social situations.

In this chapter, we examine **social psychology,** the scientific study of how individual thoughts, feelings, and behaviors are influenced by social situations. Social psychology is an important field because human beings are social creatures: We live with, work with, and seek out others—and those others shape our behavior as we shape theirs. Like other psychologists, social psychologists focus on the individual. (*Sociology* is the field that focuses on the group.) Many social psychologists take an "inside out" approach, examining how factors within a person (the "inside") interact with and influence the individual and the individual's behavior in the social world (the "out").

The history of social psychology can be traced to the early years of psychology (Goethals, 2003), and many social psychologists consider Gestalt psychology as having the strongest theoretical influence on their field (see Chapter 1 for a description of the Gestalt movement). With its emphasis on perception and the consideration of the interacting forces that determine how people see and function in the world, the Gestalt movement formed the basis for social psychology's placement of the individual within a social context. A more recent influence on social psychology has been evolutionary psychology, which explains that forming and maintaining relationships and being a member of a group has been adaptive in human evolution (Buss, 2004). Belonging to a group is a definite survival advantage, and some type of relationship is necessary for successful reproduction and child rearing.

Although social psychologists examine some of the same areas that personality psychologists do, their emphasis differs (Fiske, 2004). Personality psychologists (see Chapter 13) look for patterns of stable traits or characteristics that shape behavior in a variety of situations. Social psychologists take an alternative view, looking for the factors in the situation that shape individuals' behavior. Consistent with the "inside out" strategy, social psychologists begin with an examination of the self and how people think, feel, and behave in relation to the self. This emphasis on the self builds a foundation for considering how people relate to others and how they interact in groups.

What Is the Social Self?

Although answering the question "Who am I?" might seem like a difficult task, most people would not frame their answer in terms of their social surroundings or current situation. People tend to conceptualize "self" as something within themselves that is stable over time and in different situations. That is, the common view of the self is similar to the personality psychologists' notion of personality. Evidence from social psychology indicates otherwise—the presence of others (or even thoughts about others) can change how we see ourselves (Fiske, 2004).

The Self in Social Psychology

The self was not a topic of interest to social psychologists in the early years of psychology but became so during the 1970s (Baumeister, 1999). Social psychologists who explore issues related to the self believe that an understanding of factors within a person is necessary as a basis for exploring how people interact with each other and behave in groups.

In order to form a concept of the self, a person must be self-aware. The ability to form personal memories is necessary for the creation of self-awareness, as is the ability of the mind to turn its attention to itself (Tulving, 2002). These abilities have been crucial in the evolution of human functioning, and humans seem to have a higher degree of self-awareness than other animals (Leary & Buttermore, 2003). Self-awareness allows an individual to form a *self-concept,* what a person knows and believes about himself or herself. If you try to answer the question "Who am I?" you examine elements of your self-concept. Although self-concept draws on personal knowledge of self, it is more than what we know about ourselves. Self-concept is also how we think about ourselves, which is influenced by interactions with and reactions from others (Wilson & Dunn, 2004).

Recall that the definition of social psychology includes thoughts, feelings, and behaviors. Self-concept reflects thoughts about the self. *Self-esteem* is the aspect of self that reflects feelings; it is how a person feels about himself or herself. Personality

Self-concept ■ What an individual knows and believes about himself or herself.

Self-esteem ■ How a person feels about himself or herself.

psychologists study self-esteem as a stable trait, but social psychologists are more interested in *state self-esteem,* which changes over time and in different situations (Baumeister, 1999). For example, a student may have more positive feelings about herself after receiving a good grade on a test than she does after oversleeping and missing class. During the 1990s, many problems were attributed to low self-esteem, but other evidence indicates that high self-esteem may also bring problems.

Self-presentation ■ A person's efforts to convey an image of herself or himself to others.

The behavioral aspect of the self is *self-presentation,* a person's efforts to convey an image of herself or himself to others. Self-presentation goals may be oriented toward defining oneself to others in ways that are consistent with one's self-perceptions (Baumeister, 1999). For example, if you think of yourself as athletic, you will probably do things to show your athletic skills to others. Indeed, in order to continue to think of yourself as athletic, it is necessary to demonstrate behaviors consistent with athleticism so that others will acknowledge that part of yourself. Self-presentation efforts may also take the form of attempts to influence others' perceptions. For example, people may attempt to appear competent, likable, and moral, but they may also try to convey that they are dangerous or in need of help (Jones & Pittman, 1982). The people with whom one is interacting and the circumstances of the interaction make a difference in which self-presentation strategies a person will use; that is, people adjust their self-presentation strategies to fit their perceptions of their current situation. In general, people strive to present themselves in positive ways, even if it means engaging in some distortion and misrepresentation to do so. Indeed, distortions and misrepresentations are common in a person's thoughts about the self and about others.

Thinking about Self and Others

Social cognition ■ The process of analyzing and interpreting events, other people, oneself, and the world in general.

When we think about ourselves and others, we try to make sense of what we know and observe. We try to develop a coherent way to think about the world. *Social cognition* is the process of analyzing and interpreting events, other people, oneself, and the world in general. Social cognition draws on social information in memory, which affects judgments, choices, evaluations, and, ultimately, behavior (Fiske, 1992, 2004). For example, if you performed poorly on a test, you would probably come up with some reason for your bad grade. If you could not, you would search for an explanation, because this failure to understand your own behavior would probably be distressing for you. We also try to understand and explain the behavior of others. If your roommate dyed her hair blue, you would try to understand what prompted this behavior. One important way to understand and explain behavior is to make *attributions,* descriptions of the causes of behavior. People often make attributions to explain their own behavior and the behavior of others.

Attributions ■ Descriptions of the causes of behavior.

Internal attribution ■ A description of the cause of a behavior as originating from within the person.

External attribution ■ A description of the cause of a behavior as coming from events or situations outside the person.

When making attributions, people may believe that someone did something because of characteristics arising from the individual's personality or they may believe that the person's actions arose from the situation (Heider, 1958). Someone making an *internal attribution* thinks the behavior being observed originates from within the person, arising somehow from the individual's personality. Someone making an *external attribution* believes that the person's behavior is caused by events or situations outside the individual, such as the situation or luck. These two types of attribution lead to very different ways of interpreting behavior. For example, if you explained your poor test performance by using an internal attribution, you would conclude that you didn't study enough or that you are not intelligent enough to do well in the course. Alternatively, if you made an external attribution, you might explain your poor grade in terms of the instructor's inappropriate choice of test items, the noisy testing conditions, or your roommate's party, which kept you from sleeping the night before the exam. You may explain your roommate's new hair color by saying that she is an unconventional person (an internal attribution) or that her employer wants her to look similar to the other employees in the boutique where she works (an external attribution).

The Process of Attribution

To understand attribution, researchers have attempted to conceptualize the process and its components. Harold Kelley's (1972, 1973) theory of attribution suggests that people decide whether the causes of a behavior are internal or external based on three criteria: consensus, consistency, and distinctiveness (see **Figure 14.1**).

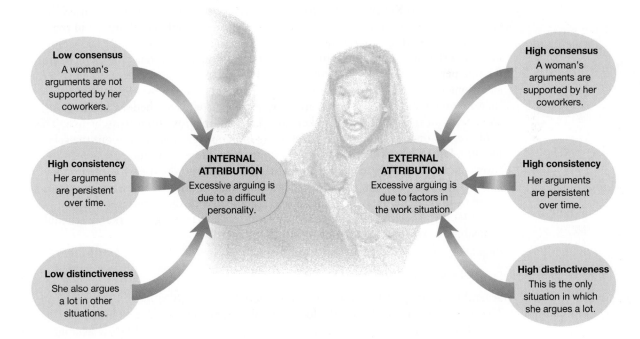

Low consensus
A woman's arguments are not supported by her coworkers.

High consistency
Her arguments are persistent over time.

Low distinctiveness
She also argues a lot in other situations.

INTERNAL ATTRIBUTION
Excessive arguing is due to a difficult personality.

EXTERNAL ATTRIBUTION
Excessive arguing is due to factors in the work situation.

High consensus
A woman's arguments are supported by her coworkers.

High consistency
Her arguments are persistent over time.

High distinctiveness
This is the only situation in which she argues a lot.

Figure 14.1
Attributional Thinking
Kelley's attributional model outlines three criteria for determining the causes of behavior: consensus, consistency, and distinctiveness. According to the theory, assigning an internal attribution to a person's behavior is usually the result of the combination of low consensus, high consistency, and low distinctiveness. When a person's behavior shows high consensus, high consistency, and high distinctiveness, others tend to attribute the causes of the behavior to external reasons.

Consensus refers to the degree of agreement among people about the situation, *consistency* reflects how similar the person's behavior is across time and situations, and *distinctiveness* describes how the person's behavior varies in different situations. According to Kelley, to decide that someone's behavior is caused by internal characteristics, you must believe that (1) most other people would not act this way in the same situation (low consensus among people about this behavior), (2) the person has acted in the same way in similar situations in the past (high consistency of the behavior for this person), and (3) the person acts in the same way in different situations (low distinctiveness of this behavior for this person). To see how Kelley's theory works, suppose that a woman in an office gets into an argument with her supervisor over the next week's schedule. She is the only one who objects, which indicates low consensus—other people in the office are not arguing about this issue. The woman has argued with the boss on other occasions, which shows high consistency for arguing. Also, the woman often argues with other people about other things, which indicates that her arguing about the schedule is low in distinctiveness. In such a case, people will be very likely to attribute the woman's argument with her supervisor to her personality; she is simply argumentative.

According to Kelley's model, to conclude that a person's behavior is caused by external factors, you must believe that (1) most people would act that way in that sort of situation (high consensus among people about the behavior); (2) the person has acted that way in similar situations in the past (high consistency of the behavior for this person in this type of situation); and (3) the person acts differently in other situations (high distinctiveness of this behavior for this situation). Again, suppose that a woman and her supervisor argue over the next week's schedule, but in this case, many of the woman's coworkers also have complaints about the schedule. This common factor reveals high consensus—lots of people are unhappy about the schedule. In addition, the woman has argued about the same issue in the past, which shows high consistency for her in this situation. However, she does not often argue in other situations, which makes this argument high in distinctiveness. In this case, people will be more likely to attribute the argument with the supervisor to situational factors, such as the supervisor's incompetence in making a workable schedule or his insensitivity to this employee's needs.

Errors in Attribution

Several years ago, a letter to the editor appeared in my (L.B.'s) local newspaper. The writer complained about the local school system, because he had heard that half of the children who had taken an achievement test had scored below average. He urged the local populace to demand higher standards for the school system so that children would do better on these important tests. Although the letter writer may have failed to "do the math," which would have told him that about half of all of us are below average in any given situation, he may also have been affected by an attributional bias. Research indicates that we tend to see ourselves (and people whom we perceive as similar to us) as above average (Klar & Giladi, 1997; Kruger, 1999). We are able to maintain such inflated estimations of our abilities more easily in situations in which the criteria for excellence are not clear (Nier, 2004). Thus, we are clearly capable of distorted attributions.

In general, we have a tendency toward *self-serving bias,* which causes us to take credit for our successes but blame others or the situation for our failures. This bias allows us to feel better about ourselves and to maintain self-esteem, resulting in an enhanced self-image and a sense of control. The self-serving bias is stronger in men than in women and more prevalent in Western than in non-Western cultures (Higgins & Bhatt, 2001). Research using brain-imaging technology has even revealed activation in a different part of the brain when people use a self-serving bias rather than an attribution in which they take responsibility for their behavior (Blackwood et al., 2003).

Two of the most common attribution errors are the fundamental attribution error and the actor–observer effect. People in Western societies have a tendency to make internal attributions for other people's behavior, explaining it in terms of stable personality characteristics rather than in terms of situations. When people commit the *fundamental attribution error,* they assume that other people's behavior is caused by their internal dispositions, and they underestimate situational influences (Ross, 1977). Suppose you observe a man in a restaurant who loses his temper, and you conclude that he is "hot tempered." You tend not to consider the possibility that he was kept waiting for his table, treated rudely by the staff, served the wrong entrée, or overcharged for his meal (or subjected to some combination of these annoying events). We often observe a behavior and tend to discount or ignore the circumstances (Sabini, Siepmann, & Stein, 2001).

However, Westerners avoid making internal attributions for their own behavior. The *actor–observer effect* is the tendency to attribute the behavior (especially the failings) of others to internal (dispositional) causes but to attribute one's own behavior (especially misbehavior or shortcomings) to situational causes (Jones & Nisbett, 1972). Individuals know that their own day-to-day behavior varies; as observers of others, they have less information to go on and are more likely to make dispositional, or internal, attributions. A child who falls off his bike may say, "The sidewalk was bumpy." When a friend does the same thing, however, the same child may say, "You're clumsy." That is, we allow ourselves excuses that we do not extend to others.

Errors in attribution can allow people to blame others inappropriately or to fail to accept responsibility for their behavior. For example, errors in attribution cause people to blame rape victims rather than rapists (Weisberg et al., 2001). Attribution can also help aggressors feel better about themselves by allowing them to attribute aggressive intention to others, which makes the aggressors feel justified in their violent behavior (MacBrayer, Milich, & Hundley, 2003). Similarly, husbands who behave aggressively toward their wives tend to attribute motives of criticism and rejection to any woman who makes a critical comment about them (not just their wives) (Schweinle, Ickes, & Bernstein, 2002). This attributional bias may underlie their tendency to react with violence, because they exaggerate the severity of the criticism.

Attributional bias has been observed in various cultures, but it does not exist to the same extent or have the same meaning in every culture (Bersoff & Miller, 1993;

Self-serving bias ■ People's tendency to take credit for their successes but to blame others or the situation for their failures.

Fundamental attribution error ■ The tendency to attribute other people's behavior to dispositional (internal) causes rather than to situational (external) causes.

Actor–observer effect ■ The tendency to attribute the behavior of others to internal (dispositional) causes but to attribute one's own behavior to situational causes.

Table 14.1

INDIVIDUALIST VERSUS COLLECTIVIST CULTURES

	Individualist Cultures	Collectivist Cultures
■ Values	Personal goals	Group goals
	Individual freedom and autonomy	Willingness to go along with the group
	Individual needs	Group needs (including family, coworkers, political groups)
■ Representative cultures	United States	Hong Kong
	Australia	Taiwan
	Great Britain	Pakistan
	Italy	Panama
	France	Guatemala

Takaku, 2000). Indeed, culture shapes attributions in important ways, and a major difference appears when contrasting individualist and collectivist cultures. Recall from Chapter 1 that *individualist cultures* stress personal rather than group goals and value individual freedom and autonomy; *collectivist cultures* stress group needs (including those of family, coworkers, religious and political groups) and value a tightly knit social fabric. **Table 14.1** lists some of the characteristics and gives examples of such cultures. An example of such a difference in attributions appeared in a study that contrasted newspaper reports concerning a dramatic crime. In 1991, a Chinese student studying at the University of Iowa killed his advisor and others who had been involved in his academic career, and then killed himself. Newspaper reports that appeared in the United States focused on his temperament and character, but reports of the same shooting in Chinese newspapers tended to emphasize the circumstances in the student's life that may have affected his behavior (Morris & Peng, 1994). When a U.S. postal worker committed a similar crime, the same attributional differences appeared in U.S. versus Chinese newspapers. Cross-cultural research has confirmed that people in an individualist culture such as that of the United States have a stronger tendency to make internal attributions to explain the actions of others than do people in collectivist cultures such as those of Korea and Japan (Choi et al., 2003; Miyamoto & Kitayama, 2002).

We not only try to make sense of our own and others' behaviors but also of our thoughts and feelings. That is, we form and try to understand our own attitudes.

Attitudes ■ Patterns of feelings and beliefs about ideas, objects, or other people that are usually evaluative, are based on a person's past experiences, and play a role in his or her future behavior.

How Are Attitudes Related to Behavior?

Attitudes are patterns of feelings and beliefs about ideas, objects, or other people that are based on a person's past experiences and play a role in his or her behavior. They are usually evaluative, and they serve certain functions, such as helping people adapt to the world effectively and develop tendencies to approach or avoid objects or situations (Ajzen, 2001). Attitudes may be long-lasting, but they are subject to change. Like other concepts in social psychology, attitudes may be analyzed in terms of thoughts, feelings, and behavior.

Dimensions of Attitudes

I (L.B.) love movies, which means that I have a very positive attitude about them. Like some movie fans, I know a great deal of movie trivia (I have even won awards in movie trivia contests). I await the release of some new movies with eager anticipation, but I especially love to find an obscure movie that surprises me with how good it is. I have "movie friends" with whom I discuss movies, and sometimes a group of us go to a movie together and then out for coffee to talk about it. Thus, all three dimensions of attitudes—cognitive, emotional, and behavioral—are represented in my attitude toward movies.

The *cognitive dimension* of an attitude consists of thoughts and beliefs. When someone forms an attitude about a group of people, a series of events, or a political philosophy, the cognitive dimension of the attitude is what helps the person categorize, process, and remember the people, events, or philosophy. My expertise in movie trivia and my analysis of movies represent this cognitive dimension. The *emotional dimension* of an attitude involves feelings, such as liking or disliking. My love of movies and anticipation of pleasure from them are clear examples of this emotional dimension. The *behavioral dimension* of an attitude determines how the beliefs and evaluative feelings are demonstrated—in my case, by going to movies, renting movies or purchasing favorite movies, and discussing movies with my friends.

Logically, attitudes should function to shape specific actions, but the relationship is not always so straightforward (Ajzen, 2001). Individuals do not always express their attitudes in behavior. For example, many people cognitively and emotionally support recycling, but they may not sort their cans and glass and take them to a recycling center. In addition, sometimes people hold two attitudes that are not completely consistent with each other. For example, there are movies that I know are terrible, and I believe that I have good critical skills in analyzing movies, but I like some of these bad movies anyway. (They are among my "guilty pleasures.") People are not always consistent in their attitudes.

People are also unaware of the full range of their attitudes. The attitudes that people are able to report and describe are called *explicit attitudes,* but people also have *implicit attitudes*. They are involuntary, uncontrollable, and not part of conscious thought (Greenwald & Banaji, 1995; Greenwald et al., 2002). Implicit attitudes are automatically activated and can affect behavior, often in subtle ways. For example, many people have negative attitudes about African Americans. Some people's negative attitudes are explicit—they acknowledge their negative bias. However, others who believe and behave in ways that indicate a lack of ethnic bias may still have negative implicit attitudes that affect their interactions with African Americans. For example, people with high scores on a measure of implicit bias (but not on a measure of explicit bias) interacted with African Americans in ways that signaled more discomfort and less friendliness, such as making less eye contact and standing farther away (Dovidio, Kawakami, & Gaertner, 2002). Implicit attitudes may be traceable to childhood and have strong emotional components, some of which originate in biases that run throughout the culture (Rudman, 2004). This developmental background for implicit attitudes combined with people's lack of awareness of them suggests that they may be resistant to change.

What variables determine how attitudes are formed, demonstrated, or changed? Why are some attitudes much harder to modify than others? What happens when people hold inconsistent attitudes?

Do Attitudes Predict Behavior?

If you believe that recycling is important to preserving the environment, will you recycle your plastic grocery bags? That is, will a favorable attitude toward recycling prompt a specific recycling behavior? Despite the logic of the relationship between attitudes and behavior, attitudes often fail to predict behavior, because other variables enter into the equation. Some of the important variables are attitude accessibility, norms, and specificity of attitudes.

Attitudes are accessible when they are strong and easily retrievable from memory. People are faster at reporting attitudes that are highly accessible, and those attitudes are better predictors of behavior than less accessible attitudes (Fazio, 2000). The more quickly an attitude comes to mind, the more likely you are to act on that attitude. However, norms are very important moderators of the link between attitudes and behavior (Ajzen, 2001). *Social norms* are the standards and values of the social group that each person internalizes. When group norms differ from personal attitudes, people are less likely to behave according to their attitudes; when group norms are consistent with personal attitudes, people are more likely to put their attitudes into action (Smith & Terry, 2003; White, Hogg, & Terry, 2002).

Social norms ■ The standards and values of the social group that each person internalizes.

Attitudes are also more likely to foretell behavior when they are specific and when the situation in which the individual will act closely matches the situation to which the attitude applies. Very general attitudes, and even stereotypes about groups of people, do not predict specific behaviors very well. For example, a person may endorse recycling in general but be unwilling to bundle newspapers together and take them to the recycling center. Therefore, attitudes are less than perfect predictors of behavior, and some researchers have approached the relationship of attitudes and behavior by turning the question around.

Does Behavior Determine Attitudes?

Is it possible that your attitudes don't determine your behavior, but just the opposite—that your behavior shapes your attitudes? Some research evidence suggests that this happens in certain circumstances. For example, people often develop positive attitudes toward a charity after making a contribution, however small. In weight control programs, alcohol abstinence programs, and many therapy groups, facilitators try to change behaviors (get people to abstain from alcohol, for example) with the idea that positive attitudes about a new life will *follow* changes in behavior.

Social psychologist Daryl Bem (1972) claims that people do not change their attitudes because of internal states such as thoughts. He has proposed *self-perception theory*—a view of attitude formation that asserts that people infer their attitudes and emotional states from their behavior. Bem holds that people don't know what their attitudes are until they stop and examine their behavior. First, they search for an external explanation, such as "Someone forced me to do this." If no such explanation is available, they seek an internal one. That is, people look at their behavior and say, "I must have felt like this if I behaved that way." See **Figure 14.2** for a comparison of Bem's view and the common-sense view of attitude formation.

Another theory also predicts that behavior affects attitudes. Leon Festinger (1919–1989) was a social psychologist who believed that people feel uncomfortable when their attitudes conflict with one another or when attitudes conflict with behavior. He also thought that this discomfort was important for attitude change, and he coined the term *cognitive dissonance* to describe a state of mental discomfort that arises from a discrepancy between two or more of a person's beliefs or between a person's beliefs and overt behavior. Festinger (1957) proposed *cognitive dissonance theory*, which predicts that when people experience conflict among their attitudes or between their attitudes and their behavior, they are motivated to change either their attitudes or their behavior.

An early study demonstrated the power of cognitive dissonance in attitude change (Festinger & Carlsmith, 1959). In this study, all participants performed an intentionally boring task for 30 minutes. Then some participants were asked to persuade potential participants to join the study by telling them that the experiment was fun and interesting. The researchers believed that making statements about how interesting the study was would create cognitive dissonance in these participants. Furthermore, the researchers paid the participants either $1 or $20 for their assistance and hypothesized that the amount of money received would affect the dissonance that participants felt and thus their attitudes about the task. Counter to most people's intuitions, these researchers predicted that those participants who received $1 would have a more favorable attitude about the task than those who received $20. The results of the study confirmed their predictions (see **Figure 14.3**).

Why should people who are paid a small amount of money change their attitudes more than those who receive a larger amount? Festinger and Carlsmith interpreted

Self-perception theory ■ A view of attitude formation that asserts that people infer their attitudes and emotional states from their behavior.

Cognitive dissonance [COG-nih-tiv DIS-uh-nents] ■ A state of mental discomfort arising from a discrepancy between two or more of a person's beliefs or between a person's beliefs and overt behavior.

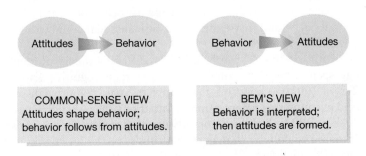

COMMON-SENSE VIEW
Attitudes shape behavior; behavior follows from attitudes.

BEM'S VIEW
Behavior is interpreted; then attitudes are formed.

Figure 14.2
Two Views of Attitudes
Does behavior follow from attitudes (the common-sense view), or do attitudes follow from behavior (Bem's view)?

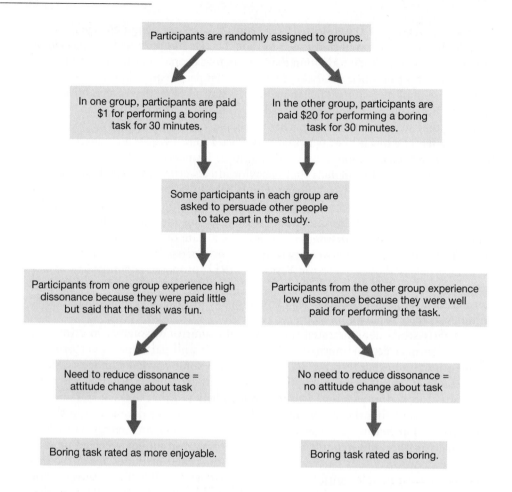

the results in terms of *cognitive dissonance reduction*. They explained that participants who received little money felt more dissonance—why they would say that the task was interesting for such a trivial amount of money. They concluded that they must really think that it was interesting, and their ratings reflected this positive attitude. The money was not a sufficient justification for their behavior, so they searched for a rationalization, and it involved changing their attitude. On the other hand, $20 was a sufficient payment to justify other participants' behavior—the task was boring, but they were well paid—and they experienced little dissonance. Their attitude about the boring task remained negative.

Cognitive dissonance theory can be considered to be a theory of motivation because it suggests that people become energized by their cognitive dissonance to do something (Tesser, 2001); in addition, the motive to avoid cognitive dissonance leads people to avoid encountering information or situations that would provoke it (D'alessio & Allen, 2002). But the theory also applies to attitudes, because what people are energized to do is to change their attitudes to reduce cognitive dissonance. Dissonance reduction produces a change of attitude that is prompted by behavior and thus demonstrates that behavior can lead to attitude change. However, dissonance reduction is more likely to change an explicit attitude than to alter an implicit attitude (Gawronski & Strack, 2004).

How Does Attitude Change Occur?

Attitudes are subject to change, and as we have just discussed, an inconsistency between attitudes and behavior may prompt people to alter their attitudes. Social psychologists have been interested in attitude change from the start. Early approaches focused on the components of persuasion, and a more modern approach examines how attitude change includes processes that are not conscious.

Attitude Change through Persuasion

In the 1950s, Carl Hovland and his colleagues (Hovland, Janis, & Kelley, 1953) were among the first social psychologists to identify key components of attitude change. Their model focused on the components of effective persuasion: the source, the communication, the medium, and the audience.

The source of the communication is the first key element of persuasion. A communicator—a person trying to effect attitude change—is more effective when he or she projects integrity, credibility, and trustworthiness. If people don't respect, believe, or trust the communicator, they are less likely to change their attitudes. For example, communicators with "mature" faces have more influence (Berry & Landry, 1997), and perceived power, prestige, expertise, celebrity, prominence, modesty, and attractiveness of the communicator are extremely important (Petty & Wegener, 1998). For example, you are more likely to believe research about weight loss strategies from university researchers than from a person who writes a column in the local paper.

The nature of the communication is also important for persuasion. A clear, well-organized, logical argument can be effective in changing attitudes, especially in Western cultures, where appeals to logic and reason are highly valued. However, communications that arouse fear are also effective in motivating attitude change, especially when they focus on health issues and the fear message is not too strong (Janis & Feshbach, 1953; Sturges & Rogers, 1996). For example, think of some of the communications about drinking and driving you've seen on television or in magazines.

If people hear a persuasive message often enough, they begin to believe it, regardless of how valid it is or even how favorably they rate it at first. This is called the *mere exposure effect*. Repeated exposure to certain situations can also change attitudes, pushing people toward favorable feelings about and even identification with people whom they see repeatedly (Greenwald, Pickrell, & Farnham, 2002). For example, after seeing numerous TV commercials that show the Energizer battery outperforming another brand, a viewer may change his or her attitude toward the product from neutral to positive. Similarly, a political candidate whose name is heard often is more likely to be viewed positively than is one whose name is heard infrequently. Thus, we get bombarded with political advertising as elections draw near.

The means by which a communication is presented—its medium—influences people's receptiveness to attitude change. Today, one of the most common avenues for attempts at attitude change is the mass media, particularly television. Television advertising is one of the most influential media for changing attitudes in the Western world, but face-to-face communication often has more impact than communication through television or in writing. Thus, even though candidates for public office rely heavily on television, radio, and printed ads, they also try to meet people face to face, often touring their districts to deliver their message directly.

The characteristics of the audience also influence how effective persuasion will be. Openness to attitude change is related in part to age and education. People are most susceptible to attitude change during the years of early adulthood (Ceci & Bruck, 1993). Changing people's attitudes can be difficult if they have well-established habits (which often come with advancing age) or are highly motivated in the direction opposite to the desired change. People of high intelligence are less likely to have their opinions changed, and those who have high self-esteem tend to be similarly unyielding (Rhodes & Wood, 1992). A change is far more likely to occur if the person trying to change another's attitude is a friend rather than a stranger (Cialdini, 2001).

Hovland's model of attitude change assumes that people are rational evaluators of information who are consciously aware of their attitudes. Subsequent research has indicated that some components of attitudes are outside conscious awareness and that individuals are not always rational in their evaluations of persuasive messages. A more recent model of attitude change takes this newer research into account.

The Elaboration Likelihood Model of Attitude Change

During the 1970s, psychologists began to concentrate on cognitive processes, and some social psychologists focused on what happens cognitively to individuals whose attitudes are being changed. One cognitive theory, proposed by Richard Petty and John Cacioppo (1985), suggests that people are influenced by the content of a message, but they are swayed by other factors as well (Petty & Wegener, 1999). This theory is called the *elaboration likelihood model*—a view suggesting that attitude change can be accomplished via two routes: a central route and a peripheral route. (See Figure 14.4 for an overview of this model.)

The *central route* emphasizes conscious, thoughtful consideration and evaluation of arguments concerning a given issue. Attitude change via this route depends on how effective, authoritative, and logical a communication is. For example, engineering and safety information about different automobiles reveals that some stand out as better examples of careful construction and dependability. People who examine this kind of information when shopping for a vehicle are processing information via the central route and tend to make rational decisions about their purchase.

The *peripheral route* emphasizes less careful and more emotional, even superficial, evaluation of the message. This route has an indirect but nevertheless

Elaboration likelihood model ■ A view suggesting that there are two routes to attitude change: the central route, which emphasizes thoughtful consideration and evaluation of arguments, and the peripheral route, which emphasizes less careful, more emotional, and even superficial evaluation.

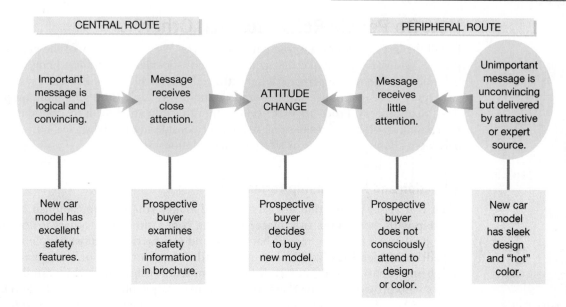

CENTRAL ROUTE

Important message is logical and convincing.

Message receives close attention.

ATTITUDE CHANGE

PERIPHERAL ROUTE

Message receives little attention.

Unimportant message is unconvincing but delivered by attractive or expert source.

New car model has excellent safety features.

Prospective buyer examines safety information in brochure.

Prospective buyer decides to buy new model.

Prospective buyer does not consciously attend to design or color.

New car model has sleek design and "hot" color.

Figure 14.4
Elaboration Likelihood Model
According to the elaboration likelihood model, attitude change can occur through the central route or the peripheral route.

powerful effect, especially when there are no logical arguments that can force the use of the central route. This peripheral route is a mainstay of advertising. Commercial messages sometimes aim to provide information, but they also include attractive images of the products and associations with other appealing people, products, or situations. For example, automobile commercials often feature not only the new car (which looks great) but also attractive people going to exciting places and having fun in it. A consumer's attitude—believing that the automobile is a great machine—often stems largely from emotional or personal rather than logical arguments and therefore may not be long-lasting (Petty et al., 1993). But by the time the attitude fades, the consumer may have already bought the car.

The fundamental idea of the elaboration likelihood model is that people can change attitudes because of thoughtful conscious decisions (central route) or because of quick, emotional choices (peripheral route). The central route dominates when people have the ability, time, and energy to think through arguments carefully; the peripheral route is more likely to be influential when motivation is low, time is short, or the ability to think through arguments is impaired (Petty et al., 1994). For example, one study showed that the peripheral cue of the ethnicity of the model in a television advertisement influenced viewers' attitudes about the product (Whittler & Spira, 2002). Therefore, evidence suggests that both direct and peripheral routes can influence attitude change.

How Do People Relate to Each Other?

Recall the last time you went to a party where you knew only a few of the people present. Did you try to make the acquaintance of someone you did not know? If so, how did you choose the person? What attracted you to the person? Social psychologists study these questions, trying to understand how people form and maintain personal relationships. Processes that occur within the individual form the foundation for relating to others, and the same strategy of considering thoughts, feelings, and behaviors allows an analysis of interpersonal relationships.

Attraction and Relationship Formation

What is it about people that attracts you and makes you want to establish a relationship with them in the first place? Forming connections with others is not only a life goal and a major source of happiness and satisfaction in most people's lives (Hendrick & Hendrick, 2003), but also an advantage for a person's survival and well-being (Kenrick et al., 2002). Infants form relationships with their families or others who provide care for them, but what attracts people to those outside their families? Social psychologists have studied the factors related to *interpersonal attraction,* the tendency of one person to evaluate another person (or a symbol or image of another person) in a positive way. Many of the answers to questions about interpersonal attraction are less dramatic than people imagine. For example, people tend to become attracted to those with whom they often come into contact.

Interpersonal attraction
▪ The tendency of one person to evaluate another person (or a symbol or image of another person) in a positive way.

Proximity

People are more likely to develop a relationship with a neighbor than with someone who lives miles away. Early research on this topic was conducted in a college dormitory (Festinger, Schachter, & Back, 1950). Fifty years of subsequent research show that the closer people are geographically, the more likely they are to become attracted to each other (Fiske, 2004). A simple explanation is that they are likely to see each other more often, and repeated exposure leads to familiarity, which leads to attraction. Thus, the mere exposure effect, whereby repeated exposure leads to positive evaluations, relates to interpersonal attraction as well as to attitude change. People who are members of the same group, such as a club, a volunteer organization, or a class, perceive themselves as sharing the same feelings, attitudes, and values as others in the group. That perception leads to attraction.

The increasing use of the Internet has changed the world in many ways, including allowing people to meet each other in cyberspace rather than face to face. It is now possible to meet and to become attracted to someone who lives thousands of miles away and whom you have never seen. Some people use Internet dating services to meet people (Donn & Sherman, 2002), and chat rooms also provide possibilities for individuals to meet others. Chat rooms furnish the electronic equivalent of proximity, and regular participation is a factor in forming relationships through this medium (Levine, 2000). But Internet relationships form without geographic proximity, which allows people to see each other. That difference is important, because physical attractiveness is a key factor in interpersonal attraction.

Physical Attractiveness

Do you believe in "love at first sight"? If so, then the basis for it must be physical attractiveness, because that is what first sight allows. Even if you do not believe in love at first sight, you usually know within seconds of seeing a person whether you find the person attractive. Physical attractiveness is an important factor in interpersonal attraction, and the basis for judging attractiveness may exist very early in life. Children as young as 6 months old show the ability to distinguish attractive from unattractive faces, making judgments similar to those of adults (Ramsey et al., 2004).

Judgments as to what constitutes an attractive face show many similarities across the world. Researchers are able to study the attractiveness of various facial characteristics by using computer technology to manipulate photographs of faces and vary characteristics. They can "masculinize" or "feminize" the faces, make them more symmetrical or asymmetrical, age them, and change them in other ways. People tend to rate symmetrical faces as more attractive than asymmetrical ones, and this preference is exhibited to people from a variety of cultures (Jones, Little, & Perrett, 2003; Rhodes et al., 2001). A preference for feminized faces is found among both U.S. and Japanese participants (Perrett et al., 1998).

The preference for more feminine-looking faces may result from the fact that such faces appear younger. Other facial characteristics typical of babies were rated as appealing in a cross-cultural study (Cunningham et al., 1995). This study contrasted the evaluations of Asian, Latino/Latina, and White participants regarding the attractiveness of faces, and the results showed consistency: Participants favored faces with large eyes, greater distance between eyes, and small noses; sexually mature, narrower female faces with smaller chins; expressive, higher eyebrows, dilated pupils, larger lower lips, larger smiles, and well-groomed, full hair. Such results are probably no surprise to Leonardo DiCaprio's agent.

Evolutionary theorists claim that facial symmetry is one indication of health and thus reproductive fitness (Jones et al., 2003). Another such indicator is the ratio of hip measurement to waist measurement in women. From an analysis of *Playboy* centerfolds and Miss America pageant winners, Singh (1993) concluded that, according to men, the ideal proportions of the female figure is a hip-to-waist ratio of 7 to 10, which approximates the "hourglass" figure, with hips wider (but not too much wider) than the waist. Subsequent studies have confirmed this preference in some but not all cultures (Furnham, Moutafi, & Baguma, 2002). Also, some research has criticized Singh for overlooking important changes in figure preferences over time (Freese & Meland, 2002). That criticism is consistent with the findings of cross-cultural researchers that some cultures show preferences for heavier women, whereas other cultures emphasize thinness (Wetsman & Marlowe, 1999).

Standards of beauty appear to be more consistent for facial than for body characteristics, which vary according to place and time period and show substantial cross-cultural differences (Matsumoto & Kudoh, 1993). For over a thousand years, Chinese women endured the suffering of foot-binding in the name of beauty, yet few Westerners see the appeal of 3-inch feet. In the United States and Europe, the current ideal female body is thin, with a small waist, slim hips, and large breasts, but 100 years ago, the standard was for fuller figures, with large hips and breasts.

How important is physical attractiveness when selecting a dating or marriage partner? Do people always want the best-looking person? Research shows that attractiveness is important, but other characteristics are more important, at least to adults. Young adolescents (14 to 16 years old) mention attractiveness as the most important characteristic for a potential dating partner (Regan & Joshi, 2003). However, college students in both the United States (Sprecher & Regan, 2002) and China (Toro-Morn & Sprecher, 2003) value warmth, kindness, openness, and a good sense of humor more highly than physical attractiveness, although the value placed on attractiveness has increased in the United States over the past 50 years (Buss et al., 2001). However, discovering that a person's personal qualities are appealing leads to alterations in the evaluation of how good-looking the person is (Kniffin & Wilson, 2004). So, a person may become more or less beautiful, depending on personality and behavior.

Physical good looks are more important when choosing a date than a mate, but the differences are not as large as many people imagine—people have similar criteria for both temporary and long-term partners (Sprecher & Regan, 2002). Physical attractiveness is less important in friends than in romantic partners, but other factors related to interpersonal attraction, including similarity of beliefs and attitudes, apply to both types of relationships.

Similarity: Liking Those Who Are Like Us

Social psychologists examine the mutual interactions that lead to relationship formation, emphasizing that the process of developing a relationship is a reciprocal one. The basic idea is simple: You like the people who like you (Katz & Beach, 2000). Real or perceived similarity in attitudes and opinions is a factor that affects the development of relationships. If you perceive someone's attitudes as being similar to your own, this perception increases the probability that you will like that person. Having similar values, interests, and backgrounds is a good predictor of a friendship or a romantic relationship (Katz & Beach, 2000).

The perception of similarity leads people to conclude that others are like them, which tends to be a positive experience. The similarity effect may be based on a cognitive evaluation about the other person (Montoya & Horton, 2004). When people learn that someone else shares one of their attitudes, they tend to make conclusions about other related attitudes that the other person may share, leading to positive perceptions about the person and thus feelings of attraction. Similarity in attitudes is not the only type of similarity that boosts attraction; similarities in ethnicity, social class, and religion can also contribute (Martin et al., 2003). People may cross some social boundaries to form relationships, but shared attitudes suggest mutual attraction (Fiske, 2004).

Friendships

Mutual liking and the sharing of ideas and values form the basis for both friend-ships and romantic relationships (Katz & Beach, 2000). *Friendship* is a type of rela-tionship that involves closeness and a commitment to continue the relationship. Children begin to develop a concept of the kind of mutual interdependence that is necessary for friendship during the preschool years (Lindsey, 2002). Older children begin to rely on friends in addition to family for companionship and emotional closeness (Cleary et al., 2002). Gender differences in friendship styles appear early in development, with girls relying more on emotional sharing and boys developing activity-based friendships. These patterns persist into adulthood, but each gender is capable of using the style typical of the other (DeLucia-Waack et al., 2001). That is, both women and men have flexible friendship styles; each can engage in the emo-tion-oriented sharing typical of women or the activity-based style typical of men.

Definitions of Love

The attempt to define love is ancient, and poets, philosophers, and lovers have tried to analyze and understand romantic feelings. Psychologists have also tried to analyze and classify love. Psychologist Robert Sternberg (1986; Barnes & Sternberg, 1997) has defined love in terms of three components: intimacy, commitment, and passion. *Intimacy* is a sense of emotional closeness. *Commitment* is the extent to which a relationship is permanent and long-lasting. *Passion* is arousal, partly sexual, partly intellectual, and partly inspirational. Sternberg proposes seven types of love having varying combinations of these three components. When the intimacy and commit-ment components are present, friendship occurs. Close friendships fit into the cate-gory of *companionate love*. When all three components are present, the highest type of love—*consummate love*—results. Another view of love (Hendrick & Hendrick, 1986) identifies six distinct varieties: passionate, game-playing, friendship, logical, possessive, and selfless. Table 14.2 shows a series of statements that are used on a test to measure the way people relate in a love relationship.

Intimate and Love Relationships

People involved in a friendship or a romantic relationship may or may not be intimate with one another. *Intimacy* is a state of being or feeling that leads each person in a relationship to self-disclose (to express important feelings and information to the other person). If the other person acknowledges the first person's feelings, then each feels valued and cared for (Katz & Beach, 2000). However, people may be in a close rela-tionship that involves mutual interdependence and yet not experience intimacy. For example, many coworkers see each other at least five days a week, get to know each other well, and depend on each other to reach common goals, but do not develop a relationship that would be described as intimate.

Research shows that the development of intimacy is related to self-disclosure (Aron et al., 1991). Intimacy tends to develop when someone discloses personal information to another and the other person reciprocates. When people engage in

Intimacy ■ A state of being or feeling that leads each person in a relationship to self-disclose (to express important feelings and information to the other person).

Table 14.2

SIX VARIETIES OF LOVE

Variety of Love	Sample Test Items
■ Passionate Love	My lover and I were attracted to each other immediately after we first met. My lover and I became emotionally involved rather quickly.
■ Game-Playing Love	I have sometimes had to keep two of my lovers from finding out about each other. I can get over love affairs pretty easily and quickly.
■ Friendship Love	The best kind of love grows out of a long friendship. Love is really a deep friendship, not a mysterious, mystical emotion.
■ Logical Love	It is best to love someone with a similar background. An important factor in choosing a partner is whether or not he (she) will be a good parent.
■ Possessive Love	When my lover doesn't pay attention to me, I feel sick all over. I cannot relax if I suspect that my lover is with someone else.
■ Selfless Love	I would rather suffer myself than let my lover suffer. Whatever I own is my lover's to use as he (she) chooses.

Source: Hendrick & Hendrick (1986)

mutual self-disclosure, they validate each other; that is, they accept each other's positive and negative attributes.

Close friendships include intimacy, but romantic love differs from friendship in the inclusion of passion (Sternberg, 1986). Although people through the centuries have experienced passionate love, it was not the basis for permanent partnerships such as marriage until relatively recently (Hatfield & Rapson, 1996; Hendrick & Hendrick, 2003). In many Western societies, people accept romance and passion as the basis for marriage, but in many societies in Asia and India, passionate love is considered to be a poor basis for a permanent relationship.

How people choose romantic or sexual partners is a major topic in evolutionary psychology, because reproduction is how people pass on their genes to offspring. According to the evolutionary view, the process of natural selection has caused women and men to develop different strategies for selecting partners (Buss, 2004; Kenrick, Ackerman, & Ledlow, 2003). Because women produce relatively few ova and must go through the lengthy and risky process of pregnancy they have more limited chances to reproduce than men do and thus must be more selective in choosing their partners. Women are best served by selecting mates who will not only contribute good genes to their offspring but also offer assistance in raising them. Men, on the other hand, benefit from trying to reproduce as often as possible as a way to perpetuate their genes. These two mating strategies produce conflicting goals for women and men, and evolutionary psychologists see many contemporary problems in relationships as a result of this evolved gender difference.

The extent to which these predictions from evolutionary psychology actually appear in contemporary behavior is a topic of heated debate. Those who take the evolutionary psychology approach see differences in sexual attitudes and behavior as confirmation of an evolved component for these behaviors, and they contend that some gender differences appear worldwide (Buss, 2004; Schmitt, 2003). Others contest not only the interpretation of gender differences in partner choice but even the existence of such differences (Gannon, 2002; Miller, Putcha-Bhagavatula, & Pedersen, 2002). Some researchers claim that variation between women and men in partner selection is too small to correspond to the mating strategies hypothesized by evolutionary psychology (Alexander & Fisher, 2003).

The existence of cultural variations in love and sexual relationships is a problem for the evolutionary view, because evolved mating strategies should be similar across cultures. In a study comparing women and men from North America and China, cultural differences in attitudes related to love and romance were larger than gender differences (Sprecher & Toro-Morn, 2002). One broad cultural difference that has an impact on the choice of mates is men's and women's social and economic circumstances (Wood & Eagly, 2002). In cultures in which women have limited access to economic resources, they tend to choose mates who seem like good providers; that is, they behave in accordance with the prediction from evolutionary psychology. In cultures in which women have greater access to economic resources, male and female mating strategies tend to be more similar (not in accordance with the evolutionary approach). Therefore, cultural differences influence the formation of romantic relationships.

Maintaining Relationships

Similarity, attractiveness, and passion contribute to relationship formation, but what factors maintain relationships? What determines whether people who get together stay together? Social psychologists have also investigated questions of relationship stability.

Equity within the relationship plays a role in maintaining close relationships. *Equity theory* states that people attempt to maintain stable, consistent interpersonal relationships in which members' contributions are in balance (Walster, Walster, & Berscheid, 1978). People in a close relationship usually feel a sense of equity in the relationship, which relates to stability. According to equity theory, when people feel that they are giving (or receiving) too much or too little, they take action to restore the balance. For example, people often give gifts as a way to apologize for neglect or bad behavior within a relationship and request (or demand) changes when they feel that their partners are contributing too little. Equity theory predicts that a relationship that is out of balance will be less stable and more likely to dissolve.

Equity theory ■ Social psychological theory that states that people attempt to maintain stable, consistent interpersonal relationships in which members' contributions are in balance.

Another way to analyze the stability of relationships is through the attachment style of the partners. John Bowlby studied attachment in children (see Chapter 4), finding that most children form *secure* attachments to their caregivers, but some children experience attachments that are *avoidant* or *ambivalent*. These styles of attachment also apply to adult relationships: People with secure attachments are comfortable in their relationships, but people with avoidant attachments are not. Individuals with ambivalent attachments are anxious and concerned about their relationships. Research indicates that attachment styles relate to relationship satisfaction and to marital problems and conflict in predictable ways. For example, individuals with secure attachments tend to be more satisfied with their relationships, although their partners' attachment style is also a factor (Banse, 2004). Partners who both have a secure attachment show more interdependence and trust, whereas those with avoidant attachment styles experience more conflict (Besharat, 2003).

In addition to conflict, aggression also arises in relationships. Therefore, aggression is an important topic in social psychology.

Aggression and Violence

Since 1995, the Verizon Wireless Company has sponsored a program called HopeLine, which helps victims of domestic violence by giving them cell phones that may allow them to summon help when they are being abused. The publicity about domestic violence has made more people aware of the frequency of this problem, which is disturbing because it demonstrates that aggression extends not only to those we hate but also to those we love. The statistics are shocking: 20% of the violent crimes against women are perpetrated by romantic partners. However, this recent figure represents a decrease; the numbers were higher 10 years ago (Bureau of Justice Statistics, 2003).

Aggression ■ Any behavior intended to harm another person or thing.

Domestic violence is only one type of aggression. Social psychologists define ***aggression*** as any behavior intended to harm another person or thing. A person may attempt to harm others physically through force, verbally through rumors or irritating comments, or emotionally by withholding attention or love. Aggression applies to groups as well as to individuals—whole countries attempt to harm others by acts of war. Theoretical explanations for aggressive behavior focus on biological influences, drives acquired through learning, and cognitions.

Is Aggression Innate?

People often talk about an "instinct for aggression," assuming that the urge to harm others is built into humans, as it is in many nonhuman animals. This thinking is incorrect, because it assumes that aggression is a common response to many situations. For humans and other animals, aggression is limited and selective. Aggressive behavior is often oriented toward specific goals, such as obtaining food or protecting offspring (Pinker, 2002). Evolutionary psychologists believe that aggression aimed at achieving these limited goals is innate to humans and other animals.

According to the evolutionary view, the competition for resources is a reason for aggression. In the environment in which humans evolved, resources were scarce, and competition for those resources provoked aggression (Pinker, 2002). Aggression can be successful as a strategy for survival and for accruing resources, both of which increase chances of reproduction. Thus, humans and other animals have an evolved capacity for aggression, which may be successful if they choose appropriate targets.

Appropriate targets include individuals who are not part of the person's immediate social group or who are competitors for resources. Thus, evolutionary psychology predicts that people are more likely to harm strangers than acquaintances. Furthermore, according to this theory, people should be hesitant to harm family members because those individuals share genetic material; harming a family member may keep a person's genes from surviving. These hypotheses do not seem consistent with the statistics on domestic violence and the number of partners and children who are harmed by family members. However, domestic abuse is more likely to be aimed at partners than at children and at stepchildren than at biological children, which is consistent with predictions from evolutionary psychology (Gaulin & McBurney, 2004). Other psychologists have very different views of the sources of aggression, including associations and learning.

Does Frustration Cause Aggression?

Another explanation for aggressive behavior is that it occurs when people feel frustrated and unable to control situations that affect their lives. The *frustration–aggression hypothesis*, initially proposed by John Dollard and colleagues (1939), holds that aggression occurs as a result of unsuccessful goal-directed behavior. This theory relies on observations that people involved in everyday goal-oriented tasks often become aggressive or angry when frustrated. For example, ordinarily, you may be unlikely to become very upset if another car pulls into traffic in front of you. However, if you are late for work because of backed-up traffic, you might honk or mutter angrily at the other driver.

Berkowitz (1964) examined the evidence for the frustration–aggression hypothesis and proposed a modified version of it. He suggested that frustration creates a *readiness* for aggressive acts rather than producing actual aggression. He showed that even when frustration is present, certain events must occur or certain conditions must exist before aggression results. For example, someone involved in a heated argument might be more likely to become aggressive if there is a weapon lying on a nearby table. In a later reformulation, Berkowitz (2000) suggested that frustrations generate aggressive inclinations to the extent that they arouse negative feelings in the individual. Many psychologists find both versions of the frustration–aggression hypothesis too simplistic, and they tend to emphasize the roles of observation and modeling and of cognition in aggression.

Do People Learn How to Be Aggressive?

Social learning theory (see Chapter 8) holds that people learn most behaviors through the processes of participation and reinforcement or observation and modeling, or some combination of these processes (Bandura, 1986, 2001). According to this view, people learn aggressive behavior from others, along with information about how successful particular aggressive actions are, who is typically aggressive, and under what circumstances aggression may be successful (Hawley & Vaughn, 2003). This view of aggressive behaviors examines the opportunities that people, especially children, have to observe aggression and connects those opportunities to the performance of aggressive acts.

Psychologists who believe that observation and learning are important factors in aggression have concerns about media violence (Anderson et al., 2003). Children have ample opportunity to observe violence on television; preschool children in the United States average about 30 hours a week of television viewing (Witt, 2000). About 61% of television programs include violence (Anderson et al., 2003). Furthermore, most televised violence tends to be either trivialized or glamorized, so children may receive positive messages about violent behavior. Violence in movies and video games is also a concern, but young children have less access to these media than do older children and adolescents.

Young children's access to violent media is a concern because age is a factor in developing aggressive behaviors. Longitudinal studies of the influence of televised violence indicate that children exposed to television violence were affected even 15 years later (Huesmann et al., 2003). However, exposure to violence on television affects immediate behaviors even more strongly than it does delayed responses (Anderson et al., 2003). The amount of exposure is also a factor, and viewers who watch a lot of violent TV programs are more likely to behave aggressively than those who watch less (Anderson & Bushman, 2002). Further, children exposed to large doses of TV violence are less likely to help a real-life victim of violence, and viewers of violence are less sympathetic to victims than are children who watch little television (Villani, 2001). That is, televised violence desensitizes people to real violence.

Clearly, violent TV programming can affect children and adults. Modeling is one of the major ways in which this medium exerts its influence. Media violence also changes how people think about the world, and cognition is another possible source of aggression.

Do Cognitions Contribute to Aggression?

The cognitive view holds that people actively engage in thoughts that lead them to violent behaviors. What thoughts go through a young man's mind when he takes a gun to school with plans to shoot classmates? What possesses people to chase someone who has cut in front of them in traffic? To try to understand how thoughts are related to aggression, Leonard Eron, Rowell Huesmann, and their colleagues (Dubow, Huesmann, & Boxer, 2003; Eron, 1987; Huesmann, Eron, & Dubow, 2002) conducted a 30-year, multigenerational longitudinal study. Beginning when participants were in the 3rd grade, these researchers studied factors related to aggression as the children grew to adolescence and then adulthood. They continued the study when the participants had children themselves. This work probed the influences in children's lives that cause them to *interpret* the world in a way that makes them aggressive. The researchers found that aggressive children respond to the world with combativeness because they have internalized aggressive views of the world. Aggressive children see others as hostile to them, and they respond in kind. In this longitudinal study, both boys and girls were identified as aggressive, but aggression was more common for boys.

Gender Differences in Aggression

Many people believe that men are naturally more aggressive than women. They refer to aggressive contact sports such as football and boxing, the aggressive behavior of men in business, the overwhelming number of violent crimes committed by men, and the traditional view that men are more likely than women to be ruthless and unsympathetic. Masculinity is stereotypically associated with aggression and femininity with victimization (Murnen, Wright, & Kaluzny, 2002). But are men really more aggressive than women?

Both crime statistics and research with college students show that men are more *physically* aggressive than women. Men's most common experience of aggression is getting into a fight with another man (Graham & Wells, 2001). Women's most common experience of physical violence is being victimized by a male partner. However, some women are physically violent, and their aggressive behavior tends to fall into the same categories as men's—that is, some defend themselves using aggression, and some use violence to control other people's behavior (Babcock & Siard, 2003).

Both men and women use psychological aggression, or ***indirect aggression,*** which consists of efforts to cause harm through indirect means, such as arranging for something bad to happen to someone or spreading rumors about someone. Men use both types of aggression more than women do (Salmivalli & Kaukiainen, 2004). Indirect aggression is much more prominent among girls than direct conflict, and those who use this tactic try to instigate fights and conflicts among friends or family members, spread false stories, and arrange for others to be ostracized by the group (Owens, Shute, & Slee, 2000; Walker, Richardson, & Green, 2000).

One interpretation of the finding about frequency and types of aggression suggests that the differences between boys and girls and men and women are directly related to the perceived consequences of the aggression. Women in many cultures are socialized to restrain their anger and aggression more than men are (Shields, 2002). In addition, women are more vulnerable to physical retaliation than men are. So women are more likely than men to use indirect aggression, which does harm but does not involve confrontation and thus carries lower risk of physical retaliation. However, when women feel justified and protected from retaliation, they can be as aggressive as men (Brannon, 2005).

Research supports the idea that the contexts in which people find themselves alter the nature and extent of aggression. For example, insults and condescending treatment provoke women more than men, but men are more angered than women by insults to their intelligence (Bettencourt & Miller, 1996). A meta-analysis of over 30 years of studies on aggression revealed gender differences that suggest that men have more trouble than women regulating their emotions (Knight et al., 2002). In situations with low levels of emotional arousal, few gender differences appear. However, in situations with high levels of emotional arousal, men respond with

Indirect aggression ▪ Aggression through indirect means, such as arranging for something bad to happen to someone or spreading rumors about someone.

higher levels of aggression than women do. The influence of context and cognition in aggressive behavior suggests that it is possible to change these factors to decrease the level of aggression.

Can Aggression Be Controlled?

Psychologists who hold an evolutionary view cite the presence of aggression in all human civilizations (and even precivilization) as evidence that aggression is part of human nature (Pinker, 2002). If this view is correct, aggression cannot be prevented. However, a look at the wide variation in levels of aggressive behavior in cultures around the world and an examination of research in psychology lead to the conclusion that a high level of aggression is not universal among human societies. Therefore, theoretically, aggression can be controlled and decreased.

One approach that is not very successful in decreasing aggression is punishment, especially physical punishment. Consistent with the social learning theory, parents' use of harsh punishment for misbehavior creates a risk of future aggression; it is not a preventative (Huesmann et al., 2002). Also consistent with this view, children who are exposed to violence in their communities and families tend to perform aggressive acts (Guerra, Huesmann, & Spindler, 2003). Therefore, limiting children's exposure to violence is one way to decrease their tendency to behave aggressively. Family and community violence may be difficult to control, but exposure to media violence is within the control of parents. Parents should also bear in mind that harsh physical punishment tends to create, rather than discourage, aggression.

Some violence prevention programs show evidence of effectiveness. One school-based intervention seems effective in decreasing children's aggression, if presented during the early elementary school years (Eron et al., 2002). This program is aimed at changing children's cognitions so that they interpret others' behavior as less hostile, developing interpersonal skills that allow children to handle conflict in a nonviolent manner, and gaining families' support for alternatives to aggression. Another school-based program targets bullying, a type of aggression that has become more recognized in recent years (Olweus, 1993, 2003). This program avoids punishment, emphasizes the power of positive models, and works toward establishing standards within the school to discourage bullying. By removing reinforcement for bullying and creating an environment that discourages this type of aggression, this program has decreased bullying by at least 50%. A major goal of these violence prevention programs is the development of prosocial behavior and finding ways to replace unacceptable aggression with prosocial behaviors.

Prosocial Behavior

Prosocial behavior ■
Behavior that benefits someone else or society.

If you are walking across campus struggling with a big stack of books, what is the likelihood that someone you don't know will help you carry them? If you drop them, will someone help you pick them up? Psychologists who try to find out when, and under what conditions, someone will help someone else are examining the likelihood of *prosocial behavior*—behavior that benefits someone else or society.

Prosocial behavior may offer no obvious benefit to the person performing it and may even involve some personal risk or sacrifice.

Altruism: Helping without Rewards

Why did two coworkers in the World Trade Center towers carry a paraplegic woman down the stairs on September 11, 2001? Their actions gave the woman a chance to live but made their own safety less likely. What compelled Mother Teresa to wander Calcutta's streets and attend to the wounds and diseases of people no one else would touch? Why did Oskar Schindler risk his life to save 1,100 Jews from the Nazi death camps during World War II? Psychologists have a name for such behaviors but have trouble explaining why they happen.

Altruism consists of behaviors that are intended to benefit another person or people, even at a cost to the person offering the assistance. Altruism is one type of prosocial behavior, and many examples exist. However, the existence of altruism has proven to be a bit of a puzzle for psychological theories. For example, many behaviorists contend that reinforcement and rewards are critically important for behavior (see Chapter 8), and altruistic behaviors seem to offer no obvious reinforcement (and may involve some aversive consequences). However, people who help others may receive social reinforcement in the form of the approval of others, high regard, or praise. They may also learn that by helping others, they are more likely to receive future help. If people help because they believe they will receive help from those they assist, then they are not really behaving altruistically (Batson et al., 2002). Their behavior is really self-centered. Such considerations have led psychologists to question whether any behavior is really altruistic.

Theorists who take an evolutionary view argue that behavior that may appear altruistic is really motivated by self-interest (Kenrick, Ackerman, & Ledlow, 2003). Consider the following scenario: An infant crawls into a busy street as a truck is approaching. The mother darts in front of the oncoming vehicle and carries her child to safety. This mother has risked her life to save the life of her child. Evolutionary psychologists argue that the mother commits her brave deed to protect her genetic investment in her child. If the child dies, then the genes passed on to that child do not survive.

The woman who puts herself in danger to save her child may not be aware of the basis for her actions, but one of the principles of natural selection is that propagation occurs at the level of the gene, not the individual (Hamilton, 1964). Many studies support the finding that degree of relationship is an important factor in how willing people are to help others (Korchmaros & Kenny, 2001). However, noting that altruism for relatives is part of our evolved heritage does not explain how that heritage is translated into behavior. The evolutionary explanation for any behavior is stated in terms of an ultimate cause, but behaviors also need to be explained in terms of more immediate (or proximate) causes. Altruism might be hypothesized as based in the emotional relationships that people form with their relatives. Alternatively, emotional feelings for others and empathy might provide the basis for the development of altruism, regardless of any biological relationship (Batson et al., 2002). People don't always help others who need it, however, and psychologists have also researched the reasons for that behavior.

Altruism ■ Behaviors that are intended to benefit another person or people, even at a cost to the person offering the assistance.

The Bystander Effect

In New York City in 1964, Kitty Genovese was walking home when a man approached her with a knife. A chase ensued, during which she screamed for help. He stabbed her, and she continued screaming. When lights came on in nearby buildings, the attacker fled. But when he saw that no one was coming to his victim's aid, he returned and stabbed her again. The assault lasted more than 30 minutes and was heard by dozens of neighbors, yet no one came to the victim's aid. Kitty Genovese died, and many people began to question why no one did anything to help her. Psychologists investigated what came to be known as the *bystander effect*, the unwillingness to help exhibited by witnesses to an event, which increases when there are more observers.

Bibb Latané and John Darley (1970) investigated the bystander effect in a series of studies. They found that people are faced with several decisions when they are in a problematic situation. First, they have to decide what is going on (whether or not there is an emergency), and they must decide whether to introduce themselves into a problematic situation. They are often misled by the *apparent* lack of concern among other bystanders, concluding that nothing really bad is going on after all—so they don't help. Latané and Darley reasoned that when people are aware of other bystanders in an emergency situation, they might also be less likely to help because they experience *diffusion of responsibility* (the feeling that they cannot be held individually responsible). To test their hypothesis, the researchers brought college students into a laboratory and told them they were going to be involved in a study of people who were interested in discussing college life in New York City. The researchers explained that in the interest of preserving people's anonymity, a group discussion would be held over an intercom system rather than face to face, and that each person in the group would talk in turn. In fact, there was only one actual participant in each experimental session. Assistants who worked for the researchers prerecorded all the other conversations.

The researchers manipulated the number of people the actual naive participant thought were in the discussion group and measured whether and how fast that participant reported that one of the other "participants" seemed to be suffering a seizure. At some point in the discussion, one of the research assistants began behaving strangely and then indicated that he needed help. At this point, the researchers began timing the speed of the real participant's response. Each participant was led to believe that his or her discussion group contained two, three, or six people, and this belief influenced the participant's response to the situation. Eighty-five percent of participants who thought they were the only bystanders responded before the end of the seizure; 62% of the participants who thought there was only one other bystander responded by the end of the seizure. When participants thought there were four additional bystanders, only 31% responded (see **Figure 14.5**).

In general, the presence of others lowers a person's probability of offering help, and even imagining other people present can prompt a diffusion of responsibility and a decreased chance of helping (Garcia et al., 2002). But bystanders will help under some conditions. People's self-concepts and previous experiences affect their willingness to intercede. Bystanders who see themselves as more competent to deal with the specific emergency are more likely to help (Pantin & Carver, 1982). If the

Bystander effect ■ The unwillingness to help exhibited by witnesses to an event, which increases when there are more observers.

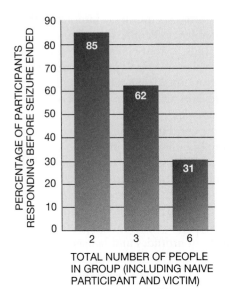

Figure 14.5
The Bystander Effect
In a classic study of the bystander effect, as the number of people in the group increased, the willingness of the naive participant to inform the experimenter that the victim had suffered a seizure decreased. (From Latané & Darley, 1970.)

person who needs help has a relationship with the person who can offer help, assistance is more likely (Batson, 1990). Research in cities of various sizes shows that people who live in smaller communities are more likely to help, and people who live in large urban areas are less likely to render help (Levine et al., 1994). Characteristics of the victim and bystander make a difference—women are more likely to be willing to intervene on behalf of children and men on behalf of women (Laner, Benin, & Ventrone, 2001). Men respond to emergencies requiring physical action more often than women do (Salminen & Glad, 1992). However, women are more likely than men to help friends and, in doing so, have a tendency to use nurturing rather than problem solving (Belansky & Boggiano, 1994).

So, if you were in need of help, your best chance of receiving it would be in a situation with only one person or a few other people present. You can increase your chances of receiving help when more people are present if you request assistance of one specific person rather than asking for help from the group in general (Markey, 2000).

Studies on the bystander effect indicate that being in a group is a different experience than being with one other person. The reluctance of bystanders to help someone in distress also hints that the influence of the group is not necessarily positive. Social psychologists study both the positive and the negative effects of becoming part of a group.

What Are the Effects of Identifying with a Group?

Membership in any group conveys certain advantages, which is why people belong to all kinds of groups. There are formal groups, such as the American Association of University Students, and informal ones, such as a lunch group of coworkers. A *group* can be any number of people who share a common purpose,

Group ■ Any number of people who share a common purpose, goals, characteristics, or interests and who interact with each other and develop some degree of interdependence.

goals, characteristics, or interests and who interact with each other and develop some degree of interdependence. People riding in an elevator together are not a group. Should they get stuck in that elevator for several hours, they would become a group, because they would experience a common goal (escape) and would interact and develop interdependence in trying to achieve that goal.

Unlike the people stuck in an elevator, most people become part of a group by joining voluntarily. Doing so indicates that a person agrees with or has a serious interest in the group's purpose. For example, a person's membership in the National Alliance for the Mentally Ill indicates an interest in ending misunderstanding and misrepresentation of mental illness. The groups we join help us clarify our own identity and show that identity to the world.

Similarity is a factor not only in interpersonal attraction but also in the formation and maintenance of groups. The people in a group tend to be similar in terms of attitudes, beliefs, and even age and gender, although people actually tend to overestimate the similarity of attitudes and beliefs within groups to which they belong (Holtz, 2004). Fraternities and sororities are good examples of groups that contain people who are similar in many ways. In addition, processes that occur within groups tend to make members more similar than they were when they joined because each group has a set of *norms* that govern behavior within the group. People who join groups soon learn what behaviors are allowed and expected and which are not, and they tend to change their behavior to be consistent with group norms. Group norms vary from group to group. For example, behavior that fits the group norm for your fraternity likely differs from behavior that seems appropriate in your church group.

Therefore, joining a group has an impact on an individual's behavior, and the mutual influences that occur in groups are of interest to social psychologists. The exploration of individual behavior in groups has revealed the positive effects of groups, such as the energizing effects of being a group member. But research has also revealed that becoming part of a group tends to foster patterns of thinking that can lead to stereotyping, prejudice, and discrimination.

Group Performance

When you work as part of a group, is your performance better or worse than when you work alone? Social psychology research on working in groups has not yielded a simple answer to this question. Some effects of working in groups tend to boost performance, but others lead to poorer outcomes.

Social Facilitation

Social facilitation ■
A change in behavior that occurs when people are (or believe they are) in the presence of other people.

Individual behavior is affected not only by membership in a group but also by the mere presence of others. *Social facilitation* is a change in behavior that occurs when people are (or believe they are) in the presence of other people. For example, people may tend to perform better when others are present. However, people's performance may also be worse in the presence of others, so the presence of others does not always produce facilitation.

Whether the presence of others is likely to change a person's behavior for better or worse is illustrated in **Figure 14.6**. This figure is based on Robert Zajonc's (1965) *drive theory of social facilitation*. According to Zajonc, the presence of others produces heightened arousal, which leads to a greater likelihood that an individual will successfully perform a simple or well-practiced behavior. Heightened arousal, however, will impair performance of more complex and less well-practiced behaviors, which explains both the facilitation and the inhibition effects of the presence of others. Although these performance effects are clear, their underlying reason is still debated among social psychologists. The ways in which people evaluate and think about observers may also help to explain social facilitation (Aiello & Douthitt, 2001).

Social Loafing

Research on social facilitation has revealed that, under some circumstances, people perform worse in a group than as individuals. Impaired performance can also occur when individuals decrease effort and productivity as a result of working in a group, an effect known as *social loafing.* Suppose you and your friends join forces in an effort to win a tug of war. Do you expend as much effort as a member of the group as you would if you had to win the tug of war alone? Probably not. Research confirms the social loafing effect. In an experiment in which participants were instructed to clap their hands and cheer, they clapped and cheered less loudly when they were part of a group (Latané, Williams, & Harkins, 1979).

Social loafing ■ The decrease in effort and productivity that occurs when individuals work in a group rather than independently.

Research indicates that social loafing tends to occur when it is difficult to identify individual performance within a group—that is, when poor performance may go undetected and exceptional performance may go unrecognized. In such a situation, people feel less pressure to work hard or efficiently (Guerin, 2003). Group size contributes to this effect, and as group size increases, individual members believe their efforts are more dispensable—that the group can function without their help.

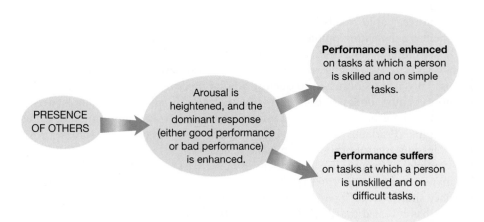

Figure 14.6
Social Facilitation
The presence of others may either help or hinder a person's performance. The presence of others heightens arousal, and heightened arousal leads to better performance on tasks a person is good at and worse performance on tasks the person finds difficult.

"Let someone else do it" becomes the prevailing view. Such findings are evident cross-culturally; for example, even Japanese students, who come from a society that stresses cohesion and group cooperation, worked less hard when they were working together than when working alone (Kugihara, 1999).

Social loafing is minimized when the task is attractive and rewarding and when the group is cohesive and committed to task performance (Karau & Williams, 2001). It is also less apparent when the group is small, when the members know one another well, and when a group leader calls on individuals by name or lets it be known that individual performance may be evaluated (Williams, Harkins, & Latané, 1981). Thus, a wide array of variables can alter the extent of social loafing, and this phenomenon may be connected to social facilitation as well as to factors that operate in group decision making. Indeed, all of these group effects may be related to the extent of individual accountability for the consequences of group performance (Guerin, 2003).

Group Decision Making

During the late 1990s, investors were making fortunes by investing in Internet-based companies (dot.coms). Some cautious investment bankers looked at the financial analyses for these companies and doubted that they were good investments, but that caution was widely questioned and often ignored (Hawn, 2002). In boardroom after boardroom, investors made the decision to give millions of dollars to companies with poor business plans and uncertain futures. Many otherwise cautious investment bankers succumbed to the pressure and enthusiasm of their colleagues and endorsed these risky investments. Their companies lost millions of dollars in the dom.com bust that put California's Silicon Valley into an economic depression. Social psychologists who have researched group interactions have discovered that group decision making may result in poorer decisions than the individuals might have made on their own.

Groupthink ■ The tendency of people in a group to seek agreement with one another when reaching a decision, rather than effectively evaluating the options.

Studies of decision making have often focused on *groupthink*—the tendency of people in a group to seek agreement with one another when reaching a decision, rather than effectively evaluating the options. Groupthink occurs when group members reinforce shared beliefs in the interest of getting along. The group discourages disagreement, dissenting opinions, and the realistic evaluation of options (Janis, 1983). Groupthink discredits or ignores information not held in common, which means that cohesive groups are more likely to exhibit groupthink than less cohesive groups. This process occurred frequently among investment bankers evaluating the option of loaning money to dot.coms (Hawn, 2002). In addition, strong leaders often insulate a group from outside information to keep the group thinking along the same line (Pratkanis & Turner, 1999; Raven, 1998). **Figure 14.7** summarizes the factors leading to groupthink and its characteristics.

Examples of groupthink are evident in many crises, such as the failed Bay of Pigs invasion of Cuba in 1961 (Janis, 1983) and NASA's ill-fated decision to launch the space shuttle *Challenger* in 1986 (Moorhead, Ference, & Neck, 1991). However, research has revealed that the effect of groupthink is not as strong as originally claimed (Paulus, 1998). Nevertheless, groupthink *can* happen, and researchers

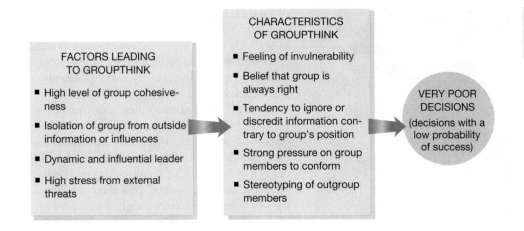

Figure 14.7
Groupthink:
Development
and Results

continue to study it because it is a defective process that people should guard against, by being aware of variables that may create it, as well as factors that help defend against it (Shelton, 2000).

Another group decision-making process pushes people toward more extreme rather than more moderate decisions. When people evaluate options on their own and then discuss those options in a group, they tend to shift their opinions, or become polarized. Shifts or exaggerations in group members' attitudes or behaviors that take place after group discussion are referred to as ***group polarization*** (Zuber, Crott, & Werner, 1992). In an individual, such a shift is known as a *choice shift*. This phenomenon was definitely a factor in the overenthusiastic investment in dot.com enterprises. Investors shifted their choices to more and more risky investments, often as a result of a group decision.

Unrestrained Group Behavior

The presence of other people can arouse people (social facilitation), can make them less active (social loafing), can lead them to make poor decisions (groupthink), or can cause them to take extreme views (group polarization). When placed in a group, normally thoughtful people have been known to make bad decisions and even to exhibit deviant behaviors.

The view that no single individual can be held responsible for the behavior of a group arises out of ***deindividuation***—the process by which individuals lose their self-awareness and distinctive personality in the context of a group, which may lead them to engage in behavior that they would not do in another context. Deindividuation (and its accompanying arousal) can lead to shifts in people's perceptions of how their behavior will be viewed—and thus to less controlled, less self-conscious, or less careful decisions about behavior. With deindividuation, people alter their thoughts about their decisions.

In an experiment conducted by Philip Zimbardo at Stanford University in 1971, normal, well-adjusted college students were asked to dress and act as either prisoners

Group polarization ■ Shifts or exaggerations in group members' attitudes or behaviors as a result of group discussion.

Deindividuation ■ The process by which individuals lose their self-awareness and distinctive personality in the context of a group, which may lead them to engage in behavior that they would not do in another context.

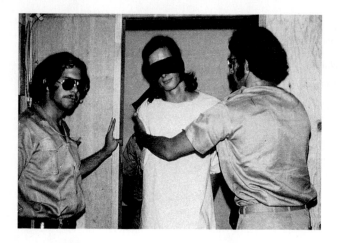

In a study that came to be known as the Stanford Prison Experiment, researchers asked normal, well-adjusted students to dress and act as prisoners and guards.

or guards. Guards were given uniforms, clubs, and whistles; prisoners were arrested, dressed in smocks, put in leg irons, and locked in cells. Although who was to be a prisoner and who was to be a guard was determined randomly, within a few days, both "guards" and "prisoners" had assumed their roles much too completely. The guards were harassing and degrading prisoners, who became obedient and even withdrawn. Let's consider this study in light of the concept of deindividuation. Both "guards" and "prisoners" lost their individuality when the researchers assigned numbers to the prisoners but allowed the guards to be identified by name. These changes stripped away many of the participants' personal characteristics and placed them in a situation that emphasized the group to which they belonged. Groups such as the military and various cults use deindividuation to encourage their members to conform. In boot camp, military recruits are made to feel that they are there to serve the group, not their own ends. In a cult, members are persuaded to go along with group beliefs and acquire a sense of obligation to the group by performing increasingly difficult acts on the group's behalf.

As the Stanford Prison Experiment demonstrated, an individual's behavior in a group often becomes distorted, more extreme, and less rational; the group makes members feel less accountable for their own actions. Researchers are increasingly asserting that people's interpretation of the setting in which they find themselves holds the key to understanding deindividuated behavior.

Identifying as a Group Member

Working in a group leads to different decisions and behavior than people would exhibit when working alone, which demonstrates the power of the group. This power includes the ability to affect the three components that social psychologists concentrate on—thoughts, feelings, and behavior. These effects appear in the processes of *stereotyping* (which is a thought process), *prejudice* (which is an attitude or a feeling), and *discrimination* (which is a behavior).

Stereotyping

Stereotypes ■ Fixed, overly simple, and often erroneous ideas about the traits, attitudes, and behaviors of groups of people, based on assumptions that all members of a given group are alike.

People's perceptions and cognitions about others are often inaccurate. *Stereotypes* are fixed, overly simple, and often erroneous ideas about the traits, attitudes, and behaviors of groups of people. Stereotypes exist for just about every type of group to which a person can belong, including many that the person did not choose. People can form stereotypes about people's religion, political affiliation, and taste in movies, all of which are choices. However, some of the strongest stereotyping applies to characteristics that are not voluntary choices, such as skin color, ethnicity, and gender.

Several types of cognitive processes underlie stereotyping. One prerequisite for stereotyping is the process of forming categories. People form hundreds of categories, which may or may not relate to stereotyping. For example, *food* is an important category, and for many college students, so is *football fan*. Stereotyping requires that individuals perceive characteristics of others and find both similarities and differences between those characteristics and their own. These perceptions and classifications allow people to form cognitive groupings into which they place other individuals.

People cannot easily analyze all the relevant data about any one thing, let alone the massive amount of information needed to sort items into categories. People thus devise mental shortcuts to help them make decisions (Fiske, 1998, 2002). One of those shortcuts is to stereotype individuals and the groups they belong to. Stereotyping involves streamlined thinking that overlooks details, which makes it easier to place items into categories—for example, all Latinos/Latinas, all homeless people, all men, all lawyers. In the process, some information is overlooked or minimized while other information is highlighted. This selective combination forms the basis for stereotyping by making categories more distinct than they really are. Items within a category become more like each other, and, at the same time, the differences between items inside and outside the category become sharper.

People are able to maintain a stereotype in part by forming an *illusory correlation,* an unsubstantiated and incorrect connection between two events or situations that appear to be related. The relationship between a group and the behavior of individual members of the group is an illusion, but the appearance of an actual relationship allows people to maintain false beliefs about group members. For example, elementary school children demonstrated illusory correlation when they exhibited memory distortion for gender-stereotypical behavior (Susskind, 2003). Children overestimated how often they saw pictures of women and men performing gender-stereotypical activities (such as a woman knitting) compared to pictures showing activities that went against gender stereotypes (such as a woman being a police officer), even when the frequencies of the activities were really equal. These 7- to 9-year-olds observed situations that involved no relationship between gender and behavior, yet they misremembered what they had seen to support their stereotypes.

Stereotypes not only influence evaluations of others, they affect how people think about themselves. A demonstration of the power of stereotypes comes from studies on the topic of *stereotype threat,* which occurs when a person is in a situation that puts her or him at risk for confirming a negative stereotype. For example, one of the negative stereotypes about African Americans is that they do not do well in school, and one of the negative stereotypes about women is that they don't do well in math. Thus, African Americans taking an important educational ability test and women taking an important math test may be affected by stereotype threat. Research indicates that this threat affects performance, making people more likely to perform poorly, which confirms the negative stereotype (Smith & White, 2002; Steele, 1997; Steele & Aronson, 1995).

In devising stereotypes, people develop ideas about people in an ***ingroup,*** a group to which they personally belong, versus those in an ***outgroup,*** a group to which they do not personally belong. The division of the world into ingroups and

Ingroup ▪ Any group to which a person belongs.

Outgroup ▪ Any group to which a person does not belong.

Social categorization ▪ The process of dividing the world into ingroups and outgroups.

outgroups—or "us" versus "them"—is known as *social categorization.* Belonging to a group affects thinking about the group members and about those not in the group. People tend to see themselves and other members of an ingroup in a favorable light and to have less positive attitudes about outgroups; these attitudes bolster members' self-esteem and may occur practically automatically (Hewstone, Rubin, & Willis, 2002). The cognitive distortions of stereotyping combined with perceptions about ingroups and outgroups can lead to prejudice.

Prejudice and Discrimination

Prejudice ▪ A negative evaluation of an entire group of people, based on unfavorable stereotypes about the group.

Prejudice is a negative evaluation of an entire group of people that is based on unfavorable stereotypes about the group. Stereotypes feed prejudice because of the thinking that underlies stereotyping—it's easier to develop negative evaluations when holding simplified and distorted thoughts about a group. Prejudice, as an attitude, is based on a cognitive belief ("All Xs are stupid") but also has an emotional element ("I hate those Xs"). When prejudice is translated into behavior, it is called *discrimination*—behavior targeted at individuals or groups and intended to hold them apart and treat them differently ("I have talked to my neighbors about keeping those Xs out"). The negative attitudes of prejudice promote the behavior of discrimination.

Discrimination ▪ Behavior targeted at individuals or groups and intended to hold them apart and treat them differently.

Several psychological theories strive to explain prejudice. Some evolutionary psychologists have suggested that the social situations of human prehistory, when our ancestors lived in hunter-gatherer groups, predisposed modern humans to certain types of group interactions (Krebs & Denton, 1997). According to this view, the advantages of cooperation within groups and the disadvantages of competition between groups resulted in an innate tendency to perceive ingroups in positive ways and outgroups in more negative terms. Thus, evolutionary psychologists see a built-in tendency toward prejudice. However, evolutionary psychologists do not accept that these tendencies will inevitably be translated into a range of negative evaluations or into the behavior of discrimination (Pinker, 2002).

Personality psychologists have investigated the *authoritarian personality,* which is characteristic of individuals who are prone to prejudice (Adorno et al., 1950; Altemeyer, 1988). Authoritarian individuals may have been fearful and anxious as children and may have been raised by cold, unloving parents who regularly used physical punishment. To gain control and mastery as adults, such individuals become aggressive and controlling toward others. They see the world in absolutes—good versus bad, black versus white. They also tend to blame others for their problems and to become prejudiced toward those they blame. Ideas about the relationship between personality and prejudice have roots in psychoanalytic theory, which many psychologists consider outdated, but people find it easy to identify examples of the authoritarian personality.

If people are placed in a situation where they must compete against others for scarce resources, the competition can foster negative feelings about those competitors. *Realistic conflict theory* asserts that individuals learn to dislike specific individuals (competitors) and then generalize that dislike to whole classes of similar individuals (people of particular races, religions, or cultures). Gordon Allport claimed that the arousal due to competition is followed by erroneous generalizations that create specific prejudice toward members of minority groups (Allport, 1954/1979; Gaines & Reed, 1995). This process turns minorities that are seen as economic competitors into scapegoats—for example, every new wave of immigrants that has come to the United States (the Italians, Chinese, and Irish in the early part of the 20th century and people from the Caribbean and Central America more recently) has been cast in this role. Research with children, adolescents, and adults shows that people who are initially seen as friends or as neutral are sometimes treated badly if they become competitors.

According to social learning theory, children learn to be prejudiced: They watch parents or other adults engage in acts of discrimination and hear their prejudiced opinions and comments. After children have observed such behaviors, they are reinforced (operant conditioning) for exhibiting similar behaviors. Thus, through imitation and reinforcement, a prejudiced view is transmitted from one generation to the next. Like the other theories of prejudice, social learning theory offers an explanation for the origin and frequency of prejudice.

Prejudice and discrimination were once widespread in U.S. society, but after the passage of the Civil Rights Act of 1964 and the laws that forbid discrimination in the workplace and housing, changes occurred. It became more difficult to discriminate openly and less acceptable to voice prejudice publicly. However, prejudice and discrimination continued, and in the late 1970s and 1980s, researchers began to look at the more subtle forms of prejudice that had developed. One branch of that research concentrates on the automatic nature of prejudice and stereotyping.

Prejudice is an attitude, and like other attitudes, it can be automatic. Stereotypes can also operate automatically, pushing people toward prejudice and discrimination. Research into the subtle manner in which stereotyped judgments are produced shows that a person may not be aware of his or her own automatic negative reactions to a racial or gender group and may even regard such negative feelings as objectionable (Greenwald & Banaji, 1995; Greenwald et al., 2002).

These unconscious effects of automatic, stereotypical associations appear in a computer-based test called the Implicit Association Test (Greenwald, McGhee, & Schwartz, 1998), which assesses implicit (unconscious or automatic) associations in a number of areas, such as ethnicity, political affiliation, and gender. For example, the Implicit Association Test can assess if participants have an implicit association that reflects the stereotype that only men (and not women) can be scientists by asking participants to respond as quickly and accurately as possible to a series of words and word pairings. Participants are asked to rapidly classify each of a number of words into the categories of *male* or *female* by pressing different keys on a computer keyboard and then to classify a number of words into either the category of *science* or the category of *humanities*. Then, they must classify combinations that include stereotypical pairings (such as *man–neuroscience* and *woman–arts*) and counter-stereotypical pairings (such as *woman–chemistry* and *man–English*). The speed of reactions measures how closely associated the concepts are; faster reactions indicate closer associations. When participants classify the gender-stereotypical pairs faster than they do the counter-stereotypical pairings, they demonstrate their implicit association of these stereotypes. (If you would like to take one of the Implicit

Association Tests, go to http://implicit.harvard.edu/implicit.) Research has even linked reactions on the Implicit Association Test with different patterns of activity in the brain.

Modern racism and subtle sexism are topics of interest to contemporary social psychologists. *Modern racism* is prejudice and discrimination by Whites against African Americans, expressed in subtle ways and in safe situations rather than blatantly or openly (McConahay, 1986). For example, Whites may rationalize their rejection of minorities with statements such as "An African American manager just wouldn't fit in well in this office" or "An African American coach would find it difficult to work with a team of mostly White players." Modern racism prevents Whites from voting for African American candidates, even when they might agree with the political views of those candidates. Modern racism consists of conscious, explicit attitudes expressed in subtle ways. However, people may hold conscious, explicit attitudes that support equality yet also hold implicit attitudes that support racism (Dovidio & Gaertner, 1998). Research indicates that people with such implicit attitudes behave in racially biased ways (Nail, Harton, & Decker, 2003). This finding demonstrates the relationship between implicit attitudes and discrimination.

Sexism is a type of prejudice based on gender, with roots in stereotyping and a long history of discrimination. Like racism, sexism has become less acceptable and has undergone changes to more subtle forms. Many people hold some negative beliefs about women (such as that they are less competent and intelligent than men), but they also hold positive beliefs that are also sexist (such as that women should be put on a pedestal and that women should be protected). Although such positive beliefs put women in a special position, they also put women at a disadvantage, because women are perceived as weak and inferior. This combination of positive and negative beliefs about women is called *ambivalent sexism*, and its effects include prejudice and discrimination (Fiske et al., 2002; Glick & Fiske, 1997, 2001).

Is it possible to combat our own prejudice when we are not aware of it? Can we overcome prejudice and discrimination? Our tendency to favor ingroups and to feel less positively about outgroups does not inspire optimism about ending prejudice and discrimination. However, research suggests that a negative attitude or stereotype does not necessarily lead to action (Fiske, 2002). Prejudice does not guarantee discrimination. The world might be a better place if we could do away with prejudice, but prejudice is an attitude, whereas discrimination is behavior. If we can treat others fairly, that may be more important than having a better opinion of them but treating them unfairly. However, decreasing prejudice may be a process of redrawing the circle of the ingroup so that it contains all of humanity (Pinker, 2002).

How Do Others Affect the Individual?

When news reports about prisoner abuse at the Abu Ghraib prison in Iraq began to appear, many people were shocked that U.S. soldiers had subjected Iraqi prisoners to humiliation and abuse. But to psychologists familiar with the Stanford Prison experiments discussed earlier in the chapter, the prison avoids brutality was predictable. What factors led the military guards at Abu Ghraib to mistreat prisoners? Both the students in Zimbardo's experiment and the military guards at Abu Ghraib may have behaved differently in other circumstances, which demonstrates the power of social influence in a given situation. *Social influence* refers to the ways in which people alter the attitudes or behaviors of others, either directly or indirectly. Important phenomena related to social influence are conformity, compliance, and obedience. All of these affected the behavior of both guards and prisoners in the Stanford Prison Experiment and at Abu Ghraib.

Social influence ■ The ways in which people alter the attitudes or behaviors of others, either directly or indirectly.

Conformity

When someone changes her or his attitudes or behaviors so that they are consistent with those of other people or with social norms, the person is exhibiting *conformity*. He or she is trying to fit in. People conform to the behaviors and attitudes of their peers or families. Conformity may prompt the adoption of positive, prosocial behaviors such as wearing seat belts, volunteering time and money to a charity, or buying only products that are safe for the environment. For example, a young man who has joined a fraternity that has a commitment to community service may volunteer to be a big brother in the Big Brothers/Big Sisters program, which he may not have done before he joined the fraternity. However, conformity may also produce deviant, antisocial behaviors, such as drug abuse, fraternity hazing, or mob violence. The new fraternity brother may also get drunk at fraternity parties, when he did not do so before joining the fraternity.

Conformity ■ People's tendency to change their attitudes or behaviors so that they are consistent with those of other people or with social norms.

Groups strongly influence conformity. Solomon Asch (1907–1996) found that people in a group adopt its standards. Imagine this situation: You have agreed to participate in an experiment and are seated at a table with four other students. The experimenter holds up a card with two straight lines printed on it and asks each of you to pick which of the two lines is longer, A or B. You quickly discover that the task is simple. The experimenter holds up successive cards showing pairs of lines; in each case, every participant correctly identifies the longer line. After several rounds, you notice that the first person has chosen line A instead of line B, although B is obviously longer. You are surprised when the second person also chooses line A, then the third, then the fourth. Your turn is next. You are sure that line B is longer. What do you do?

In 1951, Asch performed an experiment like this to explore conformity. Seven to nine people were brought together and asked to judge which of three lines matched a standard line (see **Figure 14.8**). However, only one group member—the naive participant—was unaware of the true purpose of the study. The other group members—confederates of the researcher—followed directions to give false answers to try to influence the naive participant. Asch found that some naive participants went along with the group, even though the majority answer was obviously wrong and even though the group exerted no explicit pressure to conform.

It turns out that the number of confederates a researcher uses is a critical variable in such situations. When 1 or 2 individuals collaborate with the researcher, the naive participant shows considerably less tendency to conform than when 10 do. Another important variable is the existence of dissenting votes (Asch, 1955). If even 1 of 15 collaborating participants disagrees with the others, the naive participant is more likely to choose the correct line.

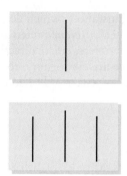

Figure 14.8
Asch's Classic Study of Conformity
Participants were shown cards like these and asked to choose the line on the lower card that was the same length as the line on the upper card. The confederates deliberately chose incorrect answers to see if the unsuspecting participant would go along with the majority.

Cultural values are an important factor in conformity. People in the United States and most of Western Europe value independence and give positive ratings to nonconformity (although they tend to conform) (Jetten, Postmes, & McAuliffe, 2002). People who live in collectivist cultures do not value nonconformity; rather, they tend to see fitting in with the group as positive and desirable. These differences lead to the prediction that people in individualist cultures should show lower levels of conformity than people in collectivist cultures, which is generally confirmed by cross-cultural research (Bond & Smith, 1996; Smith & Bond, 1999). Studies similar to Asch's line judgment procedure revealed that culture influences the amount of conformity in many countries. The difference was in the expected direction, with people living in collectivist cultures such as those of Japan, Brazil, Hong Kong, and several African nations exhibiting much higher levels of conformity than people in the United States and Western Europe. Furthermore, conformity has decreased in the United States since the time of Asch's research; people are less likely to conform now than in the past.

Asch used no obvious technique to urge participants in his study to conform to the group. But what if compliance is the goal? Do people change their behavior even more when pressured to do so?

Compliance

Bosses, salespeople, parents, and politicians all apply the principles of social psychology when they rely on tried-and-true techniques that have been used for decades to influence people, change behaviors, and obtain favors. Social psychologists have tried to understand how social influence makes these techniques work. Less work has been done on how people can successfully resist the pressures to conform and comply, but social psychologists are also beginning to research this topic.

Techniques for Inducing Compliance

One way to get someone to do as you ask is to begin by asking for a small favor. In other words, get your foot in the door. The essence of the *foot-in-the-door technique* is that a person who grants a small request is likely to comply with a larger request later. Ask to borrow a quarter today, next week ask for a dollar, and next month ask for money for your tuition. The escalation of compliance works only if the person first grants the small favor, and it works best if there is some time between the first small request and the later larger one. This is one of the standard techniques used by salespeople and telephone solicitors (Cialdini, 2004).

The *door-in-the-face technique* may seem just the opposite of foot-in-the-door, but it works too. To use this approach, first ask for something large or outrageous, and then ask for something much smaller and more reasonable. For example, ask a friend to lend you $1,000; after being turned down, ask to borrow $5. Your friend may give you the smaller amount. The door-in-the-face technique assumes that a person is more likely to grant a small request after turning down a larger one, and it works best if there is little time between requests. This technique even works in cyberspace—in an Internet solicitation, researchers found that when they used the door-in-the-face technique in presenting requests, people were more likely to give the smaller amount than when they were initially asked for the smaller amount (Guéguen, 2003).

Fund-raisers for universities, religious groups, and charitable organizations know that they often get a positive response when they simply ask, which describes the *ask-and-ye-shall-receive technique*. When people are asked for money for what they perceive as a good cause and when they have given to the cause before, the request is likely to be successful, especially if the person is in a good mood (Forgas, 2002). Research indicates that asking for a specific amount, especially an amount that corresponds to a specific denomination of printed money, boosts donations (Desmet & Feinberg, 2003).

The *low-ball technique* involves obtaining a commitment and then raising the cost of the commitment. Once the decision is made, people tend to stick with their commitment, even if the stakes increase. For example, if a man agrees to buy a car for $14,000, he may still buy it even if several options are added on, increasing the price to $15,000. The low-ball technique worked in a study that asked people to take care of a person's dog while the person visited someone in the hospital (Guéguen, Pascual, & Dagot, 2002). Those who found out after they had agreed that the visit would take 30 minutes were more likely to comply than those who found out the extent of the time commitment before they agreed.

These specific techniques use principles of social influence to get people to comply with requests. Each of these techniques can be successful, but they also may backfire. Whenever people feel their freedom of choice is being unjustly restricted, they are motivated to re-establish it. Jack Brehm (1966) termed this form of negative influence *reactance*—it is the negative response evoked when there is an inconsistency between a person's self-image as being free to choose and the person's realization that someone is trying to force him or her to choose a particular alternative. When people believe that they are being tricked or coerced, reactance may result.

However, the sales profession and the advertising industry are built around the success of techniques for gaining compliance. Clearly, these techniques often work. In addition, the broader principles of social influence that underlie these techniques apply not only to compliance but also to social interactions in groups.

Reactance ■ The negative response evoked when there is an inconsistency between a person's self-image as being free to choose and the person's realization that someone is trying to force him or her to choose a particular alternative.

The Basis for Social Influence

Psychologist Robert Cialdini (2004; Cialdini & Goldstein, 2004) has researched techniques and processes associated with conformity and compliance, and he has concluded that humans share certain tendencies that underlie the effectiveness of these types of social influence. These include the tendency to seek consistency, which operates when people change their attitudes after experiencing cognitive dissonance, and the tendency to seek social validation, which operates when people conform by matching their behavior to those around them, as Asch's study demonstrated. In addition, Cialdini has focused on how reciprocation, liking, scarcity, and authority relate to compliance.

Reciprocation occurs in situations in which people exchange something such as a gift or favor. When someone does a favor for you, you feel the urge to do something for that person. Many charitable organizations include small gifts such as address labels in their solicitations, and this technique is effective in boosting contributions, because people have the tendency to reciprocate (Cialdini, 2004). This principle extends to compliance with requests and probably explains the success of the door-in-the-face technique—the person making the large request has conceded by making a smaller one, so the other person feels the pressure to reciprocate by granting the smaller request.

Liking affects compliance in that people tend to comply with those whom they like. Therefore, the factors that govern interpersonal attraction also apply to compliance. We tend to grant the requests of people whom we find attractive more often than those of people whom we find unattractive, even if the people are strangers. However, we are more likely to grant the request of a friend than a stranger asking for the same thing. The number of successful home-based sales companies is a tribute to this tendency—Tupperware, Mary Kay cosmetics, Avon, and many other products have benefited from having sales reps sell to their friends rather than to strangers. To gain the benefits of liking, salespeople who are strangers try to be friendly and likeable.

Scarcity is also a factor in people's decisions. When people perceive a product to be scarce, they are more likely to buy it, and they value it more highly. Sales pitches that emphasize the rarity of a commodity or the limited time of an offer make use of this behavioral tendency.

Authority is another important factor in compliance. People have the tendency to accept the word of experts, and a great deal of advertising takes advantage of this tendency to promote products. Some advertising appeals use legitimate authority, but others give only the appearance of authority. For example, many commercials show actors dressed as doctors, who urge viewers to buy medications. The appearance of authority can be convincing, and consumers would benefit from developing strategies to resist such illegitimate appeals to authority.

The tendency to comply with the orders of someone in authority is strong. This tendency became apparent in one of the most famous series of experiments in social psychology.

Obedience to Authority

Obedience is compliance with the orders of another person or group of people. The studies on obedience by Stanley Milgram (1933–1984) are classic, and his results and interpretations still generate debate. Focusing on the extent to which an individual

Obedience ■
Compliance with the orders of another person or group of people.

will obey another person, Milgram's work showed that ordinary people are remarkably willing to comply with the requests of others, especially if they see the others as legitimate authority figures.

In 1963, at Yale University, Milgram placed an advertisement in the local newspaper for adult male volunteers and asked them to report to a laboratory on campus at a specified time. When each participant arrived, another person also reported. The two men were told that the study was an experiment on the effect of punishment on learning, and they drew pieces of paper to determine who was to be the teacher and who was to be the learner.

In fact, only one of the men was a participant; the other was a confederate of the experimenter and was playing a role. The drawing was rigged so that the participant was always the teacher and the confederate was the learner. Milgram was not actually interested in the effect of punishment on learning. Instead, he was investigating the extent to which the participant would obey orders that he received during the course of the experiment.

The learner/confederate was taken to a room and connected to a "shock generator." The teacher/participant went into the adjoining room, which contained a box with 30 switches, having labels that ranged from "Slight Shock" to "Danger: Severe Shock." The teacher communicated with the learner through a microphone. The learner was given a test, and the teacher/participant was instructed to listen to his answers and punish him when he answered incorrectly. The instructions directed the participant to increase the shock with each incorrect answer. As the test continued, the learner continued to give incorrect answers, and he protested as if he was suffering increasing pain; then he stopped responding and instead pounded on the wall of the room. The experimenter told the participant to treat the learner's lack of response as an error and to continue increasing the levels of shock. The learner/confederate was not actually receiving shocks, but the deception was very convincing. The participants believed that they were delivering actual shocks.

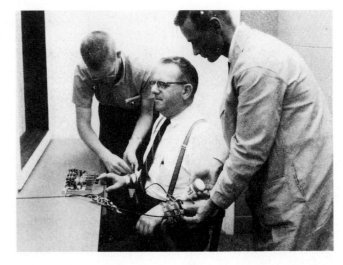

Most of Milgram's participants were obedient—65% of them continued to shock the learner until they had delivered even the highest level of shock, as **Figure 14.9** on page 552 shows. The experimenter had no real authority over the participants, yet they delivered what they believed to be severe shocks to a person whom they had just met. These results suggest that people have a tendency to obey authority.

Not all of Milgram's participants were obedient, and additional research has clarified some of the conditions under which people are more and less likely to obey. For example, the presence of another person who refuses to participate reduces the

Milgram's work focused on the extent to which an individual will obey. His studies showed that ordinary people were remarkably willing to comply with the wishes of others.

Figure 14.9
Milgram's
Obedience
Study

(Milgram, 1963)

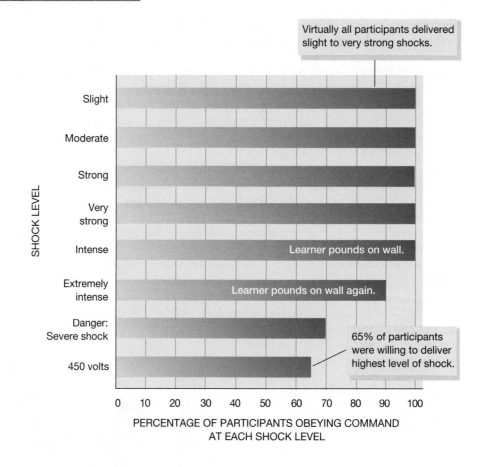

probability of obedience to as little as 10% (Milgram, 1965; Powers & Geen, 1972). These results suggest that the process of social validation operates in this situation, that people look to those around them to determine what is appropriate behavior In addition, conducting the study at the prestigious Yale University influenced the participants by creating *background authority*. A similar study in an office building showed a lower percentage of participants willing to deliver the maximum amount of shock—48% versus 65% (Milgram, 1965). However, 48% is still a high percentage of people who are willing to obey someone with no real authority over them.

When instructed to deliver a shock, most of Milgram's participants did what they were told (Blass, 2000). Why did so many participants obey the wishes of the authority figure? People in many cultures have personal histories of obeying authority figures such as teachers and parents. As adults, they maintain that respect for authority and apply it to other authority figures such as employers, judges, government leaders, and so on. This explanation suggests that Milgram's findings should apply to other cultures, and research confirms that prediction (Smith & Bond, 1999). People tend to obey those in authority, and such obedience is highly valued in cultures around the world. In studies similar to Milgram's, people in the

United States, Italy, Jordan, Spain, Germany, Austria, and the Netherlands show rates of obedience over 60%. People in Australia and Great Britain are somewhat less obedient, but still comply around 50% of the time. Milgram's findings apply to men and women, old and young.

In any psychological study, researchers worry about ethical issues, and Milgram's experimental methods certainly raised such issues. Not only was deception employed, but there was potential for psychological harm to those who completed the study. Participants did not actually harm anyone, but they believed that they were doing so until the study was over. After the study, Milgram's participants received a debriefing that presented them with the details of the study and showed them that they had not actually harmed the other person. Nevertheless, critics argued, the participants came to realize that they were capable of inflicting severe pain on other people. Milgram therefore had a psychiatrist interview a sample of his obedient participants a year later. No evidence of psychological trauma or injury was found. Moreover, one study reported that participants in an obedience experiment similar to Milgram's viewed their participation as a positive experience. They did not regret having participated, nor did they report any short-term negative psychological effects (Ring, Wallston, & Corey, 1970). Today, more stringent ethical constraints mean that studies like Milgram's are not allowed.

Studies of obedience also relate to the Abu Ghraib prison story. Some newspaper reports have contended that the guards at the military prison at Abu Ghraib were not only influenced by the situation to play the role of guard and behave viciously toward Iraqi prisoners, but they were also acting under orders to do so from military intelligence officers or others in authority (Schwartz, 2004). Thus, these military guards were influenced by two powerful forces that push people toward behaviors they might otherwise not perform. Studies of social influence show that situational components exert powerful influences on individuals, gender matters little, and the group is very important (Blass, 2000, 2002).

Summary and Review

WHAT IS THE SOCIAL SELF?

What is the role of the self in social psychology?

Social psychology is the scientific study of how individual thoughts, feelings, and behaviors are influenced by social situations. Social psychologists tend to concentrate on each of these elements and to interpret behavior in these terms. pp. 510–511

The self is the starting point for social psychologists, who see it in terms of *self-concept* (thoughts), *self-esteem* (feelings), and *self-presentation* (behavior). pp. 511–512

What does social cognition involve?

Social cognition is the process of analyzing and interpreting events, other people, oneself, and the world in general. *Attributions* are people's explanations of the causes of behavior. A person may decide that the causes of a behavior are disposi-tional (in which case he or she is making an *internal attribution*) or situational (an *external attribution*). Attribution helps people make sense of the world and under-stand their own and others' behavior. pp. 512–514

What are some common attribution errors?

Errors in attribution include the *self-serving bias*—by which people find ways to think well of themselves. The *fundamental attribution error* is the tendency to attribute other people's behavior to dispositional (internal) rather than situational (external) causes. The *actor–observer effect* is the tendency to attribute the failings of others to dispositional causes but to attribute one's own failings to situational causes. pp. 514–516

HOW ARE ATTITUDES RELATED TO BEHAVIOR?

What are the important dimensions of attitudes?

Attitudes are patterns of feelings and beliefs about other people, ideas, or objects, which are usually evaluative, are based in people's experiences, and shape their future behavior. Attitudes have cognitive, emotional, and behavioral dimensions and are formed early in life, through learning processes. Attitudes that people report and describe are explicit attitudes, and those that are involuntary and unconscious are implicit attitudes. pp. 516–518

Do attitudes determine behavior, or does behavior influence attitudes?

Although it seems logical that attitudes determine behavior, there are many situa-tions in which they do not. People are sensitive to the *social norms* of a situation, which may lead them to act in ways that are inconsistent with their attitudes. Inconsistency can prompt people to change their attitudes, and both *self-perception theory* and the theory of *cognitive dissonance* predict that behavior influences atti-tudes rather than the other way around. pp. 518–521

What are the key components of attitude change?

There are four key components of attitude change: the communicator, the communi-cation, the medium, and the audience. Each of these affects the extent of change that may take place. The *elaboration likelihood model* asserts that there are two routes to attitude change: The central route emphasizes rational evaluation and decision making; the peripheral route, which is more indirect and superficial, emphasizes less careful and more emotional evaluation. pp. 521–523

HOW DO PEOPLE RELATE TO EACH OTHER?

What is key to interpersonal attraction?

Interpersonal attraction is the tendency of one person to evaluate another person (or a symbol or image of another person) in a positive way. People tend to become attracted to people with whom they come in contact frequently and who have attitudes similar to their own. Physical attractiveness is also an important factor in attraction, and evolutionary psychology emphasizes attractiveness in mate selection. However, standards of attractiveness show cultural variations, which is not consistent with evolutionary theory. pp. 524–526

Distinguish between friendship and love.

Friendship is a relationship that involves closeness and commitment. According to Sternberg, love has three components: intimacy (a sense of emotional closeness), commitment (the extent to which a relationship is permanent), and passion (arousal, some of it sexual, some intellectual, and some inspirational). Consummate love includes all three components. *Intimacy* is a state of being or feeling that leads each person in a relationship to self-disclose. *Equity theory* holds that people attempt to maintain stable, consistent relationships in which members' contributions are balanced. Attachment style also relates to relationship stability. Individuals with secure attachment styles tend to have better and more stable relationships. pp. 527–530

Describe aggression, prosocial behavior, and the bystander effect.

Aggression is any behavior intended to harm another person or thing. Despite the assumption that aggression is innate, research evidence indicates that aggressive behavior is influenced by imitation and learning, which suggests that media violence has the potential to promote aggressive behavior in viewers. Men are more aggressive than women in some, but not all, situations, and they use direct and *indirect aggression* more than women do. Attempts to decrease aggression show some success. In addition, encouraging *prosocial behavior* can be beneficial. *Altruism*, behaviors that benefit someone else or society without personal benefit, may actually be motivated by self-interest. The *bystander effect* is the unwillingness of witnesses to an event to help, especially when there are numerous observers. pp. 530–537

WHAT ARE THE EFFECTS OF IDENTIFYING WITH A GROUP?

How is behavior affected by being in a group?

A *group* is any number of people who share a common purpose, goals, characteristics, or interests and who interact with each other and develop some degree of interdependence. *Social facilitation* is a change in behavior that occurs when people believe they are in the presence of other people. This change can be either positive or negative. *Social loafing* is a decrease in an individual's effort and productivity as a result of working in a group. pp. 537–540

Processes that may affect group decision making, positively or negatively, include *groupthink*, the tendency of people in a group to agree with one another rather than effectively evaluating options, and *group polarization*, the exaggeration of pre-existing attitudes as a result of group discussion. Groups may also contribute to unacceptable behavior, and *deindividuation*, the process by which the individuals in a group lose their self-awareness, self-perception, and concern with evaluation, is a factor in antisocial and even violent behavior. pp. 540–542

What are some results of identifying as group member?

Stereotypes are fixed, overly simple, and often erroneous ideas about traits, attitudes, and behaviors of groups of people. Stereotyping results from overly simplified cognitive processing and includes some distortion. Through the process of *social categorization*, people establish *ingroups* and *outgroups*. Stereotypes make prejudice possible. *Prejudice* is a negative evaluation of an entire group of people. Prejudice often leads to *discrimination*, behavior targeted at individuals or groups with the aim of holding them apart and treating them differently. Prejudice is complex, with explicit and implicit components. The implicit, unconscious elements of prejudice make modern racism and subtle sexism difficult to eradicate. pp. 542–546

HOW DO OTHERS AFFECT THE INDIVIDUAL?

Explain how social influence leads to conformity and compliance.

Social influence refers to the ways people alter the attitudes or behavior of others, either directly or indirectly. Social influence can result in *conformity,* which occurs when a person changes his or her attitudes or behaviors so that they are consistent with those of other people or with social norms. Compliance occurs when a person grants the request of another. The foot-in-the-door, door-in-the-face, ask-and-ye-shall-receive, and low-ball techniques have a long history of success and are based on principles of social influence such as reciprocation, liking, fear of scarcity, and perceived authority. However, feelings of coercion may lead to *reactance,* and a refusal to perform the behavior requested. pp. 546–550

What is obedience, and what did Milgram's studies of obedience demonstrate?

Obedience is compliance with the orders of another person or group of people. Milgram's studies demonstrated that an individual's ability to resist coercion is limited. However, the presence of an ally who refuses to obey reduces obedience, which underscores the importance of social influences on behavior. pp. 550–553

CHAPTER 15

Stress and Health Psychology

What Is Stress?   557
  Definition of Stress
  Sources of Stress
  Responses to Stress
  Stress and Health

How Do People Cope
with Stress?   572
  What Is Coping?
  Factors That Influence Coping
  Coping Strategies

What Is Health Psychology?   579
  How Does Behavior Affect Health and Illness?
  The Psychology of Being Sick
  Adopting a Healthier Lifestyle
  Health Psychology and the Future

Summary and Review   589

In this chapter, we examine the nature of stress, discuss how to cope with it, and consider the interrelationship of health and stress. We also look into how learned skills and personality work together to influence the ability to cope with stress in day-to-day life.

What Is Stress?

Launching into tirades at coworkers or friends, slamming doors, refusing to discuss a problem, and drinking too much alcohol are ways in which some people deal with stress. Others manage stress in more positive ways, for example, by scheduling time more effectively, getting enough sleep, or exercising. One person may have a high-pressure job that affects her social life and causes regular migraines. A coworker may experience the same amount of stress but manage it in more positive ways, without suffering negative health consequences. Such examples illustrate an important point: Different people evaluate and handle stress in different ways.

Definition of Stress

The definition of stress depends on which theory is being considered. Theorists and researchers have defined stress in terms of external forces, internal responses, and an interaction of the two. According to Hans Selye, one of the first researchers to consider its effects, *stress* is a nonspecific response to real or imagined challenges or threats. Theorists who consider stress a response define a *stressor* as an environmental stimulus that affects an organism, producing physical and psychological effects such as physical arousal and psychological tension and anxiety. According to Richard Lazarus, stress results from a cognitive appraisal of any situation involving challenge or threat. According to this view, not all people view a situation in the same way; *a person must appraise a situation as stressful for it to be stressful.* Each of these views of stress has been important in guiding psychologists' research. Let's examine them.

Stress ■ A nonspecific response to real or imagined challenges or threats, as a result of a cognitive appraisal by the individual.

Stressor ■ An environmental stimulus that affects an organism physically or psychologically, producing anxiety, tension, and physiological arousal.

Selye's General Adaptation Syndrome

In the 1930s, Hans Selye (1907–1982) began a systematic study of stressors and stress. He investigated the physiological changes in animals and people who were experiencing various amounts of stress. Selye conceptualized people's responses to stress in terms of a *general adaptation syndrome* (1956, 1976). (A *syndrome* is a set of responses; in the case of stress, these responses include behaviors and physical symptoms.) Selye's work initiated thousands of studies on stress and stress reactions, and Selye himself published more than 1,600 articles on the topic.

According to Selye, people respond to any stressor similarly, regardless of the type of stressor. This response occurs in three stages: (1) an initial short-term stage of alarm, (2) a longer period of resistance, and (3) a final stage of exhaustion (see **Figure 15.1**).

Figure 15.1
Selye's General Adaptation Syndrome
According to Hans Selye, a person's response to a stressor can be divided into three stages: alarm, resistance, and exhaustion. (Selye, 1976)

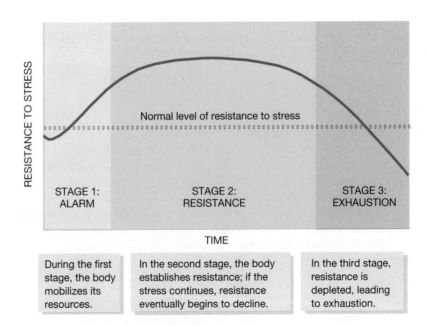

RESISTANCE TO STRESS

Normal level of resistance to stress

STAGE 1: ALARM

STAGE 2: RESISTANCE

STAGE 3: EXHAUSTION

TIME

During the first stage, the body mobilizes its resources.

In the second stage, the body establishes resistance; if the stress continues, resistance eventually begins to decline.

In the third stage, resistance is depleted, leading to exhaustion.

During the *alarm stage,* people experience increased physiological arousal. They become excited, anxious, or frightened. Bodily resources are mobilized. Metabolism speeds up dramatically, heart rate increases, and blood is diverted from the skin and extremities to the brain and internal organs. These responses involve activation of the sympathetic nervous system (see Chapter 3).

When stress continues, people's responses change. Because people cannot remain highly aroused for very long, *resistance* occurs. During this stage, physiological and behavioral responses become more moderate (but still elevated) and sustained. People in the resistance stage may appear normal, but their physiological responses are not. They continue to operate at a heightened level, and they are often irritable, impatient, and easy to anger; they may experience loss of appetite, sleep problems, headaches, or hormone imbalances. This stage can persist for a few hours, several days, or even years, although eventually resistance begins to decline.

The final stage is *exhaustion.* Stress saps psychological and physical energy, and adaptability is depleted. If people don't reduce their level of stress, they can become so exhausted physically, mentally, and emotionally that they give up. Selye believed that serious illness or even death could occur in the exhaustion stage.

This view of stress predicts that any event that requires adaptation is stressful and that illness and stress are linked; that is, stress can make people sick. To test the link between stress and illness, researchers must have ways to measure stress, and several assessment techniques have been created.

The Holmes–Rahe Scale

Among the many researchers inspired by Selye to study stressors and refine the theory were Thomas Holmes and Richard Rahe. Their basic assumption was that stressful life events, especially when they occur in combination, damage health (Holmes & Rahe, 1967; Rahe, 1989). *Stressful life events* are prominent events in a person's life that necessitate change. This change requires adaptation, which is the source of stress. Even positive events, such as getting a new job or starting college, produce stress. Building Table 15.1 contrasts Selye's view of stress with that of Holmes and Rahe.

To test their assumption, the researchers devised the Social Readjustment Rating Scale—basically, a list on which individuals circle significant life events (changes) that they've recently experienced. Holmes and Rahe developed a rating for each of

Building Table 15.1

VIEWS OF STRESS: SELYE AND HOLMES AND RAHE

Theorist(s)	Stress comes from	Consequences of stress
Selye	Stimuli in the environment	General adaptation syndrome; too much stress causes illness.
Holmes and Rahe	Life events	Stress accumulating within a limited time period requires too much adaptation, which may cause illness.

the life events on their scale. The death of a spouse, divorce, and serious illness rate high as stressors, whereas changes in eating or sleeping habits and vacations rate lower (but still require some adaptation). A person taking the test indicates the number of events experienced, typically within the past year. A person's total score reflects the cumulative impact of stressful life events, and according to Holmes and Rahe, provides an index of the likelihood that the person will suffer stress-related illness in the next 2 years. According to Holmes and Rahe, a person who scores above 300 points will be much more likely to suffer a stress-induced physical illness than a person whose score is below 150.

The Holmes–Rahe scale has been sharply criticized for a number of reasons, but it remains in wide use (Scully, Tosi, & Banning, 2000). Among the criticisms is that the scale lacks validity, because most people whose scores are high do not get sick. That is, the relationship between life events and illness is not that strong. Another criticism stems from the fact that the scale was based on a study of young male Navy personnel, whose characteristics do not necessarily match those of the general U.S. population, especially those of older people, women, and low-income individuals (Shalowitz et al., 1998). In addition, some argue that focusing on major life events is not a comprehensive way to conceptualize stress.

The Undergraduate Stress Questionnaire (Crandall, Preisler, & Aussprung, 1992) is an alternative to the Holmes–Rahe scale that includes events common in the lives of college students. Students whose scores are high are more likely to need health care than students with lower scores.

As many items on the Undergraduate Stress Questionnaire reflect, most stressors are not major events or crises; people experience stress from day-to-day irritations and difficulties. These irritations and their effects are more closely related to the conceptualization of stress formulated by Richard Lazarus.

Lazarus and Stress

Richard Lazarus (1993), a leader in the study of emotion and stress, asserts that people *actively negotiate* between the demands of the environment (stressors) and personal beliefs and behaviors. That is, stress is the result of an interaction between events and people's evaluation of those events. Cognitive researchers refer to this active negotiation as *cognitive appraisal*. Sometimes the arousal that stressors bring about is evaluated as positive, sometimes it is perceived as negative. Thinking "I can't possibly handle this!" is likely to lead to more stress than is thinking "This is my chance to really show my stuff!" (Lyubomirsky & Tucker, 1998). Lazarus's formulation recognizes that everyone experiences stress at times, but also emphasizes that stress is what people interpret; it is a response by an individual. See Figure 15.2 for an overview of the responses that occur after a cognitive appraisal has identified an event as a stressor. Building Table 15.2 contrasts Lazarus's view of stress with those of Selye and Holmes and Rahe.

What influences an individual's cognitive appraisal, determining whether a particular event will be stressful? The answer lies in the extent to which the person is familiar with the event, how much the person has anticipated the event, and how much control the person has over the event and the response to it. For example, the first day

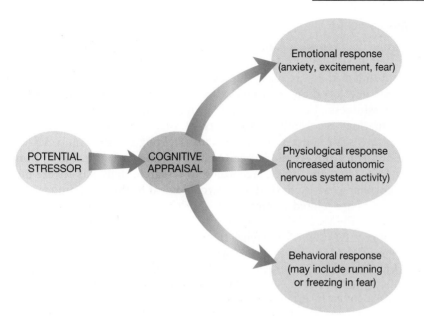

Figure 15.2
The Effect of
Cognitive
Appraisal on
Responses to
Stressors
Depending on how a potential stressor (for example, being sent into a game that is tied in overtime) is evaluated, its impact can vary emotionally, physiologically, and behaviorally.

of a new course brings both excitement and some apprehension about the instructor's expectations and whether the time commitment for the course will be burdensome. By the second or third time the class meets, going to class is usually much less worrisome. When people can predict events and are familiar with them, they feel more in control, more confident that they can have some impact on the outcome. That is, when people believe that they have the resources to cope with an event, that event is not a threat. When people believe that they lack the resources to cope with a threat, then they experience stress. Lazarus's view of stress includes a wider variety of potential stressors than either Selye's or Holmes and Rahe's, plus the individual evaluation of these events. The concept of hassles—inconveniences and annoyances in everyday life—as stressors, rather than major life events, has led to the development of an alternative assessment.

Building Table 15.2

VIEWS OF STRESS: SELYE, HOLMES AND RAHE, AND LAZARUS

Theorist(s)	Stress comes from	Consequences of stress
Selye	Stimuli in the environment	General adaptation syndrome; too much stress causes illness.
Holmes and Rahe	Life events	Stress accumulating within a limited time period requires too much adaptation, which may cause illness.
Lazarus	Appraisals of events	Consequences depend on appraisals and resources for coping.

The Hassles Scale

Even routine life events can cause stress. Indeed, Lazarus and his colleagues propose that routine events are more likely to lead to the experience of stress and physical problems than are major life events. Lazarus and his colleagues (Kanner et al., 1981) developed an assessment, the Hassles Scale, that is designed to measure the stressfulness of everyday events. People completing this assessment rated 117 life situations according to how much of a hassle each is. A streamlined revision of this scale contains only 53 items (DeLongis, Folkman, & Lazarus, 1988). Both major life events and daily hassles relate to health, but in somewhat different ways (Cassidy, 2000). According to research, daily hassles are more strongly correlated with physical and psychological health than are major life events. Hassles are related to reports of health-related symptoms among women (Erlandsson & Eklund, 2003), worsening of symptoms of a chronic disease (Pawlak et al., 2003), and headaches (Fernandez & Sheffield, 1996). Therefore, the concept of hassles adds to the explanation of the relationship between stress and health. Table 15.1 presents the ten daily hassles most frequently cited as sources of stress.

Sources of Stress

As you've seen, researchers have defined stressors in terms of both major life events and hassles. As a result, they have examined the impacts of a variety of stressors, ranging from war and earthquakes to traffic congestion and deadlines.

Table 15.1

LIFE'S LITTLE HASSLES—THE TOP TEN

1. Concerns about weight

2. Health of a family member

3. Rising prices of common goods

4. Home maintenance

5. Too many things to do

6. Misplacing or losing things

7. Yard work or outside home maintenance

8. Property, investments, or taxes

9. Crime

10. Physical appearance

Sources: Kanner et al. (1981)

Catastrophes and Stress

Throughout history, many *catastrophes*—events of massive proportion and destruction—have affected people and communities profoundly. Catastrophes can be either natural disasters, such as earthquakes or hurricanes, or events resulting from human actions, such as airplane crashes and terrorist attacks.

How do people respond to catastrophes and cope with stressors of such magnitude? People are amazingly resilient, but the impact of a catastrophe—of a natural disaster, war, or traumatic event—can be long-lasting. Mental health practitioners see many clients who continue to suffer long after an event that has changed their lives. For example, most people experienced horror in response to the terror attacks of September 11, 2001. However, some people experienced severe symptoms, and those who repeatedly watched the television replays of the attacks tended to be more severely affected (Ahern et al., 2002). Severe and prolonged responses to trauma or catastrophe constitute a psychological disorder termed *posttraumatic stress disorder (PTSD)*. Although many people were traumatized by the 9/11 terrorist attacks, most did not develop PTSD, even among residents of New York City (Galea et al., 2003). Those who did develop the disorder tended to be individuals who had a history of emotional problems, poor support from a social network of family and friends, and a tendency to see life events in a negative way (McNally, Bryant, & Ehlers, 2003).

PTSD was first recognized in military veterans who experienced combat, and the diagnosis became common among Vietnam veterans. Common symptoms of PTSD are vivid, intrusive recollections or re-experiences of the traumatic event and occasional lapses of normal consciousness (Ehlers, Hackmann, & Michael, 2004). People with PTSD may develop anxiety, depression, or exceptionally aggressive behavior (Metzger et al., 2004). Decades after the traumatic event, these individuals may still endure sleep problems, the reliving of painful experiences, difficulty in concentrating, and feelings of panic and alienation (Kagan et al., 1999; Krakow et al., 2004). Such behaviors may eventually interfere with daily functioning, family interactions, and health.

The diagnosis of PTSD was once restricted to combat veterans, but a wide variety of experiences are now known to raise the risk for PTSD. Veterans are at elevated risk (Schnurr, Lunney, & Sengupta, 2004), but victims of all types of trauma, especially those who are the victims of violence, are also at risk (Dohrenwend, 2000). An increasing number of studies focus on the psychological aftermath of natural disasters such as earthquakes, tornadoes, and floods (Wang et al., 2000), traumatic events such as rape and childhood sexual abuse (Ruggiero et al., 2004), the displacement of refugees (Kroll, 2003; Weine et al., 2001), severe accidents (Schnyder et al., 2001), and domestic abuse (Sharhabani-Arzy et al., 2003).

Despite the initial emphasis on male military veterans, women have been found to be more susceptible to PTSD than men (Stein, Walker, & Forde, 2000). Rape, violence at the hands of an intimate partner (a lover or spouse), and sexual abuse during childhood are all experiences that elevate the risk for PTSD, and women are more likely than men to have such experiences (Golding, 1999). The likelihood that a person will experience PTSD at some time during his or her life is about 10% for women and about 5% for men (Ozer & Weiss, 2004).

Posttraumatic stress disorder (PTSD) ■ A psychological disorder that may become evident in a person who has undergone extreme stress caused by some trauma or disaster and whose symptoms include vivid, intrusive recollections or re-experiences of the traumatic event and occasional lapses of normal consciousness.

Unhealthy Environments and Stress

Environmental psychology ■ The study of how physical settings affect human behavior and how people change their environment.

Environmental psychology is the study of how physical settings affect human behavior and how people change their environment. Environmental psychologists study issues such as the effects of crowding, how personal space can be changed to meet changing needs, and group reactions to environmental threats.

Environmental psychologists recognize that some environments may be hazardous to people's health. For example, a neighborhood environment may contain many factors that contribute to stress. Toxins and pollution are stressors that also carry health risks, but some neighborhoods contain other factors that produce stress. Many of these factors result from poverty. People in low socioeconomic groups often live in overcrowded and substandard housing, lack access to services such as banks and stores, experience high noise levels, and live with the threat of crime and violence (Taylor, Repetti, & Seeman, 1997). These conditions produce the type of stressors called hassles, such as having trouble cashing a check, and also the type of life events that are related to PTSD, such as witnessing or being the victim of violence. Research indicates that for those in poor inner-city neighborhoods the chances of witnessing violence are high, and this experience creates stress and anxiety (Margolin & Gordis, 2004).

Poverty-stricken environments can be detrimental in several ways—they can threaten people's safety, prevent them from forming social ties, and expose them to conflicts in schools, in families, and on the street. Thus, people who live in poverty are at higher risk for stress, anxiety, and associated health consequences.

Even people who are wealthy do not escape the stresses of urban living. Eric Graig (1993) devised the term *urban press* to describe the multitude of factors that combine in modern city life, including crowding, pollution, noise, commuting stress, and fear of crime. Graig argues that these factors are a constant presence for all city dwellers, and their combination produces a level of stress that exceeds what would result from considering each factor individually.

Although unhealthy environments produce stress, the evolutionary point of view hypothesizes that environmental stress may not be all bad. In this view, environmental stress is a force for natural selection and evolution (Hoffmann & Hercus, 2000). Just as the presence of chemical pesticides has produced changes in some insect species, making them resistant to these chemicals, the environmental stressors in modern city life may promote rapid evolution as people adapt to these stressful conditions.

Discrimination and Stress

Discrimination is an all-too-common experience; people perceive that they are discriminated against on the basis of ethnicity, sex, and sexual orientation. A survey of people in the United States showed that 33.5% of participants said they had been the targets of some major incident of discrimination (Kessler, Mickelson, & Williams, 1999). In addition, there was a substantial correlation between perception of discrimination and mental health problems. All ethnic groups are affected by life events and daily hassles, but racial discrimination adds to the stress for members of ethnic minorities.

Discrimination and unfair treatment are factors in feeling stressed, and one study of African Americans found that the combination of discrimination and poverty had a potent effect in producing stress (Schultz et al., 2000). Indeed, racism has been identified as a significant factor in the experience of stress for African American men (Bennett et al., 2004) and young adults (Sellers et al., 2003). Latinas/Latinos and Asian Americans are also victims of discrimination. Both those who have newly immigrated and those who are among the second generation to live in the United States experience this stress (Romero & Roberts, 2003).

In addition to discrimination due to their ethnicity, immigrants are subject to additional stressors. For example, language problems and the lack of familiarity with the new culture they find themselves in can turn daily tasks into hassles. Gaining familiarity with the culture eases this stress, but some immigrants do this more quickly and easily than others (Torres & Rollock, 2004). Immigrants are more likely than native-born people to be poor and thus affected by the stressors related to poverty. In addition, immigrants may have been exposed to politically related violence before leaving their country of origin, and that experience is a risk to their psychological health (Eisenman et al., 2003). Those who are second-generation Americans also must deal with becoming bicultural if they want to continue to relate to their families.

Sexism is also a stressor. Women are the targets of sexist discrimination and harassment much more often than men are (Swim et al., 2001), and these experiences produce stress (Klonoff, Landrine, & Campbell, 2000). Indeed, women who experience a high level of sexist discrimination react to it with physical as well as psychological symptoms. Discrimination is a significant factor in the lives of many women.

Gays, lesbians, and bisexuals also experience discrimination because of their sexual orientation (Meyer, 2003). Having any sexual orientation other than heterosexual can be a stigma in U.S. culture. Individuals who reveal their sexual orientation often experience rejection by or serious conflict with family, friends, or coworkers. Revealing a gay or lesbian sexual orientation puts a person in a position of facing discrimination, but being "in the closet" is also stressful (Cole et al., 1996); either choice potentially brings stress.

Personal Factors and Stress

Catastrophic events and the stressors associated with poverty and discrimination are obviously not the only sources of stress; people may also face stress in the workplace, in personal relationships, and as a result of time pressure. Stress is an unavoidable part of modern life.

The workplace environment may expose people to stressors such as toxins, noise, and crowding. However, work presents an additional array of stressors. People tend to think of executives who must make major decisions as experiencing a great deal of stress, but research indicates that the freedom to make decisions actually *decreases* a job's stress (de Jonge et al., 2000; Karasek, 1979). Demanding jobs are not necessarily stressful, because when workers feel in control of the important aspects of their jobs, they may see high demands as a challenge. In contrast, workers whose jobs impose high demands on them but give them little latitude to make decisions or to exert control are more likely to feel stressed than challenged (Grebner et al., 2004). Those whose jobs are high in stress include middle-level managers, inner-city high school teachers, customer service agents, waiters and waitresses, and emergency workers. These jobs combine high demands and low decision-making power, and this combination tends to create stress for workers.

A number of additional factors associated with work can produce stress. Workers who feel many constraints on their job-related behaviors, who work at night, who work a lot of overtime, and who are under constant deadline pressure experience increased stress (Ettner & Grzywacz, 2001). Workers who feel adequately rewarded for their job performance are less likely to feel stressed than workers who feel that their rewards are not proportional to their efforts on the job (de Jonge et al., 2000).

The stresses created by low-level jobs apply to women as well as to men (Wamala et al., 2000). A comparison of female managers and female clerks showed that the clerks evaluated stressors as more severe, less controllable, and more distressing than did the managers (Long, 1998). However, high-level jobs can be stressful as well. For example, physicians are feeling increasingly stressed by the time pressure of keeping up with scheduled appointments, the amount of work they are required to do, and the demands made by patients and administrators (Chopra, Sotile, & Sotile, 2004). Indeed, physicians are among those in the human services professions who are most vulnerable to burnout (Maslach, Schaufeli, & Leiter, 2001). *Burnout* is a state of emotional and physical exhaustion, lowered productivity, and feelings of isolation, often caused by work-related pressures. Since the origin of this concept in the 1970s, a great deal of research has indicated that people in a variety of job situations experience burnout. When a job requires some emotional commitment to people, as in counseling, health care, and teaching, burnout is more common (Baird & Jenkins, 2003; Dollard et al., 2003).

Burnout ■ A state of emotional and physical exhaustion, lowered productivity, and feelings of isolation, often caused by work-related pressures.

Therefore, all types of jobs have stressful components, and very few people escape on-the-job stress. However, despite the many possibilities for stress on the job, being without a job or being uncertain about continued employment is even more stressful (Ferrie et al., 2001).

Personal relationships are another potential source of stress, both at work and at home. At work, deterioration of relationships with coworkers is a source of stress (Sias et al., 2004), but support from supervisors and coworkers can make a critical difference in the experience of stress on the job. Supportive relationships are positive factors in work and life satisfaction.

Cultural values exert an impact on stress at work. A study of workers in Hong Kong tested the influence on workplace functioning of the Confucian cultural values of harmoniousness, collectivism, and hard work (Sui, 2003). The results showed that these values relate to higher worker satisfaction and moderate the effects of workplace stress. Thus, although job stress is not confined to Western countries, the Western values of individualism and competition may add to such stress.

Work stress and personal relationships also intersect in the balancing of job and family commitments. This balancing act is a major source of stress, especially for women. Traditionally, women have been the primary caregivers for children and family. As women have entered the workforce, they have retained the caregiver role, creating difficulties in fulfilling both roles (Cinamon & Rich, 2002; Williams, 2000). Also, men who are committed to family life and wish to devote more time to home and family experience problems in justifying this choice to their employers (Hochschild, 1997). These men are in a position similar to that of employed women who feel the time pressures and conflicts of balancing family and work demands. The need to balance family and work is an important issue for workers, and when their employers take this issue into account, work satisfaction increases (Greenhaus, Collins, & Shaw, 2003).

Marriage is celebrated as a positive event in many cultures. Nonetheless, adjusting to married life means becoming familiar with new experiences, responding in new ways, and having less control over many aspects of day-to-day life—all of which can be stressful. Even among couples married for years, disagreement and conflicts arise and create stress (Hatch & Bulcroft, 2004). Unfulfilled expectations about emotional support and sharing of responsibilities are sources of conflict. For example, when one partner feels that she or he is doing the "emotional work" to maintain the relationship, this inequity produces stress for the overburdened partner (Strazdins & Broom, 2004). Another potential source of inequity is the distribution of household chores. Few men perform as many household chores as women do, and men's lack of contribution to household work is a significant source of stress for many women (Coltrane, 2000). Finally, stresses in marriage are certainly problems, but ending a marriage creates even more stress (Hetherington & Kelly, 2002).

Lack of time is another common source of stress. Everyone faces deadlines: Students must complete tests before class ends, auto workers must keep pace with the assembly line, taxpayers must file their returns by April 15. People have only a limited number of hours each day in which to accomplish what they need to do, and people who work long hours often have little time for leisure and family. If people do not handle time pressure successfully, they may begin to feel overloaded and stressed. Employees in different work settings mention time pressure as a source of stress (Robinson, 2004; Salanova et al., 2003). People can create more time by working either on a flexible schedule or for fewer hours, but most people are unwilling to take either option, even when their employer offers them this choice (Fast & Frederick, 1996). Indeed, the trend is in the opposite direction, with people working more hours per week, creating greater time pressure in their lives (Major, Klein, & Ehrhart, 2002).

Stress affects children as well as adults. Children's stress arises from some of the same sources, including exposure to violence, time pressure, and family conflicts, but children also have to deal with school stressors such as high-stakes testing and school bullies (Hardy, 2003). In addition, children are much less able to change or control the circumstances in which they find themselves, which increases their stress. Like adults, children often show their stress response in physical symptoms (Walker et al., 2001).

Responses to Stress

People respond to stress physically as well as behaviorally and psychologically, and individuals vary in their responses on each of these levels. The basic idea underlying the work of many researchers is that stress activates responses that can result in disease. Psychologists who study stress typically divide the stress reaction into physiological and behavioral components.

The Physiology of Stress

Researchers such as James, Lange, and Cannon (discussed in Chapter 12) studied emotions, focusing on *when* an emotion was felt in response to a stressful incident—during or after the actual event. Physiologically, the response to stress is characterized by arousal of the sympathetic division of the autonomic nervous system (see Chapter 3). This arousal is evident in a host of changes, including increased heart rate, faster but shallower breathing, higher blood pressure, sweating palms, dilation of the pupils, and other changes. This array of physiological changes begins in the brain, with the activation of the pituitary gland and the hypothalamus. The pituitary releases a hormone that stimulates the adrenal glands, located above the kidneys. These glands in turn release several hormones, including cortisol and epinephrine, each of which produces specific effects. The action of epinephrine produces the variety of physiological reactions associated with stress. Cortisol allows for the mobilization of energy reserves and decreases in inflammation. **Figure 15.3** shows these responses. The arousal of the sympathetic division of the autonomic nervous system mobilizes the body for fight or flight in response to a stressor. It may be that this

Figure 15.3
Physiological Reactions to Stress
Perceiving stress initiates a cascade of effects, including arousal of the autonomic nervous system and release of hormones.

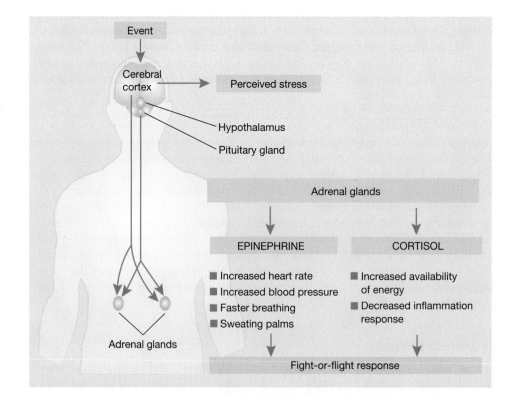

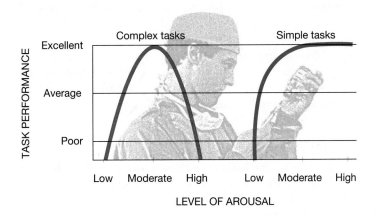

Figure 15.4
Effects of
Arousal on Task
Performance
When arousal is
low, task perfor-
mance is poor or
nonexistent.
Performance is
usually best at
moderate levels of
arousal. High levels
of arousal usually
improve perform-
ance on simple
tasks but impair
performance on
complex tasks
(such as surgery).

response was more adaptive in human evolutionary history than it is today—cortisol and epinephrine and the reactions they provoke have been implicated in the health risks related to stress.

Behavior and Stress

Behaviorally, stress and arousal are related. As we saw in Chapter 12, psychologist Donald Hebb (1972) argued that effective behavior depends on a person's state of arousal. When people are moderately aroused, they behave with optimal effectiveness. When they are underaroused, they lack the stimulation to behave effectively. Overarousal tends to produce disorganized and ineffective behavior, particularly if the tasks people undertake are complex. (**Figure 15.4** shows the effects of arousal on task performance.)

A moderate level of stress and the arousal that accompanies it may be unavoidable and even desirable. Arousal keeps people active and involved. It impels students to study, athletes to excel during competition, and workers to perform better on the job. In short, some levels of stress and arousal can be beneficial, helping people achieve their potential. However, high levels of stress are not adaptive and are related to a variety of diseases.

Stress and Health

Doctors advise many people to lower their levels of stress to avoid becoming sick, and research supports this advice. However, the effect of stress on the development of disease is not direct. Rather, stress causes a range of physiological responses that can initiate various disease processes. Stress has a relationship to many diseases, including the five major causes of death in the United States: heart disease, cancer, stroke, lung disease, and accidental injuries. However, researchers have been most interested in the link between stress and heart disease.

When I (L.B.) ask my students if stress causes heart disease, many quickly reply that it does. They know that stress elevates blood pressure and that high blood pressure creates a risk for heart disease. Their information is correct, but when I ask how a temporary elevation becomes chronic high blood pressure (hypertension), most do not have a clear explanation. Their uncertainty is warranted—there is no direct relationship between stress and chronic hypertension; the underlying cause of hypertension is currently unknown. Stress can be a problem for people with hypertension, but it is not the cause of hypertension. Therefore, the link between stress and heart disease turns out to be less obvious and more complex than most people imagine.

Heart Disease and Stress

Heart disease is the number-one killer of both men and women in the United States. Each year, more than 500,000 Americans die of heart attacks caused by coronary heart disease (U.S. Bureau of the Census, 2003). The coronary arteries furnish the blood supply to the heart muscle, and when those arteries are blocked, the heart muscle no longer gets blood, precipitating a heart attack. The most common underlying cause is the buildup of deposits inside the coronary arteries, which restricts blood flow.

The behavioral factors related to coronary artery blockage have been the subject of intensive research, and several behaviors have been found to relate to the disease process. Therefore, both physicians and psychologists accept that lifestyle factors are important to the development of heart disease (Williams, Barefoot, & Schneiderman, 2003). One of the first attempts to conceptualize the link between behavior and heart disease was the formulation of the Type A behavior pattern.

In the late 1950s, physicians Meyer Friedman and Ray Rosenman identified a pattern of behavior that they believe contributed to heart disease; they called it *Type A behavior* (Friedman & Rosenman, 1974). *Type A behavior* is the behavior pattern of individuals who are competitive, impatient, hostile, and always striving to do more in less time. *Type B behavior* is the behavior pattern exhibited by people who are calmer, more patient, less hurried, and less hostile.

Early studies of the Type A behavior pattern showed a positive association with heart disease; that is, Type A individuals were more likely than Type B individuals to have heart attacks. This association became well known, and people accepted that the combination of behaviors in the Type A pattern significantly increased the risk for heart disease. More recent research, however, casts doubt on this conclusion. This research suggests that the overall Type A behavior pattern is not a risk for heart disease (Williams et al., 2003). Friedman and Rosenman's concept has been criticized for culture and gender bias. Heart disease is a leading cause of death across the world, but the Type A behavior pattern fits middle-aged North American men better than any other group. Women exhibit Type A behavior, but some evidence suggests that this behavior pattern does not relate to heart disease in either European women (Orth-Gormér, 1998) or Japanese women (Yoshimasu et al., 2002).

Researchers began to examine components of the Type A behavior pattern for their toxic effects and found that it is the components of hostility and anger that relate to the development of heart disease (Donker & Breteler, 2004; Williams et al., 2003). Feelings of suspiciousness, mistrust of others, and thinking the worst of people are associated with increased risk for heart disease. Anger and anxiety are also associated

Type A behavior ▪
A behavior pattern characterized by competitiveness, impatience, hostility, and constant efforts to do more in less time.

Type B behavior ▪
A behavior pattern characterized by calmness, patience, and a less hurried and less hostile style.

with death from heart disease (Suinn, 2001). Even people who only experience the emotion of anger and do not express it are at increased risk for heart disease.

Heart disease may be linked to anger through the physiological changes that occur in response to this emotion, which are the same as those from the stress response—arising from activation of the sympathetic division of the autonomic nervous system. However, anger is not the same as stress. Therefore, the relationship between the experience of stress and the development of heart disease is complex. For people who have coronary heart disease, however, some experiences of stress increase the chances of death (Ketterer et al., 2004).

Another link between heart disease and stress has become apparent from a situation generated by world politics. Following the collapse of the Soviet Union, heart disease deaths skyrocketed in Russia and other countries that had been under the control of the Soviet Union. Stress and psychological factors have been implicated in this epidemic (Möller-Leimkühler, 2003; Weidner, 2000). Some researchers argue that when the communist regime collapsed, people felt optimistic about a better life—but their hopes were not fulfilled. Instead, people experienced uncertainty and economic turmoil, which generated feelings of stress, pessimism, depression, and frustration over restriction of opportunities. The incidence of heart disease rose dramatically and life expectancy decreased, especially among middle-aged men. Researchers examined other behavioral factors that relate to heart disease, such as diet and smoking, but found few differences between people in Eastern and Western Europe. Yet the death rates from heart disease in these regions were dramatically different. Researchers turned to stress and depression as the sources of the difference. Some have asserted that Eastern European countries are experiencing an epidemic of heart disease and have called on psychologists' expertise (Piko, 2004).

Stress and Infectious Disease

Does it seem as if you always get a cold just after final exams are over? Do you feel as though the stress makes you vulnerable to infection? That feeling may be correct. Stress is related to the development of disease through its effect on the immune system, the body's defense against infection. The immune system is a complex network of specialized cells and organs that has evolved to defend the body against attacks by bacteria, viruses, and fungi. These specialized cells and organs are able to distinguish these "foreign invaders" from the body's own cells and tissues. The recognition of cells that are not part of the body prompts the components of the immune system to locate, identify, and obliterate the invaders. As part of the immune response, the body acquires immunity against reinfection. That is, exposure to the same infectious agent will cause a rapid immune system response, which protects against reinfection—the body has acquired immunity against that specific infectious agent. The immune system also has cells that fight infection in more general ways, protecting against a wide range of infections.

We are exposed to many infectious agents daily and sometimes our immune systems are not 100% effective. When they are not, we can get sick. The reason that some people get sick and others do not may relate to how efficiently people's immune systems function. When researchers discovered that the immune system responds to behaviors and events through connections with the nervous system, the field of psychoneuroimmunology was born (Ader & Cohen, 1975). *Psychoneuroimmunology* is an interdisciplinary area of study that focuses on behavioral, neurological, and immune factors and their relationship to the development of disease. A basic finding from this field is that events affecting the immune system make people more vulnerable to disease (Kop, 2003).

Sheldon Cohen and his colleagues (Cohen, 1996; Cohen et al., 1998; Marsland et al., 2002) have demonstrated that stress makes people more vulnerable to the common cold. Cohen conducted a series of experiments in which he assessed the level of people's stress and their moods, made sure they were healthy, and then exposed them to a combination of cold viruses. Only one-third of the people developed colds, but those who reported high stress and negative moods were much more likely to get sick than those who reported low levels of stress and positive moods. Cohen's studies also indicate that the duration of stress may be more important than its severity in decreasing immune system function. A study on the same topic, using a naturalistic setting, confirmed the relationship between stress and vulnerability to infection with cold viruses (Takkouche, Regueira, & Gestal-Otero, 2001). Therefore, the amount, duration, and perception of stress are all important factors in vulnerability to infection.

Stress and Health-Related Behaviors

Stress has another route through which it can influence health—through behaviors that increase the risk of disease and death. Stress affects how people behave and may stimulate behaviors that can either damage or enhance health (Schneiderman et al., 2001; Strine et al., 2004). For example, many people claim that smoking helps them cope with stress. Whether or not this claim is accurate, smoking is related to the development of heart disease, cancer, and chronic lung disease. These three diseases are among the leading causes of death in the United States and many other countries (U.S. Bureau of the Census, 2003). Thus, this indirect link between stress and disease takes a substantial health toll.

Relief from stress is also one of the reasons people give for drinking alcohol, but alcohol is a risk for some types of cancer as well as a significant risk for accidents (Arias, 2004). Stress also influences eating. Some people eat more in response to stress, and this response may be more common among women than men (Klein et al., 2004). In addition, stressed people tend to eat a less healthy diet (Cartwright et al., 2003). Dietary factors are involved in heart disease and many types of cancers (Trichopoulou et al., 2003). Clearly, stress can affect health, but the extent to which it will result in disease is moderated by successful coping.

How Do People Cope with Stress?

Everyone needs a way to cope with stress, and most people use a variety of strategies. People may not be aware that they choose among various ways to cope, but they do. However, most people probably could choose more effective ways to cope. Coping strategies need to be tailored to the individual and the situation—and some strategies work better than others.

Psychoneuroimmunology [SYE-ko-NEW-ro-IM-you-NOLL-oh-gee] ■ An interdisciplinary area of study that focuses on behavioral, neurological, and immune factors and their relationship to the development of disease.

What Is Coping?

In general, *coping* means dealing with a situation. However, for a psychologist, *coping* is the process by which a person takes some action to manage, master, tolerate, or reduce environmental and internal demands that cause or might cause stress and that tax the individual's inner resources (Lazarus & Folkman, 1984). This definition of coping involves five important assumptions. First, coping is constantly being adjusted and evaluated and is therefore a process or a strategy. Second, coping involves managing demanding situations, not necessarily bringing them under complete control. Third, coping requires effort and does not happen automatically. Fourth, coping attempts to manage cognitive as well as behavioral events. Finally, coping is learned.

There are many types of coping strategies. People develop effective ones when they learn new ways of dealing with their vulnerabilities.

Coping ■ The process by which a person takes some action to manage, master, tolerate, or reduce environmental or internal demands that cause or might cause stress and that tax the individual's inner resources.

Factors That Influence Coping

People vary enormously in their ability to cope with stressors. Factors that influence coping ability include personal resources, a sense of control, and social support. Personal resources contribute to *resilience,* the extent to which people are flexible and respond adaptively to external or internal demands. A person who is resilient is able to overcome stress and risk to adapt and do well (Masten & Reed, 2002).

Resilience ■ The extent to which people are flexible and respond adaptively to external or internal demands.

Personal resources include a variety of factors, ranging from money to good health (Lazarus & Folkman, 1984). Money and other material resources can be helpful in dealing with both daily hassles, such as car problems, and with life events, such as changing one's residence. Social skills, cognitive ability, and knowledge are other personal resources that affect coping. People who are socially skilled are better at getting along with others and are at ease in social situations. They are less likely to feel stressed by, for example, having to attend a social gathering or make a speech than are individuals who are less socially skilled. Good cognitive abilities allow people to think of a variety of ways to cope. Knowledge is an important resource— someone who knows about automobile transmissions may not need the money that someone with less knowledge must have to get the transmission fixed. Being healthy is an obvious advantage in coping with stressors; healthy people have more energy and are able to endure the physical demands imposed by the stress response.

A sense of being in control is also important to resilience and coping (Zuckerman et al., 2004). People who believe that they can control important factors in their lives have an internal (rather than an external) locus of control. As we explored in Chapter 13, people who have an internal locus of control have advantages over those who have an external locus of control, and ability to cope with stress is one of those advantages. Even if the things they control are minor and even if the control is only an illusion and not an actuality, the belief in control is an advantage.

Two classic experiments demonstrated the importance of control, over even minor details. Ellen Langer and Judith Rodin (1976) demonstrated how important control could be by manipulating the amount of control residents exerted over their new rooms in a retirement home. The new residents of one floor were asked about their schedules, were encouraged to arrange the furniture to their liking, and were given a plant, which they were told was their responsibility to care for. The new residents of another floor lived in similar rooms but were not given choices or encouraged to make decisions. They also received a plant, but the staff cared for it. Residents who had more control were happier and healthier than the comparison residents, and these advantages persisted over time (Rodin & Langer, 1977).

Feeling in control is a positive state of mind that leads to optimism, which enhances coping and has a positive relation to health. Even more interesting, the feeling of being in control does not have to be real to be effective; even the illusion of control can exert a positive effect on mental and physical health (Taylor, Kemeny, et al., 2000). When people feel in control of their health and factors that relate to their health, they adopt more healthy behaviors, maintain better social relationships, and may have healthier immune systems. The personal belief in control cannot be too unrealistic, however, or people begin to think in very unrealistic ways and to take unreasonable chances, which is a health risk (Zuckerman et al., 2004). However, the benefits of feeling in control may be restricted to individuals in Western societies that value individualism and a sense of personal control. In a study that contrasted British and Japanese participants, personal control was a factor in coping only for the British participants (O'Connor & Shimizu, 2002).

Feeling in control is the opposite of learned helplessness (discussed in Chapter 8). People who experience learned helplessness find that rewards and punishments have nothing to do with their behavior, and they learn not to try to cope. Because they are young, children are less likely to have well-developed coping skills and are especially vulnerable to learned helplessness; also, stressful situations tend to discourage children from attempting to cope (Evans, 2003).

The research on resilience indicates that exposure to stressful conditions is not sufficient to produce a stressed individual. For example, some children are separated from their parents by war and must live among unfriendly strangers, and yet they grow up to be healthy, happy adults (Masten & Reed, 2002; Palmer, 2000). Similarly, some adolescents live in poverty and with the threat of violence, yet manage to function effectively (D'Imperio, Dubow, & Ippolito, 2000). Some people are resilient in the face of trauma and stress. Feelings of control, self-worth, and optimism are related to such resilience (Masten & Reed, 2002).

Studies on the development of resilience have focused on children and adolescents, and they tend to show that children who are at risk for problems because of poverty, parental absence, abuse, homelessness, or parental psychopathology may still grow up to be well adjusted and capable (Masten & Reed, 2002). One key factor in resilience is a close, supportive relationship with someone. Experiencing good parenting early in life conveys some protection against stress, but other types of supportive relationships may also be effective. For example, a group of Native American students who were attending college related their stories about the factors in their lives that allowed them to go to college (Montgomery et al., 2000). For many, tribal traditions and feeling that they were part of their community were related to their resiliency and success. Social support is a common factor in developing a sense of resiliency, and it is also an important coping resource.

Social support consists of the comfort, recognition, approval, and encouragement available from other people, including friends, family members, and coworkers. Social support can be emotional support, but people can also contribute money, knowledge, and advice. All of these forms of social support enhance the ability to deal with stress (Taylor, Dickerson, & Klein, 2002).

People receive social support from friends and family, but being part of a network includes obligations to provide support as well as opportunities to receive it. Providing social support can be stressful, so being part of a social network has costs as well as benefits (Jou & Fukada, 2002). The benefits tend to outweigh the costs, but not always equally for women and men. Women tend to have larger social networks, which may overburden them with the need to provide support (Belle & Doucet, 2003); the increased burden may outweigh the benefits of having a larger network on which they can depend.

In addition to friends and family (and sometimes in place of these), group therapy (to be examined in Chapter 17) and support groups can help people in managing stress. In group therapy and in support groups, other people who are in a similar situation can show concern and offer advice and emotional support. Therefore, people who do not have social support can find ways to obtain it, which suggests that people can also develop coping skills and strategies.

Social support ■ The comfort, recognition, approval, and encouragement available from other people, including friends, family members, and coworkers.

Coping Strategies

Stress is a universal experience, and everyone has some ways to make levels of stress more manageable. However, not everyone uses the same techniques, even in similar situations, and some people use coping strategies more effectively than other people do.

Coping strategies are the techniques people use to deal with stress. Effective coping requires that people have a variety of strategies and make appropriate choices about when to use them. No single strategy is bad or good, but some strategies tend to be more effective than others. For example, some coping strategies involve actively dealing with the stressor, whereas other strategies are more passive. Passive coping strategies include refusing to acknowledge that a problem exists, trying to ignore the problem, avoiding the situation, engaging in distracting activities, or sleeping more than usual.

Coping strategies ■ The techniques people use to deal with stress.

These approaches sound ineffective and even potentially dangerous, but under some circumstances, they can work. For example, avoiding an unpleasant person may be an effective way to cope with that person. However, this coping strategy is effective in a limited number of situations and will be disastrous in others. For example, avoiding a person with whom one must work is not effective strategy. Also, failing to accept the possibility that one is ill and avoiding medical care can be fatal. Psychologists usually view active coping strategies as more effective than passive ones, but some types of active coping are not necessarily the best choices. For example, using drugs or alcohol requires active effort, but this activity is not oriented toward solving the problem. Thus, this type of active coping is not a good strategy.

Active coping strategies can be divided into emotion-focused strategies and problem-focused strategies. Both are active ways to deal with stressful situations,

Emotion-focused coping ■ An active coping strategy that concentrates on managing the feelings that accompany stress and trying to find ways to feel better.

Problem-focused coping ■ An active coping strategy that concentrates on changing the situation to reduce the stress.

but the two types of strategies are very different. *Emotion-focused coping* concentrates on managing the feelings that accompany stress and trying to find ways to feel better, including focusing on and expressing emotions, reinterpreting events in a positive way, finding comfort in religion, and seeking social support. *Problem-focused coping* concentrates on taking action to change a situation to reduce the stress, for example, seeking more information about the problem, making a plan about what to do, and putting aside other activities to concentrate on the problem. Researchers initially believed that some people tend to choose one type of coping strategy and use it in many situations; they also hypothesized that women choose emotion-focused strategies and men select problem-focused ones. This stereotypical view is not accurate. Both women and men use both emotion-focused and problem-focused coping.

In the selection of coping strategy, situation is more important than gender. For example, a woman who deals with problems with her husband by engaging in emotional confrontations might not deal with problems with her supervisor in the same way. Based on cultural stereotypes, researchers hypothesized that Indian and Canadian students would differ in their levels of stress, attitudes about life, and preferred coping strategies (Sinha, Willson, & Watson, 2000). The students living in India did tend to use emotion-focused coping more than the Canadian students did, especially in reappraising their stresses in a positive way. Otherwise, the students in Canada and India were similar in levels of stress and attitudes about life. A study that included Japanese participants found that they also showed a preference for emotion-focused coping (O'Connor & Shimizu, 2002). Thus, situation plays a role in stress and coping—and the situation of being a student involves similar stressors in many cultures.

Emotion-Focused Coping

When you have a problem (or just a bad day), is your first thought to talk to a friend or your partner to help you ease those feelings of stress? If so, you are using emotion-focused coping. Women tend to use emotion-focused strategies more than men do (Renk & Creasey, 2003), but this preference may relate to their relationship styles and their greater reliance on social support. Seeking social support can be an adaptive coping strategy (Taylor, Klein, et al., 2000).

In addition to seeking social support, another emotion-focused technique that can be very effective is writing about stresses. James Pennebaker (Niederhoffer & Pennebaker, 2002; Pennebaker, 1989; Pennebaker & Graybeal, 2001) has researched the benefits of such writing. Pennebaker (1989) asked students to write about a traumatic event for 20 minutes for three consecutive days and compared these participants to other students who wrote about trivial events. Those students who wrote about stresses experienced physical as well as psychological benefits. These promising findings prompted additional research, which confirmed the benefits of writing about emotional events. Participants enjoyed a wide variety of benefits, from better immune system functioning to better grades. Pennebaker believes that the benefit of writing is that it helps people think differently about their stresses and problems; it is not simply a matter of "getting things out in the open." Talking about problems is the basis for many psychological treatments (see Chapter 17); writing as a coping strategy has a much shorter history but comparable effectiveness.

Some emotion-focused coping strategies are effective ways to deal with some stressors, especially if the coping strategy involves a positive, active approach rather than a passive one or a negative view (Smith, Lumley, & Longo, 2002). However, problem-focused coping is usually a better choice as a coping strategy.

Problem-Focused Coping

Most psychologists recommend problem-focused coping for managing stress. The goal of problem-focused coping is solving or managing the problem that is producing stress, and this strategy involves planning, gathering information, making decisions, and obtaining resources to deal with the problem (Folkman & Moskowitz, 2000; Penley, Tomaka, & Wiebe, 2002).

The active, task-oriented approach of problem-focused coping is associated with effective problem solving and decision making in many domains. People who use problem-focused coping tend to feel that they can effectively solve a problem involving a stressor; they have a high sense of self-efficacy for the stress-related task. As we saw in Chapter 13, a sense of self-efficacy is important, and this is particularly true in stressful situations (Jimmieson, Terry, & Callan, 2004). People with an internal locus of control tend to choose problem-focused coping. Thus, some individuals are more likely to use problem-focused coping, at least in some situations, and these individuals tend to be effective problem solvers.

Not only do problem-focused strategies tend to be more likely to solve stress-related problems, but some research also indicates that people who use such strategies tend to have a more positive outlook (Folkman & Moskowitz, 2000), to experience fewer symptoms of illness (Soderstrom et al., 2000), and to show better immune system functioning (Stowell, Kiecolt-Glaser, & Glaser, 2001). Therefore, problem-focused coping has advantages over emotion-focused coping. **Figure 15.5** compares these two approaches and also includes another strategy: proactive coping.

Proactive Coping

If you know that you are going to have a challenging semester next fall, you might try to get a full-time job over the summer so that you'll only need to work part-time when school starts. By doing so (whether you think of it that way or not), you are already coping with your tough fall semester. You are practicing *proactive coping* by anticipating a problem and taking action to prevent it or modify it.

Lisa Aspinwall and Shelley Taylor (1997) describe proactive coping as a five-stage process. First, we accumulate resources, mustering time, money, and social support and managing current situations. Next, we recognize that a stressful event is coming. Third, we appraise the event in terms of its difficulty and its potential impact. Fourth, we engage in preliminary coping, to see what we can do now to prevent or minimize any threat. And last, we elicit and use feedback to assess whether we have averted a future stressor. Using this active approach, people can avoid some stressors and modify others so that they are not so stressful. Proactive

Proactive coping ■
A strategy for dealing with stress that involves taking action in advance of a potentially stressful situation to prevent it or modify it.

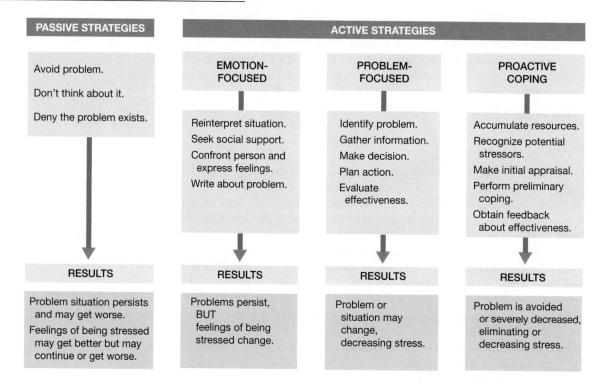

Figure 15.5
Coping Strategies and Their Effects

coping may be part of an overall positive approach to life that engenders resilience (Strumpfer, 2003). However, the process of proactive coping requires effort, and people have a limited amount of time and energy. Thus, they have to choose which situations to manage and which to try to avoid or to allow to develop. They also need to choose which strategies to use in those situations they do want to manage.

Effective Coping

Both emotion-focused and problem-focused coping can be successful—or not. Proactive coping can often prevent or decrease stress but requires time and effort. Therefore, selecting the appropriate strategy is critically important for managing stress. Emotional confrontation is obviously a strategy that needs to be chosen only after careful consideration; inappropriate choices may be not only ineffective but also dangerous. Seeking social support or writing about a distressing experience are better choices to manage the emotions generated by stress. This difference was confirmed by a study of college students' coping (Park, Armeli, & Tennen, 2004a). These students were successful in coping with controllable stressors using problem-focused coping and with uncontrollable stressors by using emotion-focused strategies, but not the reverse. First-year medical students were healthier when they used both types of coping strategies than when they used only one (Park & Adler, 2003). However, emotion-focused strategies such as smoking and drinking to avoid problems are not adaptive for college students, but positive emotion-focused coping in the form of seeking social support is (DeBerard, Spielmans, & Julka, 2004). The trick is choosing the correct strategy for the situation.

Some people are flexible and effective in dealing with the stressors in their lives, but others lack a repertoire of coping strategies. These people need help in learning to cope with stress. Biofeedback, relaxation techniques, and meditation (see Chapter 7) can help some individuals manage the physical responses that accompany stress, and psychotherapy (see Chapter 17) may also be helpful.

Stress inoculation is one therapeutic technique that can help people cope with stress by combining cognitive and behavioral approaches (Meichenbaum & Cameron, 1983). Stress inoculation is based on the same principle as inoculation against a disease: It is a technique that introduces a low, harmless level of stress and provides people with practice in using coping skills so that when more threatening stress comes along, they will know how to cope—they have become immune to stressors. This process involves three stages:

Stress inoculation [in-OK-you-LAY-shun] A therapeutic technique that teaches people ways to cope with stress and allows them to practice in realistic situations so that they develop "immunity" to stress.

1. *Conceptualization.* People develop an understanding of the stress response and their specific problems.
2. *Skills acquisition and rehearsal.* People learn relaxation and imagery techniques that can help diminish stress and anxiety; they also learn how to reinterpret stressors and regulate their feelings.
3. *Follow-through.* People apply their acquired coping skills to problems in a natural context; that is, they practice the techniques they have learned in the second stage.

Stress inoculation training provides a number of specific coping techniques, giving people a variety of strategies to manage stress. It can help people who have not devised effective strategies on their own.

In addition to having a variety of strategies to manage stress, people are better equipped to deal with the inevitable stressors of life if they lead a healthy lifestyle. Behaviors that relate to a healthy lifestyle are part of the area of health psychology, a relatively new field within psychology, which we will discuss next.

What Is Health Psychology?

In the past, infectious diseases such as influenza, tuberculosis, and pneumonia were among the leading causes of premature death in the United States. Today, at least half of all premature deaths are the result of an unhealthy lifestyle. The leading causes of death in the United States—heart disease, cancer, stroke, lung disease, and accidents—relate to behavioral and environmental variables. Psychologists know that there is a direct relationship between people's health and their behavior. *Health psychology* is the subfield of psychology concerned with the use of psychological ideas and principles to help enhance health, prevent illness, diagnose and treat disease, and improve rehabilitation. This action-oriented discipline assumes that people's ideas and behaviors contribute to the onset and prevention of illness. A closely

Health psychology Subfield of psychology concerned with the use of psychological ideas and principles to help enhance health, prevent illness, diagnose and treat disease, and improve rehabilitation.

related field, behavioral medicine, integrates behavioral science with medical knowledge and techniques; it is narrower in focus than health psychology.

Traditionally, physicians have considered health to be the absence of disease. A person who was not experiencing adverse effects from an infection, injury, or abnormal condition of some kind was considered healthy. Now, however, physicians and psychologists acknowledge that health is not just the absence of disease; an assessment of a person's health must take into account that person's total social, physical, and mental well-being (McGinnis, 2003). This orientation gives health psychology a focus on the positive—on health promotion. Health and wellness are seen as conditions people can actively pursue by eating well, exercising regularly, and managing stress effectively (Baum & Posluszny, 1999). Unlike medical science, which focuses on specific diseases, health psychology looks at the broad effects of thoughts and behaviors on health and illness, including the positive effects of health-promoting behaviors and the negative effects of risky behaviors.

How Does Behavior Affect Health and Illness?

Some people see the bright side of things, laugh at life, and wear "rose-colored glasses" to help ward off the impact of negative or difficult life events (Segerstrom, Casteñeda, & Spencer, 2003). Others worry, see the negative in everything (in the name of being "realistic"), and think of life as serious business. Our attitudes and outlook affect health and illness, and they in turn are affected by complex interrelationships among many events (Cohen, 1996; Sternberg & Gold, 2002). But health is also affected by behaviors. Research has demonstrated that many behaviors have a large influence not only on health but also on life expectancy.

Health-Related Behaviors

In 1965, researchers in Alameda County, California began a study on health practices and social variables that continues today (Berkman & Breslow, 1983). The study began with nearly 7,000 adults who were questioned about their health practices. Results indicated that five behaviors were strongly related to health and life expectancy: (1) getting 7 or 8 hours of sleep daily, (2) drinking alcohol in moderation or not at all, (3) not smoking cigarettes, (4) exercising regularly, and (5) maintaining a weight near the prescribed ideal. Follow-ups over the years have indicated that people who engage in two or fewer of these behaviors are about three times more likely to be sick or to die prematurely than people who perform all five. These behaviors reflect typical advice for maintaining a healthy lifestyle, and the Alameda County Study demonstrates the validity of such advice and how important behavior can be in determining health. Since the beginning of that study, research evidence has continued to show that failure to perform these behaviors contributes to the leading causes of death in the United States.

People engage in a wide range of self-destructive, health-impairing behaviors. For example, about 23% of Americans still smoke cigarettes, despite massive evidence that smoking ultimately leads to premature death (U.S. Bureau of the Census, 2003). Cigarette smoking is related to increased risks for heart disease, cancer, stroke, and lung disease—four of the five leading causes of death in the United States. Indeed, tobacco use is the most damaging health habit, related to more preventable deaths than any other single behavior (Mokdad et al., 2004). Health psychologists conduct research on why people begin to smoke and why smokers find it so difficult to quit so that they can devise more effective programs to help decrease this health-threatening behavior.

Americans also eat too much of the wrong things (National Center for Health Statistics [NCHS], 2003). The typical American diet is too high in fat and protein and too low in fruits, vegetables, and grains, and a high-fat diet contributes to heart disease, cancer, and stroke. This typical diet is a factor in being overweight, a problem affecting over 64% of Americans, and in obesity, which affects over 30%. Being overweight or obese can lead to a number of health problems. Health psychologists are involved in research on eating and weight control, and they devise programs to help people adopt healthier eating habits.

Health psychologists also recognize the value of exercise in promoting health and warn that Americans are too sedentary to be healthy (NCHS, 2003). A sedentary lifestyle is related to heart disease and stroke as well as some types of cancers and, of course, obesity. People who exercise regularly have better overall health and more effective immune systems, are better at coping with stress, and live longer than people who are sedentary (Baum & Posluszny, 1999; Manson et al., 2004). As computers and video games become preferred entertainment for children, the trend toward a sedentary lifestyle applies to children as well as to adults. Finding ways to boost physical activity is one challenge for health psychologists.

Preventing AIDS

Educating people about disease prevention and wellness and discovering the variables that affect health are central goals of health psychologists. The focus on disease prevention led health psychologists to be involved in addressing the AIDS epidemic from its beginning. AIDS (acquired immune deficiency syndrome) is caused by the human immunodeficiency virus (HIV), which is a virus transmitted through bodily fluids. The serious AIDS epidemic continues around the world, and the disease kills thousands of people in the United States each year. (See Figure 15.6 on p. 582 for U.S. and worldwide infection rates.) Despite developing knowledge about the virus and its methods of infection, no vaccine exists to prevent its transmission. A combination of drugs can help infected people manage AIDS, but there is no cure.

Risky behaviors spread HIV infection. High-risk behaviors are those that directly expose a person to the blood or semen of others who are likely to have been exposed to the virus—in other words, to others who are likely to have engaged in high-risk behaviors. Those behaviors include having sex with many partners, having sex with a man who has had sex with other men, and injecting drugs (U.S. Bureau of the Census, 2003). During the early years of the epidemic, AIDS was more common among gay men than in other groups, and many people developed the belief that heterosexuals were not at risk. That belief is incorrect. Heterosexuals who have had sexual contact with carriers of AIDS are at significant risk.

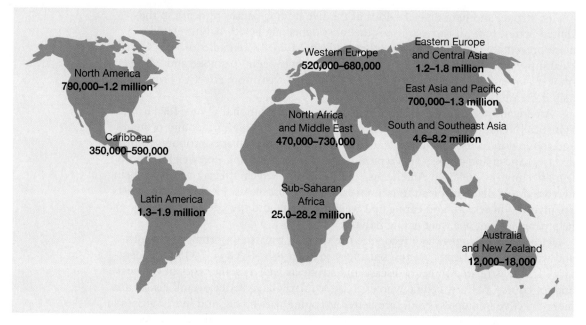

Figure 15.6
Numbers of People with HIV/AIDS in Various Parts of the World
The worldwide total of children and adults living with HIV/AIDS was estimated to be between 34 and 46 million at the end of 2003. (Source: UNAIDS, 2003, p. 41)

In the United States, almost 20% of known cases of AIDS are contracted through heterosexual sex (U.S. Bureau of the Census, 2003). But worldwide, heterosexual sex accounts for 70% of reported AIDS cases (UNAIDS, 2003). In some parts of Asia, injection drug use is the most common mode of transmission. Everywhere, adolescents are at especially high risk because they, more than adults, are likely to engage in unprotected sexual activity. Thus, adolescents have some of the highest rates of sexually transmitted diseases, including HIV.

Health psychologists attempt to prevent the spread of HIV infection by focusing on changing risky behaviors. Extensive education campaigns provide information about HIV infection and the dangers of high-risk behaviors, but such campaigns are often not sufficient to alter risky behaviors; people who are aware of the risks still engage in risky behaviors (Dodds et al., 2004; Metsch et al., 2004). One of the risky behaviors that has been resistant to change is failing to use a condom. Research shows that the most effective way to get men and women to use condoms is not by playing on their fears but by engendering positive attitudes about condoms. It is critical to persuade sexually active people throughout the world to use condoms, and this effort has been partially successful (Hearst & Chen, 2004). However, the idea of condom use may clash with cultural or religious values—in which case usage rates will suffer. In addition, the person who controls the sexual activity (typically the man in the case of heterosexual encounters) may not want to use a condom (Bowleg, Lucas, & Tschann, 2004). The challenge is to overcome these barriers, which will require different strategies targeted for specific groups (Hearst & Chen, 2004).

Barriers to Adopting Health-Promoting Behaviors

People may know in general what constitutes a healthy lifestyle but nevertheless persist in unhealthy habits that increase their risks for disease and death. It's easy to fall into bad habits, and it's often difficult to change. Social circumstances and personal attitudes can make change difficult. For example, some people find eating a healthy diet a challenge (Bray, 2004). Billions of dollars are spent on advertising to generate sales of fast foods and junk foods that are poor dietary choices. Fast-food restaurants and vending machines offer few good nutritional choices. Sometimes it is easier to make bad choices than good ones. Thus, factors in the environment can push people toward unhealthy diets.

Ways of thinking also contribute to poor health choices. Many people mistakenly think that self-destructive behaviors are likely to affect other people but not them. That is, people have an *optimistic bias* (Price, Pentecost, & Voth, 2002; Weinstein, 1980). This biased way of thinking allows people to continue risky behaviors, even if they understand the dangers intellectually. This "magical thinking" resembles teenagers' belief in the personal fable—"I am so special and unique that risky behaviors (unsafe sex or alcohol consumption or cigarette smoking) that might harm other people will not harm me." These cognitive distortions allow people to continue unsafe and unhealthy behaviors. Health psychologists must work against these thought patterns in helping people adopt healthier behaviors.

The Psychology of Being Sick

When people experience symptoms that may indicate illness, they must decide what to do. Should they ignore the symptoms, take over-the-counter medication or some home remedy, or seek medical care? No one likes being sick, and the thought of having a disease that impairs day-to-day functioning is threatening (Hagger & Orbell, 2003). Fear can make people reluctant to seek medical care. Health psychologists are concerned not only with the links between stress and illness but also with how people cope with illness when it occurs.

Seeking Medical Care

What variables prompt a person to seek medical care? Most people avoid medical care and advice except when they judge it to be necessary. The presence of visible symptoms (rashes, cuts, swellings, or fever) that are threatening, painful, or persistent is usually the deciding factor that prompts someone to seek professional help (Mechanic, 1978). However, painful symptoms alone will not necessarily motivate people to get medical care. For example, a cut or burn can be very painful, but if the injury is not judged to be serious, people tend to treat themselves rather than seek help. Also, if a person believes that a symptom does not indicate a serious condition, she or he will not seek medical help.

People are more willing to seek medical help when they believe that it will lead to a cure, but they are especially reluctant to do so when the potential diagnosis is a dreaded one. For example, people avoid cancer screenings, partly because cancer is such a dreaded disease. In addition, people try to find the least threatening explanation for a symptom—the headache must be due to a stressful day and not to brain cancer. All these tendencies point to a great deal of personal reluctance to seek medical care (Brannon & Feist, 2004).

There are gender differences in people's willingness to obtain medical attention. The female gender role is more compatible with seeking help, and women receive medical help more than men do (Chrisler, 2001). Women often visit physicians not for reasons of ill health but for consultation regarding birth control, pregnancy, and childbirth. In addition, women do report more distress and symptoms of illness than men do.

Being strong and invincible is part of the male gender role, and men may perceive seeking medical care as a sign of weakness or vulnerability (Courtenay, 2000). Ironically, men have a shorter lifespan than women do, so their tendency to avoid medical care may not serve them well (Simon, 2004). The gender difference in life expectancy results in part from men's higher rate of heart disease during middle age, leading to premature death. (Women also die of heart disease, but at older ages.) Heart disease may produce few noticeable symptoms, and men's avoidance of medical attention allows their heart disease to go undiagnosed and untreated—a potentially fatal situation.

There are also major cultural differences in decisions to seek medical care, and people tend to make these decisions in a manner that is consistent with their cultural conceptions. Most people in the United States and other Western countries have beliefs about the causes of and cures for disease that are based on principles of Western medicine; they think it is appropriate to seek help from physicians, and they expect go to a hospital for certain treatments. Other views of health and disease vary drastically from those of traditional Western medicine, leading people to use different kinds of practitioners and health-care settings. For example, traditional Chinese medicine is oriented toward understanding the body's vital energy, blood, and body fluids and maintaining a balance in the flow of these essential elements (Bassman & Uellendahl, 2003; Takeichi & Sato, 2000). This holistic concept of health has become attractive to a growing number of people in the United States and other Western countries. They are seeking health care from alternative sources, and one study found that in over two-thirds of households in the United States, someone has used some form of alternative health care (Krafft, 2003). Health care that is considered alternative includes treatments with vitamins and other nutritional supplements, herbs, acupuncture, massage therapy, and other forms of treatment. These treatments are slowly gaining acceptance by those who practice traditional medicine (Traylor, 2003), and individuals typically combine alternative and traditional medical treatments.

Health-care providers in large, ethnically diverse societies such as those of the United States, Canada, and Great Britain see people who have a variety of beliefs about the nature of health and illness, some of which differ sharply from the views of traditional practitioners (Weitz, 2001). For example, European Americans do not often seek the services of shamans or *curanderos,* but Native Americans and

Latinos/Latinas do. These practitioners provide health care that is compatible with the beliefs of those who consult them, which helps to boost healing: Patients trust and will follow the directions of these health care providers (Kim & Kwok, 1998; Padilla et al., 2001). Seeking health care from practitioners associated with specific ethnic groups is more common among immigrants and older people (Murguia, Peterson, & Zea, 2003), but beliefs about what constitutes appropriate treatment may continue to be held even by those immigrants who accept other cultural values of their adopted countries. In such situations, people often use a combination of health-care practitioners—those traditional to their society plus traditional Western physicians (Bassman & Uellandahl, 2003; Kim & Kwok, 1998). This combining of sources of health care is similar to what many individuals who use alternative health care do (Bassman & Uellandahl, 2003).

The Sick Role

When people seek medical care and receive a diagnosis, they are expected to follow medical advice and try to get well. While they try to recover, they adopt a *sick role* (Kasl & Cobb, 1966). For most people, this means taking specific steps to get well, relieving themselves of normal responsibilities, and realizing that they are not at fault for their illness. When they are in a hospital, they give the responsibility for their care to physicians and nurses. Relinquishing personal control may create a feeling of helplessness that adds stress to the experience of being ill.

Most sickness is seen as a temporary state, and so people are expected to work toward getting well—taking medication, resting, and, especially, complying with medical advice. Most infectious diseases fit into this temporary category. Chronic diseases, on the other hand, do not have cures, and people have more trouble conceptualizing how to deal with these diseases and see them as more serious (Hagger & Orbell, 2003). Heart disease, diabetes, most types of cancer, asthma, HIV, and many other conditions can be managed but not cured. This difference creates problems for people with these disorders—they cannot get well, they may have to (or want to) continue with normal responsibilities, but in order to manage their chronic illness, they must comply with medical advice.

Compliance with Medical Advice

Getting people to adhere to health regimens or to follow physicians' advice has long been a focus of health psychologists, because it is a persistent problem for medical treatment. People have trouble in following all types of medical recommendations. Much of their noncompliance arises as a result of communication problems between practitioner and patient—when patients do not understand practitioners' recommendations, they cannot follow them (Cutting Edge Information, 2004). Another problem is that patients stop taking their medications when they begin to feel better. Noncompliance with medical advice also occurs when people fail to pursue a healthy lifestyle and avoid medical check-ups and screening tests.

Following doctor's orders may be very important to people taking drugs to control hypertension or diabetes, lower cholesterol, or treat HIV infection. People are more likely to comply with recommendations about treatments designed to cure a disease than with those that prevent or manage chronic conditions (Cutting Edge Information, 2004). People are even less likely to adhere to general recommendations about behaviors for improving overall health, such as quitting smoking or getting more exercise. Overall, noncompliance is around 50%, which means that half of all people who receive medical advice fail to follow it in some way.

Compliance with medical advice is somewhat related to the severity of the problem, but the patient's perception of the severity, not the medical practitioner's, is what matters. If an illness causes pain or discomfort, people are more likely to comply with treatment to alleviate the discomfort. Also, people are more receptive to medical treatment when it is specific, simple, and easy to do, and simplifying the regimen is the most effective strategy for improving compliance (Schroeder, Fahey, & Ebrahim, 2004).

Compliance with a health-care regimen is increased when the regimen is tailored to the person's lifestyle and habits. Patients are more likely to follow the advice of a practitioner whom they like and trust than one whom they find uncaring and uncommunicative. A written agreement between the practitioner and the patient can be helpful in detailing the responsibilities and commitments of each; patients who sign such an agreement are more likely to adhere to their commitment than those who say they will but do not sign an agreement.

Patients are also more likely to adhere to treatments when the physician's influence and their own family support systems are substantial, and interventions have been devised to increase effective physician communication and to enlist the support of family members (Harrington, Noble, & Newman, 2004). Social support from family and friends turns out to be especially effective in getting even very sick people to comply with guidelines for treatment (DiMatteo & DiNicola, 1982; Safren et al., 2001). However, compliance is far from perfect, even under the best conditions, and this problem is a persistent one for health psychologists trying to help practitioners provide better health care.

Adopting a Healthier Lifestyle

In addition to conducting research on health-related behaviors, health psychologists devise and implement interventions to help people change to a healthier lifestyle. The interventions may be individual programs for people with specific health-impairing behaviors or health problems or interventions aimed at groups and even entire communities. Let's examine three interventions focusing on pain management, binge drinking among college students, and condom use.

Pain Management

We all experience pain, and if we're lucky, the experience is brief and does not present a problem for daily functioning. People with chronic headache, arthritis, back problems, or many types of cancer must live with pain that does affect their daily lives. Psychologists work to help such individuals manage their pain. Severe and disabling pain can take three forms: (1) *chronic pain,* such as the pain caused by arthritis, is long-lasting and ever-present; (2) *periodic pain*, such as headache pain, comes and goes; (3) *progressive pain*, such as cancer-related pain, is ever-present and increases in severity as an illness progresses. Drugs, surgery, or other medical interventions are usually part of treatment for chronic pain, but behavioral techniques can also offer relief (Holroyd, 2002; Wall, 2000).

Pain management interventions usually work on two fronts: trying to reduce suffering, the negative emotional experience that accompanies pain, while also decreasing the physical aspects of pain. A number of behavioral treatments have been used to manage pain, including hypnosis and biofeedback (examined in Chapter 7), behavior modification, and cognitive therapy. Behavior modification uses learning principles (see Chapter 8) to teach people new effective behaviors, to help them unlearn maladaptive behaviors, and to train those close to the patient not to reward pain behaviors (McCracken, 1997; Penzien, Rains, & Andrasik, 2002). For example, a person with back pain might be rewarded for performing normal activities and ignored when he complained about how badly his back hurts. In addition, this person might be taught to relax as a coping strategy rather than becoming tense, focusing on the pain, and thus making it worse. Chapter 17 describes how cognitive therapy can help people acquire new thoughts, beliefs, and values, which can also be helpful in managing pain.

Controlling Campus Drinking

It has long been known that many college students indulge and overindulge in alcohol. Every year there are reports of deaths from binge drinking (drinking five or more drinks in one session). Because of the dangerous effects of alcohol, such as slowed reaction time, altered judgment, and decreased coordination, every year thousands of college students are hurt or hurt others in alcohol-related automobile accidents. Alcohol abuse is considered the number-one drug problem facing young people today (NCHS, 2003).

Scott Geller and his colleagues have investigated drinking among college students and have observed that drinking is heavier at fraternity parties than at other parties (Glindemann & Geller, 2003). Interestingly, fraternity members were no more intoxicated than nonmembers who attended the same parties—indicating that the setting, and not fraternity membership, affects level of drinking. Geller and his colleagues (Timmerman et al., 2003) also investigated how the designated driver strategy works. These researchers found that larger groups of college students leaving bars were more likely to have a designated driver. However, the designated drivers were not necessarily entirely sober, which raises questions about the effectiveness of this strategy for controlling the dangers of drinking.

How, then, can dangerous drinking be controlled? Psychologists have devised several strategies that rely on changing the environment to control undesirable behavior. For example, universities can (1) change the marketing practices and service policies of student-oriented bars, (2) encourage campus bookstores to limit sales of alcohol paraphernalia (mugs, shot glasses, and the like), and (3) develop campaigns to reduce risk factors related to heavy drinking (Clapp & Stanger, 2003). It is also possible to change students' drinking by a direct intervention: rewarding them for staying sober. Geller and his colleagues (Fournier et al., 2004) demonstrated that college students who were offered rewards for drinking less did so. Therefore, it is possible to change alcohol consumption among college students by changing the environment and by changing individual behavior.

Condom Use

Behavioral interventions are important in managing health problems and preventing disease, because behaviors are the underlying cause of many health problems. Individual and campus programs can reach many people, but wide-scale campaigns are necessary to reach enough people to improve life expectancy for a community or for a nation. Health psychologists know that many problem behaviors can be modified, but they also know that traditional information campaigns are not very effective in changing behavior.

The "safer-sex" campaign is an example of an attempt to change behavior in order to decrease health risks. When researchers discovered that HIV infection was transmitted through contact with blood or semen, one obvious prevention strategy was to increase condom use. A campaign to change behavior may target an entire society or smaller risk groups. Initially, the targets of the condom use campaign were gay men, because their rate of HIV infection was very high compared to that of other groups (U.S. Bureau of the Census, 2003). Early efforts focused on educating gay men about the dangers of HIV infection and the behaviors that are risky. As psychologists know, however, education alone is not an adequate intervention, and the campaign was expanded to include persuasive techniques to increase condom use and to overcome the barriers to it (Perloff, 2001). This campaign was at least somewhat successful. Gay men did change their sexual behavior and increase their use of condoms, and their rate of HIV infection slowed more than that of other groups in the United States (Centers for Disease Control and Prevention, 2001).

The growing rate of HIV infection among heterosexuals led to an expansion of the campaign to increase condom use. Messages about condom use appeared in a variety of settings, from school-based sexuality education programs to clinic-based counseling programs and TV public service announcements in which entertainers advocated condom use (Fortenberry, 2002). Teenagers and young adults were the primary targets, because their rate of infection from sexually transmitted diseases is higher than that of older individuals (Kaplan et al., 2001). Among adolescents, condom use has increased significantly over the past two decades, suggesting that a massive nationwide health intervention oriented toward changing behavior can have some success.

Unfortunately, the development of drugs that manage HIV fairly effectively was accompanied by an increase in risky sexual behaviors, including a decrease in condom use among individuals at high risk for infection (Hamers & Downs, 2004). Continued efforts are required to maintain condom use (Yzer, Siero, & Buunk, 2000). A number of relationship factors (including level of trust and length of acquaintance) may make it difficult to ask a partner to use a condom (Elwood, Greene, & Carter, 2003; Gavin, 2000). As many as 50% of sexual encounters are unprotected, even among people who use condoms much of the time (Fortenberry, 2002).

Maintaining behavior changes requires continued efforts, even when people understand and accept the value of the new behaviors (Yzer et al., 2000). Condom use and sexual behavior are not exceptions; people have a tendency to quit exercise programs, to regain lost weight, and to start smoking again after they have quit. Maintaining a healthy lifestyle is a personal challenge, as well as a challenge for health psychologists.

Health Psychology and the Future

At the beginning of this chapter, we saw that stress has biological, psychological, and social components, and so does health. A number of biological, behavioral, and social factors interact to determine each person's state of wellness; these include genetics, biological endowment, education, social support, health habits, and medical care.

Whether studying stress and its causes and treatment or looking at ways to improve health, psychologists are taking a prosocial, action-oriented approach. In many ways, the study of stress and health can be considered the future of the discipline. If people can learn to manage stressors and adopt a healthy lifestyle, they may be able to avoid many psychological and physical problems, function at a higher and more effective level, and live longer and healthier lives.

Health psychology only emerged in the 1970s, so it has a short history. During this brief time, it has drawn on research in many areas of psychology, including biopsychology, learning, motivation, emotion, personality, developmental, social, and clinical psychology (Brannon & Feist, 2004). In addition, health psychology has integrated information from disciplines outside of psychology, such as sociology and various medical specialties, including neurology and immunology. This integration has given psychology a more prominent role in health care. As health-care practitioners come to accept the extent of psychological influences on health and disease and the value of psychologically based interventions, the field of health psychology will continue to grow.

Summary and Review

WHAT IS STRESS?

How has stress been defined and measured?

Selye defined *stress* as a nonspecific response to real or imagined challenges or threats. He characterized the stress response as a general adaptation syndrome with three stages: alarm, resistance, and exhaustion. Physiological arousal is heightened during alarm and resistance. If people do not relieve their stress, they experience exhaustion. *Stressors* are environmental stimuli that affect an organism in either physically or psychologically injurious ways. Life events scales, such as the Holmes–Rahe scale, measure the stress of major life events that require change and adaptation. pp. 558–560

According to Lazarus, stress is an interaction between stressors and a person's cognitive appraisal of threat in the situation. Whether a situation is stressful or not depends on a person's appraisal of it. The Hassles Scale is an alternative way to assess stress based on the idea that everyday annoyances are more likely to be stressors than are significant life events. pp. 560–562

What are the major sources of and responses to stress?

Stress can be created by catastrophes, such as natural disasters and events resulting from human actions, or trauma. Prolonged or very severe stress may produce *posttraumatic stress disorder (PTSD)*. Stress can also originate in unhealthy environments characterized by poverty or result from discrimination based on ethnicity, gender, or sexual orientation. The field of *environmental psychology* examines the impact of the physical environment on behavior. Personal factors such as one's job and relationships can produce satisfaction or stress. Some emotionally demanding jobs can lead to *burnout*. pp. 562–567

What characterizes the responses to stress?

Responses to stress occur on the physiological level, with arousal of the sympathetic nervous system, and on the behavioral level. pp. 567–569

How is stress related to disease?

Type A behavior is the behavior pattern of individuals who are competitive, impatient, hostile, and always striving to do more in less time. The overall Type A behavior pattern is not related to the development of heart disease, but the elements of anger and hostility seem to be. pp. 569–571

The field of *psychoneuroimmunology* focuses on the relationship of behavioral, neurological, and immune factors to the development of disease. Stress tends to alter behavior in ways that affect health. p. 572

HOW DO PEOPLE COPE WITH STRESS?

What factors influence coping?

Coping is the process by which a person takes some action to manage, master, tolerate, or reduce environmental and internal demands that cause or might cause stress and that tax the individual's inner resources. A sense of personal control, even if it is an illusion, is usually a positive factor in the ability to cope. *Social support* also increases coping ability and provides a buffer against stress. People who cope despite a great deal of stress have a high level of *resilience*. pp. 572–575

What are some coping strategies?

Coping strategies are the techniques people use to deal with stressful situations. People use both passive and active strategies to cope. Active coping strategies can be *emotion-focused* or *problem-focused*. Typically, active strategies are better than passive ones, and problem-focused strategies are more effective than emotion-focused ones, but all coping strategies can be effective in some situations. *Proactive coping* is taking action in advance of a potentially stressful situation to prevent it, modify it, or prepare for it. Ideally, people learn a variety of coping strategies and how to effectively employ them. *Stress inoculation* is a therapeutic technique for teaching people how to cope more effectively. pp. 575–579

WHAT IS HEALTH PSYCHOLOGY?

Health psychology uses psychological ideas and principles to help enhance health, prevent illness, diagnose and treat disease, and rehabilitate people. Health psychology is an action-oriented discipline that emphasizes preventive health measures as well as interventions directed at existing conditions. pp. 579–580

How does behavior affect health and illness?

Many behaviors are important to health and illness, either enhancing health (exercising, eating a healthy diet, getting enough sleep) or posing risks to health (smoking, drinking too much alcohol). The major risks for becoming infected with HIV/AIDS are behavioral, including having unprotected sex. Health psychologists devise interventions to change people's behaviors to healthier options. pp. 580–583

What are some psychological dimensions of being sick?

Health psychologists work to help people who are ill in an effort to understand the factors that relate to seeking medical care and complying with medical advice. pp. 583–586

What kinds of interventions help people adopt a healthier lifestyle?

Health psychologists are involved in interventions that promote healthy behavior for individuals and communities, such as pain management programs, efforts to control problem drinking on campuses, and the AIDS prevention campaign that focuses on condom use. pp. 586–589

CHAPTER 16

Psychological Disorders

What Is Abnormal Behavior?   592
A Definition
Perspectives on Abnormality
Diagnosing Psychopathology: The *DSM*

What Are Anxiety Disorders?   602
Defining Anxiety
Generalized Anxiety Disorder
Panic Disorder
Phobic Disorders
Obsessive-Compulsive Disorder

What Are Mood Disorders?   607
Depressive Disorders
Causes of Major Depressive Disorder
Bipolar Disorder

What Are Dissociative Disorders?   615
Dissociative Amnesia

Dissociative Identity Disorder: Multiple
   Personalities

What Is Schizophrenia?   617
Essential Characteristics of Schizophrenic
   Disorders
Types of Schizophrenia
Causes of Schizophrenia

What Are Personality Disorders?   624

How Are Violence and Mental
Disorders Related?   626
Diagnoses Associated with Violence
Violence as a Risk for Developing Mental
   Disorders

Summary and Review   631

The finding that a defendant is insane constitutes a legal judgment and not a psychological diagnosis. Psychologists do not even use the word *insane*. Instead, they concentrate on abnormal behavior and psychological disorders, trying to understand the varieties and origins of such behavior and working toward diagnoses and treatments. To do so, they must first define what constitutes abnormal behavior and differentiate it from normal behavior.

What Is Abnormal Behavior?

The first time I (L.B.) visited San Francisco a number of years ago, the street people surprised me. In other cities where I had lived, I had never seen anyone walking down the street, talking out loud to himself, and no one paying much attention. These street people kept their belongings in shopping carts or bags and lived in cardboard boxes. Starting in the 1970s, many people who were diagnosed as mentally ill were deinstitutionalized (released from hospitals). Lacking resources and coping skills, they became the core of today's homeless population, living on the streets. With their shopping carts in tow, these people have their own communities and lifestyles. Of course, not all homeless people have mental disorders or behave bizarrely.

But is walking down the street while talking out loud abnormal behavior? Before cell phones were common, talking out loud with no one else present was unusual, but now it happens regularly. Therefore, the answer depends on the culture. Every society has its own definition of abnormal behavior. (In the former Soviet Union, for example, people were once regularly placed in mental institutions for being homeless or expressing political dissent.) Generally, however, behavior classified by psychologists as abnormal is more than odd. Abnormal behavior is not uncommon, however. In any single year, between 15% and 25% of adults in the world meet the criteria for having a mental disorder; that is, they exhibit abnormal behavior (Kessler, 2000). These figures indicate that mental disorders are a source of disability for a significant portion of the world's population.

A Definition

Abnormal behavior is behavior characterized as (1) not typical, (2) socially unacceptable, (3) distressing to the person who exhibits it or to the person's friends and family, (4) maladaptive, and/or (5) the result of distorted cognitions. Let's consider these five distinguishing characteristics in turn.

Abnormal behavior ■ Behavior characterized as atypical, socially unacceptable, distressing to the individual or others, maladaptive, and/or the result of distorted cognitions.

First, abnormal behavior is *not typical*. Many behaviors are unusual; however, abnormal behaviors tend to be so unusual as to be statistically rare. For example, in April of 2000, Vadim Mieseges, a Swiss college student studying in San Francisco, came to the attention of authorities because he was trying to stab a mannequin in a department store, which is definitely unusual. Of course, some behavior that is not typical is still not abnormal. In the summer and fall of 2004, Ken Jennings broke a record for winnings on the game show *Jeopardy*. His behavior was certainly unusual, but it was acceptable, even admirable, and thus not a problem.

Second, abnormal behavior is also often *socially unacceptable*. To some degree, ideas about what is normal and abnormal vary according to cultural values. What is acceptable in one culture may be labeled unacceptable in another; what is unacceptable for one person may be allowed for another. Behavior that was considered unacceptable 25 years ago, such as a man wearing earrings, is fairly widely accepted today. A behavior that is judged abnormal, however, is one that is unacceptable to a society in general.

Third, a person's abnormal behavior often causes *distress* to the person or to those around him or her. While feelings of distress or anxiety are normal in many situations, prolonged anxiety (distress) may result from abnormal behavior. Trying to stab a mannequin is a behavior that others find distressing.

Fourth, abnormal behavior is usually *maladaptive*, or self-defeating to the person exhibiting it. Committing murder is definitely in that category. Psychologists often describe behavior as *maladjusted* rather than *abnormal*. The distinction is important, because it implies that maladaptive behavior can, with treatment, be adjusted—and become adaptive and productive. The term *maladjustment* also emphasizes specific behaviors rather than labeling the entire person as abnormal.

Last, abnormal behavior is often the result of *distorted cognitions* (thoughts). This was true for Mieseges, who believed that he was part of an alternative reality controlled by computers. His distortion in thinking was extreme, but less extreme ones may also contribute to abnormal behavior.

To summarize, abnormal behavior is not typical; it is socially unacceptable, distressing and maladaptive and may be the result of distorted cognitions. There are, of course, exceptions to this definition. For example, most people would not hesitate to label drug abuse as abnormal behavior, but it is more typical than it once was. Nevertheless, these criteria for determining abnormal behavior provide psychologists with a solid framework for studying abnormal behavior and its treatment.

Perspectives on Abnormality

In July 2004, singer and actress Courtney Love was taken to Bellevue Hospital in New York City on a stretcher and in handcuffs. Emergency medical workers had been summoned to her apartment, but she refused medical assistance, so she was taken to the hospital in restraints. Her attorney denied that the hospitalization was the result of a suicide attempt or a drug overdose, but Love has experienced a range of problems. Her behavior has been both unpredictable and unacceptable. For example, she has a history of drug problems and arrests for assaults and bizarre behavior. She claims that she is no longer addicted to drugs, but her behavior continues to fall outside the range of acceptable. Both her fans and mental health professionals are trying to understand her behavior.

Mental health practitioners want to know why a person becomes maladjusted and understand the origins of the problem, because establishing the cause of a disorder is important in defining it and formulating a treatment plan (and possibly preventing further problems before they happen). Practitioners often turn to theories and models that attempt to explain the causes of abnormality. A *model* is a set of related concepts that helps scientists organize data. Psychologists use models to make predictions about behavior. Models of maladjustment help form the basis of ***abnormal psychology,*** the subfield of psychology concerned with the assessment, treatment, and prevention of maladaptive behavior. Several models help explain abnormal behavior: medical-biological, psychodynamic, humanistic, behavioral, cognitive, sociocultural, and evolutionary.

Model ■ A set of related concepts that helps scientists organize data.

Abnormal psychology ■ The subfield of psychology concerned with the assessment, treatment, and prevention of maladaptive behavior.

The Medical-Biological Model

Thousands of years ago, people believed that abnormal behavior was caused by demons that invaded an individual's body. The "cure" was often *trephination*—drilling a hole into the skull to allow the evil force to escape. Even as recently as a few hundred years ago, people with psychological disorders were caged, like animals. Early reformers, such as Philippe Pinel, advocated the medical model and proposed that abnormal behavior could be treated and cured, like an illness. When scientists showed that syphilis could cause mental disorders, the medical model gained even greater acceptance and led to more humane treatment and better conditions for those with psychological disorders.

The *medical-biological model* of abnormal behavior focuses on the physiological conditions that initiate and underlie abnormal behaviors. This model focuses on genetic abnormalities, problems in the central nervous system, and hormonal changes. It also deals with a range of abnormal behavior caused by mercury poisoning and viral infections and helps explain and treat disorders that have a biological component, such as substance abuse, bipolar disorder, and schizophrenia. Proponents of the medical-biological model might explain Courtney Love's problems as the result of faulty metabolism of neurotransmitters that alters brain chemistry and thus behavior.

Many of the terms and concepts used in psychology and psychiatry are borrowed from medicine—among them *treatment, case, symptom, patient,* and *syndrome,* as well as *mental illness.* The medical model assumes that abnormal behavior, like other illnesses, can be diagnosed, treated, and cured or managed. This approach has not gone unchallenged, however. Its critics say that it does not take advantage of modern psychological insights, such as those of learning theory. A major—but not surprising—disadvantage of the medical model is that it emphasizes hospitalization and drug treatment rather than psychological insights into mental problems. Use of the medical model has also fostered the incorrect notion that abnormal behavior can be contagious, like an infectious disease.

The Psychodynamic Model

The *psychodynamic model* of abnormal behavior is rooted in Freud's theory of personality (discussed in Chapter 13). This model assumes that psychological disorders result from anxiety produced by unresolved conflicts and forces that lie outside a person's awareness. It asserts that maladjustment occurs when a person's ego is not strong enough to balance the demands of the id, the superego, and the outside world. According to the psychodynamic model, maintaining a healthy, functioning personality requires a careful balancing act to satisfy these often conflicting demands. Thus, even seemingly healthy people are vulnerable to maladjustment. Courtney Love's bizarre behavior might be explained as loneliness, despair, or anger turned inward, traceable to her personality development during childhood.

The Humanistic Model

Like the psychodynamic model, the *humanistic model* of abnormal behavior assumes that inner psychic forces are important in establishing and maintaining a fulfilling lifestyle. Unlike psychodynamic theorists, however, humanists believe that people have a good deal of control over their lives and are pulled toward positive development. Maladjustment occurs when people's needs are not met, because of some external circumstance or some internal, personal factor. Cases such as Courtney Love's are puzzling for humanists—her needs for food and shelter are met, but she may lack the acceptance of important others or fail to accept herself. Thus, her abnormal behavior may be determined by internal, personal factors.

The Behavioral Model

The *behavioral model* of abnormal behavior states that such behavior is learned. Behavioral theorists assume that events in a person's environment selectively reinforce or punish various behaviors and, in doing so, shape personality and may create maladjustment. They contend, for example, that an abusive husband may have learned to assert dominance over his wife through physical abuse because physical force has been effective in allowing him to dominate women. Two fundamental assumptions of behavioral (learning) theorists are that disordered behavior can be reshaped and that more appropriate, worthwhile behaviors can be substituted through traditional learning techniques (see Chapter 8). Proponents of the behavioral model might explain Courtney Love's misbehavior in terms of its reinforcement value—she gets a great deal of attention and publicity from this behavior.

The Cognitive Model

The *cognitive model* of abnormal behavior asserts that human beings engage in both healthy and maladjusted behaviors because of their thoughts. As thinking organisms, people decide how to behave. Abnormal behavior is based on false assumptions or unrealistic coping strategies. Practitioners with a cognitive perspective treat people with psychological disorders by helping them develop different ways of thinking about problems and new values. A cognitive theorist might assume that Courtney Love has developed ideas about the world that underlie her bizarre behavior or that she uses drugs that alter her cognitions in ways that affect her behavior.

The Sociocultural Model

According to the *sociocultural model* of abnormal behavior, people develop abnormalities within and because of a context—the context of the family, the community, and the society. Cross-cultural researchers have shown that personality development and psychological disorders reflect the culture and the stressors in a given society. Relying heavily on the learning and cognitive frameworks, the sociocultural model focuses on cultural variables as key determinants of maladjustment.

As researchers examine the frequency and types of disorders that occur in different societies, they note some sharp differences between societies. In China, for example, depression is relatively uncommon, but stress reactions manifested in the form of physical ailments are frequent. Americans and Europeans report guilt and shame when they are depressed; depressed individuals in Africa, on the other hand, are less likely to report these symptoms but more likely to report somatic (physical) complaints. Certain disorders seem to be highly culture-specific; for example, *amok* (as in "running amok"), a disorder that is characterized by sudden rage and homicidal aggression, is seen in some Asian countries, including Malaysia and Thailand, and is thought to be brought on by stress, sleep deprivation, and alcohol consumption.

Using the sociocultural approach, Thomas Szasz (1984, 1987) argued that maladjustment and mental illness are socially constructed and defined—abnormal behaviors are whatever the society fails to accept. Szasz contended that there is, in fact, a myth of mental illness. According to this view, once a practitioner labels a person as "abnormal," the person starts to act that way. The patient confirms the therapist's expectations about his or her abnormality, even when the expectations may not reflect the patient's real condition. In Szasz's view, a patient in therapy creates situations that lead to behaviors that the therapist has predicted, a phenomenon called the *self-fulfilling prophecy*. The creation of a self-fulfilling prophecy is a serious drawback of diagnosis and labeling. In Szasz's view, "mental illness" is a label that serves no good purpose. Although labels can have negative consequences, Szasz's view is an extreme application of the sociocultural model.

The Evolutionary Model

According to the *evolutionary model,* humans evolved in a specific type of environment and are thus best suited to function in similar environments. Modern societies are not very similar to that ancestral environment, so maladjustments may represent behavior that was normal at some point in human evolutionary history but is not today (Cosmides & Tooby, 1999; Millon, 2003). Some behavior problems are adaptive behaviors taken too far, such as fear of heights or fear of snakes. These fears were likely to keep people out of trouble in the distant past, but today, they may produce problems. Another source of maladjustment consists of the many genetic defects that all humans have. These defects do not produce problems in all environments, but in some circumstances, they do. When built-in mechanisms do not perform their adaptive function, they may instead produce harmful dysfunctions (Wakefield, 1999). The criterion of producing harm is one that evolutionary psychologists use to identify a behavior as abnormal.

Which Model Is Best?

Each of the models we've examined—medical-biological, psychodynamic, humanistic, behavioral, cognitive, sociocultural, and evolutionary—looks at maladjustment from a different perspective. Some psychologists hold to one model and use it to analyze all behavior problems, but others believe that different models explain different disorders. For example, learning theory explains the cause of phobias (unreasonable fears) and prescribes an effective course of treatment. Medical-biological theory clarifies a significant part of the problem of schizophrenia. Consequently, many psychologists use an *eclectic approach,* choosing the model that seems to best fit the problem. Other psychologists prefer a *biopsychosocial approach,* which acknowledges that a combination of biological, psychological, and social factors shape behavior. This approach differs from an eclectic approach in that it combines influences; the eclectic approach instead selects a particular model from those available.

Thinking Critically about Mental Illness

People have developed a whole range of ideas about abnormality, and a veil of misunderstanding still surrounds mental illness in many people's minds. For example, many people still think that a mental illness is "forever" and incurable. They sometimes worry that those diagnosed as mentally ill are dangerous, violent, or out of control, behaving bizarrely and wildly different from normal people. The truth is, of course, that more people recover from mental illness than do not, few people with mental illness are violent, and most people with mental illness suffer quietly and bear their pain privately. Treatment with therapy, drugs, and love and care from family members and friends helps in managing these disorders.

As you examine each psychological disorder presented in this chapter, think about whether you favor one model of maladjustment over another. Do you have a cognitive bent, or do you favor a more psychodynamic approach? Perhaps you take a more behavioral view, or the biopsychosocial model represents a combination you like. Regardless of a practitioner's predispositions, it is important that symptoms be carefully evaluated so proper diagnoses can be made. People who are suffering need appropriate help, and a wide variety of treatments are available. (We will examine some of these in Chapter 17.)

Next, we consider a system that has been developed to help practitioners make diagnoses and is presented in *The Diagnostic and Statistical Manual of Mental Disorders*.

Diagnosing Psychopathology: The *DSM*

If you ask psychologists and psychiatrists to explain homeless people or Courtney Love, they are likely to say that homeless people may be odd but not necessarily abnormal, whereas Courtney Love has received at least one diagnosis—substance abuse disorder. The process of diagnosis is complex; it must take many factors into account, and many different diagnoses are available.

The Diagnostic and Statistical Manual of Mental Disorders

The American Psychiatric Association has devised a system for diagnosing maladjusted behavior, which is presented in *The Diagnostic and Statistical Manual of Mental Disorders*, usually called the *DSM*. The current edition of the manual, published in 2000, is a text revision (TR) of the fourth edition, the *DSM–IV–TR*. Research is under way for a fifth edition, which is to appear in 2011 (Kupfer, First, & Regier, 2002). The goals of the *DSM* are to provide a system for diagnosing disorders according to observable behaviors, to improve the reliability of diagnoses, and to make diagnoses consistent with research evidence and practical experience (Kupfer et al., 2002), but many critics claim that the system is less successful than intended (Nathan & Langenbucher, 2003).

The *DSM* designates 17 major categories of disorders (see **Table 16.1**) and more than 200 subcategories. In this chapter, we will explore only a selection of these disorders, some that are common and thus relevant to many people and others that are well known but popularly misunderstood.

Table 16.1

MAJOR CLASSIFICATIONS OF *THE DIAGNOSTIC AND STATISTICAL MANUAL OF MENTAL DISORDERS,* FOURTH EDITION, TEXT REVISION

Disorders first diagnosed in infancy, childhood, and adolescence

Delirium, dementia, and other cognitive disorders

Mental disorders due to a general medical condition

Substance-related disorders

Schizophrenia and other psychotic disorders

Mood disorders

Anxiety disorders

Somatoform disorders

Factitious disorders

Dissociative disorders

Sexual and gender identity disorders

Eating disorders

Sleep disorders

Impulse control disorders

Adjustment disorders

Personality disorders

Other conditions that may receive clinical attention

Note: Each classification is further broken down into subtypes.

The *DSM* also cites the ***prevalence*** of each disorder—the percentage of the population displaying the disorder during any specified period. For most psychological disorders, the *DSM* also indicates the *lifetime prevalence*—the statistical likelihood that a person will develop the disorder during his or her lifetime. For example, a typical *DSM* statement reads, "Community-based studies reveal a lifetime prevalence for Posttraumatic Stress Disorder of approximately 8% of the adult population of the United States. ... Studies of at-risk individuals (i.e., groups exposed to specific traumatic incidents) yield variable findings, with the highest rates (ranging between one-third and more than half of those exposed) found among survivors of rape, military combat and captivity, and ethnically or politically motivated internment and genocide" (APA, 2000, p. 466). The symptoms and disorders described in the *DSM* have existed for years, but the *DSM* system of classification assigns names to the disorders that are consistent with current thought. For example, the behaviors associated with depression, schizophrenia, and attention-deficit/hyperactivity disorder have been around for years—but those specific names are part of the current *DSM*.

An important feature of the *DSM* is that diagnostic information for any disorder is divided among five different dimensions. The *DSM* refers to these dimensions as *axes,* and the manual thus uses what is called a *multiaxial system,* in which an individual is assessed on each of the five axes. Axis I describes the *clinical disorders.* Axis II describes *personality disorders and mental retardation.* Axis III describes

Prevalence ■ The percentage of a population displaying a disorder during any specified period.

current medical conditions that might be pertinent to understanding or managing the individual's mental disorder—for example, heart disease or cancer may be a pertinent factor in depression. Axis IV, *psychosocial or environmental problems,* refers to life stresses (including economic or educational problems) and familial support systems that may or may not facilitate a person's treatment or recovery. Finally, Axis V comprises a *global assessment of functioning,* which is the clinician's overall assessment of the person's functioning in the psychological, social, and occupational domains. For example, a client might be reported as occasionally truant from school but generally functioning pretty well, with some meaningful personal relationships. These five axes, when viewed together, help a clinician fully describe the nature of a person's maladjustment. It is important to note that a clinician might not use all of the axes to diagnose a client. So, for example, there may be no medical condition to report on Axis III. **Table 16.2** describes the axes of the *DSM–IV–TR.*

You might think that such a diagnostic manual would be straightforward, like an encyclopedia of mental disorders. However, because it was written by committees, the *DSM* represents various points of view and includes some biases and compromises. Therefore, it has met with resistance and engendered controversy. Some take issue with the way the *DSM* groups disorders based on symptoms rather than causes (Kihlstrom, 2002), which results in a diagnostic system without a theoretical basis. Others argue that the *DSM* is too complex, with too many categories and symptoms that overlap among them (Houts, 2002). Some say that, despite its complexity, questions remain about the reliability of the *DSM*'s diagnoses for many disorders (Nathan & Langenbucher, 2003). Some have criticized those who formulated the *DSM* for using political rather than scientific criteria in determining what

Table 16.2

THE AXES OF THE *DSM-IV-TR*

	Description
■ Axis I	Clinical disorders—symptoms that cause distress or significantly impair social or occupational functioning
■ Axis II	Personality disorders—personality patterns that are so pervasive, inflexible, and maladaptive that they impair interpersonal or occupational functioning—and mental retardation
■ Axis III	Medical conditions that may be relevant to the understanding or treatment of a psychological disorder
■ Axis IV	Psychosocial and environmental problems (such as negative life events and interpersonal stressors) that may affect the diagnosis, treatment, and prognosis of psychological disorders
■ Axis V	Global assessment of functioning—the individual's overall level of functioning in social, occupational, and leisure activities

disorders are included (Kutchins & Kirk, 1997). Many have concerns about gender and cultural bias (e.g., Hartung & Widiger, 1998; Morey, Warner, & Boggs, 2002). Many psychologists are unhappy with the use of psychiatric terms that perpetuate a medical rather than a behavioral model. Finally, a few psychologists maintain that the *DSM* pathologizes everyday behaviors, making too many behaviors into problems (Tavris, 2003). Therefore, although the *DSM* is the most widely accepted classification system for mental disorders, many object to its widespread use.

Diversity and Diagnoses

The *DSM* is by no means the final word in diagnosing maladjustment. It is a developing system of classification, and the American Psychiatric Association is continually debating new diagnoses and revisions to existing categories (Kupfer et al., 2002). *DSM–IV–TR* includes guidance for clinicians on how to be more sensitive to issues of diversity and gives examples of syndromes that are specific to various cultures, and the issue of cultural diversity will receive even more attention in the *DSM–V*.

Some psychologists, however, feel that the *DSM*'s guidance is not sufficient to assure fair diagnoses. Research does show that the likelihood of a specific diagnosis is related to ethnicity and culture. In the United States, diagnoses of African Americans, Latinos/Latinas, Asian Americans, and Native Americans differ from those of Whites for some diagnostic categories in the *DSM* (Dana, 2002; Neighbors et al., 2003). The stigma of seeking mental health care is stronger in some cultures than others, preventing individuals from seeking care until their maladjustment is severe. Thus, people from some groups are more severely pathological when they are diagnosed (Takeuchi, & Cheung, 1998). In addition, different rates of diagnosis may be due to the way in which clinicians interpret symptoms presented by various people.

Evidence also indicates that culture makes a difference in how people express maladjustment (Mesquita, 2003; Whaley, 1997). For example, in Latino/Latina cultures in the Caribbean, some individuals experience *ataque de nervios* (literally, "attack of nerves"), symptomized by screaming, crying, trembling, and often verbal or physical aggression (Lopez & Guarnaccia, 2000). When the attack has passed, individuals may have no memory of the experience. Between 16% and 23% of people in Puerto Rico report having had an *ataque de nervios,* and divorced, middle-aged women from lower socioeconomic groups are most vulnerable to it. People with *ataque de nervios* may also have disorders listed in the *DSM,* but this disorder exists in the cultural context of Latin America and is distinct from others listed in the *DSM* (Guarnaccia, Lewis-Fernández, & Marano, 2003; Lewis-Fernández et al., 2002).

The United States also has culture-bound syndromes. An analysis of eating disorders revealed that *bulimia,* the eating disorder characterized by binge eating followed by purging, occurs only in Western societies (or societies influenced by them) (Keel & Klump, 2003). However, the eating disorder *anorexia* appears in all cultures (although not with the same frequency). The prevalence rate of a specific disorder in a particular country probably reflects racial, religious, and cultural factors. Prevalence rates especially reflect the specific culture-bound behavior patterns that a society considers abnormal or normal. As suggested earlier, various cultures allow for, and perhaps encourage, the experience of specific symptoms, such as those of *ataque de nervios* or bulimia.

Understanding cultural factors in the expression of abnormal behavior is a continuing challenge for clinicians involved in making diagnoses.

The remainder of this chapter explores some of the disorders described in the *DSM*. We discuss some disorders that are common (such as phobias) as well as some that are not common but are well known yet misunderstood (such as dissociative identity disorder). We begin with a common type—anxiety disorders.

What Are Anxiety Disorders?

Everyone experiences anxiety. Most people feel anxious in specific situations, such as before taking an examination, competing in a swim meet, or delivering a speech. This experience of anxiety can be a positive, motivating force, and feelings of anxiety have a clear adaptive advantage for survival in a dangerous world. But anxiety is debilitating for some people, creating such uncertainty and fear that they cannot function. Children who experience anxiety disorders are at increased risk for suicide when they are adolescents (Rudd, Joiner, & Rumzek, 2004).

Anxiety disorders as a whole are common in the general population, affecting as many as 15% of the population of the United States (Pigott, 2003) and a similar percentage of the population of Europe (Alonso et al., 2004). Research on anxiety disorders has increased in recent years, but research on certain specific populations—for example, Asian Americans—has been sparse (Lee, Lei, & Sue, 2001). Some research investigates the genetic components in anxiety (Hariri & Weinberger, 2003); other research studies focus on how symptoms may be alleviated through various drugs that increase the availability of the neurotransmitter serotonin (Vaas, 2004).

Defining Anxiety

Anxiety ■ A generalized feeling of fear and apprehension that may be related to a particular situation or object and is often accompanied by increased physiological arousal.

Anxiety is a generalized feeling of fear and apprehension that may be related to a particular situation or object and is often accompanied by increased physiological arousal. Anxiety manifests itself in a wide range of symptoms, including fear, apprehension, inattention, heart palpitations, respiratory distress, and dizziness. Karen Horney (pronounced HORN-eye), a neo-Freudian analyst famous for her work on anxiety, described anxiety as the central factor in both normal and abnormal behavior (Horney, 1937). Horney considered anxiety a motivating force, an intrapsychic urge, and a signal of distress. She also argued that anxiety underlies many forms of maladjustment, which occurs when too many defenses against anxiety pervade the personality.

Freud, in contrast, saw anxiety as the result of constant conflict among the id, ego, and superego. He called nearly all forms of behavior associated with anxiety *neurotic*. Freud's term *neurosis* was once part of the *DSM*'s diagnostic terminology, but it was removed. (It made its way into everyday language, however, and nonpsychologists tend to describe any quirky or annoying behavior as neurotic.) Another Freudian term, *free-floating anxiety,* described persistent anxiety not clearly related to any specific object or situation and accompanied by a sense of impending doom. This term is also no longer used diagnostically.

During the 1980s, research on anxiety disorders increased dramatically, prompted in part by the recognition that these disorders are very common and not always diagnosed (Pigott, 2003). Several different types of anxiety disorders are listed in the *DSM*, including generalized anxiety disorder, phobias, and obsessive-compulsive disorder.

Generalized Anxiety Disorder

Generalized anxiety disorder is an anxiety disorder characterized by persistent anxiety occurring on more days than not for at least 6 months, sometimes with increased activity of the autonomic nervous system, apprehension, excessive muscle tension, and difficulty in concentrating (APA, 2000). In addition, people with generalized anxiety disorder find it difficult to control the anxiety they experience, so it is a persistent problem in their lives. They show three types of symptoms related to vigilance: restlessness or feeling "on edge," difficulty in concentrating, and irritability or impatience. Other symptoms are being easily fatigued and experiencing sleep difficulties or disturbances. Muscle tension and the inability to relax are also symptoms. The *DSM* states that in order to be diagnosed with generalized anxiety disorder, a person must show persistent anxiety that is not specific to one situation.

People with generalized anxiety disorder feel anxious almost constantly, even though nothing specific seems to provoke their anxiety (Gale & Oakley-Browne, 2004). Expressed fears often revolve around health, money, family, or work. Unable to relax, they have trouble falling asleep; they tend to feel tired and have trouble concentrating. They often report excessive sweating, headaches, and insomnia. They are tense and irritable, have difficulty making decisions, and may hyperventilate (Kendall, Krain, & Treadwell, 1999).

Generalized anxiety disorder ■ An anxiety disorder characterized by persistent anxiety occurring on more days than not for at least 6 months, sometimes with increased activity of the autonomic nervous system, apprehension, excessive muscle tension, and difficulty in concentrating.

Panic Disorder

People with several classifications of anxiety disorders experience *panic attacks,* characterized as acute anxiety accompanied by a sharp increase in autonomic nervous system arousal that is not triggered by a specific event. This description sounds unpleasant, but a description from one of my (L.B.'s) friends sounds even worse—he said he thought he was having a heart attack and feared he would die. His heart raced, he sweated, and he had trouble breathing, all symptoms of panic attacks.

Individuals diagnosed with panic disorder have attacks "out of the blue," with no situation or stimulus identifiable as the precipitating cause. Some people with panic disorder have frequent attacks, some experience clusters of attacks, and others have infrequent attacks. Panic attacks occur in conjunction with other anxiety disorders or other disorders more commonly than they occur as a separate disorder (APA, 2000). About 24% of people who experience panic disorder also have some type of depressive disorder, and about 10% to 20% have alcohol abuse problems (Cox & Taylor, 1999; Goodwin, Fergusson, & Horwood, 2004). However, panic attacks are most commonly associated with phobic disorders.

Panic attack ■ Acute anxiety accompanied by sharp increases in autonomic nervous system arousal that is not triggered by a specific event.

Phobic Disorders

Do you know someone who avoids crowds at all cost, who is petrified at the thought of flying in a plane, or who shudders at the sight of a harmless garter snake? That person may suffer from a *phobic disorder*—an anxiety disorder characterized by excessive

Phobic disorder ■ Anxiety disorder characterized by excessive and irrational fear of, and consequent avoidance of, some specific object or situation.

irrational fear of, and consequent avoidance of, some specific object or situation (APA, 2000). Unlike people who feel anxious almost constantly, the anxiety of those who suffer from phobic disorders is focused on a particular type of object or situation. People with a phobic disorder exhibit avoidance and escape behaviors, show increased heart rate and irregular breathing patterns, and report thoughts of disaster, severe embarrassment, or both. Many psychologists agree that once a phobia is established, it is maintained by the relief a person derives from escaping or avoiding the feared situation. Phobic disorders are common, affecting over 10% of the people in the United States (Kessler et al., 1994) and a similar percentage in Europe (Alonso et al., 2004).

One key to diagnosing phobic disorders is that the fear must be excessive and disproportionate to the situation, enough to induce a person to avoid the situation altogether. Fear alone does not distinguish a phobia; both fear and avoidance must be evident. Most people have fears, and some fears are adaptive. Phobias, however, are not normal and not adaptive. For example, many people fear heights, but this fear is not usually phobic—it is adaptive, because heights can be dangerous. Most people who fear heights would not avoid visiting a friend who lived on the top floor of a tall building, but a person with a phobia of heights would. The fears of people with phobias are unreasonable and disproportionate to the situation. An almost infinite number of objects and situations inspire fear in people. Because of the diversity and number of phobias, the *DSM* classifies three basic kinds: agoraphobia, social phobia, and specific phobia.

Agoraphobia

Agoraphobia [AG-or-uh-FOE-bee-uh] ▪ Anxiety disorder characterized by marked fear and avoidance of being alone in a place from which escape might be difficult or embarrassing.

Agoraphobia is an anxiety disorder characterized by marked fear and avoidance of being alone in a place from which escape might be difficult or embarrassing. This phobia is accompanied by avoidance behaviors that may eventually interfere with normal activities. It can become so debilitating that it prevents the individual from going into airplanes or tunnels, for example, or from being in crowds. People with severe cases may decide never to leave their homes, fearing that they will lose control, panic, or cause a scene in a public place. An episode of agoraphobia is often brought on by stress, particularly interpersonal stress. Symptoms of agoraphobia are hyperventilation, extreme tension, and even cognitive disorganization. Like most other anxiety disorders, it is far more common in women than in men (5.8% versus 2.8%) (Kessler et al., 1994). Agoraphobia may occur either with or without panic attacks.

Agoraphobia can be incapacitating and remains difficult to treat. Contemporary researchers have searched for the roots of panic attacks and the development of agoraphobia in individual learning history, family experiences, and genetics (Zuckerman, 1999). Treatment options include cognitive behavioral therapy or any of several types of drugs, or a combination of psychotherapy and drugs (Starcevic et al., 2004).

Social Phobia

Social phobia [FOE-bee-uh] ▪ Anxiety disorder characterized by fear of, and desire to avoid, situations in which one might be exposed to scrutiny by others and might behave in an embarrassing or humiliating way; sometimes called *social anxiety disorder*.

A person with a social phobia tends to avoid situations involving possible exposure to close attention from other people. A *social phobia* (sometimes called *social anxiety disorder*) is an anxiety disorder characterized by fear of, and desire to avoid, situations in which one might be exposed to scrutiny by others and might behave in an embarrassing or humiliating way. A person with a social phobia may avoid eating in public, for example, or speaking before other people. Such a person also typically refuses to become involved in any situation in which he or she might be evaluated and suffer a loss of self-esteem (Hackmann, Clark, & McManus, 2000). Common social phobias include fear of speaking in public and fear of going to parties where there will be many strangers. Many people with this disorder fail to seek treatment, which led to the misperception that it is uncommon. Social phobia is actually very common, affecting between 7% and 12% of the population (Charney, 2004). This disorder disrupts normal life and social relationships, as do many specific phobias.

Specific Phobia

A *specific phobia* is an anxiety disorder characterized by irrational and persistent fear of a particular object or situation, along with a compelling desire to avoid it. Most people are familiar with specific phobias; **Table 16.3** lists some examples, including *claustrophobia* (fear of closed spaces), *hematophobia* (fear of blood), and *acrophobia* (fear of heights). Many specific phobias develop in childhood, adolescence, or early adulthood. Most people who have fears of heights, small spaces, water, doctors, or flying can calm themselves and deal with their fears. Those who cannot—true phobics—often seek the help of a psychotherapist when the phobia interferes with their health or day-to-day functioning. Treatment using behavior therapy is typically effective.

Specific phobia ■
Anxiety disorder characterized by irrational and persistent fear of a particular object or situation, along with a compelling desire to avoid it.

Table 16.3

SOME COMMON SPECIFIC PHOBIAS

Acrophobia (fear of high places)
Ailurophobia (fear of cats)
Algophobia (fear of pain)
Anthropophobia (fear of men)
Aquaphobia (fear of water)
Astraphobia (fear of storms, thunder, and lightning)
Claustrophobia (fear of closed spaces)
Cynophobia (fear of dogs)
Hematophobia (fear of blood)
Mysophobia (fear of contamination)
Nyctophobia (fear of darkness)
Pathophobia (fear of disease)
Pyrophobia (fear of fire)
Thanatophobia (fear of death)
Xenophobia (fear of strangers)
Zoophobia (fear of animals)

Obsessive-Compulsive Disorder

Being orderly and organized is usually an asset, especially in today's fast-paced, complex society. However, when orderliness becomes an overriding concern, a person may be suffering from obsessive-compulsive disorder. *Obsessive-compulsive disorder* is an anxiety disorder characterized by persistent and uncontrollable thoughts and irrational beliefs that often cause the performance of compulsive rituals that interfere with daily life. At least for people in the United States, the unwanted thoughts, urges, and actions of people with obsessive-compulsive disorder focus on maintaining order and control. Some cultural variation occurs in the content of the obsessions, although not in other features of this disorder (Fontenelle et al., 2004). For example, a similar percentage of people are affected in the United States (about 2.5%) (Zuckerman, 1999) and in Germany (about 3.5%) (Angst et al., 2004). About 80% of affected individuals show a mixture of both obsessions and compulsions.

Most people with obsessive-compulsive disorder combat anxiety by carrying out ritual behaviors that reduce tension. They feel they have to *do* something, and their actions soothe their anxiety. For example, a man obsessed with avoiding germs may wash his hands a hundred times a day and may wear white gloves to avoid touching contaminated objects. If he does not perform these compulsive acts, he may develop severe anxiety. A woman obsessed with punctuality may become extremely anxious if she might arrive late for a dinner date. A person may compulsively write notes about every detail of every task before permitting herself or himself to take any action. Here is an account of extreme obsessive-compulsive behavior:

> I used to write notes to remind myself to do a particular job, so in my mind there was a real risk that one of these notes might go out of the window or door. . . . My fear was that if one of these papers blew away, this would cause a fatality. . . . I found it difficult to walk along the street, as every time I saw paper I wondered if it was some of mine. I had to pick it all up, unless it was brown chocolate paper, or lined paper, which I didn't use. And before I got on my bike, I checked that nothing was sticking out of my pockets and got my wife to recheck. ... I couldn't smoke a cigarette without taking it to bits and checking there was no document between the paper and tobacco. I couldn't even have sex because I thought a piece of paper might get intertwined into the mattress. (Melville, 1977, pp. 66–67)

Freud and other psychodynamic theorists believed that obsessive-compulsive disorder stems largely from difficulties during the anal stage of development, when orderliness and cleanliness are the agenda. Learning theorists argue that bringing order to the environment reduces uncertainty and risk and thus is reinforcing. Because reinforced behaviors tend to recur, these behaviors become exaggerated during times of stress. These explanations are consistent with popular views that obsessive-compulsive disorder has a psychological basis (Furnham & Buck, 2003), but growing evidence indicates a strong biological basis for this disorder. Biopsychologists have identified a genetic component for obsessive-compulsive disorder (Grados, Walkup, & Walford, 2003). In addition, biopsychologists have tried to identify brain structures associated with obsessive-compulsive disorder by using brain-imaging technology. Results indicate that several parts of the brain are

Obsessive-compulsive disorder ■ Anxiety disorder characterized by persistent and uncontrollable thoughts and irrational beliefs that often cause the performance of compulsive rituals that interfere with daily life.

Building Table 16.1

IMPORTANT CHARACTERISTICS OF ANXIETY DISORDERS

Type of Disorder	Presence of Delusions	Evidence for Biological Contribution	Main Symptoms	Higher Prevalence among Men or Women?	Typical Age of Onset
Anxiety Disorders	Not common	Yes	Anxiety, fear	Women	Any age

involved, including parts of the frontal and temporal lobes of the cerebral cortex, the basal ganglia, and the amygdala (Adler et al., 2000; Anderson & Savage, 2004). Both the functioning and the structure of an area of the frontal lobes just behind the eyes and of the amygdala (under the temporal lobes) are affected in individuals with obsessive-compulsive disorder. This evidence leads some neurologists to define this disorder as a brain disorder with behavioral symptoms (Micallef & Blin, 2001).

The increasing evidence for a biological basis for obsessive-compulsive disorder has caused greater reliance on biologically based treatments, centering on drugs. Treatment often includes drugs that affect the metabolism of the neurotransmitter serotonin, such as Prozac or Zoloft (Denys, van Megen, & van der Wee, 2004) (see Chapter 17). Drug treatments are often combined with relaxation or cognitive behavior therapy that addresses the obsessive thoughts and prevents the performance of the compulsive behaviors (Abramowitz, Franklin, & Cahill, 2003). Such treatment helps change ideas about stress and the consequences of anxiety. Family therapy is also helpful; families are taught that they should neither encourage the behaviors nor participate in the person's rituals. Today, self-help groups are also part of successful treatments. Adults with obsessive-compulsive disorder tend to show improvement over time (Angst et al., 2004), but individuals who develop the disorder as children or adolescents tend to have persistent symptoms, even with treatment (Stewart et al., 2004).

Building Table 16.1 presents some of the important characteristics of anxiety disorders. Research on these disorders has revealed that individuals diagnosed with one anxiety disorder, such as social phobia, are at elevated risk for other anxiety disorders, such as panic attacks or obsessive-compulsive disorder (Goodwin et al., 2004). In addition, anxiety disorders present a risk for mood disorders, especially depression.

What Are Mood Disorders?

Everyone experiences dark moods at one time or another. Ending a long-term intimate relationship, feeling overwhelmed during final exams, mourning the death of a close friend or relative, and experiencing serious financial problems can all give rise to bad moods. We often refer to *depression* as feeling bad. But when people become so depressed or sad that a change occurs in their outlook and overt behavior, they may be suffering from *clinical depression*, a term that has a specific meaning for psychologists. Depression is considered to be a **mood disorder**, a category of psychological disorder

Mood disorder ■ A category of psychological disorder that includes depressive disorders and bipolar disorder.

that includes depressive disorders and bipolar disorder. These disorders may sometimes be triggered by a specific event, but for many individuals the symptoms develop with no apparent cause.

Depressive Disorders

Bonnie Strickland, former president of the American Psychological Association, said during the 1988 APA annual meeting, "Depression has been called the common cold of psychological disturbances … which underscores its prevalence, but trivializes its impact." About 16% of the population of the United States will, at some time during their lives, be clinically depressed, and in any one year, 6.6% will be (Kessler et al., 2003). Those percentages translate into about 32 million Americans suffering from depression each year. As many as half of those people remain undiagnosed and do not receive treatment, despite its availability (Substance Abuse and Mental Health Services Administration, 2003).

In his 1990 memoir, *Darkness Visible*, American novelist and Pulitzer Prize–winner William Styron described his state of mind during a period of depression:

> He [a psychiatrist] asked me if I was suicidal, and I reluctantly told him yes. I did not particularize—since there seemed no need to—did not tell him that in truth many of the artifacts of my house had become potential devices for my own destruction: the attic rafters (and an outside maple or two) a means to hang myself, the garage a place to inhale carbon monoxide, the bathtub a vessel to receive the flow from my opened arteries. The kitchen knives in their drawers had but one purpose for me. Death by heart attack seemed particularly inviting, absolving me as it would of active responsibility, and I had toyed with the idea of self-induced pneumonia—a long frigid, shirt-sleeved hike through the rainy woods. Nor had I overlooked an ostensible accident, à la Randall Jarrell, by walking in front of a truck on the highway nearby …. Such hideous fantasies, which cause well people to shudder, are to the deeply depressed mind what lascivious daydreams are to persons of robust sexuality. (p. 52)

Depressed people are more than simply sad. As Styron reveals, depression is debilitating, overwhelming, and dangerous. *Depressive disorders* are mood disorders in which people show extreme and persistent sadness, despair, and loss of interest in life's usual, day-to-day activities. *Major depressive disorder* (or clinical depression) is characterized by loss of interest in almost all of life's usual activities, a hopeless or discouraged mood, sleep disturbance, loss of appetite and energy, and feelings of unworthiness and guilt.

Another depressive disorder is dysthymic disorder. People suffering from *dysthymic disorder,* experience a chronic depressed mood for more days than not for a period of at least 2 years. Dysthymic disorder often goes undiagnosed and untreated; people begin to accept this mood as part of their typical personality. Dysthymic disorder is not as severe as major depressive disorder but lasts longer and often occurs along with it. Clinicians often diagnose dysthymic disorder in persons who were initially seeking help for a major depressive episode, and the symptoms of the two types of depressive disorder are similar.

Depressive disorders ■ Mood disorders in which people show extreme and persistent sadness, despair, and loss of interest in life's usual, day-to-day activities.

Major depressive disorder ■ Depressive disorder characterized by loss of interest in almost all of life's usual activities; a sad, hopeless, or discouraged mood; sleep disturbance; loss of appetite; loss of energy; and feelings of unworthiness and guilt; also known as *clinical depression.*

Symptoms

The symptoms of depressive disorders include poor appetite, insomnia, weight loss, loss of energy, feelings of worthlessness and intense guilt, inability to concentrate, and sometimes thoughts of death and suicide (Zuckerman, 1999). Depressed people have a gloomy outlook on life, an extremely distorted view of their problems, a tendency to blame themselves, and low feelings of self-worth. People with major depression do not experience pleasure, and their brains even fail to respond to pleasurable stimuli in the way that the brains of nondepressed people do (Mitterschiffthaler et al., 2003). Depressed people often withdraw from social and physical contact with others. Every task seems to require a great effort, thought is slow and unfocused, and problem-solving abilities are impaired. Depression is associated with abnormal brain activity in the frontal lobes, the hippocampus, the amygdala, and the anterior cingulate cortex (Davidson et al., 2002).

Depressed people may also have *delusions*—false beliefs that are inconsistent with reality but are held in spite of evidence that disconfirms them. Delusions may induce feelings of guilt, shame, and persecution (Ohayon & Schatzberg, 2002). Seriously depressed people show even greater disruptions in thought and motor processes and a total lack of spontaneity and motivation. Such people typically report that they have no hope for themselves or the world; nothing seems to interest them. Their delusions may include reports of strange diseases or the sense that their bodies are disintegrating. Most people who exhibit symptoms of major depressive disorder can describe their reasons for feeling sad and dejected; however, they may be unable to explain why their response is so deep and so prolonged.

Delusions ■ False beliefs that are inconsistent with reality but are held in spite of evidence that disconfirms them.

Psychologists say that many people suffering from major depressive disorder are poor at reality testing. *Reality testing* is a person's ability to judge the demands of the environment accurately and to deal with those demands. People who are poor at reality testing are unable to cope with the demands of life in rational ways because their reasoning ability is grossly impaired.

Onset and Duration

A major depressive episode can occur at any age, but most people who experience these episodes usually undergo the first one before age 40. Symptoms may last for days, weeks, or even months, but there is a great deal of individual variation. Episodes may occur once or many times. Sometimes a depressive episode may be followed by years of normal functioning—followed by two or three brief incidents of depression a few weeks apart. Stressful life events are sometimes predictors of depression (Mazure et al., 2000). Children and adolescents can experience depression (Birmahler et al., 2004; Lewinsohn et al., 1999), and children who suffer from depression often have additional symptoms, especially anxiety and loneliness.

Prevalence

Depression imposes an enormous burden worldwide (Kessler, 2000). An examination of the rates of mood disorders in countries around the world reveals that industrialized countries show higher rates than developing countries (WHO International

Consortium in Psychiatric Epidemiology, 2000), but this difference may reflect better access to mental health services in developed countries. Depression is not restricted to industrialized, individualist cultures. It is a leading cause of disability worldwide, affecting more than 300 million people (Holden, 2000).

Women are twice as likely as men to be diagnosed as depressed and are more likely to express feelings of depression openly (Culbertson, 1997; Klose & Jacobi, 2004). In the United States, about 19%–23% of women and 8%–11% of men have experienced a major depressive episode at some time (Hollon, Thase, & Markowitz, 2002). About 6% of women and 3% of men have experienced episodes severe enough to require hospitalization. A higher rate of depression among women appears in many (but not all) cultures. The reasons for this gender difference are not clear. However, Susan Nolen-Hoeksema and her colleagues (Gonzalez, Nolen-Hoeksema, & Treynor, 2003; Nolen-Hoeksema, 2000, 2002; Nolen-Hoeksema, Larson, & Grayson, 1999) hypothesize that girls and women have more negative experiences and lower feelings of mastery and think differently about their negative life events. Specifically, they tend to engage in *rumination,* a process of dwelling on and analyzing problems and negative feelings. As **Figure 16.1** shows, this coping style tends to prolong negative feelings and to increase depression.

People between the ages of 25 and 45 are most likely to be diagnosed with depression (Ingram, Scott, & Siegle, 1999). However, the increased prevalence in this age range may be due to life events that tend to occur then and to be associated with depression, such as job and relationship problems (Nolen-Hoeksema & Ahrens, 2002). When the types of events that occur during different life phases are factored in, the rate of depression is very similar across the life span. Indeed, the expression of symptoms is similar in adolescents and adults and in women and men (Lewinsohn et al., 2003). So, although the likelihood of being diagnosed with depression varies with certain demographic factors, depressed people tend to be similar in terms of their experience of the disorder.

Causes of Major Depressive Disorder

Although major depression is "the common cold of mental disorders," its cause continues to be debated. Several different theories about the cause have research support. However, the research does not present a coherent picture, and prominent researcher Marvin Zuckerman (1999) has proposed that more than one theory may be necessary to explain all cases of depression. Let's consider the leading theories and the research support and problems with each, bearing in mind that Zuckerman may be correct—depression may have more than one cause.

Biological Theories

Both genes and neurotransmitters have been implicated as biological factors that underlie depression, and indeed, the two are probably connected. That genetic factors are at work in depression becomes apparent from research showing that children of depressed parents are more likely than other children to be depressed. Further, twin studies indicate that genetic factors play a substantial role in depression (Enam, 2003).

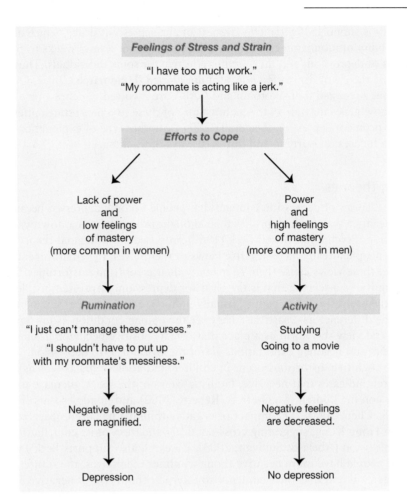

Figure 16.1
How Stress, Feelings of Mastery, and Rumination Influence Depression
Susan Nolen-Hoeksema and her colleagues hypothesize that rumination increases feelings of depression. Women are more likely than men to experience feelings of low power and low mastery, which increase rumination and magnify depression.

However, depression is not caused by a single gene, and identifying multiple interacting genes is a complex task (Zuckerman, 1999). In addition, the process through which genes affect behavior must be demonstrated. The leading possibility is that genes act by affecting the manufacture or metabolism of neurotransmitters.

You'll recall that neurotransmitters are released from the ends of neurons by an action potential, move across the synaptic space, and attach themselves at binding sites on adjacent neurons (see Chapter 3). Binding sites are specific to certain neurotransmitters, and neurons will be influenced only by those neurotransmitters for which they have receptor sites. One biological theory of depression centers on a group of neurotransmitters called *monoamines,* which includes dopamine, norepinephrine, epinephrine, and serotonin. When monoamines fail to bind to neurons, researchers find that people report feeling depressed, and when people are given drugs that promote the binding of monoamines, depression lifts. The *monoamine theory of depression* suggests that major depression results from a deficiency of monoamines or inefficient monoamine receptors (Slattery, Hudson, & Nutt, 2004; Soares & Mann, 1997).

This theory is supported by the effectiveness of antidepressant drugs, which affect the availability of monoamines. However, these drugs take several weeks to relieve symptoms of depression, and they are not effective for some individuals. Thus, the monoamine theory of depression has been questioned (Hindmarch, 2001). Other research has suggested that serotonin and GABA are involved in depression and has specified how genes may affect the manufacture of these two neurotransmitters in ways that promote depression (Sen et al., 2004). Another type of explanation for depression focuses on learning and distorted ways of thinking.

Cognitive Theories

Cognitive theories of depression contend that people become depressed because they think in negative ways, which pushes their thought processes into a downward spiral to depression. Psychiatrist Aaron Beck (1967) proposed an influential theory that depressed people already have negative views of themselves, the environment, and the future, and these views cause them to magnify their errors and misfortunes. This way of thinking forms a schema that is the basis for depression. Depressed people compare themselves to other people, usually unfairly, and when they come up short, they see the difference as disastrous. They see the human condition as universally wretched and view the world as a place that defeats positive behavior. Their poor self-concepts and negative expectations about the world lead to depression.

These cognitive distortions occur in children and adolescents as well as adults, and research indicates that negative, fatalistic views of the world increase the risk for depression in children (McGrath & Repetti, 2002) and in adolescents (Roberts, Roberts, & Chen, 2000). The impact of negative thinking has been observed in adolescents in Hong Kong, suggesting cross-cultural validation of its contribution to the risk of depression (Abela & Sullivan, 2003). Research also supports Beck's view that depressed people have more negative thoughts about themselves, the future, and the world in general and that their tendency to interpret the world in negative terms is a relatively unchanging way in which they process information (Ingram et al., 1999). This tendency is activated by negative life events.

According to Beck, cognitions underlie depression and perpetuate it by causing poor judgments, which feed back into negative cognitions. Beck's theory is influential among psychologists for two reasons: First, it is consistent with the notion that depression stems from ways of thinking. Second, it acknowledges the interaction between the cognitive schema that underlies depression and environmental variables such as stress.

A second cognitive approach to depression is based on Martin Seligman's (1976) research on *learned helplessness,* the behavior of giving up or not responding, which is exhibited by people and nonhuman animals exposed to negative consequences or punishment over which they have no control. That is, when everything that someone does fails to work, the person stops trying. Seligman suggested that people's beliefs about the causes of their failures determine whether they will become depressed. When they attribute their failures to unalterable conditions within themselves ("my own weakness, which is unlikely to change"), they set up negative thinking that may become depression. People who develop learned helplessness feel that they cannot

Learned helplessness ■ The behavior of giving up or not responding, which is exhibited by people and nonhuman animals exposed to negative consequences or punishment over which they feel they have no control.

change highly aversive life events and become pessimistic and hopeless (Abramson, Metalsky, & Alloy, 1989). For example, a man who comes to believe that his efforts to meet new people by being outgoing and friendly never work may stop trying. Eventually, he will choose not to respond to the environment because he has learned that his behavior makes no difference (Peterson & Seligman, 1984). According to Seligman, the major cause of learned helplessness is a person's (or nonhuman animal's) belief that a response will not affect what happens in the future. The result of this belief is anxiety, depression, and, eventually, nonresponsiveness. This type of negative cognitive style and a tendency to ruminate about negative events were predictors of depression among a group of college students (Alloy & Robinson, 2003).

These two views of cognition as an important component of depression have been influential in terms of therapy, prompting the widespread use of cognitive and cognitive behavior therapies for depression. However, the research on the effects of negative thinking shows that this cognitive style alone is not sufficient to prompt the development of depression. A person must also experience negative life events. In addition, depressed people may also have some biological component that predisposes them to the disorder. All of this evidence points to a biopsychosocial explanation for depression.

The Biopsychosocial Model

Many variables determine whether an individual will develop depression (or any other disorder, for that matter). Some factors, including genetic history, brain chemistry, cognitions, stress, and family environment, make some people more vulnerable to depression than others. *Vulnerability* is a person's diminished ability to deal with demanding life events. The more vulnerable a person is, the less environmental stress or other factors (such as anxiety) are needed to initiate depression. This is the vulnerability–stress hypothesis, sometimes termed the *diathesis–stress model.* (A *diathesis* is a predisposition to something.) This model hypothesizes that mental disorders occur when people with vulnerability encounter stressful situations. That is, disorders develop from the combination of factors. The vulnerability may be due either to biological factors or to learned tendencies, but vulnerable people develop problems at lower levels of stress than do less vulnerable people (Zuckerman, 1999). Several studies have demonstrated that a combination of situations is important for the development of depression.

Vulnerability ∎
A person's diminished ability to deal with demanding life events.

One combination that can lead to depression consists of negative life events and a negative view of the world (Alloy & Robinson, 2003; Osvath, Voros, & Fekete, 2004). Individuals with a negative outlook on life think about bad things that happen to them differently than do those who are more optimistic; they focus on maladaptive thoughts that promote depression. When such individuals experience few negative life events, they are fine. However, if they experience loss of some important person during childhood or adulthood, sexual abuse, or violence, they become more vulnerable to depression than people with a more positive outlook.

Another combination that is related to the development of depression is genetic vulnerability plus life stress. Avshalom Caspi and his colleagues (Caspi et al., 2003) conducted a longitudinal study to try to understand why negative life experiences affect some people more strongly than others. They found that people with a specific variation of a gene involved with the neurotransmitter serotonin were vulnerable to depression. Earlier research had not established that this genetic variation produced depression, and Caspi's study showed why: The gene alone does not create depression. However, the interaction of life events and genetic vulnerability increased the risk for symptoms of depression, diagnoses of depression, and thoughts of suicide. The concept of vulnerability also applies to another type of mood disorder—bipolar disorder.

Bipolar Disorder

Bipolar disorder ■
Mood disorder that was originally known as manic-depressive disorder because it is characterized by behavior that vacillates between two extremes: mania and depression.

Movie directors Francis Ford Coppola and Tim Burton, actors Jean-Claude Van Damme, Linda Hamilton, Margot Kidder, and Carrie Fisher, and musicians Axl Rose and Sting all have at least two things in common: artistic talent and a diagnosis of bipolar disorder. People who suffer from bipolar disorder experience depressive states similar to major depression, but they also experience the opposite feelings—excitement, confidence, and euphoria. *Bipolar disorder,* which was originally known as *manic-depressive disorder,* gets its name from the fact that people with this disorder experience two extremes: mania and depression. The *manic phase* is characterized by rapid speech, inflated self-esteem, impulsiveness, euphoria, and decreased need for sleep. People in the manic phase are easily distracted, get angry when things do not go their way, and seem to have boundless energy. A person in the *depressed phase* is moody and sad, with feelings of hopelessness. People with bipolar disorder cycle between these two mood extremes.

Bipolar disorder is much less common than major depression. Less than 1% of the population develops this disorder—although 1% works out to about 2 million

Table 16.4

BIPOLAR DISORDER: CYCLES OF MANIA AND DEPRESSION

	Manic Behavior	Depressive Behavior
■ Emotional Characteristics	Elation, euphoria, extreme sociability, expansiveness, impatience, distractibility, inflated self-esteem	Gloominess, hopelessness, social withdrawal, irritability
■ Cognitive Characteristics	Desire for action, impulsiveness, grandiosity	Indecisiveness, slowness of thought, obsessive worrying about death, negative self-image, delusions of guilt, difficulty in concentrating
■ Physical Characteristics	Hyperactivity, talkativeness, decreased need for sleep, sexual indiscretion, increased appetite	Fatigue, difficulty in sleeping, decreased sex drive, decreased appetite, decreased motor activity

Building Table 16.2

IMPORTANT CHARACTERISTICS OF ANXIETY AND MOOD DISORDERS

Type of Disorder	Presence of Delusions	Evidence for Biological Contribution	Main Symptoms	Higher Prevalence among Men or Women?	Typical Age of Onset
Anxiety Disorders	Not common	Yes	Anxiety, fear	Women	Any age
Mood Disorders	Yes	Yes	Feelings of despair	Women	Young adults

Americans (Waraich et al., 2004). Men and women are equally likely to be affected. People who suffer from bipolar disorder are often in their late 20s before they begin to manifest the symptoms, and the disorder often continues throughout their lives. Bipolar disorder may go unrecognized and be underdiagnosed in children and adolescents (Costello et al., 2002).

People with bipolar disorder may be relatively stable for a few days, weeks, or months between episodes of excitement and depression, or they may cycle rapidly between the two moods. The key component of bipolar disorder is the shift from excited states to depressive states. The disorder seems to have a biological basis with a substantial genetic component, and researchers are making progress in identifying which combination of genes makes a person vulnerable to bipolar disorder (McInnis et al., 2003; Schulze et al., 2004). People with bipolar disorder often respond fairly well to drug treatment, especially to lithium (discussed in Chapter 17) (Hollon et al., 2002). Although those who take the appropriate medications for the disorder respond fairly well, many refuse to medicate themselves because doing so means forgoing the exhilaration of the manic episodes. Without treatment, the risk of recurring episodes of mania and depression is high (Hollon et al., 2002). As many as 50% of individuals who suffer from bipolar disorder also exhibit maladaptive behaviors or personality traits, such as obsessions and compulsions, extreme dependence, or narcissism (Angst et al., 2004; Peselow, Sanfilipo, & Fieve, 1995). **Table 16.4** lists the signs and symptoms of mania and depression in bipolar disorder, and **Building Table 16.2** contrasts anxiety and mood disorders.

Depressive and bipolar disorders leave people unable to cope effectively on a day-to-day basis. Dissociative disorders, discussed next, can be even more disruptive.

What Are Dissociative Disorders?

If you watch television or go to movies, you see dissociative disorders more often than most psychologists and psychiatrists do. These disorders occur much more commonly in fictional plots than they do in real life. The relatively rare *dissociative disorders* are psychological disorders characterized by a sudden but temporary alteration in consciousness, identity, sensorimotor behavior, or memory. These disorders are easily identifiable and dramatic, which explains their frequency in fiction. They include dissociative amnesia and dissociative identity disorder.

Dissociative disorders
■ Psychological disorders characterized by a sudden but temporary alteration in consciousness, identity, sensorimotor behavior, or memory.

Dissociative Amnesia

Dissociative amnesia (formerly called *psychogenic amnesia*) is a dissociative disorder characterized by the sudden and extensive inability to recall important personal information, usually information of a stressful or traumatic nature. The memory loss is too extensive to be explained as ordinary forgetfulness. It may entail loss of all information about personal identity or only selected portions.

Dissociative amnesia is not the same as amnesia due to head injury. When people receive a blow to the head or an electric shock severe enough to produce unconsciousness, they often experience some memory loss. People with such organically based memory loss typically forget things that occurred up to the moment of injury and may lose all personal memory. They typically find that their memories return gradually, and the memory loss rarely persists for more than a few weeks. Dissociative amnesia, on the other hand, may be selective, only affecting certain types of memory. It is usually associated with traumatic events (not necessarily an injury), such as an incident involving the threat of physical injury or death. Just as it does on daytime television, dissociative amnesia can disappear suddenly, and the person's memory returns completely. How frequently this type of amnesia occurs is controversial (McNally, 2004).

Dissociative Identity Disorder: Multiple Personalities

Another form of dissociative disorder, often associated with dissociative amnesia but more extensive, is dissociative identity disorder, more commonly known as *multiple personality disorder*. *Dissociative identity disorder* is characterized by the existence within an individual of two or more distinct personalities, each of which is dominant at different times and directs the individual's behavior at those times. The person with the disorder often gives the various personalities different names, and their identities may differ quite sharply from the person's principal identity. A person with dissociative identity disorder usually cannot recall what occurs when one of the alternate personalities is controlling his or her behavior. Each personality has unique traits, memories, and behavioral patterns. For example, one personality may play the piano and speak French, while another may be like an angry, frightened child who yells and hides from other people. Some alternate personalities are of the other sex. Sometimes the alternate personalities are aware of the other ones (Putnam & Carlson, 1998; Steinberg, 1995). Each personality, when active, acknowledges that time has passed but cannot account for it. The switch from one personality to another is usually brought on by crisis or stress.

Cases of dissociative identity disorder began to receive a great deal of publicity during the 1950s, but symptoms consistent with this disorder appeared in a case reported in 1815 (Hacking, 1997). The disorder was not recognized as a diagnosis in the *DSM* until 1980, and it was considered very rare. During the 1980s, thousands of cases were identified, and controversy ensued that continues today. Despite its common portrayal in fiction, dissociative identity disorder remains poorly understood.

Building Table 16.3 adds dissociative disorders to the comparison of types of psychological disorders.

Building Table 16.3

IMPORTANT CHARACTERISTICS OF ANXIETY, MOOD, AND DISSOCIATIVE DISORDERS

Type of Disorder	Presence of Delusions	Evidence for Biological Contribution	Main Symptoms	Higher Prevalence among Men or Women?	Typical Age of Onset
Anxiety Disorders	Not common	Yes	Anxiety, fear	Women	Any age
Mood Disorders	Yes	Yes	Feelings of despair	Women	Young adults
Dissociative Disorders	Yes	Not strong	Amnesia, multiple personalities	Women	Childhood

What Is Schizophrenia?

Schizophrenia is considered the most devastating, puzzling, and frustrating of all mental disorders. People with this disorder have a distorted view of reality and are often unable to function in a world that makes no sense to them. The word *schizophrenia* comes from two Greek words that together mean "split mind," and the split refers to the fragmentation of thought processes. (Note that schizophrenia is *not* split personality. People sometimes confuse the notion of a "split mind" with dissociative identity disorder, which is characterized by the existence of two or more distinct personalities within one person.) In 1911, one of the most influential psychiatrists of the time, Eugen Bleuler, coined the term *schizophrenia* in recognition of the disorganized thinking, perceptions, emotions, and actions that characterize the disorder.

A person with schizophrenia is said to have a schizophrenic disorder, because schizophrenia is really a group of disorders. *Schizophrenic disorders* are psychological disorders characterized by a lack of reality testing and by deterioration of social and intellectual functioning. The symptoms must begin before age 45, and some disturbances in behavior must last at least 6 months, with symptoms persisting for at least 1 month (APA, 2000). People with schizophrenic disorders are said to be *psychotic*—suffering from a gross impairment in reality testing that is wide-ranging and that interferes with their ability to meet the ordinary demands of life.

Schizophrenia usually begins slowly, with more symptoms developing as time passes. It affects 1 out of every 100 people in the United States, and the rate is similar around the world (Javitt & Coyle, 2004). The disorder is associated with more lengthy hospital stays than most conditions are, so people with schizophrenia comprise a larger percentage of those receiving mental health services than people with other disorders (Carr et al., 2003). Women and men are equally likely to be affected. The diagnosis is applied more frequently to those in lower socioeconomic groups, especially to African Americans (Barnes, 2004; Nathan & Langenbucher, 1999). This finding suggests that the diagnostic process is somehow biased, and a study of bias among clinicians making diagnoses confirms this view (Trierweiler et al., 2000). As **Figure 16.2** on page 618 shows, African Americans are more likely than Whites to be diagnosed as schizophrenic.

Schizophrenic [SKIT-soh-FREN-ick] disorders ■ A group of psychological disorders characterized by a lack of reality testing and by deterioration of social and intellectual functioning, beginning before age 45 and lasting at least 6 months.

Psychotic [sye-KOT-ick] ■ Suffering from a gross impairment in reality testing that interferes with the ability to meet the ordinary demands of life.

Figure 16.2
Cultural Factors in the Diagnosis of Schizophrenia and Mood Disorders
African Americans are more likely than White Americans to be diagnosed as suffering from schizophrenia. In contrast, Whites and Latinos/Latinas are more likely than African Americans to be diagnosed as depressed.
(Based on data from Zhang & Snowden, 1999)

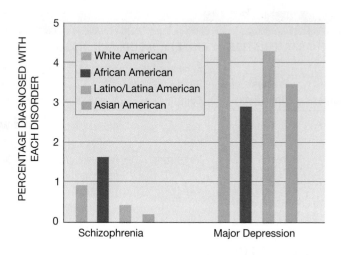

Essential Characteristics of Schizophrenic Disorders

People with schizophrenic disorders display sudden significant changes in thought, perception, mood, and overall behavior. How they think about themselves, about social situations, and about other people—their social cognition—becomes seriously distorted (Lee et al., 2004). Those changes are often accompanied by distortions of reality and an inability to respond with appropriate thoughts, perceptions, or emotions. These symptoms are classified as either positive or negative. *Positive symptoms* are those that people with schizophrenia experience that normal people do not—for example, delusions or hallucinations. *Negative symptoms* involve behaviors that occur normally but that are absent in people with schizophrenia—for example, they may lack the ability to read emotions in facial expressions. Not all of the symptoms of a schizophrenic disorder are necessarily present in any given person, although many often occur together.

Thought Distortions

One of the first signs of schizophrenia is difficulty maintaining logical thought and coherent conversation. People with schizophrenic disorders show disordered thinking, impaired language use, and memory deficits (Mueser & McGurk, 2004). They may also suffer from delusions (incorrect beliefs). For example, someone with delusions of persecution believes that someone or something is trying to harm him or her. Delusions of persecution are often accompanied by delusions of grandeur, which cause the person to believe that he or she is particularly important—important enough to be the target of persecution. Some people with schizophrenia take on the role of an important character (for example, Jesus Christ or the Queen of England) and imagine that people are conspiring to harm them. Delusional thought is often apparent in schizophrenics' speech, in which sentence structure, words, and ideas become jumbled and disordered, creating a "word salad" of thoughts. Thus, a schizophrenic person might be heard to say, "Your highness, may I more of some engine to my future food, for his lowness."

Memory is seriously disturbed in people with schizophrenia, especially verbal memory, including both working and long-term memory (Kristian Hill et al., 2004). Recall that working memory holds information for a brief period so that further processing can take place and allows a person to respond as a task demands. In addition, the attention that is critical to this process is also impaired. It is not surprising that when a system that is so important to thought and language fails, speech patterns and thinking become disorganized and people become incoherent. Recent research (Homayoun et al., 2004) suggests that the NMDA receptor, a type of receptor for the neurotransmitter glutamate, appears to be involved in both memory formation and schizophrenia, which may be a reason for the memory problems evident in schizophrenia.

Perceptual Distortions

Another sign of schizophrenic disorders is the presence of *hallucinations*—compelling perceptual (visual, tactile, olfactory, or auditory) experiences that occur without any actual physical stimulus. Auditory hallucinations are the most common (Mueser & McGurk, 2004). Hallucinations have a biological basis in brain functioning; brain-imaging studies show that the left side of the brain (the one that processes language) is more active when individuals experience auditory hallucinations (David, 2004). The person reports hearing voices originating outside his or her head; the voices may comment on the person's behavior or direct the person to behave in certain ways (Hunter, 2004). For example, convicted murderer David Berkowitz (known to the media as "Son of Sam") claimed that he was following the orders of his neighbor's dog, which told him to kill.

Distortions in Emotional Reactions

One of the most striking characteristics of schizophrenia is the display of *inappropriate affect*—emotional responses that are not appropriate in the circumstances. A person with schizophrenia may become upset and cry when her favorite food falls on the floor, yet laugh hysterically at the death of a close friend or relative. Some people with schizophrenia display no emotion (either appropriate or inappropriate) and seem incapable of experiencing a normal range of feeling (Mueser & McGurk, 2004). Their affect is constricted, or *flat*. Their faces are blank and expressionless, even when they are presented with a deliberately provocative remark or situation. Other people with schizophrenia exhibit *ambivalent* affect. They go through a wide range of emotional behaviors in a brief period, seeming happy one moment and dejected the next.

Types of Schizophrenia

People with schizophrenia display a variety of symptoms, but the *DSM* classifies schizophrenic disorders into five types: paranoid, catatonic, disorganized, residual, and undifferentiated. Each of these has different symptoms and diagnostic criteria (see **Table 16.5** on p. 620).

Table 16.5

TYPES AND SYMPTOMS OF SCHIZOPHRENIA

Type	Symptoms
■ Paranoid	Delusions of persecution or grandeur (or both) and possibly hallucinations
■ Catatonic	Either displays of excited or violent motor activity or stupor
■ Disorganized	Disturbed thought processes; frequent incoherence; disorganized behavior; blunted, inappropriate, or silly affect
■ Residual	Inappropriate affect, illogical thinking, social withdrawal, and/or eccentric behavior while remaining generally in touch with reality
■ Undifferentiated	Mixture of symptoms that do not meet the diagnostic criteria for any other type of schizophrenia

The Paranoid Type

Paranoid [PAIR-uh-noid] type of schizophrenia ■ Type of schizophrenia characterized by delusions of persecution or grandeur (or both) and possibly hallucinations.

People with the *paranoid type of schizophrenia* may seem quite normal, but their thought processes are characterized by delusions of persecution or grandeur (or both) and possibly hallucinations. Their delusions are often organized around a theme, and the hallucinations (which are most often auditory) are typically related to this theme. For example, Vadim Mieseges (discussed earlier in the chapter) believed that he had been sucked into the world of *The Matrix*, which is controlled by evil computers. These delusions led him to take actions that he believed were protecting him from harm in the dangerous place he saw as real. Mieseges's paranoid and delusional belief that his landlady was giving off "evil vibes" that would endanger him was the basis for his violent action.

Paranoid schizophrenics may be alert, intelligent, and responsive. In addition, they may be secretive concerning their delusions and hallucinations, which makes them difficult to detect and diagnose. However, delusions and hallucinations impair the ability to deal with reality, and the behavior of people with paranoid schizophrenia is often unpredictable and sometimes hostile or violent (Javitt & Coyle, 2004). The relatively low level of cognitive impairment allows people with the paranoid type of schizophrenia to have a better chance of recovery than do people with other types of schizophrenia.

The Catatonic Type

Catatonic [CAT-uh-TONN-ick] type of schizophrenia ■ Type of schizophrenia characterized either by displays of excited or violent motor activity or by stupor.

The *catatonic type of schizophrenia* is characterized either by displays of excited or violent motor activity or by stupor (APA, 2000). That is, there are actually two subtypes of the catatonic type of schizophrenia—excited and withdrawn—both of which involve extreme overt behavior. *Excited* catatonic schizophrenics show excessive activity. They may talk and shout almost continuously and engage in seemingly uninhibited, agitated, and aggressive motor activity. These episodes usually appear and disappear suddenly. *Withdrawn* catatonic schizophrenics tend to appear stuporous—mute and basically unresponsive. They usually show a high degree of muscular rigidity. They are not immobile, but they speak, move, and respond very little, although they are usually aware of events around them. Withdrawn catatonic schizophrenics may use immobility and unresponsiveness to maintain control over their environment; their behavior relieves them of the responsibility of responding to external stimuli.

Other Types of Schizophrenia

The *disorganized type of schizophrenia* is characterized by severely disturbed thought processes, frequent incoherence, disorganized behavior, and inappropriate affect (APA, 2000). People with this type of schizophrenia may exhibit bizarre emotions, with periods of giggling, crying, or irritability that have no apparent cause. Their behavior can be silly or even obscene. They show a severe disintegration of normal personality, a total lack of reality testing, and often poor personal hygiene.

People who show symptoms attributable to schizophrenia but who remain in touch with reality are said to have the *residual type of schizophrenia* (APA, 2000). Such people show inappropriate affect, illogical thinking, eccentric behavior, or some combination of these symptoms. They have a history of at least one previous schizophrenic episode.

Sometimes a person exhibits all the essential features of schizophrenia without fitting neatly into the category of paranoid, catatonic, disorganized, or residual (APA, 2000). Individuals with these characteristics are said to have the *undifferentiated type of schizophrenia.*

Causes of Schizophrenia

What causes people with schizophrenia to lose their grasp on reality with such devastating results? Are people born with schizophrenia, or does the disorder develop as a result of painful childhood experiences? Researchers have taken markedly different positions on these questions over the years, but recently, opinion has begun to converge. Biologically oriented psychologists have focused on genetics, brain structures, and chemicals in the brain—their basic argument being that schizophrenia is a brain disease. Psychodynamic and learning theorists argue that a person's environment and early experiences cause schizophrenia. Although evidence exists for both positions, neither seems adequate, and most theorists adopt a diathesis–stress model, asserting that schizophrenia is the result of an interaction between genetic predisposition or biological vulnerability and life situation. Let's look at the evidence.

Biological Factors That Contribute to Schizophrenia

Substantial evidence suggests that biological factors play some role in schizophrenia, producing a predisposition to develop the disorder. People born with that predisposition have a greater probability of developing schizophrenia than do other people, given similar circumstances.

Disorganized type of schizophrenia ■ Type of schizophrenia characterized by severely disturbed thought processes, frequent incoherence, disorganized behavior, and inappropriate affect.

Residual type of schizophrenia ■ Type of schizophrenia in which the person exhibits inappropriate affect, illogical thinking, and/or eccentric behavior but seems generally in touch with reality.

Undifferentiated type of schizophrenia ■ A schizophrenic disorder that is characterized by a mixture of symptoms and does not meet the diagnostic criteria for any one type.

Concordance rate ■
Estimate of the degree
to which a condition or
trait is shared by two or
more individuals or
groups.

A genetic contribution to the risk of developing schizophrenia is clear. Degree of family relationship relates to the level of risk. The estimate of the degree to which a condition or trait is shared by two or more individuals or groups is referred to as a *concordance rate.* The concordance rate for schizophrenia is higher for identical twins than for fraternal twins; identical twins reared apart from their natural parents and from each other show a higher concordance rate than do fraternal twins or genetically unrelated people (Cornblatt, Green, & Walker, 1999). However, if schizophrenia were totally genetic, the likelihood would be 100% that both identical (monozygotic) twins (who have identical genes) would manifest the disorder if one did. But studies of schizophrenia in identical twins show concordance rates that range from 15% to 86% (Sullivan, Kendler, & Neale, 2003). This range suggests that factors in addition to genetics are involved, and neurotransmitters are one possibility.

Researchers believe that neurotransmitters are involved in schizophrenia, because the drugs used to treat this disorder, called *antischizophrenic drugs*, alter the action of neurotransmitters. An early view of neurotransmitter involvement was the *dopamine theory of schizophrenia*, which hypothesized that too much of the neurotransmitter dopamine or too much activity at dopamine receptors causes schizophrenia (Javitt & Coyle, 2004). Additional research implicated subtypes of dopamine receptors, but, as noted earlier, more recent research has indicated that the neurotransmitter glutamate may play an important role in schizophrenia. The developing picture is complex, involving the concerted action of genes, neurotransmitters, and brain structures affected by these genes and neurotransmitters (Sawa & Kamiya, 2003; Williams et al., 2003).

Environmental Factors That Contribute to Schizophrenia

Even researchers who investigate the biological factors related to schizophrenia acknowledge that environmental factors also contribute to this disorder. Most researchers accept that the onset and development of schizophrenia are determined by an interaction of biological and environmental factors—that is, both nature and nurture contribute (see **Figure 16.3** on p. 623).

The environmental factors that contribute to schizophrenia begin before birth with difficulties during pregnancy such as prenatal infections and malnutrition; birth complications and brain injury during delivery can also contribute to the disorder (Javitt & Coyle, 2004; Walker et al., 2004). Risk is also elevated by events during infancy that affect the development of the nervous system, such as exposure to lead and other toxins (Lewis & Levitt, 2002). Other environmental factors that increase the risk for the development of schizophrenia include being born in a city rather than in a rural environment (Pederson & Mortensen, 2001) and being born into a poor family (Harrison et al., 2001).

Family environment has also been implicated as a factor, with some experiences increasing and others decreasing the risk. Loss of parents during childhood is a risk factor for the later development of schizophrenia, as are childhood depression and bipolar disorder (Agid et al., 1999). A longitudinal study of

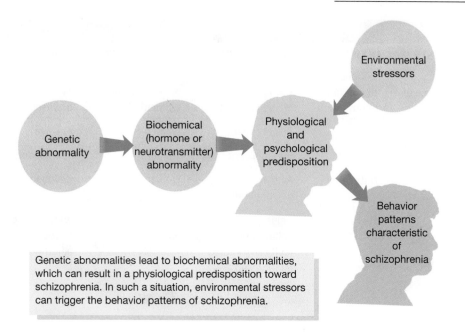

Figure 16.3
The Vulnerability–Stress View of Schizophrenia
According to the vulnerability–stress view of schizophrenia, the environment triggers behaviors in people who are predisposed to schizophrenia.

Genetic abnormalities lead to biochemical abnormalities, which can result in a physiological predisposition toward schizophrenia. In such a situation, environmental stressors can trigger the behavior patterns of schizophrenia.

children whose genetic endowment placed them at risk for the development of schizophrenia showed that positive relationships with their families decreased the risk, whereas negative relationships increased the risk (Schiffman et al., 2002). The emotional tone in families is also important in the developmental course and severity of a family member's schizophrenia. Families whose interaction style is characterized by hostility, criticism, emotional overinvolvement, and a lack of boundaries (overintrusiveness) are said to have a high level of *expressed emotions*. People with schizophrenia who are released from hospitals and return to families in which there are high levels of expressed emotion have a higher relapse rate than those whose families have low levels of expressed emotion (Widiger & Sankis, 2000). Thus, factors related to family interactions have an impact on the development of schizophrenia.

Some researchers have concentrated on events during adolescence, the developmental period in which symptoms of schizophrenia are most likely to appear. These researchers take a *neurodevelopmental view*, hypothesizing that schizophrenia develops because biological vulnerabilities due to genes and prenatal events combine with life events and stress during this important developmental period (Lewis & Levitt, 2002; Walker et al., 2004). According to this view, no single gene or event is responsible for schizophrenia, but events trigger biological vulnerabilities. Like depression, schizophrenia appears to be the product of an interaction between nature and nurture.

Building Table 16.4 on page 624 presents a comparison of the disorders on Axis I of the *DSM*, including schizophrenia.

Building Table 16.4

IMPORTANT CHARACTERISTICS OF ANXIETY, MOOD, DISSOCIATIVE DISORDERS, AND SCHIZOPHRENIA

Type of Disorder	Presence of Delusions	Evidence for Biological Contribution	Main Symptoms	Higher Prevalence among Men or Women?	Typical Age of Onset
Anxiety Disorders	Not common	Yes	Anxiety, fear	Women	Any age
Mood Disorders	Yes	Yes	Feelings of despair	Women	Young adults
Dissociative Disorders	Yes	Not strong	Amnesia, multiple personalities	Women	Childhood
Schizophrenia	Yes	Yes	Delusions, hallucinations, faulty cognitions, relationship problems	Equally prevalent	Adolescence or young adulthood

What Are Personality Disorders?

Disorders such as phobias, obsessive-compulsive disorder, depression, dissociative personality disorder, and schizophrenia are among the psychological disorders classified on Axis I of the DSM classification system. The disorders on Axis II are *personality disorders,* which are characterized by inflexible and long-standing maladaptive behaviors that typically cause distress as well as social or occupational difficulties. These disorders are conceptualized as related to personality traits and are thus stable over time and traceable to childhood or adolescence (Warner et al., 2004). This stability means that people with personality disorders are easy to spot but difficult to treat.

Categorizations of personality disorders are more controversial than those of the disorders on Axis I of *DSM,* in terms of both their reliability and their validity. The line separating normal from abnormal behavior, as well as the characteristics of each class of disorder, can sometimes be blurry. This lack of clarity may lead to problems in deciding how a person should be diagnosed and in placing an individual in one category rather than another. In addition, Axis II disorders are controversial because those diagnosed with these disorders tend to fall into stereotypical gender and ethnic categories (Iwamasa, Larabee, & Merritt, 2000; Morey et al., 2002).

People with personality disorders are divided into three broad classes (Serin & Marshall, 2003): (1) those whose behavior appears odd or eccentric, (2) those whose behavior is dramatic, emotional, and impulsive, (3) those who are fearful or anxious. We'll consider six specific personality disorders: paranoid, borderline, histrionic, narcissistic, antisocial, and dependent.

People with *paranoid personality disorder* display odd or eccentric behavior and unwarranted feelings of persecution—they mistrust almost everyone. They are

Personality disorders ■ Psychological disorders characterized by inflexible, long-standing maladaptive behaviors that typically cause distress and social or occupational problems.

hypersensitive to criticism and have a restricted range of emotional responses. They have strong fears of being exploited and of losing control and independence. Sometimes they appear cold, humorless, and even scheming. As you might expect, people with paranoid personality disorder are suspicious and seldom able to form close, intimate relationships with others.

Fitting into the second broad class, individuals with *borderline personality disorder* have trouble with relationships (Trull, Stepp, & Durrett, 2003). They show a pattern of instability in interpersonal relationships, self-image, and affect. In addition, they are often impulsive and sometimes suicidal. They report feelings of emptiness and display inappropriate anger. Easily bored and distracted, such individuals fear abandonment, and some evidence links this personality disorder to childhood attachment problems. Individuals with borderline personality disorder often sabotage or undermine themselves just before they reach a goal—for example, by dropping out of school just before graduation.

Also fitting into the second broad class, because of their dramatic, emotional, and impulsive behaviors, are people with *histrionic personality disorder*. Individuals with this disorder seek attention by exaggerating situations in their lives—they are "drama queens" (they are usually women). They have stormy personal relationships, are excessively emotional, and demand constant reassurance and praise. In addition, they are subject to a variety of physical complaints such as headache, digestive disorders, and chronic pain (Harper, 2004).

Closely related to histrionic personality disorder, and also in the second broad class, is *narcissistic personality disorder*. Indeed, this personality disorder shows a substantial overlap with histrionic personality disorder (Rivas, 2001). People with this disorder have an extremely exaggerated sense of self-importance, expect favors, and need constant admiration and attention. They exploit others and show little concern for them, and they react to criticism with shame, humiliation, and sometimes violent rage (Washburn et al., 2004).

Perhaps the most widely recognized personality disorder in the second broad class is *antisocial personality disorder*. People with antisocial personality disorder are self-centered and irresponsible, violate the rights of other people (by lying, stealing, cheating, or other violations of social rules), lack guilt feelings, are unable to understand other people, and do not fear punishment (APA, 2000). Individuals with this disorder may be superficially charming, but their behavior is destructive and often reckless.

As many as 3% of all individuals may be candidates for a diagnosis of antisocial personality disorder. Men are much more likely than women to be diagnosed with the disorder (Serin & Marshall, 2003), even though women may show similar symptoms (Nathan & Langenbucher, 1999). Researchers are exploring biological components in antisocial personality disorder and finding evidence for brain differences and genetic influence (Rogers, 2003). Brain-imaging studies suggest that people with antisocial personality disorder have less brain tissue in their frontal lobes (Raine et al., 2000) and that the frontal cortex is involved in controlling aggressive behavior (Blair, 2004). This structure is also involved in planning and impulse control, abilities that present problems for people with antisocial personality disorder. People with this disorder also fail to show normal autonomic nervous system reactions to frightening and surprising stimuli (Ortiz & Raine, 2004; van Goozen et al., 2004). As a result, people with

Antisocial personality disorder ■ Personality disorder characterized by egocentricity, irresponsible behavior that violates the rights of other people, a lack of guilt feelings, an inability to understand other people, and a lack of fear of punishment.

antisocial personality disorder may not learn to associate fear or anxiety with unacceptable behavior. Thus, their disorder may be the product of an interaction between biological endowment and factors in the environment.

Parental neglect and abuse are important factors in risk for antisocial personality disorder, and parents with antisocial personalities tend to have children with the same disorder, according to a longitudinal study over three generations (Smith & Farrington, 2004). The results suggest that genetics and parental conflict and authoritarian parenting style contribute to antisocial behavior among children.

Fitting into the third broad class of personality disorders are those who act fearful or anxious—individuals with *dependent personality disorder*. Such people are submissive and clinging; they let others make all the important decisions in their lives. They try to appear pleasant and agreeable at all times. They act meek, humble, and affectionate in order to keep their protectors. This description seems like an exaggeration of stereotypically feminine behavior, and not surprisingly, most diagnoses of this disorder are received by women (Widiger & Anderson, 2003). Battered wives are often diagnosed with dependent personality disorder, which may reflect their strategy for coping with the mistreatment they receive or may result from stereotyping and diagnostic bias. For these reasons, this personality disorder is controversial.

Several personality disorders involve a tendency toward violence. For example, people with narcissistic and antisocial personality disorder are more likely to commit violence. Other personality disorders also relate to violence—both because a person with such a disorder has an increased risk of committing aggressive acts and because the experience of violence increases the risk of exhibiting a personality disorder.

How Are Violence and Mental Disorders Related?

The media have linked mental disorders and violence. Movies show mentally disturbed individuals who "snap" and go on homicidal rampages. Television presents stories of seemingly ordinary people who are, in reality, crazed killers. An analysis of TV programming indicates that violence is shown to be common in characters with mental disorders, and the distortion is substantial—mentally ill characters are violent 10 times more often on television than in real life (Diefenbach, 1997). These images are powerful in shaping opinions about people with mental disorders and add to the stigma of having such a problem. But is there some association between mental disorders and violence? Was Vadim Mieseges exceptional? Or are people with mental disorders more dangerous than others?

The Mieseges case was unusual. Most people who have mental disorders are not violent, and most people who commit violence do not have a mental disorder. However, some mental disorders are associated with a greater likelihood of committing violent acts.

Diagnoses Associated with Violence

Several diagnoses are associated with increased risk for violence. In general, the more serious disorders carry a greater risk, and people who have delusions seem to be at high risk (Nathan & Langenbucher, 1999). In the manic phase of bipolar disorder, people can be impatient and easily angered. This anger may be expressed violently. People who question the plans and capabilities of a person experiencing a manic episode may be the target for a violent reaction.

People with schizophrenia, especially those with the paranoid type, may also commit violence. Delusions such as these people experience make them suspicious, and they feel the need to protect themselves against what they see as real danger (Junginger & McGuire, 2004). When paranoid schizophrenics react to these "dangers," their actions are difficult for others to understand and anticipate because the danger is a delusion. The actions that they take to protect themselves may be harmful, even deadly, to someone who has accidentally said or done the wrong thing. Research on people discharged from mental institutions indicates that the threat that they will commit violence is elevated, but not to the level portrayed on television.

Most schizophrenics who are violent are not killers, but some are. A 25-year longitudinal study tracked homicides committed by people who had received treatment for mental disorders and found that a diagnosis of schizophrenia created a risk, especially when combined with alcohol abuse (Schanda et al., 2004). Another study indicated that homicide was very uncommon, but young adults with schizophrenia account for a disproportionate amount of violence (Arseneault et al., 2000). However, young adults with alcohol- or drug-dependency problems are more likely than schizophrenics to be involved in violent crimes. Substance abuse alone is a risk for violence, and the combination of alcohol or drug use with a mental disorder additionally elevates the risk.

Individuals with antisocial personality disorder may be violent. In addition, they do a great deal of damage through their nonviolent criminal and amoral behavior (Zuckerman, 1999). Their disregard for the welfare of others and their resistance to change make people with antisocial personality disorder dangerous to others. When these individuals are violent, they feel no compassion or remorse. Dr. Hannibal Lecter, the character in a novel (Harris, 1988) and a series of movies, is an extreme example of an individual with antisocial personality disorder. Lecter is a serial killer who shows no sign of remorse or feelings for the people whom he murders. According to one description, he was so unfeeling that he failed to experience an elevation in heart rate when he bit off a nurse's tongue. The author of the novel drew on findings that individuals with antisocial personality disorder experience lower levels of autonomic activation under conditions of threat or fear (Ortiz & Raine, 2004; van Goozen et al., 2004).

Individuals who meet the criteria for antisocial personality disorder do not meet the legal definition of insanity. Indeed, most people with mental disorders who commit violence are not legally insane. Although Vadim Mieseges was found not guilty by reason of insanity, he was an exception. However, the concept of insanity is not a psychological one. Rather, its definition is legal. *Insanity* is the legal concept that refers to a condition that excuses people from responsibility and protects them from punishment. From the legal point of view, a person cannot be held responsible for a crime if, at the time of the crime, the person lacked the capacity to distinguish right from wrong or to obey the law.

Most people overestimate how often pleas of insanity are made. The truth is that only about 1% of all felony defendants use an insanity defense—and the plea is

Insanity ■ The legal concept that refers to a condition that excuses people from responsibility and protects them from punishment.

successful only about one-quarter of the time (Lymburner & Roesch, 1999). Despite media portrayals of the insanity defense as a mainstay of the legal system that frees guilty people, people who "get away with murder" by using the insanity plea are more common in fiction than in courtrooms. More often, a person with a mental disorder enters a plea of guilty or is found guilty and goes to prison, where appropriate mental health care is unlikely (Sentencing Project, 2002). The fictional portrayal of Hannibal Lecter reflects this reality—he had been found guilty of murder and imprisoned.

People with mental disorders are more likely to be a danger to themselves than to others. That is, violence on the part of a person with a mental disorder is more likely to be a suicide attempt or suicide than assault or homicide. Depressed people feel hopeless, and their feelings of endless misery lead to thoughts of and attempts at suicide. Each day, more than 80 people in the United States commit suicide, which means that over 30,000 people each year take their own lives (U.S. Bureau of the Census, 2003). However, many more people attempt than commit suicide (Wunderlich et al., 2001). *Attempters* try to commit suicide but are unsuccessful. They tend to be young, impulsive, more often women than men, and more likely to make nonfatal attempts such as making only shallow cuts on the wrists. *Completers* succeed in taking their lives. They tend to be White, male, and older, and they use highly lethal means, such as guns. Alcohol or drug abuse increases the risk for violence associated with mental disorders, and this increase applies to suicide. Although estimates vary with age and gender, there are an estimated 10–25 attempted suicides for every completion. **Table 16.6** (on p. 629) presents some of the many myths about suicide and counters them with facts.

Depression is the major risk for suicide, and between 60% and 70% of people with major depression at least think about suicide (Moller, 2003). In addition, people with borderline personality disorder and antisocial personality disorder are at increased risk for suicide (Trull et al., 2003). Adolescent suicide has received a great deal of attention because it is the second leading cause of death for this age group. Negative moods are common among adolescents. For college students, feelings of depression are a common experience, and thoughts of suicide are not unusual—53% of college students report that they have experienced depression, and 9% say they have considered suicide during their college years (Furr et al., 2001). However, the group with the greatest risk for suicide is White men over age 75 (National Center for Health Statistics, 2003). Preventing suicide among all age groups has become a national priority, and increased attention has been focused on depression, which is the underlying cause of most suicides and attempts.

Violence as a Risk for Developing Mental Disorders

Only a few mental disorders increase the likelihood that a person will be violent, but the targets of violence experience increased risk for many disorders. The experience of child abuse has the greatest potential for harm. *Child abuse* is physical, emotional, or sexual mistreatment of a child. This problem is a large one—over 900,000 children in the United States are the victims of abuse or neglect each year (Tenney-Soeiro, 2004). Girls are more often targets than are boys, especially of sexual abuse

Child abuse ■ Physical, emotional, or sexual mistreatment of a child.

Table 16.6

MYTHS AND FACTS ABOUT SUICIDE

Myth	Fact
1. Suicide happens without warning.	1. Suicidal individuals give many clues; 80% have to some degree discussed with others their intent to commit suicide.
2. Once people become suicidal, they remain so.	2. Suicidal persons remain so for limited periods.
3. Suicide occurs almost exclusively among affluent or very poor individuals.	3. Suicide tends to occur in the same proportion at all socioeconomic levels.
4. Virtually all suicidal individuals are mentally ill.	4. This is not so, although most are depressed to some degree.
5. Suicidal tendencies are inherited or run in families.	5. There is no evidence for a direct genetic factor.
6. Suicide does not occur in primitive cultures.	6. Suicide occurs in almost all societies and cultures.
7. In Japan, ritual suicide is common.	7. In modern Japan, ritual suicide is rare; the most common method of committing suicide is barbiturate overdose.
8. Writers and artists have the highest suicide rates because they are "a bit crazy to begin with."	8. Physicians and police officers have the highest suicide rates; they have access to the most lethal means, and their work involves a high level of frustration.
9. Once a person starts to come out of a depression, the risk of suicide dissipates.	9. The risk of suicide is highest in the initial phase of an upswing from the depth of depression.
10. People who attempt suicide fully intend to die.	10. People who attempt suicide have diverse motives.

Source: Meyer & Salmon (1988)

(Hulme & Agrawal, 2004). Children who are the victims of sexual abuse have an elevated risk of developing posttraumatic stress disorder (PTSD; see Chapter 15), depression, suicide, and sexual problems during adulthood as well as of perpetrating partner abuse and child abuse as adults (Ehrensaft et al., 2003; Salter et al., 2003). Childhood victims of abuse and neglect also face a greater risk of developing anxiety disorders, mood disorders, antisocial and borderline personality disorders, and eating disorders than children who are not abused (Johnson et al., 2003; Koss et al., 2003).

Child abusers tend to be self-centered and to lack empathy for their victims, but they usually do not have any diagnosable mental disorder (Wiehe, 2003). Most abusive parents seem quite normal by typical social standards, and sometimes they are prominent members of their communities. Most psychologists and social workers consider child abuse an interactive process involving incompetent parenting, environmental stress, and poor child management techniques. Alcohol and drug use also increase the risk of abuse (Sebre et al., 2004). Although abusers' behavior does not necessarily signal the presence of a mental disorder, it can produce both short-term and long-term problems for the abused children.

Other forms of violence within families also create mental health problems. *Intimate partner violence* is also known as spouse abuse and domestic violence. This type of violence is common throughout the world (Watts & Zimmerman, 2002). Nor is the effect limited to married partners—20% of teenage girls reported some experience of violence from a boyfriend (Silverman et al., 2001). Partner violence is more likely to occur in couples and in societies in which gender roles are rigid and inflexible and in which women have little power and few resources. In many societies, violence is seen as an effective control technique that is not associated with pathology in the perpetrator. For the victim, however, partner violence poses a substantial risk for PTSD, eating disorders, and depression. Indeed, some researchers believe that women's higher rate of depression is largely due to their more frequent experiences of childhood sexual abuse, partner violence, and rape (Golding, 1999).

Rape ■ Forcible sexual assault on an unwilling partner.

Rape is one form of violence that women experience more often than men. **Rape** is forcible sexual assault on an unwilling partner. The legal definition of rape varies from state to state, but it is generally being broadened to include any sexual assault (usually intercourse) that occurs without freely given consent. People tend to think of rape as a violent attack by a stranger, but most cases of rape involve individuals who are acquainted. That is, *date rape,* or *acquaintance rape,* is more common than stranger rape. Studies of high school girls (Ackard & Neumark-Sztainer, 2002; Silverman et al., 2001), college women (Koss, Gidycz, & Wisniewski, 1987), and women from the general U.S. population (Elliott, Mok, & Briere, 2004) indicate that around 20% have been the targets of some type of sexual violence; around 15% have been raped. Men are victims of sexual violence less often than women; around 3% of men are the victims of attempted or completed rape (Elliott et al., 2004). When men are the victims of sexual violence, their experience is similar to women's: They are likely to be raped by an acquaintance, they are not likely to report the incident, and they are likely to feel additionally victimized by their experience with the justice system.

The most common effect of rape on victims' mental health is posttraumatic stress disorder. Indeed, the *DSM* mentions rape as one of the events that may cause PTSD. In addition, rape victims are at increased risk for anxiety disorders, depression, suicide, and substance abuse disorders (Boudreaux et al., 1998; Koss et al., 2003).

Like perpetrators of child abuse, rapists are not likely to have a disorder that fits into any diagnostic category in the *DSM.* Men (and women) with personality disorders, especially antisocial personality disorder, are more likely to harm others, including committing sexual violence (Ahlmeyer et al., 2003). However, the majority of rapists do not have a personality disorder. Ten percent of men admit that they have committed acquaintance rape, and 24% of men admit that they have used force or other tactics that would meet the criteria for rape (Rubenzahl & Corcoran, 1998). These percentages are much higher than estimates of the prevalence of antisocial personality disorder, indicating that most men who commit acquaintance rape do not have this disorder. Instead, social setting is a major factor in forced sex. For example, in over half of cases of rape, the perpetrator, the victim, or both have been drinking alcohol (Abbey et al., 2004). Such situational factors and attitudes condoning the use of force are more important predictors of rape than psychopathology.

Although childhood sexual abuse, intimate partner violence, and rape are more likely to affect the mental health of women than men, no one is exempt from victimization and its effects. Being the victim of violence has a variety of short-term and long-term negative effects for mental as well as physical health (Pimlott-Kubiak & Cortina, 2003).

Summary and Review

WHAT IS ABNORMAL BEHAVIOR?

Define *abnormal behavior*.

Abnormal behavior is behavior that is not typical but is socially unacceptable, distressing, maladaptive, and/or the result of distorted cognitions. p. 593

Describe the major perspectives on abnormal behavior.

Different *models* provide alternatives that psychologists use to understand abnormal behavior. *Abnormal psychology* is the field of psychology concerned with the assessment, treatment, and prevention of maladaptive behavior. The medical–biological model focuses on the biological and physiological conditions that initiate abnormal behaviors. The psychodynamic model focuses on unresolved conflicts and forces of which a person may be unaware. The humanistic model assumes that people naturally move toward health and maladaptive behavior is the result of some force that prevents this movement. The behavioral model states that abnormal behavior is caused by faulty or ineffective learning. The cognitive model traces maladaptive behavior to people's ideas and thoughts. The sociocultural model examines abnormalities within the context of culture, the family, the community, and society. The evolutionary model sees abnormal behavior as potentially adaptive in evolutionary history but not in modern society. The biopsychosocial approach acknowledges that a combination of biological, personal, and social forces influences behavior. pp. 594–598

What are the goals of the *DSM*, and what are its advantages and disadvantages?

The *DSM–IV–TR* is the latest edition of the *Diagnostic and Statistical Manual of Mental Disorders,* which mental health practitioners use to diagnose and classify mental disorders. The *DSM* describes behavior in terms of its characteristics and its *prevalence* and uses a multiaxial system. Its goals are to improve the reliability of diagnoses and to provide a standardized diagnostic system. Some psychologists applaud the *DSM* for its recognition of social and environmental influences on behavior; others take issue with how it creates diagnoses based on political rather than research or theoretical criteria. pp. 598–602

WHAT ARE ANXIETY DISORDERS?

Define *anxiety*.

Anxiety is a generalized feeling of fear and apprehension, which is often accompanied by increased physiological arousal and may or may not be related to a specific situation or object. p. 602

What are the chief characteristics of anxiety disorders?

Generalized anxiety disorder is characterized by persistent anxiety occurring on more days than not for at least 6 months, sometimes with increased activity of the autonomic nervous system, apprehension, excessive muscle tension, and difficulty in concentrating. *Panic attacks* may occur in conjunction with *agoraphobia,* one of the *phobic disorders,* which are characterized by excessive irrational fear of and avoidance of certain objects or situations. Anxiety disorders also include *social phobia* and *specific phobia.* pp. 602–605

Individuals with *obsessive-compulsive disorder* have persistent and uncontrollable thoughts and irrational beliefs, which often cause them to perform compulsive rituals that interfere with normal daily functioning. The focus of these behaviors is often on maintaining order and control. pp. 606–607

WHAT ARE MOOD DISORDERS?

What are the characteristics of the major mood disorders?

Mood disorders include *depressive disorders* such as *major depressive disorder.* Depressed people have a gloomy outlook on life, slow thought processes, loss of appetite, sleep problems, *delusions* (such as an exaggerated view of current problems), loss of energy, and a tendency to blame themselves. pp. 607–609

What theories account for mood disorders?

The monoamine theory of depression was prompted by the effectiveness of antidepressant drugs and suggests that major depression results from deficient monoamines or inefficient monoamine receptors, but further research has implicated the role of the neurotransmitter GABA. Cognitive theorists hypothesize that depressed people have thoughts that perpetuate their negative mood. *Learned helplessness* produces feelings consistent with the experience of depression. pp. 610–613

Vulnerability is a person's diminished ability to deal with demanding life events. The more vulnerable a person is, the fewer environmental stressors are needed to initiate a depressive episode, and biological and environmental events combine to produce depression. pp. 613–614

What is bipolar disorder?

Bipolar disorder is a mood disorder that gets its name from the fact that people with this disorder show behavior that varies between two extremes: mania and depression. p. 614

WHAT ARE DISSOCIATIVE DISORDERS?

Dissociative disorders are psychological disorders characterized by a sudden but temporary alteration in consciousness, identity, sensorimotor behavior, or memory. These disorders include *dissociative amnesia* and *dissociative identity disorder.* Dissociative disorders are not well understood and are controversial; some authorities believe that they do not actually exist. pp. 615–616

WHAT IS SCHIZOPHRENIA?

Identify the essential characteristics of the major types of schizophrenia.

Schizophrenic disorders are characterized by a lack of reality testing and by deterioration of social and intellectual functioning. Individuals with these disorders often show serious personality disintegration, with significant changes in thought, mood, perception, and behavior; their symptoms are said to be *psychotic.* Positive symptoms—for example, hallucinations—are present in people with schizophrenia but not in normal people. Negative symptoms involve behaviors that are absent in people with schizophrenia but that normal people show; for example, people with schizophrenia may be unable to read facial expressions. pp. 617–691

People with the *paranoid type of schizophrenia* experience delusions of persecution—beliefs that there are plots to harm them—and/or delusions of grandeur, and possibly hallucinations. Their paranoia may make them secretive, so their behavior may seem normal, but their thought processes are not. There are actually two subtypes of the *catatonic type of schizophrenia*: excited and withdrawn. Severely disturbed thought processes characterize the *disorganized type of schizophrenia.* People with this type of schizophrenia have hallucinations and delusions and are frequently incoherent. People who show symptoms attributable to schizophrenia but who remain in touch with reality are diagnosed as having the *residual type of schizophrenia.* Those who exhibit symptoms but do not fall clearly into any of the other categories are classified as having the *undifferentiated type of schizophrenia.* pp. 619–621

What has research revealed about the causes of schizophrenia?

The *concordance rate* is an estimate of the likelihood that two or more groups or biologically related individuals will show the same trait. Research into schizophrenia shows higher concordance rates for identical twins than for fraternal twins, which suggests that schizophrenia has a genetic component. p. 621

The dopamine theory of schizophrenia asserts that problems in dopamine metabolism cause schizophrenia, and this view is bolstered by the effectiveness of antischizophrenic drugs. However, further research indicates that the neurotransmitter glutamate may play an important role. p. 622

Authorities agree that an interaction between biological and environmental factors produces schizophrenia. Biological vulnerability may be precipitated by prenatal or early childhood events, parental loss, and negative family interactions. pp. 622–633

WHAT ARE PERSONALITY DISORDERS?

Personality disorders are psychological disorders characterized by inflexible and long-standing maladaptive behaviors that typically cause distress as well as social or occupational difficulties. People who have unwarranted feelings of persecution and who mistrust almost everyone are said to be suffering from paranoid personality disorder. Those with borderline personality disorder have unstable interpersonal relationships, self-image, and affect and are often impulsive and easily distracted. Dramatic, emotional, and impulsive behaviors are characteristic of histrionic personality disorder. Narcissistic personality disorder is characterized by an extremely exaggerated sense of self-importance, an expectation of special favors, and a constant need for admiration and attention; people with the disorder show a lack of concern for others and react to criticism with shame, humiliation, or rage. *Antisocial personality disorder* is characterized by behavior that is irresponsible and destructive and violates the rights of others; persons with antisocial personality disorder experience little guilt or empathy for others. Submissive and clinging behaviors are characteristic of people with dependent personality disorder. pp. 624–626

HOW ARE VIOLENCE AND MENTAL DISORDERS RELATED?

What diagnoses are associated with increased risk for violence?

Some but not all mental disorders increase the risk of violence. More serious disorders, including schizophrenia, bipolar disorder, depression, and borderline and antisocial personality disorders, pose the highest risks for violent behavior. These disorders do not define *insanity*, which is a legal term and not a psychological one. People with mental disorders are more likely to harm themselves than others. pp. 626–627

Most depressed people do not attempt suicide, but most people who attempt suicide are depressed. Many more people think about suicide than make an attempt, and many more people attempt suicide than commit suicide. Over 30,000 people commit suicide each year in the United States, and all of these deaths are preventable. pp. 627–628

How does violence relate to the risk of developing a mental disorder?

Victims of *child abuse,* intimate partner violence, and *rape* are at increased risk for a variety of mental disorders, including posttraumatic stress disorder, depression, substance abuse, and anxiety disorders. pp. 628–630

CHAPTER 17

Therapy

What Is Psychotherapy, and What Types Are Available? 636
Is Psychotherapy Necessary and Effective?
Which Therapy, Which Therapist?
Are There Common Factors among Therapists?
What Roles Do Culture and Gender Play in Therapy?
Has Managed Care Changed Therapy?

How Do Psychodynamic Therapies Work? 647
Goals of Psychoanalysis
Techniques of Psychoanalysis
Criticisms of Psychoanalysis

What Do Humanistic Therapies Emphasize? 650
Techniques of Client-Centered Therapy
Criticisms of Client-Centered Therapy

What Are the Methods of Behavior Therapy? 654
Assumptions and Goals of Behavior Therapy
Operant Conditioning in Behavior Therapy

Counterconditioning in Behavior Therapy
Modeling in Behavior Therapy

Why Is Cognitive Therapy So Popular? 661
Assumptions of Cognitive Therapy
Types of Cognitive Therapy

How Does Therapy in a Group Work? 666
Techniques of Group Therapy
Family Therapy

How Do Psychologists Reach Out to Communities? 669

How Do Biologically Based Therapies Create Change? 671
Drugs and the Therapeutic Process
Psychosurgery and Electroconvulsive Therapy
Alternative Therapies
The Debate over Hospitalization

Summary and Review 678

The initial causes of psychological problems are not usually biological. When people have relationship or marital problems, workplace stress or conflicts, or other psychological difficulties, help from a therapist—not a drug—is usually the order of the day. After the terrorist attacks in September 2001, more than 9,000 counselors went to New York City to offer aid, guidance, and help, especially in averting the development of posttraumatic stress disorder (McNally, Bryant, & Ehlers, 2003). Today, mental health and therapy efforts are complicated by two facts: First, HMOs are putting pressure on practitioners to find fast, efficient cures that are less costly; second, some disorders, such as depression, are often left undiagnosed and untreated, which often results in the development of a more serious problem. Let's look at the available therapies to try to determine what works best, and when.

What Is Psychotherapy, and What Types Are Available?

When should a person seek out psychotherapy? According to the American Psychological Association (2004), people often consider psychotherapy, also known as therapy, under the following circumstances:

- They feel an overwhelming and prolonged sense of sadness.
- Their emotional difficulties make it hard for them to function from day to day.
- Their actions are harmful to themselves or to others.
- They are troubled by emotional difficulties facing family members or close friends.

In the past two years, 27% of American adults have received treatment for a mental health problem, in the form of therapy, medication, or a combination of the two, according to *Therapy in America 2004,* a HarrisInteractive poll (*Psychology Today,* 2004). Mental health treatment has become part of the American lifestyle. This poll also found that:

- Of Americans who need treatment, more than one in three are not getting it. The leading barriers to receiving care include cost, lack of confidence that treatment helps, and lack of health insurance.
- Of those with a treatment history, 81% report taking a prescription medication.
- Consumers lack key information for selecting a therapist.
- Of those who have received treatment, 80% have found it effective and 85% report that they are satisfied with their treatment.
- Women are disproportionately represented among those who receive treatment (making up 58% of the total).
- Almost four out of five respondents (79%) believe that if a coworker were in therapy it would make no difference in his or her ability to do the job.
- Of those who report having experienced sufficient distress to warrant treatment, 37% have not received it.
- Among those who have needed mental health treatment but not gotten it, the top reasons given for not receiving it were cost and doubt about its efficacy.
- Stigma inhibits some respondents from getting needed care; the fear that therapy would go on their "record" is mentioned by 22%.

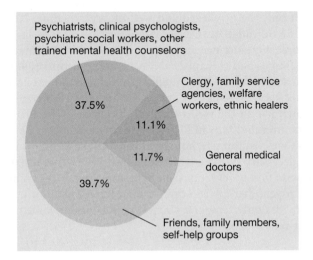

Figure 17.1
Types of
Treatment
A 1993 study of
nearly 23 million
people with mental
health or substance
abuse problems
showed that such
people seek help
from a variety of
sources. (Adapted
from Narrow et al.,
1993.)

The truth is that any number of sources and types of treatment are available to people who are having difficulty coping with their problems (see **Figure 17.1**). When a person seeks help from a physician, mental health counseling center, or drug treatment center, an initial working diagnosis is necessary. Does the person have medical problems? Should the person be hospitalized? Is the person dangerous to self or others? If talking therapy is in order, what type of practitioner is best suited for the person?

Psychotherapy is the treatment of emotional or behavioral problems through psychological techniques. It is a change-oriented process, sometimes a fairly emotional one, whose goal is to help individuals cope better with their problems and achieve more emotionally satisfying lives. Psychotherapy accomplishes its goal by teaching people how to relieve stress, improve interpersonal communication, understand previous events in their lives, and/or modify their faulty ideas about the world. Psychotherapy helps people improve their self-image and adapt to new and challenging situations.

Of course, different cultures perceive different outcomes as optimal. Thus, in the United States, enhancing a client's self-esteem may be seen as a desirable outcome of psychotherapy. In Asia, a desired outcome may be improving family harmony, which may also enhance self-esteem but involves a collective rather than a personal good. This cultural difference is recognized by professional organizations such as the American Psychological Association and the American Psychiatric Association. Also, treatment possibilities are certainly affected by a person's personality style, and some researchers, such as Theodore Millon (2003), even assert that therapists need to consider personality first. Finally, physiological factors often play a role in the decision about treatment. Some psychological problems benefit from treatments that focus on the body; such treatments are biologically based therapies, and we'll discuss them later.

Psychotherapy [SYE-ko-THER-uh-pee] ■ The treatment of emotional or behavioral problems through psychological techniques.

Is Psychotherapy Necessary and Effective?

Some people still have misunderstandings about mental illness and therapy: They believe that there is one pre-eminent therapy, that people who seek therapy are weak or pathetic, or that only the privileged and well-off seek therapy. None of these beliefs are true. A broad range of therapies are effective. They help people who are in distress and people who just need a boost in confidence or managing stress. And a wide array of therapies and therapists are available to people rich and poor.

The images presented by the mass media often shape the public's perception of psychotherapy. Talk-show psychiatrist Frasier Crane of the TV series *Frasier* bumbles through his own life. In the well-regarded 1991 movie *The Prince of Tides*, psychiatrist Barbra Streisand falls in love with her patient, played by Nick Nolte. Images like this, as well as pop psychology in general, make many ask, "Is psychotherapy really necessary or effective?" Some researchers note that many clients outgrow or otherwise find relief from their symptoms without psychotherapy. Others assert that psychotherapy is more art than science. Still others believe that psychotherapy provides only temporary relief. Let's consider some of the factors that relate to this effectiveness debate.

Placebo Effects

Placebo [pluh-SEE-bo] effect ■ An improvement that occurs as a result of a person's expectations of change rather than as a result of any specific therapeutic treatment.

A *placebo effect* is an improvement that occurs as a result of a person's expectations of change rather than as a result of any specific therapeutic treatment. Physicians report that people sometimes experience relief from their symptoms when they are given sugar pills and are told that the pills are medicine. Similarly, some patients in psychotherapy may show improvement of their symptoms simply because they have entered therapy and expect change. For some people, the attention of a therapist and the chance to express their feelings in a therapeutic environment can be helpful (Stewart-Williams & Podd, 2004).

The placebo effect complicates research on the effectiveness of therapy. Is the benefit from psychotherapy largely a placebo effect? Researchers must determine if the improvements they observe are the result of people's expectancy or of the therapy itself. The double-blind technique allows researchers to distinguish between improvement produced by expectancy versus that produced by therapy. The *double-blind technique* is a procedure in which neither the experimenter nor the participants know who is in the control and experimental groups. It helps eliminate bias by reducing the *demand characteristics*, elements of an experimental situation that might cause a participant to perceive the situation in a certain way or become aware of the purpose of the study, which might bias the participant to behave in a certain way and thus distort the results.

Double-blind technique ■ A research procedure in which neither the experimenter nor the participants know who is in the control and experimental groups.

Demand characteristics ■ Elements of an experimental situation that might cause a participant to perceive the situation in a certain way or become aware of the purpose of the study, which might bias the participant to behave in a certain way and thus distort the results.

In a study using the double-blind technique, some participants are assigned to a control condition in which they receive a placebo rather than the actual treatment; the participants assigned to the experimental group receive the treatment whose effectiveness is being tested. For example, a participant might be assigned to a group whose members are given a pill with inactive ingredients or to a group whose members are given a pill that is a new drug for treating depression. Who gets which pill is determined by a third person; the participants do not know which group they are in, and neither do the people giving out the pills. This "blinding" of both participants and researchers prevents any expectancies on their parts from contaminating the results. Both groups receive pills that look the same, so the placebo effect and demand characteristics apply to both equally; they have similar expectancies for effectiveness. The researchers who dispense the pills cannot convey their expectancies to the participants because they too are "blind" to the conditions. Thus, any differences in improvement between the experimental and control group can be attributed to the treatment effect rather than to the placebo effect. Both groups are likely to show some improvement, but there is no reason for one to show markedly *more* improvement unless the treatment is effective. Double-blind studies are the best technique for demonstrating therapy effectiveness. Research studies that compare traditional talking psychotherapies with placebo treatments like relaxation training show that the psychotherapies are consistently more effective (Kazdin, 2001).

Effectiveness of Psychotherapy

In 1952, an important paper by Hans Eysenck challenged the effectiveness of psychotherapy, claiming that it produces no greater change in maladjusted individuals than do naturally occurring life experiences. Psychologists were astonished and angry. Ultimately, thousands of studies attempted to investigate the effectiveness of therapy, and these studies showed that Eysenck was wrong. Analyses of large amounts of data using sophisticated statistical techniques have found psychotherapy to be effective (Bachar, 1998; Smith, Glass, & Miller, 1980; Tritt et al., 2000). Although some psychologists challenge the data, techniques, and conclusions of these analyses, most are convinced that psychotherapy is effective with a wide array of clients; at the end of psychotherapy, on average, patients are better off than 80% of untreated individuals (e.g., Kazdin, 2000). The effectiveness of therapy and the client's speed of response do vary with the type of problem—people suffering from anxiety and depression respond more rapidly to psychotherapy than do those with personality disorders. Nevertheless, the effects of psychotherapy are more powerful than informal support systems and placebos. Psychologists thus assert that psychotherapy is relatively efficient and effective (Lambert, 2004). **Table 17.1** on page 640 presents some generally recognized signs of good progress in therapy.

Is one type of therapy more effective than another? Many researchers contend that most psychotherapies are equally effective; that is, regardless of the approach a therapist uses, the results tend to be the same (Wampold et al., 1997). Some newer and trendier approaches—the kinds that often appear in popular magazines, such as studying Kabbalah—tend to be less reliable and to reflect a culture that is fascinated with novelty. Some therapists do not pay attention to known data, and some—often those with little training—do their clients a disservice by looking for an easy way out. But most of the traditional therapies are effective, so there must be some common underlying component that makes them successful. The American Psychological Association and many individual researchers are seeking to systematize research strategies so as to investigate the effectiveness of therapies; this research will lead to a clearer picture of which approaches work best for certain disorders and for clients of various ages and different ethnic groups (Chambless & Hollon, 1998; Kazdin, 2001). Furthermore, researchers are suggesting ways to validate therapy findings in the laboratory and in the real world (Goldfried & Wolfe, 1998) for problems as diverse as family conflict and cocaine addiction (Van Horn & Frank, 1998).

Table 17.1

SIGNS OF GOOD PROGRESS IN THERAPY

The client is providing personally revealing and significant material.

The client is exploring the meanings of feelings and occurrences.

The client is exploring material avoided earlier in therapy.

The client is expressing significant insight into personal behavior.

The client's method of communicating is active, alive, and energetic.

There is a valued client–therapist working relationship.

The client feels free to express strong feelings toward the therapist—either positive or negative.

The client is expressing strong feelings outside of therapy.

The client is moving toward a different set of personality characteristics.

The client is showing improved functioning outside of therapy.

The client indicates a general state of well-being, good feelings, and positive attitudes.

Source: Mahrer & Nadler (1986)

Which Therapy, Which Therapist?

Before 1950, there were about 15 types of psychotherapy. Today, there are dozens. Some focus on individuals, some on groups (group therapy), some on adolescents, and others on families (family therapy) (Oetzel & Scherer, 2003). Some psychologists even deal with whole communities; these *community psychologists* focus on helping members of communities develop more action-oriented approaches to individual and social problems. A therapist's training usually determines the type of treatment approach he or she takes. Rather than using just one type of psychotherapy, many therapists take an *eclectic approach*—that is, they combine several different techniques or methods when treating clients. This is a pragmatic approach that connects various approaches to fit a unique client's individual needs. Eclectic therapists often have a preferred technique or method that they draw on more often, but they are willing to use any available ones. Such a mix-and-match approach can work well because different therapies do have particular strong points; eclecticism is thus flexible and adaptive and it avoids forcing a client's treatment into a one-size-fits-all modality.

A number of systematic psychotherapeutic approaches are in use today. Each can be applied in several formats—with individuals, couples, or groups—and each will be examined in greater detail in later sections of this chapter. Some practitioners use *psychodynamically based therapies*—approaches that are derived from Freud's psychoanalytic theory, but that reject or modify some elements of that theory. These therapists' aim is to help patients understand the motivations underlying their behavior. They assume that maladjustment and abnormal behavior occur when people do not understand themselves adequately. Practitioners of *humanistic therapy* assume that people are essentially good—that they have an innate disposition to develop their potential and to seek beauty, truth, and goodness. This type of therapy tries to help people realize their full potential and find meaning in life.

In contrast, *behavior therapy* is based on the assumption that most behaviors, whether normal or abnormal, are learned. Behavior therapists encourage their clients to learn new, more adaptive behaviors. Growing out of behavior therapy and cognitive psychology (see Chapters 1 and 9) is *cognitive therapy,* which focuses on changing a client's behavior by changing her or his thoughts and perceptions.

Most of the established therapy approaches adopt a point of view that guides both research and practice. A clear example is psychoanalysis, which prescribes a strict set of guidelines for therapy. But one emerging approach, called *psychotherapy integration,* is not a single-viewpoint approach, but rather is open to using diverse theories and techniques. Psychotherapy integration differs from an eclectic approach because the goal is to integrate theories to devise new ways to solving problems. Research on psychotherapy integration is relatively rare (e.g., Castonguay et al., 2004; Fosha, 2004; O'Brien, 2004), because it is difficult to generate research hypotheses about approaches that are created by integrating theories. Goldfried (2004) argues that the success of most psychotherapies, including psychotherapy integration, depends on several key factors: the expectation that therapy can help, the presence of an optimal therapeutic relationship, the client's becoming more aware of what is creating his or her problems, corrective experiences, and the client's engaging in ongoing reality testing. The psychotherapy integration movement needs to devote clinical and research efforts to learning more about these basic elements of successful therapy. An even better avenue to explore may be research on prevention of disorders.

The effectiveness of the different kinds of therapies varies with the type of disorder being treated and the goals of the client. Research to discover the best treatment method often focuses on a specific disorder, such as depression. Such studies are usually limited to concluding that a specific method is effective for a specific problem. For example, cognitive behavior therapy has a good success rate for people with phobias or depression, but it is less successful for those with schizophrenia. Long-term group therapy is more effective than short-term individual therapy for people with personality disorders. Behavior therapy is usually the most effective approach with children, regardless of the disorder. Furthermore, researchers must be aware that many problems are tied to social, political, and/or economic conditions and must consider these variables when studying the effectiveness of any kind of therapy.

Are There Common Factors among Therapists?

An individual can receive effective treatment from a variety of therapists. One therapist might focus on the root causes of maladjustment. Another might concentrate on eliminating symptoms: sadness, anxiety, or alcohol abuse. Besides the therapeutic approach, personal characteristics of the therapist can affect treatment; among these characteristics are ethnicity, personality, level of experience, and degree of empathy.

Although there are differences among the various psychotherapies and therapists, there are also some commonalities. No matter which therapy they experience, clients usually expect a positive outcome, which helps them strive for change. (**Figure 17.2** presents an overview of outcomes when psychotherapy is combined with efforts to change.) In addition, clients receive attention, which helps them maintain a positive attitude. Moreover, no matter what type of therapy is involved, certain characteristics must be present in both therapist and client for therapeutic changes to occur. For example, good therapists communicate interest, understanding, respect, tactfulness, maturity, and ability to help. They respect clients' ability to cope with their troubles. They use suggestion, encouragement, interpretation, examples, and perhaps rewards to help clients change or rethink their situations. But clients must be willing to make some changes in their lifestyle and thinking. A knowledgeable, accepting, and objective therapist can facilitate behavior changes, but the client is the one who must make the changes (Sadock & Sadock, 2003).

In general, therapist and client must have rapport—a connection or mutual understanding—which enables them to form an alliance to work together purposefully. Such alliances are formed more readily if the therapist and the client share some values (Howe, 1999). The type of therapy a practitioner uses often turns out to be less crucial than her or his personal characteristics. Because therapy is based on the development of a unique therapist–client relationship, compatibility is especially critical to its success.

Although therapy is a collaborative effort, therapists don't make decisions for clients, and they often challenge clients to act, to take advantage of insights that are gained in therapy to bring about life changes. The change required to overcome a particular difficulty often must be effortful and deliberate, and sometimes change requires bravery and the willingness to look deep to find emotional strength. This often takes time to accomplish and rarely happens overnight or during a phone call (despite Frasier Crane's ready wisdom).

All therapists must adhere to ethical guidelines in helping clients; the following are some of the key parts of any practitioner's code. For a therapist and a patient to

Figure 17.2
Goals of Psychotherapy
An important goal of psychotherapy is engaging the client in the process of change. Once initiated, psychotherapy, along with efforts to change, can affect a host of problems, including specific maladaptive behaviors, distorted thoughts, inner conflicts, and interpersonal relationships.

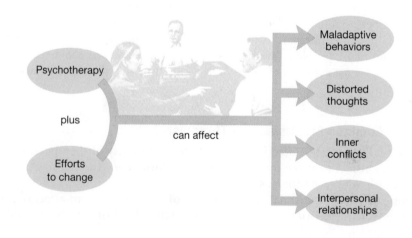

engage in a sexual relationship is unethical—whether or not both are consenting. Any business relationship with a client is problematic; even friendship should be avoided where possible, especially during treatment (in small communities, it may sometimes be unavoidable). Therapists maintain confidentiality; they avoid any conflict of interest (for example, when a client is also a student of the therapist). Last, therapists do not hire their former clients or date them.

To clarify the issues involved in psychotherapy, we'll look more closely at the four major psychotherapeutic approaches: psychodynamic, humanistic, behavioral, and cognitive therapies. Then we will examine the biologically based therapies. But first, let's look at the crucial variables of culture and gender.

What Roles Do Culture and Gender Play in Therapy?

This text has emphasized the role of culture in psychology, stressing that a person's own context and worldview affect his or her thoughts and behavior. In no situation is this more true than in therapy. When a person seeks help for problems large or small, both the therapy process and the outcome are affected by that person's ethnicity, socioeconomic status, sexuality, and disability status, among other factors. To be effective, care must be culturally congruent—there must be a match between the therapist and the client in which the therapist is sensitive to and understands the client's unique characteristics (Sadock & Sadock, 2003; Thompson Sanders, Bazile, & Akbar, 2004; Zoucha & Hustead, 2000). For example, if a Native American client is more likely to internalize new ideas and reflect on them rather than discussing them with a therapist, the practitioner needs to understand and respect this style of thought, emotion, and behavior. Similarly, in some Asian cultures, direct eye contact can be seen as confrontive, and excessive eye contact between a woman client and a male therapist may be deemed inappropriate. Finally, many Asian Americans are disinclined to express emotions openly, and thus may not reveal symptoms to a therapist.

Psychologists respect *multiculturalism*—the acceptance and celebration of distinct cultural heritages—and it continues to be the prevailing principle for appreciating ethnic identity and examining social problems. But practitioners and theorists also know that therapists must see beyond a client's specific culture (such as Vietnamese, French, or Bosnian) and see an individual made up of a confluence of different influences. This view, *transculturalism,* recognizes, for example, that a woman with an Asian family background may embrace Western values of independence and individuality and may be a single mother who runs a business. Transculturalism reflects changes that have occurred through the world as a result of globalization, increased mobility, improved communications systems (including the Internet), and intermarriage.

Therapists need to be well informed about clients' backgrounds and provide interventions that use cultural symbols, rituals, and metaphors that are meaningful to each client (Schindler-Zimmerman & Haddock, 2001; Witztum & Buchbinder, 2001). Research supports the need for such cultural sensitivity. When Costantino, Malgady, and Rogler (1986) gave Puerto Rican children therapy that involved reading folktales that featured culturally familiar characters of the same ethnicity as the children, the folktales served to motivate attentional processes. Compared to traditional therapy or no therapy, the culturally sensitive therapy using folktales as an intervention strategy yielded increased improvement in children's anxiety symptoms. As the researchers note, therapists need to "develop and critically evaluate new therapeutic alternatives that are culturally tailored to the needs of their . . . clients" (p. 661).

Clearly, not all Americans who seek therapy have the same needs. For example, in traditional Asian cultures, the *family* is the primary source of emotional support. The most important family relationship is the parent–child relationship. A person is defined by her or his generational roles in the family, including the parent role, the grandparent role, and the child role. Children of any age, including adult children, are expected to maintain a deferential and respectful relationship to their elders. These roles and the consequent responsibilities provide emotional support for individual family members. The therapeutic alliance must respect the family, its life cycle, and its traditions and recognize the types of problems that many Asian American clients present to practitioners (Tempo & Saito, 1996). Often, emphasizing family bonds—perhaps through family therapy—is an effective technique, as is relying on traditional Asian American philosophical traditions.

Therapists need to recognize that culture, even popular culture, can be used as a tool to influence clients and help them explore their values and goals (Oliver, 2000). It also helps if therapists realize that cultures have various constraints and prohibitions, for example, against self-disclosure or toward control or an acceptance of domestic violence (Thomas, 2000). Some Arab cultures are strongly patriarchal and resistant to emotional exploration, and thus, clients from these cultures may be more likely to value and adapt to therapies that are cognitive in nature (Chaleby, 2000). Cultural mistrust of therapy situations is common among African Americans (Whaley, 2001). By contrast, many Latinos/Latinas have deep-seated notions of social order, a respect for clear authoritarian social roles, and a high regard for experts like therapists (de Leff & Aco, 2000). Expectations for the therapist role often follow from these notions—so, for example, a Latina woman may expect her therapist to be highly orderly and specific. Because most Latino/Latina cultures place high value on respect and personal dignity, clients from these cultures will expect the therapist to treat them in an especially caring, confidential, and kind style, however directive.

Interestingly, the therapist's ethnicity is also a factor in therapy—Latino/Latina, African American, and Asian American therapists are viewed differently by clients than are European American therapists (Tang & Gardner, 1999). And client variables are also potent—evidence shows that there are ethnic differences in the way people respond to drugs used to treat anxiety and depression (Lin, 2001; Melfi et al., 2000; Smith, Mendoza, & Lin, 1999) as well as cultural effects on how well they comply with medical advice and maintain therapeutic drug usage (Kemppainen et al., 2001). Ethnicity—the therapist's and the client's—is an important variable and must be studied, valued, and taken into account in the therapeutic milieu (Thompson Sanders, Bazile, & Akbar, 2004; Tinsley-Jones, 2003). And last, culture is dynamic, contextual, and even political; stereotypes and oversimplifications abound (Romero, 2000). Therapists must recognize that all Asian men, Orthodox Jews, or Creoles are not the same and that therapists' own cultural values and preconceived ideas may constrain the effectiveness of therapy (Laird, 2000). Because there are relatively few minority therapists, cultural incongruity between therapist and client may be difficult to avoid, and thus therapeutic services are underused by many minority groups.

Gender is also a significant factor in therapeutic success. Women seek out therapy more often than men do, and they respond differently to therapy (Philpot, 2001; Scher, 2001), including talking therapy (Romans, 2000) and drug therapy (Martenyi et al., 2001). Therapists need to be aware of gender roles and expectations related to those roles (Papp, 2000; Scher, 2001). Therapists must also consider the way men and women talk about themselves, others, and situations. Linguist Deborah Tannen (2001) has studied language and social interactions among men and women and convincingly argues that men and women talk differently; while both try to be open and communicative, men tend to give reports and women try to establish rapport. Tannen further argues that people in therapeutic and family relationships say things that are heard quite differently than they are intended. For example, she argues that mothers who offer help are often heard to be offering criticism: "Oh, your hair would be so cute if it were short" may be heard by a daughter as "Your hair looks terrible." In the therapeutic relationship, therapists must hear what clients say and the messages that they actually intend to deliver. Therapists must also realize that they and their clients may have experienced gender bias in their families, which will affect their gender assumptions (Atwood, 2001). Gender assumptions are compounded by ethnicity—Asian men view masculinity differently than do European or American men (Sue, 2001) or Latinos (Casas et al., 2001). Women view it differently still. And gender bias can be compounded by ethnic bias. For example, African American women are seen first as women, and then considered as African American—with each designation connected to certain biases (Williams, 1999). Gay men and lesbians bring still another view to gender roles and the therapeutic situation (Biaggio et al., 2000; Gainor, 2000).

Differences occur between men and women in a variety of domains. For example, men and women tend to report similar alcohol-related psychosocial problems, but the women who do so are more likely to be diagnosed as suffering from depression and the men as having antisocial personality disorder (Parks et al., 2001). Therapists must understand how their own gender socialization affects therapy (Brooks, 2001), avoid stereotypes, and recognize the diversity of men's and women's experiences (McMahon & Luthar, 2000).

The interrelationship among culture, gender, and therapy needs empirical study, much more than has gone on to date. However, further research is difficult in a climate that seeks to limit the amount of time people spend in therapy. This constriction of research opportunities is one of the unintended consequences of managed care, our next topic.

Has Managed Care Changed Therapy?

The term *managed care* is used to describe a variety of different arrangements for insurance and health-care delivery. It emphasizes active coordination of services and usually involves three key components: oversight of the care given, contractual relationships with the providers giving the care, and control of the covered benefits. A principal aim is to control costs. Psychologists have tried to hold down costs, provide effective treatment, and be partners with managed care companies. Yet, managed care presents problems for therapy.

The first problem is that insurance companies, looking out for profits, will seek to limit the duration and/or type of psychotherapeutic services a person may receive. The second problem is that managed care policies limit a client's choice of therapists (Rupert & Baird, 2004). Not only that, but many HMOs (health maintenance organizations) require reapproval of the therapy every six sessions, which tends to make the course of therapy shorter (Liu, Sturm, & Cuffel, 2000). Also, therapists need to continually justify the treatment their clients are receiving. Some assert that the therapist–client alliance is thus compromised—either the therapist plays by the managed care rules or the client pays higher premiums for a different insurance plan that might offer a bit more flexibility in choice of doctors and length of stay in therapy (Rupert & Baird, 2004).

But there are positive outcomes of managed care. For one thing, it has led to *brief therapy,* a therapeutic approach based on a blend of psychotherapeutic orientations and skills (Cummings, 1986; Fosha, 2004). A basic goal of brief therapy is to give clients what they need—to focus on treating their problems efficiently and getting them to function on their own as quickly as possible. The time frame for brief therapy varies from therapist to therapist, client to client, and HMO to HMO, but 6 weeks is common; anything more than 16 weeks is considered lengthy. One of the objectives of this approach is to save clients time and money. Although HMOs or insurance companies may place limits on the number of sessions, clients may remain in therapy longer if they feel the need and are willing and able to continue to pay. They can also return if they need help in the future.

The primary effect of the rise in brief therapy is that more and more therapists are thinking in terms of *planned* short-term treatments (Armbruster, Sukhodolsky, & Michalsen, 2004; Hoyt, 2001). The therapist makes sure that treatment begins in the first session of brief therapy. He or she strives to perform an *operational diagnosis* that answers this question: Why is the client here today instead of last week, last month, last year, or next year? The answer helps the therapist pinpoint the specific problem for which the client is seeking help. Also, in the first session, "every client makes a therapeutic contract with every therapist" (Cummings, 1986). The goals of therapy are established and agreed on by the client and the therapist, and the therapy is precise, active, and directive, with no unnecessary steps.

Research on the use of brief therapy is encouraging, suggesting that this approach is effective and that the effects are long-lasting (Armbruster et al., 2004; Fosha, 2004; Kush & Fleming, 2000). Although research has been limited to relatively few clients with a narrow range of problems, brief therapy can be effective when treatment goals and procedures are tailored to the client's needs and the limited time frame. It can be especially effective with couples, in combination with cognitive restructuring (Brown et al., 2003), and with families that have adolescents with substance use problems (Hackett, 2003; Santisteban et al., 2003). Brief therapy is not a cure-all, however. Like all therapies, its aim is to help relieve clients' suffering, and it is effective with some clients and with some problems some of the time

(Hemphill & Littlefield, 2001; Stalker, Levene, & Coady, 1999). The future of brief therapy will depend on the results of further research.

People get good quality care—often of short duration—through managed care organizations (Armbruster et al., 2004). Still, many practitioners worry that care is terminated too quickly and is managed by people who have little or no training and who never meet patients. In some ways, the issue is one of social policy, to what extent we as a society want to provide psychotherapy for those who are in need of it (Cushman & Gilford, 2000). Many argue that managed care limits the ability to do so, especially in the delivery of traditional psychoanalysis or psychodynamic therapy.

How Do Psychodynamic Therapies Work?

Sigmund Freud believed that the exchange of words in psychoanalysis causes therapeutic change. According to Freud (1920/1966):

> The patient talks, tells of his past experiences and present impressions, complains, and expresses his wishes and his emotions. The physician listens, attempts to direct the patient's thought-processes, reminds him, forces his attention in certain directions, gives him explanations and observes the reactions of understanding or denial thus evoked. (p. 21)

Thus, Freud's approach is an *insight therapy*—a therapy that attempts to discover relationships between unconscious motivations and current abnormal behavior. Any insight therapy has two basic assumptions: (1) becoming aware of one's motivations helps one change and become more adaptable, and (2) the causes of maladjustment are unresolved conflicts that the person was unaware of and therefore unable to deal with. The goal of insight therapy is to treat the causes of abnormal behaviors rather than the behaviors themselves. In general, insight therapists try to help people see life from a different perspective so that they can choose more adaptive behaviors.

Psychoanalysis is a lengthy insight therapy that was developed by Freud and aims at uncovering conflicts and unconscious impulses through techniques such as free association and dream analysis and through the process of transference. There are about 3,300 practicing psychoanalysts in the United States. Many other psychologists use some form of therapy loosely connected to or rooted in Freudian theory. These psychologists refer to their therapies as *psychodynamically based therapies*—which use approaches or techniques derived from Freud but reject or modify some elements of Freud's theory.

Insight therapy ■ Any therapy that attempts to discover relationships between unconscious motivations and current abnormal behavior.

Psychoanalysis [SYE-ko-uh-NAL-uh-sis] ■ A lengthy insight therapy that was developed by Freud and aims at uncovering conflicts and unconscious impulses through special techniques such as free association and dream analysis and through the process of transference.

Psychodynamically [SYE-ko-dye-NAM-ick-lee] based therapies ■ Therapies that use approaches or techniques derived from Freud but reject or modify some elements of Freud's theory.

Goals of Psychoanalysis

Many individuals who seek psychotherapy are unhappy with their behavior but are unable to change it. As we saw in the discussion of Freud's theory of personality (Chapter 13), Freud believed that conflicts among a person's unconscious thoughts produce maladjusted behavior. The general goal of psychoanalysis is to help patients understand the unconscious motivations that direct their behavior.

Only when they become aware of those motivations can they begin to choose behaviors that lead to more fulfilling lives. In psychoanalysis, patients are encouraged to express healthy impulses, to strengthen their day-to-day functioning based on reality, and to perceive the world as a positive, even happy place, rather than a punishing place (Thompson, 2004).

Techniques of Psychoanalysis

In general, psychoanalytic techniques are geared toward the exploration of early experiences. In traditional psychoanalysis, the patient lies on a couch and the therapist sits in a chair out of the patient's view. Freud used this arrangement in his office in Vienna because he believed it would allow the patient to be more relaxed and feel less threatened than if the therapist was in view. Today, however, many followers of Freud prefer face-to-face interactions with patients. Psychoanalysis now exhibits a number of variations, depending on the training and theoretical emphasis of the practitioner (Schuelein, 2003).

Two major techniques used in psychoanalysis are free association and dream analysis. In *free association,* the patient is asked to report whatever comes to mind, regardless of how disorganized it might be, how trivial it might seem, or how disagreeable it might sound. A therapist might say, "I can help you best if you say whatever thoughts and feelings come to your mind, even if they seem irrelevant, immaterial, foolish, embarrassing, upsetting, or even if they're about me, even very personally, just as they come, without censoring or editing" (Lewin, 1970, p. 67). The purpose of free association is to help patients learn to recognize connections and patterns among their thoughts and to allow the unconscious to express itself freely.

In *dream analysis,* patients are asked to describe their dreams in detail. The dreams are interpreted so as to provide insight into unconscious motivations. Sometimes lifelike, sometimes chaotic, sometimes incoherent, dreams may at times replay a person's life history and at other times present the person's current problems. Freud believed that dreams represent some element of the unconscious seeking expression. Psychodynamically oriented therapists believe that dreams are full of symbolism; they assert that the content of a dream hides its true meaning. The goal of dream analysis is for the therapist to help reveal the patient's unconscious desires and motivations by discovering the meaning of the patient's dreams.

Both free association and dream analysis rely on the therapist's interpretation. *Interpretation,* in Freud's theory, is the technique of providing a context, meaning, or cause for a specific idea, feeling, or set of behaviors; it is the process of tying a set of behaviors to its unconscious influences. With this technique, the therapist tries to find common threads in a patient's behavior and thoughts. A patient's use of *defense mechanisms* (ways of reducing anxiety by distorting reality, described in Chapter 13) often points to an area that may need to be explored. For example, if a male patient avoids the subject of women, invariably deflecting the topic with an offhand remark or a joke, the therapist may wonder if the man is experiencing some kind of denial. The therapist may then encourage the patient to explore his attitudes and feelings about women in general and about his mother in particular.

Free association ■ Psychoanalytic technique in which the patient is asked to report to the therapist his or her thoughts and feelings as they occur, regardless of how disorganized, trivial, or disagreeable their content may appear.

Dream analysis ■ Psychoanalytic technique in which a patient describes her or his dreams in detail and the therapist helps to interpret them so as to provide insight into the individual's unconscious desires and motivations.

Interpretation ■ In Freud's theory, the technique of providing a context, meaning, or cause for a specific idea, feeling, or set of behaviors, thereby tying a set of behaviors to its unconscious influences.

Two phenomena are central to the process of psychoanalysis: resistance and transference. **Resistance** is an unwillingness to cooperate, which a patient signals by showing a reluctance to provide the therapist with information or to help the therapist understand or interpret a situation. Resistance can sometimes reach the point of belligerence. For example, a patient disturbed by her therapist's unsettling interpretations might become angry and start resisting treatment by missing appointments or failing to pay for therapy. Therapists usually interpret resistance as meaning either that the patient wishes to avoid discussing a particular subject or that an especially difficult stage in the therapeutic process has been reached. To minimize resistance, analysts try to accept patients' behavior. When a therapist does not judge but merely listens, a patient is more likely to describe feelings thoroughly and openly.

Transference is a psychoanalytic phenomenon in which a therapist becomes the object of a patient's emotional attitudes about an important person in the patient's life, such as a parent. For example, if a man becomes hostile toward his male therapist, a psychoanalyst would say that the patient is acting as though the therapist were his father; that is, he is directing attitudes and emotional reactions from that earlier relationship toward the therapist (Butler & Strupp, 1991). The importance of transference is that the therapist will respond differently than the parent or other important person did, so the patient can experience the conflict differently, which will lead him or her to a better understanding of the issue. By permitting transference, a therapist gives patients a new opportunity to understand their feelings and can guide them in the exploration of repressed or difficult material. The examination of thoughts or feelings that were previously considered unacceptable (and therefore were likely repressed) helps patients understand and identify the underlying conflicts that direct their behavior.

Psychoanalysis, with its slowly gained insights into the unconscious, is a gradual and continual process. Through their insights, patients learn new ways of coping with instinctual urges and develop more mature means of dealing with anxiety and guilt. The cycle of interpretation, resistance to interpretation, and transference occurs repeatedly in the process of psychoanalysis and is sometimes referred to as *working through*.

Criticisms of Psychoanalysis

Freud's therapy has not been universally accepted; even his followers have often disagreed with him. One group of psychoanalysts, referred to as *ego analysts,* or *ego psychologists,* have modified some of Freud's basic ideas. Ego analysts are psychoanalytic practitioners who assume that the ego has greater control over behavior than Freud suggested and who focus more on a patient's reality testing and self-control than on unconscious motivations and processes. Like Freud, ego analysts believe that psychoanalysis is the appropriate method for treating patients with emotional problems. Unlike Freud, however, they assume that people have voluntary control over whether, when, and in what ways their biological urges will be expressed.

A major disagreement between ego analysts and traditional psychoanalysts has to do with the role of the id and the ego. (Recall from Chapter 13 that the id is guided by the pleasure principle, while the ego operates on the reality principle and

Resistance ■ In psychoanalysis, an unwillingness to cooperate, which a patient signals by showing a reluctance to provide the therapist with information or to help the therapist understand or interpret a situation.

Transference ■ Psychoanalytic phenomenon in which a therapist becomes the object of a patient's emotional attitudes about an important person in the patient's life, such as a parent.

Working through ■ In psychoanalysis, the repetitive cycle of interpretation, resistance to interpretation, and transference.

tries to control the id's impulsivity.) A traditional Freudian asserts that the ego develops from the id and controls it—but an ego analyst asserts that the ego is independent of the id, controls memory and perception, and is not in constant conflict with the id. Whereas traditional psychoanalysts begin by focusing on unconscious material in the id and only later try to increase the patient's ego control, ego analysts begin by helping clients develop stronger egos. They may ask a client to be assertive and take control of a situation or to let reason, rather than feeling, guide a specific behavior pattern. From an ego analyst's point of view, a weak ego may cause maladjustment through its failure to control the id. Thus, by learning to master and develop their egos—including their moral reasoning and judgment—people gain greater control over their lives.

Critics of psychoanalysis contend that the approach is unscientific, imprecise, and subjective; they assert that psychoanalytic concepts such as id, ego, and superego are not linked to reality or to day-to-day behavior. Other critics object to Freud's biologically oriented approach, which suggests that a human being is merely a conflicted bundle of energy driven toward some hedonistic goal. These critics ask, "What about human free will?" Also, elements of Freud's theory are untestable, and some are sexist. Freud conceived of men and women in prescribed roles; most practitioners today find this idea objectionable.

Aside from these criticisms, the effectiveness of psychoanalysis is open to question. Research shows that psychoanalysis is more effective for some people than for others. It is more effective, for example, for people with anxiety disorders than for those diagnosed as schizophrenic. In addition, younger patients improve more than older ones. In general, studies show that psychoanalysis can be as effective as other therapies, but no more so (Kazdin, 2000, 2001). Psychoanalysis does have certain inherent disadvantages. The problems it addresses are complex, and a patient must be highly motivated and articulate to grasp the intricate and subtle relationships being explored. Further, because traditional psychoanalysis involves meeting with the analyst for an hour at a time, 5 days a week, for approximately 5 years, psychoanalysis is typically extremely time-consuming and expensive. Many people who seek therapy cannot afford this type of treatment, nor will most insurance companies foot the bill.

What Do Humanistic Therapies Emphasize?

Humanistic therapies, unlike psychodynamic therapies, emphasize the idea that human beings have free will to determine their destinies. These therapies also stress the uniqueness of the human experience and the human ability to reflect on conscious experience. Humanistic psychologists tend to focus on the present and the future rather than on the past, and they assert that human beings are creative and born with an innate desire to fulfill themselves. To some extent, humanistic approaches, being insight-oriented, are an outgrowth of psychodynamically based insight therapies. Humanistic therapies focus on helping basically healthy people understand the causes of their behavior—both well-adjusted and maladjusted—and take responsibility for their future by promoting growth and fulfillment. Client-centered therapy is a humanistic therapy that centers on self-determination.

Client-centered therapy, or *person-centered therapy,* is an insight therapy that seeks to help people evaluate the world and themselves from their own perspective. Carl Rogers (1902–1987) first developed client-centered therapy. His students and clients reported that Rogers was a quiet, caring man; he turned the psychoanalytic world upside-down when he introduced his approach. He focused on the person, listening intently to his clients and encouraging them to define their own "cures." Rogers saw people as having the potential to grow and, with a nourishing environment, to become mature, fulfilled individuals. He believed that to reach one's full potential, a person must be involved in a therapeutic relationship that includes unconditional positive regard, congruence, and empathy (described below). When people lack this experience in their lives, client-centered therapy can sometimes provide it.

Rogerian therapists hold that problem behaviors occur when the environment prevents a person from developing his or her own innate potential. If a boy is given love and reinforcement only for his achievements, for example, as an adult he may see himself almost solely in terms of his achievements. Rogerian treatment involves helping people improve their self-regard and see themselves more accurately. To this end, a Rogerian therapist might first encourage a client to explore his past goals, current desires, and expectations for the future. This approach places the client's current behavior and problems in a framework. It also allows the therapist to then ask the client whether he can achieve what he wants through his current emphasis on achievement, or if some other strategy would be more effective. **Table 17.2** presents the basic assumptions underlying Rogers's approach to treatment.

Client-centered therapy
■ An insight therapy that was developed by Carl Rogers and seeks to help people evaluate the world and themselves from their own perspective by providing them with a therapeutic relationship that includes unconditional positive regard, congruence, and empathy; also known as *person-centered therapy.*

Techniques of Client-Centered Therapy

The goal of client-centered therapy is to help clients discover their ideal selves and reconcile this ideal with their real selves. The use of the word *client* rather than *patient* is a key aspect of Rogers's approach to therapy (*patient* connotes a

Table 17.2

ROGERS'S ASSUMPTIONS ABOUT HUMAN BEINGS

1. People have an innate tendency to move toward fulfillment of their potential.

2. People have a concept of their ideal self and a self-concept; when these two are very discrepant, problems arise.

3. Healthy people are aware of all their behavior; they choose their behavior patterns.

4. A client's behavior can be understood only from the client's point of view. Even if a client has misconstrued events in the world, the therapist must understand how the client sees those events.

5. Effective therapy occurs only when a therapist creates conditions of unconditional positive regard, congruence, and empathy, allowing the client to become less defensive and more open to experiences.

medically oriented view of therapy). In psychoanalysis, the therapist directs the "cure" and helps patients understand their behavior; in client-centered therapy, the therapist *guides* clients and helps them realize what they feel is right for themselves (Merry & Brodley, 2002). Clients are viewed as the experts concerning their own experience.

The three essential characteristics of successful client-centered therapy are unconditional positive regard, congruence, and empathy (Rogers, 1957). A basic tenet of client-centered therapy is that the therapist must show *unconditional positive regard*—be an accepting person who projects positive feelings toward clients. To counteract clients' negative experiences with people who were unaccepting, and who thus have taught them to think they are bad or unlikable, client-centered therapists accept clients as they are, with good and bad points; they respect them as individuals. Of course, acceptance of a person as an individual is not the same thing as condoning actions that may be socially unacceptable or destructive. Rogers and other humanistic therapists acknowledge that sometimes good people do "bad" things. Thus, a therapist can accept the client but reject inappropriate behavior.

Congruence is the second necessary component of client-centered therapy. In the context of such therapy, this term refers to being real or genuine. Rogers believed that therapists must be more than accepting; they must be honest and aware of their own feelings. Counselors' congruence allows them to communicate more effectively and to help clients become more aware and open.

Empathy, the third characteristic of client-centered therapy, is the perception that another person accurately senses your feelings. Through *empathic listening*, therapists sense how their clients feel and communicate these feelings to clients. The therapist helps a client organize thoughts and ideas simply by asking the right questions, by giving neutral responses to encourage the client to continue, and by reflecting back the client's feelings. (That is, the therapist may *paraphrase* a client's ideas, ask the client to clarify and *restate* ideas and feelings in other words, or *reflect back* what the client has just said so that the person can hear her or his own words again.) Even a small physical movement, such as a nod or a gesture, can help a client stay on the right track. The client learns to evaluate the world from a personal vantage point, with little interpretation by the therapist.

The combination of acceptance and recognition of clients' emotions, expression of genuine feelings, and empathic listening to clients' problems is the essence of the therapeutic relationship (Weerasekera et al., 2001). Client-centered therapy can be viewed as a consciousness-raising process that helps people expand their awareness so as to construct new meanings about self-esteem and family relationships (Bott, 2001; Richert, 2002). It can also be viewed from the vantage point of positive psychology as being oriented toward strengthening clients' responsibility to self and others as well as their sense of being part of a community (Bohart & Greening, 2001; Kuhn, 2001; Resnick, Warmoth, & Selin, 2001). Positive psychology focuses on wisdom, courage, humanity, justice, forgiveness and appreciation of spirituality and hope and provides a way for therapists—especially client-centered, humanistic therapists—to focus on helping people (Baker & Stauth, 2003; Baumeister et al.,

2003; Peterson & Seligman, 2004). In many important ways, positive psychology can be seen as an outgrowth of humanistic psychology, which has similar goals (refer back to Chapter 1).

Initially, clients tend to express attitudes and ideas they have adopted from other people, to be defensive, and to show ineffective, disorganized behavior. A client might say, "I should be making top sales figures," implying "because my father expects me to be a success." As therapy progresses and the client experiences the empathy, congruence, and unconditional positive regard of the therapist, he will begin to use his own ideas and standards when evaluating himself (Rogers, 1951). As a result, he may adjust his ideal self so that it is more in line with his own (rather than his father's) goals, or his behavior may change so that his sales figures climb. Such change allows him to begin to talk about himself in more positive ways and to try to please himself rather than others, part of the process of constructing new meanings. He may then say, "I'm satisfied with my sales efforts," or "Since I've started rethinking my goals, my sales figures have improved," reflecting a more positive, more accepting attitude about himself. As this client begins to feel better about himself, he will eventually suggest to the therapist that he feels ready to deal with the world and to leave therapy. Successful client-centered therapy results in clients who are less defensive, more congruent, and more open to new experiences (Rogers, 1980).

Criticisms of Client-Centered Therapy

Client-centered therapy is acclaimed for its focus on the therapeutic relationship. No other type of therapy makes clients feel so accepted and safe. These are important characteristics of any therapy, but critics argue that they may not be enough to bring about long-lasting change (Baker & Stauth, 2003). And some critics assert that lengthy discussions about past problems do not necessarily help people with their present difficulties. They believe that client-centered therapy may be making therapeutic promises that cannot be fulfilled and that it focuses on concepts that are hard to define, such as self-actualization.

Critics of traditional therapy offer alternatives. In the view of those who promote positive psychology, which focuses on happiness, some reasons for personal problems are not part of a person's past history. Baker and Stauth (2003) call these *happiness traps*. They argue that people are ensnared by traps that keep them from being happy; that people try to buy happiness with things (the person with the most toys wins), find happiness through pleasure (for example, elaborate vacations), be happy by resolving past issues (endless therapy churning up the past), be happy by overcoming weakness (if I could only be stronger, thinner, more assertive), or force happiness (working harder, accumulating more, being the most active volunteer). Instead, positive psychologists assert, people have to focus on their strengths, listen to their hearts, stop fearing the worst, appreciate what they have, tell healthy stories about life, and live a balanced, multidimensional life. From a positive psychology viewpoint, the old ways of therapy do not focus on growth and constructing a positive, happy life.

What Are the Methods of Behavior Therapy?

Behavior therapy has assumptions and goals that differ from those of psychodynamic and humanistic therapies. It has become especially popular in the past three decades for three principal reasons. First, people sometimes have problems that may not warrant an in-depth examination of early childhood experiences, an exploration of unconscious motivations, a lengthy discussion about current feelings, or a resolution of inner conflicts. Examples of such problems are fear of heights, anxiety about public speaking, marital conflicts, and sexual dysfunction. In these cases, behavior therapy may be more appropriate than psychodynamic or humanistic therapies (Segraves & Althof, 2002). Second, behavior therapy has become popular because HMOs and insurance providers are seeking quicker, less expensive solutions to everyday problems. Last, behavior therapy can be very effective. As you will see, this type of therapy is focused on changing current behavior and on designing solutions to specific problems.

Assumptions and Goals of Behavior Therapy

Behavior therapy ■ A therapy that is based on the application of learning principles to human behavior and that focuses on changing overt behaviors rather than on understanding subjective feelings, unconscious processes, or motivations; also known as *behavior modification*.

Behavior therapy is a therapy based on the application of learning principles to human behavior. Also called *behavior modification*, it focuses on changing overt behaviors rather than on understanding subjective feelings, unconscious processes, or motivations. It uses learning principles to help people replace maladaptive behaviors with more effective ones. Behavior therapists assume that changes in people's environment affect the way they respond to that environment and the way they interact with other people—their behavior. Unlike psychodynamic therapies, behavior therapy does not aim to discover the origins of a behavior; it works only to alter it. For a person with a nervous twitch, for example, the goal would be to eliminate the twitch. Thus, behavior therapists treat people by having them first "unlearn" faulty behaviors and then learn more acceptable or effective ones.

Behavior therapy usually involves three general procedures: (1) identifying the problem behavior and its frequency by examining what people actually do; (2) treating a client with strategies that are individually tailored to the client, perhaps re-education, communication training, or some type of counterconditioning; and (3) continually assessing whether there is a behavior change. If the client exhibits a new behavior for several weeks or months, the therapist concludes that treatment was effective.

Behavior therapists do not always focus on the problem that caused the client to seek therapy. If they see that the client's problem is associated with some other situation, they may focus on changing that situation. For example, a man may seek therapy because of a faltering marriage. However, the therapist may discover that the marriage is suffering because of the client's frequent and acrimonious arguments with his wife, each of which is followed by a period of heavy drinking. The therapist may then discover that both the arguments and the drinking are brought on by stress at work, aggravated by the client's unrealistic expectations regarding his performance. In this situation, the therapist may focus on helping the client develop standards that will ease the original cause of the problem—the tension experienced at work—and that will be consistent with the client's capabilities, past performance, and realistic likelihood of future performance.

Unlike psychodynamic and humanistic therapies, behavior therapy does not encourage clients to interpret past events to find their meaning. Although a behavior therapist may uncover a chain of events leading to a specific behavior, that discovery will not generally prompt a close examination of the client's early experiences.

When people enter behavior therapy, many aspects of their behavior may change, not just those specifically being treated. For example, a woman being treated for extreme shyness may find not only that the shyness decreases, but also that she can engage more easily in discussions about emotional topics and can perform better on the job. Behaviorists argue that once a person's maladjusted behavior has changed, it may be easier for the person to manage attitudes, fears, and conflicts.

Behaviorists are dissatisfied with psychodynamic and humanistic therapies for three basic reasons: (1) Those therapies use concepts that are almost impossible to define and measure (such as the id and self-actualization); (2) some studies show that patients who do not receive psychodynamic and humanistic therapies improve anyway; and (3) once a therapist has labeled a person as "abnormal," the label itself may lead to maladaptive behavior. (Although any type of therapy has labels for various problems and behaviors, psychodynamic therapy tends to use them more than behavior therapy does.) Behavior therapists assume that people display maladaptive behaviors not because they are abnormal but because they are having trouble adjusting to their environment; if they are taught new ways of coping, the maladjustment will disappear. A great strength of behavior therapy is that it provides a coherent conceptual framework.

However, behavior therapy is not without its critics. Most insight therapists, especially those who are psychodynamically oriented, believe that if only overt behavior is treated, symptom substitution may occur. *Symptom substitution* is the appearance of one overt symptom to replace another that has been eliminated by treatment. For example, if a therapist eliminates a nervous twitch without examining its underlying causes, the client may develop some other symptom, such as a speech impediment. Behavior therapists, however, contend that symptom substitution does not occur if the treatment makes proper use of behavioral principles. Research shows that behavior therapy is at least as effective as insight therapy and in some cases more effective (Kazdin, 2000, 2001).

Symptom substitution
■ The appearance of one overt symptom to replace another that has been eliminated by treatment.

Behavior therapists use an array of techniques, often in combination, to help people change their behavior; chief among these techniques are operant conditioning, counterconditioning, and modeling. A good therapist will use whatever combination of techniques will help a client most efficiently and effectively—so, in addition to using several behavioral techniques, a behavior therapist may use some insight techniques. The more complicated the behavior being treated, the more likely it is that a practitioner will use a mix of therapeutic approaches.

Let's explore the three major behavior therapy techniques: operant conditioning, counterconditioning, and modeling.

Operant Conditioning in Behavior Therapy

Operant conditioning procedures are used with many people in a variety of settings to achieve a wide range of desirable behaviors, including increased reading speed, improved classroom behavior, and maintenance of personal hygiene. As we saw in Chapter 8, establishing new behaviors through operant conditioning often depends on a *reinforcer*—an event or circumstance that increases the probability that a particular response will recur. In behavior therapy, a client could employ operant conditioning to help herself adopt more positive responses. For example, she could ask her boyfriend to acknowledge her effort every time she tries to express her feelings openly.

One of the most effective uses of operant conditioning is with children who are antisocial, slow to learn, or in some way maladjusted. Operant conditioning is also effective with patients in mental hospitals. Ayllon and Haughton (1964), for example, instructed hospital staff members to reinforce patients for psychotic, bizarre, or meaningless verbalizations during one period and for neutral verbalizations (such as comments about the weather) during another. As expected, the relative frequency of each type of verbalization increased when it was reinforced and decreased when it was not reinforced (see **Figure 17.3**).

Token Economies

Token economy ■ An operant conditioning procedure in which individuals who display appropriate behavior receive tokens that they can exchange for desirable items or activities.

One way of rewarding adaptive behavior is to use a ***token economy***—an operant conditioning procedure in which individuals who display appropriate behavior receive tokens that they can exchange for desirable items or activities. In a hospital setting, for example, some rewards might be candy, new clothes, games, or time with important people in the patients' lives. The more tokens individuals earn, the

Figure 17.3
Reinforcement Increases Desired Behaviors
A study by Ayllon and Haughton (1964) found that reinforcement affected the frequency of psychotic and neutral verbal behavior in hospitalized patients. (Ayllon & Haughton, 1964)

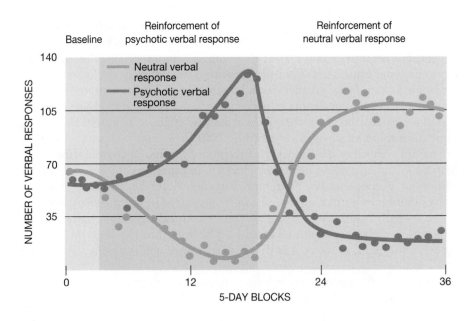

more items or activities they can obtain. Token economies have also been effective in school settings. Teachers who use a token economy often keep track of tokens publicly and reward students with some fanfare (Boniecki & Moore, 2003).

Token economies are used to modify behavior in social settings; they aim to strengthen behaviors that are compatible with social norms. As one team of researchers (LePage et al., 2003) put it, "token economies are an effective way of changing various behaviors including acquiring new skills, reducing undesired behaviors, reducing aggression, increasing treatment compliance, and improving . . . management" (p. 179). For example, a patient in a hospital might receive tokens for cleaning tables, helping in the hospital laundry, or maintaining certain standards of personal hygiene and appearance. The level of difficulty of the behavior or task determines the number of tokens earned. Thus, patients might receive 3 tokens for brushing their teeth but 40 tokens for being helpful to someone.

Ayllon and Azrin (1965) monitored the performance of a group of hospitalized patients for 45 days as they performed simple tasks. They found that when tokens (reinforcement) were contingent on performance, the patients worked about four times as long each day as when tokens were not delivered. (**Figure 17.4** presents some of the results of this research.) Token economies become especially effective when combined with other behavioral techniques. Next, we examine three of these techniques: extinction, punishment, and time-out.

Extinction

As we saw in Chapter 8, if reinforcers are withheld, extinction of a behavior will occur. Suppose a 6-year-old girl refuses to go to bed at the designated time. When

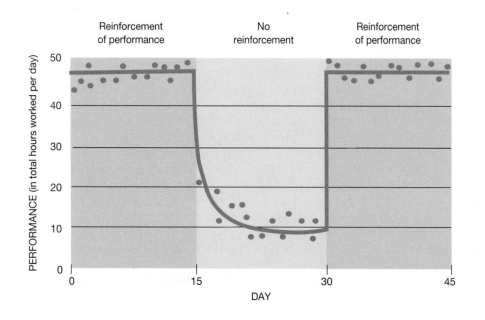

Figure 17.4
Token Economies Change Performance Effectively
Ayllon and Azrin (1965) found that tokens increased the total number of hours worked per day by a group of 44 patients. (Ayllon & Azrin, 1965)

she is taken to her bedroom, she cries and screams violently. If the parents give in and allow her to stay up, they are reinforcing the crying behavior: The child cries, and the parents give in. A therapist might suggest that the parents stop reinforcing the crying by insisting that their daughter go to bed and stay there. Chances are that the child will cry loudly and violently for two or three nights, but the behavior will eventually be extinguished (Williams, 1959), and the desired behavior will increase (Kahng, Boscoe, & Byrne, 2003).

Punishment

Another way to decrease the frequency of an undesired behavior is to punish it. Punishment often involves the presentation of an aversive stimulus. In the home, a parent might slap a child's hand to get her stop touching a delicate family heirloom. As we saw in Chapter 8, a serious limitation of punishment as a behavior-shaping device is that it only suppresses existing behaviors; it cannot be used to establish new, desired behaviors. Thus, punishment for undesired behaviors is usually combined with positive reinforcement for desired behaviors.

Research also shows that people, especially young people, imitate aggression. Thus, a child (or institutionalized person) in therapy may strike out at the therapist who administers punishment in an attempt to eliminate the source of punishment. Punishment can also bring about generalized aggression. This is especially true for prison inmates, whose hostility is well recognized, and for class bullies, who are often the children most strictly disciplined by their parents and teachers. Skinner (1988) believed that punishment is harmful; he advocated nonpunitive therapeutic techniques, which might involve developing strong bonds between clients and therapists and reinforcing specific prosocial activities. In general, procedures that lead to a perception of control on the part of an individual are much more likely to lead to the extinction of undesired behavior.

Time-Out

Time-out ■ An operant conditioning procedure in which a person is physically removed from sources of reinforcement in order to decrease the occurrence of undesired behaviors.

Another effective operant conditioning procedure, introduced in Chapter 8, is *time-out,* the physical removal of a person from sources of reinforcement in order to decrease the occurrence of undesired behaviors. Suppose a boy regularly throws a temper tantrum each time he wants a piece of candy, an ice cream cone, or his little brother's toys. With the time-out procedure, whenever the child misbehaves, he is taken to a specific place (such as a chair or a room) away from the rest of the family, without sweets, toys, other people, or any type of reinforcer. He is made to stay in the time-out area for a short period, say, 5 or 10 minutes; if he leaves, more time is added. The procedure ensures that the child not only does not get what he wants, but that he is also removed from any potential source of reinforcement. Time-out is principally used with children; it is especially effective when it is combined with positive reinforcers for appropriate behavior and is administered correctly by a parent or knowledgeable child-care specialist (Crespi, 1988).

Counterconditioning in Behavior Therapy

A second major technique used in behavior therapy is *counterconditioning,* a process of reconditioning in which a person is taught a new, more adaptive response to a familiar stimulus. For example, anxiety in response to any of a number of stimuli is one of the main reasons people seek therapy. If a therapist can condition a person to respond to a particular stimulus with something other than anxiety—that is, if the therapist can *countercondition* the person—a real breakthrough will be achieved, and the person's anxiety will be reduced.

Joseph Wolpe (1915–1997) was one of the initial proponents of counterconditioning. His work on classical conditioning, especially in situations in which animals show conditioned anxiety responses, led him to attempt to inhibit or decrease anxiety as a response in human beings. His therapeutic goal was to replace anxiety with some other response, such as relaxation, amusement, or pleasure. Behavior therapy using counterconditioning begins with a specific stimulus (S_1), which elicits a specific response (R_1). After the person undergoes counterconditioning, the same stimulus (S_1) should elicit a new response (R_2) (Wolpe, 1958). There are two basic approaches to counterconditioning: systematic desensitization and aversive counterconditioning.

Systematic Desensitization

Systematic desensitization is a multistage counterconditioning procedure in which a person is taught to relax when confronting a stimulus that formerly elicited anxiety. The client first learns how to relax, then describes the specific situations that elicit anxiety, and finally, while deeply relaxed, imagines increasingly vivid scenes of those situations. In this way, the client is gradually, step by step, exposed to the source of anxiety. With each successive experience, the client learns relaxation rather than fear as a response. Eventually, the client confronts the real-life situation.

Flying in an airplane, for example, is a stimulus situation (S_1) that can bring about a fear response (R_1). With systematic desensitization therapy, the idea of flying (S_1) can eventually be made to elicit a response of curiosity or even relaxation (R_2). The therapist might first ask the relaxed client to imagine sitting in an airplane on the ground, then to imagine the airplane taxiing down a runway, and eventually to imagine flying though the billowing clouds. As the client practices relaxation while imagining the scene, he or she becomes able to tolerate more stressful imagery and may eventually perform the behavior that previously elicited anxiety—in this case, flying in an airplane. Practicing relaxation in real-world situations produces the most lasting effects. If systematic desensitization is combined with efforts to change a person's ideas about the world—through cognitive therapy, which we examine in the next section—the person can cope better. With systematic desensitization and cognitive therapy, people can lose their fear of flying, which has been a problem for 25 million Americans, or even more since the 9/11 terrorist attacks.

Systematic desensitization is most successful for people who have impulse control problems or who exhibit particular forms of anxiety such as phobias. It is not especially effective for people who exhibit serious psychotic symptoms; nor is it the best treatment for situations involving interpersonal conflict. Although still used

Counterconditioning ■ A process of reconditioning in which a person is taught a new, more adaptive response to a familiar stimulus.

Systematic desensitization ■ A multistage counterconditioning procedure in which a person is taught to relax when confronting a stimulus that formerly elicited anxiety.

extensively, systematic desensitization is not as popular today as it was in the 1970s and 1980s (McGlynn et al., 2004).

Aversive Counterconditioning

Clients often have problems because they do not avoid a stimulus that prompts inappropriate behavior. In such cases, aversive counterconditioning may be useful. *Aversive counterconditioning* is a technique in which an unpleasant stimulus is paired with a stimulus that elicits an undesirable behavior so that the person will cease responding to the original stimulus with the undesirable behavior. As with systematic desensitization, the objective is to teach a new response to the original stimulus. A behavior therapist might use aversive counterconditioning to teach an alcoholic client to avoid alcohol. The first step might be to teach the person to associate alcohol (the original stimulus) with the sensation of nausea (a noxious stimulus). If having the client simply imagine the association is not enough, the therapist might administer a drug that causes the client to feel nauseous whenever he or she consumes alcohol. The goal is to make drinking alcohol unpleasant. Eventually, the treatment will make the client experience nausea at the *thought* of consuming alcohol, thus causing the client to avoid alcohol. Although counterconditioning is effective, it is not widely used (Paunovic, 2003; Slifer, Eischen, & Busby, 2002).

Aversive counter-conditioning ■ A technique in which an unpleasant stimulus is paired with a stimulus that elicits an undesirable behavior so that the person will cease responding to the original stimulus with the undesirable behavior.

Modeling in Behavior Therapy

Both children and adults learn behaviors by watching and imitating other people—in other words, by observing models. Children learn a whole host of behaviors—from table manners to toileting behavior to appropriate responses to animals—by observing and imitating their parents and other models. Similarly, the music you listen to, the clothing styles you wear, and the social or political causes you support are determined, in part, by the people around you.

According to Albert Bandura (1977a), as a behavior therapy technique, modeling is most effective for (1) teaching new behaviors, (2) helping to eliminate fears, especially phobias, and (3) enhancing already existing behaviors. By watching—and thinking about—the behavior of others, people learn to exhibit more adaptive and appropriate behavior. Bandura, Blanchard, and Ritter (1969), for example, asked people with snake phobia to watch other people handling snakes. Doing so reduced, the watchers' fear of snakes. This technique works because of the consequences the learner observes the model receiving. A learner may think, "Well, she didn't die when she handled the snake, so I probably won't die either." Modeling works best when the learner identifies closely with the model.

One problem with modeling is that people may observe and imitate the behavior of inappropriate models. Some people imitate violent behaviors they have observed on television and in movies. Further, many adolescents abuse alcohol and other drugs because they imitate their peers. Such imitation often occurs because of faulty thinking about situations, people, or goals.

Why Is Cognitive Therapy So Popular?

Behavior therapy and cognitive therapy have been heavily influenced by HMOs and managed care. A managed care organization usually controls the reimbursement of therapists and makes rulings about questions such as these: Does this problem qualify for reimbursement? What technique should be used to treat this client? Is this clinician the appropriate therapist for this client? Many psychologists see managed care as a crisis, a nightmare, or even the downfall of psychotherapy (Fishman & Franks, 1997). Behavior therapists and cognitive therapists, however, more than other types of therapists, have become allies of managed care organizations because of the close alignment of their goals, especially the goal of efficiency.

Assumptions of Cognitive Therapy

According to cognitive therapists, wrong, distorted, or underdeveloped ideas and thoughts often prevent a person from establishing effective coping strategies. Growing out of behavior therapy and the developing study of cognitive psychology, *cognitive therapy* focuses on changing a client's behavior by changing his or her thoughts and perceptions. Cognitive therapy is based on three basic assumptions: (1) cognitive activity affects behavior, (2) cognitive activity can be monitored, and (3) behavior changes can be effected through cognitive changes. Cognitive psychologists have had a profound impact in many areas of psychology, especially in therapy. In the past, behavior therapists were concerned only with overt behavior; today, many of these therapists address clients' thought processes in their treatments. For this reason, their work is often called **cognitive behavior therapy**. Researchers now suggest that evaluating thought processes may hold the key to managing many forms of maladjustment, including obsessive-compulsive disorder and other stress-related disorders (McGregor et al., 2004; Ong, Linden, & Young, 2004).

Cognitive behavior therapy ■ A therapy that focuses on changing a client's behavior by changing his or her thoughts and perceptions.

Therapists who use *cognitive restructuring* (another term for cognitive therapy) are interested in modifying clients' faulty thought patterns (Young, Weinberger, & Beck, 2001). This type of therapy is effective for people who have attached overly narrow or otherwise inappropriate labels to certain behaviors or situations. For example, such a person may believe that sex is dirty or that assertiveness is unwomanly. Whenever presented with a situation that involves sex or assertiveness, the person will respond in a way that is determined by his or her thoughts about the situation rather than by the facts of the situation. Those thoughts may have been established years ago and may not have ever been reevaluated or reconsidered.

Cognitive therapy typically focuses on current behavior and current thoughts. It is not especially concerned with uncovering forgotten childhood experiences, although it can be used to alter thoughts about those experiences. Cognitive therapy has been used effectively to assist in weight loss and to treat depression, bulimia, excessive anger, and adolescent behavior problems (e.g., Craighead et al., 2002; Risdale, Darbishire, & Seed, 2004). When cognitive restructuring is combined with other techniques, such as reinforcement, which help a person make behavioral changes, results are even more impressive (Franklin & Foa, 2002).

Types of Cognitive Therapy

Cognitive therapy has gone through three decades of development, and its future looks promising (Kelly & Newstead, 2004; Kubany et al., 2004). Let's look at three major types of cognitive therapy.

Rational-Emotive Therapy

Rational-emotive therapy ■ A type of cognitive therapy that was developed by Albert Ellis and emphasizes the importance of logical, rational thought processes.

The best-known cognitive therapy is *rational-emotive therapy,* which emphasizes the role of logical, rational thought processes in behavior. Researcher Albert Ellis developed this therapy more than 35 years ago. Most behavior therapists assume that abnormal behavior is caused by faulty and irrational *behavior* patterns. Ellis and his colleagues, however, assume that it is caused by faulty and irrational *thinking* patterns (Dryden & Ellis, 2001; Ellis, 1970, 1999a). They believe that if faulty thought processes can be replaced with rational ones, maladjustment and abnormal behavior will disappear.

According to Ellis, psychological disturbance is a result of events in a person's life that give rise to irrational beliefs, leading to negative emotions and maladjusted

Figure 17.5
The Foundations of Irrational Behaviors
From Albert Ellis's view, irrational beliefs about events in people's lives cause emotional distress and maladjustment. Jake has a careless roommate (or even a careless friend) who leaves a dorm room open; a roommate's wallet disappears. Jake's wrong-headed belief that he alone has to take responsibility for dorm room security leads to unhappiness and anxiety.

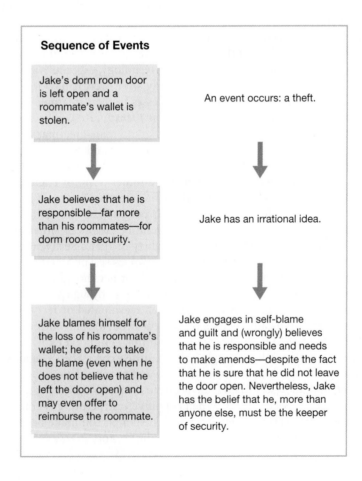

Sequence of Events

Jake's dorm room door is left open and a roommate's wallet is stolen.

An event occurs: a theft.

Jake believes that he is responsible—far more than his roommates—for dorm room security.

Jake has an irrational idea.

Jake blames himself for the loss of his roommate's wallet; he offers to take the blame (even when he does not believe that he left the door open) and may even offer to reimburse the roommate.

Jake engages in self-blame and guilt and (wrongly) believes that he is responsible and needs to make amends—despite the fact that he is sure that he did not leave the door open. Nevertheless, Jake has the belief that he, more than anyone else, must be the keeper of security.

behaviors. Moreover, these beliefs are a breeding ground for further irrational ideas (Dryden & Ellis, 1988). Ellis (1999b) argues that people make demands on themselves and on other people, and they rigidly hold on to them no matter how unrealistic and illogical they are. **Figure 17.5** portrays this sequence of events.

Thus, a major goal of rational-emotive therapy is to help people examine the past events that produced their irrational beliefs (Ellis, 2001). A therapist may try to focus on a client's basic philosophy of life and determine if it is self-defeating. That is, the therapist tries to uncover the client's thought patterns and help the client recognize that the underlying beliefs are faulty. **Table 17.3** lists ten irrational assumptions that, according to Ellis, cause emotional problems and maladaptive behaviors. They arise from people's needs to feel secure, to be competent, to be liked, or to be loved. When people assign irrational or exaggerated value to fulfilling these needs, the needs become maladaptive and lead to emotional disturbance, anxiety, and abnormal behavior. If rational-emotive therapy is successful, the client adopts different behaviors based on more rational thought processes. Research supports the effectiveness of this approach (Nucci, 2002), and Ellis (2001) asserts that rational-emotive therapy has broad applications in both therapeutic and classroom settings.

Table 17.3

ELLIS'S TEN IRRATIONAL ASSUMPTIONS

1. It is a necessity for an adult to be loved and approved of by almost everyone for virtually everything.

2. A person must be thoroughly competent, adequate, and successful in all respects.

3. Certain people are bad, wicked, or villainous and should be punished for their sins.

4. It is catastrophic when things are not going the way one would like.

5. Human unhappiness is externally caused. People have little or no ability to control their sorrows or to rid themselves of negative feelings.

6. It is right to be terribly preoccupied with and upset about something that may be dangerous or fearsome.

7. It is easier to avoid facing many of life's difficulties and responsibilities than it is to undertake more rewarding forms of self-discipline.

8. The past is all-important. Because something once strongly affected someone's life, it should continue to do so indefinitely.

9. People and things should be different from the way they are. It is catastrophic if perfect solutions to the grim realities of life are not immediately found.

10. Maximal human happiness can be achieved by inertia and inaction or by passively and without commitment "enjoying oneself."

Beck's Approach

Another cognitive therapy that focuses on irrational ideas is that of Aaron Beck (1963). As we saw in Chapter 16, Beck's theory assumes that depression is caused by people's distorted thoughts about reality, which lead to negative views about the world, themselves, and the future, and often to gross overgeneralizations. For example, people who think they have no future—that all of their options are blocked—and who undervalue their intelligence are likely to be depressed. Such individuals form appraisals of situations that are distorted and based on insufficient or wrong data. The goal of Beck's cognitive therapy, therefore, is to help people develop realistic appraisals of the situations they encounter (Beck, 1991). The therapist acts as a trainer and co-investigator, providing data to be examined and guidance in understanding how cognitions influence behavior (Beck & Weishaar, 1989).

According to Beck (1976), a successful client passes through four stages in the course of correcting faulty views and moving toward improved mental health: "First, he has to become aware of what he is thinking. Second, he needs to recognize what thoughts are awry. Then he has to substitute accurate for inaccurate judgments. Finally, he needs feedback to inform him whether his changes are correct" (p. 217).

Meichenbaum's Approach

Some researchers, among them Donald Meichenbaum, believe that what people say to themselves determines what they will do. Therefore, a key goal of therapy is to change the things people say to themselves. According to Meichenbaum, considered by many to be one of the most influential psychologists in the United States, the therapist has to change the client's appraisal of stressful events and the client's use of self-instructions, thus normalizing her or his reactions (Meichenbaum, 1993; Shaughnessy & Haight, 2003).

A strength of Meichenbaum's cognitive therapy is that self-instruction can be used in many settings for many kinds of problems. It can help people who are shy or impulsive, people with speech impediments, and even those who are schizophrenic (Meichenbaum, 1974; Meichenbaum & Cameron, 1973). Rather than attempting to change their irrational beliefs, clients learn a repertoire of activities that they can use to make their behavior more adaptive. For example, they may learn to conduct private monologues in which they work out adaptive ways of coping with situations. They may learn to organize their responses to specific situations in an orderly set of steps that can be easily carried out. They can then discuss with a therapist the quality and usefulness of their sets of self-instructional statements.

Table 17.4 provides an overall summary of the psychoanalytic, humanistic, behavioral, and cognitive approaches to individual therapy.

Cognitive therapy in its many forms has been used with individual adults and children and with groups of people with particular characteristics, such as being elderly or recently bereaved. It can be applied to problems such as anxiety disorders, marital difficulties, chronic pain, and (as is evident from Beck's work) depression. And research supports the idea that changing thoughts and behaviors alters brain chemistry (Paquette et al., 2003). Cognitive therapy continues to make enormous strides, influencing an increasing number of theorists and practitioners who conduct both long-term therapy and brief therapy (Goldfried, 2004).

Table 17.4

KEY COMPONENTS OF PSYCHOANALYTIC, HUMANISTIC, BEHAVIOR, AND COGNITIVE THERAPIES

Therapy	Nature of Psycho-pathology	Goal of Therapy	Role of Therapist	Role of Unconscious Material	Role of Patient's Insights	Techniques
■ Psycho-analytic Therapy	Maladjustment reflects inadequate conflict resolution and fixation in early development.	Attainment of maturity, strengthened ego functions, reduced control by unconscious or repressed impulses	An investigator, uncovering conflicts and resistances	Primary role in classical psycho-analysis, emphasized less in ego analysis	Includes not solely intellectual understanding but also emotional experiences	Analyst takes an active role in interpreting the dreams and free associations of patient.
■ Humanistic Therapy	Incongruity exists between real self and potential self; overdependence on others for gratification and self-esteem is also present.	Self-determination, release of human potential, expanded awareness	An empathic person, in honest encounter with a client, sharing experience	Emphasis on conscious experience	More emphasis on how and what questions than on why questions	Therapist helps client to see the world from a different perspective and focus on the present and the future instead of the past.
■ Behavior Therapy	Symptomatic behavior stems from faulty learning or learning of maladaptive behaviors.	Relief of symptomatic behavior by suppressing or replacing maladaptive behaviors	A helper, assisting the client in unlearning old behaviors and learning new ones	Not concerned with unconscious processes	Irrelevant and unnecessary	Client learns new responses in order to establish new behaviors and eliminate faulty or undesirable ones.
■ Cognitive Therapy	Maladjustment occurs because of faulty, irrational thought patterns.	Change in the way a client thinks about self and the world	A trainer and co-investigator, helping the client learn new, rational ways to think about the world	Little or no concern with unconscious processes	Not necessary but may be used if they do occur	Client learns to think situations through logically and to reconsider irrational assumptions

How Does Therapy in a Group Work?

When several people meet as a group to receive psychological help from a therapist, the treatment is referred to as *group therapy*. This technique was introduced in the early 20th century and has become increasingly popular in the United States since World War II. One reason for its popularity is that the demand for therapists exceeds the number available. Individually, a therapist can generally see up to 40 clients a week for 1 hour each. But in a group, the same therapist might see 8 to 10 clients in just 1 hour. Another reason for the popularity of group therapy is that the therapist's fee is shared among the members of the group, making treatment less expensive than with individual therapy.

Group therapy can be as effective or more effective than individual therapy (Barlow, Burlingame, & Nebeker, 2000; Ovaert, Cashel, & Sewell, 2003) because the social pressures that operate in a group can help shape the members' behavior. In addition, group members can be useful models for one another, and they can provide mutual reinforcement and support.

Techniques of Group Therapy

The techniques used in group therapy are determined largely by the nature of the group and the orientation of its therapist—psychoanalytic, client-centered, behavioral, or other. No two groups are alike, and no two therapists deal with individual group members in the same way. Many variations of group therapy have developed, including gestalt therapy, which focuses on current feelings and thoughts, as well as therapies that focus on specific problems such as weight management or smoking cessation.

In traditional group therapy, 6 to 12 clients meet regularly (usually once a week) with a therapist in a clinic, a hospital, or the therapist's office. Generally, the therapist selects members on the basis of what they can gain from and offer to the group. The goal is to construct a group whose members are compatible (though not necessarily identical) in terms of needs and problems—for example, women who were sexually abused as children (Lundqvist, Svedin, & Hansson, 2004). The duration of group therapy varies; it usually takes longer than 6 months, but there are a growing number of short-term groups that meet for fewer than 12 weeks (Miller & Slive, 2004; Rycroft, 2001). The format of a group therapy session varies, but generally each member describes her or his problems to the other members, who in turn relate their experiences with similar problems and how they coped with them. This gives individuals a chance to express their fears and anxieties to people who are accepting; each member eventually realizes that everyone has problems similar to theirs. Group members also have opportunities to try out new behaviors (role-play) in a safe environment. In a mental health center, for example, a therapist might help group members relive past traumas and cope with their continuing fears. Sometimes the therapist directs the group as people address their problems. At other times, the therapist allows group members to resolve problems independently. Members can also exert pressure on an individual to behave in more appropriate ways.

Family Therapy

Family therapy is a special form of group therapy in which two or more people who are committed to each other's well-being are treated together in an effort to change the ways they interact. (Marital, or couples, therapy is thus a subcategory of family therapy.) A *family* is defined as any group of people who are committed to one another's well-being, preferably for life (Bronfenbrenner, 1989, 1999). Today's therapists recognize that families are often nontraditional; blended families and single-parent families are very common, for example. A *blended family* is one in which at least one child is the biological or adopted child of both parents and at least one child is a stepchild of one parent; in some blended families, none of the children are biologically related to the parents. Just like traditional families, nontraditional families shape the way people respond to the world and must be considered as part of the cultural context in which psychologists view behavior (Thompson Sanders, Bazile, & Akbar, 2004). And even for traditional families, life has grown more complicated by the increasing need to juggle work and family responsibilities and cope with societal problems.

With families facing new kinds of problems, family therapy is used by a growing number of practitioners, especially social workers. In today's world of managed care and HMOs, brief family therapy is the order of the day, and symptom relief is usually the first, but certainly not the only, goal. From a family therapist's point of view, the real focus of therapy is the family's structure and organization. While family members may identify one person—perhaps a delinquent child—as the problem, family therapists believe that in many cases, that person may be a scapegoat. The so-called problem member diverts the family's attention from structural problems that are not always evident and are difficult to confront. Any clinician who works with a person who has some type of adjustment problem must also consider the impact of this problem on the people with whom the individual interacts.

Family therapists are committed to the idea that a family is more than a collection of unique individuals; family members are involved in relationships (Nichols & Schwartz, 2004). Sometimes family therapy is called *relationship therapy*, because relationships are often the focus of the intervention, especially with couples. Research indicates that family therapy and marital (couples) therapy are effective (Behr, 2000). However, the many variables operating within families complicates such research (Keitner et al., 2003; Nichols & Schwartz, 2004; Villeneuve, 2001).

Family therapists often attempt to change *family systems*. This means that treatment takes place within the dynamic social system of the marriage or the family (Fraenkel & Pinsof, 2001; Nichols & Schwartz, 2004). Therapists assume that families give rise to multiple sources of psychological influence: Individuals within a family affect family interactions, and family interactions affect individuals; a family is thus an interactive system (Sturges, 1994). For example, when a mother labels a son "lazy" because he doesn't have a job, the son may feel shame but may act out his feeling as anger. He may lash out at his father, blaming the father's poor work habits and lack of success for his own joblessness. This reaction may be followed by a squabble over who "brings home the bacon," and

Family therapy ■ A form of group therapy in which two or more people who are committed to one another's well-being are treated at once, in an effort to change the ways they interact.

so forth. The mother's attitude thus leads to a clash among all the individuals within the family system. The family systems approach has become especially popular in colleges of social work, in departments of psychology, and even in colleges of medicine, as medical doctors often must treat or deal with more than one member of a family. A useful technique in family therapy is to *restructure* the family's interactions. If a son is responding passively to his domineering mother, for example, the therapist may suggest that the son be assigned chores only by his father.

An issue that often emerges in family therapy is the involvement, or enmeshment, of all members of the family in one member's problem—for example, depression, alcoholism, drug abuse, or anxiety disorder. Such involvement often becomes devastating for the whole family. This problem is termed *codependence*. Practitioners often see patients with alcoholism or cocaine addiction whose friends or family members are codependent. Codependence is not a disorder in the *DSM*. In fact, the families of people with problems such as substance abuse have gone relatively unnoticed by psychologists. But practitioners who treat whole families, not just the person suffering from maladjustment, view codependence as a type of adjustment problem—not for the patient but for the patient's family and friends.

Codependents—family members or friends—are often plagued by intense feelings of shame, fear, anger, and pain. They cannot express those feelings, however, because they feel obligated to care for the person suffering from the disorder or addiction. Codependent children may believe their job is to take care of their maladjusted parents. Codependent adults may strive to help their maladjusted spouses, relatives, or friends with their problems. They often think that if they were perfect, they could help the maladjusted individual. In some cases, a codependent person may need the individual to stay disordered; family members sometimes unconsciously want a member with a problem to remain dependent on them so that they can remain in a controlling position.

Some researchers believe the family systems approach to be as effective as individual therapy—and more effective in some situations (Nichols & Schwartz, 2004). Not all families profit equally from such interventions, however. Family therapy is difficult with families that are chaotic, frenzied, or unstable. Younger couples and younger families seem to have better outcomes. When depression is evident, outcomes are not as good (Lebow & Gurman, 1995). In addition, some family members may refuse to participate or may drop out of therapy; this almost always has negative consequences for the family system (Prinz et al., 2001).

Family therapy is eclectic, borrowing from many schools of therapy and treating a broad range of people and problems (Guerin & Chabot, 1997). Family therapists try to help families change because they acknowledge and recognize that change of one sort or another is inevitable in a dynamic system. They further assert that only a small change for the better can make a big difference. Most family therapists believe that their clients have the strength and resources to change and that they don't need to understand the origins of a problem to solve it. Last, these therapists feel that there is no *one* solution to family problems—especially given today's nontraditional families (Selekman, 1993).

How Do Psychologists Reach Out to Communities?

If you have ever lived in a community that faced a challenge—high unemployment, a toxic spill, a hurricane, or racial upheaval—you know that people in communities can be mobilized. They can take on a school board or vote a mayor in or out of office, and they do so by pooling their resources, using their collective talent, and reaching out. Some communities are more proactive than others; people in these communities seek to prevent problems before they occur—addressing school problems, restoring decaying sections of town, or lobbying legislators for new funds for community centers. Many psychologists today are studying whole communities—they seek to influence individuals, families, and the entire social structure (Levine, 1998). They hope to help people develop resilience and a sense of purpose and nurture what is essential for survival and personal growth (Sonn & Fisher, 1998). Community psychologists work in schools, with religious groups, on planning commissions, and in prisons. They plan and set up programs to bring psychological skills and knowledge into the community. Access to information, communication within a community, and a sense of social involvement are necessary for the work of these psychologists.

The beginnings of this movement in psychology can be traced to the 1960s. In that decade, many psychologists recognized that individual therapy was inefficient for treating large numbers of people. Researchers and practitioners, as well as politicians, sought a more efficient and effective approach. President John F. Kennedy's 1963 message to Congress called for "a bold new approach" to the treatment of mental illness; it prompted legislation and funding for community mental health centers. Community psychology emerged in response to a widespread desire for a more action-oriented approach to individual and social adjustment. **Community psychology** is the branch of psychology that seeks to provide psychological services to communities, such as community mental health centers, and to effect social change by empowering individuals.

Community psychologists want to strengthen existing social support networks and to stimulate the formation of new networks to meet new challenges (Gonzales et al., 1983). These psychologists conduct community-based research and interventions, often in a community with a complex mix of religions, ethnicities, and political inclinations. They are aware of community needs and employ specialized practices to address complex social problems such as drug abuse, teen pregnancy, and decaying family structures. A crucial element in accomplishing these goals is community involvement. A church, synagogue, or mosque, for example, could mobilize its senior citizens to participate in a foster grandparent program. Or a community psychologist might help a group of residents develop better fire safety procedures in public housing. Another key element of community psychology is *empowerment*—helping people in a community enhance their existing skills, develop new ones, and acquire knowledge and motivation so that they can gain control over their lives (Rappaport, 1987).

Community psychologists work especially hard at prevention of psychological problems. Their efforts often take the form of developing neighborhood organizations to work on preventing and solving mental health problems (Wandersman &

Community psychology
■ The branch of psychology that seeks to reach out to society by providing services such as community mental health centers and to effect social change through the empowerment of individuals.

Empowerment ■
Facilitating the development and enhancement of skills, knowledge, and motivation in individuals so that they can gain control over their lives.

Nation, 1998). In creating community interventions and programs, psychologists effectively become agents of prevention in a variety of domains, such as reducing risks of teen pregnancy, preventing arson, and reducing substance abuse (Wandersman & Florin, 2003). Prevention efforts operate at three levels: primary, secondary, and tertiary.

Primary prevention means reducing the risk of *new* cases of a disorder and counteracting harmful circumstances before they lead to maladjustment. Primary prevention usually targets groups rather than individuals. It may focus on an entire community, on moderate-risk groups (such as children from families of low socioeconomic status), or on high-risk groups (such as children of schizophrenic parents). Community psychologists may help to establish drug prevention centers, safe houses for battered women, or suicide hot lines. One psychologist, Nathaniel Donson (1999), has a primary prevention model for day care. He asserts that since 5 million young children are cared for by adults other than their parents and since affordable, high-quality day care is very hard to find for those who need it most, community psychologists should take action. When such day-care centers are established, results are dramatic and positive (Peters, Petrunka, & Arnold, 2003).

In response to growing public awareness of mental health problems, a special kind of primary prevention service agency—the *neighborhood clinic*—came into being. Such clinics help communities cope with problems that may be created by mental illness, unemployment, and lack of education. They offer consultation, educational programs, and lectures and literature on topics such as therapy, family planning, and drug rehabilitation.

Secondary prevention involves identifying new cases of a mental health problem in the early stages. Community psychologists offer secondary prevention services in *crisis intervention centers,* which help people deal with short-term stressful situations requiring immediate therapeutic attention. A crisis is usually a specific event; for example, a person may be contemplating suicide, or a woman may have been raped. The focus of crisis intervention is on the immediate circumstances, not on past experiences. Like primary prevention interventions, secondary prevention services have had positive results (Cuijpers & van Lammeren, 2001).

Tertiary prevention focuses on the treatment of fully developed psychological problems. There is considerable overlap between secondary and tertiary prevention, as problems that are treated in the short term or in their early stages may sometimes have a long-standing underlying source. Community psychologists offer help to eliminate or reduce the psychological problem as well as to strengthen existing family or community resources. The emphasis is on utilizing existing community resources and empowering individuals to manage their lives and communities more effectively (e.g., Smith, 2002).

Community psychologists attempt to serve all members of a community, including people who might not otherwise be able to afford the services of a psychotherapist or counselor (Murry et al., 2004). These psychologists believe that developing individuals' sense of self and of community has a clear psychological benefit to them and a social benefit to their communities (Riger, 2001). Community psychologists are change-oriented. Because they believe that some social conditions and organizational procedures foster maladjusted behavior, they often advocate changes in community institutions (e.g., Prilleltensky, 2001)—for example, improving the court system, developing programs to prevent drug use in schools, consulting with employers about reducing stress on the job, helping religious organizations develop volunteer programs to aid the homeless, helping hospitals set up preventive medicine programs, and fostering community involvement in educational issues. They even work in universities to improve communication among faculty, students, and administrators (Huffaker et al., 2003).

How Do Biologically Based Therapies Create Change?

When a person asks a therapist for help with a psychological problem—whether it has a biological basis or not—the usual approach involves some form of talking therapy that may be based on psychodynamic, humanistic, behavioral, or cognitive theories. For some patients, however, talking therapy is not enough. Some may be too profoundly depressed; others may be exhibiting symptoms of bipolar disorder (manic depression) or schizophrenia; still others may need hospitalization because they are suicidal. This is where biologically based therapies enter the picture.

Biologically based therapy (sometimes called *somatic therapy*) refers to treating psychological disorders by treating the body, usually using drugs that affect levels of hormones and especially neurotransmitters. These therapies typically involve medication and may involve hospitalization. Such therapies are generally used in combination with traditional forms of psychotherapy. Most practitioners and theoreticians believe that the most effective treatment combines drugs and psychotherapy (Grilo, 2001; Sammons, 2001).

Biologically based therapy ■ Any treatment for psychological disorders that focuses on the body, usually through the use of drugs that affect levels of hormones and especially neurotransmitters; sometimes called *somatic therapy*.

Evolutionary psychologists think that some psychological problems are due to evolved mechanisms gone awry. They believe that some people have inborn brain abnormalities that make them susceptible to certain problems. Evolutionary psychologists assert that therapists must take into consideration the way the brain has evolved and consider both drug and talking therapies to overcome the limitations that a human brain may have developed through evolution (Bailey, 2000; Troisi & McGuire, 2000).

Biologically based therapies are of three types: drug therapy (often used), electroconvulsive therapy (occasionally used), and psychosurgery (rarely used).

Drugs and the Therapeutic Process

In modern, fast-paced societies, people seem to want quick fixes. Every few years, politicians promise a new plan to eliminate poverty or a simple solution to racial tension. Similarly, many people want to take drugs to alleviate their emotional problems. Drug therapy is an important form of treatment, especially for anxiety, depression, and schizophrenia. (See Figure 17.6 on p. 672 for recent trends in treating depression.) Drug therapy, the most widely used biologically based therapy, is effective when used correctly and carefully. Drug therapy is sometimes used in combination with traditional talking therapy (e.g., Arean & Cook, 2002; Friedman et al., 2004; Garland & Scott, 2002).

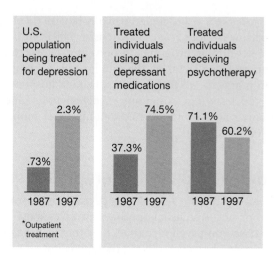

Figure 17.6
Trends in
Treatment of
Depression
More people
receive drug treat-
ment for depres-
sion than ever
before. Note the
decline in psy-
chotherapy. (Olfson
et al., 2002)

Clinicians who recommend drug therapy must be aware of several key issues. Dosages are especially important and must be monitored; too much or too little of certain drugs is dangerous. Long-term use of many drugs is ill advised. Further, no drug will permanently cure the maladjustment of people who are not coping well. Last, physicians and psychiatrists must be aware of the possibilities of overmedication and long-term dependency on drugs.

In the past decade, clinical psychologists who have been trained in psychopharmacology have been lobbying for the legal right to write prescriptions for a limited class of drugs (McGrath et al., 2004). The argument is that patients would benefit from the better integration of medications and psychological techniques (Koenigsberg, Woo-Ming, & Siever, 2002), but this is a controversial proposition even among psychologists (Tasman, Riba, & Silk, 2000). Those who do support the idea recognize that additional training would be necessary and licensing authority would need to be instituted (Klusman, 1998). This debate continues among physicians and psychologists, as well as among members of state licensing boards and legislatures.

People who do take medications prescribed by psychiatrists or other physicians may experience relief from symptoms of anxiety, mania, depression, or schizophrenia. Drugs for the relief of mental problems are sometimes called *psychotropic drugs* and are usually grouped into four classes: antianxiety drugs, antidepressant drugs, antimania drugs, and antipsychotic drugs.

Antianxiety Drugs

Antianxiety drugs ■
Any of a group of mood-altering drugs that are used to treat anxiety without causing excessive sedation; also known as *tranquilizers* or *anxiolytics*.

Antianxiety drugs, or tranquilizers (technically, *anxiolytics*), are mood-altering drugs that are used to treat anxiety without causing excessive sedation. Librium, Xanax, and Valium are the trade names of the most widely prescribed antianxiety drugs. Used by many in the United States (and probably overprescribed), these drugs reduce feelings of stress, induce calmness, and lower excitability. When taken occasionally to help a person through a stressful situation, such drugs are useful. They can also help moderate anxiety in a person who is extremely anxious, particularly when the person is also receiving some form of psychotherapy. However, long-term use of antianxiety drugs without some adjunct therapy is usually ill advised. Furthermore such drugs have side effects, including drowsiness, lightheadedness, dry mouth, depression, and nausea. Today, physicians are wary of patients who seek antianxiety drugs for management of daily stress; they worry about substance abuse and an overreliance on drugs to get through the day.

Antidepressant Drugs

As their name suggests, **antidepressant drugs** (technically, *thymoleptics*) are drugs that are used to treat depression; they are sometimes considered mood elevators. These drugs work by altering the level of specific neurotransmitters in the brain (Nemeroff & Schatzberg, 2002). With the wide availability of antidepressants, it is surprising that half of those who have been depressed for more than 20 years have never taken an antidepressant (Hirschfeld et al., 1997). Depression often goes undiagnosed and is definitely undertreated.

Antidepressant drugs Drugs used to treat depression, sometimes referred to as *mood elevators* or, more technically, as *thymoleptics*.

One kind of antidepressant, *selective serotonin reuptake inhibitors (SSRIs),* blocks the reuptake of the neurotransmitter serotonin. SSRIs work by prolonging the amount of time that serotonin stays in a synapse. According to researchers, when serotonin is released into a synapse but does not bind to receptors on the adjacent neuron, the person experiences symptoms of depression. After being released, a neurotransmitter is either neutralized in the synapse or taken back up by the neuron that released it, in the process called *reuptake* (see Chapter 3). SSRIs do not allow the serotonin molecules to be neutralized or restored to the releasing cell; more of them stay in the synapse longer and are thus more likely to bind to the receptors, and depression is averted.

Drugs such as Prozac, Zoloft, and Paxil are SSRIs. These drugs account for 60% of antidepressant sales in the United States. Extremely depressed people who take these drugs often become more optimistic and redevelop a sense of purpose in their lives after about 4 weeks on the medication. SSRIs allow many depressed people to function outside a hospital setting, and they are increasingly being given to younger patients, including adolescents (Emslie, 2004; March 2004).

Antidepressants also include two other major categories of drugs: tricyclics and monoamine oxidase (MAO) inhibitors. Both types of drugs are potent. *Tricyclics* (named for their chemical structure) act like SSRIs to block the reuptake of neurotransmitters, but *MAO inhibitors* work by breaking down monoamine oxidase, an enzyme that destroys the monoamine neurotransmitters. Tricyclics are prescribed much more often than MAO inhibitors because they pose less danger of medical complications. (Patients on MAO inhibitors have to adhere to special diets and some other restrictions to avoid adverse physical reactions.) To help a patient suffering from a severe bout of depression, a physician might prescribe a commonly used tricyclic such as imipramine (Tofranil) or amitriptyline (Elavil), which has fewer serious side effects and can alleviate depressive symptoms in most people. Note that, when researchers say that there are few or fewer side effects, they do not mean there are *no* side effects. For example, tricyclics and especially SSRIs such as Prozac have sexual side effects including decreased desire for women and erectile dysfunction for men (Albers, Hahn, & Reist, 2004; Masand & Gupta, 2002; Osvath et al., 2003; Sadock & Sadock, 2003); they may also produce nausea, decreased appetite, insomnia, and headaches (Albers et al., 2004).

Research on the effectiveness of antidepressant drugs is contradictory. Some researchers assert that these drugs have strong positive effects on depression and related disorders such as anorexia (Rivas-Vasquez, Rice, & Kalman, 2003; Zhu & Walsh, 2002); others report that antidepressants provide only modest help (Greenberg et al., 1992; Schulberg & Rush, 1994). Research using double-blind procedures and carefully controlled conditions continues, especially with drugs that have specific actions on depressive behaviors (Nemeroff & Schatzberg, 2002). The impact of new research findings will be profound because there are a great number of people with depressive disorders.

So, when is drug therapy appropriate for depression? Practitioners and researchers tend to agree that drug therapy is called for when people are seriously depressed, when they have suffered previous depressive episodes, when there is a family history of depression, when drug therapy has been used in the past, and when talk therapy is either not working or has been refused by the patient (Yapko, 1997).

Antimania Drugs

Lithium carbonate ■ An effective mood-stabilizing antimania drug that has come into wide use for treating bipolar disorder because it relieves the manic symptoms.

Lithium carbonate has long been used as an effective mood-stabilizing antimania drug (like the antidepressants, technically, a *thymoleptic*) and has come into wide use for treating bipolar (manic-depressive) disorder because it relieves the manic symptoms. Psychiatrists find that a daily maintenance dose of lithium is especially helpful in warding off patients' episodes of mania. The dosage of any drug is important, but in the case of lithium it is critical: Too much produces noxious side effects; too little has no effect. No drug will cure all individuals with bipolar disorder of all their symptoms and solve all their problems (for example, lithium is less effective with young patients); in general, however, lithium allows some bipolar patients to cope better, to control their symptoms, and to seek other therapies that allow them to manage their lives in the most productive way possible (Moncrieff, 1997). The same is true of other drugs in this class, including valproic acid, or valproate.

Antipsychotic Drugs

Antipsychotic drugs ■ Any of a group of drugs that are used to treat psychosis, especially schizophrenia; also known as *neuroleptics*.

Antipsychotic drugs (technically, *neuroleptics*) are drugs used to treat psychosis and are used mainly with people who suffer from the disabling disorder schizophrenia. These drugs reduce hostility and aggression in violent patients. They also reduce delusions and allow some patients to manage life outside a hospital setting.

Most of the antipsychotic drugs prescribed are phenothiazines; one of the most common is chlorpromazine (Thorazine). However, a number of antipsychotic drugs of other types (sometimes called *atypical antipsychotics*) have been introduced in the past decade. One of these, clozapine (Clozaril), has been shown to be especially effective but can have severe side effects. Even newer antipsychotic drugs, such as risperidone (Risperdal), are safer than either chlorpromazine or clozapine and may also be tolerated better. Risperdal is often used with older patients and is quite effective (Albers et al., 2004; Conley, 2004; Kastner & Walsh, 2004).

Antipsychotic drugs are often very effective in treating certain symptoms of schizophrenia, particularly hallucinations and delusions (Bradford, Stroup, & Liebermann, 2002). Unfortunately, they may not be as effective for other symptoms, such as reduced motivation and emotional expressiveness. As with antidepressants, dosages of antipsychotic drugs are crucial. Further, if patients take antipsychotic drugs for too long, certain problems can emerge. One such problem is *tardive dyskinesia*—a central nervous system disorder characterized by involuntary, spasmodic movements of the upper body, especially the face and fingers, and including leg jiggling and tongue protrusions, facial tics, and involuntary movements of the mouth and shoulders (Albers et al., 2004).

Table 17.5 on page 676 lists some common drugs used to treat psychiatric disorders.

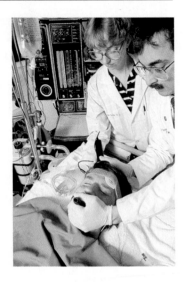

Psychosurgery and Electroconvulsive Therapy

Psychosurgery is brain surgery; it was used in the past to alleviate symptoms of serious mental disorders. A particular type of psychosurgery commonly performed in the 1940s and 1950s was the *prefrontal lobotomy,* in which the surgeon would sever parts of the brain's frontal lobes from the rest of the brain. The frontal lobes were thought to control emotions; their removal destroyed connections within the brain, making patients calm and passive. Patients lost the symptoms of their mental disorders, but they also became unnaturally calm and completely unemotional. Some became unable to control their impulses, and as many as 4% of patients died from the operation.

Today, despite advances in technology that have made such operations more precise, psychosurgery is rare. There are three reasons for this: First, drug therapy has proved more effective than surgical procedures. Second, the long-term effects of psychosurgery are questionable. Third, and most important, the procedure is irreversible and therefore morally objectionable to most practitioners and to patients and their families. Its widespread use during the 1940s and 1950s is considered by many to have been a serious mistake.

Electroconvulsive therapy (ECT), once widely employed to treat depressed individuals, is a treatment for severe mental illness in which an electric current is briefly applied to the head in order to produce a generalized seizure (convulsion). The result of the use of ECT is that patients are less depressed; bad memories and feelings are gone. The duration of the shock is less than a second, and patients are treated in 3 to 12 sessions over several weeks. In the 1940s and 1950s, ECT was routinely given to severely disturbed patients in mental hospitals. Unfortunately, it

Electroconvulsive therapy involves applying an electric current to the head briefly to produce a generalized seizure. Once widely used, it is now limited to severe depression.

Tardive dyskinesia ■ A central nervous system disorder that is characterized by involuntary, spasmodic movements of the upper body, especially the face and fingers, and that can result from taking an antipsychotic drug for too long.

Psychosurgery ■ Brain surgery used in the past to alleviate symptoms of serious mental disorders.

Electroconvulsive [ee-LECK-tro-con-VUL-siv] therapy (ECT) ■ A treatment for severe mental illness in which an electric current is briefly applied to the head in order to produce a generalized seizure (convulsion).

Table 17.5

DRUGS COMMONLY USED TO TREAT PSYCHIATRIC DISORDERS

Effect Group	Chemical Group	Generic Name	Trade Name(s)
■ Antianxiety (anxiolytic)	Benzodiazepines	Diazepam	Valium
		Chlordiazepoxide	Librium
		Alprazolam	Xanax
		Clonazepam	Klonapin
	Nonbenzodiazepine	Buspirone	Buspar
■ Antidepressant (thymoleptic)	Tricyclics	Amitriptyline	Elavil
		Imipramine	Tofranil
		Nortriptyline	Pamelor
		Desipramine	Norpramin
		Doxepin	Sinequan
		Clomipramine	Anafranil
	Monoamine oxidase inhibitors	Phenelzine	Nardil
		Tranylcypromine	Parnate
	Selective serotonin reuptake inhibitors	Fluoxetine	Prozac
		Sertraline	Zoloft
		Paroxetine	Paxil
		Fluvoxamine	Luvox
■ Antimanic (thymoleptic)	Lithium carbonate	Lithium	Eskalith, Lithonate, Lithobid
	GABA agonist	Valproic acid	Depakene
■ Antipsychotic (neuroleptic)	Phenothiazines	Chlorpromazine	Thorazine
		Trifluoperazine	Stelazine
		Fluphenazine	Prolixin
		Thioridazine	Mellaril
	Atypical antipsychotics	Clozapine	Clozaril
		Risperdal	Risperidone

was often used on patients who did not need it or administered by physicians who wished to control difficult patients. Today, ECT is not widely used. According to the National Institutes of Health, fewer than 2.5% of all psychiatric hospital patients in the United States are treated with ECT. But ECT is more prevalent in non-Western countries. In Nepal, for example, 25% of depressed inpatients received ECT (Little, 2003).

Is ECT at all effective? Could drug therapy or traditional psychotherapy be used in its place? ECT is effective in the short-term management of *severely* depressed individuals, those suffering from extreme episodes of mania, and people with psychotic depression (Prudic et al., 2004; Rohland, 2001); it is sometimes used when a particular patient is at risk of suicide (Cohen, Tyrrell, & Smith, 1997). It is effective and safe (Glass, 2001; McCall et al., 2001); however, its effects are only temporary if it is not followed by drug therapy and psychotherapy (American Psychiatric Association, 2001). Generally speaking, ECT should be used as a last option, when other forms of treatment have been ineffective and when a patient does not respond to medications (Prudic, Olfson, & Sackheim, 2001). ECT is not appropriate for treating schizophrenia or for managing unruly behaviors associated with other psychological disorders.

The risk of death during the administration of ECT is low (Coffey et al., 1991). But there are side effects, including memory loss (Lisanby et al., 2000; Prudic, Peyser, & Sackheim, 2000). In addition, ECT frightens some patients. If practitioners determine that ECT is warranted, the law requires (and medical ethics demand) that the patient be given the option to accept or reject the treatment—as is true for *any* treatment.

Alternative Therapies

There are a number of alternative therapies to which some people with emotional problems turn: irrigation of the colon, aromatherapy, spiritualism, and herbal remedies that include excessive tea drinking. What's the evidence that these therapies are effective? Many researchers feel that all practitioners should use only techniques that have proven track records based on research, those that are empirically supported. Some evidence supports the effectiveness of alternative therapeutic techniques that involve eye-movement reprocessing, massage, and other such "new approaches" (Moyer, Rounds, & Hannum, 2004). However, there is little solid, conclusive evidence; research is limited and what does exist is not controlled, not double-blind, and not systematic.

Some researchers refer to all of these approaches as fringe therapies and pseudoscience—techniques that are mistakenly held to be scientific. When you hear of a new therapy—a miracle—as a critical thinker, ask yourself what the evidence is. Does the treatment work better than no treatment at all, better than traditional treatments? Is there an intellectual, practical, or theoretical basis for the effectiveness of the treatment? Remember that testimonials may be reassuring, but evidence builds confidence. Newspaper articles are interesting; however, articles in scientific journals are believable. Keep an open mind, but stay skeptical.

The Debate over Hospitalization

Patients with mental problems are admitted to a hospital when they are at risk for hurting themselves and/or others. They are admitted to a mental hospital when their problems seem intractable and they need long-term treatment. But with the advent of managed care, the high cost of hospitalization has led to a dramatic decrease in the number of mental hospitals and the number of patients in long-term care, as well as a policy of deinstitutionalization. ***Deinstitutionalization*** is the transitioning of treatment for mental problems from inpatient facilities to outpatient or community-based facilities. While the exact number is difficult to determine because many patients are in private facilities that do not necessarily call themselves "mental hospitals," the number of inpatients has declined to less than 75,000 from its peak of 550,000 in the mid-1950s.

The benefits of deinstitutionalization are that some patients are appropriately mainstreamed into society where they continue to receive help on an outpatient basis. And costs are reduced with outpatients and those in halfway houses or other type of intermediate care facilities. But the number of untreated individuals has increased, many have nowhere to go, and a large number of the homeless population of our major cities have serious psychological problems that are left untreated. At least one-third of the estimated 600,000 homeless Americans suffer from schizophrenia or manic-depressive illness. Although it is cheaper to treat most people outside a hospital, even the best outpatient programs aren't sufficient for patients who are psychotic and don't even know they need help. This is not only a psychological issue but a social, political, and economic one. Did deinstitutionalization cause homelessness and a revolving psychiatric door at mental health facilities? This question is debated widely because there is no clear evidence. Deinstitutionalization seems like a good policy in principle, but many argue that it has been, and continues to be, poorly executed and overly applied.

Summary and Review

WHAT IS PSYCHOTHERAPY, AND WHAT TYPES ARE AVAILABLE?

What is psychotherapy?

Psychotherapy is the treatment of emotional or behavioral problems through psychological techniques. p. 637

What is the placebo effect, and how can it be avoided?

A *placebo effect* is a nonspecific therapeutic change that occurs as a result of a person's expectations of change rather than as a direct result of a certain treatment. However, any long-term therapeutic effects come from the client's and therapist's efforts. pp. 638–639

The *double-blind technique* is a procedure in which neither the experimenter nor the participants know who is in the control and experimental groups. It helps to eliminate bias and to reduce *demand characteristics*, elements of an experimental situation that might cause a participant to perceive the situation in a certain way or become aware of the purpose of the study and thus bias the participant to behave in a certain way and, in so doing, distort the results. p. 638

What is the best therapy, and what characterizes the best therapists?

The effectiveness of the different kinds of therapies varies with the type of disorder being treated and the goals of the client. Because therapy is based on the development of a unique relationship between the therapist and the client, the compatibility of the two is especially critical. Good therapists communicate interest, understanding, respect, tactfulness, maturity, and the ability to help. They respect clients' ability to cope with their troubles. They use suggestion, encouragement, interpretation, examples, and rewards to help clients change. pp. 640–643

HOW DO PSYCHODYNAMIC THERAPIES WORK?

According to psychodynamic therapists, what causes maladjustment, and what processes are involved in treatment?

According to Freud, conflicts among a person's unconscious thoughts and processes produce maladjusted behavior. Rooted in Freud's *psychoanalysis, psychodynamically based therapies,* which are one type of *insight therapy,* assume that maladjustment and abnormal behavior are caused by people's failure to understand their own motivations and needs. Psychodynamic therapists believe that once patients understand the motivations that produce maladjusted behavior, the behavior can be changed. pp. 647–648

Classical Freudian psychoanalysis uses the techniques of *free association, dream analysis,* and *interpretation.* The process involves *resistance* and *transference,* and the repetitive cycle of interpretation, resistance, and transference is referred to as *working through.* pp. 648–649

What are the main criticisms of psychoanalysis?

Ego analysts are psychoanalytic practitioners who are often critical of classical Freudian analysis and believe that the ego has greater control over behavior than Freud suggested. They are more concerned with a client's reality testing and self-control than with unconscious motivations and processes. Some critics of psychoanalysis contend that Freud's approach is unscientific, imprecise, and subjective. Other critics object to the biological orientation of psychoanalysis, which suggests that a human being is merely a conflicted bundle of energy driven toward some hedonistic goal. Further, many elements of Freud's theory are untestable or sexist. pp. 649–650

WHAT DO HUMANISTIC THERAPIES EMPHASIZE?

Humanistic therapies, unlike psychodynamic therapies, emphasize the idea that human beings have free will to determine their destinies. One humanistic therapy, *client-centered therapy,* was developed by Rogers and aims to help clients realize their full potential by being involved in a therapeutic relationship. To be effective, a client-centered therapist must convey unconditional positive regard, establish congruence, and practice empathic listening so that the client can become less defensive, more open to new experiences, and more fulfilled. pp. 650–653

What are some criticisms of client-centered therapy?

Critics assert that lengthy discussions about past problems do not necessarily help people with their present difficulties. They believe that client-centered therapy may be making therapeutic promises that cannot be fulfilled and focusing on concepts that are hard to define. As an alternative, positive psychologists assert that people have to focus on their strengths, listen to their hearts, stop fearing the worst, appreciate what they have, tell healthy stories about life, and live a balanced, multidimensional life. p. 653

WHAT ARE THE METHODS OF BEHAVIOR THERAPY?

Identify the basic assumptions and goals of behavior therapy.

Behavior therapy, or behavior modification, is a therapy based on the application of learning principles to human behavior. It focuses on changing overt behaviors rather than on understanding subjective feelings, unconscious processes, or motivations. It attempts to replace undesirable behaviors with more adaptive ones. p. 654

A criticism of behavior therapy is that there is the possibility of *symptom substitution*, the appearance of one overt symptom to replace another that has been eliminated by treatment. p. 655

What are the major techniques used in behavior therapy?

Techniques of behavior therapy include those based on operant conditioning, including *token economies* and *time-out*. pp. 656–658

Counterconditioning, a process of reconditioning in which a person is taught a new, more adaptive response to a familiar stimulus, is a second major technique of behavior therapy. *Systematic desensitization* is a three-stage counterconditioning procedure in which a person is taught to relax while imagining increasingly fearful situations. *Aversive counterconditioning* is a technique in which an unpleasant stimulus is paired with a stimulus that elicits an undesirable behavior so that the person will cease responding to the original stimulus with the undesirable behavior. pp. 659–660

As part of behavior therapy, the technique of modeling is especially effective in three areas: (1) teaching new behaviors, (2) helping to eliminate fears, especially phobias, and (3) enhancing already existing behaviors. p. 660

WHY IS COGNITIVE THERAPY SO POPULAR?

What are the basic assumptions that guide cognitive therapy?

The three basic assumptions underlying cognitive therapy are (1) cognitive activity affects behavior, (2) cognitive activity can be monitored, and (3) behavior changes can be effected through cognitive changes. Many behavior therapists consider thought processes in treating clients; their work is called *cognitive behavior therapy*. p. 661

Identify several major types of cognitive therapy.

Rational-emotive therapy emphasizes the role of logical, rational thought processes in behavior. It assumes that faulty, irrational thinking patterns are the cause of abnormal behavior. Beck's cognitive therapy assumes that depression is caused by people's distorted thoughts about reality, which lead to negative thinking and often to gross overgeneralizations. According to Meichenbaum, the therapist has to change the client's appraisal of stressful events and the client's use of self-instructions, to normalize her or his reactions. pp. 662–664

HOW DOES THERAPY IN A GROUP WORK?

What is group therapy?

Group therapy is a treatment in which several people meet as a group to receive help from a therapist for emotional or behavior problems. The techniques used in a therapy group are determined by the nature of the group and the orientation of its therapist. p. 666

What is the goal of family therapy?

Family therapy attempts to change the interactions of members of family systems, because individuals affect family processes and family processes affect individuals. This treatment takes into account that a family is a dynamic social system. pp. 667–668

HOW DO PSYCHOLOGISTS REACH OUT TO COMMUNITIES?

Community psychology is the branch of psychology that seeks to provide psychological services to communities and to effect social change by empowering individuals. Community psychologists use three levels of prevention strategies—primary, secondary, and tertiary—to help ward off, treat, or solve psychological problems in the community. *Empowerment* refers to helping people in a community enhance existing skills, develop new ones, and acquire knowledge and motivation so that they can gain control over their lives. pp. 669–670

HOW DO BIOLOGICALLY BASED THERAPIES CREATE CHANGE?

A *biologically based therapy* treats psychological disorders by focusing on the body, usually through the use of drugs. p. 671

What are the major classes of psychotropic drugs?

Drugs for the relief of mental problems are usually grouped into four classes: *antianxiety drugs, antidepressant drugs, antimania drugs* (including *lithium carbonate*), and *antipsychotic drugs*. Such drugs often work by altering the level of a key neurotransmitter in the brain. A problem that can result from taking antipsychotic drugs is *tardive dyskinesia,* a central nervous system disorder characterized by involuntary, spasmodic movements of the upper body, especially the face and fingers. pp. 672–675

What biologically based therapies do not involve drugs?

Psychosurgery (brain surgery) is a rarely used method of treatment for alleviating the symptoms of certain serious mental disorders. *Electroconvulsive therapy (ECT)* is a treatment for severe mental illness in which an electric current is briefly applied to the head in order to produce a generalized seizure (convulsion). pp. 675–677

What is the debate over hospitalization of people with mental problems?

Since the beginning of managed care, the high cost of hospitalization has led to decreases in the number of mental hospitals and the number of patients in long-term care and to the controversial policy of deinstitutionalization. *Deinstitutionalization* is the transitioning of treatment from inpatient facilities to outpatient or community-based facilities. While it is cheaper to treat most people outside of a hospital, even the best outpatient programs aren't sufficient for patients who are psychotic.
pp. 677–678

CHAPTER 18

Psychology in Action

How Is Behavior Affected by the
Work Environment? 683
    Definition of Industrial/Organizational
      Psychology
    Human Resources
    Motivation and Job Performance
    Job Satisfaction
    Teams and Teamwork
    Leadership
    The Future of I/O Psychology

How Do Human Factors Affect
Performance? 707
    Efficiency
    Behavior-Based Safety

How Do Psychology and the Law
Work Together? 710
    Psychologists in the Legal System
    Crime and Punishment
    The Law and Psychology: An Uneasy
      Partnership

What Are the Goals of Sport
Psychology? 713
    Arousal and Athletic Performance
    Anxiety and Athletic Performance
    Intervention Strategies for Athletes
    Putting It Together: Go with the Flow

Summary and Review 717

In this chapter, we consider an array of fields that apply psychology to modern life. We begin with the workplace because that is where psychological principles have been applied longest and most systematically—going as far back as 1915, when John B. Watson applied psychology to an advertising campaign for Maxwell House coffee.

How Is Behavior Affected by the Work Environment?

In *The Apprentice*, NBC's prime-time reality show starring Donald Trump, 16 aspiring contestants compete to be hired. Trump plays who he is in real life—the boss. His ways of handling employees are unique. He is forceful, focused, and yet from time to time finds himself caught in triangles involving contestants. It is important not to confuse *The Apprentice* with the way mentoring and being a boss or an apprentice actually proceed. Trump stars in a role that is about as unlike that of a personnel manager or boss as it can be. Human resources managers—the people who assist corporations in hiring new employees—play key roles in the workforce and they do not behave like Mr. Trump.

Definition of Industrial/Organizational Psychology

Work consumes a high proportion of our waking hours, and how we work and where we work are important questions. Increased global competition, new information technology, and industrial re-engineering are changing the world of work. As productivity has become increasingly important to businesses, industrial/organizational psychology has grown in importance. ***Industrial/organizational (I/O) psychology*** is the study of how individual behavior is affected by the work environment, by coworkers, and by organizational practices. It focuses not only on industry but on government and nonprofit organizations such as hospitals and universities.

I/O psychology grew out of two fields: the study of individual differences in industry (the I part of the name) and social psychology's study of group dynamics and organizational behavior (the O part of the name). The two fields still study different topics, but they often overlap (Latham, 2001). Today, I/O psychologists pay close attention to the type of company they work or consult for because companies vary widely in the people they hire and their organizational structures. They also use data and theories from various domains in the psychology literature and they recognize that here is a case where science and practice interact in fundamental ways. As Seijts and Latham (2003) point out, "I/O psychologists are pragmatic social scientists who often have to deal with concrete issues of applied psychology in real-world settings. . . . The willingness of I/O psychologists to take advantage of the social psychology literature reflects well on them and says something about the kind of person drawn to I/O psychology" (p. 237).

Given today's global economy, I/O psychologists must take into account cultural differences among organizations. Many companies adopt an organizational structure that reflects aspects of the society they operate in. Business protocols and customs differ in Eastern and Western cultures (Asia Society, 2004). Asian companies—in Korea, for example—often have a family orientation, in which people work hard for the good of the entire company and focus on interdependence. This family orientation affects hiring decisions, firing, promotions, hierarchies, and the general work ethic. In companies like Samsung, which makes liquid crystal displays among other products, a saying that might reflect the work ethic is "The nail that stands above the rest invites being hammered down." Culture especially affects how management decisions are made. In Japan, for example, in companies like Sony, new ideas often filter from the bottom up, rather than emanating from the higher levels of the organization, as they often do in the United States. In Latin American countries, some companies, for example, Venezuelan iron and steel company Sidor, are extremely hierarchical in nature, with authority figures commanding high respect. Some companies in less developed countries are more loosely organized in terms of who does what. In the United States, roles tend to be more rigid, although there is often some flexibility. Independent thought and entrepreneurial ability are valued in American companies (South America for Visitors, 2004). Sayings that reflect the American work ethic are "The squeaky wheel gets the grease" and perhaps "Nice guys finish last."

Industrial/organizational (I/O) psychology ■ The study of how individual behavior is affected by the work environment, by coworkers, and by organizational practices.

In general, I/O psychologists study five broad areas: human resources, motivation and job performance, job satisfaction, teamwork, and leadership. *Human resources* refers to the ongoing personnel functions of placing people in jobs, training and promoting them, determining benefits, and evaluating performance. *Motivation and job performance* are key areas of study for I/O psychologists—not only how rewards relate to successful performance, but also the relationships between management and employees and management's self-assessment. *Job satisfaction* is a top concern of workers and employers alike. Today, working in teams is becoming more common, and I/O psychologists are interested in the factors affecting *teamwork*. Last, the study of *leadership* focuses on the defining attributes of leaders—people who influence other people's behavior to attain agreed-upon goals.

Human Resources

Human resources psychologists, or personnel psychologists, are involved in a broad array of activities related to employment—helping employers choose among prospective job candidates, determining compensation packages, facilitating on-the-job training, and arranging termination procedures when businesses must downsize. To help organizations succeed, human resources psychologists must consider both internal conditions (the organization's size, structure, and business strategies) and external conditions (legal, social, political, and cultural factors). Among the most important tasks of these psychologists is helping organizations select qualified candidates for various positions. Today, finding the right people to do specific jobs is part of an organization's *strategic planning*. This high-level planning, which is finalized at the top levels of the organization, includes forecasting the organization's future needs, establishing specific objectives, and implementing programs to ensure that qualified job candidates will be available when needed (Jackson & Schuler, 1990). Human resources psychology is becoming more important because decisions about personnel are more complicated than ever before. New business technologies, including changes in communications technology, the global nature of many corporations, and the increasing reliance on teams to accomplish work tasks make hiring, training, and leading employees more complex.

Job Analyses

An important part of an organization's strategic planning process is taking steps to ensure that those hired to fill positions are well-qualified. Companies often prepare *job analyses*—detailed descriptions of the various tasks and activities that comprise each job, as well as the knowledge, skills, and abilities necessary to do it (the qualifications for the position). Such an analysis specifies *what* gets done and *how* it gets done. It spells out performance criteria—behaviors—that are required of employees. For example, a computer programmer might be expected to write code, debug the code of other programmers, and evaluate the efficiency of the code. The job analysis might also specify that the programmer needs a college degree in computer science, 2 or 3 years of on-the-job experience, and top-notch computing skills.

Job analysis ■ Detailed description of the various tasks and activities that comprise a job, as well as the knowledge, skills, and abilities necessary to do it.

The federal government has prepared a *functional job analysis,* or *FJA,* that describes each general type of job in some detail. An FJA is appealing to I/O psychologists because—like an operational definition of behavior in a research study—it is concrete, observable, and measurable. An FJA has three hierarchies of job functions: how workers deal with data (information), with people (coworkers, subordinates, or customers), and with things (objects). For example, employees may have to compare, contrast, or copy data. On a more complex level, they may have to analyze or synthesize data from different sources. Employees may have to take instructions from some people or help others. On a more complex level, they may have to supervise, instruct, negotiate with, or mentor others. Employees may handle, carry, sort, or tend things; on a more complex level, they may be altering, preparing, or fixing them.

There are other ways to quantify what a job entails. For example, the *position analysis questionnaire* is a widely used instrument that asks those who know a job best to analyze it. It is used to identify the duties, responsibilities, qualifications, and fiscal impact of employees. On this questionnaire, workers complete up to 194 statements describing the job they do (Jeanneret, 1992). The position analysis questionnaire covers six major areas: information sources (where the worker gets data), mental processes (what decision making is required), work output (what physical work is required), relationships with others (communication skills), job context (physical working conditions), and other (licensing, criticality of position, special clothes required, and so on).

Although the FJA and the position analysis questionnaire are widely used (for example, by the Department of Labor), many other job analysis instruments exist, and most of them work well. All have a similar goal: helping employers ensure that jobs are well defined and doable. A job should not be too big or encompass too many tasks; nor should it be too limiting or so focused that it becomes boring and too repetitive. Ideally, jobs should allow employees some level of responsibility for and control over how they do their work. Two of the main tasks of I/O psychologists are balancing the scope and complexity of jobs and helping employers make jobs as motivating as possible.

Selection Procedures

Imagine you are applying for a job. Will the employer find you an attractive applicant? Employers want to hire individuals who will enjoy their work, will fill the company's needs, and will be productive. I/O psychologists develop specific selection procedures, including tests, to produce the best match between jobs and employees. The selection procedures used at large firms are often complicated and time-consuming—such companies have the resources to do such testing and they want to "be sure."

Selection procedures all have the same basic goal—assessing the suitability of job candidates in order to help an employer determine which ones to hire. Employers use application forms, interviews, work samples, and tests to make comparisons between job candidates.

Selection procedures can also involve tests of mental ability, peer ratings, examination of experience, interest inventories, and even handwriting analysis. But research shows that the best measures for helping employers make hiring decisions are mental ability tests, work samples, and integrity tests—and when these are combined, employers are even more likely to choose the best candidates (Schmidt & Hunter, 1998).

Tests of general mental ability come in many forms, but all focus on general abilities. They may be paper-and-pencil or computerized tests and can be administered either to groups or individually. Intelligence tests are widely used as part of the selection procedures for jobs that require high-level cognitive skills. However, a continuing question for I/O psychologists is whether such tests (or any tests, for that matter) are good predictors of job performance (Sternberg, 2003a).

Work samples are hands-on simulations of all or some of a job's tasks. Depending on the job, work samples may include tests of spatial abilities (for air traffic controllers or truck drivers), perceptual accuracy (stenographers or proofreaders), or motor abilities (firefighters or drill press operators). Work samples help employers determine whether a job candidate's abilities match the job's requirements. Similar tests of managerial ability, which often present the applicant with a simulated in-box to sort through, have proven effective in evaluating managerial potential (Berman & Miner, 1985).

One type of test that is being used for many kinds of jobs is the *test of integrity.* Some tests of integrity focus on attitudes about theft, including rationalizations about "acceptably" small amounts of on-the-job theft. Others examine integrity more indirectly by assessing such characteristics as dependability, conscientiousness, and thrill seeking. Department store managers routinely query applicants about ethical values, often ruling out candidates whose answers point in the wrong direction (even after telling them that there is no "right" answer!).

As for polygraph (lie detector) tests, the federal government has laws that broadly restrict the use of polygraphs in employment screening because too often "innocent" people are seen as lying. Polygraphs are just too unreliable; nevertheless, testing employees for specific incidents is allowed—such as thefts—and they can be used as a screening device for some sensitive government positions (Oksol & O'Donohue, 2004). Most psychologists—the vast majority—agree with the report by the National Research Council (2003) that asserts that polygraph tests lack demonstrable validity.

Finally, tests such as the MMPI–2, which screens for maladjustment as well as severe mental illness and lying, are also used to evaluate job candidates' integrity. Although such tests are controversial—many believe there is a danger that prospective employees will be wrongly classified as lacking in integrity—some employers see them as an alternative that is better than not testing at all (Camara & Schneider, 1994).

In addition, many businesses in today's increasingly service-based economy want their employees to be creative, adaptable, resilient, empathic, and understanding with customers—but also to be technologically adept. Since such qualities are considered important as job qualifications, it is not surprising that the use of tests to measure elements of personality has increased markedly in the workplace in the last decade. Several million such tests are administered yearly. Personality tests tend to be used to find specific behavior patterns that make a person well suited to a type of job rather than to screen out people who may be abnormal (Hogan, Hogan, & Roberts, 1996). For example, some people who exhibit the Type A behavior pattern (discussed in Chapter 15) may do better at high-pressure jobs, such as being a commodities trader, than at more routine ones, such as meticulously checking copy for typographical errors. Tests of personality and interests, however, are difficult to correlate with job performance; for example, outgoing individuals may be good salespeople, but quiet, introspective individuals can often be just as persuasive.

Tests are just one way to gather information about applicants. Biographical data can help paint an accurate picture of an individual, as can letters of recommendation and job interviews. Interviews can be important in evaluating the fit between an applicant and a position—but research shows that interviewers often make decisions about an applicant within the first minutes of an interview! Subtle factors can be at work in employment interviews. For example, those who evaluate job applicants have to guard against being influenced by their own moods (Baron, 1993), by an applicant's clothes or looks, or by other non–job-related characteristics that have nothing to do with an applicant's true capabilities. Also, sometimes interviewers base their judgments more on negative information than on positive information. Structured interviews—in which each applicant is asked the same questions, phrased the same way, posed in a certain order, and in the same manner—work better than unstructured interviews.

Surprisingly little is known about how ethnicity may affect interview outcomes. What evidence there is suggests that African Americans receive slightly lower ratings in interviews than Whites do. Most research has been done with college students, with simulated interviews and questionnaires, rather than through observations of real-life interviews.

Allen Huffcutt and his colleagues (Huffcutt & Roth, 1998; Roth, Huffcutt, & Bobko, 2003) reviewed research studies on ethnicity and employment interviews and did a statistical analysis of all of the results. They found several things: First, African Americans and Latinos/Latinas scored lower than Whites did on ability tests. The score on such a test is strongly affected by a candidate's educational background, the school she or he attended, and socioeconomic variables. Second, for complex jobs, ethnic differences disappeared; in fact, applicants for very technical jobs were so highly sought after that minorities and Whites were recruited equally vigorously. Third, most important, and counter to expectations, group differences on *structured* interviews were small. Finally, differences in overall ability between any ethnic group and the White majority tend to be reduced when the minority pool is sufficiently large to allow comparisons and there is more variability among candidates.

What all this boils down to is that, to be fair and hire the best possible candidates, employers should make sure that their human resources departments use structured interviews because this format is more reliable and valid (Campion, Palmer, & Campion, 1998). In small businesses, particularly very small ones, hiring decisions are often made on the basis of an owner's intuition, gut feelings, and personal liking for an applicant.

If you are preparing for an interview, keep in mind several things that will make you more attractive to an employer:

- Be on time for the interview.
- Dress appropriately for the job; be well groomed.
- Demonstrate knowledge about the company, which you gained, for example, by visiting its website.
- Understand the requirements of the position for which you are applying.
- Be honest and genuine; ask questions relevant to the job's duties.
- On your résumé, and at the interview, align your experiences, skills, interests, and abilities as much as possible with the job description.
- Listen attentively and be prepared to answer questions about your previous work experience. Try not to interrupt the interviewer.
- Thank the interviewer for his or her time; it is reasonable and appropriate to ask what the next steps are in the hiring process.
- Smile. Relax—you're more likely to be perceived positively.

Education and Training

You have landed a new job and the celebration is over; now it's time to "learn the business." In small businesses, learning the job is often done one-on-one with the boss or an immediate subordinate. Job training is a process whereby companies and managers systematically teach employees knowledge and skills to improve their job performance. Many large corporations offer systematic job training, which typically begins by educating employees about the organization and its goals. In the Disney Corporation, Walt Disney World's Disney University offers training in everything from computer applications to culinary arts. Using self-paced courses and distance education, Disney U. trains its workers to be top-flight, upbeat, and service-oriented. Disney recognizes that people are at the core of its business, and a well-trained work-force is essential (when asked "How many Mickeys are in the park?" employees are told to act confused and insist that there is only one). Disney, like all employers, recognizes that a new employee may also need to learn specific skills, such as how to use a particular computer animation program.

The increasing amount of information required in today's fast-changing work-place makes employers especially concerned that employees have the necessary knowledge to perform their jobs. To help ensure this, the knowledge must be defined in job-relevant terms, knowledge areas that are relevant to the job must be identified, and the comprehensiveness of those knowledge areas must be verified (Fleishman, Costanza, & Marshall-Mies, 1999).

A variety of methods are available for educating and training employees. Among the most common are lectures, films, videotapes or DVDs, and online presentations. Self-paced instructional materials are often used. Training programs may also include discussion groups, simulations, and on-the-job demonstrations. Letting new employees observe experienced ones so that they can try to be like them is particu-larly effective. A training program can involve an apprenticeship or a mentoring relationship, with regular performance appraisals made by a more experienced or higher-ranking employee—the result is usually nothing like Donald Trump snarling, "You're fired." Finding female mentors for female employees has sometimes been difficult because of smaller numbers of women in upper management (U.S. Department of Labor, 2004).

Even seasoned employees need education and retraining. In large organizations, employee education is an ongoing process, as new products and technologies are introduced. I/O psychologists typically break down a training program into a series of learning objectives. Because such a set of objectives provides very specific goals for knowledge and skill acquisition, it can be a particularly effective method for helping employees identify their strengths and weaknesses. It can also help employees pinpoint obstacles to overcome and opportunities for improvement.

Training may be as simple as reviewing the use of a new tool or procedure—as in introducing an executive to the Internet, teaching an administrative assistant a new word-processing program, or working with custodians to promote recycling efforts. On-the-job training may also be a more elaborate process that involves the employee's active participation—in programming a robot or pitching a product to clients. Training may include repetitive practice, particularly with highly technical equipment. Last, good training—whether at the management level or in low-level positions—usually includes feedback, so that employees can learn whether they have successfully acquired the new skill or knowledge.

I/O psychologists assign great importance to education and training because business or organizational success requires well-informed employees. To help ensure good education and training, researchers attempt to determine what constitutes good job performance. That is, they begin with the desired outcome and work backward to determine how employees should be trained. I/O psychologists evaluate the effectiveness of training by examining employees' work products or test results immediately after the training procedure. Results are, after all, what employers are interested in. Effective training produces improvements in employees' ability to deliver results, whether in the form of better-quality products, clearer communications, or more effective supervision.

Performance Appraisal

Have you ever been evaluated by an employer or supervisor? Bosses are sometimes good at appraising work, but they may overlook your best efforts and remember your mistakes, or they may not accurately convey how they feel about your performance. What makes someone good at evaluating employees?

Performance appraisal ▪ The process by which a supervisor periodically evaluates the job-relevant strengths and weaknesses of a subordinate.

The process by which a supervisor periodically evaluates the job-relevant strengths and weaknesses of subordinates is called *performance appraisal*. Performance appraisals are important because they are often used to determine salaries, layoffs, firings, transfers, and promotions (Harris, Gilbreath, & Sunday, 1998). In many states, employees have the right to view their personnel files, which include performance appraisals. A supervisor or human resources manager may use performance appraisals to decide whether to hire or promote employees (Who has the right, 2004). It is important to realize that performance appraisals enhance the functioning of organizations and improve decision making by employees. Performance appraisals affect employees' view of their organization. Finally, performance appraisals help companies provide a rational basis for personnel decisions, including promotions, changes in job titles, and even dismissals. Researchers have tried to find ways to do performance appraisals systematically and effectively.

Evaluating others in the work setting is uncomfortable for many people. Supervisors generally report that they dislike conducting appraisals—especially face-to-face ones (McDaniel, 2003). They don't like to judge their subordinates, and many acknowledge that they do not have strong evaluative skills. Further, supervisors have just as many inappropriate biases as anyone else (Swim et al., 1989), including the tendency to make attribution errors (pointed out in Chapter 14). And even when performance appraisals are done well, research shows that people's pay is more often associated with the quantity of their work than with its quality (Jenkins et al., 1998).

Increasingly, performance appraisals are being done by more than one individual, even many (Fletcher & Perry, 2002). An employee may be rated on different behavioral dimensions by a number of people who have interactions with the employee and knowledge of his or her skills and performance. This multi-source, multi-rater type of appraisal is sometimes called *360-degree feedback*. The feedback can come from managers, coworkers, clients, and/or customers (Facteau & Craig, 2001; Roberts, 2003).

First, a well-done appraisal must be based on specific criteria, or standards, on which a worker should be judged. There is usually no single performance criterion, no comprehensive yardstick, by which to evaluate a worker. Second, a worker's quantity of work is important, but so is the quality. Also, relationships with other workers often affect performance. Researchers have devised scales to measure performance variables such as sales volume, relationship with customers, and quality of communication with coworkers; these scales can be helpful diagnostic tools. But because skills often overlap, composite scales have been devised (Facteau & Craig, 2001).

Because of the "soft" nature of some performance criteria, such as how well people "get along," most I/O psychologists recommend focusing on the best available criteria. This means giving first attention to those elements that *best* describe satisfactory performance, recognizing that many criteria can be used. For example, a manager would look first at measurable criteria, such as a salesperson's sales volume, a keyboarder's number of words or characters typed, a bank teller's number of shortages, or a nursery worker's number of saplings planted. The manager would then assess other elements of performance that may be important, such as customer relations or coworker communication.

Performance appraisals should use objective measures. Managers often compare employees, ranking them from best to worst or rating them in percentile groups (the top 10%, the next 20%, and so on). Such ratings help differentiate among employees, but they sometimes fall short of fairness. What if workers doing the same job are evaluated by different supervisors, one of them easygoing and the other demanding? What if supervisors use, even if unintentionally, subjective, "soft" criteria, such as how friendly they feel employees are? Might that discriminate against workers who don't have personal interests in common with the supervisors? Research shows that subjective measures do not always have more potential for bias than objective measures. Instead, Roth, Huffcutt, and Bobko (2003) found that there may be some pressure to minimize (rather than accentuate) ethnic group differences with subjective ratings. The performance appraisal process is complicated further by certain factors: who is doing the appraisal and how much power or status this person has, as well as the type of company and its culture. For example, in Asian companies, whose cultures tend to be more collectivist, performance appraisals and resulting changes in job performance are a result of respect for authority more so than in companies in individualist Western cultures. So, culture can affect performance appraisal and subsequent work-related behavior (Fletcher & Perry, 2002).

Many companies establish goals at the beginning of the year to guide year-end performance evaluations. Accurate and systematic evaluations leave employees feeling appreciated and comfortable with the system (Lam, Yik, & Schaubroeck, 2002). Of course, employees can help facilitate the appraisal process by recording their monthly accomplishments, sales totals, or objectives achieved. This allows them to show managers how well they have met company goals and objectives.

Motivation and Job Performance

What would motivate you more—money or satisfying work? New lawyers are often faced with such a choice, between jobs in successful firms that offer very high pay or public interest work that is often low paid but personally quite satisfying.

I/O psychologists help people work together in organizations; they seek ways to make jobs more satisfying, to improve work environments, and to help organizations motivate employees. One obvious motivator is a paycheck—people need money to live. But both employers and psychologists know that people are motivated by many things. Monetary rewards are important, of course—but so is the likelihood of praise for success. Motivators are culturally determined. The value placed on hard work varies from culture to culture. Some cultures stress a person's duty to contribute to society; others stress the right to meaningful work; still others stress the need for job satisfaction. I/O psychologists are especially interested in studying the impact of workplace rewards within the context of culture.

When Hofstede (1983) examined attitudes in more than 50 countries, he found that cultures and organizations vary on four main dimensions. *Power distance* is the extent to which there is a rigid hierarchy, or "pecking order," in a company, limiting employees' freedom of actions. Individuals in high power distance cultures are comfortable with a larger status discrepancy than those in low power distance cultures. *Uncertainty avoidance* is a lack of tolerance for ambiguity or vagueness in the workplace; uncertainty avoidance occurs especially frequently in risk-averse countries such as Japan and Greece. In such cultures, it is never good to break laws or go outside the chain of command, whatever the motive. Cultures vary in the extent to which they value *individualism* as opposed to the collective good. Finally, Hofstede found that emphasis on work goals as opposed to interpersonal goals, a trait he labeled *masculinity,* also varies from culture to culture. Not surprisingly, Hofstede found that most Western companies foster a combination he called independent individualism, while most Asian companies foster collectivism. And companies in

Israel reflect dependent collectivism (high power distance, low individualism). Such cultural values will affect employees' needs and goals, their perceptions of equitable treatment, and how they can most effectively be managed. Interestingly, small shared activities—even eating lunch together in a group—can stimulate group cohesion and willingness to work toward shared goals.

In the United States at least, job performance is to some degree affected by whether the job involves *intrinsically motivated behavior*—engaged in because it brings pleasure. (We examined intrinsic and extrinsic motivation in Chapters 8 and 12.) Recall that when intrinsically motivated behaviors are reinforced with direct external rewards (such as money), productivity often drops. Money is often not that important to job performance. A well-paid computer programmer may do her job well as much for the challenge and personal gratification as for the money, and a lower-paid clerical worker who finds his job important and challenging will perform well. With the help of I/O psychologists, employers can find ways to motivate their employees to be more productive (and thus increase profits).

So what are the top characteristics of jobs that cause stress and unhappiness? They are:

- Work overload (too much to do, too little time to do it)
- Underutilization of employee knowledge and skills
- Dangerous work conditions
- Overly complex work
- Interpersonal conflict in the job setting
- Lack of control of work

In the end, as in many areas studied by psychologists, job performance is affected by an array of variables. Tett and Burnett (2003) assert that five situational features—job demands, distracters, job constraints, things that release or ease job constraints, and facilitators—all operate at task, organizational, and social levels. The task of sorting out how and when each of these variables affects job performance lies ahead for researchers.

Goal-Setting Theory

Workers often perform difficult tasks for long hours, not for pay or for praise, but merely to reach a goal or to compare their present performance with past performance (Locke & Latham, 2002). Mountain climbers tackle a new peak "because it's there." In business and in personal life, people often set goals based on a larger vision and then tackle the specific activities needed to accomplish them. Goals should be SMART—Specific, Motivational, Attainable, Relevant, and Trackable. *Goal-setting theory* asserts that setting specific, clear, attainable goals for a given activity leads to better performance. For example, I (L.L.) challenge myself to ride my mountain bike harder and longer, not to break records for middle-aged men but to meet goals I have set for myself.

Goal-setting theory states that the best job goals are those that are somewhat challenging but attainable and that a worker has agreed to (Locke & Latham, 2002).

Goal-setting theory ■
The theory that asserts that setting specific, clear, attainable goals for a given activity leads to better performance.

Figure 18.1
Goal-Setting
Theory

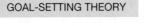

For example, if a sales manager and her staff agree to generate a 50% increase in annual sales, rather than an unrealistic 200% increase, they are likely to perform better (see **Figure 18.1**). Goals work especially well when they enhance a worker's sense of self-esteem or self-efficacy. Research supports goal-setting theory. As Locke and Latham (2002) say, "With goal-setting theory, specific difficult goals have been shown to increase performance on well over 100 different tasks involving more than 40,000 participants in at least eight countries working in laboratory, simulation, and field settings. The dependent variables have included quantity, quality, time spent, costs, job behavior measures, and more" (p. 714).

Goal-setting theory can account for some work behaviors, but it will not explain why people will work on projects for years, at low pay or under difficult conditions. More fully developed expectancy theories take the next step—explaining the motivation for this type of performance.

Expectancy Theories

A successful employer–employee relationship relies on many factors beyond economic motivation. **Expectancy theories,** which we discussed in Chapter 12, suggest that a worker's effort and desire to maintain goal-directed behavior (in other words, to work) are determined by expectations regarding the outcomes of that behavior.

One expectancy theory, proposed by Victor Vroom (1964), suggests that both motivation and ability determine job performance. Vroom's proposal is considered an expectancy theory because it states that motivation is determined by what people expect to experience in performing a task—a rewarding outcome or a frustrating one. Vroom's theory holds that motivation can be determined from a three-part equation made up of expectancy, instrumentality, and valence. *Expectancy* is the belief that hard or extra work will lead to good or improved performance; *instrumentality* refers to the belief that good performance will be rewarded; *valence* refers to the value placed on the rewards that are offered (see **Figure 18.2**). A person who gets a big raise but then gets the cold shoulder from coworkers because of it may give the raise lower valence.

It turns out that ability, effort, *and* role perceptions—the ways people believe they should be doing their jobs—are the key variables that determine performance (see Figure 18.2). Edward Lawler and Lyman Porter (1967) believed that workers must fully understand the nature of their positions and exactly what is required of them. Too often, people fail not because of lack of effort or ability, but because they do not know what is expected of them or how to achieve a sense of control over

Expectancy theories ▪
Theories that suggest that a worker's effort and desire to maintain goal-directed behavior (to work) are determined by expectations regarding the outcomes of that behavior.

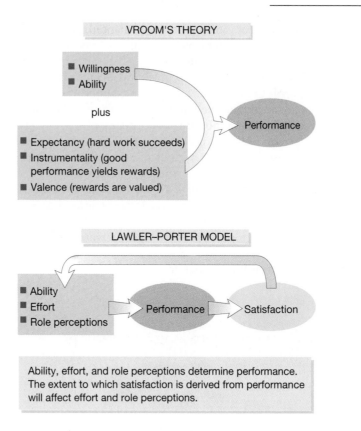

Figure 18.2
Expectancy
Theories

their work situation. So an employee may burn a great deal of midnight oil, but if he or she has misread what it really takes to succeed in the organization (say, team-work rather than long hours), performance may not be rated highly.

Researchers assert that the motivation to work can be best explained by integrative theories that focus on goals, experiences, and thoughts (Locke & Latham, 2002). When employees receive incentives, when they think that their contributions are important, and when the effort required of them is not excessive, productivity tends to be high (Locke & Latham, 2002). When performance is high, job satisfaction is likely; job satisfaction then increases the employee's commitment to the organization and its goals.

Equity Theory

People want to be compensated for their work and to earn as much as they can, but most people feel that they are worth more than they are paid. What happens when people think they aren't being treated fairly?

In I/O psychology, *equity theory* asserts that what people bring to a work situation should be balanced by what they receive compared to other workers; that is, workers' input (what they do) should be reflected in their compensation (what they

Equity theory ■ In I/O psychology, the theory that asserts that what people bring to a work situation should be balanced by what they receive compared to other workers; that is, input should be reflected in compensation.

receive). If input and compensation are not well balanced, people will adjust their work level, and their job satisfaction and performance may be affected. According to equity theory, each individual privately assesses her or his ratio of input to compensation and compares it to other people's input/compensation ratio. When the ratios are similar, people are relatively happy. For example, if my (L.L.'s) workload and compensation are at certain levels and other faculty members seem to have similar levels, our input/compensation ratios are about equal.

But what if a person feels that his or her ratio is out of kilter with those of coworkers? In such cases (especially in cases of underpayment), people may slow down their efforts and gripe and groan, causing the quality of their work to decrease (see **Figure 18.3**). If people perceive such an inequity, they will choose one of several alternatives to alter the situation (Greenberg, 1996; Hellriegel & Slocum, 1992):

- They can increase their inputs to justify higher rewards (when they feel overrewarded).
- They can decrease their inputs (loaf on the job or leave work early) to compensate for low rewards.

Figure 18.3
Equity Theory

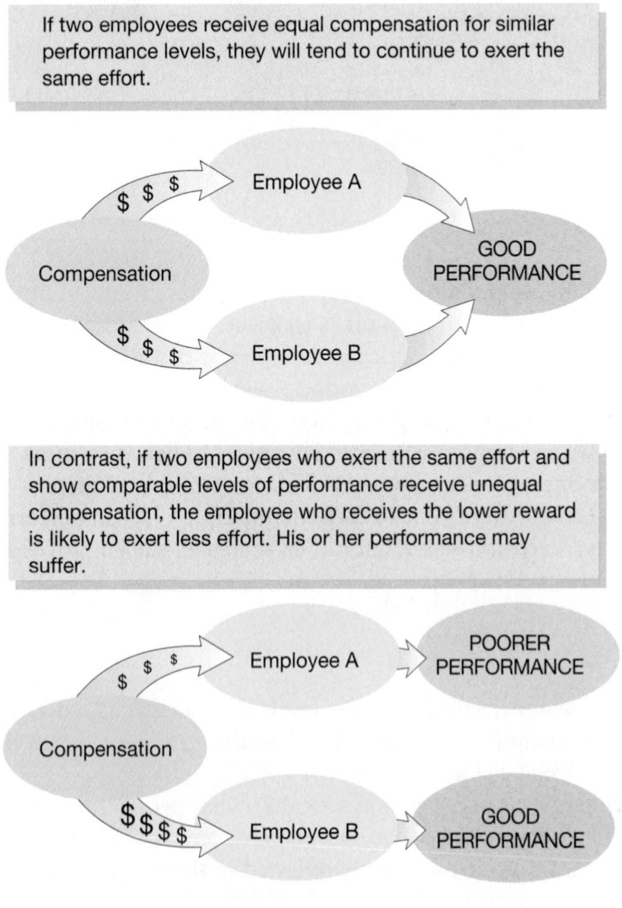

If two employees receive equal compensation for similar performance levels, they will tend to continue to exert the same effort.

$ $ $ → Employee A → GOOD PERFORMANCE

Compensation

$ $ $ → Employee B → GOOD PERFORMANCE

In contrast, if two employees who exert the same effort and show comparable levels of performance receive unequal compensation, the employee who receives the lower reward is likely to exert less effort. His or her performance may suffer.

$ $ $ → Employee A → POORER PERFORMANCE

Compensation

$$$$ → Employee B → GOOD PERFORMANCE

- They can change their rewards through legal actions or illegal ones (stealing company assets).
- They can distort reality by rationalizing inequities, and thus feel better.
- They can quit.

There are hidden costs of inequity in pay and benefits. When Greenberg (1990) examined employee theft rates in manufacturing plants, he found that rates of theft increased after pay reductions. However, when supervisors explained the basis for pay cuts to workers, the theft rate decreased. Thus, explanations of changes in compensation can minimize the perception of unfairness.

Self-Efficacy and Work

How well you expect to execute a series of actions required to deal with a particular situation is a measure of your belief in your abilities, or your *self-efficacy*. People who view themselves as competent tend to do better at work than others (but this is especially true for easier tasks). This leads researchers to some practical suggestions for employers: Managers should provide accurate descriptions of work to be performed; managers should indicate to employees what techniques should be used to complete tasks; employers should provide tasks that employees can accomplish to enhance their self-efficacy; rewards should be timed to enhance workers' self-efficacy. Knowing what the goals are—and the rewards associated with them—can enhance self-efficacy and, ultimately, effectiveness (Latham, Daghighi, & Locke, 1997).

Motivation Management: Three Approaches

I/O psychologists have identified three basic approaches to managing motivation in the workplace: paternalistic, behavioral, and participatory. The fundamental idea underlying the *paternalistic approach* to workplace motivation is that a company takes care of its employees' needs and desires as a protective father would. Early in this century, this approach was common in the company mining towns of Appalachia and in the mills of Massachusetts. The company owners provided housing, schools, recreation, and churches for employees. This approach is still followed in some Japanese and Chinese companies, which promote lifelong employment and fill employees' needs, from recreation to drug rehabilitation (Cheng et al., 2004; Wu & Lee, 2001). As Cheng and colleagues note, this approach assumes that a powerful authority shows consideration for subordinates and provides moral leadership. However, this approach is contrary to many American psychologists' views on behavior. Operant conditioning studies show that for a behavior (such as good performance of job tasks) to be established and maintained—at least in Western cultures—reinforcement must be contingent on performance. In a paternalistic system, all employees, productive as well as nonproductive, are reinforced. As equity theory predicts, reinforcement without the need for good performance does not encourage people to work hard.

The *behavioral approach* to workplace motivation assumes that people will work only if they receive tangible rewards for specific task performance. Examples include paying a factory worker by the piece and a typist by the page. In such a system, hardworking employees obtain more rewards—commissions, salary increases, bonuses, and so on—because they produce more, with fewer errors or faster (Roetting et al., 2003). However, little attention is paid to the emotional needs of workers. Goal-setting theory and, to some extent, expectancy theory thus argue that the behavioral approach to motivation is incomplete.

The *participatory approach* to workplace motivation is based on the belief that individuals who have a say in the decisions that affect their work lives are motivated to work harder and smarter. Participation, it is argued, allows managers and employees to exchange information to solve problems (Pearce & Randel, 2004; Mikkelsen & Gundersen., 2003). Supporters of this approach believe that a sense of competence and self-determination is likely to increase individuals' levels of motivation (Wagner, Parker, & Christiansen, 2003). *Quality circles,* in which workers at all levels meet to discuss ways to improve product quality and promote excellence, constitute one technique employers use to involve workers in the management process (Joffe & Glynn, 2002). Lovett & Gilmore (2003) showed that quality circles can also be used effectively to empower teachers to become agents of change. The campus-like settings built by many corporations—Microsoft and Oracle, for example—are intended to create a team-oriented, participatory environment.

Many variables affect the success of participatory management programs: the work setting, the individuals involved, the kinds of decisions to be made, and the company's hiring policies, for example. Truly participatory programs have positive effects on workers' values, thoughts, and motivation. These changes lead to less conflict among workers, increased productivity, and better overall job performance (see **Figure 18.4**). When workers feel involved in their work and their organization, they are more likely to be spontaneous, to help coworkers, to look out for the organization's best interests, and so on. Many of these behaviors depend on employees having positive feelings about the work environment and having a good job attitude (George & Brief, 1992). In many firms, where workers feel a lack of participatory management, the result is low self-esteem among them—and a resulting lack of a good work ethic.

Job Satisfaction

If you have a positive view of your abilities and feel competent and in control at your workplace (at least most of the time), chances are good that you will like your job and that you will feel satisfied with it (Schleicher, Watt, & Greguras, 2004). It is important to realize that job satisfaction is different from job motivation. Motivation is always shown in behavior; job satisfaction (a person's attitude about the work and workplace) may not be shown in behavior. A tired, bored, overworked electrician may feel discouraged and angry—and may even hate her job—but still be motivated to work. Her motivation may stem from the high pay she receives, from her sense of obligation to get the job done, or from some other source. Thus, although her job satisfaction is low, it does not affect her performance. In general, however, a satisfied worker is a high-performing worker who will remain in the organization. This is why organizations want I/O psychologists to identify the sources of job satisfaction.

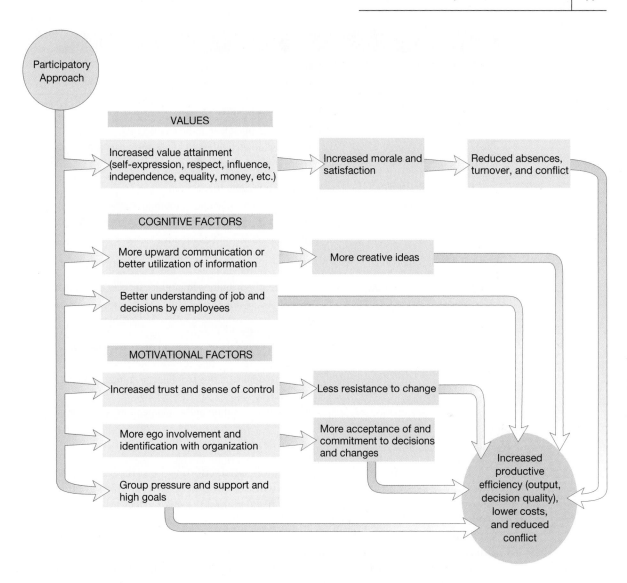

Figure 18.4
The Participatory Approach to Motivation Leads to Increased Work Effectiveness
(Locke & Schweiger, 1979)

There are probably more sources of job satisfaction than can be listed here, but they cluster in five basic categories: the work itself, the perceived rewards of the work, the quality of supervision, the support of coworkers, and the work setting (e.g. Hodson, 2004; Hsieh, 2004; Peterson & Wilson, 2004). These categories, with examples, are presented in **Table 18.1** (on p. 700). The overall level of satisfaction depends on the extent to which people's expectations are matched by their actual feelings.

Table 18.1

KEY FACTORS RELATED TO JOB SATISFACTION

Area	Positive Factors
■ The Work Itself	The work is interesting.
	The work is perceived to be challenging.
	There are opportunities to apply one's own judgment.
	There is some degree of autonomy.
■ Perceived Rewards	There is adequate recognition.
	The pay is adequate and equitable.
	The work contributes to self-esteem and self-efficacy.
	There are opportunities for advancement.
■ Quality of Supervision	Supervisors offer encouragement, support, and help.
■ Support from Coworkers	There are opportunities to interact socially and in teams.
	Coworkers are supportive and compatible.
■ The Work Setting	There is job security.
	The work environment is viewed positively (seen as pleasant, attractive, and comfortable).
	There are opportunities to influence company policy and procedures.
	Adequate information and equipment are available.

Pay and benefits have an impact on job satisfaction, to be sure. But support from coworkers and feelings about the work environment have an even greater impact. A person's dispositions—his or her personality—also affect job satisfaction, as do his or her mood and emotions. The key here is that a mood, a bad day, an especially challenging task, or a disagreeable coworker may—but also may not—affect a person's job satisfaction. Moods and emotions at work are not precisely equated with job satisfaction (Brief & Weiss, 2002). However, job satisfaction is not totally separable from a person's underlying feelings about life and typical approaches to day-to-day tasks. People who are chronically unhappy are likely to be unhappy at work. By contrast, the optimists among us tend to find ways to make work satisfying. Thus, an employer can provide a comfortable, satisfying work environment and give an employee control over her or his work and support and encouragement, but a person who is depressed or chronically unhappy is rarely going to find a job satisfying (Thoresen et al., 2003).

In the end, when people feel good about their work, believe what they are doing is important, and have some control over their work, then their job performance is usually better. When job performance is better, people usually do better—this is a reinforcing cycle of feelings, beliefs, and productivity (Schleicher et al., 2004). One factor affecting feelings about work is the extent to which people work in teams.

Teams and Teamwork

Many individuals who work in companies work with others in groups or teams. A *team* is a group of individuals who interact with one another on a regular basis to accomplish a shared objective or responsibility. Teams have a defined membership—for example, a group of junior account executives who work on the Brand X account. Team members may have different but complementary skills—some focus on branding and others on visual design, for example. Team members meet, work on shared tasks, share information and resources, are often dependent on one another, and are rewarded as a team when they accomplish their short-term and long-term goals. Some teams focus on specific, limited problems; others work on developing more general or innovative solutions.

Team ■ A group of individuals who interact with one another on a regular basis to accomplish a shared objective or responsibility.

Because a team is a group of people, it is important to remember that its dynamics are complex and will change over time (McGrath & Argote, 2004). Teamwork requires team members to periodically share information, to provide and get feedback, and to follow along when a group makes a decision. A team needs to see itself as a group, with leaders and members. In larger organizations, teams often have a defined structure with specified roles: leaders, facilitators, finishers, and evaluators, among others. The number of roles within a team is dependent on its size, complexity, and the nature of the organization's mission.

It is no surprise that work in teams is a bit more complicated than working individually. Individuals need to be socialized into a team; they have to accommodate team differences and personalities. This means managing conflict, building trust, sharing ideas, developing group cohesiveness, and working toward team goals, which sometimes requires putting aside personal goals. Team composition is important and teams need to have authority over a task—that is, the ability to make decisions and get the job done. For all these reasons, working in teams is full of twists and turns; team building, evaluation, and delegation of authority are also complex. *Social loafing* can occur and so can *groupthink*, two phenomena that can impede good group performance, as we saw in Chapter 14. But companies are finding that teamwork is making employees happier and more productive and companies more profitable.

The idea behind teams is that many tasks cannot be accomplished by a single person but require the skills and abilities of more than one person (Cannon-Bowers & Salas, 1998). Today, more than ever before, companies are relying on teams of workers to accomplish complex tasks. Surprisingly, as teamwork has increased, research on what makes a good team, how teams work, and how to best utilize teams has decreased (Ilgen, 1999). When teams are put together carefully, job satisfaction is bound to increase. Workers enjoy collaborating with their colleagues toward a shared goal. Identifying the shared goals—such as developing the best precision-drilling-systems device—and setting up the teams often require the leadership that comes from managers.

Leadership

Perhaps one of the most admired corporate leaders in the United States was Jack Welch, the CEO of General Electric. Welch reshaped GE through more than 600 acquisitions and brought about record earnings. He devoted the most time to personnel issues—50%, he says. In real-life organizations, large and small, leaders like Welch work to persuade, encourage, and inspire. They try to build cohesion and facilitate goal-oriented teamwork. In every organization, some individuals emerge as *leaders*—people who influence the behavior of others toward the attainment of agreed-upon goals. But there is no "right" type of leader. In fact, leadership styles fluctuate widely, from autocratic leaders, who say "My way or the highway," to democratic leaders, whose motto is "Let's decide this together." An early researcher in social psychology, Kurt Lewin (1890–1947), argued that that there was more originality, group-mindedness, and friendliness in groups led by democratic leaders and more aggression, hostility, scapegoating, and discontent in groups led by auto-cratic managers (Lewin & Lippitt, 1938; Reid, 1981).

In any work setting, informal leaders may emerge spontaneously; higher management may also formally designate leaders. Leaders are expected to help further the purposes of their organizations. Thus, one of their primary roles is to persuade and motivate employees to perform well. Note, however, that not all managers are leaders; nor are all leaders managers. Truly effective leadership is so close to being an art that it should come as no surprise that I/O psychologists have made intensive efforts to understand it.

Psychologists have learned a great deal about leadership. Yet there are a number of questions still pending: Can people choose a good leader? Is it possible to predict who will provide effective leadership? Why do some leaders succeed and others fail? The study of leadership has gone through three major phases, each with a different focus: traits, behaviors, or situations. The right combination of these elements ultimately produces an effective leader.

Trait Approach to Leadership

The specific personality traits of individual organizational leaders were studied inten-sively in the early 1950s. This research tried to isolate the characteristics that make individuals good or poor leaders; for example, are good leaders assertive, directive, or authoritarian? But the trait approach troubles some researchers. Leaders cannot be universally characterized by traits such as assertiveness, self-confidence, and drive. Many good business leaders are assertive, but other equally good ones are not. In fact, although an individual leader's personality traits can tell psychologists something about leadership, the differences among leaders tend to be greater than the similarities. One reason that trait studies have been unable to find a common denominator is that each leader and each organization have different goals. Today, researchers recognize that one defining trait of effective business leaders is *flexibility*—the ability to adapt to a rapidly changing work environment and global economy. Other key traits are intelli-gence, maturity, inner motivation, vision, and employee orientation.

Leadership Behaviors

Another focus of research on leadership is specific behaviors of leaders. Many researchers try to find characteristic ways in which leaders interact with other members of their organizations. Some of the pioneering work on leadership was done at the University of Michigan's Institute for Social Research. The Michigan studies (as they are often called) found that many business leaders tend to be either employee-oriented or task-oriented—but many show both orientations. Whether a leader is principally employee- or task-oriented has to do with how the leader chooses to influence behavior. An employee-oriented leader acts to maintain and enhance individual employees' feelings of self-worth or self-esteem. Such leaders try to empower employees and make them feel valued and important. A task-oriented leader focuses on getting the job done as efficiently and quickly as possible.

In general, a *transactional leader* is a leader who seeks to motivate others by appealing to their self-interest—the focus is on performance outcomes, or real results. A transactional leader concentrates on getting the job done and done well—such leaders often focus on specific (often short-term) goals. Transactional leaders motivate by the *exchange process*. For example, business owners exchange status and wages (rewards) for the work effort of the employee. Sometimes they use correction or punishment as a response to unacceptable performance, but other times, they actively monitor the work and use remedial approaches. Transactional leadership is effective. As well-respected leadership researcher Bernard Bass (Bass et al., 2003) put it, "It appears that transactional leadership is needed to establish clear standards and expectations of performance. Transactional leadership can build a base level of trust in the leader as he or she reliably executes what has been agreed to over time. When clarity exists around expectations and performance objectives, followers come to learn that their leaders and peers, when asked to execute a task, do so reliably" (p. 216).

As more women enter leadership roles, the possibility that they might carry out these roles differently than men do is attracting increasing attention (Eagly, Johannesen-Schmidt, & van Engen, 2003). Leadership styles are somewhat related to gender; generally, women are more employee-oriented, and men are more task-oriented; women value connectedness more and fear evaluation more than do men (Boatwright & Egidio, 2003). Recent studies show that the gender of a leader has other important effects. For example, female leaders or managers tend to be evaluated as positively as their male counterparts. However, when they behave in "alpha male," dominating ways (physical, aggressive, forceful), women in leadership roles are devalued—especially if the evaluators are men (Eagly et al., 2003). Also, culture and gender interact. Women continue to be underrepresented in management globally, including in the so-called developing countries. Research in culturally diverse contexts in Africa shows that women leaders are treated differently: In Ghana, men encourage both men and women, but women do not respond well to female leaders; in Tanzania, men responded negatively toward women, but women responded positively to women—the exact opposite result (Akuamoah-Boateng et al., 2003).

Other research has confirmed that behavioral differences among leaders are sometimes determined by characteristics of the people being led (without taking gender into account). Some groups of individuals have characteristics that demand an employee orientation on the leader's part. For example, underpaid, overworked, but dedicated social workers may have a great need to maintain a high level of self-esteem, to feel that their work is worthwhile. A supervisor must motivate these

Transactional leader ■
A leader who seeks to motivate others by appealing to their self-interest and who focuses on performance outcomes.

people not with task-oriented directions but with concern for their sense of self-worth. Highly paid executives, however, may be better motivated by a leader taking a task-oriented approach because they assume that their salaries reflect their higher levels of ability, creativity, and/or productivity. Job performance, job satisfaction, and the way a worker is treated are closely related. In motivating workers, leaders must consider their own personal traits, the various possible behaviors they might use to influence others, and the conditions in which the work is being done.

Situational Leadership Theory

In the 1980s, many researchers shifted from investigating leaders' behaviors to investigating the *situations* in which these behaviors are performed. Some situations lend themselves to leadership, and even to specific forms of leadership; others call for little leadership. Thus, a warm, friendly, employee-oriented leader (or supervisor) is generally very useful for a group of service workers. But if the organization encounters financial trouble and decides to lay off some employees, and if the supervisor has no control over who is let go, the climate of uncertainty may undermine the effects of the warmth and friendliness.

A number of interacting factors determine the most effective style of leadership for a given situation. Effective leaders may simply be those who are best at perceiving the current goals and needs of their organizations and fitting their style to those needs. A major theory that accounts for leadership effectiveness is *Vroom's leadership model*.

Victor Vroom and his colleagues Phillip Yetton and Arthur Jago focused on the various ways in which leaders may make decisions in organizations. As part of the leader–participation model, Vroom created a flowchart for determining the amount of advice a leader should seek, depending on the task to be accomplished. A leader can make an authoritarian decision and simply announce it; a leader can present a problem, solicit advice, and then make the final decision; or a leader can allow other people to make the decision. As a leader's use of authority increases, the freedom of others in the group decreases. That is, when a manager makes a decision and announces it, subordinates have little freedom of choice; this style of leadership is called *boss-centered* (Vroom, 1974; Vroom & Jago, 1995; Vroom & Yetton, 1973). According to Vroom's leadership model, each time a decision is to be made, managers can ask themselves a series of questions to arrive at the best possible leadership approach for the situation. For example, a prototypical question is "Is the quality of the final result important?" (The answer had better be yes!)

The strength of Vroom's model is that it recognizes that leaders have options—that they can choose how to behave in light of their previous experiences and knowledge and the current situation or conditions (Vroom, 1997). Vroom's model has received some research support, but its practical implications in the workplace have not been evaluated systematically (Brockner & Higgins, 2001; Lord, Hanges, & Godfrey, 2003). It emphasizes the important role of situational variables in determining which leadership approach is most appropriate at any given time.

Transformational Leadership

If a person took charge of a faltering organization and provided it with direction, a new vision, and a sense of purpose, that person would be considered a first-rate leader. Such leaders are hard to find, but occasionally someone emerges who is charismatic and has extraordinary effects on others. These leaders are often called *transformational leaders*; they provide inspiration, intellectual stimulation, and individual attention to followers and are able to draw extra effort out of them (Bass, 1997). Often such individuals do not have formal authority; because of their personality, style, and interpersonal skills, however, they seem to be able to influence and empower others. Examples of transformational leaders are Martin Luther King, Margaret Mead, and Germaine Greer. Transformational leaders have a strong sense of moral purpose and an aura of authority and dignity; they define people's roles in terms of their own ideological and moral values (Hoyt et al., 2003; Turner et al., 2002). Such leaders often use unconventional techniques or novel ideas to frame their vision for the future, and they communicate extreme confidence in their own abilities to lead and to solve problems. Business examples include Lee Iacocca, formerly of Chrysler, GE's Jack Welch, and Carly Fiorina of Hewlett-Packard. They all led their companies through good and bad times, never lacked confidence, and always inspired commitment, loyalty, and a sense of well-being in employees (Hoyt et al., 2003; van Dierendonck et al., 2004). In the political arena, Abraham Lincoln and Franklin D. Roosevelt were both transformational leaders who acted daringly and decisively in spite of contrary public opinion and political opposition. Many feel that transformational leaders are born, not made, and are individually unique. Bernard Bass (2001) asserts that the unique combination of three types of intelligence—cognitive, social, and emotional—contributes to transformational leadership. It is unclear whether transformational leadership skills can be learned.

We can contrast transformational leaders with transactional ones described earlier. Remember that transactional leaders focus on achievable shorter-term goals; they manage by exchange processes and focus on getting the job done and done well. Transformational leaders tend to think longer-term and to focus on values, missions, and overarching long-term goals. They energize people to persist when conditions are unpredictable, difficult, and/or stressful (Bass et al., 2003); they empower employees to be successful (Kark, Shamir, & Chen, 2003). They create a sense of trust (Dirks & Ferrin, 2002).

Although gender differences among transformational leaders are small, women's typical leadership styles tend to be more transformational than those of men. According to Alice Eagly and her colleagues (Eagly et al., 2003), "It appears that female leaders are somewhat more likely than their male counterparts to have a repertoire of the leadership behaviors that are particularly effective under contemporary conditions ..." (p. 587).

Transformational leaders often create opportunities to change an organization and its employees or constituents. Transformational leaders are often able to instill in others a willingness to go along with their ideas and a reluctance to criticize those ideas and to create situations that allow them to be seen as charismatic—they manage impressions well (Gardner & Avolio, 1998). A transformational leader inspires followers to rank

Transformational leader ■ A leader who is typically charismatic and able to effect change by inspiring and providing intellectual stimulation and individual attention to followers, who respond with extra effort.

organizational goals above self-interest. Some researchers assert that transformational leaders don't have to be charismatic but can be effective using inspiration, intellectual stimulation, and individual consideration—they have heart (Looman, 2003). With such leadership, the members of an organization adopt new values, ideas, and ways of operating (Sosik, Kahai, & Avolio, 1998). When new values are adopted, higher levels of performance are often expected.

What Constitutes Effective Leadership?

Psychologists' knowledge of how people influence and manage others has grown dramatically. Researchers now know that effective leadership depends not only on personal traits and specific techniques or behaviors, but also on the situation. Lord, Brown, and Freiberg (1999) assert that leadership effectiveness arises from a dynamic interplay between leaders and followers that involves leaders' behavior but also followers' perceptions. Workers may exaggerate a boss's leadership effectiveness if they are productive and happy (Shamir, 1992). Thus, leadership, workers' perceptions of leadership, and motivation are interrelated.

Although the research results are not unanimous, several ideas are widely agreed on (Bass et al., 2003; van Dierendonck et al., 2004). To be an effective leader, follow these guidelines:

- Know the job, and be practical when making decisions.
- Be an active leader—passive leadership is not effective.
- Set up good personnel selection policies—carefully selected workers help establish a favorable working situation.
- Act in ways consistent with the organization's vision—this builds a strong organization.
- Foster listening and well-being among all levels of employees.
- Create an organization that allows for choices.
- Be sensitive to workers' motivation, satisfaction, and performance—be nurturing.
- Be both task-oriented *and* relationship-oriented

Through carefully conducted research, I/O psychologists can help organizations seek out effective leaders who can persuade, motivate, build confidence, and create a better workplace with more satisfied workers and stockholders (Hogan, Curphy, & Hogan, 1994).

The Future of I/O Psychology

I/O psychologists are presented with a whole range of new opportunities as the work world is changing very quickly. Riggio (2003) has suggested that we live in a brave new world of work, a world where I/O psychologists can and are making a big difference.

First, *work is changing*—organizations are moving toward fewer levels in their hierarchies. In addition, people are working from remote locations using telecommunications technology (Hoogervorst, Koopman, & van der Flier, 2002). Thus, I/O psychologists are helping reshape organizational structures, including downsizing, and helping workers deal with new ways of communicating and new forms of stress.

Second, there *is a new focus on human resources*—organizations are trying, more than ever before, to hire only the best workers. Medical benefits and family-friendly environments are prime considerations for both workers and organizations. As business has become more competitive, companies are focusing on how to cope with the whole person and his or her problems, not just how to increase productivity.

Third, *there is a much more diverse workforce*—more than ever before, the workforce contains women and ethnic minorities. While the advantages of diversity in terms of having more viewpoints and reflecting the demographics of society are obvious, diversity also presents challenges. Work teams are no longer homogenous; special interests and needs of subgroups now have to be factored in. Flexible work scheduling for young mothers and dads—even grandparents—is becoming an issue. I/O psychologists are helping companies develop policies and procedures to address such issues.

Last, *business has gone global*—this requires that employees be flexible about travel, have knowledge of other cultures, and also be able to think from the viewpoint of workers and managers in other cultures.

So, the nature of work is changing, and how we work is in part determined by our interactions with computers and other devices that we use on a day-to-day basis. We'll look at this interaction next.

How Do Human Factors Affect Performance?

When I (L.L.) sit at my computer paying bills, I often recall how time-consuming it used to be to write checks, address envelopes, buy stamps, and mail the bills. Now I can pay bills at home at my convenience. In addition, I can check my bank balance and move money between accounts rather easily. Applied psychologists who study human factors have played an important role in streamlining banking procedures as well as many other day-to-day routine tasks. Donald Norman, a psychologist who has studied applied issues, wrote what is now considered a classic, which I regularly recommend to my students: *Design of Everyday Things* (1990). Entertaining and enlightening, this book focuses on how cleverly designed machines and software make life easier.

Human factors (sometimes called *ergonomics*) is the study of the relationship of human beings to machines and to workplaces and other environments. A human factors psychologist might focus on the creation of health-care products for use by handicapped people, the design of cooking utensils or educational products, or the interaction between robots and people. Most human factors research focuses on the work environment, especially on the issues of efficiency and safety.

Human factors ■ The study of the relationship of human beings to machines and to workplaces and other environments; sometimes called *ergonomics*.

Efficiency

Human factors researchers have examined workers' ability to operate machines efficiently and effectively. Much of this research centers on the fit between human anatomy or physiology, the demands of a particular task or piece of equipment, and the environment in which the task is done. Human factors researchers seek to develop person–machine interfaces that minimize frustration and errors, maximize output, and are reliable. (*Person–machine interfaces* are devices, often computer screens, that provide the links between a human user and a machine, often a computer.) Human factors researchers study how machines can be used to ensure that speed and accuracy of work are optimized and that workers' fatigue and stress are minimized (Westgaard, 2000).

A key difference between a human factors psychologist and an I/O psychologist is that the I/O psychologist tends to focus on getting human beings to change their behavior to improve efficiency. A human factors psychologist, on the other hand, looks at how the equipment or tools or machines used by people can be improved to increase efficiency. It is often easier to change a machine than to change a human being!

In the early part of the 20th century, working with machinery meant reading dials, turning wheels, pulling levers, and so on. Today, working with machinery often means operating a computer, monitoring computer-controlled devices, or programming them. To a great extent, *controlling* equipment, rather than operating it, has become a focus of human factors research. If equipment is to be properly controlled, switches, buttons, dials, computer screens, and other display devices have to be designed to minimize errors. For example, a pilot must be able to read a computer screen accurately, under all possible conditions, in order to land a plane safely; a nuclear power plant operator must be able to read the temperature of nuclear devices.

As you know, computer displays are everywhere—at work and school, at computerized cash registers, and at ATMs (automated teller machines). Well-designed computer interfaces minimize errors, but the ability to create good interfaces depends on knowledge of how human beings perceive and interact with machines. This means studying human perception, information processing, and decision making (Sommerich, Joines, & Psihogios, 2001). The ATM is an example of an interface that has been studied extensively by human factors researchers. My local bank has an ATM that is easy to operate—I have never made a mistake there. But the ATM at the bank down the street has a confusing, overly complicated interface, and I have seen many users kick or curse it and lose their cards. It is usually a human factors psychologist who can take the credit for a well-designed interface that minimizes errors, confusion, and anger on the part of users.

Even the tools of carpenters, tailors, and data-entry operators can be designed using human factors principles. For example, what is the best weight for a hammer? How tall should a drill press be? Today, computer keyboards have been designed to be easy to type on, to minimize typing errors, and to reduce carpal tunnel syndrome. The human factors psychologists who help design such keyboards attempt to meet the important human considerations of accuracy, productivity, and safety. (Interestingly, keyboard designs that rearrange the letters on the keyboard so that the more frequently used letters are closer together make typing more efficient than with the standard keyboards.)

Behavior-Based Safety

The goal of any safety practice is injury prevention. *Behavior-based safety* refers to effective safety management through a wide range of programs that focus on changing the behavior of workers *and* companies to prevent occupational injuries and illnesses. An organizational culture that fosters safety minimizes the use of shortcuts and the violations of rules, encourages open communication among workers and management, and thus reduces the probability of on-the-job injuries. In fact, the failure of employees and management to communicate about safety issues is itself a safety issue—safety is more than just common sense, and safety management is more than just a way to shift responsibility onto workers (Geller, 2001a, 2001b).

Safety violations are related to the occurrence of incidents that jeopardized the quality of aircraft maintenance (Hobbs & Williamson, 2002). Geller (2001c) argues that corporations—aircraft builders and all others—must develop cultures that value and reinforce safety. Safety has to be part of the work ethic; safety management is a continuous process, and companies must develop a total safety culture. However, many industrial accidents occur despite attempts to protect workers' safety. Human factors psychologists can help reduce accidents through design improvements and can also help estimate how quickly people become fatigued and then design work schedules that optimize the safe use of potentially dangerous equipment. Such psychologists can help promote safety through programs that improve people's attitudes about safety and therefore promote safer work behavior. Only when workers believe that the company values their safety are they likely to make safety-promoting changes.

It is often easier to design a safe, or nearly safe, work environment than to influence workers to work safely. Researchers classify efforts to design safe work environments into three categories (Sanders & McCormick, 1993): *exclusion designs* make it impossible for a specific error to occur; *prevention designs* make it difficult though not impossible for an error to happen; *fail-safe designs* do not reduce the likelihood of an error, but do lessen its consequences should it occur. For a nuclear power plant, for example, human factors psychologists might develop prevention designs that greatly decrease the likelihood of an accident. To ensure safe work environments, the federal government enacted the Occupational Safety and Health Act (OSHA), which established standards for health and safety in the workplace. These standards function as prevention designs. Workers must accept safety standards before they can be effective, and the government does not have adequate staff to regulate, enforce, or inspect all places of business. Since OSHA was enacted in 1971, however, the death rate from workplace accidents has been cut in half.

While very few people are actually killed in accidents involving airplanes, these accidents receive significant media attention. When a team of researchers looked into the causes of crash circumstances (Li et al., 2002), they found that psychological factors were very important. Pilot error was a contributing factor in 73% of the crashes involving younger pilots and in 69% of the crashes involving older pilots. Overall, 23% of pilot errors were attributable to inattentiveness, 20% to flawed decisions, 18% to mishandled judgments of the forces of wind on the aircraft, and 18% to mishandled wind/runway conditions.

Research in several other subdisciplines of psychology has also helped establish and maintain workplace safety—in airplanes, auto factories, or insurance companies. *Perceptual research* investigates topics such as appropriate light levels for reading computer screens. Which color is most visible in the dark? (Yellow.) Is it easier to see white letters on a dark background, or the reverse? (White letters on dark backgrounds are easier.) *Environmental research* focuses on variables such as temperature and noise. When the temperature or noise level is too high, performance decreases. Moderate temperatures and noise levels improve both efficiency and safety. Warnings, labels, and compliance techniques are also helpful in establishing safety. Environmental research reveals that signs and warnings help motivate people to follow regulations. Specific instructions for a specific user—for example, using that person's name as part of the instructions—work better still (Elliott, Armitage, & Baughan, 2003). A warning label is especially effective when the user has to remove it before using a machine. Even when people are given specific warnings about equipment safety and clear directions, incentives and proper reinforcements boost their compliance; the use of social influence and reinforcements to induce worthwhile and helpful behaviors is the domain of social and learning psychologists.

In the workplace and elsewhere, the laws that govern society help regulate both public and private behavior. People's thoughts and behaviors shape laws, and laws in turn shape people's behaviors; there is a reciprocal relationship between the two.

How Do Psychology and the Law Work Together?

Most people have few reasons to be in a courtroom. Yet we read courtroom dramas in John Grisham novels, watch movie stars such as Tom Cruise portray lawyers in films like *A Few Good Men*, and are big fans of TV shows featuring lawyers, such as *Law and Order* or reruns of *Ally McBeal*. In any media portrayal like these, the attorney tends to use a mix of psychology and the law to win cases.

The interaction between the fields of psychology and law has increased greatly over the past few decades. *Forensic psychology* is the study of the integration of psychology and the law and focuses on such topics as the insanity defense, competence to stand trial, and commitment to mental hospitals. Forensic psychology is an interesting career choice that usually requires a PhD or a PsyD in clinical psychology with a concentration in forensic psychology. With such training, forensic psychologists perform a number of tasks, including these:

Forensic psychology ■
The study of the integration of psychology and the law, focusing on such topics as the insanity defense and competence to stand trial.

- Evaluate and testify about a defendant's competency to waive rights to confess (Miranda rights)
- Evaluate and testify on sanity and insanity issues
- Determine the impact of intoxication on mental abilities
- Provide evidence on death penalty issues
- Assess family members for parental fitness
- Assess child abuse
- Assess individuals' competency to enter into and carry out legal contracts
- Administer and evaluate neuropsychological inventories

Forensic psychologists might help a judge decide which parent should have custody of a child or might evaluate an accident victim to determine if he or she suffered psychological or neurological damage. Some forensic psychologists counsel prison inmates; others counsel the victims of crimes and help them prepare to testify, cope with emotional distress, and resume their normal activities. Forensic psychologists also conduct empirical research on psychological issues that have an impact on the legal system, such as eyewitness accuracy, selection of law enforcement personnel, decision making in juries, and assumptions about human behavior relevant to the legal rights of defendants, victims, children, and mental patients.

Psychologists in the Legal System

Psychologists play several roles in the legal system: researchers, policy or program evaluators, advocates, and expert witnesses. As *researchers,* they look at legal issues from a psychological perspective (for example, how juries decide cases) and at psychological questions in a legal context (for example, how jurors assign blame or responsibility for a crime). They also help determine why individuals behave in ways that are unacceptable to society; for instance, they do basic research on intelligence, personality, and the role of genetics in determining aggressiveness. This basic research often helps solve practical problems. For example, some researchers look for the causes of aggressiveness in order to develop programs to avert it or to help people channel their aggressive impulses productively. Others develop tests to determine who is mentally ill or to evaluate the truthfulness and integrity of defendants and witnesses.

Psychologists often serve as *policy or program evaluators,* helping governments and other institutions determine whether various policies, agencies, or programs actually work. For example, psychologists assess what remedial education has accomplished and interpret whether IQ testing has been valid. When legislators wondered whether Head Start programs were making a difference, they turned to psychologists. When new laws calling for equal educational opportunities for handicapped people were being considered, lawyers and judges turned to psychologists for insight into how well various proposed programs might work. Psychologists advise government agencies at all levels on how to help those who suffer from anxiety, fear, grief, and even posttraumatic stress after a natural disaster or other traumatic events such as airplane crashes and terrorist attacks. They also advise on how to respond more effectively to such disasters in the future.

Psychologists are also often asked to be *advocates,* helping to shape social policy on issues such as education of the gifted and remedial education. When state and federal governments trim budgets for social programs affecting children, they turn to psychologists to ascertain what the impact of such acts might be. Boards of education consult psychologists to determine how best to mainstream students with disabilities (Köhnken, Fiedler, & Möhlenbeck, 2004).

Finally, psychologists often serve as *expert witnesses,* bringing their knowledge to courtrooms. They do not try to address legal issues directly or to make decisions for the courts. Rather, they offer help in their area of competence—psychology. Psychologists might be asked to determine who is a good eyewitness (we examined this topic in Chapter 9). They also address specific questions: Is this person insane? What are the implications of a divorce for this child? Is this woman competent to stand trial? Psychologists can help determine whether there is a link between a person's mental state or mental disorder and the crime the person committed (Brogdon, Adams, & Bahri, 2004; Köhnken et al., 2004). From a legal standpoint, a person who deliberately plans a crime is more accountable for it than one who accidentally commits one. In many states, for example, Pennsylvania and South Carolina, when an accused person is convicted of a serious crime, a jury can judge the person "guilty, but mentally ill." (In fact, a person can even plead "guilty, but mentally ill.") This verdict is seen by many as a reasonable alternative to the verdict "not guilty by reason of insanity" (a finding that many find unsatisfying); it encourages treatment for people with serious mental illness and takes a potentially dangerous offender off the street (Roesch, Viljoen, & Hui, 2004). There is a widespread belief that criminals are getting off left and right, but the truth is that very few people are judged not guilty by reason of insanity. Those who are mentally ill need treatment; otherwise, we as a society face the risk of their becoming repeat offenders (Walker & Shapiro, 2003).

Psychologists may also be hired as expert witnesses by individuals who sue their employers. In this capacity, they help an aggrieved individual establish that an employer engaged in bias, discrimination, unfair practices, or some combination of these. They may question the validity of a particular employment criterion (such as attractiveness and youthfulness for flight attendants). Of course, employers hire their own expert witnesses. In court, these I/O psychologists testify to the validity, reliability, and predictability of various tests and selection procedures, including polygraphs (which we know are unreliable and often wrong) (Oksol & O'Donohue, 2004).

Crime and Punishment

An example of an issue that links psychology and the law directly is whether severe punishment is a deterrent to violent crime—especially whether capital punishment deters murder. The majority of countries in Western Europe, North America, and South America—more than 95 nations worldwide—have abandoned capital punishment. In contrast, support for capital punishment for convicted murderers has grown in the United States since the 1960s (Baer, 2001), and "three-strikes" laws for repeat felons have become increasingly common at the state level. These get-tough approaches have resulted in a growing U.S. prison population, as more criminals are jailed than ever before (Moss, 2001; Shaw et al., 1998). In 2003, 65 inmates were executed in the United States, 6 fewer than in 2002.

The murder rate in the United States was at its lowest in 35 years in 2001: 5.5 per 100,000 people. Also, annual murder rates in states with the death penalty are significantly higher than those in states that have abolished it. For example, in 1993, the murder rate per 100,000 residents was 9.35 for states with the death penalty and 5.22 for states without the death penalty. In 1997, the average murder rate in states without the death penalty was 3.5 per 100,000 residents; in Texas (with capital punishment), the rate was nearly twice that, at 6.8 per 100,000 residents. When researchers examined states that had capital punishment, abolished it, and then reinstated it, the results were identical—the annual murder rates were higher when the death penalty was in force. In the states that instituted capital punishment after the Supreme Court reaffirmed it in 1976, homicide rates have gone up (Lester, 2000).

The fact is that most murders are crimes of passion—committed because of rage, hatred, or jealousy. Psychologists try to help legislators and courts understand that deterrence of violent crime through capital punishment depends on uncertain assumptions. Interestingly, Acker (1993) argues that the courts have often ignored such research studies. One faulty assumption is that capital punishment actually deters crime (e.g., Bailey & Peterson, 1999); another is that violent criminals will view the possibility of execution in the future as a substantially harsher punishment than life imprisonment. A final faulty assumption is that harsh sentencing of criminals is a deterrent when evidence suggests that sentencing is unrelated to deterrence and that individual sentencing decisions seemed driven mostly by jurors' and judges' wanting criminals to get their "just desserts" (Carlsmith, Darley, & Robinson, 2002). In the end, there is consensus among criminologists and psychologists that the death penalty does little to lessen rates of violence.

The Law and Psychology: An Uneasy Partnership

Psychology deals with human behavior and mental process; the legal system is the means by which society tries to live in an orderly fashion. But these two disciplines overlap on a broad array of social issues. For example, the law helps establish boundaries for the ethical treatment of elders. There is far too much elder abuse in the United States (Henderson, Varable, & Buchanan, 2004). The law and psychology also partner in trying to reduce child abuse and neglect (Azar & Olsen, 2004). They collaborate in determining who should be committed involuntarily to mental hospitals (Johnson, 2004) and how to evaluate youths in the juvenile justice system (Otto & Borum, 2004).

But this partnership is an uneasy one. The psychologists who conduct research on controversial social issues such as capital punishment are, to be sure, in the eye of a storm. Most people's views on capital punishment—and other similar issues— are informed by religious beliefs, anecdotal experiences, media portrayals, and common sense. Psychologists try to provide the judicial system with data and theory to make predictions about crime and criminals a more exact process. Lawyers assert that psychology is an inexact, or "fuzzy," science and that psychologists should not be allowed to testify as expert witnesses. Psychologists argue that lawyers want simple answers to complicated human questions. For example, in a divorce case, a clinical psychologist might be asked to testify as to which of the parents should have custody of the children and what the psychological consequences of living with one parent or the other would be. Yet because the legal system is adversarial, each side is likely to have its own psychologist testifying that the children will do best with that parent. In fact, there may be no right or wrong answer in some cases. Unfortunately, the legal system cannot generally tolerate such ambiguity.

What Are the Goals of Sport Psychology?

Rick Ankiel is one of the best left-handed pitchers in baseball. He's especially tough against left-handed hitters, who hit only one homer off him in 95 at-bats in a recent season. He received a $2.5 million bonus for signing with the Cardinals. In his 20s, he is young, athletic, and focused on one thing and one thing only—winning. But Ankiel isn't always consistent. In one playoff game, he threw five wild pitches in one inning—a record. Ankiel has had to put a bad season and a couple of really bad games behind him. He now realizes it's all about attitude. Ankiel "got his groove back" after some rest, relaxation with family, and a lot of talking about the game. He has been heard to say "Let's turn the page"—meaning "Let's move on." Confident that everything will come up fastballs, he is going to focus on each day, one day at a time—and not ponder the past or what went wrong.

Psychologists know that Rick Ankiel is right. Top performance in sports has a lot to do with attitude—and preparation, skill, and a little luck. But having a proper frame of mind turns out to be a key component of athletic success. In using a mental strategy to improve his performance, Ankiel is applying the principles of sport psychology.

Sport psychology is the systematic application of psychological principles to several aspects of sports. Sport psychologists are interested in how participating in sports or any physical activity may enhance a person's well-being. These psychologists work to help athletes in a number of areas: First and foremost, they help *improve sports performance*. In general, performance may be enhanced through mental strategies that either refine the effective performers or help ineffective performers overcome obstacles. Second, sport psychologists try to *enhance the sports experience for young participants*. Third, they provide *assistance with injury rehabilitation*.

Sport psychologists, like any psychologists, recognize that athletic performance is a matter of behavior and is affected by the individual athlete, the athlete's team, the team leader or coach, and the environment in which these individuals interact. The characteristics of athlete, team, coach, and environment are multidimensional. People's personal characteristics, how they interact with others, and how the environment affects them are all influenced by past events, relationships, and successes or failures. Nevertheless, sport psychologists have tried to bring some order to the study of athletic performance.

To obtain certification from the Association for the Advancement of Applied Sport Psychology, an individual may be trained primarily in the sport sciences with additional training in counseling or clinical psychology *or* primarily in clinical psychology with supplemental training in the sport sciences. Sport psychologists study the behaviors associated with sports in the traditional ways that psychologists go about things: some do basic research on athletic performance; others take an educational role, teaching about sport psychology; still others are applied practitioners who help athletes overcome obstacles to achieve their highest potential. Researchers consider a whole range of topics associated with athletic performance, among which are those we consider here: motivation, activation and arousal, anxiety and performance, and intervention strategies (Cox, Qiu, & Liu, 1993).

Sport psychology ■ The systematic application of psychological principles to several aspects of sports.

Arousal and Athletic Performance

The discussion of motivation in Chapter 12 revealed that, with moderate levels of arousal and moderately difficult tasks, as arousal increased, performance improved. Arousal is generally viewed as stimulation and excitement—a performance enhancer. But excessive levels of arousal are associated with poor performance. Yerkes and Dodson characterized such a learning curve as an inverted U (see Chapter 12 for a review of the Yerkes–Dodson principle). You don't need to be a psychologist to recognize that when people are extremely frightened or nervous, performance suffers. This is certainly true in sports; dozens of research studies have shown that being aroused improves athletic performance—but only up to a point.

The inverted U relationship between arousal and performance is not always consistent, especially in sports situations that involve intensive cognitive activity, such as quarterbacking in football or catching in baseball. Researchers know that for every increase in a person's arousal, a corresponding increase (or decrease) in performance is not necessarily evident. A small increase in arousal can push some people "over the top" to acute anxiety and poor performance. Young children are less affected by pressure; older children, in contrast, think about options ("Our second baseman doesn't catch very well, so it makes more sense to throw to first") and are more affected by pressure (French, Spurgeon, & Nevett, 1995). How then is arousal distinct from anxiety?

Anxiety and Athletic Performance

Think back to Rick Ankiel, the terrific left-handed pitcher. Ankiel recognizes that it is never good to overtrain or overanalyze, either physiologically or psychologically—such overtraining can lead to intense anxiety (Kreider, Fry, & O'Toole, 1998). When an athlete is tense and apprehensive, and such feelings are associated with arousal, the athlete is experiencing anxiety. Some people, including some athletes, feel this way most of the time—trait personality theorists would say that such people have a strong, or dominant, anxiety trait. A whole range of tests has been developed to measure anxiety in athletes and to discern whether anxiety is related to specific events or is a trait of a given athlete.

Unlike weekend athletes, those who participate in sports occasionally or just for exercise or enjoyment, competitive athletes often reach their peak of anxiety significantly before an athletic event begins, and their level of anxiety may diminish immediately before the event. As they step up to the plate or onto the court or field, professional athletes often become cool, collected, and in control. Three hours earlier, they may have felt overwhelmed by their anxiety, but when they have to perform, it is gone.

If the relationship between anxiety and performance were predictable, psychologists wouldn't be quite so interested in precompetitive anxiety. But like so many other psychological phenomena, anxiety is affected by many aspects of a person's life (Ferraro, 2001). If an athlete's arousal exceeds the level needed for effective performance, anxiety can take over. Similarly, an underaroused athlete may also become anxious and stay that way throughout an event. So arousal and anxiety are hard to separate. But a separation can be achieved through good intervention strategies.

Intervention Strategies for Athletes

When an athlete's level of anxiety is sufficiently high that arousal leads to lower performance, certain interventions can help relieve the anxiety. Stress management approaches described in Chapter 15 have proved to be effective. There are a broad array of such anxiety-reducing techniques (Humara, 2001).

One widely used technique is *progressive relaxation*, in which athletes are taught to relax slowly and progressively. Relaxation of individual muscles, focusing on progressively larger muscle groups, is the goal. Typically, the trainer or psychologist instructs the person to relax in steps: to relax the limbs, to feel heaviness or warmth in the arms and legs, to feel a reduced heart rate, and to sense coolness on the forehead.

Hypnosis, which can facilitate uncritical acceptance of suggestions, has been widely used to help athletes achieve deep relaxation, as well as to help them focus their energy and attention. Closely associated with hypnosis is *meditation*, a technique that can help an athlete relax and focus. Meditation involves focusing one's attention on a single thought, idea, sound, or object. (Although hypnosis and meditation can help athletes relax and focus, they will never make a bad athlete into a good one.) Closely associated with meditation are the physical and mental techniques involved in yoga. Practitioners of yoga claim that it is capable of causing profound physiological and psychological changes. When Phil Jackson was head coach of the Chicago Bulls, he made his players attend yoga sessions!

Using *mental imagery* to promote relaxation has been shown to be worthwhile in many sports activities and combining mental imagery with other relaxation strategies has proved especially effective (Murphy & Jowdy, 1992). Athletes also use mental imagery to "psyche themselves up" or to practice a sports activity mentally.

Cognitive interventions that focus on changing thought patterns about a sport, an event, one's abilities, or one's strategies have been especially helpful to some athletes (Boutcher, 1992). Cognitive strategies often combine education about aspects of the sport with training in relaxation, such as thinking calm thoughts just before a pole vault. Cognitive interventions may teach athletes to think positively, to block out distractions, and to focus on the one part of their body that is crucial in their sport (Eubank, Collins, & Smith, 2000).

Putting It Together: Go with the Flow

In Chapter 13, we discussed the concept of flow. *Flow* occurs when a person becomes totally engrossed in overcoming a challenge. It occurs when people are deeply engaged in an activity that they enjoy. For athletes, flow resembles what many call "being in the zone." Mihaly Csikszentmihalyi (1997) argued that there is a relationship between experience and performance, especially in competitive sports. That is, there is a balance between an athlete's perception and her or his skill; there is also a merging of the athlete's actions and awareness. An athlete experiencing flow receives unambiguous feedback, is better able to concentrate, and develops not only confidence but momentum. All of this leads to a loss of self-consciousness and a sense that the sports event takes place in "a split second." Flow is more likely when the sports event has intrinsic value to the athlete (Jackson & Csikszentmihalyi, 1999). As Seligman and Csikszentmihalyi (2000) argue, sport psychology attempts to adapt what is best about the scientific method and to apply scientific knowledge to the problems of athletes. They assert that sport psychology can help athletes transform their performance and experience flow, and then achieve success through complete engagement with their various sports activities.

The Future of Sport Psychology

As sport psychologists gain a stronger sense of the variables that affect athletic performance, they will develop more comprehensive theories to help explain success in various sports. Sport psychologists will begin to specialize, focusing on areas such as motivation, personality variables, coaching, specific behavioral training, relaxation, imagery, and aggression. Since people all over the world play sports, there will be significant growth in cross-cultural research in sport psychology. Environments and cultural expectations in various countries shape athletic performance in different ways. For example, Chinese athletes see the causes of their failures as being more internal and controllable than do German athletes (Si, Rethorst, & Willimczik, 1995). Researchers need to understand how factors such as locus of control (discussed in Chapter 13) operate in sports, how the family environment affects an athlete's development, and how such factors vary crossculturally (Hellstedt, 1995). Such research may begin to reveal why Russian athletes are such wonderful ice dancers, why Canadians play hockey so well, and why rugby and soccer are not the national sports of the United States. Sport psychologists also need to pay attention to ethical issues, for example, limiting college athletes to a certain number of hours of practice per week, as specified by the NCAA (Moore, 2003). The field has many challenges ahead.

Summary and Review

HOW IS BEHAVIOR AFFECTED BY THE WORK ENVIRONMENT?

What is industrial/organizational psychology?

Industrial/organizational (I/O) psychology is the study of how individual behavior is affected by the work environment, coworkers, and organizational practices. I/O psychologists study broad areas: human resources, motivation of job performance, job satisfaction, teamwork, and leadership. pp. 683–685

How are job analyses, selection procedures, and training used in today's workplaces?

The functional job analysis and the position analysis questionnaire are instruments that have been developed by I/O psychologists for *job analyses*. All such analyses are intended to help ensure that jobs are well defined and doable. Two important tasks of an I/O psychologist are to balance the scope and complexity of jobs and to help employers create jobs that will be motivating. pp. 685–686

Selection procedures are means of evaluating job candidates in order to help an employer determine which ones to hire. Application forms, interviews, samples of work, and ability tests are some of the instruments used in employee selection. Training is the process by which organizations systematically teach employees skills to improve their job performance. pp. 686–690

What is a performance appraisal?

A *performance appraisal* is a process whereby a supervisor periodically evaluates the job-relevant strengths and weaknesses of subordinates. The problem with performance appraisals is that they are often done inaccurately by people with few evaluative skills and with few diagnostic aids. Multiple performance criteria must enter into an appraisal. pp. 690–691

How have I/O psychologists helped employees motivate workers?

I/O psychologists help employers find ways to motivate employees to be more productive. *Goal-setting theory* asserts that setting specific, clear, attainable goals for a given task leads to better performance. pp. 692–694

Expectancy theories assert that a worker's effort and desire to work are determined by expectations about the outcome of the work. Vroom suggested that work motivation is determined by expectancy (the belief that hard or extra work will lead to good or improved performance); instrumentality (the belief that good performance will be rewarded); and valence (the value put on rewards that are offered). Lawler and Porter contended that performance is determined by ability, effort, and role perceptions—the ways people believe they should be doing their jobs. p. 694

The view that what people bring to a work situation should be balanced by what they receive there compared to others constitutes *equity theory*. Thus, workers' input (what they do) should be reflected in the rewards they receive. If input is not balanced with compensation, people will adjust their work input accordingly. pp. 695–697

I/O psychologists have identified three basic approaches to motivation management: paternalistic, behavioral, and participatory. pp. 697–698

What determines job satisfaction?

There are many sources of job satisfaction, including the work itself, the perceived rewards of the work, the quality of supervision, the support of coworkers, and the work setting. The overall level of satisfaction depends on the extent to which people's expectations are matched by their actual feelings. pp. 698–700

What is the role of teams in the workplace?

Teams are groups of two or more people who work together toward some common goal. The idea behind teams is that many tasks require the skills and abilities of more than one person. Today, companies are relying on teams of workers to accomplish a wide array of tasks. p. 701

What makes a good leader?

A leader is a person who influences other people's behavior toward the attainment of agreed-upon goals. Business leaders can be employee-oriented or task-oriented; the situation is a key determinant of which type of leader will be more effective. A *transactional leader* seeks to motivate others by appealing to their self-interest and tends to focus on performance outcomes. *Transformational leaders*—charismatic leaders who inspire and provide intellectual stimulation and individual attention—can transform an organization. pp. 701–706

HOW DO HUMAN FACTORS AFFECT PERFORMANCE?

Describe the field of human factors.

Human factors is the study of the relationship of human beings to machines and to workplaces and other environments. It focuses on the fit between human anatomy or physiology, the demands of a particular task or piece of equipment, and the environment in which the task occurs. Human factors research can help design work environments that are both efficient and safe. Warnings, labels, and compliance techniques are all helpful in improving safety. pp. 707–708

What is behavior-based safety?

Behavior-based safety refers to effective safety management through a wide range of programs that focus on changing the behavior of workers *and* companies to prevent occupational injuries and illnesses. pp. 708–710

HOW DO PSYCHOLOGY AND THE LAW WORK TOGETHER?

Forensic psychology is the study of the interaction of psychology and the law. As researchers, forensic psychologists help determine why individuals behave in ways that are unacceptable to society. Psychologists also act as policy or program evaluators, helping governments and other institutions determine whether various policies, agencies, or programs actually work. Psychologists work as advocates for individuals and society, helping shape social policy in areas such as remedial and gifted education. Finally, psychologists often serve as expert witnesses, bringing their knowledge to court as consultants. pp. 710–713

WHAT ARE THE GOALS OF SPORT PSYCHOLOGY?

What is sport psychology?

Sport psychology is the systematic application of psychological principles to several aspects of sports. Sport psychologists recognize that athletic performance is affected by the athlete, the team, the leader or coach, and the environment. pp. 713–714

Sport psychologists study factors such as level of arousal and have found that the inverted U-shape relationship between arousal and performance identified by Yerkes and Dodson is not always consistent in sports; that is, as arousal increases, athletic performance may or may not increase or decrease smoothly. When anxiety is too high and arousal lowers performance, interventions can help lower arousal and relieve anxiety. pp. 714–715

Identify some intervention strategies that can help athletes improve their performance.

One widely used technique to improve sports performance is progressive relaxation, in which athletes are taught to relax muscles slowly and progressively. Another technique, hypnosis, has been widely used to help athletes achieve deep relaxation, as well as to help them focus their energy and attention. Closely associated with hypnosis is meditation, which can also help athletes relax. Last, mental imagery to promote relaxation and focus is worthwhile in many sports activities. pp. 715–716

Statistical Methods

How Do Psychologists Use Descriptive Statistics? p. 720
    Organizing Data: Frequency Distributions
    Measures of Central Tendency
    Measures of Variability
    The Normal Distribution
    Correlation

How Do Psychologists Use Inferential Statistics? p. 736
    Significant Differences
    Testing Group Differences

Statistics ■ The branch of mathematics that deals with classifying and analyzing data.

Clearly, scientific progress is linked to researchers' ability to measure and quantify observations—that is, to collect data in the form of numbers. Large collections of numbers can be very confusing, and the data that researchers gather are not useful without some interpretation. *Statistics* is the branch of mathematics that deals with classifying and analyzing data. Although we examined the basics of statistics and statistical thinking in Chapter 2, this appendix presents a fuller exploration.

To understand behavior, psychologists use a number of different methods for investigation (discussed in detail in Chapter 2); then, they use statistics to describe, summarize, interpret, and present their results. The statistics that psychologists use consist of two different types: descriptive and inferential statistics.

How Do Psychologists Use Descriptive Statistics?

Descriptive statistics ■ A set of mathematical procedures used to summarize, condense, and describe sets of data.

Psychologists use *descriptive statistics* to organize their data by summarizing, condensing, and describing sets of numbers. Descriptive statistics make it possible to understand important factors about data. For example, your professors use descriptive statistics to interpret exam results. A statistical description of a 100-point midterm exam may show that 10% of a class scored more than 60 points, 70% scored between 40 and 60 points, and 20% scored fewer than 40 points. On the basis of this statistical description, the professor might conclude that the test was very difficult and adjust the grading so that anyone who earned 61 points or more receives an A (rather than the standard grading scale of 90 points or more). But, before the professor can make conclusions or assign grades, the exam scores must be organized in a meaningful way.

Organizing Data: Frequency Distributions

An educational psychologist was interested in study habits and grades in college. She selected 80 students for her study—20 students each from psychology, chemistry, art, and nursing majors—obtained their consent and cooperation, and asked them to furnish information about their study habits and techniques as well as their grades. She asked all 80 students to keep a record for a week of several behaviors related to school, including how many class meetings they missed and how many hours they studied or did schoolwork outside of class. Here is a list of the numbers of hours of studying or schoolwork reported by the 80 students for the week:

It's very difficult to get any overall impression from this set of numbers, partly

11	18	5	9	22	11	9	7	15	10
15	17	6	10	4	4	5	8	8	8
10	10	13	12	15	9	4	3	9	13
10	5	6	12	8	2	14	12	6	9
8	4	10	7	14	13	7	4	10	17
11	13	16	7	15	11	9	11	16	8
14	7	10	10	12	8	11	12	7	6
9	10	19	18	9	8	5	7	9	14

because they are not organized. So, the first step in interpreting these numbers is to arrange them in an array, organized from the highest to the lowest and showing how many times each number occurs. This type of organization, shown in Table A.1, is known as a *frequency distribution.*

The frequency distribution allows the educational psychologist who collected these data to see a pattern. As the frequency distribution in Table A.1 shows, very few students fell at the extremes, and many are in the middle. Ten students reported that they studied 10 hours during this particular week—the most frequent number of hours reported by this group of students. However, some students studied a great deal more, and others spent less time on studying.

Another way to see the pattern in these numbers is to construct a graph, and researchers often construct graphs from the data in frequency distributions. One type of graph they use is a bar graph, called a *histogram.* To construct a histogram of the frequency distribution of hours spent studying for the 80 college students, the data are plotted on two dimensions: One dimension, represented on the horizontal axis (or *abscissa*), consists of categories that represent the numbers of hours spent studying. The frequency for each category, or score, is the number of students who studied for that number of hours; this frequency is represented on the vertical axis (the *ordinate*). Figure A.1 (on p. 723) shows a histogram of the data from the frequency distribution in Table A.1.

Frequency distribution
■ An array of scores, usually arranged from the highest to the lowest, showing the number of instances for each score.

Histogram ■ A bar graph that displays the data in a frequency distribution.

Table A.1

A FREQUENCY DISTRIBUTION OF THE NUMBER OF HOURS STUDIED IN A WEEK BY 80 COLLEGE STUDENTS

Number of Hours of Studying	Individuals Studying for That Number of Hours	Total Numbers of Individuals
2	I	1
3	I	1
4	I I I I I	5
5	I I I I	4
6	I I I I	4
7	I I I I I I I	7
8	I I I I I I I I	8
9	I I I I I I I I I	9
10	I I I I I I I I I I	10
11	I I I I I I	6
12	I I I I I	5
13	I I I I	4
14	I I I I	4
15	I I I I	4
16	I I	2
17	I I	2
18	I I	2
19	I	1
22	I	1
		80

Note that few individuals score very high or very low—most score in the middle range.

Frequency polygon ■ Graph of a frequency distribution that shows the range of scores obtained and the number of instances of each score, usually with the data points connected by straight lines.

Another possibility for graphing such data is a *frequency polygon,* which also shows the range of possible results, or scores, and the frequency of each score. In a frequency polygon, the points are connected by lines rather than represented by bars. Figure A.2 (on p. 724) shows a frequency polygon of the data on college students' hours of studying.

These visual representations provide a way of condensing the data into a form that is easier to understand. For further interpretation of these data, the psychologist would probably also compute a measure of central tendency and a measure of variability.

Measure of central tendency ■ A descriptive statistic that tells which score best represents an entire set of scores.

Measures of Central Tendency

A descriptive statistic that tells which score best represents an entire set of scores is a *measure of central tendency.* It is a way to summarize data—all the numbers in the distribution are condensed into one number. Also, because almost every group has members who score higher or lower than the rest of the group, researchers often use a measure of central tendency to describe the group *as a whole*.

People often use the word *average* in a casual way. A woman asks a clerk to help her find a sweater for her "average-sized" husband. A man boasts that his new car "averages" 40 miles per gallon. A doctor tells her patient that his serum cholesterol level is "average" because it is in neither the low nor the high range. In each of these cases, the person is using *average* to depict a type of norm, and others understand what the person means, even though not all of these examples are technically "averages."

Consider this statement: Psychology majors make better grades than chemistry majors. Because you know that some chemistry majors make better grades than some psychology majors, you assume that the statement means: *On the average,* psychology majors make better grades than chemistry majors. In other words, comparing the grade point averages of all psychology majors and all chemistry majors in

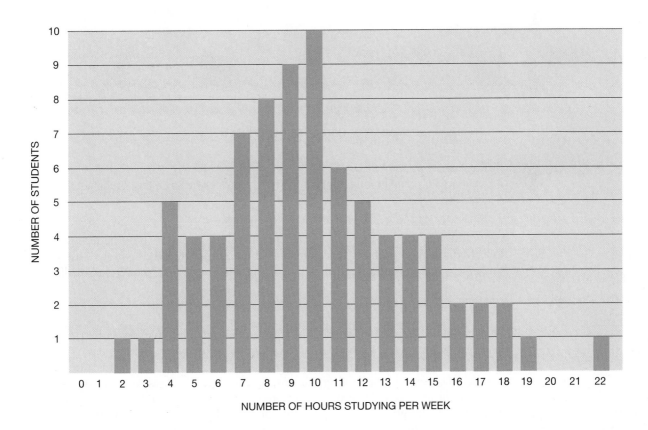

Figure A.1
A Histogram Showing Hours of Studying per Week for 80 College Students.

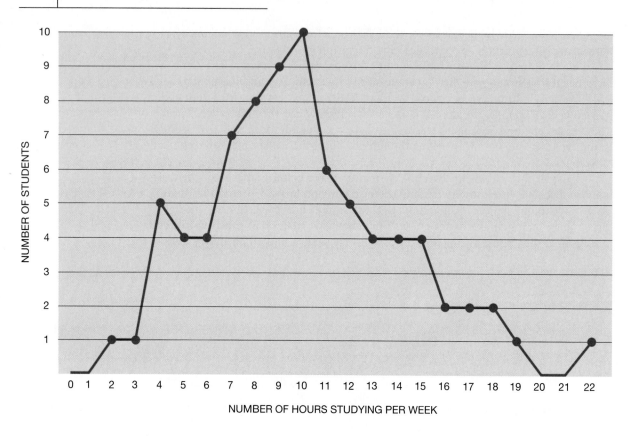

Figure A.2
A Frequency Polygon Showing Hours of Studying per Week by 80 College Students.

the world would show that, *on the average*, psychology majors have better grades. Let's find a way to evaluate this statement about grades by looking more closely at three measures of central tendency: mean (arithmetic average), mode, and median.

Mean

How could a researcher investigate the truth of the statement that psychology majors get better grades? One way would be to obtain the grade point averages (GPAs) of thousands of psychology majors and thousands of chemistry majors, being careful to sample each geographical area, ethnic group, and gender. The researcher could then calculate the average GPA of psychology majors in the sample and plot the results on a graph. The educational psychologist of our example took a sample of 20 (rather than thousands of) students from several majors. Table A.2 lists GPAs from those students, focusing on the psychology and chemistry majors. For each of these groups, the GPAs were added together and divided by the number of people in the group. The resulting number is the *mean*, or *arithmetic average*, the measure of central tendency

Mean ■ The measure of central tendency that is calculated by dividing the sum of the scores by the total number of scores; also known as the *arithmetic average*.

Table A.2

CALCULATION OF MEAN GRADE POINT AVERAGE FOR 20 PSYCHOLOGY AND 20 CHEMISTRY MAJORS

Psychology Majors		Chemistry Majors	
Brandon	2.0	Jay	1.8
Cyndi	2.2	Rob	2.0
Wyatt	2.3	Jesse	2.0
Mauri	2.5	Pam	2.1
Tonya	2.7	Pat	2.2
Marg	3.0	Duncan	2.5
Kendra	3.0	Gayla	2.5
Diane	3.2	Dorry	2.7
Anne	3.2	Laurette	2.8
Mike	3.2	Trey	2.9
Brenda	3.2	Deené	2.9
Tiffany	3.3	Jamie	3.0
Rosita	3.3	Cinamon	3.0
Brad	3.4	Miquel	3.0
Chris	3.4	James	3.2
Gwen	3.5	Iris	3.2
Tonio	3.5	Florette	3.4
Christine	3.6	Aaron	3.5
Koren	3.7	Darin	3.6
Toni	3.8	Constance	3.7
	$\overline{62}$		$\overline{56}$

Mean GPA: $\dfrac{\Sigma S}{N} = \dfrac{62}{20} = 3.1$ $\qquad$ Mean GPA: $\dfrac{\Sigma S}{N} = \dfrac{56}{20} = 2.8$

Overall mean GPA: $\dfrac{\Sigma S}{N} = \dfrac{118}{40} = 2.95$

Note: ΣS means the sum of all the scores; N is the number of scores.

calculated by dividing the sum of scores (the total of all GPAs) by the total number of scores (in this case, the number of psychology majors or chemistry majors). The mean GPA is higher for the psychology than for the chemistry majors.

The mean is the most frequently used measure of central tendency, but not the only one, and other measures of central tendency may yield somewhat different results.

Mode

Another statistic used to describe the central tendency of a set of data is the mode. The *mode* is the most frequently observed data point. Table A.3 (on p. 726) shows the

Mode ■ The measure of central tendency that is the most frequently observed data point.

Table A.3

CALCULATING THE MODE FOR GPAS OF PSYCHOLOGY AND CHEMISTRY MAJORS

1.8	I
2.0	III
2.1	I
2.2	II
2.3	I
2.5	III
2.7	II
2.8	I
2.9	II
3.0	IIIII
3.2	IIIIII—Mode
3.3	II
3.4	III
3.5	III
3.6	II
3.7	II
3.8	I

Median ■ The measure of central tendency that is the data point with 50% of all the observations (scores) above it and 50% below it.

Variability ■ The extent to which scores differ from one another, or especially from the mean.

Range ■ A measure of variability that describes the spread between the highest and the lowest scores in a distribution.

frequencies of all the GPAs from Table A.2. It shows, for example, that only one person has a GPA of 1.8 or 3.8, five have 3.0, and six have 3.2. Therefore, the mode of the GPAs is 3.2. Looking back at Table A.2, find the mode for the psychology majors and the mode for the chemistry majors. Are they the same? Does comparing the modes for the two groups reveal the same pattern as examining the means?

Median

The *median* is the 50% point in a distribution of data. Half the observations (or scores) fall above the median, and the other half fall below it. You have probably read news reports that refer to medians, for example: "According to the U.S. Census Bureau, the median family income in United States rose to $36,000 this year." What this statement means is that half of American families earned more than $36,000 and half earned less.

Table A.4 presents all the GPAs from Table A.2 arranged from lowest to highest. It shows that half fall above 3.0 and half fall below 3.0. The median of this data set, therefore, is 3.0. Looking back at Table A.2, find the median GPA for the psychology majors and for the chemistry majors. How do these numbers compare with the mode and the mean for each of these groups?

Table A.5 (on p. 728) presents the entire set of data gathered by the educational psychologist, with the nursing and art majors added to the psychology and chemistry majors, and shows computation of the mean and median GPA for all four groups. The psychology and art majors have the same mean GPA (3.1), the nursing majors' mean GPA is a little lower (3.0), and the chemistry majors' mean GPA is the lowest (2.8) of the four groups. The medians show a pattern similar to that of the means, but the values of the two statistics are not the same. The art majors have the highest median GPA (3.35), followed by the psychology majors (3.2). The nursing majors' median GPA (3.0) is the same as their mean GPA. The median GPA for chemistry majors (2.9) is the lowest of the medians, but it is higher than the group's mean.

The differences between median and mean scores occur because mean scores are influenced by extreme scores, whereas median scores are not. The median discounts very high and very low scores. For example, if an art major was on the way to flunking out and had a GPA of 1.0, that low score would affect the mean for the art majors but not the median. It would bring down the mean for the entire group but leave the median unaffected. The fact that the mean is sensitive to all scores and the median is not may be either an advantage or a disadvantage, depending on the researcher's goals in using these descriptive statistics.

Each measure of central tendency tells something about the typical person, score, or data item in a set. You might use the mean if you had to guess the height of a woman you had never met; a good guess would be the mean, or average, height for women. However, if you were a buyer for a clothing store and had to pick one dress size or one shoe size to order, you would be wiser to use the mode, picking the size that occurs more often than any other. If someone needs a size 16 shoe, you would not have it, but you would have the size that more people request than any other.

Measures of Variability

A measure of central tendency is a single number that embodies a statistical "average." In real life, however, people or data can vary so much that any average is misleading. Consequently, knowing an average data item or score is more useful when it is accompanied by knowledge of how all the items or scores in the group are distributed relative to one another. If you know that the mean of a set of numbers is 150, you still do not know how widely dispersed the numbers that were averaged to calculate that mean are. For example, the mean on the final exam in your psychology class may be 150, and you may have scored 170 (above the mean), but you still do not know how much you can celebrate. Are there few other scores above your score? If there are many others, how much better are those scores than yours?

Statistics that describe the extent to which scores in a distribution differ from one another are called *measures of variability*. *Variability* is the extent to which scores differ from one another, or especially from the mean. If all scores in a data set are the same, there is no variability. However, this situation is unlikely to occur. Usually, in any group of people being tested or measured in some way, personal and situational characteristics will cause some to score high and some to score low. If researchers know the variability, they can estimate the extent to which participants' scores differ from the mean, or "average." Two measures of variability are the range and the standard deviation.

Range

The *range* shows the spread of scores in a distribution; it is calculated by subtracting the lowest score from the highest score. For the psychology majors in Table A.2, the lowest GPA is 2.0 and the highest is 3.8, which makes the range 1.8 points. Because it is a measure of variability, not of central tendency, the range is unaffected by the mean. The values in between the highest and lowest scores

Table A.4

CALCULATING THE MEDIAN FOR GPAS OF PSYCHOLOGY AND CHEMISTRY MAJORS

The median is the score in the middle of the range of GPAs measured—half of the GPAs are above the median and half are below.

GPA	
1.8	
2.0	
2.0	
2.0	
2.1	
2.2	
2.2	
2.3	
2.5	
2.5	
2.5	
2.7	
2.7	
2.8	
2.9	
2.9	
3.0	
3.0	
3.0	
3.0	Median
3.0	
3.2	
3.2	
3.2	
3.2	
3.2	
3.2	
3.3	
3.3	
3.4	
3.4	
3.4	
3.5	
3.5	
3.5	
3.6	
3.6	
3.7	
3.7	
3.8	

Table A.5

COMPUTATIONS OF MEAN AND MEDIAN GPAS FOR FOUR GROUPS OF COLLEGE STUDENTS

Psychology Majors		Chemistry Majors		Nursing Majors		Art Majors	
Brandon	2.0	Jay	1.8	Jeanne	2.2	Michelle	1.7
Cyndi	2.2	Rob	2.0	Brett	2.5	Angelique	1.8
Wyatt	2.3	Jesse	2.0	Donna	2.5	Bethany	2.0
Mauri	2.5	Pam	2.1	Martin	2.5	Raymond	2.3
Tonya	2.7	Pat	2.2	Heidi	2.6	Amanda	2.5
Marg	3.0	Duncan	2.5	Barton	2.7	Jeannette	2.8
Kendra	3.0	Gayla	2.5	Ramona	2.8	Gina	2.9
Diane	3.2	Dorry	2.7	Luis	2.9	Shonda	3.0
Anne	3.2	Laurette	2.8	Stephanie	3.0	Glen	3.2
Mike	3.2	Trey	2.9	Janet	3.0	Carolita	3.3
Brenda	3.2	Deené	2.9	Jon	3.0	Helene	3.4
Tiffany	3.3	Jamie	3.0	Melanie	3.0	Marianne	3.5
Rosita	3.3	Cinamon	3.0	Rizzi	3.2	Evan	3.5
Brad	3.4	Miquel	3.0	Medina	3.3	Tyree	3.6
Chris	3.4	James	3.2	Bridgette	3.3	Taylor	3.6
Gwen	3.5	Iris	3.2	Vince	3.4	Bev	3.7
Tonio	3.5	Florette	3.4	Sandra	3.4	Darla	3.7
Christine	3.6	Aaron	3.5	Suzanne	3.5	Mekka	3.8
Koren	3.7	Darin	3.6	David	3.6	Ellyn	3.8
Toni	3.8	Constance	3.7	Sarah	3.6	Theresa	3.9
Total =	62		56		60		62
Mean =	3.1		2.8		3.0		3.1
Median =	3.2		2.9		3.0		3.35

Psychology Majors

Mean

$$2.0 + 2.2 + 2.3 + 2.5 + 2.7 + 3.0 + 3.0 + 3.2 + 3.2 + 3.2 + 3.2 + 3.3 + 3.3 + 3.4 + 3.4 + 3.5 + 3.5 + 3.6 + 3.7 + 3.8 = \frac{62}{20} = 3.1$$

Median

2.0 2.2 2.3 2.5 2.7 3.0 3.0 3.2 3.2 $\boxed{3.2\ \ 3.2}$ 3.3 3.3 3.4 3.4 3.5 3.5 3.6 3.7 3.8

Median = 3.2

Chemistry Majors

Mean

$$1.8 + 2.0 + 2.0 + 2.1 + 2.2 + 2.5 + 2.5 + 2.7 + 2.8 + 2.9 + 2.9 + 3.0 + 3.0 + 3.0 + 3.2 + 3.2 + 3.4 + 3.5 + 3.6 + 3.7 = \frac{56}{20} = 2.8$$

Median

1.8 2.0 2.0 2.1 2.2 2.5 2.5 2.7 2.8 $\boxed{2.9\ \ 2.9}$ 3.0 3.0 3.0 3.2 3.2 3.4 3.5 3.6 3.7

Median = 2.9

(Continued)

Nursing Majors

Mean

$$2.2 + 2.5 + 2.5 + 2.5 + 2.6 + 2.7 + 2.8 + 2.9 + 3.0 + 3.0 + 3.0 + 3.0 + 3.2 + 3.3 + 3.3 + 3.4 + 3.4 + 3.5 + 3.6 + 3.6 = \frac{60}{20} = 3.0$$

Median

2.2 2.5 2.5 2.5 2.6 2.7 2.8 2.9 3.0 $\boxed{3.0 \; 3.0}$ 3.0 3.2 3.3 3.3 3.4 3.4 3.5 3.6 3.6

Median = 3.0

Art Majors

Mean

$$1.7 + 1.8 + 2.0 + 2.3 + 2.5 + 2.8 + 2.9 + 3.0 + 3.2 + 3.3 + 3.4 + 3.5 + 3.5 + 3.6 + 3.6 + 3.7 + 3.7 + 3.8 + 3.8 + 3.9 = \frac{62}{20} = 3.1$$

Median

1.7 1.8 2.0 2.3 2.5 2.8 2.9 3.0 3.2 $\boxed{3.3 \; 3.4}$ 3.5 3.5 3.6 3.6 3.7 3.7 3.8 3.8 3.9

Median = 3.35

may be any assortment of intermediate values, and the range will not be affected. It's the extremes that determine the range—the lowest score and the highest.

The range is a relatively crude measure of the extent to which participants vary within a group because it is only sensitive to the endpoints of a distribution and overlooks all the numbers in between. More precise measures of the spread of scores within a group indicate how the scores are distributed as well as the extent of their spread.

Standard Deviation

Consider the 20 psychology majors' GPAs in Table A.2. We know that the mean GPA is 3.1, but the GPAs vary from 2.0 to 3.8. Statisticians say that these data are variable, or that variability exists within this set of data. To find out how much variability exists among data and to quantify it in a meaningful manner, researchers use a statistic called the standard deviation. A *standard deviation* is a descriptive statistic that measures the variability of data from the mean of the distribution—that is, the extent to which each score differs from the mean.

The calculation of a standard deviation for these scores appears in Table A.6 (on p. 730). Here is the general procedure: First, subtract the mean from each score, and then square that difference. Next, add up the squared differences and divide that sum by the number of scores minus 1. (For a small sample, to get a better estimate of the sample's standard deviation, researchers divide by 1 less than the number of scores.) Last, take the square root of that result. You have now calculated a standard deviation.

A standard deviation represents information about all the members of a group, not just an "average" member. Knowing the standard deviation—that is, the variability with respect to the mean—enables a researcher to understand more about the distribution. As Table A.5 shows, the psychology majors and the art majors have the same mean GPA (3.1). But a calculation of the standard deviation for the art majors,

Standard deviation ■ A descriptive statistic that measures the variability of data from the mean of the distribution.

Table A.6

COMPUTATION OF THE STANDARD DEVIATION FOR PSYCHOLOGY MAJORS' GPAS

GPA	Score – Mean	(Score – Mean)²
2.0	2.0 − 3.1 = − 1.1	1.21
2.2	2.2 − 3.1 = − 0.9	0.81
2.3	2.3 − 3.1 = − 0.8	0.64
2.5	2.5 − 3.1 = − 0.6	0.36
2.7	2.7 − 3.1 = − 0.4	0.16
3.0	3.0 − 3.1 = − 0.1	0.01
3.0	3.0 − 3.1 = − 0.1	0.01
3.2	3.2 − 3.1 = 0.1	0.01
3.2	3.2 − 3.1 = 0.1	0.01
3.2	3.2 − 3.1 = 0.1	0.01
3.2	3.2 − 3.1 = 0.1	0.01
3.3	3.3 − 3.1 = 0.2	0.04
3.3	3.3 − 3.1 = 0.2	0.04
3.4	3.4 − 3.1 = 0.3	0.09
3.4	3.4 − 3.1 = 0.3	0.09
3.5	3.5 − 3.1 = 0.4	0.16
3.5	3.5 − 3.1 = 0.4	0.16
3.6	3.6 − 3.1 = 0.5	0.25
3.7	3.7 − 3.1 = 0.6	0.36
3.8	3.8 − 3.1 = 0.7	0.49
62		4.92

Standard deviation = $\sqrt{\dfrac{\Sigma(x-\bar{x})^2}{N-1}}$, where Σ means 'sum up," x is a score, $\bar{x}$ is the mean of the scores, and N is the number of scores.

Sum of scores = 62.

$\bar{x}$ = sum of scores ffi 20 = 3.1

Sum of squared differences from mean = 4.92

Average of square differences from mean (dividing by the number of scores −1)

= 4.92 ÷ 19 = 0.259.

Square root of average square difference from the mean = 0.51 = standard deviation.

performed just like the one in Table A.6, yields a standard deviation of 0.70. This is larger than the standard deviation for the psychology majors (0.51). The art majors show a larger degree of variability than the psychology majors: The GPAs differ from the mean more for the art majors than for the psychology majors.

The Normal Distribution

The *normal distribution* is the approximate distribution of scores expected when a sample is drawn from a large population. When the normal distribution is drawn as a frequency polygon, it takes the form of a bell-shaped curve, known as a *normal curve*. Normal distributions have few scores at each extreme and progressively more scores toward the middle. Although the 80 GPAs for students from four different majors show few scores toward the extremes and more scores in the middle, this sample is too small for the distribution of scores to be a normal distribution. A distribution of 1,000 GPAs would more closely match a normal distribution. Height is a measure that is approximately normally distributed: More people are closer to average height than are very tall or very short. Weights, shoe sizes, IQ scores, psychology exam scores, and many other variables tend to be normally distributed when data sets are large.

Normal distribution ▪
The approximate distribution of scores expected when a sample is taken from a large population; when drawn as a frequency polygon, it takes the form of a bell-shaped curve, known as a *normal curve.*

Characteristics of a Normal Curve

A normal curve has certain characteristics. One important characteristic is that the mean, mode, and median of the sample are the same, and the distribution of scores around that central point is symmetrical. Another important characteristic is that most individuals' scores fall within 6 standard deviations—3 above the mean and 3 below it (see Figure A.3).

To understand this phenomenon, look at Figure A.4 (on p. 732), which shows a normal curve for heights of men. The mean height is 70 inches, and the standard deviation is 4 inches. Note how each increment of 4 points above or below the mean accounts for fewer and fewer individuals. Scores between 70 and 74 account for 34.13% of those measured, scores between 74 and 78 account for 13.59%, and scores

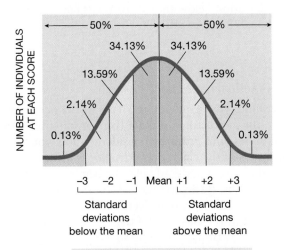

Figure A.3
Percentages of Population for a Normal Curve

On a normal curve, most individuals score within 6 standard deviations, 3 on either side of the mean.

Figure A.4

A Normal Curve with a Mean of 70 and a Standard Deviation of 4 Inches On this normal curve, Dennis's height of 74 inches is 1 standard deviation above the mean height of 70 inches. Rob's height is 66 inches, which is 1 standard deviation below the mean.

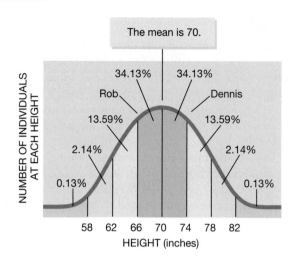

above 78 account for under 2.5%. The sum of these percentages (34.13 + 13.59 + 2.14 + 0.13) represents 50% of the scores. The other 50% fall below the mean in the same proportions.

When you know the mean and the standard deviation of a set of scores *and* you know that the scores are normally distributed, you can estimate where an individual in the sample population stands relative to others. Figure A.4 also shows two individuals and their heights relative to each other in the distribution. Dennis is 74 inches tall. His height is 1 standard deviation above the mean, which means that he is taller than 84% of the population (0.13 + 2.14 + 13.59 + 34.13 + 34.13 = 84.12%). Rob, who is 66 inches tall, is taller than only 16% of the population. His height is 1 standard deviation below the mean. What percentage of the population is taller than a man who is 78 inches tall? How many standard deviations is his height from the mean?

Normal Curves: A Practical Example

If an instructor determines your grade on the basis of the percentage of exam questions you get correct, the instructor is using a fixed grading scale (with no "curve"). If an instructor determines your grade by considering how you perform on the exam relative to other members of the class, the instructor is using a sliding scale, or grading on a "curve." In this case, your grade may be better (or worse) than the percentage of answers you got right. If the average student in a class answers only 50% of the questions correctly, a student who answers 70% correctly has done a good job in comparison to the rest of the class. But if the average student scores 85%, then someone who scores only 70% has not done so well.

Before they assign grades on a sliding scale, instructors generally calculate a mean and a standard deviation. They then inspect the scores and "slide the scale" to an appropriate level based on those descriptive statistics. Figure A.5 shows scores achieved and grades assigned on a calculus test. The average score was 65%, and

Grades assigned

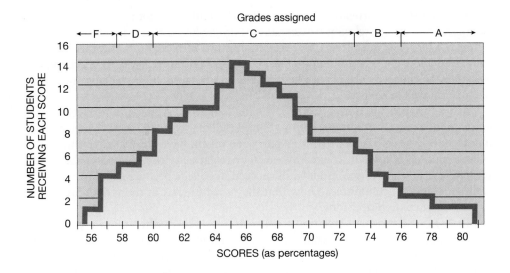

Figure A.5

Grading on a Sliding Scale
To calculate grades on a sliding scale, instructors often draw a graph like this one, showing the number of individuals who received each score. They then figure out the cutoff points for assigning letter grades (A, B, C, D, and F).

the instructor decided to give students who scored 65% a C, an average grade. Those students who did better got an A or a B, depending on how much better than the mean they scored. Those who did worse got a D or an F, depending on how much below the mean they scored. Is this scale advantageous to the calculus students?

Correlation

Sometimes a researcher wants to know about the relationship between two sets of scores. For example, the educational psychologist who conducted the research on studying wanted to know the relationship between number of hours studied and GPA as well as the relationship between number of class absences (both excused and unexcused) and GPA. To determine these relationships, she calculated correlations.

A correlation exists when an increase in the value of one variable is regularly accompanied by either an increase or a decrease in the value of a second variable. The degree and direction of the relationship between two variables is expressed by a numerical value called the ***correlation coefficient*** (and symbolized by *r*). Correlation coefficients range from −1, through 0, to +1. Any correlation coefficient greater or less than 0, regardless of its sign, indicates that the variables are somehow related. Correlation coefficients close to −1 or +1 indicate strong relationships, and those close to 0 indicate weak relationships. A correlation coefficient of +0.8 is no stronger than one of −0.8. That is, the plus or minus sign changes the *direction*, but not the strength, of a relationship. The strength is shown by the number: The larger the number, the greater the strength of the correlation. A correlation coefficient of −0.8 is stronger than one of +0.7; a correlation coefficient of +0.6 is stronger than one of −0.5.

When the correlation coefficient is 1.00, the variables are perfectly correlated, and knowing the value of one variable allows a researcher to predict *precisely* the value of the second. A perfect correlation is, of course, a rare occurrence in psychological

Correlation coefficient
■ A number that expresses the degree and direction of a relationship between two variables, ranging from −1 (a perfect negative correlation) to +1 (a perfect positive correlation).

research. But strong correlations allow predictions (although not perfect ones). For example, there is a correlation between scores on the SAT and grade point average during the first year in college. The correlation is not perfect (1.00), but it is high enough to allow colleges and universities to use SAT scores as a way to select students. They tend to choose students with high SAT scores because those students are more likely to do well in college.

Most variables are not perfectly correlated, and SAT scores and first-year college grade point averages are no exception. Some students receive high scores on the SAT but do poorly in college because they party too much, have trouble adapting to the college routine, become distracted by extracurricular activities, and so forth. Other students get lower SAT scores and still succeed in college because they work hard. College admission committees know that they need to look at more than SAT scores in making admission decisions.

Before calculating a correlation coefficient, researchers often plot, or graph, their data in a scatter plot. A *scatter plot* is a diagram of data points that shows the relationship between two variables. An individual's score on one variable is measured on the horizontal axis, or *x* axis, and the score on the second variable is measured on the vertical axis, or *y* axis.For example, a scatter plot might show the relationship between students' GPAs and the number of hours they study. For each student, there is a point that represents GPA and amount of studying. If a student studies 10 hours per week and has a GPA of 3.2, a dot appears on the graph at the point where 10 hours (on the *x* axis) and 3.2 (on the *y* axis) intersect, as shown in Figure A.6(a). Plotting all 20 points for the psychology majors in this way gives a graphic illustration of the extent to which these two variables are related. The graph

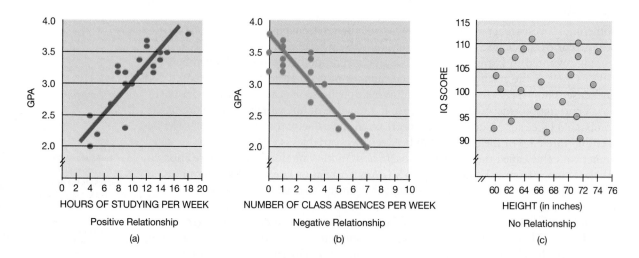

Figure A.6

Three Types of Correlation: A Summary

(a) With a positive correlation, an increase in one variable is associated with an increase in the other variable. (b) With a negative correlation, an increase in one variable is associated with a decrease in the other variable. (c) No correlation exists when changes in one variable are not associated in any systematic way with changes in the other variable.

shows that as study time increases, so does GPA (at least most of the time), indicating a correlation. When one variable shows an increase in value and a second also shows an increase, as studying and GPA do, the two variables are said to be positively related. The relationship is known as a *positive correlation*.

Knowing how much time a student spends studying does not allow someone to predict his or her GPA precisely, but it allows for an approximation. For example, given the correlation between hours studied and GPA for the 20 psychology students, if you were given information about study time for a 21st psychology major, you could make a good guess about the student's GPA. For a student who says she studies about 4 hours a week, what is your best guess about her GPA? What about a student who reports studying 15 hours per week?

The scatter plot in Figure A.6(a) shows a positive direction overall—upward and to the right. The correlation coefficient is $r = .80$, which is a high value, indicating a strong relationship between these two variables. Do you think that the correlation would also be positive for the art, chemistry, and nursing majors? Do you think that the value of r would be as high?

On the other hand, when a decrease in one variable is accompanied by an increase in the other, the relationship is known as a *negative correlation*. For example, the relationship between the number of class meetings missed per week and GPA shows a negative correlation—that is, as the number of classes a students misses per week increases, grades decrease. The scatter plot in Figure A.6(b) shows this negative correlation for the psychology majors; the trend of the points is downward and to the right. In this case, $r = -.90$, which is a high value for a correlation and indicates a strong negative relationship between these two variables. The interpretation: Don't miss class. Do you think that the correlation between classes missed and GPA would be negative for the art, chemistry, and nursing majors? Would the relationship be as strong?

Some variables show absolutely no correlation; absence of correlation is expressed by a correlation coefficient of 0. Figure A.6(c) plots data for IQ and height. There is no pattern in the scatter plot, and thus no correlation between IQ and height—that is, $r = 0$.

The positive correlation ($r = .80$) for the relationship between number of hours studying and students' grade point averages means that as study time increases, so do grades. However, some people make good grades with less studying than others, just as you have observed and as you can see by examining Figure A.6(a). These variations prevent the correlation from being perfect. In general, however, studying is positively related to good grades; there is a high positive correlation between the two. These results also demonstrate that missing class is a bad strategy for making good grades. The correlation between grades and absences is negative and strong, which means that as absences increase, grades decrease. This researcher did not differentiate between students who had a good excuse for missing class and those who did not; only the number of class meetings missed during the week of the study was measured. Thus, we can conclude that students who miss class tend to have lower grades, regardless of their reasons for missing class.

As we saw in Chapter 2, a correlation in no way demonstrates a cause-and-effect relationship. A correlation between two variables simply indicates that if there is an increase in one variable, there will probably be an increase (or a decrease) in the other variable. Even if the variables do have a causal relationship, the correlational technique will not allow researchers to determine that relationship. Do you think that studying and grades are causally related? What about absences and grades?

It is only through experimental studies that researchers can make cause-and-effect statements. To analyze the data from experimental studies, they use a different type of statistic—inferential statistics.

How Do Psychologists Use Inferential Statistics?

Inferential statistics
A set of mathematical procedures used to interpret data and draw reasonable conclusions.

Inferential statistics are procedures used to interpret data and draw reasonable conclusions. Researchers want to be able to tell whether a difference observed between groups in an experiment is due to manipulation of the independent variable. Researchers must be careful to include the proper controls in their experiments so that they will not introduce extraneous factors into their design. If a researcher does a good job in designing an experiment and the variability is due to the manipulation of the independent variable, then the researcher will use inferential statistics to determine if there are group differences and if those differences are statistically significant.

Significant Differences

Significant difference
An experimentally obtained difference that is statistically unlikely to have occurred because of chance alone.

Psychology researchers hope to find a *significant difference*—a difference that is statistically unlikely to have occurred because of chance alone and thus is more likely to be due to experimental manipulation. To claim that a difference between two or more groups is significant, a researcher must show that the difference is not a result of chance variations. Statistically significant differences can be repeated experimentally because they have a basis that is known; thus, an experimenter can create that difference again. If the difference were due to chance, it would not be likely to occur again.

Generally, psychologists assume that a difference is statistically significant if the likelihood of its occurring by chance is less than 5%—that is, if it would occur by chance less than 5 out of 100 times. But many researchers set a more strict criterion, assuming that a difference is significant only if the likelihood of its occurring by chance is less than 1%.

Inferential statistics are necessary for analyzing data because it is difficult to decide if a difference is significant by looking at the scores. Look back at Table A.2, which shows calculations of the mean grade point averages for psychology and chemistry majors. To determine whether psychology majors make better grades than chemistry majors, we considered these data from a study performed by an educational psychologist, who collected information that would allow a test of that question. This study was not an experiment because this researcher did not manipulate the independent variable, college major. Rather, she selected students in each of four majors. Thus, this study had an *ex post facto* design (see Chapter 2 for more information about this design), which prevents the researcher from making any conclusion about cause and effect. The ex post facto design also has more limitations on the interpretation of results than does an experiment.

An examination of the mean, mode, and median scores indicated that the psychology majors had higher grades than the chemistry majors. But do the psychology majors have *significantly* better grades than the chemistry majors? Is the difference between the mean GPA of 3.2 for psychology majors and that of 2.8 for chemistry majors big enough to be a significant difference? It is difficult to determine if this difference is a significant difference by just looking at the two sets of scores. We need to apply a statistical test to evaluate the significance of the difference between these two groups.

Testing Group Differences

Researchers use inferential statistics in making decisions about the data they have gathered—to determine if their results have turned out as hypothesized. Researchers form a hypothesis before they begin a study, and they design the study and collect data to test the hypothesis. For example, the hypothesis we considered earlier was that psychology majors have better grades than chemistry majors. However, the logic of statistical testing requires the use of a ***null hypothesis,*** which is a hypothesis of no difference between groups. The null hypothesis for this study would be: There is no significant difference between the grades of psychology and chemistry majors.

Null hypothesis ■ A hypothesis of no difference between groups in a study.

Researchers hope to find evidence to reject the null hypothesis and accept their *alternative hypothesis* that a difference between groups does exist. They begin with the assumption that no difference exists. Then, they look for evidence to reject that null hypothesis. The evidence comes from the application of an appropriate statistical test and an interpretation of its results.

Dozens of statistical tests exist, so selecting one that is appropriate requires an understanding of the type of analysis required. The ***t-test*** is a statistical test consisting of a mathematical formula that allows researchers to determine if the means of two groups differ significantly, making this test appropriate for the study of psychology and chemistry majors. The result of the *t*-test is a *t*-statistic, which reveals how much the means of the two groups differ and allows the researcher to determine if this difference is likely to be due to chance. By using the *t*-test, it is possible to determine if the difference between the GPAs of the two groups of students is statistically significant. Researchers can calculate a *t*-statistic without using a computer program, but most researchers use such programs to calculate their statistics (it's not only easier but produces fewer mistakes).

t-test ■ An inferential statistical formula that allows researchers to determine if the means of two groups differ significantly.

Large values of the *t*-statistic indicate an increasing likelihood of a significant difference and a decreasing likelihood that the difference is based on chance. That is, large values of *t* indicate statistically significant differences between the groups being compared. The calculation of the *t*-statistic for the psychology versus chemistry majors results in $t = 2.169$. This value indicates that the means of the two groups are significantly different because the probability of this difference occurring on the basis of chance is less than 5%. Therefore, the difference in mean GPA between these groups of psychology and chemistry majors is significant.

What does this difference mean? Does it mean that psychology majors are generally better students than chemistry majors? Does it mean that they are smarter? Researchers must be very careful in interpreting their results so as to avoid overgeneralizations and invalid conclusions. The results of this statistical test show that this group of psychology majors has a significantly higher mean GPA than this group of chemistry majors. However, this sample of students was rather small, which limits our ability to generalize the result. If this sample represents the characteristics of the psychology and chemistry majors at this university, then we can generalize this result to all of those majors at this one university. We should hesitate to generalize this finding to other universities because students vary from school to school. We have not discovered a basic truth about all psychology and chemistry majors in the world; we have only learned something about these two groups at this university.

Abaya, C. (2004). The sandwich generation. Retrieved November 23, 2004, from http://www.sandwichgeneration.com/

Abbey, A., Zawacki, T., Buck, P. O., Clinton, A., & McAuslan, P. (2004). Sexual assault and alcohol consumption: What do we know about their relationship and what types of research are still needed? *Aggression & Violent Behavior, 9,* 271–303.

Abbott, L. F., Varela, J. A., Sen, K., & Nelson, S. B. (1997). Synaptic depression and cortical gain control. *Science, 275,* 220–224.

Abbott, M. L., & Joireman, J. (2001). *The relationship among achievement, low income, and ethnicity across six groups of Washington state students.* Washington School Research Center, Technical Report #1.

Abel, M. H., & Hester, R. (2002). The therapeutic effects of smiling. In M. H. Abel (Ed.). *An empirical reflection on the smile* (pp. 217–253). Lewiston, NY: Edwin Mellen Press.

Abela, J. R. Z., & Sullivan, C. (2003). A test of Beck's cognitive diathesis-stress theory of depression in early adolescents. *Journal of Early Adolescence, 23,* 384–404.

Abraham, W. C., & Williams, J. M. (2003). Properties and mechanisms of LTP maintenance. *Neuroscientists, 9,* 463–474.

Abramowitz, J. S., Franklin, M. E., & Cahill, S. P. (2004). Approaches to common obstacles in the exposure-based treatment of obsessive-compulsive disorder. *Cognitive & Behavioral Practice, 10,* 14–22.

Abramson, L. Y., Metalsky, G. I., & Alloy, L. B. (1989). Hopelessness depression: A theory-based subtype of depression. *Psychological Review, 96,* 358–372.

Ackard, D. M., & Neumark-Sztainer, D. (2002). Date violence and date rape among adolescents: Associations with disordered eating behaviors and psychological health. *Child Abuse and Neglect, 26,* 455–473.

Acker, J. R. (1993). A different agenda: The Supreme Court, empirical research evidence, and capital punishment decisions, 1986–1989. *Law & Society Review, 27,* 65–88.

Acocella, J. (1999). *Creating hysteria: Women and multiple personality disorder.* San Francisco: Jossey-Bass.

Addis, M. E., & Mahalik, J. R. (2003). Men, masculinity, and the contexts of help seeking. *American Psychologist, 58,* 5–14.

Ader, R. (1997). The role of conditioning in pharmacotherapy. In A. Harrington (Ed.). *The placebo effect: An interdisciplinary exploration* (pp. 138–165). Cambridge, MA: Harvard University Press.

Ader, R. (2001). Psychoneurolmmunology. *Current Directions in Psychological Science, 10,* 94–98.

Ader, R., & Cohen, N. (1975). Behaviorally conditioned immunosuppression. *Psychosomatic Medicine, 37,* 333–340.

Ader, R., & Cohen, N. (1993). Psychoneuro-immunology: Conditioning and stress. *Annual Review of Psychology, 44,* 53–85.

Adeyemo, S. A. (2002). A review of the role of the hippocampus in memory. *Psychology & Education: An Interdisciplinary Journal, 39,* 46–63.

Adler, A. (1927). *Understanding human nature.* New York: Greenberg.

Adler, A. (1929/1964). *Problems of neurosis.* New York: Harper Torchbooks.

Adler, C. M., McDonough-Ryan, P., Sax, K. W., Holland, S. K., Arndt, S., & Strakowski, S. M. (2000). FMRI of neuronal activation with symptom provocation in unmedicated patients with obsessive compulsive disorder. *Journal of Psychiatric Research, 34,* 317–324.

Adolphs, R., & Damasio, A. R. (2000). Neurobiology of emotion at a systems level. In J. C. Borod (Ed.). *The neuropsychology of emotion: Series in affective science* (pp. 194–213). New York: Oxford University Press.

Adolphs, R., & Tranel, D. (2003). Amygdala damage impairs emotion recognition from scenes only when they contain facial expressions. *Neuropsychologia, 41,* 1281–1289.

Adolphs, R., & Tranel, D. (2004). Impaired judgments of sadness but not happiness following bilateral amygdala damage. *Journal of Cognitive Neuroscience, 16,* 453–462.

Adorno, T., Frenkel-Brunswick, E., Levinson, D., & Sanford, R. (1950). *The authoritarian personality.* New York: Harper and Row.

Adrian, M. (2002). A critical perspective on cross-cultural contexts for addiction and multiculturalism: Their meanings and implications in the substance use field. *Substance Use & Misuse, 37,* 853–900.

Agarguen, M. Y., Oener, A. F., & Akbayram, S. (2001). Hypnotic intervention for pain management in a child with sickle cell anemia. *Sleep & Hypnosis, 3 (3),* 127–128.

Agid, O., Shapira, B., Zislin, J., Ritsner, M., Hanin, B., Murad, H., et al. (1999). Environment and vulnerability to major psychiatric illness: A case control study of early parental loss in major depression, bipolar disorder and schizophrenia. *Molecular Psychiatry, 4,* 163–172.

Ahern, J., Galea, S., Resnick, H., Kilpatrick, D., Bucuvalas, M., Gold, J., et al. (2002). Television images and psychological symptoms after the September 11 terror attacks. *Interpersonal & Biological Processes, 65,* 289–300.

Ahlmeyer, S., Kleinsasser, D., Stoner, J., & Retzlaff, P. (2003). Psychopathology of incarcerated sex offenders. *Journal of Personality Disorders, 17,* 306–318.

Aiello, J. R., & Douthitt, E. A. (2001). Social facilitation from Triplett to electronic performance monitoring. *Group Dynamics, 5,* 163–180.

Aiken, L. R. (1988). *Psychological testing and assessment* (6th ed.). Boston: Allyn and Bacon.

Ainsworth, M. D. S. (1979). Infant-mother attachment. *American Psychologist, 34,* 932–937.

Ajzen, I. (2001). Nature and operation of attitudes. *Annual Review of Psychology, 52,* 27–58.

Akuamoah-Boateng, R., Bolitho, F. H., Carr, S. C., Chidgey, J. E., O'Reilly, B., Phillips, R., et al. (2003). Psychosocial barriers to female leadership: Motivational gravity in Ghana and Tanzania. *Psychology & Developing Societies, 15,* 201–221.

Albers, L. J., Hahn, R. K., & Reist, C. (2004). *Handbook of psychiatric drugs.* Laguna Hills, CA: Current Clinical Strategies Publishing.

Alcock, J. E. (1988). *A comprehensive review of major empirical studies in parapsychology involving random event generators or remote viewing.* Washington, DC: National Academy Press.

Alcock, J. E., Burns, J. E., & Freeman, A. (Eds.). (2003). *Psi-wars: Getting to grips with the paranormal.* Charlottesville, VA: Imprint Academic.

Alexander, G. M., Altemus, M., Peterson, B. S., & Wexler, B. E. (2002). Replication of a premenstrual decrease in right-ear advantage on language-related dichotic listening tests of cerebral laterality. *Neuropsychologia, 40,* 1293–1299.

Alexander, M. G., & Fisher, T. D. (2003). Truth and consequences: Using the bogus pipeline to examine sex differences in self-reported sexuality. *Journal of Sex Research, 40,* 27–35.

739

Allen, G. L., (2000). Men and women, maps and minds: Cognitive bases of sex-related differences in reading and interpreting maps. In S. O. Nuallain (Ed.), *Spatial cognition: Foundations and applications: Selected papers from Mind Ill, Annual Conference of the Cognitive Science Society of Ireland, 1998: Advances in Consciousness Research* (pp. 3–18). Amsterdam: John Benjamins.

Allen, W. (1983). *Without feathers*. New York: Ballantine.

Allison, T., Ginter, H., McCarthy, G., Nobre, A. C., Puce, A., Luby, M., & Spencer, D. D. (1994). Face recognition in human extrastriate cortex. *Journal of Neurophysiology, 71,* 821–825.

Alloy, L. B., & Robinson, M. S. (2003). Negative cognitive styles and stress-reactive rumination interact to predict depression: A prospective study. *Cognitive Therapy & Research, 27,* 275–291.

Allport, G. W. (1961). *Pattern and growth in personality*. New York: Holt, Rinehart & Winston.

Allport, G. W. (1979). *The nature of prejudice*. Cambridge, MA: Addison-Wesley. (Original work published in 1954).

Alonso, J., Angermeyer, M. C., Bernert, S., Bruffaerts, R., Brugha, T. S., Bryson, H., et al. (2004). Prevalence of mental disorders in Europe: Results from the European Study of the Epidemiology of Mental Disorders (ESEMeD) project. *Psychiatrica Scandinavica, 109* (Suppl. 420), 21–27.

Altemeyer, B. (1988). *Enemies of freedom: Understanding right-wing authoritarianism*. San Francisco, CA: Jossey-Bass.

Althoff, R. R., & Cohen, N. J. (1999). Eye-movement-based memory effect: A reprocessing effect in face perception. *Journal of Experimental Psychology: Learning, Memory, and Cognition, 25,* 997–1010.

American Association of University Women Educational Foundation. (1998). *Gender gaps: Where schools still fail our children [Special report]*. Washington, DC: Author.

American Association on Mental Retardation. (2002). *Mental retardation: Definition, classification, and systems of supports* (10th ed.). Washington, D. C.: Author.

American Dietetic Association. (2000). Nutrition, aging and the continuum of care. *Journal of the American Dietetic Association, 10,* 580–595.

American Psychiatric Association. (2002). *Diagnostic and statistical manual of mental disorders* (4th ed., text revision). Washington, DC: Author.

American Psychiatric Association. (2001). *The practice of electronconvulsive therapy: Recommendalions for treatment, training, and privileging: A task force report of the American Psychiatric Association* (2nd ed.). Washington, DC: Author.

American Psychological Association [APA]. (2001). A new look at adolescent girls: Strengths and stresses. *American Psychological Association Research Report*, unique identifier 315542004–000. Retrieved July 4, 2004, from www.apa.org

American Psychological Association. (2002). Ethical principles of psychologists and code of conduct. *American Psychologist, 57,* 1060–1073.

American Psychological Association. (2003). The wage gap favoring men doesn't just hurt women's pay, according to new research: Pay of both men and women managers is less when managers' subordinates, peers and supervisors are women, study finds. *American Psychological Association Conference paper*, unique identifier 306612004–000. Retrieved July 4, 2004, from www.apa.org.

American Psychological Association. (2004). *How therapy helps*. Retrieved April 24, 2004, from http://helping.apa.org./theraphy/psychotherapy.html

Amrein, A. L., & Berliner, D. C. (2002, March 28). High-stakes testing, uncertainty, and student learning. *Education Policy Analysis Archives, 10(18)*. Retrieved April 4, 2004, from http://epaa.asu.edu/epaa/v10n18/

Anderson, C. A. & Bushman, B. J. (2002). The effects of media violence on society. *Science Magazine, 295,* 2377–2379.

Anderson, C. A., Berkowitz, L., Donnerstein, E., Huesmann, L. R., Johnson, J. D., Linz, D., Malamuth, N. M., & Wartella, E. (2003). The influence of media violence on youth. *Psychological Science in the Public Interest, 4,* 81–110.

Anderson, J. R., & Schooler, L. J. (2000). The adaptive nature of memory. In E. Tulving & F. I. Craik (Eds.). *The Oxford handbook of memory* (pp. 557–570). New York: Oxford University Press.

Anderson, J. S., Lampl, I., Gillespie, D. C., & Ferster, D. (2000). The contribution of noise to contrast invariance of orientation tuning in cat visual cortex. *Science, 290,* 1968–1972.

Anderson, K. E., & Savage, C. R. (2004). Cognitive and neurobiological findings in obsessive-compulsive disorder. *Psychiatric Clinics of North America, 27,* 37–47.

Anderson, M. C., Ochsner, K. N., Brice, K., Cooper, J., Robertson, E., Gabrielie, S. W., et al. (2004). Neural systems underlying the suppression of unwanted memories. *Science, 303,* 232–235.

Anderson, R. N., & Smith, B. L. (2003). Deaths: Leading causes for 2001. *National Vital Statistics Report, 52(9),* 1–86.

Andrejevic, M. (2003). *Reality TV: The work of being watched*, New York: Rowman & Littlefield.

Andresen, J. (2000). Meditation meets behavioural medicine: The story of experimental research on meditation, *Journal of Consciousness Studies, 7* (11–12), 17–73.

Angst, J., Gamma, A., Endrass, J., Goodwin, R., Ajdacic, V., Eich, D., & Rössler, W. (2004). Obsessive-compulsive severity spectrum in the community: Prevalence, comorbidity, and course. *European Archives of Psychiatry & Clinical Neuroscience, 254,* 156–164.

Anstey, K. J., Luszcz, M. A., Giles, L. C., & Andrews, G. R. (2001). Demographic, health, cognitive, and sensory variables as predictors of mortality in very old adults. *Psychology and Aging 16,* 3–11.

APA Committee on Animal Research and Ethics. (1996). *Research with animals in psychology*. Retrieved January 11, 2004. from http://www.apa.org/science/animal2.html?CFID=2826293&CFTOKEN=27745608

APA Research Office, (2001). *Demographic, education and employment data*. Retrieved November 28, 2003, from http://research.apa.org/datanew.html?CFID=282

Apter, T. (1995). *Secret paths: Women in the new midlife*. New York: Norton.

Archibald, A. B. (2000). Moody girls: Is puberty to blame? *Dissertation Abstracts International: Section B: The Sciences & Engineering, 60(12–B),* 6394.

Arean, P. A., & Cook, B. L. (2002). Psychotherapy and combined psychotherapy pharmacotherapy for late life depression. *Biological Psychiatry, 52,* 293–303.

Arias, D. C. (2004). Road safety, traffic systems global public health concerns. *Nation's Health, 34(5),* 13.

Ariely, D. (2001). Seeing sets: Representation by statistical properties. *Psychological Science, 12,* 157–162.

Ariznavarreta, C., Cardinali, D. P., Villanua, M. A., Granados, B., Martin, M., Chiesa, J. J., & Tresguerres, J. A. F. (2002). Circadian rhythms in airline pilots submitted to long-haul transmeridian flights. *Aviation, Space, & Environmental Medicine, 73,* 445–455.

Armbruster, P., Sukhodolsky, D., & Michalsen, R. (2004). The impact of managed care on children's outpatient treatment: A comparison study of treatment outcome before and after managed care. *American Journal of Orthopsychiatry, 74,* 5–13.

Armstrong, L., with S. Jenkins. (2000). *It's not about the bike: My journey back to life.* New York: Putnam.

Armstrong, L., with S. Jenkins. (2003). *Every second counts.* New York: Putnam.

Arnedt, J. T., Wilde, G. J. S., Munt, P. W., & MacLean, A. W. (2001). How do prolonged wakefulness and ness alcohol compare in the decrements they produce on a simulated driving task? *Accident Analysis and Prevention, 33,* 337–344.

Aron, A., Aron, E. M., Tudor, M., & Nelson, G. (1991). Close relationships as including other in the self. *Journal of Personality and Social Psychology, 60,* 241–253.

Aronin, L., & Toubkin, L., (2002). Language interference and language learning techniques transfer in L2 and L3 immersion programmes. *International Journal of Bilingual Education & Bilingualism, 5,* 267–278.

Arriaza, C. A., & Mann, T. (2001). Ethnic differences in eating disorder symptoms among college students: The confounding role of body mass index. *Journal of American College Health, 49,* 309–315.

Arseneault, L., Moffitt, T. E., Caspi, A., Taylor, P. J., & Silva, P. A. (2000). Mental disorders and violence in a total birth cohort: Results from the Dunedin Study. *Archives of General Psychiatry, 57,* 979–986.

Asbjornsen, A. E., Helland, T., Obrzut, J. E., & Boliek, C. A. (2003). The role of dichotic listening performance in tasks of executive functions: A discriminant function analysis. *Child Neuropsychology, 9,* 277–288.

Asch, S. E. (1955, November). Opinions and social pressure. *Scientific American,* 31–35.

Aserinsky, E., & Kleitman, N. (1953). Regularly occurring periods of eye motility, and concomitant phenomena, during sleep. *Science, 118,* 273–274.

Asia Society. (2004). *Business protocol.* Retrieved May 20, 2004, from http://www.asiasource.org/ business/2know/index.cfm

Aspinwall, L. G., & Taylor S. E. (1997). A stitch in time: Self-regulation and proactive coping. *Psychological Bulletin, 121,* 417–436.

Astin, J. A. (2004). Mind-body therapies for the management of pain. *Clinical Journal of Pain, 20,* 27–32.

Astington, J. (1999). What is theoretical about the child's theory of mind? A Vygotskian view of its development. In P. Lyoyd, C. Fernhough, et al. (Eds.). *Leo Vygotsky: Critical assessments, future directions,* Vol. IV (401–418). New York: Routledge.

Atwood, N. C. (2001). Gender bias in families and its clinical implications for women. *Social Work, 46,* 23–36.

Aube, J., Fichman, L., Saltaris, C., & Koestner, R. (2000). Gender differences in adolescent depressive symptomalology: Towards an integrated social–developmental model. *Journal of Social & Clinical Psychology, 19,* 297–313.

Austin, J. S., & Partridge, E. (1995). Prevent school failure: Treat text anxiety. *Preventing School Failure, 40,* 10–13.

Averett, S. L., Gennetian, L. A., & Peters, H. E. (2000). Patterns and determinants of paternal child care during a child's first three years of life. *Marriage & Family Review, 29 (2/3),* 115–136.

Avis, N. E. (1999). Women's health at midlife. In S. L., Willis & J. D. Reid (Eds.). *Life in the middle: Psychological and social development in middle age.* (pp. 105–146). San Diego, CA: Academic Press.

Ayllon, T., & Azrin, N. H. (1965). The measurement and reinforcement behavior of psychotics. *Journal of the Experimental Analysis of Behavior, 8,* 357–383.

Ayllon, T., & Haughton, E. (1964). Modification of symptomatic verbal behavior of mental patients. *Behavior Research and Therapy, 2,* 87–97.

Azar, S. T., & Olsen, N. (2004). Legal issues in child abuse and neglect. In W. O'Donohue & E. Levensky (Eds.). *Handbook of forensic psychology: Resource for mental health and legal professionals* (pp. 685–711). London: Elsevier Academic Press.

Baars, B. (2003). How brain reveals mind: Neural studies support the fundamental role of conscious experience. *Journal of Consciousness Studies, 10,* 100–114.

Babcock, J. C., & Siard, C. (2003). Toward a typology of abusive women: Differences between partner-only and generally violent women in the use of violence. *Psychology of Women Quarterly, 27,* 153–161.

Bachar, E. (1998). Psychotherapy—an active agent: Assessing the effectiveness of psychotherapy and its curative factors. *Israel Journal of Psychiatry and Related Sciences, 35,* 128–135.

Baddeley, A. D. (2002). Is working memory still working? *European Psychologist, 7,* 85–97.

Baddeley, A. D., & Hitch, G. (1947). Working memory. In G. Bower (Ed.). *Recent advances in learning and motivating* (Vol. 8). New York: Academic Press.

Baddeley, A. D., & Longman, D. J. (1978). The influence of length and frequency of training session on the rate of learning to type. *Ergonomics, 21,* 627–635.

Bader, C. D. (2003). Supernatural support groups: Who are the UFO abductees and ritual-abuse survivors? *Journal for the Scientific Study of Religion, 42,* 669–678.

Bae, Y., Choy, S., Geddes, C., Sable, J., & Snyder, sT. (2000). *Trends in educational equity for girls and women.* Washington, DC: U.S. Department of Education, National Center for Education Statistics.

Baer, M (2001). Chair's corner. *Annals of the American Psychotherapy Association, 4(5),* 5.

Baie, J. S., Sampson, P. D., Barr, H. M., Connor, P. D., & Streissgulh, A. P. (2003). A 21-year longiludinal analysis on the effects of prenatal alcohol exposure on young drinking. *Archives of General Psychiatry, 60,* 377–385.

Bailey, D. S. (2004, February). Number of psychology PhDs declining. *Monitor on Psychology, 35,* 18–19.

Bailey, J. M., Dunne, M. P., & Martin, N. G. (2000). Genetic and environmental influences on sexual orientation and its correlates in an Australian twin sample. *Journal of Personality and Social Psychology, 78,* 524–536.

Bailey, K. G. (2000). Evolution, kinship, and psychotherapy: Promoting psychological health through human relationships. In P. Gilbert & K. G. Bailey (Eds.), *Genes on the couch: Explorations in evolutionary psychotherapy* (pp. 42–67). New York: Brunner-Routledge.

Bailey, W. C., & Peterson, R. D. (1999). Capital punishment, homicide, and deterrence: An assessment of the evidence and extension to female homicide. In M. D. Smith, M. Zahn, (Eds.). *Homicide: A sourcebook of social research* (pp. 257–276). Thousand Oaks, CA: Sage.

Baillargeon, R. (1998). Infants' understanding of the physical world. In M. Sabourin, F. Craik, et al. (Eds.). *Advances in psychological science, Vol. II: Biological and cognitive aspects* (503–529). Hove, England: Psychology Press/Erlbaum, Taylor & Francis.

Baillargeon, R., & Wang, S. (2002). Event categorization in infancy. *Trends in Cognitive Sciences, 6,* 85–93.

Baird, J. C., Wagner, M., & Fuld, K. (1990). A simple but powerful theory of the moon illusion. *Journal of Experimental Psychology: Human Perception and Performance, 16,* 675–677.

Baird, S., & Jenkins, S. R. (2003). Vicarious traumalization, secondary traumatic stress, and burnout in sexual assault and domestic violence agency staff. *Violence & Victims, 18,* 71–86.

Baker, D., & Stauth, C. (2003). *What happy people know.* New York: St. Martin's Griffin.

Bakermans-Kranenburg, M. J., van Lizendoorn, M. H., & Juffer, F. (2003). Less is more: Meta-analyses of sensitivity and attachment intervention in early childhood. *Psychological Bulletin, 129*, 195–215.

Bakken, L., Thompson, J., Clark, F. L., Johnson, N., & Dwyer, K. (2001). Making conservationists and classifiers of preoperational fifth-grade children. *Journal of Educational Research, 95*, 56–61.

Balay, J., & Shevrin, H. (1988). The subliminal psychodynamic activation method. *American Psychologist, 3*, 161–174.

Ball, K., & Lee, C. (2000). Relationship between psychological stress, coping and disordered eating: A review. *Psychology & Health, 14*, 1007–1035.

Bamshad, M. J., & Olson, S. E. (2003). Does race exist? *Scientific American, 289*(6), 78–85.

Bancroft, J. (2002). Biological factors in human sexuality. *Journal of Sex Research, 39*, 15–21.

Bandura, A. (1969). *Principles of behavior modification*. New York: Holt, Rinehart & Winston.

Bandura, A. (1977a). Self-efficacy: Toward a unifying theory of behavioral change. *Psychological Review, 84*, 191–215.

Bandura, A. (1977b). *Social learning theory*. Englewood Cliffs, NJ: Prentice-Hall.

Bandura, A. (1986). *Social foundations of thought and action: A social cognitive theory*. Englewood Cliffs, NJ: Prentice-Hall.

Bandura, A. (1999). Social cognitive theory of personality. In L. A. Pervin & O. P. John (Eds.), *Handbook of personality: Theory and research* (pp. 154–196). New York: Guilford Press.

Bandura, A. (2000). Exercise of human agency through collective efficacy. *Current Directions in Psychological Science, 9*, 75–78.

Bandura, A. (2001). Social cognitive theory: An agentic perspective. *Annual Review of Psychology, 52*, 1–26.

Bandura, A. (2004). Swimming against the mainstream: The early years from chilly tributary to transformative mainstream. *Behaviour Research & Therapy, 42*, 613–630.

Bandura, A., Blanchard, E. B., & Ritter, B. (1969). Relative efficacy of desensitization and modeling approaches for inducing behavioral, affective, and attitudinal changes. *Journal of Personality and Social Psychology, 13*, 173–199.

Bandura, A., & Locke, E. A. (2003). Negative self-efficacy and goal effects revisited. *Journal of Applied Psychology, 88*, 87–99.

Bandura, A., Ross, D., & Ross, S. A. (1963). Imitation of film-mediated aggressive models. *Journal of Abnormal and Social Psychology. 66*. 3–11.

Banks-Wallace, J., & Parks, L., (2004). It's all sacred: African American women's perspective on spirituality. *Issues in Mental Health Nursing, 25*, 25–45.

Banse, R. (2004). Adult attachment and marital satisfaction: Evidence for dyadic configuration effects. *Journal of Social and Personal Relationships, 21*, 273–282.

Barash, D. P. (2001, April 20). Deflating the myth of monogamy. *Chronicle of Higher Education, 47* (32), Section 2, B16–17.

Barber, J. (1991). The locksmith model: Accessing hypnotic responsiveness. In S. J. Lynn & J. W. Rhue (Eds.), *Theories of hypnosis: Current models and perspectives* (pp. 241–274). New York: Guilford Press.

Barber, T. X. (1999). Hypnosis: A mature view. *Contemporary Hypnosis, 16* 123–127.

Barco, A., Alarcon, J. M., & Kandel, E. R. (2002). Expression of constitutively active CREB protein facilitates the late phases of long-term potentiation by enhancing synaptic capture. *Cell, 108*,689–703.

Bard, P. (1934). Emotion: The neuro-humoral basis of emotional reactions. In C. Murchison (Ed.), *Handbook of general experimental psychology*. Worcester, MA: Clark University Press.

Bargh, J. A., Gollwitzer, P. M., Lee-Chai, A., Barndollar, K., & Troetschel, R. (2001). The automated will: Nonconscious activation and pursuit of behavioral goals. *Journal of Personality and Social Psychology, 81*, 1014–1027.

Barlow, S. H., Burlingame, G. M., & Nebeker, R. S. (2000). Meta-analysis of medical self-help groups. *International Journal of Group Psychotheraphy, 50*, 53–69.

Barnes, A. (2004). Race, schizophrenia, and admission to state psychiatric hospitals. *Administration & Policy in Mental Health, 31*, 241–252.

Barnes, M. L., & Sternberg, R. J. (1997). A hierarchical model of love and its prediction of satisfaction in close relationships. In R. J. Sternberg, & M. Hojjat (Eds), *Satisfaction in close relationships* (pp. 79–101). New York: Guilford Press.

Barnier, A.J., & McConkey, K.M. (1998). Posthypnotic responding away from the hypnotic setting. *Psychological Science, 9*, 256–262.

Baron, R. A. (1993). Interviewers' moods and evaluations of job applicants: The role of applicant qualifications. *Journal of Applied Social Psychology, 23*, 253–271.

Baron, R.S. (2000). Arousal, capacity, and intense indoclrination. *Personality & Social Psychology Review, 4*, 238–254.

Barr, H. M., Streissguth, A. P., Darby, B. L., & Sampson, P. D. (1990). Prenatal exposure to alcohol, caffeine, tobacco, and aspirin: Effects on fine and gross motor performance in 4-year-old children. *Developmental Psychology, 26*, 339–348.

Barrelt, L., Dunbar, R., & Lycett, J. (2002). *Human evolutionary psychology*. Princeton, NJ: Princeton University Press.

Bartholomew, K., & Horowitz, L. M. (1991). Attachment styles among young adults: A test of a four category model. *Journal of Personality and Social Psychology, 61*, 226–244.

Bartlett, T. (2004, February 27). Ecstasy agonistes. *Chronicle of Higher Education, 50*(25), A14–A16.

Bartoshuk, L. M. (2000). Comparing sensory experiences across individuals: Recent psychophysical advances illuminate genetic variation in taste perception. *Chemical Senses, 25*, 447–460.

Bass, B. M. (1997). Does the transactional–transformational leadship paradigm transcend organizational and national boundaries? *American Psychologist, 52*, 130–139.

Bass, B. M. (2001). Cognitive, social, and emotional intelligence of transformational leaders. In R. E. Riggio & S. E. Murphy (Eds.) *Multiple intelligences and leadership LEA's organization and management series* (pp. 105–118). Mahwah, NJ: Erlbaum.

Bass, B. M., Avolio, B. J., Jung, D. I., & Berson, Y. (2003). Predicting unit performance by assessing transformational and transactional leadership. *Journal of Applied Psychology, 88*, 207–218.

Bassman, L. E., & Uellendahl, G. (2003). Complementary/alternative medicine: Ethical, professional, and practical challenges for psychologists. *Professional Psychology: Research and Practice, 34*, 264–270.

Bat-Chava, Y., & Martin, D. (2002). Sibling relationships for deal children: The impact of child and family characteristics. *Rehabilitation Psychology, 41*(1), 73–91.

Bates, E., & Dick, F. (2002). Language, gesture, and the developing brain. *Developmental Psychology, 40*, 293–310.

Bates, E., Thal, D., Whitesell, K., Fenson, L., & Oakes, L. (1989). Integratng language and gesture in infancy. *Developmental Psychology, 25*, 1004–1019.

Batson, C. D. (1990). How social an animal? *American Psychologist, 45*, 336–346.

Batson, C.D., Ahmad, N., Lishner, D. A., & Tsang, J. A. (2002). Empathy and altruism. In C. R. Snyder & S. J. Lopez (Eds.), *Handbook of positive psychology* (pp. 485–498). New York: Oxford University Press.

Baum, A., & Posluszny, D. M. (1999). Health psychology: Mapping biobehavioral contributions to health and illness. *Annual Review of Psychology, 50,* 137–164.

Baum, A., & Valins, S. (1977). Suite-style dorm and traditional corridor dorm figure. Architecture and Social Behavior. Mahwah: NJ: Erlbaum.

Baumeister, R. F. (1999). The nature and structure of the self: An overview. In R. F. Baumeister (Ed.). *The self in social psychology* (pp. 1–20). Philadelphia: Taylor & Francis.

Baumeister, R. F. (2001, April). Violent pride. *Scientific American, 284,* 96–101.

Baumeister, R. F., Campbell, J. D., Krueger, J. I., & Vohs, K. D. (2003). Does high self-esteem cause better performance, interpersonal success, happiness, or healthier lifestyles? *Psychological Science in the Public Interest, 4,* 1–44.

Baumeister, R. F., Catanese, K. R., & Vohs, K. D. (2001). Is there a gender difference in strength of sex drive? Theoretical views, conceptual distinctions and a review of the relevant evidence. *Personality & Social Psychology Review, 5,* 242–273.

Baumeister, R. F., & Leary, M. R. (1995). The need to belong: Desire for interpersonal attachments as a fundamental human motivation. *Psychological Bulletin, 117,* 497–529.

Baumeister, R. F., Smart, L., & Boden, J. M. (1996). Relation of threatened egotism to violence and aggression: The dark side of high self esteem. *Psychological Review, 103,* 5–33.

Baumeister, R. F., & Tice, D. M. (2001). *The social dimension of sex.* Boston: Allyn and Bacon.

Baumrind, D., Larzelere, R. E., & Cowan, P.A. (2002). Ordinary physical punishment: Is it harmful? Comment on Gershoff (2002). *Psychological Bulletin, 128,* 580–589.

Bavelier, D., Tomann, A., Hutton, C., Mitchell, T., Corina, D., Liu, G., & Neville, H. (2000). Visual attention to the periphery is enhanced in congenitally deaf individuals. *The Journal of Neuroscience, 20* (RC93), 1–6.

Bayley, N. (1969). Consistency and variability in the growth of intelligence from birth to eighteen years. *Journal of Genetic Psychology, 25,* 165–196.

Bayster, P.G., & Ford, C. M. (2000). The impact of functional issue classification on managerial decision processes: A study in the telecommunications industry. *Journal of Managerial Issues, 12,* 468–483.

Bean, M. (2003, May 21). *Matrix* makes its way into courtrooms as defense strategy. *Court TV.com.* Retrieved March 20, 2004, from http://www.cnn.com/2003/LAW/05/21/clv.matrix.insanity/

Beauchesne, M. A., Barnes, A., Palsdaughter, C., & Beauchesne, M. (2004). Children with disabilities need a Head Start too. *Journal of Learning Disabilities, 8(1),* 41–45.

Beck, A. T. (1963). Thinking and depression: I. Idiosyncratic content in cognitive distortions. *Archives of General Psychiatry, 9,* 324–333.

Beck, A.T. (1967). *Depression: Clinical, experimental, and theoretical aspects.* New York: Hober.

Beck, A.T. (1976). *Cognitive therapy and emtional disorders.* New York: International Universities Press.

Beck, A. T. (1991). Cognitive therapy. *American Psychologist, 46,* 368–375.

Beck, A.T., & Weishaar, M. (1989). Cognitive therapy. In A. Freeman, K. M. Simon, L. E. Beutler, & H. Arkowitz (Eds.), *Comprehensive handbook of cognitive therapy.* New York: Plenum.

Beck, J. (1966). Effects of orientation and of shape similarity on perceptual grouping. *Perception and Psychophysics, 1,* 311–312.

Bednar, D. E., & Fisher, T. D. (2003). Peer referencing in adolescent decision making. *Adolescence, 38,* 607–621.

Beeghley, L. (2000). *The structure of social stratification in the United States* (3rd ed.). Boston:Allyn & Bacon.

Beers, T. M. (2000). Flexible schedules and shift work: Replacing the "9-to-5" workday? *Monthly Labor Review, 123,* 33–40.

Begg, I. M., Needham, D. R., & Bookbinder, M. (1993). Do backward messages unconsciously affect listeners? No. *Canadian Journal of Experimental Psychology, 47,* 1–14.

Behr, H. (2000). Families and group analysis. In D. Brown & L. Zinkin, (Eds.). *The psyche and the social world: Developments in group-analytic theory.* International Library of Group Analysis (pp. 163–179). London, UK: Jessica Kingsley.

Belansky, E. S., & Boggiano, A. K. (1994). Predicting helping behaviors: The role of gender and instrumental/expressive self-schemata. *Sex Roles, 30,* 647–662.

Belgrave, F. Z., Brome, D. R., & Hampton, C. (2000). The contribution of africentric values and racial identity to the prediction of drug knowledge, attitudes, and use among African American youth. *Journal of Black Psychology, 26,* 386–401.

Belle, D., & Doucet, J. (2003). Poverty, inequality, and discrimination as sources of depression among U.S. women. *Psychology of Women Quarterly, 27,* 101–113.

Belsky, J., Jaffee, S., Hsieh, K., & Silva, P. (2001). Child-rearing antecedents of intergenerational relations in young adulthood: A prospective study. *Developmental Psychology, 37,* 801–813.

Bem, D. J. (1972). Self-perception theory. In L. Berkowitz (Ed.), *Advances in experimental social psychology* New York: Academic Press.

Bem, D. J. (1996). Exotic becomes erotic: A developmental theory of sexual orientation. *Psychological Review,103,* 320–335.

Bem, D. J. (2000). Exotic becomes erotic: Interpreting the biological corelates of sexual orientation. *Archives of Sexual Behavior, 29,* 531–548.

Bem, S. L. (1985). Androgyny and gender schema theory: A conceptual and empirical integration. In T. B. Sonderegger (Ed.), *Nebraska symposium on motivation* (pp 179–226). Lincoln, NE: University of Nebraska Press.

Bem, S. L. (1993). *The lenses of gender.* New Haven, CT: Yale University Press.

Bender, S. T. (1999). Attachment style and friendship characteristics in college students. *Dissertation Abstracts International: Section B: The Sciences & Engineering, 60* (5-B), 2407.

Benet-Martinez, V., & Waller, N. G. (1997). Further evidence for the cross-cultural generality of the Big Seven Factor model: Indigenous and imported Spanish personality constructs. *Journal of Personality, 65,* 567–598.

Benjamin, L. T, Jr., & Baker, D. B. (2004). *From séance to science: A history of the profession of psychology in America.* Belmont, CA: Wadsworth.

Bennett, G. G., Merritt, M. M., Edwards, C. L., & Sollers, J. J., Ill. (2004). Perceived racism and affective responses to ambiguous interpersonal interactions among African American men. *American Behavioral Scientist, 47,* 963–976.

Berardi, N., Pizzorusso, T., Rallo, G. M., & Maffei, L., (2003). Molecular basis of plasticity in the visual cortex. *Trends in Neuroscience, 26,* 369–378.

Berk, L. E. (1994). *Child Development* (3rd ed.). Boston: Allyn and Bacon.

Berkley, K. J. (1997). Sex differences in pain. *Behavioral and Brain Sciences, 20,* 371–380.

Berkman, L. F., & Breslow, L. (1983). *Health and ways of living: The Alameda County Study.* New York: Oxford University Press.

Berkowitz, L., (1964). *The effects of observing violence.* San Francisco: Freeman.

Berkowitz, L., (2000). *Causes and consequences of feelings: Studies in emotion and social interaction.* New York; Cambridge University Press.

Berman, F. E., & Miner, J. B. (1985). Motivation to manage at the top executive level: A test of the hierarchic role-motivation theory. *Personal Psychology, 38,* 377–391.

Bernal, G., &Berger, S. M. (1976). Vicarious eyelid conditioning. *Journal of Personality and Social Psychology, 34,* 62–68.

Bernard, M. M., Maio, G. R., & Olson, J. M. (2003). The vulnerability of values to attack: Inoculation of values and value-relevant attitudes. *Personality and Social Psychology Bulletin, 29,* 63–75.

Bernardo, A. B., Zhang, L-F., & Callueng, C. M. (2002). Thinking styles and academic achievement among Filipino students. *Journal of Genetic Psychology, 163,* 149–164.

Bernstein, D., & Ebbesen, E. (1978). Reinforcement and substitution in humans: A multiple-response analysis. *Journal of the Experimental Analysis of Behavior, 30,* 243–253.

Bernstein, G. A., Carroll, M. E., Thuras, P. D., Cosgrove, K. P., & Roth, M. E. (2002). Caffeine dependence in teenagers. *Drug & Alcohol Dependence, 66,* 1–5.

Bernstein, I. L., (1988, September). *What does learning have to do with weight loss and cancer?* Paper presented at a science and public policy seminar sponsored by the Federation of Behavioral, Psychological, and Cognitive Sciences, Washington, DC.

Bernstein, I. L. (1991). Aversion conditioning in response to cancer and cancer treatment. *Clinical Psychology Review, 11,* 185–191.

Bernstein, K. S. (2000). The experience of acupuncture for treatment of substance dependence. *Journal of Nursing Scholarship, 32,* 267–272.

Bernstein, L. R., Trahiotis, C., Akeroyd, M. A., & Hartung, K. (2001). Sensitivity to brief changes of interaural time and interaural intensity. *Journal of the Acoustical Society of America, 109,* 1604–1615.

Berry, D. S., & Landry, J. C. (1997). Facial maturity and daily social interaction. *Journal of Personality and Social Psychology, 72,* 570–580.

Bersoff, D. M., & Miller, J. G. (1993). Culture, context, and the development of moral accountability judgments. *Developmental Psychology, 29,* 664–676.

Bertenthal, B. I., Campos, J. J., & Kermoian, R. (1994). An epigenetic perspective on the development of self-produced locomotion and its consequences. *Current Directions in Psychological Science, 3,* 140–145.

Berthier, N. E., DeBlois, S., Poirier, C. R., Novak, M. A., & Clinton, R. K. (2001). Where's the ball? Two-and three-year-olds reason about unseen events. *Developmental Psychology, 36,* 394–401.

Besharat, M. A. (2003). Relation of attachment style with marital conflict, *Psychological Reports, 92,* 1135–1140.

Bettencourt, B. A., & Miller, N. (1996). Gender differences in aggression as a function of provocation: A meta-analysis. *Psychological Bulletin, 119,* 422–447.

Bexton, W. H., Heron, W., & Scott, T. H. (1954). Effects of decreased variation in the sensory environment. *Canadian Journal of Psychology, 8,* 70–76.

Beyer, S. (2002). The effects of gender, dysphoria, and performance feedback on the accuracy of self-evaluations. *Sex Roles, 47,* 453–464.

Biaggio, M., Roades, L. A., Staffelbach, D., Cardinali, J., & Duffy, R. (2000). Intracultural and intercultural. Dialogue in psychoanalytic psychotherapy and psychoanalysis. *Journal of Applied Social Psychology, 30,* 1657–1669.

Bickerton, D. (1998). The creation and re-creation of language. In C. B. Crawlord & D. L. Krebs (Eds.). *Handbook of evolutionary psychology: Ideas, issues, and applications* (pp. 613–634). Mahwah, NJ: Erlbaum.

Binet, A., & Simon, T. (1905/1916). New methods for the diagnosis of the intellectual level of sub-normals. In H. H. Goddard (Ed.) and E. S. Kite (trans.), *Development of intelligence in children (the Binet-Simon Scale)* (pp.37–90). Baltimore: Williams & Wilkins.

Birmahler, B., Williamson, D. E., Dahl, R. E., Axelson, D. A., Kaufman, J., Dorn, L. D., & Ryan, N. D. (2004). Clinical presentation and course of depression in youth: Does onset in childhood differ from onset in adolescence? *Journal of the American Academy of Child & Adolescent Psychiatry, 43,* 63–70.

Bjorklund, D. E. & Pellegrini, A. D. (2000). Child development and evolutionary psychology. *Child development, 71*(6), 1678–1708.

Blackwood, N. J., Bentall, R. P., ffytche, D. H., Simmons, A., Murray, R. M., & Howard, R. J. (2003). Self-responsibility and the self-serving bias: An [MR] investigation of causal attributions. *NeuroImage, 20,* 1076–1085.

Blair, R. J. R. (2004). The roles of orbital frontal cortex in the modulation of antisocial behavior *Brain & Cognition, 55,* 198–208.

Blake, R. J., & Zyzik, E. C. (2003). Who's helping whom?: Learner/heritage-speakers' networked discussions in Spanish. *Applied Linguistics, 24,* 519–544.

Blakemore, C., & Campbell, F. W. (2000). On the existence of neurons in the human visual system selectively sensitive to the orientation and size of retinal images. In S. Yantis, *Visual perception: Essential readings: Key readings in cognition* (pp. 172–189). Philadelphia: Psychology Press/Taylor & Francis.

Blakemore, J. E. O. (2003). Children's beliefs about violating gender norms: Boys shouldn't look like girls, and girls shouldn't act like boys. *Sex Roles, 48,* 411–419.

Blass, T. (2000). The Milgram Paradigm after 35 years: Some things we now know about obedience to authority. In T. Blass (Ed.), *Obedience to authority: Current perspectives on the Milgram paradigm* (pp. 35–59). Mahwah, NJ: Erlbaum.

Blass, T. (2002). Perpetrator behavior as destructive obedience: An evaluation of Stanley Milgram's perspective, the most influential social-psychological approach to the Holocaust. In L. S. Newman & R. Erber (Eds.). *Understanding genocide: The social psychology of the Holocaust* (pp. 91–109). London: Oxford University Press.

Blazina, C., & Watkins, C. E., (2000). Separation/individuation, parental attachment, and male gender role conflict: Attitudes toward the feminine and fragile masculine self. *Psychology of Men & Masculinity, 1,* 126–132.

Bleak, J. L., & Frederick, C. M. (1998). Superstitious behavior in sport: Levels of effectiveness and determinants of use in three collegiate sports. *Journal of Sport Behavior, 21,* 1–15.

Bleeker, M. M., & Jacobs, J. E. (2004). Achievement in math and science: Do mothers' beliefs matter 12 years later? *Journal of Educational Psychology, 96,* 97–109.

Bleske, A. L., & Buss, D. M. (2000). Can men and women be just friends? *Personal Relationships, 7,* 131–151.

Bliss, T. V. P., & Lømø, T. (1973). Long-lasting potentiation of synaptic transmission in the dentate area of the anaesthetized rabbit following stimulation of the perforant path. *Journal of Physiology, 232,* 331–356.

Bloom, M., & Michel, J. G. (2002). The relationships among organizational context, pay dispersion, and managerial turnovers.

Academy of Management Journal, 45, 33–42.

Bloomfield, K., Stockwell, T., Gmel, G., & Rehn, N. (2003). *International comparisons of alcohol consumption*. National Institute on Alcohol Abuse and Alcoholism (NIAAA). Retrieved May 26, 2004, from http://www.niaaa.nih.gov/publications/arh27–1/95–109.htm

Blount, S., & Larrick, R. P. (2002). Framing the game: Examining frame choice in bargaining. *Organizational Behavior & Human Decision Processes, 81,* 43–71.

Blum, K., Braverman, E. R., Holder, J. M., Lubar, J. F., Monastra, V. J., Miller, D., Lubar, J. O., Chen, T. H., & Comings, D. E. (2000). Reward deficiency syndrome: A biogenetic model for the diagnosis and treatment of impulsive, addictive, and compulsive behaviors. *Journal of Psychoactive Drugs, 32,* 1–68.

Boake, C. (2002). From the Binet-Simon to the Wechsler-Bellvue: Tracing the history of intelligence testing. *Journal of Clinical and Experimental Neuropsychology, 24,* 383–405.

Boatwright, K. J., Egidio, R. K., & Kalamazoo College Women's Leadership Research Team. (2003). Leadership aspirations of women college students. *Journal of College Student Development, 44,* 653–699.

Bodamer, M. D., & Gardner, R. A. (2002). How cross-fostered chimpanzees (*Pan troglodytes*) initiate and maintain conversations. *Journal of Comparative Psychology, 116,* 12–26.

Bodenhorn, N., & Lawson, G. (2003). Genetic counseling: Implications for community counselors, *Journal of Counseling and Development, 81,* 497–501.

Bodnar, A. G., Ouellette, M., Frolkis, M., Holt, S. E., Chiu, C. P., Morin, G. B., Harley, C. B., Shay, J. W., Lichisteiners, S., & Wright, W. E. (1998). Extension of life-span by introduction of telomerase into normal human cells. *Science, 279,* 349–352.

Bohart, A. C., & Greening, T. (2001). Humanistic psychology and positive psychology. *American Psychologist, 56,* 81–82.

Boivin, D. B., & James, F. O. (2002). Phase-dependent effect of room light exposure in a 5-h advance of the sleep-wake cycle: Implications for jet lag. *Journal of Biological Rhythms, 17,* 266–276.

Bolanowski, S. J., Maxfield, L. M., Gescheider, G. A., & Apkarian, A. V. (2000). The effect of stimulus location on the gating of touch by heat- and cold-induced pain. *Somatosensory & Motor Research, 17,* 195–204.

Bolt, M. (2003, January). *Incorporating positive psychology themes into your course.*

Paper presented at the 25th annual National Institute on the Teaching of Psychology,. St. Petersburg Beach, FL.

Bond, C. F., Jr., & Titus, L. J. (1983). Social facilitation: A meta-analysis of 241 studies. *Psychological Bulletin, 94,* 265–292.

Bond, R. A., & Smith, P. B. (1996). Culture and conformity: A meta-analysis of studies using Asch's (1952b, 1956) line judgment task. *Psychological Bulletin, 119,* 111–137.

Boniecki, K. A., & Moore, S. (2003). Breaking the silence: Using a token economy to reinforce classroom participation. *Teaching of Psychology, 30,* 224–227.

Bookheimer, S. (2002). Functional MRI of language: New approaches to understanding the cortical organization of semantic processing. *Annual Review of Neuroscience, 25,* 151–188.

Booth, A., Johnson, D. R., Granger, D. A., Crouter, A. C., & McHale, S. (2003). Testosterone and child and adolescent adjustment: The moderating role of parent-child relationships. *Developmental Psychology, 39,* 85–98.

Booth, C. L., Clarke-Stewart, K. A., Vandell, D. L., McCartney, K. O., & Owen, M. T. (2002). Child-care usage and mother-infant "quality-time." *Journal of Marriage & Family, 64,* 16–26.

Bor, D., Duncan, J., Wiseman, R. J., & Owen, A. M, (2003). Encoding strategies dissociate prefrontal activity from working memory demand. *Neuron, 37,* 361–367.

Boraas, S., & Rodgers, W. M. (2003). How does gender play a role in the earnings gap? An update. *Monthly Labor Review, 3,* 9–15.

Borg, E., & Counter, S. A. (1989, August). The middle-ear muscles. *Scientific American,* 74–80.

Boring, E. G. (1950). *A history of experimental psychology* (2nd ed.). New York: Appleton-Century-Crofts.

Borkenau, P., & Ostendorf, F. (1998). The Big Five as states: How useful is the five-factor model to describe intraindividual variations over time? *Journal of Research in Personality, 32,* 202–221.

Boronat, C. B., & Logan, G. D. (1997). The role of attention in automatization: Does attention operate at encoding, or retrieval, or both? *Memory and Cognition, 25,* 36–46.

Borrie, R. A. (1991). The use of restricted environmental stimulation therapy in treating addictive behaviors. *International Journal of the Addictions, 25,* 995–1015.

Bosacki, S. L. (2003). Psychological pragmatics in preadolescents: Sociomoral understanding, self-worth, and school behavior. *Journal of Youth & Adolescence, 32*(2), 141–155.

Botschner, J. V. (1996). Reconsidering male friendships: A social-development perspective. In C. W. Tolman, F. Cherry, R. Van Hezewijk, & I. Lubek (Eds.), *Problems of theoretical psychology* (pp. 242–253). North York, Ontario: Captus Press.

Bolt, D. (2001). Towards a family-centered therapy. Postmodern developments in family therapy and the person-centered contribution. *Counseling Psychology Quarterly, 14,* 111–118.

Bouchard, T. J., & Loehlin, J. C. (2001). Genes, evolution, and personality. *Behavior Genetics, 31,* 243–273.

Bouchard, T. J., Jr., & McGue, M. (1981). Familial studies of intelligence: A review. *Science, 212,* 1055–1058.

Boudreaux, E., Kilpatrick, D. G., Resnick, H. S., Best, C. L., & Saunders, B. E. (1998). Criminal victimization, posttraumatic stress disorder, and comorbid psychopathology among a community sample of women. *Journal of Traumatic Stress, 11,* 665–678.

Boutcher, S. H. (1992). Attention and athletic performance: An integrated approach. In T. S. Horn (Ed.), *Advances in sport psychology* (pp. 251–265). Champaign, IL: Human Kinetics.

Bower, G. H. (1981). Mood and memory. *American Psychologist, 36,* 126–148.

Bowlby, J. (1977). The making and breaking of affectional bonds: Etiology and psychopathology in the light of attachment theory. *British Journal of Psychiatry, 130,* 201–210.

Bowlby, J. (1988). *A secure base*. New York: Basic Books.

Bowleg, L., Lucas, K. J., & Tschann, J. M. (2004). "The ball was always in his court": An exploratory analysis of relationship scripts, sexual scripts, and condom use among African American women. *Psychology of Women Quarterly, 28,* 70–82.

Boynton, D. M. (2003). Superstitious responding and frequency matching in the positive bias and gambler's fallacy effects. *Organizational Behavior & Human Decision Processes, 91,* 119–127.

Boynton, R. M. (1988). Color vision. *Annual Review of Psychology, 39,* 69–101.

Brackett, M. A., Mayer, J. D., & Warner, R. M. (2004). Emotional intelligence and its relation to everyday behaviour. *Personality and Individual Differences, 36,* 1387–1402.

Bradford, D., Stroup, S., & Lieberman, J. (2002). Pharmacological treatments for schizophrenia. In P. E. Nathan & J. M. Gorman (Eds.), *A guide to treatments that work* (pp. 169–199). New York: Oxford Press.

Bradley, C. L., & Marcia, J. E. (1998). Genera-tivity-stagnation: A five-category model. *Journal of Personality, 66*(1), 39–44.

Braffman, W., & Kirsch, I. (1999). Imaginative suggestibility and hypnotizability: An empir-ical analysis. *Journal of Personality and Social Psychology, 77*, 578–587.

Branje, S. J. T., van Aken, M. A. G., & van Lieshout, C. F. M. (2002). Relational sup-port in families with adolescents. *Journal of Family Psychology, 16*, 351–362.

Brannon, L. (2005). *Gender: Psychological per-spectives* (4th ed.). Boston: Allyn & Bacon.

Brannon, L., & Feist, J. (2004). *Health psy-chology: An introduction to behavior and health* (5th ed.). Belmont, CA: Wadsworth.

Bray, G. A. (2004). The epidemic of obesity and changes in food intake: The fluoride hypothesis. *Physiology & Behavior, 82*, 115–121.

Breger, L. (2000). *Freud: Darkness in the midst of vision.* New York: Wiley.

Brehm, J. W. (1966). *A theory of psychological reactance.* New York: Academic Press.

Brems, C., & Johnson, M. E. (1997). Compari-son of recent graduates of clinical versus counseling psychology programs. *Journal of Psychology, 131*, 91–99.

Brennan, K. A., Clark, C. L., & Shaver, P. R. (1998). Self-report measurement of adult attachment: An integrative overview. In J. A. Simpson, W. S. Rholes, and others. *Attachment Theory and Close Relationships.* (46–76). New York, NY: Guilford Press.

Bretschneider, J. G., & McCoy, N. L. (1988). Sexual interest and behavior in healthy 80- to 102-year-olds. *Archives of Sexual Behavior, 17*, 109–129.

Brelt, M., Johnsrude, I. S., & Owen, A. M. (2002). The problem of functional localiza-tion in the human brain. *Nature Reviews: Neuroscience, 3*, 243–249

Brewer, C. L. (1991). Perspectives on John B. Watson. In G. A. Kimble, M. Wertheimer, & C. White (Eds.), *Portraits of pioneers in psy-chology* (pp. 171–186). Washington, DC: American Psychological Association.

Bridges, K. M. B. (1932). Emotional develop-ment in early infancy. *Child Development, 3*, 324–341.

Bridges, R. S., & Kunselman, J. C. (2004). Gun availability and use of guns for suicide, homicide, and murder in Canada. *Perceptual & Motor Skills, 98*, 594–599.

Brief, A. P., & Weiss, H. M. (2002). Organiza-tional behavior: Affect in the workplace. *Annual Review of Psychology, 53*(1), 279–307.

Broberg, A. G., Wessels. H., Lamb, M. E., & Hwang, C. P. (1997). Effects of day care on

the development of cognitive abilities in 8-year-olds: A longitudinal study. *Developmental Psychology, 33*(1), 62–69.

Brockner, J., & Higgins, E. T. (2001). Regula-tory focus theory: Implications for the study of emotions at work. *Organizational Behavior & Human Decision Processes, 86*, 35–66.

Bröder, A. (2003). Decision making with the "adaptive toolbox": Influence of environ-mental structure, intelligence, and working memory load. *Journal of Experimental Psy-chology: Learning, Memory, and Cognition, 29*, 611–625.

Brody, G. H. (1998). Sibling relationship qual-ity: Its causes and consequences. *Annual Review in Psychology, 49*, 1–24.

Brogdon, M. G., Adams, J. H., & Bahri, R. (2004). Psychology and the law. In W. O'Donohue & E. Levensky (Eds.). *Handbook of forensic psychology: Resource for mental health and legal professionals* (pp. 3–26). London: Elsevier Academic Press.

Brofenbrenner, U. (1979). *The ecology of human development: Experiments by nature and design.* Cambridge, MA: Harvard University Press.

Bronfenbrenner, U. (1989, September). Who cares for children? Invited address, UNESCO, Paris.

Bronfenbrenner, U. (1999). Environments in developmental perspective: Theoretical and operational models. In S. L. Friedman & T. D. Wachs (Eds.). *Measuring environment across the life span: Emerging methods and concepts* (pp. 3–28). Washington, DC: American Psychological Association.

Brooks, G. R. (2001). Developing gender awareness: When therapist growth promotes family growth. In S. H. McDaniel, D. D. Lusterman, & C. Philpot (Eds.). *Casebook for integrating family therapy: An ecosys-temic approach* (pp. 265–274). Washington, DC: American Psychological Association.

Brooks, R., & Meltzoff, A. (2002). The impor-tance of eyes: How infants interpret adult looking behavior. *Developmental Psychology, 38*, 958–966.

Brooks-Gunn, J., Han, W., & Waldfogel, J. (2002). Maternal employment and child cognitive outcomes in the first three years of life: The NICHD study of early child care. *Child Development, 73*, 1052–1072.

Brown, A. S. (1991). The tip of the tongue experience: A review and evaluation. *Psychological Bulletin, 10*, 204–223.

Brown, B., Moore, K., & Bzostek, S. (2003). A portrait of well being in early adulthood. *A Report to the William and Flora Hewlett Foundation.* Retrieved July 6, 2004, from http://www.hewlett.org/NR/

rdonlyres/B0DB0AFI-02A4-455A-849A-AD582B767AF3/0/ FINALCOM-PLETEPDF.pdf

Brown, G. S., Jones, E. R., Betts, E., & Wu, J. (2003). Improving suicide risk assessment in a managedcare environments. *Crisis: The Journal of Crisis Intervention and Suicide Prevention, 24*, 49–55.

Brown, J. M., Mehler, P. S., & Harris, R. H. (2000). Medical complications occuring in adolescents with anorexia nervosa. *Western Journal of Medicine, 172*, 189–193

Brown, K. W., & Moskowitz, D. S. (1998). Dynamic stability of behavior: The rhythms of our interpersonal lives. *Journal of Personality, 66*, 105–108.

Brown, R. (1970). The first sentences of child and chimpanzee. In R. Brown (Ed.), *Psycholinguistics: Selected papers* (pp. 208–231). New York: Free Press.

Brown, R. (1973). *A first language: The early stages.* Cambridge, MA: Harvard University Press.

Brown, R., & Kulik, J. (1977). Flashbulb memories. *Cognition, 5*, 73–99.

Brown, S. C., & Craik, F. I. M. (2000). Encoding and retrieval of information. In E. Tulving & F. I. M. Craik (Eds.). *The Oxford handbook of memory* (pp. 93–107). New York: Oxford University Press.

Bruner, J. (1997). Celebrating divergence: Piaget and Vygotsky. *Human Development, 40*, 63–73.

Buccino, G., Lui, F., Canessa, N., Pastteri, I., Lagravinese, G., Benuzzi, F., et al. (2004). Neural circuits involved in the recognition of actions performed by nonconspecifics: An [MR] study. *Journal of Cognitive Neuro-science, 16*, 114–126.

Bumpus, M. F., Crouter, A. C., & McHale, S. M. (2001). Parental autonomy granting during adolescence: Exploring gender differ-ence in context. *Developmental Psychology, 37*, 163–173.

Bureau of Justice Statistics. (2003). *Intimate partner violence, 1993–2001.* Retrieved June 15, 2004, from http://www.ojp.usdoj.gov/bjs/abstract/ipv01.htm

Burroughs, S. M., & Eby, L. T. (1998). Psychological sense of community at work: A measurement system and explanatory framework. *Journal of Community Psychol-ogy, 26*, 509–532.

Busato, V. V., Prins, F. J., Elshout, J. J., & Hamaker, C. (1999). The relation between learning styles, the Big Five personality traits and achievement motivation in higher edu-cation. *Personality and Individual Differ-ences, 26*, 129–140.

Bush, G., Shin, L. M., Holmes, J., Roseb, B. R., & Vogt, B. A. (2003). The multi-source interference task: Validation study with [MR] in individual subjects. *Molecular Psychiatry, 8*, 60–70.

Bushman, B. J., & Anderson, C. A. (2001). Media violence and the American public: Scientific facts versus media misinformation. *American Psychologist, 56*, 477–489.

Bushman, B. J., & Baumeister, R. F. (1998). Threatened egotism, narcissism, self-esteem, and direct and displaced aggression: Does self-love or self-hate lead to violence? *Journal of Personality & Social Psychology, 75*, 219–229.

Bushman, B. J., & Baumeister, R. F. (2002). Does self-love or self-hate lead to violence? *Journal of Research in Personality, 36*, 543–545.

Bushman, B. J., & Cantor, J. (2003). Media ratings for violence and sex implications for policymakers and parents. *American Psychologist, 58*, 130–141.

Buss, D. M. (1999). *Evolutionary psychology* Boston: Allyn & Bacon.

Buss, D. M. (2000a). *The dangerous passion: Why jealousy is as necessary as love and sex.* New York: Free Press.

Buss, D. M. (2000b). The evolution of happiness. *American Psychologist, 55*, 15–23.

Buss, D. M. (2004). *Evolutionary psychology: The new science of the mind* (2nd ed.). Boston: Allyn & Bacon.

Buss, D. M., Shackelford, T. K., Kirkpatrick, L. A., & Larsen, R. J. (2001). A half century of mate preference: The cultural evolution of values. *Journal of Marriage and Family, 63*, 491–503.

Bussey, K., & Bandura, A. (1999). Social cognitive theory of gender development and differentiation. *Psychological Review, 106*, 676–713.

Butler, S. F., & Strupp, H. H. (1991). Psychodynamic psychotherapy. In M. Hersen, A. E. Kazdin, & A. S. Bellack (Eds.), *The clinical psychology handbook* (2nd ed., pp. 519–533). New York: Pergamon Press.

Cabeza, R., Rao, S. M., Wagner, A. D., Mayer, A. R., & Schacter, D. L. (2001). Can medial temporal lobe regions distinguish true from false? An event-related functional MRI study of veridical and illusory recognition memory. *Proceedings of the National Academy of Sciences of the United States, 98*, 4805–4810.

Cacioppo, J. T., Berntson, G. G., Lorig, T. S., Norris, C. J., Rickett, E., & Nusbaum, H. (2003). Just because you're imaging the brain doesn't mean you can stop using your head: A primer and set of first principles. *Journal of Personality and Social Psychology, 85*, 650–661.

Cacioppo, J. T., Berntson, G. G., Sheridan, J. F., & McClintock, M. K. (2000). Multilevel

integrative analyses of human behavior: Social neuro-science and the complementing nature of social and biological approaches. *Psychological Bulletin, 126*, 829–843.

Cacioppo, J. T., & Gardner, W. L. (1999). Emotion. *Annual Review of Psychology, 50*, 191–214.

Cairns, R. B., & Cairns, B. D. (1994). *Lifelines and risks: Pathways of youth in our time.* Cambridge, UK: Cambridge University Press.

Cairns, R. B., & Cairns, B. D. (2000). The natural history and developmental functions of aggression. In A. J. Sameroff, M. Lewis, S. M. Miller (Eds.), *Handbook of developmental psychopathology* (pp. 403–429). New York: Kluwer/Plenum.

California Task Force to Promote Self-Esteem and Personal and Social Responsibility. (1990). *Toward a State of self-esteem*, Sacramento: California State Department of Education.

Call, M. J. (1999). Transgenerational attachment, life stress, and the development of disruptive behavior in preschool children. *Dissertation Abstracts International: Section B: The Sciences & Engineering, 60* (4-B), 1884.

Camara, W. J., & Schneider, D. L. (1994). Integrity tests: Facts and unresolved issues. *American Psychologist, 49*, 112–119.

Cameron, P., & Cameron, K. (1998). "Definitive" University of Chicago sex survey overestimated prevalence of homosexual identity. *Psychological Reports, 82*(3, Pt.1), 861–862.

Campbell, F. A., Ramey, C. T., Pungello, E., Sparling, J., & Miller-Johnson, S. (2002). Early childhood education: Young adult outcomes from the Abecedarian Project. *Applied Developmental Science, 6*, 42–57.

Campion, M. A., Palmer, D. K., & Campion, J. E. (1998). Structuring employment interviews to improve reliability, validity, and users' reactions. *Current Directions in Psychological Science, 7*, 77–82.

Cannon, W. B. (1927). The James-Lange theory of emotion: A critical examination and an alternative theory. *American Journal of Psychology, 39*, 106–124.

Cannon-Bowers, J. A., & Salas, E. (1998). Team performance and training in complex environments: Recent findings from applied research. *Current Directions in Psychological Science, 7*, 83–87.

Cantwell, R. H., & Andrews, B. (2002). Cognitive and psychological factors underlying secondary school students' feelings toward group work. *Educational Psychology, 22*, 75–91.

Caporael, L. R. (2001). Evolutionary psychology: Toward a unifying theory and a hybrid science. *Annual Review of Psychology, 52*, 607–628.

Caputo, R. K. (2003). Head Start, other preschool programs and life success in a youth cohort. *Journal of Sociology and Social Welfare, 30*, 105–126.

Carello, C., & Turvey, M. T. (2004). Physics and the psychology of the muscle sense. *Current Directions in Psychological Science, 13*, 25–28

Carlsmith, K. M., Darley, J. M., & Robinson, P. H. (2002). Why do we punish? Deterrence and just desserts as motives for punishment. *Journal of Personality and Social Psychology, 83*, 284–299.

Carlson-Radvansky, L. A., Covey, E. S., & Lattanzi, K. M. (1999). "What" effects on "Where": Functional influences on spatial relations. *Psychological Science, 10*, 516–521.

Carmena, J. M., Lebedev, M. A., Crist, R. E., O'Doherty, J. E., Santucci, D. M., Dimitrov, D. F., & et. al. (2003). Learning to control a brain–machine interface for reaching and grasping by primates. *Public Library of Psychology, 1*, 193–208.

Caron, A. J., Butler, S., & Brooks, R. (2002). Gaze following at 12 and 24 months: Do the eyes matter? *British Journal of Developmental Psychology, 20*, 225–240.

Carr, M., Borkowski, J. G., & Maxwell, S. E. (1991). Motivational components of underachievement. *Developmental Psychology, 27*, 108–118.

Carr, V. J., Johnston, P. J., Lewin, T. J., Rajkumar, S., Carter, G. L., & Issakidis, C. (2003). Patterns of service use among persons with schizophrenia and other psychotic disorders. *Psychiatric Services, 54*, 226–235.

Carruth, B. R., Ziegler, P. J., Gordon, A., & Hendricks, K. (2004). Developmental milestones and self-feeding behaviors in infants and toddlers. *Journal of the American Dietetic Association*. Retrieved June 25, 2004, from http://articles.findarticles.com/p/articles/mi_m0822/is_1_104/ai_112801025

Carstensen, L. L., & Charles, S. T. (1998). Emotion in the second half of life. *Psychological Science, 7*, 144–149.

Cartwright, M., Wardle, J., Steggles, N., Simon, A. E., Croker, H., & Jarvis, M. J. (2003). Stress and dietary practices in adolescents. *Health Psychology, 22*, 362–369.

Carver, C. S., & Scheier, M. F. (2002). Optimism. In C. R. Snyder & S. J. Lopez (Eds.), *Handbook of positive psychology* (pp. 231–243). New York: Oxford University Press.

Carver, P. R., Peny, D. G., & Egan, S. K. (2004). Children who question their heterosexuality. *Developmental Psychology, 40*, 43–53.

Casagrande, M., Violani, C., Lucidi, F., & Buttinelli, E. (1996). Variations in sleep mentation as a function of time of night. *International Journal of Neuroscience, 85,* 19–30.

Casas, J. M., Turner, J. A., Ruiz, de, E., & Christoper, A. (2001). Machismo revisited in a time of crisis: Implications for understanding and counseling Hispanic men. In G. R. Brooks, R. Gary, G. E. Good (Eds.). *The new handbook of psychotherapy and counseling with men: A comprehensive guide to settings, problems, and treatment approaches,* 1 & 2 (pp. 754–779). San Francisco: Jossey-Bass.

Casey, B. J., Giedd, J. N., & Thomas, K. M. (2000). Structural and functional brain development and its relation to cognitive development. *Biological Psychology, 54,* 241–257.

Casino, S., Maquet, P., Dolan, R. J., & Rugg, M. D. (2002). Brain activity underlying encoding and retrieval of source memory. *Cerebral Cortex, 12,* 1048–1056.

Caspi, A., McClay, J., Moffill, T. E., Mill, J., Martin, J., Craig, I. W., Taylor, A., & Poulton, R. (2002). Role of genotype in the cycle of violence in maltreated children. *Science, 297,* 851–854.

Caspi, A., & Roberts, B. W. (2001). Target article: Personality development across the life course: The argument for change and continuity. *Psychological Inquiry, 12,* 49–66.

Caspi, A., Sugden, K., Moffitt, T. E., Taylor, A., Craig, I. W., Harrington, H., et al. (2003). Influence of life stress on depression: Moderation by a polymorphism in the 5-HTT gene. *Science, 301,* 386–389.

Cassia, V. M., Simion, F., & Umilta, C. (2001). Face preference at birth: The role of an orienting mechanism. *Developmental Science, 4,* 101–108.

Cassia, V. M., Simion, F., Milani, I., & Umiltà, C. (2002). Dominance of global visual properties at birth. *Journal of Experimental Psychology: General, 131(3),* 398–411.

Cassidy, T. (2000). Stress, healthiness, and health behaviours: An exploration of the role of life events, daily hassles, cognitive appraisal, and the coping process. *Counselling Psychology Quarterly, 13,* 293–311.

Castonguay, L. G., Schul, A. J., Aikins, D. E., Constantino, M. J., Laurenceau, J. P., Bologh, L., et al. (2004). Integrative cognitive therapy for depression: A preliminary investigation. *Journal of Psychotherapy Integration, 14,* 4–20.

Cattell, R. B. (1949). *Manual for forms A and B: Sixteen personality factors questionnaire.* Champaign, IL: IPAT.

Cattell, R. B. (1950). *Personality: A systematic, theoretical and factual study.* New York: McGraw-Hill.

Cavalier, A. R., Ferretti, R. P., & Hodges, A. E. (1997). Self-management within a classroom token economy for students with learning disabilities. *Research in Development Disabilities,18,* 167–178.

Ceci, S. J. (2000). So near and yet so far: Lingering questions about the use of measures of general intelligence for college admission and employment screening. *Psychology, Public Policy, & Law, 6,* 233–252.

Ceci, S. J., & Bruck, M. (1993). Suggestibility of the child witness: A historical review and synthesis. *Psychological Bulletin, 113,* 403–439.

Ceci, S. J., & Williams, W. M. (1997). Schooling, intelligence, and income. *American Psychologist, 52,* 1051–1058.

Center on Aging and Aged. (2004). *Aging trends.* Retrieved July 6, 2004, from http://www.indiana. edu/-caa/gai_trends.html

Centers for Disease Control and Prevention. (1997). Regional variations in suicide rates—United States 1990–1994. *Mortality and Morbidity Weekly Report, 34,* 789–792. Retrieved July 8, 2004, from http://www.cdc.gov/mmwr/ preview/ mmwrhtml/00049117.htm

Centers for Disease Control and Prevention. (2001). HIV and AIDS—United States, 1981–2000. *Morbidity and Mortality Weekly Report, 50,* 430–433.

Centers for Disease Control and Prevention. (2004). *Suicide and attempted suicide.* Retrieved November 23, 2004, from http://www.cdc.gove/mmwr/ preview/mmwrhtml/mm5322al.htm

Cervantes, J.M., & Lechuga, D. M. (2004). The meaning of pain: A key to working with the Spanish-speaking patients with work-related injuries, *Professional Psychology: Research and Practice, 35,* 27–35.

Chaleby, K. (2000). Forensic psychiatry and Islamic law.In I.Al-Issa (Ed.), *Al-Junun: Mental illness in the Islamic world* (pp. 71–98). Madison, CT: International Universities Press.

Chall, J. S., & Jacobs, V. A. (2003). Poor children's fourth-grade slump. *American Educator.* Retrieved [July 4, 2004, from http://www.aft.org/american_educator/spring2003/chall.html

Chalmers, D. J. (1996). *Conscious mind: In search of a fundamental theory.* New York: Oxford University Press.

Chalmers, D. J. (2002). The puzzle of conscious experience. *Scientific American, 12(1),* 90–99.

Chambless, D. L., & Hollon, S. D. (1998). Defining empirically supported therapies. *Journal of Consulting and Clinical Psychology, 66,* 7–18.

Chan, J., Edman, J. C., & Koltai, P. J. (2004). Obstructive sleep apnea in children. *American Family Physician, 69,* 1147–1153.

Changizi, M. A., McGehee, R. M. F., & Hall, W. G. (2002). Evidence that appetitive responses for dehydration and food-deprivation are learned. *Physiology & Behavior, 75,* 295–304.

Channouf, A. (2000). Subliminal exposure to facial expressions of emotion and evaluative judgements of advertising messages. *European Review of Applied Psychology, 50,* 19–25.

Charles, S. T., Reynolds, C. A., & Gatz, M. (2001). Agerelated differences and change in positive and negative affect over 23 years. *Journal of Personality and Social Psychology, 80,* 136–151.

Charney, D. S. (2004). Discovering the neural basis of human social anxiety: A diagnostic and therapeutic imperative. *American Journal of Psychiatry, 161,* 1–2.

Chase, V. M. (2000). Where to look to find out why: Rational information search in causal hypothesis testing. *Dissertation Abstracts International: Section B: The Sciences & Engineering, 60(11-B),* 5800.

Chassin, L., Collins, R. L., Ritter, J., & Shirley, M. C. (2001). Vulnerability to substance use disorders across the lifespan. In R. E. Ingram, J. M. Price, *Vulnerability to Psychopathology: Risk Across the Lifespan* (pp. 165–172). New York: Guilford Press.

Chassin, L., Pitts, S. C., & Prost, J. (2002). Binge drinking trajectories from adolescence to emerging adulthood in a high-risk sample: Predictors and substance abuse outcomes. *Journal of Consulting & Clinical Psychology, 70,* 67–78.

Chen, I. (1999). Local enhancing connections among spatial frequency filters might mediate Gestalt grouping principles. *Chinese Journal of Psychology, 41(1)* 19–37.

Chen, T., Han, B. M., & Wang, J. (2003). A review of the aging of working memory. *Psychological Science (China), 26,* 127–129.

Chen, X. (2000). Growing up in a collectivist culture: Socialization and socioemotional development in Chinese children. In A. L. Comunian, U. P. Gielen, *International Perspectives on Human Development* (331–353). Lengerich, Germany: Pabst Science Publishers.

Chen, X., Zhang, D., Zhang, X., Xiaochu, L., Zhilrao, M., Meng, X., et al. (2003). A lunctional MRI study of high-level cognition. II. The game of GO. *Cognitive Brain Research, 16,* 32–37.

Cheng, B. S., Chou, L. F., Wu, T. Y., Huang, M. P., & Farh, J. L. (2004). Paternalistic leadership and subordinate responses: Establishing a leadership model in Chinese organizations. *Asian Journal of Social Psychology, 7,* 89–117.

Chess, S., & Thomas, T. (1996). *Temperament: Theory and practice.* New York: Brunner-Rutledge.

Chiara, G. D. (2002). Nucleus accumbens shell and core dopamine: Differential role in behavior and addiction. *Behavioural Brain Research, 137,* 75–114.

Choi, I., Dalal, R., Kim-Prieto, C., & Park, H. (2003). Culture and judgment of causal relevance. *Journal of Personality and Social Psychology, 84,* 46–59.

Chomsky, N. (1957). *Syntactic structures.* The Hague, Netherlands; Mouton.

Chomsky, N. (1999). On the nature, use, and acquisition of language. In W. Ritchie & T. Bhatia (Eds.), *Handbook of child language acquisition.* New York: Academic Press.

Chopra, S. S., Sotile, W. M., & Sotile, M. O. (2004). Physician burnout. *Journal of the American Medical Association, 219,* 633.

Chrisler, J. C. (2001). Gendered bodies and physical health. In Rhoda K. Unger (Ed.), *Handbook of psychology of women and gender* (pp. 289–302). New York: Wiley.

Christenfeld, N., Gerin, W., Linden, W., & Sanders, M. (1997). Social support effects on cardiovascular reactivity: Is a stranger as effective as a friend? *Psychosomatic Medicine, 59,* 388–398.

Christensen, L. B. (2004). *Experimental methodology* (9th ed.). Boston: Allyn & Bacon.

Christoffersen, M. N., Poulsen, H. D., & Nielsen, A. (2003). Attempted suicide among young people: Risk factors in a prospective register based study of Danish children born in 1966. *Acta Psychiatrica Scandinavica, 108,* 350–358.

Chusmir, L. H. (1989). Behavior: A measure of motivation needs. *Psychology: A Journal of Human Behavior, 26,* 1–10.

Cialdini, R. B. (2001). *Influence: Science and practice* (4th ed.), Boston: Allyn & Bacon.

Cialdini, R. B. (2004, January). The science of persuasion. *Scientific American, 14* (Special Edition), 70–77.

Cialdini, R. B., & Goldstein, N. J. (2004). Social influence: Compliance and conformity. *Annual Review of Psychology, 55,* 591–521.

Cicogna, P., & Bosinelli, M. (2001). Consciousness during dreams. *Consciousness & Cognition: An International Journal, 10,* 26–41.

Cinamon, R. G., & Rich, Y. (2002). Gender differences in the importance of work and family roles: Implications for work-family conflict. *Sex Roles, 47,* 531–541.

Cioffi, J. (2001). A study of the past experiences in clinical decision making in emergency situations. *International Journal of Nursing Studies, 38,* 591–599.

Clancy, S. A., McNally, R. J., Schacter, D. L., Lenzenweger, M. F., & Pitman, R. K. (2002). Memory distortion in people reporting abduction by aliens. *Journal of Abnormal Psychology, 111,* 455–461.

Clapp, J. D., & Stanger, L. (2003). Changing the college AOD environment for primary prevention. *Journal of Primary Prevention, 23,* 515–523.

Clark, D. M., Ehlers, A., McManus, F., Hackman, A., Fennell, M., Campbell, H. et al. (2003). Cognitive therapy versus fluoxetine in generalized social phobia: A randomized placebo-controlled trial. *Journal of Consulting & Clinical Psychology, 71,* 1058–1067.

Clark, R. E., Manns, J. R., & Squire, L. R. (2002). Classical conditioning, awareness, and brain systems. *Trends in Cognitive Sciences, 6,* 524–531.

Clarke-Stewart, A., Friedman, S., & Koch, J. B. (1985). *Child development: A topical approach.* New York: Wiley.

Claxon, G. (1975). Why we can't tickle ourselves. *Perceptual and Motor Skills, 41,* 335–338.

Clay, R. A. (2002, September). A renaissance for humanistic psychology. *Monitor on Psychology, 33(8),* 42–43.

Cleary, D. J., Ray, G. E., LoBello, S. G., & Zachar, P. (2002). Children's perceptions of close peer relationships: Quality, congruence and meta-perception. *Child Study Journal, 32,* 179–192.

Clutton-Brock, T. H., & Parker, G. A. (1995). Punishment in animal societies. *Nature, 373,* 209–216.

CNN, (2004, April 5). Osbournes: Kelly in drug rehab. Retrieved May 28, 2004, from http://www.cnn.com/2004/SHOWBIZ/Music/04/02/osbournes.lkl/

Coffey, C. W., Weiner, R. D., Djang, W. T., Figiel, G. S., Soady, S. A. R., Patterson, L. J., Holt, P. D., Spritzer, C. E., & Wilinson, W. E. (1991). Brain anatomic effects of electroconvulsive therapy. *Archives of General Psychiatry, 48,* 1013–1021.

Cohen, D., & Gunz, A. (2002). As seen by the other . . . : Perspectives on the self in the memories and emotional perceptions of Easterners and Westerners. *Psychological Science, 13,* 55–59.

Cohen, K. M. (2002). Relationships among child-hood sex-atypical behavior, spatial ability, handedness, and sexual orientation in men. *Archives of Sexual Behavior, 31,* 129–143.

Cohen, S. (1996). Psychological stress, immunity, and upper respiratory infections. *Current Directions in Psychological Science, 5,* 86–90.

Cohen, S., Doyle, W. J., Turner, R., Alper, C. M., & Skoner, D. P. (2003). Sociability and susceptibility to the common cold. *Psychological Science, 14,* 389–395.

Cohen, S., Frank, E., Doyle, W.J., Skoner, D.P., Rabin, B. S., & Gwallney. J. M., Jr. (1998). Types of stressors that increase susceptibility to the common cold in healthy adults. *Health Psychology, 17,* 214–223.

Cohen, S., Tyrrell, D. A. J., & Smith, A. P. (1997). Psychological stress in humans and susceptibility to the common cold. In T. W. Miller et al. (Eds.), *Clinical disorders and stressful life events* (pp. 217–235). Madison, CT. International University Press.

Cohn, L. (1991). Sex differences in the course of personality development: A meta-analysis. *Psychological Bulletin, 109,* 252–266.

Cole, S. W., Kemeny, M. E., Taylor, S. E., Visscher, B. R., & Fahey, J. L. (1996). Accelerated course of human immunodeficiency virus infection in gay men who conceal their homosexual identity. *Psychosomatic Medicine, 58,* 219–231.

Coley, R. L., & Chase-Lansdale, P. L. (1998). Adolescent pregnancy and parenthood: Recent evidence and future directions. *American Psychologist, 53,* 152–166.

Colledge, E., Bishop, D. V. M., Koeppen-Schomerus, G., Price, T. S., Happé, F. G. E., Eley, T. C., et al. (2002). The structure of language abilities at 4 years: A twin study. *Developmental Psychology, 38,* 749–757.

Collette, F., & Van der Linden, M. (2002). Brain imaging of the central executive component of working memory. *Neuroscience & Biobehavior Reviews, 26,* 105–125.

Colley, A., Ball, J., Kirby, N., Harvey, R., & Vingelen, I. (2002). Gender-linked differences in everyday memory performance: Effort makes the difference. *Sex Roles, 47,* 577–562.

Collins, W. A., & Laursen, B. (2000). Adolescent relationships: The art of fugue. In C. Hendrick & S. S. Hendrick (Eds.), *Close relationships: A source-book* (pp. 59–69). Thousand Oaks, CA: Sage.

Collins, W. A., Maccoby, E. E., Steinberg, L., Hetherington, E. M., & Bornstein, M. H. (2000). Contemporary research on parenting: The case for nature and nurture. *American Psychologist, 55,* 218–232.

Colman, H., Nabekura, J., & Lichtman, J. W. (1997). Alternations in synaptic strength preceding axon withdrawal. *Science, 275,* 356–361.

Colom, R., Abad, F. J., García, L. F., & Juan-Espinosa, M. (2002). Education, Wechsler's full scale IQ, and g. *Intelligence, 30,* 449–462.

Colom, R., & Lynn, R. (2004). Testing the developmental theory of sex differences in intelligence on 12–18 year olds. *Personality & Individual Differences, 36,* 75–62.

Coltrane, S. (2000). Research on household labor: Modeling and measuring the social embeddedness of routine family work. *Journal of Marriage and the Family, 62,* 1208–1233.

Comer, J. P., & Woodruff, D. W. (1998). Mental health in schools. *Child & Adolescent Psychiatric Clinics of North America, 7,* 499–513.

Compas, B. E., Connor-Smith, J. K., Saltzman, H., Thomsen, A. H., & Wadsworth, M. E. (2001). Coping with stress during childhood and adolescence; Problems, progress, and potential in theory and research. *Psychological Bulletin, 127,* 87–127.

Conger, R. D., Neppl, T., Kim, K. J., & Scaramella, L. (2003). Angry and aggressive behavior across three generations: A prospective, longitudinal study of parents and children. *Journal of Abnormal Child Psychology, 31,* 143–160.

Conley, R. R. (2004). Monitoring patients who take long-acting Risperidone. *Journal of Clinical Psychiatry, 65,* 127–130.

Conyers, L. M., Enright, M. S., & Strauser, D. R. (1998). Applying self-efficacy theory to counseling college students with disabilities. *Journal of Applied Rehabilitation Counseling, 29,* 25–30.

Cook, D. L., Schwindt, P. C., Grande, L. A., & Spain, W. J. (2003). Synaptic depression in the localized sound. *Nature, 421*(6918), 66–70.

Cook, K. V., Larson, D.C., & Boivin, M. D. (2003). Moral voices of women and men in the Christian liberal arts college: Links between views of self and views of God. *Journal of Moral Education, 32,* 77–89.

Cooper, R. S. (2004). Race and IQ: Molecular genetics as deus ex machina. *American Psychologist, 59,* 174–178.

Corbetta, D., & Vereijken, B. (1999). Understanding development and learning of motor coordination in sport: The contribution of dynamic systems theory. *International Journal of Sport Psychology, 30,* 507–530.

Corina, D. P., San Jose-Robertson, L., Guillemin, A., High, J., & Braun, A. K. (2003). Language lateralization in a bimanual language. *Journal of Cognitive Neuroscience, 15,* 718–730.

Cornblatt, B. A., Green, M. F., & Walker, E. F. (1999). Schizophrenia: Etiology and neurocognition. In T. Millon, P. H. Blaney, & R. D. Davis (Eds.), *Oxford textbook of psychopathology* (pp. 277–310). New York: Oxford University Press.

Cosmides, L. (1989). The logic of social exchange: Has natural selection shaped how humans reason? Studies with the Wason selection task. *Cognition, 31,* 187–276.

Cosmides, L., & Tooby, J. (1997). Evolutionary psychology: A primer. Retrieved May 13, 2001, http://www.psych.ucsb.edu/research/cep

Cosmides, L., & Tooby, J. (1999). Toward an evolutionary taxonomy of treatable conditions. *Journal of Abnormal Psychology, 108,* 453–464.

Cosmides, L., & Tooby, J. (2000). Evolutionary psychology and the emotions. In M. Lewis & J. M. Haviland-Jones (Eds.), *Handbook of emotions* (2nd ed., pp. 91–115). New York: Guilford Press.

Cosmides, L., & Tooby, J. (2002). Unraveling the enigma of human intelligence: Evolutionary psychology and the multimodular mind. In R. J. Sternberg & J. C. Kaufman (Eds.), *The evolution of intelligence* (pp. 145–198). Mahwah, NJ: Erlbaum.

Costa, P. T., & McCrae, R. R. (1992). *The NEO Personality Inventory (NEO-PI-R) and NEO Five-Factor (NEO-FF) Inventory professional manual.* Odessa, FL: Psychological Assessment Resources.

Costa, P. T., & McCrae, R. R. (1995). Domains and facets: Hierarchical personality assessment using the Revised NEO Personality Inventory. *Journal of Personality Assessment, 64,* 21–50.

Costantino, G., Malgady, R. G., & Rogler, L. H. (1986). Cuento therapy: A culturally sensitive modality for Puerto Rican children. *Journal of Consulting & Clinical Psychology, 54,* 639–645.

Costello, B. J., & Dunaway, R. G. (2003). Egotism and delinquent behavior. *Journal of Interpersonal Violence, 18,* 572–590.

Costello, E. J., Pine, D. S., Hammen, C., March, J. S., Plotsky, P. M., Weissman, M. M., et al. (2002). Development and natural history of mood disorders. *Biological Psychiatry, 52,* 529–542.

Courage, M. L., & Howe, M. L. (2002). From infant to child: The dynamics of cognitive change in the second year of life. *Psychology Bulletin, 128,* 250–277.

Courtenay, W. H. (2000). Behavioral factors associated with disease, injury, and death among men: Evidence and implications for prevention. *Journal of Men's Studies, 9,* 81–142.

Coward, L., & Sun, R. (2004). Criteria for an effective theory of consciousness and some preliminary attempts. *Consciousness & Cognition, 13,* 268–281.

Cox, B. J., & Taylor, S. (1999). Anxiety disorders: Panic and phobias. In T. Millon, P. H. Blaney, & R. D. Davis (Eds.), *Oxford textbook of psychopathology* (pp. 81–113). New York: Oxford University Press.

Cox, R. H., Qiu, Y., & Liu, Z. (1993). Overview of sport psychology. In R. N. Singer, M. Murphey, & L. K. Tennant (Eds.), *Handbook of research on sport psychology* (pp. 3–31). New York: Macmillan.

Coyne, J. A. (2000, April 3). Of vice and men—the fairy tales of evolutionary psychology. *New Republic, 222,* 27–34.

Crabbe, J. C. (2002). Genetic contributions to addiction. *Annual Review of Psychology, 53,* 435–463.

Craft, L. L., Pleiller, K. A., & Pivarnik, J. M. (2003). Predictors of physical competence in adolescent girls. *Journal of Youth & Adolescence, 32*(6), 431–438.

Craighead, W. E., Hart, A. B., Craighead, L. W., & Ilardi, S. S. (2002). Psychosocial treatments for major depressive disorder. In P. E. Nathan & J. M. Gorman (Eds.), *A guide to treatments that work* (pp. 245–261). New York: Oxford Press.

Craik, F. I. M. (2002). Levels of processing: Past, present … and future? *Memory, 10,* 305–318.

Craik, F. I. M., & Lockhart, R. S. (1972). Levels of processing: A framework for memory research. *Journal of Verbal Learning and Verbal Behavior, 11,* 671–784.

Cramer, R. E., Abraham, W., Johnson, L., & Manning-Ryan, B. (2002). Gender differences in subjective distress to emotional and sexual infidelity. *Current Psychology: Developmental, Learning, Personality, Social, 20,* 327–336.

Crandall, C. S., Preisler, J. J., & Aussprung, J. (1992). Measuring life event stress in the lives of college students: The Undergraduate Stress Questionnaire (USQ). *Journal of Behavioral Medicine, 15,* 627–662.

Cray, D., Fowler D., Julie Grace, J., Jones, A., & Thompson, D. (2000, October 30). Teens before their time. *Time,* 44–53.

Crespi, T. D. (1988). Effectiveness of time-out: A comparison of psychiatric, correctional, and day-treatment programs. *Adolescence, 23,* 805–811.

Crews, F. (1996). The verdict on Freud. *Psychological Science, 7,* 63–68.

Crick, F., & Mitchison, G. (1983). The function of dream sleep. *Nature, 304,* 111–114.

Cross, T. L. (2003). Culture as a resource for mental health. *Cultural Diversity & Ethnic Minority Psychology, 9*(4), 354–359.

Crosson, B. (2000). Systems that support language processes: Verbal working memory. In S. E. Nadeau, L. J. Gonzalez Rothi, &

B. Crosson (Eds.), *Aphasia and language: Theory to practice. The science and practice of neuropsychology* (pp. 399–418). New York: Guilford Press.

Csikszentmihalyi, M. (1997). *Finding flow: The psychology of engagement with everyday life.* New York: Basic Books.

Csikszentmihalyi, M. (2000). *Beyond boredom and anxiety.* San Francisco: Jossey-Bass.

Csikszentmihalyi, M. (2001). The context of creativity. In W. Bennis, G. M. Spreitzer, & T. G. Cummings (Eds.), *The future of leadership: Today's top leadership thinkers speak to tomorrow's leaders* (pp. 116–124). San Francisco: Jossey-Bass.

Cuijpers, P., & Van Lammeren, P. (2001). Secondary prevention of depressive symptoms in elderly inhabitants of residential homes. *International Journal of Geriatric Psychiatry, 16*(7), 702–708.

Culbertson, F. M. (1997). Depression and gender: An international review. *American Psychologist, 52*, 25–31.

Cummings, N. A. (1986). The dismantling of our health system: Strategies for the survival of psychological practice. *American Psychologist, 41*, 426–431.

Cunningham, C. L., Dickinson, S. D., Grahame, N. J., Okorn, D. M., & McMullin, C. S. (1999). Genetic differences in cocaine-induced conditioned place preference in mice depend on conditioning trial duration. - *Psychopharmacology, 146*, 73–80.

Cunningham, M. (2001). Parental influences on the gendered division of housework. *American Sociological Review, 66*, 184–203.

Cunningham, M. R., Roberts, A. R., Bargee, A. P., Druen, P. B., Wu, C. H. (1995). "Their ideas of beauty are, on the whole, the same as ours": Consistency and variability in the cross-cultural perception of female physical attractiveness. *Journal of Personality and Social Psychology, 68*, 261–279.

Curtis, S. (2004, March/April). Freedom fighters. *Crisis, 111*(2).

Cushman, P., & Gilford, P. (2000). Will managed care change our way of being? *American Psychologist, 55*, 985–996.

Cutting, A. L., & Dunn, J. (1999). Theory of mind, emotion understanding, language, and family background: individual differences and interrelations. *Child Development, 70* (4), 853–865.

Cutting, J. (2001). The speech acts of the in-group. *Journal of Pragmatics, 33*, 1207–1233.

Cutting Edge Information. (2004). *Pharmaceutical patient compliance and disease management.* Retrieved July 18, 2004, from http://www.pharmadiseasemanagement.com/metrics.htm

Czeisler, C., Duffy, J. F., Shanahan, T. L., Brown, E. N., Mitchell, J. F., Rimmer, D. W., et al. (1999). Stability, precision, and near-24-hour period of the human circadian pacemaker. *Science, 284*, 2177–2181.

Dadds, M. R., Bovbjerg, D. H., Redd, W. H., & Cutmore, T. R. (1997). Imagery in human classical conditioning. *Psychological Bulletin, 122*, 89–103.

d'Agincourt-Canning, L. (2001). Experiences of genetic risk: Disclosure and the gendering of responsibility. *Bioethics, 15*, 231–247.

D'alessio, D., & Allen, M. (2002). Selective exposure and dissonance after decisions. *Psychological Reports, 91*, 527–532.

Damak, S., Rong, M., Yasumalsu, K., Kokrashvili, Z., et al. (2003). Detection of sweet and unami taste in the absence of taste receptor T1r3. *Science, 301*(5634), 850–851.

Damasio, A. R. (1994). *Descartes' error: Emotion, reason, and the human brain.* New York: Putnam.

Damasio, A. R. (1999). *The feeling of what happens.* New York: Harcourt Brace & Company.

Damasio, A. R. (2000). A neurobiology for consciousness. In T. Metzinger (Ed.), *Neural correlates of consciousness: Empirical and conceptual questions* (pp. 111–120). Cambridge, MA: The MIT Press.

Damasio, A. R. (2003). *Looking for Spinozo: Joy, sorrow, and the feeling brain.* New York: Harcourt.

Damian, M. F. (2001). Congruity effects evoked by subliminally presented primes: Automaticity rather than semantic processing. *Journal of Experimental Psychology: Human Perception and Performance, 27*, 154–165.

Dana, R. H. (2002). Examining the usefulness of *DSM-IV*. In K. S. Kurasaki, S. Okazaki, & S. Sue (Eds.), *Asian American mental health: Assessment theories and methods* (pp. 29–46). New York: Kluwer Academic/Plenum.

Daniel, M. H. (2000). Interpretation of intelligence test scores. In R. J. Sternberg (Ed.). *Handbook of intelligence* (pp. 477–491). New York: Cambridge University Press.

Danner, D. D., Snowdon, D. A., & Friesen, W. V. (2001). Positive emotions in early life and longevity: Findings from the nun study. *Journal of Personality and Social Psychology, 80*, 804–813.

Dantzer, R. (2001). Innate immunity at the forefront of psychoneuroimmunology. *Brain, Behavior, & Immunity, 18*, 1–6.

Darley, J. M., & Gross, P. H. (2000). A hypothesis-confirming bias in labeling effects. In C. Stangor (Ed.), *Stereotypes and prejudice:*

Essential readings (pp. 212–225). Philadelphia: Psychology Press/Taylor & Francis.

Darwin, C. (1859). *On the origin of species by means of natural selection.* London: Murray.

Darwin, C. (1872). *The expression of the emotions in man and animals.* London: Murray.

Davachi, L., Mitchell, J. P., & Wagner, A. D. (2003). Multiple routes to memory: Distinct medial temporal lobe processes build item and source memories. *Proceedings of the National Academy of Sciences of the United States of America, 100*, 2157–2162.

David, A. S. (2004). The cognitive neuropsychiatry of auditory verbal hallucinations: An overview. *Cognitive Neuropsychiatry, 9*, 107–123.

Davidson, R. J. (2003). Affective neuroscience and psychophysiology: Toward a synthesis. *Psychophysiology, 40*, 655–665.

Davidson, R. J., Jackson, D. C., & Kalin, N. H. (2000). Emotion, plasticity, context, and regulation: Perspectives from affective neuroscience. *Psychological Bulletin, 126*, 890–909.

Davidson, R. J., Kabat-Zinn, J., Schumacher, J., Rosenkranz, M., Muller, D., Santorelli, S., et al. (2003). Alternations in brain and immune function produced by mindfulness meditation. *Psychosomatic Medicine, 65*, 564–570.

Davidson, R. J., Pizzagalli, D., Nitschke, J. B., & Putnam, K. (2002). Depression: Perspectives from affective neuroscience. *Annual Review of Psychology, 53*, 545–576.

Davis, D., & Follette, W. C. (2003). Toward an empirical approach to evidentiary ruling. *Law & Human Behavior, 27*(6), 661–684.

Davis, K. D. (2001). Studies of pain using functional magnetic resonance imaging. In K. Casey & C. Bushnell (Eds.), *Pain imaging: Progress in pain research and management* (pp. 195–210). Seattle, WA: IASP Press.

Davis, K. D., Kiss, Z. H. T., Luo, L., Tasker, R. R., Lozano, A. M., & Dostrovsky, J. O. (1998). Phantom sensations generated by thalamic microstimulation. *Nature, 391*, 385–387.

Davison, H. K., & Burke, M. J. (2000). Sex discrimination in simulated employment contexts: A meta-analytic investigation. *Journal of Vocational Behavior, 56*, 225–248.

Daw, J. (2002, March). Steady and strong progress in the push for Rx privileges. *Monitor on Psychology, 33*(3), 56–58.

Deakin, J. M., & Proteau, L. (2000). The role of scheduling in learning through observation. *Journal of Motor Behavior, 32*, 268–276.

Deary, l. J., Whiteman, M. C., Starr, J. M., Whalley, L. J., & Fox, H. C. (2004). The impact of childhood intelligence on later life: Following up the Scottish Mental Surveys of 1932 and 1947. *Journal of Personality and Social Psychology, 86*, 130–147.

DeBeni, R., & Palladino, P. (2004). Decline in working memory updating through ageing: Intrusion error analyses. *Memory, 12*, 75–89.

DeBerard, M. S., Speilmans, G. I., & Julka, D. C. (2004). Predictions of academic achievement and retention among college freshmen: A longitudinal study. *College Student Journal, 38*, 66–80.

Deci, E. L. (1975). *Intrinsic motivation*. New York: Plenum.

Deci, E. L., Koestner, R., & Ryan, R. M. (1999). A meta-analytic review of experiments examining the effects of extrinsic rewards on intrinsic motivation. *Psychological Bulletin, 125*, 627–668.

Deco, G., & Schurmann, B. (2000). A neurocognitive visual system for object recognition based on testing of interactive attentional top-down hypotheses. *Perception, 29*, 1249–1264.

de Jong, N., Mulder, I., De Graff, C., & van Staveren, W. (1999). Impaired sensory functioning in elders: The relation with its potential determinants and nutritional intake. *Journals of Gerontology: Series A: Biological Sciences & Medical Science, 54A*(8), B324–B331.

De Jong, P. F., & van der Leij, A. (2003). Developmental changes in the manifestation of a phonological deficit in dyslexic children learning to read a regular orthography. *Journal of Educational Psychology, 95*, 22–40.

de Jonge, J., Bosma, H., Peter, R., & Siegrist, J. (2000). Job strain, effort-reward imbalance, and employee well-being: A large-scale cross-sectional study. *Social Science & Medicine, 50*, 1317–1327.

Dekker, A., & Schmidt, G. (2002). Patterns of masturbatory behaviour: Changes between the sixties and the nineties. *Journal of Psychology & Human Sexuality, 14*, 35–48.

De La Casa, L. G., & Lubow, R. E. (2000). Super-latent inhibition with delayed conditioned taste aversion testing. *Animal Learning & Behavior, 28*, 389–399.

DeLamater, J., & Friedrich, W. N. (2002). Human sexual development. *Journal of Sex Research, 39*, 10–14.

de Leff, J. F., & Aco, E. E. (2000). Cultural myths and social relationships in Mexico: A context for therapy. *Journal of Family Psychotherapy, 11*, 79–92.

DeLongis, A., Folkman, S., & Lazarus, R. S. (1988). The impact of daily stress on health and mood: Psychological and social

resources as mediators. *Journal of Personality and Social Psychology, 54*, 486–495.

DeLucia-Waack, J. L., Gerrity, D. A., Taub, D. J., & Baldo, T. D. (2001). Gender, gender role identity, and type of relationship as predictors of relationship behavior and beliefs in college students. *Journal of College Counseling, 4*, 32–48.

DeMarco, S. C., Clements, M., Vichienchom, K., Liu, W., Humayun, M., & Weiland, J. (1999). An epiretinal visual prosthesis implementation. *Proceedings of the First Joint BMES/EMBS Conference, 1*, 475.

Dement, W. C. (1972). *Some must watch while some must sleep*. New York: Norton.

Dement, W. C., & Wolpert, E. A. (1958). The relation of eye movements, body motility, and external stimuli to dream content. *Journal of Experimental Psychology, 55*, 543–553.

Dement, W. C., with C. Vaughan. (1999). *The promise of sleep*. New York: Delacorte Press.

Dennett, D. (2003). Who's on first? Heterophenomenology explained. *Journal of Consciousness Studies, 10*, 19–30.

Dennett, D. C. (1991). *Consciousness explained*. Boston: Little, Brown.

Dennett, D. C. (1996). *Kinds of minds: Toward an understanding of consciousness*. New York: Basic Books.

Denys, D., van Megen, H. J. G. M., & van der Wee, N. (2004). A double-blind switch study of Paroxetine and Ventafaxine in obsessive-com.pulsive disorder. *Journal of Clinical Psychiatry, 65*, 37–43.

Desmet, P., & Feinberg, F. M. (2003). Ask and ye shall receive: The effect of the appeals scale on consumers' donation behavior. *Journal of Economic Psychology, 24*, 349–376.

Dessler, G. (Ed.). (2003). *Human resource management*. Delhi, India: Pearson Education.

DeValois, R. L., & Jacobs, G. H. (1968). Primate color vision. *Science, 162*, 533–540.

Devoto, A., Lucidi, F., Violani, C., & Bertini, M. (1999). Effects of different sleep reductions on day-time sleepiness. *Sleep, 22*, 336–343.

Diamond, A., Lee, E., & Hayden, M. (2003). Early success in using the relation between stimuli and rewards to deduce an abstract rule: Perceived physical connection is key. *Developmental Psychology, 39*, 825–847.

Dickens, W. T., & Flynn, J. R. (2001). Heritability estimates versus large enviromental effects: The IQ paradox resolved. *Psychological Review, 108*, 346–369.

Dickhaeuser, O., & Stiensmeier-Pelster, J. (2003). Gender differences in the choice of computer courses: Applying an expectancy-value model. *Social Psychology of Education, 6*, 173–189.

Diedrich, F. J., Highlands, T. M., Spahr, K. A., Thelan, E., & Smith, L. B. (2001). The role of target distinctiveness in infant perseverative reaching. *Journal of Experimental Child Psychology, 78*(3), 263–290.

Diefenbach, D. L. (1997). The portrayal of mental illness on prime-time television. *Journal of Community Psychology, 25*, 289–302.

Diener, E., & Biswas-Diener, R. (2002). Will money increase subjective well-being? *Social Indicators Research, 57*, 119–169.

Diener, E., Lucas, R. E., & Oishi, S. (2002). Subjective well-being: The science of happiness and life satisfaction. In C. R. Snyder & S. J. Lopez (Eds.). *Handbook of positive psychology* (pp. 63–73). New York: Oxford University Press.

Diener, E., Oishi, S., & Lucas, R. E. (2003). Personality, culture, and subjective well-being: Emotional and cognitive evaluations of life. *Annual Review of Psychology, 54*, 403–425.

Diener, E., & Seligman, M. E. P. (2004). Beyond money: Toward an economy of well-being. *Psychological Science in the Public Interest, 5*, 1–31.

DiLalla, L. F., & Jones, S. (2000). Genetic and environmental influences on termperament in preschoolers. In V. J. Molfese, D. L. Molfese, and others, *Temperament and Personality Development Across the Life Span* (33–55). Mahwah, NJ: Erlbaum.

DiMatteo, M. R., & DiNicola, D. D. (1982). *Achieving patient compliance: The psychology of the medical practitioner's role*. New York: Pergamon.

D'Imperio, R. L., Dubow, E. F., & Ippolito, M. F. (2000). Resilient and stress-affected adolescents in an urban setting. *Journal of Clinical Child Psychology, 29*, 129–142.

Din-Dzietham, R., Nembhard, W. N., Collins, R., & Davis, S. K. (2004). Perceived stress following race-based discrimination at work is associated with hypertension in African-Americans. *Social Science & Medicine, 58*, 449–461.

Dinges, N. G., Atlis, M. M., & Vincent, G. M. (1997). Cross-cultural perspectives on antisocial behavior. In D. M. Stoff, J. Breiling, & J. Wohl (Eds.). *Handbook of antisocial behavior* (pp. 463–473). New York: Wiley.

DiPietro, J. A. (2004). The role of prenatal maternal stress in childhood development. *Current Directions in Psychological Science, 13*, 71–74.

Dirks, K. T., & Ferrin, D. L. (2002). Trust in leadership: Meta-analytic findings and implications for research and practice. *Journal of Applied psychology, 87*, 611–628.

Disaster Center, (2004). *Death rates from 12 age groups.* Retrieved July 5, 2004, from http://disastercenter.com/cdc/

Dodds, J. P., Mercey, D. E., Parry, J. V., & Johnson, A. M. (2004). Increasing risk behaviour and high levels of undiagnosed HIV infection in a community sample of homosexual men. *Sexually Transmitted Infections, 80,* 236–240.

Dohrenwend, B. P. (2000). The role of adversity and stress in psychopathology: Some evidence and its implications for theory and research. *Journal of Health and Social Behavior, 41,* 1–19.

Dollard, J., Doob, L. W., Miller, N. E., Mowrer, O. H., & Sears, R. R. (1939). *Frustration and aggression.* New Haven, CT: Yale University Press.

Dollard, J., & Miller, N. E. (1950). *Personality and psychotherapy: An analysis in terms of learning, thinking, and culture.* New York: McGraw-Hill.

Dollard, M. F., Dormann, C., Boyd, C. M., Winefield, H. R., & Winefield, A. H. (2003). Unique aspects of stress in human service work. *Australian Psychologist, 38,* 84–91.

Domhoff, G. W. (2004). Why did empirical dream research reject Freud? A critique of historical claims by Mark Solms. *Dreaming, 14,* 3–17.

Domijan, D. (2003). A neural model for visual selection of grouped spatial arrays. *Neuroreport: For Rapid Communication of Neuroscience Research, 14,* 367–370.

Donker, F. J. S., & Breteler, M. H. M. (2004). Blood lipids: A shortcut from hostility to CHD? *Psychology & Health, 19,* 197–212.

Donn, J. E., & Sherman, R. C. (2002). Attitudes and practices regarding the formation of romantic relationships on the Internet. *CyberPsychology & Behavior, 5,* 107–123.

Donson, N. (1999). Caring for day care: Models for early intervention and primary prevention. In T. B. Cohen, M. H. Etezady, B. L. Pacella (Eds.), *The vulnerable child* (Vol. 3, pp. 181–212). Madison, CT: International Universities Press.

Doty, R. W. (1999). Two brains, one person. *Brain Research Bulletin, 50*(5/6), 423.

Dovidio, J. F., & Gaertner, S. L. (1998). On the nature of contemporary prejudice: The causes, consequences, and challenges of aversive racism. In J. L. Eberhardt & S. T. Fiske (Eds.), *Confronting racism: The problem and the response* (pp. 3–32). Thousand Oaks, CA: Sage.

Dovidio, J. F., Kawakami, K., & Gaertner, S. L. (2002). Implicit and explicit prejudice and interracial interaction. *Journal of Personality and Social Psychology, 82,* 62–68.

Dowling, J. E., & Boycott, B. B. (1966). Proceedings from the Royal Society (London). B166, 80–111.

Downey, D. B. (2001). Number of siblings and intellectual development: The resource dilution explanation. *American Psychologist, 56,* 497–504.

Dryden, W., & Ellis, A. (1988). Rational-emotive therapy. In K.S. Dobson (Ed.), *Handbook of cognitive-behavioral therapies.* New York: Guilford.

Dryden, W., & Ellis, A. (2001). Rational emotive behavior therapy. In K. S. Dobson (Ed.). *Handbook of cognitive-behavioral therapies* (2nd ed.), (pp. 295–348). New York: Guilford Press.

DuBois, D. L., & Silverthorn, N. (2004). Do deviant peer associations mediate the contributions of self-esteem to problem behavior during early adolescence? A 2-year longitudinal study. *Journal of Clinical Child & Adolescent Psychology, 33,* 382–388.

Dubow, E. F., Huesmann, L. R., & Boxer, P. (2003). Theoretical and methodological considerations in cross-generational research on parenting and child aggressive behavior. *Journal of Abnormal Child Psychology, 31,* 185–192.

Duff, C. (2003). The importance of culture and context: Rethinking risk and risk management in young drug using populations. *Health, Risk, & Society, 5,* 285–299.

Duman, R. S., Malberg, J., Nakawaga, S., & D'Sa, C. (2000). Neuronal plasticity and survival in mood disorders. *Biological Psychiatry, 48,* 732–739.

Duncan, J., Seitz, R. J., Kolodny, J., Bor, D., Herzog, H., Ahmed, A., Newell, F. N., & Emslie, H. (2000). A neural basis for general intelligence. *Science, 289,* 457–460.

Duncan, R. M., & Tarulli, D. (2003). Play as the leading activity of the preschool period: Insights from Vygotsky, Leont'ev, and Bakhtin. *Early Education and Development, 14,* 271–292.

Dunning, D., & Perretta, S. (2002). Automaticity and eyewitness accuracy: A 10-to-12 second rule for distinguishing accurate from inaccurate positive identifications. *Journal of Applied Psychology, 87,* 951–962.

Durand, K., Lecuyer, R., & Frichtel, M. (2003). Representation of the third dimensions: The use of perspective cues by 3- and 4-month-old infants. *Infant Behavior and Development, 26,* 151–166.

D'Zurilla, T. J., Chang, E. C., & Sanna, L. J. (2003). Self-esteem and social problem solving as predictors of aggression in college students. *Journal of Social & Clinical Psychology, 22,* 424–440.

Eagly, A. H. (2003). The rise of female leaders. *Seitschrift fur Sozialpsychologie, 34*(3), 123–132.

Eagly, A. H., Johannesen-Schmidt, M. C., & van Engen, M. L. (2003). Transformational, transactional, and laissez-faire leadership styles: A meta-analysis comparing woman and men. *Psychological Bulletin, 129,* 569–591.

Easterbrook, G. (1996). It's unreal: How phony realism in film and literature is corrupting and confusing the American mind. *Washington Monthly, 28*(10), 41–43.

Ebbinghaus, H. (1885). *On memory.* Leipzig: Duncker & Humblot.

Ebrecht, M., Hextall, J., Kirtley, L. G., Taylor, A., Dyson, M., & Weinman, J. (2004). Perceived stress and cortisol levels predict speed of wound healing in healthy male adults. *Psychoneuro-endocrinology, 29,* 798–809.

Eccles, J. S., & Wigfield, A. (2002). Motivational beliefs, values, and goals. *Annual Review of Psychology, 53,* 109–132.

Edelheit, S., & Meiri, N. (2004). Cyclin S: A new member of the cyclin family plays a role in long-term memory. *European Journal of Neuroscience, 19,* 365–375.

Edenberg, H.J., Dick, D. M., Xuei, Z., Tian, H., Almasy, L., Bauer, L. O., et al. (2004). Variations in GABRA2, encoding the alpha-2 subunit of the GABA(A) receptor, are associated with alcohol dependence and with brain oscillations. *American Journal of Human Genetics, 74,* 705–714.

Edery-Halpern, G., & Nachson, I. (2004). Distinctiveness in flashbulb memory: Comparative analysis of five terrorist attacks. *Memory, 12,* 147–157.

Edwards, K. (1998). The face of time: Temporal cues in facial expressions of emotion. *Psychological Society, 9,* 270–276.

Edwards, L. C. (2003). Candidacy and the Children's Implant Profile: Is our selection appropriate? *International Journal of Audiology, 42*(7), 426–431.

Egan, S. K. & Perry, D. G. (2001). Gender identity: A multidimensional analysis with implications for psychosocial adjustment. *Developmental Psychology, 37*(4), 451–463.

Ehlers, A., Hackmann, A., & Michael, T. (2004). Intrusive re-experiencing in post-traumatic stress disorder: Phenomenology, theory, and therapy. *Memory, 12,* 403–415.

Ehrensaft, M. K., Cohen, P., Brown, J., Smailes, E., Chen, H., & Johnson, J. G. (2003). Intergenerational transmission of partner violence: A 20-year prospective study. *Journal of Consulting & Clinical Psychology, 71,* 741–753.

Eich, E., Macaulay, D., & Ryan, L. (1994). Mood dependent memory for events of the personal past. *Journal of Experimental Psychology: General, 123,* 201–215.

Einsenberg, N., Shepard, S. A., Faves, R. A., Murphy, B. C., & Guthrie, I. K. (1998). Shyness and children's emotionality, regulation, and coping: Contemporaneous, longitudinal, and across-context relations. *Child Development 69*(3), 767–790.

Eisenberger, R., & Cameron, J. (1996). Detrimental effects of reward. *American Psychologist, 51,* 1153–1166.

Eisenman, D. P., Gelberg, L., Liu, H., & Shapiro, M. F. (2003). Mental health and health-related quality of life among adult Latino primary care patients living in the United States with previous exposure to political violence. *Journal of the American Medical Association, 290,* 627–634.

Ekman, P. (1992). Facial expressions of emotion: New findings, new questions. *Psychological Science, 3,* 34–38.

Ekman, P. (1993). Facial expression and emotion. *American Psychologist, 48,* 384–392.

Ekman, P., & Friesen, W. V. (1975). *Unmasking the face: A guide to recognizing emotions from facial cues.* Englewood Cliffs, NJ: Prentice-Hall.

Elfenbein, H. A., & Ambady, N. (2002). On the universality and cultural specificity of emotion recognition; A meta-analysis. *Psychological Bulletin, 128,* 203–235.

Elfenbein, H. A., & Ambady, N. (2003). When familiarity breeds accuracy: Cultural exposure and facial emotion recognition. *Journal of Personality and Social Psychology, 85,* 276–290.

Elias, L. J., Saucier, D. M., Hardie, C., & Sarty, G. E. (2003). Dissociating semantic and perceptual components of synaesthesia: Behavioral and functional neuroanatomical investigations. *Cognitive Brain Research, 16,* 232–237.

Eliot, L. (1999). *What's going on in there? How the brain and mind develop in the first five years of life.* New York: Bantam Books.

Elliott, D. M., Mok, D. S., & Briere, J. (2004). Adult sexual assault: Prevalence, symptomatology, and sex differences in the general population. *Journal of Traumatic Stress, 17,* 203–211.

Elliott, M. A., Armitage, C. J., & Baughan, C. J., (2003). Drivers' compliance with speed limits: An application of the theory of planned behavior. *Journal of Applied Psychology, 88,* 964–972.

Ellis, A. (1970). *The essence of rational psychotherapy: A comprehensive approach to treatment.* New York: Institute for Rational Living.

Ellis, A. (1999). Early theories and practices of rational emotive behavior therapy and how they have been augmented and revised during the last three decades. *Journal of Rational Emotive and Cognitive Behavior Therapy, 17,* 69–93.

Ellis, A., & Harper, R. A. (1961). *A guide to rational living.* North Hollywood, CA: Wilshire.

Ellis, M. V. (2001). Harmful supervision, a cause for alarm: Comment on Gray et al. (2001) and Nelson and Friedlander (2001). *Journal of Counseling Psychology, 48*(4), 401–406.

Elsner, B., & Aschersteben, G. (2003). Do I get what you get? Learning about the effects of self-performed and observed actions in infancy. *Consciousness & Cognition, 12,* 732–752.

Elwood, W. N., Greene, K., & Carter, K. K. (2003). Gentlemen don't speak: Communication norms and condom use in bathhouses. *Journal of Applied Communication Research, 31,* 277–297.

Emslie, G. (2004, June). *The treatment of adolescents with depression study (TADS): Primary safety outcomes.* Paper presented at New Clinical Drug Evaluation Unit meetings, Phoenix, AZ.

Enam, S. (2003). A review of genetic factors in depressive affects. *Social Behavior & Personality: An International Journal, 31,* 657–665.

Engel, S. A. (1999). Using neuroimaging to measure mental representations: Finding color-opponent neurons in visual cortex. *Psychological Science, 8,* 23–26.

Engen, T., & Engen, E. A. (1997). Relationship between development of odor perception and language, *Enfance, 1,* 125–140.

Epstein, H. T. (2001). An outline of the role of brain in human cognitive development. *Brain & Cognition, 45*(1), 44–51.

Epstein, L. H., Truesdale, R., Wojcik, A., Paluch, R., & Raynor, H. A. (2003). Effects of deprivation on hedonics and reinforcing value of food. *Physiology & Behavior, 78,* 212–227.

Erdelyi, M. H. (2004). Subliminal perception and its cognates: Theory, indeterminancy, and time. *Consciousness & Cognition, 13,* 73–91.

Erel, O., Oberman, Y., & Yirmiya, N. (2000). Maternal versus nonmaternal care and seven domains of children's development. *Psychological Bulletin, 126*(5), 727–747.

Ergene, T. (2003). Effective interventions on test anxiety reduction. *School Psychology International, 24,* 313–328.

Erikson, E. H. (1964). *Childhood and society* (2nd ed.). Oxford, England: Norton.

Erikson, E. H. (1975). *Life history and the historical moment.* Oxford, England: Norton.

Erikson, E. H. (1984). Reflections on the last stage—and the first. *Psychoanalytic Study of the Child, 39,* 155–165.

Erlandsson, L. K., & Eklund, M. (2003). The relationships of hassles and uplifts to experience of health in working women. *Women & Health, 38,* 19–37.

Erlenmeyer-Kimling, L., & Jarvik, L. F. (1963). Genetics and intelligence: A review. *Science, 142,* 1477–1479.

Eron, L. D. (1987). The development of aggressive behavior from the perspective of a developing behaviorism. *American Psychologist, 42,* 435–442.

Eron, L., Huesmann, L., R., Spindler, A., Guerra, N., Henry, D., & Tolan, P. (2002). A cognitive-ecological approach to preventing aggression in urban settings: Initial outcomes for high-risk children. *Journal of Consulting & Clinical Psychology, 70,* 179–194.

Ettner, S. L., & Grzywacz, J. G. (2001). Workers' perceptions of how jobs affect health: A social ecological perspective. *Journal of Occupational Health Psychology, 6,* 101–113.

Eubank, M., Collins, D., & Smith, N. (2000). The influence of anxiety direction on processing bias. *Journal of Sport and Exercise Psychology, 4,* 292–306.

Evans, G. W. (2003). A multimethodological analysis of cumulative risk and allostatic load among rural children. *Developmental Psychology, 39,* 924–933.

Evans, G.W. (2004). The environment of childhood poverty, *American Psychologist, 59,* 77–92.

Exner, J. E. (1974). *The Rorschach: A comprehensive system. Vol I: Basic Foundations* (2nd ed.). New York: Wiley.

Eysenck, H. J. (1970). *The structure of human personality* (3rd ed.), London: Methuen.

Eysenck, H. J. (1994). Personality: Biological foundations. In P.A. Vernon (Ed.), *The neuropsychology of individual differences* (pp. 151–207). San Diego, CA: Academic Press.

Eysenck, H. J. (1998). *A new look at intelligence.* London: Transaction Publishers.

Eysenck, H. J., & Eysenck, S. B. G. (1993). *The Eysenck Personality Questionnaire-Revised.* London: Hodder & Stoughton.

Ezzo, J., Berman, B., Hadhazy, V.A., Jadad, A. R., Lao, L., & Singh, B. B. (2000). Is acupuncture effective for the treatment of chronic pain? A systematic review. *Pain, 86,* 217–225.

Fabiani, M., Stadler, M. A., & Wessels, P. M. (2000). True but not false memories produce a sensory signature in human laterlized brain potentials. *Journal of Cognitive Neuroscience, 12,* 941–949.

Facteau, J. D., & Craig, S. B. (2001). Are performance appraisal ratings from different rating sources comparable? *Journal of Applied Psychology, 86*, 215–227.

Fagan, C. (2001a). The temporal reorganization of employment and the household rhythm of work schedules: The implications for gender and class relations. *American Behavioral Scientist, 44*, 1199–1212.

Fagan, C. (2001b). Time, money and the gender order: Work orientations and working-time preferences in Britain. *Gender, Work & Organization, 8*, 239–266.

Fagot, B. I., Rodgers, C. S., & Leinbach, M. D. (2000). Theories of gender socialization. In T. Eckes & H. M. Trautner (Eds.), *The developmental social psychology of gender* (pp. 65–89). Mahwah, NJ: Eribaum.

Faludi, S. (1999). *Stiffed: The betrayal of the American man*. New York: Morrow.

Fan, X., Chen, M., & Matsumoto, A. R. (1997). Gender differences in mathematics achievement: Findings from the National Education Longitudinal Study of 1988. *Journal of Experimental Education, 65*, 229–242.

Fang, C. Y., & Myers, H. F. (2001). The effects of racial stressors and hostility on cardiovascular reactivity in African American and Caucasian men. *Health Psychology, 20*, 64EN70.

Fantz, R. L. (1961, May). The origin of form perception. *Scientific American*, 66–72.

Farah, M. J., Wilson, K. D., Drain, M., & Tanaka, J. N. (1998). What is special about face perception? *Psychological Review,105*, 482–498.

Farmer, T. W., Estell, D. B., Bishop, J. L., O'Neal, K. K., & Cairns, B. D. (2003). Rejected bullies or popular leaders? The social relations of aggressive subtypes of rural African American early adolescents. *Developmental Psychology, 39*, 992–1004.

Farmer-Dougan, V. (1998). A disequilibrium analysis of incidental teaching: Determining reinforcement effects. *Behavior Modification, 22*, 78–95.

Farver, J. M., Narang, S. K., & Bhadha, B. R. (2002). East meets west: Ethnic identity, acculturation, and conflict in Asian Indian families. *Journal of Family Psychology, 16*, 338–350.

Fast, J. E., & Frederick, J. A. (1996). Working arrangements and time stress. *Canadian Social Trends, 43*, 14–19.

Fausto-Sterling, A. (2000). *Sexing the Body*. New York, NY: Basic Books.

Fazio, R. H. (2000). Accessible attitudes as tools for objects appraisal: Their costs and benefits. In G. Maio & J. Olson (Eds.),

Why we evaluate: Functions of attitudes (pp. 1–36). Mahwah, NJ: Erlbaum.

Feist, J., & Feist, G. J. (2006). *Theories of personality* (6th ed.). Boston: McGraw-Hill.

Fernandes, M.A., & Moscovitch, M. (2002). Factors modulating the effect of divided attention during retrieval of words. *Memory & Cognition, 30*, 731–744.

Fernandez, E., & Sheffield, J. (1996). Relative contributions of life events versus daily hassles to the frequency and intensity of headaches. *Headache, 36*, 595–602.

Ferraro, T. (2001). A psychoanalytic perspective on anxiety in athletes. *Athletic Insight: Online Journal of Sport Psychology* (2). Retrieved from www.athleticinsight.com/vollssw/Psychoanalytic-Anxiety.htm.

Ferrie, J. E., Martikainen, P., Shipley, M. J., Marmot, M. G., Stansfeld, S. A., & Smith, G. D. (2001). Employment status and health after privatisation in white collar civil servants: Prospective cohort study. *British Medical Journal, 322*, 647–651.

Festinger, L. (1957). *A theory of cognitive dissonance*. Evanston, IL: Row, Petersen.

Festinger, L., & Carlsmith, J. M. (1959). Cognitive consequences of forced compliance. *Journal of Abnormal and Social Psychology, 58*, 203–210.

Festinger, L., Schachter, S., & Back, L. (1950). *Social pressures in informal groups: A study of human factors in housing*. New York: Harper.

Fiebach, C. J., & Friederici, A. D. (2004). Processing concrete words: MRI evidence against a specific right-hemisphere involvement. *Neuropsychologia, 42*, 62–70.

Field, A. E., Austin, S. B., Taylor, C. B., Malspeis, S., Rossner, B., Rockett, H. R., et al. (2003). Relation between dieting and weight change among preadolescents and adolescents. *Pediatrics, 112*, 900–906.

Fillingim, R. B. (2003). Sex-related influences on pain: A review of mechanisms and clinical implications. *Rehabilitation Psychology, 48*, 165–174.

Finch, S. J., Farberman, H. A., Neus, J., Adams, R. E., & Price-Baker, D. (2002). Differential test performance in the American educational system: The impact of race and gender. *Journal of Sociology & Social Welfare, 29*, 89–108.

Fine, M. (2002). 2001 Carolyn Sherif award address: The presence of an absence. *Psychology of Women Quarterly, 26*, 9–24.

Finegold, K.,& Wherry, L. (2004) *Race, ethnicity, and economic well-being*. Retrieved July 7, 2004, from http://www.urban.org/url.cfm?ID=310968

Finkel, D., Pedersen, N. L., Berg, S., & Johansson, B. (2000). Quantitative genetic analysis

of biobehavioral markers of aging in Swedish studies of adult twins. *Journal of Aging & Health, 12*, 47–68.

Finkel, D., Pedersen, N. L., Plomin, R., & McClearn, G. E. (1998). Longitudinal and cross-sectional twin data on cognitive abilities in adulthood: The Swedish Adoption/Twin Study of Aging. *Developmental Psychology, 34*, 1400–1413.

Finney, E. M., Clementz, B. A., Hickok, G., & Dobkins, K. R. (2003). Visual stimuli activate auditory cortex in deaf subjects: Evidence from MEG. *Neuroreport: For Rapid Communication of Neuroscience Research, 14*, 1425–1427.

Fischer, A. H., Mosquera, P. M. R., van Vianen, A. E. M., & Manstead, A. S. R. (2004). Gender and culture differences in emotion. *Emotion, 4*, 87–94.

Fischhoff, B., Downs, J., & de Bruin, W. B. (1998). Adolescent vulnerability: A framework for behavioral interventions. *Applied and Preventive Psychology, 9*, 77–94.

Fish, J. M. (2002). The myth of race. In J. M. Fish (Ed.), *Race and intelligence: Separating science from myth* (pp. 113–141). Mahwah. NJ: Erlbaum.

Fishbain, D. A. (2000). Non-surgical chronic pain treatment outcome: A review. *International Review of Psychiatry, 12*, 170–180.

Fisher, C. B., & Fryberg, D. (1994). Participant partners: College students weigh the costs and benefits of deceptive research. *American Psychologist, 49*. 417–427.

Fisher, L. A., & Bredemeier, B. J. (2000). Caring about injustice: The moral self-perceptions of professional female bodybuilders. *Journal of Sport & Exercise Psychology, 22*(4), 327–344.

Fishman, D. B., & Franks, C. M. (1997). The conceptual evolution of behavior therapy. In P. L. Wachiel & S. B. Messer (Eds.), *Theories of psychotherapy: Origins and evolution* (pp. 131–180). Washington, DC: American Psychological Association.

Fiske, S. T. (1992). Thinking is for doing: Portraits of social cognition from daguerreotype to laser-photo. *Journal of Personality and Social Psychology, 63*, 877–889.

Fiske, S. T. (1998). Stereotyping, prejudice, and discrimination. In D. T. Gilbert, S. T. Fiske, & G. Lindzey (Eds.), *The handbook of social psychology* (pp. 357–411). New York: McGraw Hill.

Fiske, S. T. (2002). What we know now about bias and intergroup conflict, the problem of the century. *Current Directions in Psychological Science, 11*, 123–128.

Fiske, S. T. (2004). *Social beings: A care motives approach to social psychology*. New York: Wiley.

Fiske, S. T., Cuddy, A. J. C., Glick, P., & Xu, J. (2002). A model of (often mixed) stereotype content: Competence and warmth respectively follow from perceived status and competition. *Journal of Personality and Social Psychology, 82,* 878–902.

Fitch, W. T., & Hauser, M. D. (2004). Computational constraints on syntactic processing in a non-human primate. *Science, 303,* 377–380.

Flammer, E., & Bongartz, W. (2003) On the efficacy of hypnosis: A meta-analytic study. *Contemporary Hypnosis, 20(4),* 179–197.

Flavell, J. H., Green, F. L., & Flavell, E. R. (2000). Development of children's awareness of their own thoughts. *Journal of Cognition & Development. l(1).* 97–112.

Fleishman, E. A., Costanza, D. C., & Marshall-Mies, J. (1999). Abilities. In N. G. Peterson, M. D. Mumford, W. C. Borman, P. R. Jeanneret, and E. A. Fleishman (Eds.), *An occupational information system for the 21st century: The development of O * NET.* Washington, DC: American Psychological Association.

Fletcher, A. C., Darling, N. E., Steinberg, L., & Dornbusch, S. (1995). The company they keep: Relation of adolescents' adjustment and behavior to the perceptions of authoritative parenting in the social network. *Developmental Psychology, 31,* 300–310.

Fletcher, C., & Perry, E. L. (2002). Performance appraisal and feedback: A consideration of national culture and a review of contemporary research and future trends. In N. Anderson, D.S. Ones, H. K. Sinangil, & C. Viswesvaran (Eds.), *Handbook of industrial, work & organizational psychology* (pp. 127–144). London: Sage publications.

Flowers, L. A., Milner, H., R., & Moore, J. L., Ill, (2003). Effects of locus of control on African American high school seniors' educational aspirations: Implications for preservice and inservice high school teachers and counselors. *High School Journal, 87,* 39–50.

Flynn, G. (2002). A legal examination of testing. *Workforce, 81,* 92–93.

Flynn, J. R. (1987). Massive gains in 14 nations: What IQ tests really measure. *Psychological Bulletin, 101,* 171–191.

Flynn, J. R. (1999). Searching for justice: The discovery of IQ gains over time. *American Psychologist, 54,* 5–20.

Flynn, J. R. (2003). Movies about intelligence: The limitations of *g. Current Directions in Psychological Science, 12,* 95–99.

Fogel, A., Nelson-Goens, G. C., Hsu, H., & Shapiro, A. F. (2000). Do different infant smiles reflect different positive emotions? *Social Development, 9,* 497–520.

Folkman, S., & Moskowitz, J. T. (2000). Positive affect and the other side of coping. *American Psychologist, 55,* 647–654.

Fonlenelle, L. F., Mendlowicz, M. V., Marques, C., & Versiani, M. (2004). Trans-cultural aspects of obsessive-compulsive disorder: A description of a Brazilian sample and a systematic review of international clinical studies. *Journal of Psychiatric Research, 38,* 403–411.

Foote, R., Eyberg, S., & Schuhmann, E. (1998). Parentchild interaction approaches to the treatment of child behavior problems. *Advances in Clinical Child Psychology, 20,* 125–151.

Forbes, G. B., Adams-Curtis, L. E., Rade, B., & Jaberg, P. (2001). Body dissatisfaction in women and men: The role of gender-typing and self-esteem. *Sex Roles, 44,* 461–484.

Forbes, G. B., Doroszewicz, K., Card, L., & Adams-Curtis, L. (2004). Association of thin ideal body, ambivalent sexism, and self-esteem with body mass index and the preferred body size of college women in Poland and the United States. *Sex Roles, 50,* 331–345.

Ford, C. S., & Beach, F. A. (1951). *Patterns of sexual behavior.* New York: Harper.

Forest, G., & Godbout, R. (2000). Effects of sleep deprivation on performance and EEG spectral analysis in young adults. *Brain and Cognition, 43,* 195–200.

Forgas, J. P. (2002). Feeling and doing: Affective influences on interpersonal behavior. *Psychological Inquiry, 13,* 1–28.

Forman, D. R., & Kochanska, G. (2001). Viewing imitation as child responsiveness: A link between teaching and discipline domains of socialization. *Developmental Psychology, 37(2),* 198–206.

Fornai, F., & Orzi, F. (2001). Sexual pheromone or conventional odors increase extracellular lactate without changing glucose utilization in specific brain areas of the rat. *Neuroreport: An International Journal for the Rapid Communication of Research in Neuroscience, 12,* 63–69.

Fortenberry, J. D. (2002). Clinic-based service programs for increasing responsible sexual behavior. *Journal of Sex Research, 39,* 63–66.

Fosha, D. (2004). Brief integrative therapy comes of age: A commentary. *Journal of Psychotherapy Integration, 14,* 66–92.

Fossati, P., Hevenor, S., Graham, S. J., Grady, C., Keightley, M. L., Craik, F., et al. (2003). In search of the emotional self: An [MR] study using positive and negative emotional words. *American Journal of Psychiatry, 160,* 1938–1945.

Fosse, R., Stickgold, R., & Hobson, J. A. (2004). Thinking and hallucinating: Reciprocal changes in sleep. *Psychophysiology, 41,* 298–305.

Foulkes, D. (1985). *Dreaming: A cognitive-psychological analysis.* Hillsdale, NJ: Eribaum.

Foulkes, D. (1990). Dreaming and consciousness. *European Journal of Cognitive Psychology, 2,* 39–55.

Foulkes, D. (1996). Dream research. *Sleep, 19,* 609–624.

Foulkes, D., Meier, B., Strauch, I., & Kerr, N. H. (1993). Linguistic phenomena and language selection in the REM dreams of German–English bilinguals. *International Journal of Psychology, 28,* 871–891.

Fournier, A. K., Ehrhart, I. J., Glindemann, K. E., & Geller, E. S. (2004). Intervening to decrease alcohol abuse at university parties. *Behavior Modification, 28,* 167–181.

Fox, N., Kagan, J., & Weiskopf, S. (1979). The growth of memory during infancy. *Genetic Psychology Monographs, 99,* 91–130.

Frable, D. E. (1989). Sex typing and gender ideology: Two facets of the individual's gender psychology that go together. *Journal of Personality and Social Psychology, 56,* 95–108.

Fraenkel, P., & Pinsof, W. M. (2001). Teaching family therapy-centered integration: Assimilation and beyond. *Journal of Psychotherapy Integration, 11,* 59–85.

Fraley, R. C., & Spieker, S. J. (2003). Are infant attachment patterns continuously disturbed? A taxometric analoysis of strange situation behavior. *Developmental Psychology, 39,* 387–404.

Franken, R. E. (2002). *Human motivation* (5th ed.). Belmont, CA: Wadsworth.

Frankenberger, K. D. (2000). Adolescent egocentrism: A comparison among adolescents and adults. *Journal of Adolescence, 23,* 343–354.

Franklin, M. E., & Foa, E. B. (2002). Cognitive behavioral treatments for obsessive compulsive disorder. In P. E. Nathan & J. M. Gorman (Eds.). *A guide to treatments that work* (pp. 367–410). New York: Oxford Press.

Franks, J. J., Bilbrey, C. W., Lein, K. G., & McNamara, T. P. (2000). Transfer-appropriate processing (TAP) and repetition priming. *Memory and Cognition, 28,* 1140–1151.

Frederick, C. M. (2000). Competitiveness: Relations with GPA, locus of control, sex, and athletic status. *Perceptual and Motor Skills, 90,* 413–414.

Fredriksen, K., Reddy, R., & Way, N. (2004). Sleepless in Chicago: Tracking the effects of adolescent sleep loss during the middle school years. *Child Development, 75,* 84–95.

Freese, M., & Meland, S. (2002). Seven tenths incorrect: Heterogeneity and change in the waist-to-hip ratios of Playboy centerfold models and Miss America pageant winners. *Journal of Sex Research, 39*, 133–138.

French, K. E., Spurgeon, J. H., & Nevett, M. E. (1995). Expert-novice differences in cognitive and skill execution components of youth baseball performance. *Research Quarterly for Exercise and Sport, 66*, 194–201.

Freud, S. (1900/1953). The interpretation of dreams. In J. Stachey (Ed.), *The standard edition of the complete psychological works of Sigmund Freud* (Vols. 4 and 5). London: Hogarth. (Original work published 1900.)

Freud, S. (1901/1960). The psychopathology of everyday life. In J. Strachey (Ed. and Trans.), *The standard edition of the complete psychological works of Sigmund Freud* (Vol. 6). London: Hogarth Press.

Freud, S. (1915/1957). The unconscious. In J. Strachey (Ed. And Trans.). *The standard edition of the complete psychological works of Sigmund Freud* (Vol. 14). London: Hogarth Press.

Freud, S. (1920/1955). Beyond the pleasure principle. In J. Strachey (Ed. And Trans.). *The standard edition of the complete psychological works of Sigmund Freud* (Vol. 18). London: Hogarth Press.

Freud, S. (1920/1966). *A general introduction to psychoanalysis* (J. Riviere, Trans.). New York: Washington Square (Original work published 1920.)

Freud, S. (1925/1961). Some physical consequences of the anatomical distinction between the sexes. In J. Strachey (Ed. and Trans.). *The standard edition of the complete psychological works of Sigmund Freud* (Vol. 19). London: Hogarth Press.

Freud, S. (1926/1959). Inhibitions, symptoms, and anxiety. In J. Strachey (Ed. and Trans.). *The standard edition of the complete psychological works of Sigmund Freud* (Vol. 20). London: Hogarth Press.

Freud, S. (1933/1964). *New introductory lectures on psychoanalysis.* New York: Norton. (Original work published 1933.)

Freud, S. (1985). *The complete letters of Sigmund Freud to Wilhelm Fliess, 1887–1904* (J. M. Masson, Ed. and Trans.), Cambridge, MA: Harvard University Press.

Frey, B. J., & Hinton, G. E. (1999). Variational learning in nonlinear gaussian belief networks. *Neural Computation, 11*, 193–213.

Frezza, M., di Padova, C., Pozzato, G., Terpin, M., Baraona, E., & Lieber, C. S. (1990). High blood alcohol levels in women. *New England Journal of Medicine, 322*, 95–99.

Friedman, D. P. (1990). Perspectives on the medical use of drugs of abuse. *Journal of Pain and Symptom Management, 5*, S2–S5.

Friedman, M., & Rosenman, R. H. (1974). *Type A behavior and your heart.* Greenwich, CT: Fawcett.

Friedman, M. A., Detweiler-Bedell, J. B., Leventhal, H. E., Horne, R., Keitner, G. I., & Miller, I. W. (2004). Combined psychotherapy and pharmacotherapy for the treatment of major depressive disorder. *Clinical Psychology: Science & Practice, 11*, 47–68.

Friedrich, R. W., & Laurent, G. (2001). Dynamic optimization of odor representations by slow temporal patterning of mitral cell activity. *Science, 291*, 889–894.

Frieze, I. H., Boneva, B. S., šarlija N., Horvat, J., Ferligoj, A. Kolgovšek T., et al. (2004). Psychological differences in stayers and leavers: Emigration desires in central and eastern European university students. *European Psychologist, 9*, 15–23.

Frost, J. A., Binder, J. R., Springer, J. A., Hammeke, T. A., Bellgowan, P. S. F., Rao, S. M., & Cox, R. W. (1999). Language processing is strongly left lateralized in both sexes: Evidence from functional MRI, *Brain, 122*, 199–208.

Frost, L. (2003). Doing bodies differently? Gender, youth, appearance and damage. *Journal of Youth Studies, 6*(1), 53–70.

Fujiki, N., Riederer, K. A., Jousmaki, V., Makela, J. P., & Hari, R. (2002) Human cortical representation of virtual auditory space: Differences between space and elevation. *European Journal of Neuroscience, 16*, 2207–2213.

Fuller, B., Caspary, G., Kagan, S., Gautier, C., Huang, D., Carroll, J., & McCarthy, J. (2002). Does maternal employment influence poor children's social development? *Early Childhood Research Quarterly, 17*, 470–490.

Fullmer, C. E. (1999). Infant responses to changes in parental behavior: A comparison to two still-faced situations. *Dissertation Abstracts International: Section B: The Sciences & Engineering, 60*(6-B), 2983.

Fundudis, T. (2003). Consent issues in medicolegal procedures: how competent are children to make their own decisions. *Child & Adolescent Mental Health, 8*(1), 18–22.

Furman, W., Simon, V. A., Shaffer, L., & Bouchey, H. A. (2002). Adolescents' working models and styles for relationships with parents, friends, and romantic partners. *Child Development, 73*, 241–255.

Furnham, A., & Buck, C. (2003). A comparison of lay-beliefs about autism and obsessive-compulsive disorder. *International Journal of Social Psychiatry, 49*, 287–307.

Furnham, A., Moutafi, J., & Baguma, P. (2002). A cross-cultural study o the role of weight and waist-to-hip ratio on female attractiveness. *Personality & Individual Differences, 32*, 729–745.

Furnham, A., Moutafi, J., & Crump, J. (2003). The relationship between the revised NEO-Personality Inventory and the Myers-Briggs Type Indicator. *Social Behavior & Personality: An International Journal, 31*, 577–584.

Furnham, A., Reeves, E., & Budhani, S. (2002). Parents think their sons are brighter than their daughters: Sex differences in parental self-estimations and estimations of their children's multiple intelligences. *Journal of Genetic Psychology, 163*, 24–39.

Furr, S. R., Westefeld, J. S., McConnell, G. N., & Jenkins, J. M. (2001). Suicide and depression among college students: A decade later. *Professional Psychology: Research and Practice. 32*, 97–100.

Gaines, S. O., Jr., & Reed, E. S. (1995). Prejudice: From Allport to DuBois. *American Psychologist, 50*, 96–103.

Gainor, K. A. (2000). Including transgender issues in lesbian, gay, and bisexual psychology: Implications for clinical practice and training. In B. Greene & G. L. Croom (Eds.), *Education, research, and practice in lesbian, gay, bisexual, and transgendered psychology: A resource manual, 5* (pp. 131–160). Thousand Oaks, CA: Sage.

Galambos, N. L., & Tilton-Weaver, L. C. (2000). Adolescents' psychosocial maturity, problem behavior, and subjective age: In search of the adultoid. *Applied Developmental Science, 4*(4), 178–192.

Gale, C., & Oakley-Browne, M. (2004). EBMH note-book: Generalised anxiety disorder. *Evidence-Based Mental Health, 7*, 32–33.

Galea, S., Vlahov, D., Resnick, H., Ahern, J., Susser, E., Gold, J., et al. (2003). Trends of probable post-traumatic stress disorder in New York City after the September 11 terrorist attacks. *American Journal of Epidemiology, 158*, 514–524.

Gallager, A., Bridgeman, B., & Cahalan, C. (2002). The effect of computer-based tests on racial-ethnic and gender groups. *Journal of Educational Measurement, 39*(2), 133–147.

Gallopin, T., Fort, P., Eggerman, E., Cauli, B., Luppi, P. H., Rossier, J., Audinal, E., Muhlethaler, M., & Seralin, M. (2000). Identification of sleep-promoting neurons in vitro, *Nature, 404*, 992–995.

Galloway, R., Dusch, E., Elder, L., Achadi, E., Grajeda, R., Hurtado, R., et al. (2002) Women's perceptions of iron deficiency and anemia prevention and control in eight developing countries. *Social Science and Medicine, 55,* 529–544.

Gannon, L. (2002). A critique of evolutionary psychology. *Psychology, Evolution & Gender, 4,* 173–218.

Gao, F., Levine, S. C., Huttenlocher, J. (2000). What do infants know about continuous quantity? *Journal of Experimental Child Psychology, 77*(1), 20–29.

Garcia, J., Gustavson, C. R., Kelly, D. J., & Sweeney, M. (1976). Prey-lithium aversions: I. Coyotes and wolves. *Behavioral Biology, 16,* 61–72.

Garcia, J., & Koelling, R. A. (1971). The use of ionizing rays as a mammalian olfactory stimulus. In H. Autrum, R. Jung, W. R. Loewenstein, D. M. MacKay, & H. L. Teuber (Eds.), *Handbook of sensory physiology: Vol. 4. Chemical senses (Pt. 1).* New York: Springer-Verlag.

Garcia, S. M., Weaver, K., Moskowitz, G. B., & Darley, J. M. (2002). Crowded minds: The implicit by-stander effect. *Journal of Personality and Social Psychology, 83,* 843–853.

Garcia, W. J. (2002). *Sign with your baby: How to communicate with infants before they can speak.* Seattle, WA: Northlight Communications.

Gardner, H. (1983/1993). *Frames of mind: The theory of multiple intelligences.* New York: Basic Books. (Original worked published in 1983).

Gardner, H. (1999). *Intelligence reframed: Multiple intelligences for the 21st century.* New York: Basic Books.

Gardner, H. (2003). Three distinct meanings of intelligence. In R. J. Sternberg, J. Laulrey, & T. I. Lubart (Eds.), *Models of intelligence: International perspectives* (pp. 43–54). Washington, DC: American Psychological Association.

Gardner, H., & Hatch, T. (1989). Multiple intelligences go to school: Educational implications of the theory of multiple intelligences. *Educational Researcher, 18,* 6.

Gardner, R. A., & Gardner, B. T. (1969). Teaching sign language to a chimp. *Science, 165,* 664–672.

Gardner, W. L., & Avolio, B. J. (1998). The charismatic relationship: A dramaturgical perspective. *Academy of Management Review, 23,* 32–58.

Garland, A., & Scott, J. (2002). Cognitive therapy for depression in women. *Psychiatric Annals, 32,* 465–476.

Garnet, K. E. (1998). Jumpstart: An evaluation of program efficacy for an intensive intervention with high-risk preschool children. *Dissertation Abstracts International: Section B: The Sciences and Engineering, 58*(9-B), 5517.

Gatchel, R. J., & Turk, D. C. (1999). Interdisciplinary treatment of chronic pain patients. In R. J. Gatchel & D. C. Turk (Eds.), *Psychosocial factors in pain: Critical perspectives* (pp. 435–444). New York: Guilford Press.

Gates, G. J., & Sonenstein, F. L. (2000). Heterosexual genital sexual activity among adolescent males: 1988 and 1995. *Family Planning Perspectives, 32,* 295–297.

Gathercole, S. J., Pickering, S. J., Ambridge, B., & Wearing, H. (2004). The structure of working memory from 4 to 15 years of age. *Developmental Psychology, 40,* 177–190.

Gaulin, S. J. C., & McBurney, D. H. (2001). *Psychology: An evolutionary approach.* Upper Saddle River, NJ: Prentice-Hall.

Gaulin, S. J. C., & McBurney, D. H. (2004). *Psychology: An evolutionary approach* (2nd ed). Upper Saddle River, NJ: Prentice-Hall.

Gavin, J. (2000). Arousing suspicion and violating trust: The lived ideology of safe sex talk. *Culture, Health, and Sexuality, 2,* 117–134.

Gawne, T. J., & Woods, J. M. (2003). The responses of visual cortical neurons encode differences across saccades. *Neuroreport: For Rapid Communication of Neuroscience Research, 14*(1), 105–109.

Gawronski, B., & Strack, F. (2004). On the propositional nature of cognitive consistency: Dissonance changes explicit, but not implicit attitudes. *Journal of Experimental Social Psychology, 40,* 535–542.

Gazzaniga, M. S. (1967). The split brain in man. *Scientific American, 217,* 24–29.

Gazzaniga, M. S. (2000). Right hemisphere language following brain bisection: A 20-year perspective. In M. S. Gazzaniga (Ed.), *Cognitive neuro-science* (pp. 411–430). Malden, MA: Blackwell.

Ge, X., Conger, R. D., & Elder, G. H. (2001). The relation between puberrty and psychological distress in adolescent boys. *Journal of Research on Adolescence, 11*(1), 49–70.

Geary, D. C. (1998). *Male, female: The evolution of human sex differences.* Washington, DC: American Psychological Association.

Geary, D. C. (2000). Evolution and proximate expression of human paternal investment. *Psychological Bulletin, 126,* 55–77.

Geary, D. C., & Bjorklund. D. F. (2000). Evolutionary developmental psychology. *Child Development, 71*(1), 57–65.

Geary, D. C., & Huffman, K. J. (2002). Brain and cognitive evolution forms of modularity and functions of mind. *Psychological Bulletin, 128,* 667–698.

Geary, D. C., Liu, F., Chen, G., Saults, S. J., & Hoard, M. K. (1999). Contributions of computational fluency to cross-national differences in arithmetical reasoning abilities. *Journal of Educational Psychology, 91,* 716–719.

Gee, T., Allen, K., & Powell, R. A. (2003). Questioning premorbid dissociative symptomatology in dissociative identity disorder: Comment on Gleaves, Hernandez, and Warner (1999). *Professional Psychology: Research and Practice, 34,* 114–116.

Geher, G. (2000). Perceived and actual characteristics of parents and partners: A test of a Freudian model of mate selection. *Current Psychology, 19,* 194–213.

Geller, B., Zimerman, B., Williams, M., Bolhofner, K., & Craney, J. L. (2004). Adult psychosocial outcome of prepubertal major depressive disorder. *Journal of the American Academy of Child & Adolescent Psychiatry, 40*(6), 673–677.

Geller, E. S. (2001a). The future of safety: From conversation to commitment. *Occupational Health & Safety, 1,* 58–63.

Geller, E. S. (2001b). *The psychology of safety handbook* (2nd ed.). Boca Raton, FL: CRC Press LLC.

Geller, E. S. (2001c). Sustaining participation in a safety improvement process: 10 relevant principles from behavioral science. *American Society of Safety Engineers,* 24–29.

George, J. M., & Brief, A. P. (1992). Feeling good—doing good: A conceptual analysis of the mood at work—organizational spontaneity relationship. *Psychological Bulletin, 112,* 310–329.

Georgopoulos, A. P., Whang, K., Georgopoulos, M. A., Tagaris, G. A., Amirikian, B., Richter, W., Kim, S. G., & Ugurbil, K. (2001). Functional magnetic resonance imaging of visual object construction and shape discrimination: Relations among task, hemispheric lateralization, and gender. *Journal of Cognitive Neuroscience, 13,* 72–89.

German, T. P., & Defeyter, M. A. (2000). Immunity to functional fixedness in young children. *Psychonomic Bulletin & Review, 7,* 707–712.

Gerra, G., Angioni, L., Zaimovic, A., Moi, G., Bussandri, M., Bertacca, S., et al. (2004)-Substance use among high-school students: Relationships with temperament, personality traits, and parental care perception. *Substance Use & Misuse, 39,* 345–367.

Gershoff, E. T. (2002). Corporal punishment by parents and associated child behaviors and experience: A meta-analysis and theoretical review. *Psychological Bulletin, 128,* 539–579.

Geschwind, N. (1972, April). Language and the brain. *Scientific American, 226*(4), 76–83.

Gest, S. D., Graham-Bermann, S. A., & Hartup, W. W. (2001). Peer excellence: Common and unique features of number of friendships, social centrality, and socioeconomic status. *Social Development, 10*(1), 23–40.

Ghetti, S., Schaaf, J. M., Qin, J., & Goodman, G. S. (2004). Issues in eyewitness testimony. In W. O' Donohue & E. Levensky (Eds.), *Handbook of forensic psychology: Resource for mental health and legal professionals* (pp. 513–554). London: Elsevier Academic Press.

Gibson, L. (2004). Newer hypnotics no better for insomnia that short-acting benzodiazepines. *British Medical Journal, 328,* 1093.

Giddens, A., Dunier, M., & Applebaum, R. (2001). *Introduction to sociology* (4th ed.). New York: Norton.

Gilligan, C. (1982). *In a different voice: Psychological theory and women's development.* Cambridge, MA: Harvard University Press.

Gilligan, C. (1995). In a different voice: Women's conceptions of self and of morality. In B. Puka et al. (Eds.), *Caring voices and women's moral frames: Gilligan's view.* New York: Garland.

Gilligan, C. (1997). Remembering Iphigenia: Voice, resonance, and a talking cure. In B. Mark (Ed.), *The handbook of infant, child, and adolescent psychotherapy.* Northvale, NJ: Jason Aronson.

Ginandez, C., Brooks, P., Sando, W., Jones, C., & Aker, J. (2003). Can medical hypnosis accelerate post-surgical wound healing? Results of a clinical trial. *American Journal of Clinical Hypnosis, 45,* 333–351.

Glass, R. M. (2001). Electroconvulsive therapy: Time to bring it out of the shadows. *Journal of the American Medical Association, 285*(10), special issue.

Gleaves, D. H. (1996). The sociocognitive model of dissociative identity disorder: A reexamination of the evidence. *Psychological Bulletin, 120,* 42–59.

Gleaves, D. H., Smith, S. M., Butler, L. D., & Spiegel, D. (2004). False and recovered memories in the laboratory and clinic: A review of experimental and clinical evidence. *Clinical Psychology: Science & Practice, 11,* 3–28.

Glenmullen, J. (2001). *Prozac backlash: Overcoming the dangers of Prozac, Zoloft, Paxil, and other antidepressants with safe, effective alternatives.* New York: Touchstone Books/Simon & Schuster, Inc.

Glick, P., & Fiske, S. T. (1997). Hostile and benevolent sexism: Measuring ambivalent sexism toward women. *Psychology of Women Quarterly, 21,* 119–135.

Glick, P., & Fiske, S. T. (2001). An ambivalent alliance: Hostile and benevolent sexism as complementary justification for gender inequality. *American Psychologist, 56,* 109–118.

Glindemann, K. E., & Geller, E. S. (2003). A systematic assessment of intoxication at university parties: Effects of the environmental context. *Environment & Behavior, 35,* 655–663.

Goerke, M., Möller, J., Schultz-Hardt, S., Naplersky, U., & Frey, D. (2004). "It's not my fault—but only I can change it": Counterfactual and prefactual thoughts of managers. *Journal of Applied Psychology, 89,* 279–282.

Goethals, G. R. (2003). A century of social psychology: Individuals, ideas, and investigations. In M. A. Hogg & J. Cooper (Eds.), *The Sage handbook of social psychology* (pp. 3–23). London: Sage.

Goldfried, M. R. (2004). Integrating integratively oriented brief Psychotherapy. *Journal of Psychotherapy Integration, 14,* 93–105.

Goldfried, M. R., & Wolfe, B. E. (1998). Toward a more clinically valid approach to therapy research. *Journal of Consulting and Clinical Psychology, 66,* 143–150.

Golding, J. (1999). Intimate partner violence as a risk factor for mental disorders: A meta-analysis. *Journal of Family Violence, 14,* 99–101.

Goldin-Meadow, S. (2000). Learning with and without a helping hand. In B. Landau, J. Sabini, J. Jonides, & E. L. Newport (Eds.), *Perception, cognition, and language: Essays in honor of Henry and Lila Gleitman* (pp. 121–137). Cambridge, MA: The MIT Press.

Goldstein, J. M., Seidman, L. J., Horton, N. J., Makris, N., Kennedy, D. N., Caviness, V. S., Jr., Faraone, S. V., & Tsuang, M. T. (2001). Normal sexual dimorphism of the adult human brain assessed by in vivo magnetic resonance imaging. *Cerebral Cortex, 11,* 490–497.

Goleman, D. (1995). *Emotional intelligence.* New York: Bantam.

Gonzales, L. R., Hays, R. B., Bond, M. A., & Kelly, J. G. (1983). Community mental health. In M. Hersen, A. E. Kazdin, & A. S. Bellack (Eds.), *The clinical psychology handbook.* New York: Pergamon Press.

Gonzalez, R., Nolen-Hoeksema, S., & Treynor, W. (2003). Rumination reconsidered: A psychometric analysis. *Cognitive Therapy &Research, 27,* 247–259.

Goodwin, R. D., Fergusson, D. M., & Horwood, L. J. (2004). Panic attacks and the risk of depression among young adults in the community. *Psychotherapy & Psychosomatics, 73,* 158–165.

Gortmaker, S. L., Kagan, J., Caspi, A., & Silva, P. A. (1997). Daylength during pregnancy and shyness in children: Results from Northern and Southern hemispheres. *Developmental Psychobiology, 31* (2), 107–114.

Gottman, J. M. (1998). Psychology and the study of marital processes. *Annual Review of Psychology, 49,* 169–187.

Gould, S. J. (1996). *The mismeasure of man* (rev. ed.). New York: Norton.

Gowaty, P. A. (2001). Women, psychology, and evolution. In R. K. Unger (Ed.), *Handbook of the psychology of women and gender* (pp. 53–65). New York: Wiley.

Graber, J. A., Britto, P. R., & Brooks-Gunn, J. (1999). What's love got to do with it? Adolescents' and young adults' beliefs about sexual and romantic relationships. In W. Furman, B. B. Brown, & C. Feiring (Eds.), *Self, social identity, and physical health: Interdisciplinary explorations, Rutgers Series on Self and Social Identity* (pp. 364–395). New York: Cambridge University Press.

Grachev, I. D., & Apkarian, A. V. (2000). Chemical mapping of anxiety in the brain of healthy humans: An in vivo-sup-1H-MRS study on the effects of sex, age, and brain region. *Human Brain Mapping, 11,* 261–272.

Grados, M. A., Walkup, J., & Walford, S. (2003). Genetics of obsessive-compulsive disorders: New findings and challenges. *Brain & Development, 25* (January Suppl.), S55.

Graham, K., & Wells, S. (2001). The two worlds of aggression for men and women. *Sex Roles, 45,* 595–622.

Graig, E. (1993). Stress as a consequence of the urban physical environment: In L. Goldberger & S. Breznitz (Eds.), *Handbook of stress: Theoretical and clinical aspects* (2nd ed., pp. 316–332). New York: Free Press.

Graven-Nielsen, T., & Mense, S. (2001). The peripheral apparatus of muscle pain: Evidence from animal and human studies. *Clinical Journal of Pain, 17*(1), 2–10.

Gray, R., & Regan, D. (2000). Risky driving behavior a consequence of motion adaptation for visually guided motor action. *Journal of Experimental Psychology: Human Perception and Performance, 26,* 1721–1732.

Graziano, M. S. A., & Gross, C. G. (1994). Mapping space with neurons. *Current Directions in Psychological Science, 3,* 164–167.

Grebner, S., Elfering, A., Semmer, N. K., Kaiser-Probst, C., & Schlapbach, M.-L. (2004). Stressful situations at work and in private life among young workers: An event sampling approach. *Social Indicators Research, 67,* 11–49.

Green, J. P. (2003). Beliefs about hypnosis: Popular beliefs, misconceptions, and the importance of experience. *International Journal of Clinical & Experimental Hypnosis, 51*, 369–381.

Greenberg, D. L. (2004). President Bush's false flash-bulb memory of 9/11/01. *Applied Cognitive Psychology, 18*, 363–370.

Greenberg, J. (1990). Employee theft as a reaction to underpayment inequity: The hidden cost of pay cuts. *Journal of Applied Psychology, 75*, 561–568.

Greenberg, J. (1996). "Forgive me, I'm new": Three experimental demonstrations of the effects of attempts to excuse poor performance. *Organizational Behavior & Human Decision Process, 66*(2), 165–178.

Greenberg, R. P., Bornstein, R. F., Greenberg, M. D., Fiser, S., & Seymour, F. (1992). A meta-analysis of antidepressant outcome under "blinder" conditions. *Journal of Consulting and Clinical Psychology, 60*, 664–669.

Greenfield. P. M., Keller, H., Fuligni, A., & Maynard, A. (2003). Cultural pathways through universal development. *Annual Review of Psychology, 54*, 461–490.

Greenhaus, J. H., Collins, K. M., & Shaw, J. D. (2003). The relation between work-family balance and quality of life. *Journal of Vocational Behavior, 63*, 510–531.

Greenough, W. T., & Chang, F. F. (1989). Plasticity of synapse structure and pattern in the cerebral cortex. In A. Peters & E. G. Jones (Eds.), *Cerebral cortex: Vol. 7* (pp. 391–440). New York: Plenum Press.

Greenshaw, A. J. (2003). Neurotransmitter interactions in psychotropic drug action: Beyond dopamine and serotonin. *Journal of Psychiatry & Neuroscience, 28*, 247–250.

Greenspan, S. I. (2003). Child care research: A clinical perspective. *Child Development, 74*, 1064–1068.

Greenwald, A. G. (2003). On doing two things at once Ill. Confirmation of perfect time-sharing when simultaneous tasks are ideomotor compatible. *Journal of Experimental Psychology: Human Perception and Performance, 29*, 859–868.

Greenwald, A. G., & Banaji, M. R. (1995). Implicit social cognition: Attitudes, self-esteem, and stereotypes. *Psychological Review, 102*, 1–27.

Greenwald, A. G., Banaji, M. R., Rudman, L. A., Farnham, S. D., Nosek, B. A., & Mellot, D. S. (2002). A unified theory of implicit attitudes, stereotypes, self-esteem, and self-concept. *Psychological Review, 109*, 3–25.

Greenwald, A. G., McGhee, D. E., & Schwartz, J. L. K. (1998). Measuring individual differences in implicit cognition: The Implicit

Association Test. *Journal of Personality and Social Psychology, 74*, 1464–1480.

Greenwald, A. G., Pickrell, J. E., & Farnham, S. D. (2002). Implicit partisanship: Taking sides for no reason. *Journal of Personality and Social Psychology, 83*, 367–379.

Grice, H. P., Cole, P., & Morgan, J. (1975). Logic and conversation. In P. Cole & J. Morgan (Eds.), *Syntax and semantics* (Vol. 3, pp. 41–58), San Diego, CA: Academic Press.

Griffin, Z. M., & Bock, K. (2000). What the eyes say about speaking. *Psychological Science 11*, 274–279.

Grigorenko, E. L. (2003). Intraindividual fluctuations in intellectual functioning: Selected links between nutrition and the mind. In R. J. Sternberg, J. Lautrey, & T. I. Lubart (Eds.), *Models of intelligence: International perspectives* (pp. 91–115). Washington, DC: American Psychological Association.

Grigson, P. S. (2000). Drugs of abuse and reward comaprison: A brief review. *Appetite, 35*, 89–91.

Grilo, C. M. (2001). Pharmacological and psychological treatments of obesity and binge eating disorder. In M. T. Sammons & N. B. Schmidt (Eds.), *Combined treatments for mental disorders* (pp. 239–269). Washington, DC: American Psychological Association.

Groffman, S. (2000). Seeing a sound, hearing a sight. *Journal of Optometric Vision Development, 30*, 177–180.

Grön, G., Schul, D., Bretschneider, V., Wunderlich, A. P. & Riepe, M. W. (2003). Alike performance during nonverbal episodic learning from diversely imprinted neural networks. *European Journal of Neuroscience, 18*, 3112–3120.

Grunbaum, J. A., Kann, L., Kinchen, S. A., Williams, B., Ross, J. G., Lowry, R., & Kolbe, L. (2002). Youth Risk Behavior Surveillance—United States, 2001. *Morbidity and Mortality Weekly Report, 51*, No. ss-4.

Grusec, J. F., Goodnow, J. J., & Kuczynski, L. (2000). New directions in analyses of parenting contributions to children's acquisition of values. *Child Development, 71*, 205–211.

Grych, J. H., Fincham, F. D., Jouriles, E. N., & McDonald, R. (2000). *Child Development, 71*(6), 1648–1661.

Guarnaccia, P. J., Lewis-Fernández, R., & Marano, M. R. (2003). Toward a Puerto Rican popular nosology: Nervios and ataque de nervios. *Culture, Medicine & Psychiatry, 27*, 339–351.

Guéguen, N. (2003). Fund-raising on the web: The effect of an electronic door-in-the-face technique on compliance to a request, *CyberPsychology & Behavior, 6*, 189–193.

Guéguen, N., Pascual, A., & Dagot, L. (2002). Low-ball and compliance to a request: An

application in a field setting. *Psychological Reports, 91*, 81–84.

Guerin, B. (2003). Social behaviors as determined by different arrangements of social consequences: Diffusion of responsibility effects with competition. *Journal of Social Psychology, 143*, 313–329.

Guerin, P. J., Jr., & Chabot, D. R. (1997). Development of family systems theory, In P. L. Wachtel & S. B. Messer (Eds.), *Theories of psychotherapy: Origins and evolution* (pp. 181–226). Washington, DC: American Psychological Association.

Guerra, N. G., Huesmann, L. R., & Spindler, A. (2003). Community violence exposure, social cognition, and aggression among urban elementary school children. *Child Development, 74*, 1561–1576.

Guilford, J. P. (1976). *The nature of human intelligence,* New York: McGraw-Hill.

Gulevich, G., Dement, W., & Johnson, L. (1966). Psychiatric and EEG observations on a case of prolonged (264 hours) wakefulness. *Archives of General Psychiatry, 15*, 29–35.

Gump, L. S., Baker, R. C., & Roll, S. (2000). Cultural and gender differences in moral judgement: A study of Mexican Americans and Anglo-Americans. *Hispanic Journal of Behavioral Sciences, 22*(1), 78–93.

Gur, R. C., Turetsky, B. I., Matsui, M., Yan, M., Bilker, W., Hughett, P., & Gur, R. E. (1999). Sex differences in brain gray and white matter in healthy young adults: Correlations with cognitive performance. *Journal of Neuroscience, 19*, 4065–4072.

Gur, R. E., McGrath, C., Chan, R. M., Schroeder, L., Turner, T., Turetsky, B. I., et al. (2003). An [MR] study of facial emotion processing in patients with schizophrenia. *American Journal of Psychiatry, 159*, 1992–1999.

Guthrie, R. V. (2004). *Even the rat was white: A historical view of psychology* (2nd ed.). Boston: Allyn & Bacon.

Guttmacher Institute. (2003). Religious teenagers may have a lowered risk of engaging in unsafe sexual behavior. *Perspectives on Sexual and Reproductive Health, 35*(6).

Gwinn, H. M., Fernando, S., James, S., & Wilson, J. F. (2002). Do landmarks help or hinder women in route learning? *Perceptual & Motor Skills, 95*, 713–718.

Habib, R., Nyberg, L., & Tulving, E. (2003). Hemispheric asymmetries of memory: The HERA model. *Trends in Cognitive Sciences, 7*, 241–245.

Hackett, P. (2003). Utilizing media competence. *Journal of Family Psychotherapy, 14*, 101–104.

Hacking, I. (1997). *Rewriting the soul: Multiple personality and the sciences of memory*. Princeton, NJ: Princeton University Press.

Hackmann, A., Clark, D. M., & McManus, F. (2000). Recurrent images and early memories in social phobia. *Behavior Research and Therapy, 38*, 601–610.

Haggbloom, S. J., Warnick, R., Warnick, J. E., Jones, V. K., Yarbrough, G. L., Russell, T. M., et al. (2002). The 100 most eminent psychologists of the 20th century. *Review of General Psychology, 6*, 139–152.

Hagger, M. S., Chatzisarantis, N. L. D., Culverhouse, T., & Biddle, S. J. H. (2003). The processes by which perceived autonomy support in physical education promotes leisure-time physical activity intentions and behavior: A trans-contextual model. *Journal of Educational Psychology, 95*(4), 784–795.

Hagger, M.S., & Orbell, S. (2003). A meta-analytic review of the common-sense model of illness representations. *Psychology & Health, 18*, 141–184.

Hakuta, K., Bialystok, E., & Wiley, E. (2003). Critical evidence: A test of the critical-period hypothesis for second-language acquisition. *Psychological Science, 14*, 31–38.

Halford, J. C. G., Cooper, G. D., & Dovey, T. M. (2004). The pharmacology of human appetite expression. *Current Drug Targets, 5*, 221–240.

Halford, J. C. G., Gillespie, J., Brown, V., Pontin, E. E., & Dovey, T. M. (2004). Effect of television advertisements for foods on food consumption in children. *Appetite, 42*, 221–225.

Hall, J. M. (2003). Dissociative experiences of women child abuse survivors. Trauma, Violence & Abuse, 4, 283–308.

Halpern, D. F. (2000). *Sex differences in cognitive abilities* (3rd ed.). Mahwah, NJ: Erlbaum.

Hamer, D. (2002). Rethinking behavior genetics. *Science, 298*, 71–72.

Hamers, F. F., & Downs, A. M. (2004). The changing face of the HIV epidemic in Western Europe: What are the implications for public health policies? *Lancet, 364*, 83–94.

Hamilton, W. D. (1964). The genetical evolution of social behaviour. I, II. *Journal of Theoretical Biology, 7*, 1–52.

Hampton, N. A., & Mason, E. (2003). Learning disabilities, gender, sources of efficacy, self-efficacy beliefs, and academic achievement in high school students. *Journal of School Psychology, 41*, 101–112.

Han, S., Humphreys, G. W., & Chen, L. (1999). Uniform connectedness and classical Gestalt principles of perceptual grouping. *Perception & Psychophysics, 61*(4), 661–674.

Hanauer, D. I. (2001). The task of poetry reading and second language learning. *Applied Linguistics, 22(3)*, 295–323.

Haney, C., Banks, W., & Zimbardo, P. (1973). Interpersonal dynamics in a simulated prison. *International Journal of Criminology and Penology, 1*, 69–97.

Hanley, S. J., & Abell, S. C. (2002). Maslow and relatedness: Creating an interpersonal model of self-actualization. *Journal of Humanistic Psychology, 42*, 37–57.

Hannover, B. (2000). Development of the self in gendered contexts. In T. Eckes, H. M. Trautner, and others, *The Developmental Social Psychology of Gender* (pp. 177–206). Mahwah, NJ: Erlbaum.

Hanson, K. L. (2004). Neurocognitive function in users of MDMA: The importance of clinically significant patterns of use. *Psychological Medicine, 34*, 229–246.

Harandi, A. A., Esfandani, A., & Shakibaei, F. (2004). The effect of hypotherapy on procedural pain and state anxiety in women hospitalized in a burn unit. *Contemporary Hypnosis, 21*(1), 28–34.

Hardy, L. (2003). Helping students de-stress. *Education Digest, 68*, 10–17.

Hariri, A. R., & Weinberger, D. R. (2003). Functional neuroimaging of genetic variation in serotonergic neurotransmission. *Genes, Brain & Behavior, 2*, 341–349.

Harlow, H. W., (1958). The nature of love. *American Psychologist, 13*, 673–685.

Harlow, H. F. (1962). The heterosexual affectional system in monkeys. *American Psychologist, 17*, 1–9.

Harlow, H. F., & Zimmerman, r. R. (1958). The development of affectional responses in infant monkeys. *Proceedings of the American Philosophic Society, 102*, 501–509.

Harper, R. G. (2004). Histrionic personality. In R. G. Harper, *Personality-guided therapy in behavioral medicine* (pp. 111–131). Washington, DC: American Psychological Association.

Harrington, J., Noble, L. M., & Newman, S. P. (2004). Improving patients' communication with doctors: A systematic review of intervention studies. *Patient Education & Counseling, 52*, 7–16.

Harris, C. R., & Christenfeld, N. (1997). Humor, tickle, and the Darwin–Hecker hypothesis. *Cognition and Emotion, 11*, 103–110.

Harris, J. R. (1998). *The nurture assumption: Why children turn out the way they do*. New York: Free Press.

Harris, M. M., Gilbreath, B., & Sunday, J. A. (1998). A longitudinal examination of a merit pay system: Relationships among performance ratings, merit increases, and total pay increases. *Journal of Applied Psychology, 83*, 825–831.

Harris, T. (1998). *The silence of the lambs*. New York: St. Martin's Press.

Harrison, G., Gunnell, D., Glazebrook, C., Page, K., & Kwiecinski, R. (2001). Association between schizophrenia and social inequality at birth: Case-control study. *British Journal of Psychiatry, 179*, 346–350.

Harrison, J. R., & Barabasz, A. F. (1991). Effects of restricted environmental stimulation therapy on the behavior of children with autism. *Child Study Journal, 21*, 153–166.

Harrison, L. J., & Ungerer J. A. (2002). Maternal employment and infant–mother attachment security at 12 months postpartum. *Developmental Psychology, 38*, 758–773.

Hartman, R. G. (2002). Coming of age: Devising legislation for adolescent decision making. *American Journal of Law and Medicine, 28*(4), 1–55.

Hartung, C. M., & Widiger, T. A. (1998). Gender differences in the diagnosis of mental disorders: Conclusions and controversies of the *DSM-IV. Psychological Bulletin, 123*, 260–278.

Hartup, W. W., & Stevens, N. (1997). Friendships and adaptation in the life course. *Psychological Bulletin, 121*, 355–370.

Harvey, E. (1999). Short-term and long-term effects of early parental employment on children of the National Longitudinal Survey of Youth. *Developmental Psychology, 35*, 445–459.

Harvey, M. (2000, July). Sleepless in America: A lack of rest reaches epidemic proportions. *American Demographics, 22*, 9–10.

Haskell, T. R., MacDonald, M. C., & Seidenberg, M. S. (2003). Language learning and innateness: Some implications of compounds research. *Cognitive Psychology, 47*, 119–163.

Haskins, R., & Sawhill, l. (2003). The future of Head Start. *The Brookings Institution Policy Brief*, July, 2003. Retrieved June 25, 2004, from http://www.brookings.edu

Haslam, N. (1997). Evidence that male sexual orientation is a matter of degree. *Journal of Personality and Social Psychology, 73*, 862–870.

Hatch, L. R., & Bulcroft, K. (2004). Does long-term marriage bring less frequent disagreements? Five explanatory frameworks. *Journal of Family Issues, 25*, 465–495.

Hatfield, E., & Rapson, R. L. (1996). *Love and sex: Cross-cultural perspectives* Boston: Allyn & Bacon.

Haugaard, J. J. (2004). Recognizing and treating uncommon behavioral and emotional disorders in children and adolescents who have been severely maltreated: Dissociative disorders. *Child Maltreatment, 9*, 146–153.

Haveman, R. B., Wolf, K., Wilson, & Peterson, E. (1997). *Do teens make rational choices? The case of teen nonmarital chilbearning* Discussion Paper 1137–97. Institute for Research on Poverty, University of Wisconsin, Madison.

Hawkins, B. A. (1999). Population ageing: Perspectives from the United States. *World Leisure Recreation Journal, 41(2)*, 11–51.

Hawkins, E. H., Cummins, L. H., & Marlatt, G. A. (2004). Preventing substance abuse in American Indian and Alaska native youth: Promising strategies for healthier communities. *Psychological Bulletin, 130*, 304–323.

Hawks, S. R., Madanat, H. N., Merrill, R. M., Goudy, M. B., & Miyagawa, T. (2003). A cross-cultural analysis of "Motivation for eating" as a potential factor in global obesity: Japan and the United States. *Health Promotion International, 18*, 153–162.

Hawley, P. H., & Vaughn, B. E. (2003). Aggression and adaptive functioning: The bright side to bad behavior. *Merrill-Palmer Quarterly, 49*, 239–242.

Hawn, C. (2002, March 25). Fear and posing. *Forbes, 169*, 22+.

Hay, D. F., Payne, A., & Chadwick, A. (2004). Peer relations in childhood. *Journal of Child Psychology & Psychiatry & Allied Disciplines. 45(1)*, 84–108.

Hayes, E. A., Warrier, C. M., Nicol, T. G., Zecker, S. G., & Kraus, N. (2003). Neural plasticity following auditory training with learning problems. *Clinical Neurophysiology, 114*, 673–684.

Hayflick, L. (1996). *How and why we age.* New York: Ballantine Books, Inc.

Hearst, N., & Chen, S. (2004). Condom promotion for AIDS prevention in the developing world: Is it working? *Studies in Family Planning, 35*, 39–47.

Hebb, D. O. (1949). *Organization of behavior* New York: Witey.

Hebb, D. O. (1955). Drive and the C. N. S. (conceptual nervous system). *Psychological Review, 62*, 243–254.

Hebb, D. O. (1972). *Textbook of Psychology* (3rd ed.). Philadelphia: Saunders.

Hedley, A. A., Ogden, C. L., Johnson, C. L., Carroll, M. D., Curtin, L. R., & Flegal, K. M. (2004). Prevalence of overweight and obesity among U.S. children, adolescents, and adults, 1999–2002. *Journal of the American Medical Association, 291*, 2847–2850.

Heeger, D. J. (1999). Linking visual perception with human brain activity. *Current Opinion in Neurobiology, 9*, 474–479.

Heider, F. (1958). *The psychology of interpersonal relations.* New York: Wiley.

Hellriegel, D., & Slocum, J. (1992). *Management* (6th ed.). Reading, MA: Addison-Wesley.

Hellstedt, J. C. (1995). Invisible players: A family systems model. In S. M. Murphy (Ed.), *Sport psychology interventions* (pp. 117–146). Champaign, IL: Human Kinetics.

Hemphill, S. A., & Littlefield, L. (2001). Evaluation of a short-term group therapy program for children with behavior problems and their parents. *Behavior Research & Therapy, 39(7)*, 823–841.

Henderlong, J., & Lepper, M. R. (2002). The effects of praise on children's intrinsic motivation: A review and synthesis. *Psychological Bullentin, 128*, 774–795.

Henderson, D., Varable, D., & Buchanan, J. A. (2004). Elder abuse: Guidelines for treatment. In W. O'Donohue & E. Levensky (Eds.), *Handbook of forensic psychology: Resource for mental health and legal professionals* (pp. 743–766). London: Elsevier Academic Press.

Hendrick, C., & Hendrick, S. S. (1986). A theory and method of love. *Journal of Personality and Social Psychology, 50*, 392–402.

Hendrick, S., & Hendrick, C. (2003). Love. In C. R. Snyder & S. J. Lopez (Eds.). *Handbook of positive psychology* (pp. 472–484). New York: Oxford University Press.

Hendrie, H. C., Hall, K. S., Ogunniyi, A., & Gao, S. (2004). Alzheimer's disease, genes, and environment: The value of international studies. *Canadian Journal of Psychiatry, 49*, 92–99.

Hendriks, A. J., Perugini, M., Angleitner, A., Ostendorf, F., Johnson, J. A., De Fruyt, F., et al. (2003). The five-factor personality inventory: Cross-cultural generalizability across 13 countries. *European Journal of Personality, 17*, 347–373.

Henkel, L. A. (2004). Erroneous memories arising from repeated attempts to remember. *Journal of Memory and Language, 50*, 26–46.

Herman, L. M., Richards, D. G., & Wolz, J. P. (1984). Comprehension of sentences by bottlenosed dolphins. *Cognition, 16*, 129–219.

Hermann, D. J., Crawford, M., & Holdsworth, M. (1992). Gender-linked differences in everyday memory performance. *British Journal of Psychology, 83*, 221–231.

Hermans, D., Spruyt, A., De Houwer, J., & Eelen, P. (2003). Affective priming with subliminally presented pictures. *Canadian Journal of Experimental Psychology, 2*, 97–114.

Hernandez, P. J., Sadeghian, K., & Kiley,. A. E. (2002). Early consolidation of instrumental learning requires protein synthesis in the nucleus accumbens. *Nature Neuroscience, 5*, 1327–1331.

Herrmann, C. S., & Bosch, V. (2001). Gestalt perception modulates early visual processing. *Neuroreport: For Rapid Communication of Neuroscience Research, 12*, 901–904.

Herrnstein, R. J., & Murray, C. (1994). *The bell curve: Intelligence and class structure in American life.* New York: Free Press.

Hertzog, N. B., & Bennett, T. (2004). In whose eyes? Parent' perspectives on the learning needs of their gifted children. *Roeper Review, 26*, 96–104.

Herxheimer, A. (2004). Coping with jet lag. *Clinical Pulse, 64(8)*. 59–60.

Hespos, S. J., & Baillargeon, R. (2001). Reasoning about containment events in very young infants. *Cognition, 78(3)*, 207–245.

Hesse, E., & Main, M. (2000). Disorganized infant, child and adult attachment: Collapse in behavioral and attentional strategies. *Journal of the American Psychoanalytic Association, 48(4)*, 1097–1127.

Hetherington, E. M., & Kelly, J. (2002). For better or for worse. In E. M. Hetherington & J. Kelly (Eds). *Divorce reconsidered* (pp. 1–293). New York: W. W. Norton.

Hewitt, J. P. (2003). The social construction of self-esteem. In C. R. Snyder & S. J. Lopez (Eds.), *Handbook of positive psychology* (pp. 135–147). New York: Oxford University Press.

Hewstone, M., Rubin, M., & Willis, H. (2002). Intergroup bias. *Annual Review of Psychology, 53*, 575–604.

Heyman, G. D., & Legare, C. H. (2004). Children's beliefs about gender differences in the academic and social domains. *Sex Roles, 50*, 227–236.

Higgins, N. C., & Bhatt, G. (2001). Culture moderates the self-serving bias: Etic and emic features of causal attributions in India and in Canada. *Social Behavior and Personality, 29*, 49–61.

Hilgard, E. R. (1965). *Hypnotic susceptibility.* New York: Harcourt, Brace & World.

Hilgard, E. R. (1994). Neodissociation theory. In S. J. Lynn & J. W. Rhue (Eds.). *Dissociation: Clinical and theoretical perspectives* (pp. 32–51). New York: Guilford Press.

Hill, J. (2004). Sleep deprivation. *Lancet, 363*, 996.

Hill, J. O., & Peters, J. C. (1998). Environmental contributions to the obesity epidemic. *Science, 280*, 1371–1374.

Hindmarch, I. (2001). Expanding the horizons of depression: Beyond the monoamine hypothesis. *Human Psychopharmacology: Clinical and Experimental, 16*, 203–218.

Hinkle, D. A., & Connor, C. E. (2002). Three-dimensional orientation tuning in macaque area V4. *Nature Neuroscience, 5*, 665–670.

Hinsz, V. B., Matz, D. C., & Patience, R. A. (2001). Does women's hair signal reproductive potential? *Journal of Experimental Social Psychology, 37*, 166–172.

Hirschfeld, R. M. A., Keller, M. B., Panico, S., Arons, B. S., Barlow, D., Davidoff, F., et al. (1997). The National Depressive and Manic Depressive Association consensus statement on the undertreatment of depression. *Journal of the American Medical Association, 277*, 333–340.

Ho. C. S. H., Chan, D. W., Tsang, S. M., & Lee, S. H. (2002). The cognitive profile and multipledeficit hypothesis in Chinese developmental dyslexia. *Development Psychology, 38*, 543–553.

Hobbs, A., & Williamson, A. (2002). Unsafe acts and unsafe outcomes in aircraft maintenance. *Ergonomics, 45*, 866–882.

Hobbs, P. (2003). The medium is the message: Politeness strategies in men's and women's voice mail messages. *Journal of Pragmatics, 35*, 243–262.

Hobson, J. A. (1989). *Sleep.* New York: Freeman.

Hobson, J. A. (1999). *Consciousness.* New York: Freeman.

Hobson, J. A. (2004). Freud returns? Like a bad dream. *Scientific American, 290*(5), 89.

Hobson, J. A., & McCarley, R. W. (1977). The brain as a dream state generator: An activation-synthesis of the dream process. *American Journal of Psychiatry, 134*, 1335–1348.

Hobson, J. A., & Pace-Schott, E. F. (2002). The cognitive neuroscience of sleep: Neuronal systems, consciousness and learning. *Nature Reviews Neuroscience, 3*, 679–693.

Hobson, J. A., Pace-Schott, E. F., & Stickgold, R. (2003). Dreaming and the brain: Toward a cognitive neuroscience of conscious states. In E. F. Pace-Schott, M. Solms, M. Blagrove, & S. Harnad (Eds.). *Sleep and dreaming: Scientific advances and reconsiderations* (pp. 1–50). New York: Cambridge University Press.

Hochschild, A. (1997). *The time bind.* New York: Metropolitan Books.

Hodges, J. R. (2000). Memory in the dementias. In E. Tulving & F. I. M. Craik (Eds.), *The Oxford handbook of memory* (pp. 441–459). New York: Oxford University Press.

Hodson, R. (2004a). A meta-analysis of workplace ethnographies: Race, gender, and employee attitude and behavior. *Journal of Contemporary Ethnography, 33*(1), 4–38.

Hodson, R. (2004b). Work life and social fulfillment: Does social affiliation at work reflect a carrot or a stick? *Social Science Quarterly, 85*, 221–239.

Hoffmann, A. A., & Hercus, M. J. (2000). Environmental stress as an evolutionary force. *BioScience, 50*, 217–226.

Hoffmann, M. L., & Powlishta, K. K. (2001). Gender segregation in childhood: A test of the interaction style theory. *Journal of Genetic Psychology, 162*, 298–313.

Hofstede, G. (1983). National cultures revisited. *Behavior Science Research, 18*, 285–305.

Hofstede, G., & McCrae, R. R. (2004). Personality and culture revisited: Linking traits and dimensions of culture. *Cross-Cultural Research, 38*, 52–88.

Hogan, R., Curphy, G. J., & Hogan, J. (1994). What we know about leadership: Effectiveness and personality. *American Psychologist, 49*, 493–504.

Hogan, R., Hogan, J., & Roberts, B. W. (1996). Personality measurement and employment decisions. *American Psychologist, 51*, 469–477.

Holden, C. (2000, April 7). Global survey examines impact of depression. *Science, 288*, 39–40.

Hollis, K. L. (1997). Contemporary research on Pavlovian conditioning: A "new" functional analysis. *American Psychologist, 52*, 956–965.

Hollon, D. F., Thase, M. E., & Markowitz, J. C. (2002). Treatment and prevention of depression. *Psychological Science in the Public Interest, 3*, 39–77.

Holloway, M. (2003). The mutable brain. *Scientific American, 289*(3), 78–85.

Holmes, T. H., & Rahe, R. H. (1967). The Social Readjustment Rating Scale. *Journal of Psychosomatic Research, 11*, 213–218.

Holroyd, K. A. (2002). Assessment and psychological management of headache disorders. *Journal of Consulting and Clinical Psychology, 70*, 656–677.

Holthoff, V. A., Beuthien-Baumann, B., Zündori, G., Triemer, A., Lüdecke, S., Winiecki, P., et al. (2004). Changes in brain metabolism associated with remission in unipolar major depression. *Acta Psychiatrica Scandinavica, 110*, 184–194.

Holtz, R. (2004). Group cohesion, attitude projection, and opinion certainty: Beyond interaction. *Group Dynamics, 8*, 112–125.

Holtzer, G. (2002). Learning culture by communicating: Native—non-native speaker telephone interactions. *Language, Culture & Curriculum, 15*, 235–242.

Homayoun, H., Stefani, M. R., Adams, B. W., Tamagan, G. D., & Moghaddan, B. (2004). Functional interaction between NMDA and mGlu5 receptors: Effects on working memory, instrumental learning, motor behaviors, and dopamine release. *Neuropsychopharmacology, 29*, 1259–1269.

Hong, Y., Morris, M., Chiu, C., & Benet-Martinez, V. (2000). Multicultural minds: A dynamic constructivist approach to culture and cognition. *American Psychologist, 55*, 709–720.

Hoogervorst, J. A. P., Koopman, P. L., & van der Flier, H. (2002). Human resource strategy for the new ICT-driven business context. *International Journal of Human Resource Management, 13*, 1245–1265.

Hoon, M. A., Adler, E., Lindemeier, J., Battey, J. F., Ryba, N. J., & Zuker, C. S. (1999). Putative mammalian taste receptors: A class of taste-specific GPCRs with distinct topographic selectivity. *Cell, 96*, 541–551.

Horne, J. A. (1988). *Why we sleep: The functions of sleep in humans and other mammals.* Oxford, England: Oxford University Press.

Horney, K. (1937). *The neurotic personality of our time.* New York: Norton.

Hornstein, G. A. (1992). The return of the repressed. *American Psychologist, 47*, 254–263.

Houston, D. M., Santelmann, L. M., & Jusczyk, P. W. (2004). English-learning infants' segmentation of trisyllabic words from fluent speech. *Language & Cognitive Processes, 19*, 97–136.

Hout, M. (2002). Test scores, education, and poverty. In J. M. Fish (Ed.), *Race and intelligence: Separating science from myth* (pp. 329–354). Mahwah, NJ: Erlbaum.

Houts, A. C. (2002). Discovery, invention, and the expansion of the modern *Diagnostic and Statistical Manuals of Mental Disorders.* In L.E. Beutler & M. L. Malik (Eds.), *Rethinking the DSM: A psychological perspective* (pp. 17–65). Washington, DC: American Psychological Association.

Hovland, C. I., Janis, I. L., & Ketley, H. H. (1953). *Communication and persuasion: Psychological studies of opinion change.* New Haven, CT: Yale University Press.

Howe, D. (1999). The main change agent in psychotherapy is the relationship between therapist and client. In C. Feltham (Ed.), *Controversies in psychotherapy and counseling* (pp. 95–103). London: Sage.

Hoyt, C. L., Murphy, S. E., Halverson, S. K., & Watson, C. B. (2003). Group leadership efficacy and effectiveness. *Group Dyanmics: Theory, Research, and Practice, 4*, 259–274.

Hoyt, M. F. (2001). Constructing managed care, constructing brief therapy. *American Psychologist, 56*, 763–765.

Hrdy, S. B. (1999). *Mother nature: A history of mothers, infants, and natural selection.* New York: Pantheon.

Hsieh, T. (2004). The relationship between employees' personal work standards and perceived stress. *International Journal of Stress Management, 11,* 177–187.

Hubbard, E. M., & Ramachandran, V. S. (2003). Refining the experimental lever: A reply to Shannon and Pribram. *Journal of Consciousness Studies, 10,* 77–84

Hubel, D. H., & Wiesel, T. N. (1962). Receptive fields, binocular interaction, and functional architecture in the cat's visual cortex. *Journal of Physiology, 160,* 106–164.

Hubel, D. H., & Wiesel, T. N. (2000). Receptive fields and functional architecture of monkey straite cortex. In S. Yantis (Eds.), *Visual perception: Essential readings, key readings in cognition* (pp. 147–167). Philadelphia: Psychology Press/Taylor & Francis.

Hudak, M. A. (1993). Gender schema theory revisted: Men's stereotypes of American women. *Sex Roles, 28,* 279–293.

Hudspeth, A. J. (1983, January). The hair cells of the inner ear. *Scientific American,* 54–73.

Huesmann. L. R., Eron, L. D., & Dubow, E. F. (2002). Childhood predictors of adult criminality: Are all risk factors reflected in childhood aggressiveness? *Criminal Behaviour & Mentol Health, 12,* 185–208.

Huesmann, L. R., Moise-Titus, J., Podolski, C. L., & Eron, L. D. (2003). Longitudinal relations between children's exposure to TV violence and their aggressive and violent behavior in young adulthood: 1977–1992. *Developmental Psychology, 39,* 201–221.

Huff, D. J. (1997). *To live heroically: Institutional racism and American Indian education.* New York: State University of New York.

Huffaker, R., Mittelhammer, R., Barkley, P., & Folwell, R. (2003). Community dynamics in a university environment. *Nonlinear Dynamics, Psychology, & Life Sciences, 7(2),* 181–203.

Huffcutt, A. I., & Roth, P. L. (1998). Racial group differences in employment interview evaluations. *Journal of Applied Psychology, 83,* 179–189.

Huffman, L. C., Bryan, Y. E., del Carmen, R., Pedersen, F. A., Doussard-Roosevelt, J. A., & Porgess, S. W. (1998). Infant temperament and cardiac vagal tone: Assessments at twelve weeks of age. *Child Development, 69(3),* 624–635.

Hugdahl, K., Ek, M., Takio, F., Rintee, T., Tuomainen, J., Haarala, C., & Hämäläinen, H. (2004). Blind individuals show enhanced perceptual and alentional sensitivity for

identical speech sounds. *Cognitive Brain Research, 19(1),* 28–32

Hull, C. L., (1943). *Principles of behavior.* New York: Appleton.

Hull, C. L. (1951). *Essentials of behavior.* New Haven, CT: Yale University Press.

Hulme, P. A., & Agrawal, S. (2004). Patterns of childhood sexual abuse characteristics and their relationships to other childhood abuse and adult health. *Journal of Interpersonal Violence, 19,* 389–405.

Humara, M. (2001). The relationship between anxiety and performance: A cognitive-behavioral perspective. *Athletic Insight: Online Journal of Sport Psychology, 2,* NP.

Hunsley, J., Lee, C. M. & Wood, J. M. (2003). Controversial and questionable assessment techniques. In S. O. Lilienfeld, S. J. Lynn, & J. M. Lohr (Eds.), *Science and pseudoscience in clinical psychology* (pp. 39–76). New York: Guilford Press.

Hunt, G., & Evans, K. (2003). Dancing and drugs: A cross-national perspective. *Contemporary Drug Problems, 30,* 779–794.

Hunt, M. (1974). *Sexual behavior in the 1970s.* New York: Dell.

Hunt, R. R., & Lamb, C. A. (2001). What causes the isolation effect? *Journal of Experimental Psychology: Learning, Memory, and Cognition, 27,* 1359–1366.

Hunter, M. D. (2004). Locating voices in space: A perceptual model for auditory allucinations? *Cognitive Neuropsychiatry, 9,* 93–105.

Hurlbert, A. (2003). Colour vision: Primary visual cortex shows its influence. *Current Biology, 13(7),* R270–R272.

Hurvich, L., & Jameson, D. (1974). Opponent processes as a model of neural organization. *American Psychologist, 30,* 88–102.

Huurre, T., Aro, H., & Rahkonen, O. (2003). Well-being and health behavior by parental socioeconomic status: A follow-up study of adolescents aged 16 until age 32 years. *Social Psychiatry & Psychiatric Epidemiology, 38(5),* 249–255.

Hyde, J. S. (1996). Gender and cognition: A commentary on current research. *Learning & Individual Differences,8,* 33–38.

Hyde, J. S. & Kling, K. C. (2001). Women, motivation, and achievement. *Psychology of Women Quarterly, 25(4),* 364–378.

Hyde, J. S., & Oliver, M. B. (2000). Gender differences in sexuality: Results from meta-analysis. In C. B. Travis & J. W. White (Eds.), *Sexuality, society, and feminism* (pp. 57–77). Washington, DC: American Psychological Association.

IIgen, D. R. (1999). Teams embedded in organizations: Some implications. *American Psychologist, 54,* 129–139.

Ingram, D. (2002). The measurement of whole-word productions. *Journal of Child Language, 29,* 713–732.

Ingram, R. E., Scott, W., & Siegle, G. (1999). Depression: Social and cognitive aspects. In T. Millon, P. H. Blaney, & R. D. Davis (Eds.). *Oxford textbook of psychopathology* (pp. 203–226). New York: Oxford University Press.

Ingrassia, R. (2003, May 21). "The Matrix" and murder. *New York Daily News.* Retrieved July 28, 2004, from http://www.nydailynews.com/entertainment/movies/story/85563p-78010c.html

Inhelder, B., & Piaget, J. (1958). *The growth of logical thinking from childhood to adolescence.* New York: Basic Books.

Inhoff, A. W., Starr, M., & Shindler, K. L. (2000). Is the processing of words during eye fixations in reading strictly serial? *Perception & Psychophysics, 62,* 1474–1484.

Ionescu, M. D. (2000). Sex differences in memory estimates for pictures and words. *Psychological Reports, 87,* 315–322.

Issacs, J., Card., N. A., & Hodges, E. V. E. (2001). Victimization by peers in the school context. *NYS Psychologist, 13,* 21–24.

Iwamasa, G. Y., Larrabee, A. L., & Merritt, R. D. (2000). Are personality disorder criteria ethnically biased? A cord-sort analysis. *Cultural Diversity and Ethnic Minority Psychology, 6,* 284–296.

Izard, C. E. (1990). Facial expressions and the regulation of emotions. *Journal of Personality and Social Psychology, 58,* 487–498.

Izard, C. E. (1997). Emotions and facial expressions: A perspective from differential emotions theory. In J. A. Russell, J. M. Fernandez-Dols & J. Miguel (Eds.). *The psychology of facial expression. Studies in emotion and social interaction, 2nd series* (pp. 57–77). New York: Cambridge University Press.

Jackson, L., A., von Eye, A., & Biocca, F. (n.d). Children and Internet use: Social, psychological and academic consequences for low-income children. Retrieved December 21, 2003, from http://www.apa.org/science/psa/sbjackson.html

Jackson, O., Ill, & Schacter, D. L., (2004). Encoding activity in anterior medial temporal lobe supports subsequent associative recognition. *NeuroImage, 21,* 456–462.

Jackson, S. A., & Csikszentmihalyi, M. (1999). Flow in sports: The key to optimal experiences and performances. In E. Cashmore (Ed.), *Sport psychology: The key concepts* (pp. 114–116). London and New York: Routledge Key Guides.

Jackson, S. E., & Schuler, R. S. (1990). Human resource planning: Challenges for industrial/organizational psychologists. *American Psychologist, 45*, 223–239.

Jacob, S., & McClintock, M. K. (2000). Psychological state and mood effects of steroidal chemosignals in women and men. *Hormones & Behavior, 37*, 57–78.

Jacobs, B., Schall, M., & Scheibel, A. B. (1993). A quantitative dendritic analysis of Wernicke's area. II. Gender, hemispheric, and environmental factors. *Journal of Comprehensive Neurology, 237*, 97–111.

Jacobson, S. W. (1997). Assessing the impact of maternal drinking during and after pregnancy. *Alcohol Health & Research World, 21(3)*, 199–203.

Jaffee, S., & Hyde, J. S. (2000). Gender differences in moral orientation: A meta-analysis. *Psychological Bulletin, 126*, 703–726.

James, W. (1884). What is an emotion? *Mind, 9*, 188–205.

James, W. *Principles of psychology*. New York: Dover.

Janik, V. M. (2000). Whistle matching in wild bottlenose dolphins. *Science, 289*, 1355–1357.

Janis, I. L. (1983). *Groupthink* (2nd ed.). Boston: Houghton Mifflin.

Janis, I. L., & Feshbach, S. (1953). Effects of leararousing communications. *Journal of Abnormal and Social Psychology, 48*, 78–92.

Janssen, T., & Carton, J. S. (1999). The effects of locus of control and task difficulty on procrastination. *Journal of Genetic Psychology, 160*, 436–442.

Javitt, D. C., & Coyle, J. T. (2004). Decoding schizophrenia. *Scientific American, 290(1)*, 48–55.

Jayakody, R., & Kalil, A. (2002). Social fathering in low-income, African American families with preschool children. *Journal of Marriage and Family, 64*, 504–516.

Jazwinski, S. M. (1996). Longevity, genes, and aging. *Science, 273*, 54–59.

Jeanneret, R. P. (1992). Applications of job component/synthetic validity to construct validity. *Human Performance, 5*, 81–96.

Jeffery, R. W., Epstein, L. H., Wilson, G. T., Drewnowski, A., Stunkard, A. J., & Wing, R. R. (2000). Long-term maintenance of weight loss: Current status. *Health Psychology, 19*, 5–16.

Jenkins, G. D., Jr., Mitra, A., Gupta, N., & Shaw, J. D. (1998). Are financial incentives related to performance? A meta-analytic review of empirical research. *Journal of Applied Psychology, 83*, 777–787.

Jenkins, H. M., & Harrison, R. H. (1960). Effect of discrimination training on auditory generalization. *Journal of Experimental Psychology, 59*, 244–253.

Jensen, A. R. (1969). How much can we boost IQ and scholastic achievement? *Harvard Educational Review, 39*, 1–123.

Jensen, M. P., Turner, J. A., & Romano, J. M. (2001). Changes in beliefs, catastrophizing, and coping are associated with improvement in multidisciplinary pain treatment. *Journal of Consulting and Clinical Psychology, 69*, 655–662.

Jensvold, M. L. A., & Gardner, R. A. (2002). Interactive use of sign language by cross-fostered chimpanzees (*Pan troglodytes*). *Journal of Comparative Psychology, 114*, 335–346.

Jerome, L., & Segal, A. (2001). Benefit of long-term stimulants on driving in adults with ADHD. *Journal of Nervous & Mental Disease, 189* (1), 63–64.

Jetten, J., Postmes, T., & McAuliffe, B. J. (2002). "We're all individuals": Group norms of individualism and collectivism, levels of identification and identity threat. *European Journal of Social Psychology, 32*, 189–207.

Jimmieson, N. L., Terry, D. J., & Callan, V. J. (2004). A longitudinal study of employee adaptation to organizational change: The role of change-related information and change-related self-efficacy. *Journal of Occupational Health Psychology, 9*, 11–27.

Joffe, M., & Glynn, S. (2002). Facilitating change and empowering employees. *Journal of Change Management, 2*, 369–379.

Johnson, B. P. (2004). Involuntary commitment. In W. O'Donohue & E. Levensky (Eds.), *Handbook of forensic psychology: Resource for mental health and legal professionals* (pp. 767–780). London: Elsevier Academic Press.

Johnson, D. M., Shea, M. T., Yen, S., Battle, C. L., Zlotnick, C., Sanislow, C. A., et al. (2003). Gender differences in borderline personality disorder: Findings from the Collaborative Longitudinal Personality Disorders Study. *Comprehensive Psychiatry, 44*, 284–292.

Johnson, J. (2001, February). "I'm too busy!" *Campus Life, 66+*.

Johnson, L. G., Cohen, P., Smailes, E. M., Kasen, S., & Brook, J. S. (2002). Television viewing and aggressive behavior during adolescence and adulthood. *SCIENCE Magazine, 295*, 2468–2471.

Johnson, L. C., Slye, E. S., & Dement, W. (1965). Electroencephalographic and autonomic activity during and after prolonged sleep deprivation. *Psychosomatic Medicine, 27*, 415–423.

Johnson, S. D., Phelps, D. L., & Cottler, L. B. (2004). The association of sexual dysfunction and substance use among a community epidemiological sample. *Archives of Sexual Behavior, 33*, 55–63.

Johnson, S. H. (1998). Cerebral organization of motor imagery: Contralateral control of grip selection in mentally represented prehension. *Psychological Science, 9*, 219–222.

Johnston, T. D., & Edwards, L. (2002). Genes, interactions, and the development of behavior. *Psychological Review, 109*, 26–34.

Jonas, E., Schulz-Hardt, S., Frey, D., & Thelen, N. (2001). Confirmation bias in sequential information search after preliminary decisions: An expansion of dissonance theoretical research on selective exposure to information. *Journal of Personality and Social Psychology, 80*, 557–571.

Jones, B. C., Little, A. C., & Perrett, D. L. (2003). Why are symmetrical faces attractive? In S. P. Shohov (Ed.), *Advances in psychology research* (pp. 145–166). Hauppauge, NY: Nova Science.

Jones, C. J., & Meredith, W. (2000). Developmental paths of psychological health from early adolescence to later adulthood. *Psychology and Aging, 15*, 351–360.

Jones, E. E., & Nisbett, R. E. (1972). The actor and the observer: Divergent perceptions of the causes of behavior. In E. E. Jones, D. E. Kanouse; H. H. Kelley, R. E. Nisbett, S. Valins, & B. Weiner (Eds.), *Attribution: Perceiving the causes of behavior* (pp. 79–94). Morristown, NJ: General Learning Press.

Jones, E. E., & Pitman, T. S. (1982). Toward a general theory of strategic self-presentation. In J. Suts (Ed.), *Psychological perspectives on the self* (Vol. 1, pp. 231–262). Hillsdale, NJ: Erlbaum.

Jones, M. C. (1924). A laboratory study of fear: The case of Peter. *Pedagogical Seminary, 31*, 308–315.

Josse, G., & Tzourio-Mazoyer, N. (2004). Hemispheric specialization for language. *Brain Research Reviews, 44*, 1–11.

Jou, Y. H., & Fukada, H. (2002). Stress, health, and reciprocity and sufficiency of social support: The case of university students in Japan. *Journal of Social Psychology, 142*, 353–370.

Jouvet, M. (1999). *The paradox of sleep: The story of dreaming* (L. Garey, Trans.). Cambridge, MA: The MIT Press.

Judge, T. A., & Colquitt, J. A. (2004). Organizational justice and stress: The mediating role of work-family conflict. *Journal of Applied Psychology, 89*, 395–404.

Julien, R. M. (2004). *A primer of drug action* (8th ed.). New York: Freeman.

Jung, C. G. (1937/1959). The concept of the collective unconscious. In H. Read, M. Fordham, & G. Adler (Eds.), R. F. C. Hull (Trans.), *The collected works of C. G. Jung* (Vol. 9, Pt. l), New York: Pantheon.

Jung, C. G. (1951/1959). Aion: Researches into the phenomenology of the self. In H. Read,

M. Fordham, & G. Adler (Eds.), R. F. C. Hull (Trans.), *The collected works of C. G. Jung* (Vol. 9, Pt. 2), New York: Pantheon.

Jung, C. G. (1954/1959). Archetypes and the collective unconscious. In H. Read, M. Fordham, & G. Adler (Eds.), R. F. C. Hull (Trans.), *The collected works of C. G. Jung* (Vol. 9, Pt. l). New York: Pantheon.

Jung, C. G. (1961). *Memories, dreams, reflections* (A. Jaffe, Ed.). New York: Random House.

Junginger, J., & McGuire, L. (2004). Psychotic motivation and the paradox of current research on serious mental illness and rates of violence. *Schizophrenia Bulletin, 30,* 21–30.

Kabat-Zinn, J. (1993). Mindfulness meditation: health benefits of an ancient Buddhist practice. In D. Goleman & J. Gurin (Eds.), *Mind/body medicine: How to use your mind for better health* (pp. 259–275). Yonkers, NY: Consumer Reports Books.

Kagan, B. L., Leskin, G., Haas, B., Wilkins, J., & Foy, D. (1999). Elevated lipid levels in Vietnam veterans with chronic posttraumatic stress disorders. *Biological Psychiatry, 45,* 374–377.

Kahneman, D. (2003). A perspective on judgment and choice mapping bounded rationality. *American Psychologist, 58,* 697–720.

Kahng, S., Boscoe, J. H., & Byrne, S. (2003). The use of an escape contingency and a token economy to increase food acceptance. *Journal of Applied Behavior Analysis, 36,* 349–353.

Kail, R., & Hall, L. K. (2001). Distinguishing short-term memory from working memory. *Memory and Cognition, 29,* 1–9.

Kallio, A., & Revonsuo, A. (2003). Hypnotic phenomena and altered states of consciousness: A multilevel framework of description and explanation. *Contemporary Hypnosis, 20,* 111–164.

Kanaya, T., Scullin, M. H., & Ceci, S. J. (2003). The Flynn effect and U.S. policies: The impact of rising IQ scores on American society. *American Psychologist, 58,* 778–790.

Kanazawa, S. (2004). General intelligence as a domain-specific adaptation. *Psychological Review, 11,* 512–523.

Kancelbaum, B., Singer, B., & Wong, N. (2004). *Therapy in America 2004.* Retrieved May 5, 2004, from http://cms.psychologytoday.com/pto

Kandel, E. R. (2001). The molecular biology of memory storage: A dialogue between genes and synapses, *Science, 294,* 1030–1038.

Kanner, A. D., Coyne, J. C., Schaefer, C., & Lazarus, R. S. (1981). Comparison of two modes of stress measurement: Daily hassles and uplifts versus major life events. *Journal of Behavioral Medicine, 4,* 1–39.

Kansi, J., Wichstrom, L., & Bergman, L. R. (2003). Eating problems and the self-concept: Results based on a representative sample of Norwegian adolescent girls. *Journal of Youth & Adolescence, 32,* 325–335.

Kaplan, D. W., Feinstein, R. A., Fisher, M.M., Klein, J. D., Olmedo, L. E., Rome, E. S., & Yancy, W. S. (2001). Condom use by adolescents. *Pediatrics, 107,* 1463–1469.

Karasek, R.A. (1979). Job demands, job decision latitude, and mental strain: Implications for job redesign. *Administrative Science Quarterly, 24,* 285–308.

Karau, S. J., & Williams, K. D. (2001). Understanding individual motivation in groups: The collective effort model. In M. E. Turner (Ed.). *Groups at work: Theory and research. Applied social research* (pp. 113–141). Mahwah, NJ: Erlbaum.

Kark, R., Shamir, B., & Chen, G. (2003). The two faces of transformational leadership: Empowerment and dependency. *Journal of Applied Psychology, 88,* 246–255.

Kasl, S. V., & Cobb, S. (1966). Health behavior, illness behavior, and sick role behavior I. Health and illness behavior. *Archives of Environmental Health 12,* 331–341.

Kastner, S., De Eerd, P., Desimone, R., & Ungerleider, L. G. (1998). Mechanisms of directed attention in the human extrastriate cortex as revealed by functional MRI. - *Science, 282,* 108–111.

Kastner, T., & Walsh, K. K. (2004). A retrospective analysis of efficacy of Risperidone in people with developmental disabilities living in institutional settings. *Mental Health Aspects of Developmental Disabilities, 7,* 10–20.

Katsuki, Y. (1961). Neutral mechanisms of auditory sensation in cats. In W. A. Rosenblith (Ed.), *Sensory communication.* Cambridge, MA: The MIT Press.

Katz, J., & Beach, S. R. H. (2000). Looking for love? Self-verification and self-enhancement effects on initial romantic attraction. *Society for Personality and Social Psychology, 26,* 1526–1539.

Kaufman, G., & Phua, V. C. (2003). Is ageism alive in date selction among men? Age requests among gay and lesbians in internet personal ads. *Journal of Men's Studies, 11(2),* 225–235

Kazdin, A. E. (2000). *Psychotherapy for children and adolescents: Directions for research and practice.* New York: Oxford University Press.

Kazdin, A. E. (2001). Bridging the enormous gaps of theory with therapy research and practice. *Journal of Clinical Child Psychology, 30,* 59–66.

Kazdin, A. E., & Benjet, C. (2003). Spanking children: Evidence and issues. *Current Directions in Psychological Science, 12,* 99–103.

Kazul, H., Hashimoto, M., Hirono, N., & Mori, E. (2003). Nature of personal semantic memory: Evidence form Alzheimer's disease. *Neuropsychologia, 41,* 981–988.

Keefe, K., & Berndt, T.J. (1996). Relations of friendship quality to self-esteem in early adolescence. *Journal of Early Adolescence, 16,* 110–129.

Keel, P.K., & Klump, K.L. (2003). Are eating disorders culture-bound syndromes? Implications for conceptualizing their etiology. *Psychological Bulletin, 129,* 747–769.

Keita, G. P., Cameron, L., & Burrwell, T. (2003). *Women in the American Psychological Association.* Washington, DC: Women's Program Office, American Psychological Association.

Keitner, G. I., Archambault, R., Ryan, C. E., & Miller, I. W. (2003). Family therapy and chronic depression. *Journal of Clinical Psychology, 59,* 873–884.

Kelemen, W. L., & Creeley, C. E. (2003). State-dependent memory effects using caffeine and placebo do not extend to metamemory. *Journal of General Psychology, 130* 70–86.

Keller, J. (2002). Blatant stereotype threat and women's math performance: Self-handicapping as a strategic means to cope with obtrusive negative performance expectations, *Sex Roles, 47,* 193–198.

Kelley, H. H. (1972). Attribution in social interaction. In E. E. Jones & D. E. Kanouse (Eds.), *Attribution: Perceiving the causes of behavior* (pp. 1–37). Morristown, NJ: General Learning Press.

Kelley, H. H. (1973). Process of causal attribution. *American Psychologist, 28,* 107–128.

Kelly, G. A. (1955). *The psychology of personal constructs* (Vols. 1 and 2). New York: Norton.

Kelly. M., & Newstead, L. (2004). Family intervention in routine practice: It is possible! *Journal of psychiatric & Mental Health Nursing, 11,* 64–72.

Kelly, S. J., Day, N., & Streissguth, A. P. (2000). Effects of prenatal alcohol exposure on social behavior in humans and other species. *Neurotoxicology & Teratology, 22 (2),* 143–149.

Keltner, D. (2004) Ekman, emotional expression, and the art of empirical epiphany. *Journal of Research in Personality, 38,* 37–44.

Keltner, D., & Ekman, P. (2000). Facial expressions and emotion. In M. Lewis &

J. M. Haviland-Jones (Eds.), *Handbook of emotions* (2nd ed., pp. 236–249). New York: Guilford Press.

Kemppainen, J. K., Levine, R. E., Mistal, M., & Schmidgall, D. (2001). HAART adherence in culturally diverse patients with HIV/AIDS: A study of male patients from a Veterans Administration hospital in Northern California. *AIDS Patient Care and STD's, 15,* 117–127.

Kendall, P. C., Krain, A., & Tradwell, K. R. H. (1999). Generalized anxiety disorder. In R. T. Ammerman, M. Hersen, & C. J. Last (Eds.). *Handbook of prescriptive treatments for children and adolescents* (2nd ed., pp. 155–171). Boston: Allyn and Bacon.

Kennedy, M. B. (2000, October 27). Signal-processing machines at the postsynaptic density. *Science, 290,* 750–754.

Kennedy, R. B., & Kennedy, D. A. (2004). Using the Myers-Briggs Type Indicator in career counseling. *Journal of Employment counseling, 41,* 38–44.

Kenrick, D. (2001). Evolutionary psychology, cognitive science, and dynamical systems: building an integrative paradigm. *Current Directions in Psychological Science, 10*(1), 13–17.

Kenrick, D., Ackerman, J., & Ledlow, S. (2003). Evolutionary social psychology: Adaptive predispositions and human culture. In J. Delamater (Eds.). *Handbook of social psychology* (pp. 103–122). New York: Kluwer.

Kenrick, D. T., Maner, J. K., Butner, J., Li, N. P., Vaughn Becker, D., & Schaller, M. (2002). Dynamical evolutionary psychology: Mapping the domain of the new interactionist paradigm. *Personality and Social Psychology Review, 6,* 347–356.

Kerns, K. A. (1998). Individual differences in friendship quality: Links to child-mother attachment. In W. M. Bukowski, A. F. Newcomb, & W. W. Hartup (Eds.). *The company they keep: Friendship in childhood and adolescence* (pp. 137–157). New York: Cambridge University Press.

Kessler, R. C. (2000). Pasychiatric epidemiology: Selected recent advances and future directions. *Bulletin of the World Health Organization, 78,* 464–474.

Kessler, R. C., Berglund, P., Demler, O., Jin, R., Koretz, D., Merikangas, K. R. et al. (2003). The epidemiology of major depressive disorders: Results from the National Comorbidity Survey Replication (NCS-R). *Journal of the American Medical Association, 289,* 3095–3105.

Kessler, R. C., McGonagle, K. A., Zhao, S., Nelson, C. B., Hughes, M., Eshleman, S., Wittchen, H. U., & Kendler, K. S. (1994).

Lifetime and 12-month prevalence of *DSM-III-R* psychiatric disorders in the United States. *Archives of General Psychiatry, 51,* 8–19.

Kessler, R. C., Mickelson, K. D., & Williams, D. R. (1999). The prevalence, distribution,a nd mental health correlates of perceived discrimination in the United States. *Journal of Health and Social Behavior, 40,* 208–230.

Ketelaar, T., & Ellis, B. J. (2000). Are evolutionary explanations unfalsifiable? Evolutionary psychology and the Lakatosian philosophy of science. *Psychological Inquiry, 11,* 1–21.

Ketterer, M. W., Denollet, J., Chapp, J., Thayer, B., Keteyian, S., Clark, V., et al. (2004). Men deny and women cry, but who dies? Do the wages of "denial" include early ischemic coronary heart disease? *Journal of Psychosomatic Research, 56,* 119–123.

Keyes, C. L. M., & Magyar-Moe, J. L. (2003). The measurement and utility of adult subjective well-being. In S. L. Lopez & C. R. Snyder (Eds.). *Positive psychological assessment: A handbook of models and measures* (pp. 411–425). Washington, DC: American Psychological Association.

Khan, S. (2003). Gender equity in Bangladesh: An intentional perspective. *American Psychological Association Conference paper,* unique identifier 355332004–000. Retrieved July 4, 2004, from http://www.apa.org

Kida, S., Josselyn, S. A., de Ortiz, S. P., Kogan, J. H., Chevere, I., Masushige, S., & Silva, A. J. (2002). CREB required for the stability of new and reactivated fear memories. *Nature Neuroscience, 5,* 348–355.

Kiecolt-Glaser, J. K., & Glaser, R. (2002). Depression and immune function: Central pathways to mobidity and mortality. *Journal of Psychosomatic Research, 53,* 873–876.

Kiecolt-Glaser, J. K., & Newton, T. L. (2001). Marriage and health: His and hers. *Psychological Bulletin, 127,* 472–503.

Kiecolt-Glaser, J. K., Page, G. G., Marucha, P. T., MacCallum, R. C., & Glaser, R. (1998). Psychological influences on surgical recovery: Perspectives from psychoneuroimmunology. *American Psychologist, 53,* 1209–1218.

Kihlstrom, J. F. (2002). To honor Kraepelin. . . . From symptoms to pathology in the diagnosis of mental illness. In L. E. Beutler & M. L. Malik (Eds.). *Rethinking the DSM: A psychological perspective* (pp. 279–303). Washington, DC: American Psychological Association.

Kilgard, M. P., & Merzenich, M. M. (1998). Cortical map recorganization enabled by nucleus basalis activity. *Science, 279,* 1714–1718.

Kilpatrick, D. G., Acierno, R., Saunders, B., Resnick, H. S., Best, C. L., & Schnurr, P. P. (2000). Risk factors for adolescent substance abuse and dependence data from a national sample. *Journal of Consulting and Clinical Psychology, 68,* 19–30.

Kilpatrick Demaray, M., & Kerres Malecki, C. (2003). Importance ratings of socially supportive behaviors by children and adolescents. *School Psychology Review, 32*(1), 108–131.

Kim, C., & Kwok, Y. S. (1998). Navajo use of native healers. *Archives of Internal Medicine, 158,* 2245–2249.

Kim, H., & Markus, H. R. (1999). Deviance or uniqueness, harmony or conformity? A cultural analysis. *Journal of Personality and Social Psychology, 77,* 785–800.

Kim, S. G., & Ogawa, S. (2002). Insight into new techniques for high resolution functional MRI. *Current Opinion in Neurobiology, 12,* 607–615.

Kimbrough, O. D., Eliers, R. E., Rebecoa, N. A., & Cobo-Lewis, A. B. (1998). Late onset canortical babbling: A possible early market for abnormal development. *American Journal on Mental Retardation, 103,* 249–263.

King, J. E. (2003). The structure of personality differences is not uniquely human. *International Review of Sociology, 13,* 533–544.

Kinsey, A. C., Pomeroy, W. B., & Martin, C. E. (1948). *Sexual behavior in the human male.* Philadelphia: Saunders.

Kinsey, A. C., Pomeroy, W. B., Martin, C. E., & Gebhard, P. H. (1953). *Sexual behavior in the human female.* Philadelphia: Saunders.

Kirk, K. M., Bailey, J. M., & Martin, N. G. (2000). Etiology of male sexual orientation in an Australian twin sample. *Psychology, Evolution & Gender, 2,* 301–311.

Kirkcaldy, B. D., Shephard, R. J., & Siefen, R. G. (2002). The relationship between physical activity and self-image and problem behaviour among adolescents. *Social Psychiatry & Psychiatric Epidemiology, 37*(11), 544–550.

Kisker, E. E., Paulsell, D., Love, J. M., & Raikes, H. (2002). *Pathways to quality and full implementation in early Head Start Programs.* Washington, DC: U.S. Department of Health & Human Services.

Kivilu, J. M., & Rogers, W. T. (1998). A multi-level analysis of cultural experience and gender influences on causal attributions to perceived performance in mathematics. *British Journal of Educational Psychology, 68,* 25–37.

Kjellgren, A., Sundequist, U., Sundholm, U., Norlander, T., & Archer, T. (2004). Altered consciousness in flotation-rest and chamber-rest: Experience of experimental pain and subjective stress. *Social Behavior & Personality: An International Journal, 32,* 103–116.

Klar, Y., & Giladi, E. E. (1997). No one in my group can be below the group's average: A robust positivity bias in favor of anonymous peers. *Journal of Personality and Social Psychology, 73,* 885–901.

Klassen, R. M. (2004). Optimism and realism: A review of self-efficacy from a cross-cultural perspective. *International Journal of Psychology, 39,* 205–230.

Klein, L. C., Faraday, M. M., Quigley, K. S., & Grunberg, N. E. (2004). Gender differences in biobehavioral aftereffects of stress on eating, frustration, and cardiovascular responses. *Journal of Applied Social Psychology, 34,* 538–562.

Klein, S. B., Cosmides, L., Tooby, J., & Chance, S. (2002). Decisions and the evolution of memory: Multiple systems, multiple functions. *Psychological Review, 109,* 306–329.

Kliegl, R., Philipp, D., Luckner, M., & Krampe, R. (2001). Face memory skill acquisition. In N. Charness, D. C. Parks, & B. A. Sable (Eds.), *Communication, technology, and aging: Opportunities and challenges for the future* (pp. 169–186). New York: Springer.

Klinke, R., Kral, A., Heid, S., Tillein, J., & Hartmann, R. (1999). Recruitment of the auditory cortex in congenitally deaf cats by long-term cochlear electrostimulation. *Science, 285,* 1729–1733.

Klonoll, E. A., Landrine, H., & Campbell, R. (2000). Sexist discrimination may account for well-known gender differences in psychiatric symptoms. *Psychology of Women Quarterly, 24,* 93–99.

Klose, M., & Jacobi, F. (2004). Can gender differences in the prevalence of mental disorders be explained by sociodemographic factors? *Archives of Women's Mental Health, 7* 133–13.

Kluger, J. (2001, May 21). Can gays switch sides? *Time, 157,* 62.

Klusman, L. E. (1998). Military health care providers' views on prescribing privileges for psychologists. *Professional Psychology: Research and Practice, 29,* 223–229.

Kmietowicz, Z. (2002). US and UK are top in teenage pregnancy rates. *British Medical Journal, 324,* 1354.

Knapp, S., & VandeCreek, L. (2000). Recovered memories of childhood abuse: Is there an underLyinhg professional consensus? *Professional Psychology: Research and Practice, 31,* 365–371.

Kniffin, K. M., & Wilson, D. S. (2004). The effect of nonphysical traits on the perception of physical attractiveness: Three naturalistic

studies. *Evolution & Human Behavior, 25,* 88–101.

Knight, D. C., Nguyen, H. T., & Bandettini, P. A. (2003). Expression of conditional fear with and without awareness. *Proceedings of the National Academy of Sciences of the United States of America, 100,* 15280–15285.

Knight, G. P., Guthrie, I. K., Page, M. C., & Fabes, R. A. (2002). Emotional arousal and gender differences in aggression: A meta-analysis. *Aggressive Behavior, 28,* 366–393.

Knoblich, G., & Ohlsson, S. (1999). Constraint relaxation and chunk decomposition in insight problem solving. *Journal of Experimental Psychology: Learning, Memory, & Cognition, 25,* 1534–1555.

Kobayashi, F., Schallert, D. L., & Ogren, H. A. (2003). Japanese and American folk vocabularies for emotions. *Journal of Social Psychology, 143,* 451–478.

Koenigsberg, H. W., Woo-Ming, A. M., Siever, L. J. (2002). Pharmacological treatments for personality disorders. In P. E. Nathan J.& J.M. Gorman (Eds.), *A guide to treatments that work* (pp. 367–410). New York: Oxford Press.

Kollka, K. (1935). *Principles of gestalt psychology.* New York: Harcourt Brace.

Kohlberg, L. (1969). The cognitive-developmental approach to socialization. In D. A. Goslin (Ed.), *Handbook of socialization theory and research.* Chicago: Rand McNally.

Köhler, W. (1927). *The mentality of apes.* New York: Harcourt Brace.

Köhler, W. (1947). Gestalt psychology: An introduction to new concepts in modern psychology. New York: Liveright Publishing.

Köhnken, G., Fiedler, M., & Möhlenbeck, C. (2004). Psychology and law. In M. Brewer (Ed.), *Applied social psychology* (pp. 113–135). Malden, MA: Blackwell Publishing.

Kohout, J., & Wicherski, M. (2003). 1999 doctorate employment survey. Retrieved November 26, 2003, from http://research. apa.org/ doctoralemp04.html.

Kolb, B., & Gibb, R. (1999). Neuroplasticity and recovery of function after brain injury. In D. T. Stuss, G. Winocur, & I. H. Robinson (Eds.), *Cognitive neurorehabilitation* (pp. 9–25). New York: Cambridge University Press.

Kolb, B., Gibb, R., & Gorny, G. (2003). Experience-dependent changes to dendritic arbor and spine density in neocortex vary with age and sex. *Neurobiology of Learning & Memory, 79,* 1–10.

Kolb, B., Gibb, R., & Robinson, T. E. (2003). Brain plasticity and behavior. *Current Directions in Psychological Science, 12,* 1–5.

Koob, G. F., Wall, T. L., & Bloom, F. E. (1989). Nucleus accumbens as a substrate for the aversive stimulus effects of opiate withdrawal. *Psychopharmacology, 98,* 530–534.

Kop, W. J. (2003). The integration of cardiovascular behavioral medicine and psychoneuroimmunology: New developments based on converging research fields. *Brain, Behavior, & Immunity, 17,* 233–237.

Korchmaros, J. D., & Kenny, D. A. (2001). Emotional closeness as a mediator of the effect of genetic relatedness on altruism. *Psychological Science, 12,* 262–265.

Kornhaber, M. L., Fierros, E. G., & Veenema, S. A. (2004). *Multiple intelligences: Best ideas from research and practice.* Boston: Allyn & Bacon.

Koski, L., & Petrides, M. (2001). Time-related changes in task performance after lesions restricted to the frontal cortex. *Neuropsychologia, 39,* 268–281.

Koss, M. P., Bailey, J. A., Yuan, N. P., Herera, V. M., & Lichter, E. L. (2003). Depression and PTSD in survivors of male violence: Research and training initiatives to facilitate recovery. *Psychology of Women Quarterly, 27,* 130–142.

Koss, M. P., Gidycz, C. A., & Wisniewski, N. (1987). The scope of rape: Incidence and prevalence of sexual aggression and victimization in a national sample of higher education students. *Journal of Consulting and Clinical Psychology, 55,* 162–170.

Kosslyn, S. M. (1975). Information representation in visual images. *Cognitive Psychology, 7,* 341–370.

Kosslyn, S. M. (2003). Understanding the mind's eye . . . and nose. *Nature Neuroscience, 6,* 1124–1125.

Kotimaa, A. J., Moianen, I., Taanila, A., Ebeling, H., Smalley, S. L., McGough, J., Hartikainen, A. L., & Jaervelin, M. R. (2003). Maternal smoking and hyperactivity in 8-year-old children. *Journal of the Academy of Children and Adolescent Psychiatry, 42,* 826–833.

Kouider, S., & Dupoux, E. (2004). Partial awareness creates the "illusion" of subliminal semantic priming. *Psychological Science, 15*(2), 75–81.

Krafft, J. (2003, October 29). Alternative medicine use increases in acceptance. *American's Intelligence Wire.* Retrieved July 18, 2004, from http://www.m2.com

Kraft, L. L., Pfeiffer, K. A., & Pivarnik, J. M. (2003). Predictors of physical competence in adolescent girls. *Journal of Youth & Adolescence, 32,* 431–438.

Krakow, B., Haynes, P. L., Warner, T. D., Santana, E., Melendrez, D., Johnston, L., et al. (2004). Nightmares, insomnia, and sleep-disordered breathing in fire evacuees seeking treatment for posttraumatic sleep disturbance. *Journal of Traumatic Stress, 17,* 257–268.

Kranitz, L. (2004). Biofeedback applications in the treatment of cardiovascular diseases. *Cardiology in Review, 12,* 177–181.

Krebs, D. L., & Denton, K. (1997). Social illusions and self-deception: The evolution of biases in person perception. In J. A. Simpson & D. T. Kenrick (Eds.), *Evolutionary social psychology* (pp. 21–48), Mahwah, NJ: Erlbaum.

Kreeger, K. Y. (2002, May 13). Sex-based longevity: Societal and lifestyle issues—not biology—appear to have the greatest influences on whether men or women live longer. *Scientist, 16*(10), 34–35.

Kreider, R. B., Fry, A. C., & O'Toole, M. L., (1998). Overtraining in sport. *International Journal of Sport Psychology, 27,* 269–285.

Kreiman, G., Koch, C., & Fried, J. (2000). Imagery neurons in the human brain. *Nature, 408,* 357–361.

Kremen, A. M., & Block, J. (1998). The roots of ego-control in young adulthood: Links with parenting in early childhood. *Journal of Personality and Social Psychology, 75,* 1062–1075.

Kring, A. M., & Gordon, A. H. (1998). Sex differences in emotion: Expression, experience, and physiology, *Journal of Personality and Social Psychology, 74,* 686–703.

Krippner, S., & Thompson, A. (1996). A 10-facet model of dream applied to dream practices of sixteen Native American cultural groups. *Dreaming, 6,* 71–96.

Krisel, W. (2001). Letter to the editor. *Archives of Sexual Behavior, 30,* 457.

Kristian Hill, S., Beers, S. R., Kmiec, J. A., Keshavan, M., & Sweeney, J. A. (2004). Impairment of verbal memory and learning in antipsychotic-naïve patients with first-episode schizophrenia. *Schizophrenia Research, 68,* 127–136.

Kroger, J. (2000). Ego identity status research in the new millennium. *International Journal of Behavioral Development, 24,* 145–148.

Kroll, J. (2003). Posttraumatic symptoms and the complexity of responses to trauma. *Journal of the American Medical Association, 290,* 667–670.

Kroll, N. E. A., Yonelinas, A. P., Kishiyama, M. M., Baynes, K., Knight, R. T., & Gazzaniga, M. S. (2003). The neural substrates of visual implicit memory: Do the two hemispheres play different roles? *Journal of Cognitive Neuroscience, 15,* 833–842.

Kruger, J. (1999). Lake Wobegon be gone! The "below-average effect" and the egocentric nature of comparative ability judgments.

Journal of Personality and Social Psychology, 77, 221–232.

Kubany, E. S., Hill, E. E., Owens, J. A., Iannce-Spencer, C., McCaig, M. A., Tremayne, K. J., et al. (2004). Cognitive trauma therapy for battered women with PTSD (CTT-BW), *Journal of Consulting & Clinical Psychology, 72,* 3–18.

Kubicek, E. B. (2000). Women in middle management: The impact of an involuntary job change. *Dissertation Abstracts International, A (Humanities and Social Sciences), 60* (9-A), 3235.

Kugihara, N. (1999). Gender and social loafing in Japan. *Journal of Social Psychology, 139,* 516–526.

Kuhn, D. (2000). Metacognitive development. *Current Directions in Psychological Science, 9,* 178–181.

Kuhn, J. L., (2001). Toward an ecological humanistic psychology. *Journal of Humanistic Psychology, 41,* 9–24.

Kuncel, N. R., Hezlell, S. A., & Ones, D. S. (2001). A comprehensive meta-analysis of the predictive validity of the graduate record examinations: Implications for graduate student selection and performance. *Psychological Bulletin, 127,* 162–181.

Kung, H. E (2004). Imaging of AB plaques in the brain of Alzheimer's disease. *International Congress Series, 1264,* 3–9.

Kupfer, D, J., First, M. B., & Regier, D. A. (Eds.). (2002). *A research agenda for DSM-V.* Washington, DC: American Psychiatric Association.

Kush, E. R., & Fleming, L. M. (2000). An innovative approach to short-term cognitive therapy in the combined treatment of anxiety and depression. *Group Dynamics: Theory, Research, and Practice, 4,* 176–183.

Kutchins, H., & Kirk, S. A. (1997). *Making us crazy. DSM: The psychiatric bible and the creation of mental disorders.* New York: Free Press.

Kuther, T. L. (2003). Medical decision-making and minors: issues of consent and assent. *Adolescence, 38*(150), 343–358.

Kvavilashvili, L., Mirani, J., Schlagman, S., & Kornbrot, D. E. (2003). Comparing flashbulb memories of September 11 and the death of Princess Diana: Effects of time delays and nationality. *Applied Cognitive Psychology, 17,* 1017–1031.

Labelle, R., & Lachance, L. (2003). Locus of control and academic efficacy in the thoughts of life and death of young Quebec university students, *Crisis, 24,* 68–72.

LaBerge, S., & Gackenbach, J. (2000). Lucid dreaming. In E. Cardeña, S. J. Lynn, & S. Krippner (Eds.), *Varieties of anomalous experience: Examining the scientific*

evidence (pp. 151–182). Washington, DC: American Psychological Association.

Lachman, R., Lachman, J. R., & Butterfield, E. C. (1979), *Cognitive psychology and information processing: An introduction,* Hillsdale, NJ: Erlbaum.

Lachter, J., Durgin, E., & Washington, T. (2000). Disappearing percepts: Evidence for retention failure in metacontrast masking. *Visual Cognition, 7,* 269–279.

Ladegaard, H. J., & Blese, D. (2003). Gender differences in young children's speech: The acquisition of sociolinguistic competence. *International Journal of Applied Linguistics, 13,* 222–223.

Laible, D. J., & Thompson, R. A. (2000). Mother-child discourse, attachment security, shared positive affect, and early conscience development. *Child Development, 71*(5), 1424–1440.

Laird, J. (2000). Culture and narrative as central metaphors for clinical practice with families. In D. H. Demo, K. R. Allen, & M. A. Fine (Eds.). *Handbook of family diversity* (pp. 338–358). New York: Oxford University Press.

Lakoff, R. T. (2000). *The language war.* Los Angeles: University of California Press.

Lam, S. S. K., Yik, M. S. M., & Schaubroeck, J. (2002). Responses to formal performance appraisal feedback: The role of negative affectivity. *Journal of Applied Psychology, 87,* 192–201.

Lamberg, L. (2004). Promoting adequate sleep finds a place on the public health agenda. *Journal of the American Medical Association, 291,* 2415–2417.

Lambert, M. J. (2004). *The effectiveness of psychotherapy: What has a century of research taught us about the effects of treatment?* Retrieved April 25, 2004, from http://www.cwru.edu/affil/div29/lambert.htm

Landau, B., Sabini, J., Jonides, J., Newport, F. L. (2000). *Perception, Cognition, and Language: Essays in Honor of Henry and Lila Gleitman.* Cambridge, MA: The MIT Press.

Laner, M. R., Benin, M. H., & Ventrone, N. A. (2001). Bystander attitudes toward victims of violence: Who's worth helping? *Deviant Behavior, 22,* 23–42.

Lang, A. J., Craske, M. G., Brown, M., & Ghaneian, A. (2001). Fear-related state dependent memory. *Cognition & Emotion, 15,* 695–703.

Lang, P. J. (1994). The varieties of emotional experience: A meditation on James–Lange theory. *Psychological Review, 101,* 211–221.

Lang, S. L. (2001). American and Chinese recall memories differently. *Human Ecology, 29,* 23+.

Lange, C. G. (1922). *The emotions* (English translation). Baltimore: Williams & Wilkins. (Original work published 1885).

Langer, E. J., & Rodin, J. (1976). The effects of choice and enhanced personal responsibility for the aged: A field experiment in an institutional setting. *Journal of Personality and Social Psychology, 34,* 191–198.

Lanza, S. T., & Collins, L. M. (2002). Pubertal timing and the onset of substance use in females during early adolescence. *Prevention Science, 3(1),* 69–82.

LaRossa, R., Jaret, C., Gadgil, M., & Wynn, G. R. (2000). The changing culture of fatherhood in comic-strip families: A six-decade analysis. *Journal of Marriage & the Family, 62(2),* 375–387.

Larson, R. W. (2000). Toward a psychology of positive youth development. *American Psychologist, 55,* 170–183.

Larsson, M., Lövdén, M., & Nilsson, L. -G. (2003). Sex differences in recollective experience for olfactory and verbal information. *Acta Psychologica, 112,* 89–104.

Lashley, K. S. (1950). In search of the engram. *In Society of Experimental Biology Symposium No. 4: Physiological mechanisms in animal behavior* (pp. 478–505). Cambridge, England: Cambridge University Press.

Latané, B., & Darley, J. M. (1970). *The unresponsive bystander: Why doesn't he help?* New York: Meredith.

Latané, B., Williams, K., & Harkins, S. (1979). Many hands make light work: The causes and consequences of social loafing. *Journal of Personality and Social Psychology, 37,* 822–832.

Latham, G. P. (2001). The reciprocal effects of science on practice: Insights from the practice and science of goal setting. *Canadian Psychology, 42(1),* 1–11.

Latham, G. P., Daghighi, S., & Locke, E. A. (1997). Implications of goal-setting theory for faculty motivation. In J. L. Bess (Ed.), *Teaching well and liking it: Motivating faculty to teach effectively* (pp. 125–142). Baltimore, MD: Johns Hopkins University Press.

Laumann, E. O., Gagnon, J. H., Michael, R. T., & Michaels, S. (1994). *The social organization of sexuality: Sexual practices in the United States.* Chicago: The University of Chicago Press.

Laumann, E. O., Paik, A., & Rosen, R. C. (1999). Sexual dysfunction in the United States: Prevalence and predictors. *Journal of the American Medical Association, 281,* 537–544.

Laurent, G. (1999). A systems perspective on early olfactory coding. *Science, 286,* 723–728.

Lavie, P. (2001). Sleep-wake as a biological rhythm. *Annual Review of Psychology, 52,* 277–303.

Lavoie, K. L., & Fleet, R. P. (2002). Should psychologists be granted prescription privileges? A review of the prescription privilege debate for psychiatrists. *Canadian Journal of Psychology, 47,* 443–449.

Lawler, E. E., & Porter, L. W. (1967). Antecedent attitudes of effective managerial performance. *Organizational Behavior and Human Performance, 2,* 122–142.

Lawler, J. J., & Elliot, R. (1996). Artificial intelligence in HRM: An experimental study of an expert system. *Journal of Management, 22,* 85–111.

Lazarus, R. S. (1991). *Emotion and adaptation.* New York: Oxford University Press.

Lazarus, R. S. (1993). From Psychological stress to the emotions: A history of changing outlooks. *Annual Review of Psychology, 44,* 1–21.

Lazarus, R. S., & Folkman, S. (1984). Stress, appraisal, and coping. New York: Springer.

Leary, M. R., & Buttermore, N. R. (2003). The evolution of the human self: Tracing the natural history of self-awareness. *Journal for the Theory of Social Behavior, 33,* 365–404.

Leary, M. R., Herbst, K. C., & McCrary, F. (2003). Finding pleasure in solitary activities: Desire for aloneness or disinterest in social contact? *Personality & Individual Differences, 35,* 59–68.

Lebow, J. L., & Gurman, A. S. (1995). Research assessing couple and family therapy. *Annual Review of Psychology, 46,* 27–57.

LeDoux, J. (2002). *Synaptic self.* New York: Viking.

LeDoux, J. (2003). The emotional brain, fear, and the amygdata. *Cellular & Molecular Neurobiology, 23,* 727–738.

LeDoux, J. E. (1995). Emotion: Clues from the brain. *Annual Review of Psychology, 46,* 209–235.

LeDoux, J. E. (1996). *The emotional brain: The mysterious underpinnings of emotional life.* New York: Simon & Schuster.

LeDoux, J. E. (2002). *Synaptic self: How our brains become who we are.* New York: Viking.

LeDoux, J. E., & Phelps, E. A. (2000). Emotional networks in the brain. In M. Lewis & J. M. Haviland-jones (Eds.), *Handbook of emotions* (2nd ed., pp. 157–172). New York: Guilford Press.

Lee, B. P. H. (2001). Mutual knowledge, background knowledge and shared beliefs: Their roles in establishing common ground. *Journal of Pragmatics, 33(1),* 21–44.

Lee, K. -H., Farrow, T. F. D., Spence, S. A., & Woodruff, P. W. R. (2004). Social cognition, brain networks and schizophrenia. *Psychological Medicine, 34,* 391–400.

Lee, M., Lei, A., & Sue, S. (2001). The current state of mental health research on Asian Americans. *Journal of Human Behavior in the Social Environment, 3,* 159–178.

Lee, R. M., Keough, K. A., & Sexton, J. D. (2002). Social connectedness, social appraisal, and perceived stress in college women and men. *Journal of Counseling and Development, 80,* 355–361.

Lee, T. S. (2002). Top down influence in early visual processing: A Bayesian perspective. *Physiology & Behavior, 77,* 645–650.

Lefcourt, H. M. (1992). Durability and impact of the locus of control construct. *Psychological Bulletin, 112,* 411–414.

Lefcourt, H. M., & Davidson-Katz, K. (1991). Locus of control and health. In C. R. Snyder & D. R. Forsyth (Eds.), *Handbook of social and clinical psychology* (pp. 246–266). New York: Pergamon.

Lehrer, P., Feldman, J., Giardino, N., Song, H. S., & Schmaling, K. (2002). Psychological aspects of asthma. *Journal of Consulting and Clinical Psychology, 70,* 691–711.

Leibowitz, H. W. (1971). Sensory, learned, and cognitive mechanisms of size perception. *Annals of the New York Academy of Sciences, 1988,* 47–62.

Lende, D. H., & Smith, E. O. (2002). Evolution meets biopsychosociality: An analysis of addictive behavior. *Addiction, 97,* 447–458.

Lenneberg, E. H. (1967). *Biological foundations of language.* New York: Wiley.

Lenz, B. K. (2004). Tobacco, depression, and lifestyle choices in the pivotal early college years. *Journal of American College Health, 52,* 213–219.

Leonard, H., & Wen, X. (2002). Epidemiology of mental retardation: Challenges and opportunities in the new millennium. *Mental Retardation and Developmental Disabilities Research Reviews, 8,* 117–134.

LePage, J. P., DelBen, K., Pollard, S., McGhee, M., VanHorn, L., Murphy, J., et al. (2003). Reducing assaults on an acute psychiatric unit using token economy: A 2-year foollow-up. *Behavioral Interventions, 18,* 179–190.

Lerman, C., Croyle, R. T., Tercyak, K. P., & Hamann, H. (2002). Genetic testing: Psychological aspects and implications. *Journal of Consulting and Clinical Psychology, 70,* 784–797.

Lesaux, N. K., & Siegel, L. S. (2003). The development of reading in children who speak English as a second language. *Developmental Psychology, 39,* 1005–1019.

Leslie, M. (2000). The vexing legacy of Lewis Terman. *Stanford Magazine.* Retrieved April 4, 2004, from http://www.stanfordalumni.org/

news/magazine/2000/julaug/articles/terman.html

Lester, D. (2000). Executions as a deterrent to homicide. *Perceptual and Motor Skills, 91,* 696.

Leventhal, T., & Brooks-Gunn, J. (2000). The neighborhoods they live in: The effects of neighborhood residence on child and adolescent outcomes. *Psychological Bulletin, 126,* 309–337.

Levine, D. (2000). Virtual attraction: What rocks your boat. *CyberPsychology & Behavior, 3,* 565–573.

Levine, M. (1998). Prevention and community. *American Journal of Community Psychology, 26(2),* 189–206.

Levine, R. L., & Standtman, E. R. (1992). Oxidation of proteins during aging. *Generations, 16,* 39–42.

Levine, R. V., Martinez, T. S., Brase, G., & Sorenson, K. (1994). Helping in 36 U.S. cities. *Journal of Personality and Social Psychology, 67,* 69–82.

Levinson, D. J. (1978). *The seasons of a man's life.* New York: Knopf.

Levinson, D. J. (1980). Toward a conception of the adult life course. In N. J. Smelser & E. H. Erikson (Eds.), *Themes of work and love in adulthood.* Cambridge, MA: Harvard University Press.

Levinson, D. J. (1996). *The seasons of a woman's life.* New York: Knopf.

Levitt, M. J., Weber, R. A., Clark, M. C., & Mc Donell, P. (1985). Reciprocity or exchange in toddler behavior. *Developmetal Psychology, 21,* 122–123.

Levy, G. D. (1999). Gender-typed and non-gender-typed category awareness in toddlers. *Sex Roles, 41,* 851–873.

Levy, G. D., Sadovsky, A. L., & Troseth, G. L. (2000). Aspects of young children's perceptions of gender-typed occupations. *Sex Roles, 42(11/12),* 993–1006.

Lewald, J. (2004). Gender-specific hemispheric asymmetry in auditory space perception. *Cognitive Brain Research, 19(1),* 92–99.

Lewin, K., & Lippill, R. (1938). An experimental approach to the study of autocracy and democracy. A preliminary note. *Sociometry, 1,* 292–300.

Lewin, K. K. (1970). *Brief psychotherapy.* St. Louis, MO: Warren H. Green.

Lewin, M. (1984). "Rather worse than lolly?" Psychology measures feminity and masculinity: I. From Terman and Miles to the Guilfords. In M. Lewin (Ed.), *In the shadow of the past: Psychology portrays the sexes* (pp. 155–178). New York: Columbia University Press.

Lewinsohn, P. M., Pettit, J. W., Joiner, T. E., & Seeley, J. R. (2003). The symptomatic expression of major depressive disorder in adolescents and young adults. *Journal of Abnormal Psychology, 112,* 244–252.

Lewinsohn, P. M., Rohde, P., Klein, D. N., & Seeley, J. R. (1999). Natural course of adolescent major depressive disorder: I. Continuity into young adulthood. *Journal of the American Academy of Child and Adolescent Psychiatry, 38,* 56–63.

Lewis, D. A., & Levitt, P. (2002). Schizophrenia as a disorder of neurodevelopment. *Annual Review of Neuroscience, 25,* 409–432.

Lewis, M. (1998). Altering fate: Why the past does not predict the future. *Psychological Inquiry, 9(2),* 105–108.

Lewis, M., Feiring, C., & Rosenthal, S. (2000). Attachment over time. *Child Development, 71(3),* 707–720.

Lewis, S., Richards, D., Bryunner, J., Butler, N., & Britton, J. (1995). Prospective study of risk factors for early and persistent wheezing in childhood. *European Respiratory Journal, 8,* 349–356.

Lewis-Fernández, R., Guarnaccia, P. J., Martinez, I. E., & Salmán, E. (2002). Comparative phenomenology of ataques de nervios, panic attacks, and panic disorder. *Culture, Medicine & Psychiatry, 26,* 199–223.

Li, G., Baker, S. P., Lamb, M. W., Grabowski, J. G., & Rebok, G. W. (2002). Human factors in aviation crashes involving older pilots. *Aviation, Space, & Environmental Medicine, 73,* 134–138.

Lichtenberg, P. S., Bachner-Melman, R. S., Ebstein, R. P., & Crawford, H. J. (2004). Hypnotic susceptibility: Multidimensional relationships with Cloninger's Tridimensional Personality Questionnaire, COMT polymorphisms, absorption, and attentional characteristics. *International Journal of Clinical & Experimental Hypnosis, 52,* 47–52.

Lickliter, R., & Honeycutt, H. (2003). Developmental dynamics toward a biologically plausible evolutionary psychology. *Psychological Bulletin, 129,* 819–835.

Liddell, A., & Locker, D. (2000). Changes in levels of dental anxiety as a function of dental experience. *Behavior Modification, 24(1),* 57–68.

Lidow, M. S. (2002). Long-term effects of neonatal pain on nociceptive systems. *Pain, 99,* 377–383.

Lilienfield, S. O., Lynn, S. J., Kirsch, I., Chaves, J. F., Sarbin, T. R., Ganaway, G. K., & Powell, R. A. (1999). Dissociative identity disorders and the sociocognitive model: Recalling the lessons of the past. *Psychological Bulletin, 125,* 507–523.

Lilienfeld, S. O., Wood, J. M., & Garb, H. N. (2000). The scientific status of projective techniques. *Psychological Science in the Public Interest, 1,* 27–66.

Lilly, J. C. (1956). Mental effects of reduction of ordinary levels of physical stimuli in intact, healthy persons. *Psychiatric Research Reports, 5,* 1–28.

Lin, K. (2000). Neurobiological correlates in prenatally stressed rats: In comparison with human schizophrenia. *Dissertation Abstracts International: Section B: The Sciences & Engineering, 60(12-B),* 5959.

Lin, K. M. (2001). Biological differences in depression and anxiety across races and ethnic groups. *Journal of Clinical Psychiatry, 62*(Suppl. 13), 13–19.

Lin, Y.-H. (2003). Interphonology variability: Sociolinguistic factors affecting L2 simplification strategies. *Applied Linguistics, 24,* 439–464.

Lindblom, J., & Ziemke, T. (2003). Social situatedness of natural and artificial intelligence: Vygotsky and beyond. *Adaptive Behavior, 11,* 79–96.

Lindsay, D. S., Hagen, S., Read, J. D., Wade, K. A., & Garry, M. (2004). True photography and false memories. *Psychological Science, 15,* 149–154.

Lindsey, E. W. (2002). Preschool children's friendship and peer acceptance: Links to social competence. *Child Study Journal, 32,* 145–156.

Lips, H. M. (2004). The gender gap in possible selves: Diverence of academic self-views among high school and university students. *Sex Roles, 50,* 357–371.

Lisanby, S. H., Maddox, J. H., Prudic, J., Devanand, D. P., & Sackeim, H. A. (2000). The effects of electroconvulsive therapy on memory of autobiographical and public events. *Archives of General Psychiatry, 57,* 581–590.

Little, B. R. (2000). Persons, contexts, and personal projects: Assumptive themes of methodological transactionalism. In S. Wapner, J. Demick, et al., *Theoretical Perspectives in Environment-Behavior Research: Underlying Assumptions, Research Problems, and Methodologies* (pp. 79–88). New York, NY: Kluwer Academic/Plenum.

Little, J. D. (2003). ECT in the Asia Pacific region: What do we know? *Journal of ECT, 19,* 93–97.

Liu, H. M., Kuhl, P. K., & Tsao, F. M. (2003). An association between mothers' speech clarity and infants' speech discrimination skills. *Developmental Science, 6,* F1–F10.

Liu, X., Sturm, R., & Cuffel, B. J. (2000). The impact of prior authorization on outpatient utilization in managed behavioral health plans. *Medical Care and Review, 57,* 182–195.

Liu, Y., Gao, J.-H., Fox, P.T., & Liu, H.-L. (2000). The temporal response of the brain after eating revealed by functional MRI. *Nature, 405,* 1058–1062.

Livingston, R. H. (1998). Growing up hearing with deaf parents: The influences on adult patterns of relating and on self/other awareness. *Dissertation Abstracts International: Section B: The Sciences & Engineering, 58*(9-B), 5127.

Lobel, T. E., Gruber, R., Govrin, N., & Masshraki-Pedhatzur, S. (2001). Children's gender-related inferences and judgments: A cross-cultural study. *Developmental Psychology, 37,* 839–846.

Lock, J., & Steiner, H. (1999). Gay, lesbian, and bisexual youth risks for emotional, physical, and social problems: Results from a community-based survey. *Journal of the American Academy of Child and Adolescent Psychiatry, 38,* 297–304.

Locke, E. A., & Latham, G. P. (2002). Building a practically useful theory of goal setting and task motivation: A 35-year odyssey. *American Psychologist, 57,* 705–717.

Locke, E. A., & Schweiger, D. M. (1979). Participation in decision-making: One more look. In B. M. Staw (Ed.), *Research in organizational behavior, I.* Greenwich, CT: JAI Press.

Loeb, S., Fuller, B., Kagan, S. L., & Carrol, B. (2004). Child care in poor communities: Early learning effects of type, quality, and stability. *Child Development, 75,* 47–65.

Loehlin, J. C. (1992). *Genes and environment in personality development.* Newbury Park, CA: Sage.

Loehlin, J. C., McCrae, R. R., Costa, P. T., Jr., & John, O. P. (1998). Heritabilities of common and measure-specific components of the Big Five personality factors. *Journal of Research in Personality, 32,* 431–453.

Loftus, E. F. (1975). Leading questions and the eye-witness report. *Cognitive Psychology, 7,* 560–572.

Loftus, E. F. (1979). *Eyewitness testimony.* Cambridge, MA: Harvard University Press.

Loftus, E. F. (2000). Remembering what never happened. In E. Tuvling (Ed.), *Memory, consciousness, and the brain: The Tallinn conference* (pp. 106–118). Philadelphia: Taylor & Francis.

Logan, C. A. (2002). When scientific knowledge becomes scientific discovery: The disappearance of classical conditioning before Pavlov. *Journal of History of the Behavioral Sciences, 38,* 393–403.

Logie, R. H., Venneri, A., Della Sala, S., Redpath, T. W., & Marshall, I. (2003). Brain activation and the phonological loop: The impact of rehearsal. *Brain & Cognition, 53,* 293–296.

Lokko, P., Kirkmeyer, S., & Mattes, R. D. (2004). A cross-cultural comparison of appetitive and diatary responses to food challenges. *Food Quality & Preference, 15,* 129–136.

LoLordo, V. M., & Taylor, T. L. (2001). Effects of uncontrollable aversive events: Some unsolved puzzles. In R. R. Mowrer & S. B. Klein (Eds.), *Handbook of contemporary learning theories* (pp. 119–154). Mahwah, NJ: Erlbaum.

Long, B. C. (1998). Coping with workplace stress: A multiple-group comparison of female managers and clerical workers. *Journal of Counseling Psychology, 45,* 65–78.

Long, D. L., & Baynes, K. (2002). Discourse representation in the two cerebral hemispheres. *Journal of Cognitive Neuroscience, 14,* 228–242.

Looman, M. D. (2003). Reflective leadership: Strategic planning from the heart and soul. *Consulting Psychology Journal: Practice and Research, 55,* 215–221.

Loop, M. S., Shows, J. F., Mangel, S. C., & Kuyk, T. K. (2003). Colour thresholds in dichromats and normals. *Vision Research, 43,* 983–992.

Lopez, S. R., & Guarnaccia, P. J. J. (2000). Cultural psychopathology: Uncovering the social world of mental illness. *Annual Review of Psychology, 51,* 571–598.

Lord, R. G., Brown, D. J., & Freiberg, S. J. (1999). Understanding the dynamics of leadership: The role of follower self-concepts in leader/follower relationship. *Organizational Behavior & Human Decision Processes, 78,* 167–203.

Lord, R. G., Hanges, P. J., & Godfrey, E. G. (2003). Integrating neural networks into decision-making and motivational theory: Rethinking VIE theory. *Canadian Psychology, 44,* 21–38.

Louie, K., & Wilson, M. A. (2001). Temporally structured replay of awake hippocampal ensemble activity during rapid eye movement sleep. *Neuron, 29,* 145–156.

Louis, W., & Taylor, D. M. (2001). When the survival of a language is at stake: The future of Inuttitut in arctic Quebec. *Journal of Language & Social Psychology, 20,* 111–143.

Love, J. M., Harrison, L., Sagi-Schwartz, A., Van IJzendoorn, M., Ross, C., Ungerer, J., Raikes, H., et al. (2003). Child care quality matters: How conclusions may vary with context. *Child Development, 84*(4), 1021–1033.

Lovett, S., & Gilmore, A. (2003). Teachers' learning journeys: The quality learning circle as a model of professional development. *School Effectiveness & School Improvement, 14,* 189–211.

Lowden, A., Akerstedt, T., & Wibom, R. (2004). Suppression of sleepiness and melatonin by bright light exposure during breaks in night work. *Journal of Sleep Research, 13,* 37–43.

Lowe, P. A., Mayfield, J. W., & Reynolds, C. R. (2003). Gender differences in memory test performance among children and adolescents. *Archives of Clinical Neuropsychology, 18,* 865–878.

Lowell, E. L. (1952). The effect of need for achievement on learning and speed of performance. *Journal of Psychology, 33,* 31–40.

Lubart, T. I. (1999). Creativity across cultures, In R. J. Sternberg (Ed.), *Handbook of creativity* (pp. 339–350). Cambridge, MA: Cambridge University Press.

Lubinski, D., Webb, R. M., Morelock, M. J., & Benbow, C. P. (2001). Top 1 in 10,000: A 10-year follow-up of the profoundly gifted. *Journal of Applied Psychology, 86,* 718–729.

Lundin, R. W. (1961). *Personality: An experimental approach.* New York: Macmillan.

Lundqvisi, G., Svedin, C. G., & Hansson, K. (2004). Childhood sexual abuse. Women's health when starting in group therapy. *Nordic Journal of Psychiatry, 58,* 25–32.

Luo, Y., Baillargeon, R., Brueckner, L., & Munakata, Y. (2003). Reasoning about hidden object after a delay: Evidence for robust representations in 5-month-old infants. *Cognition, 88,* B23–B32.

Lykken, D. T., Bouchard, T. J., McGue, M., & Tellegen, A. (1993). Heritability of interests: A twin study. *Journal of Applied Psychology, 78,* 649–661.

Lymburner, J. A., & Roesch, R. (1999). The insanity defense: Five years of research (1993–1997). *International Journal of Law and Psychiatry, 22,* 213–240.

Lynn, R. (1999). Sex differences in intelligence and brain size: A developmental theory. *Intelligence, 27,* 1–12.

Lynn, R. (2002). Skin color and intelligence in African Americans. *Population & Environment, 23,* 365–375.

Lynn, R., & Martin, T. (1997). Gender differences in extraversion, neuroticism, and psychoticism in 37 nations. *Journal of Social Psychology, 137,* 369–373.

Lyubomirsky, S., & Tucker, K. L. (1998). Implications of individual differences in subjective happiness for perceiving, interpreting, and thinking about life events. *Motivation and Emotion, 22,* 155–186.

Ma, J., & Leung, L. S. (2004). Schizophrenia-like behavioral changes after partial hippocampal kindling. *Brain Research, 997,* 111–118.

Macaluso, E., Frith, C. D., & Driver, J. (2000). Modulation of human visual cortex by cross-model spatial attention. *Science, 289,* 1206–1208.

MacBrayer, E. K., Milich, R., & Hundley, M. (2003). Attributional biases in aggressive children and their mothers. *Journal of Abnormal Psychology, 112,* 698–708.

Maccoby, E. E. (1998). *The two sexes: Growing up apart, coming together.* Cambridge, MA: Harvard University Press.

Maccoby, E. E. (2000). Perspectives on gender development. *International Journal of Behavioral Development, 24,* 398–406.

Maccoby, E. E. (2002). Gender and group process: A developmental persepctive. *Current Directions in Psychological Science, 11,* 54–58.

MacDonald, S., Uesiliana, K., & Hayne, H. (2000). Cross-cultural and gender differences in child-hood amnesia. *Memory, 8,* 365–376.

MacFadden, A., Elias, L., & Saucier, D. (2003). Males and females scan maps similarly, but give directions differently. *Brain & Cognition, 53,* 297–300.

Mack, A. (2003). Inattentional blindness: Looking without seeing. *Current Directions in Psychological Science, 12,* 180–184.

Mackain, J., Tedeschi, R. G., Durham, T. W., & Goldman, V. J. (2002). So what are master's-level psychology practitioners doing? Surveys of employers and recent graduates in North Carolina. *Professional Psychology: Research and Practice, 33,* 408–412.

MacNeilage, P. F., & Davis, B. L. (2000). On the origin of internal structure of word forms. *Science, 288*(5465), 527–531.

MacNichol, E. F., Jr. (1964). Retinal mechanisms of color vision. *Vision Research, 4,* 119–133.

Maddux, J. E. (2002). Self-efficacy: The power of believing you can. In C. R. Snyder & S. J. Lopez (Eds.), *Handbook of positive psychology* (pp. 277–287). New York: Oxford University Press.

Maguire, E. A., Burgess, N., Donnett, J. G., Frackowiak, R. S. J., Frith, C. D., & O'Keefe, J. (1998). Knowing where and getting there: A human navigation network. *Science, 280,* 921–924.

Maguire, E. A., & Frith, C. D. (2004). The brain network associated with acquiring semantic knowledge. *NeuroImage, 22,* 171–178.

Mahoney, J. L., Cairns, B. D., & Farmer, T. W. (2003). Promoting interpersonal competence and educational success through rough extracurricular activity participation. *Journal of Educational Psychology, 95,* 409–418.

Mahrer, A. R., & Nadler, W. P. (1986). Good moments in psychotherapy: A preliminary review, a list, and some promising research avenues. *Journal of Consulting and Clinical Psychology, 54,* 10–15.

Maier, N. R. F., & Klee, J. B. (1941). Studies of abnormal behavior in the rat: 17. Guidance versus trial and error and their relation to convulsive tendencies. *Journal of Experimental Psychology, 29,* 380–389.

Maier, S. F., Peterson, C., & Schwartz, B. (2000). From helplessness to hope: The seminal career of Martin Seligman. In J. E. Gillham (Ed.), *The science of optimism and hope: Research essays in honor of Martin E. P. Seligman. Laws of Life Symposia Series* (pp. 11–37). Philadelphia: Templeton Foundation Press.

Major, V. S., Klein, K. J., & Ehrhart, M. G. (2002). Work time, work interference with family, and psychological distress. *Journal of Applied Psychology, 87,* 427–436.

Malinowski, J. C. (2001). Mental rotation and realworld wayfinding. *Perceptual and Motor Skills, 92,* 19–30.

Malt, B. C., & Sloman, S. A. (2003). Linguistic diversity and object naming by non-native speakers of English. *Bilingualism: Language & Cognition, 6,* 47–67.

Maner, J. K., Kenrick, D. T., Becker, D. V., Delton, A. W., Hofer, B., Wilbur, C. J., et al. (2003). Sexually selective cognition: Beauty captures the mind of the beholder. *Journal of Personality and Social Psychology, 85,* 1107–1120.

Manlove, J. (1998). The influence of high school dropout and school disengagement on the risk of school-age pregnancy. *Journal of Research on Adolescence, 8,* 187–220.

Manson, J. E., Skerrett, P. J., Greenland, P., & Vanitallie, T. B. (2004). The escalating pandemics of obesity and sedentary lifestyle: A call to action for clinicians. *Archives of Internal Medicine, 164,* 249–258.

Maquet, P., Peigneaux, P., Laureys, S., Desseilles, M., Boly, M., & Dang-Vu, T. (2003). Off-line processing of memory traces during human sleep: Contributions of functional neuroimaging. *Sleep & Biological Rhythms, 1,* 75–83.

March, J. S. (2004). *The Treatment of Adolescents with Depression Study (TADS): Primary efficacy outcomes.* Paper presented at New Clinical Drug Evaluation Unit meetings, Phoenix, AZ, June 2004.

Margolin, G., & Gordis, E. B. (2004). Children's exposure to violence in the family and community. *Current Directions in Psychological Science, 13,* 152–155.

Margolis, R. L. (2002). Psychiatric and cognitive complications of diseases affecting the cerebellum. *Generations, 30*(4), 8–11.

Marino, L. (2002). Convergence of complex cognitive abilities in cetaceans and primates. *Brain, Behavior, & Evolution, 59,* 21–32.

Markey, P. M. (2000). Bystander intervention in computer-mediated communication. *Computers in Human Behavior, 16,* 183–188.

Markowitsch, H. J. (2000). Neuroanatomy of memory. In E. Tulving & F. I. M. Craik (Eds.), *The Oxford handbook of memory* (pp. 465–484). New York: Oxford University Press.

Marks, J. (1979). *The search for the Manchurian candidate.* New York: Times Books.

Marks, L. E. (2000). Synesthesia. In E. Cardena, S. J. Lynn, & S. Krippner (Eds.), *Varieties of anomalous experience: Examining the scientific evidence* (pp. 121–149). Washington, DC: American Psychological Association.

Marks, W. B., Dobell, W. H., & MacNichol, J. R. (1964). The visual pigments of single primate cones. *Science, 142,* 1181–1183.

Markus, H. R. (2004). Culture and personality: Brief for an arranged marriage. *Journal of Research in Personality, 38,* 75–83.

Marquis, D. P. (1931). Can conditioned responses be established in the newborn infant? *Journal of Genetic Psychology, 39,* 479–492.

Marsland, A. L., Bachen, E. A., Cohen, S., Rabin, B., & Manuck, S. B. (2002). Stress, immune reactivity and susceptibility to infectious disease. *Physiology & Behavior, 77,* 711–716.

Martenyi, F., Dossenbach, M., Mraz, K., & Metcalfe, S. (2001). Gender differences in the efficacy of fluoxetine and maprotiline in depressed patients. A double-blind trial of antidepressants with serotonergic reuptake inhibition profile. *European-Neuropsychopharmacology, 11,* 227–232.

Martin, C. L. (2000). Cognitive theories of gender development. In T. Eckes & H. M. Trautner (Eds.), *The developmental social psychology of gender* (pp. 91–121). Mahwah. NJ: Erlbaum.

Martin, C. L., & Ruble, D. (2004). Children's search for gender cues. *Current Directions in Psychological Science, 13,* 67–70

Martin, C. L., Ruble, D. N., & Szkrybalo, J. (2002). Cognitive theories of early gender development. *Psychological Bulletin, 128,* 903–933.

Martin, J. N., Bradford, L. J., Drzewiecka, J. A., & Chitgopekar, A. S. (2003). Intercultural dating patterns among young White U.S. Americans: Have they changed in the past 20 years? *Howard Journal of Communications, 14,* 53–73.

Martin, K. C., Bartsch, D., Bailey, C. H., & Kandel, E. R. (2000). Molecular mechanisms underlying learning-related long-lasting synaptic plasticity. In M. S. Gazzaniga (Ed.), *The new cognitive neurosciences* (pp. 121–137). Cambridge, MA: The MIT Press.

Martin, S. (2002, October). Norman B. Anderson is APA's new chief. *Monitor on Psychology, 33*(9), 22–26.

Martino, G., & Marks, L. E. (2000). Cross-modal interaction between vision and touch: The role of synesthetic correspondence. *Perception, 29*, 745–754.

Martino, G., & Marks, L. E. (2001). Synesthesia: Strong and weak. *Current Directions in Psychological Science, 10*, 61–65.

Mas Nieto, M., Wilson, J., Walker, J., Benavides, J., Fournié-Zaluski, M., Roques, B. P., & Noble, F. (2001). Facilitation of encephalins, catabolism inhibitor-induced antinociception by drugs used in pain management. *Neuropharmacology, 41*, 496–506.

Masand, P. S., & Gupta, S. (2002). Long-term side effects of newer-generation antidepressants: SSRIs, venlafaxine, nefazodone, bupropion, and mirtazapine. *Annals of Clinical Psychiatry, 14*, 175–182.

Masia, C. L., & Chase, P. N. (1997). Vicarious learning revisited: A contemporary behavior analytic interpretation. *Journal of Behavior Therapy and Experimental Psychiatry, 28*, 41–51.

Maslach, C., Schaufeli, W. B., & Leiter, M. P. (2001). Job burnout. *Annual Review of Psychology, 52*, 397–422.

Maslow, A. B. (1950). Self-actualizing people: A study of psychological health. *Personality Symposia, Symposium #1 on Values* (pp. 11–34). New York: Gruen & Stratton.

Maslow, A. H. (1970). *Motivation and personality* (2nd ed.). New York: Harper & Row.

Maslow, S. E. (2002). Prozac and crime: Who is the victim? *American Journal of Orthopsychiatry, 72*, 445–455.

Masten, A. S., & Reed, M. -G. J. (2002). Resilience in development. In C. R Snyder & S. J. Lopez (Eds.), *Handbook of positive psychology* (pp. 74–88). New York: Oxford University Press.

Masters, W. H., Johnson, V. E., & Kolodny, R. C. (1994). *Heterosexuality*. New York: HarperCollins.

Matlin, M. W. (2003). From menarche to menopause: Misconceptions about women's reproductive lives. *Psychology Science, 45*, 106–122.

Matsumoto, D. (2000). Culture and self: An empirical assessment of Markus and Kitayama's theory of independent and interdependent self-construal. *Asian Journal of Social Psychology, 2*, 289–310.

Matsumoto, D., Consolacion, T., Yamada, H., Suzuki, R., Franklin, B., Paul, S., et al. (2002). American-Japanese cultural differences in judgments of emotional expressions of different intensities. *Cognition & Emotion, 16*, 721–747.

Matsumoto, D., & Kudoh, T. (1993). American-Japanese cultural differences in attributions of personality based on smiles. *Journal of Nonverbal Behavior, 17*, 231–243.

Max, D. T. (2001, May 6). To sleep no more. *New York Times*. Retrieved May 10, 2001 from the World Wide Web: www.nytimes.com/2001/05/06/magazine/06INSOMNIA.html.

May, J., Christopher, D., Maurico, R., Dahl, R. E., Stenger, V., Andrew, R., Neal, D., Carter, J. A., & Cameron, S. (2004). Event-related functional magnetic resonance imaging of reward related brain circuitry in children and adolescents. *Biological Psychiatry, 55*, 359–366.

Mayer, D. M., & Hanges, P. J. (2003). Understanding the stereotype threat effect with "culture-free" tests: An examination of its mediators and measurement. *Human Performance, 16*, 207–230.

Mayer, J. D., & Salovey, P. (1997). What is emotional intelligence? In P. Salovey & D. Sluyter (Eds.), *Emtional development and emotional intelligence: Implications for educators* (pp. 3–31). New York: Basic Books.

Mayer, J. D., Salovey, P., & Caruso, D. (2000). Models of emotional intelligence. In R. J. Sternberg (Ed.). *Handbook of intelligence* (pp. 396–420). New York: Cambridge University Press.

Mazur, A. (2002). Take a chimp, add language, melt glaciers. *Journal for Theory of Social Behaviour, 32*, 29–39.

Mazure, C. M., Bruce, M., Maciejewski, P. K., & Jacobs, S. C. (2000). Adverse life events and cognitive-personality characteristics in the prediction of major depression and antidepressant response. *American Journal of Psychiatry, 157*, 896–903.

McBurney, D. H., Collings, V. B., & Glanz, L. H. (1973). Temperature dependence of human taste responses. *Physiology & Behavior, 11*, 89–94.

McBurney, D. H., Gaulin, S. J. C., Deviveni, T., & Adams, C. (1997). Superior spatial memory of women: Stronger evidence for the gathering hypothesis. *Evolution & Human Behavior, 18*, 165–174.

McCain, G., & Segal, E. M. (1988). *The game of science* (5th ed.). Pacific Grove, CA: Brooks/Cole.

McCall, V. W., Reboussin, B. A., Cohen, W., & Lawton, P. (2001). Electroconvulsive therapy is associated with superior symptomatic and functional change in depressed patients after psychiatric hospitalization. *Journal of Affective Disorders, 63*, 17–25.

McCartney K., Owen, M., Booth, C. L., Clarke-Stewart, A., Vandell, D. L., & McCartney, K. (2004). Testing a maternal attachment model of behavior problems in early childhood. *Journal of Child Psychology & Psychiatry, 45*, 765–778.

McCarty, R. (January/February, 1998). APA launches decade of behavior. *Psychological Science Agenda, 11*, American Psychological Association, p. 1.

McClellan, J. A. & Youniss, J. (2003). Two systems of youth service: Determinants of voluntary and required youth community service. *Journal of Youth & Adolescence, 32*(1), 47–58.

McClelland, D. C. (1958). Methods of measuring human motivation. In J. W. Atkinson (Ed.), *Motives in fantasy, action, and society*. Princeton, NJ: Van Nostrand.

McClelland, D. C. (1961). *The achieving society*. Princelon, NJ: Van Nostrand.

McClelland, D. C. (1985). *Human motivation*. New York: Scott Foresman.

McClelland, D. C., & Koestner, R. (1992). The achievement motive. In C. P. Smith, J. W. Atkinson, D. C. McClelland, & J. Veroff (Eds.), *Motivation and personality: Handbook of the matic content analysis* (pp. 143–152). New York: Cambridge University Press.

McClintock, M. K. (1971). Menstrual synchrony and suppression. *Nature, 229*, 244–245.

McConahay, J. B. (1986). Modern racism, ambivalence, and the Modern Racism Scale. In J. F. Dovidio & S. L. Gaertner (Eds.), *Prejudice, discrimination and racism* (pp. 91–125). Orlando, FL: Academic Press.

McConatha, J. T., Schnell, F., Volkwein, K., Riley, L., & Leach, E. (2003). Attitudes toward aging: A comparative analysis of young adults from the United States and Germany. *International Journal of Aging & Human Development, 57*, 203–221.

McCourt, K., Bouchard, T. J., Lykken, D. T., Tellegen, A., & Keyes, M. (1999). Authoritarianism revisited: Genetic and environmental influences examined in twins reared apart and together. *Personality & Individual Differences, 27*(5), 985–1014.

McCracken, L. M. (1997). "Attention" to pain in persons with chronic pain: A behavioral approach. *Behavior Therapy, 28*, 271–284.

McCrae, R. R. (2004). Human nature and culture: A trait perspective. *Journal of Research in Personality, 38*, 3–14.

McCrae, R. R., & Allik, J. (Eds.) (2002). *The five-factor model of personality across cultures*. New York: Kluwer.

McCrae, R. R., & Costa, P. T. (1999). A Five Factor theory of personality. In L. A. Pervin & O. P. John (Eds.). *Handbook of personality theory and research* (pp. 139–153). New York: Guilford Press.

McCrae, R. R., & Costa, P. T. (2003). *Personality in adulthood: A five-factor theory perspective* (2nd ed.). New York: Guilford.

McCrae, R. R., & Costa, P. T. (2004). A contemplated revision of the NEO Five-Factor Inventory. *Personality & Individual Differences, 36,* 587–596.

McCrae, R. R., Costa, P. T., Del Pilar, G. H., Rolland, J. P., & Parker, W. D. (1998). Cross-cultural assessment of the five-factor model: The revised NEO personality inventory. *Journal of Cross-Cultural Psychology, 29,* 171–188.

McCrae, R. R., Costa, P. T., Hrebickova, M., Ostendorf, F., Angleitner, A., Avia, M. D., Sanz, J., Sanchez-Bernardos, M. L., Kusdil, M. E., Woodfield, R., Saunders, P. R., & Smith, P. B. (2000). Nature over nurture: Temperament, personality, and life span development. *Journal of Personality and Social Psychology, 78,* 173–186.

McCrae, R. R., Costa, P. T., Martin, T. A., Oryol, V. E., Rukavishnikov, A. A., Senin, I. G., et al. (2004). Consensual validation of personality traits across cultures. *Journal of Research in Personality, 38,* 179–191.

McCrae, R. R., Costa, P. T., Terracciano, A., Parker, W. D., Mills, C. J., De Fruyt, F., & Mervielde, I. (2002). Personality trait development from age 12 to 18: Longitudinal, cross-sectional, and cross-cultural analyses. *Journal of Personality and Social Psychology, 83,* 1456–1468.

McCubbin, M., & Cohen, D. (1999). Empirical, ethical, and political perspectives on the use of methylphenidate. *Ethical Human Sciences and Services, 1,* 81–101.

McDaniel, J. G. (2003). Don't put off employee performance appraisals. *Optometry: Journal of the American Optometric Association, 74,* 123–127.

McDermott, D. (2001). Parenting and ethnicity. In Marvin J. Fine, S. W. Lee, *Handbook of Diversity in Parent Education: The Changing Faces of Parenting and Parent Education* (pp. 73–96). San Diego, CA: Academic Press.

McDonald, J. J., & Ward, L. M. (2000). Involuntary listening aids seeing: Evidence from human electrophysiology. *Psychological Science, 11,* 167–171.

McEwen, B. S. (1999). The natural course of shyness and related syndromes. In L. A. Schmidt, J. Schulkin, *Extreme Fear, Shyness, and Social Phobia: Origins, Biological Mechanisms, and Clinical Outcomes* (pp. 173–192). New York, NY: Oxford University Press.

McGaugh, J. L. (1999). The perseveration-consolidation hypothesis: Mueller and Pilzecker 1900. *Brain Research Bulletin, 50,* 445–446.

McGinn, C. (1999). *The mysterious flame: Conscious minds in a material world.* New York: Basic Books.

McGinnis, J. M. (2003). A vision for health in our new century. *American Journal of Health Promotion, 18,* 146–150.

McGlynn, F. D., Smitherman, T. A., & Gothard, K. D. (2004). Comment on status of systematic desensitization. *Behavior Modification, 28,* 194–205.

McGlynn, R. P., McGurk, D., Effland, V. S., Johll, N. L., & Harding, D. J. (2004). Brainstorming and task performance in groups constrained by evidence. *Organizational Behavior & Human Decision Processes, 93,* 75–87.

McGrath, E. P., & Repetti, R. L. (2002). A longitudinal study of children's depressive symptoms, selfperceptions, and cognitive distortions about the self. *Journal of Abnormal Psychology, 111,* 77–87.

McGrath, J. E., & Argote, L. (2004). Group processes in organizational contexts. In M. Brewer & M. Hewstone (Eds.), *Applied social psychology* (pp. 318–341). Malden, MA: Blackwell.

McGrath, R. E., Wigginsm, J. G., Sammons, M. T., Levant, R. F., Brown, A., & Stock, W. (2004). Professional issues in pharmacotherapy for psychologists. *Professional Psychology: Research and Practice, 35,* 158–163.

McGregor, B. A., Antoni, M. H., Boyers, A., Alferi, S. M., Bloomberg, B. B., & Carver, C. S. (2004). Cognitive-behavioral stress management increase benefit finding and immune function among women with early-stage breast cancer. *Journal of Psychosomatic Research, 56,* 1–8.

McGue, M., & Bouchard, T. J. (2000). Genetic and environmental influences on human behavioral differences. *Annual Review of Neuroscience, 21,* 1–24.

McGuffin, P., Riley, B., & Plomin, R. (2001, February 16). Toward behavioral genomics. *Science, 291,* 1232–1249.

McHale, S. M., Crouter, A. C., & Whiteman, S. D. (2003). The family contexts of gender development in childhood and adolescence. *Social Development, 12,* 125–148.

McHale, S. M., Updegraff, K. A., Helms-Erikson, H., & Crouter, A. C. (2001). Sibling influences on gender development in middle childhood and early adolescence: A longitudinal study. *Developmental Psychology, 37,* 115–125.

McInnis, M. G., Dick, D., Willour, V. L., Avramopoulos, D., MacKinnon, D. F., Simpson, S. G., et al. (2003). Genome-wide scan and conditional analysis in bipolar disorder: Evidence for genomic interaction in the National Institute of Mental Health genetics initiative bipolar pedigrees. *Biological Psychiatry, 54,* 1265–1273.

McIntyre, C. K., Marriott, L. K., & Gold, P. E. (2003). Patterns of brain acetylcholine release predict individual differences in preferred learning strategies in rats. *Neurobiology of Learning & Memory, 79,* 177–183.

McKelvey, M. W., & McKenry, P. C. (2000). The psychosocial well-being of black and white mothers following marital dissolution. *Psychology of Women Quarterly, 24,* 4–14.

McKim, W. A. (2003). *Drugs and behavior: An introduction to behavioral pharmacology* (5th ed.). Upper Saddle River, NJ: Prentice Hall.

McLynn, F. (1997). *Carl Gustau Jung: A biography.* New York: St. Martin's Press.

McMahon, D. B. T., Shikata, H., & Breslin, P. A. S. (2001). Are human taste thresholds similar on the right and left sides of the tongue? *Chemical Senses. 26,* 875–883.

McMahon, T. J., & Luthar, S. S. (2000). Women in treatment: Within gender differences in the clinical presentation of opioid-dependent women. *Journal of Neruous and Mental Disease, 88,* 679–687.

McNally, R. J. (2003). Recovering memories of trauma: A view from the laboratory. *Current Directions in Psychological Science, 12,* 32–35.

McNally, R. J. (2004). Is traumatic amnesia nothing but psychiatric folklore? *Cognitive Behaviour Therapy, 33,* 97–101.

McNally, R. J., Bryant, R. A., & Ehlers, A. (2003). Does early psychological intervention promote recovery from posttraumatic stress? *Psychological Science in the Public Interest, 4,* 45–79.

McNally, R. J., Lasko, N. B., Clancy, S. A., Macklin, M. L., Pitman, R. K., & Orr, S. P. (2004). Psychophysiological responding during script-driven imagery in people reporting abduction by space aliens. *Psychological Science, 15,* 493–497.

McNeil, J. E., & Warrington, E. K. (1993). Prosopagnosia: A face-specific disorder. *The Quarterly Journal of Experimental Psychology, 46A*(1), 1–10.

McNeill, D. (1970). Explaining linguistic universals. In J. Morton (Ed.), *Biological and social factors in psycholinguistics.* London: Logos.

McVitte, C., McKinlay, A., & Widdicombe, S. (2003) Committed to (un)equal opportunitles?: "New Ageism" and the older worker.

British Journal of Social Psychology, 42, 595–612.

Meadows, S. (1998). Children learning to think: Learning from others? Vygotskian theory and educational psychology. *Educational and Child Psychology, 15*(2), 6–13.

Mechanic, D. (1978). *Medical sociology* (2nd ed.). New York: Free Press.

Mecklinger, A. (2000). Interfacing mind and brain: A neurocognitive model of recognition memory. *Psychophysiology, 37,* 565–582.

Medland, S. E., Geffen, G., & McFarland, K. (2002). Lateralization of speech production using verbal/manual dual tasks: Meta-analysis of sex differences and practice effects. *Neuropsychologia, 40,* 1233–1239.

Mehlhorn, G., Holborn, M., & Schliebs, R. (2000). Induction of cytokines in glial cells surrounding cortical beta-amyloid plaques in transgenic Tg2576 mice with Alzheimer pathology. *International Journal of Developmental Neuroscience, 18,* 423–431.

Mehlum, L. (2004). A suicide prevention strategy for England. *Crisis: The Journal of Crisis Intervention and Suicide Prevention, 25,* 69–73.

Meichenbaum, D. (1974). *Cognitive behavior modification.* Morristown, NJ: General Learning.

Meichenbaum, D. (1993). Changing conceptions of cognitive behavior modification: Retrospect and prospect. *Journal of Consulting and Clinical Psychology, 61,* 202–204.

Meichenbaum, D., & Cameron, R. (1973). Training schizophrenics to talk to themselves: A means of developing attentional controls. *Behavior Therapy, 4,* 515–534.

Meichenbaum, D., & Cameron, R. (1983). Stress inoculation training: Toward a general paradigm for training coping skills. In D. Meichenbaum & M. E. Jaremko (Eds.), *Stress reduction and prevention* (pp. 115–154). New York: Plenum.

Melara, R. D., & Algom, D. (2003). Driven by information: A tectonic theory of Stroop effects. *Psychological Review, 110,* 422–471.

Melfi, C. A., Croghan, T. W., Hanna, M. P., & Robinson, R.L. (2000). Racial variation in antidepressant treatment in a Medicaid population. *Journal of Clinical Psychiatry, 61,* 16–21.

Meltzoff, A. N., & Moore, M. K. (2001). "Discovery procedures" for people and things—The role of representation and identity. In F. Lacerda, C. von Hofsten, & M. Heimann (Eds.), *Emerging cognitive abilities in early infancy* (pp. 213–230). Mahwah, NJ: Eribaum.

Melville, J. (1977). *Phobias and compulsions.* New York: Penguin.

Melzack, R. (1999). From the gate to the neuromatrix. *Pain* (Suppl.6), S121–S126.

Merckelbach, H., Muris, P., de Jong, P.J., & de Jongh, A. (1999). Disgust sensitivity, blood-injection-injury fear, and dental anxiety. *Clinical Psychology & Psychotherapy, 6* 279–285.

Merrill, S. S., & Verbrugge, L. M. (1999). Health and disease in midlife. In S. L. Willis & J. D. Reid (Eds.), *Life in the middle: Psychological and social development in middle age* (pp. 77–103). San Diego, CA: Academic Press.

Merry, T., & Brodley, B.T. (2002). The nondirective attitude in client-centered therapy: A response to Kahn. *Journal of Humanistic Psychology, 42,* 66–77.

Mesquita, B. (2001). Emotions in collectivist and individualist contexts. *Journal of Personality and Social Psychology, 80,* 68–74.

Mesquita, B. (2003). Cultural differences in emotions: A context for interpreting emotional experiences. *Behaviour Research & Therapy, 41,* 777–793.

Metcalfe, J., Funnell, M., & Gazzaniga, M. S. (1995). Right-hemisphere memory superiority: Studies of a split-brain patient. *Psychological Science, 6,* 157–164.

Metsch, L. R., McCoy, C. B., Miles, C. C., & Wohler, B. (2004). Prevention myths and HIV risk reduction by active drug users. *AIDS Education & Prevention, 16,* 150–159.

Metzger, L. J., Paige, S. R., Carson, M. A., Lasko, N. B., Paulus, L. A., Pitman, R. K., et al. (2004). PTSD arousal and depression symptoms associated with increased right-side parietal EEG asymmetry. *Journal of Abnormal Psychology, 113,* 324–329.

Meyer, I. H. (2003). Prejudice, social stress, and mental health in lesbian, gay, and bisexual populations: Conceptual issues and research evidence. *Psychological Bulletin, 129,* 674–697.

Meyer, R. G., & Salmon, P. (1988). *Abnormal psychology* (2nd ed.). Boston: Allyn & Bacon.

Micallef, J., & Blin, O. (2001). Neurobiology and clinical pharmacology of obsessive-compulsive disorder. *Clinical-Neuropharmacology, 24,* 191–207.

Michael, R. T., Wadsworth, J., Feinleib, H., Johnson, A. M., Laumann, E. O., & Wellings, K. (1998). Private sexual behavior, public opinion, and public health policy related to sexually transmitted diseases: A U.S.—British comparison. *American Journal of Public Health, 88,* 749–754

Middleton, B., Arendt, J., & Stone, B. M. (1997). Complex effects of melatonin on human circadian rhythms in constant dim light. *Journal of Biological Rhythms, 12,* 467–477.

Mikkelsen, A., & Gundersen, M. (2003). The effect of a participatory organizational intervention on work environment, job stress, and subjective health complaints. *International Journal of Stress Management, 10,* 91–110.

Milgram, S. (1963). Behavioral study of obedience. *Journal of Abnormal and Social Psychology, 67,* 371–378.

Milgram, S. (1965). Liberating effects of group pressure. *Journal of Personality and Social Psychology, l,* 127–134.

Miller, G.A. (1956). The magical number seven plus or minus two: Some limits on our capacity for processing information. *Psychological Review, 63,* 81–97.

Miller, G. A. (1965). Some perliminaries to psycholinguistics. *American Psychologist, 20,* 15–20.

Miller, J. K., & Slive, A. (2004). Breaking down the barriers to clinical service delivery: Walk-in family therapy, *Journal of Marital & Family Therapy, 30,* 95–103.

Miller, K.E., & Baillargeon, R. (1990). Length and distance: Do preschoolers think that occlusion brings things together? *Developmental Psychology, 26,* 103–114.

Miller, L. C., Putcha-Bhagavatula, A., & Pedersen, W. C. (2002). Men's and women's mating preferences: Distinct evolutionary mechanisms? *Current Directions in Psychological Science, 11,* 88–93.

Miller, M. N., & Pumariega, A. (1999). Culture and eating disorders. *Psychiatric Times, 16*(2), 1–6.

Miller, N. E. (1944). Experimental studies of conflict. In J. M. Hunt (Ed.), *Personality and behavioral disorders* (Vol. New York: Ronald Press.

Miller, N. E. (1959). Liberalization of basic S–R concepts: Extensions to conflict behavior, motivation, and social learning. In S. Koch (Ed.), *Psychology: A study of a science* (Vol. 2). New York: McGraw-Hill.

Miller, N.E. (1969). Learning of visceral and glandular responses. *Science, 163,* 434–445.

Miller, P.J. O., & Bain, D. E. (2000). Within-pod variation in the sound production of a pod of killer whales, *Orcinus orca. Animal Behavior, 60,* 617–628.

Millon, T. (2003). It's time to rework the blue-prints: Building a science for clinical psychology. *American Psychologist, 58,* 949–961.

Mills, C. B., Viguers, M. L., Edelson, S. K., Thomas, A. T., Simon-Deck, S. L., & Innis, J. A. (2002). The color of two alphabets for a multilingual synesthete. *Perception, 31,* 1371–1394.

Milner, B. (1966). Amnesia following operation on the temporal lobes. In C. W. M. Whilly & O. L. Zangwill (Eds.), *Amnesia*. London: Butter-worth.

Mischel, W. (1999). Personality coherence and dispositions in a cognitive-affective personality system (CAPS) approach. In D. Cervone & Y. Shoda (Eds.), *The coherence of personality: Social- cognitive bases of consistency, variability, and organization* (pp. 37–66). New York: Guilford Press.

Mischel, W. (2004). Toward an integrative science of the person. *Annual Review of Psychology, 55*, 1–22.

Mischel, W., & Ayduk, O, (2002). Self-regulation in a cognitive-affective personality system: Attentional control in the service of the self. *Self and Identity, 1*, 213–220.

Mischel, W., & Shoda, Y. (1999). Integrating dispositions and processing dynamics within a unified theory of personality: The cognitive-affective personality system. In L. A. Pervin & O. P. John (Eds.), *Handbook of personality: Theory and research* (pp. 197–218). New York: Guilford Press.

Mitchell, K. J., Johnson, M. K., Raye, C. L., & D'Esposito, M. (2000). FMRI evidence of age-related hippocampal dysfunction in feature binding in working memory. *Cognitive Brain Research, 10*(1–2), 197–206.

Mitler, M. M., Miller, J. C., Lipsitz, J. J., & Walsh, J. K. (1997). The sleep of long-haul truck drivers. *New England Journal of Medicine, 337*, 755–761.

Mitterschiffthaler, M. T., Kumari, V., Malhi, G. S., Brown, R. G., Giampietro, V. P., Brammer, M. J. et al. (2003). Neural response to pleasant stimuli in anhedonia: An IMRI study. *Neuroreport: For Rapid Communication of Neuroscience Research, 14*, 177–182.

Miyamoto, Y., & Kitayama, S. (2002). Cultural variation in correspondence bias: The critical role of attitude diagnosticity of socially constrained behavior. *Journal of Personality and Social Psychology, 83*, 1239–1248.

Mokdad, A. H., Marks, J. S., Stroup, D. F., & Gerberding, J. L. (2004). Actual causes of death in the United States, 2000. *Journal of the American Medical Association, 291*, 1238–1245.

Moller, H. J. (2003). Suicide, suicidality and suicide prevention in affective disorders. *Acta Psychiatrica Scandinavica, 108*(Suppl. 418), 73–80.

Möller-Leimk¨hler, A. M. (2003). The gender gap in suicide and premature death or: Why are men so vulnerable? *European Archives of Psychiatry & Clinical Neuroscience, 253*, 1–8.

Monahan, J. L., Murphy, S. T., & Zajonc, R. B. (2000). Subliminal mere exposure: Specific, general, and diffuse effects. *Psychological Science, 11*, 462–466.

Moncrieff, J. (1997). Lithium: Evidence reconsidered. *British Journal of Psychiatry, 171*, 113–119.

Mondloch, C. J., Lewis, T. L., Budreau, D. R., Maurer, D., Dannemiler, J. L., Stephens, B. R., & Kleiner-Gathercoal, K. A. (1999). Face perception during early infancy. *Psychological Science, 10*, 419–422.

Montague, D. P., & Walker-Andrews, A. S. (2001). Peekaboo: A new look at infants' perception of emotion expressions. *Developmental Psychology, 37*, 826–838.

Monteleone, P., Luisi, M., Colurcio, B., Casarosa, E., Monteleone, P., Ioime, R., Genazzani, A. R., & Maj, M. (2001). Plasma levels of neuroactive steroids are increased in untreated women with anorexia nervosa or bulimia nervosa. *Psychosomatic Medicine, 63*, 62–68.

Monlgomery, D., Miville, M. L., Winterowd, C., Jeffries, B., & Baysden, M. F. (2000). American Indian college students: An exploration into resiliency factors revealed through personal stories. *Cultural Diversity and Ethnic Minority Psychology, 6*, 387–398.

Montgomery, G. H., & Bovbjerg, D. H. (1997). The development of anticipatory nausea in Patients receiving adjuvant chemotherapy for breast cancer. *Psychology & Behavior, 61*, 737–741.

Montgomery, G. H., Tomoyasu, N., Bouojerg, D. H., Andrykowski, M. A., Currie, V. E., Jacobsen, P. B., & Redd, W. H. (1998). Patients' pretreatment expectations of chemotherapy-related nausea are an independent predictor of anticipatory nausea. *Annals of Behaviora Medicine, 20*, 104–108.

Montoya, M., & Horion, R. S. (2004). On the importance of cognitive evaluation as a determinant of interpersonal attraction. *Journal of Personality and Social Psychology, 86*, 696–712.

Moore, T. E. (1995). Subliminal self-help auditory tapes: An empirical test of perceptual consequences. *Canadian Journal of Behavioral Science, 27*, 9–20.

Moore, Z. E. (2003). Ethical dilemmas in sports psychology: Discussion and recommendations for practice. *Professional Psychology: Research and Practice, 34*, 601–610.

Moorhead, G., Ference, R., & Neck, C. P. (1991). Group decision fiascoes continue: Space shuttle *Challenger and a revised groupthink frame-work. Human Relations, 44*, 539–550.

Morey, L. C., Warner, M. B., & Boggs, C. D. (2002). Gender bias in the personality disorders criteria: An investigation of five bias indicators. *Psychopathology & Behavioral Assessment, 24*, 55–65.

Morris, C. D., Bransford, J. D., & Franks, J. J. (1977). Levels of processing versus transfer appropriate processing. *Journal of Verbal Learning and Verbal Behavior, 16*, 519–533.

Morris, M. W, & Peng, K. (1994). Culture and cause: American and Chinese attributions for social and physical events. *Journal of Personality and Social Psychology, 67*, 949–971.

Morrish, E., King, M. A., Smith, I. E., & Shneerson, J. M. (2004). Factors associated with a delay in the diagnosis of narcolepsy. *Sleep Medicine, 5*, 37–41.

Morrison, T. G., Morrison, M. A., & Hopkins, C. (2003). Striving for bodily perfection? An exploration of the drive for muscularity in Canadian men. *Psychology of Men & Masculinity, 4*, 111–120.

Morrongiello, B. A., Lasenby, J., & Lee, N. (2003). Infants' learning, memory, and generalization of learning for bimodal events. *Journal of Experimental Child Psychology, 84*, 1–19.

Mor-Sommerfield, A. (2002). Language mosaic, Developing literacy in a second-new language: A new perspective. *Reading, Literacy & Language, 36*, 99–105.

Mosier, C. E., & Rogoff, B. (2003). Privileged treatment of toddlers: Cultural aspects of individual choice and responsibility. *Developmental Psychology, 39*, 1047–1060.

Moskowitz, R. A. (1978). The acquisition of language. *Scientific American, 239*(5), 92–108.

Moss, D. (2001) Civilization and its discontents: An ongoing update. Part I: The death penalty. *Psychoanalytic Review, 88*, 87–94.

Most, S. B., Simons, D. J., Scholl, B. J., Jimenez, R., Clifford, E., & Chabris, C. F. (2001). How not to be seen: The contribution of similarity and selective ignoring to sustained inattentional blindness. *Psychological Science, 12*, 9–17.

Mounts, N. S. (2002). Parental management of adolescent peer relationships in context: The role of parenting style. *Journal of Family Psychology, 16*, 58–69.

Mouras, H., Stoléru, S., Bittoun, J., Glutron, D., Pélégrini-Issac, M., Paradis, A.-L., & Burnod, Y. (2003). Brain processing of visual sexual stimuli in healthy men: A functional magnetic resonance imaging study. *Neurolmage, 20*, 855–869.

Moyer, C. A., Rounds, J., & Hannum, J. W. (2004) A meta-analysis of massage therapy research. *Psychological Bulletin, 130*, 3–18.

Mueser, K. T., & McGurk, S. R. (2004). Schizophrenia. *Lancet, 363*, 2062–2072.

Muir, H. (2002, February 23). Bigger ain't better. *New Scientist, 173,* 15.

Mumford, M. D., Feldman, J. M., Hein, M. B., & Nagao, D. J. (2001). Tradeoffs between ideas and structure: Individuals versus group performance in creative problem solving. *Journal of Creative Behavior, 35*(1), 1–23.

Munato, M. R., Clark, T. G., Moore, L. R., Payne, E., Walton, R., & Flint, J. (2003). Genetic polymorphisms and personality in healthy adults: A systematic review and meta-analysis, *Molecular Psychiatry, 8,* 471–484.

Munk, M. H. J. (2003). The principle of controlling neuronal dynamics in neocortex: Rapid reorganization and consolidation of neural assemblies. In R. H. Kluew, G. Lueer, & F. Roesler (Eds.), *Principles of learning and memory* (pp. 187–205). Cambridge, MA: Birkhaeuser.

Murguia, A., Peterson, R., & Zea, M. C. (2003). Use and implications of ethnomedical health care approaches among Central American immigrants. *Health & Social Work, 28,* 43–51.

Murnen, S. K., Wright, C., & Kaluzny, G. (2002). If "boys will be boys," then girls will be victims? A meta-analytic review of the research that relates masculine ideology to sexual aggression. *Sex Roles, 46,* 359–375.

Murphy, F. C., Nimmo-Smith, I., & Lawrence, A. D. (2003). Functional neuroanatomy of emotions: A meta-analysis. *Cognitive, Affective & Behavioral Neuroscience, 3,* 207–233.

Murphy, S. M., & Jowdy, D. P. (1992). Imagery and mental practice. In T. S. Horn (Ed.), *Advances in sport psychology* (pp. 221–250). Champaign, IL: Human Kinetics.

Murray, B. (2002a, June). Good news for bachelor's grads. *Monitor on Psychology, 33*(6), 30–32.

Murray, B. (2002b, June). More students blend business and psychology. *Monitor on Psychology, 33*(6), 34–35.

Murray, J. B. (1995). Evidence for acupuncture's analgesic effectiveness and proposals for the physiological mechanisms involved. *Journal of Psychology, 129,* 443–461.

Murry, V. M., Kotchick, B. A., Wallace, S., Ketchen, B., Eddings, K., Heller, L., & Collier, I. (2004). Race, culture, and ethnicity: implications for a community intervention. *Journal of Child & Family Studies, 13*(1), 81–99.

Musher-Eizenman, D. R., & Kulick, A. D. (2003). An alcohol expectancy-challenge prevention program for at-risk college women. *Psychology of Addictive Behaviors, 17,* 163–166.

Myers, D. G. (2000). The funds, friends, and faith of happy people. *American Psychologist, 55,* 56–67.

Myers, I. B. (1962). *Myers-Briggs type indicator manual.* Princeton, NJ: Educational Testing Service.

Nail, P. R., Harton, H. C., & Decker, B. P. (2003). Political orientation and modern versus aversive racism: Tests of Dovidio and Gaertner's (1998) integrated model. *Journal of Personality and Social Psychology, 84,* 754–770.

Najjar, L. (2003). Age and gender bias in psychiatric diagnosis: A vignette study. *American Psychological Association Conference paper,* unique identifier 347262004–000, Retrieved July 4, 2004, from www.apa.org

Nakamura, J., & Csikszentmihalyi, M. (2002). The concept of flow. In C. R. Snyder & S. J. Lopez (Eds.), *Handbook of positive psychology* (pp. 89–105). New York: Oxford University Press.

Nannini, D. K., & Meyers, L. S. (2000). Jealousy in sexual and emotional infidelity: An alternative to the evolutionary explanation. *Journal of Sex Research, 37,* 117–122.

Napholz, L. (2000). Balancing multiple roles among a group of urban midlife American Indian working women. *Health Care for Women International, 21,* 255–266.

Nardi, P. M. (2003). *Doing survey research: A guide to quantitative methods,* Boston: Allyn & Bacon.

Narrow, W. E., Regier, D. A., & Rae, D. S. (1993). Use of services by persons with mental and addictive disorders: Findings from the National Institute of Mental Health Epidemiologic Catchment Area Program. *Archives of General Psychiatry, 50,* 95–107

Nasar, S. (2002, March 11). The man behind *A Beautiful Mind. Newsweek,* 52+.

Nash, R. A. (1996). The serotonin connection. *Journal of Orthomolecular Medicine, 11,* 35–44.

Nathan, P. E., & Langenbucher, J. (2003). Diagnosis and classification. In G. Stricker, T. A. Widiger, & E. B. Weiner (Eds.), *Handbook of psychology: Clinical psychology* (Vol 8, pp. 3–26). New York: Wiley.

Nathan, P. E., & Langenbucher, J. W. (1999). Psychopathology: Description and classification. *Annual Review of Psychology, 50,* 79–108.

Nathans, J. (1989, February). The genes for color vision. *Scientific American,* 42–49.

Nation, M., Crusto, C., Wandersman, A., Kumpfer, K. L., Seybolt, D., Morrissey-Kane, E., et al. (2003). What works in prevention: Principles of effective prevention programs. *American Psychologist, 58,* 449–456.

National Academy on an Aging Society, (1999). *Hearing loss: A growing problem that affects quality of life.* Retrieved November 23, 2004, from http://www.agingsociety.org/agingsociety/pdf/hearing.pdf

National Alliance for the Mentally Ill. (2004). *About mental illness.* Retrieved June 25, 2004, from http://www.nami.org/Content/NavigationMenu/Ingorm_Yourself/About_Mental_Illness/About_Mental_Illness.htm

National Association for the Deal, (2004). *NAD prosition statement on cochiear implants.* Retrieved July 11, 2004, from http://www.nad.org/infocenter/newsroom/positions/CochlearImplants.html

National Association of Anorexia Nervosa and Associated Disorders. (2004). *We help those with eating disorders—anorexia nervosa, bulimia, compulsive overeating.* Retrieved April 18, 2004, from http://www.anad.org/site/anadweb/content.php

National Center for Health Statistics. (2003). *Health, United States, 2003.* Hyattsville, MD: U.S. Government Printing Office.

National Center for Health Statistics. (2004a). *Deaths—leading causes.* Retrieved July 4, 2004, from http://www.cdc.gov/nchs/fastats/lcod.htm

National Center for Health Statistics. (2004b). Estimated pregnancy rates for the United States, 1990–2000: An Update. *NVSR 52*(23), 1–10.

National Center for Injury Prevention and Control. (2004). *Community-based interventions to reduce motor vehicle-related injuries: Evidence of effectiveness from systematic reviews.* Retrieved July 6, 2004, from http://www.cdc.gov/ncipc/duip/mvsafety.htm

National Center on Birth Defects and Developmental Disabilities. (2004). *Mental retardation.* Retrieved April 22, 2004, from http://www.cdc.gov/ncbddd/dd/ddmr.htm

National Council on Aging. (1998, September 28). Half of older Americans report they are sexually active; 4 in 10 want more sex, says new survey. Washington, DC: NCOA [Online press release]. Retrieved from http://www.ncoa.org/ press/sexsurvey.htm

National Eating Disorders Association. (2004). *Anorexia nervosa.* Retrieved April 20, 2004, from http://www.nationaleatingdisorders.org/p.asp

National Institute on Deafness and Other Communication Disorders. (2004). *Hearing loss and older adults.* Retrieved July 11, 2004, from http://www.nided.nih.gov/ health/hearing/older.asp

National Institute on Drug Abuse. (2002). *NIDA research report: Marijuana abuse.* NIH Publication No. 02–3859. Washington, DC: U.S. Government Printing Office.

National Institutes of Health. (1995). Consensus statements. Cochlear implants in adults and children. Retrieved October 25, 2004, from http://consensus,nih.gov/cons/100/100_statement.htm

National Institutes of Health. (1997). Acupuncture. Retrieved October 28, 2004, from http://nccam.nih.gov/health/acupuncture

National Institutes of Health. (1998). Diagnosis and treatment of attention deficit hyperactivity disorder. *Consensus Statement Online, 16*(2), 1–37.

National Institutes of Health (2004a). *The dementias: Hope through research.* Retrieved November 23, 2004, from http://www.ninds.nih.gov/disorders/alzheimersdisease/detail_alzheimersdisease.htm

National Institutes of Health (2004b). *The Dementias: hope through research.* Retrieved November 23, 2004, from http://www.ninds.nih.gov/disorders/alzheimersdisease/detail_alzhemersdisease.htm

National Network for Women's Employment. (2004). What is the wage gap? *Fighting the Wage Gap.* Retrieved April 24, 2004, from http://www.womenwork.org/pdfresources/wagegap.pdf

National Research Council. (2003). *The polygraph and lie detection.* Washington, DC: National Academies Press. Retrieved August 7, 2004, from http://www.nap.edu/execsumm/0309084369.html

National Research Council, Committee to Review the Scientific Evidence on the Polygraph, (2002). *The polygraph and lie detection.* Washington, DC: National Academies Press.

National Sleep Foundation. (2004). *For promoting a healthy lifestyle.* Retrieved May 28, 2004, from http://www.sleepfoundation.org/sleeptips.clm

National Task Force on the Prevention and Treatment of Obesity. (2000). Overweight, obesity, and health risks. *Archives of Internal Medicine, 160,* 898–904.

Naumann, A., & Daum, I. (2003). Pathophysiology and neuropsychological changes. *Behavioral Neurology, 14,* 89–98.

Neighbors, H. W., Trierweiler, S. J., Ford, B. C., & Muroff, J. R. (2003). Racial differences in DSM diagnosis using a semistructured instrument: The importance of clinical judgment in the diagnosis of African Americans. *Journal of Health & Social Behavior, 44,* 237–256.

Neiss, M., & Rowe, D. C. (2000). Parental education and child's verbal IQ in adoptive and biological families in the National Longitudinal Study of Adolescent Health. *Behavior Genetics, 30,* 487–495.

Neisser, U., & Libby, L. K. (2000). Remembering life events. In E. Tulving & F. I. M. Craik (Eds.), *The Oxford handbook of memory* (pp. 315–332). New York: Oxford University Press.

Neitz, M., & Neitz, J. (2001). A new mass screening test for color-vision deficiencies in children. *Color Research & Application. 26*(Suppl.), S239–S249.

Nelson, D. L., McKinney, V. M., & Gee, N. R. (1998). Interpreting the influence of implicity activated memories on recall and recognition. *Psychological Review, 105,* 299–324.

Nelson, K., & Fivush, R. (2004). The emergence of autobiographical memory: A social cultural developmental theory. *Psychological Review, 111,* 486–511.

Nemeroll, C. B., & Schatzberg, A. F. (2002). Pharmacological treatments for unipolar depression. In P. E. Nathan & J. M. Gorman (Eds.). *A guide to treatments that work* (pp. 229–243). New York: Oxford Press.

Ness Research Team. (2004). The national evaluation of Sure Start local programmes in England. *Child & Adolescent Mental Health, 9*(1), 2–8.

Nesse, R. M. (1997, October 3). Psychoactive drug use in evolutionary perspective. *Science, 278,* 63–66.

Nestler, E. J., & Malenka, R. C. (2004, March). The addicted brain. *Scientific American, 290,* 78–85.

Netzer, N. C., Hoegel, J. J., Loube, D., Netzer, C. H., Hay, B., Alvarez-Sala, R., & Stohl, K. P. (2003). Prevalence of symptoms and risk of sleep apnea in primary care. *Chest, 124,* 1406–1414.

Neubauer, A. C. (2000). Physiological approaches to human intelligence: A review. *Psychologische Beitrage, 42,* 161–173.

Neubatter, A. C., Fink, A., & Schrausser, D. G. (2002). Intelligence and neural efficiency: The influence of task content and sex on the brain-IQ relationship. *Intelligence, 30,* 515–536.

Neumark-Sztainer, D., Story, M., Hannan, P. J., Beuhring, T., & Resnick, M. D. (2000). Disordered eating among adolescents: Associations with sexual/physical abuse and other familial/psychosocial factors. *International Journal of Eating Disorders, 28,* 249–258.

Neville, H. J., & Bavelier, D. (2000). Specilicity and plasticity in neurocognitive development in humans. In M. S. Gazzaniga (Ed.). *The new cognitive neurosciences* (pp. 83–98). Cambridge, MA: The MIT Press.

Newcomb, A. F., Bukowski, W. M., & Bagwell, C. L. (1999). Knowing the sounds: Friendship as a developmental context. In W. A. Collins, B. Laursen, et al. (Eds.), *Relationships as developmental contexts. The Minnesota Symposia on Child Psychology* (pp. 63–84). Mahwah, NJ: Erlbaum.

Newcombe, N. S. (2003). Some controls too much. *Child Development, 74,* 1050–1052.

Newcombe, N. S. & Huttenlocher, J. (2000). *Making Space: the Development of Spatial Representation and Reasoning.* Cambridge, MA: The MIT Press.

Newell, B. R., & Bright, J. E. H. (2003). The subliminal mere exposure effect does not generalize to structurally related stimuli. *Canadian Journal of Experimental Psychology, 57,* 61–68.

Newman, L. S., Dulf, K. J., & Baumeister, R. F. (1997). A new look at defensive projection: Thought suppression, accessibility, and biased person perception. *Journal of Personality and Social Psychology, 72,* 980–1001.

Niaura, R., Spring, B., Borrelli, B., Hedeker, D., Goldstein, M. G., Keuthen, N., et al. (2002). Multicenter trial of fluoxetine as an adjunct to behavioral smoking cessation treatment. *Journal of Consulting & Clinical Psychology, 70,* 887–896.

NICHD Early Child Care Research Network. (2000). Factors associated with fathers' caregiving activities and sensitivity with young children. *Journal of Family Psychology, 14,* 200–219.

NICHD Early Child Care Research Network. (2003). Does quality of child care affect child outcomes at age 4? *Developmental Psychology, 39,* 451–469.

Nichols, M. P., & Schwartz, R. C. (2004). *Family therapy concepts and methods.* Boston, MA: Allyn & Bacon.

Nicol. J., & Greth, D. (2003). Production of subjectverb agreement in Spanish as a second language. *Experimental Psychology, 50,* 196–203.

Niederholfer, K. G., & Pennebaker, J. W. (2002). Sharing one's story: On the benefits of writing or talking about emotional experience. In C. R. Snyder & S. J. Lopez (Eds.) *Handbook of positive psychology* (pp. 573–583). New York: Oxford University Press.

Niedzwienska, A. (2003). Gender differences in vivid memories. *Sex Roles, 49,* 321–331.

Nier, J. A. (2004). Why does the "above average effect" exist? Demonstrating idiosyncratic trait definition. *Teaching of Psychology, 31,* 53–54.

Nisbet, R. E. (1972). Hunger, obesity, and the ventromedial hypothalamus. *Psychological Review, 79,* 433–453.

Nisbett, R. E. (2003). *The geography of thought.* New York: Free Press.

Nishino K., & Nayar, S. K. (2004). The world in an eye. *Proceedings of Computer Vision and Pattern Recognition CVPR*, II, 1444–1451.

Nolen-Hoeksema, S. (2000). The role of rumination in depressive disorders and mixed anxiety/depressive symptoms. *Journal of Abnormal Psychology, 109,* 504–511.

Nolen-Hoeksema, S. (2002). Gender differences in depression. In I. H. Gotlib & C. Hammen (Eds.), *Handbook of depression* (pp. 492–509). New York: Guilford.

Nolen-Hoeksema, S., & Ahrens, C. (2002). Age differences and similarities in the correlates of depressive symptoms. *Psychology and Aging, 17,* 116–124.

Nolen-Hoeksema, S., Larson, J., & Grayson, C. (1999). Explaining the gender difference in depressive symptoms. *Journal of Personality and Social Psychology, 77,* 1061–1072.

Norman, D. A. (1990), *Design of everyday things.* New York: Doubleday.

Nosek, B. A., Banaji, M. R., & Greenwald, A. G. (2002). Math = male,me = female, therefore math? me. *Journal of Personality and Social Psychology, 83,* 44–59.

Nourkova, V., Bernstein, D. M., &Loftus, E. F. (2004). Biography becomes autobiography: Distoring the subjective past. *American Journal of Psychology, 117,* 65–80.

Novins, D. K., & Baron, A. E. (2004). American Indian substance use: The hazards for substance use initiation in adolescents aged 14–20 years. *Journal of the American Academy of Child Psychiatry, 43,* 316–322.

Nucci, C. (2002). The rational teacher: Rational emotive behavior therapy in teacher education. *Journal of Rational-Emotive & Cognitive Behavior Therapy, 20,* 15–32.

Nyberg, L., Cabeza, R., & Tulving, E. (1996). PET studies of encoding and retrieval: The HERA model. *Psychonomic Bulletin and Review, 3,* 135–148.

Oakland, T., Mpofu, E., Glasgow, K., & Jurnel, B. (2003). Diagnosis and administrative interventions for students with mental retardation in Australia, France, United States, and Zimbabwe 98 years after Binet's first intelligence test. *International Journal of Testing, 3,* 59–75.

O'Brien, M. (2004). An integrative therapy frame-work: Research and practice. *Journal of Psychotherapy Integration, 14,* 21–37.

Occhionero, M. (2004). Mental processes and the brain during dreams. *Dreaming, 14,* 54–64.

Ochsner, K., & LIeberman, M. (2001). The emergence of social cognitive neuroscience. *American Psychologist, 56,* 717–734.

O'Connor, D. B., & Shimizu, M. (2002). Sense of personal control, stress and coping style:

A cross-cultural study. *Stress & Health: Journal of the International Society for the Investigation of Stress, 18,* 173–183.

O'Connor, L., Brooks-Gunn, J., & Graber, J. (2000). Black and white girls' preferences in media and peer choices and the role of socialization for black girls. *Journal of Family Psychology, 14,* 510–521.

Oelveczky, B. P., Baccus, S. A., & Meister, M. (2003). Segregation of object and background motion in the retina. *Nature, 423*(6938), 401–408.

Oetzel, K. B., & Scherer, D. G. (2003). Therapeutic engagement with adolescents in psychotherapy. *Psychotherapy: Theory, Research, Practice, Training, 40,* 215–220.

Ogawa, K., Niltono, H., & Hori, T. (2002). Brain potentials associated with the onset and offset of rapid eye movement (REM) during REM sleep. *Psychiatry & Clinical Neurosciences, 56,* 259–260.

Ohayon, M. M., & Schatzberg, A. F. (2002). Prevalence of depressive episodes with psychotic features in the general population. *Journal of Psychiatry, 159,* 1855–1861.

Ohio State University. (2004). Alcohol and pregnancy don't mix. *Ohio State University Extension Fact Sheet*, Retrieved June 25, 2004, from http://ohioline.osu.edu/hyg-fact/5000/5534.html

Öhman, A. (2002). Automaticity and the amygdala: Nonconscious responses to emotional faces. *Current Directions in Psychological Science, 11,* 62–66.

Öhman, A., & Mineka, S. (2003). The malicious serpent: Snakes as a prototypical stimulus for an evolved module of fear. *Current Directions in Psychological Science, 12,* 5–9.

Okagaki, L., & Bojezyk, K. E. (2002). Perspectives on Asian American development. In G. C. Nagayama Hall & S. Okazaki (Eds.), *Asian American psychology* (pp. 67–104). Washington, DC: American Psychological Association.

Okagaki, L., & Sternberg, R. J. (1993). Parental beliefs and children's school performance. *Child Development, 64,* 36–56.

Oksol, E. M., & O'Donohue, W. T. (2004). A critical analysis of the polygraph. In W. O'Donohue & E. Levensky (Eds.), *Handbook of forensic psychology: Resource for mental health and legal professionals* (pp. 601–634). London: Elsevier Academic Press.

Okuda-Ashitaka, E., Minami, T., Tachibana, S., Yosihara, Y., Nishiuchi, Y., Kimura, T., & Ito, S. (1998). Nocistatin, a peptide that blocks nonciceptin action in pain transmission. *Nature, 392,* 286–289.

Olausson, B., & Sagvik, J. (2000). Pain threshold changes following acupuncture, measured with cutaneous argon laser and

electrical tooth pulp stimulation, a comparative study. *Progress in Neuro-Psychopharmacology & Biological Psychiatry, 24,* 385–395.

Olds, J. (1955). Physiological mechanisms of reward. Nebraska Symposium on Motivation, 3, 73–139.

Olds, J. (1969). The central nervous system and the reinforcement of behavior. *American Psychologist, 24,* 114–132.

Olds, J., & Milner, P. (1954). Positive reinforcement produced by electrical stimulation of septal area and other regions of rat brain. *Journal of Comparative and Physiological Psychology, 47,* 419–427.

Olfson, M., Marcus, S. C., Druss, B., & Pincus, H. A. (2002). National trends in the use of outpatient psychotherapy. *American Journal of Psychiatry, 159,* 1914–1920.

Olivardia, R., Pope, H. G., & Phillips, K. A. (2000). *The Adonis complex: The secret crisis of male body obsession.* New York: Free Press.

Oliver, W. (2000). Preventing domestic violence in the African American community: The rational for popular culture interventions. *Violence Against Women, 6,* 533–549.

Olsen, R. A. (1997). Desirability bias among professional investment managers: Some evidence from experts. *Journal of Behavioral Decisian Making, 10,* 65–72.

Olweus, D. (1993). *Bullying at school: What we know and what we can do.* Cambridge, MA: Blackwell.

Olweus, D. (2003). A profile of bullying at school. *Educational Leadership, 60*(6), 12–17.

O'Mara, S. M., Commins, S., & Anderson, M. (2000). Synaptic plasticity in the hippocampal area CAI-subiculum projection: Implications for theories of memory. *Hippocampus, 10,* 447–456.

Ones, D. S., & Anderson, N. (2002). Gender and ethnic group differences on personality scales in selection: Some British data. *Journal of Occupational & Organizational Psychology, 75,* 255–276.

Ong, L., Linden, W., & Young, S. (2004). Stress management: What is it? *Journal of Psychosomatic Research, 56*(1), 133–137.

Oppenheimer, D. M. (2004). Spontaneous discounting of availability in frequency judgment tasks. *Psychological Science, 15,* 100–105.

Ortega, L. (2003). Syntactic complexity measures and their relationship to L2 proficiency: A research synthesis of college-level L2 writing. *Applied Linguistics, 24,* 492–518.

Orth-Gomér, K. (1998). Psychosocial risk factor profile in women with coronary heart disease. In K. Orth-Gomér, M. Chesney, & N. K. Wenger (Eds.), *Women, stress, and heart disease* (pp. 25–38). Mahwah, NJ: Erlbaum.

Ortiz, J., & Raine, A. (2004). Heart rate level and antisocial behavior in children and adolescents: A meta-analysis. *Journal of the American Academy of Child & Adolescent Psychiatry, 43,* 154–162.

Oshodi, J. E. (1999). The construction of an Africentric sentence completion test to assess the need for achievement. *Journal of Black Studies, 30,* 216–231.

Osorio, L. C., Cohen, M., Escobar, S. E., Salkowski-Bartlett, A., & Compton, R. J. (2003). Selective attention to stressful distractors: Effects of neurolicism and gender. *Personality and Individual Differences, 34,* 831–844.

Ostroff, C., & Atwater, L. E. (2003). Does whom you work with matter? Effects of referent group gender and age composition on managers' compensation. *Journal of Applied Psychology, 88,* 725–740.

Osvath, P., Fekete, S., Voros, V., & Vitrai, J. (2003). Sexual dysfunction among patients treated with antidepressants—a Hungarian retrospective study. *European Psychiatry, 18,* 412–414.

Osvath, P., Voros, V., & Fekete, S. (2004). Life events and psychopathology in a group of suicide attempters. *Psychopathology, 37,* 36–40.

Otten, L. J., Henson, R. N. A., & Rugg, M. D. (2002). State-related and item-related neural correlates of successful memory encoding. *Nature Neuroscience, 5,* 1339–1345.

Otto, L. B. (2000). Youth perspectives on parental career influence. *Journal of Career Development, 27*(2), 111–118.

Otto, R., & Borum, R. (2004). Evaluation of youth in the juvenile system. In W. O'Donohue & E. Levensky (Eds.), *Handbook of forensic psychology: Resource for mental health and legal professionals* (pp. 873–895). London: Elsevier Academic Press.

Ovaert, L. B, Cashel, M. L., & Sewell, K. W. (2003). Structured group therapy for posttraumatic stress disorder in incarcerated male juveniles. *American Journal of Orthopsychiatry, 73,* 294–301.

Owens, L., Shute, R., & Slee, P. (2000). Guess what I just heard: Indirect aggression amongst teenage girls. *Aggressive Behavior, 26,* 67–83.

Oyserman, D., Coon, H. M., & Kemmelmeier, M. (2002). Rethinking individualism and collectivism: Evaluation of theoretical assumptions and meta-analyses. *Psychological Bulletin, 128,* 3–72.

Ozer, E. J., & Weiss, D. S. (2004). Who develops postraumatic stress disorder? *Current Directions in Psychological Science, 13,* 169–172.

Pace-Schott, E. F., & Hobson, J. A. (2002). The neuro-biology of sleep: Genetics, cellular physiology and subcortical networks. *Nature Reviews Neuroscience, 3,* 591–605.

Padilla, R., Gomez, V., Biggerstaff, S. L., & Mehler, P. S. (2001). Use of curanderismo in a public health care system. *Archives of Internal Medicine, 161,* 1336–1340.

Pagel, J. F. (2003). Non-dreamers. *Sleep Medicine, 4,* 235–241.

Pagel, J. F., Crow, D., & Sayles, J. (2003). Filmed dreams: Cinematographic and story line characteristics of the cinematic dreamscapes of John Sayles. *Dreaming: Journal of the Association for the Study of Dreams, 13,* 43–48.

Paivio, A. (1971). *Imagery and verbal processes.* New York: Holt, Rinehart & Winston.

Palmer, B., Gardner, L., & Stough, C. (2003). The relationship between emotional intelligence, personality and effective leadership. *Australian Journal of Psychology, 55* (Suppl.), 140–144.

Palmer, G. (2000). Resilience in child refugees: An historical study. *Australian Journal of Early Childhood, 25*(3), 39+.

Palmore, E. (2001). The ageism survey: First findings. *Gerontologist 41,* 572–575.

Pan, C., Morrison, R. S., Ness, J., Fugh-Berman, A., & Leipzig, R. M. (2000). Complementary and alternative medicine in the management of pain, dyspnea, and nausea and vomiting near the end of life: A systematic review. *Journal of Pain & Symptom Management, 20,* 374–387.

Pani, M., & Parida, S. K. (2000). Effects of culture on cognitive development. *Psycho-Lingua, 30,* 51–55.

Panksepp, J. (2000a). Emotions as natural kinds within the mammalian brain. In M. Lewis & J. M. Haviland-Jones (Eds.), *Handbook of emotions* (2nd ed., pp. 137–156). New York: Guilford.

Panksepp, J. (2000b) The riddle of laughter: Neural and psychoevolutionary underpinnings of joy. *Current Directions in Psychological Science, 9,* 183–186.

Pantin, H. M., & Carver, C. S. (1982). Induced competence and the bystander effect. *Journal of Applied Social Psychology, 12,* 100–111.

Paolucci, E. O., Genuis, M. L., & Violato, C. (2001). A meta-analysis of the published research on the effects of child sexual abuse. *Journal of Psychology, 135,* 17–36.

Papp, P. (2000). Gender differences in depression: His or her depression. In P. Papp (Ed.). *Couples on the fault line: New directions for therapists* (pp. 130–151). New York: Guilford Press.

Paquette, V., Lévesque, J., Mensour, B., Leroux, J. M., Beaudoin, G., Bourgouin, P., & Beauregard, M. (2003). "Change the mind and you change the brain": Effects of cognitive-behavioral therapy on the neural correlates of spider phobia. *Neurolmage, 18,* 401–409.

Paradiso, S., Andreasen, N. C., Crespo-Facorro, B., O'Leary, S. D., Watkins, G., Leonard, P., et al. (2003). Emotions in unmedicated patients with schizophrenia during evaluation with positron emission tomography. *American Journal of Psychiatry, 160,* 1775–1783.

Pargament, K. l., & Mahoney, A. (2002). Spirituality: Discovering and conserving the sacred. In C. R. Snyder & S. J. Lopez (Eds.), *Handbook of positive psychology* (pp. 646–659). New York: Oxford University Press.

Park, C. L., & Adler, N. E. (2003). Coping style as a predictor of health and well-being across the first year of medical school. *Health Psychology, 22,* 627–631.

Park, C. L., Armeli, S., & Tennen, H. (2004a). Appraisal-coping goodness of fit: A daily Internet study. *Personality & Social Psychology Bulletin, 30,* 558–569.

Park, C. L., Armeli, S., & Tennen, H. (2004b). The daily stress and coping process and alcohol use among college students. *Journal of Studies on Alcohol, 65,* 126–135.

Park, H,-J., Levitt, J., Shenton, M. E., Salisbury, D. F., Kubicki, M., Kikinis, R., et al. (2004). An MRI study of spatial probability brain map differences between first-episode schizophrenia and normal controls. *Neurolmage, 22,* 1231–1246.

Park, H. S., Bauer, S. C., & Sullivan, L. M. (1998). Gender differences among top-performing elementary school students in mathematical ability. *Journal of Research and Development in Education, 31,* 133–141.

Park, J., & Liao, T. F. (2000). The effect of multiple roles in South Korean married women professors: Role changes and the factors which influence potential role gratification and strain. *Sex Roles, 43,* 571–591.

Parker, J. D. A., Summerfeldt, L. J., Hogan, M. J., & Majeski, S. A. (2004). Emotional intelligence and academic success: Examining the transition from high school to university. *Personality and Individual Differences, 36,* 163–172.

Parks, C. A., Hesselbrock, M. N., Hesselbrock, V. M., & Segal, B. (2001). Gender and reported health problems in treated alcohol-dependent Alaska natives. *Journal of Studies on Alcohol, 62,* 286–293.

Parvizi, J., & Damasio, A. (2001). Consciousness and the brainstem. *Cognition, 79,* 135–159.

Pasquini, P., Liotti, G., Mazzotti, E., Fassone, G., & Picardi, A. (2002). Risk factors in the early family life of patients suffering from dissociative disorders. *Acta Psychiatrica Scandinavica, 105,* 110–116.

Patenaude, A. F., Guttmacher, A. E., & Collins, F. S. (2002). Genetic testing and psychology: New roles, new responsibilities. *American Psychologist, 57,* 271–282.

Patterson, D. R., & Jensen, M. P. (2003). Hypnosis and clinical pain. *Psychological Bulletin, 129,* 495–521.

Paulesu, E., Demonet, J., Faxio, F., McCrory, E., Chanoine, V., Brunswick, N., Cappa, S. F., Cossu, G., Habib, M., Frith, C. D., & Frith, U. (2001). Dyslexia: Cultural diversity and biological unity. *Science, 16,* 2165–2167.

Paulus, P. B. (1998). Developing consensus about groupthink after all these years. *Organizational Behavior & Human Decision Processes, 73,* 362–374.

Paunovic, N. (2003). Prolonged exposure counter-conditioning as a treatment for chronic post-traumatic stress disorder. *Journal of Anxiety Disorders, 17,* 479–499.

Pavlov, I. P. (1927). *Conditioned reflexes.* London: Oxford University Press.

Pawlak, C. R., Witte, T., Heiken, H., Hundt, M., Schubert, J., Wiese, B., et al. (2003). Flares in patients with systemic lupus erythematosus are associated with daily psychological stress. *Psychotherapy & Psychosomatics, 72,* 159–165.

Pearce, J. L., & Randel, A. E. (2004). Expectations of organizational mobility, workplace social conclusion, and employee performance. *Journal of Organizational Behavior, 25,* 81–98.

Pedersen, D. M., & Wheeler, J. (1983). The Mülller-Lyer illusion among Navajos. *Journal of Social Psychology, 121,* 3–6.

Pedersen, N. L., & Reynolds, C. A. (1998). Stability and change in adult personality: Genetic and environmental components. *European Journal of Personality, 12,* 365–386.

Pedersen, N. L., & Svedberg, P. (2000). Behavioral genetics, health, and aging. *Journal of Adult Development, 7,* 65–71.

Pederson, C. B., & Mortensen, P. B. (2001). Family history, place and season of birth as risk factors for schizophrenia in Denmark: A replication and reanalysis. *British Journal of Psychiatry, 179,* 46–52.

Pekala, R. J., Angelini, F., & Kumar, V. K. (2001). The importance of fantasy-proneness in dissociation: A replication. *Contemporary Hypnosis, 18,* 204–214.

Pelkonen, M., Marttunen, M., & Arno, H. (2003). Risk for depression: A 6-year follow-up of Finnish adolescents. *Journal of Affective Disorders, 77,* 41–51.

Pelli, D. G. (1999). Close encounters—an artist shows that size affects shape. *Science, 285,* 844–846.

Peltzer-Karpl, A., & Zangl, R. (2001). Figure-ground segregation in visual and linguistic development: A dynamic systems account. In K. E., Nelson, A. Aksu-Koc, and others, *Children's Language: Interactional Contributions to Language Development* (197–226). Mahwah, NJ: Erlbaum.

Penfield, W. (1977). *No man alone: A neurosurgeon's life.* Boston: Little, Brown.

Peng, K., & Nisbett, R. (1999). Culture, dialectics, and reasoning about contradiction. *American Psychologist, 54,* 741–754.

Penley, J. A., Tomaka, J., & Wiebe, J. S. (2002). The association of coping to physical and psychological health outcomes: A meta-analytic review. *Journal of Behavioral Medicine, 25,* 551–603.

Pennebaker, J. W. (1989). Confession, inhibition, and disease. In L. Berkowitz (Ed.), *Advances in experimental social psychology* (Vol. 22, pp. 211–244). New York: Academic Press.

Pennebaker, J. W., & Graybeal, A. (2001). Patterns of natural language use: Disclosure, personality, and social integration. *Current Directions in Psychological Science, 10,* 90–93.

Penzien, D. B., Rains, J. C., & Andrasik, F. (2002). Behavioral management of recurrent headache: Three decades of experience and empiricism. *Applied Psychophysiology & Biofeedback, 27,* 163–181.

Peper, L., Bootsma, R. J., Mestre, D. R., & Bakker, F. C. (1994). Catching balls: How to get the hand to the right place at the right time. *Journal of Experimental Psychology: Human Perception and Performance, 20,* 591–612.

Peplau, L. A. (2003). Human sexuality: How do men and women differ? *Current Directions in Psychological Science, 12,* 37–40.

Perloff, R. M. (2001). *Persuading people to have safer sex: Applications of social science to the AIDS crisis.* Mahwah, NJ: Erlbaum.

Perner, J., & Dienes, Z. (2003). Developmental aspects of consciousness: How much theory of mind do you need to be consciously aware? *Consciousness & Cognition, 12,* 63–82.

Perrett, D. I., Lee, K. J., Penton-Voak, I., Rowland, D., Yoshikawa, S., Burt, D. M., Henzi, S. P., Castles, D. L., & Akamatsu, S. (1998). Effects of sexual dimorphism on facial attractiveness. *Nature, 394,* 884–887.

Perrow, C. (1999). *Normal accidents.* Princeton, NJ: Princeton University Press.

Pert, C. B., & Snyder, S. H. (1973). Opiate receptor: Demonstration in nervous tissue. *Science, 179,* 1011–1014.

Peselow, E. D., Sanfilipo, M. P., & Fieve, R. R. (1995). Relationship between hypomania and personality disorders before and after successful treatment. *American Journal of Psychiatry, 152,* 232–238.

Peters, R. D., Petrunka, K., & Arnold, R. (2003). The better beginnings, better futures project: A universal, comprehensive, community-based prevention approach for primary school children and their families. *Journal of Clinical Child & Adolescent Psychology, 32(2),* 215–227.

Peterson, C., & Chang, E. C. (2003). Optimism and flourishing. In C. L. M. Keyes & J. Haidt (Eds.), *Flourishing: Positive psychology and the life well-lived* (pp. 55–79). Washington, DC: American Psychological Association.

Peterson, C., & Seligman, M. E. P. (1984). Causal explanations as a risk factor for depression: Theory and evidence. *Psychological Review, 91,* 347–374.

Peterson, C., & Seligman, M. E. P. (2004). *Character strengths and virtues.* New York: Oxford University Press.

Peterson, L. R., & Peterson, M. J. (1959). Short-term retention of individual verbal items. *Journal of Experimental Psychology, 58,* 193–198.

Peterson, M., & Wilson, J. F. (2004). Work stress in America. *International Journal of Stress Management, 11,* 91–113.

Petrides, K. V., Frederickson, N., & Furnham, A. (2004). The role of trait emotional intelligence in academic performance and deviant behavior at school. *Personality and Individual Differences, 36,* 277–293.

Petrill, S. A. (2003). The development of intelligence: Behavioral genetic approaches. In R. J. Sternberg, J. Lautrey, & T. I. Lubart (Eds.), *Models of intelligence: International perspectives* (pp. 81–89). Washington, DC: American Psychological Association.

Petrinovich, L. (1997). Evolved behavioral mechanisms. In M. E. Bouton & M. S. Fanselow (Eds.), *Learning, motivation, and cognition: The functional behavioralism of Robert C. Bolles* (pp. 13–30). Washington, DC: American Psychological Association.

Petrosini, L., Graziano, A., Mandolesi, L., Neri, P., Molinari, M., & Leggio, M. G. (2003). Watch how to do it! New advances in learning by observation. *Brain Research Reviews, 42*, 252–264.

Petty, R. E., & Cacioppo, J. T. (1985). The elaboration likelihood model of persuasion. In L. Berkowitz (Ed.), *Advances in experimental social psychology* (Vol. 19). New York: Academic Press.

Petty, R. E., Cacioppo, J. T., Strathman, A. J., & Priester, J. R. (1994). To think or not to think: Exploring two routes to persuasion. In S. Shavitt & T. C. Brock (Eds.), *Persuasion: Psychological insights and perspectives* (pp. 113–148). Boston: Allyn & Bacon.

Petty, R. E., Schumann, D. W., Richman, S. A., & Strathman, A. J. (1993). Positive mood and persuasion: Different roles for affect under high-and low-elaboration conditions. *Journal of Personality and Social Psychology, 64*, 5–20.

Petty, R. E., & Wegener, D. T. (1998). Attitude change: Multiple roles for persuasion variables. In D. T. Gilbert, S. T. Fiske, & G. Lindzey (Eds.), *The hand-book of social psychology* (pp. 323–371). Boston: McGraw-Hill.

Petty, R. E., & Wegener, D. T. (1999). The elaboration likelihood model: Current status and controversies. In S. Chaiken & Y. Trope (Ed.), *Dual process theories in social psychology* (pp. 37–72). New York: Guilford Press.

Phelps, E. A., Cannistraci, C. J., & Cunningham, W. A. (2003). Intact performance on an indirect measure of race bias following amygdala damage. *Neuropsychologia, 41*, 203–208.

Phelps, E. A., O'Conner, K. J., Cunningham, W. A., Funayama, E. S., Gatenby, J. C., Gore, J. C., & Banaji, M. R. (2000). Performance in indirect measure of race evaluation predicts amygdala activation. *Journal of Cognitive Neuroscience, 12*, 729–738.

Phillips, D. P., Liu, G. C., Kwok, K., Jarvinen, J. R., Zhang, W., & Abramson, I. S. (2001). The Hound of the Baskervilles effect: Natural experiment on the influence of psychological stress on timing of death. *British Medical Journal, 323*, 1443–1446.

Phillips, D., Mekos, D., Scarr, S., McCartney, K., & Abott-Shim, M. (2000). Within and beyond the classroom door: Assessing quality in child care centers. *Early Childhood Research Quarterly, 15*, 475–496.

Philpot, C. L. (2001). Family therapy for men. In G. R. Brooks (Ed.), *The new handbook of psychotherapy and counseling with men: A comprehensive guide to settings, problems, and treatment approaches, 1 &2* (pp. 622–636). San Franciscio: Jossey-Bass.

Piaget, J. (1932). *The moral judgment of the child*, London: Routledge & Kegan Paul.

Piaget, J. (1936). The origins of intelligence in children. New York: Norton.

Piaget, J. (1970). *Genetic epistemology*. New York: Norton.

Piaget, J. (1980). *Adaptation and intelligence: Organic selection and phenocopy*, Chicago: University of Chicago Press.

Pickel, K. L., (2004). When a lie becomes the truth: The effects of self-generated misinformation on eyewitness memory. *Memory, 12*, 14–26.

Pigott, T. A. (2003). Anxiety disorders in women. *Psychiatric Clinics of North America, 26*, 621–672.

Piko, B. F. (2004). Interplay between self and community: A role for health psychology in Eastern Europe's public health. *Journal of Health Psychology, 9*, 111–120.

Pillemer, D. B., Wink, P., DiDonato, T. E., & Sanborn, R. L. (2003). Gender differences in autobiographical memory styles of older adults. *Memory, 11*, 525–532.

Pimlott-Kubiak, S., & Cortina, L. M. (2003). Gender, victimization, and outcomes: Reconceptualizing risk. *Journal of Consulting and Clinical Psychology, 71*, 528–539.

Pincus, T., & Morley, S. (2001). Cognitive-processing bias in chronic pain: A review and integration. *Psychological Bulletin, 27*, 599–617.

Pine, K. J., & Nash, A. (2003). Barbie or Betty? Preschool children's preference for branded products and evidence for gender-linked differences. *Journal of Developmental & Behavioral Pediatrics, 24*, 219–224.

Pinel, J. P. J. (2003). *Biopsychology* (5th ed.). Boston: Allyn & Bacon.

Pinel, J. P. J., Assanand, S., & Lehman, D. R. (2000). Hunger, eating, and ill health. *American Psychologist, 55*, 1105–1116.

Pinker, S. (1997). *How the mind works*. New York: Norton.

Pinker, S. (1999). *Words and rules*. New York: Basic Books.

Pinker, S. (2002). *The blank state: The denial of human nature in modern intellectual life*. New York: Viking.

Pirenne, M. H. (1967). *Vision and the eye*. London: Chapman & Hall.

Pittenger, D. J. (1997). Reconsidering the overjustification effect: A guide to critical resources. *Teaching of Psychology, 23*, 234–236.

Pittenger, D. J. (2002). Deception in research: Distinctions and solutions from the perspective of utilitarianism. *Ethics & Behavior, 12*, 117–132.

Place, U. T. (2000). Consciousness and the zombie within: A functional analysis of the blind-sight evidence. In Y. Rossetti & A. Revonsuo (Eds.). *Beyond dissociation: Interaction between dissociated implicit and explicit processing. Advances in consciousness research* (pp. 295–329). Amsterdam: John Benjamins.

Plant, E. A., Hyde, J. S., Keltner, D., & Devine, P. G. (2000). The gender stereotyping of emotions. *Psychology of Women Quarterly, 24*, 81–92.

Plomin, R. (2003). Genetics, genes, genomics and g. *Molecular Psychiatry, 8*, 1–5.

Plomin, R., & Caspi, A. (1999). Behavior genetics and personality. In L. A. Pervin & O. P. John (Eds). *Handbook of personality: Theory and research* (pp. 251–276). New York: Guilford Press.

Plomin, R., & Colledge, E. (2001). Genetics and psychology: Beyond heritability. *European Psychologist, 6*, 229–240.

Plomin, R., & DeFries, J. C. (1999). The genetics of cognitive abilities and disabilities. In S. J. Ceci & W. M. Williams (Eds.), *The nature-nurture debate: The essential readings. Essential readings in developmental psychology* (pp. 177–195). Malden, MA: Blackwell Publishers.

Plomin, R., DeFries, J. C., Craig, I. W., & McGuffin, P. (2003a). Behavioral genetics. In R. Plomin, J. C. DeFries, I. W. Craig, & P. McGuffin (Eds.). *Behavioral genetics in the postgenomic era* (pp. 3–15). Washington, DC: American Psychological Association.

Plomin, R., DeFries, J. C., Craig, I. W., & McGuffin, P. (2003b). Behavioral genomics. In R. Plomin, J. C. DeFries, I. W. Craig, & P. McGuffin (Eds.). *Behavioral genetics in the postgenomic era* (pp. 531–540). Washington, DC: American Psychological Association.

Plomin, R., Fulker, D. W., Corley, R., & DeFries, J. C. (1997). Nature, nurture, and cognitive development from 1 to 16 years: A parent-offspring adoption study. *Psychological Science, 8*, 442–447.

Plomin, R., & McGuffin, P. (2003). Psychopathology in the postgenomic era. *Annual Review of Psychology, 54*, 205–228.

Plomin, R., & Spinath, F. M. (2004). Intelligence: Genetics, genes, and genomics. *Journal of Personality and Social Psychology, 86*, 112–129.

Plous, S. (1996). Attitudes toward the use of animals in psychology research and education: Results from a national survey of psychologists, *American Psychologist, 51*, 1167–1180.

Polivy, J., & Herman, C. P. (2002). Causes of eating disorders. *Annual Review of Psychology, 53*, 187–214.

Pollack, W. (1998). *Real boys: Rescuing our sons from the myths of boyhood*. New York: Random House.

Polonsky, A., Blake, R., Braun, J., & Heeger, D. J. (2000). Neuronal activity in human primary visual cortex correlates with perception during binocular rivalry. *Nature Neuroscience, 3*, 1153–1159.

Ponnappa, B. C., & Rubin, E. (2000). Modeling alcohol's effects on organs in animal models. *Alcohol Health & Research World, 24*(2), 93–104.

Pope, J. S. (2000). Pseudoscience, cross-examination, and scientific evidence in the recovered memory controversy. *Psychology, Public Policy, and Law, 4*, 1160–1181.

Posada, G., Jacobs, A., Richmond, M. K., Carbonell, O. A., Alzate, G., Bustamante, M. R., & Quiceno, J. (2002). Maternal caregiving and infant security in two cultures. *Developmental Psychology, 38*, 67–78.

Posner, M. I., & Pavese, A. (1998). Anatomy of word and sentence meaning. *Proceedings of the National Academy of Sciences, 95*, 899–905.

Postma, A., Jager, G., Kessels, R. P. C., Koppeschaar, H. P. F., & van Honk, J. (2004). Sex differences for selective forms of spatial memory. *Brain & Cognition, 54*, 24–34.

Poulsen, B. C., & Mathews, W. J., Jr. (2003). Correlates of imaginative and hypnotic suggestibility in children. *Contemporary Hypnosis, 20*, 198–208.

Povinelli, D. J., Theall, L. A., Reaux, J. E., & Dunphy-Lelii, S. (2003). Chimpanzees spontaneously alter the location of their gestures to match the attentional orientation of others. *Animal Behaviour, 66*, 71–79.

Power, A. E., Vazdarjanova, A., & McGaugh, J. L. (2003). Muscarinic cholinergic influences in memory consolidation. *Neurobiology of Learning & Memory, 80*, 178–193.

Powers, P. C., & Geen, R. G. (1972). Effects of the behavior and the perceived arousal of a model on instrumental aggression. *Journal of Personality and Social Psychology, 23*, 175–184.

Powledge, T. M. (1999). Addiction and the brain. *BioScience, 49*, 513–519.

Pozzi, M. E. (2000). Ritalin for whom? Understanding the need for Ritalin in psychodynamic counseling with families of under 5s. *Journal of Child Psychotherapy, 26*(1), 25–43.

Pratkanis, A. R. (2001). Propaganda and deliberate persuasion: The implications of Americanized mass media for established and emerging democracies. In W. Wosinska, R. B. Cialdini, D. W. Barrett, & J. Reykowski (Eds.), *The practice of social influence in multiple cultures.*

Applied social research (pp. 259–285). Mahwah, NJ: Erlbaum.

Pratkanis, A. R., & Turner, M. E. (1999). Groupthink and preparedness for the Loma Prieta earth-quake: A social identity maintenance analysis of causes and preventions. In R. Wageman (Ed.), *Research on managing group and teams: Groups in context* (pp. 115–136). Stamford, CT: JAI Press.

Premack, D. (1971). Language in chimpanzees? *Science, 172*, 808–822.

Premack, D. (2004). Is language the key to human intelligence? *Science, 303*, 318–320.

Price, P. C., Pentecost, H. C., & Voth, R. D. (2002). Perceived event frequency and the optimistic bias: Evidence for a two-process model of personal risk judgments. *Journal of Experimental Social Psychology, 38*, 242–252.

Price, R. A., Li, W. D., & Kilker, R. (2002). An X-chromosome scan reveals a focus for fat distribution in chromosome region Xp21–22. *Diabetes, 51*, 1989–1991.

Price, T. S., Eley, T. C., Dale, P. S., Stevenson, J., Saudino, K., & Plomin, R. (2000). Genetic and environmenal covariation between verbal and non-verbal cognitive development in infancy. *Child Development, 71*(4), 948–959.

Prickaerts, J., Koopmans, G., Blokland, A., & Scheepens, A. (2004). Learning and adult neurogenesis: Survival with or without proliferation? *Neurobiology of Learning & Memory, 81*, 1–10.

Prilleltensky, 1. (2001). Value-based praxis in community psychology: moving toward social justice and social action. *American Journal of Community Psychology, 29*(5), 747–778.

Prinz, R. J., Smith, E. P., Dumas J. E., Laughlin, J. E., White, D. W., & Barron, R. (2001). Recruitment and retention of participants in prevention trials involving family-based interventions. *American Journal of Preventive Medicine, 20*(Suppl. 1), 31–37.

Prinzmental, W., & Beck, D. (2001). The tilt-constancy theory of visual illusions. *Journal of Experimental Psychology: Human Perception and Performance, 27*, 206–217.

Prokopcakova, A. (1998). Drug experimenting and pubertal maturation in girls, *Studio Psychologica, 40*, 287–290.

Prudic, J., Olfson, M., Marcus, S. C., Fuller, R. B., & Sackeim, H. A. (2004). Effectiveness of electro-convulsive therapy in community settings. *Biological Psychiatry, 55*, 301–312.

Prudic, J., Olfson, M., & Sackeim, H. A. (2001). Electro-convulsive therapy practices in the community. *Psychological Medicine, 31*, 929–934.

Prudic, J., Peyser, S., & Sackeim, H. A. (2000). Subjective memory complaints: A review of

patient self-assessment of memory after electroconvulsive therapy. *Journal of ECT: 16*, 121–132.

Psychology Today. (2004). Therapy in America 2004. Poll shows: Mental health treatment goes mainstream. Retrieved December 7, 2004, from http://cms.psychologytoday.com/pto/press_release_050404.html

Puhl, R. M., & Schwartz, M. B. (2003). If you are good you can have a cookie: How memories of childhood food rules link to adult eating behaviors. *Eating Behaviors, 4*, 283–293.

Punamaki, R. L., & Joustie, M. (1998). The role of culture, violence, and personal factors affecting dream content. *Journal of Cross-Cultural Psychology, 29*, 320–342.

Purves, D., Augustine, G. J., Fitzpatrick, D., Katz, L. C., LaMantia, A.-S., McNamara, J. O., & Williams, S. M. (2001). *Neuroscience* (2nd ed.). Sunderland, MA: Sinauer.

Putnam, F. W., & Carlson, E. B. (1998). Trauma, memory, and dissociation, *Progress in Psychiatry, 54*, 27–55.

Quinlan, R. J. (2003). Father absence, parental care, and female reproductive development. *Evolution & Human Behavior, 24*, 376–390.

Raber, J., Huang, Y., & Ashford, J. W. (2004). ApoE genotype accounts for the vast majority of AD risk and AD pathology. *Neurobiology of Aging, 25*, 641–650.

Radach, R., & Kennedy, A. (2004). Preface. *European Journal of Cognitive Psychology, 16*, 1–2.

Rahe, R. H. (1989). Recent life change stress and psychological depression. In T. W. Miller (Ed.), *Stressful life events* (pp. 5–11). Madison, CT: International Universities Press.

Rahola, J. G. (2001). Antidepressants: Pharmacological profile and clinical consequences. *International Journal of Psychiatry in Clinical Practice, 5*(Suppl. 1), S19–S28.

Raine, A., Lenczk, T., Bihrle, S., LaCasse, L., & Colletti, P. (2000). Reduced prefrontal gray matter volume and reduced autonomic activity in antisocial personality disorder. *Archives of General Psychiatry, 57*, 119–127, 128–129.

Rainville, P. (2002). Brain mechanisms of pain, affect and pain modulation. *Current Opinian in Neurobiology, 12*, 195–204.

Rainville, P., Hofbauer, R. K., Paus, T., Duncan, G. H., Bushnell, M. C., & Price, D. D. (1999). Cerebral mechanisms of hypnotic induction and suggestion. *Journal of Cognitive Neuroscience, 11*, 110–125.

Raj, P., Steigerwald, I., & Esser, S. (2003). Socioeconomic and cultural influences on pain management in practice. *Pain Practice, 3*(1), 80–83.

Rajaram, S., Srinivas, K., & Roediger, H. L., Ill. (1998). A transfer-appropriate processing account of context effects in word-fragment completion. *Journal of Experimental Psychology: Learning, Memory and Cognition, 24*, 993–1004.

Ramachandran, V. S. (2000). Memory and the brain: New lessons from old syndromes. In D. L. Schacter & E. Scarry (Eds.), *Memory, brain, and belief* (pp. 87–114). Cambridge, MA: Harvard University Press.

Ramachandran, V. S., & Hubbard, E. (2001a). Psychophysical investigations into the neural basis of synesthesia. Proceedings of the Royal Society of London. Series B. *Biological Sciences, 268*, 979–983.

Ramachandran, V. S., & Hubbard, E. M. (2001b). Synaesthesia—a window into perception, thought, and language. *Journal of Consciousness Studies, 12*, 3–34.

Ramachandran, V. S., & Hubbard, E. M. (2003, May 1). Hearing colors, tasting shapes. *Scientific American, 288*, 53–59.

Ramey, C. T., & Campbell, F. A. (1984). Preventive education for high-risk children: Cognitive consequences of the Carolina Abecedarian Project. *American Journal of Mental Deficiency, 88*, 515–523.

Ramey, C. T., & Campbell, F. A. (1992). Povert early childhood education, and academic competence: The Abecedarian experiment. In A. Huston (Ed.), *Children in poverty* (pp. 190–221). New York: Cambridge University Press.

Ramey, C. T., Campbell, F.A., Burchinal, M., Skinner, M. L., Gardner, D. M., & Ramsey, S. L. (2000). Persistent effects of early intervention on high-risk children and their mothers. *Applied Developmental Science, 4*, 2–14.

Ramey, C. T., Ramey, S. L., & Lanzi, R. G. (2001). Intelligence and experience. In R. J. Sternberg & E. L. Grigorenko (Eds.), *Environmental effects on cognitive abilites* (pp. 83–115). Mahwah, NJ: Erlbaum.

Ramey, S. L. (1999). Head Start and preschool education. *American Psychologist, 54*(5), 344–346.

Ramey, S. L., & Sackett, G. P. (2000). The early care-giving environment: Expanding veiws on non-parental care and cumulative life experiences. In A. J. Sameroff, M. Lewis, & S. M., Miller (Eds.), *Handbook of developmental psychopathology* (2nd ed., pp. 365–380). New York: Kluwer/Plenum.

Ramsey, J. L., Langlois, J. H., Hoss, R. A., Rubenstein, A., & Griffin, A. M. (2004). Origins of a stereo-type: Categorization of facial attractiveness by 6-month-old infants. *Developmental Science, 7*, 201–211.

Ranelli, P. L., Bartsch, K., & London, K. (2000). Pharmacists' perceptions of children and families as medicine consumers. *Psychology & Health, 15*(6), 829–840.

Rao, K. R. (ed.). (2001). *Basic research in porapsychology* (2nd ed.). Jefferson, NC: McFarland & Co.

Rappaport, J. (1987). Terms of empowerment/exemplars of prevention: Toward a theory for community psychology: *American Journal of Community Psychology, 2*, 121–143.

Rasmussen, L. E. L., & Krishnamurthy, V. (2000). How chemical signals integrate Asian elephant society: The known and the unknown. *Zoo Biology, 19*, 405–423.

Rauf, D., Mosser, T., & O'Hagan, C. (2004, March/April). Reality check: Freshman survivors tell all. *Careers & Colleges, 24*(4), 30–33.

Rauschecker, J. P., & Shannon, R. V. (2002). Sending sound to the brain. *Science, 295*, 1025–1029.

Raven, B. H. (1998). Groupthink, Bay of Pigs, and Watergate reconsidered. *Organizational Behavior and Human Decision Processes, 73*, 352–361.

Ravussin, E., Lillioja, S., Knowler, W. C., Christin, L., Freymond, D., Abbott, W. G. H., Boyce, V., Howard, B. V., & Bogardus, C. (1988). Reduced rate of energy expenditure as a risk factor for body-weight gain. *New England Journal of Medicine, 318*, 467–472.

Ray, O., & Ksir, C. (1993). *Drugs, society, and human behavior* 6th ed.). St. Louis, MO: Mosby-Year Book.

Rayna, S. (2001). The very beginning of togetherness in shared play among young children. *International Journal of Early Years Education, 9*, 109–115

Rayner, K., Liversedge, S. P., White, S. J., & Vergilino-Perez, D. (2003). Reading disappearing text: Cognitive control of eye movements. *Psychological Science, 14*, 385–388.

Rayner, K., Reichle, E. D., & Pollatsek, A. (2000). Eye movement control in reading: Updating the E-Z reader model to account for initial fixation locations and refixations. In A. Kennedy, R. Radach, D. Heller, & J. Pynte (Eds.), *Reading as a perceptual process* (pp. 701–719). Amsterdam: North-Holland/Elsevier Science.

Raynor, H. A., & Epstein, L. H. (2001). Dietary variety: Energy regulation and obesity. *Psychological Bulletin, 127*, 325–341.

Rechtschaffen, A. (1998). Current perspectives on the function of sleep. *Perspectives in Biology and Medicine, 41*, 359–370.

Rechtschaffen, A., & Bergmann, B. M. (2002). Sleep deprivation in the rat: An update of

the 1989 paper. *Journal of Sleep & Sleep Disorders Research, 25*, 18–24.

Reed, B., & Railsback, J. (2003). *Strategies and resources for mainstream teachers of English language learners*. Portland, OR: Northwest Regional Educational Laboratory.

Reed, C. F. (1984). Terrestrial passage theory of the moon illusion. *Journal of Experimental Psychology: General, 113*, 489–516.

Regan, P. C., & Joshi, A. (2003). Ideal partner preferences among adolescents. *Social Behavior & Personality, 31*, 13–20.

Reichle, E. D., Carpenter, P.A., & Just, M. A. (2000). The neural bases of strategy and skill in sentence-picture verification. *Cognitive Psychology, 40*, 261–295.

Reichmuth, C., & Schusterman, R. J. (2002). Sea lions and equivalence: Expanding classes by exclusion. *Journal of the Experimental Analysis of Behavior, 78*, 449–465.

Reid, K. E. (1981). *From character building to social treatment: The history of the use of groups in social work*. Westpoint, CT: Greenwood Press.

Reilly, J. S., & Wulfeck, B. B. (2004). Issues in plasticity and development: Language in atypical children. *Brain & Language, 88*, 163–166.

Reis, H. T., & Gable, S. L. (2003). Toward a positive psychology or relationships. In C. L. M. Keyes & J. Haidt (Eds.), *Flourishing: Positive psychology and the life well-lived* (pp. 129–159). Washington, DC: American Psychological Association.

Reis, S. M., & Renzulli, J. S. (2004). Current research on the social and emotional development of gifted and talented students: Good news and future possibilities. *Psychology in the Schools, 41*, 119–130.

Reisenzein, R. (1983). The Schachter theory of emotion: Two decades later. *Psychological Bulletin, 94*, 239–130.

Reiss, D., Neiderhiser, J. M., Hetherington, E. M., & Plomin, R. (2000). *The relationship code*. Cambridge, MA: Harvard University Press.

Renault, B., Signoret, J. L., Debruille, B., Broton, F., & Bolgert, F. (1989). Brain potentials reveal covert facial recognition in prosopagnosia. *Neuropsychologica, 27*, 905–912.

Reneman, L., Booij, J., de Bruin, K., Reitsma, J. B., de Wolff, F. A., Gunning, W. B., den Heeten, G. J., & van den Brink, W. (2001). Effects of dose, sex, and long-term abstention from use on toxic effects of MDMA (ecstasy) on brain serotonin neurons. *Lancet, 358*, 1864–1869.

Renk, M., & Creasey, G. (2003). The relationships of gender, gender identity, and coping strategies in late adolescents. *Journals of Adolescence, 26*, 159–168.

Renzulli, J. S. (2002). Emerging conceptions of giftedness: Building a bridge to the new century. *Exceptionality, 10,* 67–75.

Renzulli, J. S. (2004). Expanding the umbrella: An interview with Joseph Renzulli. *Roeper Review, 26,* 65–67.

Rescorla, R. A. (1977). Pavlovian 2nd-order conditioning: Some implications for instrumental behavior. In H. Davis & H. Herwit (Eds.), *Pavlovian-operant interactions.* Hillsdale, NJ: Erbaum.

Rescorla, R. A. (1988). Pavlovian conditioning: It's not what you think it is. *American Psychologist, 43,* 151–160.

Rescorla, R. A. (1998). Instrumental learning: Nature and persistence. In M. Sabourin, F. Craik, & M. Robert (Eds.), *Advances in psychological scienece* (pp. 239–257). Hove, UK: Psychology Press/Erlbrum (UK)/Taylor & Francis.

Rescorla, R. A. (2001a). Experimental extinction. In R. R. Mowrer & S. B. Klein (Eds.), *Handbook of contemporary learning theories* (pp. 119–154). Mahwah, NJ: Erlbaum.

Rescorla, R. A. (2001b). Retraining of extinguished Pavlovian stimuli. *Journal of Experimental Psychology: Animal Behavior Processes, 27,* 115–124.

Resnick, S., Warmoth, A., & Selin, I. A. (2001). The humanistic psychology and positive psychology connection: Implications for psychotherapy. *Journal of Humanistic Psychology, 41,* 73–101.

Ressler, K., & Davis, M. (2003). Genetics of childhood disorders: I. Learning and memory, part 3: Fear conditioning. *Journal of the American Academy of Child & Adolescent Psychiatry, 42,* 612–615.

Restle, F. (1970). Moon illusion explained on the basis of relative size. *Science, 167,* 1092–1096.

Revonsuo, A. (2003). The reinterpretation of dreams: An evolutionary hypothesis of the function of dreaming. In E. F. Pace-Schott, M. Solms, M. Blagrove, & S. Harnad (Eds.), *Sleep and dreaming: Scientific advances and reconsiderations* (pp. 85–109). New York: Cambridge University Press.

Reynolds, J. R., Donaldson, D. I., Wagner, A. D., & Braver, T. S. (2004). Item- and task-level processes in the left inferior prefrontal cortex: Positive and negative correlates of encoding. *Neurolmage, 21,* 1472–1483.

Reznick, J. S., Chawarska, K., & Betts, S. (2000). The development of visual expectations in the first year. *Child Development, 71(5),* 1191–1204.

Rhodes, G., Yoshikawa, S., Clark, A., Lee, K., McKay, R., & Akamatsu, S. (2001). Attractiveness of facial averageness and symmetry in non-Western cultures: In search of biologically based standards of beauty. *Perception, 30,* 611–625.

Rhodes, N., & Wood, W. (1992). Self-esteem and intelligence affect influenceability: The mediating role of message reception. *Psychological Bulletin, 111,* 156–171.

Ribalow, M. Z. (1998). Script doctors. *The Sciences, 38(6),* 26–31.

Rice, G., Anderson, C., Risch, N., & Ebers, G. (1999). Male homosexuality: Absence of linkage to microsatellite markers at Xq28. *Science, 284,* 665–667.

Richards, J. M. (2004). The cognitive consequences of concealing feelings. *Current Directions in Psychological Science, 13,* 131–134.

Richardson, J. T. E., & Woodley, A. (2001). Perception of academic quality among students with a hearing loss in distance education. *Journal of Educational Psychology, 93,* 563–570.

Richert, A. J. (2002). The self in narrative therapy: Thoughts from a humanistic/existential perspective. *Journal of Psychotherapy Integration, 12,* 77–104.

Ridsdale, L., Darbishire, L., & Seed, P. T. (2004). Is graded exercise better than cognitive behavior therapy for fatigue? A U.K. randomized trial in primary care. *Psychological Medicine, 34,* 37–49.

Riegel, B., & Bennett, J. A. (2000). Cardiovascular disease in elders: Is it inevitable? *Journal of Adult Development, 7,* 101–112.

Rieger, E., Touyz, S. W., Swain, T., & Beumont, P. J. V. (2001). Cross-cultural research on anorexia nervosa: Assumptions regarding the role of body weight. *International Journal of Eating Disorders, 29,* 205–215.

Riger, S. (2001). Transforming community psychology. *American Journal of Community Psychology, 29(1),* 69–81.

Riggio, R. S. (2003). *Introduction to industrial/organizational psychology* (4th ed.). Upper Saddle River, NJ: Prentice Hall.

Ring, K., Wallston, K., & Corey, M. (1970). Mode of debriefing as a factor affecting subjective reaction to a Milgram-type obedience experiment: An ethical inquiry. *Representative Research in Social Psychology, 1,* 67–88.

Rivas, L. A. (2001). Controversial issues in the diagnosis of narcissistic personality disorder. A review of the literature. *Journal of Mental Health Counseling, 23,* 22–35.

Rivas-Vazquez, R. A., Rice, J., & Kalman, D. (2003). Pharmacotherapy of obesity and eating disorders. *Professional Psychology: Research and Practice, 34,* 562–566.

Roane, H. S., Fisher, W. W., & McDonough, E. M. (2003). Progressing from programmatic to discovery research: A case example with the over-justification effect. *Journal of Applied Behavior Analysis, 36,* 35–46.

Robbins, S. B., Lauver, K., Le, H., Davis D. Langley, R., & Carlstrom, A. (2004). Do psychosocial and study skill factors predict college outcomes? A meta-analysis. *Psychological Bulletin, 130,* 261–288.

Roberts, C., Kane, R., Thompson, H., Bishop, B., & Hart, B. (2003). The prevention of depressive symptoms in rural school children. A randomized controlled trial. *Journal of Consulting and Clinical Psychology, 71,* 622–628.

Roberts, G. C. (1992). *Motivation in sport and exercise: Conceptual constraints and convegence* (pp. 3–29). Champaign, IL: Human Kinetics.

Roberts, G. E. (2003). Employee performance appraisal system participation: A technique that works. *Public Personnel Management, 32,* 89–97.

Roberts, R. E., Roberts, C. R., & Chen, I. G. (2000). Fatalism and risk of adolescent depression. *Psychiatry: Interpersonal and Biological Processes, 63,* 239–252.

Robertson, E. M., Pascual-Leone, A., & Press, D. Z. (2004). Awareness modifies the skill-learning benefits of sleep. *Current Biology, 14,* 208–212.

Robins, R. W., Trzesniewset, K. H., Tracy, J. L., & Gosling, S. D. (2002). Global self-esteem across the life span. US *Psychology & Aging, 17(3),* 423–434.

Robinson, G. E. (2004). Career satisfaction in female physicians. *Journal of the American Medical Association, 291,* 635

Robinson, T. E., & Berroge, K. C. (2000). The psychology and neurobiology of addiction: An incentive-sensitization view. *Addiction, 95,* 91–117.

Robinson, T. N., Wilde, M. L., Navracruz, L. C., Haydel, K. E., & Varady, A. (2001). Effects of reducing children's television and video game use on aggressive behavior: A randomized controlled trial. *Archives of Prediatrics and Adolescent Medicine, 155,* 17–23.

Robinson-Riegler, G., & Robinson-Riegler, B. (2004). *Cognitive psychology: Applying the science of the mind.* Boston: Allyn & Bacon.

Rock, I., & Palmer, S. (1990). The legacy of Gestalt psychology. *Scientific American, 263(6),* 84–90.

Rodin, J., & Langer, E. J. (1977). Long-term effects of a control-relevant intervention with the institutionalized aged. *Journal of Personality and Social Psychology, 35,* 897–902.

Rodriguez, C. M. (2003). Parental discipline and abuse potential effects on child depression, anxiety, and attributions. *Journal of Marriage & the Family, 65,* 809–817.

Roediger, H. L., & McDermott, K. B. (1995). Creating false memories: Remembering words not presented in lists. *Journal of Experimental Psychology: Learning, Memory, and Cognition, 21,* 803–814.

Roesch, R., Viljoen, J. L., & Hui, I. (2004). Assessing intent and criminal responsibility. In W. O'Donohue & E. Levensky (Eds.), *Handbook of forensic psychology: Resource for mental health and legal professionals* (pp. 157–174). London: Elsevier Academic Press.

Roeser, R. W., Eccles, J. S., & Sameroff, A. J. (2000). School as a context of early adolescents' academic and social-emotional development: A summary of research findings. *Elementary School Journal, 100,* 443–471.

Roetting, M., Huang, Y. H., McDevitt, J. R., & Melton, D. (2003). When technology tells you how you drive—truck drivers' attitudes towards feedback by technology. *Transportation Research Part F: Traffic Psychology & Behaviour, 6,* 275–287.

Roffwarg, H. P., Muzio, J. N., & Dement, W. C. (1966). Ontogenetic development of human sleepdream cycle. *Science, 152,* 604–619.

Rogers, C. R. (1951). *Client-centered therapy.* Boston: Houghton Mifflin.

Rogers, C. R. (1957). The necessary and sufficient conditions of therapeutic personality change. *Journal of Consulting Psychology, 21,* 95–103.

Rogers, C. R. (1959). A theory of therapy, personality, and interpersonal relationships, as developed in the client-centered framework. In S. Koch (Ed.), *Psychology: A study of a science* (Vol. 3). New York: McGraw-Hill.

Rogers, C. R. (1961). *On becoming a person: A therapist's view of psychotherapy.* Boston: Houghton Mifflin.

Rogers, C. R. (1980). *A way of being.* Boston: Houghton Mifflin.

Rogers, M. A., Kasai, K., Koji, M., Fukuda, R., Iwanami, A., Nakagome, K. et al. (2004). Executive and prefrontal dysfunction in unipolar depression: A review of neuropsychological and imaging evidence. *Neuroscience Research, 50,* 1–11.

Rogers, R. D. (2003). Neuropsychological investigations of the impulsive personality disorders. *Psychological Medicine, 33,* 1335–1340.

Rohland, B. M. (2001). Self-report of improvement following hospitalization for electroconvulsive therapy: Relationship to functional status and service use. *Administration and Policy in Mental Health, 28,* 193–203.

Rollmann, S. M. (2000). Courtship pheromone effects on female receptivity in a plethodontid salamander, *Dissertation Abstracts International: Section B: The Sciences & Engineering, 61(1-B),* 144.

Romans, S. E. (2000). Gender issues in psychiatry. *Hong Kong Journal of Psychiatry, 10(4),* 7–11.

Romero, A. J. (2000). Assessing and treating Latinos: Overview of research. In I. Cuellar & F. A. Paniagua (Eds.), *Handbook of multicultural mental health* (209–223). San Diego, CA: Academic Press.

Romero, A. J., & Roberts, R. E. (2003). Stress within a bicultural context for adolescents of Mexican descent. *Cultural Diversity and Ethnic Minority Psychology, 9,* 171–184.

Rosch, E. (1978). Principles of categorization. In E. Rosch & B. B. Lloyd (Eds.), *Cognition and categorization* (pp. 27–48). Hillsdale, NJ: Erlbaum.

Rose, S. A., Feldman, J. F., & Jankowski, J. J. (2001). Visual short-term memory in the first year of life: Capacity and recency effects. *Developmental Psychology, 37,* 539–549.

Rose, S. A., Feldman, J. F., & Jankowski, J. J. (2003). Infant visual recognition: Memory independent contributions of speed and attention. *Developmental Psychology, 39,* 563–571.

Rosen, A. C., Prull, M. W., Gabrieli, J. D., Stoub, T., O'Hara, R., Friedman, L., Yesavage, J. A., & de Toledo-Morrell, L. (2003). Differential associations between entorhinal and hippocampal volumes and memory performance in older adults. *Behavioral Neuroscience, 117,* 1150–1160.

Rosenberg, H. (1993). Prediction of controlled drinking by alcoholics and problem drinkers. *Psychological Bulletin, 113,* 129–139.

Rosenberg, S. D., Rosenberg, H. J., & Farrell, M. P. (1999). The midlife crisis revisited. In S. L. Willis & J. D. Reid (Eds.), *Life in the middle: Psychological and social development in middle age* (pp. 47–73). San Diego, CA: Academic Press.

Rosenbluth, R., Grossman, E. S., & Kaitz, M. (2000). Performance of early-blind and sighted children on olfactory tasks. *Perception, 29,* 101–110.

Rosenthal, R., & Jacobson, L. (1966). Teachers' expectancies: Determinates of pupils' I.Q. gains. *Psychological Reports, 19,* 115–118.

Roser, M., & Gazzaniga, M. S. (2004). Automatic brains—interpretive minds. *Current Directions in Psychological Science, 13,* 56–59.

Ross, H. S., & Lollis, S. P. (1987). Communication within infant social games. *Developmental Psychology, 2,* 241–248.

Ross, L. (1977). The intuitive psychologist and his shortcomings: Distortions in the attribution process. In L. Berkowitz (Ed.), *Advances in experimental social psychology* (Vol. 10, pp. 173–220). New York: Academic Press.

Rossier, J., Meyer de Stadelholen, F., & Berthoud, S. (2004). The hierarchicat structures of the NEO P1-R and the 16 PF 51. *European Journal of Psychological Assessment, 20,* 27–38.

Roth, G. (2004, January, Special Edition). The quest to find consciousness. *Scientific American, 14,* 32–39.

Roth, P. L., Huffcultt, A. I., & Bobko, P. (2003). Ethnic group differences in measures of job performance: A new mela-analysis. *Journal of Applied Psychology, 88,* 697–706.

Rotter, J. B. (1990). Internal versus external control of reinforcement. *American Psychologist, 45,* 489–493.

Rotter, J. C. (1954). *Social learning and clinical psychology.* Englewood Cliffs, NJ: Prentice-Hall.

Rotter, J. C. (1966). Generalized expectancies for internal versus external control of reinforcement. *Psychological Monographs, 80*(Whole No. 609).

Rowe, D. C. (2001). The nurture assumption persists. *American Psychologist, 56,* 168–169.

Rozin, P. (1999). Food is fundamental, fun, frightening, and far-reaching. *Social Research, 66,* 9–30.

Rozin, P. (2003). Five potential principles for understanding cultural differences in relation to individual differences. *Journal of Research in Personality, 37,* 273–283.

Rozin, P., & Cohen, A. B. (2003). High frequency of facial expressions corresponding to confusion, concentration, and worry in an analysis of naturally occurring facial expressions of Americans. *Emotion, 3,* 68–75.

Rozin, P., & Zellner, D. (1985). The role of Pavlovian conditioning in the acquisition of food likes and dislikes. *Annals of the New York Academy of Sciences, 443,* 189–202.

Rubenzahl, S. A., & Corcoran, K. J. (1998). The prevalence and characteristics of male perpetrators of acquaintance rape: New research methodology reveals new findings. *Violence Against Women, 4,* 713–725.

Rudd, M. D., Joiner, T. E., Jr., Rumzek, H. (2004). Childhood diagnoses and later risk for multiple suicide attempts. *Suicide & Life Threatening Behavior, 34,* 113–125.

Rudman, L. A. (2004). Sources of implicit attitudes. *Current Directions in Psychological Science, 13,* 79–82.

Rudy, D., & Grusec. J. F. (2001). Correlates of authoritarian parenting in individualist and collectivist cultures and implications for understanding the transmission of values. *Journal of Cross-Cultural Psychology, 32,* 202–212.

Ruggieri, V., Milizia, M., Sabatini, N., & Tosi, M. T. (1983). Body perception in relation to muscular tone at rest and tactile sensitivity. *Perceptual and Motor Skills, 56,* 799–806.

Ruggiero, K. J., Smith, D. W., Hanson, R. F., Resnick, H. S., Saunders, B. E., Kilpatrick, D., et al. (2004). Is disclosure of childhood rape associated with mental health outcome? Results from the National Women's Study. *Child Maltreatment, 9,* 62–77.

Rumbaugh, D. M., Gill, T. V., & Von Glaserfeld, E. D. (1973). Reading and sentence completion by a chimpanzee (Pan troglodytes). *Science, 182,* 731–733.

Rumelhart, D. E., & McClelland, J. L. (1986). *Parallel distributed processing: Explorations into the microstructure of cognition.* Cambridge, MA: MIT Press.

Rumiati, R. I., & Humphreys, G. W. (1997). Visual object agnosia without alexia or propagnosia: Arguments for separate knowledge stores. *Visual Cognition, 4,* 207–217.

Rupert, P. A., & Baird, K. A. (2004). Managed care and the independent practice of psychology. *Professional Psychology: Research and Practice, 35,* 185–193.

Rushton, J. P., & Jensen, A. R. (2003). African-White IQ differences from Zimbabwe on the Wechsler Intelligence Scale for Children-Revised are mainly on the g factor. *Personality & Individual Differences, 34,* 177–183.

Rushton, J. P., & Rushton, E. W. (2003). Brain size, IQ, and racial-group differences: Evidence from musculoskeletal traits. *Intelligence, 31,* 139–155.

Russell, J. A., Bachorowski, J. -A., & Fernandez-Dols, J. -M. (2003). Facial and vocal expressions of emotion. *Annual Review of Psychology, 54,* 329–349.

Ruzgis, P. M., & Grigorenko, E. L. (1994). Cultural meaning systems, intelligence and personality. In R. J. Sternberg & P. Ruzgis (Eds.), *Personality and intelligence* (pp. 248–270). New York: Cambridge University Press.

Ryalls, B. O., & Ryalls, K. R. (2000). Infant imitation of peer and adult models: Evidence for a peer model advantage. *Merrill-Palmer Quarterly, 46,* 188–202.

Ryan, R. M., & Deci, E. L. (2001). On happiness and human potentials: A review of research on hedonic and eudaimonic well-being. *Annual Review of Psychology, 52,* 141–166.

Rybak, I. A., Gusakova, V. I., Golovan, A. V., Podladchikova, L. N., & Shevtsova, N. A. (1998). A model of attention-guided visual perception and recognition. *Vision Research, 38,* 2387–2400.

Rycroft, P. J. (2001). An evaluation of short-term group therapy for battered women. *Dissertation Abstracts International: Section B: The Sciences & Engineering, 61*(7-B). Univ. Microfilms International.

Sabbagh, M. N., Lukas, R. J., Sparks, D. L., & Reid, R. T. (2002). The nicotinic acetyl-choline receptor, smoking, and alzheimer's disease. *Journal of Alzheimer's Disease, 4,* 317–325.

Sabini, J., Siepmann, M., & Stein, J. (2001). The really fundamental attribution error in social psychological research. *Psychological Inquiry, 12*(1), 1–15.

Sachs, G., Steger-Wuchse. D., Kryspin-Exner, I., Gur, R. C., & Katschnig, H. (2004). Facial recognition deficits and cognition in schizophrenia. *Schizophrenia Research, 68,* 27–35.

Sackeim, H. A. (2001). Functional brain circuits in major depression and remission. *Archives of General Psychiatry, 58,* 649–650.

Sadock, B. J., & Sadock, V. A. (Eds.). (2003). *Synopsis of psychiatry: Behavioral sciences/clinical psychiatry.* Philadelphia: Lippincott Williams & Wilkins.

Safren, S. A., Otto, M. W., Worth, J. L., Salomon, E., Johnson, W., Mayer, K., & Boswell, S. (2001). Two strategies to increase adherence to HIV antiretroviral medication: Life-Steps and medication monitoring. *Behavior Research & Therapy, 39,* 1151–1162.

Sagarin, R. B., Cialdini, R. B., Rice, W. E., & Serna, S. B. (2002). Dispelling the illusion of invulnerability: The motivations and mechanisms of resistance to persuasion. *Journal of Personality and Social Psychology, 83,* 526–541.

Salanova, M., Llorens, S., Cifre, E., Martinez, I., & Schaufeli, W. B. (2003). Perceived collective efficacy, subjective well-being and task performance among electronic work groups: An experimental study. *Small Group Research, 34,* 43–73.

Salminen, S., & Glad, T. (1992). The role of gender in helping behavior. *The Journal of Social Psychology, 132,* 131–133.

Salmivalli, C., & Kaukiainen, A. (2004). "Female aggression" revisited: Variable- and person-centered approaches to studying gender differences in different types of aggression. *Aggressive Behavior, 30,* 158–163.

Salovey, P., & Mayer, J. D. (1990). Emotional intelligence, *Imagination, Cognition, and Personality, 9,* 185–211.

Salovey, P., & Pizarro, D. A. (2003). The value of emotional intelligence. In R. J. Sternberg, J. Lautrey, & T. I. Lubart (Eds.), *Models of intelligence: International perspectives* (pp. 263–278). Washington, DC: American Psychological Association.

Salter, D., McMillan, D., Richards, M., Talbot, T., Hodges, J., Bentovim, A., et al. (2003). Development of sexually abusive behaviour in sexually victimised males: A longitudinal study. *Lancet, 361,* 471–476.

Salthouse, T. A. (1999). Theories of cognition. In V. L. Bengtson & K. W. Schale (Eds.), *Handbook of theories of aging* (pp. 196–208). New York: Springer.

Salthouse, T. A. (2001). A research strategy for investigating group differences in a cognitive construct: Application to ageing and executive processes. *European Journal of Cognitive Psychology, 13,* 29–46.

Salthouse, T. A., Atkinson, T. M., & Berish, D. E. (2003). Executive functioning as a potential mediator of age-related cognitive decline in normal adults. *Journal of Experimental Psychology: General, 132,* 566–594.

Sammons, M. T. (2001). Combined treatments for mental disorders: Clinical dilemmas. In M. T. Sammons & N. B. Schmidt (Eds.), *Combined treatments for mental disorders* (pp. 11–32.). Washington, DC: American Psychological Association.

Sammons, M. T., Gorny, S. W., Zinner, E. S., & Allen, R. P. (2000). Prescriptive authority for psychologists: A consensus of support. *Professional Psychology: Research & Practice, 31,* 604–609.

Samoriski, G. M., & Gross, R. A. (2000). Functional compartmentalization of opioid desensitization in primary sensory neurons. *Journal of Pharmacology & Experimental Therapeutics, 294,* 500–509.

Sampson, E. (2000). Reinterpreting individualism and collectivism: Their religious roots and monologic versus dialogic person-other relationship. *American Psychologist, 55,* 1425–1432.

Sanchez, F. J. (2002). The lost men: Life stories from the IMCC. *American Psychological Association Newsletter,* unique identifier 308512004–000. Retrieved July 4, 2004, from www.apa.org.divisions/div51

Sanders, C. (2004). Conjoined twins. Essay on twinstuff.com. Retrieved June 25, 2004, from http://twinstuff.com/conjoined.htm

Sanders, C. E., Field, T. M., Diego, M., & Kaplan, M. (2000). The relationship of Internet use to depression and social isolation among adolescents. *Adolescence, 35,* 237–242.

Sanders, M. S., & McCormick, E. J. (1993). *Human factors in engineering and design* (7th ed.). New York: McGraw-Hill.

Sanders, R. E., & Delin, P. S. (2000). Transliminality and the telepathic transmission of emotional states: An exploratory study. *Journal of the American Society for Psychical Research, 94(1–2),* 1–24.

Sanderson, S., & Thompson, V. L. S. (2002). Factors associated with perceived paternal involvement in childrearing. *Sex Roles, 46,* 99–111.

Sandkuehler, J. (2002). Fear the pain. *Lancet, 360(9331),* 426.

Santisteban, D. A., Coatsworth, J. D., Perez-Vidal, A., Kurtines, W. M., Schwartz, S. J., LaPerriere, A., et al. (2003). Efficacy of brief strategic family therapy in modifying Hispanic adolescent behavior problems and substance use. *Journal of Family Psychology, 17,* 121–133.

Sato, N., & Nakamura, K. (2003). Visual response properties of neurons in the parahypocampal cortex of monkeys. *Journal of Neurophysiology, 90,* 876–886

Sattler, J. M. (1992). *Assessment of children: Revised and updated* (3rd ed.), San Diego: Jerome M. Sattler.

Saucier, D. M., Green, S. M., Leason, J., MacFadden, A., Bell, S., & Elias, L. J. (2002). Are sex differences in navigation caused by sexually dimorphic strategies or by differences in the ability to use the strategies? *Behavioral Neuroscience, 116,* 403–410.

Sawa, A., & Kamiya, A. (2003). Elucidating the pathogenesis of schizophrenia: DISC-I gene may predispose to neurodevelopmental changes underlying schizophrenia. *British Medical Journal, 327,* 632–633.

Scarr, S. (1998). American child care today. *American Psychologist, 53(2),* 95–108.

Schachter, S. L. (1959). *The psychology of affiliation.* Stanford, CA: Stanford University Press.

Schachter, S., & Singer, J. E. (1962). Cognitive, social, and physiological determinants of emotional state. *Psychological Review, 69,* 379–399.

Schacter, D. L. (2001). *The seven sins of memory: How the mind forgets and remembers.* Boston: Houghton Mifflin.

Schafe, G. E., & Bernstein, I. L. (1996). Taste aversion learning. In E. D. Capaldi (Ed.) *Why we eat what we eat: The psychology of eating* (pp.31–51). Washington, DC: American Psychological Association.

Schaie, K. W. (1993). The Seattle longitudinal studies of adult intelligence. *Current Directions in Psychological Science, 2,* 171–175.

Schall, U., Johnston, P., Todd, J., Ward, P., & Michie, P. T. (2003). Functional neuroanatomy of auditory sensory memory: An event-related fMRI study. *Australian Journal of Psychology, 55* (Suppl.), 90.

Schanda, H., Knecht, G., Schreinzer, D., Stompe, Th., Ortwein-Swoboda, G., & Waldhoer, Th. (2004). Homicide and major mental disorders: A 25-year study. *Acta Psychiatrica Scandinavica, 110,* 98–107.

Schelbel, A. B., Conrad, T., Perdue, S., Tomiyasu, U., & Wechsler, A. (1990). A quantitative study of dendrite complexity in selected areas of the human cerebral cortex. *Brain Cognition, 12,* 85–101.

Scher, A., & Mayseless, O. (2000). Mothers of anxious/ambivalent infants: Maternal characteristics and child-care context. *Child Development, 71(6),* 1629–1639.

Scher, M. (2001). Male therapist, male client: Reflections on critical dynamics. In G. R. Brooks & G. E. Good (Eds.), *The new handbook of psychotherapy and counseling with men: A comprehensive guide to settings, problems, and treatment approaches, 1 & 3* (pp. 719–733). New York: Jossey-Bass.

Scherer, K. R. (1997). The role of culture in emotionantecedent appraisal. *Journal of Personality and Social Psychology, 73,* 902–922.

Schiffman, J., LaBrie, J., Carter, J., Cannon, T., Schulsinger, F., Parnas, J., & Mednick, S. (2002). Perception of parent-child relationship in highrisk families, and adult schizophrenia outcome of offspring. *Journal of Psychiatric Research, 36,* 41–47.

Schiller, P. H. (1998). The neural control of visually guided eye movements. In J. E. Richards (Ed.), *Cognitive neuroscience of attention: A development perspective* (pp. 3–50). Mahwah, NJ: Erlbaum.

Schindler-Zimmerman, T., & Haddock, S. A. (2001). The weave of gender and culture in the tapestry of a family therapy training program: Promoting social justice in the practice of family therapy. *Journal of Feminist Family Therapy, 12,* 1–31.

Schinka, J. A., Dye, D. A., & Curtiss, G. (1997). Correspondence between five-factor and RI-ASEC models of personality. *Journal of Personality Assessment, 68,* 355–368.

Schleicher, D. J., Watt, J. D., & Greguras, G. J. (2004). Reexamining the job satisfaction-performance relationship: The complexity of attitudes. *Journal of Applied Psychology, 89,* 165–177.

Schmidt, D. F., & Boland, S. M. (1986). Struture of perceptions of older adults: Evidence for multiple stereotypes. *Psychology and Aging, 1,* 255–260.

Schmidit, E.M., Bak, M. J., Hambrecht, Et., Kufta, C. V., O'Rourke, D. K., & Vallabhanath, P. (1996). Feasibility of a visual prosthesis for the blind based on intracortical microstimulation of the visual cortex. *Brain, 119,* 507–522.

Schmidt, F. L., & Hunter, J. E. (1998). The validity and utility of selection methods in personnel psychology: Practical and theoretical implications of 85 years of research findings. *Psychological Bulletin, 124,* 262–274.

Schmitt, D. P., & 118 members of the International Sexuality Description Project. (2003). Universal sex differences in the desire for sexual variety: Tests from 52 nations, 6 continents, and 13 islands. *Journal of Personality and Social Psychology, 85,* 85–104.

Schmitt, D. P., Shackelford, T. K., Duntley, J., Tooke, W., Buss, D. M., Fisher, M. L., Lavellee, M., & Vasey, P. (2002). Is there an early-30s peak in female sexual desire? Cross-sectional evidence from the United States and Canada. *Canadian Journal of Human Sexuality,* 111–18.

Schmitt, K. L., Anderson, D. R., & Collins, P. A. (1999). Form and content: Looking at visual features of television. *Developmental Psychology, 35(4),* 1156–1167.

Schmitz, J. M., Averill, P., Stotts, A. L., Moeller, F. G., Rhoades, H. M., & Grabowski, J. (2001). Fluoxetine treatment of cocaine-dependent patients with major depressive disorder. *Drug & Alcohol Dependence, 63,* 207–214.

Schmitz, S. (1999). Gender differences in acquisition of environmental knowledge related to wayfinding ability, spatial anxiety, and self-estimated environmental competencies. *Sex Roles, 41,* 71–94.

Schneider, I. (1987). The theory and practice of movie psychiatry. *American Journal of Psychiatry, 144,* 996–1002.

Schneiderman, N., Antoni, M. H., Saab, P. G., & Ironson, G. (2001). Health psychology: Psychosocial and biobehavioral aspects of chronic disease management. *Annual Review of Psychology, 52,* 555–580.

Schneier, F. R. (2003). Social anxiety disorder. *British Medical Journal, 327,* 515–516.

Schnur, E., Brooks-Gunn, J., & Shipman, V. C. (1992). Who attends programs serving poor children? The case of Head Start attendees and nonattendees. *Journal of Applied Developmental Psychology, 13,* 405–421.

Schnurr, P. P., Lunney, C. A., & Sengupta, A. (2004). Risk factors for the development versus maintenance of posttraumatic stress disorder. *Journal of Traumatic Stress, 17,* 85–95.

Schnyder, U., Moergeli, H., Klaghofer, R., & Buddeberg, C. (2001). Incidence and prediction of posttraumatic stress disorder symptoms in severely injured accident victims. *American Journal of Psychiatry, 158,* 594–599.

Scholl, B. J. (2000). Attenuated change blindness for exogenously attended items in a flicker paradigm. *Visual Cognition, 7,* 377–396.

Scholz, U., Gutiérrez Doña, B., Sud, S., & Schwarzer, R. (2002). Is general self-efficacy a universal construct? Psychometric findings from 25 countries, *European Journal of Psychological Assessment, 18,* 242–251.

Schooler, J. W., & Eich, E. (2000). Memory for emotional events. In E. Tulving and F. I. Craik (Eds.). *The Oxford handbook of memory* (pp. 379–392). New York: Oxford University Press.

Schrauf, R. W. (2000). Bilingual autobiographical memory: Experimental studies and clinical cases. *Culture and Psychology, 6,* 387–417.

Schredl, M., Ciric, P., Bishop, A., Golitz, E., & Buschtons, D. (2003). Content analysis of German students' dreams: Comparison to American findings. *Dreaming, 13,* 237–243.

Schredl, M., Dombrowe, C., Bozzer, A., & Morlock, M. (1999). Do subliminal stimuli affect dream content? Methodological issues and empirical data. *Sleep & Hypnosis, 1,* 181–185.

Schredl, M., & Hofmann, F. (2003). Continuity between waking activities and dream activities. *Consciousness & Cognition, 12,* 298–299.

Schroeder, K., Fahey, T., & Ebrahim, S. (2004). How can we improve adherence to blood pressure-lowering medication in ambulatory care? Systematic review of randomized controlled trials. *Archives of Internal Medicine, 164,* 722–732.

Schuelein, J.A. (2003). On the logic of psychoanalytic theory. *International Journal of Psychoanalysis, 84,* 315–330.

Schulberg, H. C., & Rush, A. J. (1994). Clinical practice guidelines for managing major depression in primary care practice: Implications for psychologists. *American Psychologist, 49,* 34–41.

Schultz, A., Williams, D., Israel, B., Becker, A., Parker, E., James, S.A., & Jackson, J. (2000). Unfair treatment, neighborhood effects, and mental health in the Detroit metropolitan area. *The Journal of Health and Social Behavior, 41,* 314–333.

Schultz, D.P., & Schultz, S. E. (2004). *A history of modern psychology* (8th ed). Belmont, CA: Wadsworth.

Schultz, G., & Melzack, R. (1999). A case of referred pain evoked by remote light touch after partial nerve injury. *Pain, 81,* 199–202.

Schulze, T.G., Buervenich, S., Badner, J.A., Steele, C.J. M., Detera-Wadleigh, S. D., Dick, D., et al. (2004). Loci on chromosomes 6q and 6p interact to increase susceptibility to bipolar affective disorder in the National Institute of Mental Health genetics initiative pedigrees. *Biological Psychiatry, 56,* 18–23.

Schwartz, B. (2000). Pitfalls on the road to a positive psychology of hope. In J.E. Gillham (Ed.). *The science of optimism and hope: Research essays in honor of Martin E. P. Seligman* (399–412). Philadelphia, PA: Templeton Foundation Press.

Schwartz, J. (2004, May 6). Simulated prison showed fine line between "normal" and "monster." *New York Times,* Sec. A, P.2.

Schwartz, S., & Maquet, P. (2002). Sleep imaging and the neuro-psychological assessment of dreams. *Trends in Cognitive Science, 6,* 23–30.

Schweinle, W. E., Ickes, W., & Bernstein, J. H. (2002). Empathic inaccuracy in husband to wife aggression: The overattribution bias. *Personal Relationships, 9,* 141–158.

Scientists study body's hunger signals. (2003, Jan. 1). *Biotech Week,* 136–138.

Schifiwire. (2002, October 17). Poll reveals UFO belief. *Scifiwire,* Retrieved March 1, 2004, from http://www.scifi.com/scifiwire/art-main.html?2002-10/17/11.00sic

Scollon, C. N., Diener, E., Oishi, S., & Biswas-Diener, R. (2004). Emotions across cultures and methods. *Journal of Cross-Cultural Psychology, 35,* 304–326.

Scott, K., Brady, R., Cravchik, A., Morozov, P., Rzhetsky, A., Zuker, C., & Axel, R. (2001). A chemosensory gene family encoding candidate gustatory and olfactory receptors in *Drosophila, Cell, 104,* 661–673.

Scott, S. D., Mandryk, R. L., & Inkpen, K. M. (2003) Understanding children's collaborative interactions in shared environments. *Journal of Computer Assisted Learning, 19,* 220–228.

Scrimsher, S., & Tudge, J. (2003). The teaching/learning relationship in the first years of school: Some revolutionary implications of Vygotsky's theory. *Early Education and Development, 14,* 293–312.

Scully, J.A., Tosi, H., & Banning, K. (2000). Life event checklists: Revisiting the Social Readjustment Rating Scale after 30 years. *Educational & Psychological Measurement, 60,* 864–876.

Sebre, S., Sprugevica, I., Novotni, A., Bonevski, D., Pakalniskiene, V., Popescu, D., et al. (2004). Cross-cultural comparisons of child-reported emotional and physical abuse: Rates, risk factors and psychosocial symptoms. *Child Abuse & Neglect, 28,* 113–127.

Segerstrom, S. C., Castañeda, J.O., & Spencer, T. E. (2003). Optimism effects on cellular immunity: Testing the affective and persistence models. *Personality & Individual Differences, 35,* 1615–1624.

Segraves, T., & Althol, S. (2002). Psychotherapy and pharmacotherapy for sexual dysfunctions. In P. E. Nathan & J. M. Gorman (Eds.). *A guide to treatments that work* (pp. 367–410). New York: Oxford Press.

Seidman, S. M. (2003). The aging male: Androgens, erectile dysfunction, and depression. *Journal of Clinical Psychiatry, 64,* 31–37.

Seijts, G. H., & Latham, B. W. (2003). Creativity through applying ideas from fields other than one's own: Transferring knowledge from social psychology to industrial/organizational psychology. *Canadian Psychology, 44,* 232–239.

Selekman, M.D. (1993). Solution-oriented brief therapy with difficult adolescents. In S. Friedman (Ed.), *The new language of change: Constructive collaboration in psychotherapy* (pp. 138–157). New York: Guilford Press.

Self, D. (2003). Dopamine as chicken and egg. *Nature, 422,* 573–574.

Seligman, M. E. P. (1976). *Learned helplessness and depression in animals and humans.* Morristown, NJ: General Learning.

Seligman, M.E.P., & Csikszentmihalyi, M. (2000). Positive psychology. *American Psychologist, 55,* 5–14.

Selkoe, D. J. (1992, September). Aging brain, aging mind. *Scientific American,* 135–142.

Sell, R. L., Wells, J.A., & Wypij, D. (1995). The prevalence of homosexual behavior and attraction in the United States, the United Kingdom, and France: Results of national population-based samples. *Archives of Sexual Behavior, 24,* 235–248.

Sellers, R. M., Caldwell, C. H., Schmeelk-Cone, K. H., & Zimmerman, M. A. (2003). Racial identity, racial discrimination, perceived stress, and psychological distress among African American young adults. *Journal of Health and Social Behavior, 44,* 302–316.

Selye, H. (1956). *The stress of life.* New York: McGraw-Hill.

Selye, H. (1976). *Stress in health and disease.* London: Butterworth.

Sen, M. G., Yonas, A., & Knill, D. C. (2001). Development of infants' sensitivity to surface contour information for spatial layout. *Perception, 30,* 167–176.

Sen, S., Villafuerte, S., Nesse, R., Stoltenberg, S. F., Hopcian, J., Gleiberman, L., et al. (2004). Serotonin transporter and GABA (?) alpha 6 receptor variants are associated with neuroticism. *Biological Psychiatry, 55,* 244–249.

Sentencing Project. (2002). *Mentally ill offenders in the criminal justice system: An analysis and prescription.* Retrieved July, 27, 2004, from http://www.soros.org/initiatives/justice/articles_publications/publications/mi_offenders_20020101/mentallyill.pdf

Serin, R. C., & Marshall, W. L. (2003). Personality disorders. In M. Hersen & S. M. Turner (Eds.). *Adult psychopathology and diagnosis* (4th ed., pp. 615–650). New York: Wiley.

Shalowitz, M. U., Berry, C. A., Rasinski, K. A., & Dannhausen-Brun, C. A. (1998). A new measurement of contemporary life stress: Development, validation, and reliability of the CRISYS (Crisis in Family Systems). *Health Services Research, 33*, 1381–1382.

Shamir, B. (1992). Attribution of influence and charisma to the leader: The romance of leadership revisited. *Journal of Applied Social Psychology, 22*, 386–407.

Sharhabani-Arzy, R., Amir, M., Kotler, M., & Liran, R. (2003). The toll of domestic violence. *Journal of Interpersonal Violence, 18*, 1335–1346.

Shatz, M., & Gelman, R. (1973). The development of communication skills: Modifications in the speech of young children as a function of listener. *Monographs of the Society for Research in Child Development, 38* (2, Serial No. 152).

Shatz, S. M. (2000). The relationship of locus of control and social support to adult nursing home residents. *Dissertation Abstracts International: Section B: The Sciences & Engineering, 61*(3-B), 1655.

Shaughnessy, M. F., & Haight, M. (2003). Interview with Donald Meichenbaum. *North American Journal of Psychology, 5*, 213–222.

Shaw, G. M., Shapiro, R. Y., Lock, S., & Jacobs, L. R. (1998). Trends: Crime, the police, and civil liberties. *Public Opinion Quarterly, 62*, 405–426.

Shaywitz, S. E., Shaywitz, B. A., Fulbright, R. K., Skudlarski, P., Menel, W.E., Constable, R. T., et al. (2003). Neural systems for compensation and persistence: Young adult outcome of childhood reading disability. *Biological Psychiatry, 54*, 25–33.

Sheets, V.L., & Wolfe, M. D. (2001). Sexual jealousy in heterosexuals, lesbians, and gays. *Sex Roles, 44*, 255–276.

Sheldon, A. B. (1969). Preference for familiar versus novel stimuli as a function of the familiarity of the environment. *Journal of Comparative & Physiological Psychology, 67*, 516–521.

Shelton, C. M. (2000). *Achieving moral health: An exercise plan for your conscience.* New York: Crossroad.

Sherin, J. E., Shiromani, P.J., McCarley, R. W., & Saper, C. B. (1996). Activation of ventrolateral preoptic neurons during sleep. *Science, 271*, 216–219.

Sherrington, R., Rogaev, E.I., Liang, Y., Rogaeva, E. A., Levesque, G., lkeda, M., et al. (1995).

Cloning of a gene bearing missense mutations in early-onset familial Alzheimer's disease. *Nature, 375*, 754–760.

Shields, S. A. (1975). Functionalism, Darwinism, and the psychology of women: A study in social myth. *American Psychologist, 30*, 852–857.

Shields, S. A. (2002). *Speaking from the heart: Gender and the social meaning of emotion.* Cambridge, England: Cambridge University Press.

Shiner, R. L. (1998). How shall we speak of children's personalities in middle childhood? A preliminary taxonomy. *Psychological Bulletin, 124*, 308–332.

Shoda, Y., LeeTiernan, S., & Mischel, W. 2002). Personality as a dynamic system: Emergence of stability and distinctiveness from intra- and interpersonal interactions. *Personality and Social Psychology Review, 6*, 316–326.

Shonkoff, J. P. (2000, October). *From neurons to neighborhoods: The science of early childhood development.* Briefing presented at the National Research Council and Institute of Medicine, Washington, DC.

Shostrom, E. L. (1974). *Manual for the Personal Orientation Inventory.* San Diego, CA: Educational and Industrial Testing Service.

Shukla-Mehta, S., & Albin, R. W. (2003). Twelve practical strategies to prevent behavioral escalation in classroom settings. *Clearing House, 77*, 50–56.

Si, G., Rethorst, S., & Willimczik, K. (1995). Causal attribution perception in sports achievement: A Cross-Cultural study on attributional concepts in Germany and China. *Journal of Cross-Cultural Psychology, 26*, 537–553.

Sias, P.M., Heath, R. G., Perry, T., Silva, D., & Fix, B. (2004). Narratives of workplace friendship deterioration. *Journal of Social & Personal Relationships, 21* 321–340.

Siegel, J. M. (2003). Why we sleep. *Scientific American, 289*, 92–97.

Siegel, J. M. (2004). Hypocretin (orexin): Role in normal behavior and neuropathology. *Annual Review of Psychology, 55*, 125–152.

Siegel, S. (1999). Drug anticipation and drug addiction: The 1998 H. David Archibald lecture. *Addiction, 94*, 1113–1124.

Siegel, S., Baptista, M. A. S., Kim, J.A., McDonald, R. V., & Weise-Kelly, L. (2000). Pavlovian psychopharmacology: The associative basis of tolerance. *Experimental & Clinical Psychopharmacology, 8*, 276–293.

Siegel, S., & Ramos, B. M. C. (2002). Applying laboratory research: Drug anticipation and the treatment of drug addiction. *Experimental and Clinical Psychopharmacology, 10*, 162–183.

Silk, J. S., Morris, A. S., Kanaya, T., & Steinberg, L. S (2003), Psychological control and autonomy granting: Opposite ends of a continuum of constructs. *Journal of Research on Adolescence, 13(1)*, 113–118.

Silverman, I., Choi, J., Mackewn, A., Fisher, M., Moro, J., & Olshansky, E. (2000). Evolved mechanisms underlying wayfinding: Further studies on the hunter-gatherer theory of spatial sex differences. *Evolution & Human Behavior, 21*, 201–213.

Silverman, J. G., Raj, A., Mucci, L. A., & Hathaway, J. E. (2001). Dating violence against adolescent girls and associated substance use, unhealthy weight control, sexual risk behavior, pregnancy, and suicidality. *Journal of the American Medical Association, 286*, 572–579.

Silvers, J. M., Tokunaga, S., Berry, R. B., White, A. M., & Matthews, D. B. (2003). Impairments in spatial learning and memory: Ethanol, allopregnanolone, and the hippocampus. *Brain Research Reviews, 43*, 275–284.

Simion, F., & Butterworth, G. (1998). *The development of sensory, motor and cognitive capacities in early infancy: From perception to cognition.* Hove, England: Psychology Press/Erlbaum, Taylor & Francis.

Simon, H. B. (2004). Longevity: The ultimate gender gap. *Scientific American*, Special Edition 14(3), 18–23.

Simon, L., (1998). *Genuine reality: A life of William James.* New York: Harcourt Brace.

Simon, R. W., & Nath, L. E. (2004). Gender and emotion in the United States: Do men and women differ in self-reports of feelings and expressive behavior? *American Journal of Sociology, 109*, 1137–1176.

Simons, D. J., & Chabris, C. F. (1999). Gorillas in our midst: Sustained inattentional blindness for dynamic events. *Perception, 28*, 1059–1074.

Simons, D. J., Franconeri, S. L., & Reimer, R. L. (2000). Change blindness in the absence of a visual disruption. *Perception, 29*, 1143–1154.

Singer, T., Lindenberger, U., & Baltes, P. B. (2003). Plasticity of memory for new learning in very old age: A story of major loss? *Psychology & Aging, 18*, 306–317.

Singh, D. (1993). Adaptive significance of female physical attractiveness: Role of waist-to-hip ratio. *Journal of Personality and Social Psychology, 65*, 293–307.

Singh, S., Wulf, D., Samara, R., & Cuca, Y. P. (2000). Gender differences in the timing of first intercourse: Data from 14 countries. *International Family Planning Perspectives, 26*, 21–28, 43.

Singleton, D., Tate, A., & Randall, G. (2003). *Salaries in psychology, 2001: Report of the 2001 APA salary survey.* American Psychological Association Research Office. Retrieved January 14,2004, from http://research.apa.org/01salary/index.html#intro

Sinha, B. K., Willson, L. R., & Watson, D. C. (2000). Stress and coping among students in India and Canada. *Canadian Journal of Behavioural Science, 32,* 218–225.

Skegg, K., Nada-Raja, S., Dickson, N., Paul, C., & Williams, S. (2003). Sexual orientation and self-harm in men and women. *American Journal of Psychiatry, 160,* 541–546.

Skinner, B. F. (1938). *The behavior of organisms.* New York: Appleton

Skinner, B. F. (1987). *Upon further reflection.* Englewood Cliffs, NJ: Prentice-Hall.

Skinner, B. F. (1988, June). Skinner joins aversives debate. *APA Monitor,* p. 22.

Slater, A., Quinn, P. C., Hayes, R., & Brown, E. (2000). The role of facial orientation in newborn infants' preference for attractive faces. *Developmental Science, 3(2),* 181–185.

Slattery, D. A., Hudson, A. L., & Nutt, D. J. (2004). The evolution of antidepressant mechanisms. *Fundamental & Clinical Pharmacology, 18,* 1–21.

Sleeter, C. E., & Grant, C. A. (2002). *Making choices for multicultural education: Five approaches to race class and gender.* New York: Wiley.

Slifer, K. J., Eischen, S. E., & Busby, S. (2002). Using counterconditioning to treat behavioural distress during subcutaneous injections in a pediatric rehabilitation patient. *Brain Injury, 16,* 901–916.

Smith, A. G. (2004). Behavioral problems in dementia. *Postgraduate Medicine, 115,* 47–54.

Smith, A., Vollmer-Conna, U., Bennett, B., Wakefield, D., Hickie, I., & Lloyd, A. (2004). The relationship between distress and the development of a primary immune response to a novel antigen. *Brain, Behavior, & Immunity, 18,* 65–75.

Smith, C. A., & Farrington, D. P. (2004). Continuities in antisocial behavior and parenting across three generations. *Journal of Child Psychology & Psychiatry & Allied Disciplines, 45,* 230–247.

Smith, D. (2002, October). The theory heard 'round the world. *Monitor on Psychology, 33,* 30–32.

Smith, J. (2002). Brief encounters and available places to land. *Psychodynamic Practice: Individuals, Groups & Organizations, 8(4),* 463–482.

Smith, J. A., Lumley, M. A., & Longo, D. J. (2002). Contrasting emotional approach coping with passive coping for chronic myofascial pain. *Annals of Behavioral Medicine, 24,* 326–335.

Smith, J. C. (2004). Alterations in brain and immune function produced by mindfulness meditation: Three caveats. *Psychosomatic Medicine, 66,* 148–149.

Smith, J. L., & White, P. H. (2002). An examination of implicitly activated, explicitly activated, and nullified stereotypes on mathematical performance: It's not just a woman's issue. *Sex Roles, 47,* 179–191.

Smith, J. R., & Terry, D. J. (2003). Attitude-behavior consistency: The role of group norms, attitude accessibility, and mode of behavioural decision-making. *European Journal of Social Psychology, 33,* 591–608.

Smith, L. B., Quittner, A. L., Osberger, M. J., & Miyamoto, R. (1998). Audition and visual attention: The developmental trajectory in deaf and hearing populations. *Developmental Psychology, 34(5),* 840–850.

Smith, M. L., Glass, G. V., & Miller, T. l. (1980). *The benefits of psychotherapy.* Baltimore: Johns Hopkins University Press.

Smith, M. W., Mendoza, R. P., & Lin, K. M. (1999). Gender and ethnic differences in the pharmacogenetics of psychotropics. In M. Herrera & W. B. Lawson (Eds.). *Cross-cultural psychiatry* (pp. 323–341). New York: Wiley.

Smith, P. B., & Bond, M. H. (1999). *Social psychology across cultures* (2nd ed.). Boston: Allyn & Bacon.

Smith, R. (2002). Professional educational psychology and community relations education in Northern Ireland. *Educational Psychology Service, Londonderry, United Kingdom, 18,* 275–295.

Smith, R. A. & Davis, S. F. (2003). *The psychologist as detective* (3rd ed.). Upper Saddle River, NJ: Prentice Hall.

Sneed, C. D., McCrae, R. R., & Funder, D. C. (1998). Lay conceptions of the five-factor model and its indicators. *Personality & Social Psychology Bulletin, 24,* 115–126.

Snelders, H. J., & Lea, S. E. (1996). Different kinds of work, different kinds of pay: An examination of the overjustification effect. *Journal of Socio-Economics, 25,* 517–535.

Snider, V. E., Frankenberger, W., Aspenson, M. R. (2000). The relationship between learning disabilities and Attention Deficit Hyperactivity Disorder: A national survey. *Developmental Disabilities Bulletin, 28(1),* 18–38.

Snyder, C. R., & Lopez, S. J. (Eds.) (2002). *Handbook of positive psychology,* New York: Oxford University Press.

Snyder, C. R., Rand, K. L., & Sigmon, D. R. (2002). Hope theory: A member of the positive psychology family. In C. R. Snyder & S. J. Lopez (Eds.), *Handbook of positive psychology* (pp. 257–276). New York: Oxford University Press.

Soares, C. (2002, July). Inner turmoil: Prescription privileges make some psychologists anxious. *Scientific American, 287(1),* 25–26.

Soares, J. C., & Mann, J. (1997). The functional neuroanatomy of mood disorders. *Journal of Psychiatric Research, 31,* 393–432.

Sobell, L. C., Cunningham, J. A., & Sobell, M. B. (1996). Recovery from alcohol problems with and without treatment: Prevalence in two population surveys. *American Journal of Public Health, 86,* 966–972.

Soderstrom, M., Dolbier, C., Leiferman, J., & Steinhardt, M. (2000). The relationship of hardiness, coping strategies, and perceived stress to symptoms of illness. *Journal of Behavioral Medicine, 23,* 311–328.

Sohlberg, S., & Birgegard, A. (2003). Persistent complex subliminal activation effects: First experimental observations. *Journal of Personality and Social Psychology, 85,* 302–316.

Soken, N. H., & Pick, A. D. (1999). Infants' perception of dynamic affective expressions: Do infants distinguish specific expressions? *Child Development, 70,* 1275–1282

Sokolov, R. (1999). Culture and obesily. *Social Research, 66,* 31–38.

Sokolowski, K., Schmalt, H. D., Langens, T. A., & Puca, R. M. (2000). Assessing achievement, affiliation, and power motives all at once: The Multi-Motive Grid (MMG). *Journal of Personality Assessment, 74,* 126–145.

Solms, M. (2003). Dreaming and REM sleep are controlled by different brain mechanisms. In E. F. Pace-Schott, M. Solms, M. Blagrove, & S. Harnad (Eds.), *Sleep and dreaming: Scientific advances and reconsiderations* (pp. 51–58). New York: Cambridge University Press.

Solms, M. (2004). Freud returns. *Scientific American, 290(5),* 82–88.

Solms, M., & Turnbull, O. (2002). *The brain and the inner world.* New York: Other Press.

Solomon, P. R., Flynn, D., Mirak, J., Brett, M., Coslov, N., & Groccia, M. E. (1998). Five-year retention of the classically conditioned eyeblink response in young adult, middle-aged, and older humans. *Psychology and Aging, 13,* 186–192.

Sommerhalder, J., Oueghlani, E., Bagnoud, M., Leonards, U., Safran, A. B., & Pelizzone, M. (2003). Simulation of artificial vision: Eccentric reading of isolated words, and perceptual learning. *Vision Research, 43,* 269–283.

Sommerich, C. M., Joines, S. M. B., & Psihogios, J. P. (2001). Effects of computer monitor viewing angle and related factors on strain, performance, and preference outcomes. *Human Factors, 43*, 39–55.

Sonn, C. C., & Fisher, A. T. (1998). Sense of community: Community resilient responses to oppression and change. *Journal of Community Psychology, 26*, 457–472.

Sonnenborg, F. A., Andersen, O. K., & Arendt-Nielsen, L. (2000). Modular organization of excitatory and inhibitory reflex receptive fields elicited by electrical stimulation of the foot sole in man. *Clinical Neurophysiology, 11*, 2160–2169.

Sosik, J. J., Kahai, S. S., & Avolio, B. J. (1998). Transformational leadership and dimensions of creativity: Motivating idea generation in computer-mediated groups, *Creativity Research Journal, 11*, 111–121.

Soto-Faraco, S., Spence, C., Lloyed, D., & Kingstone, A. (2004). Moving multisensory research along: Motion perception across sensory modalities. *Current Directions in Psychological Science, 13*, 29–32.

Soussignan, R. (2002). The Duchenne smile, emotional experience, and autonomic reactivity: A test of the facial feedback hypothesis. *Emotion, 2*, 52–74.

South America for visitors, (2004). Retrieved May 20, 2004, from http://gosouthamerica. about.com/cs/culturel/

Spangler, W. D. (1992). Validity of questionnaire and TAT measures of need for achievement: Two meta-analyses. *Psychological Bulletin, 112*, 140–154.

Spanos, N. P. (1994). Multiple identity enactments and multiple personality disorder: A sociocognitive perspective. *Psychological Bulletin, 116*, 143–165.

Spelke, E. S. (2000). Core knowledge. *American Psychologist, 55*, 1233–1243.

Spelke, E. S., Breinlinger, K., Jacobson, K., & Phillips, A. (1993). Gestalt relations and object perception: A developmental study. *Perception, 22*, 1483–1501.

Spencer, R. M. C., Zelaznik, H. N., Diedrichsen, J., & lvry, R. B. (2003). Disrupted timing of discontinuous but not continuous movements by cerebellar lesions. *Science, 300*, 1437–1439.

Sperling, G. (1960). The information available in brief visual presentations. *Psychological Monographs, 74*(11, Whole No. 498).

Spiegel, D. (1998). Hypnosis. *Harvard Mental Health Letter, 15*(3), 5–6.

Sprecher, S., & Regan, P. C. (2002). Liking some things (in some people) more than others: Partner preference in romantic relationships and friendships. *Journal of Social and Personal Relationships, 19*, 463–481.

Sprecher, S., & Toro-Morn, M. (2002). A study of men and women from different sides of earth to determine if men are from Mars and women are from Venus in their beliefs about love and romantic relationships. *Sex Roles, 46*, 131–147.

Springer, P. J. (2000). The relationship between learned helplessness and work performance in registered nurses. *Dissertation Abstracts International: Section B: The Sciences & Engineering, 60*(12-B), 6407.

Springer, S. P., & Deutsch, G. (1998). *Left brain, right brain: Perspectives from cognitive neuroscience* (5th ed.). New York: Freeman.

Squire, L. R., & Kandel, E. R. (1999). *Memory: From mind to molecules*. New York: Freeman.

Sroufe, A. A. (2003). Attachment categories as reflections of multiple dimensions: Comment on Fraley and Spieker. *Developmental Psychology, 39*, 413–416.

Stalker, C. A., Levene, J. E., & Coady, N. F. (1999). Solution focused brief therapy—one model fits all? *Families in Society, 80*, 468–477.

Stanton-Salazar, R. D., & Spina, S. U. (2003). Informal mentors and role models in the lives of urban Mexican-origin adolescents. *Anthropology & Education Quarterly, 34*, 231–254.

Starcevic, V., Linden, M., Uhlenhuth, E. H., Kolar, D., & Latas, M. (2004). Treatment of panic disorder with agoraphobia in an anxiety disorders clinic: Factors influencing psychiatrists' treatment choices. *Psychiatry Research, 125*, 41–52.

Steele, C. M. (1997). A threat in the air: How stereotypes shape intellectual identity and performance. *American Psychologist, 52*, 613–629.

Steele, C. M. (1999). The psychology of self-affirmation: Sustaining the integrity of the self. In R. F. Baumeister (Ed.). *The self in social psychology* (pp. 372–390). Philadelphia: Psychology Press/Taylor & Francis.

Steele, C. M., & Aronson, J. (1995). Stereotype threat and the intellectual test performance of African Americans. *Journal of Personality and Social Psychology, 69*, 797–811.

Steele, C. M., & Aronson, J. (2000). Stereotype threat and the intellectual test performance of African Americans. In C. Stangor (Ed.), *Stereotypes and prejudice: Essential readings* (pp. 369–389). Philadelphia: Psychology Press/ Taylor & Francis.

Stein, H. H. (2003). Good psychoanalytic psychotherapy in film: Three unorthodox examples. *Psychoanalytic Psychology, 20*, 701–709.

Stein, M. B., Walker, J. R., & Forde, D. R. (1996). Public-speaking fears in a community sample: Prevalence, impact on

functioning, and diagnostic classification, *Archives of General Psychiatry, 53*, 169–174.

Stein, M. B., Walker, J. R., & Forde, D. R. (2000). Gender differences in susceptibility to posttraumatic stress disorder. *Behaviour Research and Therapy, 38*, 619–628.

Steinberg, L. (2001). We know some things: Parent-adolescent relationships in retrospect and prospective. *Journal of Research on Adolescence, 11*(1), 1–19.

Steinberg, L., Lamborn, S. D., Dornbusch, S. M., & Darling, N. (1992). Impact of parenting practices on adolescent achievement: Authoritative parenting, school involvement, and encouragement to succeed. *Child Development, 63*, 1266–1281.

Steinberg, M. (1995). *Handbook for the assessment of dissociation: A clinical guide*. Washington, DC: American Psychiatric Press.

Steinkamp, F. (2000). Does precognition foresee the future? A postal experiment to assess the possibility of precognition. *Journal of Parapsychology, 64*(1), 3–18.

Stephan, N., Vozarova, B., Del Parigi, A., Ossowski, V., Thompson, D. B., Hanson, R. L., Ravussin, E., et al., (2002). The Gln223Arg polymorphism of the leptin receptor in Pima Indians: Influence on energy expenditure, physical activity and lipid metabolism. *International Journal of Obesity, 26*, 1629–1632.

Stern, K., & McClintock, M. K. (1998). Regulation of ovulation by human pheromones. *Nature, 392*, 126–127.

Sternberg, E. M., & Gold, P. W. (2002). The mind-body interaction in disease. *Scientific American, 12*(Special Ed., 1), 82–89.

Sternberg, R. J. (1986). A triangular theory of love. *Psychological Review, 93*, 119–135.

Sternberg, R. J. (2000a). Identifying and developing creative giftedness. *Roeper Review, 23*, 60–64.

Sternberg, R. J. (2000b), Implicit theories of intelligence as exemplar stories of success: Why intelligence test validity is in the eye of the beholder. *Psychology, Public Policy, & Law, 6*, 159–167.

Sternberg, R. J. (2001a). Successful intelligence: A unified view of giftedness. In C. F. M. van Lieshout & P. G. Heymans (Eds.), *Developing talent across the life span* (pp. 43–65). Philadelphia: Psychology Press/ Taylor & Francis.

Sternberg, R. J. (2001b). What is the Common thread of creativity?: Its dialectical relation to intelligence and wisdom. *American Psychologist, 56*, 360–362.

Sternberg, R. J. (2002, August). *Wisdom, schooling, and society*. Paper presented at the annual meeting of the American Psychological

Association, Chicago, IL. Retrieved January 4, 2004, from http://www.gallup.hu/ pps/sternberg_long.htm

Sternberg, R. J. (2003a). A broad view of intelligence: The theory of successful intelligence. *Consulting Psychology Journal: Practice and Research, 55,* 139–154.

Sternberg, R. J. (2003b). Construct validity of the theory of successful intelligence. In R. J. Sternberg, J. Lautrey, & T. I. Lubart (Eds.), *Models of intelligence: International perspectives* (pp. 55–77). Washington, DC: American Psychological Association.

Sternberg, R. J. (2003c). *Wisdom, intelligence, and creativity synthesized.* Cambridge, England: Cambridge University Press.

Sternberg, R. J., Castegon, J. L., Prieto, M. D., Hautamki, J., & Grigorenko, E. L. (2001). Confirmatory factor analysis of the Sternberg Triarchic Abilities Test in three international samples: An empirical test of the triarchic theory of intelligence. *European Journal of Psychological Assessment, 17*(1), 1–16.

Sternberg, R. J., & Grigorenko, E. L. (2000a). Practical intelligence and its development. In R. Bar-On, & J. D. A. Parker (Eds.), *The handbook of emotional intelligence: Theory, development, assessment, and application at home, school, and in the workplace* (pp. 215–243). San Francisco: Jossey-Bass.

Sternberg, R. J., & Grigorenko, E. L. (2000b). Theme-park psychology: A case study regarding human intelligence and its implications for education. *Educational Psychology Review, 12*(2), 247–268.

Sternberg, R. J., Grigorenko, E. L., & Bundy, D. A. (2001). The predictive value of IQ. *Merrill-Palmer Quarterly, 47,* 1–41.

Sternberg, R. J., Lautrey, J., & Lubart, T. I. (2003). Where are we in the field of intelligence, how did we get here, and where are we going? In R. J. Sternberg, J. Lautrey, & T. I. Lubart (Eds.), *Models of intelligence: International perspectives* (pp. 3–25). Washington, DC: American Psychological Association.

Sternberg, R. J., & Lubart, T. I. (1999). The concept of creativity: Prospects and paradigms. In R. J. Sternberg (Ed.), *Handbook of creativity* (pp. 3–15). New York: Cambridge University Press.

Sternberg, R. J., & Williams, W. M. (1997). Does the Graduate Record Examination predict meaningful success in the graduate training of psychologists? *American Psychologist, 52,* 630–641.

Sterr, A. M. (2004). Attention performance in young adults with learning disabilities. *Learning and Individual Differences, 14*(2), 125–133.

Stevens, G. (2004). Using census data to test the critical-period hypothesis for second-language acquisition. *Psychological Science, 15,* 215–216.

Stewart, A. J., & Ostrove, J. M. (1998). Women's personality in middle age: Gender, history, and midcourse corrections. *American Psychologist, 53,* 1185–1194.

Stewart, A. J., Ostrove, J. M., & Helson, R. (2001). Middle aging in women: Patterns of personality change from the 30s to the 50s. *Journal of Adult development, 8*(1), 23–27.

Stewart, A. J. & Vandewater, E. A. (1998). The course of generativity. In D. P. McAdams, & E. de St. Aubin, (Eds.), *Generativity and adult development: How and why we care for the next generation* (pp. 75–100). Washington, DC: American Psychological Association.

Stewart, S. E., Geller, D. A., Jenike, M., Pauls, D., Shaw, D., Mullin, B., & Farone, S. V. (2004). Long-term outcome of pediatric obsessive-compulsive disorder: A meta-analysis and qualitative review of the literature. *Acta Psychiatrica Scandinavica, 110,* 4–13.

Stewart-Williams, S., & Podd, J. (2004). Placebo psychotherapies and nonconscious learning in the placebo effect: Reply to Kirsh (2004). *Psychological Bulletin, 130,* 344–345.

Stice, E., & Shaw, H. (2004). Eating disorder prevention programs: A meta-analytic program. *Psychological Bulletin, 130,* 206–227.

Stickgold, R. A., & Walker, M. (2004). To sleep, perchance to gain creative insight? *Trends in Cognitive Sciences, 8,* 191–192.

Stickgold, R. A., Winkelman, J. W., Wehrwein, P., & Ulick, J. (2004, January 19). You will start to feel very sleepy . . . *Newsweek, 143,* 58–59.

Stickgold, R., James, L., & Hobson, J. A. (2000). Visual discrimination learning requires sleep after training. *Nature Neuroscience, 3,* 1237–1238.

Stigler, J. W., & Baranes, R. (1988). Culture and mathematics learning. In E. Rothkopi (Ed.), *Review of research in education, 15* (pp. 253–306). Washington, DC: American Educational Research Association.

Stilwell, B. M., Galvin, M. R., & Kopta, S. M. (2000). *Right us Wrong: Raising a Child With a Conscience.* Bloomington, IN: Indiana University Press.

Stoolmiller, M. (1999). Implications of the restricted range of family environments for estimates of heritability and nonshared environment in behavior-genetic adoption studies. *Psychological Bulletin, 125,* 392–409.

Stough, C., & De Guara, D. (2003). Examining the relationship between emotional intelligence and job performance. *Australian Journal of Psychology, 55* (Suppl.), 145–148.

Stowell, J. R. (2003). Use and abuse of academic examinations in stress research. *Psychosomatic Medicine, 65,* 1055–1057.

Stowell, J. R., Kiecolt-Glaser, J. K., & Glaser, R. (2001). Perceived stress and cellular immunity: When coping counts. *Journal of Behavioral Medicine, 24,* 323–339.

Straus, M. A., & Yodanis, C. L. (1996). Corporal punishment in adolescence and physical assaults on spouses in later life: What accounts for the link? *Journal of Marriage & the Family, 58,* 825–841.

Strayer, D. L., Drews, F. A., & Johnston, W. A. (2003). Cell phone-induced failures of visual attention during stimulated driving. *Journal of Experimental Psychology: Applied, 9,* 23–32.

Strazdins, L., & Broom, D. H. (2004). Acts of love (and work): Gender imbalance in emotional work and women's psychological distress. *Journal of Family Issues, 25,* 356–378.

Striegel-Moore, R. H., & Cachelin, F. M. (1999). Body image concerns and disordered eating in adolescent girls: Risk and protective factors. In N. G. Johnson, M. C. Roberts, & J. Worell (Eds.), *Beyond appearance; A new look at adolescent girls* (pp. 85–108). Washington, DC: American Psychological Association.

Strine, T. W., Greenfund, K. J., Brown, D. W., Mokdad, A., & Balluz, L. (2004). Characteristics of people aged 45 years or older with heart disease by frequent mental distress status, 2001. *Preventive Medicine, 39,* 191–196.

Stroganova, T. A., Tsetlin, M. M., Malykh, S. B., Malakhovskaya, E. V. (2000). Biological principles of individual differences of children of the second half-year of life: Communication II. The nature of individual differences in temperamental features. *Human Physiology, 26*(3), 281–289.

Stroop, J. R. (1935). Studies of interference in serial verbal reactions. *Journal of Experimental Psychology, 18,* 643–662.

Strumpfer, D. J. W. (2003). Resilience and burnout: A stitch that could save nine. *South African Journal of Psychology, 33,* 69–79.

Stunkard, A. J., Faith, M. S., & Allison, K. C. (2003). Depression and obesity. *Biological Psychiatry, 54*(3), 330–337.

Sturges, J. S. (1994). Family dynamics. In J. L. Ronch, W. V. Ornum, & N. C. Stilwell (Eds.), *The counseling sourcebook: A practical reference on contemporary issues* (pp. 358–372). New York: Crossroad.

Sturges, J. W., & Rogers, R. R. (1996). Preventive health psychology from a developmental perspective: An extension of protection motivation theory. *Health Psychology, 15,* 158–166.

Subhi, T. (1999). The impact of LOGO on gifted children's achievement and creativity. *Journal of Computer Assisted Learning, 15,* 98–108.

Substance Abuse and Mental Health Services Administration. (2003a). *The NHSDA Report: Treatment among adults with serious mental illness.* Retrieved August 1, 2004, from http://www.DrugAbuseStatistics. gov

Substance Abuse and Mental Health Services Administration (SAMHSA). (2003b). *Overview of findings from the 2002 National Survey on Drug Use and Health.* (NHSDA Series H-21, DHHS Publication No. SMA 03-3774). Washington, DC: U.S. Government Printing Office.

Sue, D. (2001). Asian American masculinity and therapy: The concept of masculinity in Asian American males. In G. R. Brooks & G. E. Good (Eds.), *The new handbook of psychotherapy and counseling with men: A comprehensive guide to settings, problems, and treatment approaches, 1 & 2* (pp. 780–795). San Francisco: Jossey-Bass.

Suedfeld, P. (1998). What can abnormal environments tell us about normal people? Polar stations as natural psychology laboratories. *Journal of Environmental Psychology, 18,* 95–102.

Suedfeld, P. (2001). Applying positive psychology in the study of extreme environments. *Journal of Human Performance in Extreme Environments, 6,* 21–25.

Suedfeld, P. (2003). Canadian space psychology: The future may be almost here, *Canadian Psychology, 44(2),* 85–92.

Suh, E., Diener, E., Oishi, S., & Triandis, H. C. (1998). The shifting basis of life satisfaction judgments across cultures: Emotions versus norms. *Journal of Personality and Social Psychology, 74,* 482–493.

Sui, O. L. (2003). Job stress and job performance among employees in Hong Kong: The role of Chinese work values and organizational commitment. *International Journal of Psychology, 38,* 337–347.

Suinn, R. M. (2001). The terrible twos—anger and anxiety: Hazardous to your health. *American Psychologist, 56,* 27–36.

Suizzo, M. A. (2002). French parents' cultural models and childrearing beliefs. *International Journal of Behavioral Development, 26,* 297–307.

Sullivan, P. F., Bulik, C. M., Fear, J. L., & Pickering, A. (1998). Outcome of anorexia nervosa: A case-control study. *American Journal of Psychiatry, 155(7),* 939–946.

Sullivan, P. F., Kendler, K. S., & Neale, M. C. (2003). Schizophrenia as a complex trait: Evidence from a meta-analysis of twin studies. *Archives of General Psychiatry, 60,* 1187–1192.

Surguladze, S. A., Young, A. W., Senior, C., Brébion, G., Travis, M. J., & Phillips, M. L. (2004). Recognition accuracy and response bias to happy and sad facial expressions in patients with major depression. *Neuropsychology, 18,* 212–218.

Susskind, J. E. (2003). Children's perception of gender-based illusory correlations: Enhancing preexisting relationships between gender and behavior. *Sex Roles, 48,* 483–494.

Suzuki, K. (1998). The role of binocular viewing in a spacing illusion arising in a darkened surround. *Perception, 27,* 355–361.

Swim, J., Borgida, E., Maruyama, G., & Myers, D. G. (1989). Joan McKay versus John McKay: Do gender stereotypes bias evaluations? *Psychological Bulletin, 105,* 409–429.

Swim, J. K., Hyers, L. L., Cohen, L. L., & Ferguson, M. J. (2001). Everyday sexism: Evidence for its incidence, nature, and psychological impact from three daily diary studies. *Journal of Social Issues, 57(1),* 31–53.

Szasz, T. (1984). *The therapeutic state: Psychiatry in the mirror of current events.* Buffalo, NY: Prometheus.

Szasz, T. (1987). *Insanity: The idea and its consequences.* New York: Wiley.

Szeszko, P. R., MacMillan, S., McMeniman, M., Chen, S., Baribault, K., Lim, K. O., et al. (2004). Brain structural abnormalities in psychotropic drugnaïve pediatric patients with obsessive-compulsive disorder. *American Journal of Psychiatry, 161,* 1049–1056.

Tacon, A. M., McComb, J., Caldera, Y., & Randolph, P. (2003). Mindfulness meditation, anxiety reduction, and heart disease. *Family & Community Health, 26,* 25–33.

Tafarodi, R. W., Marshall, T. C., & Katsura, H. (2004). Standing out in Canada and Japan. *Journal of Personality, 72,* 785–814.

Tagaya, H., Uchiyama, M., Ohida, T., Kamei, Y., Shibui, K., Ozaki, A., et al. (2004). Sleep habits and factors associated with short sleep duration among Japanese high-school students: A community study. *Sleep & Biological Rhythms, 2,* 57–64.

Taglialatela, J. P., Savage-Rumbaugh, S., & Baker, L. A. (2003). Vocal production by a language-competent Pan paniscus. *International Journal of Primatology, 24,* 1–17.

Takahashi, J. S. (1999). Narcolepsy genes wake up the sleep field. *Science, 285,* 2076–2077.

Takaku, S. (2000). Culture and status as influences on account giving: A comparison between the United States and Japan. *Journal of Applied Social Psychology, 30,* 371–388.

Takeichi, M., & Sato, T. (2000). Studies on the psychosomatic functioning of ill-health according to Eastern and Western medicine: 4. The verification of possible links between ill-health, lifestyle illness and stress-related disease. *American Journal of Chinese Medicine, 28,* 9–24.

Takeuchi, D. T., & Cheung, M. K. (1998). Coercive and voluntary referrals: How ethnic minority adults get into mental health treatment. *Ethnicity and Health, 3,* 149–158.

Takeuchi. J. (2000). Treatment of a biracial child with schizophreniform disorder: Cultural formulation. *Cultural Diversity and Ethnic Minority Psychology, 6,* 93–101.

Takkouche, B., Regueira, C., & Gestal-Olero, J. J. (2001). A cohort study of stress and the common cold. *Epidemiology, 12,* 345–349.

Talarico, J. M., & Rubin, D. C. (2003). Confidence, not consistency, characterizes flash bulb memories. *Psychological Science, 14,* 455–461.

Talbot, M. (2002, October 27). Supermom fictions. *New York Times Magazine,* 23–41.

Tang, N., & Gardner, J. (1999). Race, culture, and psychotherapy: Transference to minority therapists. *Psychoanalytic Quarterly, 68(1),* 1–20.

Tangney, J. P. (2002). Humility. In C. R. Snyde & S. J. Lopez (Eds.), *Handbook of positive psychology* (pp. 411–419). New York: Oxford University Press.

Tangney, J. P., Baumeister, R. F., & Boone, A. L. (2004). High self-control predicts good adjustment, less pathology, better grades, and interpersonal success. *Journal of Personality, 72,* 271–324.

Tannen, D. (2001) *I only say this because I love you: How the way we talk can make or break family relationships throughout our lives* New York: Random House.

Tannen, D. (2002). *I only say this because I love you.* New York, NY: Ballantine Books.

Tannen, D., Holmes, J., & Meyerhoff, M. (2003). Gender and family interaction. In J. Holmes & M. Meyerhoff (Eds.). *Handbook on Language and Gender.* Oxford, England and Cambridge, MA: Basil Blackwell.

Tanner, L. R., Haddock, S. A., Zimmerman, T. S., & Lund, L. K. (2003). Images of couples and families in Disney feature length an nated films. *American Journal of Family Therapy, 31,* 355–373.

Tardif, T., & Wellman, H. M. (2000). Acquistion of mental state language in Mandarin and Cantonese speaking children. *Developmental Psychology, 36(1),* 25–43.

Task Force on Promotion and Dissemination of Psychological Procedures. (1995). Training in and dissemination of empirically-validated psychological treatments: Report and recommendations. *The Clinical Psychologist, 48(1),* 3–23

Task Force on Women in Academe. (2000). *Women in academe: Two steps forward, one step back*. Washington, DC: American Psychological Association.

Tasman, A., Riba, M. B., & Silk, K. R. (2000). *The doctor-patient relationship in pharmacotherapy: Improving treatment effectiveness*. New York: Guilford Press.

Tataranni, P. A., Harper, I. T., Snitker, S., Del Parigi, A., Vozarova, B., Bunt, J., Bogardus, C., & Ravussin, E. (2003). Body weight gain in free-living Pima Indians: Effect of energy intake vs expenditure. *International Journal of Obesity, 27*, 578–583.

Tate, D. F., Wing, R. R., & Winett, R. A. (2001). Using Internet-based technology to deliver a behavioral weight loss program. *Journal of the American Medical Association, 285*, 1172–1177.

Taubman-Ben-Ari, O. (2000). The effects of reminders of death on reckless driving: A terror management perspective. *Current Directions in Psychological Science, 9*, 196–199.

Tavris, C. (2003). Rethinking the DSM [book review]. *Journal of Sex & Marital Therapy, 29*, 83–86.

Taylor, S. E., Dickerson, S. S., & Klein, L. C. (2002). Toward a biology of social support. In C. R. Snyder & S. J. Lopez (Eds.), *Handbook of positive psychology* (pp. 556–569). New York: Oxford University Press.

Taylor, S. E., Kemeny, M. E., Reed, G. M., Bower, J. E., & Gruenwald, T. L. (2000). Psychological resources, positive illusions, and health. *American Psychologist, 55*, 99–109.

Taylor, S. E., Repetti, R. L., & Seeman, T. (1997). Health psychology: What is an unhealthy environment and how does it get under the skin? *Annual Review of Psychology, 48*, 411–447.

Taylor, W. R., He, S., Levick, W. R., & Vaney, D. I. (2000). Dendritic computation of direction selectivity by retinal ganglion cells. *Science, 289*, 2347–2350.

Tedlock, B. (2004). The poetics and spirituality of dreaming: A Native American enactive theory. *Dreaming, 14*, 183–189.

Teevan, R. C., & McGhee, P. E. (1972). Childhood development of fear of failure motivation. *Journal of Personality and Social Psychology, 21*, 345–348.

Teichman, Y. (2001). The development of Israeli children's images of Jews and Arabs and their expression in human figure drawings. *Developmental Psychology, 37*, 749–761.

Tempo, P. M., & Saito, A. (1996). Techniques of working with Japanese-American families. In G. Yeo, D. Gallagher-Thompson,

et al. (Eds.), *Ethnicity and the dementias* (pp. 109–112). Washington, DC: Taylor & Francis.

Tenenbaum, H. R., & Leaper, C. (2003). Parent-child conversations about science: The socialization of gender inequities? *Developmental Psychology, 39*, 34–47.

Tenenbaum, J. B., de Silva, V., & Langford, J. C. (2000). A global geometric framework for nonlinear dimensionality reduction. *Science, 290*, 2319–2323.

Tenney-Soeiro, R. (2004). An update on child abuse and neglect. *Current Opinion in Pediatrics, 16*, 233–237.

Tentative approvals granted for Modafinil, topiramate. (2004, February 6). *Drug Week*, 164–165.

Tepper, B. J. (1998). 6-n-propylthiouracil: A genetic marker for taste, with implication for food preference and dietary habits. *American Journal of Human Genetics, 63*, 1271–1276.

Terman, L. (1916). *The measure of intelligence: An explanation of and a complete guide for the use of the Standford Revision and Extension of the Binet-Simon Intelligence Scale*. Boston, MA: Houghton Millin.

Terman, L. M. (1939). The gifted student and his academic environment. *School and Society, 49*, 65–73.

Terrace, H. S. (1985). In the beginning was the "name." *American Psychologist, 40*, 1011–1028.

Tesser, A. (2001). On the plasticity of self-defense. *Current Directions in Psychological Science, 10*, 66–69.

Telt, R. P., & Burnelt, D. D. (2003). A personality trait based integrationist model of job performance. *Journal of Applied Psychology, 88*, 500–517.

Thalbourne, M. A., Houran, J., Alias, A. G., & Brugger, P. (2001). Transliminality, brain function, and synesthesia. *Journal of Nervous & Mental Disease, 189*, 190–192.

Theeuwes, J., Alferdinck, J. W. A. M., & Perel, M. (2002). Relation between glare and driving performance. *Human Factors, 44*(1), 95–107.

Thiel, C. M. (2003). Cholinergic modulation of learning and memory in the human brain as detected with functional neuroimaging. *Neurobiology of Learning & Memory, 80*, 234–244.

Thomas, A., & Chess, S. (1977). *Temperament and development*. New York: Brunner/Mazel.

Thomas, E. K. (2000). Domestic violence in African-American communities: A comparative analysis of two racial/ethnic minority cultures and implications for mental health service provision for women of color. *Psychology: A Journal of Human Behavior, 37*, 32–43.

Thomas, S. P. (2003). Anger: The mismanaged emotion. *Dermatology Nursing, 15*, 351–357.

Thompson, B. R., & Thornton, H. J. (2002). The transition from extrinsic to intrinsic motivation in the college classroom: A first-year experience. *Education, 122*, 785–792.

Thompson, D. (2004, January 22). *Dean's meltdown haunts his campaign*. Retrieved May 13, 2004, from http://www.capitolhillblue.com/artman/publish/article_3937.shtml

Thompson, J. R., McGrew, K. S., & Bruininks, R. H. (2002). Pieces of the puzzle: Measuring the personal competence and support needs of persons with intellectual disabilities. *Peabody Journal of Education, 77*, 23–39.

Thompson, M. G. (2004). Happiness and chance: A reappraisal of the psychoanalytic conception of suffering. *Psychoanalytic Psychology, 21*, 134–153.

Thompson, M. S. & Keith, V. M. (2001). The blacker the berry: Gender, skin tone, self-esteem and self-efficacy, *Gender & Society, 15*(3), 336–357.

Thompson, R. (2000). The legacy of early attachments. *Child Development, 71*(1), 145–152.

Thompson, R., Gupta, S., Miller, K., Mills, S., & Orr, S. (2004). The effects of vasopressin on human facial responses related to social communication. *Psychoneuroendocrinology, 29*, 35–48.

Thomson, R., Murachver, T., & Green, J. (2001). Where is the gender in gendered relationships? *Psychological Science, 12*, 171–175.

Thompson, R., & Nelson, C. (2001). Developmental science and the media: Early brain development. *American Psychologist, 56*(1), 5–15.

Thompson Sanders, V. L., Bazile, A., & Akbar, M. (2004). African Americans' perception of psychotherapy and psychotherapists. *Professional Psychology: Research and Practice, 35*, 19–26.

Thoresen, C. J., Kaplan, S., Barsky, A., Warren, C., & de Chermont, K. (2003). The affective underpinnings of job perceptions and attitudes: A meta-analytic review and integration. *Psychological Bulletin, 129*, 914–945.

Tice, D. M., Bratslavsky, E., & Baumeister, R. F. (2001). Emotional distress regulation takes precedence over impulse control: If you feel bad, do it! *Journal of Personality and Social Psychology, 80*, 53–67.

Tiedemann, J. (2000). Parents gender stereotypes and teachers' beliefs as predictors of children's concept of their mathematical ability in elementary school. *Journal of Educational Psychology, 92*, 144–151.

Tieso, C. L. (2003). Ability grouping is not just tracking anymore. *Roeper Review, 26,* 29–36.

Tiggemann, M., & Ruutel, E. (2004). Gender role concerns in Estonian and Australian young adults. *Journal of Social Psychology, 144*(1), 93–95.

Tiggemann, M., & Williamson, S. (2000). The effect of exercise on body satisfaction and self-esteem as a function of gender and age. *Sex Roles, 43,* 119–127.

Timmerman, M. A., Geller, E. S., Glindemann, K. E., & Fournier, A. K. (2003). Do the designated drivers of college students stay sober? *Journal of Safety Research, 34,* 127–133.

Tinsley-Jones, H. (2003). Racism. *Psychotherapy: Theory, Research, Practice, Training, 40,* 179–186.

Tkachuk, G. A., & Martin, G. L. (1999). Exercise therapy for patients with psychiatric disorders: Research and clinical implications. *Professional Psychology: Research & Practice, 30,* 275–282.

Tolman, E. C. (1948). Cognitive maps in rats and men. *Psychological Review, 55,* 189–209.

Tolman, E. C., & Honzik, C. H. (1930). Introduction and removal of reward, and maze performance in rats. *University of California Publications in Psychology, 4,* 257–275.

Tomasello, M. (2000). *Culture and cognitive development: Psychological science* (pp. 37–40). Malden, MA: Blackwell Publishers.

Tomes, H. (2002, December). Recognizing Kenneth B. Clark's legacy. *Monitor on Psychology, 33*(11), 56.

Tooby, J., & Cosmides, L. (1997, June 26). On Stephen Jay Gould's *"Darwinian Fundamentalism"* and *"Evolution: The Pleasures of Pluralism"* [Letter to the editor]. *The New York Review of Books.*

Toro-Morn, M., & Sprecher, S. (2003). A cross-cultural comparison of mate preferences among university students: The United States vs. the People's Republic of China (PRC). *Journal of Comparative Family Studies, 34,* 151–170.

Torres, L., & Rollock, D. (2004). Acculturative distress among Hispanics: The role of acculturation, coping, and intercultural competence. *Journal of Multicultural Counseling & Development, 32,* 155–167.

Tourangeau, R., & Ellsworth, P. C. (1979). The role of facial response in the experience of emotion. *Journal of Personality and Social Psychology, 37,* 1519–1531.

Trachtenberg, J. T., Trepel, C., & Stryker, M. P. (2000). Rapid extragranular plasticity in the absence of thalamocortical plasticity in the developing primary visual cortex. *Science, 287,* 2029–2032.

Tranel, D., Damasio, H., Eichhorn, G. R., Grobowski, T., Ponto, L. L. B., & Hichwa, R. D. (2003). Neural correlates of naming animals from their characteristic sounds. *Neuropsychologia, 41,* 847–854.

Trappey, C. (1996). A meta-analysis of consumer choice and subliminal advertising. *Psychology and Marketing, 13,* 517–530.

Traylor, P. S. (2003). Beyond the conventional. *Modern Physician, 7*(2), 34–35.

Triandis, H. C., & Gelfand, M. J. (1998). Converging measurement of horizontal and vertical individualism and collectivism. *Journal of Personality and Social Psychology, 74,* 118–128.

Triandis, H. C., & Suh, E. M. (2002). Cultural influences on personality. *Annual Review of Psychology, 53,* 133–160.

Trichopoulou, A., Costacou, T., Bamia, C., & Trichopoulos, D. (2003). Adherence to a Mediterranean diet and survival in a Greek population. *New England Journal of Medicine, 348,* 2599–2608.

Trierweiler, S. J., Neighbors, H. W., Munday, C. Thompson, E. E., Binion, V. J., & Gomez, J. P. (2000). Clinician attributions associated with the diagnosis of schizophrenia in African American and non-African American patients. *Journal of Consulting and Clinical Psychology, 68,* 171–175.

Trimble, J. E. (2000). Social psychological perspectives on changing self-identification among American Indians and Alaska Natives. In R. H. Dana (Ed.), *Handbook of cross-cultural and multicultural personality assessment* (pp. 197–222). Mahwah, NJ: Erlbaum.

Tritt, K., Loew, T. H., Meyer, M., Werner, B., & Peseschkian, N. (2000). Positive psychotherapy: Effectiveness of an interdisciplinary approach. *European Journal of Psychiatry, 13,* 231–242.

Troisi, A., & McGuire, M. T. (2000). Psychotherapy in the context of Darwinian psychiatry. In P. Gilbert & K. G. Bailey (Eds.), *Genes on the couch: Explorations in evolutionary psychotherapy* (pp. 3–27). Philadelphia: Brunner-Routledge.

Tronick, E. Z., Morelli, G. A., & Ivey, P. K. (1992). The Efe forager infant and toddler's pattern of social relationships: Multiple and simultaneous. *Developmental Psychology, 28,* 568–577.

Trull, T. J., Stepp, S. D., & Durrett, C. A. (2003). Research on borderline personality disorder: An update. *Current Opinion in Psychiatry, 16,* 77–82.

The truth about dieting. (2002, June). *Consumer Reports, 67*(6), 26–31.

Tucker, C. J., McHale, S. M., & Crouter, A. C. (2001). Conditions of sibling support in adolescence. *Journal of Family Psychology, 15,* 254–271.

Tuckman, B. (2003, August). *The strategies-for-achievement approach for teaching study skills.* Paper presented at the Annual Meeting of the American Psychological Association, Toronto.

Tulananda, O., & Roopnarine, J. L. (2001). Mothers' and fathers' interactions with preschoolers in the home in northern Thailand: Relationships to teachers' assessments of children's social skills. *Journal of Family Psychology, 15,* 676–687.

Tulving E. (1972). Episodic and semantic memory. In E. Tulving & W. Donaldson (Eds.), *Organization of memory* (pp. 381–403). New York: Academic Press.

Tulving, E. (2002). Episodic memory: From mind to brain. *Annual Review of Psychology, 53,* 1–25.

Tulving, E., & Thompson, D. M. (1973). Encoding specificity and retrieval processes in episodic memory. *Psychological Review, 80,* 352–373.

Tural, U., & Onder, E. (2003). Fluoxetine once every third day in the treatment of major depressive disorder. *European Archives of Psychiatry & Clinical Neuroscience, 253,* 307–312.

Turati, C. (2004). Why faces are not special to newborns: An alternative account of the face preference. *Current Directions in Psychological Science, 13*(1) 5–12.

Turati, C., Simion, F., Milani, l., & Umiltà, C. (2002). Newborns' preference for faces: What is crucial? *Developmental Psychology, 38,* 875–882.

Turkheimer, E., Haley, A., Waldron, M., D'Onofrio, B., & Gottesman, I. I. (2003). Socioeconomic status modifies heritability of IQ in young children. *Psychological Science, 14,* 623–628.

Turner, N., Barling, J., Epitropaki, O., & Milner, V. B. C. (2002). Transformational leadership and moral reasoning. *Journal of Applied Psychology, 87,* 304–311.

Tweed, R. G., & Lehman, D. R. (2002). Learning considered within a cultural context: Confucian and Socratic apprachaes. *American Psychologist, 57,* 89–99.

U.S. Bureau of the Census. (2002). Demographic trends in the 20th century. *Special Reports, Series CENR-4.* Washington, DC: U.S. Government Printing Office.

U.S. Bureau of the Census. (2003). *Statistical abstract of the United States, 2003* (124th ed.). Washington, DC: U.S. Government Printing Office.

U.S. Census Bureau. (2004a). *Sixty-five plus in the United States.* Retrieved November 24,

2004, from http://www.census.gov/population/ socdemo/statbriefs/agebrief.html

U.S. Census Bureau. (2004b). *Sixty-five plus in the United States*. Retrieved November 24, 2004, from http://www.census.gov/population/ socdemo/statbriefs/agebrief.html

U.S. Department of Education. (2003). *Twenty-third annual report to Congress on the implementaion of the Individuals with Disabilities Education Act*. Washington, DC: Author.

U.S. Department of Health and Human Services. (2001). *National strategy for suicide prevention: Goals and objectives for action*. Rockville, MD: U.S. Government Printing Office.

U.S. Department of Justice. (1999). *Eyewitness evidence: A guide for law enforcement*. Rockville, MD: U.S. Government Printing Office.

U.S. Department of Labor. (2004a). *Occupational outlook handbook 2002–2003*. Washington, DC: Author.

U.S. Department of Labor. (2004b). Usual weekly earning of wage and salary workers: First quarter 2004. *Bureau of Labor Statistics*. Retrieved July 4, 2004, from http://www.bls.gov/cps

Ueda, K., & Matsumoto, Y. (2003). National strategy for suicide prevention in Japan. *Lancet, 361*, 882.

Uhl, G. H., Sora, I., & Wang, Z. (1999). The μ opiate receptor as a candidate gene for pain: Polymorphisms, variations in expression, nociception, and opiate responses. *Proceedings of the National Academy of Sciences USA, 96*, 7752–7755.

Ukkolal, O., & Bouchard, D. (2004). Role of candidate genes in the responses to long-term overfeeding: Review of findings. *Obesity Reviews, 5*, 3–12.

Ulanovsky, N., Lars, L., & Nelken, I. (2003). Processing of low-probability sounds by cortical neurons. *Nature Neuroscience, 6*, 391–398.

Ullian, E. M., Sapperstein, S. K., Christopherson, K. S., & Barres, B. A. (2001, January 26). Control of synapse number by glia. *Science, 291*, 657–661.

UNAIDS. (2003). *AIDS epidemic update*. Geneva: World Health Organization.

Ungar, M. T. (2000). The myth of peer pressure. *Adolescence, 35*, 167–180.

Unterrainer, J., Wranek, U., Staffen, W., Gruber, T., & Landurner, G. (2000). Lateralized cognitive visuospatial processing: Is it primarily gender-related or due to quality of performance? *Neuropsychobiology, 41*, 95–101.

Utsey, S. O., Chae, M. H., Brown, C. F., & Kelly, D. (2002). Effect of ethnic group membership on ethnic identity, race-related stress, and quality of life. *Cultural Diversity and Ethnic Minority Psychology, 8*, 366–377.

Uttal, W. R. (2001). *The new phrenology*. Cambridge, MA: MIT Press.

Vaas, R. (2004). Fear not. *Scientific American, 14*(1), 62–69

Vahava, O., Morell, R., Lynch, E. D., Weiss, S., Kagan, M. E., Ahituv, N., et al. (1998). Mutation in transcription factor POU4F3 associated with inherited progressive hearing loss in humans. *Science, 279*, 1950–1954.

Valdez, P., Ramirez, C., & Garcia, A. (2003). Adjustment of the sleep-wake cycle to small (1–2 hour) changes in schedule. *Biological Rhythm Research, 34*, 145–155.

Valenstein, E. S. (1998). *Blaming the brain: The truth about drugs and mental health*. New York: Free Press.

Van Boven, L., & Gilovich, T. (2003). To do or to have? That is the question. *Journal of Personality and Social Psychology, 85*, 1193–1202.

Van der Lugt, R. (2002). Brain sketching and how it differs from brainstorming. *Current Directions in Psychological Science, 11*, 208–212.

van Dierendonck, D., Haynes, C., Borrill, C., & Stride, C. (2004). Leadership behavior and subordinate well-being. *Journal of Occupational Health Psychology, 9*, 165–175.

van Goozen, S. H. M., Snoek, H., Matthys, W., van Rossum, I., & van Engeland, H. (2004). Evidence of fearlessness in behaviorally disordered children: A study on startle reflex modulation. *Journal of Child Psychology & Psychiatry & Allied Disciplines, 45*, 884–892.

van Hess, M., & Anand, P. (2003). New choices: Genomics, freedom, and morality. *Social Theory and Practice, 29*, 607–630.

van Horn, D. H. A., & Frank, A. F. (1998). Psychology of addictive behaviors. *Educational Publishing Foundation, 12*, 47–61.

van Schie, H. T., Mars, R. B., Coles, M. G. H., & Bekkering, H. (2004). Modulation of activity in medial frontal and motor cortices during error observation. *Nature Neuroscience, 7*, 549–554.

Vartanian, L. R. (2001). Adolescents' reactions to hypothetical peer group conversations: Evidence for imaginary audience? *Adolescence, 36*, 347–380.

Vartanian, L. R., & Powlishta, K. K. (2001). Demand characteristics and self-report measures of imaginary audience sensitivity: Implications for interpreting age differences in adolescent egocentrism. *Journal of Genetic Psychology, 162*, 187–200.

Vasquez, M. J. T., & Lopez, S. (2002). Martha E. Bernal (1931–2001). *American Psychologist, 57*, 362–363.

Vaughan, P. W., Rogers, E. M., Singhal, A., & Swalehe, R. M. (2000). Entertainment-education and HIV/AIDS prevention: A field experiment in Tanzania. *Journal of Health Communication, 5*(3), 81–100.

Vazsonyi, A. T., Hibbert, J. R., & Snider, J. B. (2003). Exotic enterprise no more? Adolescent reports of family and parenting processes from youth in four countries. *Journal of Research on Adolescence, 13*(2), 129–160.

Vecera, S. P., & Rizzo, M. (2003). Spatial attention: Normal processes and their breakdown. *Neurologic Clinics, 21*, 575–607.

Vello, J., & Cohen, D. (1999). Patterns of individualism and collectivism across the United States. *Journal of Personality and Social Psychology, 77*, 279–292.

Venter, J. C., Adams, M. D., Myers, G. W., Li, P. W., Mural, R. J., Sutton, G. W., et al. (2001, February 16). The sequence of the human genome. *Science, 291*, 1304–1351.

Vermersch, P. (1999). Introspection as a practice. *Journal of Consciousness Studies, 6*(2/3), 17–42.

Viggiano, D., Vallone, D., Ruocco, L. A., & Sadile, A. G. (2003). Behavioural, pharmacological, morpho-functional molecular studies reveal a hyperfunctioning mesocortical dopamine system in an animal model of attention deficit and hyperactivity disorder. *Neuroscience & Biobehavioral Reviews, 27*, 683–689.

Villa, R. A., & Thousand, J. S. (2003). Making inclusive education work. *Educational Leadership, 61*, 19–23.

Villani, S. (2001). Impact of media on children and adolescents: A 10-year review of the research. *Journal of the American Academy of Child and Adolescent Psychiatry, 40*, 392–401.

Villeneuve, C. (2001). *Emphasizing the interpersonal in psychotherapy: Families and groups in the era of cost containment*. Philadelphia: Brunner-Routledge.

Visser, M. (1999). Food and culture: Interconnections. *Social Research, 66*, 117–132.

Voelker, R. (2004). Stress, sleep loss, and substance abuse create potent recipe for college depression. *Journal of the American Medical Association, 291*, 2177–2179.

Vogel, J. J., Bowers, C. A., & Vogel, D. S. (2003). Cerebral lateralization of spatial abilities: A meta-analysis. *Brain & Cognition, 52*, 197–204.

Voisin, T., Reynish, E., Portet, F., Feldman, H., & Vellas, B. (2004). What are the treatment options for patients with severe Alzeimer's disease? *CNS Drugs, 18*, 575–583.

Volkow, N. D., Fowler, J. S., Wang, O.-J., & Goldstein, R. Z. (2002). Role of dopamine, the frontal cortex and memory circuits in drug addiction: Insight from imaging studies. *Neurobiology of Learning & Memory, 78*, 610–624.

Vroom, V. H. (1964). *Work and motivation.* New York: Wiley.

Vroom, V. H. (1974). A new look at managerial decision making. *Organizational Dynamics, 5*, 66–80.

Vroom, V. H., & Jago, A. G. (1995). Situation effects and levels of analysis in the study of leader participation. *Leadership Quarterly, 6*, 169–181.

Vroom, V. H., & Yetton, P. W. (1973). *Leadership and decision-making.* Pittsburgh: University of Pittsburgh Press.

Vroon, P. (1997). *Smell: The secret seducer.* New York: Farrar, Straus & Giroux.

Vygotsky, L. S. (1930/1978). *Mind in society: The development of higher mental processes.* Cambridge, MA: Harvard University Press. (Original works published 1930, 1933, and 1935).

Vygotsky, L. S. (1934/1962). *Thought and language* (E. Hanfmann & G. Vakar, Ed and Trans.): Cambridge, MA: The MIT Press. Original work published in 1934).

Vygotsky, L. S. (1985). *Thought and language.* Cambridge, MA: MIT Press.

Wadden, T. A., Brownell, K. D., & Foster, G. D. (2002). Obesity: Responding to the global epidemic. *Journal of Consulting and Clinical Psychology, 70*, 510–525.

Wagar, B. M., & Cohen, D. (2003). Culture, memory, and the self: An analysis of the personal and collective self in long-term memory. *Journal of Experimental Social Psychology, 39*, 468–475.

Wagner, E. E. (2003). Defining projective techniques: Finding common ground for discourse. *Psychological Reports. 92*, 951–956.

Wagner, J. D., Flinn, M. V., & England, B. G. (2002). Hormonal response to competition among male coalitions. *Evolution & Human Behavior, 23*, 437–442.

Wagner, S. H., Parker, C. P., & Christiansen, N. D. (2003). Employees that think and act like owners: Effects of ownership beliefs and behaviors on organizational effectiveness. *Personnel Psychology, 56*, 847–871.

Wagner, T. D., & Smith, E. E. (2003). Neuroimaging studies of working memory: A meta-analysis. *Cognitive, Affective & Behavioral Neuroscience, 3*, 255–274.

Wagstaff, G. F., MacVeigh, J., Boston, R., Scolt, L., Brunas-Wagstaff, J., & Cole, J. (2003). Can laboratory findings on eyewitness testimony be generalized to the real world? An archival analysis of the influence of violence, weapon presence, and age on eyewitness accuracy. *Journal of Psychology, 137*, 17–28.

Wakefield, J. C. (1999). Evolutionary versus prototype analyses of the concept of disorder. *Journal of Abnormal Psychology, 108*, 374–399.

Wakefield, M., Flay, B., Nichter, M., & Giovino, G. (2003). Role of the media in influencing trajectories of youth smoking. *Addiction, 98*(5, suppl.), 79–103.

Waldie, K., & Mosley, J. L. (2000). Hemispheric specialization for reading. *Brain & Language, 75*(1), 108–122.

Walker, A. R. P., Walker, B. F., & Adam, F. (2003). Nutrition, diet, physical activity, smoking, and longevity: From primitive hunter-gather to present passive consumer— how far can we go? *Nutrition, 19*, 169–173.

Walker, E., Kestler, L., Bollini, A., & Hochman, K. M. (2004). Schizophrenia: Etiology and course, *Annual Review of Psychology, 55*, 401–430.

Walker, L. A., & Shapiro, D. L. (2003). *Introduction to forensic psychology: Clinical and social psychological perspectives.* New York: Kluwer Academic/ Plenum Publishers.

Walker, L. J., Hennig, K. H., & Krettenauer, T. (2000). Parent and peer contexts for children's moral reasoning development. *Child Development, 71(4)*, 1033–1048.

Walker, L. J., & Pitts, R. C. (1998). Naturalistic conceptions of moral maturity. *Developmental Psychology, 34* (3), 403–419.

Walker, L. S., Garber, J., Smith, C. A., Van Slyke, D. A., & Claar, R. L. (2001). The relation of daily stressors to somatic and emotional symptoms in children with and without recurrent abdominal pain. *Journal of Consulting and Clinical Psychology, 69*, 85–91.

Walker, S., Richardson, D. S., & Green, L. R. (2000). Aggression among older adults: The relationship of interaction networks and gender role to direct and indirect responses. *Aggressive Behavior, 26*, 145–154.

Walker-Andrews, A. S. (1986). Intermodal perception of expressive behaviors: Relation of eye and voice? *Developmental Psychology, 22*, 373–377.

Wall, P. (2000). *Pain: The science of suffering.* New York: Columbia University Press.

Walla, P., Lindinger, G., Deecke, L., & Lang, W. (2001). Physiological evidence of gender differences in word recognition: A magnetoencephalographic (MEG) study. *Cognitive Brain Research, 12*, 49–54.

Wallerstein, J. S., Lewis, J. M., & Blakeslee, S. (2000). *The unexpected legacy of divorce: A 25 year landmark study.* New York: Hyperion.

Walsh, B. T., & Devlin, M. J. (1998). Eating disorders: Progress and problems. *Science, 280*, 1387–1390.

Walsh, V. (2000). Hemispheric asymmetries: A brain in two minds. *Current Biology, 10*(12), 460–462.

Walster, E. M., Walster, G. W., & Berscheid, E. (1978). *Equity: Theory and research.* Boston: Allyn & Bacon.

Wamala, S. P., Mittleman, M. A., Horsten, M., Schenck-Gustalsson, K., & Orth-Gómer, K. (2000). Job stress and the occupational gradient in coronary heart disease risk in women: The Stockholm Female Coronary Risk Study. *Social Science & Medicine, 51*, 481–489.

Wampold, B. E., Monding, G. W., Moody, M., Stich, F., Benson, K., & Ahn, H. (1997). A meta-analysis of outcome studies comparing bona fide psychotherapies: Empirically, "all must have prizes." *Psychological Bulletin, 122*, 203–215.

Wandell, B. A., & Movshon, J. A. (2003). Cognitive neuroscience. *Current Opinion in Neurobiology, 13*, 141–143.

Wandersman, A., & Florin, P. (2003). Community interventions and effective prevention. *American Psychologist, 58*(6–7), 441–448.

Wandersman, A., & Nation, M. (1998). Urban neighborhoods and mental health: Psychological contributions to understanding toxicity, resilience, and interventions. *American Psychologist, 53*, 647–656.

Wang, A., Gao, L., Shinfuku, N., Zhang, H., Zhao, C., & Shen, Y. (2000). Longitudinal study of earth-quake-related PTSD in a randomly selected community sample in North China. *American Journal of Psychiatry, 157*, 1260–1266.

Waraich, P., Goldner, E. M., Somers, J. M., & Hsu, L. (2004). Prevalence and incidence studies of mood disorders: A systematic review of the literature. *Canadian Journal of Psychiatry, 49*, 124–138.

Ward, R., & Jackson, S. R. (2002). Visual attention in blindsight: Sensitivity in the blind field increased by targets in the sighted field. *Neuroreport: For Rapid Communication of Neuroscience Research, 13*, 301–304.

Warner, M. B., Morey, L. C., Finch, J. F., Gunderson. J. G., Skodol, A. E., Sanislow, C. A. et al. (2004). The longitudinal relationship of personality traits and disorders. *Journal of Abnormal Psychology, 113*, 217–227.

Washburn, J. J., McMahon, S. D., King, C. A., Reinecke, M. A., & Silver, C. (2004). Narcissistic features in young adolescents: Relations to aggression and internalizing symptoms. *Journal of Youth & Adolescence, 33*, 247–260.

Watanabe, T. (2003). Lucid dreaming: Its experimental proof and psychological conditions. *Journal of the International Society of Life Information Society of Life Information Science, 21*, 159–162.

Waterhouse, J., Edwards, B., Carvalho-Bos, S., Buckely, P., & Reilly, T. (2002). Circadian rhythms, jet lag, and shift work, with particular reference to athletes. *European Journal of Sport Science, 2*, 1–18.

Waters, E., Hamilton, C. E., & Weinfield, N. S. (2000). The stability of attachment security from infancy to adolescence and early adulthood: General introduction. *Child Development, 71(3)*, 678–683.

Watson, J. B. (1913). Psychology as the behaviorist views it. *Psychological Review, 20*, 158–177.

Watson. J. B., & Rayner, R. (1920). Conditioned emotional responses. *Journal of Experimental Psychology, 3*, 1–14.

Watson, J. M., McDermott, K. B., & Balota, D. A. (2004). Attempting to avoid false memories in the Deese/Roediger-McDermott paradigm: Assessing the combined influence of practice and warnings in young and old adults. *Memory & Cognition, 32*, 135–142.

Watts, C., & Zimmerman, C. (2002). Violence against women: Global scope and magnitude. *Lancet, 359*, 1232–1237.

Webb, W. B., & Agnew, H. W., Jr. (1975). The effects on subsequent sleep of an acute restriction of sleep length. *Psychophysiology, 12*, 367–370.

Webster, R. (1995). *Why Freud was wrong: Sin, science, and psychoanalysis.* New York: Basic Books.

Wechsler, D. (1958). *The measurement and appraisal of adult intelligence.* Baltimore: Johns Hopkins University Press.

Weddle, D. O., & Fanelli-Kuczmarski, M. (2000). Position of the American Dietetic Association: Nutrition, aging and the continuum of care. *Journal of the American Dietetic Association, 100(5)*, 580–595.

Weerasekera, P., Linder, B., Greenberg, L., & Watson, J. (2001). The working alliance in client-centered and process-experiential therapy of depression. *Psychotherapy Research, 11*, 221–223.

Weidner, G. (2000). Why do men get more heart disease than women? An international perspective. *Journal of American College Health, 48*, 291–294.

Weine, S. M., Kuc, G., Dzudza, E., Razzano, L., & Pavkovic, I. (2001). PTSD among Bosnian refugees: A survey of providers' knowledge, attitudes and service patterns (posttraumatic stress disorder). *Community Mental Health Journal, 37*, 261–272.

Weingartner, H., Adefris, W., Eich, J. E., & Murphy, D. L., (1976). Encoding-imagery specificity in alcohol state-dependent learning. *Journal of Experimental Psychology, 2*, 83–87.

Weinstein, N. D. (1980). Unrealistic optimism about future life events. *Journal of Personality and Social Psychology, 39*, 806–820.

Weisberg, R. B., Brown, T. A., Wineze, J. P., & Barlow, D. H. (2001). Casual attributions and male sexual arousal: The impact of attributions for a bogus erectile difficulty on sexual arousal, cognitions, and affect. *Journal of Abnormal Psychology, 110*, 324–334.

Weiser, S., & Weiser, H. G. (2003). Event-related brain potentials in memory: Correlates of episodic, semantic and implicit memory. *Clinical Neurophysiology, 114*, 1144–1149.

Weisfeld, G. E. (1993). The adaptive value of humor and laughter. *Ethology and Sociobiology, 14*, 141–169.

Weitz, R. (2001). *The sociology of health, illness, and health care: A critical approach* (2nd ed.). Belmont, CA: Wadsworth.

Wellings, K., Nanchahal, K., Macdowall, W., McManus, S., Erens, B., Mercer, C. H., et al. (2001). Sexual behaviour in Britain: Early heterosexual experience. *Lancet, 358*, 1843–1860.

Wellman, H. M., Phillips, A. T., & Rodriguez, T. (2000). Young children's understanding of perception, desire, and emotion. *Child Development, 71(4)*, 895–912.

Wells, G. L., & Olson, E. A. (2003). Eyewitness testimony. *Annual Reveiw of Psychology, 54*, 277–295.

Wells, G. L., Olson, E.A., & Charman, S. D.(2002). The confidence of eyewitnesses in their identifications from lineups. *Current Directions in Psychological Science, 11*, 151–154.

Werker, J. F., & Vouloumanos, A. (1999). Speech and language processing in infancy: A neurocognitive approach. In C. A. Nelson & M. Luciana (Eds.), *Handbook of developmental cognitive neuroscience* (pp. 269–280). Cambridge, MA: The MIT Press.

Werking, K. (1997). *We're just good friends.* New York: Guilford Press.

Werner, W. L. (2004). *Where have the women attorneys gone?* Retrieved November 23, 2004, from http://www.mobar.org/local_bars/werner.pdf

Wertheimer, M. (1923). Untersuchungen zur Lehre von der Gestalt, II. *Psychologische Forschung, 4*, 301–350. Translated as "Laws of organization in perceptual forms," in Ellis, W. D. (1955). *A source-book of Gestalt psychology.* London: Routledge & Kegan Paul.

Westen, D. (1998). The scientific legacy of Sigmund Freud: Toward a psychodynamically informed psychological science. *Psychological Bulletin, 124*, 333–371.

Westgaard, R. H. (2000). Work related musculoskeletal complaints: Some ergonomics challenges upon the start of a new century. *Applied Ergonomics, 6*, 569–580.

Wetsman, A., & Marlowe, F. (1999). How universal are preferences for female waist-to-hip ratios? Evidence from the Hadza of Tanzania. *Evolution & Human Behavior, 20*, 219–228.

Whaley, A. L. (1997). Ethnicity/race, paranoia, and psychiatric diagnoses: Clinician bias versus sociocultural differences. *Journal of Psychopathology and Behavioral Assessment, 19*, 1–20.

Whaley, A. L. (2001). Cultural mistrust and mental health services for African Americans: A review and meta-analysis. *Counseling Psychologist, 29*, 513–531.

Whalley, L. J. (2001). *The aging brain.* New York: Columbia University Press.

Wharry, C. (2003). Amen and hallelujah preaching: Discourse functions in African American sermons. *Language in Society, 32*, 203–225.

Wheeler, M. A. (2000). Episodic memory and autonoetic awareness. In E. Tulving & F. I. M. Craik (Eds.), *The Oxford handbook of memory* (pp. 597–608). New York: Oxford University Press.

White, J. D. (2000). Correlates of children's anxiety in the dental setting. *Dissertation Abstracts International: Section B: The Sciences & Engineering, 60(12-B)*, 6388.

White, K. M., Hogg, M. A., & Terry, D. J. (2002). Improving attitude-behavior correspondence through exposure to normative support from a salient ingroup. *Basic & Applied Social Psychology, 24*, 91–103.

Whittler, T. E., &Spira, J. S. (2002). Model's race: A peripheral cue in advertising messages? *Journal of Consumer Psychology, 12*, 291–301.

Who has the right to view personnel files? (2004). Retrieved May 25, 2004, from http://www.nolo.com/lawcenter/ency/article.cfm

WHO International Consortium in Psychiatric Epidemiology. (2000). Cross-national comparisons of the prevalences and correlates of mental disorders. *Bulletin of the World Health Organization, 78*, 413–426.

Widiger, T. A., & Anderson, K. G. (2003). Personality and depression in women. *Journal of Affective Disorders, 74*, 59–66.

Widiger, T. A., & Sankis, L. M. (2000). Adult psychopathology: Issues and controversies. *Annual Review of Psychology, 51*, 377–404.

Wiehe, V. R. (2003). Empathy and narcissism in a sample of child abuse perpetrators and a comparison sample of foster parents. *Child Abuse & Neglect, 27,* 541–555.

Wiley, J. (1998). Expertise as mental set: The effects of domain knowledge in creative problem solving. *Memory & Cognition, 26,* 716–730.

Willhite, R., & Eckstein, D. (2003). The angry, the angrier, and the angriest: Relationship implications. *The Family Journal, 11,* 76–83.

Williams, C. B. (1999). African American women, Afrocentrism, and feminism: Implications for therapy. *Women and Therapy, 22,* 1–16.

Williams, C. D. (1959). Case report: The elimination of tantrum behavior by extinction procedures. *Journal of Abnormal and Social Psychology, 59,* 269.

Williams, J. (2000). *Unbending gender: Why family and work conflict and what to do about it.* New York: Oxford University Press.

Williams, J. N., Moebius, P., & Kim, C. (2001). The task of poetry reading and second language learning. *Applied Linguistics, 22,* 295–323.

Williams, K., Harkins, S., & Latané, B. (1981). Identifiability as a deterrent to social loafing: Two cheering experiments. *Journal of Personality and Social Psychology, 40,* 303–311.

Williams, N. M., Norton, N., Williams, H., Ekholm, B., Hamshere, M. L., Lindbolm, Y., et al. (2003). A systematic genomewide linkage study in 353 sib pairs with schizophrenia. *American Journal of Human Genetics, 73,* 1355–1367.

Williams, R. B., Barefoot, J. C., & Schneiderman, N. (2003). Psychosocial risk factors for cardiovascular disease: More than one culprit at work. *Journal of the American Medical Association, 290,* 2190–2192.

Williams, W. M., & Ceci, S. J. (1997). Are Americans becoming more or less alike? Trends in race, class, and ability differences in intelligence. *American Psychologist, 52,* 1226–1235.

Williams-Nickelson, C. (2000, Winter). Prescription privileges fact sheet: What students should know about the APA's pursuit of prescription privileges for psychologists (RxP). *American Psychological Association of Graduate Students Newsletter.* Retrieved November 30, 2003, from http://www.apa.org/apags/profdev/prespriv.html?CFID=2826293&CFTOKEN=27745608

Williamson, D. A., Allen, H. R., Martin, P. D., Alfonso, A., Gerald, B., & Hunt, A. (2004). Digital photography: A new method for estimating food intake in cafeteria settings. *Eating and Weight Disorders, 9*(1), 24–28.

Williamson, D. A., Thaw, J. M., & Varnado-Sullivan, P. J. (2001). Cost-effectiveness analysis of a hospital-based cognitive-behavioral treatment program for eating disorders. *Behavior Therapy, 32,* 459–470.

Willingham, D. T., & Dunn, E. W. (2003). What neuroimaging and brain localization can do, cannot do, and should not do for social psychology. *Journal of Personality and Social Psychology, 85,* 662–671.

Willis, S. L., & Schaie, K. W. (1999). Intellectual functioning in midlife. In S. L. Willis & J. D. Reid (Eds.). *Life in the middle: Psychological and social development in middle age* (pp. 233–247). San Diego, CA: Academic Press.

Willough by, T., Wood, E., Desmaris, S., Sims, S., & Kalra, M. (1997). Mechanisms that facilitate the effectiveness of elaboration strategies. *Journal of Educational Psychology, 89,* 682–685.

Wills, L., & Garcia, J. (2002). Parasomnias: Epidemiology and management. *CNS Drugs, 16,* 803–810.

Wills, T. A. (1998). Social support. In E. A. Blechman & K. D. Brownell (Eds.), *Behavioral medicine and women: A comprehensive handbook* (pp. 118–128). New York: Guilford Press.

Wilson, D. A. (2000). Comparison of odor receptive field plasticity in the rat olfactory bulb and anterior piriform cortex. *Journal of Neurophysiology, 84,* 3036–3042.

Wilson, G. T., Fairburn, C. C., Agras, W. S., Walsh, B. T., & Kraemer, H. (2002). Cognitive-behavioral therapy for bulimia nervosa: Time course and mechanisms of change. *Journal of Consulting and Clinical Psychology, 70,* 267–274.

Wilson, H. W., & Donnenberg, G. (2004). Quality of parent communication about sex and its relationship to risky sexual behavior among youth in psychiatric care: A pilot study. *Journal of Child Psychology & Psychiatry & Allied Disciplines, 45,* 387–395.

Wilson, M. E. (1992). Factors determining the onset of puberty. In A. A. Gerall, H. Moltz, A. A. Gerall, H. Moltz, & I. L., Ward (Eds.), *Sexual differentiation: Handbook of behavioral neurobiology* (pp. 275–312). New York: Plenum.

Wilson, T. D., & Dunn, E. W. (2004). Self-knowledge: Its limits, value and potential for improvement. *Annual Review of Psychology, 55,* 493–518.

Wing, R. R., & Jeffery, R. W. (1999). Benefits of recruiting participants with friends and increasing social support for weight loss and maintenance. *Journal of Consulting & Clinical Psychology, 67,* 132–138.

Winsler, A., Carlton, M. P., & Barry, M. J. (2000). Age-related changes in preschool children's systematic use of private speech in a natural setting. *Journal of Child Language, 27*(3), 665–687.

Winson, J. (2002, August). The meaning of dreams. *Scientific American, 12*(1), 54–61.

Winterich, J. A. (2003). Sex, menopause, and culture: Sexual orientation and the meaning of menopause for women's sex lives. *Gender & Society, 17,* 627–642.

Winters, K. C., Stinchfield, R. D., Botzet, A., & Anderson, N. (2002). A prospective study of youth gambling behaviors. *Psychology of Addictive Behavior, 16,* 3–9.

Wise, R. A. (1996). Neurobiology of addiction. *Current Opinion in Neurobiology, 6,* 243–251.

Wise, R. A., & Safer, M. A. (2004). What U.S. judges know and believe about eyewitness testimony. *Cognitive Psychology, 18,* 427–443.

Witt, S. D. (2000). The influence of television on children's gender role socialization. *Childhood Education, 76,* 322–324.

Wittig, V. R. (2001). AMA's scope of practice for nonphysicians. *Perspectives in Psychiatric Care, 37,* 38.

Witztum, E., & Buchbinder, J. T. (2001). Strategic culture sensitive therapy with religious Jews. *International Review of Psychiatry, 13,* 117–124.

Wolpe, J. (1958). *Psychotherapy by reciprocal inhibition.* Stanford, CA: Stanford University Press.

Wood, J. J., & Repelti, R. L. (2004) What gets dad involved? A longitudinal study of change in parental child caregiving involvement. *Journal of Family Psychology, 18*(1), 237–249.

Wood, J. M., Garb, H. N., Lilienfeld, S. O., & Nezworski, M. T. (2002). Clinical assessment. *Annual Review of Psychology, 53,* 519–543.

Wood, W., & Eagly, A. H. (2002). A cross-cultural analysis of the behavior of women and men: Implications for the origins of sex differences. *Psychological Bulletin, 128,* 699–727.

Woodhill, B. M., & Samuels, C. A., (2003). Positive and negative androgyny and their possible relationship with psychological health and well-being. *Sex Roles, 48,* 555–565.

Woods, S. C., Schwartz, M. W., Baskin, D. G., & Seeley, R. J. (2000). Food intake and the regulation of body weight. *Annual Review of Psychology, 51,* 255–278.

Woods, S. C., & Seeley, R. J. (2002). Hunger and energy homeostasis. In H. Pashler & R. Gallistel (Eds.). *Steven's handbook of experimental psychology* (3rd ed., pp. 633–688). New York: Wiley.

Woodward, S. A., Lenzenweger, M. F., Kagan, J., Snidman, N., & Arcus, D. (2000). Taxonic structure of infant reactivity: Evidence from a taxometric perspective. *Psychological Science, 11*(4), 296–301.

Woodward, W. R. (1982). The "discovery" of social behaviorism and social learning theory, 1870–1980. *American Psychologist, 37*, 396–410.

Worsdell, A. S., Iwata, B. A., Conners, $ Kahng, S. W., & Thompson, R. H. (2000). Relative influences of establishing operations and reinforcement contingencies on self-injurious behavior during functional analyses. *Journal of Applied Behavior Analysis, 33*(4), 451–461.

Worthman, C. M., & Melby, M. K. (2002). Toward a comparative developmental ecology of human sleep. In M. A. Carskadon (Ed.). *Adolescent sleep patterns: Biological, social, and psychological influences* (pp. 69–117). New York: Cambridge University Press.

Wrightsman, L. S., & Fulero, S. M. (2005). *Forensic psychology* (2nd ed.). Belmont, CA: Wadsworth.

Wu, W., & Lee, Y. (2001). Participatory management and industrial relations climate: A study of Chinese, Japanese, and U.S. firms in Taiwan. *International Journal of Human Resource Management, 12*, 827–844.

Wunderlich, U., Bronisch, T., Wittchen, H. -U., & Carter, R. (2001). Gender differences in adolescents and young adults with suicidal behavior. *Acta Psychiatrica Scandinavica, 104*, 332–339.

Wundt, W. (1896). *Lectures on human and animal psychology*. New York: Macmillan.

Wynn, K., Bloom, P. & Chiang, W. (2002). Enumeration of collective entities by 5-month-old infants. *Cognition, 83*, B55–B62.

Wyszecki, G., & Stiles, W. S. (1967). *Color science: Concepts and methods, quantitative data, and formulas*. New York: Wiley.

Xie, H., Swift, D. J., Cairns, B., & Cairns, R. B. (2002). Aggressive behaviors in social interaction and developmental adaptation: A narrative analysis of interpersonal conflicts during early adolescence. *Social Development, 11*, 205–224.

Yan, L., & Silver, R. (2004). Resetting the brain clock: Time course and localization of mPERI and mPER2 protein expression in suprachiasmatic nuclei during phase shifts. *European Journal of Neuroscience, 19*, 1105–1109.

Yang, S., & Sternberg, R. J. (1997). Conceptions of intelligence in ancient Chinese philosophy. *Journal of Theoretical and Philosophical Psychology, 17*, 101–119.

Yang, S. C., & Lin, W. C. (2004). The relationship among creative, critical thinking and thinking styles in Taiwan high school students. *Journal of Instructional Psychology, 31*, 33–45.

Yapko, M. D. (Ed.). (1997). *Breaking the pattern of depression*. New York: Broadway Books.

Yarmey, A. D. (2004). Eyewitness recall and photo identification: A field experiment. *Psychology, Crime & Law, 10*, 53–68.

Yeung, N., & Monsell, S. (2003). Switching between tasks if unequal familiarity: The role of stimulus-attribute and response-set selection. *Journal of Experimental Psychology: Human Perception & Performance, 29*, 455–469.

Yonan, C. A., & Wegener, S. T. (2003). Assessment and management of pain in older adults. *Rehabilitation Psychology, 48*, 4–13.

Yonelinas, A. P., Kroll, N. E. A., Baynes, K., Dobbins, I. G., Fredrick, C. M., Knight, R. T., et al. (2001). Visual implicit memory in the left hemisphere: Evidence from patients with callosotomies and right occipital lode lesions. *Psychological Science, 12*, 293–298.

Yoshimasu, K., Washio, M., Tokunaga, S., Tanaka, K., Liu, Y., Kodama, H., et al. (2002). Relation between Type A behavior pattern and the extent of coronary atherosclerosis in Japanese women. *International Journal of Behavioral Medicine, 9*, 77–93.

Young, J. E., Weinberger, A. D., & Beck, A. T. (2001). Cognitive therapy for depression. In D. H. Barlow (Ed.), *Clinical handbook of psychological disorders* (pp. 264–308). New York: Guilford Press.

Young, L. R., & Nestle, M. (2002). The contribution of expanding portion sizes to the U.S. obesity epidemic. *American Journal of Public Health, 92*, 246–249.

Young, S. N. (2003). Lifestyle drugs, mood, behaviour and cognition. *Journal of Psychiatry & Neuroscience, 28*, 87–89.

Young, S. N., Hoffer, L. J., & Jones, P. J. (2002). Clinical nutrition: 3. The fuzzy boundary between nutrition and psychopharmacology. *Canadian Medical Association Journal, 166*, 205–209.

Young, T., Skatrud, J., & Peppard, P. E. (2004). Risk factors for obstructive sleep apnea in adults. *Journal of the American Medical Association, 291*, 2013–2016.

Youngstedt, S. D., O'Connor, P. J., & Dishman, R. K. (1997). The effects of acute exercise on sleep: A quantitative synthesis. *Sleep, 20*, 203–214.

Youniss, J., Bales, S., Christmas-Best, V., Diversi, M., McLaughlin, M., & Silbereisen, R. (2002). Youth civic engagement in the twenty-first century. *Journal of Research on Adolescence, 12*(1). 121–148.

Yu, H., & Miller, P. (2003). The generation gap and cultural influence—A Taiwan empirical investigation. *Cross Cultural Management, 10*(3), 23–41.

Yurgelun-Todd, D. A., Killgore, W. D. S., & Young, A. D. (2002). Sex differences in cerebral tissue volume and cognitive performance during adolescence. *Psychological Reports, 91* (3, Pt. 1), 743–757.

Yzer, M. C., Siero, F. W., & Buunk, B. P. (2000). Can public campaigns effectively change psychological determinants of safer sex? An evaluation of three Dutch campaigns. *Health Education Research, 15*, 339–352.

Zahn, P., & Collins, S. (2004, April 17). Profile of Christopher Reeve, Lance Armstrong. Part 1. *America's Intelligence Wire* (no page).

Zajonc, R. B. (1965). Social facilitation. *Science, 149*, 269–274.

Zajonc, R. B. (1976, April 16). Family configuration and intelligence. *Science, 192*, 227–236.

Zajonc, R. B. (2001). The family dynamics of intellectual development. *American Psychologist, 56*, 490–496.

Zangwill, O. L., & Blakemore, C. (1972). Dyslexia: Reversal of eye movements during reading. *Neuropsychologia, 10*, 371–373.

Zarcone, J. R., Crosland, K., Fisher, W. W., Worsdell, A. S., & Herman, K. (1999). A brief method for conduction a negative-reinforcement assessment. *Research in Developmental Disabilities, 20*, 107–124.

Zeineh, M. M., Engel, S. A., Thompson, P. M., & Bookheimer, S. Y. (2003). Dynamics of the hippocampus during encoding and retrieval of face-name pairs. *Science, 299*, 577–580.

Zentall, T. R. (2003). Imitation by animals: How do they do it? *Current Directions in Psychological Science, 12*, 91–95.

Zettle, R. D. (2003). Acceptance and commitment therapy (ACT) vs. systematic desensitization in treatment of mathematics anxiety. *Psychological Record, 53*, 197–215.

Zhang, A. Y., & Snowden, L. R. (1999). Ethnic characteristics of mental disorders in five U.S. communities. *Cultural Diversity and Ethnic Minority Psychology, 5*, 134–146.

Zhang, L. I. Tan, A. Y. Y., Schreiner, C. E., & Merzenich, M M.. (2003). Topography and synaptic shaping of direction selectivity in primary auditory cortex. *Nature, 424*(6945), 201–205.

Zheng, M., & Goldin-Meadow, S. (2002). Thought before language: How deaf and hearing children express motion events across cultures. *Cognition, 85,* 145–175.

Zhou, Z. (2001). American and Chinese children's knowledge of basic relational concepts. *School Psychology International, 22,* 5–21.

Zhu, A. J., & Walsh, B. T. (2002). In review: Pharmacologic treatment of eating disorders. *Canadian Journal of Psychiatry, 47,* 227–234.

Zimbardo, P. G., Maslach, C., & Haney, C. (2000). *Reflections on the Standard prison experiment: Genesis, transformations, consequences.* Mahwah, NJ: Erlbaum.

Zimmerman, L. (2000). *The SE switch: Evolution and our self-esteem.* Orlando, FL: Rivercross.

Zoucha, R., & Husted, G. L. (2000). Culturally congruent care to individual patients by health care professional: The differences between transculturalism and multiculturalism are explored. *Issues in Mental Health Nursing, 21,* 324–340.

Zuber, J. A., Crolt, H. W., & Werner, J. (1992). Choice shift and group polarization: An analysis of the status of arguments and social decision schemes. *Journal of Personality and Social Psychology, 62,* 50–61.

Zucker, A. N., Ostrove, J. M., & Stewart, A. J. (2002). College educated women's personality development in adulthood: Perceptions of differences. *Psychology & Aging, 17*(2), 236–244.

Zuckerman, M. (1969). Variables affecting deprivation results and hallucinations, reported sensations, and images. In J. P. Zubek (Ed.), *Sensory deprivation.* New York: Appleton-Century-Crofts.

Zuckerman, M. (1999). *Vulnerability to psychopathology: A biosocial model.* Washington, DC: American Psychological Association.

Zuckerman, M. (2004). The shaping of personality: Genes, environments, and chance encounters. *Journal of Personality Assessment, 82,* 11–22.

Zuckerman, M., Knee, C. R., Kieffer, S. C., & Gagne, M. (2004). What individuals believe they can and cannot do: Explorations of realistic and unrealistic control beliefs. *Journal of Personality Assessment, 82,* 215–232.

Abnormal behavior Behavior characterized as atypical, socially unacceptable, distressing to the individual or others, maladaptive, and/or the result of distorted cognitions.

Abnormal psychology The subfield of psychology concerned with the assessment, treatment, and prevention of maladaptive behavior.

Absolute threshold The statistically determined minimum level of stimulation necessary to excite a perceptual system.

Accommodation (1) According to Piaget, the process by which existing mental structures and behaviors are modified to adapt to new experiences. (2) In visual perception, the change in the shape of the lens of the eye that enables the observer to keep an object in focus on the retina when the object is moved or when the observer focuses on an object at a different distance.

Acetylcholine An excitatory neurotransmitter that was the first to be identified and is the most well-studied.

Achievement tests Tests designed to measure how well students have learned specific content.

Action potential An electrical current that travels along the axon of a neuron and is initiated by a rapid reversal of the polarization of the cell membrane; also known as a *spike discharge*.

Actor-observer effect The tendency to attribute the behavior of others to internal (dispositional) causes but to attribute one's own behavior to situational causes.

Adaptation A trait or inherited characteristic that has increased in a population because it solved a problem of survival or reproduction.

Adolescence The period extending from the onset of puberty to early adulthood.

Afferent neurons Neurons that send messages to the spinal cord and brain;sensory neurons.

Ageism Prejudice toward, stereotyping of, and/or discrimination against any person or persons solely because of age.

Aggression Any behavior intended to harm another person or thing.

Agnosia An inability to recognize a sensory stimulus that should be recognizable, despite having normal, intact perceptual systems for detecting color, shape, and motion and no verbal, memory, or intellectual impairments.

Agonist [AG-oh-nist] Chemical that mimics or facilitates the actions of a neurotransmitter.

Agoraphobia [AG-or-uh-FOE-bee-uh] Anxiety disorder characterized by marked fear and avoidance of being alone in a place from which escape might be difficult or embarrassing.

Algorithm [AL-go-rith-um] A procedure for solving a problem by implementing a set of rules over and over again until the solution is found.

All-or-none Either at full strength or not at all; the basis on which neurons fire.

Altruism Behaviors that are intended to benefit another person or people, even at a cost to the person offering the assistance.

Alzheimer's [ALTZ-hy-merz] **disease** A chronic and progressive disorder of the brain that is the most common cause of degenerative dementia in the United States.

Amnesia [am-NEE-zhuh] Inability to remember information (typically all events within a specific period), usually because of physiological trauma.

Amplitude The total energy of a sound wave, which determines the loudness of the sound; also known as *intensity*.

Amygdala One of a pair of oval structures in the forebrain that are part of the limbic system and are involved in emotional behaviors.

Anal stage Freud's second stage of personality development, from about age 2 to about age 3, during which children learn to control the immediate gratification they obtain through defecation and to become responsive to the demands of society.

Androgynous Having both stereotypically male and sterotypically female characteristics.

Androgyny Behavior and attitudes that incorporate qualities traditionally considered masculine as well as those traditionally considered feminine.

Anorexia nervosa An eating disorder characterized by an obstinate and willful refusal to eat, a distorted body image, and an intense fear of being fat.

Antagonist Chemical that opposes the actions of a neurotransmitter.

Anterograde amnesia, Inability to remember events and experiences that occur after brain damage.

Antianxiety drugs Any of a group of mood-altering drugs that are used to treat anxiety without causing excessive sedation; aslo known as *tranquilizers* or *anxiolytics*.

Antidepressant drugs Drugs used to treat depression, sometimes referred to as *mood elevators* or, more technically, as *thymoleptics*.

Antipsychotic drugs Any of a group of drugs that are used to treat psychosis, especially schizophrenia; also known as *neuroleptics*.

Antisocial personality disorder Personality disorder characterized by egocentricity, irresponsible behavior that violates the rights of other people, a lack of guilt feelings, an inability to understand other people, and a lack of fear of punishment.

Anxiety A generalized feeling of fear and apprehension that may be related to a particular situation or object and is often accompanied by increased physiological arousal.

Appraisal A person's evaluation of the significance of a situation or an event in terms of the person's well-being.

Approach-approach conflict Conflict that results from having to choose between two attractive alternatives.

Approach-avoidance conflict Conflict that results when facing a single alternative that has both attractive and unappealing aspects.

Aptitude tests Psychological tests designed to measure the ability to learn specific types of material.

Archetypes [AR-ki-types] In Jung's theory, the inherited ideas and images that exist within the collective unconscious and are emotionally charged with rich meaning and symbolism.

Arousal, Physical activation, including activation of the central nervous system, the autonomic nervous system, and the muscles and glands.

Artificial intelligence (AI) The branch of computer science concerned with making a device or machine (a computer) behave like a human being, especially in reasoning abilities.

Assessment The process of evaluating individual differences among human beings by means of tests, interviews, observations, and recordings of physiological responses.

Assimilation According to Piaget, the process by which new ideas and experiences are absorbed and incorporated into existing mental structures and behaviors.

Attachment The strong emotional bond or connection that a person feels toward special people in his or her life.

Attitudes Patterns of feelings and beliefs about ideas, objects, or other people that are usually evaluative, are based on a person's past experiences, and play a role in his or her future behavior.

Attributions Descriptions of the causes of behavior.

Autonomic [au-toe-NOM-ick] nervous system, The part of the peripheral nervous system that controls physiological actions and reactions that proceed automatically, such as heart-rate, digestive processes, regulation of blood pressure, and the functioning of internal organs.

Availability heuristic The tendency to judge the probability of an event by how easy it is to think of examples of it.

Aversive counterconditioning A technique in which an unpleasant stimulus is paired with a stimulus that elicits an undesirable behavior so that the person will cease responding to the original stimulus with the undesirable behavior.

Avoidance-avoidance conflict Conflict that results from having to choose between two distasteful alternatives.

Axon A thin, elongated structure that transmits signals from a neuron's cell body to the axon terminals, which pass the signals on to adjacent neurons.

Babinski reflex Reflex that causes a newborn to fan out the toes when the sole of the foot is touched.

Backward search Heuristic procedure in which a problem solver works back from the goal to the current position, in order to analyze the problem and reduce the steps needed to get to the goal.

Behavior therapy A therapy that is based on the application of learning principles to human behavior and that focuses on changing overt behaviors rather than on understanding subjective feelings, unconscious processes, or motivations; also known as *behavior modification*.

Behaviorism The approach to psychology that focuses on describing and measuring only what is observable, either directly or through assessment instruments.

Belief in small numbers The willingness to draw conclusions from a small sample and to assume that such a sample is representative.

Belief perseverance People's tendency, once they have decided to believe something, to keep on accepting it as true, even in the face of conflicting data.

Binocular depth cues Cues for depth perception that require the use of both eyes.

Biofeedback A process through which people receive information about the status of a phsical function and use this feedback to learn to alter that function.

Biologically based therapy Any treatment for psychological disorders that focuses on the body, usually through the use of drugs that affect levels of hormones and especially neurotransmitters; sometimes called *somatic therapy*.

Biopsychology perspective The psychological perspective that examines how biological factors affect mental processes and behavior and how behavior can change brain function and structure; also known as the *neuro-science perspective*.

Bipolar disorder Mood disorder that was originally known as manic-depressive disorder because it is characterized by behavior that vacillates between two extremes: mania and depression.

Blood-brain barrier A mechanism that prevents certain molecules from entering the brain but allows others to cross.

Bottom-up analysis Analysis of the perceptual process that begins at the most fundamental level of sensation—where a stimulus meets receptors—and works up to more complex perceptual tasks involving interpretation.

Brain The part of the central nervous system that is located in the skull and that regulates, monitors, processes, and guides other nervous system activity.

Brainstorming A problem-solving technique that involves considering all possible solutions without any initial judgments about the worth of those solutions.

Brightness The lightness or darkness of a hue, determined in large part by the intensity of reflected light.

Broca's area The area of the left frontal lobe that Paul Broca discovered to be critical for language production.

Bulimia nervosa An eating disorder characterized by repeated episodes of binge eating (and by a fear of not being able to stop eating), followed by purging.

Burnout A state of emotional and physical exhaustion, lowered productivity, and feelings of isolation, often caused by work-related pressures.

Bystander effect The unwillingness to help exhibited by witnesses to an event, which increases when there are more observers.

Case study A descriptive research method that involves intensive observation and analysis of a single individual.

Catatonic [CAT-uh-TONN-ick] type of schizophrenia Type of schizophrenia characterized either by displays of excited or violent motor activity or by stupor.

Central nervous system OneF of the two major divisions of the nervous system, consisting of the brain and the spinal cord.

Cerebellum [seh-rah-BELL-um] A structure in the hindbrain that influences balance, coordination, and movement.

Cerebral cortex The convoluted exterior covering of the brain's hemispheres, which is about 2–3 millimeters thick and is divided into several lobes.

Child abuse Physical, emotional, or sexual mistreatment of a child.

Chromosomes Microscopic strands of DNA that are found in the nucleus of every cell in the body and that carry the genetic information in the genes.

Chunks Manageable and meaningful units of information organized in a familiar way for easy encoding, storage, and retrieval.

Circadian [sir-KAY-dee-an] rhythms Internally generated patterns of body functions, including hormone levels, sleep and wakefulness, blood pressure, and body temperature, which vary over approximately a 24-hour cycle and occur even in the absence of normal cues about whether it is day or night.

Classical conditioning Conditioning process in which an originally neutral stimulus, through repeated pairing with a stimulus that naturally elicits a response, comes to elicit a similar or even identical response; also known as *Pavlovian conditioning*.

Client-centered therapy An insight therapy that was developed by Carl Rogers and seeks to help people evaluate the world and themselves from their own perspective by providing them with a therapeutic relationship that includes unconditional positive regard, congruence, and empathy; also known as *person-centered therapy*.

Clinical psychologist Mental health practitioner who provides diagnosis and treatment of emotional and behavioral problems in hospitals, clinics, or private practices.

Cognitive behavior therapy A therapy that focuses on changing a client's behavior by changing his or her thoughts and perceptions.

Cognitive dissonance [COG-nih-tiv DIS-uh-nents] A state of mental discomfort arising from a discrepancy between two or more of a person's beliefs or between a person's beliefs and overt behavior.

Cognitive maps Mental representations that enable people to navigate from a starting point to an unseen destination.

Cognitive psychology The psychological perspective that focuses on the mental processes involved in perception, learning, memory, and thinking, with an emphasis on how people attend to, acquire, transform, store, and retrieve knowledge.

Cognitive theories In the study of motivation, explanations of behavior that assert that people use thought processes to actively determine their own goals and the means of achieving them.

Collective unconscious Jung's concept of a shared storehouse of primitive ideas and images (archetypes) that humans have inherited from our ancestors and that are emotionally charged and rich in meaning and symbolism.

Color blindness The inability to perceive different hues.

Community psychology The branch of psychology that seeks to reach out to society by providing services such as community mental health centers and to effect social change through the empowerment of individuals.

Concept A mental category people use to classify events or objects according to their common properties or features.

Concordance rate Estimate of the degree to which a condition or trait is shared by two or more individuals or groups.

Concrete operational stage Piaget's third stage of cognitive development (lasting from approximately age 6 or 7 to age 11 or 12), during which the child develops the ability to understand constant factors in the environment, rules, and higher-order symbolic systems.

Conditioned response The response elicited by a conditioned stimulus.

Conditioned stimulus A neutral stimulus that, through repeated association with an unconditioned stimulus, begins to elicit a conditioned response.

Conditioning A systematic procedure through which associations and responses to specific stimuli are learned.

Conduction deafness Deafness resulting from interference with the transmission of sound to the inner ear.

Cones Cone-shaped receptors in the retina that are primarily responsible for vision at high levels of illumination and are responsive to fine details and to variations in wavelength (color).

Confirmation bias The tendency of people to discount information that does not fit with their preexisting views.

Conflict The emotional state or condition that arises when a person must choose between two or more competing motives, behaviors, or impulses.

Conformity People's tendency to change their attitudes or behaviors so that they are consistent with those of other people or with social norms.

Conscious According to Freud, the level of the mind that consists of those experiences that a person is aware of at any given time.

Consciousness The general state of being aware of and responsive to events in the environment, as well as one's own mental processes.

Conservation Ability to recognize that objects can be transformed in some way, visually or physically, yet still be the same in number, weight, substance, or volume.

Consolidation [kon-SOL-ih-DAY-shun] The process of changing a temporary (short-term) memory to a permanent (long-term) one.

Content validity The ability of a test to measure the knowledge or behavior it is intended to measure, determined through a detailed examination of the contents of the test items.

Control group In an experiment, the comparison group—the group of participants who are tested on the dependent variable in the same way as the experimental group but who receive the standard treatment.

Convergence (1) In the nervous system, the synapsing of electrochemical signals from many rods or cones onto one bipolar cell. (2) In visual perception, the movement of the eyes inward, toward each other, to keep visual stimulation at corresponding points on the retinas as an object moves closer to the observer.

Convergent thinking In problem solving, the process of narrowing down choices and alternatives to arrive at a suitable solution.

Convolutions Folds in the cortical tissue and in the underlying cerebral hemispheres.

Coping The process by which a person takes some action to manage, master, tolerate, or reduce environmental or internal demands that cause or might cause stress and that tax the individual's inner resources.

Coping strategies The techniques people use to deal with stress.

Corpus callosum A thick band of nerve fibers that forms the main connection between the left and right cerebral hemispheres.

Correlation coefficient A descriptive statistic used to assess the degree of relationship between the two variables of interest in a correlational study.

Correlational study A descriptive research method that attempts to determine the strength of a relationship between two variables.

Counselling psychologist Mental health practitioner who assists people who have emotional or behavioral problems, through the use of testing, psychotherapy, and other therapies; this profession is very similar to clinical psychology.

Counterconditioning A process of reconditioning in which a person is taught a new, more adaptive response to a familiar stimulus.

Creativity The ability to generate or recognize high-quality ideas that are original, novel, and appropriate, along with the tendency to do so.

Critical period A time in the development of an organism when it is especially sensitive to certain enviornmental influences; outside of that period, the same influences will have far less effect.

Cross-sectional research design A method for conducting a research study that compares individuals of different ages to determine if and how they differ on some dimension.

Dark adaptation The increase in sensitivity to light that occurs when the illumination level changes from high to low, causing the photopigments in the rods and cones to regenerate.

Debriefing A procedure to inform participants about the true nature of a research study after its completion.

Decay Loss of information from memory as a result of disuse and the passage of time.

Decentration Process of changing from a totally self-oriented point of view to one that recognizes other people's feelings and viewpoints.

Decision making Assessing and choosing among alternatives.

Declarative memory Memory for specific information.

Defense mechanism An unconscious way of reducing anxiety by distorting perceptions of reality.

Deindividuation The process by which individuals lose their self-awareness and distinctive personality in the context of a group, which may lead them to engage in behavior that they would not do in another context.

Deinstitutionalization The transitioning of treatment for mental problems from inpatient facilities to outpatient or community-based facilities.

Delusions False beliefs that are inconsistent with reality but are held in spite of evidence that disconfirms them.

Demand characteristics Elements of an experimental situation that might cause a participant to perceive the situation in a certain way or become aware of the purpose of the study, which might bias the participant to behave in a certain way and thus distort the results.

Dementia An impairment of mental functioning and global cognitive abilities in an otherwise alert individual, causing memory loss and related symptoms and typically having a progressive nature.

Dendrites Thin, bushy, widely branching fibers that extend outward from a neuron's cell body and that receive signals from neighboring neurons and carry them back to the cell body.

Denial Defense mechanism by which people refuse to accept reality or recognize the true source of anxiety.

Dependence The condition that occurs when a drug becomes part of the body's functioning in such a way that the user suffers withdrawal symptoms when the drug is discontinued.

Dependent variable, The behavior or response that is expected to change because of the manipulation of the independent variable.

Depressants Another term for sedative-hypnotics, used because these drugs depress many body responses.

Depressive disorders Mood disorders in which people show extreme and persistent sadness, despair, and loss of interest in life's usual, day-to-day activities.

Descriptive research methods The type of research that involves describing existing events rather than performing a manipulation of an independent variable and observing change.

Descriptive statistics A category of statistics that includes procedures to summarize, condense, and describe sets of data.

Developmental psychology The study of the lifelong, often age-related processes of change in the physical, cognitive, moral, emotional, and social domains of functioning; such changes are rooted in biological mechanisms that are genetically controlled but are also influenced by social interactions.

Deviation IQ A standard IQ test score whose mean and standard deviation remain constant for all ages.

Dichromats [DIE-kroe-MATZ] People who can distinguish only two of the three basic colors.

Discrimination Behavior targeted at individuals or groups and intended to hold them apart and treat them differently.

Disorganized type of schizophrenla Type of schizophrenia characterized by severely disturbed thought processes, frequent incoherence, disorganized behavior, and inappropriate affect.

Displacement Defense mechanism by which people divert sexual or aggressive feelings for one person onto another person or thing.

Display rules The rules that govern the display of emotion, which vary according to age, culture, and gender, thus creating wide differences in emotional expression.

Dissociative amnesia Dissociative disorder characterized by the sudden and extensive inability to recall important personal information, usually information of a stressful or traumatic nature; formerly called *psychogenic amnesia.*

Dissociative disorders Psychological disorders characterized by a sudden but temporary alteration in consciousness, identity, sensorimotor behavior, or memory.

Dissociative identity disorder Dissociative disorder characterized by the existence within an individual of two or more distinct personalities, each of which is dominant at different times and directs the individual's behavior at those times; commonly known as *multiple personality disorder.*

Divergent thinking In problem solving, the process of widening the range of possibilities and expanding the options for solutions.

Dopamine One of the monoamine neurotransmitters that plays a role in movement, thought processes, emotion, feelings of reward and pleasure, and several behavior problems.

Double-blind technique A research procedure in which neither the experimenter nor the participants know who is in the control and experimental groups.

Dream A state of consciousness that occurs during sleep, usually accompanied by vivid visual, tactile, or auditory imagery.

Dream analysis Psychoanalytic technique in which a patient describes her or his dreams in detail and the therapist helps to interpret them so as to provide insight into the individual's unconscious desires and motivations.

Drive An internal aroused condition that directs an organism to satisfy a physiological need.

Drive theory An explanation of behavior that assumes that an organism is motivated to act because of a need to attain, reestablish, or maintain some goal that aids survival.

Drug Any chemical substance that, in small amounts, alters biological or mental processes, or both.

Efferent neurons Neurons that send messages from the brain and spinal cord to other structures in the body; motor neurons.

Ego In Freud's theory, the mental force that seeks to satisfy instinctual needs in accordance with reality.

Egocentrism [ee-go-SENT-rism] Inability to perceive a situation or event except in relation to oneself; self-centeredness.

Elaboration likelihood model A view suggesting that there are two routes to attitude change: the central route, which emphasizes thoughtful consideration and evaluation of arguments, and the peripheral route, which emphasizes less careful, more emotional, and even superficial evaluation.

Elaborative rehearsal Rehearsal involving repetition and analysis, in which a stimulus may be associated with (linked to) other information and further processed.

Electroconvulsive [ee-LECK-tro-con-VUL-siv] therapy (ECT) A treatment for severe mental illness in which an electric current is briefly applied to the head in order to produce a generalized seizure (convulsion).

Electroencephalogram [ee-LECK-tro-en-SEFF-uh-low-gram] (EEG), A graphical record of brain-wave activity obtained through electrodes placed on the scalp.

Electromagnetic [ee-LEK-tro-mag-NET-ick] radiation The entire spectrum of waves initiated by the movement of charged particles.

Embryo [EM-bree-o] The prenatal organism from the 5th through the 49th day after conception.

Emotion A subjective response, accompanied by a physiological change, which is interpreted in a particular way by the individual and often leads to a change in behavior.

Emotion-focused coping An active coping strategy that concentrates on managing the feelings that accompany stress and trying to find ways to feel better.

Emotional intelligence The ability to both perceive and express emotions in accurate and adaptive ways.

Empiricism The idea that knowledge should be acquired through careful observation.

Empowerment Facilitating the development and enhancement of skills, knowledge, and motivation in individuals so that they can gain control over their lives.

Encoding The organizing of sensory information so that the nervous system can process it.

Encoding specificity principle The principle that the effectiveness of a specific retrieval cue depends on how well it matches up with the originally encoded information.

Endocrine [END-oh-krin] glands Ductless glands that secrete hormones into the bloodstream (rather than into a duct that goes to the target organ).

Endorphins [en-DOR-finz] Neuropeptides that are produced naturally in the brain and the pituitary gland and exert effects similar to those of opiate drugs.

Environmental psychology The study of how physical settings affect human behavior and how people change their environment.

Episodic [ep-ih-SAW-dick] memory Memory for specific personal events and situations (episodes), tagged with information about time.

Equity theory (1) Social psychological theory that states that people attempt to maintain stable, consistent interpersonal relationships in which members' contributions are in balance. (2) In I/O psychology, the theory that asserts that what people bring to a work situation should be balanced by what they receive compared to other workers; that is, input should be reflected in compensation.

Ethics Rules concerning proper and acceptable conduct that investigators use to guide their studies and that govern the treatment of animals, the rights of human beings, and the responsibilities of researchers.

Ethnic identity A feeling of membership in an ethnic or cultural group.

Ethnocentrism The tendency to believe that one's own ethnic or cultural group is the standard, the reference point against which other people and groups should be judged.

Evolutionary psychology The psychological perspective that seeks to explain and predict behaviors by analyzing how the human brain developed over time and how that evolutionary history affects brain functions and behaviors today.

Ex post facto study A descriptive research method that allows researchers to describe differences among groups of participants.

Excitatory postsynaptic potential (EPSP), Postsynaptic change in the polarization of a neuron that pushes the neuron toward its threshold and firing.

Excitement phase The first phase of the sexual response cycle, during which there are increases in heart rate, blood pressure, and respiration.

Expectancy theories (1) In the area of motivation, explanations of behavior that focus on people's expectations about reaching their goals and their need for achievement. (2) In I/O psychology, theories that suggest that a worker's effort and desire to maintain goal-directed behavior (to work) are determined by expectations regarding the outcomes of that behavior.

Experiment A procedure in which a researcher systematically manipulates and observes elements of a situation in order to test a hypothesis and try to establish a cause-and-effect relationship.

Experimental group In an experiment, the group of participants who receive some level of the independent variable as a treatment.

Explicit memory Conscious memory that a person is aware of.

External attribution A description of the cause of a behavior as coming from events or situations outside the person.

Extinction (1) In classical conditioning, the procedure of withholding the unconditioned stimulus and presenting the conditioned stimulus alone, which gradually reduces the probability that the conditioned response will occur. (2) In operant conditioning, the process by which the probability of an organism's emitting a response is reduced when reinforcement no longer follows the response.

Extrinsic [ecks-TRINZ-ick] motivation Motivation supplied by rewards or threats of punishment that come from the external environment.

Factor analysis A statistical procedure designed to discover the independent elements (factors) in any set of data or to detect which are related.

Factorial research design A type of experimental design that includes two independent variables with conditions arranged so that participants are subject to all possible combinations of the variables.

Family therapy A form of group therapy in which two or more people who are committed to one another's well-being are treated at once, in an effort to change the ways they interact.

Fetal alcohol syndrome A set of physical, mental, and neurobehavioral birth defects that is associated with alcohol consumption during pregnancy and is the leading known and preventable cause of mental retardation.

Fetus [FEET-us] The prenatal organism from the 8th week after conception until birth.

Fixation An excessive attachment to some person, object, or behavior that was appropriate only at an earlier stage of development.

Fixed-interval schedule A schedule of reinforcement in which a reinforcer (reward) is delivered after a specified interval of time, provided that the required response occurs at least once in the interval.

Fixed-ratio schedule A schedule of reinforcement in which a reinforcer (reward) is delivered after a specified number of responses has occurred.

Flashbulb memory A detailed memory for circumstances at the time of some dramatic event.

Flow The experience of becoming completely and pleasurably absorbed in an intrinsically motivated behavior.

fMRI (functional magnetic resonance imaging) Imaging technique that allows observation of functioning brains by registering changes in the metabolism (energy consumption) of neurons.

Forebrain The largest and most complex of the three main divisions of the brain, which has many interconnected structures, including the thalamus, hypothalamus, limbic system, basal ganglia, corpus callosum, and cortex.

Forensic psychology The study of the integration of psychology and the law, focusing on such topics as the insanity defense and competence to stand trial.

Formal operational stage Piaget's fourth and final stage of cognitive development (beginning at about age 12), during which the individual can think hypothetically, can consider future possibilities, and can use deductive logic.

Fraternal twins Twins who occur when two sperm fertilize two eggs and who are no more genetically similar than other brothers and sisters; dizygotic twins.

Free association Psychoanalytic technique in which the patient is asked to report to the therapist his or her thoughts and feelings as they occur, regardless of how disorganized, trivial, or disagreeable their content may appear.

Frequency The number of complete sound waves passing a point per unit of time; measured in hertz (Hz), or cycles per second.

Frequency distribution An array of scores, usually arranged from the highest to the lowest, showing the number of instances for each score.

Frequency polygon Graph of a frequency distribution that shows the range of scores obtained and the number of instances of each score, usually with the data points connected by straight lines.

Fulfillment In Rogers's theory of personality, an inborn tendency directing people toward actualizing their essential nature and thus attaining their potential.

Functional fixedness The inability to see that an object can have a function other than its stated or usual one.

Functionalism The school of psychological thought that was an outgrowth of structuralism and was concerned with how the mind functions and how this functioning is related to consciousness.

Fundamental attribution error The tendency to attribute other people's behavior to dispositional (internal) causes rather than to situational (external) causes.

Gambler's fallacy The belief that the chances of an event's occurring increase if the event has not recently occurred.

Gamma-aminobutyric acid (GABA) An important inhibitory neurotransmitter.

Gender A socially and culturally constructed set of distinctions between masculine and feminine behaviors that are promoted and expected by society.

Gender identity A person's sense of being male or female.

Gender intensification The exaggeration of traditional male or female behaviors seen in some adolescents.

Gender role A set of expectations in a given society about behaviors and responsibilities that are appropriate for males or females.

Gender schema theory The theory that children and adolescents use gender as an organizing theme to classify and interpret their perceptions about the world and themselves.

Gender stereotype A fixed, overly simple, sometimes incorrect idea about traits, attitudes, and behaviors of males or females.

Gene The functional unit of hereditary transmission, which provides a template for protein production.

Generalized anxiety disorder An anxiety disorder characterized by persistent anxiety occurring on more days than not for at least 6 months, sometimes with increased activity of the autonomic nervous system, apprehension, excessive muscle tension, and difficulty in concentrating.

Genetics The study of heredity, the process through which physical traits and behavioral characteristics are transmitted from parents to offspring.

Genital [JEN-it-ul] stage Freud's last stage of personality development, from the onset of puberty through adulthood, during which the sexual conflicts of childhood resurface (at puberty) and are often resolved (during adolescence).

Genome The total sequence of the genes on an organism's DNA.

Genomics The study of the entire pattern of generes in an individual.

Genotype A person's genetic makeup, which is fixed at conception.

Gestalt [gesh-TALT] psychology The school of psychological thought that argued that it is necessary to study a person's total experience, not just parts of the mind or behavior, since conscious experience is more than simply the sum of its parts.

Glial cells Cells in the nervous system that nourish the neurons and provide support functions.

Goal-setting theory The theory that asserts that setting specific, clear, attainable goals for a given activity leads to better performance.

Grammar The linguistic description of how a language functions, especially the rules and patterns used for generating appropriate and comprehensible sentences.

Grasping reflex Reflex that causes a newborn to grasp vigorously any object touching the palm or fingers or placed in the hand.

Group Any number of people who share a common purpose, goals, characteristics, or interests and who interact with each other and develop some degree of interdependence.

Group polarization Shifts or exaggerations in group members' attitudes or behaviors as a result of group discussion.

Group therapy Any psychotherapeutic treatment in which several people meet as a group with a therapist to receive psychological help.

Groupthink The tendency of people in a group to seek agreement with one another when reaching a decision, rather than effectively evaluating the options.

Halo effect The tendency for one noticeable characteristic of an individual (or a group) to influence the evaluation of other characteristics.

Health psychology Subfield of psychology concerned with the use of psychological ideas and principles to help enhance health, prevent illness, diagnose and treat disease, and improve rehabilitation.

Heritability The genetically determined proportion of a trait's variation among individuals in a population.

Heuristics [hyoo-RISS-ticks] Sets of strategies that serve as flexible guidelines for discovery-oriented problem solving.

Higher-order conditioning The process by which a neutral stimulus takes on conditioned properties through pairing with a conditioned stimulus.

Hindbrain The lowest of the three main divisions of the brain, consisting of the medulla, the reticular formation, the pons, and the cerebellum.

Hippocampus A structure in the forebrain that is part of the limbic system and is involved in learning and memory.

Histogram A bar graph that displays the data in a frequency distribution.

Homeostasis Maintenance of a steady state of inner stability or balance.

Hormones Chemicals that are produced by the endocrine glands and that regulate the activities of specific organs or cells.

Hue The psychological property referred to as "color," determined by the wavelengths of reflected light.

Human factors The study of the relationship of human beings to machines and to workplaces and other environments; sometimes called *ergonomics*.

Humanistic psychology The psychological perspective that emphasizes positive human values and people's inherent tendency toward personal growth.

Humanistic theory An explanation of behavior that emphasizes the entirety of life rather than individual components of behavior and focuses on human dignity, individual choice, and self-worth.

Hyperopic [HY-per-OH-pick] Able to see objects at a distance clearly but having trouble seeing things up close; farsighted.

Hypnosis A state of consciousness during which a person's sensations, perceptions, thoughts, or behaviors change because of suggestions made to the person.

Hypothalamus A relatively small structure of the forebrain, lying just below the thalamus, that affects many complex behaviors, such as eating, drinking, and sexual activity.

Hypothesis A tentative statement or idea expressing a relationship between events or variables that is to be evaluated in a research study.

Id In Freud's theory, the mental force that is the source of a person's instinctual energy and that works mainly on the pleasure principle.

Ideal self In Rogers's theory of personality, the self a person would ideally like to be.

Identical twins Twins who occur when one fertilized egg splits into two identical cells, which then develop independently into twins with exactly the same genes; monozygotic twins.

Illusion A perception of a physical stimulus that differs from measurable reality or from what is commonly expected.

Imagery The creation or recreation of a mental picture of a sensory or perceptual experience.

Imaginary audience A cognitive distortion experienced by adolescents, in which they feel that they are always "on stage" with an audience watching.

Implicit memory Memory a person is not aware of possessing.

Inclusion The integration of children with special needs into regular classroom settings, whenever appropriate, with the support of professionals who provide special education services.

Independent variable The condition that the experimenter directly and intentionally manipulates to see what changes occur as a result of the manipulation.

Indirect aggression Aggression through indirect means, such as arranging for something bad to happen to someone or spreading rumors about someone.

Industrial/organizational (I/O) psychology The study of how individual behavior is affected by the work environment, by co-workers, and by organizational practices.

Inferential statistics A category of statistics that allows researchers to conclude whether the results they have obtained from experiments form meaningful patterns.

Information-processing approach A model of human memory that proposes that information is processed and stored in three stages, moving in a sequential manner from one stage to the next.

Informed consent The agreement of participants to take part in a research study and their acknowledgement, expressed through their signature on a document, that they have been fully informed about the general nature of the research, its goals, and its methods.

Ingroup Any group to which a person belongs.

Inhibitory postsynaptic potential (IPSP) Postsynaptic change in the polarization of a neuron that pushes the neuron away from its threshold, making it less likely to fire.

Insanity The legal concept that refers to a condition that excuses people from responsibility and protects them from punishment.

Insight The process of finding a solution to a problem by thinking about the problem in a new way.

Insight therapy Any therapy that attempts to discover relationships between unconscious motivations and current abnormal behavior.

Insomnia Problems in getting to sleep or remaining asleep.

Instinct A fixed behavioral pattern that occurs in all members of a species and appears without learning or practice.

Insulin Hormone that is produced by the pancreas and that facilitates the transport of sugar (glucose) from the bloodstream into body cells.

Intelligence The overall capacity of an individual to act purposefully, to think rationality, and to deal effectively with the environment.

Intelligence quotient (IQ) A child's mental age (intellectual ability) divided by the child's chronological age and multiplied by 100.

Intelligence tests Tests designed to measure general mental abilities rather than specific learned content.

Interaction effect An effect of the combination of two variables that is separate from the influence of either variable.

Interference The suppression of one bit of information by another that is received either earlier or later or the confusion caused by the input of more than one piece of information.

Internal attribution A description of the cause of a behaviour as originating from within the person.

Interneurons Neurons that connect sensory neurons to motor neurons.

Interpersonal attraction The tendency of one person to evaluate another person (or a symbol or image of another person) in a positive way.

Interpretation In Freud's theory, the technique of providing a context, meaning, or cause for a specific idea, feeling, or set of behaviors, thereby tying a set of behaviors to its unconscious influences.

Intimacy A state of being or feeling that leads each person in a relationship to self-disclose (to express important feelings and information to the other person).

Intrinsic [in-TRINZ-ick] motivation Motivation that arises from the pleasure and satisfaction gained by engaging in a particular behavior.

Introspection The self-examination of one's mental processes, a technique used by the structuralists.

Job analysis Detailed description of the various tasks and activities that comprise a job, as well as the knowledge, skills, and abilities necessary to do it.

Kinesthesis [kin-iss-THEE-sis] The awareness aroused by movements of the muscles, tendons, and joints.

Language A system of symbols, usually words, that convey meaning, along with a set of rules for combining the symbols to generate an infinite number of messages, usually sentences.

Latency [LAY-ten-see] stage Freud's fourth stage of personality development, from about age 7 until puberty, during which sexual urges are inactive.

Latent content The deeper meaning of a dream, usually involving symbolism, hidden meaning, and repressed or obscure ideas and wishes.

Latent learning Learning that occurs in the absence of direct reinforcement and that is not necessarily demonstrated through observable behavior.

Lateralization The localization of a particular brain function primarily in one hemisphere.

Law of Prägnanz [PREG-nants] The Gestalt notion that when items or stimuli can be grouped together and seen as a whole, they will be.

Learned helplessness The behavior of giving up or not responding, which is exhibited by people and nonhuman animals exposed to negative consequences or punishment over which they feel they have no control.

Learning A relatively permanent change in an organism that occurs as a result of experiences in the environment.

Levels-of-processing approach Theory of memory that suggests that the brain encodes and processes stimuli (information) in different ways, to different extents, and at different levels.

Lexicon The entire set of morphemes in a language or in an individual's linguistic inventory.

Libido [lfh-BEE-doe] In Freud's theory, the instinctual (and sexual) life force that, working on the pleasure principle and seeking immediate gratification, energizes the id.

Life expectancy The average number of years a newborn can expect to live.

Light The small portion of the electromagnetic spectrum that is visible to the human eye.

Limbic system An interconnected group of structures in the forebrain that includes parts of the cortex, the thalamus, and the hypothalamus and that influences emotions, memory, social behavior, and brain disorders such as epilepsy.

Linguistics [ling-GWIS-ticks] The study of language, including speech sounds, meaning, and grammar.

Lithium carbonate An effective mood-stabilizing antimania drug that has come into wide use for treating bipolar disorder because it relieves the manic symptoms.

Logic The system of principles of reasoning that is used to reach valid conclusions or make inferences.

Longitudinal research design A method for conducting a research study that follows individuals over a period of time to examine changes that have occurred with aging.

Long-term memory The storage mechanism that keeps a relatively permanent record of information.

Long-term potentiation An increase in responsiveness of a neuron after it has been stimulated.

Lucid [LOO-sid] dream Dream in which the dreamer is aware of dreaming while it is happening.

Maintenance rehearsal Repetitive review of information with little or no interpretation.

Major depressive disorder Depressive disorder characterized by loss of interest in almost all of life's usual activities; a hopeless, sad, or discouraged mood; sleep disturbance; loss of appetite; loss of energy; and feelings of unworthiness and guilt; also known as *clinical depression*.

Manifest content The overt story line, characters, and setting of a dream—the obvious, clearly discernible events of the dream.

Mean A measure of central tendency that reflects the average of a set of scores.

Means-end analysis Heuristic procedure in which the problem solver compares the current situation or position with a desired goal to determine the most efficient way to get from one to the other.

Measure of central tendency A descriptive statistic that tells which score best represents an entire set of scores.

Median The point in the ordered distribution of a set of scores that has 50% of the scores above it and 50% of the scores below it.

Meditation The use of a variety of techniques, including concentration, restriction of incoming stimuli, and attention to breathing and muscle tension, to produce a state of consciousness characterized by a sense of detachment and deep relaxation.

Medualla [meh-DUH-lah] The part of the hindbrain that controls heartbeat and breathing.

Memory The ability to recall past events, images, ideas, or previously learned information or skills; the storage system that allows for retention and retrieval of previously learned information.

Memory span The number of items that a person can reproduce from short-term memory, usually consisting of one or two chunks.

Mental age The age at which children of average ability are able to perform various tasks on an intelligence test.

Mental retardation A disability defined by significant limitations in both intellectual functioning and adaptive skills.

Mental set Limited ways of thinking about possibilities and a tendency to approach situations the same way because that way worked in the past.

Meta-analysis A statistical procedure used to combine and evaluate results from multiple studies that addressed the same topic or question.

Midbrain The second of the three main divisions of the brain, which receives neural signals from other parts of the brain and from the spinal cord, interprets the signals, and either relays the information to the forebrain or causes the body to act at once.

Mode The most frequent score in a set of scores.

Model An analogy or a perspective that helps scientists discover relationships among data.

Modeling The process, critical to observational learning, in which an observer matches his or her behavior to that of the model through an internal representation of the behavior, which is stored in memory in symbolic form.

Monochromats [MON-o-kroe-MATZ] People who cannot perceive any color, usually because their retinas lack cones.

Monocular [mah-NAHK-you-ler] depth cues, Cues for depth perception that do not depend on the use of both eyes.

Mood disorder A category of psychological disorder that includes depressive disorders and bipolar disorder.

Morality A system of learned attitudes about social practices, institutions, and individual behavior used to evaluate situations and behavior as right or wrong, good or bad.

Moro reflex Reflex that causes a newborn to stretch out the arms and legs and cry in response to a loud noise or an abrupt change in the environment.

Morpheme [MORE-feem] A basic unit of meaning in a language.

Motivation Any condition, usually an internal one, that initiates, activates, or maintains an organism's goal-directed behavior.

Motive A specific (usually internal) condition, typically involving some form of arousal, which directs an organism's behavior toward a goal.

MRI (magnetic resonance imaging) Imaging technique that uses magnetic fields to produce scans of great clarity and high resolution, distinguishing brain parts as small as 1 or 2 millimeters.

Mutations Unexpected changes in genes that result in unusual, and sometimes harmful, characteristics of body or behavior.

Myelin sheath A thin, white, fatty layer that covers some large motor neurons and speeds neural transmission.

Myopic [my-OH-pic] Able to see things that are close clearly but having trouble seeing objects at a distance; nearsighted.

Narcolepsy A sleep disorder characterized by sudden, uncontrollable episodes of sleep.

Natural selection The principle that those characteristics and behaviors that help organisms adapt, be fit, and survive will be passed on to successive generations, because flexible, fit individuals have a greater chance of reproducing.

Naturalistic observation A descriptive research method that involves observation of behavior in a naturally occurring situation rather than in a laboratory.

Nature A person's biological makeup, including inherited characteristics determined by genetics.

Need A state of physiological imbalance that is usually accompanied by arousal.

Need for achievement The social need that directs a person to strive for excellence and success.

Need for affiliation The social need that motivates a person to be with and to establish positive relationships with others.

Negative reinforcement Removal of an unpleasant stimulus after a particular response in order to increase the likelihood that the response will recur.

Nervous system The structures and organs that facilitate electrical and chemical communication in the body and allow all behavior and mental processes to take place.

Neuron The type of cell that is the basic building block of the nervous system and functions through specialized structures, including dendrites (which receive neural signals), an axon (which transmits neural signals), and axon terminals (which relay signals to adjacent neurons); also known as a *nerve cell*.

Neurotransmitter Chemical substance that is stored within a synaptic vesicle in the axon terminal vesicles and that, when released, moves across the synaptic space and binds to a receptor site on an adjacent cell.

Night terrors A sleep disorder in which a person experiences a high degree of arousal and symptoms of panic that occur within 60–90 minutes after he or she falls asleep.

Non-rapid eye movement (NREM) sleep Four distinct stages of sleep during which no rapid eye movements occur.

Norepinephrine One of the monoamine neurotransmitters that plays a role in arousal reactions and possibly in hunger, eating, and sexual activity.

Normal curve A bell-shaped graphic representation of normally distributed data showing what percentage of the population falls under each part of the curve.

Normal distribution The approximate distribution of scores expected when a sample is taken from a large population; when drawn as a frequency polygon, it takes the form of a bell-shaped curve, known as a *normal curve*.

Norms The scores and corresponding percentile ranks of a large and representative sample of individuals from the population for which a test was designed.

Null hypothesis A hypothesis of no difference between groups in a study.

Nurture A person's experiences in the environment.

Obedience Compliance with the orders of another person or group of people.

Object permanence The realization that objects continue to exist even when they are out of sight.

Obsessive-compulsive disorder Anxiety disorder characterized by persistent and uncontrollable thoughts and irrational beliefs that often cause the performance of compulsive rituals that interfere with daily life.

Oedipus [ED-i-pus] complex A group of unconscious wishes to have sexual intercourse with the parent of the opposite sex and to kill or remove the parent of the same sex, which arise during Freud's phallic stage and are ultimately resolved through identification with the parent of the same sex.

Olfaction [ole-FAK-shun] The sense of smell.

Operant [OP-er-ant] conditioning Conditioning in which an increase or decrease in the probability that a behavior will recur is affected by the delivery of reinforcement of punishment as a consequence of the behavior; also known as *instrumental conditioning*.

Operational definition A definition of a variable in terms of the set of methods or procedures used to measure or study it.

Opiates Sedative-hypnotic drugs that are derived from the opium poppy and include opium, morphine, and heroin.

Opponent-process theory Theory, proposed by Herring, that there are six basic colors and color is coded by varying responses of three types of paired receptors: red-green, blue-yellow, and white-black.

Optic chiasm [KI-azm] The point at which half of the optic nerve fibers from each eye cross over and connect to the other side of the brain.

Oral stage Freud's first stage of personality development, from birth to about age 2, during which the instincts of the infant are focused on the mouth as the primary pleasure center.

Orgasm phase The third phase of the sexual response cycle, during which autonomic nervous system activity reaches its peak and muscle contractions occur in spasms throughout the body, but especially in the genital area.

Osteoporosis A condition characterized by low bone mass and deterioration of bone tissue, which increases the risk of a break or fracture.

Outgroup Any group to which a person does not belong.

Overconfidence phenomenon The tendency of individuals who are highly committed to their ideas and beliefs, especially political ones, to be more certain than correct and, when challenged, to become even more rigid and inflexible.

Overjustification effect The decrease in likelihood that an intrinsically motivated task, after having been extrinsically rewarded, will be performed when the reward is no longer given.

Panic attack Acute anxiety accompanied by sharp increases in autonomic nervous system arousal that is not triggered by a specific event.

Paranoid [PAIR-uh-noid] type of schizophrenia, Type of schizophrenia characterized by delusions of persecution or grandeur (or both) and possibly hallucinations, and sometimes irrational jealousy.

Parasympathetic [PAIR-uh-sim-puh-THET-ick] nervous system The part of the autonomic nervous system that controls the normal operations of the body, including digestion, blood pressure, and respiration.

Participant An individual who takes part in an experiment and whose behavior is observed and recorded.

Percentile score A score indicating what percentage of the population taking a test obtained a lower score.

Perception Process by which an organism selects and interprets sensory input so that it acquires meaning.

Performance appraisal The process by which a supervisor periodically evaluates the job-relevant strengths and weaknesses of a subordinate.

Peripheral [puh-RIF-er-al] nervous system, The part of the nervous system that carries information to and from the central nervous system through spinal nerves attached to the spinal cord and through 12 cranial nerves.

Personal constructs Ways of understanding the world based on personal interpretation.

Personal fable A cognitive distortion experienced by adolescents, in which they believe that they are so special and unique that other people cannot understand them and that risky behaviors will not harm them.

Personality A pattern of relatively permanent traits, dispositions, or characteristics that give some consistency to an individual's behavior.

Personality disorders Psychological disorders characterized by inflexible, long-standing maladaptive behaviors that typically cause distress and social or occupational problems.

PET (positron emission tomography) Imaging technique that tracks radioactive substances injected into the bloodstream, allowing researchers to view how brain activity varies in response to different sensations, perceptions, emotions, and cognitive tasks.

Phallic [FAL-ick] stage Freud's third stage of personality development, from about age 4 through age 7, during which children obtain gratification primarily from the genitals.

Phenotype A person's observable characteristics.

Phobic disorder Anxiety disorder characterized by excessive and irrational fear of, and consequent avoidance of, some specific object or situation.

Phoneme [FOE-neem] A basic unit of sound that combines with others to compose the words in a language.

Phonology The study of the patterns and distribution of speech sounds in a language and the commonly accepted rules for their pronunciation.

Photoreceptors The light-sensitive cells in the retina—the rods and the cones.

Pitch The psychological experience that corresponds with the frequency of an auditory stimulus; also known as *tone.*

Pituitary [pit-YOU-th-tare-ee] gland The body's so-called master gland, which is located at the base of the brain and closely linked to the hypothalamus and which regulates the actions of many other endocrine glands.

Placebo [pluh-SEE-bo] effect An improvement that occurs as a result of a person's expectations of change rather than as a result of any specific therapeutic treatment.

Placenta [pluh-SENT-uh] A mass of tissue that is attached to the wall of the uterus and connected to the developing fetus by the umbilical cord; it supplies oxygen, nutrients, and antibodies and eliminates waste products.

Plasticity The capability of the brain to grow and develop throughout the life span.

Plateau phase The second phase of the sexual response cycle, during which physical arousal continues to increase as the partners' bodies prepare for orgasm.

Pons A structure in the hindbrain that provides a link to the rest of the brain and that affects sleep and dreaming.

Positive psychology The subfield of psychology that combines an emphasis on positive human values such as optimism and well-being with an emphasis on research and assessment.

Positive reinforcement Presentation of a stimulus after a particular response in order to increase the likelihood that the response will recur.

Posthypnotic suggestion A suggestion that a participant in hypnosis should perform a particular action after the hypnotic session has ended.

Posttraumatic stress disorder (PTSD) A psychological disorder that may become evident in a person who has undergone extreme stress caused by some trauma or disaster and whose symptoms include vivid, intrusive recollections or re-experiences of the truamatic event and occasional lapses of normal consciousness.

Pragmatics The study of how the social context in which words are used affects their meaning.

Preconscious According to Freud, the level of the mind that contains those experiences of which a person is not currently conscious but may become so, with varying degrees of difficulty.

Predictive validity The ability of a test to predict a person's future achievement with at least some degree of accuracy.

Prejudice A negative evaluation of an entire group of people, based on unfavorable stereotypes about the group.

Properational stage Piaget's second stage of cognitive development (lasting from about age 2 to age 6 or 7), during which the child begins to represent the world symbolically.

Prevalence The percentage of a population displaying a disorder during any specified period.

Primacy effect The more accurate recall of items presented at the beginning of a series.

Primary punisher Any stimulus that is naturally painful or unpleasant to an organism.

Primary reinforcer Reinforcer (such as food, water, or the termination of pain) that has survival value for an organism.

Proactive coping A strategy for dealing with stress that involves taking action in advance of a potentially stressful situation to prevent it or modify it.

Proactive [pro-AK-tiv] interference A decrease in accurate recall of information as a result of the effects of previously learned or presented information; also known as proactive inhibition.

Problem-focused coping An active coping strategy that concentrates on changing the situation to reduce the stress.

Problem solving The behavior of individuals when confronted with a situation or task that requires insight or determination of some unknown elements.

Procedural memory Memory for skills, including the perceptual, motor, and cognitive skills required to complete complex tasks.

Projection Defense mechanism by which people attribute their own undersirable traits to others.

Projective tests Assessment instruments made up of a standard set of ambiguous stimuli that are presented to examinees, who are asked to respond to the stimuli in their own way.

Prosocial behavior Behavior that benefits someone else or society.

Prototype An abstraction, an idealized pattern of an object or idea that is stored in memory and used to decide whether similar objects or ideas are members of the same class of items.

Psychedelic drug Consciousness-altering drug that affects moods, thoughts, memory, judgement, and perception and that is consumed for the purpose of producing those results.

Psychiatrist Physician (medical doctor) specializing in the treatment of mental or emotional disorders.

Psychoactive [SYE-koh-AK-tiv] drug A drug that affects biochemical reactions in the nervous system, thereby altering behavior, thought, or perceptions and thus consciousness.

Psychoanalysis [SYE-ko-uh-NAL-uh-sis] A lengthy insight therapy that was developed by Freud and aims at uncovering conglicts and unconscious impulses through special techniques such as free association and dream analysis and through the process of transference.

Psychoanalyst Mental health practitioner, generally a psychiatrist, who has studied the technique of psychoanalysis and uses it in treating people with mental or emotional problems.

Psychoanalytic [SYE-ko-an-uh-LIT-ick] approach The perspective developed by Freud, which assumes that emotional problems are due to anxiety resulting from unresolved conflicts that reside in the unconscious and treats these problems using the therapeutic technique of psychoanalysis.

Psychodynamic theory An approach to personality that focuses on how unconscious processes direct day-to-day behavior and affect personality formation.

Psychodynamically [SYE-ko-dye-NAM-ick-lee] based therapies, Therapies that use approaches or techniques derived from Freud but reject or modify some elements of Freud's theory.

Psycholinguistics The study of how language is acquired, perceived, understood, and produced.

Psychologist Professional who studies behavior and mental processes and uses behavioral principles in scientific research or in an applied setting.

Psychology The science of behavior and mental processes.

Psychoneuroimmunology [SYE-ko-NEW-ro-IM-you-NOLL-oh-gee] An interdisciplinary area of study that focuses on behavioral, neurological, and immune factors and their relationship to the development of disease.

Psychopharmacology The study of how drugs affect behavior.

Psychophysics Subfield of psychology that focuses on the relationship between physical stimuli and people's conscious experiences of them.

Psychosexual stages The oral, anal, phallic, latency, and genital stages of personality development described by Freud, through which all people pass.

Psychosurgery Brain surgery used in the past to alleviate symptoms of serious mental disorders.

Psychotherapy [SYE-ko-THER-uh-pee] The treatment of emotional or behavioral problems through psychological techniques.

Psychotic [sye-KOT-ick] Suffering from a gross impairment in reality testing that interferes with the ability to meet the ordinary demands of life.

Puberty The period during which the reproductive system matures; it begins with an increase in the production of sex hormones, which signals the end of childhood.

Punishment Process of presenting an undersirable or noxious stimulus, or removing a desirable stimulus, in order to decrease the probability that a preceding response will recur.

Range A measure of the variability of a set of scores that is calculated by substracting the lowest score from the highest score.

Rape Forcible sexual assault on an unwilling partner.

Rapid eye movement (REM) sleep Stage of sleep characterized by high-frequency, low-amplitude brain-wave activity, rapid eye movements, more vivid dreams, and postural muscle paralysis.

Rational-emotive therapy A type of cognitive therapy that was developed by Albert Ellis and emphasizes the importance of logical, rational thought processes.

Rationalization Defense mechanism by which people reinterpret undesirable feelings or behaviors in terms that make them seem acceptable.

Raw score A test score that simply gives the number of correct answers not converted or transformed in any way.

Reactance The negative response evoked when there is an inconsistency between a person's self-image as being free to choose and the person's ralization that someone is trying to force him or her to choose a particular alternative.

Reaction formation Defense mechanism by which people behave in a way opposite to what their true (but anxiety-provoking) feelings would dictate.

Reasoning The purposeful process by which a person generates logical and coherent ideas, evaluates situations, and reaches conclusions.

Recall A method of measuring memory in which participants have to retrieve previously presented information by reproducing it.

Recency effect The more accurate recall of items presented at the end of a series.

Receptive fields Areas of the retina that, when stimulated, produce a change in the firing of cells in the visual system.

Recognition A method of measuring memory in which participants select previously presented information from other unfamilar information.

Reflex Automatic behavior that occurs involuntarily in response to a stimulus, without prior learning, and usually shows little variability from one instance to another.

Refractory period The time needed for a neuron to recover after it fires; during this period, an action potential will not occur.

Regression Defense mechanism by which a person is driven by anxiety to return to an earlier stage of psychosexual development.

Rehearsal The process of repeatedly verbalizing, thinking about, or otherwise acting on or transforming information in order to keep that information active in memory.

Reinforcer Any event that increases the probability of a recurrence of the response that preceded it.

Relearning A method of assessing memory by measuring how long it takes participants to relearn material they have learned previously.

Reliability The ability of a test to yield very similar scores for the same individual over repeated testings.

Representative sample A sample that reflects pertinent characteristics of the population from which it was drawn.

Repression Defense mechanism by which anxiety-provoking thoughts and feelings are forced into the unconscious, where they remain but are inaccessible to conscious memory.

Residual type of schizophrenia Type of schizophrenia in which the person exhibits inappropriate affect, illogical thinking, and/or eccentric behavior but seems generally in touch with reality.

Resilience The extent to which people are flexible and respond adaptively to external or internal demands.

Resistance In psychoanalysis, an unwillingness to cooperate, which a patient signals by showing a reluctance to provide the therapist with information or to help the therapist understand or interpret a situation.

Resolution phase The fourth phase of the sexual response cycle, following orgasm, during which the body returns to its resting, or normal, state.

Reticular formation An interconnected network of nerve cells that stretches from the hindbrain into the midbrain, with connections to the pons and projections toward the cortex, and that is involved in the regulation of arousal.

Retina A multilayered network of neurons that line the back of the eyeball and generate signals in response to light.

Retinal disparity The slight difference between the visual images projected on the two retinas.

Retrieval The process by which stored information is recovered from memory.

Retroactive [RET-ro-AK-tiv] interference A decrease in accurate recall of information as a result of the subsequent presentation of different information; also known as *retroactive inhibition*.

Retrograde [RET-ro-grade] amnesia, Inability to remember events and experiences that preceded a blow to the head or other event causing brain damage.

Rods Rod-shaped receptors in the retina that are primarily responsible for vision at low levels of illumination and are not especially responsive to either fine details or variations in wavelength (color).

Rooting reflex Reflex that causes a newborn to turn the head toward a light touch on lip or cheek.

Saccades [sack-ADZ] Rapid voluntary movements of the eyes.

Sample A group of individuals who participate in a study and are assumed to be representative of the larger population.

Saturation The depth and richness of a hue, determined by the homogeneity of the wavelengths of the reflected light; also known as *purity*.

Schedule of reinforcement The pattern of presentation of a reinforcer over time.

Schema [SKEEM-uh] (1) In Piaget's view, a specific mental structure; an organized way of interacting with the environment and experiencing it; a generalization a child makes based on comparable occurrences of various, usually physical or motor, actions (plural, *schemata*). (2) In cognitive psychology, a conceptual framework that organizes information and allows a person to make sense of the world.

Schizophrenic [SKIT-soh-FREN-ick] disorders A group of psychological disorders characterized by a lack of reality testing and by deterioration of social and intellectual functioning, beginning before age 45 and lasting at least 6 months.

Scientific method The technique used in psychology and other sciences to discover knowledge about human behavior and mental processes.

Secondary punisher Any neutral stimulus that initially has no negative value for an organism but acquires punishing qualities when linked with a primary punisher.

Secondary reinforcer Any neutral stimulus that initially has no value for an organism but that becomes rewarding when linked with a primary reinforcer.

Secondary sex characteristics The genetically determined physical features that differentiate the sexes but are not directly involved with reproduction.

Sedative-hypnotic Any of a class of drugs that relax and calm a user and, in higher doses, induce sleep; also known as a *sedative* or a *depressant*.

Sedatives Another term for sedative-hypnotics.

Selective attention The purposeful focusing of conscious awareness on a specific stimulus or event in the environment to the (relative) exclusion of other stimuli or events.

Self In Rogers's theory of personality, the perception an individual has of himself or herself and of his or her relationships to other people and to various aspects of life.

Self-actualization In humanistic theory, the highest level of psychological development, in which one strives to realize one's uniquely human potential—to achieve everything one is capable of achieving.

Self-concept (1) In Rogers's theory of personality, how a person sees his or her own behavior and internal characteristics. (2) In social psychology, what an individual knows and believes about himself or herself.

Self-efficacy A person's belief about whether he or she can successfully engage in and execute a specific behavior.

Self-esteem How a person feels about himself or herself.

Self-fulfilling prophecy A situation in which personal expectations unintentionally influence people's behavior.

Self-perception theory A view of attitude formation that asserts that people infer their attitudes and emotional states from their behavior.

Self-presentation A person's efforts to convey an image of herself or himself to others.

Self-serving bias People's tendency to take credit for their successes but to blame others or the situation for their failures.

Semantic memory Memory for ideas, rules, words, and general concepts about the world.

Semantics [se-MAN-ticks] The analysis of the meaning of language, especially of individual words, the relationships among them, and their significance within particular contexts.

Sensation Process in which the sense organs' receptor cells are stimulated and relay initial information to the brain for further processing.

Sensorimotor stage The first of Piaget's four stages of cognitive development (covering roughly the first 2 years of life), during which the child develops some motor coordination skills and a memory for past events.

Sensorineural [sen-so-ree-NEW-ruhl] deafness Deafness resulting from damage to the cochlea, the auditory nerve, or auditory processing areas in the brain.

Sensory memory The mechanism that performs initial encoding of sensory stimuli and provides brief storage of them; also known as the *sensory reigster*.

Separation anxiety The distress or fear response that children feel when they are separated from a primary caregiver.

Serial position curve A bow-shaped curve that represents the probability of recall as a function of an item's position in a list (series) of presented items.

Serotonin One of the monoamine neurotransmitters that plays a role in sleep, mood, and appetite.

Sex The biologically based category of male or female.

Shape constancy Ability of the visual perceptual system to recognize a shape despite changes in its orientation or the angle from which it is viewed.

Shaping Selective reinforcement of behaviors that gradually come closer and closer to (approximate) a desired response.

Signal detection theory Theory that holds that an observer's perception depends not only on the intensity of a stimulus but also on the observer's motivation, on the criteria he or she sets for the stimulus, and on the background noise.

Significant difference A difference that is unlikely to have occurred because of chance alone and is thus inferred to be most likely due to the systematic manipulation of a variable in a research study.

Size constancy Ability of the visual perceptual system to recognize that an object remains constant in size regardless of its distance from the observer or the size of its image on the retina.

Skinner box Named for its developer, B. F. Skinner, a box that contains a responding mechanism and a device capable of delivering a consequence to an animal in the box whenever it makes a desired response.

Sleep apnca A life-threatening sleep disorder in which airflow into the lungs stops for at least 15 seconds, causing the sleeper to choke and then awaken briefly.

Social categorization The process of dividing the world into ingroups and outgroups.

Social cognition The process of analyzing and interpreting events, other people, oneself, and the world in general.

Social facilitation A change in behavior that occurs when people are (or believe they are) in the presence of other people.

Social influence The ways in which people alter the attitudes or behaviors of others, either directly or indirectly.

Social interest In Adler's theory of individual psychology, a feeling of oneness with all humanity.

Social learning theory Bandura's theory that suggests that organisms learn new responses by observing the behavior of a model and then imitating it; also known as *observational learning theory*.

Social loafing The decrease in effort and productivity that occurs when individuals work in a group rather than independently.

Social need An aroused condition that directs people to behave in ways that allow them to feel good about themselves and others and to establish and maintain relationships.

Social norms The standards and values of the social group that each person internalizes.

Social phobia [FOE-bee-uh] Anxiety disorder characterized by fear of, and desire to avoid, situations in which one might be exposed to scrutiny by others and might behave in an embarrassing or humiliating way; sometimes called *social anxiety disorder*.

Social psychology The scientific study of how individual thoughts, feelings, and behaviors are influenced by social situations.

Social support Assistance from others, in the form of either emotional support or tangible help.

Socialization The process by which a person's behaviors, values, skills, plans, and attitudes conform to and are adapted to those desired by society.

Somatic [so-MAT-ick] **nervous system** The part of the peripheral nervous system that carries information from sense organs to the brain and from the brain and spinal cord to skeletal muscles, and thereby allows bodily movement; it controls voluntary sensory and motor functions.

Sound The psychological experience that occurs when changes in air pressure stimulate the receptive organ for hearing.

Specific phobia Anxiety disorder characterized by irrational and persistent fear of a particular object or situation, along with a compelling desire to avoid it.

Spinal cord The portion of the central nervous system that is contained within the spinal column and relays signals from the sensory organs, muscles, and glands to the brain, controls reflexive responses, and transmits signals from the brain to the peripheral nervous system.

Split-brain individuals People whose corpus callosum, which normally connects the two cerebral hemispheres, has been surgically severed.

Spontaneous recovery The recurrence of an extinguished conditioned response, usually following a rest period.

Sport psychology The systematic application of psychological principles to several aspects of sports.

Standard deviation A measure of the variability of the scores in a set from the mean of the set.

Standard score A score that expresses an individual's position to those of other test takers, based on the mean score and on how scores are distributed around it.

Standardization The process of developing uniform procedures for administering and scoring a test and for establishing norms.

State-dependent learning The tendency to recall information learned while in a particular physiological or emotional state most accurately when one is again in that state.

Statistics The branch of mathematics that deals with classifying and analyzing data.

Stereotype threat The fear that one's performance on a task will confirm a negative stereotype about one's group.

Stereotypes Fixed, overly simple, and often erroneous ideas about the traits, attitudes, and behaviors of groups of people, based on assumptions that all members of a given group are alike.

Stimulant A drug that increases alertness, reduces fatigue, and elevates mood.

Stimulus discrimination The process by which an organism learns to respond only to a specific stimulus and not to other similar stimuli.

Stimulus generalization The process by which a conditioned response becomes associated with a stimulus that is similar but not identical to the original conditioned stimulus.

Storage The process of maintaining or keeping information readily available, as well as the locations where information is held, also known as *memory stores*.

Strange situation technique A procedure in which infants are observed with parents, separated from them briefly, and then reunited with them in order to assess attachment patterns.

Stress A nonspecific response to real or imagined challenges or threats, as a result of a cognitive appraisal by the individual.

Stress inoculation [in-OK-you-LAY-shun] A therapeutic technique that teaches people ways to cope with stress and allows them to practice in realistic situations so that they develop "immunity" to stress.

Stressor An environmental stimulus that affects an organism physically or psychologically, producing anxiety, tension, and physiological arousal.

Structuralism The school of psychological thought that considered the structure and elements of immediate, conscious experience to be the proper subject matter of psychology.

Subgoal analysis Heuristic procedure in which a problem is broken down into smaller steps, each of which has a subgoal.

Sublimation [sub-it-MAY-shun] Defense mechanism by which people redirect socially unacceptable impulses toward acceptable goals.

Subliminal perception Perception that occurs below the threshold of awareness.

Substance abuse Overuse of and reliance on a drug in order to deal with everyday life.

Sucking reflex Reflex that causes a newborn to make sucking motions when a finger or nipple is placed in the mouth.

Superego [sue-pur-EE-go] In Freud's theory, the mental force that comprises the ego ideal (what a person would ideally like to be) and the conscience (taught by parents and society).

Superstitious behavior Behavior learned through its co-incidental association with reinforcement.

Suprachiasmatic nucleus A structure in the anterior hypothalamus, just above where the two optic nerves meet and cross in the brain.

Survey A descriptive research method in which a set of questions is posed to a large group of participants.

Sympathetic nervous system The part of the autonomic nervous system that responds to emergency situations by activating certain physiological changes to prepare the body to respond.

Symptom substitution The appearance of one overt symptom to replace another that has been eliminated by treatment.

Synapse [SIN-apps] The microscopically small space between the axon terminals of one neuron and the dendrites, cell body, or axons of other neurons.

Synaptic vesicles Small structures that are found in every axon terminal and store neurotransmitters.

Syntax [SIN-tacks] The way words and groups of words can be combined to form phrases, clauses, and sentences.

Systematic desensitization A multistage counterconditioning procedure in which a person is taught to relax when confronting a stimulus that formerly elicited anxiety.

Tardive dyskinesia A central nervous system disorder that is characterized by involuntary, spasmodic movements of the upper body, especially the face and fingers, and that can result from taking an antipsychotic drug for too long.

Team A group of individuals who interact with one another on a regular basis to accomplish a shared objective or responsibility.

Telegraphic speech A condensed form of speech used by young children, which often consists of almost all nouns and verbs, arranged in an order that makes sense.

Temperament Early-emerging and long-lasting pattern in an individual's disposition and in the intensity and especially the quality of his or her emotional reactions.

Teratogen [ter-AT-oh-jen] Substance that can produce developmental malformations (birth defects) during the prenatal period.

Thalamus A large structure of the forebrain that acts primarily as a routing station for sending sensory information to other parts of the brain but probably also performs some interpretive functions.

Thanatology The study of the psychological and medical aspects of death and dying.

Theory A collection of interrelated ideas and observations that together describe, explain, and predict behavior or mental processes.

Theory of mind A set of ideas about mental states such as feelings, desires, beliefs, and intentions and about the causal role they play in human behavior.

Threshold A level of stimulation required for activation of a neuron.

Time-out An operant conditioning procedure in which a person is physically removed from sources of reinforcement in order to decrease the occurrence of undesired behaviors.

Token economy An operant conditioning procedure in which individuals who display appropriate behavior receive tokens that they can exchange for desirable items or activities.

Tolerance The condition in which higher and higher doses of a drug are required to procedure the same effect.

Top-down analysis Analysis of perceptual phenomena that begins at the more complex level of the perceptual process, with aspects such as attention, concentration, and decision making, to see how these affect the identification of sensory stimuli.

Trait Any readily identifiable stable quality that characterizes how an individual differs from other individuals.

Transactional leader A leader who seeks to motivate others by appealing to their self-interest and who focuses on performance outcomes.

Transduction Process by which a perceptual system converts stimuli into electrical impulses; also known as *coding*.

Transfer-appropriate processing Processing of information that is similar for both encoding and retrieval of the information.

Transference Psychoanalytic phenomenon in which a therapist becomes the object of a patient's emotional attitudes about an important person in the patient's life, such as a parent.

Transformational leader A leader who is typically charismatic and able to effect change by inspiring and providing intellectual stimulation and individual attention to followers, who respond with extra effort.

Trichromatic [try-kroe-MAT-ick] theory Theory that proposed that different types of cones provide the basis for color coding in the visual system and that all colors can be made by mixing three basic colors (red, green, and blue); also known as the *Young-Helmholtz theory*.

Trichromats [TRY-kroe-MATZ] People who can perceive all three basic colors and thus can distinguish any hue.

***t*-test** An inferential statistical formula that allows researchers to determine if the means of two groups differ significantly.

Type A category or broad collection of personality traits that are loosely interrelated.

Type A behavior A behavior pattern characterized by competitiveness, impatience, hostility, and constant efforts to do more in less time.

Type B behavior A behavior pattern characterized by calmness, patience, and a less hurried and less hostile style.

Unconditional positive regard Complete and unconditional acceptance by another person.

Unconditioned response An unlearned or involuntary response to an unconditioned stimulus.

Unconditioned stimulus A stimulus that normally produces an involuntary response.

Unconscious According to Freud, the level of the mind that consists of thoughts, urges, and memories that are not within a person's awareness.

Undifferentiated type of schizophrenia A schizophrenic disorder that is characterized by a mixture of symptoms and does not meet the diagnostic criteria for any one type.

Validity The ability of a test to measure only what it is supposed to measure and to predict only what it is supposed to predict.

Variability The extent to which scores differ from one another, or especially from the mean.

Variable A condition or a characteristic of a situation or a person that is subject to change or that differs either within or across situations or individuals.

Variable-interval schedule A schedule of reinforcement in which a reinforcer (reward) is delivered after predetermined but varying amounts of time, provided that the required responses occurs at least once a after each interval.

Variable-ratio schedule A schedule of reinforcement in which a reinforcer (reward) is delivered after a predetermined but variable number of responses has occurred.

Vasocongestion Engorgement of the blood vessels, particularly in the genital area, due to increased blood flow.

Vestibular [ves-TIB-you-ler] sense The sense of bodily orientation and postural adjustment.

Visual cortex The most important area of the brain's occipital lobe, which receives and further processes visual information from the lateral geniculate nucleus; also known as the *striate cortex*.

Vulnerability A person's diminished ability to deal with demanding life events.

Wernicke's area The area of the left temporal lobe that Karl Wernicke discovered to be important for language comprehension.

Withdrawal symptoms The reactions experienced when a person with a drug dependence stops using the drug.

Working memory The storage mechanism that temporarily holds current or recent information for immediate or short-term use.

Working through In psychoanalysis, the repetitive cycle of interpretation, resistance to interpretation, and transference.

Zone of proximal development The gap or difference between a child's current abilities and what he or she might accomplish with the help and guidance of a more skilled individual.

Zygote [ZY-goat] A fertilized egg.

Abad, F. J., 416
Abbey, A., 631
Abbott, L. F., 61
Abbott, M. L., 150
Abel, M. H., 456
Abela, J. R. Z., 612
Abell, S. C., 439
Abraham, W. C., 317
Abraham, W., 163
Abramowitz, J. S., 607
Abramson, L. Y., 613
Achadi, E., 103
Acierno, R., 147
Ackard, D. M., 630
Acker, J. R.,713
Ackerman, J., 86, 314, 528, 535
Aco, E. E., 644
Acocella, J., 126
Adams, B. W., 619
Adams, J. H., 711
Addis, M. E., 48
Ader, R., 288, 572
Adeyemo, S. A., 334
Adler, A., 481, 482, 484
Adler, C. M., 607
Adler, E., 220
Adolphs, R., 372, 459
Adorno, T., 544
Agarguen, M. Y., 229
Agid, O., 622
Agrawal, S., 629
Ahern, J. , 562
Ahern, J., 562
Ahlmeyer, S., 630
Ahmed, A., 400
Aiello, J. R., 539
Aiken, L. R., 503
Aikins, D. E., 641
Ainsworth, M. D. S., 125, 126
Ajdacic, V., 607, 615
Ajzen, I.,517, 518
Akbayram, S., 229
Aker, J., 229
Akeroyd, M. A., 217
Åkerstedt, T., 241
Akuamoah–Boateng, R., 703
Alarcon, J. M., 317
Albers, L. J., 674, 675
Alcock, J. E., 231
Alexander, G. M., 45
Alexander, M. G., 529
Algom, D., 349
Allen, G. L., 236
Allen, M., 520
Allen, W., 314
Allik, J., 490
Allison, T., 196

Alloy, L. B., 613
Allport, G. W., 487, 488, 489, 544, 545
Almasy, L., 270
Alonso, J., 602, 604
Alper, C. M., 454
Altemeyer, B., 544
Alzheimer, A., 174
Ambady, N., 463
Ambridge, B., 330
American Association on Mental Retardation,
    50, 421–422
American Psychiatric Association, 14, 677
American Psychological Association (APA), 8,
    10,14, 51, 156, 270, 599, 603, 617, 620,
    621, 625, 636, 677
Amirikian, B., 80
Anastasi, A., 10
Anderson, C. A., 135
Anderson, C. A., 532
Anderson, J. S., 75, 194, 195
Anderson, K. E., 607
Anderson, N., 10
Anderson, R. N., 153, 532
Andresen, J., 261
Andrews, B., 454
Andrews, G. R., 164
Angermeyer, M. C., 602, 604
Angioni, L., 268
Angleitner, A., 472
Angst, J., 607, 615
Anstey, K. J., 164
Antoni, B. H., 661
Applebaum, R., 151
Apter, T., 169
Archambault, R., 667
Archibald, A. B., 146, 148
Arean, P. A., 671
Arendt, J., 241
Argote, L., 701
Arias, D. C., 572
Ariely 2001, 358
Ariznavarreta, C., 241
Armbruster, P., 646, 647
Armitage, C. J., 710
Armstrong, L., 224, 428
Arndt, S., 607
Arndt, J. T., 246
Aro, H., 152
Aron, A., 527
Aron, E. M., 527
Arseneault, L., 627
Asbjornsen, A., E., 185
Asch, S. E., 547
Aschersleben, G., 309, 312
Aserinsky, E., 242
Asia Society, 684
Aspinwall, L. G., 577

Astin, J. A., 258, 260
Astington, J., 122
Atlis, M. M., 378
Atwood, N. C., 645
Audinat, E., 249
Aussprung, J., 560
Austin, S. B., 445
Averett, S. L., 136
Avis, N. E., 162
Avolio, B. J., 703, 705, 706
Avolio, B. J., 705
Axelson D. A., 609
Ayduk, O., 500
Ayllon, T., 656, 657
Azar, S. T., 713

Baars, B., 237
Babcock, J. C., 533
Bachar, E., 639
Bachen, E. A., 572
Bachner–Melman, R. S., 259
Back, L., 524
Baddeley, A. D., 328, 330, 334
Bae, Y., 418
Baer, M., 712
Baguma, P., 525
Bahri, R., 711
Baie, J. S., 106
Bailey, C. H., 81
Bailey, D. S., 10, 671
Bailey, W. C., 713
Baillargeon, R., 116, 120
Baird, J. C., 208
Baird, S., 566
Baker, D. B., 394
Baker, D., 652, 653
Baker, R. C., 134
Baker, S. P., 709
Bakermans–Kranenburg, M. J., 126
Bakken, L., 119
Baldo, T. D., 527
Ball, J., 344
Ballargeon, R., 116
Bamshad, M. J. 46
Banaji, M. R., 517, 545
Bancroft, J., 447
Bandettini, P. A., 279
Bandura, A., 297, 308, 310, 311, 452, 497,
    498, 499, 531, 660
Banks–Wallace, J., 147
Banse, R., 530
Barabasz, A. F., 187
Baraona, E., 263
Barco, A., 317
Bard, P., 456, 458
Bargee, A. P., 525
Barkley, P., 671

Barlow, S. H., 666
Barnes, A., 123, 617
Barnes, M. L., 527
Barnier, A. J., 260
Baron, R. S., 688
Barr, H. M., 106
Barrera, M., 11
Barrett, L., 458, 459
Bartlett, T., 266, 346
Bartoshuk, L. M., 220
Bartsch, D., 81
Bass, B. M., 703, 705, 706
Bassman, L. E., 584, 585
Batson, C. D., 535, 537
Bauer, L. O., 270
Baughan, C. J., 710
Baum, A., 580, 581
Baumeister, R. F., 152, 158, 162, 454, 455,
    511, 512, 652, 653
Baumrind, D., 299
Bavelier D., 212
Bayley, N., 409
Baynes, K., 384
Bayster, P. G., 368
Beach, S. A., 446
Beach, S. R. H., 526, 527
Beauchesne, M. A., 123
Beauchesne, M., 123
Beck, A. T., 211, 612, 664
Becker, D. V., 181
Beckham, A. S., 10
Bednar, D. E., 151
Beeghley, L., 47
Beers, S. R., 619
Beers, T. M., 240
Behr, H., 667
Belansky, E. S., 537
Belgrave, F. Z., 166
Belle, D., 575
Bellgowan, P. S. F., 80
Belsky, J, 135
Bem, D. J., 155, 156, 519
Bender, S. T., 157
Benet–Martinez, V., 490
Benin, M. H., 537
Benjamin, L. T., Jr., 394
Benjet, C., 297
Bennett, T., 420
Bennett. G. G., 565
Bentall R. P., 515
Berger, S. M., 309
Berkeley, K. J., 224
Berkman, L. F., 580
Berkowitz, L., 531
Berman, B., 228
Berman, F. E., 687
Bernal, G., 309
Bernal, M., 11
Bernardo, A. B., 150
Berndt, T. J., 157
Bernert, S., 604

Bernstein, D., 306
Bernstein, G. A., 265
Bernstein, I. L., 288
Bernstein, L. R., 217
Berntson, G. G., 14, 223, 522
Berry, D. S., 521
Bersoff, D. M., 515
Berson, Y., 703, 705, 706
Bertacca, S., 268
Bertenthal, B. I., 110
Bertheir, N. E., 116
Bertini, M., 246
Besharat, M. A., 530
Best, C. L., 630
Bettencourt, B. A., 533
Betts, E., 646
Bexton, W. H., 186
Beyer, S., 499
Bhadha, B. R., 147
Bhatt, G., 515
Biaggio, M., 645
Bialystok, E., 384
Biddle, S. J. H., 152
Bilbrey, C. W., 324
Binder, J. R., 80
Binet, A., 394
Birmahler, B., 609
Bishop, D. V. M., 382
Bishop, J. L., 150
Biswas–Diener, R., 494
Bjorklund, D. F., 100
Bjorklund, D. F., 100
Blackwood, N. J., 515
Blair, R. J., R., 625
Blakemore, C., 194
Blakemore, J.. E. O., 312
Blanchard, E. B., 660
Blass, T., 552, 553
Blazina, C., 138
Bleak, J. L., 306
Bleeker, M. M., 499
Bleses, D., 376
Bleske, A. L., 169
Blin, O., 607
Bliss, T. V. P., 316
Bloom, F. E., 228
Bloomfield, K. 270
Blount, S,, 368
Blum, K., 228
Boake, C., 394, 395, 396, 397, 421
Bock, K., 197
Bodamer, Gardner, 387
Boden, J. M., 152
Bodnar, A. G., 163
Boggiano, A. K., 537
Bohart, A. C., 652
Boivin, D. B., 241
Boivin, M. D., 134
Boliek, C. A., 185
Bolitho, F. H., 703
Bologh, L., 641

Bolt, M., 15, 494
Bond, M. A., 669
Bond, R. A., 472, 548
Boneva, B. S., 451
Bongartz, W., 229
Boniecki, K., 657
Bookheimer, S., 75, 79
Booth, A., 83, 127
Booth, C. L., 126
Bor, D., 330, 400
Borg, E., 216
Boring, E. G., 3
Borkenau, P., 490
Borkowski, J. G., 452
Bornstein, M. H., 138, 148
Boronat, C. B., 334
Borrie, R. A., 187
Bosacki, S. L., 152
Bosch, V., 211
Bosinelli, M., 255
Bosma, H., 565, 566
Botschner, J. V., 169
Bott, D., 652
Bouchard, T. J., 99, 100, 128, 415
Bouchey, H. A., 157
Boudreaux, E., 630
Boutcher, S. H., 716
Bovbjerg, D. H., 287
Bower, G., 339
Bowlby, J., 125
Bowleg, L., 582
Boxer, P., 532
Boyd, C. M., 566
Boynton, D. M., 368
Boynton, R. M., 202
Brackett, M. A., 406
Bradford, D., 675
Bradford, L. J.,526
Bradley, C. L., 166
Braffman, W., 259
Branje, S. J. T., 146
Brannon, L., 9, 14, 48, , 454, 533, 584, 589
Bransford, J. D., 324
Braun, A. K., 384
Braverman, E. R., 228
Bray, G. A., 583
Bredemeier, B. J., 134
Breger, L., 473, 478
Brehm, J., 549
Brennan, K. A., 126
Breslin, P. A. S., 220
Breslow, L., 580
Breteler, M. H. M., 570
Bretschneider, J. G., 172
Brett, M., 50
Brewer, C. L., 6
Bridgeman, B., 149
Bridges, K. M. B., 456
Brief, A. P., 698, 700
Briere, J., 630
Britto, P. R., 158

Broberg, A. G., 127
Broca, P. 73, 77
Brockner, J., 704
Bröder, A., 361
Brodgon, M. G., 711
Brodley, B. T., 652
Brome, D. R., 166
Bronfenbrenner, U., 120, 667
Brooks, G. R., 645
Brooks, P., 229
Brooks, R., 109
Brooks–Gunn, J., 123, 127, 147, 158
Brown, A. S., 337
Brown, B., 159
Brown, G. D., 706
Brown, G. S., 646
Brown, J., 629
Brown, K. W., 500
Brown, R., 343
Brown, S. C. 323, 329, 349, 381
Brown, V., 443, 445
Bruce, M., 609
Bruck, M., 522
Bruffaerts, R., 604
Brugha, T. S., 604
Bruner, J., 121
Bryan, Y. E., 130
Bryant, R. A., 562
Bryson, T. S., 604
Buchanan, J. A., 713
Buck, C., 606
Buck, P. O., 631
Bucuvalas, M., 562
Budhani, S., 417
Bulcroft, K., 567
Bumpus, M. F., 146
Bureau of Justice Statistics, 530
Burlingame, G. M., 666
Burns, J. E., 231
Burroughs, S. M., 454
Burrwell, T., 9
Busato, V. V., 490
Bushman, B. J., 135, 532
Buss, D. M., 16, 90, 92, 93, 169, 459, 526, 528, 529
Bussandri, M., 268
Bussey, K., 311, 499
Butler, S. F., 649
Butner, J., 524
Butterfield, E. C., 322
Buttermore, N. R., 511
Buttinelli, E., 251
Bzostek, S., 159

Cabeza, R., 75
Cacioppo, J. T., 14, 223, 458, 522
Cahalan, C., 149
Cahill, S. P. 607
Cairns, B. D., 150, 151, 152
Cairns, R. B., 151, 152
Calkins, M. W., 9, 10

Call, M. J., 126
Callan, V. J., 577
Calleung, C. M., 150
Camara, W. J. 687
Cameron, J., 438
Cameron, K., 450
Cameron, P., 9, 450
Cameron, R., 579, 664
Campbell, F. W., 194
Campbell, J. D., 652, 653
Campbell, R., 565
Campion, J. E., 688
Campion, M. A., 688
Campos, J. J., 110
Cannon, W., 457
Cantor, D. W., 10
Cantor, J., 135
Cantwell, R. H., 454
Caporael L. R., 16, 93
Caputo, R. K., 123
Cardinali, D. P., 241
Carello, C., 230
Carlsmith, J. M., 520
Carlsmith, K. M., 713
Carlson–Radvansky, L. A., 196
Carmena, J. M., 374
Carr, M., 452
Carr, S. C., 703
Carr, V. J., 617
Carroll, M. E., 265
Carruth, B. R., 107
Carstensen, L. L., 171, 172
Carter, G. L., 617
Carter, K.. K., 588
Carton, J. S., 497
Cartwright, M., 572
Caruso, D., 406
Carver, C. S., 494
Casagrande, M., 251
Casas, J. M., 645
Casey, B. J., 148
Casino, S., 325
Caspi, A., 87, 129, 613, 627
Cassia, V. M., 106, 109
Cassidy, T., 562
Castonguay, L. G., 641
Catanese, K. R., 158
Cattell, R. B., 471, 488, 489, 504
Cauli, B., 249
Cavaleir, A. R., 307
Cavanagh, 207
Ceci, S. J., 416, 522
Centers for Disease Control and Prevention, 153, 158, 161, 163, 165, 588
Cervantes, J. M., 226
Chabot, D. R., 668
Chadwick, A., 157
Chaleby, K., 644
Chall, J. S., 123
Chalmers, D. J., 237, 238, 239
Chambless, D. L., 639

Chan, J., 250
Chan, R. M., 75
Chang, F. F., 81
Changizi, M. A., 442
Charles, S. T., 171, 172
Charney, D. S., 605
Chase, P. N., 310
Chase, V, M., 367
Chase–Lansdale, F. L., 158
Chassin, L., 130, 146
Chatzisarantis, N. L. D., 152
Chayefsky, P., 186
Chen G., 50, 705
Chen, H., 629
Chen, I., 130, 211
Chen, L., 212
Chen, S., 582
Chen, T. H., 228
Chen, T., 164
Cheng, B. S., 697
Chess, S., 129
Chidgey, J. E., 703
Chiesa, J. J., 241
Chiu, C. P., 163
Chiu, C., 370
Choi, I., 516
Chomsky, N., 382, 383
Chopra, S. S., 566
Chou, L. F., 697
Choy, S., 418
Chrisler, J. C., 584
Christenfeld, N., 225
Christopher, A., 645
Chusmir, L. H., 451, 454
Cialdini, R. B., 522, 549, 550
Cicogna, P., 255
Cinamon, R. G., 567
Cioffi, J., 368
Clapp, J. D., 587
Clark, C. L. 126
Clark, D. M., 605
Clark, F. L., 119
Clark, K., 10
Clark, M. P., 10
Clark, R. E., 279, 288
Claxon, G., 225
Clay, 13
Clay, R. A., 7
Cleary, D. J., 527
Clements, M., 194
Clinton, A., 631
Clinton, R. K., 116
Clutton–Brock, T. H., 297
Cobb, S., 585
Coffey, C. W., 677
Cohen, D., 464
Cohen, N., 288, 572
Cohen, P., 629
Cohen, S., 454, 572, 580
Cohn, L., 154
Cole, P., 377

Cole, S. W., 565
Coley, R. L., 158
Colledge, E., 382
Collette, F., 335
Colley, A., 344
Collings, V. B., 220
Collins, D., 716
Collins, K. M., 567
Collins, L. M., 148
Collins, R. L., 130
Collins, W. A., 138, 147, 148
Colman, H., 81
Colom, R., 416
Coltrane, S., 567
Comer, J. P., 298
Comings, D. E., 228
Compas, B. E., 146
Conger, R. D., 148, 309
Conley, R. R., 675
Connor, K., 195
Connor, P. D., 106
Connor-Smith, J. K., 146
Consolacion, T., 463, 464
Constantino, M. J., 641
Conyers, I. M., 498
Cook, B. L., 671
Cook, D. L., 217
Cook, K. V., 134
Cooper, G. D., 441
Corbetta, D., 196
Corina, D. P., 212, 384
Cornblatt, B. A., 622
Cosgrove, K. P., 265
Cosmides L., 90, 93, 239, 371, 413, 430, 458, 597
Costa, P. T., 489, 490, 504
Costantino, G., 643
Costanza, D. C., 689
Costello, B. J., 152
Costello, E. J., 615
Cottler, L. B., 449
Counter, S. A., 216
Courage, M. L., 120
Courtenay, W. H., 584
Covey, E. S., 196
Cowan, P. A., 299
Coward, L., 237
Cox, B. J., 603
Cox, R. H., 714
Cox, R. W., 80
Coyle, J. T., 62, 617, 620, 622
Coyne J. C., 562
Crabbe, J. C., 84, 87, 88, 89
Craft, L. L., 148
Craig, I. W., 87
Craig, S. B., 691
Craighead, I. W., 661
Craighead, W. E., 661
Craik, F. I. M., 323, 329, 349
Cramer, R. E., 163
Crandall, C. S., 560

Craske, M. G., 339
Crawford, M., 344
Cray, D., 148
Creeley, C. E., 339
Crespi, T. D., 658
Crick, F., 248
Crist, R. E., 374
Croker, H., 572
Cross, T. L., 151
Crosson, B., 373
Crouter, A. C., 83, 127, 146, 311
Crump, J., 504
Csikszentmihalyi, M., 15, 365, 437, 716
Cuddy, A. J. C., 546
Cuffel, B. J., 646
Cuijpers, P., 670
Culbertson, F. M., 610
Culverhouse, T., 152
Cummings, N. A., 646
Cunningham, C. L., 281
Cunningham, M. R., 525
Cunningham, M., 311
Cushman, P., 647
Cutting Edge Information, 585
Cutting, A. L., 123
Cutting, J., 377
Czeusker, T., 249

D'alessio, D., 520
D'Imperio, R. L., 574
D'Sa, C., 317
Dadds et al 1997, 289
Daghighi, S., 697
Dagot, L., 549
Dahl, R. E., 609
Dalal, R., 516
Dalton, J., 201
Damak, S., 219
Damasio, A. R., 70, 239, 372
Dana, R. H., 601
Daniel, M. H., 411
Danner, D. D., 15
Darby, B. L., 106
Darley, J. M., 410, 536, 713
Darwin, C., 4, 16, 430
Davachi, L., 325
David, A. S., 619
Davidson, R. J., 64, 70, 261, 609
Davidson-Katz, K., 497
Davis, B. L., 379
Day, N., 106
De Eerd, P., 185
de Jonge, J., 565, 566
De La Casa, L. G., 287
de Leff, J. F., 644
Deakin, J. M., 310
DeBeni, R., 165
DeBerard, M. S., 579
DeBlois, S., 116
Deci, E. L., 15, 437, 438

Deco, G., 196
Defeyter, M. A., 362
DeJong et al, 220
Dekker, Schmidt, 448
del Carmen, R., 130
DeLamater, J., 449
DeLongis, A., 562
DeLucia-Waack, J. L., 527
DeMarco, S. C., 194
Dement, W. C., 241, 242, 244, 246, 247, 248, 250, 252
Denmark, F. L., 9, 10
Dennett, D., 239
Denton, K., 544
Denys, D., 607
Desimone, R., 185
Desmet, P., 549
Detweiler-Bedell, J. B., 671
DeValois, R. L., 201
Devoto, A., 246
Di Padova, C., 263
Diamond, A., 120
Diaz-Guerrero, R., 11
Dick, D. M., 270
Dick, D., 615
Dickens, W., 418
Dickinson, S. D., 281
Diedrich, F. J., 115
Diefenbach, D. L., 626
Diener, E., 15, 436, 459, 464, 494
DiLalla, L. F., 130
DiMatteo, M. R., 586
Dimitrov, D. F., 374
Dinges, N. G., 378
DiNicola, D. D., 586
Dirks, K. T., 705
Disaster Center, 161
Disckhaeuser, F., 138
Djang, W. T., 677
Dobell, W. H., 200
Dodds, J. P., 582
Dodson, J. D., 434
Dohrenwend, B. P., 563
Dolan, R. J., 325
Dollard, J., 432, 531
Dollard, M. F., 566
Domhoff, G. W., 244, 255
Domijan, D., 185
Donker, F. J. S., 570
Donn, J. E., 524
Donson, N., 670
Dormann, C., 566
Dorn, L. D., 609
Doty, R. W., 79
Doucet, J., 575
Douthitt, E. A., 539
Dovey, T. M., 441
Dovey, T. M., 443, 445
Dovidio, J. F., 518, 546
Downey, D. B., 417
Downs, A. M., 588

Doyle, W. J., 454, 572
Drain, M., 210, 459
Driver, J., 182, 210
Druen, P. B., 525
Dryden, W., 662, 663
Dubow, E. F., 532, 534, 574
Duff, C., 270
Duman, R., S., 317
Dunaway, R. G., 152
Dunbar, R., 458, 459
Duncan, J., 330
Duncan, J., 400
Duncan, R. M., 121
Dunier, M., 151
Dunn, J., 123
Dunning, D., 350
Durand, K., 110
Durgin, F., 187
Dusch, E., 103
Dwyer, K., 119

Eagan, C. W., 153
Eagly, A. H., 703, 705
Ebbesen, E., 306
Ebbinghaus, H., 345
Ebstein, R. P., 259
Eby, L. T., 454
Eccles, J., 435
Edelheit, S., 317
Edenberg, H. J., 270
Edery–Halpern, G., 343
Edman, J. C., 250
Edwards, K., 459
Edwards, L. C., 565
Eggerman, E., 249
Ehlers, A., 562, 563
Ehrensaft, M. K. 629
Ehrhart, I. J., 588
Ehrhart, M. G., 567
Eich, D., 607, 615
Eider, L., 103
Eisenberg, N., 129
Eisenberger, R., 438
Eisenman, D. P., 565
Eishout, J. J., 490
Ek, M., 186
Eklund, M., 562
Ekman P., 455, 456, 459, 463
Elder, G. H., 148
Eley, T. C., 382
Elfenbein, H. A., 463
Elfering, A., 566
Elias, L., 197
Elliott, D. M., 630
Elliott, M. A., 710
Elliott, R., 372
Ellis, A., 662, 663
Ellis, B. J., 93
Elsner, B., 309
Elwood, W. N., 588
Emslie, G., 673

Emslie, H., 400
Enam, S., 610
Endrass, J., 607, 615
Engel, S. A., 201
Engen, E. A., 222
Engen, T., 222
Enright, M. S., 498
Epstein, L. H., 293, 307
Erdelyi, M. H., 238
Erel, O., 127
Erikson, E. H., 139, 140, 166
Erlandsson, L.–K., 562
Eron L., 532, 534
Esfandani, A, 229
Estell, D. B., 150
Esté C. P., 11
Ettner, S. L., 566
Eubank, M., 716
Evans, G. W., 123, 574
Evans, K., 266
Exner, J. E., 503
Eyberg, S., 126
Eysenck, H. J., 415, 471, 489, 504, 639
Eysenck, S. B. G., 504
Ezzo, J., 228

Fabes, R. A., 48, 533
Facteau, J. D., 691
Fagan, C., 135
Fahey, J. L., 565
Fahr, J. L., 697
Faludi, S., 156
Fantz, R., 109
Faraday, M. M., 351
Farah, M. J., 210, 459
Farmer, T. W., 150, 151
Farmer–Dougan, V., 293
Farnham, S. D., 521, 545
Farrow, T. F., D., 618
Farver, J. M., 147
Fast, J. E., 567
Fausto–Sterling, A., 133
Faves, R. A., 129
Fazio, R. H., 518
Fechner G., 183
Feinberg, F. M., 549
Feinstein, R. A., 588
Feiring, C., 126
Feist, G. J., 485, 492, 496
Feist, J., 454, 485, 492, 496, 584, 589
Ference, R., 540
Fergusson, D. .M., 603, 607
Ferlgoj, A., 451
Fernandes, M. A., 349
Fernandez, E., 562
Fernando, S., 197
Ferraro, T., 715
Ferretti, R. P., 307
Ferrin, D. L.. 705
Feshbach, S., 521
Festinger, L., 519, 520, 524

Fiedler, M., 710
Field, A. E., 445
Fierros, E. G., 402
Figiel, G. S., 677
Fillingim, R. B., 227
Fincham, F. D., 126
Fine, M., 48
Finegold, K., 151
Finkel, D., 415
First, M. B., 598, 601
Fischer, A. H., 465
Fishbain, D. A., 229
Fisher C. B., 52
Fisher, L. A., 134
Fisher, M. M., 588
Fisher, T. D., 151, 529
Fishman, D. B., 661
Fisk, S. T., 546
Fiske, S. T., 511, 512, 524, 526, 543, 546
Fitch, W. T., 375
Flammer, E., 229
Flavell, E. R., 117
Flavell, J. H., 117
Fleishman, E. A., 689
Fleming, L. M., 646
Fletcher, C., 692
Flindemann, B. J., 587
Flowers, L. A., 497
Flynn, J., 418
Foa, E. B., 661
Fogel, A., 225
Folkman, S., 562, 573, 577
Folwell, R., 671
Fontenelle, L. F., 606
Foote, R., 126
Ford, C. S., 368, 446
Forest, G., 246
Forgas, J. P., 549
Forman, D. R., 111
Fornai, F., 223
Fort, P., 249
Fortenberry, J. D., 588
Fosha, D., 641, 646
Fosse, R., 251
Foulkes, D., 244, 255
Fournier, A., K., 588
Fowler, D., 148
Fox P. T., 442
Fox, H. C., 409
Frable, D. E., 376
Fraley, R. C., 126
Frank, E., 572
Franken, R. F., 452
Franken–Berger, K. D., 149
Franklin, M. E., 607, 661
Franks, C. M., 661
Franks, J. J., 324
Frederick, C, M., 306, 497
Frederick, J. A., 567
Fredriksen, K., 247
Freeman, A., 231

Freese, M., 525
Freiberg, S. J., 706
Freidman M. A., 671
Freidrich, R. W., 221, 222
French, K. E., 715
Frenkel–Brunswick, E., 544
Freud, S., 2, 6, 11–12, 18, 237, 254, 351, 472, 473, 474, 476, 477, 479, 647
Frey, D., 324
Frey, Hinton, 196
Frezza, M., 263
Frichtel, M., 110
Fried, I., 196
Friedman, M., 229, 570
Friedrich, W. N., 449
Friesen, W. V., 15, 455, 459
Frieze, I. H., 451
Frith, C. D., 182, 210, 325
Frolkis, M., 163
Frost, J. A., 80
Frost, L., 155
Fry, A. C., 715
Fryberg, D., 52
Fujiki, N., 217
Fukada, H., 575
Fuld, K., 208
Fuller, B., 128
Fullmer, C. E., 109
Funnell, M., 79
Furman, W., 157
Furnham, A., 417, 504, 525, 606
Furr, S. R., 628

Gackenbach, J., 252
Gaertner, S. L., 518, 546
Gagnon, J. H., 449
Gaines, S. O., Jr., 545
Gainor, K. A., 645
Galambos, N. L., 146
Gale, C., 603
Galea, S., 562
Gallager, A., 149
Gallopin, T., 249
Galloway, R., 103
Galton, F., 393
Gamma, A., 314, 607, 615
Gannon, L., 430, 529
Gao, J. H., 442
Garb, H. N., 502
Garcia, J., 116, 286
Garcia, J., 287
Garcia, J., 287
Garcia, L. F., 416
Garcia, S. M., 536
Gardner, A., 385
Gardner, B., 385
Gardner, H., 401, 402
Gardner, R. A., 387
Gardner, W. L., 458, 705
Garland, A., 671
Gatchel, R. J., 229

Gates, G. J., 158
Gathercole, S. J., 330
Gaulin, S. J. C., 239, 439, 531
Gavin, J., 588
Gawne, T. J., 196
Gawronski, B., 521
Gazzaniga, M. S., 77
Gazziniga, M. S., 79
Ge, X., 148
Geary, D. C., 50, 90, 100, 154, 371
Geddes, C., 418
Geffen, G., 79
Geher, G., 478
Gelberg, L., 565
Geller, E. S., 587, 588, 709
Gelman, R., 120
Gennetian, L. A., 136
George, J. M. 698
Georgopoulos, A. P., 80
Georgopoulos, M. A., 80
German, T. P., 362
Gerra, G., 268
Gerrity, D. A.,527
Gershoff, E. T., 297, 298
Geschwind, N., 384
Gest, S. D., 157
Ghrelin, G. G., 441–442
Gibb, R., 81
Gibson, L., 110, 250
Giddens, A., 151
Gidycz, C. A., 630
Giedd, J. M., 148
Giladi, E. E., 514
Gilbreath, B., 690
Giles, L. C., 164
Gilford, P., 647
Gillespie, D. C., 75, 194, 195
Gillespie, J., 443, 445
Gilligan, C., 48, 133–134, 143
Gilmore, A., 698
Ginandez, C., 229
Ginter, H., 196
Glanz, L. H., 220
Glass, R., M., 677
Glazebrook, C., 622
Glick, P., 546
Glindemann, K. E., 588
Glynn, S., 698
Gmel, G., 270
Godbout, R., 246
Goddard, H. H., 394
Godfrey, E. G., 704
Gold J., 562
Gold, P. E., 62
Goldfried, M. R., 639, 641, 664
Golding, J., 563, 630
Goldman–Rakic, P., 9
Goldstein, N. J., 550
Goleman, D., 405
Gones, A., 148
Gonzales, L. R., 669

Gonzalez, R., 610
Goodnow, J. J., 297
Goodwin, R. D., 603, 607
Goodwin, R., 607, 615
Gordis, E. B., 564
Gordon, A. H., 465
Gordon, A., 107
Gorny, G., 81
Gottman, J. M., 465
Gould, S. J., 28
Gowaty, P., 93
Graber, J. A., 158
Grados, M. A., 606
Graham, K., 533
Graham–Bermann, S. A., 157
Grahame, N. J., 281
Graig, E., 564
Grajeda, R., 103
Granados, B., 241
Grande, L. A., 217
Granger, D. A., 83, 127
Graven–Nielsen, T., 229
Gray, R., 184
Graziano, M. S. A., 185
Grebner, S., 566
Green, F. L., 117
Green, J. P., 259
Green, M. F., 622
Greenberg, J., 343, 696
Greene, K., 588
Greenfield, P. M., 312
Greenhaus, J. H., 567
Greening, T., 652
Greenough, W. T., 81
Greenshaw, A. J., 62
Greenspan, S. I., 130
Greenwald, A. G., 186, 517, 521, 545
Grice, H.P., 377
Griffin, Z. M., 197
Grigorenko, E. L., 418
Grigson, P. S., 287
Grilo, C. M., 671
Gross, C. G., 185
Gross, R. H., 410
Grusec, J. F., 297
Grych, J. H., 126
Grzywacz, J. G., 566
Guarnaccia, P. J. J., 601
Guarnaccia, P. J., 601
Guéguen, N., 549
Guerin, B., 539, 540
Guerin, P. J., Jr., 668
Guerra, N. G. , 534
Guilford, J. P., 365
Guillemin, A., 384
Gulevich, G., 246
Guligni, A., 312
Gump, L. S., 134
Gundersen, M., 698
Gunnell, D., 622
Gunz, A., 464

Gupta, N., 691
Gupta, S., 674
Gur, R. C., 75
Gurman, A. S., 668
Gustavson, C. R., 287
Guthrie, E. K., 48, 533
Guthrie, I. K., 129
Guthrie, R. V., 10, 28
Guttmacher Institute, 158
Gwaltney, J. M., Jr., 572
Gwinn, H. M., 197

Haas, B., 563
Habib, R., 325
Hackett, P., 646
Hacking, I., 616
Hackmann, A., 563, 605
Hadhazy V. A., 228
Hagen, S., 351
Haggbloom, S. J., 7, 290
Hagger, M. S., 583, 585
Hagger, M. S., 152
Hahn, R. K., 674, 675
Hakuta, K., 384
Halford, J. C. G., 441, 443
Hall, L. K., 328
Hall, W. G., 442
Halpern, D. F., 10, 154
Halverson, S. K., 705
Hamaker, C., 490
Hamer, D., 87
Hamers, F. F., 588
Hamilton, W. D., 535
Hammeke, T. A., 80
Hammen, C., 615
Hampton, C., 166
Hampton, N. A., 498
Han, B. M., 164
Han, S., 212
Han, W., 127
Hanges, P. J., 411, 704
Hanin, B., 622
Hanley, S. J., 439
Hannover, B., 138
Hanson, K. L., 266
Hansson, K., 666
HappéF. G. E., 382
Harandi, A. A., 229
Hardi, S. S., 661
Hardy, L., 567
Hari, R., 217
Harkins, S., 539, 540
Harley, C. B., 163
Harlow, H. F., 124, 125
Harper, R. G., 625
Harrington, J., 586
Harris, C. R., 225
Harris, M. M., 690
Harris, T., 152, 627
Harrison, G., 622
Harrison, J. R., 187

Harrison, L. J., 127
Harrison, L., 127
Hart, A. B., 661
Hartung, C. M., 601
Hartung, K., 217
Hartup, W. W., 157
Harvey, E., 127
Harvey, M., 246, 247
Harvey, R., 344
Haskell, T. R., 388
Haslam, N., 450
Hatch, L. R., 567
Hatch, T., 401
Hatfield, E., 528
Haughton, E., 656, 657
Hauser, M. D., 375
Hawley, P. H., 532
Hawn, C., 540
Hay, D. F., 157
Hayden, M., 120
Hayflick, L., 164
Hayne, H., 345
Haynes, P. L. 563
Hays, R. B., 669
Hearst, N., 582
Hebb, D. O., 316, 335, 434, 435, 569
Heid, S., 218
Heider, F., 512
Helland, T., 185
Hellriegel, D., 696
Hellstedt, J. C., 717
Hemphill, S. A., 647
Henderlong, J., 438
Henderson, D., 713
Hendrick, C., 524, 527, 528
Hendrick, S., 524, 527, 528
Hendricks, K., 107
Hendriks, A. J., 472
Henkel, L. A., 350
Henry, D., 534
Hensen, L., 226
Herbst, K. C., 453
Hercus, M. J., 564
Herman, L. M., 387
Hermann, D. J., 344
Hernandez, P. J., 316
Heron, W., 186
Herring, E., 200
Herrmann, C. S., 211
Hertzog, N. B., 420
Herxheimer, A., 241
Herzog, H., 400
Hespos, S., J. 116
Hesse, E., 130
Hester, R., 456
Hetherington, E. M., 9, 138, 148, 567
Hewstone, M., 544
Hezlett, S. A., 410
Higgins, E. T., 704
Higgins, N. C., 515
High, J., 384

Highlands, T. M., 115
Hill, E. E., 662
Hill, J. O, 445
Hill, J., 241
Hindmarch, I., 612
Hinsz, V. B., 162
Hirschfeld, R. M. A., 673
Hitch, G., 330
Hoard, M. K., 50
Hobbs, A., 709
Hobbs, P., 376
Hobson, J. A., 243, 255, 256
Hobson, J. A., 251
Hochschild, A., 567
Hodges, A. E., 307
Hodson, R., 454, 699
Hoffmann, A. A., 564
Hofstede, G., 472, 490, 692
Hogan, J., 688
Hogan, R., 688
Hokrashvili, Z., 219
Holden, C., 610
Holder, J. M, 228
Holdsworth, M., 344
Holland S. K., 607
Hollingworth, L. S., 9
Hollis, K. L., 287
Hollon, D. F., 610, 615
Hollon, S. D., 639
Holloway, M., 80, 81
Holmes, T. H., 559
Holroyd, K. A., 587
Holt, P. D., 677
Holt, S. E., 163
Holtz, R., 538
Homayoun H., 619
Honeycutt, H., 100, 371
Hong, Y., 370
Hoogervorst, J. A. P., 706
Hoon, M. A., 220
Hopkins, C., 445
Horne, R., 671
Horney, K., 602
Hornstein, G. A., 12
Horton, F., 526
Horvat, J., 451
Houston, D. M., 383
Houts, A. C., 600
Hovland, C. I., 521
Howard, R. J., 515
Howe, D., 642
Howe, M. L., 120
Hoyt, C. L., 705
Hoyt, M. F., 646
Hrdy, S. B., 90
Hsieh, K., 135
Hsieh, T., 699
Hsu, H., 225
Huang, M. P., 697
Hubel, D., 194, 195, 216
Hudak, M. A., 155

Hudspeth, A. J., 216
Huesman, L. R., 532, 534
Huff, D. J., 46
Huffaker, R., 671
Huffcutt, A. I., 688
Huffman, K. J., 371
Huffman, L. C., 130
Hugdahl, K., 185
Hull, C., 430, 431
Hulme, P. A., 629
Humara, M., 715
Humayun, M., 194
Humphreys, G. W., 212
Hundley, M., 515
Hunt, G., 266
Hunt, M., 448
Hunt, R. R., 341
Hunter, M. D., 619
Hurlburt, A., 195
Hurtado, R., 103
Hurvich, L., 200
Hutton, C., 212
Huurre, T., 152
Hwang, C., 127
Hyde, J. S., 134, 418
Hyde, J. S., 149, 418, 449
Hytche, D. H., 515

Ilgen, D. R., 701
Ingram, R. E., 612
Inhelder, B., 118, 149
Inhoff, A. W., 198
Ionescu, M. D., 344
Ippolito, M. F., 574
Issakidis, C., 617
Iwamasa, G. Y., 624
Izard, C. E., 456, 463

Jackson, O. III, 325
Jackson, S. A., 716
Jackson, S. E., 685
Jacob, S., 223
Jacobi, F., 610
Jacobs, B., 316
Jacobs, G. H., 201
Jacobs, J. E., 499
Jacobs, V. A., 123
Jacobson, S. W., 106
Jadad, A. R., 228
Jaffee, S., 134, 135, 418
James, F. O., 241
James, S., 197
James, W., 5, 9, 236, 456
Jameson, D., 200
Jamison, K. R., 9
Janik, V. M., 387
Janis, I. L., 521, 540
Janssen, T., 497
Jarvis, M., 572
Javitt, D. C., 62, 617, 620, 622
Jayakody, R., 135, 136

Jazwinski, S. M., 163
Jeanneret, R. P., 686
Jeffery, R. W., 307, 691
Jenkins, G. D., Jr., 691
Jenkins, J. M., 628
Jenkins, S. R., 566
Jensvold, M. L. A., 387
Jetten, J., 548
Jimmieson, N. L., 577
Joffe, M., 698
Johannesen–Schmidt, M. C., 703, 705
Johnson, A. M., 582
Johnson, B. P., 713
Johnson, D. M., 629
Johnson, D. R., 83, 127
Johnson, J. G., 629
Johnson, L. C., 163, 246
Johnson, N. G., 10, 119
Johnson, S. D., 449
Johnson, S. H., 77
Johnson, V., 448
Johnsrude, I. S., 50
Johnston, P. J., 617
Joireman, J., 150
Jonas, E., 324
Jones V. K., 7, 290
Jones, B. C., 525
Jones, C. J., 160, 171, 172, 229
Jones, E. E., 512, E. E., 515
Jones, E. R., 646
Jones, G. H., 10
Jones, S., 130
Josse, G., 79
Jou, Y. H., 575
Jouriles, E. N., 126
Jousmaki, V., 217
Jouvet, M., 244
Juan–Espinosa, M., 416
Juffer, F., 126
Julie Grace, J., 148
Julien, R. M., 64, 264, 265
Julka, D. C., 579
Jung, C. G., 254
Jung, C. G., 484, 485
Jung, D. I., 703, 705, 706
Junginger, J., 627
Jusczyk, P. W., 383

Kabat–Zinn, J., 261
Kagan, B., 563
Kagan, J., et al, 129
Kahneman, D., 361, 363
Kail, R., 328
Kaiser–Probst, C., 566
Kalil, A., 135, 136
Kanazawa, S., 413
Kandel, E. R., 317, 335
Kanner, A. D., 562
Kaplan, D. W., 588
Karasek, R. A., 565
Karau, S. J., 540

Kark, R. 705
Kasl, S. V., 585
Kastner, S., 185
Kastner, T., 675
Katsuki, Y., 216
Katz, J., 526, 527
Kaufman, G., 173
Kaufman, J., 609
Kawakami, K., 518
Kazdin, A. E., 297, 639, 650, 655
Keefe, K., 157
Keel, P. K., 601
Keita, G. P., 9
Keitner, G. I., 667
Keitner, G. I., 671
Kelemen, W. L., 339
Kelin et al 2004, 572
Keller, H., 312
Keller, M. B., 673
Kelley, H. H., 521
Kelley, H., 513
Kelly, D. J., 287
Kelly, G. A., 495, 496
Kelly, J. G., 669
Kelly, J., 567
Kelly, M., 662
Kelly, S. J., 106
Keltner, D., 459, 463
Kemeny, M. E., 565
Kemppainen, J. K., 644
Kendall, P. C., 603
Kennedy, D. A., 504
Kennedy, M. B., 57
Kennedy, R. B., 504
Kenny, D. A., 535
Kenrick, D., 86, 93, 181, 314, 524, 528, 535
Kermoian, R., 110
Kerns, K. A., 157
Kerres Malecki, C., 153
Kessler, R. C., 564, 593, 604, 609
Ketelaar, T., 93
Ketterer, M. W., 571
Keyes, C. L. M., 454
Khan, S., 156
Kiecolt–Glaser, J. K., 454
Kiley, L. E., 316
Kilgard, M. P., 196
Kilpatrick Demaray, M., 153
Kilpatrick, D. G., 147, 630
Kilpatrick, D., 562
Kim, C., 585
Kim, H., 472
Kim, K. J., 309
Kim, S–G., 80
Kim-Prieto, C., 516
Kinkle, C., 195
Kinsey, A. C., 448, 450
Kirby, N., 344
Kirk, S. A., 601
Kirkcaldy, B. D., 152
Kirkmeyer, S., 443

Kirkpatrick, L. A., 526
Kirsch, I., 259
Kishiyama, M. M., 384
Kisker, E. E., 123
Kitayama, S., 516
Kivilu, J. M. 150
Kjellgren, A., 434
Klar, Y., 514
Klassen, R. M., 499
Klee, J. B., 285
Klein, K. J., 567
Klein, L. C., 351
Kleinsasser, D., 630
Kleitman, N., 242
Kliegl, R., 165
Kling, K. C., 149
Klinke, R., 218
Klonoff, E. A., 565
Klose, M., 610
Klump, K. L., 601
Klusman, L. E., 672
Kmietowicz, Z., 449
Kniffin, K. M., 526
Knight, D. C., 279
Knight, G. P., 48, 533
Knoblich, G., 360
Kobayashi, F.. 463
Koch, C., 196
Kochanska, G., 111
Koelling, R. A., 287
Koenigsberg, H. W., 672
Koeppen-Schomerus, G., 382
Koestner, R., 438
Koestner, R., 454
Koffka, K., 5, 211
Kogovšek, T., 451
Kohlberg, L., 131
Köhler, 211, 312
Kohnken, G., 710, 711
Kohout, J., 9, 17, 21
Kolb, B., 81
Kolodny, J., 400
Kolodny, R., 448
Koltai, P. J., 250
Kontoya, S. 526
Koob, G. F., 228
Koopman, P. L., 706
Kop, W. J., 572
Korchmaros, J. D., 535
Kornhaber, M. L., 402
Koski, L. 75
Koss, M. P., 629, 630
Kosslyn, S. M., 341
Kotimaa, A. J., 106
Krain, A., 603
Krakow, B., 563
Kral, A., 218
Krampe, R., 165
Kranitz, L., 258
Krebs, D. L., 544
Kreeger, K. Y., 48

Kreider, R. B., 715
Kreiman, G., 196
Kring, A. M., 465
Krippner, S., 254
Kristian Hill, S., 619
Kroger, J., 170
Kroll, J., 563
Kroll, N. E. A., 384
Krueger, J. I., 514, 652, 653
Kubany, E. S., 662
Kubicek, E. B., 169
Kuczynski, L., 297
Kudoh, T., 526
Kugihara, N., 540
Kuhl, P. K., 388
Kuhn, J. L., 238, 652
Kulik, J., 343
Kuncel, N. R., 410
Kupfer, D. J., 598, 601
Kush, F. R., 646
Kutchins, H., 601
Kvavilashvili, L., 343
Kwiecinski, R., 622
Kwok, Y. S., 585

Labelle, R., 497
LaBerge, S., 252
Lachance, L., 497
Lachman, J. R., 322
Lachman, R., 322
Lachter, J., 187
Ladegaard, H. J., 376
Laible, D. J., 131
Laird, J., 645
Lakoff, R. T., 376
Lam, S. S., K., 692
Lamb, C. A., 341
Lamb, M. E., 127
Lambert, M. J., 639
Lampl, I., 75, 194, 195
Landrine, H., 545
Landry, J. C., 521
Laner, M. R., 537
Lang, A. J., 339
Lang, P. J., 460
Lang, S. L., 344
Lange, C., 456
Langer, E., 573, 574
Lanza, S. T., 148
Lao, L., 228
Larabee, A. L., 624
Larrick, R. P., 368
Larsen, R. J., 526
Larson, D. C., 134, 146
Larsson, M., 344
Larzelere, R. E., 299
Lasenby, J., 111
Lashley, K. S., 336
Latané, B., 536, 539, 540
Latham, G. F., 693, 694, 695
Latham, G. P., 684, 697

Lattanzi, K. M., 196
Laumann, E. O., 448, 449
Laurenceau, J. P., 641
Laurent, G., 221, 222
Laursen, B., 147
Lavie, P., 240
Lawler, E., 694
Lawler, J. J., 372
Lazarus, R. S., 461, 560, 562, 573
Lazarus, R., 562
Leary, M. R., 453, 454, 455, 511
Lebedev, M. A., 374
Lebow, J. L., 668
Lechuga, D. M., 226
Leclerc, C., 207
Lecuyer, R., 110
Ledlow, S., 86, 314, 528, 535
LeDoux, J. E., 239, 315
Lee, B. P. H., 137
Lee, E., 120
Lee, K.-H., 618
Lee, M., 602
Lee, N., 111
Lefcourt, H. M., 496, 497
Lehrer, P., 288
Lei, A., 602
Leibowitz, H. W., 209
Lein, K. G., 324
Leiter, N. P., 566
Lende, D. H., 270
Lenneberg, E., 384
Leonard, H., 421
LePage, J. P., 657
Lepper, M. R., 438
Lesaux, N. K., 378
Leskin, G., 563
Leslie, M., 416
Leung, L. S., 70
Levanthal, T., 124, 147
Leventhal, H. E., 671
Levine, D., 525
Levine, M., 669
Levine, R. E., 644
Levine, R. L., 164
Levine, R. V., 537
Levinson, D., 167-168, 169, 544
Levitt, M. J., 137
Levitt, P., 622, 623
Levy, G. D., 155
Lewald, J., 197
Lewin, K., 648, 702
Lewin, M., 417
Lewin, T. J., 617
Lewinsohn, P. M., 609
Lewis, D. A., 622, 623
Lewis, M. 126
Lewis, S., 106
Lewis-Fernández, R., 601
Li, G, 709
Lichtenberg, P. S., 259
Lichtenstein, S., 163

Lichtman, J. W., 81
Lickliter, R., 100, 371
Liddell, A., 276
Lidow, M. S., 226
Lieber, C. S., 263
Liebermann, J., 675
Lilienfeld, S. O., 502, 503
Lilly, J., 186, 187
Lin, K. M., 644
Linberg, C. D., 287
Lindblom, J. 121
Lindemeier, J., 220
Lindsay, D. S., 351
Lindsey, E. W., 527
Lippitt, R., 702
Lisanby, S. H., 677
Little 2000, 100
Little, A. C., 525
Little, B. R., 676
Littlefield, L., 647
Liu, F., 50
Liu, G., 212
Liu, H. M., 388
Liu, H., 565
Liu, W., 194
Liu, X., 646
Liu, Y., 442
Liu, Z., 714
Livingston, R. H., 124
Lobel, T. E., 133
LoBello, S. G., 527
Lock, J., 450
Locke, E. A., 498, 693, 694, 695, 697
Locker, D., 276
Lockhart, R., 323
Loeb, S., 128
Loftus, E., 9, 260, 350
Logan, G. D., 276, 334
Lokko, P., 443
LoLordo, V. M., 298
Lømø,T., 316
Long, B. C., 566
Long, D. L., 384
Long, H. H., 10
Long, T. S., 14
Longman, D. J., 334
Looman, M. D., 706
Loop, M. S., 201, 202
Lopez, S. R., 11, 601
Lord, R. D., 704, 706
Louis, W., 377
Lövdén, M., 344
Love, J. M., 123, 127
Lovett, S., 698
Lowden, A., 241
Lowe, P. A., 344
Lowell, E. L., 452
Lubar, J. F., 228
Lubar, J. O., 228
Lubart, T. I., 365
Lubinski D., 421

Lubow, R. E., 287
Luby, M., 196
Lucas, K. J., 582
Lucas, R. E., 436, 494
Lucidi F., 246, 251
Luckner, M., 165
Lundin, R. W., 285
Lundqvist, G., 666
Luo, Y., 120
Luppi, P-H., 249
Luszcz, M. A., 164
Luthar, S. S., 645
Lycett, J., 458, 459
Lykken, D. T., 99, 128
Lymburner, J. A., 628
Lynn, R., 472
Lynn, S. J., 503
Lyubomirsky, S., 560

Ma, J., 70
Macaluso, F., 182, 210
MacBrayer, E, K., 515
Maccoby, E. E., 136, 138, 148, 154, 155, 312
MacDonald, M. C., 388
MacDonald, S., 345
MacFadden, A., 197
Mack, A., 187
MacKain, J., 21
MacNeilage, P. F., 379
MacNichol, J. R., 200
Maddox, J. H., 677
Maddux, J. E., 452
Maguire, E. A., 325
Magyar-Moe, J. L., 454
Mahalik, J. R., 48
Mahoney, J. L., 151
Maier, N. R. F., 285
Maier, S. F., 298
Main, M., 130
Major, V. S., 567
Makela, J. P., 217
Malberg, J., 317
Malgady, R. G., 643
Malinowski, J. C., 197
Malspels, S., 445
Maner, J. K., 181, 524
Manlove, J., 158
Manning-Ryan, B., 163
Manns, J. R., 279, 288
Manstead, A. S. R., 465
Maquet, P., 256, 325
Marano, M. R., 601
March, J. S., 615
Marcia, J. E., 166
Margolin, G., 564
Margolis, R. L., 69
Marino, L., 384
Markey, P. M., 537
Markowitsch, H. J., 336
Markowitz, J. C., 610, 615
Marks, L. E., 185

Marks, W. B., 200
Markus, H. R., 472
Marques, C., 606
Marquis, D. P., 279
Marriott, L. K., 62
Marshall-Mies, J., 689
Marsland, A. L., 572
Martin, C. E., 448
Martin, C. L., 138
Martin, J. N., 526
Martin, J., 87
Martin, K. C., 81
Martin, M., 241
Martin, S., 10
Martin, T., 472
Martinez, T. S., 537
Martino, G., 185
Mas Nieto, M., 229
Masand, P. S., 674
Masia, C. L., 310
Maslach, C., 566
Maslow, A., 438, 439, 491
Mason, E., 498
Masten, Reed, 573, 574
Masters, W., 448
Matlin, M. W., 162
Matsumoto, D., 377, 463, 464, 526
Mattes, R. D., 443
Matz, D. C., 162
Maxwell, S. E., 452
Mayer, D. M., 411
Mayer, J. D., 405, 406
Mayfield, J. W., 344
Maynard, A., 312
Mazur, A., 385
Mazure, C. M., 609
McAuliffe, B. J., 548
McAuslan, P., 631
McBurney, D. H., 197, 229, 239, 430, 531
McCain, G., 26
McCall, V. W., 677
McCarley, R., 255
McCarthy, G., 196
McCartney, K., 126
McCarty, R., 199
McClay, J., 87
McClearn, G. E., 415
McClellan, J. A., 152
McClelland, D. C., 435, 451, 454
McClintock, M. K., 223
McConahay, J. B., 546
McConatha, J. T., 173
McConkey, K. M., 260
McConnell, G. N., 628
McCourt, K., 100
McCoy, N. L., 172
McCracken, L. M., 587
McCrae, R. R., 472, 489, 490
McCrae, R. R., 472, 490, 504
McCrary, F., 453
McDaniel, J. G., 691

McDermott, D., 135
McDonald, J. J., 185
McDonald, R., 126
McDonough-Ryan, P., 607
McEwen, B. S., 130
McFarland, K., 79
McGaugh, J. L., 316
McGehee, R. M. E., 442
McGhee, D. E., 545
McGinn, C., 238
McGinnis, J. M., 580
McGlynn, R. P. 365, 660
McGonagle, K A., 604
McGrath, C., 75
McGrath, E. P., 612
McGrath, J. E., 672, 701
McGregor, B. A., 661
McGue, M., 415
McGuffin, P., 88
McGuire, L., 627
McGurk, D., 365, 660
McHale, S. M., 83, 127, 146, 311
McInnis, M. G., 615
McIntyre, C. K., 62
McKim, W. A., 263
McKinlay, A., 173
McLean, A. W., 246
McLynn, F., 254
McMahon, D. B. T., 220
McMahon, T. J., 645
McManus, F., 605
McMullin, C. S., 281
McNalley, R. J., 562, 616
McNamara, T. P., 324
McNeil, J. E., 210
McNeill, D., 381
McVittie, C., 173
Meadows, S., 121
Mechanic, D., 583
Medland, S. E., 79
Meichenbaum, D., 579, 664
Meiri, N., 317
Meland, S., 525
Melara, R. D., 349
Melfi, C. A., 644
Meltzoff, A., 109, 116
Melville, J., 606
Melzack, R., 227
Mendlowicz, M. V., 606
Mense, S., 229
Mercey, D. E., 582
Merckelbach, H., 275
Meredith, W., 160, 171, 172
Merrill, S. S., 161
Merritt, M. M., 565
Merritt, R. D., 624
Merry, T., 652
Merzenich, M. M., 196
Mesquita, B., 464, 601
Metalsky, G. I., 613
Metcalfe, J., 79

Metsch, L. R., 582
Metzger, L. J., 563
Meyer, I. H., 450, 565
Micallef, J., 607
Michael, R. T., 448, 449
Michael, T., 563
Michalsen, R., 646
Mickelson, K. D., 564, 698
Middleton, B., 241
Mikkelsen, A., 698
Milani, I., 106
Milgram, S., 550, 552
Milich, R., 515
Mill, J., 87
Miller, D., 228
Miller, G., 328, 383, 387
Miller, I. W., 671
Miller, J. G., 515
Miller, J. K., 666
Miller, K. F., 120
Miller, L. C., 529
Miller, N. E., 432
Miller, N., 258, 432, 533
Millon, T., 637
Milner, B., 335
Milner, H. R., 497
Miner, J. B., 687
Minuchin, S., 11Mischel, W., 500
Mistal, M., 644
Mitchell, J. P., 325
Mitchell, T., 212
Mitchison, G., 248
Mitler, M. M. 247
Mitra, A., 691
Mittelhammer, R., 671
Mitterschiffthaler, M. T., 609
Miyamoto, Y., 516
Moffitt, T. E., 87, 627
Mohlenbeck, C., 710
Moi, G., 268
Moise-Titus, J., 532
Mok, D. S., 630
Mokdad, A. H., 265, 369, 581
Moller, H. J., 628
Mör-Leimkü A. M., 571
Monastra, V. J., 228
Moncrieff, J., 674
Mondloch, C. J., 210
Montague, D. P., 110
Montgomery, D., 574
Montgomery, G. H., 287
Moore, J. L. III, 497
Moore, K., 159
Moore, M. K., 116
Moore, S., 657
Moore, Z. E., 717
Moorhead, G., 540
Moran, J., 377
Morey, 601, 624
Morin, G. B., 163
Morris, C. D., 324

Morris, M. W., 516
Morris, M., 370
Morrish, E., 251
Morrison, M. A., 445
Morrison, T. G., 445
Morrongiello, B. A., 111
Moscovitch, M., 349
Mosier, Rogoff, 137
Moskowitz, D. S., 500
Moskowitz, G. B., 536
Moskowitz, J. T., 577
Mosquera, P. M. R., 465
Moss, 712
Most, 187
Mounts, 146
Mouras, 447
Moutafi, J., 504, 525
Moyer, 677
Mueser, 619
Muhlethaler, M., 249
Muller, D. 261
Mumford, 365
Munk, 317
Munt, P. W., 246
Murad H., 622
Muris, P., 275
Murnen, 533
Murphy, B. C., 129
Murphy, Jowdy, 716
Murphy, S. E., 705
Murray, R. M., 16, 228, 515, 670
Myers, 459, 464, 503

Nabekura, J., 81
Nachson, I., 343
Nail, P. R., 546
Najjar, L., 156
Nakamura, J., 437
Nakawaga, S., 317
Nannini, D. K., 92
Napholz, L., 169
Narang, S. K., 147
Nardi, P. M., 37
Nash, R. A., 228
Nashino, 189
Nathan, P. E., 598, 600, 617, 625, 626
Nathans, J., 202
National Academy on an Aging Society, 161
National Center for Health Statistics, 158, 175, 581, 628
National Council on Aging, 162
National Institute on Deafness and Other Communication Disorders, 218
National Institute on Drug Abuse, 266
National Institutes of Health, 174, 175, 228
National Research Council, 457
Naumann, A., 249
Nebeker, R. S., 666
Neck, C. P., 540
Neiderhoffer, P., 576
Neighbors, H. W., 601

Neiss, M., 416
Neisser, U., 333
Neitz, J., 201, 202
Neitz, M., 201, 202
Nelson, D. L., 334
Nelson, G., 527
Nelson, K., 333
Nelson, S. B., 61
Nelson-Goens, G. C., 225
Nemeroff, C. B., 673
Neppi, T., 309
Ness Research Team, 123, 124
Nesse, R. M., 270
Netzer, N. C., 250, 251
Neubauer, A. C., 401
Neumark-Sztainer, D., 153, 630
Nevett, M. E., 715
Neville, H. J., 81, 212
New York Longitudinal Study, 129
Newcomb, A. F., 137
Newell, F. N., 400
Newman, L. S., 481
Newman, S. P., 586
Newstead, L., 662
Newton, T. L., 454
Nguyen, H. T., 279
NICHD Early Child Care Research Network, 128, 135
Nichols, M. P., 667, 668
Nicol, J., 378
Niedzwienska, A., 343
Nier, J. A., 515
Nilsson, L.-G., 344
Nisbett, R., 47, 441
Nisbett, R. E., 451, 515
Nitschke, J. B., 64, 609
Noble, L. M., 586
Nobre, A. C., 196
Nolen-Hoeksema, S., 610
Norman, D., 707
Norris, C., 14
Nosek, B. A. 499
Nourkova, V., 351
Novak, M. A., 116
Novins, D. V., 148
Nucci, C., 663
Nusbaum, J., 14
Nyberg, L., 325

Oakland, T., 421, 422
Oakley-Browne, M., 603
Oberman, Y., 127
O'Brien, M., 641
Obrzut, J. E., 185
Occhionero, M., 247, 252
O'Connor, D. B., 574, 576
O'Connor, L., 135
O'Doherty, J. E., 374
Oelveczky, B., 196
Oener, A. F., 229
Oetzel, K. B., 640

Ogawa, K., 256
Ogren, H. A., 463
Ohio State University 2004, 106
Ohlsson, S., 360
öhman, A., 458
Oishi, S., 15, 436, 494
Okagaki, L., 399, 451
Okorn, D. M., 281
Oksol, E. M., 687, 711
Okuda-Ashitaka. E., 228
Olausson, B., 228
Olds, J., 315
Oliver, M. B., 449
Oliver, W., 644
Olsen, N., 713
Olsen, R. A., 368
Olson, S. E., 46
Olweus, D., 534
O'Mara, S. M, 316
O'Neal, K. K., 150
Ones, D. S., 503
Ong, L. 661
Oppenheimer, D. M., 368
O'Reilly, B., 703
Orth-Gormér, K., 570
Ortiz, J., 625, 627
Orzi, F., 223
Oshodi, J. E., 452
Osorio, L. C., 185
Ostendorf, F., 490
Ostroff, C., 154
Osvath, P., 613, 674
O'Toole, M. L., 715
Otten, L. B., 152, 325
Otto, R., 713
Ouelette, M., 163
Ovaert, Cashel, Sewell, 666
Owen, A. M., 50, 330
Owen, M., 126
Owens, L., 533
Oyserman, D., 47
Ozer, E. J., 563

Pace-Schott, E. E., 240, 243, 248, 249,256
Padilla R., 585
Page, K., 622
Page, M. C., 48, 533
Pagel, J. F., 251
Paik, A., 449
Paivio, A., 342
Palladino, P., 165
Palmer, D. K., 574, 688
Palmer, B., 406
Palmore, E., 173
Paluch, R., 293
Pan, C., 228
Pani, M., 209
Panico, S., 673
Panksepp, J., 225, 455
Pantin, H. M., 536
Papp, P., 645

Paquette, V., 75, 664
Pargament, K. I., 494
Park, C. L., 578, 579
Park, H. S., 149
Park, H., 516
Park, J., 169
Parker, J. D. A., 406
Parker, G. A., 297
Parks, C. A., 645
Parks, L., 147
Parry, J. V., 582
Parvizi, J., 372
Pascual, A., 549
Patience, R. A., 162
Patsdaughter, C., 123
Patterson, D. R., 229, 259, 260
Patterson, L. J., 677
Paulsell, D., 123
Paulus, P. B., 540
Paunovic, N., 660
Pavlov, I., 276, 280
Pawlak, C. R., 562
Payne, A., 157
Pearce, J. L., 698
Pederson, C. B., 622
Pedersen, D. M., 209
Pedersen, N. L, 173, 176, 415
Pedersen, W., 529
Pellegrini, A. D., 100
Pelli, D. G., 204
Peltzer-Karpf, A., 111
Penfield, W., 72
Peng, K., 370, 516
Penley, J. A., 577
Pennebaker, J., 576
Penzien, D. B., 587
Peper, L., 195
Peplau, L. A., 48
Perloff, R., M., 588
Perner, J., 238
Perrett, D. L., 525
Perretta, S., 350
Perry, E. D., 153
Perry, E. L., 692
Pert, 62
Perugini, M., 472
Peselow, 615
Peter, R., 565, 566
Peters, H. E., 136
Peters, J. C., 445
Peters, R. D., 670
Peterson, C., 298, 494, 613, 653
Peterson, L., 328
Peterson, M., 328, 699
Peterson, R. D., 713
Petrides, K., 406
Petrides. M., 75
Petrill, S., 414, 417
Petrinovich, L., 314
Petrosini, L., 69
Pettit, J. W., 609

Vingelen, I., 344
Violani, C., 246
Violani, C., 251
Vishow, D., 562
Visscher, B. R., 565
Visser, 443
Voelker, 247
Vogel, J. J., 79
Vohs, K. D., 158, 652, 653
Volkow, N. D., , 70
von Helmholtz, H., 199
von Hofsten, F. , 116
Von Senden, T., 194
Vroom, V. H., 694, 704
Vroon, P., 221
Vygotsky, L., 120, 121, 122, 400

Wadden, T. A., 444
Wadsworth, M. E., 146
Wagar, B. M., 344
Wagner, A. D., 325
Wagner, E. E., 502
Wagner, J. D., 83
Wagner, M., 208
Wagner, S. H., 698
Wagner, T. D., 335
Wagstaff, G. E., 350
Wakefield, J. C., 308, 597
Waldfogel, J., 127
Waldie, K., 79
Walford, S., 606
Walker, A. R. P., 444
Walker, E., 622, 623
Walker, L. A., 711
Walker, L. J., 131, 132
Walker, L. S., 567
Walker, S., 533
Walker-Andrews, A. S., 2001
Walkup, J., 606
Wall, P., 225, 226, 228, 229, 587
Wall, T. L., 228
Walla, P., 80
Waller, N. G., 490
Wallerstein, J., 9
Walsh, V., 79
Walsh, K. K., 675
Walster, E. M., 529
Wamala, S. P., 566
Wampold, B. E., 639
Wandersman, A., 669, 670
Wang, A., 563
Wang, J., 164
Waraich, P., 615
Ward, L. M., 185
Ward, R., 373
Wardle, J., 572
Warner, M. B., 406, 624
Warner, R. M., 406
Warnick J. E., 7, 290
Warnick, R., 7, 290
Warrington, E. K., 210

Washburn, J. J., 625
Washburn, M. F., 9, 10
Washington, T., 187
Watanabe, T., 252
Waterhouse. J., 241
Waters, E., 126, 139
Watkins, C. E., 138
Watson, J. B., 6, 279, 283
Watts, C., 630
Way, N., 247
Wearing, H., 330
Weaver, K., 536
Webb, R. M., 250, 420
Weber, E., 183
Webster, R., 478, 481
Wechsler, D., 395, 416
Weddle, D. O., 164
Weerasekera, P., 652
Weidner, G., 571
Weiland, J., 194
Weine, S. M., 563
Weiner R. D., 677
Weingartner, H., 339
Weinstein, N. D., 583
Weisberg, R. B., 515
Weiser, S., 326
Weisfeld, G. E., 225
Weiss, H. M., 700
Weissman, M. M., 615
Weitz, R., 584
Wellings, K., 448
Wellman, H. M., 122, 137
Wells, G. L., 350
Wells, S., 533
Wen, X., 421
Werker, J. F., 382
Werner, W. L., 169
Wernicke, K. 73, 77
Wertheimer, M., 5, 211
Wessels, H., 127
Westefeld, J. S., 628
Westgaard, R. H., 708
Wetsman, A., 525
Whaley, A. L., 57, 81, 601, 644
Whalley, L. J., 409
Whang, K., 80
Wharry, 376
Wheeler, 333
Wherry, L., 151
White, J. D., 275
White, K. M., 518
Whiteman, M. C., 409
Whiteman, S. D., 311
Whittler, T. E., 523
WHO International Consortium in Psychiatric
    Epidemiology, 609-610
Wibom, R., 241
Wicherski, M., 9, 17, 21
Widdicombe, S., 173
Widfield, A., 435
Widiger, T. A., 601, 623, 626

Wiehe, V. R., 630
Wiesel, T., 194, 195, 216
Wilde, G., J. S., 246
Wiley, J., 362, 366, 384
Wilinson, W. E., 677
Williams, R. B., 567, 570, 622
Williams, D. R., 564
Williams, J. M., 317
Williams, K. D., 540
Williams, K., 539, 540
Williams, W. M., 416
Williamson, A., 709
Williamson, D. E., 609
Willingham, D. T., 73, 75, 76
Willis, H., 544
Willis, S. L., 164
Willoughby, T., 342
Wills, L., 250
Wills, T. A., 454
Wilson, D. S., 526
Wilson, G. T., 307
Wilson, H. W., 148
Wilson, J. F., 197
Wilson, J., 229
Wilson, K. D., 210, 459
Wilson, T. D., 511
Windler, C., 121
Winefield, A. H., 566
Winefield, H. R., 566
Winsler, A., 307
Winson, J., 244, 251
Winterich, J. A., 162
Wise, R. A., 70, 350
Wiseman, R. J., 330
Wisniewski, N., 630
Witt, S. D., 532
Witztum, E., 643
Wojcik, A., 293
Wolfe, B. E., 639
Wolpe, J., 659
Wolpert, E. A., 252
Wolz, A. P., 387
Wood, J. J., 135, 136
Wood, J. M., 452, 502
Wood, W., 529
Woodhill, B. M., 156
Woodruff, D. W., 298
Woods, J. M., 196
Woods, S. C., 441, 444
Woodward, W. R., 129, 308
Woo-Ming, A. M., 672
Wordsell, A. S., 301
Worthman, C. M., 245
Wright, W. E., 163
Wu, C-H., 525
Wu, J., 646
Wu, L., 697
Wu, T. Y., 697
Wunderlich, U., 628
Wundt, W., 3-4, 236, 456
Wyatt, G. E., 10

Wynn, K., 115
Wyszecki, G., 202

Xie, H., 151
Xu, J., 546
Xuei, Z., 270

Yan, L., 241
Yang, S., 399, 504
Yapko, M. D., 674
Yarbrough, G. L., 7, 290
Yarmey, A. D., 350
Yasumatsu, K., 219
Yen, S., 629
Yerkes, R. M., 434
Yeung, N., 185
Yik, M. S. M., 692
Yirmiya, N., 127

Yonan, C. A., 226
Yonelinas, A. P., 384
Yoshimasu, K., 570
Young, J. E., 661
Young, L. R., 445
Young, S. N., 62
Young, T., 199, 250
Youngstedt, S. D., 248
Youniss, J., 152
Yu, H., 150
Yzer, M. C., 588, 589

Zachar, P., 527
Zaimovic, A., 268
Zajonc, R., 417, 539
Zangwill, B., 197
Zarcone, F., 301
Zawacki, T., 631

Zeineh, M. M., 75, 335
Zentall, T. R., 309
Zhang, L.F., 150
Zhang, L. I., 196
Zhao, S., 604
Zheng, M., 382
Ziegler, P. J., 107
Ziemke, T., 121
Zimbardo, P., 541
Zimmerman, R. R., 92, 125
Zislin, J., 622
Zoucha, R., 643
Zuber, J. A., 541
Zucker, A. N., 169, 170
Zuckerman, 490, 573, 574, 604, 606, 609,
    610, 611, 613, 627

Ablation, 73
Abnormal behavior, 593–598, 631. *See also* Psychopathology
  behavioral model of, 596
  biophysical approach to treatment, 597
  characteristics of, 594–594
  cognitive model of, 596
  eclectic approach to treatment of, 597
  evolutionary model, 597
  humanistic model of, 595–596
  medical-biological model, 594–595
  models of, 594–597
  psychodynamic model of, 595
  sociocultural model of, 596–597
Abnormal psychology, 631. *See also* Psychopathology
Absolute threshold, 183, 231
Abu Ghraib prison story, 553
Access (to thought), 239
Accommodation, 113–114, 233
  visual, 207
Acetylcholine, 62, 64, 94
Achievement tests, 406–407, 424
Acquaintance rape, 630
Acquisition process, 278
Acrophobia, 605
Action potential, 59, 94
Activation-synthesis theory of dreaming, 256
Actor-observer effect, 515, 554
Acupuncture, 228
Adaptations (behavioral), 90–92, 97, 113–114
Addiction, 262
Adolescence, 146–159, 168, 176
  cognitive development in, 149–151
  emotional and social development in, 151–159
  in Erikson's stage theory, 166
  ethnic identity in, 152
  friendship and sexual behavior in, 157–159
  gender identity development in, 154–155
  multiple contexts of, 146–147
  physical development in, 147–148
  suicide in, 153–154
Adrenal glands, 83
Adrenaline, 65, 83
Adulthood, 159–176. Adulthood. *See also* Aging
  ageism and, 173
  changes in important domains of functioning, 160
  cognitive changes in, 164–165
  fitness changes in, 161
  gender differences in adult stages, 169
  health and aging, 173–174
  physical changes in, 160–164
  sensory changes in, 161

sexual behavior in, 162–163
sexual changes in, 162
social and personality development in, 165–166
stage theories of adult development, 166–170
Afferent neurons, 56, 65, 94
  action of, 57
African Americans
  in psychology, 10–11, 24
  represented in U.S. population, 47
  schizophrenic disorders in, 617
  stress in, 565
Age/aging
  bias based on, 46, 49, 54
  as factor in brain plasticity, 81
  genetic theory of, 164
  health and, 173–174
  heredity and, 163
  homeostatic theory of, 164
  myths regarding, 171–173
  physiological explanations for, 164
  prevalence of depressive disorders and, 610
  stereotypes regarding, 171–173
  theories of, 163–164
  wear-and-tear theory of, 164
Ageism, 173, 178
Aggression, 530–534, 555
  cognitive view of, 532–533
  controlling, 533
  gender differences in, 533–534
  as learned behavior, 531–532
  readiness state, 531
  research on, 48
  testosterone and, 83
Agnosia, 210, 233
Agonists, 63–64, 94
Agoraphobia, 604
AIDS (acquired immune deficiency syndrome), 581–583
Alarm stage of stress, 558–559
Alcohol
  as a psychoactive drug, 263–264, 273
  behavioral effects associated with blood levels, 264
  effects on prenatal development, 106
  relationship between consumption and blood level, 263
  use on college campuses, 587–588
Algorithm(s), 360–361, 389
All-or-none (action potential), 60, 94
Allport's personal disposition theory of personality, 487–488
Alpha waves, 74
Altered state of consciousness, 238
  sleep as, 239
  psychoactive drugs and, 263–264

Alternative therapy, 677
Altruism, 535–536, 555
Alzheimer's disease, 174, 178
Ambivalent attachments, 530
Ambivalent sexism, 546
American Psychiatric Association, 49
American Psychological Association (APA), 8, 9, 26, 49, 636
American Sign Language (ASL), 375
Amitriptyline, 673
Amnesia, 352, 355
Amok, 596
Amphetamines, 265
Amplitude, 213, 233
Amygdala, 69– 70, 95
Anal stage, 476
Analytic dimension (of intelligence), 402, 403
Analytical psychology, 484
Androgens, 82, 446
Androgyny, 377, 391
Androgynous behaviors, 156
Anorexia, 601
Antagonists, 63–64, 94
Anterograde amnesia, 352, 355
Antianxiety drugs, 672–673, 681
Antidepressant drugs, 612, 673–674, 681
  effectiveness of, 674
  side effects from, 673–674
Antimania drugs, 674, 681
Antipsychotic drugs, 674–675, 681
  side effects from, 675
Antischizophrenic drugs, 622
Antisocial personality disorder, 624–626, 634
  violence associated with, 627
Anvil (ossicle), 214–216
Anxiety, 602, 632
  and pain, 229
Anxiety disorders, 602, 632
  generalized anxiety disorder, 603
  obsessive-compulsive disorder, 606–607
  panic disorder, 603
  phobic disorders, 603–605
Anxiolytics, 672
Apoptosis, 163
Appraisal, 461
Approach-approach conflict, 466
Approach-avoidance conflict, 432–433
Approach-avoidance conflict, 467
Appropriate response, 365
Aptitude tests, 406–407, 424
Archetypes, 484
Archetypes, 506
Army Intelligence Test, 397
Aromatherapy, 677
Arousal, 434, 467
Arousal theory of motivation, 434–435
Artificial intelligence (AI), 371, 390

Asian Americans (in psychology), 10–11
Ask-and-ye-shall-receive technique, 549, 556
Assessment, 500–502, 509
Assimilation, 113–114
Ataque de nervios, 601
Athletic performance
    anxiety and, 715
    arousal and, 714–715
    intervention strategies to improve,
        715–716
Atmospheric perspective, 207
Attachment, 124, 143
    child care and, 127–128
    evolutionary perspective on, 128
    in infants, 125–127
Attachment theory, 530
Attention, 309, 323
    interference with, 349
Attitudes, 554
    and behavior, 516–523
    dimensions of, 517–518
    explicit and implicit, 517–518
    mechanisms of changing, 521–523
Attribution, 512–516, 553
    cultural shaping of, 516
    errors in, 514–515
    external, 512, 554
    internal, 512, 554
    process of, 513, 554
Atypical antipsychotic drugs, 674
Audiometer, 218
Audition
    ear structure and function, 214–216
    hearing impairments, 218
    sound localization, 217
    theories of hearing, 216–217
Auditory hallucinations, 619
Authoritarian personality, 544
Authority
    compliance and, 550
    obedience to, 550–553
Autobiographical memories, 333
Autoimmune disease, 288–289
Autonomic nervous system, 65, 94
    divisions of, 66
Autonomy (vs. shame and doubt), 139
Availability heuristic, 369, 390
Aversive counterconditioning, 660, 680
Avoidance conditioning, 292
Avoidance-approach conflict, 432–433
Avoidance-avoidance conflict, 432–433,
    466–467
Avoidant attachments, 530
Axes (of mental disorders), 599–601
Axon(s), 57, 94
Axon terminals, 57, 94
    synaptic vesicles in, 60

Babinski reflex, 108, 142
Baby boomer generation, 49
Background authority, 552

Backward search, 361–362, 389
Balance, 235
Barbiturates, 250, 264, 273
Basal ganglia, 70, 95
Basic trust (vs. basic mistrust), 139
Basilar membrane, 216
Beck's theory of cognitive therapy, 664
Behavior
    abnormal. *See* Abnormal behavior
    effect of attitudes on, 516
    evolutionary history and, 89–93
    genetic influences on, 84–89
    hormonal influences on, 81–84
    human universals, 92–93
Behavior therapy, 641, 654, 680
    counterconditioning in, 659–660
    criticisms of, 655
    goals of, 654
    modeling in, 660
    operant conditioning in, 656–658
    procedures in, 654–655
    techniques of, 656
Behavioral analysis, 486
Behavioral approach (to workplace
    motivation), 697
Behavioral dimension of attitude, 517
Behavioral genetics, 86–88
Behavioral genomics, 89, 96–97
Behavioral production, 310–311
Behavior-based safety, 708–710
Behaviorism, 6–7, 23
Behaviorist perspective, 13, 15
Belief in small numbers, 368, 389–390
Belief perseverance, 369, 389–390
Bell-shaped curve, 425
Beta waves, 74
Bias
    attributional, 515–516
    class, 47–48
    confirmation, 324
    cultural bias, 46–47
    ethnicity, 46–47
    gender, 45–46, 48, 54
    optimistic, 583
    in research, 28, 33, 54
    self-serving, 515, 554
    sexist bias in language, 376–377
Bimodal neurons, 185
Binet-Simon intelligence test, 394
Binocular depth cues, 207, 233
Biofeedback, 65, 258, 272
    and pain, 229
Biological theories of intelligence, 401
Biologically based therapy, 671–677, 681
    alternative therapy, 676
    drug therapy, 671–675
    electroconvulsive therapy, 671, 676–677
    psychosurgery, 671, 675
Biopsychology perspective, 14
Biopsychology theme, 22, 25
Bipolar cells, 190

Bipolar disorder, 614–615, 633
    antimania drugs for, 674
    violence in manic phase, 627
Bisexual orientation, 49, 450
Blended family, 667
Blood-brain barrier, 262, 273
Body-self neuromatrix (BSN), 227, 234
Borderline personality disorder, 624–625, 628
Boss-centered leadership, 704
Bottom-up analysis, 181–182, 231
Boy Code, 156
Brain, 68–81
    divisions of, 68–72
    gender and, 79–80
    gender differences in function, 95
    imaging techniques, 73–77
    individuals with damage to, 73
    lobes of, 71
    methods for determining function of, 73–77
    plasticity of, 80–81, 96
    specialization in, 77, 95
Brain waves
    amplitude, 74
    frequency, 74
    types of, 74
Brainsketching, 365
Brainstorming, 365, 389
Brief therapy, 646
Brightness, 199
Broca's area, 73
Broca's area, 95
Bulimia, 601
Burnout, 566, 590
Bystander effect, 536–537, 555

Caffeine, 265
Cannabis sativa, 266
Cannon-Bard theory of emotion, 456–457
Cardinal traits, 488
Case study, 35–36, 53
Catastrophes, 563
Catatonic type of schizophrenia, 620–621, 633
Cattell's trait theory, 488
Causality conclusions, 38
Central nervous system, 67–68, 94
Central route, 522–523
Central traits, 488
Cephalocaudal trend, 107
Cerebellum, 69, 95
Cerebral cortex, 71–72, 95
    mapping, 72
Cerebral hemispheres, 70, 95
    functions of each of, 77–79
Cerebrum, 70
Child abuse, 628–630
Child development
    cognitive theories of, 111–123
    early enrichment programs and,
        123–124
    moral reasoning and, 130–134
    neonatal, 106–111

prenatal, 103–106
psychology of, 99–103
research designs in studies of, 101–103
social and emotional, 124–130. *See also*
Social development; Psychosocial
development stages
Vygotsky's sociocultural theory, 120–122
Chlorpromazine, 674
Choice shift, 541
Cholecystokinin, 441
Christensen 2004, 38
Chromosomes, 85
Chronic pain, 586–587
Chunks (memory), **328–329**, 353
Cigarette smoking, 106
Circadian rhythms, 240–241, 271
Clairvoyance, 230–231
Class bias, 47–48
Classical conditioning, 275, 276–289, 317
extinction, 282–283
frequency of unconditioned stimulus,
282
Garcia effect, 286–287
higher-order conditioning, 280
in humans, 279–280
imagined stimuli and, 289
immune system function and, 288–289
important concepts in, 286
key variables in, 281–289
predictability of stimuli, 282
spontaneous recovery, 282–283
stimulus discrimination, 285
stimulus generalization, 283–285
strength of unconditioned stimulus, 281
terms and procedures in, 276–279
timing of unconditioned stimulus, 281
Classification, 358
Claustrophobia, 605
Client (vs. "patient"), 651
Client-centered therapy, 651–653, 679
Client-centered therapy, 8
criticisms of, 653
successful, 652
techniques of, 651–652
Clinical depression. *See* Depressive disorders;
Major depressive disorder
Clinical psychologists, 17–18, 24
Clozapine, 674–675
Clozaril, 675–675
Cocaine, 265
Cochlea, 216
Cocktail party phenomenon, 185
Codependence, 668
Coding (visual), 190
Cognition, 357
artificial intelligence and, 371–374
computer model of neural networks,
372–374
Cognitive approach to personality,
495–500
key cognitive concepts, 495

Cognitive behavior therapy, 661–668, 680
assumptions of, 661
types of, 662–664
Cognitive development. *See under* Child
development
Cognitive dimension of attitude, 517
Cognitive dissonance, 519–521, 554
Cognitive dissonance reduction, 519–520
Cognitive interventions (in sports), 716
Cognitive maps, 313–314, 320
Cognitive neuroscience, 181
Cognitive perspective, 13, 15
Cognitive psychology, 8, 23, 357, 388
Cognitive theories of emotion, 459–462
Cognitive theories of motivation, 435–438,
467
Cognitive therapy, 641
Cognitive-affective personality units, 500
Collecting and analyzing data, 31
Collective unconscious, 254, 272, 484, 506
Collectivist cultures, 47, 516
Colon irrigation, 677
Color blindness, 201–202, 232
Color coding, 200
Color vision
dimensions of, 198–199
theories of, 199–201, 232
three psychological dimensions of, 232
Commitment, 527, 555
Common fate principle, 211
Communication
as an adaptive behavior, 90–91
role of smell in, 222–223
Community psychologists, 19, 640
Community psychology, 669–671, 681
Compassionate love, 527
Compliance, 548–550
with medical advice, 585–586
obedience and, 550–553
Computerized tomography (CT) scanning,
74, 95
Concentrative meditation, 261
Concept formation, 358–360
laboratory studies of, 359
Concept(s), 358, 388
Concordance rate, 622, 633
Concrete operational stage, 117–118, 142
Conditioned response, 278, 317
Conditioned stimulus, 278, 317
Conditioned taste aversion, 286–287, 318
chemotherapy and, 287–288
Conditioning, 275, 317. *See also* Classical
conditioning; Operant conditioning
Conduction deafness, 218, 233
Cones (visual receptors), **190**–192, 232
in color perception, 200–201
Confidentiality, 51
Confirmation bias, 324, 369
Conflict, 431, 466
Conformity, 547–548, 556
Confounding variables, 33

Congruence, 652
Conscious, 474, 506
Consciousness, 5, 237–238, 271
altered states of, 238
biofeedback and, 258
drugs and. *See* Drugs/drug use
hypnosis and, 259–260
levels of, 238
meditation and, 260–261
theories of, 238–240
Consensus, 514
Conservation, 117–118
Consistency, 514
Consolidation, 316, 335, 354
Constancy, 202–205
Consummate love, 527, 555
Content validity, 410, 425
Context of development, 120
Continuous reinforcement, 300
Control group, 33, 53
Conventional morality, 132
Convergence, 207, 233
of electrochemical signals, **190**
zone, 372–374
Convergent thinking, 365, 389
Convolutions, 71
Coping, 573, 590
effective strategies, 578–579
emotion-focused coping, 576, 590
factors that influence, 573–575
proactive, 577–578, 590
problem-focused, coping, 576, 590
resilience and, 573
social support and, 575
strategies for, 575–579
stress inoculation, 579
Cornea, 192
Corpus callosum, 70, 72, 77–78, 95
split-brain individuals and, 77–78
Correlation coefficient, 43, 53
Correlational study(ies), **38**, 53
Cortex, 70. *See also* Cerebral cortex
Counseling psychologists, 17–18
Counterconditioning, 680
in behavior therapy, 659–660
Creative dimension (of intelligence), 403–404
Creative power, 482
Creativity, 364, 389
investment theory of, 366
Critical periods of development), 141, **106**
Critical thinking, 53
Cross-sectional research design, 102–103, 141
CT. *See* Computerized tomography scanning
Cultural bias, 46–47
Culture, 47
effects on maladjustment, 601–602
emotion and, 463–464
influence on child development, 101
interaction with language, 377–378
medical care-seeking behavior and, 585–586
memory and, 344–345

Dark adaptation, 191–192
 curve, 192
Data collection and analysis, 31
Date rape, 630
Deafness, 218
Debriefing, 51, 54
Decade of Behavior (2000–2010), 26–27
Decay (of information), 347, 355
Decentration, 117, 142
Deception (in research), 51–52, 54
Decibels, 213
Decision-making, 366–368, 389
 barriers to sound, 368–370
 uncertainty, 367–368
Declarative memory, 332, 354
Decontextualized thought, 122
Defense mechanisms, 479–481, 506, 648
Deindividuation, 541–542, 555
Deinstitutionalization, 678, 681
Delta waves, 242
Delusions, 609
 antipsychotic drug treatment for, 675
Demand characteristics, 638, 678
Dementia, 174, 178
Dendrites, 56–57, 94
Dendritic spines, 316
Denial, 506
Dependence (drug), 262, 273
Dependent personality disorder, 624, 626
Dependent variable, 32, 53
Depolarization, 59
Depressants, 263, 273
Depressed phase (in bipolar disorder), 614
Depression. See also Depressive disorders;
 Major depressive disorder
 monoamine theory of, 611
Depressive disorders, 608–614, 632
 biopsychosocial model of, 613–614
 diathesis-stress model, 613
 onset and duration of, 609
 prevalence of, 609–610
 symptoms of, 609
Depth perception, 204–207
 infants', 110–111
Descriptive research methods, 35–40, 53
 examples of, 40
Descriptive statistics, 41–43, 53
Design (study), 30–31
Develop a hypothesis, 29–30
Developmental psychology, 99, 141
 issues in, 99–101
 research designs in, 101–103
Deviation IQ, 408, 425
Diabetes mellitus, 83–84
Diagnostic and Statistical Manual of Mental
 Disorders (DSM), 631–632
 axes of diagnoses, 599–601
 classifications of disorders in, 598–599
 criticisms of, 600–601
 dimensions of disorders in, 599–600
Diathesis, 613

Diathesis-stress hypothesis, 613
Dichromats, 202
Difference threshold, 183
Differentiation, 104
Disability bias, 49–50, 54
Discrimination, 544–546
 as a stressor, 564–565
Disorganized type of schizophrenia,
 621, 633
Displacement, 480, 506
Display rules, 455, 468
Dissociative amnesia, 616, 633
Dissociative disorders, 615–617, 633
 dissociative amnesia, 616
 dissociative identity disorder, 616–617
 multiple personality disorder, 616–617
Dissociative identity disorder, 616–617, 633
Distinctiveness, 514
Divergent thinking, 365, 389
Diversity, in research samples, 50
Dizygotic twins, 87
DNA (deoxyribonucleic acid), 86–87
Doctrine of dualism, 237
Door-in-the-face technique, 549, 556
Dopamine, 62, 315, 320, 611
 Parkinson's disease and, 63
 theory of schizophrenia, 622, 633
Double-blind technique, 638
Draw conclusions and report results,
 31–32
Dream analysis, 648, 679
Dreams, 6, 244, 252–257, 272
 biological views of, 255–256
 cognitive view of, 254
 content of, 252
 lucid, 252
 psychodynamic views of, 254
 REM and NREM sleep and, 253
 theories of, 252–257
Drive, 431, 466
Drive theory, 430–434, 466
 of social facilitation, 539
Drug(s) use, 262–270
 dependence, 262
 effects on prenatal development, 106
 psychoactive drugs, 262–266
 substance abuse, 269–270
 use of legal, 266–269
 use vs. abuse, 269
DSM. See Diagnostic and Statistical Manual of
 Mental Disorders
Duplexity theory of vision, 190–191
Duplicity theory of vision, 190–191
Dying, 175–176
Dysthymic disorder, 608

Ear structure and function, 214–216
Early recollections, 483
Echoic storage, 327
Eclectic approach, 640
Ecological systems theory, 120

Ecstasy (MDMA), 63, 266
Educated guess, 367
EEG. See Electroencephalogram
Efferent neurons, 56, 65, 94
 action of, 57
Ego, 474–475, 506
Ego analysts, 649
Ego psychologists, 649
Egocentrism, 116–117, 142
 adolescent, 149
Elaboration likelihood model (of attitude
 change), 522
Elaborative rehearsal, 328, 353
Elavil, 673
Electroconvulsive therapy (ECT), 675–677,
 681
Electroencephalogram (EEG), 74, 95,
 242, 271
Electroencephalograph, 74
Electromagnetic radiation, 188
Ellis's ten irrational assumptions, 663
Embryo, 103–104
Emotion, 455–456
Emotion(s), 468
 control of, 465–466
 culture and, 463–464
 effects on behavior, 463–467
 gender and, 464–465
 physiological theories of, 456–458
 theories of, 456–462
Emotional dimension of attitude, 517
Emotional intelligence, 405–406, 424
Emotion-focused coping, 576–577, 590
Empathic listening, 652
Empathy, 652
Empiricism, 27, 52
Empowerment, 669
Encoding, 322, 323, 352
 failure, 323, 347
 neuroscience and, 324
Encoding-specificity principle, 324, 353
 role in memory retrieval, 339
Endocrine glands, 82–83, 96
Endocrine system, 82
Endorphins, 62, 94, 228, 234
Enkephalin, 228
Environmental psychology, 564, 590
Environmental research, 709–710
Epidermis, 224
Epinephrine, 65, 83, 611
Episodic buffer, 330–331
Episodic memory, 332–333, 354
EPSP. See Excitatory postsynaptic potential
Equity theory, 555, 695–697, 718
Ergonomics, 707
Erikson's stage theory of psychosocial
 development, 144
 adolescence through adulthood, 166–167,
 178
Estrogens, 446
Ethics, 51, 54

Ethnic diversity in psychology, 10–11
Ethnic identity, 152, 176
Ethnicity, 46–47
 academic success and, 150–151
 job interview outcomes and, 687
 bias based on, 46–47
Ethnocentrism, 46, 54
Evolutionary psychology, 16–17, 24,
  89–93, 97
 and adult sexual behavior, 162–163
 aggression and, 530
 and intelligence theory, 413
 consciousness and, 239
 controversies about, 92–93, 97
 human development and, 100
 human nature and determinism
   controversy, 93
 learning theory and, 314–315
 natural selection principle and, 90
 prejudice and, 544
 theories of emotion, 458–459
 theories of motivation, 430
Ex post facto study(ies), 39–40, 53
Exchange process, 703
Excitatory postsynaptic potential (EPSP),
  61, 94
Excited catatonic schizophrenics, 620
Excitement phase, 447, 468
Exclusion designs, 709
Exhaustion stage of stress, 558–559
Expectancy theories of motivation, 467
Expectancy theories, 435, 694–695, 718
Experiment, 32, 53
 steps in conducting (flow chart), 34
Experimental group, 33, 53
Experimental method, 32–35
Experimental psychologists, 19
Expert witnesses, 712–713
Explicit attitudes, 516–517
Explicit memory, 333–334, 354
External attribution, 512, 554
Extinction, 282– 283, **303**–304, 318, 319
 in behavior therapy, 657–658
 resistance to, 303–304
Extraneous variables, 33, 53
Extrasensory perception (ESP), 230–231
 types of, 230–231
Extraversion-intraversion dimension,
  488, 489
Extreme sensory restriction, 232
Extrinsic motivation, 437, 467
Eye movements, 198–199
Eyewitness testimony, 349–350
Eysenck Personality Questionnaire, 504
Eysenck's factor theory, 489

Facial feedback hypothesis, 456
Factor analysis, 400, 424, 488–489, 507
Factor theory of intelligence, 400
Fail-save designs, 709
False memories, 351

Family constellations, 483
Family systems, 667–668
Family, 667
Family therapy, 667–668, 681
Fantz's viewing box, 109–110
 study results, 109
Farsightedness, 190
Fathers' role in child development,
  135–136
Feature detectors, 194
Fetal alcohol syndrome, 106, 142
Fetus, 103–104, 141
Fight-or-flight response, 65, 83
Firing (neuronal), 59
Fissures (cortical), 71
Five-Factor Model of personality traits,
  489–490, 504, 507
Fixation, 480, 506
Fixed-interval schedule (of reinforcement),
  300–301, 319
Fixed-ratio schedule (of reinforcement),
  301, 319
Flashbulb memory, 342– **343,** 355
Flow, 437, 467
 athletic performance and, 716
fMRI. *See* Functional magnetic resonance
  imaging MRI (fMRI)
Foot-in-the-door technique, 548–549, 556
Forebrain, 68, 69–72, 95
Forensic psychology, 710–711, 719
Forgetting, 355
 amnesia, 352
 early studies in, 345–352
 eyewitness testimony and, 349–350
 key causes of, 347–349
 motivated, 351
Formal operational stage, 118–119, 142
Fraternal twins, 87, 96
Free association, 648, 679
Free nerve endings, 226
Free recall tasks, 337–338
Free-floating anxiety, 602
Frequency, 213, 233
Frequency theories, 217
Freudian slips, 6, 474
Friendship, 177, 527, 555
 in adolescence, 157
Frontal lobe, 71
Frustration-aggression hypothesis, 531
Fulfillment, 492, 508
Functional fixedness, 362, 389
Functional job analysis (FJA), 686
Functional magnetic resonance imaging MRI
  (fMRI), 75–76, 95
 in memory research, 324–326, 334–335, 353
Functionalism, 4–5, 23
Fundamental attribution error, 515, 554
Fuzzy concepts, 359

GABA. See Gamma-aminobutyric acid
Gambler's fallacy, 368, 389

Gamma-aminobutyric acid (GABA), 62, 94
 depressive disorders and, 612, 632
 role in sleep-wake cycle, 249
Ganglion cells, 190
Garcia effect, 286–287
Gardner's multiple intelligences theory,
  401–402, *403*
Gates (of neural cell membranes), 59
Gay, 49
Gender, 133
 aggression and, 533–534
 emotion and, 464–465
 intelligence and, 417–418
 medical care-seeking behavior and, 585
 prevalence of depressive disorders and, 610
 visual abilities and, 197
Gender bias, 45–46, 48, 54
Gender identity, 154–155, 177
Gender intensification, 154–155, 177
Gender role(s), 137–138, 144, 155–156, 177
Gender schema theory, 155, 177
Gender stereotypes, 144, 156
Generalized anxiety disorder, 603
Generativity vs. stagnation, 166
Genes, 85–86, 96
 example of interaction with environment, *88*
Genetics, 96
 color blindness and, 202
 depressive disorders and, 613–614
 drug abuse and, 270
 overview of, 85–86
 schizophrenia and, 622
 taste sensitivity and, 220
Genetic predisposition, 270
Genital stage, 478–479
Genome, 88, 96
Genomics, 88–89, 96–97
Genotype, 85–86, 96
Gestalt psychology, 5–6, 23
Gifted and Talented Children's Act (1978)
Giftedness, 419, 426
Glial cells, 56, 94
Goal-setting theory, 693–694, 718
Grammar, 375, 381
Grasping reflex, 108, 142
Great mother, 484
Group(s), 537–553, 555
 conformity in, 547–548
 deindividuation in, 541–542
 groupthink in, 540–541
 identification with, 537–553
 impaired individual performance in,
   539–540
 polarization in, 541
 poor decision making by, 540–541
 prejudice and discrimination against,
   544–546
 social facilitation in, 538–539
 social influence and, 547–553
 Stanford Prison Experiment, 542
 stereotyping in, 542–544

Group polarization, 541, 555
Group therapy, 666–668, 681
  family therapy, 667–668
  techniques of, 666–668
Groupthink, 540–541, 555
  in the workplace, 701

Hallucinations, 619
  antipsychotic drug treatment for, 675
Halo effect, 410–411, 425
Hammer (ossicle), 214–216
Happiness traps, 653
Hassles Scale, 562
Head Start program, 123, 124
Health psychology, 579, 590. See also Health-
  related behaviors
  future of, 589
Health-related behaviors. See also Illness
  AIDS prevention, 581–583
  alcohol use/abuse on college campuses,
    587–588
  compliance with medical advice,
    585–586
  condom use, 588–589
  health-impairing behaviors, 581
  health-promoting behaviors, 580
  research on, 48
  stress and, 572
Hearing. See Audition
Heart disease
  anger and, 571
  political influence on, 571
  and stress, 570–571
Heart meanings, 377
Hematophobia, 605
Hemispheric specialization, 79
  gender differences in, 79–80
Herbal remedies, 677
Heredity, 163
Heritability, 87, 96
  of intelligence, 413–415, 426
Heterosexism, 49
Heterosexual orientation, 49, 449
Heuristics, 361–362, 389
Higher-order conditioning, 280, 317
Hindbrain, 68–69, 95
Hippocampus, 69– 70, 95
  role in memory, 335
Histrionic personality disorder, 624–625
HIV. See Human immunodeficiency virus
Holmes-Rahe scale of life stressors,
  559–560
Holophrases, 380
Homeostasis, 431, 466
  hunger and, 441
Homeostatic theory of aging, 164
Homophobia, 49
Homosexual orientation, 49, 450
Hormones, 81, 96
  behavior and, 81–84
  steroid, 82–83

Hue, 198–199
Human diversity theme, 22, 25
Human factors, 707–710, 719
  behavior-based safety, 708–710
  efficiency, 707–708
Human immunodeficiency virus (HIV),
  581–583
Human resources, 685–692
  education and training, 689–690
  job analyses and, 685–686
  performance appraisal, 690–692
  selection procedures and, 686–689
Humanistic perspective, 13
Humanistic psychology, 7–8, 23
Humanistic theory of motivation, 432, 467
Humanistic therapies, 640, 650–654
Hunger, 441–446, 467
  eating and obesity, 443–446
  environmental and cultural influences on,
    442–443
  psychological determinants of, 441–442
Hypercomplex cells, 194
Hyperopia, 190
Hypnosis, 259–260, 272–273
  age regression and, 260
  athletic performance and, 716
  as pain management strategy, 229, 260
  recovered memories and, 260
Hypodermis, 224
Hypoglycemia, 84
Hypothalamus, 69–70, 95
  influence on eating, 442
Hypothesis, 29–30, 52
  development of, 29–30

Iconic storage, 327
Id, 474–475, 506
Ideal self, 492
Identical twins, 87, 96
Identity vs. role confusion, 166
Illness
  avoidance of diagnosis, 584
  compliance with medical advice, 585–586
  pain management and, 586–587
  seeking medical care, 583–585
  sick role, 586
Illusion (optical), 207, 208–210, 233
Illusory correlation, 543
Imagery, 341–342, 354
Imaginary audience, 149, 176
Imipramine, 673
Immigrants' stress, 565
Implicit Association Test, 545–546
Implicit attitudes, 516–517
Implicit memory, 333–334, 354
Impulse (neural), 59
Inattentional blindness, 187–188, 232
Inclusion (classrooms), 423
Independent variable, 32, 39, 53
Indirect aggression, 533, 555
Individual difference variable, 39

Individual psychology theory of personality,
  481–484
Individualism, 692
Individualist cultures, 47, 516
Individualized Education Program (IEP),
  423
Individuals with Disabilities Education Act
  (IDEA), 422–423, 427
Industrial/organizational (I/O) psychology,
  15–16, 24, 684, 717. See also Human
  resources; Job satisfaction; Leadership;
  Motivation and job performance;
  Teamwork
  areas of study of, 685–706
  focus of, 684
  future of, 706–707
  human factors and performance, 707–710
Industry vs. inferiority, 140
Infancy, 107
Inferential statistics, 43, 45, 53
Information processing, 322
  encoding-specific principle, 324
  levels-of-processing approach, 323–324
  transfer-appropriate processing, 324
Information-processing approach, 371–372,
  390
Informed consent, 51, 54
Ingroups, 543–544, 556
Inhibitory postsynaptic potential (IPSP),
  61, 94
Initiative vs. guilt, 139
Insanity, 627–628
Insight, 312–313, 319
Insight therapy, 647, 679
Insomnia, 250, 271
Instincts, 466
Instrumental conditioning/behaviors, 290
Instrumentality, 694
Insulin, 83–84, 441
Integrity vs. despair, 167
Intellectual disability, 421–423, 426
  types of support required for, 422
Intelligence, 399–406, 424
  biology and, 412–413
  cultural factors and, 415
  emotional, 405–406
  environmental factors and, 415, 416–417
  evolution and, 413
  gender and, 417–418
  genetics and, 413–415
  giftedness, 419
  intellectual disability, 421–423
  socioeconomic status and, 418
  theories of, 399–405
Intelligence quotient (IQ), 394–395, 424
Intelligence tests, 393–398 (395), 424
  Binet-Simon intelligence test, 394
  cultural bias in, 415
  development of, 406–412
  environmental influence, 416–417
  group tests, 397–398

increases in scores on, 418–419
misconceptions about, *412*
performance skills and, 396
standardization in, 407
Stanford-Binet Intelligence Scale, 394–395
The Psychological Corporation and, 398
Intensity (of sound), 213
Interactionists, 500
Interaural intensity differences, 217
Interaural time differences, 217
Interference (in memory), **347**–349, 355
Internal attribution, 512, 554
Interneurons, 56, 94
Interpersonal attraction, 524–525, 554–555
Interposition, 205
Interpretation, 648, 679
Intimacy, 527, 555
    vs. isolation, 166
Intimate partner violence, 630
Intrinsic motivation, 437, 467
Intrinsically motivated behavior, 693
Introspection, 4
Investment theory of creativity, 366
IPSP. *See* Inhibitory postsynaptic potential
I/O. *See* Industrial/organization psychology
IQ. *See* Intelligence quotient
Irreversible dementias, 174
Isolation tanks, 186

James-Lange theory of emotion, 456
Jealousy, 92
Job analyses, 685–686, 717
Job satisfaction, 698–700
    key factors related to, 700
    sources of, 699–700
Journal of Humanistic psychology, 8
JUMPSTART program, 123

Kinesthesis, 230, 235
Kinetic depth effect, 205
Kohlberg's levels of moral development,
    131–132

Lana, 386
Language, 375, 390
    American Sign Language (ASL), 375
    biological and evolutionary basis of, 382
    biological theories of, 383–384
    brain lateralization and, 384
    chimpanzees and, 384–387
    dolphins and whales and, 387
    elements of, 375
    gender stereotypes and, 376–377
    human acquisition of, 382–383
    interaction with culture, 377–378
    interaction with thought, 377
    learning approach to, 383
    learning readiness and, 384
    linguistic milestones, 381
    linguistics, 378
    phonology, 378–379

semantics, 379–380
social interaction theory of, 388
as a social tool, 375–376
structure of, 375–376, 378–381
syntax, 380–381
Language acquisition device, 383
Latency stage, 478
Latent content (of dreams), **254,** 272
Latent learning, 313, 319–320
Lateralization, 384, 391
Latinos/Latinas
    in psychology, 10–11, 24
    represented in U.S. population, 47
Law of closure, 211
Law of continuity, 211
Law of Prägnanz, 211, 233
Law of proximity, 211
Law of similarity, 211
Leadership, 701–706
    behaviors, 702–704
    guidelines for effective, 706
    situational leadership theory, 704
    trait approach to, 702
    transformational, 705–706
    Vroom's leadership model, 704
Learned helplessness, 298, 319, **612**–613,
    632
    vs. feeling in control, 574
Learning, 317
    approach to language, 383
    biological basis for, 314–317
    brain changes and, 316–317
    by neural networks, 374
    observation and, 307–314
    operant condition and, 290–307
    Pavlovian (classical) conditioning, 275–289
    types of, *305, 310*
Learning theory (evolutionary theory and),
    314–315
Left hemisphere functions, 79
Lens, 189
Leptin, 442
Lesbian, 49
Leveling process, 345
Levels-of-processing approach, 323–324,
    353
Levinson's life structures, 167–168
Levinson's stage theory of adult development,
    178
Lexicon, 379, 391
Libido, 479, 506
Librium, 672
Licensing (of psychologists), 21
Life expectancy, 170, 178
Light (visible), **188**
Liking (compliance and), 550
Limbic system, 69–70, 95
Linear perspective, 205
Linguistics, 378, 391. *See also* Language
Lithium carbonate, 674, 681
Locus coeruleus, 249

Locus of control, 496–497, 508
Logic, 367, 389
Longitudinal research design, 102–103, 141
Long-term memory, 332–334, 353
Long-term potentiation (LTP), 316, 335,
    354
Love
    components of, 527
    varieties of, 527, 528
Lower class, 47–48
LSD, 266
Lucid dream, 252
Lysergic acid diethylamide (LSD), 266

Macular degeneration, 190
Magnetic resonance imaging (MRI), 74–75,
    95. *See als* Functional magnetic resonance
    imaging (fMRI)
Mainstreaming, 423
Maintenance rehearsal, 328, 353
Major depressive disorder, 608, 632. *See also*
    Depressive disorders
    biological theories of, 610–613
    causes of, 610
    cognitive theories of, 612–613
    learned helplessness and, 612–613
    monoamine theory of depression, 611
Mandala, 485
Manic phase (in bipolar disorder), 614
Manic-depressive disorder, 614–615
Manifest content (of dreams), **254,** 272
Mantra, 261
Marijuana, 266
Market research, 38
Marriage (as a life stressor), 567
Maslow's hierarchy of needs, 438
Maslow's theory of self-actualization,
    491–492, 508
Materialism, 237–238
MDMA. *See* Ecstasy
Mean, 41–42, 53
Means-end analysis, 361, 389
Measures of central tendency, 41–42, 53
    example, 42
Measures of variability, 42–43, 53
    example, 44
Median, 41–42, 53
Medical model of disability, 49–50
Meditation, 260– 261
    athletic performance and, 716
Medulla, 68, 95
Meichenbaum's theory of cognitive therapy,
    664
Melatonin, 241
Memory, 352
    culture and, 344–345
    early research on short-term memory,
        328–329
    failures. *See* Forgetting
    gender and, 343–344
    information processing in the brain, 322

information-processing approach to, 371–372
key processes in the three stages of, 336
long-term, 332–334
neurobiological bases for, 324–326
neuroscience and storage of, 334–336
practice as a factor in storage, 334
retrieval, 337–345
short-term, 328–331
types of storage of, 326–336
Memory span, 328, 353
Menarche, 148
Menopause, 162
Mental age, 394, 424
Mental disorders. *See also* Anxiety disorders; *Diagnostic and Statistical Manual of Mental Disorders (DSM)*; Mood disorders; Dissociative disorders; Schizophrenic disorders; Personality disorders; *and under specific disorders*
deinstitutionalization and, 678
hospitalization in, 677–678
suicide risk in individuals with, 628
suicide risk in individuals with, 628
violence and, 634
violence as a risk for developing, 628
Mental imagery, 716
Mental retardation, 421, 426
Mental set, 362–363, 389
Mental structure, 113
Mere exposure effect, 521–522
Meta-analysis, 688
Metamessages, 377
Method of constant stimuli, 184
Method of limits, 184
Method of successive approximations, 294
Methylene-dioxymethamphetamine (MDMA). *See* Ecstasy
Midbrain, 68, 69, 95
Middle class, 48
Midlife crisis, 168
Midlife transition, 168
Milgram's obedience study, 550–553
Mindfulness meditation, 261
Minnesota Multiphasic Personality Inventory (MMPI; MMPI-2), 505
use in job selection procedures, 687
Misinformation effect, 350
Mode, 41–42, 53
Modeling, 308, 319, 680
Modern racism, 546
Monoamine oxidase (MAO) inhibitors, 673
Monoamine(s), 62, 611
theory of depression, 632
Monochromats, 202
Monocular depth cues, 205– 207, 233
Monocultural beliefs, 46
Monogamy, 163
Monozygotic twins, 87
Mood disorders, 607–615, 632
bipolar disorder, 614–615

depressive disorders, 608–614
major depressive disorder, 608–613,
Moral model of disability, 49
Moral reasoning/development
gender differences in, 133–134
social development and, 130–134
Moral relativity, 131
Morality, 131, 143–144
gender and, 133–134
research on, 48
Moro reflex, 108, 142
Morphemes, 379
Morphine, 228
Motion parallax, 205
Motivated forgetting, 351
Motivation, 311, 429, 466
effects on behavior, 441–455
theories of, 429–*440*
Motivation and job performance, 692–698
equity theory and, 695–697
expectancy theories and, 694–695
goal-setting theory and, 693–694
motivation management, 697–698
self-efficacy and work, 697
Motor neurons, 65, 94
MRI. *See* Magnetic resonance imaging
Müller-Lyer illusion, 208, 209
Multiaxial system, 599–600
Multiculturalism, 643
Multi-Move Grid (MMG), 452
Multinodal neurons, 185
Multiple infarct dementias, 174
Multiple personality disorder, 616–617
Mutations (gene), **86,** 96
Myelin sheath, 56, 94
Myers-Briggs Type Indicator (MBTI), 503–504
Myopia, 190
Mysterians, 238

Narcissism, 488
Narcissistic personality disorder, 624–625
Narcolepsy, 249, 271
National Institute of Child Health and Human Development, 135
Native Americans
in psychology, 10–11
represented in U.S. population, 47
Nativist view (of language), 383
Natural illusion, 208
Natural selection, 90, 97
Naturalistic observation, 36, 53
Nature, 84
nature-nurture interaction theme, 22, 25
vs. nurture, 84–85, 99–100
Nearsightedness, 190
Need for achievement, 450, 468
Need for affiliation, 450, 453–455, 468
Need(s), 431, 450–455, 466
Negative instance, 359
Negative punishment, 295

Negative reinforcement, 292, 318
Negative symptoms (in schizophrenic disorders), 618
Neonatal development
depth perception, 110–111
perceptual and cognitive milestones, 112
physical, 106–111
reflexes, 108–109
visual perception, 109–110
Nervous system, 56–81, 94
cellular structure and function, 56–64
central nervous system, 56
divisions of, 64–68, 67
peripheral nervous system, 56
Neural impulse, 59
Neural signal, 59
Neural transmission
major steps in, 60
role of neurotransmitters in, 60
sequence of events in, 61
Neurogenesis, 80
Neuroleptic drugs, 674
Neuromatrix theory of pain, 227
Neuron(s), 56, 94
afferent, 65, 94
basic components of, 58
bimodal, 185
depolarization in, 59
efferent, 65, 94
functioning of, 59–60
genesis of new, 80
monitoring activity of, 73–77
motor, 65, 94
multimodal, 185
polarization in, 59
sensory, 65, 94
threshold of, 59
transmission across. *See* Neuronal transmission
Neuropeptides, 62
Neuroscience perspective, 14
Neurosignature, 227
Neurosis, 602
Neurotransmitter(s), 60–64, 94
agonists, 63–64
antagonists, 63–64
excitatory and inhibitory action on receiving neurons, 61, 62–63
receptor site binding, 60
Neutral stimulus, 277
Nicotine, 64, 265
Night terrors, 250, 271–272
Nim Chimpski, 386
Nocistatin, 228
Non-rapid eye movement sleep, 242–245, 271
brain wave patterns in, 242
Norepinephrine, **62,** 611
reuptake inhibitors, 64
Normal curve, 408, 425
Norms, 407, 425

NREM. *See* Non-rapid eye movement sleep
Nurture, 84
  nature vs., 84–85, 99–100

Obedience, 550–553, 556
Object permanence, 115–116, 142
Objectivity, 28, 52
Observation
  naturalistic, 36, 53
  systematic, 28, 52
Observational learning
  cognitive maps and, 313–314
  gender role development and, 311–312
  insight, 312–313
  key processes in, 309–311
  latent learning, 313
  learning cultural values and, 311–312
  modeling, 308–309
Obsessive-compulsive disorder, 606–607
Occipital lobe, 71
Occupational Safety and Health Act (OSHA),
  709
Oedipus complex, 473, 478, 506
Olfaction, 221–223
  theories of smell, 222
Olfactory
  bulbs, 222
  epithelium, 221
  hallucinations, 619
  nerve, 222
  receptor cells, 221–222
Operant conditioning, 290–307, 318
  behavioral self-regulation, 306–307
  in behavior therapy, 656–658
  four important concepts in, *305*
  frequency of consequences, 299–302
  intrinsically motivated behavior, 306
  key variables in, 298–307
  in personality development, 485–486
  pioneers in, 290–291
  punishment and, 295–298
  reinforcement in, 291–293
  shaping, 294–295
  strength of consequences, 298–299
  superstitious behaviors, 305–306
  timing of consequences, 299
Operational definition, 32, 53
Operational diagnosis, 646
Opiates, 264
Opponent-process theory, 201, 232
Optic chiasm, 193–194
Optic nerve, 190
Optical illusions, 207–210
  cross-cultural research on, 209–210
Oral stage, 476
Orexin, 249
Organismic self, 493
Organizational psychology, 16
Orgasm phase, 447–448, 468
OSHA. *See* Occupational Safety and
  Health Act

Oshodi Sentence Completion Test, 452
Ossicles, 214
Osteoporosis, 161, 177
Outgroups, 543–544, 556
Overconfidence phenomenon, 369
Overgeneralization, in research, 46
Overintrusiveness, 623
Overjustification effect, 438, 467
Overt behaviors, 26–27

Pain, 224, 225–229
  acupuncture and, 228
  cultural differences regarding, 226
  endorphins and, 228
  management of, 228–229
  in personality development, 485–486
  neuromatrix theory of, 227
  physical and psychological nature of, 226
  receptors for, 226
  types of severe and disabling, 586–587
  variables that affect perception of, 227
Paired associate tasks, 338
Pancreas, 83
Panic attacks, 603
Papillae (tongue), 219
Paradoxical sleep, 244
Parallel distributed processing (PDP),
  373, 390
Parallel processing, 196
Paranoid personality disorder, 624–625
Paranoid type of schizophrenia, 620, 633
Paraphrasing, 652
Parasympathetic nervous system, 66, 94
Parietal lobe, 71
Parkinson's disease, 70
  dopamine and, 63
Participants, 33, 53
Participatory approach (to workplace
  motivation), 697
Passion, 527
Paternalistic approach (to workplace
  motivation), 697
Pavlovian conditioning. *See* Classical
  conditioning
Paxil, 673
Peptide YY, 442
Percentile score, 408, 425
Perception, 181–182, 231
  balance, 230
  bottom-up and top-down analyses, 181
  electrochemical basis of, 194–202
  extrasensory, 230–231
  Gestalt laws of organization and,
    211–212
  information-processing approach to,
    371–372
  pain, 223, 225–229
  vs. sensation, 181
  of shape constancy, 204
  of size constancy, 203–204
  smell (olfaction), 221–223

of sound. *See* Audition
  taste, 219–221
  touch, 224–225
  vision. *See* Vision
Perceptual distortions, 619
Perceptual research, 709
Perceptual thresholds, 183–184
Performance appraisal, 690–692, 718
Periodic pain, 587
Peripheral nervous system, 68–66, 94
Peripheral route, 522–523
Personal constructs, 495–496, 508
Personal fable, 149, 176
Personal Orientation Inventory (POI), 504
Personality, 471, 505
  assessment of, 500–505
  behaviorist approach to, 485–486
  cognitive approach to, 495–500
  disorders. *See* Personality disorders
  humanistic approach to, 490–495
  in cultural context, 471–473
  positive psychology approach to, 493
  psychodynamic approach to, 473–485
  trait and type theories of, 487–490
Personality disorders, 624–627, 634
  antisocial, 624–626, 627, 628
  borderline, 624–625, 628
  classifications of, 624–625
  dependent, 624, 626
  histrionic, 624–625
  narcissistic, 624–625
  odd or eccentric behaviors in, 624
  paranoid, 624–625
Personality inventories, 503–508, 509
Person-centered therapy, 651–653
Persuasion, 521
PET. *See* Positron emission tomography
Phallic stage, 476–477
Phantom pain, 227
Pharmacology, 63
Phenomenological approach, 490
Phenotype, 85–86, 96
Pheromones, 222–223
Phobic disorders, 603–605
Phonemes, 379
Phonological loop, 330–331
Phonology, 378–379, 391
Phosphenes, 194
Photopigments, 190
Photoreceptors, 190, 232
Phrenology, 72
Physical attractiveness, 525–526
Physiological theories of emotion, 456–458
Piaget's stages of cognitive development,
  114–119
Piaget's theory of moral development,
  131–132
Pitch, 213
Pituitary gland, 82
Place theories, 216–217
Placebo effect, 638, 678

Placenta, 104, 141
Plasticity (of brain), 80–81, 95
    learning and, 317
Plateau phase, 447, 468
Pleasure centers, 70
Polarization, 59
Political polls, 38
Polygraph testing, 457, 687
Pons, 68–69, 95
Ponzo illusion, 208, 209
Position analysis questionnaire, 686
Positive instance, 359
Positive psychology, 15, 24, 452–453,
    493–495
Positive punishment, 295
Positive reinforcement, 292, 318
Positive symptoms (in schizophrenic
    disorders), 618
Positron emission tomography (PET) scanning,
    74, 75, 95
    in memory research, 324–325, 334–335,
        353
Postconventional morality, 132
Posthypnotic suggestion, 259–260, 273
Postsynaptic potential, 61
Posttraumatic stress disorder (PTSD), 563,
    564, 590
    child abuse and, 629
    rape and, 630
Poverty (as a stressor), 564
Power distance, 692
Practical dimension (of intelligence), 403
Pragmatics, 375, 390
Precognition, 230–231
Preconscious, 474, 506
Preconventional morality, 132
Prefrontal lobotomy, 675
Prejudice, 544–546
Prenatal physical development, 103–106
    environmental effects on, 104–106
    major milestones during, 105
Preoperational stage, 116–117, 142, 142
Prevalence, 599
Primacy effect, 340–341, 354
Primary aging, 164
Primary prevention, 670
Primary punisher, 295–296
Primary reflexes, 108
Primary reinforcers, 293, 318
Primary sex characteristics, 147
Principles of Psychology, 5
Private speech, 400
Proactive coping, 577–578
Proactive inhibition, 348
Proactive interference, 348–349, 355
Probability estimating, 367–368
Problem-focused coping, 576, 577, 590
Problem-solving, 360–362, 389
    avoiding barriers to, 363–364
    barriers to, 362–364
    creative approaches to, 364–365

expertise in, 365–366
    information-processing approach to
        371–372
Procedural memory, 332, 353
Progressive pain, 587
Projection, 480, 506
Projective tests, 502–503, 509
Proprioceptive cues, 230
Prosocial behavior, 534–537, 555
Prosopagnosia, 210, 233
Prototype, 359, 373, 389
Proximate causes, 314
Proximity, 524–525
Proximodistal trend, 107
Prozac, 673
Psychedelic drugs, 265–266, 273
Psychiatrists, 18, 24
Psychoactive drugs, 262–266, 273
Psychoanalysis, 6, 473 647–650, 679
    criticisms of, 649–650
    goals of, 647–648
    techniques of, 648–649
Psychoanalysts, 18, 24
Psychoanalytic approach, 11–13, 15, 24
Psychoanalytic theory, 473–481
    personality development and, 475–479
    sex and aggression, 479–481
    and structure of the mind, 474–475
    three levels of mental life, 474
Psychodynamic theory, 473, 505
Psychodynamically based therapies,
    640, 647, 679
Psychokinesis, 230–231
Psycholinguistics, 378, 391
Psychological Corporation, The, 398
Psychological testing
    intelligence testing, 393–398
    IQ test development, 406–412
    origins and history of, 393–398
Psychologists, 17–19, 24. See also specific
    types
    demographic profile of, 19, 21
    differences among types of professionals,
        24–25
    in the legal system, 711–713
    licensing of, 21
Psychology, 3. See also specific subfields
    as action-oriented discipline of research and
        practice, 22, 25
    careers in, 19–22
    crime and punishment and, 712–713
    current trends in, 15–17
    description of, 3, 23
    early traditions in, 3–6
    empiricism in, 27
    ethnic diversity in, 10–11
    four key organizing themes in, 22–23
    history of, 3–8
    images of, 2
    in the legal system, 711–712
    major perspectives in, 11–15

popular images of, 2, 23
    principles of scientific endeavor in, 27–29
    research bias in, 28
    research methods in, 32–40
    as science, 26–54
    scientific method in, 29–32
    as social and behavioral science, 26–27
    subfields of, 20
    theory development in, 27
    women in, 9–10
Psychoneuroimmunology, 572
Psychopathology. See also Anxiety disorders;
    Mood disorders; Dissociative disorders;
    Schizophrenic disorders; Personality
    disorders; and under specific disorders
    cultural effects on maladjustment,
        601–602
    diagnoses associated with increased risk for
        suicide, 628
    diagnoses associated with violence,
        626–628
Psychopharmacology, 63–64, 94
Psychophysics, 183–184, 231
    vs. metaphysics, 183
Psychosexual stages (of personality
    development), 475–479, 506
Psychosocial development stages, 138–141
Psychosurgery, 675, 681
Psychotherapists, 641
    ethical guidelines for, 642–643
Psychotherapy, 636– 637, 678. See also
    Psychotherapists
    approaches to, 640–641
    behavior therapy, 654–660. See also Behavior
        therapy
    brief, 646
    cognitive therapy, 661–668. See also Cognitive
        behavior therapy
    culture and, 643–645
    effectiveness of, 637–640
    gender and, 645
    group therapy, 666–668
    humanistic therapies, 650–654. See also
        Client-centered therapy
    managed care and, 645–647
    need for, 637
    psychodynamic therapy, 647–650. See also
        Psychoanalysis
    signs of good progress in, 640
    types of, 636–637
Psychotherapy integration, 641
Psychotropic drugs, 672
PTSD, 563, 564
Puberty, 146, 147, 176
Punishers
    nature of, 295
    types of, 295–296
Punishment, 295–298, 319
    in behavior therapy, 658
    limitations of, 297–298
    negative, 295

plus reinforcement, 298
positive, 295
Pupil, 188–189

Race, 46–47
Racial bias, 46
Racism, 546
Railroad illusion, 208
Random assignment, 33
Range, 43, 53
Rape, 630–631
Rapid eye movement sleep (REM), 242–245,
   271
   brain wave patterns in, 242
Rational-emotive therapy, 662–663, 680
Rationalization, 480, 506
Raw score, 408, 425
Reactance, 549, 556
Reaction formation, 480, 506
Realistic conflict theory, 544–545
Reality principle, 475
Reality testing, 609
Reasoning, 366–368, 389
   culture and, 370
   evolutionary perspective on, 370–371
Recall, 337–338, 354
Recency effect, 340–341, 354
Receptive fields, 194–196, 232
Receptors
   neuronal receptor sites, 60
   sensory, 181
Reciprocation (compliance and), 550
Recognition, 338, 354
Reflecting back, 652
Reflex(s), 275
   neonatal, 108–109
   spinal, 67
Refractory period
   neuronal, 60
   in sexual response, 448
Regression, 480, 506
Rehearsal, 328, 353
Reinforcement schedules, 300
   types of, 300–302
Reinforcer(s), 291, 318, 656
   electrical brain stimulation as, 315–316
   nature of, 293
   types of, 292–293
Relationship maintenance, 529–530
Relationship therapy, 667
Relearning, 338, 345, 354
Reliability, 409, 425
REM. *See* Rapid eye movement sleep
Replicability, 29, 52
Representation, 310
Representative sample, 37, 53, **407,** 425
Repression, 349, 355, **479–480,** 506
Research
   bias in, 28
   ethical guidelines for, 54
   ethical principles of, 51–52

evaluating findings in, 40–51
five basic steps in, 29–32
methods of, 32–40
scientific method in, 29–32
study designs, 102–103
twin studies, 87–88
Residual type of schizophrenia, 621
Resilience, 573
Resistance, 648, 679
   to extinction, 303–304
Resistance stage of stress, 558–559
Resolution phase, 448, 468
Restating, 652
Restricted environment stimulation,
   186–187
Reticular formation, 68, 69, 95
Retina, 189, 232
   role in color perception, 201
Retinal disparity, 207, 233
Retrieval (of information), 322, **337–345,**
   354
   factors that facilitate, 340–342
   measures of, 337–338
   role of encoding specificity, 338–339
   state-dependent learning and, 339
Retroactive interference, 348–349, 355
Retrograde amnesia, 352, 355
Reverberating circuit, 316
Reversible dementias, 174
Revised NEO-Personality Inventory (NEO-
   PI-R), 504
Right hemisphere functions, 79
Risperdal, 675
Risperidone, 675
Robotics, 374
Rods (visual receptors), 190–192, 232
Rogers's self theory of personality, 492–493
Rogers's assumptions about human beings,
   651
Rooting reflex, 108, 142
Rorschach Inblot Test, 502–503

Saccades, 198
Sadism, 488
Sample, 32, 53
   representative, 37, 53
Sarah, 385
Saturation, 199
Savings method, 345
Scaffolding, 121
Scarcity (compliance and), 550
Schedule of reinforcement, 300, 319
Schema/schemata, 113, 142, 155, **345,** 355
Schizophrenia, 64. *See also* Schizoprenic
   disorders
   dopamine and, 64
Schizophrenic disorders, 617–623, 633
   antipsychotic drug treatment for,
      674–675
   biological factors contributing to,
      621–622

catatonia in, 620–621
causes of schizophrenia, 621–623
distortions in emotional reactions in, 619
dopamine theory of schizophrenia, 622
environtmental contributors to schizophrenia,
   622–623
essential characteristics of, 618–619
neurodevelopmental view of schizophrenia, 623
paranoia in, 620
perceptual distortions in, 619
thought distortions in, 618–619
types of schizophrenia, 619–621
violence associated with, 627
School psychologists, 19
Scientific method, 28, 52
   five basic steps of, 29–32
Scrooge, 488
Secondary aging, 164
Secondary prevention, 670
Secondary punisher, 296
Secondary reinforcers, 293, 318–319
Secondary sex characteristics, 147, 176
Secondary traits, 488
Secure attachments, 530
Sedative-hypnotics, 63, 263–264, 273
Selection procedures, 686–689
Selective attention, 185–186, 231
Selective serotonin reuptake inhibitors (SSRIs),
   673
Self, 485
Self-actualization, 8, 438–439, 467, **491–492,**
   508
Self-awareness, 138–139
Self-concept, 492, 508, 511
Self-efficacy, 452, 468, **498–499,** 508
   and work, 697
   gender and cultural influences on, 499
Self-esteem, 511–512, 553
Self-examination, 5
Self-fulfilling prophecy, 596
Self-knowledge, 238
Self-perception theory, 519, 554
Self-presentation, 512, 553
Self-regulation, 500
Self-serving bias, 515, 554
Selye's general adaptation syndrome,
   558–559
Semantic memory, 333
Semantics, 379–380, 391
Sensation, 181–182, 231
   bottom-up and top-down analyses, 181
   vs. perception, 181
Sensorimotor stage, 115–116, 142
Sensorineural deafness, 218, 233
Sensory adaptation, 221
Sensory memory, 326–327, 353
Sensory neurons, 65, 94. *See also* Neuron(s);
   Sensation
Sensory receptors, 181
Sensory register, 326
Sentience, 237, 239

Separation anxiety, 125–126
Serial position curve, 341–341, 354
Serial processing, 196
Serial recall tasks, 337–338
Serotonin, 62, 611, 612
Set point theory, 441
Sex, 133
Sex hormones, 446–447
Sexism, 546
    as a stressor, 565
Sexual attitudes research, 48
Sexual behavior, 446–450
    in adolescence, 158–159
    research, 48
    sexual orientation, 449–450
    sexual response cycle, 447–448
    understanding, 448–449
Sexual dysfunction, 449
Sexual orientation, 449–450
    bias based on, 49, 54
    vs. sexual behavior, 49
    types of, 49
Sexual response cycle, 447–448, 468
Shading, 205, 207
Shadow, 484
Shape constancy, 204, 232
Shaping, 294–295
    punishment and, 297–298
Sharing, 137
Sharpening process, 345
Short-term memory, 328–331
Short-term storage, 328
Sick role, 586
Signal detection theory, 184
Signal (neural), 59
Significant difference, 43, 45
Similarity (effect on interpersonal attraction), 526
Simple cells, 194
Single-unit recording, 73
Situational leadership theory, 704
Sixteen Personality Factor Test (16 PF), 504
Size constancy, 203–204, 232
Skinner box, 294, 319
Sleep
    as altered state of consciousness, 239
    circadian rhythms and, 240–241
    consequences of sleep deprivation, 245–247
    disorders of, 249–251
    dreaming, 244, 252–257
    need for, 247–248
    physiology of onset of, 248–249
    "sleep switch," 248–249
    sleep-wake cycle, 240–241
    slow wave, 242
    stages of, 242–245
Sleep apnea, 250, 271
Sleep debt, 247
Sleep deprivation, 245–247, 271
Sleep laboratories, 245

Sleep-wakefulness cycle, 240–241
Sleepwalking, 244, 250–251
Slow wave sleep, 242
SMART goals, 693–694
Smell. See also Olfaction
    communication and, 222–223
    theories of, 222
Social and cultural perspective, 14
Social categorization, 544, 556
Social classes, 47–48
Social cognition, 512, 553
Social development, 124–130
    characteristics of, 144
    environmental factors and, 134–141
    Erikson's theory of, 138–141
    in first two years of life, 136
    gender roles, 137–138
    moral reasoning and, 130–134
    role of child rearing in, 134–135
    role of fathers in, 135–136
    sharing, 137
Social facilitation, 538–539, 555
Social influence, 547–553, 556
    basis for, 550
    compliance and, 548–550
    conformity and, 547–548
Social interest, 482, 490, 506
Social learning theory, 308, 319
Social loafing, 539–540, 555
    in the workplace, 701
Social model of disability, 49, 50
Social need, 436, 450–455, 467
Social norms, 518, 554
Social phobia, 604–605
Social psychology, 554
    groups, 537–553
    interpersonal relationships and, 524–537
    social self and, 511–516
    the self in, 511
Social self, 511
Social support, 575, 590
Socialization, 124
Somatic nervous system, 65, 94
Sound localization, 233
Sound, 213–218, 233. See also Audition
    dimensions of, 213–214
Spanking, 295–296
Specific phobia(s), 605
    list of some common, 605
Spike discharge, 59
Spinal cord, 67
    functions of, 67–68
Spinal reflexes, 67
Spiritualism, 677
Split–brain individuals, 77–78
Spontaneous recovery, 282–283, 304, 318
Sport psychology, 714–717, 719. See also
    Athletic performance
    future of, 717
SSRIs. See selective serotonin reuptake
    inhibitors

Standard deviation, 43, 53
Standard score, 425
Standardization (of psychological tests), 407, 425
Stanford Prison Experiment, 542
Stanford-Binet Intelligence Scale, 394–395
Startle response, 279
State the problem, 29
State-dependent learning, 339, 354
Statistic(s), 40–45
    descriptive, 41–43
    inferential, 43, 45
Statistical difference, 53
Statistical significance, 43, 45
Stereotype, 556
Stereotype threat, 411, 425, 543
Stereotyping, 542–544
Sternberg's theory of successful intelligence, 402, 403–405
Steroid hormones, 82–83
Stimulant (drugs), 63, 265
Stimulation
    restricted environment, 186–187
    role in neuronal firing, 59–60
Stimulus discrimination, 285, 302–303, 318
Stimulus generalization, 284–285, 302–303, 318
Stirrup (ossicle), 214–216
Storage (memory), 322, 326–336, 353
Strange situation technique, 125–126
Strategic planning, 685
Stream of consciousness, 5
Stress, 558–579, 589
    behavior and, 569
    catastrophes and, 563
    in children, 567
    cognitive appraisal of, 560–561
    coping with, 572–579
    discrimination and, 564–565
    Hassles Scale, 562
    and health, 569–572
    health behaviors and, 572
    and heart disease, 570–571
    and infectious disease, 571–572
    Holmes-Rahe scale of life stressors, 559–560
    life events and, 560
    personal factors and, 565–567
    physiology of, 568–569
    posttraumatic stress disorder, 563
    poverty and, 564
    responses to, 567–569
    Selye's general adaptation syndrome, 558–559
    sources of, 562–567
    three stages of, 558–559
    toxins and pollutants, 564
    Undergraduate Stress Questionnaire, 560
    unhealthy environments and, 564
    urban press, 564
    work stress, 566–567

Stress inoculation, **579**, 590
Stroop effect, 349
Stroop test, 349
Structuralism, 3– 4, 23
Study
  case study, 38, 53
  correlational, 38, 53
  design, 30–31
  ex post facto, 39–40, 53
Subcultures, 47
Subgoal analysis, 361
Subject, 33
Subject variable, 39
Sublimation, 481
Subliminal perception, 183, 231
Substance abuse, 269–270, 273, 273
Successful intelligence theory, 402, 403–405
Sucking reflex, 108, 142
Suicide, 628
  attempters, 628
  completers, 629
  in adolescence, 153–154
Sulci, 71
Superego, 475, 506
Superior colliculus, 69
Superstitious behavior, 305– 306, 319
Supertasters, 220
Suprachiasmatic nucleus, 240, 249, 271
Sure Start program, 123–124
Survey(s), 36–38, 53
Sympathetic nervous system, 69, 94
Symptom substitution, 655, 680
Synapse(s), 57, *58*
  brain plasticity and, 81
Synaptic vesicles, 60
Synchronous menstruation, 223
Syndrome, 558
Syntax, 380– 381, 391
Systematic desensitization, 659–660, 680
Systematic observation, 28, 52

Tactile hallucinations, 619
Tardive dyskinesia, 675, 681
Taste, 219–221
  basic types of, 220
  sensory adaptation in, 221
Taste buds, 219
Team(s), 701, 718
  and teamwork, 701
Telegraphese, 380–381, 391
Telegraphic speech, 380–381, 391
Telepathy, 230–231
Telomeres, 163
Temperament, 128–130, 143
Temporal lobe, 71
Teratogens, 141–142, 106
Terminal drop, 175–176
Tertiary prevention, 670
Test of integrity, 687
Testosterone, 83
Test-retest method, 409

Tests of general mental ability, 687
Tetrahydrocannabinol (THC), 266
Texture gradient, 205
Thalamus, 69–70, 95
Thanatology, 176, 179
Thematic Apperception Test (TAT), 451–452,
  454, 503
Theory, 27, 52
Theory of mind, 122–123, 143
Therapy. *See* Alternative therapy; Biologically
  based therapy; Psychotherapy
Therapy in America 2004, 636
Thorazine, 674
Thought distortions, 618–619
360-degree feedback, 691
Threshold
  absolute, 183
  difference, 183
  neuronal, 59
  perceptual, 183–184
  sensory, 183
Thymoleptics, 673, 674
Tickling, 225
Timbre, 214
Time-out, 295, **658**, 680
Tofranil, 673
Token economy, 656–657
Tolerance (to drugs), **262**, 273
Top note (smell), 222
Top-down analysis, 181–182, 231
Touch, 224–225. *See also* Pain
  tickling, 225
Trait, 487, 507
Trance states, 186
Tranquilizers, 264, 273
Transaction model, 100
Transactional leader, 703, 718
Transculturalism, 643
Transduction, 190
Transfer-appropriate processing, 324, 353
Transference, 648, 679
Transformational leaders, 705–706, 718
Trephination, 594
Trichromatic theory, 200–201
Trichromats, 202
Tricyclic antidepressants, 673
Tryptophan, 62
Two-factor theory of intelligence, 400
Tympanic membrane, 214
Type A behavior, 570, 590
Type B behavior, 570
Type, 487

U.S. population, ethnic makeup of, 47
Ultimate causes, 314
Umbilical cord, 104
Uncertainty avoidance, 692
Unconditional positive regard, 492, 508
  as essential characteristic of client-centered
  therapy, 652
Unconditioned response, 276–278, 317

Unconditioned stimulus, 276–278, 317
Unconscious, 6, 474, 506
Undergraduate Stress Questionnaire, 560
Undifferentiated arousal, 457
**Undifferentiated type of schizophrenia,
  621**, 633
Upper class, 48

Validity, 410–411, 425
Valium, 672
Variable, 32, 53
Variable-interval schedule (of reinforcement),
  301, 319
Variable-ratio schedule, 301, 319
Vasocongestion, 447, 468
Ventrolateral preoptic area (VLPO), 249,
  271
Vestibular sense, 230, 235
Viagra, 162
Violence
  child abuse, 628–630
  in individuals with personality disorders, 626
  intimate partner, 630
  mental disorders and, 634
  rape, 630–631
Vision
  brain pathways and, 192–194
  color blindness, 201–202
  color vision, 198–202
  constancy in perception, 196, 202
  depth perception, 204–207
  eye movements, 198–199
  eye structures and function, 188–192
  form perception, 202–212
  image processing, 196
  optical illusions, 207–210
  prosopagnosia, 210
  structures of the visual system, 188–194
Visual acuity test, 191
Visual cliff method, 110–111
Visual cortex, 192
Visual hallucinations, 619
Visual-spatial scratchpad, 330–331
Vocabulary, 380
Vroom's leadership model, 704
Vulnerability, 613, 632
Vygotsky's theory of intelligence, 400–401
  Vs. Piaget's approach, 142

WAIS. *See* Wechsler Adult Intelligence Scale
Washoe, 385
Wear-and-tear theory of aging, 164
Wechsler scales, 395–397
  Wechsler Adult Intelligence Scale (WAIS),
    397, 398
  Wechsler-Bellvue Intelligence Scale, 397
  Wechsler Intelligence Scale for Children
    (WISC), 397
  Wechsler Preschool and Primary Scale of
    Intelligence (WPPSI), 397
Wernicke's area, 73, 95

Wise old man, 484
Withdrawal symptoms, 262, 273
Withdrawn catatonic schizophrenics, 620
Women (in psychology), 9–10, 19
Women Who Run With the Wolves, 11
Work samples, 687
Work stress, 566–567

Working class, 48
Working memory, 328, 330–331, 353
Working through, 648, 679
Workplace motivation. *See* Motivation and job
  performance

Xanax, 672

Yerkes-Dodson principle, 434–435
Young-Helmholtz theory, 200

Zollner illusion, 209
Zoloft, 673
Zone of proximal development, 121, 143
Zygote, 103–104

CREDITS

Photo Credits

Page 7: Nina Leen /Time Life Pictures/Getty Images; page 36: Spencer Grant/PhotoEdit; page 58: Omikron/Science Source/Photo Researchers; page 74: AJPhoto/Photo Researchers; page 75: Scott Camazine/Photo Researchers; page 77: Roger Ressmeyer/Corbis; page 85: CNRI Photo Researchers; page 105 (top): Petit Format/Photo Researchers; page 105 (middle): Petit Format/Photo Researchers; page 105 (bottom): James Stevenson/Photo Researchers; page 110: Mark Richards/PhotoEdit; page 112 (TL): Superstock; page 112 (TR): Laura Dwight/Peter Arnold; page 112 (ML): James A. Sugar/Black Star; page 112 (MR): Laura Dwight/Peter Arnold; page 112 (BL): Andy Cox/Getty Images; page 112 (BR): Richard Hutchings/Photo Researchers; page 186: Benjamin Ailes; page 190: Ralph C. Eagle, Jr, MD/Science Source/Photo Researchers; page 204: Mike Yamashita/Woodfin Camp and Associates; page 205 (left): Corbis Digital Stock; page 205 (right): Bettmann/Corbis; page 221: Omikron/Photo Researchers; page 242: Will & Deni McIntyre/ Photo Researchers; page 245: Ted Spagna/Science Source/Photo Researchers; page 254: Granger Collection; page 258: Will and Deni McIntyre/Photo Researchers; page 259: Brian Phillips/Image Works; page 261: Bill Aron/PhotoEdit; page 276: Blair Seitz/Science Source/Photo Researchers; page 280: Archives of the History of American Psychology; page 290: AP Images; page 292: Tony Freeman/PhotoEdit; page 296 (TL): Brian Smith; page 296 (TR): Omikron/Science Source/Photo Researchers; page 296 (BL): Kevin Horan/Stock Boston; page 296 (BM): Elizabeth Crews Photography; page 309: Albert Bandura; page 360: Michael Newman/PhotoEdit; page 374: AP Images; page 395: Bob Daemmrich/ Image Works; page 437: Tobi Corney/Stone/Getty Images; page 542: Philip G. Zimbardo; page 551: Alexandra Milgram; page 675: Will & Deni McIntyre/Science Source/Photo Researchers.

Figures and Tables

Figure 4.2, p. 107: From Berk, Laura (1993). *Infants, children, and adolescents,* 166. Copyright © 1993 by Allyn and Bacon. Used by permission. Figure 4.3, p. 108: From Frankenberg, W. K., & Dobbs, J. B. (1967). The Denver Developmental Screening Tests. *Journal of Pediatrics,* 71, 191. St. Louis, MO: Mosby–Year Book, Inc. Used by permission. Figure 4.5, p. 112: From Clarke-Stewart, A., Friedman, S., & Koch, J. (1985). *Child development: A topical approach,* 191. Copyright © 1985 by John Wiley & Sons, Inc. Used by permission. Figure 4.6, p. 115: From Fox, N.A., Kagan, J., & Weiskopf, S. (1979).The growth of memory during infancy. *Genetic Psychology Monographs,* 99, 91–130. Reprinted with permission of the Helen Dwight Reid Education Foundation. Published by Heldref Publications, 1319 Eighteenth St., NW, Washington, DC 20036–1802. Copyright © 1979. Figure 6.4, p. 189: Neural interconnections figure from Dowling, J. E., & Boycott, B. B. (1966). *Proceedings of the Royal Society (London),* B166, 80–111. Figure 6.5, p. 191: From Pirenne, M. H. (1967). *Vision and the eye,* 32. London: Chapman & Hall, Ltd. Used by permission. Figure 6.13, p. 200: From MacNichol, Edward F., Jr. (1964). Retinal mechanisms of color vision. Vision Research, 4, 119–133. Copyright 1964. Used by permission. Figure 6.17, p. 212 (bottom right): From Beck, Jacob (1966). Effects of orientation and of shape similarity on perceptual grouping. *Perception and Psychophysics,* 1, 300–302. Used by permission. Figure 7.2, p.244: From Dement, William C. (1972). *Some must watch while some must sleep.* Copyright © 1972 by William C. Dement. Used by permission of the Stanford Alumni Association and William C. Dement. Figure 7.3, p.246: From Roffwarg, Howard P., Muzio, Joseph N., & Dement, William C. (1966). Ontogenetic development of human sleep–dream cycle. *Science,* 152, 604–619. Figure 7.4, p. 263: From Ray, Oakley, & Ksir, Charles (1993). *Drugs, society, and human behavior,* 6th ed. St. Louis, MO: Mosby–Year Book, Inc., 192. Used by permission. Table 7.2, p.264: From Ray, Oakley, & Ksir, Charles (1993). *Drugs, society, and human behavior,* 6th ed. St. Louis, MO: Mosby–Year Book, Inc., 194. Used by permission. Figure 9.7, p. 341: From Kosslyn, Stephen. M. (1975). Information representation in visual images. *Cognitive Psychology,* 7, 341–370. Used by permission. Figure 10.5, p. 386: From Premack, David (1977). Language in chimpanzees? Science, 172, 808–822. Table 11.3, p. 403: Adapted from Gardner & Hatch (1989). Multiple intelligences go to school. *Educational Researcher,* Vol. 18, No. 8, 6. Reprinted by permission of Howard Gardner. Table 11.5, p.412: Adapted from Sattler, Jerome M. (1992). *Assessment of children,* revised and updated, 3rd edition, by Jerome M. Sattler, 79. San Diego, CA: Sattler. Used by permission. Table 14.2, p. 528: Adapted from Hendrick, C., & Hendrick, S. (1986). A theory and method of love. *Journal of Personality and Social Psychology,* 50, 392–402. Figure 14.9, p. 552: Adapted from Milgram, S.(1963).Behavioral study of obedience. *Journal of Abnormal and Social Psychology,* 67, 371–378. Used by permission. Figure 15.1, p. 558: From Selye, Hans (1976). *The stress of life,* revised edition. Used by permission. Table 15.1, p. 562: From Kanner, A. D., Coyne, J. C., Schaefer, C., & Lazarus, R. S. (1981). Comparison of two modes of stress measurement: Daily hassles and uplifts versus major life events. *Journal of Behavioral Medicine,* 4, 1–39. Figure 15.6, p. 582: From AIDS Epidemic Update, December 2003. Reproduced by kind permission of UNAIDS. www.unaids.org. Table 16.6, p. 619: From Meyer, Robert. G., and Salmon, Paul. *Abnormal psychology,* 2nd ed., 333, and the work of Edwin Shneidman and Norman Farberow. Copyright © 1988 by Allyn and Bacon. Used by permission. Table 17.1,

p. 640: Adapted from Mahrer, A. R.,& Nadler, W. P. (1986). Good moments in psychotherapy: A preliminary review, a list, and some promising research avenues. *Journal of Consulting and Clinical Psychology, 54,* 10–15. Figure 17.3, p. 656: From Ayllon, T., & Haughton, T. (1964). Modification of symptomatic verbal behavior of mental patients. *Behavior Research and Therapy,* 2, 87–97. Figure 17.4, p. 657: From Ayllon, T., & Azrin, N. H. (1965).The measurement and reinforcement of behavior of psychotics. *Journal of the Experimental Analysis of Behavior, 8,* 357–383. Copyright 1965 by the Society for the Experimental Analysis of Behavior, Inc. Used by permission. Table 17.3, p. 663: From Ellis, Albert, and Harper, Robert A. *A guide to rational living.* © 1989, 1961. Used by permission. Figure 18.4, p. 699: From Locke, E. A., & Schweiger, D. M. (1979). Participation in decision-making: One more look. In B. M. Staw (Ed.), *Research in organizational behavior.*